Psychology

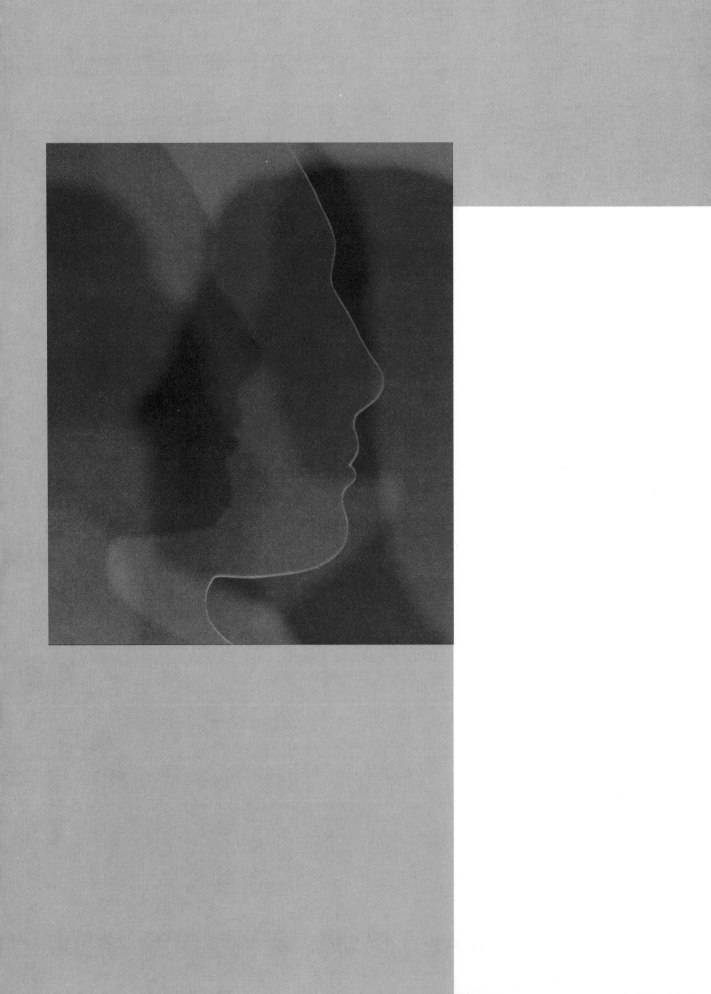

SECOND EDITION

Psychology

David G. Myers

HOPE COLLEGE, HOLLAND, MICHIGAN

WORTH PUBLISHERS, INC.

Psychology, Second Edition

Copyright © 1986, 1989 by Worth Publishers, Inc.

All rights reserved

Manufactured in the United States of America

Library of Congress Catalog Card Number: 88-50722

ISBN 0-87901-400-8

First printing, December 1988

Editors: Anne Vinnicombe and Deborah Posner

Production: Barbara Anne Seixas

Design: Malcolm Grear Designers

Art director: George Touloumes

Layout design: Patricia Lawson and David Lopez

Illustrators: Warren Budd and Demetrios Zangos

Picture editors: Elaine Bernstein and David Hinchman

Cover design: Demetrios Zangos

Composition: York Graphic Services, Inc.

Printing and binding: R. R. Donnelley & Sons Company

Illustration credits begin on page IC-1, and constitute an extension of the
copyright page.

Worth Publishers, Inc.

33 Irving Place

New York, New York 10003

TO CAROL

Preface

Preface

My goals in writing this book can be reduced to one overriding aim: *to merge rigorous science with a broad human perspective in a book that engages both the mind and the heart.* I wanted to set forth clearly the principles and processes of psychology and at the same time to remain sensitive to students' interests and to their futures as individuals. My aim was a book that helps students to gain insight into the phenomena of their everyday lives, to feel a sense of wonder about seemingly ordinary human processes, and to see how psychology addresses deep intellectual issues that cross disciplines. I also wanted to produce a book that conveys to its readers the inquisitive, compassionate, and sometimes playful spirit in which psychology can be approached. Believing with Thoreau that "Anything living is easily and naturally expressed in popular language," I sought to communicate scholarship with crisp narrative and vivid story telling.

To achieve these goals, I established, and have steadfastly tried to follow, eight principles:

1. *To exemplify the process of inquiry.* The student is repeatedly shown not just the outcome of research, but how the research process works. Throughout, the book tries to excite the reader's curiosity. It invites readers to imagine themselves as participants in classic experiments. Several chapters introduce research stories as mysteries that are progressively unraveled as one clue after another is put into place.

2. *To teach critical thinking.* By presenting research as intellectual detective work, I have tried to exemplify an inquiring, analytical mind set. The reader will discover how an empirical approach can help evaluate competing ideas and claims for highly publicized phenomena ranging from subliminal persuasion, ESP, and mother-infant bonding to astrology, basketball streak shooting, and hypnotic age regression. And whether they are studying memory, cognition, or statistics, students learn principles of critical reasoning.

3. *To put facts in the service of concepts.* My intention has been not to fill students' intellectual file drawers with facts but to reveal psychology's major concepts. In each chapter I have placed the greater emphasis on the concepts that students should carry with them long after they have forgotten the details of what they have read.

4. *To be as up-to-date as possible.* Few things dampen students' interest as quickly as the sense that they are reading stale news. While doing justice to the classic contributions of prior years, I therefore sought to present the most important recent

developments in the discipline. Accordingly, 73 percent of the references in this edition are from the 1980s, and 47 percent of these were published between 1986 and 1989.

5. *To integrate principles and applications.* Throughout—by means of anecdotes, case histories, and the posing of hypothetical situations—I have tried to relate the findings of basic research to their applications and implications. Where psychology can illuminate pressing human issues—be they racism and sexism, health and happiness, or violence and war—I have not hesitated to shine its light.

6. *To enhance comprehension by providing continuity.* Many chapters have a significant issue or theme that links the subtopics, forming a thread through the chapter. The "Learning" chapter, for example, conveys the idea that bold thinkers (Pavlov, Skinner, Bandura) can serve as intellectual pioneers. The "Thinking and Language" chapter raises the issue of human rationality and irrationality. Other threads, such as the nature-nurture issue, weave throughout the whole book.

7. *To reinforce learning at every step.* Everyday examples and rhetorical questions encourage students to process the material actively. Concepts are frequently applied and reinforced in later chapters. Pedagogical aids in the margins augment learning without diluting or interrupting the text narrative. Each chapter concludes with a narrative summary, a glossary of defined key terms, and suggested readings that are attuned to students' interests and abilities.

8. *To provide organizational flexibility.* I have chosen an organization in which developmental psychology is covered early because students usually find the material of particular interest and because it introduces themes and concepts that are used later in the text. Nevertheless, many instructors will have their own preferred sequence. Thus the chapters were written to anticipate other approaches to organizing the introductory course. Statistics, for example, is covered in an appendix, thus facilitating its being covered at any time.

SECOND EDITION FEATURES

This new edition retains the first edition's basic organization, format, and voice. It is, however, thoroughly updated (more than 40 percent of the references are new to this edition), painstakingly revised and polished paragraph by paragraph, and there are dozens of fresh examples. Without watering down the content, new learning aids summarize or diagram difficult concepts. Research related to biopsychology, gender, and industrial/organizational psychology is integrated throughout the text, with a cross-reference guide to these topics at the ends of the chapters on biological foundations, gender, and motivation.

There are numerous changes within chapters:

To increase the appeal of biological psychology, Chapter 2—formerly the longest and most arduous chapter—has been shortened by moving material on evolution and behavior genetics to later chapters. Without reducing overall coverage of biological foundations, this reduces redundant coverage and enables students to get more quickly to inherently interesting neuroscience research.

Chapter 3 treats infancy and childhood within a single section, lending more coherence to its coverage of physical, cognitive, and social development. Chapter 4 similarly unifies the coverage of adulthood and aging. Now, for example, we explore changes in memory, intelligence, and other traits across all of the adult years.

Chapter 5, Gender, is reorganized, and now emphasizes more strongly the social construction of gender.

Among the major changes in other chapters you will find new material on the biology of memory, on the biological and cognitive underpinnings of depression, on teen sexual activity and pregnancy, on the psychological effects of AIDS, on well-being across the life span, on drugs and behavior, and on managerial motivation. Coverage of obesity has been moved to the chapter on health, pain to the chapter on sensation, and the ethics of animal research are now discussed in the introductory chapter. The discussion of TV, pornography, and aggression has been carefully revised and updated.

SUPPLEMENTS

Psychology is accompanied by a comprehensive and widely acclaimed teaching and learning package. For students, there is a successful study guide, *Discovering Psychology,* prepared by Richard Straub (University of Michigan, Dearborn). Using the SQ3R (study, question, read, recite, review) method, each chapter contains overviews, guided study and review questions, and progress tests. In this new edition, *all* answers to test questions are explained and page-referenced—enabling students to know why each possible answer is right or wrong. *Discovering Psychology* is available as a paperback and *Diskcovering Psychology* is a microcomputer version for use on IBM PC, Macintosh, or Apple II.

The masterfully improved computer software prepared by Thomas Ludwig (Hope College) brings some of psychology's concepts and methods to life. *PsychSim II: Computer Simulations in Psychology* contains eleven revised programs and five new ones for use on the IBM PC or true compatibles, Macintosh, and the Apple II family. Some simulations engage the student as experimenter, by conditioning a rat or electrically probing the hypothalamus. Others engage the student as subject, as when responding to tests of memory or visual illusions. Still others provide a dynamic tutorial/demonstration of, for example, hemispheric processing or cognitive development principles. Student worksheets are provided.

The *Instructor's Resources,* created by Martin Bolt (Calvin College), have been acclaimed by users everywhere. The resources include ideas for organizing the course, chapter objectives, lecture/discussion topics, classroom exercises, student projects, film suggestions, and ready-to-use handouts for student participation. The new resources package is 30 percent bigger, now includes approximately 140 transparencies, and offers many new demonstration handouts.

The *Test Bank,* by John Brink (Calvin College), builds upon the first edition *Test Bank,* which was written and edited by Brink with the able assistance of Martin Bolt, Nancy Campbell-Goymer (Birmingham-Southern College), James Eison (Southeast Missouri State University), and Anne Nowlin (Roane State Community College). The new edition includes definitional/factual questions, more conceptual questions than previous versions, and adds a new section of essay questions. All questions are keyed to learning objectives and are page-referenced to the textbook. The *Test Bank* questions are available on *Computest,* a user-friendly computerized test-generation system for IBM PC, Macintosh, and the Apple II family of microcomputers.

IN APPRECIATION

Aided by nearly 150 consultants and reviewers over the last six years, this has become a far better, more accurate book than one author alone (this author, at least) could have written. It gives me pleasure, therefore, to thank, and to exonerate from blame, the esteemed colleagues who contributed criticisms, corrections, and creative ideas.

This new edition benefited from careful reviews at several stages. Nearly a thousand students at seven colleges and universities critiqued the first edition. Fourteen sensitive and knowledgeable teachers offered their page-by-page critique of the first edition after using it in class. This resulted in hundreds of small and large improvements, for which I am indebted to:

Lisa J. Bishop, *Indiana State University*

Laurie Braidwood, *Indiana State University*

William Buskist, *Auburn University*

Thomas H. Carr, *Michigan State University–East Lansing*

Richard N. Ek, *Corning Community College*

Roberta A. Eveslage, *Johnson County Community College*

Larry Gregory, *New Mexico State University*

Michael McCall, *Monroe Community College–Rochester*

James A. Polyson, *University of Richmond*

Donis Price, *Mesa Community College*

Walter Swap, *Tufts University*

Linda L. Walsh, *University of Northern Iowa*

Rita Wicks-Nelson, *West Virginia Institute of Technology*

Mary Lou Zanich, *Indiana University of Pennsylvania*

Additional reviewers critiqued individual first edition chapters and/or successive second edition drafts. For their generous help and countless good ideas, I thank:

David Barkmeier, *Bunker Hill Community College*

John B. Best, *Eastern Illinois University*

Martin Bolt, *Calvin College*

Richard Bowen, *Loyola University of Chicago*

Kenneth S. Bowers, *University of Waterloo*

David W. Brokaw, *Azusa Pacific University*

Freda Rebelsky Camp, *Boston University*

Linda Camras, *DePaul University*

Bernardo J. Carducci, *Indiana University Southeast–New Albany*

Dennis Clare, *College of San Mateo*

Timothy DeVoogd, *Cornell University*

Alice A. Eagly, *Purdue University*

Mary Frances Farkas, *Lansing Community College*

Larry Gregory, *New Mexico State University*

Richard A. Griggs, *University of Florida–Gainesville*

Joseph H. Grosslight, *Florida State University–Tallahassee*

Diane F. Halpern, *California State University–San Bernardino*

Janet Shibley Hyde, *University of Wisconsin–Madison*

Mary Jasnoski, *George Washington University*

Carl Merle Johnson, *Central Michigan University*

John Kounios, *Tufts University*

Robert M. Levy, *Indiana State University*

T. C. Lewandowski, *Delaware County College*

A. W. Logue, *State University of New York–Stony Brook*

Nancy Maloney, *Vancouver Community College–Langara Campus*
Matthew Margres, *Saginaw Valley State University*
Donald H. McBurney, *University of Pittsburgh*
Donna Wood McCarty, *Clayton State College*
Mark McDaniel, *Purdue University*
Elizabeth C. McDonel, *University of Alabama–Tuscaloosa*
Douglas Mook, *University of Virginia*
James A. Polyson, *University of Richmond*
Oakley Ray, *Vanderbilt University*
Duane M. Rumbaugh, *Georgia State University*
Neil Salkind, *University of Kansas*
Nancy L. Segal, *University of Minnesota*

William Siegfried, *University of North Carolina–Charlotte*
John Simpson, *University of Washington–Seattle*
Shelly E. Taylor, *University of California–Los Angeles*
Ross A. Thompson, *University of Nebraska–Lincoln*
Janet J. Turnage, *University of Central Florida*
Ko Vandonselaar, *University of Saskatchewan*
Nancy J. Vye, *Vanderbilt University*
Mary Roth Walsh, *University of Lowell*
Wilse B. Webb, *University of Florida*
Rita Wicks–Nelson, *West Virginia Institute of Technology*

In preparing the first edition, consultants helped me reflect the most current thinking in their specialties, and expert reviewers critiqued the various chapter drafts. Because the result of their guidance is carried forward into this new edition, I remain indebted to:

T. John Akamatsu, *Kent State University*
Harry H. Avis, *Sierra College*
Bernard J. Baars, *The Wright Institute*
John K. Bare, *Carleton College*
Jonathan Baron, *University of Pennsylvania*
Andrew Baum, *Uniformed Services University of the Health Sciences*
Kathleen Stassen Berger, *Bronx Community College, City University of New York*
Allen E. Bergin, *Brigham Young University*
George D. Bishop, *University of Texas–San Antonio*
Douglas W. Bloomquist, *Framingham State College*
Kenneth S. Bowers, *University of Waterloo*
Robert M. Boynton, *University of California–San Diego*
Ross Buck, *University of Connecticut*
Timothy P. Carmody, *San Francisco Veterans Administration Medical Center*
Stanley Coren, *University of British Columbia*
Donald Cronkite, *Hope College*
Peter W. Culicover, *The Ohio State University*

Richard B. Day, *McMaster University*
Edward L. Deci, *University of Rochester*
Timothy DeVoogd, *Cornell University*
David Foulkes, *Georgia Mental Health Institute and Emory University*
Larry H. Fujinaka, *Leeward Community College*
Robert J. Gatchel, *University of Texas Southwestern Medical Center–Dallas*
Mary Gauvain, *Oregon State University*
Alan G. Glaros, *University of Missouri–Kansas City*
Judith P. Goggin, *University of Texas–El Paso*
Marvin R. Goldfried, *State University of New York–Stony Brook*
William T. Greenough, *University of Illinois at Urbana–Champaign*
Joseph H. Grosslight, *Florida State University–Tallahassee*
James V. Hinrichs, *University of Iowa*
Douglas Hintzman, *University of Oregon*
Nils Hovik, *Lehigh County Community College*
I. M. Hulicka, *State University College–Buffalo*

Janet Shibley Hyde, *University of Wisconsin–Madison*

Carroll E. Izard, *University of Delaware*

John Jung, *California State University–Long Beach*

John F. Kihlstrom, *University of Arizona*

Kathleen Kowal, *University of North Carolina–Wilmington*

Richard E. Mayer, *University of California–Santa Barbara*

Donald H. McBurney, *University of Pittsburgh*

Timothy P. McNamara, *Vanderbilt University*

Donald Meichenbaum, *University of Waterloo*

Donald H. Mershon, *North Carolina State University*

Carol A. Nowak, *Center for the Study of Aging, State University of New York–Buffalo*

Anne Nowlin, *Roane State Community College*

Jacob L. Orlofsky, *University of Missouri–St. Louis*

Willis F. Overton, *Temple University*

Daniel J. Ozer, *Boston University*

Joseph J. Palladino, *University of Southern Indiana*

Herbert L. Petri, *Towson State University*

Robert Plutchik, *Albert Einstein College of Medicine*

Ovide F. Pomerleau, *School of Medicine at the University of Michigan–Ann Arbor*

Dennis R. Proffitt, *University of Virginia*

Judith Rodin, *Yale University*

Alexander J. Rosen, *University of Illinois at Chicago Circle*

Kay F. Schaffer, *University of Toledo*

Alexander W. Siegel, *University of Houston*

Ronald K. Siegel, *School of Medicine at the University of California–Los Angeles*

Donald P. Spence, *School of Medicine at Rutgers The State University of New Jersey*

Richard A. Steffy, *University of Waterloo*

Leonard Stern, *Eastern Washington University*

Robert J. Sternberg, *Yale University*

George C. Stone, *University of California–San Francisco*

Elliot Tanis, *Hope College*

Don Tucker, *University of Oregon*

Rhoda K. Unger, *Montclair State College*

Richard D. Walk, *George Washington University*

George Weaver, *Florida State University*

Wilse B. Webb, *University of Florida*

Merold Westphal, *Fordham University*

David A. Wilder, *Rutgers The State University of New Jersey*

Joan Wilterdink, *University of Wisconsin–Madison*

Jeffrey J. Wine, *Stanford University*

Joseph Wolpe, *The Medical College of Pennsylvania, Eastern Pennsylvania Psychiatric Institute*

Gordon Wood, *Michigan State University*

Fourteen individuals read the whole first edition manuscript and provided me not only with a critique of each chapter but also with their sense of the style and balance of the whole book. For their advice and warm encouragement, I am grateful to:

John B. Best, *Eastern Illinois University*

Martin Bolt, *Calvin College*

Cynthia J. Brandau, *Belleville Area College*

Sharon S. Brehm, *University of Kansas*

Steven L. Buck, *University of Washington*

James Eison, *Southeast Missouri State University*

Robert M. Levy, *Indiana State University*

G. William Lucker, *University of Texas–El Paso*

Angela P. McGlynn, *Mercer County Community College*

Carol Myers, *Holland, Michigan*

Bobby J. Poe, *Belleville Area College*

Catherine A. Riordan, *University of Missouri–Rolla*

Richard Straub, *University of Michigan–Dearborn*

Robert B. Wallace, *University of Hartford*

Through both editions, I have benefited from the meticulous critique, probing questions, and constant encouragement of Charles Brewer (Furman University).

At Worth Publishers—a company whose entire staff is devoted to the highest quality in everything they do—a host of people played key supportive roles. Alison Meersschaert commissioned this book, envisioned its goals and a process to fulfill them, and nurtured the book nearly to the end of the draft first edition. I am also indebted to Managing Editor Anne Vinnicombe, leader of a dedicated editorial team, for her prodigious effort in bringing both editions to fulfillment and meticulously scrutinizing the accuracy, logical flow, and clarity of every page. For this edition, developmental editor Barbara Brooks's careful analysis and thoughtful suggestions improved every chapter. Debbie Posner demonstrated exceptional commitment and competence in coordinating the transformation of manuscript into book, as did Christine Brune, who supervised countless editorial details. Thanks also go to Worth's production team, led by George Touloumes, for once again crafting a final product that exceeds my expectations.

At Hope College, the supporting team members for this edition included Julia Zuwerink, Wendy Braje, and Richard Burtt, who researched, checked, and proofed countless items; Kathy Adamski, who typed hundreds of dictated letters without ever losing her good cheer; Phyllis and Richard Vandervelde, who processed thousands of pages of various chapter drafts with their customary excellence; and my psychology colleagues, Les Beach, Jane Dickie, Charles Green, Thomas Ludwig, James Motiff, Patricia Roehling, John Shaughnessy, and Phillip Van Eyl, whose knowledge and personal libraries I have tapped on hundreds of occasions. The influence of my writing coach, poet-essayist Jack Ridl, continues to be evident in the voice you will be hearing in the pages that follow.

David Myers

Contents in Brief

Contents

Psychology

PART 1

Foundations of Psychology

We begin by laying a foundation for our exploration of psychology. In Chapter 1, we introduce psychology and its methods and consider what psychology is and how it is conducted. Understanding how psychologists ask questions will prepare us to understand their research findings and to think more critically about events in everyday life. In Chapter 2, we consider the biological foundations of our behavior. We will see how our nervous system, body chemistry, and brain play a vital role in virtually everything else this book describes—our development as individuals, our abilities to perceive, learn, and think, and our normal and sometimes disordered behavior and emotions.

CHAPTER 1

Introducing Psychology

I was relaxing in the barber's black leather chair, enjoying my last haircut before leaving Seattle, when the barber struck up a conversation:

"What do you do?"

"Next week I'll be moving to Iowa to begin graduate school," I replied.

"What are you studying?"

"Psychology."

The haircutting ceased as the friendly barber took a step back, and then timidly wondered aloud:

"So what do you think of me?"

For the barber, as for many people whose exposure to psychology comes mostly from popular books, magazines, and TV, psychologists analyze personality, practice psychotherapy, and dispense child-rearing advice. Do they? Yes, and much more. Consider some of psychology's questions, questions that from time to time you may wonder about:

Have you ever found yourself reacting to something just as one of your parents would—perhaps in a way you've vowed you never would—and then wondered how much of your personality is inherited? To what degree are you really like your mother or your father? *To what extent is their influence transmitted through their genes and to what extent through the environment they provided for you?*

Have you ever played peekaboo with a 6-month-old infant and wondered why the baby finds the game so delightful? The baby reacts as if, when you momentarily move behind a door, you actually disappear—only to reappear later out of thin air. *What do babies actually perceive and think?*

Have you ever awakened from a nightmare and, with a great wave of relief, wondered why we have such crazy dreams? *How often do we dream? What function is served by dreaming?*

Have you ever been to a circus and wondered how the poodles were trained to dance, how the lions were taught to jump through hoops, how the chimps learned to ride bikes—and *whether there are any limitations on what animals can be taught to do?*

Have you ever suffered periods of depression or anxiety and wondered *what triggers such states and how they might be alleviated?*

Have you ever brooded over having lost an election or having not been invited to a party and wondered how you might better "win friends and influence people"? *What makes some people so influential and socially attractive?*

Such questions provide grist for psychology's mill, for psychology is a science that seeks to answer all sorts of questions about us all: how we think, feel, and act.

WHAT IS PSYCHOLOGY?

How did psychology arise? From what perspectives do psychologists analyze behavior? What do they study and do?

PSYCHOLOGY'S ROOTS

Psychology is a fairly young science, with roots in many disciplines, from physiology to philosophy. Wilhelm Wundt, who founded the first psychology laboratory in 1879 at Germany's University of Leipzig, was both a physiologist and a philosopher. Ivan Pavlov, who pioneered the study of learning, was a Russian physiologist. Sigmund Freud, renowned personality theorist, was an Austrian physician. Jean Piaget, this century's most influential observer of children, was a Swiss biologist. William James, author of an important 1890 psychology textbook, was an American philosopher (Figure 1–1).

As this list of pioneering psychologists illustrates, psychology has its origins not only in many disciplines but also in many countries. In the last few decades, psychology has especially flourished in the United States, which currently has more than 100,000 psychologists (Stapp & others, 1985). But the field is now growing rapidly in other countries as well (Rosenzweig, 1984b). Psychology's researchers and students, like its historic pioneers, are citizens of many nations.

With current research that ranges from recording nerve cell activity to studying the effects of psychotherapy, and with perspectives that range from basic science to philosophy, psychology is difficult to define. A century ago, psychology was defined as the science of mental life. In establishing his psychology laboratory, Wilhelm Wundt focused on the *inner* (covert) experiences of consciousness—sensations, feelings, and thoughts. Introspection, the examination of one's own emotional states and mental processes, was the basic research tool at that time. Psychologists of that era therefore relied on people's introspective reports of their conscious experiences in response to various stimuli. Then, from about 1920 to 1960, American psychologists led by John Watson redefined psychology as the science of behavior. After all, they said, science is rooted in observation. You cannot observe a sensation, a feeling, or a thought; but you *can* observe how people's *outer* (overt) behaviors are affected by external stimuli.

Since the 1960s, psychology has recaptured its initial interest in conscious and unconscious mental processes. Many psychologists now study how our minds process and retain information. To encompass psychology's concern with both overt behavior and covert thoughts and feelings we will define ***psychology*** as *the science of behavior and mental processes.*

One big issue today is whether our behavior and mental processes are best explained by *internal* or *external* influences: Are eating and sexual behavior mostly "pushed" by internal drives or "pulled" by external incentives? Is social behavior better explained by the presence of enduring inner traits or by the temporary demands of external situations? Are personality and intelligence influenced more by our genes or by our experience?

Clearly, the influences on us are both internal and external. The

"I'm a social scientist, Michael. That means I can't explain electricity or anything like that, but if you ever want to know about people I'm your man."

The membership of the American Psychological Association (which includes seven in ten doctoral psychologists in the United States) more than doubled during the 1950s, nearly doubled again during the 1960s, and has doubled again since 1970.

Throughout this book, important concepts will be set in boldface italic type. As a study aid, these terms are repeated with their definitions at the end of each chapter.

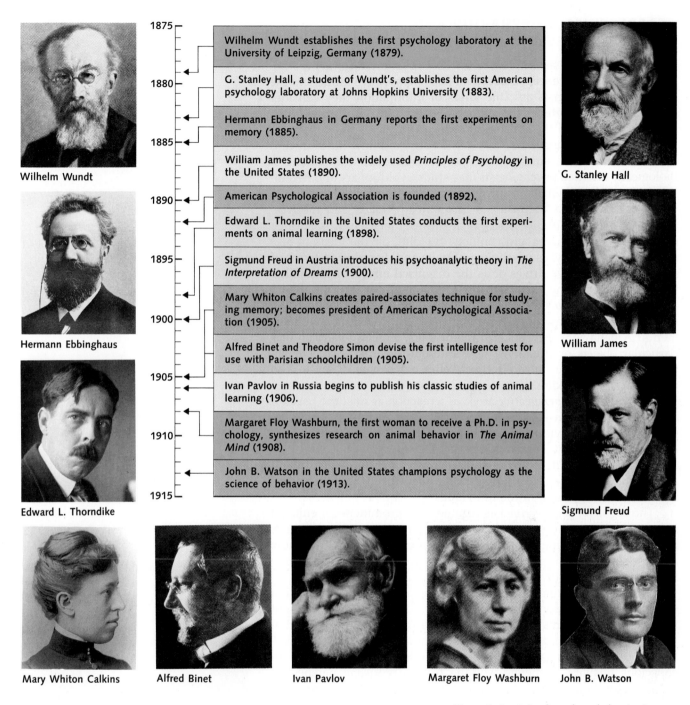

Wilhelm Wundt

Hermann Ebbinghaus

Edward L. Thorndike

Wilhelm Wundt establishes the first psychology laboratory at the University of Leipzig, Germany (1879).

G. Stanley Hall, a student of Wundt's, establishes the first American psychology laboratory at Johns Hopkins University (1883).

Hermann Ebbinghaus in Germany reports the first experiments on memory (1885).

William James publishes the widely used *Principles of Psychology* in the United States (1890).

American Psychological Association is founded (1892).

Edward L. Thorndike in the United States conducts the first experiments on animal learning (1898).

Sigmund Freud in Austria introduces his psychoanalytic theory in *The Interpretation of Dreams* (1900).

Mary Whiton Calkins creates paired-associates technique for studying memory; becomes president of American Psychological Association (1905).

Alfred Binet and Theodore Simon devise the first intelligence test for use with Parisian schoolchildren (1905).

Ivan Pavlov in Russia begins to publish his classic studies of animal learning (1906).

Margaret Floy Washburn, the first woman to receive a Ph.D. in psychology, synthesizes research on animal behavior in *The Animal Mind* (1908).

John B. Watson in the United States champions psychology as the science of behavior (1913).

G. Stanley Hall

William James

Sigmund Freud

Mary Whiton Calkins   **Alfred Binet**   **Ivan Pavlov**   **Margaret Floy Washburn**   **John B. Watson**

Figure 1–1   A timeline of psychology's pioneers.

issue is their relative importance and how they interact. This issue is basic and longstanding. The Greek philosopher Plato (428–348 B.C.) assumed that character and intelligence are largely inherited and that ideas are inborn (Robinson, 1981). Aristotle (384–322 B.C.), on the other hand, argued that there is nothing in the mind that does not first come from the external world through the senses. In the seventeenth century, this issue was revived by the philosophers John Locke, who believed that the mind is a blank slate at birth and that most knowledge comes through sense experience, and René Descartes, who thought that knowledge is not dependent on sense experience. Thus, the question of internal and external influences weaves a thread from the ancient past to our time. Psychology is a young science but an old subject.

PERSPECTIVES ON BEHAVIOR AND MENTAL PROCESSES

Whether psychologists emphasize internal or external influences depends on their theoretical perspective. Each perspective influences the questions psychologists ask, the kinds of information they consider important, and sometimes the method of study utilized. Consider five such perspectives in their historical order.

The *biological perspective* helps us understand how the body and brain work to create emotions, memories, and sensory experiences. Biologically oriented psychologists may study evolutionary and hereditary influences on behavior, how messages are transmitted within the body, or how blood chemistry is linked with moods and motives.

The *psychoanalytic perspective* assumes that behavior springs from unconscious drives and conflicts. Building on the ideas of Sigmund Freud, it analyzes psychological traits and disorders in terms of sexual and aggressive drives or as the disguised effects of unfulfilled wishes and childhood traumas.

The *behavioral perspective* studies the mechanisms by which observable responses are acquired and modified in particular environments. A behavioral psychologist might study how we learn to fear particular objects or situations, how external rewards shape our actions, or how we can most effectively alter our behavior, say to lose weight or stop smoking.

The *humanistic perspective* arose as a reaction against the psychoanalytic view, which sees people as driven by unconscious internal forces, and the behavioristic view, which sees people as shaped by the external environment. Humanistic psychologists emphasize our capacities to choose our life patterns and to grow to greater maturity and fulfillment. They also seek to understand behavior more subjectively, in terms of its meaning to the individual.

The *cognitive perspective* has regained the prominence it enjoyed in psychology's early history. (*Cognition* refers to our remembering, thinking, and knowing.) Hundreds of researchers are exploring how we process, store, and retrieve information, and how we use information to reason and solve problems.

Consider how from each perspective we might view an emotion such as anger. Someone working from a *biological* perspective might study the brain circuits that trigger the physical state of being "red in the face" and "hot under the collar." Someone working from a *psychoanalytic* perspective might view an angry outburst as an outlet for unconscious hostility. Someone working from a *behavioral* perspective might study the facial expressions and body gestures that accompany anger, or attempt to determine which external stimuli result in angry responses or aggressive acts. Someone working from a *humanistic* perspective might want to understand what it means to experience and express anger—from the individual's own point of view. Someone working from a *cognitive* perspective might study how the different ways we perceive a frustrating situation affect the intensity of our anger, and how an angry mood affects our thinking.

The biological, psychoanalytic, behavioral, humanistic, and cognitive perspectives describe and explain anger very differently. This doesn't necessarily mean that they contradict one another. Rather, they are five useful ways of looking at the same psychological state. By using all five, we gain a richer, fuller understanding of anger than that provided by any single perspective.

This important point—that different perspectives can complement

An emotion such as anger can be studied from several perspectives, each of which explores different aspects. Taken together, these studies provide a fuller understanding of the emotion.

one another—is also true for all the academic disciplines, each of which provides a different perspective on nature and our place in it. The basic sciences investigate nature's building blocks—atoms, energy forces, living cells—seeking principles based on objective observation. The humanities (literature, philosophy, and the like) address questions of meaning and value in human life and use more subjective methods. Psychology lies near the middle of this continuum; it usually uses scientific methods to explore our subjective thoughts and actions.

Each discipline, like each perspective within psychology, has its questions and its limits. They can be like different two-dimensional views of a three-dimensional object (see Figure 1–2).

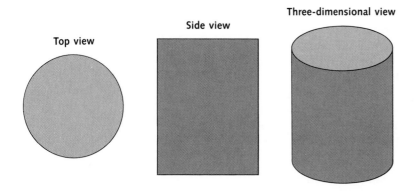

Top view   **Side view**   **Three-dimensional view**

Figure 1–2   What is this object? One person, looking down from the top, says it is a circular disk. Another, looking at it from the side, says it is a rectangle. Their differing perspectives seem contradictory. In fact, they are complementary, for their respective images can be assembled into a more complete three-dimensional view of the object, a cylinder. The views of behavior and mental processes offered by psychology's different perspectives are often like this: A lot depends on the observer's point of view.

Each two-dimensional view is a helpful perspective that can be compatible with the others; none by itself reveals the whole picture. If you ignore psychology's limits and expect it to answer the ultimate questions posed by the Russian novelist Leo Tolstoy (1904)—"Why should I live? Why should I do anything? Is there in life any purpose which the inevitable death that awaits me does not undo and destroy?"—you are destined for disappointment. If instead you expect that psychology will help you better understand why people, yourself included, feel, think, and act as they do—or if you enjoy exploring such questions—then you should find the study of psychology both fascinating and applicable to life.

"Science can no more answer the questions of how we ought to live than religion can decree the age of the earth."
Stephen Jay Gould (1987)

BASIC AND APPLIED PSYCHOLOGY

To many people, psychology is a mental health profession devoted to such practical issues as how to achieve marital happiness, how to overcome anxiety and depression, and how to raise children. For such people it often comes as a surprise to learn that only about 60 percent of America's professional psychologists work in the mental health fields (Stapp & others, 1985). What are the others doing? Most are conducting *basic* research (which builds psychology's base of knowledge) or *applied* research (which tackles practical problems) and teaching students what has been learned from this research.

Later chapters will introduce psychology's specialists. We will, for example, meet:

> ***Biological psychologists,*** also called *behavioral neuroscientists, neuropsychologists, physiological psychologists,* or *biopsychologists.* They explore the links between biology and behavior, including hereditary influences on behavior; the effects of hormones, drugs, and neurotransmitters on our moods and behavior; and the functioning of various components of the nervous system.

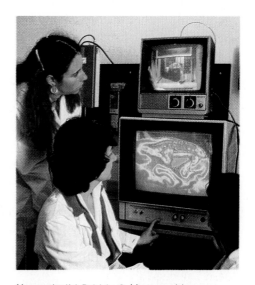

Neuroscientist Patricia Goldman and her colleagues at Yale observe metabolic activity in different regions of a monkey's brain while it performs a task for a study on memory.

Developmental psychologists, who study the processes that result in physical, mental, and social changes throughout the life cycle. We will encounter one group of developmental psychologists who have used eye-tracking machines, pacifiers wired to electronic instruments, and other such devices to reveal the surprising abilities of newborn babies to, say, recognize their mothers' odors and voices. We will find other developmental psychologists studying how young animals and humans become attached to their parents, and what happens when a closely attached parent and child are separated. We will see yet another group debating which aspects of intelligence change as we age.

General experimental psychologists, who conduct experiments on, among other things, sensation and perception, learning, memory, and thought, motivation and emotion. Peering over the shoulders of experimental psychologists at work in their laboratories, we will observe some of them flashing syllables, words, and faces on a screen to see how people remember and how much and why they forget. We will find others studying the elements of learning by teaching animals to perform simple acts. We will see still others presenting various problems to people and recording the speed and accuracy of their responses in order to discover how the mind processes information.

Personality and social psychologists, who study how individuals are influenced by enduring inner factors (personality psychology) and how they influence and are influenced by other people (social psychology). Such psychologists might be found observing people in a variety of situations to see whether their behavior reflects a consistent personality or whether it varies, depending on the people they are with and on the situation.

Clinical psychologists, who study, assess, and treat psychologically troubled people. During and after graduate school, clinical psychologists are trained to assess and assist those with psychological disorders. Unlike *psychiatrists,* who have earned a medical degree and then undertaken a residency in psychiatry, clinical psychologists neither diagnose physical causes of psychological disorders nor prescribe drugs. But clinicians are prepared to administer tests, provide psychotherapy, manage mental health programs, and conduct research and training. Other helping professionals include *counseling psychologists,* with jobs ranging from vocational guidance and rehabilitation, to working with the disabled and handicapped, to staffing the student mental health clinics at colleges and universities, and *school psychologists,* who evaluate children and work with their teachers and parents.

Industrial/organizational psychologists, who study and manage human behavior in the workplace and in the marketplace. These psychologists assist organizations in selecting and training employees, boosting morale and productivity, and assessing consumer responses to new products.

A clinical psychologist and a teenager interact intently during a therapy session.

With perspectives ranging from the physiological to the philosophical and new subfields continuing to emerge, psychology has become the meeting place for different disciplines. More and more, psychology connects with fields ranging from mathematics and biology to sociology and philosophy. And more and more, psychology's methods and findings assist other disciplines. Psychologists teach in medical schools, law schools, and theological seminaries; they work in hospitals, factories, and corporate offices; they engage in interdisciplinary studies such as *psychohistory*, the psychological analysis of historical characters, and *psycholinguistics*, the study of the relationship between language and the cognitive or behavioral characteristics of its users.

After some of the events of the 1980s, one is tempted to propose a new interdisciplinary field: *psychoceramics*, the study of crackpots.

SCIENTIFIC ATTITUDES AND APPROACHES

What unifies psychology? Psychology is the *science* of behavior and mental processes, but what scientific ideals unite psychology's perspectives and its subfields? All scientific inquiry—psychological inquiry included—involves certain attitudes and certain methods of creating theories that organize, explain, and predict observations.

SKEPTICISM AND HUMILITY

The first scientific attitude, *skepticism*, spurs us to check our ideas against observation. Because our intuitive hunches are prone to error, scientists typically approach them with an attitude of open-minded doubt. Do parents and infants "bond" more closely with one another if allowed body contact during the first hour after birth (see page 71)? Can movie theater owners motivate you to buy popcorn by flashing an imperceptibly brief image of the words "eat popcorn" on the screen (see page 141)? Can astrologers analyze character and predict your future based on the positions of the planets at the moment of your birth (see pages 436–437)?

All such claims can be tested with open-minded skepticism: If they are refuted—as the above claims have been—we can reject them; if they are confirmed, we can reject the skepticism. It is by careful scrutiny of competing ideas that we sift profound insights from believable fantasies. Over and over again we will see that the scientist's attitude is like a detective's. The energetic scientist is a sleuth who checks various leads, dismissing most, but verifying some.

"Truth is arrived at by the painstaking process of eliminating the untrue."
Arthur Conan Doyle's Sherlock Holmes

The scientific ideal is also one of *humility*. Scientists know that their personal opinions are never the last word. So they test their ideas and then report their research precisely enough to allow others to **replicate** (repeat) their observations, usually by recreating the essence of a study and seeing whether they get the same results. If, when tested, nature does not conform to our ideas, then so much the worse for our ideas. If animals or people do not behave in accord with the expectations of a psychological theory, then so much the worse for the theory. This is the attitude expressed in one of experimental psychology's early mottos: "The rat is always right."

This attitude of humility before nature is not always apparent in the behavior of scientists who, like anyone else, can have big egos and may cling stubbornly to their pet theories (Greenwald & others, 1986). Nevertheless, historians of science tell us that the attitudes of skepticism and humility helped make modern science possible. Many of the founders of modern science were people like mathematician-physicist Isaac Newton, people whose religious convictions emboldened them to think that the created world was worth exploring and that, owing no ultimate allegiance to any human authority, they should humbly accept whatever truths nature revealed (Hooykaas, 1972; Merton, 1938).

"My deeply held belief is that if a god anything like the traditional sort exists, our curiosity and intelligence are provided by such a god. We would be unappreciative of those gifts . . . if we suppressed our passion to explore the universe and ourselves."
Carl Sagan (1979a)

THE SCIENTIFIC METHOD

Psychologists apply these scientific attitudes as they make observations, form theories, and then refine their theories in the light of new observations.

In everyday conversation, we sometimes use "theory" to mean "mere hunch." In science, a ***theory*** *explains;* it does so through an integrated set of principles that *organizes* and *predicts* observable behaviors or events. A good theory of depression, for example, will first organize countless observations concerning depression into a much shorter list of coherent principles. Say we observe over and over that depressed people are down on themselves—that they recall their past, describe their present, and predict their future in gloomy terms. We might therefore theorize that low self-esteem is a prime cause of depression. So far so good: Our self-esteem principle summarizes an otherwise long list of disorganized observations concerning depressed people.

A good theory also implies *testable predictions,* called ***hypotheses.*** Such predictions give direction to research by enabling us to test and revise the theory. Without a guiding theory, scientists lack direction; they just haphazardly gather isolated facts. Charles Darwin put it more strongly: "Without the making of theories, I am convinced there would be no observations."

No matter how reasonable a theory may sound—and low self-esteem certainly seems a reasonable cause of depression—it cannot be considered "true" or "valid" until it has been tested. To test our self-esteem theory of depression we might assess people's self-esteem and see whether, as we hypothesize, people who have poorer self-images are in fact more depressed.

In so doing, we should be aware that our theory itself may bias our observations. For example, once we've theorized that depression springs from low self-esteem, we may be tempted to perceive depressed people's comments as self-disparaging. Nevertheless, our theory will be useful if it (1) effectively organizes a wide range of observations and (2) implies clear predictions that anyone can use to check the theory or to derive practical applications. (If we could boost people's self-esteem, might we alleviate their depression?) Eventually, our theory will probably give way to a revised theory (such as the one on pages 460–462) that organizes, explains, and predicts even better what we know about depression.

A theory implies hypotheses, which predict observable behaviors and events; these observations, in turn, are used to refine the theory.

PSYCHOLOGY'S METHODS AND AIMS

Psychologists test their theories and hypotheses with three research methods—observation, correlation, and experimentation—that help them to describe, predict, and explain behavior.

OBSERVATION YIELDS DESCRIPTION

The starting point of any science is the systematic observation and description of events of interest. In everyday life, all of us observe and describe people, often forming hunches about why they behave as they do. Professional psychologists are doing much the same, only more objectively and systematically.

The Case Study Method   Psychologists sometimes use a ***case study*** approach, in which they study individuals in great depth and detail in the hope of revealing things true of us all. Much of our early knowledge about the brain came from case studies of individuals who suffered a particular impairment after damage to a particular brain region. Sigmund Freud constructed a monumental theory of personality by studying individual cases in depth. The great developmental psychologist Jean Piaget taught us a great deal about children's thinking through the careful questioning and observation of his own three children.

The Survey   The *survey* method of observation looks at many cases in less depth. In a survey, people are asked specific questions about their behavior or opinions. Questions about everything from sexual practices to opinions about policies and politicians have been put to the public. It's hard to think of a significant question that has not been asked: Louis Harris (1987) reports that 89 percent of Americans say that they have high stress, 95 percent believe in God, 70 percent favor hand gun registration, and 96 percent say that there is something about their appearance they would like to change. Yet surveys have limitations. They are only valid if the questions are clear and unbiased, if the respondents will answer them honestly, and if the respondents are representative of the total population being studied.

Like the Harris polls, most surveys are taken of a sample of the target population. If you wished to survey the students at your college you could question them all, but probably there are too many. Instead, you survey a representative sample of the total student population. How can you make your sample representative of the whole population under study? By making it a *random sample,* one in which every person in the entire group has an equal chance of being included.

To randomly sample the students at your institution, you would *not* send them all a questionnaire, because the conscientious people who return it would not represent a random sample. Rather, you would aim for a representative sample by starting at a random point and selecting, say, every tenth person from an alphabetical listing and then making sure you obtain responses from virtually all of them. Better to have a small representative sample of 100 than a haphazard, unrepresentative sample of 500.

The random-sampling principle is also used in national surveys. If you had a giant barrel containing 60 million white beans that were thoroughly mixed with 40 million green beans, a scoop that randomly sampled 1500 of them would contain about 60 percent white and 40 percent green beans, give or take 2 or 3 percent. Sampling voters in a national election survey is like sampling those beans; 1500 randomly sampled people can provide a remarkably accurate snapshot of the opinions of a nation.

But obtaining a random sample can be an enormous task. Some people will not be home and others—often 30 percent or more in urban areas—may refuse to cooperate. University of Michigan researchers Philip Converse and Michael Traugott (1986) report that one of their 1984 election surveys gave President Reagan a mere 3 percent edge over candidate Walter Mondale among those reached on the first attempt. When those who answered callbacks were included, the Reagan lead increased to 13 percent. (He won the election by 18 percent.) Why? Democrats apparently spend more time at home. This illustrates the bias that can result if survey researchers do not go to the trouble (and expense) of gaining full participation of their random sample.

The pitfalls of sampling bias sound pretty obvious. But consider: As recently as October 1987, writer Shere Hite's latest book, *Women and*

" 'Well my dear,' said Miss Marple, 'human nature is very much the same everywhere, and of course, one has opportunities of observing it at closer quarters in a village.' "
   Agatha Christie,
   The Tuesday Club Murders, 1933

Psychologists use the survey method to gain information about specific groups of people. Well-done surveys use random sampling to obtain information representative of the entire population being studied.

Following the Carter-Reagan presidential debate in 1980 (after 11 P.M. in the East, after 8 P.M. in the more pro-Reagan West), ABC television invited viewers to place a 50-cent long-distance call to indicate who they thought won the debate. Among the more than 700,000 callers, Mr. Reagan had a better than 2 to 1 edge. However, surveys of *random* samples of likely voters indicated the debate outcome as a virtual draw. Why might the ABC result have been misleading? (Are Republicans or Democrats more likely to own phones and make long-distance calls? To be up after 11 P.M. Eastern time? To have been eager to voice support of their candidate in this election?)

Love, reports survey findings based only on a 4.5 percent response rate from mailings to an unrepresentative sample of 100,000 American women. Doubly unrepresentative, because not only do we have a self-selected return, but also the women initially contacted were members of women's organizations. Nonetheless, "It's 4,500 people. That's enough for me," reported Hite. And it was apparently enough for *Time* magazine, which made her findings—that 70 percent of women married five years or more were having affairs, and that 95 percent of women feel emotionally harassed by the men they love—a cover story (Wallis, 1987). Evidently it didn't matter that on less publicized surveys, *randomly* sampled American women express much higher levels of satisfaction: Half or more report feeling "very happy" or "completely satisfied" with their marriage, and only 3 percent say they are "not at all happy" (Peplau & Gordon, 1985). The moral: Before believing survey findings, consider the sample.

Naturalistic Observation   Watching and recording the behavior of organisms in their natural environment is known as **naturalistic observation.** Studies range from watching chimpanzee societies in the jungle, to observing parent-child interactions in different cultures, to recording students' self-seating patterns in the lunchrooms of desegregated schools.

Such studies do not explain behavior, they simply describe it. Nevertheless, descriptions can be revealing. It was once thought, for example, that tool use is a distinguishing feature of human behavior. However, naturalistic observation has revealed that another tool user is the chimpanzee, which will sometimes insert a stick in a termite mound and then withdraw it, eating the stick's load of termites. Through naturalistic observations we have also learned that culture shapes child-rearing. In the Soviet Union, children are taught to "get along" and "go along" with their group. American child-rearing is more likely to emphasize individual achievement and to reward assertiveness. Naturalistic observation has also revealed that in many desegregated schools, students of different races shun each other outside the classroom (see page 606). (The latter finding implies that unless special efforts are made to engage students in cooperative play and work, school desegregation may not foster social integration.)

Although naturalistic observations do not explain behavior they are a rich source of testable hypotheses.

Naturalistic observation can involve activities as disparate as studying langurs in their natural habitat, as this researcher is doing, or watching children in the playground or classroom.

CORRELATION YIELDS PREDICTION

Describing events is a first step toward predicting them. When changes in one event are accompanied by changes in another, we say the two are correlated. A *correlation* is a statistical measure of relationship: It indicates the extent to which two factors vary together and thus how well one factor *predicts* the second factor. A positive correlation indicates a *direct* relationship, meaning that two factors increase together or decrease together. Thus, if amount of violence viewed on television positively correlates with aggressive social behavior (which it does), then people's TV viewing habits will predict their aggressiveness. A negative correlation—equally predictive—indicates an *inverse* relationship, meaning that as one factor increases the other decreases. Our findings on self-esteem and depression provide a good example of a negative correlation: People who score low on self-esteem tend to score high on depression.

So, does TV violence *cause* aggression and low self-esteem *cause* depression? If, based on the correlational evidence, you assume that

Psychology's statistical tools are described more fully in the Appendix.

they do, you have much company. Perhaps the most irresistible thinking error made both by lay people and by professional psychologists is assuming that correlation proves causation. It does not! If watching TV violence is positively correlated with aggressiveness, does this mean that observing televised violence influences aggressive behavior? It may, but it may also be that aggressive people prefer violent programs. And what about the negative correlation between self-esteem and depression? Perhaps low self-esteem does cause depression. But perhaps instead depression causes people to disparage themselves. Or perhaps self-esteem and depression are causally unrelated; as Figure 1–3 suggests, *both* low self-esteem and depression might be caused by some underlying third factor, such as distressing events or a biological predisposition. Among males, marriage is positively correlated with hair loss—because both are associated with a third factor, age.

The moral: Although correlation provides the basis for prediction, it does not provide an explanation. *Knowing that two events are correlated does not tell us what is causing what.* Remember this principle and you will be the wiser as you read reports of scientific studies in the news and in this book.

Figure 1–3 People low in self-esteem tend to be more depressed than those high in self-esteem. One possible explanation of this negative correlation is that a bad self-image causes depressed feelings. But, as the diagram indicates, other combinations of cause-effect relationships among these factors are possible.

EXPERIMENTATION IDENTIFIES CAUSE AND EFFECT

To isolate cause and effect, psychologists conduct **experiments.** Experiments enable a researcher to focus on the possible effects of a single factor or two *by holding constant those factors not being tested and manipulating the one or two being studied.* If behavior changes when only the manipulated experimental factor is varied, then that factor is having an effect. Note that unlike correlation studies, which uncover naturally occurring relationships, experiments manipulate something to see its effect. To illustrate, consider two experiments, one a 200-year-old study on magnetism and mental health, the other a modern experiment on spectator response to the color of athletic uniforms.

The Experimental Method: A Classic Study   The need for experimentation was recognized by an investigative team headed by Benjamin Franklin while he was the U.S. ambassador to France. The king of France established the Franklin Commission in 1784 to investigate the claims of Franz Anton Mesmer, a physician whose spectacular "magnetic" cures for various disorders had become the talk of Paris (Bowers, 1983). Within two years of his arrival in the city, several thousand Parisians had applied for an opportunity to touch Mesmer's specially prepared metal bars. By transferring "magnetism" to their bodies, the treatment was said to restore their own "animal magnetism" to its proper balance.

Mesmer's procedure produced dramatic reactions, including convulsions and blackouts, followed by a relief of symptoms. "Mesmerized" patients who had lost feeling in a limb regained it; patients who had become paralyzed in some part of their bodies resumed normal functioning. Franklin's commission, however, found no magnetism or electricity in the metal bars. Moreover, the commissioners themselves were not noticeably affected by undergoing the treatments.

Though now more skeptical than ever, the commissioners still had to account for the patients' dramatic reactions—or at least to rule out the effects of magnetism, which their tests had failed to detect. So, they undertook controlled experiments with five people who Mesmer's assistant said were especially susceptible to the magnetism effect. In one experiment, a 12-year-old boy was taken to the garden of Benjamin

Parisians flocked to Franz Anton Mesmer to undertake his "magnetic" cure for a variety of ills. Scientific investigation by the Franklin Commission showed the popular success of Mesmer's treatment to be due to the powers of the human imagination rather than to "animal magnetism."

Franklin's house where the assistant "magnetized" an apricot tree and claimed that anyone who touched it would be cured.

Instead of bringing the boy to this "magnetized" fruit tree, the commissioners exposed him to what we today call *control conditions.* A control condition is identical to the *experimental condition* in all respects except one: The experimental treatment (in this case, contact with the "magnetized" apricot tree) is absent. The control condition of an experiment therefore provides a baseline against which one can compare the effect of the treatment found in the experimental condition. Blindfolded, the boy was led to a tree that he thought was magnetized but which actually was 27 feet away from the "magnetized" apricot tree. Within a minute he was profusely perspiring and coughing. At a second tree, even farther away, he reported a headache. These symptoms grew stronger until at the fourth control tree the boy fainted. When tested, the other subjects also reacted as strongly to the unmagnetized control-condition trees as to the "magnetized" experimental tree. The commissioners had news for the king of France!

The effects of Mesmer's treatments, the commissioners reported, were due not to "animal magnetism," but to the powers of imagination. In solving one riddle, the Franklin Commission had created another: Today, more than 200 years later, these remarkable powers of imaginative involvement are still being explored in research on hypnosis. And so it frequently happens: Scientific inquiry is a voyage of discovery toward a horizon, beyond which yet another horizon often beckons.

The Franklin Commission experiment was simple. It manipulated just one factor, "magnetism." This experimental factor is called the *independent variable* because it can be varied independently of other factors. Experimenters examine the effect of one or more independent variables on some measurable behavior, which is called the *dependent variable* because it can vary depending on what takes place during the experiment. In the Franklin Commission experiment (see Table 1–1), the dependent variable was the subjects' physical symptoms in response to the control (unmagnetized) and to the experimental ("magnetized") trees. A point to remember: Every experiment has at least two different conditions, a comparison or control condition and an experimental condition; in this way it tests the effect of at least one independent variable (the experimental factor) on at least one dependent variable (the response that is measured).

"In solving one discovery we never fail to get an imperfect knowledge of others of which we had no idea before, so that we cannot solve one doubt without creating several new ones."

Joseph Priestley,
Experiments and Observations on Different Kinds of Air, 1775–1786

Table 1–1

THE DESIGN OF THE FRANKLIN COMMISSION EXPERIMENT

(Most experiments are more complex than this, but the logic of the design remains the same.)

Condition	Independent variable	Dependent variable
Experimental condition	Touching "magnetized" tree	Physical symptoms
Control condition	Touching nonmagnetized trees	Physical symptoms

Summary of Experimental Design

Independent variable The experimental factor you manipulate; the treatment itself.

Dependent variable The behavior you are observing; the factor that might be changed by changes in the independent variable.

Experimental condition The condition in which subjects are exposed to the independent variable.

Control condition A condition identical to the experimental one, except subjects are not exposed to the independent variable.

Random Assignment   Some experiments, including the Franklin Commission's, expose all the participants to all the conditions of an experiment, to see how they respond to each. Other experiments assign people to the different conditions using *random assignment.* If enough individuals of different ages and opinions are randomly assigned to two groups, the random assignment will make the two groups approximately equal in age, opinion, and every other characteristic that could possibly affect the results. With random assignment, we can therefore say that if the two groups behave or feel differently at the end of the experiment, it very probably has something to do with the effect of the experiment's independent variable.

The Experimental Method: A Modern Study   To review the essentials of psychological theory and research, let's look at some studies recently conducted by Cornell University psychologists Mark Frank and Thomas Gilovich (1988). Frank and Gilovich noticed that in virtually all cultures from the Orient to Western Europe to central Africa, the color black connotes evil. In movies, the bad guys wear black. It's a "black day" when we get "blackballed" or "blackmailed." Iran's Ayatollah Khomeini reportedly refers to the residence of the American president as the "Black House."

Summarizing these varied observations, Frank and Gilovich proposed a simple theory: Black garb suggests evil, cuing us to perceive people dressed in black as evil and cuing those who wear black to act out their evil image. Knowing that a useful theory must offer predictions that allow us to test it, Frank and Gilovich derived several hypotheses. First, they predicted that people who were unfamiliar with football and hockey would rate the black uniforms of National Football League and National Hockey League teams as more evil. Indeed, for both sports, people rated black uniforms as bad, mean, and aggressive.

Second, Frank and Gilovich hypothesized, and found, a positive correlation between the blackness of a team's uniforms and its total penalties for aggressive play. In all but one of the seventeen seasons between 1970 and 1986, the football teams with black uniforms were penalized a disproportionate number of yards. Likewise, in all sixteen hockey seasons between 1970–1971 and 1985–1986, the teams wearing black uniforms spent more time in the penalty box. Moreover, when the Pittsburgh Penguins switched to black uniforms during the middle of the 1979–1980 season, their penalties increased from an average of 8 minutes per game to 12 minutes. So, in these two sports at least, there definitely has been a correlation between black uniforms and penalized play.

Because a correlation is simply an association between two variables—in this case uniform color and penalties—it cannot prove a cause-effect relationship. Maybe there is no cause-effect connection; that is, maybe organizations wanting an aggressive image simply choose black outfits and hire aggressive players. (For the Hell's Angels, white outfits just won't do.) But can you imagine *possible* causes of this correlation? Frank and Gilovich discerned at least two possibilities: Maybe the correlation results from referees *perceiving* acts by players in black as more violent than similar acts by players not wearing black. Or maybe players who wear black uniforms *enact* the expected tough image.

To evaluate these two possibilities, Frank and Gilovich needed to experiment. They did so first by videotaping two staged football plays in which black- or white-clad defenders drove the ball carrier back sev-

In traditional westerns you can always tell the good guys from the bad guys by the color of their outfits.

eral yards and then threw him to the ground, or hit the ball carrier violently in midair. When the color was taken out of the picture and all jerseys appeared dull gray, raters judged the tackles of the white- and black-clad defenders as equally aggressive. With the color on, the raters (knowledgeable fans and professional referees) were more likely to judge the tackles as illegal when committed by players wearing black. So the uniform color did indeed seem to affect perceptions (see Figure 1–4).

In a second experiment (see Table 1–2), Cornell students came to an experiment on "the psychology of competition." They were randomly assigned to wear either black or white jerseys and then were invited to choose some games. They preferred more aggressive games if they had donned black rather than white jerseys. So, *on average* (such findings tell us only about group trends), wearing black also seems to affect behavior.

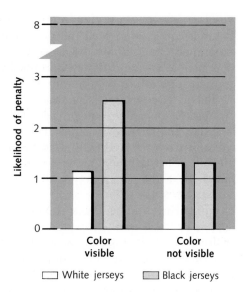

Figure 1–4   Perceptions of violence. People judged videotaped midair tackles as more likely to be declared illegal when enacted by a player wearing black—but only when the color of the jersey was visible.

Table 1–2
THE DESIGN OF THE SECOND FRANK AND GILOVICH EXPERIMENT

	Condition	Independent variable	Dependent variable
Random assignment of subjects	Experimental condition	Black jerseys	Aggressiveness
	Control condition	White jerseys	Aggressiveness

In the *first* Frank and Gilovich experiment, what was the independent variable? The dependent variable? (See page 18.)

Note that in this series of studies a simple *theory*, inspired by everyday observations, generated a *hypothesis* that was confirmed by the *correlation* between uniforms and penalties, which in turn stimulated *experiments* that examined causation. How freely can we generalize the findings? Surely the Catholic clergy and Hassidic Jews are not perceived as aggressive, nor does wearing black cause them to act more aggressively. Frank and Gilovich suspect—but can't know without further research—that the effects occur only in situations involving competition and aggressive confrontation. As usual, the answering of one question leads to the asking of another.

COMMONLY ASKED QUESTIONS ABOUT PSYCHOLOGY

We have discussed psychology's historical roots, its current perspectives, and its research methods. We have seen how case studies, surveys, and naturalistic observations allow us to describe behavior. We have noted that correlational studies assess the extent of relationship between two factors, thus indicating how well we can predict one thing, knowing another. And we have examined the logic that underlies experiments, which use control conditions and random assignment of subjects to isolate the effects of an independent variable on a dependent variable.

This is reasonable preparation for understanding what lies ahead. Yet, knowing this much, students often approach psychology with a mixture of curiosity and apprehension. So before we plunge into the subject matter, let us address some typical questions and concerns.

Aren't Laboratory Experiments Artificial?   Perhaps when reading or hearing a report of psychological research you have wondered whether people's behavior in an artificial laboratory situation has anything to do with their behavior in real life. Does being able to detect the blink of a faint red light in a dark room have anything useful to say about the ability to fly planes at night? Does the fact that people remember best the first and last items in a list of unrelated words tell us anything about our recall of the names of people we meet at a party? After viewing a sexually violent film, does an angered man's increased willingness to push buttons that he thinks deliver electric shocks to a woman really say anything about whether violent pornography makes men more prone to abuse women? Where on earth but a psychological laboratory does someone squint at red lights in a dark room, watch unrelated words flash on a video screen, or push buttons that supposedly deliver an electric shock to someone?

Before you answer, consider the intent of laboratory experiments. Far from considering artificiality to be a problem, the experimenter *intends* the laboratory environment to be a simplified reality where important features of everyday life can be simulated and controlled. Like an aeronautical wind tunnel that recreates atmospheric forces under controlled conditions, an experiment enables a psychologist to recreate psychological forces under controlled conditions. Obviously, deciding whether to push a button that delivers shock is not literally the same as slapping someone in the face. But the principle is the same. The purpose of the experiment is not to recreate the exact behavior that a person may perform in everyday life; rather, it is to evaluate theoretical principles (Mook, 1983). *It is the resulting principles—not the specific findings—that help explain everyday behaviors.* When psychologists apply laboratory research on aggression to actual sexual violence, they are applying theoretical *principles* of aggressive behavior, principles that have been tested and refined in many experiments. Similarly, it is the *principles* of the visual system, developed from countless experiments in artificial settings (such as looking at red lights in the dark), that we cautiously apply to more complex behaviors such as night flying.

It is also the underlying principles, not the specific behaviors, that we assume to be universal. Principles can usually be generalized from one situation or culture to another. To check this assumption, psychologists attempt to replicate their findings: By repeating the essence of a study with new subjects in new situations, psychologists can see whether the process presumably at work generalizes to other people and circumstances. When Warren Jones and his colleagues (1985) replicated loneliness research done on U.S. mainland college students with college students in Puerto Rico, they found that the Puerto Rican students reported more intense feelings of loneliness than did their counterparts on the mainland. Nevertheless, in both cultures, the same processes influenced loneliness. People who were shy, uncertain about their purpose in life, and low in self-esteem reported feeling more lonely. Much the same point could be made regarding racial attitudes, sexual behaviors, and other psychological attributes: Even when the specific attitudes and behaviors vary across cultures, as they often do, the underlying processes are much the same.

"When a man has discovered why men in Bond Street wear black hats he will at the same moment discover why men in Timbuctoo wear red feathers."
G. K. Chesterton,
Heretics, 1909

What Do Animal Experiments Have to Do with People?   Many psychologists study animals because they find animals inherently interesting and want to discover what their behavior can tell us about them. Psychologists also study animals because such studies can tell us about ourselves. The human physiological system is like that of many other animals. That is why animal experimentation has led to treatments for human diseases—insulin for diabetes, vaccines to prevent polio and rabies, transplants to replace defective organs. Likewise, the processes by which humans see, exhibit emotion, and become obese operate in rats and monkeys. To discover more about the basics of human learning, researchers are even studying sea slugs. To understand how a combustion engine works you would do better to study a lawn mower's engine than a Cadillac's. Humans, like Cadillacs, are more complex, but it is precisely the simplicity of the sea slug's nervous system that makes it so revealing.

Is It Ethical to Experiment on Animals?   Each year, some 20 million animals are used in scientific research in America and 30 million more are used in European experiments (Dickson, 1986; Fisher, 1986a). All told, about 7 percent of the studies compiled by *Psychological Abstracts* used animals, 95 percent of which are rats, mice, or birds. About 10 percent of these animal studies involve electric shock (Coile & Miller, 1984; Gallup & Suarez, 1985).

During the 1980s, a growing animal rights movement has protested the use of animals in psychological, biological, and medical research. To rally support for a protest at one American Psychological Association convention, Mobilization for Animals, a network of some 400 animal protection organizations, declared that in psychological experiments animals are shocked "until they lose the ability to even scream in pain," "deprived of food and water to suffer and die slowly from hunger and thirst," "put in total isolation chambers until they are driven insane or even die from despair and terror," and made "the victims of extreme pain and stress, inflicted upon them out of idle curiosity." After analyzing every animal research article published in the American Psychological Association journals during the preceding 5 years, psychologists Caroline Coile and Neal Miller (1984) found not one study in which any of these allegations was true. Even when shock was used, it usually was of a mild intensity that humans can easily endure on their fingers.

Moreover, say researchers, does anyone who cares about the millions of people who are alive thanks to animal research wish that scientists had heeded the advice of the president of the American Anti-Vivisection Society: that animals not be used in an experiment if the experiment "is not for the benefit of the animals involved" (Goodman, 1982)? How many of us would have attacked Pasteur's experiments with rabies, which in causing some dogs to suffer led to a vaccine that spared millions of dogs and people from agonizing death? And would we really wish to deprive ourselves of the knowledge, gleaned from psychological research with animals, that has led to new methods of training retarded children, relieving fears and depression, and controlling stress-related pain and disease?

Out of the heated debate on this subject, two issues emerge. The basic one is whether it is right to place the well-being of humans above that of animals. In experiments on stress and cancer, is it right that mice get tumors so that people might not? Defenders of research on animals argue that anyone who has eaten a hamburger, tolerated hunt-

Answer to question on page 16: The independent variable is the color of the player's jersey; the dependent variable is the rater's assessment of the legality of the play.

Is it right that animals be used to advance our understanding of how humans function? For animal rights activists, no purpose justifies hurting, frightening, or (as here) manipulating an animal. However, most psychologists and medical researchers believe that animal research is necessary and ethically justified so long as strict standards for the animals' care are observed and no unnecessary pain is inflicted.

"I believe that to prevent, cripple, or needlessly complicate the research that can relieve animal and human suffering is profoundly inhuman, cruel, and immoral."
Psychologist Neal Miller (1983b)

ing and fishing, or supported the extermination of pests that destroy crops or carry plague has already agreed that, yes, it is sometimes permissible to sacrifice animals for the sake of human well-being. Acts that appear unjustifiable in themselves may be excusable if they are essential means to a justifiable end, they maintain.

Assuming that human life is given first priority, the second issue is what priority should be given to the well-being of animals. With what safeguards should they be protected? Researchers generally agree that pointless exploitation of animals is *not* justified. They may stop short of agreeing with Michael Fox, vice president of the bioethics division of the Humane Society of the United States, that scientists "have no God-given right to inflict pain on animals" (Fields, 1984). But most researchers today agree that the needless suffering of animals is inexcusable. They therefore welcome the Animal Welfare Act updated by Congress in 1985 and the regulations and laboratory inspections that enforce it. And animals have themselves benefited: Psychological research has helped improve the care of animals in laboratories and zoos. By demonstrating our behavioral kinship with animals, experiments have served to increase our empathy with them. At its best, a psychology that is concerned for humans and sensitive to animals can serve the welfare of both.

Is It Ethical to Experiment on People?   If the image of people delivering what they think are electric shocks troubles you, you may find it reassuring that most psychological research involves no such stress. Blinking lights, flashing words, and pleasant social interactions are the rule.

But, occasionally, researchers do temporarily stress or deceive people. This is only done when judged essential to achieving a justifiable end, such as understanding and controlling violent behavior or studying the effects of mood swings. If the participants in such experiments knew all there was to know about the experiment beforehand, either the procedures would be ineffective or the participants, wanting to be helpful, might try to confirm the researchers' predictions.

Ethical principles developed by the American Psychological Association urge investigators (1) to obtain the consent of potential participants, explaining enough for them to be able to make an informed decision about whether to take part, (2) to protect participants from harm and discomfort, (3) to treat information about individual participants confidentially, and (4) to explain the research fully afterward. Moreover, in most universities today research proposals are screened by an ethics committee that safeguards participants' well-being.

Is Psychology Free of Value Judgments?   Psychology is definitely not value-free. Researchers' values influence their choice of research topics—whether to study worker productivity or worker morale, sex discrimination or sex differences, conformity or independence. Values can also color "the facts." Our preconceptions can bias our observations and interpretations; sometimes we see what we are predisposed to see. Even the words we use to describe a phenomenon can reflect our values. Whether we label sex acts we do not practice as "perversions" or as "sexual variations" conveys a value judgment. The same is true in everyday speech, as when one person's "terrorists" are another person's "freedom fighters." Both in and out of psychology, labels describe and labels evaluate.

Popular applications of psychology also contain hidden values.

"Please do not forget those of us who suffer from incurable diseases or disabilities who hope for a cure through research that requires the use of animals."
Paraplegic psychologist
Dennis Feeney (1987)

"The greatness of a nation can be judged by the way its animals are treated."
Mahatma Gandhi, 1869–1948

People interpret ambiguous information to fit their preconceptions.

When people defer to "professional" guidance about how to live— how to raise children, how to achieve self-fulfillment, what to do with sexual feelings, how to get ahead at work—they are accepting value-laden advice. A science of behavior can help us reach our goals, but it cannot decide our goals for us.

Aren't Psychology's Theories Mere Common Sense?   Perhaps the most common criticism of psychology is that it merely documents the obvious by dressing in jargon what people already know, prompting the reaction, "So what else is new—you get paid for this?"

In several experiments, psychologist Baruch Fischhoff and others (Slovic & Fischhoff, 1977; Wood, 1979) have found that, actually, events seem far less obvious and predictable beforehand than in hindsight. Once people are told the outcome of an experiment, or of a historical episode, it suddenly seems less surprising to them than it is to people who are asked to guess the outcome. Finding out that something has happened makes it seem inevitable. Psychologists now call this 20/20 hindsight vision the *I-knew-it-all-along phenomenon,* or *hindsight bias.*

This phenomenon can be demonstrated by giving half the members of a group some purported psychological finding and the other half an opposite result. For example, imagine that you are told, "Psychologists have found that separation weakens romantic attraction. As the old adage says, 'Out of sight, out of mind.'" Could you imagine why this might be? Most people can, and nearly all will then report that the finding is unsurprising.

What if you are told the opposite: "Psychologists have found that separation intensifies romantic attraction. As the old adage says, 'Absence makes the heart grow fonder.'" People given this result can also easily explain it and overwhelmingly see *it* as unsurprising common sense. Obviously, when both a statement and its opposite can seem like common sense, there is a problem.

Nevertheless, it would be surprising if many of psychology's findings had *not* been anticipated. As the English philosopher Alfred North Whitehead (1861–1947) once remarked, "Everything important has been said before." Regardless of whether psychological studies reveal that "you're never too old to learn" or that "you can't teach an old dog new tricks," their findings will have been anticipated. Should a psychologist discover that we are attracted to people whose traits are different from our own, someone is sure to chortle, "Of course! My grandmother could have told you that 'opposites attract.'" Should it instead turn out that we are attracted to people whose traits are similar to our own, the same person may remind the psychologist, "Everyone knows that 'birds of a feather flock together.'" Thus the problem with common sense is not that it is necessarily wrong (in centuries of casual observation some wisdom is bound to have accumulated),but that it is so often a judgment we make after we know the results.

Even the keen observations and ingenious deductions of Arthur Conan Doyle's detective Sherlock Holmes would sometimes fail to impress his clients, once they understood them. "Anything seems commonplace, once explained," noted his friend Dr. Watson. "When I hear you give your reasons, the thing always appears to me to be so ridiculously simple that I could easily do it myself, though at each successive instance of your reasoning I am baffled, until you explain your process." (You may have noticed this hindsight phenomenon when reading or watching a mystery: The solution, once revealed, seems obvious.)

"It is doubtless impossible to approach any human problem with a mind free from bias."
Simone de Beauvoir,
The Second Sex, 1953

"Life is lived forwards, but understood backwards."
Søren Kierkegaard, 1813–1855

But then again, sometimes psychological findings *do* jolt our common sense. Throughout this book we will see how research has both inspired and overturned popular ideas—about aging, about sleep and dreams, about personality assessment—and how it has surprised us with discoveries about how the brain's chemical messengers control our moods and memories, about animal abilities, about the effects of stress on our body's capacity to fight diseases. If some people see psychology as mere common sense, others have an opposite concern—that psychology is becoming dangerously powerful.

Isn't Psychology Potentially Dangerous? Students often approach psychology with two apprehensions. First, they are concerned that psychology will reveal them to be mere robots. Are we driven by forces beyond our control? Are we therefore devoid of real choice and able to evade responsibility for our actions? In fact, the human image that emerges from much of contemporary psychology is not that of a robot; it is instead the picture of a highly evolved, self-conscious agent whose thoughts and perceptions include a sense of personal choice and control.

Second, students know that psychologists attempt to describe, explain, and predict behavior and mental processes. In their apprehension they wonder whether psychology can also be used to manipulate people. Might it become the tool of someone seeking to create a totalitarian *Brave New World* or *Nineteen Eighty-Four*?

Knowledge is a power that, like all powers, can be used for good or evil. Nuclear power has been used to light up cities—and to destroy them. Persuasive power has been used to educate people—and to deceive them. The power of mind-altering drugs has been used to restore sanity—and to destroy it.

Although it has the power to deceive, psychology strives to enlighten. Psychologists are exploring ways to enhance moral development, perceptual accuracy, learning, creativity, and compassion. And psychology speaks to many of the world's great problems—war, overpopulation, prejudice, and crime—all of which are problems of attitudes and behavior. Psychology also speaks to humanity's deepest longings—for love, for happiness, even for food and water. Psychology cannot address all the great questions of life, but it speaks to some mighty important ones. So read on, and enjoy.

SUMMING UP

WHAT IS PSYCHOLOGY?

Psychology's Roots Beginning with the first psychological laboratory, founded in 1879 by German philosopher and physiologist Wilhelm Wundt, psychology's modern roots can be found in many disciplines and countries. Psychology's historic perspectives and current activities lead us to define the field as the science of behavior and mental processes.

Perspectives on Behavior and Mental Processes There are many disciplines that study human nature, of which

psychology is one. Within psychology, the biological, behavioral, psychoanalytic, humanistic, and cognitive perspectives are complementary. Each has its own purposes, questions, and limits; together they provide a fuller understanding of mind and behavior.

Basic and Applied Psychology Psychologists' activities are widely varied, ranging from studies of the links between biology and behavior, to experimental studies of perception and memory, to the diagnoses and therapies of clinical psychology.

SCIENTIFIC ATTITUDES AND APPROACHES

Skepticism and Humility Scientific inquiry requires a mixture of skeptical scrutiny of competing ideas and humility before nature.

The Scientific Method Observations stimulate the construction of theories, which organize the observations and imply predictive hypotheses. These hypotheses (predictions) are then tested to validate and refine the theory and to suggest practical applications.

PSYCHOLOGY'S METHODS AND AIMS

To describe, predict, and explain behavior and mental processes, psychologists use three basic research methods: observation, correlation, and experimentation.

Observation Yields Description Through case studies, surveys, and naturalistic observations, psychologists observe and describe phenomena.

Correlation Yields Prediction The strength of relationship between one factor and another is expressed in their correlation. Knowing how closely two things are correlated tells us how much one predicts the other. But correlation is only a measure of relationship; it does not indicate cause and effect.

Experimentation Identifies Cause and Effect To examine cause-and-effect relationships more directly, psychologists conduct experiments. By constructing a miniature reality, experimenters can manipulate one or two factors and discover how these independent variables affect a particular behavior, the dependent variable. In many experiments, control is achieved by randomly assigning people either to be experimental subjects who are exposed to the treatment, or control subjects who are not.

COMMONLY ASKED QUESTIONS ABOUT PSYCHOLOGY

Aren't Laboratory Experiments Artificial? By intentionally creating a controlled, artificial environment, experimenters aim to test theoretical principles. These principles help us to understand, describe, explain, and predict everyday behaviors.

What Do Animal Experiments Have to Do with People? Some psychologists study animals out of an interest in animal behavior. Others do so because knowledge of the physiological and psychological processes of animals enables them to better understand the similar processes that operate in humans.

Is It Ethical to Experiment on Animals? Only about 7 percent of all psychological experiments involve animals, mostly rats, mice, and birds. In only a few of these experiments do they experience pain. Nevertheless, opposition to animal experimentation by animal rights groups has raised two important issues: Is the temporary suffering of even a few animals in medical and psychological research justified if it leads to the relief of human suffering? And if indeed human well-being is given first priority, what safeguards should protect animal well-being?

Is It Ethical to Experiment on People? Occasionally researchers temporarily stress or deceive people in order to learn something important. Professional ethical standards provide guidelines concerning the treatment of human subjects.

Is Psychology Free of Value Judgments? Psychology is not value-free. Psychologists' own values can influence their choice of research topics, their theories and observations, their labels for behavior, and their professional advice.

Aren't Psychology's Theories Mere Common Sense? Experiments reveal a hindsight bias called the I-knew-it-all-along phenomenon: Learning the outcome of a study can make it seem like obvious common sense. But things seldom seem so obvious before the results are known.

Isn't Psychology Potentially Dangerous? Knowledge is power that can be used for good or evil. Applications of psychology's principles have so far been mostly for the good, and psychology addresses some of humanity's greatest problems and deepest longings.

TERMS AND CONCEPTS TO REMEMBER

behavioral perspective Emphasizes environmental influences on observable behaviors.

biological perspective Emphasizes the influences of heredity and physiology upon our behaviors, emotions, memories, and sensory experiences.

biological psychology A branch of psychology concerned with the links between biology and behavior. (Some biological psychologists call themselves *behavioral neuroscientists, neuropsychologists, physiological psychologists,* or *biopsychologists.*)

case study An observational technique in which one person is studied in depth in the hopes of revealing things universally true.

clinical psychology A branch of psychology involving the assessment and treatment of those with psychological disorders.

cognitive perspective Emphasizes how we process, store, and retrieve information and how we use it to reason and solve problems.

control condition The condition of an experiment in

which the experimental treatment is absent; serves as a comparison for evaluating the effect of the treatment.

correlation A statistical index that indicates the extent to which two factors vary together and thus how well one factor can be predicted from knowing the other.

dependent variable The variable that is being measured; in an experiment, the variable that may change in response to manipulations of the independent variable.

developmental psychology A branch of psychology that studies physical, cognitive, and social change throughout the life cycle.

experiment A research method in which the investigator manipulates one or more factors (independent variables) to observe their effect on some behavior (the dependent variable) while controlling other relevant factors.

experimental condition The condition of an experiment in which subjects are exposed to the treatment, that is, to the independent variable.

general experimental psychology A branch of psychology that uses experimental methods to discover principles of behavior, such as those underlying sensation and perception, learning and memory, motivation and emotion.

humanistic perspective Emphasizes people's capacities for choice and growth; studies people's subjective experiences.

hypothesis A testable prediction, often derived from a theory.

I-knew-it-all-along phenomenon The tendency to believe one would have foreseen how something turned out, *after* learning the outcome. (Also known as *hindsight bias*.)

independent variable The experimental factor; the manipulated variable whose effect is being studied.

industrial/organizational psychology A branch of psychology that studies behavior in the workplace and the marketplace; it seeks to enhance the former and influence the latter.

naturalistic observation Observing and recording behavior in naturally occurring situations, without trying to manipulate and control the situation.

personality psychology A branch of psychology that studies how individuals are influenced by relatively enduring inner factors.

psychiatry A branch of medicine dealing with psychological disorders practiced by physicians and sometimes involving medical (for example, drug) treatments as well as psychological therapy.

psychoanalytic perspective Builds on Freud's ideas that behavior arises from unconscious drives and conflicts, many of which may stem from childhood experiences.

psychology The science of behavior and mental processes.

random assignment Assigning subjects to experimental and control conditions by chance, thus minimizing preexisting differences between those assigned to the different groups.

random sample A sample that is representative of some larger group because every person has an equal chance of being included.

replication Repeating the essence of an experiment, usually with different subjects in different situations, to see whether the basic finding generalizes to other people and circumstances.

social psychology The study of how people influence and relate to one another.

survey A technique for ascertaining the self-reported attitudes or behaviors of people by questioning a representative (random) sample of them.

theory An integrated set of principles that organizes, explains, and predicts observations.

FOR FURTHER READING

> The best effect of any book is that it excites the reader to self-activity.
>   Thomas Carlyle, 1795–1881

At the conclusion of each chapter I suggest several books or articles you could explore for further information.

For many students, the most helpful supplementary source will be *Discovering Psychology* by Richard Straub, the innovative study guide that accompanies this text. It begins with a helpful summary of how best to study this (or any other) textbook. For each text chapter, *Discovering Psychology* provides learning objectives, a programmed review of the chapter, multiple-choice practice quizzes (with answers—including explanations of what is wrong with the incorrect choices), and a discussion of key terms. My students who have trouble with exams find it a valuable study aid—almost like a tutor.

For an informative free booklet that describes psychology's fields and careers, you can write the American Psychological Association, 1200 Seventeenth Street N.W., Washington, D.C. 20036, and request ''Careers in Psychology.''

Psychology Today magazine provides entertaining and readable information about current trends and research in psychology.

CHAPTER 2

Biological Roots of Behavior

On the time scale of human existence, the last 150 years are only a few ticks of the clock. But that's how recently a scientific understanding of the biological roots of our behavior began to emerge. We have come far since the early 1800s, when a German physician named Franz Gall invented an ill-fated theory, called *phrenology,* which held that bumps on the skull could reveal our mental abilities and character traits.

Despite its wrong-headedness, phrenology did help focus attention on the idea that various brain regions might have specific functions. In little more than a century, we have also realized that the body is composed of cells, among which are nerve cells that conduct electricity and "talk" to one another by sending chemical messages across a tiny gap that separates them, and that specific areas of the brain serve specific functions (though not the functions Gall supposed). You and I are privileged to be living at a time when scientific discoveries about the most basic aspects of our biology and behavior are occurring at an exhilarating pace.

Throughout this book you will find examples of how our biology underlies our thoughts, emotions, and behaviors. Every idea, every mood, every memory, every urge that you or I have ever experienced is fundamentally a biological phenomenon. By studying how the nervous system and brain operate, scientists are gaining new clues to sleep and dreams, depression and schizophrenia, hunger and sex, stress and disease. We therefore begin our study of psychology with a look at its biological foundation.

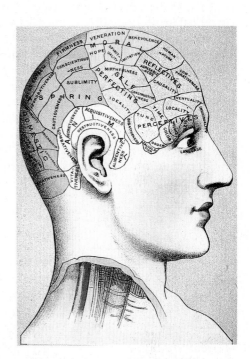

In his theory called *phrenology,* Gall speculated that the brain's functions were linked to various bumps on the skull.

THE NERVOUS SYSTEM

Our *nervous system* is the electrochemical communication system that enables us to think, feel, and behave. For scientists, it is a happy fact of nature that the nervous systems of humans and other animals operate similarly. All animals with nervous systems have essentially identical building blocks, called *neurons,* or nerve cells. Neurons are organized in remarkably similar ways, so similar, in fact, that small samples of brain tissue from a person and a monkey are indistinguishable. These facts allow researchers to study simple animals, such as squids and sea slugs, to discover how neurons operate and communicate, and to study mammals' brains in order to understand the organization of our own brains. Human brains are more complex, but our nervous systems operate according to the same principles that govern the rest of the animal world.

DIVISIONS OF THE NERVOUS SYSTEM

The human nervous system is complex beyond comprehension, yet its basic organization is simple (Figure 2–1). It consists of two systems, the *central nervous system (CNS),* which includes all the neurons in the brain and spinal cord, and the *peripheral nervous system (PNS),* which connects the central nervous system to the rest of the body.

The peripheral nervous system has two components, the somatic and the autonomic nervous systems. The *somatic nervous system* transmits *sensory input* (touch, temperature, taste, for example) to the CNS from the outside world and directs *motor output,* the voluntary movements of our skeletal muscles. As you reach the bottom of the next page, the somatic nervous system will report to your brain the current state of your skeletal muscles and carry instructions back, triggering your hand to turn the page.

The *autonomic nervous system* controls the glands and the muscles of our internal organs. It is to the central nervous system roughly what an automatic pilot is to a pilot. It can be overridden. But usually it operates on its own (autonomously) to control our internal functioning, including our heartbeat, digestion, and glandular activity.

The autonomic nervous system is a dual system (Figure 2–2). One part, the *sympathetic nervous system,* arouses. If something alarms or enrages you, the sympathetic system will accelerate your heartbeat,

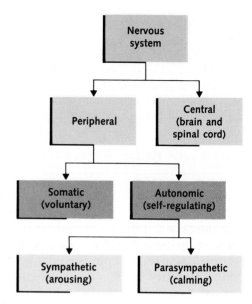

Figure 2–1 The divisions of the human nervous system.

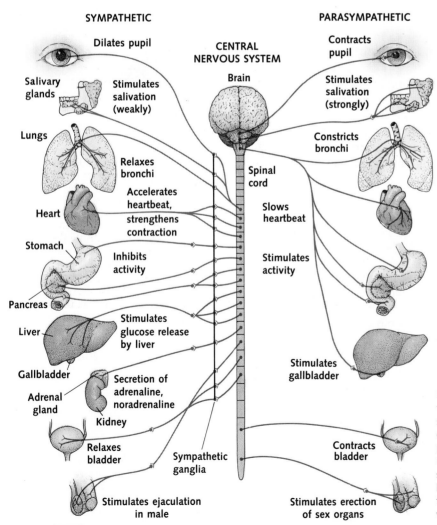

Figure 2–2 The autonomic nervous system controls the more autonomous (or self-regulating) internal functions, and consists of the sympathetic and parasympathetic divisions. The sympathetic system usually arouses and the parasympathetic system calms. Most organs are affected by both divisions. For example, sympathetic stimulation accelerates heartbeat while parasympathetic stimulation slows it.

slow your digestion, raise your blood sugar, dilate your arteries, and produce perspiration to cool you, making you alert and ready for action. When the emergency is over, the ***parasympathetic nervous system*** produces the opposite effects. In general, it calms you down, by decreasing your heartbeat, lowering your blood sugar, and so forth. In everyday situations, the sympathetic and parasympathetic nervous systems work together to keep us in a steady internal state.

NEURONS AND THEIR MESSAGES

Neural Pathways   Information travels in the nervous system through three types of neurons. The ***sensory*** ("afferent," meaning inward) ***neurons*** transmit information from the body's tissues inward to the central nervous system, where the information is processed. This processing usually involves a second class of neurons, the ***interneurons*** of the brain and spinal cord. Instructions from the central nervous system are then relayed to the body's tissues via the ***motor*** ("efferent," meaning outward) ***neurons.***

To illustrate, consider the simplest of neural pathways, those that govern our ***reflexes,*** our automatic responses to stimuli. A simple reflex pathway is composed of a single sensory neuron and a single motor neuron, which often communicate through an interneuron. One such pathway is involved in the pain reflex (Figure 2–3). When your fingers touch a hot stove, neural activity excited by the heat travels via sensory neurons to interneurons in your spinal cord. These interneurons respond by activating motor neurons to the muscles in your arm, causing you to jerk your hand away.

Because the simple pain reflex pathway runs through the spinal cord and out, you instantly jerk your hand from the hot stove *before* your brain receives and responds to the information that causes you to feel pain. Information travels to and from the brain mostly by way of the spinal cord. Were the top of your spinal cord to be severed, you would not feel such pain. Or pleasure. If a person's spinal cord is severed, the person loses all sensation and voluntary movement in the body regions whose sensory and motor neurons enter the spinal cord

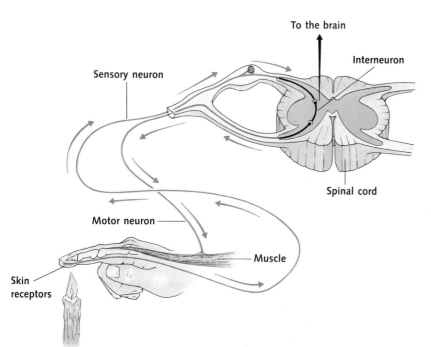

Figure 2–3   In this simple reflex, information from the skin receptors travels via a sensory neuron to an interneuron in the spinal cord, which sends a signal to the muscles in the arm via a motor neuron. Because this reflex involves only the spinal cord, you would jerk your hand away from the candle flame *before* your brain had responded to the information that caused you to experience pain.

below the injury. Male paraplegics (whose legs are paralyzed) are usually capable of an erection (a simple reflex) if their genitals are stimulated, but, depending on where the spinal cord is severed, they may have no genital feeling. To feel bodily pain or pleasure, the sensory information must reach the brain.

Generating a Neural Impulse   Each neuron consists of a cell body and one or more branchlike fibers (Figure 2–4). The fibers are of two types, the *dendrites*, which receive information from sensory receptors or other neurons, and the *axons*, which transmit it to other neurons. Unlike the short dendrites, axons may project through the body up to several feet. The cell body and axon of a motor neuron can be thought of as roughly on the scale of a basketball attached to a rope 4 miles long. Some axons are insulated by a layer of fatty cells, called the *myelin sheath*, which looks somewhat like sausage links separated from each other by tiny gaps. The sheath helps speed the neural, or nerve, impulses.

"If the nervous system be cut off between the brain and other parts, the experiences of those other parts are nonexistent for the mind. The eye is blind, the ear deaf, the hand insensible and motionless."
William James,
Principles of Psychology, 1890

"Dendrite" is derived from the Greek word *dendron*, meaning tree.

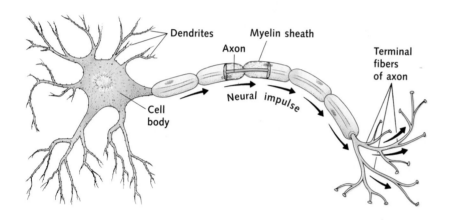

Figure 2–4   A simplified diagram of a motor neuron. Each neuron consists of a cell body and one or more branchlike extensions or fibers. Information from sensory receptors or other neurons is received by the dendrites and cell body and is summed in the cell body; if the threshold is exceeded, the neuron fires an electrical impulse down its axon, whose terminal fibers transmit this outgoing information to other neurons or to the body's muscles or glands.

A neural impulse is generated when a neuron is stimulated in some way—by pressure, by heat, by light, or by messages from adjacent neurons. The neuron, a miniature decision-making device, receives signals on its dendrites and cell body from hundreds or even thousands of other neurons. The signals are combined in the cell body, and an impulse is triggered if the sum of all the individual signals exceeds a minimum intensity, called the *threshold.* (The signals may be either positive—*excitatory*—or negative—*inhibitory*.) If the threshold is reached, the neuron fires an electrical impulse down its axon, which branches into junctions with the body's muscles and glands or with the dendrites and cell bodies of hundreds or thousands of other neurons.

Increasing the stimulus above the threshold, however, will not increase the intensity of the impulse. The neuron's reaction is therefore called an *all-or-none response;* neurons, like guns, either fire or they don't. Nor does the strength of the stimulus affect the speed of the impulse, which, depending on the type of fiber, travels at speeds ranging from a sluggish 2 miles per hour to a breakneck 200 miles or more per hour along the myelinated axons. But even this top speed is 3 million times slower than the speed of electricity through a wire. That helps to explain why, unlike the nearly instantaneous reactions of a high-speed computer, it takes a quarter-second for you to react to a sudden event, such as a child darting in front of your car.

How then is information about the intensity of a stimulus transmitted? How do we distinguish between a gentle touch and a firm hug?

You can remember the dendrite-axon sequence as DA—District Attorney.

Although a strong stimulus cannot trigger a stronger or faster impulse in a neuron, it can trigger more neurons to fire and to fire more often.

How Do Nerve Cells Communicate?   Neurons interweave so intricately that even with a microscope it is hard to see where one neuron ends and another begins. A hundred years ago many scientists believed that the branching axons of one cell were actually fused with the dendrites of another in an uninterrupted fabric. But then British physiologist Sir Charles Sherrington (1857–1952) noticed that neural impulses were taking more time to travel a reflex pathway than they should. Sherrington inferred that there must be a brief interruption in the transmission.

We now know that the axon terminal of one neuron is indeed separated from the receiving neuron by a tiny gap less than a millionth of an inch wide. This junction is called the *synapse* or *synaptic gap.* To the Nobel laureate Spanish neuroanatomist Santiago Ramón y Cajal (1832–1934), these near-unions of neurons were one of nature's marvels— "protoplasmic kisses," he called them. How does the nerve impulse execute the protoplasmic kiss? How does it cross the tiny synaptic gap? The answer has been one of the most important scientific discoveries of our age.

By an elegant mechanism, the axon's knoblike terminals release chemical messengers, called *neurotransmitters,* into the synaptic gap (see Figure 2–5). Within 1/10,000th of a second, the neurotransmitter molecules cross the gap and bind to receptor sites on the receiving neuron—as precisely as a key fits a lock. For an instant, the neurotransmitter unlocks tiny "gates" at the receiving site, allowing ions (electrically charged atoms) to enter the receiving neuron, thereby influencing its "decision" to fire.

"All information processing in the brain involves neurons 'talking to' each other at synapses."
   Solomon H. Snyder (1984a)

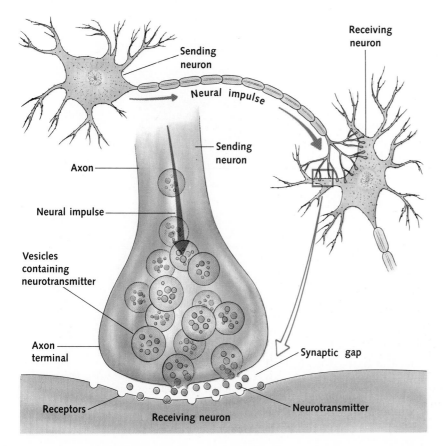

Figure 2–5   Electrical impulses travel from one neuron to another across a junction known as the synaptic gap. When a signal reaches the axon terminal, it stimulates the release of neurotransmitter molecules from the sacs, or *vesicles,* containing them. These molecules cross the synaptic gap and bind to receptor sites on the receiving neuron. This allows ions—electrically charged atoms—to enter the receiving neuron, thereby influencing its rate of firing.

If this influence is excitatory it will increase the likelihood of the neuron's firing; if inhibitory, it will decrease the likelihood. (Most neurons have a resting rate of random firing that can be increased or decreased by input from other neurons and by chemicals that affect their sensitivity.) Roughly speaking, the neuron is democratic: If more excitatory than inhibitory messages are being received, the cell fires more often. More electrical impulses flash down the axon, releasing more packets of neurotransmitters, which zip across their synaptic gaps to other cells.

The discovery of over fifty different neurotransmitters has created a neuroscience revolution. Why are there so many neural messengers? Are certain neurotransmitters found only in specific places? What are their effects? Can they be increased or diminished through drugs or nutritional changes? Could such changes affect our moods, memories, or mental abilities? These are questions that intrigue neuroscience researchers and fascinate those of us who are their spectators.

We now know that a particular neuron terminal generally produces only one neurotransmitter, that a particular neural pathway in the brain may use only one or two neurotransmitters, and that particular neurotransmitters may have particular effects on behavior and emotions. For example, one of the best understood neurotransmitters, *acetylcholine (ACh)*, is the messenger at every junction between a motor neuron and muscle. With powerful electron microscopes, neurobiologists can magnify thinly sliced specimens of the synaptic tissue enough to see the sacs that store and release ACh molecules. When ACh is released to the muscle cells, the muscle contracts.

If the transmission of ACh is blocked, muscles cannot contract, a fact made dramatically clear by the effects of curare, a poison that certain South American Indians put on the tips of their darts. When introduced into the body, curare occupies and blocks ACh receptor sites, leaving the neurotransmitter unable to affect the muscles. The result: total paralysis. Botulin, a poison that can form in improperly canned food, causes paralysis by blocking the release of ACh. Some nerve gases and insecticides similarly interfere with ACh transmission. By contrast, the venom of the black widow spider causes a flood of ACh to be released, inducing violent muscle contractions.

Therapeutic drugs, such as those used to alleviate depression, similarly influence neurotransmission. They do so sometimes by mimicking a natural neurotransmitter and blocking receptor sites, and sometimes by hampering a neurotransmitter's natural breakdown or its reuptake—the process by which brain cells take the molecules out of circulation.

One of the most exciting discoveries about neurotransmitters occurred at Johns Hopkins University. Candace Pert and Solomon Snyder (1973) attached a radioactive tracer to morphine, allowing them to observe exactly where in an animal's brain it was taken up. Morphine, an opiate, elevates mood and eases pain, and, sure enough, Pert and Snyder discovered that the morphine was taken up by receptor sites in areas that have been linked to mood and pain sensations.

It was difficult to imagine why the brain would contain these "opiate receptors" unless it had its own naturally occurring opiates. Why would the brain have a chemical lock, unless it also had a key that would fit it? Soon researchers confirmed that the brain does indeed contain neurotransmitter molecules very similar to morphine. Named **endorphins** (short for *end*ogenous [produced within] m*orphin*e), these natural opiates are released in response to pain and vigorous exercise (Farrell & others, 1982; Lagerweij & others, 1984). They have therefore

The increased release of pain-killing endorphins contributes to "runner's high," that feeling of increased emotional well-being that sometimes comes to long-distance runners.

been proposed as an explanation for all sorts of good feelings, such as the pain-killing effects of acupuncture, the "runner's high," and the indifference to pain in some badly injured people, such as David Livingstone reported in his 1857 *Missionary Travels:*

> I heard a shout. Starting, and looking half round, I saw the lion just in the act of springing upon me. I was upon a little height, he caught my shoulder as he sprang, and we both came to the ground below together. Growling horribly close to my ear, he shook me as a terrier does a rat. The shock produced a stupor similar to that which seems to be felt by a mouse after the first shake of the cat. It caused a sort of dreaminess in which there was no sense of pain nor feeling of terror, though [I was] quite conscious of all that was happening. . . . This peculiar state is probably produced in all animals killed by the carnivora; and if so, is a merciful provision by our benevolent creator for lessening the pain of death.

If indeed the endorphins alleviate pain and boost mood, could we flood the brain with artificial opiates, thereby intensifying the brain's own "feel good" chemistry? One problem seems to be that when the brain is flooded with such opiate drugs as heroin and morphine, it may stop producing its own natural opiates. Thus, when the drug is withdrawn, the brain may be deprived of any form of opiate. The result, according to this theory, is pain and agony that persists either until the brain resumes production of its natural opiates or until more of the drug is administered.

This illustrates the risks inherent in trying to improve our mental state by altering our brain's chemistry. Alert to these dangers, researchers try to understand the effects of specific neurotransmitters by experimenting first with animals and only then verifying the results on people. In this way they are discovering how neurotransmitter abnormalities are linked with depression and schizophrenia.

THE ENDOCRINE SYSTEM

Chemical messengers travel not just between nerve cells but throughout the body. *Hormones* are chemical messengers produced in one tissue that travel through the bloodstream and affect another tissue. The best known hormones are secreted by the glands of the *endocrine system* (see Figure 2–6), the second of the body's communication systems. Unlike the speedy nervous system, which zips messages from eyes to brain to hand in a fraction of a second, endocrine messages use the slow lane: Several seconds or more may elapse before the bloodstream carries a hormone from an endocrine gland to its target tissue.

Hormones influence many aspects of our lives, from growth to reproduction, from metabolism to mood, keeping everything in balance while responding to stress, exertion, and internal thoughts (Clark & Gelman, 1987). In a moment of danger, for example, the autonomic nervous system will order the *adrenal glands* atop the kidneys to release *epinephrine* and *norepinephrine* (also called *adrenaline* and *noradrenaline*), hormones that increase heart rate, blood pressure, and blood sugar, providing us with a surge of energy. When the emergency passes, the hormones—and the feelings of excitement—linger awhile. If stress occurs repeatedly, surging hormones may, as we will see in a later chapter, depress the body's immune system, one of our primary defenses against disease.

Our most influential gland is the *pituitary,* a pea-sized structure at the base of the brain. One of its hormones has the important task of regulating body growth. Too little of this hormone will produce a

Physician Lewis Thomas on the endorphins: "There it is, a biologically universal act of mercy. I cannot explain it, except to say that I would have put it in had I been around at the very beginning, sitting as a member of a planning committee."
The Youngest Science, 1983

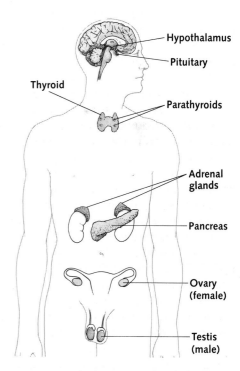

Figure 2–6 The body's major endocrine glands. The pituitary releases hormones that, in turn, regulate the hormone secretions of the thyroid, the adrenal cortex (the outer layer of the adrenal gland), and the sex glands. The pituitary's master is the hypothalamus, which is sensitive to the concentration of circulating substances in the blood, including hormones. The hypothalamus thus is a major link between the nervous system and the endocrine system.

dwarf; too much, a giant. Since 1985, genetic engineering has made possible the commercial production of the pituitary growth hormone, making it available to children who suffer dwarfism (Kolata, 1986a).

The pituitary used to be called the "master gland" because some of its secretions influence the release of hormones by other endocrine glands. But these other glands may also be influenced by the chemistry of the blood. For example, when you eat a candy bar the increasing sugar in your bloodstream directly triggers the pancreas to release the hormone insulin, which helps convert blood sugar into stored fat.

The pituitary's secretions are regulated by the hypothalamus, a part of the brain that lies above the pituitary. The hypothalamus, in turn, monitors blood chemistry and receives information from other brain areas that regulate its secretions. This feedback system illustrates the close interaction of the nervous and endocrine systems: The nervous system directs the endocrine glands, and the secretions of these glands in turn affect neural activity. The maestro that conducts and coordinates this orchestra is the brain. Understanding how the brain functions is therefore the ultimate scientific challenge: the mind seeking to understand the brain.

Imagine that synthetic pituitary growth hormone is found effective with no harmful side effects. Knowing that taller people tend to be more successful in business, politics, and sports, would you give this drug to your children?

THE BRAIN

In a jar on a display shelf in Cornell University's psychology department resides the well-preserved brain of Edward Bradford Titchener, a great turn-of-the-century experimental psychologist and proponent of the study of consciousness. Imagine yourself gazing at that wrinkled mass of gray tissue. Is there any sense in which Titchener is still in there?[1]

Your answer might be that without the living whir of electrochemical activity there could be nothing of Titchener in his preserved brain. Consider then an experiment about which the inquisitive Titchener might himself have daydreamed. Imagine that before his death, Titchener's brain had been removed from his body and kept alive by pumping enriched blood through it as it floated in a tank of cerebral fluid. Would Titchener now still be in there? If, to carry our fantasy to its limit, the still-living brain were successfully transplanted into the body of a badly brain-damaged person, to whose home should the recovered patient return?

That we can imagine such questions illustrates how completely we have been convinced that we live in our heads. And for good reason. The brain makes possible the functions we attribute to the mind: seeing, hearing, remembering, thinking, feeling, speaking, dreaming. But precisely where and how are such mind functions tied to the brain? Let us first see how scientists explore such questions.

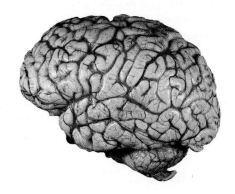

The human brain.

"The living body and its brain, on the one hand, and behavior and the mind, on the other, are indissoluble. Therefore, studying and learning about one necessarily implies studying and learning about the other."
Mortimer Mishkin (1986)

THE TOOLS OF DISCOVERY

It is exciting to consider how fast and far the neurosciences have progressed within a lifetime. For centuries, the study of the human brain lay largely beyond the reach of science. The neuron is too small to study with the naked eye, its electrical signals too faint to record with ordinary electrodes. We were able to feel bumps on the skull and dissect and analyze lifeless brains, but there were no tools high-powered enough and gentle enough to explore the living brain. Now, that has all changed. Whether in the interests of science or medical practice, we

[1]Carl Sagan's *Broca's Brain* (1979a) inspired this question.

can selectively destroy tiny clusters of normal or defective brain cells, leaving their surroundings unharmed. We can probe the brain with tiny electrical pulses. We can snoop on the messages of individual neurons and on the mass action of billions. We can see color representations of the brain's energy-consuming activity. These new tools and techniques have made possible what can most certainly be called the neuroscientific revolution.

Clinical Observations   The oldest method of studying brain-mind connections is by observing the effects of brain diseases and injuries. Although such observations were first recorded some 5000 years ago, it was not until the last two centuries that physicians began to systematically record the results of damage to specific brain areas. Some noted that damage to one side of the brain often caused numbness or paralysis on the body's opposite side. Others noticed that damage to the back of the brain disrupted vision, and that damage to the left front part of the brain produced speech difficulties. Gradually, the brain was being mapped.

Manipulating the Brain   Now, however, scientists need not wait for brain injuries to occur randomly; researchers can surgically produce a brain *lesion* (destruction of tissue) or electrically stimulate specific brain areas in animals. For example, a lesion in one well-defined region of a rat's brain reduces eating, causing the rat to starve unless force-fed. Conversely, a lesion in a nearby area produces overeating.

Recording the Brain's Electrical Activity   Modern researchers have also learned to eavesdrop on the brain. Modern microelectrodes have tips so small that they can detect the electrical activity in a single neuron. Microelectrodes make possible some astonishingly precise findings; for example, we can now detect exactly where the information goes after a cat's whisker is stroked.

The electrical activity of the brain's approximately 100 billion neurons is orchestrated in regular waves that sweep across its surface. In the 1920s, Hans Berger, a young German psychiatrist, discovered this when he placed electrically sensitive disks on the head of his son, Klaus. When he attached the disks to a recording device, Berger observed that faint waves (changes in electrical activity in large portions of the brain) peaked about 10 times per second when Klaus was relaxed with his eyes closed. If Klaus opened his eyes and concentrated on a mental problem, the waves would speed up, indicating a more excited brain state. The *electroencephalogram (EEG)* is simply an amplified tracing of such waves by an instrument called an electroencephalograph. This method for measuring the gross activity of the whole brain is roughly like studying the activity of a car engine by listening to the hum of its motor.

It is now possible to detect by EEG the brain's response to a sound, a flash of light, or even a thought (Figure 2–7). By presenting a stimulus repeatedly and having a computer filter out electrical activity unrelated to the stimulus, one can identify the electrical wave evoked by the stimulus. Observing abnormalities in such brain-wave responses is an easy, painless way to diagnose certain forms of brain damage.

Computers are also being used to analyze EEG data, providing information that was inconceivable 10 years ago. A high-tech instrument, called a brain mapper, neurometric analyzer, or brain-state analyzer, analyzes the brain's electrical activity. The resulting "brain maps" provide valuable diagnostic information to psychiatrists, allow the effects of certain medications to be monitored, and increase the safety of brain surgery (Schwarz, 1987).

Figure 2–7   An electroencephalograph provides amplified tracings of waves of electrical activity in the brain. Here it is being used to detect brain response to sound, making possible an early evaluation of what may be a hearing impairment.

Brain Scans   Other new windows into the brain similarly allow re-searchers to scan the brain without lesioning or probing it. For exam-ple, the *CAT (computerized axial tomograph) scan* examines the brain by taking x-ray photographs that can reveal brain damage (Figure 2–8). Even more dramatic is the *PET (position emission tomograph) scan.* A PET scan depicts the levels of activity of different areas of the brain by showing each area's consumption of its chemical fuel, the sugar glu-cose (Figure 2–9). The more active the neurons of a particular area, the more glucose they burn. When a person is given a temporarily radioac-tive form of glucose, the PET scan measures and locates the radioactiv-ity, thereby detecting where this "food for thought" goes. In this way, researchers can see which areas are most active as the person performs mathematical calculations, listens to music, or daydreams (Phelps & Mazziotta, 1985).

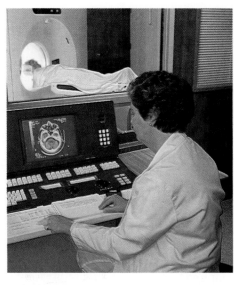

Figure 2–8   The CAT scan examines the brain by taking a series of x-rays from dif-ferent positions. A computer analyzes the data and arranges it into an image repre-senting a slice through the brain at what-ever angle the operator requests.

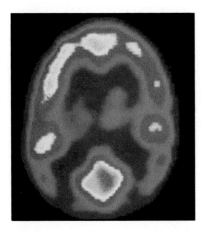
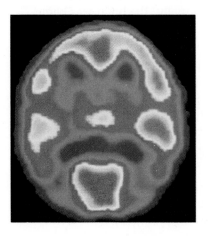

Figure 2–9   The PET scan detects the activity of different areas of the brain by measuring their relative consumption of a temporarily radioactive form of the brain's normal fuel, glucose. The PET scan visual-izes how much of this radioactive glucose is being consumed in different areas of

the brain. In these scans, differences in glucose consumption patterns while rest-ing (left) and while listening to music (right) are evident. The red blotches indi-cate where the brain is most rapidly con-suming glucose.

Refinements of a technique borrowed from analytic chemistry have given brain investigators a new look into the skull. Using powerful magnetic fields and radio waves, *MRI (magnetic resonance imaging)* produces computer-generated images that better distinguish between different types of soft tissue, enabling us to see more clearly the struc-tures of the brain (Figure 2–10).

These new tools have indeed triggered a scientific revolution, most of whose pioneers are still active. To be learning about the neurosci-ences now is like studying world geography while Magellan was ex-ploring the seas. Every year the explorers announce new discoveries, which also generate new interpretations of old discoveries. Such times can be unsettling, but they are never dull.

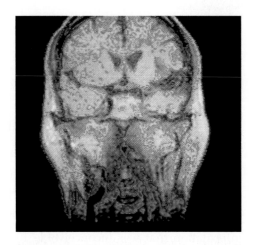

Figure 2–10   MRI image of a frontal section of a stroke victim's brain.

HOW THE BRAIN GOVERNS BEHAVIOR

With our tool kit in hand, we are ready to explore the brain's interior. The beauty of this organ lies not in its appearance but in its intricacy.

In primitive vertebrate animals, such as frogs, the brain is primarily involved with basic survival functions: breathing, resting, and feeding.

In lower mammals, such as rodents, the brain has expanded capacities for emotion and memory. In advanced mammals, such as humans, the brain has an increased ability to process information and to act with foresight.

Corresponding to these three stages of brain evolution are the three principal layers of the vertebrate brain—the brainstem, the limbic system, and the cerebral cortex (Figure 2–11). With the evolution of each succeeding layer, the tight genetic control of behavior relaxes and the adaptability of the organism increases. Thus, lower vertebrates, such as frogs, operate mostly on preprogrammed genetic instructions; higher mammals' increased capacities for learning and thinking enable them to be more adaptable.

Figure 2–11   The structures of the human brain with a simplified view of its three principal regions—the brainstem (spinal cord, cerebellum, medulla, reticular activating system), the limbic system (hypothalamus, amygdala, hippocampus), and the cerebral cortex. Each of these three overlapping layers of the brain can be thought of as representing a stage in brain evolution. The brainstem region is responsible for automatic survival functions. The limbic system is linked to memory, emotion, and behaviors that meet basic needs. The cerebral cortex receives, processes, and retrieves information, makes decisions, and directs voluntary actions.

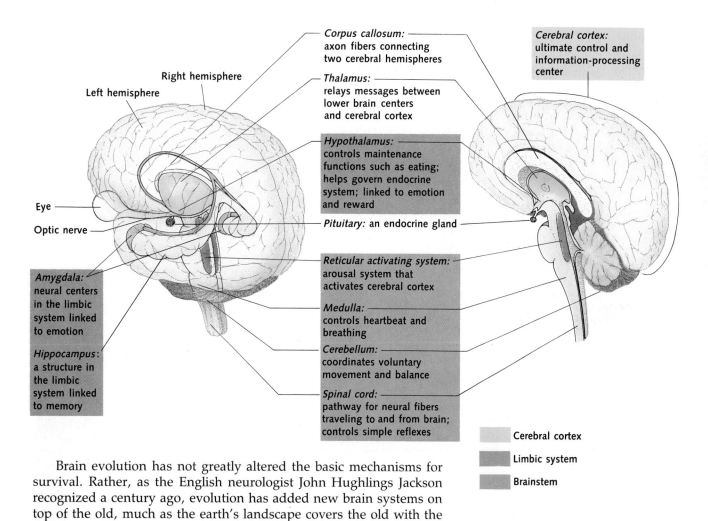

Corpus callosum: axon fibers connecting two cerebral hemispheres

Right hemisphere

Left hemisphere

Thalamus: relays messages between lower brain centers and cerebral cortex

Hypothalamus: controls maintenance functions such as eating; helps govern endocrine system; linked to emotion and reward

Cerebral cortex: ultimate control and information-processing center

Eye

Optic nerve

Pituitary: an endocrine gland

Amygdala: neural centers in the limbic system linked to emotion

Hippocampus: a structure in the limbic system linked to memory

Reticular activating system: arousal system that activates cerebral cortex

Medulla: controls heartbeat and breathing

Cerebellum: coordinates voluntary movement and balance

Spinal cord: pathway for neural fibers traveling to and from brain; controls simple reflexes

Cerebral cortex

Limbic system

Brainstem

Brain evolution has not greatly altered the basic mechanisms for survival. Rather, as the English neurologist John Hughlings Jackson recognized a century ago, evolution has added new brain systems on top of the old, much as the earth's landscape covers the old with the new. Digging down, one discovers the fossil remnants of the past—brainstem components still performing much as they did for our distant ancestors.

The Brainstem and Basic Survival   The *brainstem* is the brain's oldest and innermost region, and is therefore sometimes called the "old brain" or "central core." It begins where the spinal cord enters the skull and swells slightly, forming the *medulla.* Here lie the controls for your heartbeat and breathing. Here also is the crossover point, where nerves to and from each side of the brain mostly connect with the opposite side of the body. This peculiar cross-wiring is but one of many surprises the brain has to offer.

"No one has the remotest idea why there should be this amazing tendency for nervous system pathways to cross."
David H. Hubel and Torsten N. Wiesel (1979)

Extending from the rear of the brainstem is the *cerebellum*, which has two wrinkled hemispheres. The cerebellum has been linked to learning and memory, but its most obvious function is muscular control. On orders from the cortex, the cerebellum coordinates voluntary movement. If your cerebellum were injured, you would probably have difficulty walking, keeping your balance, or shaking hands.

Atop the brainstem sits a joined pair of egg-shaped structures called the *thalamus.* This is the brain's sensory switchboard: It receives information from the sensory neurons, and routes it to the higher brain regions that deal with seeing, hearing, tasting, and touching. We can think of the thalamus as being to neural traffic what Chicago's O'Hare Airport is to midwestern air traffic: Sensory input passes through it en route to various destinations. The thalamus also processes a portion of the higher brain's replies, which are then directed to the cerebellum and medulla.

Inside the brainstem, extending from the spinal cord right up to the thalamus, is a finger-shaped network of neurons called the *reticular activating system* (also known as the *reticular formation*). Most of the spinal cord's sensory input travels up to the thalamus (Figure 2–12). Along the way, some of it branches off to and activates the reticular system, which filters incoming stimuli, relaying important information to other areas of the brain. What do you suppose would happen if the reticular system of a sleeping cat were electrically stimulated?

The people who first dissected and labeled the brain used the language of scholars, Latin and Greek. Their words are actually attempts at graphic description: For example, "cerebellum" means little brain, "thalamus" is inner chamber, and "cortex" is bark.

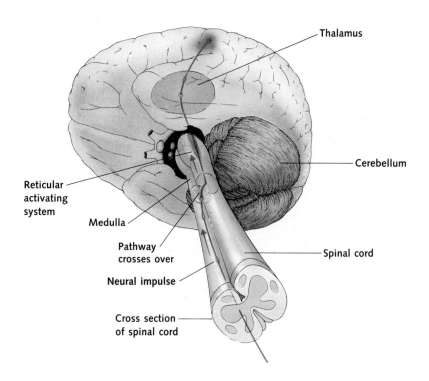

Figure 2–12   We can imagine looking up at the brain from the bottom. First, we see the spinal cord, which then swells to form a tube (the medulla), on which rests a pair of egg-shaped structures (the thalamus), surrounding which, as we will see, are additional layers. Hanging at the back is the baseball-sized cerebellum. Sensory information from, say, the pen in your right hand travels up the spinal cord, crosses over to the left side at the medulla, and is routed to higher brain regions through the thalamus.

In 1949, Giuseppe Moruzzi and H. W. Magoun discovered that electrical stimulation of the reticular system would almost instantly produce an awake, alert cat. Magoun also was able to sever a cat's reticular system from higher brain regions without damaging the nearby sensory pathways. The effect? The cat lapsed into a coma from which it could never be awakened. Magoun could clap his hands at its ear, even pinch it; still no response.

Under the influence of the cortex, the reticular activating system controls not only arousal but also attention. While you are concentrating on this paragraph (or for that matter when you are asleep), you are, thanks to your reticular system, less sensitive to the sound of someone talking nearby. In the same way, a sleeping cat's brain sorts through countless noises, blocking out the irrelevant ones and arousing the animal if it detects a significant sound. This illustrates one of the recurring themes of this book: the brain's capacity to process information without conscious awareness. Remarkably, these life-sustaining functions are so well managed by the brain that they require little or no conscious effort. Whether one is asleep or awake, life functions go on, freeing the higher brain regions to dream, to think, to talk, to savor a memory.

You can check your understanding of the essential functions of each of these four brainstem areas by answering these questions: Within what brain region would damage most likely disrupt your ability to skip rope? Your ability to sense tastes or sounds? In what brain region would damage perhaps leave you in a coma? Without the very breath and heartbeat of life? (See page 38.)

The Limbic System: Emotion, Motivation, and Memory At the border (or "limbus") of the brainstem and the cerebral hemispheres is a doughnut-shaped neural structure called the *limbic system.* As we will see in Chapter 10, two limbic system components, the amygdala and the hippocampus, play a role in memory. Here, we will look at the limbic system's links to emotions, such as fear and anger, and to basic drives, such as those for food and sex.

The Amygdala Two almond-shaped neural clusters in the limbic system, called the *amygdala,* influence aggression and fear. In 1939, psychologist Heinrich Kluver and neurosurgeon Paul Bucy reported that a lesion in a part of the brain that included the amygdala would transform a normally ill-tempered rhesus monkey into the most mellow of creatures. Poke it, pinch it, do virtually anything that normally would trigger a ferocious response, and still the animal would remain placid. In later studies with other wild animals, such as the lynx, wolverine, and wild rat, the same effect was observed. What then might happen if we electrically stimulated the amygdala in a normally placid domestic animal, like a cat? Do so in one spot and the cat prepares to attack, hissing with its back arched, its pupils dilated, its hair on end. Move the electrode only slightly within the amygdala and the cat cowers in terror when caged with a small mouse.

These experiments persuasively testify to the amygdala's role in such emotions as rage and fear. Still, we must be careful not to think of the amygdala as *the* control center for aggression and fear. The brain is not neatly organized into structures that correspond to our categories of behavior. Aggressive and fearful behavior involve neural activity in all levels of the brain—brainstem, limbic system, and cerebral cortex. Even within the limbic system, such behavior can be evoked by stimulating neural structures other than the amygdala. Similarly, if you manipulate your car's carburetor, you can affect how the car runs, but that does not mean that the carburetor by itself runs the car. It is merely one link in an integrated system.

Given that amygdala lesions change violent monkeys into mellow ones, might such lesions do the same in violent humans? *Psychosurgery* has been tried, with varied results (Mark & Ervin, 1970; Valenstein, 1986). In a few cases involving patients who suffer brain abnormalities, fits of rage have been reduced, though sometimes with devastating side effects on the patient's ability to function in everyday life. For ethical reasons, and also because of the uncertainties involved, psychosurgery is highly controversial and seldom used. Perhaps, though, as we learn more about how the brain controls behavior, we will learn to alleviate brain disorders without creating new ones.

What division of the autonomic nervous system—sympathetic or parasympathetic —has been activated? (See page 38.)

Electrical stimulation of the amygdala provokes physical reactions in cats such as the ones shown here.

The Hypothalamus   Another of the limbic system's fascinating structures lies below *(hypo)* the thalamus, and so is called the **hypothalamus.** By lesioning and stimulating different areas in the hypothalamus, neuroscientists have isolated groups of neurons within it that perform amazingly specific bodily maintenance duties. Some of these neural clusters influence hunger; still others regulate thirst, body temperature, and sexual behavior. The hypothalamus exerts its control in two ways: electrochemically, by triggering activity in the autonomic nervous system, and chemically, by secreting hormones that influence the nearby pituitary gland, which in turn produces hormones that circulate to other endocrine glands.

The story of a remarkable discovery about the hypothalamus illustrates how progress in scientific research often occurs—when curious, open-minded investigators make an unexpected observation. Two young McGill University neuropsychologists, James Olds and Peter Milner (1954), were trying to implant electrodes in the reticular systems of white rats. One day they made a magnificent mistake. In one rat, they incorrectly placed an electrode in what was later discovered to be the region of the hypothalamus (Olds, 1975). Curiously, the rat kept returning to the place on its tabletop enclosure where it had been when stimulated by this misplaced electrode, as if it were seeking more stimulation. Upon discovering their mistake, the alert investigators recognized that they had stumbled upon a brain center that provides a pleasurable reward. In a meticulous series of experiments, Olds (1958) then went on to locate other "pleasure centers," as he called them. (What the rats actually experience only they know, and they aren't telling.) When rats were allowed to trigger their own stimulation in these areas by pressing a pedal, they would sometimes do so at a feverish pace—up to 7000 times per hour—until they dropped from exhaustion. Moreover, they would do anything to obtain this stimulation, even cross an electrified floor that a starving rat would not cross to reach food (Figure 2–13).

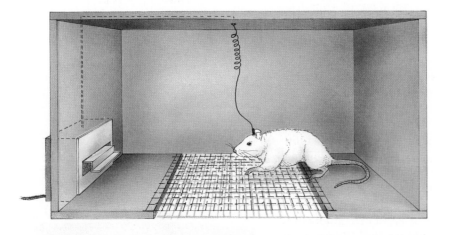

Similar pleasure centers in or near the hypothalamus were later discovered in many other species, including goldfish, dolphins, and monkeys. In fact, animal research reveals that there are specific centers associated with the pleasures of eating, drinking, and sex. Animals, it seems, come equipped with built-in reward systems for activities essential to survival.

These dramatic findings made people wonder whether humans, too, might have limbic centers for pleasure. Indeed they do. One neu-

Answers to questions at top of page 37: the cerebellum, the thalamus, the reticular system, and the medulla.

Answer to question at middle of page 37: the sympathetic nervous system.

Figure 2–13   A rat willingly crosses an electrified grid, accepting the painful shocks, in order to press a lever that sends electrical impulses to its "pleasure centers."

"If you were designing a robot vehicle to walk into the future and survive, . . . you'd wire it up so that behavior that ensured the survival of the self or the species—like sex and eating—would be naturally reinforcing."

Candace Pert (1986)

rosurgeon has used electrodes to calm some previously violent patients. Stimulated patients find that their anger is replaced by feelings of mild pleasure; unlike rats they are not driven to a frenzy by it (Deutsch, 1972; Hooper & Teresi, 1986).

The Cerebral Cortex and Information Processing   To review, our brainstems are organized much like those of other vertebrates, and our limbic systems are similar to those of other mammals. Most of what makes us distinctively human is linked to the complex functions of our highly developed cerebral cortex. When the cortex ceases to function, a person vegetates without voluntary movement, without the experiences of sight, sound, and touch, without consciousness.

Structure of the Cortex   Opening a human skull and exposing the brain, we would see a wrinkled, pinkish gray organ, shaped rather like the meat of an oversized walnut. Covering the brain is the *cerebral cortex,* a ⅛-inch sheet of cells composed of billions of nerve cells and their countless interconnections. With at least 10^{10} neurons, each having roughly 10^4 contacts with other neurons, we end up with something like 10^{14} (100 trillion or more) cortical synaptic connections. Being human takes a lot of nerve.

Glancing at the human cortex, the first thing we notice is its wrinkled appearance. The folds increase the surface area, enabling the skull to encase "lots of gray matter." In rats and other lower mammals, the surface of the cortex is much smoother, which means there is less of this neural fabric.

The cortex is only the thin outer layer of the ballooning left and right cerebral hemispheres. The hemispheres, which account for about 80 percent of the brain's weight, are filled with myelin-sheathed axons that interconnect the neurons of the cortex with those of other brain regions.

Each hemisphere can be viewed as divided into four regions, or lobes (Figure 2–14). Starting at the front of your brain and going around over the top, these are the *frontal lobes* (behind your forehead), the *parietal lobes* (at the top and to the rear), the *occipital lobes* (at the very back of your head), and the *temporal lobes* (just above your ears). These lobes are convenient "geographic" subdivisions rather than distinct operating units. They are separated by fissures, or grooves. The *central fissure* separates the frontal and parietal lobes, while the *lateral fissure* separates the frontal and temporal lobes. As we will see, each lobe carries out many functions, and some functions require the interplay of several lobes.

Functions of the Cortex   More than a century ago, autopsies of partially paralyzed or speechless individuals revealed damage to specific areas of the cortex. But this rather crude evidence did not convince everyone that specific parts of the cortex perform specific functions. After all, if control of speech and movement were diffused across the entire cortex, damage to almost any area might produce the same effect. Likewise, a television would go dead with its power cord cut, but we would be deluding ourselves if we were to think that we had "localized" the source of the picture in the cord. This analogy suggests how easy it is to err when seeking to localize functions within the brain.

Motor Functions   In 1870, German physicians Gustav Fritsch and Eduard Hitzig applied mild electrical stimulation to the cortexes of dogs and made an important discovery: Different body parts could be made to move. The effects were selective: Only in an arch-shaped region at

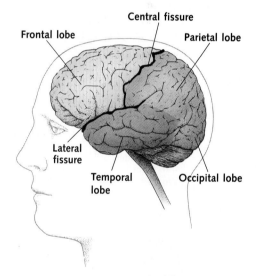

Figure 2–14   The basic subdivisions of the cortex. The cortex can be viewed as divided into four lobes in each hemisphere, separated by fissures, or grooves.

"We have to remember that what we observe is not nature herself, but nature exposed to our method of questioning."
Werner Heisenberg, 1901–1976

the back of the frontal lobe that runs roughly from ear to ear across the top of the brain did stimulation cause movement. This arch is now called the *motor cortex* (Figure 2–15). Moreover, when they stimulated specific parts of this region in the left or right hemisphere, specific body parts moved on the *opposite* side of the body.

More recently, neuroscientist José Delgado demonstrated that motor behavior can be controlled mechanically. In one monkey, he evoked a smiling response over 400,000 times. In one human patient, stimulation of a certain spot on the left motor cortex made him close his right hand into a fist. Asked to keep the fingers open during the next stimulation, the patient, whose fingers still closed, remarked, "I guess, Doctor, that your electricity is stronger than my will" (Delgado, 1969, p. 114).

In the 1940s, similar results were obtained in explorations of the brains of patients with severe seizures. Montreal brain surgeon Wilder Penfield (1958) would painlessly (the brain has no sensory receptors) remove the damaged cortical tissue that caused the disorder. To learn the possible side effects of such surgery, he needed to know the function of the cortical areas to be removed, so he mapped the cortex during surgery by stimulating different cortical areas and observing body responses in hundreds of his wide-awake patients. Like Fritsch and Hitzig, he found that when he stimulated different areas of the motor cortex at the back of the frontal lobe, different body parts moved. Penfield was therefore able to map the motor cortex according to the body parts it controlled (see Figure 2–16). Interestingly, he discovered that those areas of the body requiring precise control, such as the fingers and mouth, occupied the greatest amount of cortical space.

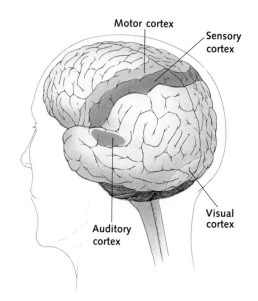

Figure 2–15 The motor cortex, directly in front of the central fissure, controls voluntary muscle movements. The sensory cortex, directly to the rear of the central fissure, receives input from the skin and muscles. The occipital lobes at the rear receive input from the eyes, while an area of the temporal lobes receives information from the ears.

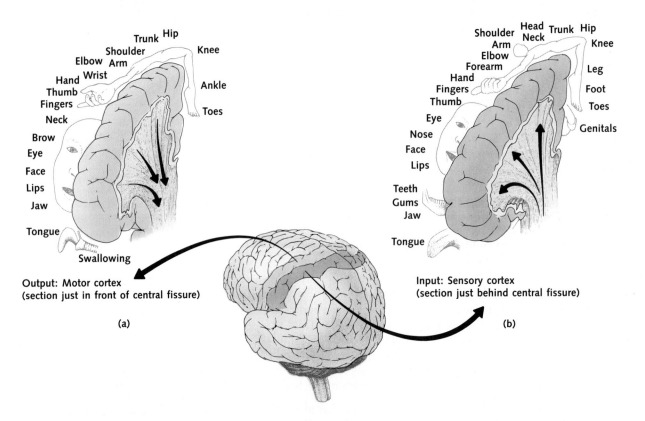

Figure 2–16 A depiction of the proportion of tissue devoted to each body part in (a) the motor cortex and (b) the sensory cortex. As you can see, the amount of cortex devoted to a body part is not proportional to that part's size. Major representation is given to sensitive areas and to areas requiring precise control. For example, the fingers have a larger representation in the cortex than the upper arm.

Sensory Functions   If the motor cortex sends messages out to the body, where do incoming messages reach the cortex? Penfield identified a cortical area that specializes in receiving information from the skin senses and from the movement of body parts. This area, parallel to the motor cortex and just behind it at the front of the parietal lobes, we now call the **sensory cortex** (Figure 2–15). Stimulate a point on the top of this band of tissue, and the person may report being touched on the shoulder; stimulate some point on the side, and perhaps the person will feel something on the face. The more sensitive a body region, the greater the area of the sensory cortex devoted to it; your supersensitive lips project to a larger brain area than do your toes (Figure 2–16). Similarly, rats have a large brain area devoted to whisker sensation, owls to hearing sensations, and so forth. If a monkey or a human loses a finger, the region of the sensory cortex devoted to receiving input from that finger becomes available to receive sensory input from the adjacent fingers, which now become more sensitive (Fox, 1984). This finding illustrates a principle to which we will return: The brain is sculpted not only by our genes but also by our experience.

Further exploration has identified where the cortex first receives messages from the other senses (Figure 2–15). Visual information is being received at this moment in the occipital lobes at the very back of your brain. Stimulated there, you might see flashes of light or dashes of color. So, in a sense, we *do* have eyes in the back of our head. In fact, research is progressing on artificial visual systems that link the "eyes" of a computer-based video system to electrodes in the occipital lobes, allowing a blind person to "see," at least crudely. (In Chapter 6, Sensation, we will look more closely at how this region of our occipital lobes manages to transform neural impulses into a visual perception.) Information from the ear travels to the auditory areas in the temporal lobes. Most of this auditory information travels a circuitous route from one ear to the auditory receiving area above the opposite ear. Stimulated there, you might hear a sound.

Association Areas   So far we have pointed out small areas of the cortex that either receive sensory information or direct muscular responses. In humans, that leaves some three-fourths of the thin wrinkled layer, the cerebral cortex, uncommitted. Neurons in these **association areas** (the beige areas in Figure 2–17) communicate mainly with one another and with the cortical neurons of the sensory and motor areas.

No response is observed in or by the subject when these areas are electrically probed, so their functions are not so easily specified as are those of the sensory and motor areas. The silence of the association areas seems to be what someone had in mind when formulating one of the most widespread pop psychology myths: that we ordinarily use only 10 percent of our brains. The myth implies that were we to activate our whole brain we would be far smarter than those who drudge along on 10 percent brain power. But from observations of lesioned animals and brain-damaged humans, we know that the association areas are not dormant. Rather, they interpret, integrate, and act on information that has been received and processed by the sensory areas. We might compare the functions of the association areas of the cortex to a group of switchboard operators monitoring incoming and outgoing calls, but mostly conversing among themselves.

Frontal lobe association areas seem linked to judging and planning. People with damaged frontal lobes may have intact memories, score high on intelligence tests, and be well able to bake a cake—yet they may be unable to plan ahead in order to *begin* baking the cake for a birthday party.

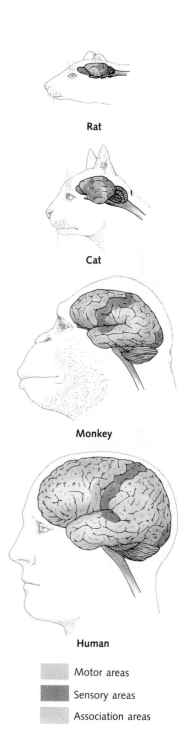

Rat

Cat

Monkey

Human

Motor areas

Sensory areas

Association areas

Figure 2–17   As animals increase in complexity, there is an increase in the amount of "uncommitted" or association areas of the cortex. These vast areas of the brain seem to be responsible for integrating and acting on information received and processed by sensory areas.

Frontal lobe damage can also alter personality, leaving a person uninhibited, coarse, and even promiscuous. The classic case is Phineas Gage, a railroad worker. One afternoon in 1848, 25-year-old Gage was packing gunpowder into a rock with a tamping iron. A spark ignited the gunpowder, shooting the rod up through his left cheek and out the top of his skull, leaving his left frontal lobe massively damaged. To everyone's amazement, Gage was still able to sit up and speak, and after the wound healed he returned to work. His mental abilities and memories were preserved, but his personality was not. The affable, soft-spoken Phineas Gage was now an irritable, profane, capricious person who lost his job and ended up earning his living as a fairground exhibit. This person, said his friends, was "no longer Gage."

The association areas of the other lobes also perform mental functions. For example, an area on the underside of the right temporal lobe enables us to recognize faces. But by and large, complex mental functions such as learning and memory are not localized in any one place. There is no one spot in a rat's (admittedly small) association cortex that, when damaged, will obliterate its ability to learn or remember a maze. Such functions seem spread throughout much of the cortex.

Language   It is curious that **aphasia,** an impaired use of language, can be caused by damage to any one of several cortical areas. It is even more curious that some aphasic people can speak fluently but are unable to read (despite good vision), while others can comprehend what they read but are unable to speak. Still others are able to write but not to read, to read numbers but not letters, or to sing but not speak. These observations are puzzling because we tend to think of speaking and reading, or writing and reading, or singing and speaking, as merely different examples of the same general ability. The unraveling of the mystery of language illustrates an important principle: Complex human abilities result from the intricate coordination of many brain areas. Consider the clues that led to the solving of this mystery:

> *Clue 1:* In 1865, French physician Paul Broca reported that damage to a specific area of the left frontal lobe, later called *Broca's area,* left a person struggling to form words, yet often able to sing familiar songs with ease.
>
> *Clue 2:* In 1874, German investigator Carl Wernicke discovered that damage to a specific area of the left temporal lobe *(Wernicke's area)* would leave people able to babble words but in a meaningless way. Asked to describe a picture that showed two boys stealing cookies behind a woman's back, one patient responded: "Mother is away here working her work to get her better, but when she's looking the two boys looking the other part. She's working another time" (Geschwind, 1979).
>
> *Clue 3:* It was later discovered that when we read, a third brain area, the *angular gyrus,* receives the visual information from the visual area and recodes it into the auditory form in which the word is understood in Wernicke's area.
>
> *Clue 4:* These areas of the brain are interconnected by nerve fibers.

Norman Geschwind assembled these clues into an explanation of how we use language. When you read aloud (Figure 2–18), the words (1) register in the visual area, (2) are relayed to the angular gyrus, which then transforms the words into an auditory code that is (3) received and understood in the nearby Wernicke's area, and (4) transmit-

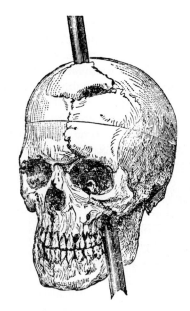

Phineas Gage's skull pierced by tamping rod.

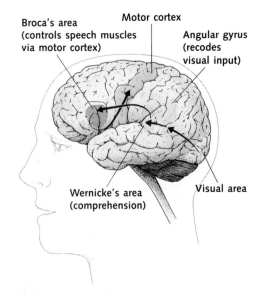

Figure 2–18   Speaking a written word requires the coordination of several brain areas. The arrows show the movement of information in the brain from the time the word is read until it is spoken. (Adapted from "Specialization of the human brain" by N. Geschwind. Copyright ©1979 Scientific American, Inc. All rights reserved.)

ted to Broca's area, which (5) controls the motor cortex, creating the pronounced word. Depending on which link in this chain is damaged, a different form of aphasia occurs. Damage to the angular gyrus leaves the person able to speak and understand but unable to read. Damage to Wernicke's area disrupts understanding. Damage to Broca's area disrupts speaking.

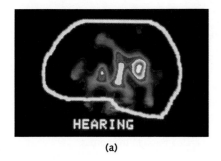
(a)

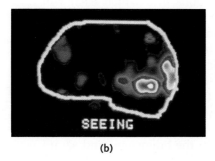
(b)

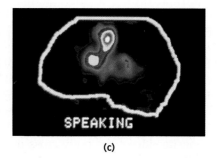
(c)

This series of side-view PET scans shows levels of increased brain activity in specific areas: (a) when hearing a word—auditory cortex and Wernicke's area; (b) when seeing a word—visual cortex and angular gyrus; and (c) when repeating a word—Broca's area and the motor cortex.

Normal conversation involves even more brain centers. The auditory receiving area transmits information directly to Wernicke's area, which passes it on to association areas to be processed and acted upon. Broca's area sends directions to the motor cortex, which in turn transmits commands on down the brainstem to the mouth. The sequence of brain events quickly becomes overwhelming, yet this description is simplified. There is a continuous interplay of still other brain areas, and we have hardly begun to explore the internal operation of any one of them. How does Wernicke's area create meaning out of a sound? How does Broca's area play the keyboard of the motor cortex? More generally, how can we best describe the coordinated function of the whole brain? Mechanically, as a hierarchy of extremely sophisticated and unbelievably miniaturized computers? Artistically, as an enchanted loom of billions upon billions of interconnected neurons? Such images help us to think about the brain, but they do not diminish our sense of wonder.

Question: If your Broca's area were damaged, could you write a letter? (See page 46.)

OUR DIVIDED BRAINS

We have seen that while certain attributes of mind, such as language, are localized in particular brain regions, the brain nevertheless acts as a unified whole. Both principles of brain functioning—specialization and integration—are apparent in research on the two brain hemispheres.

For more than a century, clinical evidence has shown that the two sides of the brain serve differing functions. Accidents, strokes, and tumors in the left hemisphere generally impair reading, writing, speaking, arithmetic reasoning, and understanding. Similar lesions in the right hemisphere do not have such dramatic effects. A recent analysis of 520 brain-injured Vietnam war veterans revealed that those with right hemisphere damage were less likely to suffer prolonged unconsciousness (Fischman, 1986). Small wonder, then, that the left hemisphere came to be known as the "dominant" or "major" hemisphere, and its silent companion to the right as the "subordinate" or "minor" hemisphere. (With some left-handers, this is reversed—see page 48.)

By 1960, the assumption of left hemisphere superiority was well accepted. But in science today's facts are often replaced tomorrow by a fuller understanding. So it was when the "minor" right hemisphere was found not to be so limited after all (Sperry, 1982). The story of this discovery is a fascinating chapter in the history of psychology.

Splitting the Brain   Back in 1860, one of the founders of experimental psychology, Gustav Fechner, wondered what would happen if the brain's hemispheres were divided. Would not the person be duplicated? "The two cerebral hemispheres," he wrote, will ". . . develop differently according to the external relations into which each will enter."

During the 1950s, one of Fechner's intellectual descendants, psychologist Roger Sperry, made Fechner's imaginary experiment a reality. Working with Ronald Myers and Michael Gazzaniga, Sperry "divided the brains" of cats and monkeys by severing the *corpus callosum,* the wide band of axon fibers that connects the two hemispheres (Figure 2–19). In these experiments, the operation seemed not to be seriously incapacitating. (Recall that the brain's connections to the opposite side of the body cross over in the brainstem, and so are not injured by the operation.)

In 1961, Los Angeles neurosurgeons Philip Vogel and Joseph Bogen developed a theory. Perhaps major epileptic seizures were caused by an amplification of abnormal brain activity that reverberated back and forth across the corpus callosum. If so, epilepsy might be controlled by cutting communication between the two hemispheres. The surgeons decided to sever the corpus callosum in severely afflicted patients as a last resort. The result? Seizures were nearly eliminated and the patients seemed surprisingly normal, their personalities and intellect hardly affected. Waking from the surgery, one patient even managed to quip that he had a "splitting headache" (Gazzaniga, 1967).

If you chatted with one of these *split-brain* patients you would probably not notice anything unusual. Given this result, one can understand why only a decade earlier neuropsychologist Karl Lashley jested that maybe the corpus callosum served only "to keep the hemispheres from sagging." But surely a band of 200 million nerve fibers capable of transferring more than a billion bits of information per second between the hemispheres must have a more significant purpose. It does, and the ingenious experiments of Sperry and Gazzaniga revealed its purpose and provided a key to understanding the special functions of the two hemispheres.

Shortly after one of the split-brain operations, the researchers noted that when an unseen object was placed in a patient's left hand he denied it was there. This came as no surprise to Sperry and Gazzaniga. They knew that information from the left hand goes to the right hemisphere, and their animal experiments led them to expect that the right hemisphere would be unable to transmit this information to the speech-controlling areas of the left hemisphere. More extraordinary results came when Sperry and Gazzaniga conducted some perceptual tests.

Our eyes are connected to our brains in such a way that, when we look straight ahead, the left half of our field of vision transmits to our right hemisphere and the right half transmits to our left hemisphere (Figure 2–20). In those of us with intact corpus callosums, something that is presented only to our right hemisphere is quickly transmitted to our left hemisphere, which names it. But what happens in a person whose corpus callosum has been severed? By asking the split-brain patient to look at a designated spot and then flashing information in the right or left half of the visual field, the experimenter can communicate solely with the right or left hemisphere and so find out.

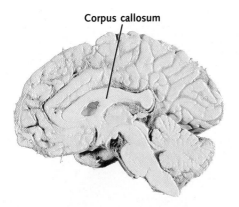

Figure 2–19   The corpus callosum is a large band of neural fibers that connects the two brain hemispheres. In the side view of a brain, the hemispheres have been separated through the corpus callosum.

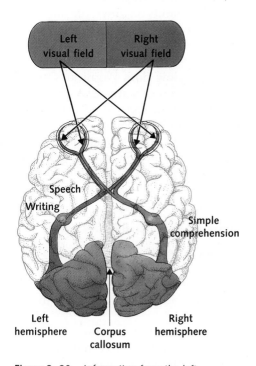

Figure 2–20   Information from the left half of your field of vision is received only by your right hemisphere, and information from the right half of your visual field is received only by your left hemisphere. (Note, however, that each eye receives sensory information from *both* the right and left visual fields.) The data received by either hemisphere is quickly transmitted to the other across the corpus callosum. In a split-brain patient, whose corpus callosum has been severed, this sharing of information does not take place.

See if you can guess the results of an experiment using this procedure (Gazzaniga, 1967). While the patients stared at a dot the word HEART was flashed across the visual field with HE in the left visual field and ART in the right. What did the patients *say* they saw? Asked to identify with their *left* hands what they had seen, HE or ART, what did they point to?

As Figure 2–21 shows, the patients *said* they saw ART, and so were surprised when their left hands *pointed* to HE. When given an opportunity to express itself, each hemisphere reported only what *it* had seen.

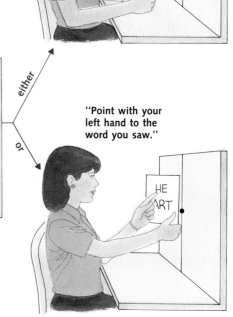

"What word did you see?"

"Art."

"Point with your left hand to the word you saw."

"Look at the dot."

Figure 2–21 Testing the divided brain. When an experimenter flashes the word HEART across the visual field, the split-brain patient reports seeing the portion of the word transmitted to her left hemisphere. However, if asked to indicate with her left hand what she saw, she points to the portion of the word transmitted to her right hemisphere.

Similarly, when a picture of a spoon was flashed to the right hemisphere, the patients could not say what they saw; but when asked to identify what they had seen by feeling with their left hands an assortment of objects hidden behind a screen, they were readily able to select the spoon (Figure 2–22). If the experimenter said "Right!" the patient might reply, "What? Right? How could I possibly pick out the right object when I don't know what I saw?" It is, of course, the left hemisphere doing the talking here, bewildered by what its other half knows. It was as if the patients had "two separate inner visual worlds," noted Sperry (1968).

Figure 2–22 The nonverbal right hemisphere sees the spoon flashed on the screen and directs the left hand to locate it among the objects hidden behind the screen. But the split-brain patient cannot say what he has seen.

"With your left hand, select the object you saw from those behind the screen."

"What did you see?"

"I don't know."

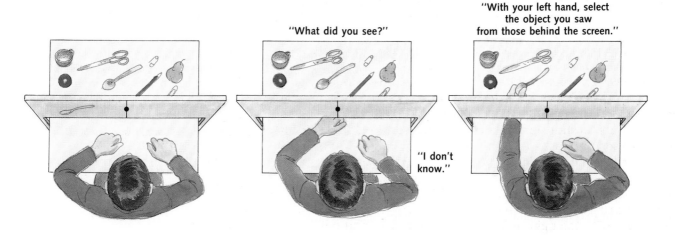

These experiments demonstrated that the right hemisphere understands simple requests and easily perceives objects. In fact, the right hemisphere is superior to the left at copying drawings and at recognizing faces. Its perceptual superiority is also demonstrated in one of Sperry's films. A split-brain patient's left hand (directed by the right hemisphere) easily rearranges some blocks to match a drawing. When the right hand (directed by the left hemisphere) tries to perform the same perceptual task, it makes many errors. The bumbling performance frustrates the right hemisphere, which is observing all this. So it triggers the left hand to interrupt the bumbling right hand. Outside the laboratory, a few split-brain patients have occasionally been bothered by the unruly independence of their left hand, which may unbutton a shirt while the right hand buttons it. Split-brain surgery, said Sperry (1964), seems to leave people rather as Fechner imagined—''with two separate minds.''

Answer to question on page 43: Yes. Broca's area produces a program for controlling the muscles of speech. If damaged, a victim can still understand speech and communicate through gestures or writing.

''I am at two with nature.''
Woody Allen

IS THE RIGHT HEMISPHERE INTELLIGENT?

Researchers who have studied split-brain patients concur on many findings: for example, the function of the corpus callosum, the logical and linguistic superiority of the left hemisphere, and the superiority of the right hemisphere on at least some simple perceptual tasks. But on other issues, disagreement prevails. Does the right hemisphere possess language, too? No, concludes Michael Gazzaniga (1983): ''Right hemisphere language is not common.'' Fellow researcher Jerre Levy (1983) partially disagrees; the right hemisphere often can grasp the meanings of words, she believes. Eran Zaidel (1983) even more strongly disputes the right hemisphere's alleged linguistic incompetence: ''Evidence for right hemisphere involvement in normal language is becoming increasingly prominent.''

Assuming that the right hemisphere is inferior in language, is it correspondingly superior in other abilities? Again, the experts disagree. Gazzaniga (1983) states, ''It could well be argued that the cognitive skills of a normal disconnected right hemisphere without language are vastly inferior to the cognitive skills of a chimpanzee.'' Here, Levy

(1983) clearly parts company with Gazzaniga. She wonders, ''Why is the right hemisphere so large if it is so stupid?'' From her research she concludes that ''the evidence is overpowering [that the right hemisphere] is active, responsive, highly intelligent, thinking, conscious, and fully human with respect to its cognitive depth and complexity.'' It also, she believes, makes instant, preconscious, executive decisions that direct our conscious attention (Levy, 1987).

What makes these disagreements so striking is that all three researchers have collaborated with Roger Sperry in the same laboratory, have observed many of the same patients, and have read the same research literature. Their clashing conclusions therefore sharply illustrate a point made in Chapter 1: The theorist must always make a leap from factual data to interpretations and conclusions that are consistent with the data. When researchers arrive at different conclusions, their disagreements are a driving force for further scientific inquiry, for all agree that their disagreements should be resolved not by opinion but by further research.

''Conciliatory smoothness is the lifeblood of diplomacy; it is the death of science. Diplomacy consists of producing agreement. . . . Science consists of organizing controversy or, if need be, generating it.''
E. A. Murphy (1982)

Hemispheric Specialization   Split-brain patients have enabled us to observe the special functions of each hemisphere: The left is more verbal, the right excels at visual perception. (Perhaps because of its perceptual ability, the right hemisphere also helps us to perceive subtle expressions of emotion [Tucker, 1981].)

When Sperry (1968) flashed a picture of a nude woman to the right hemisphere, split-brain patients would blush, grin, and giggle, yet could not correctly explain the emotion. The left hemisphere, which acts as the brain's press agent, then would often do mental gymnastics to rationalize the reactions (see Figure 2–23). Thus if the patient follows an order sent to the right hemisphere ("Go into the house"), the left hemisphere will offer a ready explanation ("I'm going to get a drink"). (In other tests, the right hemisphere would sometimes cause the patient to frown or wince when it heard the left hemisphere speak a wrong answer. Awareness by the left hemisphere of this facial reaction occasionally cued the person to correct the answer.)

Figure 2–23   When an experimenter flashes simple commands to the right hemisphere of split-brain patients, they comply. But when asked about their response, their left hemisphere, which controls speech and is unaware of what the right hemisphere has seen, invents—and seemingly believes—plausible explanations for what it does not comprehend. Thus Michael Gazzaniga (1986) concludes that the left hemisphere is an "interpreter" that instantly constructs theories to explain our behavior.

So, the left hemisphere specializes in language and in the fine muscle control that enables us to speak and write, and the right hemisphere specializes in visual and emotional tasks. Does this mean that the right hemisphere is speechless and the left emotionless? Although controversy remains (see page 46), many neuropsychologists have concluded that the left hemisphere is usually more logical, rational, and able to deal with things in sequence, and that the right is more intuitive, nonverbal, and able to deal with things all at once. But neuropsychologists also advise us to beware the fad of locating complex human capacities, such as abilities in science or art, in either hemisphere. Popularized descriptions of the left-right dichotomy have tended to outrun the scientific findings. "The left-right dichotomy in cognitive mode is an idea with which it is very easy to run wild," observes Sperry (1982). True, the cortex does have specialized regions for performing certain subtasks (Allen, 1983), but complex activities such as practicing science or creating art emerge from the *integrated* activity of both hemispheres. Even when simply reading a story, both hemispheres are at work—the left understanding the words and finding meaning, the right appreciating humor, imagery, and emotional content (Levy, 1985).

Studying the Normal Brain   What about the 99.99+ percent of us with undivided brains? Have scientists found our hemispheres to be similarly specialized? They have indeed, by evidence from several different types of studies. For example, when a person performs a *perceptual* task, the brain waves, bloodflow, and glucose consumption of the *right* hemisphere indicate increased activity; when a person speaks or performs calculations, the left hemisphere becomes more active (Springer & Deutsch, 1985).

"Foster here is the left side of my brain, and Mr. Hoagland is the right side of my brain."

"In the normal state, the two hemispheres appear to work closely together as a unit, rather than one being turned on while the other idles."

Roger Sperry (1982)

On occasion, hemispheric specialization has been even more dramatically demonstrated by briefly sedating an entire hemisphere. To check for the locus of language before surgery, a physician may inject a sedative into the neck artery that feeds blood to the hemisphere on its side of the body. Just before the drug is administered the patient is lying down, arms in the air, conversing easily. Can you predict what happens when the drug is injected in the artery going to the left hemisphere? Within seconds, the right arm falls limp, and, assuming the person's left hemisphere controls language, the subject becomes speechless until the drug wears off. When the drug is injected into the artery going to the right hemisphere, the *left* arm falls limp, but speech is still possible.

LEFT-HANDEDNESS: IS BEING A LEFTY ALL RIGHT?

Judging by our everyday conversation, left-handedness is not all right. To be "coming from left field," or to offer a "left-handed compliment" is hardly more complimentary than to be "sinister" or "gauche" (words derived from the Latin and French for left). On the other hand, right-handedness is "right on," which any "righteous" "right-hand man" "in his right mind" usually is.

How Many People Are Left-handed?

Almost 10 percent (somewhat more among males, somewhat less among females) of the human population is left-handed. Judging from cave drawings and the tools of prehistoric humans, this veer to the right occurred long long ago in the development of our species.

Is Handedness Inherited?

Observing 150 babies during the first 2 days after birth, George Michel (1981) found that two-thirds consistently preferred to lie with their heads turned to the right. When he restudied a sample of these babies at age 5 months, almost all of the "head right" babies reached for things with their right hands, and almost all of the "head left" babies reached with their left hands. Such findings, along with the universal prevalence of right-handers, suggest that handedness is genetically influenced.

Is the Brain Organization of Left-handers Opposite That of Right-handers?

Tests reveal that about 95 percent of right-handers process speech primarily in the left hemisphere (Springer & Deutsch, 1985). Left-handers are more diverse. More than half process speech in the left hemisphere, just as right-handers do. About one-quarter process language in the right hemisphere; the other quarter use both hemispheres more or less equally. Such left-handers may therefore require better communication between the hemispheres. This might explain the recent discovery that the corpus callosum averages 11 percent larger in left-handers (Witelson, 1985).

So, Is It All Right to Be Left-handed?

Left-handers are disproportionately numerous among those afflicted with reading disabilities, allergies, and migraine headaches (Geschwind & Behan, 1984). But left-handedness is also more common among musicians, mathematicians, professional baseball players, architects, and artists, including such luminaries as Michelangelo, Leonardo da Vinci, and Picasso. If one can tolerate elbow-jostling at dinner parties, right-handed desks, and awkward scissors, then apparently the pros and cons of being a lefty are roughly equal.

Hemispheric specialization has also been verified by tests in which most people recognize pictures faster and more accurately when they are flashed to the right hemisphere, but recognize words faster and more accurately when flashed to the left hemisphere. (If a word is flashed to your right hemisphere, perception takes a fraction of a second longer—the length of time it takes to transmit the information through the corpus callosum to the more verbal left hemisphere.)

Doreen Kimura (1973) refined a technique that further confirmed hemispheric specialization. As we noted earlier, input from the right ear goes mostly to the left hemisphere, and vice versa. If a dual-track tape recorder were to present simultaneously the spoken number "one" to your left ear and "nine" to your right ear, which would you more likely hear? Kimura observed that with verbal information your right ear (left hemisphere) wins this "dichotic listening" contest, but that the left ear (right hemisphere) is superior at perceiving nonspeech sounds, such as melodies, laughing, and crying.

So, a variety of observations—of people with "split" brains and people with "normal" brains—converge beautifully. There is now little doubt that we have unified brains with specialized parts, and that infants are born with their brains "prewired" accordingly (Hahn, 1987). From looking at the two hemispheres, which appear nearly identical to the naked eye, who would suppose that they contribute so uniquely to the harmony of the whole?

Brain Reorganization   If brain tissue is destroyed through injury or illness, are its special functions forever lost? If you scrape your knee, new cells will be generated to repair the damage. Not so with the neurons of the central nervous system. If the spinal cord is severed or if brain tissue is destroyed, the injured neurons normally will not be replaced.

That is the bad news. The good news concerns the brain's *plasticity.* When one brain area is damaged, other areas may in time reorganize and take over its functions. If some neurons are destroyed, nearby neurons may partly compensate for the damage by making new connections that replace the lost ones (Cotman & Nieto-Sampedro, 1982). These new connections are one way in which the brain struggles to recover from, say, a minor stroke. They are also the brain's way of compensating for the gradual loss of neurons with age.

Before the functions of young children's cortical regions become fixed, their brains are especially plastic. If the speech areas of an infant's left hemisphere are damaged, the right hemisphere will usually take over, with no noticeable impairment of language. Left hemisphere damage does not permanently disrupt language until about age 8.

As an extreme example, consider a 5-year-old boy whose severe seizures, caused by a deteriorating left hemisphere, require removing the *entire* hemisphere. What hope for the future would such a child have? Is there any chance he might attend school and lead a normal life, or would he be permanently retarded?

This is an actual case, and, astonishingly, the individual was at last report an executive. Half his skull is filled with nothing but cerebrospinal fluid—functionally it might as well be sawdust—yet he has scored well above average on intelligence tests, has completed college, and attended graduate school part-time (Smith & Sugar, 1975; A. Smith, 1987). Although paralyzed on the right side, this individual (along with other such cases of "hemispherectomy") testifies to the brain's extraordinary powers of reorganization, especially when damaged before it is fully developed.

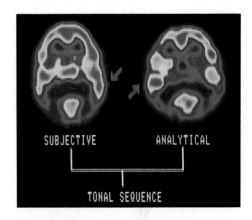

Subjects have been asked to compare sequences of notes. PET scans revealed that (right) activity was heightened in the left hemisphere of subjects who, using visual imagery, mentally constructed charts as a comparison strategy; and that (left) other kinds of listening stimulated activity in the right hemisphere.

"My suspicion is that the universe is not only queerer than we suppose, but queerer than we can suppose."
J. B. S. Haldane,
Possible Worlds, 1927

Could we enhance the brain's self-repair by transplanting brain tissue? Even in this era of heart transplants and skin grafts, transplanting neural tissue still sounds like science fiction. But in experiments with animals, neuroscientists are now attempting, with some success, to mend the brain by replacing destroyed nerve cells with healthy ones (Gash & others, 1986). In one dramatic experiment, Randy Labbe and her colleagues (1983) removed a portion of the frontal lobes from a group of rats and gave them replacement tissue from the frontal lobes of rat fetuses. Later, compared to rats who had similar portions removed but had not received the transplanted fetal cortical tissue, they learned a maze twice as fast. So it seems that transplants of appropriate brain tissue may in some cases partially replace lost or damaged tissue.

Might transplants of human brain tissue someday enable neurosurgeons to repair the brain? The tremors of Parkinson's disease and the progressive deterioration of Alzheimer's disease, for example, involve a degeneration of brain tissue that normally produces vital neurotransmitters—dopamine in Parkinson's disease, acetylcholine in Alzheimer's. If dopamine-producing tissue were transplanted into the brains of Parkinson's patients, would the tissue survive and release the needed neurotransmitters? Using such tissue from patients' own adrenal glands or from miscarried fetuses, experimental surgery on several dozen patients in Sweden, Mexico, the United States, and elsewhere has raised hopes that it might (Lewin, 1987; Maugh, 1988).

From the phrenology of just the last century to today's neuroscience we have come a long way. Yet what is unknown dwarfs what is known. We can describe the brain. We can learn the functions of its parts. We can study how the parts communicate. But how does this electrochemical whir give rise to a feeling of elation, a creative idea, or a memory of grandmother's freshly baked cookies?

To judge from one series of interviews with leading brain scientists, feelings of wonder are commonplace, and sometimes lead to mystical and spiritual inspirations. In the words of Candace Pert (1986, p. 390), "I see in the brain all the beauty of the universe and its order— constant signs of God's presence." Others ponder philosophical mysteries: How does the material brain give rise to consciousness? And to what extent can a thing understand itself?

"If the human brain were so simple that we could understand it, we would be so simple that we couldn't."

Emerson M. Pugh, quoted by George E. Pugh, *The Biological Origin of Human Values*, 1977

SUMMING UP

As the first step in understanding our behavior and mental processes, we have examined the biological roots of how we think, feel, and act.

THE NERVOUS SYSTEM

Divisions of the Nervous System The body's circuitry, the nervous system, consists of billions of nerve cells, called neurons. These are organized into the central nervous system (CNS) neurons in the brain and spinal cord, which communicate with the sensory and motor neurons of the peripheral nervous system (PNS). The PNS consists of the somatic nervous system, which directs voluntary movements and reflexes, and the autonomic nervous system, whose sympathetic and parasympathetic divisions control our involuntary muscles and our glands.

Neurons and Their Messages Neurons usually receive signals from other neurons through their branching dendrites and cell body, then combine these signals in the cell body and transmit electrical impulses down their axon. When these signals reach the end of the axon, they stimulate the release of chemical messengers, called neurotransmitters. These molecules traverse the tiny synaptic gap between neurons and combine with receptor sites on neighboring neurons, thus passing on their excitatory or inhibitory messages. Over fifty neurotransmitters have been isolated, and are now being studied in the hope of understanding their importance for human thought and emotion.

THE ENDOCRINE SYSTEM

The endocrine system is the second of the body's communication systems. Under the influence of the autonomic nervous system and the hypothalamus, endocrine glands, such as the adrenals and the pituitary, release hormones. Hormones travel through the bloodstream to various target organs, where they affect emotional states, growth, and other body functions.

THE BRAIN

The Tools of Discovery Although clinical observations have long revealed the effects of damage to various brain areas, powerful new technologies reveal brain structures and activities that once were invisible. By lesioning or stimulating specific brain areas, by recording the brain's surface electrical activity, and by displaying neural activity with computer-aided brain scans, neuroscientists are exploring the connections between brain, mind, and behavior.

How the Brain Governs Behavior Each of the brain's three basic regions—the brainstem, the limbic system, and the cerebral cortex—represents a stage of brain evolution.

The brainstem begins where the spinal cord swells to form the medulla, which controls heartbeat and breathing. The cerebellum, which is attached to the rear of the brainstem, coordinates muscle movement. On top of the brainstem is the thalamus, the brain's sensory switchboard. Within the brainstem, the reticular activating system controls arousal.

At the border of the brainstem and cerebral cortex is the limbic system, which has been linked primarily to memory, emotions, and drives. For example, one of its neural centers, the amygdala, is involved in aggressive and fearful responses. Another, the hypothalamus, has been linked to various bodily maintenance functions, to pleasurable rewards, and to the control of the pituitary gland.

The cerebral cortex can be viewed as having four geographical areas: the frontal, parietal, occipital, and temporal lobes. Small, well-defined regions within these lobes control muscle movement and receive information from the body senses. However, most of the cortex—its association areas—is uncommitted to such functions and is therefore free to process other information.

Some brain regions are known to serve specific functions. In general, however, human emotions, thoughts, and behaviors result from the intricate coordination of many brain areas. Language, for example, depends on a chain of events in several brain regions.

Our Divided Brains Clinical observations long ago revealed that the left cerebral hemisphere is crucial for language. More recent experiments on split-brain patients have refined our knowledge of each hemisphere's special functions. By testing the two hemispheres separately, researchers have confirmed that for most people the left hemisphere is indeed the more verbal, and that the right hemisphere excels in visual perception and the recognition of emotion. Controversy still exists regarding the capacities of the right hemisphere, but studies of normal people with intact brains confirm that each hemisphere makes unique contributions to the integrated functioning of the brain. Nevertheless, if one hemisphere is damaged early in life, the other will pick up many of its functions, thus demonstrating the brain's plasticity.

TERMS AND CONCEPTS TO REMEMBER

acetylcholine [ah-seat-el-KO-leen] **(ACh)** A neurotransmitter that, among its functions, triggers muscle contraction.

adrenal [ah-DREEN-el] **glands** A pair of endocrine glands just above the kidneys. The adrenals secrete the hormones epinephrine (adrenaline) and norepinephrine (noradrenaline), which help to arouse the body in times of stress.

all-or-none response The principle that at any moment, like a gun, a neuron either fires or does not.

amygdala [ah-MIG-dah-la] Two almond-shaped neural centers in the limbic system that are linked to emotion.

aphasia Impairment of language, usually caused by left hemisphere damage either to Broca's area (impairing speaking) or to Wernicke's area (impairing understanding).

association areas Areas of the cerebral cortex that are involved not in primary motor or sensory functions, but rather in higher mental functions such as learning, remembering, thinking, and speaking.

autonomic [aw-tuh-NAHM-ik] **nervous system** The part of the peripheral nervous system that controls the glands and the muscles of the internal organs (such as the heart). Its sympathetic division arouses; its parasympathetic division calms.

axon The extension of a neuron ending in branching terminal fibers through which messages are sent to other neurons or to muscles or glands.

brainstem The central core of the brain, beginning where the spinal cord swells as it enters the skull; it is the oldest part of the brain, and is responsible for automatic survival functions.

Broca's area   An area of the left frontal lobe that directs the muscle movements involved in speech.

CAT (computerized axial tomograph) scan   A series of x-ray photographs taken from different angles and combined by computer into a composite three-dimensional representation of a slice through the body at whatever angle is desired.

central nervous system (CNS)   The brain and spinal cord.

cerebellum [sehr-uh-BELL-um]   The "little brain" attached to the rear of the brainstem; it helps to coordinate voluntary movement and balance.

cerebral [seh-REE-bruhl] **cortex**   The intricate fabric of interconnected neural cells that covers the cerebral hemispheres; the body's ultimate control and information-processing center.

corpus callosum [kah-LOW-sum]   The largest bundle of nerve fibers connecting and carrying messages between the two brain hemispheres.

dendrite   The bushy, branching extensions of a neuron that receive messages and conduct impulses toward the cell body.

electroencephalogram (EEG)   An amplified recording of the waves of electrical activity that sweep across the brain's surface. These waves are measured by placing electrodes on the scalp.

endocrine [EN-duh-krin] **system**   The body's "slow" chemical communication system; a set of glands that secrete hormones into the bloodstream.

endorphins [en-DOR-fins]   "Morphine within"—natural, opiatelike neurotransmitters linked to pain control and pleasure.

frontal lobes   The portion of the cerebral cortex lying behind the forehead; involved in speaking and muscle movements and in making plans and judgments.

hormones   Chemical messengers, such as those manufactured by the endocrine glands, that are produced in one tissue and affect another.

hypothalamus [hi-po-THAL-uh-muss]   A neural structure lying below (*hypo*) the thalamus; it directs several maintenance activities (eating, drinking, body temperature), helps govern the endocrine system via the pituitary gland, and is linked to emotion and reward.

interneurons   Central nervous system neurons that intervene between the sensory inputs and motor outputs.

lesion [LEE-zhuhn]   Tissue destruction. A brain lesion is a naturally or experimentally caused destruction of brain tissue.

limbic system   A doughnut-shaped system of neural structures at the border of the brainstem and cerebral hemispheres; associated with emotions such as fear and aggression and drives such as those for food and sex.

medulla [muh-DUL-uh]   The base of the brainstem; controls heartbeat and breathing.

motor cortex   An area at the rear of the frontal lobes that controls voluntary movements.

motor neurons   The neurons that carry outgoing information from the central nervous system to the muscles and glands.

myelin [MY-uh-lin] **sheath**   A layer of fatty cells segmentally encasing the axons of many neurons; makes possible vastly greater transmission speed of neural impulses.

nervous system   The body's electrochemical communication system, consisting of all the nerve cells of the peripheral and central nervous systems.

neuron   A nerve cell; the basic building block of the nervous system.

neurotransmitters   Chemical messengers that traverse the synaptic gaps between neurons. When released by the sending neuron, neurotransmitters travel across the synapse and bind to receptor sites on the receiving neuron, thereby influencing whether it will fire.

occipital [ahk-SIP-uh-tuhl] **lobes**   The portion of the cerebral cortex lying at the back of the head; includes the visual areas, each of which receives visual information from the opposite visual field.

parasympathetic nervous system   The division of the autonomic nervous system that calms the body, conserving its energy.

parietal [puh-RYE-uh-tuhl] **lobes**   The portion of the cerebral cortex lying at the top of the head and toward the rear; includes the sensory cortex.

peripheral nervous system (PNS)   The part of the nervous system that lies outside of the central nervous system. It consists of the sensory neurons, which carry messages to the central nervous system from the body's sense receptors, and the motor neurons, which carry messages from the central nervous system to the muscles and glands.

PET (position emission tomograph) scan   A visual display of brain activity that detects where a radioactive form of glucose goes while the brain performs a given task.

phrenology   A discarded nineteenth-century theory, proposed by Franz Gall, that the shape of the skull reveals one's abilities and character.

pituitary gland   The endocrine system's most influential gland. Under the influence of the hypothalamus, the pituitary regulates growth and controls other endocrine glands.

plasticity   The brain's capacity for modification, as evident in brain reorganization following damage (especially in children) and in experiments on the effects of experience on brain development.

reflex A simple, automatic, inborn response to a sensory stimulus, such as the knee-jerk response.

reticular activating system A nerve network (also called the *reticular formation*) in the brainstem that plays an important role in controlling arousal and attention.

sensory cortex The area at the front of the parietal lobes that registers and processes body sensations.

sensory neurons Neurons that carry incoming information from the body's sense receptors to the central nervous system.

somatic [so-MAT-ik] **nervous system** The division of the peripheral nervous system that receives information from various sense receptors and controls the skeletal muscles of the body.

split-brain Describing a condition in which the two hemispheres of the brain are isolated by cutting the connecting fibers between them (mainly those of the corpus callosum).

sympathetic nervous system The division of the autonomic nervous system that arouses the body, mobilizing its energy in stressful situations.

synapse [SIN-aps] The junction (also called the *synaptic gap*) between the axon tip of the sending neuron and the dendrite or cell body of the receiving neuron.

temporal lobes The portion of the cerebral cortex lying roughly above the ears; includes the auditory areas, each of which receives auditory information primarily from the opposite ear.

thalamus [THAL-uh-muss] The brain's sensory switchboard, located on top of the brainstem; directs messages to the sensory receiving areas in the cortex and transmits replies to the cerebellum and medulla.

threshold The level of stimulation required to trigger a neural impulse.

Wernicke's area An area of the left hemisphere involved in language comprehension.

FOR FURTHER READING

Bloom, F. E., Lazerson, A., & Hofstadter, L. (1988). *Brain, mind, and behavior* (2nd ed.). New York: Freeman.

A lavishly illustrated summary of recent brain research written to accompany the 1984 PBS television series "The Brain."

Hooper, J., & Teresi, D. (1986). *The three-pound universe.* New York: Macmillan.

Science journalists Hooper and Teresi queried dozens of brain researchers. The result is a personalized picture of how the neurosciences are revealing new insights into emotion, memory, madness, and even spirituality.

Ornstein, R., & Thompson, R. F. (1984). *The amazing brain.* Boston: Houghton Mifflin.

An excellent introduction to recent brain research, written by two psychologists involved in it.

Springer, S. P., & Deutsch, G. (1985). *Left brain, right brain* (2nd ed.). New York: Freeman.

An award-winning description of research on the two hemispheres of brain-damaged, split-brain, and normal subjects. Discusses handedness, gender differences, learning disabilities, and theories of consciousness.

For further information in this text regarding the biology of behavior, see:

Genes and
    aggression, p. 576
    altruism, pp. 589–590
    depression, p. 459
    development, pp. 58, 59, 80–85
    fearfulness, p. 391
    gender, pp. 118–120, 128
    intelligence, pp. 335–337
    learning, pp. 236–238, 248–249
    obesity, p. 537
    schizophrenia, pp. 466–67
    sociobiology, pp. 119–120

Neurotransmitters and
    depression, p. 460
    drugs, pp. 217–218

    exercise, p. 521
    hunger, p. 355
    memory, p. 268
    schizophrenia, p. 466
    smoking, p. 531
    therapy, p. 499–500

Hormones and
    aggression, p. 130
    development, pp. 90–91
    emotion, p. 382
    gender, pp. 118–119
    hunger, p. 355
    memory, p. 268
    sex, pp. 363–364
    stress, pp. 508–510

Brain activity and
    aggression, pp. 576–577
    development, pp. 62–65
    dreams, pp. 204–206
    emotion, p. 383
    hunger, p. 356
    hypnosis, pp. 212–213
    intelligence, p. 331
    memory, pp. 266–269
    sensation, Chapter 6
    psychosurgery, pp. 497–498
    sex, p. 364
    sleep, pp. 197–200
    stress and health, Chapter 18

PART 2

Development over the Life Span

How, over time, do we come to be the persons we are, and how might we expect to change in the future? In the next two chapters we consider how we develop— physically, cognitively, and socially—during infancy and childhood (Chapter 3) and during adolescence, adulthood, and later life (Chapter 4). Then, in Chapter 5, we examine how our development is affected by whether we were born male or female.

CHAPTER 3

The Developing Child

In mid-1978, the newest astonishment in medicine, covering all the front pages, was the birth of an English baby nine months after conception in a dish. The older surprise, which should still be fazing us all, is that a solitary sperm and a single egg can fuse and become a human being under any circumstance, and that, however implanted, [this multiplied] cell affixed to the uterine wall will grow and differentiate into eight pounds of baby; this has been going on under our eyes for so long a time that we've gotten used to it; hence the outcries of amazement at this really minor technical modification of the general procedure—nothing much, really, beyond relocating the beginning of the process from the fallopian tube to a plastic container.

Lewis Thomas,
The Medusa and Snail, 1979

The developing child is no less a wonder after birth than in the womb. As we journey through life from womb to tomb, when and how do we change?

As psychologists Clyde Kluckhohn and Henry Murray (1956) noted, each person develops in certain respects like all other persons, like some other persons, and like no other persons. Usually, our attention is drawn to the ways in which we are unique. But to developmental psychologists our commonalities are as important as our uniquenesses. Virtually all of us—Michelangelo, Queen Elizabeth, Martin Luther King, Jr., you, and I—began walking around age 1, talking by age 2, and as children we engaged in social play in preparation for life's serious work. We all smile and cry, love and hate, and occasionally ponder the fact that someday we will die. As preparation for considering both the similarities and differences in our physical, cognitive, and social development, let us first confront three overriding developmental issues.

In male or female, young or old, development is a process of physical, mental, and social growth that continues throughout life.

DEVELOPMENTAL ISSUES

Three major issues pervade developmental psychology:

1. How much is our development influenced by our genetic inheritance and how much by our experience?

2. Is development a gradual, continuous process, or does it proceed through a sequence of separate stages?

3. Do our individual traits persist or do we become different persons as we age?

Let's briefly consider each of these issues and then return to them later in this and the next chapter.

GENES OR EXPERIENCE?

Our *genes* are the biochemical units of heredity that make each of us a distinctive human being. The genes we share are what make us people rather than dogs or tulips. But might our individual genetic makeups explain why one person is outgoing, another shy, or why one person is slow-witted and another smart? Questions like these raise an issue of profound importance: Are we influenced more by our genes or by our life experience?

This *nature-nurture* (or genes-experience) debate has long been one of psychology's chief concerns. Is behavior, like eye color, pretty much fixed, or is it changeable? Our answer affects how we view certain social policies. Suppose that you presume people are the way they are "by nature." You probably will not have much faith in programs that try to rehabilitate prisoners or compensate for educational disadvantage. And you will probably agree with developmental psychologists who emphasize the influence of our genes. As a flower unfolds in accord with its genetic blueprint, so our genes design an orderly sequence of biological growth processes called *maturation.* Maturation decrees many of our commonalities: standing before walking, using nouns before adjectives. Although extreme deprivation or abuse will retard development, the genetic growth tendencies are inherent.

If you take the nurture side of the debate, you probably will agree with the developmentalists who emphasize external influences. As a potter shapes a lump of clay, our experiences are presumed to shape us. This view was argued by the seventeenth-century philosopher John Locke, who proposed that at birth the child in some ways is an empty page on which experience writes its story. Although few today wholeheartedly support Locke's proposition, research provides many examples of nurture's effects.

In reality, nearly everyone agrees that our behaviors are a product of the interaction of (1) our genes, (2) our past experience, and (3) the present situation to which we are responding. Moreover, these factors sometimes *interact.* For example, if an attractive, athletic teenage boy has been treated as a leader and is now sought out by girls, shall we say his positive self-image is due to his genes or his environment? It's both, because his environment is reacting to his genetic endowment. Asking which factor is more important is like asking whether the area of a football field is due more to its length or to its width.

CONTINUITY OR STAGES?

Everyone agrees that adults are vastly different from infants. But do they differ as a giant redwood differs from its seedling—a difference created by gradual, cumulative growth? Or do they differ as a butterfly differs from a caterpillar—a difference of distinct stages?

Generally speaking, researchers who emphasize experience and learning tend to see development as a slow, continuous shaping process. Those who emphasize biological maturation tend to see development as a sequence of genetically predetermined stages or steps. They believe that, depending on an individual's heredity and experiences, progress through the various stages may be quick or slow, but everyone passes through the same stages in the same order.

More than 98 percent of our genes are identical to those of chimpanzees. Not surprisingly, the physiological systems and even the brain organizations of humans and chimpanzees are quite similar.

"Maturation (read the genetic program, largely) sets the course of development, which is modified by experience, especially if that experience is deviant from what is normal for the species."
    Sandra Scarr (1982)

Nature or nurture? Stability or change? For example, how much is this outgoing baby's temperament due to her heredity and how much to her upbringing? And how likely is it that she will be an outgoing adult? These questions define two fundamental issues of developmental psychology.

STABILITY OR CHANGE?

For most of this century, psychologists have taken the position that once a person's personality is formed, it hardens and usually remains set for life. Researchers who have followed lives through time are now in the midst of a spirited debate over the extent to which our past reaches into our future. Is development characterized more by *stability* over time or by *change?* Are the effects of early experience enduring or temporary? Will the cranky infant grow up to be an irritable adult, or is such a child just as likely to become a placid, patient person? Do the differences among classmates in, say, aggressiveness, aptitude, or strivings for achievement persist throughout the life span? In short, to what degree do we grow to be merely older versions of our early selves and to what degree do we become new persons?

Most developmentalists today believe that for certain traits, such as basic temperament, there is an underlying continuity, especially in the years following early childhood. Yet, as we age we also change— physically, cognitively, socially. Thus we have today's life-span view: Human development is a lifelong process.

PRENATAL DEVELOPMENT AND THE NEWBORN

FROM LIFE COMES LIFE

Nothing is more natural than a species reproducing itself. Yet nothing is more wondrous. Consider human reproduction: The process starts when a mature *ovum* (egg) is released by a woman's ovary and the some 300 million sperm deposited during intercourse begin their race upstream toward it. When a girl is born, she carries all the eggs she will ever have, although only a few will ever mature and be released. A boy, in contrast, begins producing sperm at puberty. The manufacturing process continues 24 hours a day for the rest of his life, although the rate of production—over 1000 sperm a second—does slow down with age.

New life is created when egg and sperm unite, and the twenty-three *chromosomes* carried in the egg are paired with the twenty-three chromosomes brought to it by the sperm. These forty-six chromosomes contain the master plan for your body (Figure 3–1). Each chromosome is composed of long threads of a molecule called *DNA (deoxyribonucleic acid)*. DNA in turn is made up of thousands of segments, called genes, that are capable of synthesizing specific proteins (the biochemical building blocks of life).

Your sex is determined by the twenty-third pair of chromosomes, the sex chromosomes. The member of the pair that came from your mother was, invariably, an **X** *chromosome.* From your father, you had a fifty-fifty chance of receiving an X chromosome, making you a female, or a **Y** *chromosome,* making you a male. Biology has become so advanced that scientists have pinpointed the single tiny gene on the *Y* chromosome that seems responsible for throwing the master switch leading to the production of *testosterone*, and thus to maleness (Roberts, 1988).

Like space voyagers approaching a huge planet, the sperm approach a cell 85,000 times bigger than themselves. The relatively few sperm that make it to the egg release digestive enzymes that eat away

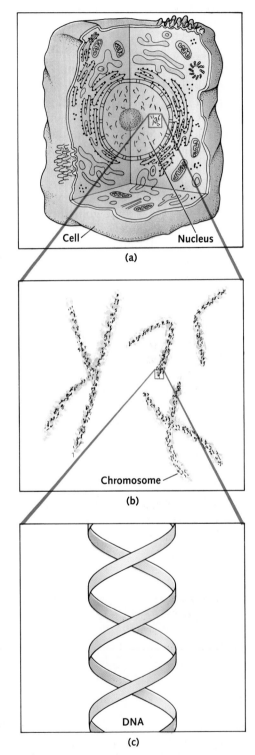

Figure 3–1 The genes: their location and composition. Contained in the nucleus of each of the trillions of cells (a) in your body are chromosomes (b). Each chromosome is composed in part of the molecule DNA (c). Genes, which are segments of DNA, form templates for the production of proteins. By directing the manufacture of proteins, the genes determine our individual biological development.

the egg's protective coating, allowing one sperm to penetrate (Figure 3–2). As it does so, an electrical charge shoots across the ovum's surface, blocking out other sperm during the minute or so that it takes the egg to form a barrier. Meanwhile, fingerlike projections sprout around the successful sperm and pull it inward. The egg nucleus and the sperm nucleus move toward each other and, before half a day has elapsed, they fuse. The two have become one.

But even at that moment, when one lucky sperm has won the 1 in 300 million lottery, an individual's destiny is not assured. Fewer than half of fertilized eggs, called **zygotes**, survive beyond the first week (Grobstein, 1979), and only a fourth survive to birth (Diamond, 1986). If human life begins at conception, then most people die without being born.

But for you and me good fortune prevailed. Beginning as one cell, each of us became two cells, then four—each cell just like the first. Then, within the first week, when this cell division had produced a zygote of approximately 100 cells, the cells began to *differentiate*—to specialize in structure and function. Within 2 weeks, the increasingly diverse cells became attached to the mother's uterine wall, beginning approximately 37 weeks of the closest human relationship (see Figure 3–3).

During the ensuing 6 weeks, the developing human is called an **embryo.** In this embryonic period the organs begin to form and may begin to function: The heart begins to beat and the liver begins to make red blood cells. By the ninth week, the embryo has become unmistakably human and is called a **fetus.** By the end of the sixth month, internal organs such as the stomach have become sufficiently formed and functional that they allow a prematurely born fetus a chance of survival.

Nutrients and oxygen in the mother's blood pass through the *placenta* into the blood of the fetus. If the mother is severely malnourished during the last third of the pregnancy, when the demand for nutrients reaches a peak, the baby may be born prematurely—or even be stillborn.

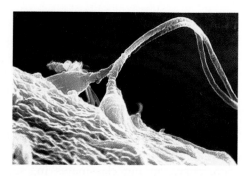

Figure 3–2 Development begins when a sperm unites with an egg. The resulting zygote is a single cell that, if all goes well, will become a 100-trillion-cell human being.

Prenatal stages

Zygote: conception to 2 weeks.

Embryo: 2 weeks through 8 weeks.

Fetus: 9 weeks to birth.

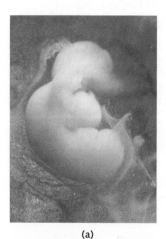

(a)

(b)

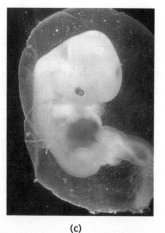

(c)

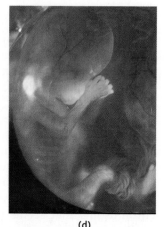

(d)

Figure 3–3 Prenatal development. (a) The embryo grows and develops rapidly. At 40 days, the spine is visible and the arms and legs are beginning to grow. (b) Five days later the embryo's proportions have begun to change. The rest of the body is now bigger than the head, and the arms and legs have grown noticeably. (c) By the end of the second month, when the fetal period begins, facial features, hands, and feet have formed. (The placenta, which attaches the fetus to the wall of the uterus and through which the fetus is nourished, is clearly visible in this photo.) (d) As the fetus enters the fourth month, it weighs about 3 ounces.

Along with nourishment, harmful substances, called *teratogens,* can pass through or harm the placenta—with potentially tragic effects. If the mother is a heroin addict, her baby is born a heroin addict. If she is a heavy smoker, her newborn is likely to be underweight, sometimes dangerously so (U.S. Department of Health and Human Services, 1983a). If she drinks much alcohol, her baby is at greater risk for birth defects and mental retardation (Raymond, 1987). If she carries the AIDS virus, her baby will often be infected as well (Minkoff, 1987).

THE COMPETENT NEWBORN

Newborns come equipped with reflexes that are ideally suited for survival. The infants will withdraw a limb to escape pain; if a cloth is put over their faces, interfering with their breathing, they will turn their heads from side to side and swipe at it. New parents are often awed by the coordinated sequence of reflexes by which babies obtain food. The *rooting reflex* is one example: When their cheeks are touched, babies will open their mouths and vigorously "root" for a nipple. Finding one, they will automatically close on it and begin sucking—which itself requires a coordinated sequence of tonguing, swallowing, and breathing. Failing to find satisfaction, the hungry baby may cry—a behavior that parents are predisposed to find highly unpleasant to hear and very rewarding to relieve.

The pioneering American psychologist William James (who once said, "The first lecture on psychology I ever heard was the first I ever gave") presumed that the newborn experiences a "blooming, buzzing confusion." Until the 1960s few people disagreed. It was said that, apart from a blur of meaningless light and dark shades, newborns could not see. Then, just as the development of new technology led to a surge of progress in the neurosciences, so too did new investigative techniques enhance the study of infants. Scientists discovered that babies can tell you a lot—if you know how to ask. To ask, you must capitalize on what the baby can do—gaze, suck, turn the head. So, equipped with eye-tracking machines, pacifiers wired to electronic gear, and other such devices, researchers set out to answer parents' age-old question: What can my baby see, hear, smell, and think?

They discovered that a baby's sensory equipment is "wired" to facilitate social responsiveness. Newborns turn their heads in the direction of human voices, but not in response to artificial sounds. They gaze more at a drawing of a human face than at a bull's-eye pattern; yet they gaze more at a bull's-eye pattern—which has contrasts much like that of the human eye—than at a solid disk (Fantz, 1961). They focus best on objects about 9 inches away, which, wonder of wonders, just happens to be the typical distance between a nursing infant's eyes and the mother's. Newborns, it seems, arrive perfectly designed to see their mothers' eyes first of all.

Babies' perceptual abilities are continuously developing during the first months of life. Within days of birth, babies can distinguish their mothers' facial expression, odor, and voice. A week-old nursing baby, placed between a gauze pad from its mother's bra and one from another nursing mother, will generally turn toward the smell of its own mother's pad (MacFarlane, 1978). At 3 weeks of age, an infant who is allowed to suck on a pacifier that sometimes turns on recordings of its mother's voice and sometimes that of female stranger, will suck more vigorously when it hears its mother's voice (Mills & Melhuish, 1974). So not only can infants see what they need to see, and smell and hear well, but they are already using their sensory equipment to learn.

Tera literally means "monster"; teratogens are "monster-producing" agents, such as chemicals and viruses, that may harm the fetus.

"It is a rare privilege to watch the birth, growth, and first feeble struggles of a living human mind."
 Annie Sullivan, in Helen Keller's
 The Story of My Life, 1903

Studies like the one under way in this MIT lab are exploring infants' abilities to perceive, think, and remember. This infant is being tested on pattern perception. Experiments have demonstrated that even very young infants are capable of sophisticated visual discrimination. They often show a marked preference for one picture over another, and will also look much longer at an unfamiliar pattern than at one which they have seen before. Such tests have changed psychologists' ideas of what the world looks like to a baby.

Two teams of investigators have reported the astonishing and controversial finding that, in the second week—or even the first hour of life—infants tend to imitate facial expressions (Field & others, 1982; Meltzoff & Moore, 1983, 1985).

If such findings can be substantiated by additional research, it will be a further tribute to the newborn's competence. Consider: How do newborn babies relate their own facial movements to those of an adult? And how can they coordinate the movements involved? The findings are controversial because they contradict what most people have presumed to be the newborn's very limited sensory and motor abilities.

Researcher Tiffany Field (1987) notes that "Our knowledge of infancy was in its infancy 20 years ago, but what we have learned since then has dramatically changed the way we perceive and treat infants." More and more, psychologists see the baby as "a very sophisticated perceiver of the world, with very sensitive social and emotional qualities and impressive intellectual abilities." The "helpless infant" of the 1950s has become the "amazing newborn" of the 1980s.

Imitation? When Andrew Meltzoff shows his tongue, an 18-day-old boy responds similarly. "As our experimental techniques have become more and more sophisticated," reports Meltzoff (1987), "the infants themselves have appeared more and more clever."

INFANCY AND CHILDHOOD

During infancy, a baby grows from newborn to toddler, and during childhood from toddler to teenager. Beginning in this chapter with infancy and childhood and continuing in the next chapter with adolescence through old age, we will see how people of all ages are continually developing—physically, cognitively, and socially.

PHYSICAL DEVELOPMENT

Brain Development   While you resided in your mother's womb, your body was forming nerve cells at the rate of about one-quarter million per *minute*. On the day you were born you had essentially all the brain cells you were ever going to have. However, the human nervous system is immature at birth; the neural networks that enable us to walk, talk, and remember are only beginning to form (see Figure 3–4).

Along with the development of neural networks we see increasing myelinization of neurons. (As we saw in Chapter 2, myelin is a fatty cell that encases the axon, enabling messages to speed many times faster.) The nerve fibers that monitor and coordinate bladder control, for example, are not fully myelinated until the second year. To expect a toddler to do without a diaper before then is to court disaster.

The storage of permanent memory also requires neural development. Our earliest memories go back only to between our third and fourth birthdays (Kihlstrom & Harachkiewicz, 1982). For parents, this "infantile amnesia," as Freud called it, can be disconcerting. After all the hours we spend with our babies—after all the frolicking on the rug, all the diapering, feeding, and rocking to sleep—what would they consciously remember of us if we died? Nothing!

But if nothing is consciously recalled, something has still been gained. From birth (and even before), infants can learn. They can learn to turn their heads away to make an adult "peekaboo" at them, to pull a string to make a mobile turn, to turn their heads to the left or right to receive a sugar solution when their forehead is stroked (Blass, 1987; Bower, 1977; Lancioni, 1980). Such learning tends not to persist unless

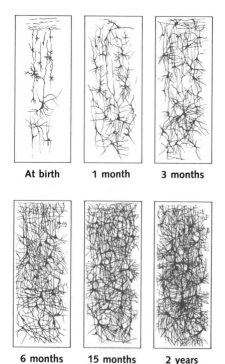

| At birth | 1 month | 3 months |
| 6 months | 15 months | 2 years |

Figure 3–4   In humans, the brain is immature at birth. These drawings of sections of brain tissue from the cerebral cortex illustrate the increasing complexity of the neural networks in the maturing human brain.

reactivated. Nevertheless, early learning may prepare our brains for those later experiences that we *do* remember. For example, children who become deaf at age 2, after being exposed to speech, are later more easily language trained than those deaf from birth (Lenneberg, 1967). It has been suggested that the first 2 years are therefore critical for learning language.

Animals such as guinea pigs, whose brains are mature at birth, more readily form permanent memories from infancy than do animals with immature brains, such as rats (Campbell & Coulter, 1976). Because human brains are also immature at birth, these findings cast doubt on the idea that people subconsciously remember their prenatal life or the trauma of their birth. But, given occasional reminders, 3-month-old infants who learn that moving their leg propels a mobile will indeed remember the association for at least a month (Rovee-Collier, 1988)—so some infant memory does exist.

Does experience, as well as biological maturation, help develop the brain's neural connections? Although "forgotten," early learning may help prepare our brains for thought and language, and for later experiences. Surely our early learning must somehow be recorded "in there."

If early experiences affect us by leaving their "marks" in the brain, then it should be possible to detect evidence of this. The modern tools of neuroscience allow us a closer look. Working at the University of California, Berkeley, Mark Rosenzweig caged some rats in solitary confinement, while others were caged in a communal playground (Figure 3–5). Rats living in the deprived environment usually developed a lighter and thinner cortex with smaller nerve cell bodies, as well as fewer glial cells (the "glue cells" that support and nourish the brain's neurons). Rosenzweig (1984a; Renner & Rosenzweig, 1987) reported being so surprised by these effects of experience on brain tissue that he repeated the experiment several times before publishing his findings—findings that have led to improvements in the environments provided for laboratory and farm animals and for institutionalized children.

Other recent studies extended these findings. Several research teams have found that infant rats and premature babies benefit from the stimulation of being touched or massaged (Field & others, 1986; Meaney & others, 1988). "Handled" infants of both species gain weight more rapidly and develop faster neurologically. In adulthood, handled rat pups also secrete less of a stress hormone that during aging causes neuron death in the hippocampus, a brain center important for memory. William Greenough and his University of Illinois coworkers (1987) further discovered that repeated experiences sculpt a rat's neural tissue—at the very spot in the brain where the experience is processed. This sculpting seems to work by preserving activated neural connections while allowing unused connections to degenerate.

More and more, researchers are becoming convinced that the brain's neural connections are dynamic; throughout life our neural tissue is changing. Our genes dictate our overall brain architecture, but experience directs the details. If a monkey is trained to push a lever with a finger several thousand times a day, the brain tissue that controls the finger changes to reflect the experience. The wiring of Michael Jordan's brain reflects the thousands of hours he has spent shooting baskets. Experience, it seems, helps nurture nature.

Motor Development   As the infant's muscles and neural networks mature, ever more complicated skills emerge. Although the age at

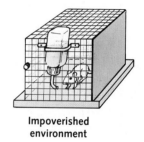

**Impoverished
environment**

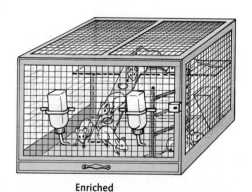

**Enriched
environment**

Figure 3–5 Experience affects the brain's development. In experiments pioneered by Mark Rosenzweig and David Krech, rats were reared either alone in an environment without playthings or with others in an environment enriched with playthings that were changed daily. In fourteen out of sixteen repetitions of this basic experiment, the rats placed in the enriched environment developed significantly more cerebral cortex relative to the rest of the brain's tissue than those in the impoverished environment. (From ''Brain changes in response to experience'' by M. R. Rosenzweig, E. L. Bennett, and M. C. Diamond. Copyright © 1972 Scientific American, Inc. All rights reserved.)

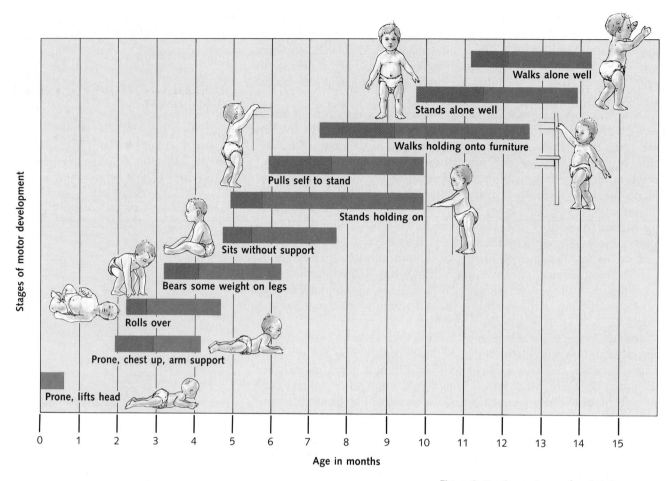

Stages of motor development

Walks alone well

Stands alone well

Walks holding onto furniture

Pulls self to stand

Stands holding on

Sits without support

Bears some weight on legs

Rolls over

Prone, chest up, arm support

Prone, lifts head

0   1   2   3   4   5   6   7   8   9   10   11   12   13   14   15

Age in months

Figure 3–6 Some stages of motor development in infants. Although some infants reach each stage ahead of others, the order of the stages is the same for all infants. The colored bars show age ranges for the development of each stage. The far left side of the bar is the age by which 25 percent have mastered this movement; the far right side is the age by which 90 percent have mastered it. The point on the bar where blue meets red is the age by which half of the infants have mastered the movement.

which infants sit, stand, and walk varies from child to child, the sequence in which babies pass these developmental milestones (Figure 3–6) is universal.

Can experience retard or speed up the maturation of physical skills? If babies were bound to a cradleboard for much of their first year—the traditional practice among the Hopi Indians—would they walk later than do unbound infants? If allowed to spend an hour a day in a walker chair after age 4 months, would they walk earlier? Amazingly, in view of what we now know about the effects experience has on the brain, the answer to both questions seems to be no (Dennis, 1940; Ridenour, 1982).

Biological maturation—including the rapid development of the cerebellum at the rear of the brain—creates a readiness to learn walking at about 1 year of age. Experience before that time has no more than a small effect, although restriction later may retard development (Super, 1981). This is true for other physical skills, including bowel and bladder control. Until the necessary muscular and neural maturation has occurred, no amount of pleading, harassment, or punishment can lead to successful toilet training.

After a spurt during the first 2 years, growth slows to a steady 2 to 3 inches per year through childhood. With all of the neurons and most of their interconnections in place, brain development after age 2 similarly proceeds at a slower pace. The sensory and motor cortex areas continue to mature relatively rapidly, enabling fine motor skills to develop further (R. Wilson, 1978). The association areas of the cortex—those associated with thinking, memory, and language—are the last brain areas to develop.

To predict a girl's adult height, double her height at 18 months. To predict a boy's adult height, double his height at 2 years.

COGNITIVE DEVELOPMENT

Brain scans and brain wave analyses reveal that the development of different brain areas during infancy and childhood corresponds closely with cognitive development (Chugani & Phelps, 1986; Thatcher & others, 1987). Brain and mind develop together. *Cognition* refers to all the mental activities associated with thinking, knowing, and remembering. Few questions have intrigued developmental psychologists more than these: When can children begin to remember? See things from another's point of view? Reason logically? Think symbolically? Simply put, how does a child's mind grow? Such were the questions posed by developmental psychologist Jean Piaget (pronounced Pea-ah-ZHAY).

"Who knows the thoughts of a child?" wondered poet Nora Perry. As much as anyone of his generation, Piaget knew. His interest in children's cognitive processes began in 1920, when he was working in Paris to develop questions for children's intelligence tests. In the course of administering tests to find out at what age children could answer certain questions correctly, Piaget became intrigued by children's *wrong* answers. Where others saw childish mistakes, Piaget saw intelligence at work. He observed that the errors made by children of a given age were often strikingly similar.

The more than 50 years Piaget spent in such informal activities with children convinced him that *the child's mind is not a miniature model of the adult's:* Young children actively construct their understandings of the world in radically different ways than adults do, a fact that we overlook when attempting to teach children by using our adult logic. Piaget further believed that the child's mind develops through a series of stages, in an upward march from the sensorimotor simplicity of the newborn to the abstract reasoning power of the adult. An 8-year-old child therefore comprehends things that a 3-year-old *can*not. An 8-year-old might grasp the analogy "getting an idea is like having a light turn on in your head," but trying to teach the same analogy to a 3-year-old would be fruitless.

How the Mind of a Child Grows   The driving force behind this intellectual progression is the unceasing struggle to make sense out of one's world. To this end, the maturing brain builds concepts, which Piaget called *schemas.* Schemas are ways of looking at the world that organize our past experiences and provide a framework for understanding our future experiences. We start life with simple schemas— those involving sense-driven reflexes such as sucking and grasping. By adulthood we have built a seemingly limitless number of schemas that range from knowing how to tie a knot to knowing what it means to be in love.

Piaget proposed two concepts to explain how we use and adjust our schemas. First, we interpret our experience in terms of our current understandings; in Piaget's terms, we incorporate, or *assimilate,* new experiences into our existing schemas.

Assimilation is interpreting new experiences in light of one's schemas, as when a toddler calls all four-legged animals "doggies." But we also adjust, or *accommodate,* our schemas to fit the particulars of new experiences. The child learns fairly quickly that the original "doggie" schema is too broad, and accommodates by refining the category. When new experiences just will not fit our old schemas, our schemas may change to accommodate the experiences. When prejudiced people perceive a minority person through their preconceived ideas, they are assimilating. When experience forces them to modify their former schemas, they are accommodating.

Jean Piaget (1930, p. 237): "If we examine the intellectual development of the individual or of the whole of humanity, we shall find that the human spirit goes through a certain number of stages, each different from the other."

"For everything there is a season, and a time for every matter under heaven."
   Ecclesiastes 3:1

Look carefully at the "devil's tuning fork" below.

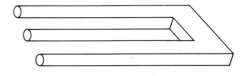

Now look away—no, better first study it some more—and *then* look away and draw it. Not so easy, is it? Because this tuning fork is an impossible object, you have no schema into which you can assimilate what you see.

Highly realistic art is easy to assimilate; it requires for interpretation only those schemas already available from observing the world. Highly abstract art is difficult to assimilate, which may explain the frustration it sometimes causes. When art combines realism with abstraction, it allows observers to impose meaning by stimulating them to stretch their schemas.

Science itself is a process of assimilation and accommodation. Scientists interpret nature using their preconceived theories—for example, that newborns are passive, incompetent creatures—to *assimilate* what would otherwise be a bewildering body of disconnected observations. Then, as new observations collide with these theories, the theories must be changed or replaced to *accommodate* the findings. Thus the new concept of the newborn as competent and active replaces the old schema. That, Piaget believed, is how children (and adults) construct reality using *both* assimilation and accommodation. What we know is not reality exactly as it is, but our constructions of it.

Piaget's Theory of Cognitive Stages   Piaget went on to describe cognitive development as occurring in four major stages (Table 3–1).

Table 3–1
PIAGET'S STAGES OF COGNITIVE DEVELOPMENT

Approximate age	Description of stage	Developmental milestones
Birth–2 years	**Sensorimotor** Infant experiences the world through senses and actions (looking, touching, mouthing).	Object permanence (page 67); stranger anxiety (page 68).
2–6 years	**Preoperational** Child represents things with words and images, but cannot reason with logic.	Ability to pretend (page 67); egocentrism (page 68).
7–12 years	**Concrete operational** Child thinks logically about concrete events; can grasp concrete analogies and perform arithmetical operations.	Conservation (page 69); mathematical transformations (page 69).
Teen years	**Formal operational** Teenager develops abstract reasoning.	Scientific reasoning (page 92); potential for mature moral reasoning (pages 92–95).

The sensorimotor stage of development begins in infancy and continues until about age 2. Very young children explore the world through their senses, enjoying the smell, feel, and taste of almost anything they can get their hands on. As the child moves into the preoperational stage, at the age of about 18 months, pretending becomes possible. This child's imagination is still expressed through simple care-giving; in another year the pretend activities will become much more elaborate.

The developing child, he believed, moves from one age-related plateau to the next. Each plateau has distinctive characteristics that permit specific kinds of thinking. The differences between these kinds of thinking are qualitative: They involve changes in the *way* the child thinks.

During the first stage, which occurs between birth and approximately age 2, infants are limited to *sensorimotor intelligence:* Their understanding of the world is restricted to their interactions with objects through their senses and motor activity—through looking, touching, sucking, grasping, and the like. In the preschool years of 2 to 6 most children demonstrate *preoperational intelligence:* They can think about objects without physically interacting with them, which means they can begin to think about objects in a simple symbolic way.

This new type of thinking is reflected in the preschooler's ability to pretend, to think about past events and anticipate future ones, and to begin to use language. Children in the preoperational stage are not able, however, to think in a truly logical fashion. They may figure out that five plus three is eight and not instantly realize that three plus five is also eight.

Beginning at about age 7, children demonstrate *concrete operational intelligence:* They can perform the mental operations that produce logical thought, but they are able to think logically only about concrete things. It is not until about age 12, when children enter the stage of *formal operational intelligence,* that they are able to begin to think hypothetically and abstractly. To appreciate how the mind of a child grows, let's look more closely at each of these stages.

Sensorimotor Stage   During the **sensorimotor stage,** infants understand their world in terms of their senses and the effects of their actions; they are aware only of what they can see, smell, suck, taste, and grasp, and at first they seem to be unaware that things continue to exist apart from their perceptions.

In one of his tests, Piaget would show an infant an appealing toy and then flop his beret over it to see whether the infant searched for the toy. Before the age of 8 months, they did not. They lacked **object permanence**—the awareness that objects continue to exist when not perceived. The infant lives in the present. What is out of sight is out of mind. By 8 months, infants begin to develop what psychologists now believe is a memory for things no longer seen. Hide the toy and the

"Children think not of what is past, nor what is to come, but enjoy the present time, which few of us do."
La Bruyère, 1645–1696
Les caractères: De l'homme

Object permanence. Younger children lack the sense that things continue to exist when not in sight; but for this 8½-month-old child, out of sight is not out of mind.

infant will momentarily look for it. Within another month or two, the infant will look for it even after being restrained for several seconds.

This flowering of recall occurs simultaneously with the emergence of a fear of strangers, called *stranger anxiety.* Watch how infants of different ages react when handed over to a stranger and you will notice that, beginning at 8 or 9 months, they often will cry and reach for their familiar caregivers. Is it a mere coincidence that object permanence and stranger anxiety develop together? Probably not. After about 8 months of age, the child has schemas for familiar faces; when a new face cannot be assimilated into these remembered schemas, the infant becomes distressed (Kagan, 1984). This link between cognitive development and social behavior illustrates the interplay of brain maturation, cognitive development, and social development.

Preoperational Stage   Seen through the eyes of Piaget, preschool children are still far from being short grownups. Although aware of themselves, of time, and of the permanence of objects, they are, he said, *egocentric:* They cannot perceive things from another's point of view. The preschooler who blocks your view of the television while trying to see it herself and the one who asks a question while you are on the phone both assume that you see and hear what they see and hear. When relating to a young child, it may help to remember that such behaviors reflect a cognitive limitation: The egocentric preschooler has difficulty taking another's viewpoint.

Preschoolers also find it easier to follow positive instructions ("Hold the puppy gently") than negative ones ("Don't squeeze the puppy"). One characteristic of parents who abuse their children is that they generally have no understanding of these limits. They perceive their children as junior adults who are in control of their behavior (Larrance & Twentyman, 1983). Thus children who stand in the way, spill food, disobey negative instructions, or cry may be perceived as willfully malicious.

Just before age 3 children do, however, become more capable of thinking symbolically. Judy DeLoache (1987) discovered this when she showed a group of 2½-year-olds a model of a room and hid a model toy in it (say a miniature stuffed dog behind a miniature couch). The children could easily remember where to find the miniature toy, but could not readily locate the actual stuffed dog behind the couch in the real room. When 3-year-olds were given a look at the model room, however, they would usually go right to the actual stuffed animal in the real room, showing that they could think of the model as a symbol for the room.

Piaget believed that during this preschool period and up to about age 7, children are in what he called the *preoperational stage*—unable to perform mental operations. For a 5-year-old, the quantity of milk that is "too much" in a tall, narrow glass may become an acceptable amount if poured into a short, wide glass. This is because the child focuses only on the height dimension, and is incapable of reversing the operation by mentally pouring it back. The child lacks the concept of *conservation*—the principle that the quantity of a substance remains the same despite changes in its shape. Children's conversations confirm this inability to reverse information (Phillips, 1969, p. 61):

> "Do you have a brother?"
> "Yes."
> "What's his name?"
> "Jim."
> "Does Jim have a brother?"
> "No."

Concrete Operational Stage   With older children, Piaget would roll one of two identical balls of clay into a rope shape and ask whether there was more clay in the rope or the ball. Children who are in the preoperational stage almost always say that the rope has more clay because they assume "longer is more." They cannot mentally reverse the clay-rolling process to see that the amount of clay is the same in both shapes. But children who are in the *concrete operational stage* realize that a given quantity remains the same no matter how its shape changes. Piaget contended that during the stage of concrete operations (roughly ages 7 to 12) children acquire the mental operations needed to comprehend mathematical transformations and conservation. When my daughter Laura was age 6, I was astonished at her inability to reverse arithmetic operations—until considering Piaget. Asked, "What is eight plus four?" she required 5 seconds to compute "twelve," and another 5 seconds to then compute twelve minus four. By age 8, she could reverse the process and answer the second question instantly.

The preoperational child cannot perform the mental operations essential to understanding conservation. A glass of milk seems to be "more" after being poured into a tall, narrow glass.

Although the operations usually must involve concrete images of physical actions or objects, not abstract ideas, preteen children exhibit logic. Eleven-year-olds can mentally pour the milk back and forth between different-shaped glasses, so they realize that change in shape does not mean change in quantity. They also enjoy jokes that allow them to utilize their recently acquired concepts, such as conservation:

> Mr. Jones went into a restaurant and ordered a whole pizza for his dinner. When the waiter asked if he wanted it cut into 6 or 8 pieces, Mr. Jones said, "Oh, you'd better make it 6, I could never eat 8 pieces!" (McGhee, 1976)

If Piaget was correct that children construct their understandings through assimilation and accommodation, and that in early childhood their thinking is radically different from adult thinking, what are the implications for preschool and elementary school teachers? Might teachers capitalize on what comes naturally to children? Believing that children actively construct their own understandings, Piaget contended that teachers should strive to "create the possibilities for a child to invent and discover." Build on what children already know, allow them to touch and see, to witness concrete demonstrations, to think for themselves. Exploit their natural ways of thinking and learning. Because the young child is incapable of adult logic, teachers must under-

Piaget's writings have influenced many educators to provide children with situations and encouragement that will prompt them to do their own exploring and discovering. For younger children, especially, direct observation has proved an effective learning tool.

stand how children think, and therefore realize that what is simple and obvious to them—that subtraction is the reverse of addition—may be incomprehensible to a 6-year-old.

Reflections on Piaget's Theory   Piaget's stage theory is controversial. Do children's cognitive abilities really go through distinct stages? Does object permanence in fact appear rather abruptly, much as a tulip blossoms in spring? Today's researchers contend that we have underestimated the competence of young children. Given very simple tasks, preschoolers are *not* purely egocentric; they will adjust their explanations to make them clearer to a listener who is blindfolded, and will show a toy or picture with the front side facing the viewer (Gelman, 1979; Siegel & Hodkin, 1982). If questioned in a way that makes sense to them, 5- and 6-year-olds will exhibit some understanding of conservation (Donaldson, 1979). It seems, then, that the abilities to take another's perspective and to perform mental operations are not utterly absent in the preoperational stage—and then suddenly appear. Rather, these abilities begin earlier than Piaget believed and develop more gradually.

What remains of Piaget's ideas about the mind of the child? Plenty. For Piaget identified and named important cognitive phenomena and helped stimulate interest in studying how the mind develops. That we today are adapting his ideas to accommodate new findings would not surprise him.

SOCIAL DEVELOPMENT

As we have seen, babies are social creatures from birth. Almost from the start, parent and baby communicate through eye contact, touch, smiles, and voice. The end result is social behavior that promotes infants' survival and their emerging sense of self, so that they, too, eventually may bear and nurture a new generation.

In all cultures, infants develop an intense bond with those who care for them. Beginning with newborns' attraction to humans in general, infants soon come to prefer familiar faces and voices and then to coo and gurgle when given their mothers' or fathers' attention. By 8 months, when they are dealing with the linked milestones of object permanence and stranger anxiety, they will crawl wherever mother or father goes and will become distressed when separated from them. At 12 months many infants cling tightly to a parent when frightened or anticipating separation and, when reunited, shower the parent with smiles and hugs. No social behavior is more striking than this intense infant love, called *attachment,* a powerful survival impulse that keeps infants close to their caregivers. Among the early social responses— love, fear, aggression—the first and greatest is this bond of love.

Origins of Attachment   How does this parent-infant bond develop? A number of elements work together to create this relationship.

Body Contact   For many years developmental psychologists reasoned that infants became attached to those who satisfied their need for nourishment. It makes perfect sense. But an accidental finding revealed this explanation of attachment to be incomplete. For his 1950s studies of the development of learning abilities, University of Wisconsin psychologist Harry Harlow needed to breed monkeys. To equalize the infant monkeys' early experiences and to prevent the spread of disease, he separated the monkeys from their mothers shortly after birth and raised them in sanitary, individual cages, which included a cheesecloth baby blanket (Harlow & others, 1971). Surprisingly, the infants became intensely attached to their blankets: When the blankets were taken to be laundered, the monkeys were greatly distressed. They acted as if they had been separated from their mothers.

Harlow soon recognized that this attachment to the blanket contradicted the idea that attachment is derived from the association with nourishment. But could he demonstrate this more convincingly? Doing so would require some way to pit the drawing power of a food source against the contact comfort of the blanket. Harlow's creative solution consisted of two artificial mothers—one a bare wire cylinder with a wooden head, the other a similar cylinder wrapped with foam rubber and covered with terrycloth. Either could be associated with feeding through an attached bottle.

Even when reared with a nourishing wire mother and a nonnourishing cloth mother, the monkeys overwhelmingly preferred the cloth mother (Figure 3–7). Like human infants clinging to their mothers, they would cling to the cloth mother when anxious and would use her as a base of security from which to venture out into the environment, as if attached to the mother by an invisible elastic band that stretches so far and then pulls the infant back. Further studies with Margaret Harlow and others revealed that other qualities— rocking, warmth, and feeding—could boost the magnetism of the comfortable cloth mother.

In human infants, too, attachment usually grows from body contact with parents who are soft and warm and who rock, pat, and feed. This may help explain the recent finding that infants whose parents were instructed to carry them for at least 3 hours a day cried less than other infants (Hunziker & Barr, 1986). The net result of Harlow's research should also reassure the fathers of breast-fed infants: Attachment does not depend on feeding alone.

Familiarity   Another key to attachment is familiarity (Rheingold, 1985). Infants prefer faces and objects with which they are familiar. In certain animals, attachments based on familiarity form during a *critical period*—a restricted time period during which certain events must take

Figure 3–7   When Harry Harlow reared monkeys with two artificial mothers—one a bare wire cylinder with a wooden head and an attached feeding bottle and the other a cylinder covered with foam rubber and wrapped with terrycloth but without a feeding bottle—they preferred the comfortable cloth mother to the nourishing wire mother. It is interesting that monkeys also prefer the texture of terrycloth to the unmonkey-like smoothness of satins and silks, and that human infants are similarly more soothed by a textured than a smooth blanket (Maccoby, 1980).

place if proper development is to occur—shortly after birth. The first moving object that a gosling, duckling, or chick sees during the hours shortly after hatching is normally its mother, and thereafter the young fowl follows her, and her alone. Konrad Lorenz (1937) explored this rigid attachment process, called *imprinting.* He wondered what ducklings would do if *he* were the first moving creature they observed. What they did was follow him around. Further tests revealed that baby birds would imprint to a variety of moving objects—an animal of another species, a box on wheels, a bouncing ball—and that, once formed, this attachment was often difficult to reverse (Colombo, 1982).

The attachment of infants to their parents is reciprocated. Most mammals lick and groom their newborns during the first hours after birth and, if prevented from doing so, may later reject their offspring. Might there be a critical period during which contact triggers such bonding in humans?

Proponents of bonding maintain that physical contact during the first hours after birth boosts parent-infant attachment (Kennell & Klaus, 1982). But developmental psychologists Michael Lamb (1982), Susan Goldberg (1983), and Barbara Myers (1984a, 1984b) scrutinized the research on mother-infant bonding and each came away unconvinced. Either the studies were seriously flawed, they reported, or the effects of physical ''bonding'' are both minimal and temporary. Humans *don't* have a precise critical period for becoming attached.

Critics of the bonding notion welcome the trend toward involving parents in the childbirth process. The danger, they suggest, comes in making parents who have not experienced early contact—including mothers who have had cesareans or parents who have adopted children—feel inadequate. These parents may be led by proponents of bonding to fear that they and their child have missed out on something terribly important. And that, say the critics, is simply not true.

Likewise, there is little evidence that breast-feeding is psychologically more advantageous to an infant than bottle-feeding. Bottle-fed infants usually enjoy nearly the same cuddling, eye contact, and sensory experience as nursing infants. To be sure, breast-feeding is commendable as an intimate and pleasurable way of providing ideal nutrition—as ideal as cow's milk is for calves. But to be bottle-fed is not to be psychologically handicapped (Ferguson & others, 1987).

Responsive Parenting   How are children's attachments linked with parental behavior? Placed in a strange situation (usually a laboratory playroom), some children show *secure attachment:* In the mother's presence they play comfortably, happily exploring their new environment; when she leaves, they are distressed; when she returns, they seek contact with her. Other infants show *insecure attachment:* They are less likely to explore their surroundings and may even cling to their mother; when the mother leaves, they cry loudly; and when she returns, they may be indifferent or even hostile toward her (Ainsworth, 1973; Ainsworth & others, 1978). What accounts for these differences?

The innate differences among infants is one likely answer. Some babies may be more disposed to forming a secure attachment just as, from birth, some babies are more easily held, cuddled, and comforted. But there is more to infant differences than biology. Mary Ainsworth (1979) explored another possible influence on attachment: the mother's behavior. She observed mother-infant pairs at home during the first 6 months and then later observed the 1-year-old infants in a strange situation without their mother. Sensitive, responsive mothers—mothers who continually noticed what their babies were doing and

When imprinting studies go awry . . .

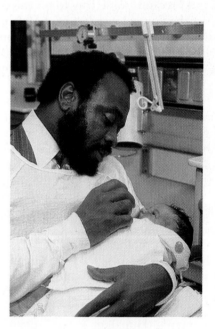

Although breast-feeding provides babies with superior nutrition and can increase a mother's sense of intimacy with her infant, fathers, too, love to feed their babies, and there is little evidence that breast-feeding significantly affects the infant's psychological development. The intimacy evident in this photo will benefit both infant and father.

responded appropriately—tended to have infants who became securely attached. Insensitive, unresponsive mothers—mothers who attended to their babies when they felt like doing so but ignored them at other times—tended to have infants who became insecurely attached. The Harlows' monkey studies, in which the artificial mothers were the ultimate in unresponsiveness, produced even more striking consequences. When put in strange situations without their artificial mothers, the deprived infants were more than distressed—they were terrified.

Although informative, such studies would probably not be conducted in today's climate of concern for the welfare of animals.

Monkeys raised by artificial mothers were terror-stricken when placed in strange situations without their surrogate mothers.

FATHER CARE

Michael Lamb (1979): "Mothers and fathers can be equally effective as parents. They just have different styles."

Perhaps you are wondering why the focus of so much research has been on mothers and not on fathers, too. The common assumption, long evident in court child-custody decisions, has been that fathers are less interested and less competent in child care than are mothers. In both subtle and not-so-subtle ways, psychologists have accepted this assumption. Infants who lack mother care are said to suffer "maternal deprivation"; those lacking father care are said merely to experience "father absence."

It is true that across the world mothers tend to assume more responsibility for infant care, and that a breast-feeding mother and nursing infant have wonderfully coordinated biological systems that predispose their responsiveness to one another (Maccoby, 1980). Nevertheless, many modern fathers are becoming more involved in infant care, and researchers are becoming more interested in fathers.

One of the leading father-watchers, Ross Parke (1981), reported that fathers can be just as interested in, sensitive to, and affectionate toward their infants as mothers are. Although mothers typically do most of the infant care, fathers are as capable (at least when researchers are watching). It also seems that although most infants prefer their mothers when anxious, when left alone they are as distressed by their fathers'

departure as by their mothers'. Moreover, infants whose fathers have shared in their care, for example, by changing diapers, are more secure when left with a stranger.

Looking for differences, research psychologists have also uncovered several distinctive ways in which fathers and mothers interact with their infants. Fathers tend to smile less at their babies (males smile less at everyone), to spend more of their interaction in play rather than caretaking (especially with sons), and to play with more physical excitement (Parke, 1981).

However, when fathers are the primary caregivers, they interact with their babies more as mothers typically do. This suggests that father-mother differences are not biologically fixed, but have social roots as well. Animal research confirms this. When the Harlows caged mothers and fathers with their infant monkeys, the fathers were protective and affectionate toward their infants and more likely than mothers to engage in physical play.

Within two-parent families, both parents have yet another gift to offer: their support of one another. Mothers and fathers who support one another and who sense this mutual support and agreement in child-rearing also tend to be more responsive to their infants and to feel more competent as parents (Dickie, 1987).

Effects of Attachment   What have researchers learned about the effects of attachment on later development?

Secure Attachment Breeds Social Competence   If a trusting, secure attachment has lasting benefits, then the quality of an infant's attachments should predict the child's social competence in the years that follow. Even adult romantic love styles exhibit childlike secure or insecure attachment (Hazen & Shaver, 1987). But do our early attachment patterns actually predict our later social behavior?

At the University of Minnesota, Alan Sroufe and his co-workers (Sroufe, 1978; Sroufe & others, 1983) confirmed that infants' attachments do predict their later social competence. Sroufe reported that infants who are securely attached at 12 to 18 months of age—those who use their mother as a base for comfortably exploring the world and as a haven when distressed—function more confidently as 2- to 3½-year-olds. Given challenging tasks, they are more enthusiastic and persistent. When with other children, they are more outgoing and responsive.

Developmental theorist Erik Erikson, whose ideas we will consider further in Chapter 4, would say that such children approach life with a sense of *basic trust*—a sense that the world is predictable and reliable—rather than mistrust. Erikson theorized that infants whose needs are well met by sensitive caregivers form a lifelong attitude of trust rather than fear. Basic trust is the first of Erikson's proposed stages in children's social development (see Table 3–2).

"Out of the conflict between trust and mistrust, the infant develops hope, which is the earliest form of what gradually becomes faith in adults."
Erik Erikson (1983)

Table 3–2
ERIKSON'S STAGES OF PSYCHOSOCIAL DEVELOPMENT (to adolescence)

Approximate age	Description of stage
Infancy (1st year)	**Trust vs. mistrust** If needs are met, infant develops a sense of basic trust.
Toddler (2nd year)	**Autonomy vs. shame and doubt** Toddler strives to learn independence and self-confidence.
Preschooler (3–5 years)	**Initiative vs. guilt** Preschooler learns to initiate tasks and grapples with self-control.
Elementary School (6 years to puberty)	**Competence vs. inferiority** Child learns either to feel effective or inadequate.

Other psychologists believe the child's social competence reflects not the early parenting but the continued responsive parenting that these children are still receiving when retested (Lamb, 1987). The genes shared by competent parents and their competent children may also predispose their similar behavior (Goldsmith & Alansky, 1987; Plomin & others, 1985).

The attachments of early childhood in time relax. Whether raised entirely at home or also in a day care center, whether living in America, Guatemala, or the Kalahari Desert, anxiety over being separated from parents peaks at around 13 months and then gradually declines (Kagan, 1976; see Figure 3–8). With time, children become familiar with a wider and wider range of situations, and with the advent of language they communicate with strangers more freely.

Does this mean that, as we develop, our need for and love of others fades away? Hardly. In other ways our capacity for love grows, and our pleasure in touching and holding those we love never ceases. The powerful parental love nonetheless gradually relaxes, allowing children to move out into the world. One might even say that much of the life cycle story—from fetus to birth and infancy, to adolescence, to marriage and parenthood, to old age and death—boils down to two realities: attachment and separation.

Deprivation of Attachment   If social competence is affected by a secure attachment, what are the outcomes of parental deprivation or prolonged separation? One way to study the benefits of positive early nurturing experiences is to observe the development of children denied such experiences. In all of psychology, no research literature is more saddening. Children reared in institutions without the stimulation and attention of a regular caregiver, or locked away at home under conditions of extreme neglect, are frequently pathetic creatures—withdrawn, frightened, speechless. Adopted into a loving home, they usually progress rapidly, especially in their cognitive development. They are particularly likely to do well if they were in the company of other children while they were deprived of adult contact. Nevertheless, they often bear scars from their early neglect (Rutter, 1979).

Most abusive parents report being battered or neglected as children (Kempe & Kempe, 1978). Although most abused children do *not* later become abusive parents, 30 percent do abuse their children—a rate six times higher than the national rate of child abuse (Kaufman & Zigler, 1987). Moreover, young children who have been terrorized through sexual abuse or wartime atrocities (beatings, witnessing torture, and living in constant fear) also suffer scars; nightmares, depression, and a troubled adolescence are frequent outcomes (Browne & Finkelhor, 1986; Goleman, 1987).

These findings were underscored by the Harlows. They reared monkeys not only with artificial mothers but also alone in barren cages or, worse, in total isolation from even the sight and sound of other monkeys. If socially deprived in these ways for 6 months or longer (corresponding to the first 2 years or more of human life), the monkeys were socially devastated. They either cowered in fright or lashed out in aggression when placed with other monkeys their age. Upon reaching sexual maturity, most were incapable of mating. Females who were artificially impregnated often were neglectful, sadistically cruel, or even murderous toward their firstborn offspring. The unloved had become the unloving.

The new generation of unloved animals would nevertheless persistently approach and cling to their abusive mothers. In fact, so powerful was the infant monkey's drive for attachment that even artificial "monster mothers"—mothers constructed to occasionally blast compressed air, poke spikes through their terrycloth bodies, or fling their infant off—could only temporarily break their infant's attachment. When the monster mother calmed down, the pitiful infant would re-

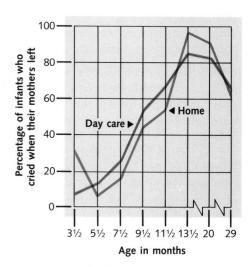

Figure 3–8   Infants' anxiety over separation from parents. In an experiment, groups of infants who had and had not experienced day care were left alone by their mothers in an unfamiliar room. In both groups, the percentage who cried when the mother left peaked at about 13 months. (From Kagan, 1976.)

Monkeys raised in total isolation from the sight or sound of other monkeys for more than 6 months were terrified of other monkeys and either lashed out aggressively or cowered in fright.

turn, clinging again, as if all were forgiven. Indeed, the distress of abuse seemed even to intensify the infant's clinging, a phenomenon sometimes observed among abused human children.

Disruption of Attachment   What happens to an infant when attachment is disrupted? Does being uprooted, even from neglectful or abusive parents, predispose the child to later emotional difficulties? These questions bear heavily on custody decisions in cases of child neglect or abuse.

Separated from their families, both monkey and human infants become agitated and, before long, withdrawn and even despairing (Bowlby, 1973; Mineka & Suomi, 1978). Fearing that such extreme stress might cause lasting damage (and when in doubt acting to protect parents' rights), the courts have generally been very reluctant to remove children from their homes. However, it seems that infants generally recover from the distress of separation if placed in a more positive and stable environment. In studies of adopted children, Leon Yarrow and his co-workers (1973) found that when children over 6 months of age were removed from their foster mothers they initially had difficulties eating, sleeping, and relating to their new mothers. But by 10 years of age there was little discernible difference in the adjustment of children who had been placed before the age of 6 months (with little accompanying distress) and those who had been adopted between the ages of 6 and 16 months (with much more distress). Although adoptions at later ages might more often be permanently disruptive, it seems that most year-old infants can form new attachments without permanent emotional scars. Foster care with a series of foster families, or repeated removal from a mother and then reunion with her, can be very disruptive, however.

Does Day Care Disrupt Attachment?   In 1950, when only 14 percent of American mothers worked outside the home, society's Perfect Mom was at the door with cookies, milk, and a sympathetic ear when her children arrived home from school. Today, with half of mothers of American children under age 5 employed, society's Supermom pursues a successful career while sharing parental duties with Dad. Where are these children of mothers who work full-time? Almost 50 percent are cared for in someone else's home. The rest are nearly evenly divided between day care centers and being cared for in their own homes. Of this last group, 20 percent are cared for by sitters, 44 percent by fathers, and 36 percent by another relative (Bureau of the Census, 1987).

During the 1950s and '60s, when Perfect Mom was the social norm, the research questions were, "Is day care bad for children? Does it disrupt children's attachments to their parents?" For the high-quality day care programs most commonly studied, the answers were no (Belsky, 1984). In *Mother Care/Other Care*, developmental psychologist Sandra Scarr (1986) explains that children are "biologically sturdy individuals . . . who can thrive in a wide variety of life situations." Today, the questions have therefore shifted to the effect that different forms of day care may have on different types and ages of children. We now know enough about the consequences of child neglect to distinguish good from poor day care. Scarr and Richard Weinberg (1986) explain: "Good care means three or four infants and toddlers per care giver and six to eight preschoolers. . . . Good care also means a cheerful, stimulating, and safe physical environment. . . ." The ideal, then, is a verbally stimulating environment in which any child can frequently be seen talking with an adult caregiver (Phillips, McCartney, & Scarr, 1987).

"We can hazard a tentative conclusion: The child's later adjustment will be primarily determined by the quality of the relationship with the new caretakers, not by the experience of separation."
Eleanor Maccoby (1980)

Drawing by Chast; © 1987 The New Yorker Magazine, Inc.

High-quality day care provides a safe, stimulating environment and a caregiver for every six to eight toddlers.

Although parents of children 2 years and older may gain some relief from knowing that day care *can* mean high-quality child care, the scientific jury is still debating infant day care. Many developmentalists, including Scarr, believe that high-quality infant care does not hinder secure attachments. Fellow developmental psychologists Jay Belsky (1988) and Edward Zigler (1986) caution that, in Belsky's words, "Children growing up in families using more than 20 hours per week of non-parental care in their first year of life are at heightened risk of seeming insecure as 1-year-olds and of being disobedient and aggressive at older ages."

One striking outcome of research on mother care and other care is how *little* quality time children receive from parents, employed or not. One national survey revealed that employed mothers average only 11 minutes and fathers 8 minutes per weekday in child-centered activities such as reading, conversing, and playing with their children; home-maker mothers devote not much more—only about 30 minutes per day—to such activities (Timmer & others, 1985–1986). Moreover, there is little disagreement that the half million preschool children actually left *alone* for part of the time their parents are at work deserve better! So do those children who merely exist for 9 hours a day in minimally equipped, understaffed centers with untrained and poorly paid care-givers. What all children need is a consistent, warm relationship with people whom they can learn to trust.

Self-Concept   If attachment is the number one social achievement of infancy, for childhood it is the construction of a positive sense of self. By the end of childhood, at about age 12, most children have developed a clear self-concept—a sense of their own personal worth and social identity. When and how does this sense of self develop, and how can parents foster a child's self-esteem?

"Is my baby aware of herself—does she know that she is a person distinct from others?" The baby cannot talk, so we cannot ask her. Perhaps, however, the infant's *behavior* could provide clues to the beginnings of her self-awareness. But what sorts of behavior? In 1877, biologist Charles Darwin offered one idea: Self-awareness begins when a child recognizes herself in a mirror. By this indicator, self-recognition emerges gradually over about a year, starting in roughly the sixth month, when the child reaches toward the mirror to touch her image as if it were another child (Damon & Hart, 1982).

How can we know when the infant recognizes that the girl in the mirror is indeed herself and not just an agreeable playmate? In a simple variation of the mirror procedure, researchers surreptitiously dabbed rouge on their subjects' noses before placing them in front of the mirror. Beginning at 15 to 18 months, children, upon seeing the red spot, will touch their noses (Gallup & Suarez, 1986). Apparently, 18-month-olds have a schema of how their faces should look; it is as if they wonder, "What is that spot doing on *my* face?"

Beginning with this simple self-awareness, the child's self-concept gradually becomes stronger. By school age, children begin to describe themselves in terms of their gender, their group memberships, and their psychological traits. They come to see themselves as good and skillful in some ways but not others. They form a concept of which traits, ideally, they would like to have, and by age 8 or 10 their self-image has become quite stable.

Children's views of themselves affects their actions. Children who have formed a positive self-concept tend to be more confident, independent, optimistic, assertive, and sociable (Maccoby, 1980). All this raises a profoundly important question: How can parents encourage a positive self-concept?

Mirror images are fascinating to infants from the age of about 6 months, but the recognition that the child in the mirror is "me" does not happen until about 18 months.

Child-Rearing Practices   Some parents spank, some reason; some parents are strict, some are lax; some parents seem indifferent to their children, some liberally hug and kiss them. Whether such differences in parenting affect children's behavior has been the subject of much research. The most heavily researched aspect of parenting has been how, and to what extent, parents seek to control their children.

Several investigators have identified three specific styles of child management: (1) permissive, (2) authoritarian, and (3) authoritative. *Permissive* parents tend to submit to their children's desires, make few demands, and use little punishment. *Authoritarian* parents impose rules and expect obedience: "Don't interrupt." "Don't leave your room a mess." "Don't stay out late or you'll be grounded." "Why? Because I said so." *Authoritative* parents exert control by establishing rules and consistently enforcing them, but also by explaining the reasons for their rules and, especially with older children, encouraging open discussion when making the rules. Studies by Stanley Coopersmith (1967), Diana Baumrind (1983), and John Buri and others (1988) reveal that the children with the highest self-esteem and most self-reliance tend to have warm, concerned, authoritative parents.

What might account for this finding? As later chapters will explain, many experiments indicate that people become more motivated and self-confident if they experience control over their lives; those who experience little control tend to see themselves as somewhat helpless and incompetent. Moreover, children who sense enough control to be able to attribute their behaviors to their own choices ("I obey because I am good") internalize their behaviors more than do children who comply solely because they are coerced ("I obey or I get in bad trouble").

Of the three parenting styles studied, it seems that authoritative parenting provides children with the greatest sense of control over their own lives for two reasons. First, authoritative parents openly discuss family rules, by explaining them to younger children and reasoning about them with older children. When such rules seem not so

Studies suggest that consistency in enforcing rules, combined with calm discussion and explanation, helps children achieve self-control.

much imposed as negotiated, older children feel more self-control (Baumrind, 1983; Lewis, 1981). Second, when parents enforce rules with consistent, predictable consequences, the child controls the outcome. Recall that infants become more attached to parents who sensitively and predictably respond to their behaviors. Such infants experience control.

It is when the consequences become extreme—perhaps a threatened spanking for noncompliance—that the child of authoritarian parents is left with no feeling of choice. Similarly, children may lose their sense of control when their parents nag or explode unpredictably. Given permissive parents, children learn early that their own coercive behavior—whining, yelling, tantrums—brings desired results (Patterson, 1986). Thus Eleanor Maccoby (1980, p. 389) concluded that "skillful parents must operate within a very delicate balance of forces. They need to obtain compliance to reasonable demands—for the child's, the parents', and the family's sake—without . . . destroying their children's sense of [choice]."

Before jumping to any conclusions about the consequences of different parenting styles, we must heed a caution. The evidence is correlational. It tells us that certain child-rearing practices (say, being firm but open) are associated with certain childhood outcomes (say, social competence). But as we have seen before, correlation does not necessarily reveal cause and effect. There may be other possible explanations (see Figure 3–9). Perhaps socially mature, agreeable children *elicit* greater trust and more reasonable treatment from their parents than do less competent and less cooperative children. Or perhaps some other unnoted characteristic of authoritative parents produces their children's competence. For example, such parents are less likely to be enduring the stresses of poverty or recent divorce (Hetherington, 1979), and they are more likely to be well educated—factors that might also be linked with children's competence. Or, as was suggested earlier, maybe competent parents and their competent children share genes that predispose social competence. Thus, knowing that parents' behavior is related to their children's behavior does not prove cause and effect.

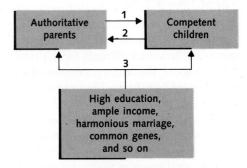

Figure 3–9   Three possible explanations of the correlation between parental authoritativeness and social competence in children.

When considering "expert" child-rearing advice—of which there seems to be no shortage—we should also remember that it inevitably reflects the advice-giver's values. Even if we knew exactly how to encourage the development of any given trait in children, we could not advise parents without assuming that some traits are to be preferred over others. But which? Should the chief end of childhood be unquestioning obedience? Then an authoritarian style could be recommended. Are sociability and self-reliance a higher end? Then firm but open authoritative parenting is advisable. Different experts have different values, which, along with the uncertainties of cause and effect, helps explain their disagreements.

Parents struggle with conflicting advice and with the other stresses of child-rearing. Indeed, the tens of thousands of dollars it costs to raise a child buys 20 years of not only joy and love but also worry and irritation. Yet for most parents, a child is a personal investment in the human future. To paraphrase psychiatrist Carl Jung, we reach backward into our parents and forward into our children, and through their children into a future that we will never see, but about which we must nonetheless care.

REFLECTIONS ON A DEVELOPMENTAL ISSUE: GENES AND EXPERIENCE

Our journey through developmental psychology is set in the context of three pervasive issues: whether development is (1) steered more by genes or experience, and whether it is characterized (2) by continuous growth or distinct stages, and (3) by stability or by change. Let's step back for a moment and take stock of current thinking on the nature-nurture issue.

Everyone agrees: Each of us is influenced by genes *and* experience working together. The real question is: How important is each? For physical attributes such as hair color, the genetic factor predominates. For psychological attributes, the answer is less obvious. In Chapter 12, Intelligence, we will examine the thorny debate over genetic and environmental determinants of intelligence. Here, let us consider the provocative findings of several recent investigations into the inheritance of personal and social traits.

TEMPERAMENT

Infants and young children cannot take personality tests, so investigators observe their actual behavior and infer their temperament. *Temperament* is a catchall term for the rudiments of personality and generally refers to the child's emotional excitability—whether the child is reactive (responds readily to stimuli), intense, and fidgety, or easygoing, quiet, and placid.

From the first weeks of life, "easy" babies are cheerful, relaxed, and predictable in feeding and sleeping. "Difficult" babies are more irritable, intense, and unpredictable (Thomas & Chess, 1986). Moreover, the most emotionally reactive newborns tend also to be the most reactive 9-month-olds (Wilson & Matheny, 1986), and the most emotionally intense preschoolers tend to be relatively intense as young adults (Larsen & Diener, 1987). Physiological tests reveal that these temperamental qualities are linked to a reactive sympathetic nervous system (Kagan & others, 1988). Infant monkeys also vary in tempera-

Faced with a mild stress, some children are characteristically more anxious, just as some monkeys are naturally more fearful.

ment; from birth, some are timid and fearful, others more relaxed (Suomi, 1983).

Are such temperamental differences hereditary? Several lines of evidence indicate they are indeed. Animal breeders selectively mate dogs, horses, and other animals to be either highly reactive or easygoing. In one selective breeding study, Finnish psychologist Kirsti Lagerspetz (1979) took normal albino mice and bred the most aggressive ones with one another and the least aggressive ones with one another. After repeating this for twenty-six generations, she had one set of fierce mice and one of placid mice.

When researcher Stephen Suomi placed genetically predisposed "uptight" versus "easygoing" monkeys with foster mothers who were themselves uptight or easygoing, heredity tended to override rearing. The naturally uptight infant monkeys later reacted more anxiously to the stress of separation from their mother, even if they had been raised by easygoing, nurturant foster mothers (Asher, 1987).

To judge from twin studies (see below), genes help determine human temperament, too. Moreover, newborns of different racial groups exhibit differing temperaments. Babies of Caucasian and African descent tend to be more reactive and irritable than Chinese and Native American babies (who share a common Asian descent). For example, if restrained, undressed, or covered with a cloth, Caucasian babies will typically respond more intensely (Freedman, 1979).

Most Navajo babies calmly accept the cradleboard; Caucasian babies protest vigorously. Findings like these suggest that the rudiments of personality are to some extent genetically influenced.

STUDIES OF TWINS

Selective breeding experiments seek to vary heredity but not environment, thereby revealing an effect of heredity. Could we also do the reverse—vary environment but not heredity—to seek the effect of environment? Happily for our purposes, in three or four human births out of every thousand, nature has given us ready-made subjects for this experiment. *Identical twins* develop from a single fertilized egg that splits into two genetically identical replicas, each of which becomes a person (Figure 3–10). *Fraternal twins,* who develop from separate eggs, are genetically no more similar than ordinary brothers and sisters.

Curiously, twinning rates vary by race. Caucasians have twins roughly twice as often as Asians, and half as often as blacks (Diamond, 1986).

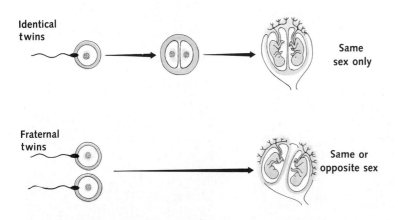

Figure 3–10   Identical twins develop from a single fertilized egg; fraternal twins from two.

Do identical twins, being genetic replicas of one another, develop more similar personalities than fraternal twins? To find out, Birgitta Floderus-Myrhed and her colleagues (1980) administered tests of extraversion (outgoingness) and neuroticism (psychological instability) to nearly 13,000 pairs of Swedish identical and fraternal twins, as did Richard Rose and his colleagues (1988) with 7000 pairs of Finnish twins. Their findings: On both of these personality dimensions identical twins were much more similar than fraternal twins, suggesting that there is substantial genetic influence on both traits.

Other dimensions of personality also reflect genetic influences. John Loehlin and Robert Nichols (1976) gave a battery of questionnaires to 850 identical and fraternal twin pairs who were identified while competing for National Merit scholarships. Once again, identical twins were substantially more similar, and in a variety of ways—in abilities, personality, and even interests. However, most of the identical twins also reported being treated more alike than did fraternal twins, raising the possibility that their experience rather than their genes accounts for their similarity. Not so, said Loehlin and Nichols, because identical twins whose parents treated them alike were *not* psychologically more alike than identical twins who were treated less similarly.

The Minnesota Twin Study Better than studying identical twins who *recall* being reared differently would be to study identical twins who were reared in different environments. To the extent that such twins differ from one another (more than do identical twins reared together), one could only credit their differing environments. Thus in 1979 when University of Minnesota psychologist Thomas Bouchard read a newspaper account of the reuniting of 39-year-old twins who had been separated from infancy, he seized the opportunity and flew them to Minneapolis for extensive tests. Bouchard was looking for differences; what "the Jim twins," Jim Lewis and Jim Springer, presented were amazing similarities (Holden, 1980a, 1980b). Both had married women named Linda, divorced, and married women named Betty. One had a son James Alan, the other a son James Allan. Both had dogs named Toy, chain-smoked Salems, served as sheriff's deputies, drove Chevrolets, chewed their fingernails to the nub, enjoyed stock car racing, had basement workshops, and had built circular white benches around trees in their yards. They also had similar medical histories: Both gained 10 pounds at about the same time and then lost it; both suffered what they mistakenly believed were heart attacks, and both began having late-afternoon headaches at age 18.

Equally striking similarities were presented by identical twins Oskar Stohr and Jack Yufe, one of whom was raised by his grand-

Identical twins: 6 years ago these two girls shared the same fertilized egg.

"The Jim twins." Despite having been separated at birth, these identical twins have remarkable similarities. Here each is shown in his basement carpentry workshop, only one of the "coincidences" psychologist Thomas Bouchard discovered.

mother in Germany as a Catholic and a Nazi, while the other was raised by his father in the Caribbean as a Jew. Nevertheless, they share traits and habits galore: They like spicy foods and sweet liqueurs, have a habit of falling asleep in front of the television, flush the toilet before using it, store rubber bands on their wrists, and dip buttered toast in their coffee. Stohr is domineering toward women and yells at his wife, as did Yufe before he was separated.

Aided by publicity in magazine and newspaper stories, Bouchard, David Lykken, Auke Tellegen, and their colleagues have located and studied some four dozen pairs of identical twins reared apart. They continue to be impressed by the similarities not only of tastes and physical attributes but also of assessments of personality, abilities, and even fears (Tellegen & others, 1988). The more bizarre similarities—such as flushing the toilet before using it—exist not because we have genes for specific behaviors, contends Bouchard; rather, presented with a similar range of options, similarly disposed people tend to make similar choices. Even in the domains where heredity strongly influences personality (such as "social potency"—having an assertive, take-charge nature), it does so not through a single gene but through a complex combination of genes.

> "In some domains it looks as though our identical twins reared apart are . . . just as similar as identical twins reared together. Now that's an amazing finding and I can assure you none of us would have expected that degree of similarity."
>   Thomas Bouchard (1981)

Criticism of Twin Studies   The cute stories do not impress Bouchard's critics. They contend that if any two strangers of the same sex and age were to spend hours comparing their behaviors and life histories, they would probably discover a string of coincidental similarities. Even the more impressive data from the personality assessments (Bouchard, 1984) are clouded by the fact that many of the separated twins were actually together for several months before adoption, or had been reunited for some years before being tested. Moreover, adoption agencies tend to place separated twins in similar homes. When people come from a narrow range of environments, the hereditary factor will play a bigger role. Nevertheless, the Swedish, National Merit, and Minnesota twin studies illustrate why scientific opinion is shifting toward a greater appreciation of genetic influences, and why further research is needed.

> Coincidences are not unique to twins. Patricia Kern of Colorado was born March 13, 1941 and named Patricia Ann Campbell. Patricia DiBiasi of Oregon also was born March 13, 1941 and named Patricia Ann Campbell. Both had fathers named Robert, worked as bookkeepers, and have children ages 21 and 19. Both studied cosmetology, enjoy oil painting as a hobby, and married military men, within 11 days of each other. They are not genetically related. (From an AP report, May 2, 1983.)

ADOPTION STUDIES

Adoption studies offer additional clues. For any given trait we can ask whether adopted children are more like their adoptive parents, who contributed a home environment, or their biological parents, who contributed their genes. Sandra Scarr (Scarr, 1982; Scarr & Weinberg, 1983), John Loehlin and his colleagues (1982, 1985, 1987), and Robert Plomin and John DeFries (1985) therefore studied hundreds of adoptive families in Minnesota, Texas, and Colorado, respectively. The stunning finding of these studies is that people who grow up together do *not* much resemble one another in personality, whether they are biologically related or not (Rowe, 1987). Moreover, in many studies of families without twins, the personalities of parents have been astonishingly unrelated to the personalities of their children. Sandra Scarr and her colleagues (1981) summarized the findings vividly:

> "Two children in the same family [are on average] as different from one another as are pairs of children selected randomly from the population."
>   Robert Plomin and Denise Daniels (1987)

> It would have to be concluded that upper-middle class brothers who attended the same school and whose parents took them to the same plays, sporting events, music lessons, and therapists and used similar child-rearing practices on them would be found to be only slightly more similar to each other in personality measures than to working-class or farm boys, whose lives would be totally different.

What we have here is developmental psychology's newest and one of its biggest puzzles: Why are children in the same family so different? Why do the shared genes and the shared family environment (the family's social class, the parents' personalities, the neighborhood) have so little discernible effect on children's personalities? Is it because even though siblings share genes, each sibling has a very different combination of genes? Is it because the different siblings of a family experience different environments (differing peer influences, birth orders, and so forth)? Might sibling differences be triggered by brothers and sisters comparing themselves with one another, perhaps unconsciously distancing themselves in an effort to create their own identities?

And why are identical twins so much alike in personality when biological parent-child and sibling pairs are so little alike? Is it because identical twins share not only the same individual genes but also the same combinations of genes? Is it because they tend not only to be treated alike by parents and friends but, being the same age, also to experience the same cultural influences simultaneously? All these possibilities have been suggested. (Notice how in hindsight we begin to transform into tomorrow's common sense a finding that has stunned today's psychologists.)

Adoption studies show that, although the personalities of adopted children do not much resemble those of their adoptive parents, adoption has many positive effects. First, in their values and social attitudes, adopted children are demonstrably influenced by their home environments. Second, in the adoptive homes studied, child neglect and abuse were virtually unheard of. So it is not surprising that nearly all the adoptive children thrived. They scored higher than their biological parents on intelligence tests, and many became happier and more stable people than they surely would have in a neglectful environment. Children need not resemble their adoptive parents to have benefited greatly from adoption.

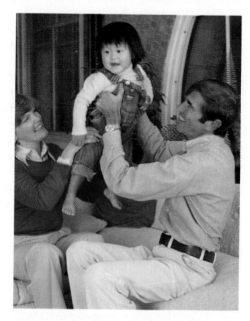

Studies of adopted families have provided new clues to hereditary and environmental influences on development. How similar would you expect these children to be to their adoptive parents and siblings? To their biological parents and siblings?

HOW MUCH CREDIT (OR BLAME) DO PARENTS DESERVE?

Parents typically feel enormous pride in their children's successes, and guilt or shame over their failures. They beam when folks offer congratulations for the child who wins an award. They wonder where they went wrong with the child who repeatedly is called into the principal's office. Society reinforces such feelings: Believing that parents shape their children as a potter molds clay, people readily praise parents for their children's virtues and blame them for their children's vices.

This chapter has provided some confirmation of the power of parenting. The extremes provide the sharpest examples—the abused who become abusive, the loved but firmly handled children who become self-confident and socially competent. Given our readiness to praise or blame, and to feel pride or shame, we do well also to remember a simple principle: Within the normal range of environments, children's genetically predisposed tendencies will assert themselves. Children are not so easily molded as clay. Moreover, as our next chapter illustrates, lives also are formed by environmental influences beyond parents' control—by peer influences, by chance events, by all sorts of life experiences.

It may be scary to realize how risky is the business of having and raising children. In procreation a woman and a man shuffle their gene decks and deal a life-forming hand to their child-to-be, who thereafter is subject to countless influences beyond their control. Remembering that lives are formed by influences both under *and* beyond parents' control, we had best be restrained in crediting parents for their children's achievements and slower still to blame them for their children's problems.

To say that genes and experience are *both* important is true, but an oversimplification. More precisely, their effects are intertwined. Imagine two babies, one genetically predisposed to be attractive, sociable, and easygoing, the other less so. Assume further that the first baby attracts more affectionate and stimulating care than the second, and so develops into a warmer and more outgoing person. Moreover, as the two children grow older, the more naturally outgoing one seeks out activities and friends that encourage further social confidence.

What has caused their resulting personality difference? One cannot truthfully say that their personalities are formed of *x* percent genes and *y* percent experience, for the gene-experience effect is combined. In fact, *genes direct experience* (Scarr & McCartney, 1983). As in our imaginary example, one's genetically influenced traits may *evoke* significant responses in others. Moreover, as we grow older we *select* environments well suited to our natures. In such ways, our genes influence the experiences that shape us.

SUMMING UP

Developmental psychologists examine how we develop physically, cognitively, and socially by studying the human life span from conception to death.

DEVELOPMENTAL ISSUES

Three issues pervade developmental psychology. First, to what extent is each of our traits influenced by our genes and to what extent by our experiences? Second, is development a continuous process, or do we develop through distinct stages? Third, are our lives characterized more by stability of traits or by change?

PRENATAL DEVELOPMENT AND THE NEWBORN

From Life Comes Life The life cycle begins as one sperm, out of the some 300 million ejaculated, unites with an egg to form a zygote. Two weeks later, the developing embryo attaches to the uterine wall, and after 2 months is a recognizably human fetus. Along with nutrients, teratogens ingested by the mother can reach the developing child and possibly place it at risk.

The Competent Newborn With the aid of new methods for studying babies, researchers have discovered that newborns are surprisingly competent. They are born with sensory equipment and reflexes that facilitate their interacting with adults and securing nourishment; they

quickly learn to discriminate the smell and sound of their mothers; and they may even be capable of imitating simple gestures.

INFANCY AND CHILDHOOD

Physical Development Within the brain, nerve cells form before birth and, sculpted by experience, their interconnections continue to multiply after birth. Infants' more complex physical skills—sitting, standing, walking—develop in a predictable sequence whose actual timing is a function of individual maturation rate. Childhood—from toddlerhood to the teen years—is a period of slow, steady physical development.

Cognitive Development Jean Piaget's observations of children convinced him—and almost everyone else—that the mind of the child is not that of a miniature adult. Piaget theorized that the mind develops by forming schemas that help us assimilate our experiences and that must occasionally be altered to accommodate new information. In this way, children progress from the sensorimotor simplicity of the infant to more complex stages of thinking. For example, at about 8 months, an infant becomes aware that things still exist even when out of sight. This sense of object permanence coincides with the development of stranger anxiety, which requires the ability to remember who is familiar and who is not.

Piaget believed that preschool children are egocentric

and unable to perform simple logical operations. However, he thought that at about age 7 children become capable of performing concrete operations, such as those required to comprehend the principle of conservation. Recent research indicates that young children are not so incapable as Piaget believed. It seems that the cognitive abilities that emerge at each stage are developing in a rudimentary form in the previous stage.

Social Development   Although the experiences of infancy are not for long consciously remembered and their effects may largely be reversed by later experiences, they can nevertheless have a lasting influence on social development.

A social response of infancy that can critically affect later social development is attachment. Infants become attached to their mothers and fathers not simply because mothers and fathers gratify biological needs, but, more important, because they are comfortable, familiar, and responsive. If denied such care, both monkey and human infants may become pathetically withdrawn, anxious, and eventually abusive. Once an attachment forms, infants who are separated from their caregiver will, for a time, be distressed. Human infants who display secure attachment to their mothers generally become socially competent preschoolers.

As with cognitive abilities, the concept of self develops gradually. At about age 18 months, infants will recognize themselves in a mirror. By age 10, children's self-images are quite stable, and are linked with their independence, optimism, and sociability. Children who develop a positive self-image and a happy, self-reliant manner tend to have been reared by parents who are neither permissive nor authoritarian, but authoritative without depriving their children of a sense of control over their own lives. Decisions about child-rearing involve value judgments about what traits in children should be encouraged.

REFLECTIONS ON A DEVELOPMENTAL ISSUE: GENES AND EXPERIENCE

Studies of the inheritance of temperament, along with adoption studies and studies of twins, provide scientific support for the idea that genes influence one's developing personality. Developmentalists generally agree that genes *and* environment, biological *and* social factors, direct our life courses, and that their effects often intertwine, partly because our genetic predispositions influence our formative experiences.

TERMS AND CONCEPTS TO REMEMBER

accommodation   Adapting one's current understandings (schemas) to incorporate new information.

assimilation   Interpreting one's new experience in terms of one's existing schemas.

attachment   An emotional tie with another person; evidenced in young children by their seeking closeness to the caregiver and showing distress on separation.

basic trust   According to Erik Erikson, a sense that the world is predictable and trustworthy; said to be formed during infancy by experiences with responsive caregivers.

chromosomes   Threadlike structures made of DNA molecules that contain the genes. A human cell has twenty-three pairs of chromosomes, one member of each pair coming from each parent.

cognition   All the mental activities associated with thinking, knowing, and remembering.

concrete operational stage   In Piaget's theory, the stage of cognitive development (from about 7 to 12 years of age) during which children acquire the mental operations that enable them to think logically about concrete events.

conservation   The principle (which Piaget believed to be a part of concrete operational reasoning) that properties such as mass, volume, and number remain the same despite changes in the forms of objects.

critical period   A restricted time period during which an organism must be exposed to certain influences or experiences if proper development is to occur; in humans there appear to be critical periods for the formation of attachments and the learning of language.

DNA (deoxyribonucleic acid)   In cells, a complex molecule containing genetic information.

egocentrism   In Piaget's theory, the inability of the preoperational child to take another's point of view.

embryo   The early developmental stage of an organism after fertilization; in human development, the prenatal stage from about 2 weeks to 2 months.

fetus   The developing human organism from 9 weeks after conception to birth.

fraternal twins   Twins who develop from separate eggs and sperm cells, thus ordinary brothers and sisters who have shared the fetal environment.

genes   The biochemical units of heredity that make up the chromosomes; a segment of DNA capable of synthesizing a protein.

identical twins   Twins who develop from a single fertilized egg that splits in two, creating two genetic replicas.

imprinting   The process by which certain birds and mammals form attachments during a critical period very early in life.

maturation   Biological growth processes that enable orderly changes in behavior, relatively uninfluenced by experience.

nature-nurture issue   The longstanding controversy over the relative contributions of genes and experience to the development of psychological traits and behaviors.

object permanence   The awareness that things continue to exist even when they are not perceived.

ovum   The female reproductive cell, or egg, which after fertilization develops into a new individual.

preoperational stage   In Piaget's theory, the stage (from about 2 to 7 years of age) during which a child learns to use language but does not yet comprehend the mental operations of concrete logic.

rooting reflex   A baby's tendency, when touched on the cheek, to open the mouth and search for the nipple.

schema   A concept or framework that organizes and interprets information.

sensorimotor stage   In Piaget's theory, the stage (from birth to about 2 years of age) during which infants know the world mostly in terms of their sensory impressions and motor activities.

stranger anxiety   The fear of strangers that infants commonly display beginning at about 8 months of age.

temperament   A person's characteristic emotional reactivity and intensity.

teratogens   Agents, such as chemicals and viruses, that can reach the embryo or fetus during prenatal development and cause harm.

X sex chromosome   The sex chromosome found in both men and women. Females have two X chromosomes; males have one. An X chromosome from each parent produces a female.

Y sex chromosome   The sex chromosome found only in males. When it pairs with an X sex chromosome from the mother, a male is produced.

zygote   The fertilized egg; it enters a 2-week period of rapid cell division and develops into an embryo.

FOR FURTHER READING

Berger, K. (1986). *The developing person through childhood and adolescence* (2nd ed.). New York: Worth.

A comprehensive, and readable textbook summarizing what we know about infancy, childhood, and adolescence.

Chess, S., & Thomas, A. (1987). *Know your child.* New York: Basic Books.

A respected wife-and-husband child psychiatrist team discuss how effective child-rearing adjusts to the temperamental traits of the individual child.

Flavell, J. H. (1985). *Cognitive development* (2nd ed.). Englewood Cliffs, NJ: Prentice-Hall.

A comprehensive overview of intellectual growth from infancy through adolescence. Includes discussions of the development of perception, memory, and language.

Park, R. D. (1981). *Fathers.* Cambridge, MA: Harvard University Press.

A prominent developmental psychologist describes his own and others' studies of fathering.

Scarr, S. (1986). *Mother care/Other care.* New York: Basic Books.

An award-winning guide to child care by a leading developmental researcher.

CHAPTER 4

Adolescence and Adulthood

For much of this century, psychologists echoed William Wordsworth's sentiment that "the child is father of the man." In this view, by the end of childhood one's traits have nearly set, like clay. Although it remains for life experiences to smooth the rough edges, the really pliable period of development is over. The heritage of infancy and childhood will reach decades into the future, for the characteristic features of one's personality have been set.

So long as psychologists held this view, they focused their attention on the "critical" early years. Now, among a new generation of developmental psychologists, the belief that no important changes in personality occur after childhood is giving way to a growing sense that development is *lifelong*. Yes, we are shaped during infancy and childhood, but the shaping continues during adolescence and well beyond. At a 5-year high school reunion, friends may be surprised at the divergence of their paths. A decade after college, two former soul mates may have trouble communicating. As long as we live, we develop.

ADOLESCENCE

Adolescence extends from the beginnings of sexual maturity to the achievement of independent adult status. In preindustrial societies, the adolescent transition from childhood to adulthood typically lasts but a few days or weeks (Baumeister & Tice, 1986). Adult status and responsibilities are bestowed rather abruptly at the time of sexual maturation, often marked by an initiation ceremony. In pre-twentieth-century North America, young teenagers often labored as adults but were expected to behave as obedient children until marriage (Kett, 1977). Not until this century, when biological maturity began occurring earlier (because of improved nutrition) and adult labor was largely postponed until after compulsory schooling, did people begin to think of adolescence as a distinct period of life.

What are the teen years like? To St. Augustine, these years were a time of fiery passions involving

> the hot imagination of puberty. . . . Both love and lust boiled within me and swept my youthful immaturity over the precipice.

In Leo Tolstoy's *Anna Karenina*, the teenage years were, rather,

> that blissful time when childhood is just coming to an end, and out of that vast circle, happy and gay, a path takes shape.

In her diary, written as she and her family hid from the Nazis, teenager Anne Frank observed,

Not until this century were young teenagers routinely spared the demands of adult labor. Adolescents were expected to work as soon as they were physically able.

My treatment varies so much. One day Anne is so sensible and is allowed to know everything; and the next day I hear that Anne is just a silly little goat who doesn't know anything at all and imagines that she's learned a wonderful lot from books. . . . Oh, so many things bubble up inside me as I lie in bed, having to put up with people I'm fed up with, who always misinterpret my intentions.

To G. Stanley Hall (1904), the first American psychologist to describe adolescence, it was a period of "storm and stress"—of emotional turbulence caused by the tension between biological maturity and emotional and economic dependence. Indeed, after age 30, many people look back on their teenage years as a time they would not like to relive (Macfarlane, 1964). They recall those years as a period when the social approval of peers was imperative, pressures for achievement were nerve-racking, one's sense of direction in life was in flux, and alienation from parents was deepest.

Other psychologists have noted that for many, adolescence is often as Tolstoy described it—a time of vitality without the cares of adulthood, a time of congenial family relationships punctuated by only occasional tensions, a time of rewarding friendships, a time of heightened idealism and a growing sense of life's exciting possibilities (Coleman, 1980). These psychologists would not be surprised that nine out of ten high school seniors agreed with the statement, "On the whole, I'm satisfied with myself" (*Public Opinion*, 1987a).

Despite such conflicting observations, we can make some general statements about the most common physical, cognitive, and social changes of the adolescent years.

PHYSICAL DEVELOPMENT

Adolescence begins at *puberty*, the time of rapid growth and sexual maturation. Puberty commences with a surge of hormones, which triggers a 2-year period of rapid development that usually begins in girls at about age 11 and in boys at about age 13. Boys grow as much as 5 inches a year, compared with about 3 inches for girls—propelling the average male, for the first time in his life, to become noticeably taller than the average female (Figure 4–1). During this growth spurt, the reproductive organs, or *primary sex characteristics*, develop dramatically. So do the *secondary sex characteristics*, the nonreproductive traits of females and males, such as enlarged breasts and hips in girls, facial hair and a deepened voice in boys, pubic and underarm hair in both sexes (Figure 4–2).

The landmarks of puberty are the first ejaculation in boys, which usually occurs by about age 14, and the first menstrual period in girls, by about age 13. (These events do not necessarily signify fertility; it may be another year or more before ejaculations contain sufficient live sperm and the menstrual cycle includes ovulation [Tanner, 1978].)

The first menstrual period, called *menarche* (meh-NAR-key), is an especially memorable event, one that is recalled by nearly all adult women. Most recall it with a mixture of feelings—pride, excitement, embarrassment, and apprehension (Greif & Ulman, 1982; Woods & others, 1983). Girls who are well prepared for menarche are the most likely to experience it as a positive life transition. And a transition it is: Regardless of the age at which their menarche occurs, shortly afterward most girls increasingly see and present themselves as different from boys and function more independently of their parents (Golub, 1983).

Have you any idea how you will look back on your life 10 years from now? Are you doing the things and making the choices that someday you will recollect with satisfaction?

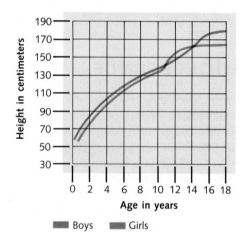

Figure 4–1 Throughout childhood, boys and girls are similar in height. At puberty, girls surge ahead briefly, but then boys overtake them at about age 14. (From Tanner, 1978.)

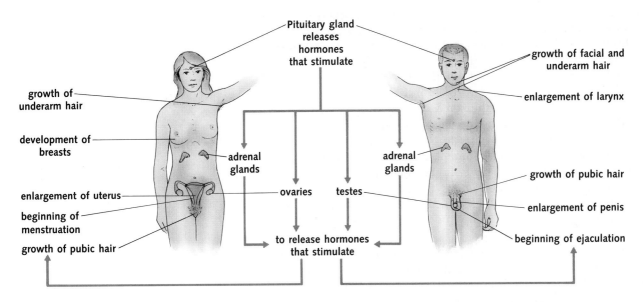

Pituitary gland
releases
hormones
that stimulate

growth of facial and
underarm hair

enlargement of larynx

growth of
underarm hair

development of
breasts

adrenal
glands

adrenal
glands

enlargement of uterus

ovaries

testes

growth of pubic hair

enlargement of penis

beginning of
menstruation

to release hormones
that stimulate

beginning of ejaculation

growth of pubic hair

Figure 4–2   Puberty commences with a surge of hormones that trigger a variety of physical changes.

As in the earlier life stages, the *sequence* of physical changes (for example, breast buds before visible pubic hair before menarche) is far more predictable than their *timing*. Some girls start their growth spurt at 9, some boys as late as age 16. Such variations have little effect on height at maturity. However, they may have psychological consequences. Studies performed in the 1950s by Mary Cover Jones and her colleagues revealed that for boys early maturation pays dividends. Early-maturing boys, being stronger and more athletic during their early teen years and seemingly less childlike, tend to be more popular, self-assured, and independent, and some of their greater sociability may continue into early adulthood.

For girls, early maturation is less advantageous (Petersen, 1987). The 11-year-old who towers over her classmates and becomes sexually attractive before her peers do may temporarily suffer embarrassment and be the object of teasing. But as her peers catch up, in junior and senior high school, her postpubertal experience helps her to enjoy greater prestige and self-confidence. In some situations—dance training, for example—girls are more successful if they mature late (late-maturing girls tend to have physical characteristics, such as leanness, preferred by dance masters [Brooks-Gunn, 1986]). This illustrates what makes for smooth adjustment: It's not only when we mature that counts, but also how people around us react to our physical development. This exemplifies a recurring theme: Heredity and environment interact. In this case, how the environment responds to the youngster depends on the timing of maturation, as programmed by heredity.

COGNITIVE DEVELOPMENT

Adolescents' developing ability to reason allows a new level of social awareness and moral judgment. As young teenagers become capable of thinking about their own thinking, and thinking about what other people are thinking, they become prone to imagining what other people are thinking about *them*. As their cognitive abilities continue to grow, many adolescents begin to think about what is ideally possible and become quite critical of their society, their parents, and even their own shortcomings.

Girls often begin their "ascent" into puberty earlier than boys. This can lead to social embarrassment for early and late bloomers alike.

Formal Operations   According to Piaget, preadolescents are restricted to reasoning about the concrete, but adolescents become capable of thinking logically about abstract propositions. They can reason hypothetically and deduce consequences: *if* this, *then* that. Unlike children, adolescents can deduce that when an investigator hides a poker chip and says, "Either this chip is green or it is not green," the statement logically must be true (Osherson & Markman, 1974–1975). These developing reasoning skills define Piaget's final stage of cognitive growth, ***formal operations.***

Formal operations are the summit of intellectual development. Early adolescents may already have enough command of formal operations to learn algebra. But their ability to reason systematically, as a scientist might in testing hypotheses and deducing conclusions, awaits the full development of their ability for formal reasoning (Inhelder & Piaget, 1958).

Piaget's critics have raised a number of objections to his depiction of formal operational intelligence. They maintain that the rudiments of logic can begin earlier than Piaget believed. Given a simple problem such as "If John is in school, then Mary is in school. John is in school. What can you say about Mary?," many 7-year-olds have no trouble answering correctly (Patrick Suppes, cited by Ennis, 1982).

Another criticism, which Piaget (1972) acknowledged, is that he overestimated the number of people who attain the level of formal logic. Many adolescents and adults seldom achieve formal operational reasoning, particularly if they are uneducated in the logic of science and mathematics. Consider this conversation between researcher Sylvia Scribner (1977) and an illiterate Kpelle farmer in a Liberian village:

> ***Sylvia Scribner:***   *All Kpelle men are rice farmers. Mr. Smith is not a rice farmer. Is he a Kpelle man?*
>
> ***Kpelle farmer:***   *I don't know the man. I have not laid eyes on the man myself.*

Kpelle villagers who had had formal schooling could answer Scribner logically.

Nevertheless, it seems fair to conclude that the mind usually becomes capable of such reasoning in adolescence. One of the ways this new cognitive power manifests itself most frequently is in adolescents' pondering and debating such abstract topics as human nature, good and evil, truth and justice. Adolescents' logical thinking enables them to detect logical inconsistencies in others' reasoning, which can lead to heated debates with parents (Peterson & others, 1986). As Roger Brown (1965, p. 233) observed,

> As an adolescent one is amazed at adults who do not seem to realize the logical implications of their own ideas and who, still more unaccountably, do not make their actions consistent with their beliefs. The adolescent vows that he will never get to be like that; he will fight off whatever it is that clouds the adult intelligence. And suddenly he is ten years older, uncertain about everything and thoroughly compromised, trying to recall what it was he vowed to preserve.

Moral Thinking   A crucial task of childhood is learning right from wrong. But how do our notions of right and wrong develop?

Following Piaget's (1932) contention that children's moral development is tied to their cognitive development, Lawrence Kohlberg (1981, 1984) proposed that moral thought also develops through stages. To study people's moral thinking, Kohlberg (1981, p. 12) posed stories to children, adolescents, and adults in which the characters face a moral dilemma. Ponder for a moment his best known dilemma:

"The principal novelty of this period is the capacity to reason in terms of verbally stated hypotheses and no longer merely in terms of concrete objects and their manipulation."
    Jean Piaget (1972)

More on logical thinking in Chapter 11, Thinking and Language.

The adolescent's growing ability to think logically about abstract propositions illustrates Piaget's final stage of cognitive growth, formal operations.

In Europe, a woman was near death from a very bad disease, a special kind of cancer. There was one drug that the doctors thought might save her. It was a form of radium that a druggist in the same town had recently discovered. The drug was expensive to make, but the druggist was charging ten times what the drug cost him to make. He paid $200 for the radium and charged $2,000 for a small dose of the drug. The sick woman's husband, Heinz, went to everyone he knew to borrow the money, but he could get together only about $1,000, which was half of what it cost. He told the druggist that his wife was dying and asked him to sell it cheaper or let him pay later. But the druggist said, "No, I discovered the drug and I'm going to make money from it." Heinz got desperate and broke into the man's store to steal the drug for his wife.

What do you think: Should Heinz have stolen the drug? Why was what he did right or wrong? Kohlberg would not have been interested in whether you judged Heinz's behavior as right or wrong—either answer could be justified—but rather in the reasoning process by which you arrived at your judgment. We all are moral philosophers, Kohlberg proposed, and our moral reasoning helps guide our judgments and behavior (Berkowitz & others, 1986; Candee & Kohlberg, 1987).

On the basis of his research, Kohlberg argued that as we develop intellectually we pass through as many as six stages of moral reasoning (see Table 4–1). These six stages are divided into three basic levels:

Table 4–1

KOHLBERG'S LEVELS AND STAGES OF MORAL DEVELOPMENT

Stage description	Examples of moral reasoning in support of Heinz's stealing	Examples of moral reasoning against Heinz's stealing
Preconventional morality: morality of self-interest		
1. Avoids punishment	"If you let your wife die, you will get in trouble."	"You shouldn't steal the drug because you'll get caught and sent to jail if you do."
2. Gains concrete rewards	"If you steal the drug, your wife will live."	"He may not get much of a jail term if he steals the drug, but his wife will probably die before he gets out."
Conventional morality: morality of law and social convention		
3. Gains approval/ avoids disapproval	"If you steal the drug, your wife will live and you'll be a hero."	"It isn't just the druggist who will think you're a criminal, everyone else will, too."
4. Does duty to society/avoids dishonor or guilt	"If you have any sense of honor, you won't let your wife die because you're afraid to do the only thing that will save her."	"You'll always feel guilty for your dishonesty and lawbreaking."
Postconventional morality: morality of abstract principles		
5. Affirms agreed-upon rights	"His obligation to save his wife's life must take precedence. The value of human life is logically prior to the value of property."	"It is so hard for people to live together unless there are some laws governing their actions."
6. Affirms own ethical principles	"If you don't steal the drug, you would have lived up to the outside rule of the law but you wouldn't have lived up to your own standards of conscience."	"If you steal the drug, you won't be blamed by other people but you'll condemn yourself because you won't have lived up to your own conscience and standards of honesty."

Source: Second and third columns adapted from *The philosophy of moral development: Essays on moral development* (Vol. I) by L. Kohlberg, 1984, San Francisco: Harper & Row.

preconventional, conventional, and postconventional. Before age 9, most children have a "preconventional morality" of self-interest: One obeys to avoid punishment (Stage 1) or to gain concrete rewards (Stage 2). By early adolescence, morality usually evolves to a more "conventional morality" that upholds laws and conventions simply because they are the laws and conventions. Being able to take others' perspectives, adolescents may approve actions that will gain social approval (Stage 3) or that will help maintain the social order (Stage 4). Those who become sophisticated in the abstract reasoning of formal operational thought may come to a "postconventional morality" that affirms people's socially agreed-upon rights (Stage 5) or that follows what their individual conscience perceives as universal ethical principles that may sometimes conflict with society's rules (Stage 6).

Kohlberg's controversial claim was that these six stages form a moral ladder that extends from the immature, preconventional morality typical of the 7-year-old to, at its top rung, a recognition of what the person perceives to be fundamental ethical principles. As with all stage theories, the sequence is assumed to be unvarying. People begin at the bottom rung, and ascend to varying heights.

Kohlberg's theory of moral development is provocative. It spells out some of the ways people determine right from wrong. It suggests why people who operate from different levels of moral thinking often clash in their political and social judgments. And it implies a strategy for moral education. In the tradition of Piaget, Kohlberg believes that moral thinking matures as children's minds actively confront moral challenges. Moral education is therefore consciousness-raising—raising a person's moral consciousness to a higher stage through dialogue concerning rules and moral issues.

Provocative, yes. But is the theory valid? Does it accurately and helpfully describe moral development? Kohlberg's detractors offer two criticisms. The first emphasizes that, though our moral reasoning may largely determine our moral *talk,* it is but one of several influences on our *actions.* Morality, some critics say, involves what you *do* as well as what you think, and what we do is powerfully influenced by the social situation as well as by our inner attitudes. Many of the guards in the Nazi concentration camps were rather ordinary people who were corrupted by a powerfully evil system (Arendt, 1963). Given the imperfect link between moral reasoning and moral action, say the critics, we should also concentrate on instructing children how to *act* morally in given situations and on setting a good example ourselves (Blasi, 1980; Gibbs & Schnell, 1985).

The relationships between attitudes and actions are explored in Chapter 19, Social Influence.

Those who conform to society's rules often do not take kindly to those who seek to change those rules. Kohlberg contends that Stage 6 moral thinking, embodied here by Martin Luther King, Jr., may be rejected by those who, not comprehending, feel threatened by it.

The second criticism is that Kohlberg's theory has a Western cultural bias. Children in various cultures do seem to progress sequentially through the first three or four of Kohlberg's stages (Edwards, 1981, 1982; Snarey, 1985, 1987). However, the postconventional stages are most frequently found in educated, middle-class people in countries, such as the United States, Canada, Britain, and others that value individualism. The schema may therefore be biased against the moral reasoning of those in communal societies such as China and Papua New Guinea. Moreover, who is to say that the nonconformity of what Kohlberg calls the "highest" and most "mature" postconventional level is indeed morally preferable?

Because Kohlberg's formative studies involved male subjects only, Carol Gilligan (1982) offered another critique: Stage 6 is morality from a male perspective. For women, she argues, moral maturity is less an impersonal morality of abstract ethical principles and more a morality of responsible social relationships. Thus, measured by Kohlberg's yardstick, women's moral differences are seen as moral deficits. Actually, contends Gilligan (1982, p. 173), women's concern for social responsibilities is a moral strength that complements men's concern with abstract ethics: "In the different voice of women lies the truth of an ethic of care."

The accumulating evidence has provided little direct support for Gilligan's views (Blake & Cohen, 1985; Friedman & others, 1987; Rothbart & others, 1986; Thoma, 1986; Walker, 1986). Nevertheless, polls continue to find that women are more likely than men to favor the Democratic party, which generally promotes programs for the poor and disadvantaged. Might an "ethic of care" also help explain why women are more likely than men to select helping professions such as child care and social work, and why daughters rather than sons so often take primary responsibility for their elderly parents (Troll, 1987)?

Kohlberg's critics agree that moral reasoning is linked with cognitive development. Nevertheless, they caution that moral reasoning is but one determinant of moral action and that Kohlberg's postconventional moral stages may be those of individualists in a Western culture.

SOCIAL DEVELOPMENT

Theorist Erik Erikson (1963) contended that each stage of life has its own "psychosocial" task. As we saw in Chapter 3 (Table 3–2, page 74), young children deal with issues of *trust,* then *autonomy,* then *initiative.* Later, between the ages of 7 and 11, they develop *industry,* the sense that they are competent and productive human beings. For adolescents, the task is to synthesize their past, their present, and their future possibilities into a clear sense of self. Erikson calls this attempt to establish a sense of self the adolescent's search for **identity.**

Forming an Identity "Who am I as an individual? What do I want to do with my life? What values should I live by? What do I believe in?" According to Erikson, arriving at answers that provide a stable and consistent identity is essential to the adolescent's finding a meaningful place in society.

To gain this sense of identity, adolescents usually try out different "selves" in different situations—perhaps acting out one self at home, another with friends, and still another at school and work. If two of these situations overlap—as when a teenager brings home friends with whom he is Joe Cool—the discomfort can be considerable. The teen asks, "Which self should I be? Which is the real me?" Often, this role

What would happen to society if everyone adopted Stage 6 moral reasoning and acted according to their own perception of universal ethical principles, with little regard for society's conventions?

"It is obvious that the values of women differ very often from the values which have been made by the other sex."
Virginia Woolf,
A Room of One's Own, 1929

"This might not be ethical. Is that a problem for anybody?"

"I am becoming still more independent of my parents; young as I am, I face life with more courage than Mummy; my feeling for justice is immovable, and truer than hers. I know what I want, I have a goal, an opinion, I have a religion, and love. Let me be myself and then I am satisfied. I know that I'm a woman, a woman with inward strength and plenty of courage."
Anne Frank,
Diary of a Young Girl, 1947

confusion gets resolved by the gradual forging of a self-definition that unifies the various selves into a consistent and comfortable sense of who one is—an identity.

But not always. Erikson believes that some adolescents form their identity early, simply by taking on their parents' values and expectations. Others may form a negative identity, one that defines itself in opposition to parents and society, complete perhaps with shaved head or multicolored, spiked hair. Still others never quite seem to find themselves or to develop strong commitments. For most, the struggle for identity continues throughout the teen years and reappears at turning points during adult life.

The late teen years, when many people begin attending college or working full-time, provide new opportunities for trying out possible roles. As college seniors, many students have achieved a clearer identity than they had as first-year students (Waterman & others, 1974). This identity tends to incorporate a more positive self-concept than existed before. In several nationwide studies, researchers have given young Americans tests of self-esteem (sample item: ''I am able to do things as well as most other people''). Between ages 13 and 23, the sense of self usually becomes more positive (O'Malley & Bachman, 1983). A clearer, more self-affirming identity is forming.

During the teen years identity also becomes more personalized. Daniel Hart (1988) asked youth of various ages to imagine a machine that would copy either (a) what you think and feel, (b) your exact appearance, or (c) your relationships with friends and family. Asked ''Which of these persons is closest to being you?,'' three-fourths of seventh graders chose the clone with the same social network; three-fourths of ninth graders chose the clone with their individual thoughts and feelings.

Erikson contends that the adolescent identity stage is followed in young adulthood by a developing capacity for **intimacy**, the ability to form emotionally close relationships. But to Carol Gilligan (1982), the ''normal'' struggle to create one's separate identity characterizes individualistic males more than relationship-oriented females. Gilligan believes that females are less concerned than males with viewing themselves as separate individuals, and more concerned with intimate relationships. Thus females are less likely to exhibit Erikson's identity-before-intimacy sequence (Kahn & others, 1985).

By trying out different roles, adolescents try out different ''selves.'' Although some of their roles are uncomfortable for both the adolescents and their parents, most teenagers eventually forge a consistent and comfortable identity.

''How about that? I recently became my own person, too.''

Drawing by Lorenz; © 1984 The New Yorker Magazine, Inc.

Relationships with Parents and Peers   Are adolescents indeed pre-occupied with separating themselves from their parents in order to form their own identities? Is adolescence a time of undeclared war between restrictive parents and their rebellious, independence-seeking, identity-craving offspring? In Western cultures, adolescence is typically a time of growing peer influence and diminishing parental influence, especially on matters of personal taste and life-style. For example, the best predictor of whether a high school student smokes marijuana is simply how many of the student's friends smoke it (Oetting & Beauvais, 1987). Another predictor is working long hours at a job; high school students who do so are more likely to use drugs, perhaps because they spend more time with older co-workers who use drugs; perhaps, too, the need for cash to purchase drugs motivates them to work long hours (Bachman, 1987). Those who continue to live with their parents after high school show little change in drug use, while those who move in with peers become more likely to use drugs (Bachman & others, 1984). As peer influences grow, parental influences diminish.

Does this mean that parents and their adolescents are estranged? For a small minority, it does. But for most, disagreement at the level of bickering is not destructive. "We usually get along but . . . ," adolescents often report (Steinberg, 1987). Positive relations with parents actually support positive peer relations. High school girls who have the most affectionate relationships with their mothers tend also to enjoy the most intimate friendships with girlfriends (Gold & Yanof, 1985).

Moreover, in most families the generation gap is easily bridged because it is rather narrow. In response to a 1977 Gallup poll that asked adolescents how they got along with their parents, 56 percent—the "teen angels," we might call them—said they got along with them "very well," 41 percent indicated "fairly well," and only 2 percent indicated they got along "not at all well." Indeed, researchers have been surprised at how closely most adolescents reflect the social, political, and religious views of their parents (Gallatin, 1980). As often as not, what "generation gaps" there were on such issues merely involved differences in the strength with which adolescents and their parents held their shared opinions and values (Figure 4–3).

Most teenagers say they generally have a good relationship with their parents.

"When I was a boy of 14 my father was so ignorant I could hardly stand to have the old man around. But when I got to be 21, I was astonished at how much he had learnt in seven years."
   Mark Twain, 1835–1910

Figure 4–3   High school seniors' attitudes appear to be in much closer agreement with their parents' than many suppose. Agreement is greater, however, on basic values than on life-style choices. (From Bachman & others, 1987.)

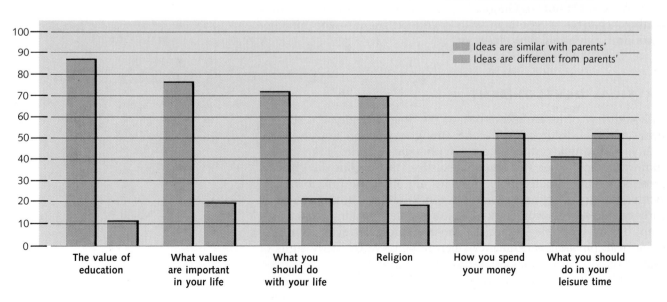

ADULTHOOD AND AGING

Until recently, adulthood, especially the center-of-life years between adolescence and old age, was commonly viewed as one long plateau. No longer. As we will see, those who have closely followed the unfolding of people's adult lives have been impressed by the degree to which development continues. Physically, cognitively, and especially socially, people at age 50 are quite different from their 25-year-old selves.

Recognizing that adults do change, developmental theorists have proposed various stages of adult development, complete with transition periods. When people become independent of their parents and assume work roles, a transition from adolescence to *early adulthood* occurs—at about age 20, give or take a few years depending on the culture and the individual. This period extends to about age 40, at which time a transition to *middle adulthood* is said to occur. Within the later adult years, many developmentalists distinguish the "young-old" postretirement years (65 to 75) from the "old-old" years (after 75) of more rapid physical decline.

The labeling of life's phases is a convenient way to organize the adult years. But the labels are arbitrary, and the transition points are fuzzy. Moreover, by itself, age causes nothing. People do not get wiser with age; they get wiser with experience. People do not die because of old age; they die of the physical deterioration that accompanies aging. For that matter, during the adult years, age only modestly predicts people's traits. If you know only that Maria is a 1-year-old and Meredith is a 10-year-old, you could say a great deal about each. Not so with adults who differ similarly in age. The boss may be 30 or 60; the marathon runner may be 20 or 50; the reader of this book may be a teenager or a grandparent. Likewise, to be 19 can mean that one is a parent who supports young children or a student who still gets an allowance.

The unpredictability of adult lives reflects the increasing importance of individual experiences. During the first 2 years of life, biological maturation narrowly restricts our course. The infant who is strapped on a cradleboard and the one who moves freely will both walk and talk at about the same age. But as the years pass, we sail a widening channel, allowing the winds of experience to diverge our courses more and more.

Individual life experiences make it much more difficult to generalize about adulthood than about life's early years. Yet our life courses are in some ways similar. Our bodies, our minds, and our relationships undergo changes in common with childhood friends who in other ways now may seem very different.

"I am still learning."
Michelangelo's motto, 1560, at age 85

"I'm just getting around to sowing my wild oats."

Drawing by Koren; © 1987 The New Yorker Magazine, Inc.

PHYSICAL DEVELOPMENT

Although few of us are aware of it at the time, our physical abilities peak in early adulthood. Muscular strength, reaction time, sensory acuity, and cardiac output all crest by the mid-twenties. Like the declining daylight after the summer solstice, the decline in physical prowess begins imperceptibly. Athletes are often the first to notice. World-class sprinters and swimmers generally peak in their teens or early twenties, with women (who mature earlier) peaking earlier than men. But most people—especially those whose daily lives do not require peak physical performance—hardly perceive the early signs of decline.

Physical Changes in Middle Adulthood In middle adulthood, physical decline gradually accelerates (Figure 4–4), but even diminished vigor is sufficient for normal activities. Moreover, during early and middle adulthood a person's health and exercise habits have more to say about physical vigor than does aging. Many of today's physically fit 50-year-olds can run several miles with ease, while sedentary 25-year-olds find themselves huffing and puffing on a jog around the block.

The physical changes of adult life can trigger psychological responses, which vary depending on how one views growing older. In some Eastern cultures where respect and power come with age, outward signs of one's advancing years are generally accepted, even welcomed. In Western cultures where the perceived ideal is youthful, smooth skin and a slim torso, the wrinkles and bulges that frequently accompany middle age can be a threat to self-esteem—something to try to avoid. But nature will not be denied; inevitably the lines appear, the youthful form begins to change its shape.

For women, the most definite biological change related to aging is *menopause,* the cessation of the menstrual cycle, usually beginning within a few years of age 50. Menopause is caused by a reduction in the hormone estrogen and is sometimes accompanied by physical symptoms such as hot flashes and profuse perspiring. Some women also experience periods of anxiety, emotional instability, or depression. But like the stereotype of adolescent storm and stress, the image of menopausal upheaval has given way to a recognition that menopause usually does not create significant psychological problems for women, nor does it greatly diminish sexual appetite or appeal (Newman, 1982).

What determines the emotional impact of menopause is the woman's attitude toward it. Does she see menopause as a sign that she is losing her femininity and sexual attractiveness and beginning to grow old? Or does she look on it as liberation from contraceptives, menstrual periods, fears of pregnancy, and the demands of children? To ascertain women's attitudes toward menopause, Bernice Neugarten and her colleagues (1963) did what, amazingly, no one had bothered to do: They asked questions of women, including those whose experience of menopause had not led them to seek treatment. When asked, for example, whether it is true that after menopause "women generally feel better than they have for years," only one-fourth of the premenopausal women under age 45 guessed yes; of the older women who had experienced menopause, two-thirds said yes. As one woman said, "I can remember my mother saying that after her menopause she really got her vigor, and I can say the same thing myself." Social psychologist Jacqueline Goodchilds (1987) quips: "If the truth were known, we'd have to diagnose [older women] as having P.M.F.—Post-Menstrual Freedom."

Men experience no equivalent to the menopause—no cessation of fertility, no sharp drop in sex hormones. But they do experience a gradual decline in sperm count and testosterone level. Some may also experience psychological distress related to their perception of decreased virility and declining physical capacities.

Physical Changes in Later Life Is old age "more to be feared than death" (Juvenal, *Satires*)? Or is life "most delightful when it is on the downward slope" (Seneca, *Epistulae ad Lucilium*)? What have we to look forward to? What is it like to be old? To gauge your own attitudes, take the following true/false quiz:

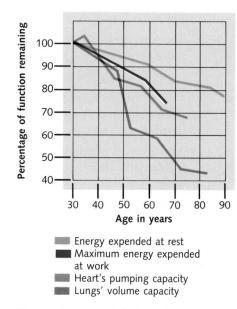

Energy expended at rest
Maximum energy expended at work
Heart's pumping capacity
Lungs' volume capacity

Figure 4–4 The body's physical capacities decline slowly during adulthood. (Adapted from Insel & Roth, 1976.)

During middle adulthood, physical vigor depends more on exercise than on age. Kareem Abdul-Jabbar (left), who turned 40 in 1987, remains in great shape.

1. By 2030, 1 in 9 Americans will be 65 or older (see below).

2. The average life expectancy for a person 65 years old is 10 more years (see page 101).

3. During old age there usually occurs a substantial loss of neurons in the brain (see page 101).

4. Older people become more susceptible to short-term illnesses (see below).

5. Approximately one-fourth of people age 65 and older live in institutions (nursing homes, hospitals, and homes for the aged) (see page 101).

6. If they live long enough—to be 90 or more—most elderly people eventually become senile (see page 101).

7. Recognition memory—the ability to identify things previously experienced—declines with age (see page 102).

8. Life satisfaction peaks in one's fifties and then gradually declines after age 65 (see page 109).

9. Among the elderly, there are twice as many widows than widowers (see page 110).

10. Many older people are preoccupied with a fear of death (see page 111).

Life Expectancy   The above statements—all false—are among the myths about aging that have been exploded by current research on North America's most rapidly growing population group. In 1900, those 65 and older accounted for 1 in 25 Americans; by 1987, thanks partly to strides in combating childhood diseases, the proportion increased to 1 in 8. By 2030, when living members of the baby-boom generation born in the 1950s and early 1960s will all have reached 65, the 65 and over group will include 1 in 5 Americans. In the Third World, the elderly population is rising even faster—and will have doubled between 1980 and 2000. The number of childless adults also is rising. Consider China, where there were 5 children per elderly person in 1955. In 2040, there will be but 2 children per elderly person (Hugo, 1987). Clearly, countries that depend on children to look after elderly persons are destined for major social changes.

Sensory Abilities   As we have seen, physical decline begins in early adulthood, but it is usually not until later in life that people become acutely aware of it. As visual acuity diminishes and the speed of one's adaptation to changes in light level slows, older people tend to have more accidents. Most stairway falls taken by older persons occur on the top step, precisely where the person typically descends from a window-lit hallway into the darker stairwell (Fozard & Popkin, 1978). Muscle strength, hearing, reaction time, and stamina also diminish noticeably. Thus, in later life it may seem as if the stairs are getting steeper, the newspaper print smaller, and people are mumbling more than they used to.

Health   Despite these signs of aging, the "young-old," especially those in good health with a positive attitude, continue to enjoy the vitality to maintain an active life. Indeed, although older people are more subject to long-term ailments, such as arthritis, they *less often* suffer short-term ailments, such as flu (Palmore, 1981). The similar good health in the preretirement years helps explain why older workers have lower absenteeism than do young workers (Rhodes, 1983).

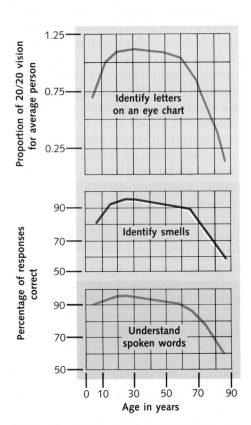

The senses of sight, smell, and hearing all decline in later life. (From Doty & others, 1984.)

Although at birth the average American has a 75-year life expectancy, current statistics show that those who survive to age 65 can expect to live until they are 82—or even longer if they are women, had parents who lived past 80, and maintain a healthy way of life, free of cigarettes and with regular exercise. One survey revealed that most elderly people think that the majority of their peers have some sort of serious health problem—although when asked about their own health fewer than one in four report that *they* have such a problem (National Council on the Aging, 1976). So it should not surprise us that only 5 percent of all those over 65 are residing in institutions such as nursing homes.

Bear in mind, too, that age-linked changes need not be age-determined. For example, blood pressure and blood cholesterol are affected not so much by age per se as by age-linked changes in nutrition and exercise, and by the accumulated effects of smoking and drinking (Rowe & Kahn, 1987). To the extent that consumption and activity patterns rather than age itself determine "usual aging," we have it within our power to age in good health.

However, aging does slow neural processes, and with age there is a small, gradual loss of brain cells, contributing to a 5 percent or so reduction of brain weight by age 80. But the proliferation of neural connections, especially in people who remain active, helps compensate for the cell loss (Coleman & Flood, 1986). Perhaps this helps explain the common finding that adults who remain active—physically, sexually, and mentally—tend to retain more of their functional capacity for such activities in later years (Jarvik, 1975; Pfeiffer, 1977). In general, "use it or lose it" appears to be sound advice. We are more likely to rust from disuse than wear out from overuse.

A small number of adults do, however, suffer a tragic loss of brain cells. A series of small strokes, a brain tumor, or alcoholism can result in progressive brain damage causing senility. The most feared of all brain diseases, *Alzheimer's disease,* strikes 10 percent of the aging by age 75, and 20 percent of those 85 and older (Heckler, 1985). Some 2 million Americans are afflicted at a cost of some $40 billion a year, and the numbers are expected to double by the year 2000 as the population ages (Holden, 1987c).

Alzheimer's destroys even the brightest of minds. Memory, and eventually reasoning and language, gradually deteriorate. As the disease runs its course, after some 3 to 20 years, the patient may become disoriented, then incontinent, and progressively lose mental function—a sort of living death preceding actual death.

In its early stages, Alzheimer's disease is easily mistaken for mental laziness. Robert Sayre (1979) recalls his father shouting at his afflicted mother to "think harder" when she could not remember where she had put something, while his mother, confused, embarrassed, on the verge of tears, randomly searched the house. Caregiving family members of increasingly confused and helpless sufferers can themselves easily become Alzheimer's exasperated and exhausted hidden victims.

We now know that underlying the disease is a deterioration in neurons that produce the neurotransmitter acetylcholine, and that drugs that block the normal activity of this neurotransmitter produce Alzheimer-like symptoms (Weingartner, 1986). Investigators have also located on the twenty-first chromosome the genetic defect that causes one form of Alzheimer's. With continuing advances in our understanding of the genetics, brain chemistry, and neural underpinnings of Alzheimer's, hopes for an eventual treatment grow.

Most older people are in good enough health to maintain an active life. And the more active they remain, the more vigor they retain.

COGNITIVE DEVELOPMENT

One of the most controversial questions in the study of human development is whether cognitive abilities such as memory, creativity, and intelligence follow a similar course of gradually accelerating decline during adulthood. Employers may wonder what they should do with their older workers. Retire them—or capitalize on their experience? Voters may wonder if a 75-year-old person retains the agility of mind, the flexibility of thought, and the judgment required to lead a nation.

Aging and Memory   We do know that early adulthood provides the peak years for some types of learning and remembering (Craik, 1977). For example, David Schonfield and Betty-Anne Robertson (1966) asked adults of various ages to learn a list of twenty-four words. Some were then asked, without being given any clues, to *recall* as many words as they could from the list. As Figure 4–5 indicates, younger adults had better recall—a finding that parallels the greater ease with which younger adults recall new names and process complicated information (Zacks & Hasher, 1988). Others, given multiple-choice questions that asked them simply to *recognize* which words they had seen, exhibited no memory decline with age. So it seems that while our ability to recall new learning gradually declines during adulthood, our ability to recognize what we have learned remains strong. Moreover, part of the recall difficulty that the elderly often complain of is attributable to normal forgetting. When Grandpa forgets where he put his car keys, he and we are more likely to blame his age than when his 20-year-old granddaughter mislays hers.

The proficiency of adults in retaining newly acquired learning is also evident in classrooms. In recent years, American adults have returned to school and turned to leisure education programs in increased numbers. Since 1973 the percentage of college students 35 years and older has nearly doubled (Grant & Snyder, 1986). By 1985, 38 percent of college students were age 25 and older (Center for Education Statistics, 1987). Despite occasional difficulties in adjusting to the demands of coursework and testing, older students are generally successful in their academic efforts. In fact, most older students do better than the typical 18-year-old, perhaps because they have clearer goals and are better motivated (Badenhoop & Johansen, 1980).

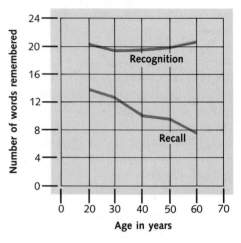

Figure 4–5   In this experiment of recall and recognition in adulthood, the ability to *recall* new information declined during early and middle adulthood but the ability to *recognize* new information showed little decline. (From Schonfield & Robertson, 1966.)

College enrollments of post-35-year-olds are rising. Despite occasional adjustment problems, older students usually do better than the typical 18-year-old.

Aging and Intelligence   Describing the cognitive abilities of older people is complicated. As we just noted, how well they remember depends: Are they being asked simply to *recognize* what they have tried to memorize (little decline) or to *recall* it without clues (greater decline)?

Actually, the truth is even more complicated. If the information being recalled is meaningless—remembering nonsense syllables or saying five digits backward—then the older you are, the more errors you are likely to make. But the elderly's rich web of existing knowledge helps them catch meaningful information; thus their capacity to learn and remember meaningful material shows little decline with age (Labouvie-Vief & Schell, 1982; Perlmutter, 1983).

What happens to our broader intellectual powers as we age? Do they gradually decline, like our ability to remember nonsense material, or do they remain nearly constant, like our ability to recall meaningful material? The evolving answer to this question makes an interesting research story, one that illustrates psychology's self-correcting process. At any stage of scientific inquiry, conclusions may be reached that seem sound, that meet ready social acceptance, and that shape social policy. But then an awareness grows of shortcomings in the research, and new studies must be done. This particular research story has progressed through several phases (Woodruff-Pak, 1989).

Phase I: Cross-Sectional Evidence for Intellectual Decline   In *cross-sectional studies,* people of various ages are tested at the same time. When administering intelligence tests to representative samples of people, researchers consistently found that older adults gave fewer correct answers than younger adults (Figure 4–6). As David Wechsler (1972), creator of the widely used adult intelligence test, put it, "the decline of mental ability with age is part of the general [aging] process of the organism as a whole."

Until the 1950s, this rather dismal view of intelligence declining with age remained essentially unchallenged. Many corporations established mandatory retirement policies under the presumption that the company would benefit by replacing aging workers with younger, presumably more capable, employees. As everyone "knew," you can't teach an old dog new tricks.

Phase II: Longitudinal Evidence for Intellectual Stability   Colleges began administering intelligence tests to entering students about 1920. So by the 1950s it was possible to find 50-year-olds who had taken an intelligence test 30 years earlier. Several psychologists saw their chance to study intelligence *longitudinally,* by retesting the same people over a period of years. What they expected to find was the usual decrease in intelligence after about age 30 (Schaie & Geiwitz, 1982). What they actually found was a surprise: Until very late in life, intelligence remained stable, and on some tests it even increased (Figure 4–7).

How then are we to account for the previous findings from the cross-sectional studies? In retrospect, researchers saw the problem. Whenever a cross-sectional study compares people of different ages, age is not the only factor that influences the result. A cohort (generation) factor is also at work. The average 70-year-old and the average 30-year-old who were tested in 1950 were born and raised in different eras and circumstances, offering different educational opportunities. So when comparing 70- and 30-year-olds, one compares not only people of two different ages and eras, but also generally less educated people with more educated people, people raised in large families with people raised in smaller families, and so forth.

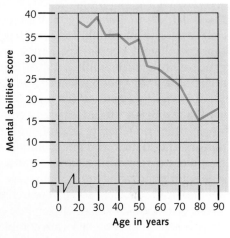

Figure 4–6   When intelligence tests were administered to representative samples of adults of various ages (the cross-sectional method), older adults consistently got fewer questions correct than younger adults. But see Figure 4–7. (From Geiwitz, 1980.)

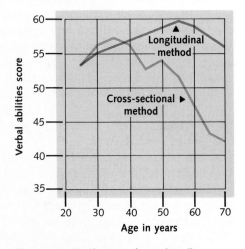

Figure 4–7   In this test of verbal intelligence, when the cross-sectional method was used (the same method as in the Figure 4–6 studies), scores were observed to drop with age. But when the longitudinal method was used (in which the same people were retested over a period of years) scores rose until late adulthood. (From Schaie & Strother, 1968.)

According to this more optimistic view, the myth that intelligence sharply declines with age had been laid to rest. As everyone "knows," you're never too old to learn. Witness Dr. John Rock, who at age 70 developed the birth control pill, Grandma Moses, who at age 78 took up painting and was still painting after age 100, and architect Frank Lloyd Wright, who at age 89 designed New York's Guggenheim Museum. Moreover, when people have kept alive their expertise—typing, playing chess, playing the piano—their abilities often remain intact well into their eighties (Schaie, 1987). As psychologist David Krech (1978) said, "He who lives by his wits, dies with his wits."

Phase III: It All Depends   But the controversy was not, and still is not, over. For one thing, longitudinal studies have their own pitfalls. More intelligent people live longer and suffer less decline in intelligence with age (Botwinick, 1977). Thus longitudinal studies may be selecting the very people whose intelligence is least likely to decline. If so, such studies underestimate the average decline in intelligence.

Psychologists are increasingly convinced that intelligence is not a single trait (see Chapter 12, Intelligence). Intelligence tests that were designed to assess academic abilities—including speed of thinking—may place older adults at a disadvantage, because their neural mechanisms for processing information are slower than those of younger people. And, in fact, some researchers find that on tests involving speed of response, senior citizens do perform relatively poorly, especially when the mental tasks are complex (Cerella, 1985; Poon, 1987). A 70-year-old is generally no match for a 20-year-old at video games.

But slower need not mean less intelligent. Given other tests that assess general vocabulary, knowledge, and ability to integrate information, older adults generally hold their own. Researcher Paul Baltes (1987) is developing tests of "wisdom" that assess traits such as expertise and sound judgment in the problems of daily life. His results suggest that older adults more than hold their own on such tests.

Building on a distinction originally suggested by intelligence expert Raymond Cattell, John L. Horn (1982) proposed that we all possess two distinct types of intelligence, and that these are quite differently affected by age. *Crystallized intelligence* is basically the accumulation of stored information that comes with education and experience. For example, tests of verbal ability, such as vocabulary tests, tend to reflect crystallized intelligence. *Fluid intelligence* reflects one's ability to reason abstractly, and is less closely associated with one's stored knowledge. For example, being able to identify the next letter in the series *d f i m r x e* ___ reflects fluid intelligence. It turns out that crystallized intelligence *increases* with age, while fluid intelligence *decreases*. Perhaps this helps to explain why mathematicians and scientists often do their most notable work during their late twenties or early thirties and psychologists peak about age 40, while those in literature, history, and philosophy tend to produce their best work later—in their forties, fifties, and beyond, after more knowledge has accumulated (Denney, 1982; Horner & others, 1986). So, whether intelligence increases or decreases with age depends on what type of intellectual performance is measured.

SOCIAL DEVELOPMENT

Most of the differences between early and middle adulthood are created not by the physical and cognitive changes linked to aging but by life events—events often associated with family relationships and

Born in 1898, Armand Hammer continues his lifelong involvement in bettering Soviet-American relations through his friendships with leaders in both countries—and still guides a successful major corporation.

"In youth we learn, in age we understand."
Marie von Ebner-Eschenbach,
Aphorisms, 1883

Erik and Joan Erikson have focused their attention on the end of the life cycle as they themselves have aged. Now in their eighties, the Eriksons maintain that wisdom has little to do with formal learning: "What is real wisdom? It comes from life experience, well digested. It's not what comes from reading great books. When it comes to understanding life, experiential learning is the only worthwhile kind; everything else is hearsay."

work. A new job means new relationships, new expectations, and new demands. Marriage brings the potential for both the joy of intimacy and the stress of merging your life with someone else's. The birth of children introduces new responsibilities and significantly alters your life focus. A sudden shift in economic fortune may turn your world upside down, for better or for worse. The death of a loved one creates a sense of irreplaceable loss, and generally produces a need to reaffirm your own life. Any such life event represents a challenge that may significantly change you. To the extent that these major events of adult life are common, we may expect their influence to shape a predictable sequence of life changes.

Ages and Stages of Adulthood   As we have seen, Erikson (1963) theorized that the challenge facing the individual in young adulthood is that of achieving *intimacy,* of forming close, loving relationships. In middle age, the challenge is to achieve *generativity*—to become less self-absorbed, more productive, more caring for the world and its future generations. This is generally experienced through the raising of a family and building of a career or business.

The final task, or crisis, of adulthood is achieving a sense of *integrity*—that is, arriving at a feeling that one's life has been worthwhile. Those who cannot do this—who feel that they have failed to realize their goals or to make a contribution to others' well-being—are likely to approach their final days with a sense of despair. Those who do achieve integrity look back on their lives with a sense of completion. Keenly aware of their mortality, they review their relationships and accomplishments and judge that, yes, life has been good (Table 4–2).

"Perhaps middle-age is, or should be, a period of shedding shells; the shell of ambition, the shell of material accumulations and possessions, the shell of the ego."
Anne Morrow Lindbergh,
Gift from the Sea, 1955

"It is a blessed thing to dispatch the business of life before we die, and then to expect death in the possession of a happy life."
Seneca,
Of a Happy Life, A.D. 54

Table 4–2
ERIKSON'S STAGES OF PSYCHOSOCIAL DEVELOPMENT

Approximate age	Description of stage
Infancy (1st year)	**Trust vs. mistrust** If needs are met, infant develops a sense of basic trust.
Toddler (2nd year)	**Autonomy vs. shame and doubt** Toddler strives to learn independence and self-confidence.
Preschooler (3–5 years)	**Initiative vs. guilt** Preschooler learns to initiate tasks and grapples with self-control.
Elementary School (6 years to puberty)	**Competence vs. inferiority** Child learns either to feel effective or inadequate.
Adolescence (teen years)	**Identity vs. role confusion** Teenager works at developing a sense of self by testing roles, then integrating them to form a single identity.
Young Adulthood (20–40 years)	**Intimacy vs. isolation** Young adult struggles to form close relationships and to gain the capacity for intimate love.
Middle Adulthood (40–65 years)	**Generativity vs. stagnation** Middle-aged person seeks a sense of contributing to the world, through, for example, family and work.
Late Adulthood (65 years and up)	**Integrity vs. despair** Reflecting on life, the elderly person may experience satisfaction or a sense of failure.

Other developmental psychologists have attempted to describe more precisely how people feel and act at various stages of adulthood. In the best known of these investigations, psychiatrist Daniel Levinson and his associates (1978) spent 10 to 20 hours talking with each of forty successful middle-aged men. Based partly on his impressions of their recollections, Levinson proposed a series of distinct stages of adult development (Figure 4–8), which he considers confirmed by his more recent interviews with forty-five women (1986).

Levinson believes that after a transitional time of breaking away from their preadult world, people devote their twenties to entering and exploring the adult world and "to creating a stable life structure" by embarking on careers and beginning a family. At the end of their twenties, most begin a stressful transitional period in which they take stock of their lives and seek to restructure them in more satisfying ways. This accomplished, they settle down, tending to family life and seeking advancement in their careers. Then the cycle of stability and turbulence repeats. As they enter their forties they undergo a transition to middle adulthood, which for many is a crisis, a time of great struggle or even of feeling struck down by life. The dream of fame and fortune (or the illusion that such brings happiness) is given up, work and family commitments are called into question, and turmoil and despair may result. They realize that they are no longer starting out, but rather drawing closer to the end. When this painful growth period is concluded, at about age 45, they again settle into new or deepened attachments, set about completing their careers, and become more compassionate and reflective without being tyrannized by external demands.

Levinson's basic idea, then, is that life progresses in a predictable cycle of stability followed by rapid change. "Everyone goes through the same basic sequence," says Levinson (1986), and each "developmental period begins and ends at a well-defined [average] age, with a range of about two years above and below this average."

Other researchers are skeptical about any attempt at defining adult life as a series of neatly packaged stages, especially one based merely on interviews with a select few people, most of them high achievers. To generalize from their career-oriented lives or to use their "midlife crises" to explain or justify the renouncing of old relationships is both misleading and dangerous (Gilligan, 1982). The fact is that job dissatisfaction, marital dissatisfaction, divorce, anxiety, and suicide do *not* surge during the early forties (Costa & McCrae, 1980; Scanzoni & Scanzoni, 1981; Schaie & Geiwitz, 1982).

Moreover, the *social clock*—the cultural prescription of "the right age" to leave home, get a job, marry, have children, and retire—varies from culture to culture and era to era. In Turkey, 76 percent of brides are in their teens; in Belgium, only 35 percent are (United Nations, 1980). In Western nations, contemporary women are increasingly entering the workplace and college classroom during middle adulthood, if not before. In earlier times, such ventures outside the home were often frowned on.

Life Events and Commitments   Given variations in the social clock and individual experience, the critics suspect that any proposed timetable of adult ages and stages will have limited generality. More important than one's chronological age are life events and the historical and cultural setting (being divorced in 1989 does not mean what it meant in 1955) (Harris & others, 1986). Marriage, childbearing, vocational changes, divorce, nest-emptying, relocation, and retirement mark transitions to new life stages whenever they occur—and increasingly

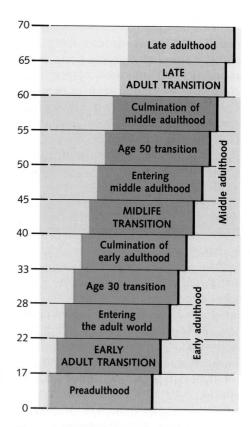

Figure 4–8   Developmental periods in early and middle male adulthood as proposed by Levinson. (Adapted from Levinson, 1986.)

Transitions in adult lives tend to be work- or family-related. Just as marriage, at age 28, 48, or 68, heralds significant changes, so does the attainment of a college degree.

they are occurring at unpredictable ages. The social clock is still ticking, but people feel freer to be out of sync with it.

Even chance encounters with people and events can have lasting significance, deflecting us down one road rather than another (Bandura, 1982). The 1950s actress Nancy Davis might never have met her future husband had she not, through a mix-up, begun to receive announcements of communist meetings intended for another person of the same name. Fearing that her career might be jeopardized by this mistaken identity, she went to see the president of the Screen Actors Guild. Before long she married this man, Ronald Reagan, and the rest is history (Reagan & Libby, 1980). Given the impact of chance encounters, it is small wonder that researcher Bernice Neugarten (1979, 1980) concludes that "adults change far more, and far less predictably, than the oversimplified stage theories suggest." It is therefore "a distortion to describe adulthood as a series of discrete and nearly bounded stages, as if adult life were a staircase."

Two basic aspects of our lives do, however, dominate adulthood. Erikson called them intimacy and generativity. Personality theorist Abraham Maslow (1968) described them as a need to love and belong. Researchers have chosen various terms—affiliation and achievement, attachment and productivity, commitment and competence. But Sigmund Freud (1935) put it most simply: The healthy adult, he said, is one who can love and work. For most adults, *love* is centered on family commitments toward spouse, parents, and children. *Work* is one's other productive activities, whether for pay or not.

Love   "Traditional" families—father, mother, and children under 18—compose only 28 percent of U.S. households (Bureau of the Census, 1987). Who are the other 72 percent? They are the divorced and their children, the widowed, the older couples with an empty nest, the singles, the cohabiting men and women, and the childless or voluntarily child-free married people. To judge from the U.S. divorce rate—now one-half the marriage rate—marriage has become a union that often defies management.

Despite the alternatives to marriage and the celebration of single life, most adults marry and most who divorce remarry. Indeed, 95 percent of U.S. citizens age 40 and older have been married, and among women of this age group 9 in 10 have had a child (Bureau of the Census, 1987). At the same time, in many countries women are having fewer children. Since 1960, the proportion of American women in their

"Two roads diverged in a wood, and I—
I took the one less traveled by,
And that has made all the difference."
    Robert Frost,
    The Road Not Taken, 1916

The growing number of single-parent households has altered the picture of the North American family. Single parents must find new social supports, as these mothers have done with communal dinners, and learn new skills, as this father has done.

late twenties who are childless has more than doubled, from 20 percent to over 40 percent, while the average fertility rate has dropped from 3.6 children per woman to 1.8 (Kantrowitz, 1986; *Public Opinion*, 1986a).

Perhaps the most enduring and significant of all life changes, having a child is a happy event for most people. As children begin to absorb one's time, money, and emotional energy, however, satisfaction with the marriage itself often declines, especially among employed women who find themselves bearing the traditional burden of increased chores at home (Belsky & others, 1986).

Another significant event in family life is the children leaving home. Consider your parents' experience: If you have left home, did your parents suffer an "empty nest syndrome"—was either of them distressed by a loss of purpose and relationship? Or did your parents discover renewed freedom, relaxation, and satisfaction with their own relationship?

Contrary to the myth, the empty nest for most couples is a happy place. As Neugarten (1974) commented,

> Just as the major problem of middle-aged women is not the menopause, it is also not the empty nest. Most women are glad to see their children grow up, leave home, marry, and have their careers. The notion that they mourn the loss of their reproductive ability and their mother role does not seem to fit modern reality. No matter what the stereotypes tell us, it is not the way women talk when you listen.

Work   A large part of the answer to "Who are you?" is the answer to "What do you do?" Much of what adults do to fulfill their need to feel productive and competent is (1) to raise children and (2) to undertake a career.

Predicting people's career choices and guiding them toward satisfying occupations is a complex matter. Because it often takes time for people to settle into an occupation and because of the impact of chance encounters, there will always remain a large element of unpredictability in career choices. During the first 2 years of college, most students cannot accurately predict their later career path. Most students shift from their initially intended majors while in college, many find their postcollege employment in fields not directly related to their majors, and most will change careers (Rothstein, 1980). To many career counselors, this means that the best education is not a narrow vocational

"Appearances notwithstanding, for women, at least, midlife is not a stage tied to chronological age. Rather, it belongs to that point in the life cycle of the family when the children are grown and gone, or nearly so—when, perhaps for the first time in her adult life, a woman can attend to her own needs, her own desires, her own development as a separate and autonomous being."
  Sociologist Lillian B. Rubin (1979)

Work is a major focus of adulthood.

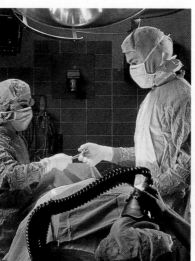

training, but rather a broad liberal education, an education that fosters "the critical qualities of mind and the durable qualities of character that will serve [people] in circumstances we cannot now even predict" (Gardner, 1984).

Does work, including a career, indeed contribute to personal fulfillment as Freud supposed? During the 1970s and 1980s, one approach to answering this question has compared self-reported happiness among the roughly equal numbers of North American women who have or have not been employed. Despite changing employment rates (see Figure 4–9) and shifts in social attitudes regarding women's roles, the happiness difference between the two groups—which slightly favors employed women—has always been far smaller than the person-to-person differences within each group (Adelmann, 1988; Campbell, 1981). Grace Baruch and Rosaline Barnett (1986) of the Wellesley College Center for Research on Women have found that what matters is not which role a woman occupies—as paid worker, wife, and/or mother—but the quality of her experience in that role. Happiness is having work that fits your interests and provides a sense of competence and accomplishment; having a partner who is a close, supportive companion and who sees you as special; having loving children whom you like and feel proud of.

Well-Being Across the Life Span Researchers have also compared the sense of well-being among young and old. Who do you suppose are the happiest? The carefree youth? The up-and-coming young adults? The successful and secure middle aged? Or those enjoying the leisurely retired life?

To live is to grow older, which means that all of us can look backward with satisfaction or sorrow and forward with hope or dread. Adolescents are buffeted by mood swings and insecurity, parental power and peer pressures, identity confusions and career worries. In later life, income shrinks, work has been taken away, the body deteriorates, recall fades, energy wanes, family members and friends die or move away, and the great enemy, death, looms ever closer. Small wonder that we presume the teen and over-65 years to be the worst of times (Freedman, 1978).

Surprisingly, they are not. When people of all ages describe *their own* feelings of happiness or sense of life satisfaction, there is no tendency for people of any particular age to report greater feelings of well-being. One statistical digest of results from 119 studies revealed that less than 1 percent of the person-to-person variation in well-being was attributable to age (Stock & others, 1983). Illustrative are the pooled data from 5 years of recent surveys in eight Western European countries. How many Europeans reported themselves "very happy"? By age group, 19 percent of the 15- to 24-year-olds, 17 percent of the 35- to 40-year-olds, and 19 percent of those 65 and older! And how many were "satisfied" or "very satisfied" with life as a whole? Equal proportions: 78 percent of the 15- to 24-year-olds, 78 percent of the 35- to 44-year-olds, and 78 percent of those over 65 (Ingelhart & Rabier, 1986).

Whatever the explanation—reduced stress, lowered aspirations, newfound sources of pleasure—the bottom line from hundreds of thousands of interviews with people of all ages in many countries is this: Older people report as much happiness and satisfaction with life as younger people do. Given that growing older is one sure consequence of living, an outcome that most of us prefer to its alternative, we can all take comfort in this.

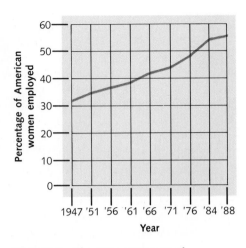

Figure 4–9 The rising percentage of employed American women as reported by the U.S. Bureau of Labor Statistics.

"One can live magnificently in this world if one knows how to work and how to love."
Leo Tolstoy, 1856

"How many of us older persons have really been . . . prepared for the second half of life, for old age, death and eternity?"
Carl Jung,
Modern Man in Search of a Soul, 1933

"*I used to be old, too, but it wasn't my cup of tea.*"

With the tasks of the earlier adult years behind them, many older adults have more time to enjoy pursuing their personal interests. No wonder their satisfaction with life is generally high, especially if they are healthy.

The astonishing stability of well-being across the life span obscures some interesting age-related emotional differences. As the years go by, feelings mellow (Costa & others, 1987; Diener & others, 1986). Highs become less high, lows less low. Thus while the *average* feeling level may remain stable, with age we find ourselves less often feeling excited, intensely proud, and on top of the world, but also less often depressed. Compliments provoke less elation and criticisms less despair as both become merely additional feedback atop a mountain of accumulated praise and blame. University of Chicago psychologists Mihalyi Csikszentmihalyi and Reed Larson (1984) mapped people's emotional terrain by periodically signaling them with electronic beepers to report their current activities and feelings. They found that teenagers typically come down from elation or up from gloom in less than an hour. Adult moods are less extreme but more enduring. Old age offers less intense joy but more feelings of contentment.

"Grow old along with me! The best is yet to be."
Robert Browning,
Rabbi Ben Ezra, 1864

Death and Dying   Most of us will suffer and cope with the deaths of relatives and friends. Usually, the most difficult separation is from one's spouse—a loss suffered by five times more women than men. Grief is especially severe when the death of a loved one comes before its expected time on the social clock. The accidental death of a child or the sudden illness that claims a 45-year-old spouse may trigger a year or more of mourning flooded with memories, eventually subsiding to a mild depression that sometimes continues for several additional years (Lehman & others, 1987). Contrary to popular myths, those who express the strongest grief immediately do not resolve their grief more quickly (Wortman & Silver, 1987).

The death of a child is one of the most traumatic events imaginable; especially if the child was healthy, the mother's anguish can be excruciating (Littlefield & Rushton, 1986). Although most parents emerge from the tragedy intact, for some the shadow of separation and loss endures; many become less materialistic and more religious (Knapp, 1987).

Those who suffer a terminal illness live with the realization of their impending death. In analyzing how people cope with the prospect of death, the stage theorists have once again arrived ahead of us. From

For survivors, such as this grieving widow on Memorial Day, death is the ultimate separation.

her interviews with dying patients, Elizabeth Kübler-Ross (1969) proposed that the terminally ill pass through a sequence of five stages: *denial* of the terminal condition, *anger* and resentment ("Why me?"), *bargaining* with God (or physicians) for more time, *depression* stemming from the impending loss of everything and everyone, and, finally, peaceful *acceptance* of one's fate.

The critics of Kübler-Ross's proposal first question the generality of the stages, stressing that each dying person's experience is unique. Moreover, they argue, the simplified stages ignore many important factors; for example, that people who are old usually view death with less expressed fear and resentment (Wass & others, 1978–1979). Critics also express concern about the eagerness with which the death-and-dying formula has been popularized in courses and books. The danger, they fear, is that rather than having their feelings respected, dying people may be analyzed or manipulated in terms of the stereotyped stages: "She's just going through the anger stage."

Nevertheless, the death-education movement has enabled us to deal more openly and humanely with death and grief. A growing number of individuals are aided by *hospice* organizations, whose staff and volunteers work in special facilities and in people's homes to support the terminally ill and their families. We can be grateful that death-denying attitudes are being dislodged. Facing death with dignity and openness helps a person to complete the life cycle with a sense of the meaningfulness and unity of life—the sense that their existence has been good and that life and death have their places in an ongoing cycle. Although death may be unwelcome, life itself can be affirmed even at death.

"Do not go gentle into that good night,
Old age should burn and rave at close of day;
Rage, rage against the dying of the light."

Dylan Thomas,
Do Not Go Gentle into That Good Night, 1952, a poem written to his father as he lay dying peacefully

Hospice workers seek to enable those who are dying to live and die with dignity and to aid their families in dealing with the impending loss. The hospice movement is but one sign of the more open and understanding attitudes toward death and grief in North America today.

REFLECTIONS ON DEVELOPMENTAL ISSUES

Our survey of developmental psychology began in Chapter 3 by identifying three pervasive issues: (1) whether development is steered more by genes or experience, (2) whether development is a gradual, continuous process or a discrete series of stages, and (3) whether development is characterized more by stability over time or by change. We concluded there that heredity and environment jointly affect human development. Let's now take stock of current thinking on the latter two issues.

CONTINUITY AND STAGES

Chapters 3 and 4 have described three major stage theories: Jean Piaget's theory of cognitive development, Lawrence Kohlberg's theory of moral development, and Erik Erikson's theory of psychosocial development. As we have seen, these stage theories have been vigorously criticized as failing to recognize the early rudiments of later abilities (Piaget), as biased by a worldview characteristic of educated people in individualistic cultures (Kohlberg), or as contradicted by research demonstrating that adult life does not progress up a fixed series of steps (Erikson and Levinson). Nevertheless, there do seem to be some spurts of brain growth during childhood and puberty, corresponding roughly to Piaget's stages (Thatcher & others, 1987). Moreover, stage theories have served to encourage a developmental perspective on the whole life span by suggesting how people of one age think and act differently when they arrive at a later age.

STABILITY AND CHANGE

This leads us to the final question: Over time, are people's personalities consistent, or do they change? If reunited with a long-lost grade school friend, would you instantly recognize that "it's the same old Andy"? Or is a person during one period of life likely to be quite different at a later period? Obviously, either extreme is false: If there were no stability, we could not hope that the person we marry today would be the same person a decade later, or that the promising management trainee would in the future remain suited for management. If there were no change possible, all juvenile delinquents would become career criminals; all alcoholics would drink themselves into the grave; and life would be one long rut, without growth or the possibility of betterment.

Still the issue is real: How well do infants' traits predict their childhood characteristics? Is the troubled adolescent likely to have a rocky adulthood? Will the assertive young woman still be noticeably assertive at age 60? Researchers who have followed lives through time are debating the extent to which our past reaches into our future.

For most of this century it was assumed that once personality is formed by life's early experiences, it remains set for life. Then, during the late 1960s and 1970s, new findings suggested that throughout much of life one's personality can still be shaped. Let us allow some of the researchers to speak for themselves.

Jerome Kagan and Howard Moss related observations made of several dozen Ohio children during their first 14 years of life to their adult traits. Kagan (1978) found "little relation between psychological qualities during the first 3 years of life—fearfulness, irritability, or activity—and any aspect of behavior in adulthood." Not until 6 to 10 years of age did the child's behavior begin to predict the kind of adult the child would become. Kagan (1982, 1988) sums up: "The first two or three years of life generally represent a poor basis from which to predict anything important about adulthood. . . . The capacity for change in an ordinary child is enormous."

Jean Macfarlane (1964) followed 166 lives from babyhood to age 30 and discovered that "many of our most mature and competent adults had severely troubled and confusing childhoods and adolescences." Often, the unhappy, rebellious adolescent became a stable, successful, and happy adult. Alexander Thomas and Stella Chess (1986) similarly followed 133 people from infancy to early adulthood and found that the troubled children among them usually became stable adults.

In addition, some researchers have found that even adults may undergo surprising and unpredictable changes. Reflecting on her studies of such changes during the life cycle, for example, Bernice Neugarten (1980) reported that "the primary consistency we have found is a lack of consistency."

So, shall we conclude that later experience records over early experience, erasing the voices of the past? If so, we can counsel parents of difficult babies and teenagers to be patient and hopeful. The depressed, lonely young adult can be reassured that development never ends: The struggles of the present may lay the foundation for a happier future than now seems possible.

On the other hand, a considerable body of recent research has found that there is also consistency to personality. After painstakingly comparing people in their forties with ratings of the same people as junior high students, Jack Block (1981) concluded that there is an underlying stability to our *basic social and emotional style*. The troubled adolescent sometimes turned out better than we would have guessed, but on the whole, it was the cheerful teenager who tended to become the most cheerful 40-year-old.

"Mr. Coughlin over there was the founder of one of the first motorcycle gangs."

"Whether one is an extreme hereditarian, an environmentalist, a constitutionalist, or an orthodox psychoanalyst, he is not likely to anticipate major changes in personality after the first few years of life."
E. Lowell Kelly (1955)

"I've thoroughly enjoyed my life, except when I was thirty-one and fifty-eight."

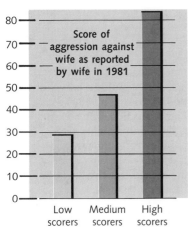
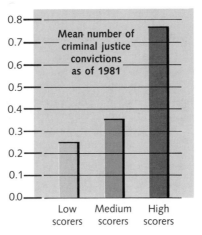

Boys' 1960 aggression score

Figure 4–10 The stability of aggressiveness. Leonard Eron and Rowell Huesmann (1984) found that the degree of aggressiveness displayed by 8-year-old boys (low, medium, or high—as shown by the colored bars) helped predict their aggressiveness two decades later, as testified to both by their wives' reports and by the number of their criminal convictions.

Similarly, Avshalom Caspi and his colleagues (1987) found that 9-year-olds with explosive temper tantrums were more likely than others to have trouble keeping good jobs during adulthood. Compared to children who did not have tantrums, they were also more than twice as likely to have divorced by age 40. And Leonard Eron (1987) and others found that the most physically aggressive 8-year-olds often became the most aggressive (and potentially violent) 30-year-olds (Figure 4–10).

Once people reach adulthood, their dispositions become more stable. From their periodic retesting of Boston and Baltimore area adults, Robert McCrae and Paul Costa (1982) concluded: "For the great majority of people, the self-concept at age 30 is a good guide to personality at age 80." During the adult years, people's outgoingness and emotional instability are equally persistent (Conley, 1985; Finn, 1986).

So, what should we conclude from these somewhat conflicting findings—that we retain throughout the life span a considerable capacity for change but that our basic social and emotional style becomes more ingrained as we grow older? Whatever their disagreements, researchers agree that:

1. The first 2 years of life provide a poor basis for predicting a person's eventual traits. As people grow older, predictability increases. For example, there is less stability from age 14 to 18 than from 18 to 22 (Stein & others, 1986).

2. The greater the span of years between assessments, the greater the likelihood that personality will have changed. From assessments of the traits of 25-year-olds, psychologists can better predict their personalities as 35-year-olds than as 55-year-olds (Conley, 1984).

3. Some characteristics, such as temperament, are more stable than others, such as social attitudes (Moss & Susman, 1980).

4. In some ways, we all change with age. Most shy, fearful toddlers begin opening up by age 4, and during adulthood most of us mellow. Such changes can occur without modifying a person's position *relative* to others of the same age. The hard-driving young adult may have mellowed by later life but may still be recognized as a relatively hard-driving senior citizen.

Finally, it is important to remember that life contains *both* stability and change. The fact of stability enables us to depend on others and motivates our concern for the healthy development of children. The fact of change motivates our concerns about present influences and sustains our hope for a brighter future.

"At 70, I would say the advantage is that you take life more calmly. You know that 'this, too, shall pass!'"
Eleanor Roosevelt, 1954

SUMMING UP

The overriding assumption of modern developmental psychology is that development is lifelong. We grow and change and adapt during infancy and childhood, *and* during adolescence and adulthood.

ADOLESCENCE

Physical Development   Adolescence typically begins at puberty with the onset of rapid growth and developing sexual maturity. Depending on how other people react, early or late maturation can influence adjustment; this illustrates how genes and environment interact in shaping our development.

Cognitive Development   Piaget theorized that adolescents develop the capacity for formal operations, which enables them to reason abstractly. However, some developmentalists believe that the development of formal logic depends on schooling as well, and that the rudiments of logic appear earlier than Piaget believed.

Following Piaget, Lawrence Kohlberg contended that moral thinking likewise proceeds through a sequence of stages, from a preconventional morality of self-interest, to a conventional morality concerned with gaining others' approval or doing one's duty, to (in some people) a post-conventional morality of agreed-upon rights or universal ethical principles. Other theorists respond that morality also lies in one's actions, which are influenced by one's social situation and inner attitudes as well as by one's moral reasoning. Moreover, say Kohlberg's critics, the postconventional stages represent morality from the perspective of individualistic, liberal-minded males.

Social Development   Erik Erikson theorized that a chief task of adolescence is to form one's sense of self—one's identity. For many people the struggle for identity continues in the adult years as new relationships emerge and new roles are assumed. While adolescence has traditionally been viewed as a time of storm and stress, researchers have found that most teenagers relate to their parents reasonably well and generally affirm their parents' beliefs and attitudes.

ADULTHOOD AND AGING

During early life, we sail a narrow channel, constrained by maturation. As the years pass, the channel widens, allowing us to diverge more and more. By adulthood, age no longer neatly predicts a person's experiences and traits. Yet in some ways our bodies, minds, and relationships still undergo predictable changes. As long as we live, we develop.

Physical Development   The barely perceptible physical declines of early adulthood begin to accelerate during middle adulthood. For women, a significant physical change of adult life is menopause, which generally seems to be a smooth rather than rough transition. After 65, declining perceptual acuity, strength, and stamina are evident, but short-term ailments are fewer. Although neural processes slow, the brain nevertheless remains healthy, except for those who suffer brain disease, such as the progressive deterioration of Alzheimer's disease.

Cognitive Development   As the years pass, recognition memory remains strong, although recall memory begins to decline, especially for novel types of information.

Research on how intelligence changes with age has progressed through several phases: cross-sectional studies suggesting a steady intellectual decline after early adulthood; longitudinal studies suggesting intellectual stability until very late in life; and an alternative view that, while fluid intelligence declines in later life, crystallized intelligence does not.

Social Development   Several theorists maintain that adults progress through an orderly sequence of stages. Erikson proposes that after the formation of an identity, the young adult must deal with intimacy. The developmental tasks that follow involve generativity in middle adulthood, and in later adulthood a sense of integrity. Daniel Levinson contends that moving from one stage to the next entails recurring times of crisis, such as the early-forties time of transition to midlife. Critics contend that people are not so predictable; life events involving love and work, and even chance events and encounters, influence adult life in unanticipated ways.

Although few grow old gratefully, most do so gracefully, retaining a sense of well-being throughout the life span. Those who live to old age must, however, cope with the deaths of friends and family members and with the prospect of their own deaths.

REFLECTIONS ON THE DEVELOPMENTAL ISSUES

Chapters 3 and 4 (and Chapter 5, Gender, which follows) touch three pervasive issues in developmental psychology: nature versus nurture, continuity versus discrete stages, and stability versus change in personality. Although the stage theories of Piaget, Kohlberg, and Erikson have been modified in light of later research, the theories usefully alert us to differences among people of different ages. The discovery that people's traits continue to change in later life has helped create the new emphasis that development is lifelong. Nevertheless, research demonstrates that there is also an underlying consistency to most people's temperaments and personality traits, especially after infancy and early childhood.

TERMS AND CONCEPTS TO REMEMBER

adolescence   The period from puberty to independent adulthood; in industrialized nations, roughly the teen years.

Alzheimer's disease   A progressive and irreversible brain disorder characterized by gradual deterioration of memory, reasoning, language, and finally, of physical function.

cross-sectional study   A study in which people of different ages are tested or observed at a given time.

crystallized intelligence   One's accumulated information and verbal skills; tends to increase with age.

fluid intelligence   One's ability to reason abstractly; tends to decrease during later adulthood.

formal operational stage   In Piaget's theory, the stage of cognitive development (normally beginning about age 12) during which people learn to think logically about abstract concepts.

generativity   In Erikson's theory, the impulse to be productive, such as by raising children and doing creative work; a major focus during middle adulthood.

hospice   Organizations whose largely volunteer staff members provide support for dying people and their families either in special facilities or in people's own homes.

identity   One's sense of self. According to Erikson, the adolescent's task is to form a sense of self by integrating various roles.

integrity   In Erikson's theory, the positive outcome of later life: a nondespairing sense that one's life has been meaningful and worthwhile.

intimacy   In Erikson's theory, the ability to form close, loving relationships; the primary developmental task of early adulthood.

longitudinal study   Research in which the same people are restudied over a long period of time.

menarche [meh-NAR-key]   The first menstrual period.

menopause   The cessation of menstruation. Also used loosely to refer to the biological and psychological changes during the several years of declining ability to reproduce.

primary sex characteristics   The body structures (ovaries and gonads) that make sexual reproduction possible.

puberty   The early adolescent period of rapid growth and sexual maturation.

secondary sex characteristics   Nonreproductive sexual characteristics such as female breasts and hips, male voice quality, and body hair.

social clock   The culturally preferred timing of social events such as marriage, childbearing, and retirement.

FOR FURTHER READING

Berger, K. (1988). *The developing person through the life span* (2nd ed.). New York: Worth.

A comprehensive, current, and readable textbook summary of what we know about infancy, childhood, adolescence, and adulthood.

Butler, R. N. (1975). *Why survive? Being old in America.* New York: Harper & Row.

A Pulitzer prize-winning book that portrays the experience of older people in the United States.

Damon, W. (1988). *The moral child: Nurturing children's natural moral growth.* New York: Free Press.

Drawing on recent research, a developmental psychologist charts the course of moral development, stressing the value of authoritative rather than authoritarian parenting.

Henig, R. M. (1981). *The myth of senility.* New York: Anchor Press/Doubleday.

Discusses memory and intelligence changes with age and describes the causes of "senility," including Alzheimer's disease.

Silverstone B., & Hyman, H. K. (1981). *You and your aging parent: The modern family's guide to emotional, physical, and financial problems* (2nd ed.). New York: Pantheon.

A useful book that provides information and practical advice on how, without feeling trapped, to care responsibly for one's aging parents.

CHAPTER 5

Gender

Of all the aspects of our development, none is more central to our identity, or to how others regard and treat us, than our sex. When you were born, the first thing most people asked about you was, "Boy or girl?" Children's biological sex dictates their *gender,* their social category of male or female. By age 3, you had acquired a strong *gender identity*—a sense of being male or female—and your play reflected this. From preschool at least through junior high school, most of your playmates were probably children of your sex. As you played with friends and interacted with family, you learned a *gender role,* a set of expectations that prescribed how you, as a female or a male, should act. Today, the first thing a stranger notices about you is whether you are female or male.

Psychologists study gender development because our maleness or femaleness is indeed so fundamental to our personal identity and social relations. It is a curious fact of life that whether you were born a girl or a boy helps to predict your future social power and how you will ultimately spend much of your time. In the United States today, women devote more than twice as many hours to housework than do men, more than three times as many hours to child care (Fuchs, 1986). But for an hour's employment they earn only 68 cents for every $1 earned by the average man (Bureau of the Census, 1987). When surveyed, 82 percent of married women report doing most or all of the housework (and nearly all their husbands concur) (*Public Opinion,* 1986b). Women constitute 51 percent of the population, but only 1.7 percent of the officers of major corporations (Von Glinow, 1986) and 2 percent of the 1988 U.S. Senate. Except in prisons, men are seldom victimized by rape, nor are they the ones injured by domestic violence, incest, or sexual harassment.

Such disregard for women is not true only in the United States. Although female infants are no longer left out on a hillside to die of exposure, as was the practice in ancient Greece, even today we find evidence from around the world that male offspring are held in higher regard than their sisters. For example, during the 1976–1977 famine in Bangladesh, preschool-age girls were more malnourished than boys, and in many developing countries death rates are higher for girls than for boys (Bairagi, 1987).

Can you anticipate, then, the replies of 2000 Colorado schoolchildren when asked how their lives would be different if they woke up tomorrow and discovered they were the other sex? Virtually no boys envied girls (Tavris & Baumgartner, 1983). "If I woke up and I was a girl, I would hope it was a bad dream and go back to sleep," said one boy. Girls were more likely to think the switch a good deal: "If I were a boy, my whole life would be easier." There was no doubt in these children's minds that it is "better" to be a boy than a girl. Why? What is

"As the man beholds the woman,
As the woman sees the man,
Curiously they note each other,
As each other only can."
  Bryan Waller Procter, 1787–1874
  The Sexes

On some occasions, your identity is your gender.

society telling them about gender differences? What kinds of gender differences are there? Are our gender-related behavioral differences ordained by biology? By culture? By an intricate interplay between biology and culture?

BIOLOGICAL INFLUENCES ON GENDER: IS BIOLOGY DESTINY?

Obviously, men and women differ physically. In the United States, the average man is 40 percent muscle, 15 percent fat, and 5 feet 9 inches tall; the average woman is 23 percent muscle, 25 percent fat, and 5 feet 4 inches tall. Do men and women vary in physical ways that also influence their gender identities and roles? The "biosocial" view of gender says yes—perhaps indirectly, through the social consequences of physical differences, but yes.

HORMONES

Males and females are variations on a single form. Eight weeks after conception, they are anatomically indistinguishable. (Thus both sexes have nipples, although only females will ever develop a use for them.) Then, our genes activate our biological sex: *XY* sex chromosomes direct development of a male; in the absence of a *Y* chromosome, a female develops. After a male embryo's testes form internally they begin to secrete **testosterone,** the principal male sex hormone. Testosterone triggers the development of external male sex organs; lacking testosterone, the embryo continues its course toward the development of female sex organs.

Note to computer geeks: The sex variable has a default value of female.

What, then, do you suppose happens when, due to a glandular malfunction or injections received by the mother, a female embryo is exposed to excess testosterone? Genetically female infants are born with masculine-appearing genitals, which can be corrected surgically. Until puberty, such females typically act in more aggressive "tomboyish" ways than most girls, and dress and play in ways more typical of boys than girls (Ehrhardt, 1987; Money, 1987).

Is their behavior due to the prenatal hormones? Perhaps. (Experiments with many species, from rats to monkeys, confirm that female embryos given male hormones later exhibit more masculine appearance and behavior [Hines, 1982].) But the girls frequently look masculine and are known to be "different," so perhaps people also treat them more like boys. Genes and hormones can affect gender identity indirectly, by predisposing the expectations and life experiences that shape us. Biological appearances have social consequences.

SOCIOBIOLOGY: DOING WHAT COMES NATURALLY?

A century ago, the English novelist Samuel Butler remarked that "A hen is only an egg's way of making another egg." In the same vein, the relatively new and controversial field of *sociobiology*—the study of the evolution of social behavior—views organisms as but their genes' way of making more genes. We are elaborate survival machines for our immortal genes: When we die, our genes live on in our biological relatives.

Sociobiologists study how evolution may predispose the behavior of social animals, whether ants, dogs, or humans. The underlying rationale is simple: If a behavior tendency is genetically influenced and if it helps an organism to survive and reproduce, then the relevant genes will be favored in the competition for gene survival. Through *natural selection*—the process by which evolution favors organisms best equipped to survive and reproduce—such genes become more common.

As an example of a sociobiological explanation, consider: Why are men quicker than women to perceive sexual intent in friendly behavior (Abbey, 1987; Shotland & Craig, 1988)? And why do males of most mammalian species, including our own, tend to initiate sexual relations more frequently and with more partners than do females (Hinde, 1984; Kenrick & Trost, 1987)? To maximize the survival and spread of their genes, each male and female must maximize the number of their offspring that survive to reproduce. Because of their limited number of eggs and the reproductive time it takes to carry and nurse their young, female mammals have far fewer potential offspring than do males. Sociobiologists suggest that to ensure survival of the maximum number, females tend to be cautiously selective in their choice of a mate. They look for evidence of health and vitality and, in some species, for a commitment in time and resources to help in raising their young.

On the other hand, sperm are abundant, giving males a much larger number of potential offspring. (If you are male, you will have produced about 2000 new sperm during the time it takes to read this sentence.) Because their success at reproducing depends partly on the number of females they fertilize, males that most successfully seek out and compete for females should leave more offspring. And if, as sociobiologists suppose, social behaviors in humans are genetically predisposed, then the continued reproductive success of these individuals should, over time, favor the increase of sexually assertive males.

What is controversial here? Not the idea that inherited behaviors which help organisms survive are selected for over the generations. Most scientists agree with that. But many object when this idea is applied to complex social behaviors, such as marital fidelity. Critics contend that two problems exist with sociobiological explanations.

First, they question whether genetic evolution really explains very much of human social behavior. Thanks to our common biology, we do share some universal behaviors: A smiling face can be read across cul-

Note: Sociobiology is not just the biology of social behavior, but the *evolutionary* biology of social behavior.

Sociobiologists attempt to explain the evolutionary development of social behaviors, such as grooming. Among primates such as baboons, grooming is the most time-consuming mode of social interaction. It averts aggression, reveals social dominance, and indicates sexual partnership. The development of grooming behaviors to replace fighting benefits both the individual and the group.

Secretariat's reward for being the greatest racehorse of modern times was the opportunity to sire more than 400 foals.

A universal behavior. You know the meaning of these facial expressions, and each of these people would understand the same expression on your face.

tures. But there is also great diversity in such behaviors as fathers' involvement in infant care. Marriage patterns vary, too—from monogamy (one spouse) to serial monogamy (a succession of spouses) to polygamy (multiple wives) to polyandry (multiple husbands) to spouse-swapping. Our shared biological heritage does not predict such diversity, nor does it explain rapid cultural changes in behavior.

Second, after-the-fact explanations may sound convincing, but as we saw in Chapter 1, you can hardly lose at this game. Given a sexual double standard, we can, in hindsight, imagine how natural selection might explain it. Now let's explain the opposite—men who mate with but one woman. Could we not just as easily claim that natural selection favors the genes of males who are loyal to their mates? Of course— such behavior helps to protect and support the young, thereby perpetuating the parents' genes. (Indeed, sociobiologists support this view, saying it helps explain why humans tend to pair off.) So we are left with two plausible explanations of men's sexual behavior: that men are genetically programmed to be promiscuous, and that men are genetically programmed to be faithful. The moral? Unless a theory makes *testable* predictions, such after-the-fact explanations should be viewed with a healthy skepticism.

There is yet a third objection to the application of sociobiology to humans. Some critics fear that if we explain human behavior in terms of our genes, some people may assume, wrongly, that certain gender roles, sexual tendencies, or racial hostilities are natural—adaptive, genetic, inevitable, and unchangeable. For example, someone may excuse a sexual double standard that tolerates male promiscuity with "Men will be men—it's in their genes!"

No one disputes that men and women are the products of our mammalian, primate, and human history. But neither does anyone dispute that nature has endowed us with an enormous capacity to learn and to adapt.

"My own guess is that the genetic bias is intense enough to create a substantial division of labor even in the most free and most egalitarian of future societies. . . . Even with identical education and equal access to all professions, men are likely to continue to play a disproportionate role in political life, business and science."
Sociobiologist E. O. Wilson (1975)

THE SOCIAL CONSTRUCTION OF GENDER

What biology initiates, culture accentuates. Social expectations mold our experiences as males or females. And when social expectations vary, so do gender role behaviors. In earlier decades, when ambiguous genitals made an infant's genetic sex uncertain, the physician and parents had to choose the baby's gender. (Note that even when one's biological sex is ambiguous, human beings cannot tolerate ambiguity about gender—one must be considered either female or male.) What do you suppose the child's gender identity usually became—would the child's self-image as boy or girl agree with the socially assigned gender, even if tests later revealed it to be wrong? Or would the child be more likely to have a confused gender identity?

Most of these children comfortably accepted whatever gender they were assigned, whether genetically correct or not (Ehrhardt & Money, 1967; Money & others, 1957). Like other children, by age 3 they knew themselves as boys or girls, and this identity was thereafter difficult to reverse. Our gender identity, it seems, is socially constructed.

THEORIES OF GENDER-TYPING

During childhood we gain not only our gender identity but also many masculine and feminine behaviors and attitudes. Although nearly everyone has the gender identity associated with their sex, some children become more strongly **gender-typed** than others. That is, some boys exhibit more traditionally masculine traits and interests than other boys, and some girls become more distinctly feminine than other girls. By what process do girls become feminine and boys masculine? Four theories of gender-typing attempt to explain how gender is socially constructed from the biological base of sex. (Table 5–1 on page 123 summarizes these explanations.)

Identification Theory   The best known theory is also the oldest: Sigmund Freud's (1933) theory of **identification.** Freud proposed that 3- to 5-year-olds develop a sexual attraction to the parent of the other sex. By age 5 or 6, he said, such feelings make them anxious. So they renounce the feelings by identifying with the same-sex parent, unconsciously adopting his or her characteristics.

Although historically influential and still well known outside psychology, Freud's theory is now disputed by most researchers and many clinical psychologists. Children become gender-typed well before age 5 or 6 and may become strongly feminine or masculine even in the absence of a same-sex parent (Frieze & others, 1978). Moreover, children tend to imitate familiar people who are powerful yet warm, which generally includes both parents (Jackson & others, 1986).

Social Learning Theory   In contrast to Freud's assumption that gender-typing comes from within the child as the child identifies with the same-sex parent, **social learning theory** assumes that children are molded (socialized) by their social environment. Children learn behaviors deemed appropriate for their sex by observation and imitation, and by being rewarded and punished. Parents use rewards and punishments to teach their daughters to be feminine ("Susie, you're such a good mommy to your dolls") and their sons to be masculine ("Big boys don't cry, Dick"). Children are rewarded for imitating people of their

Gender   The social definition of male and female.

Gender identity   One's sense of being male or female.

Gender-typing   The acquisition of a masculine or feminine gender identity and role.

Gender roles   Expected behaviors for males and females.

For more information on Freud's theory of personality, see Chapter 15.

Is this child identifying with the same-sex parent? Is he being socialized into traditional gender-typed behaviors?

own sex. When Dick dresses up in Daddy's clothes, his parents are more amused than when he dons Mommy's dress and shoes. Moreover, by observing others in the home, the neighborhood, and on television, children learn the consequences of various behaviors without having to experience them.

Children learn gender-typed behaviors by observing and imitating, and being rewarded or punished.

Critics complain that children are not so passive as social learning theory assumes. Whether their social worlds encourage or discourage traditional gender-typing, children inevitably seem to know that "boys are boys and girls are girls." They organize their worlds accordingly and create and enforce their own somewhat rigid rules for socially acceptable behavior.

Cognitive Developmental Theory   To account for the child's active participation in the gender-typing process, Lawrence Kohlberg (1966) proposed a theory of gender-typing that applied Piaget's principles of cognitive development. As children struggle to comprehend themselves and their worlds, one of the first concepts, or schemas, they form is that of their own gender. Having identified themselves as male or female, they soon begin to organize their worlds on the basis of gender. As their cognitive machinery matures, so does their understanding of what defines the genders—their schema accommodates to the more sophisticated understanding. To a preschool girl, short hair may define a man and long hair a woman, in which case the girl may insist on having long hair. By the concrete operational stage, when a child knows that the amount of milk remains constant after being poured from a tall, narrow glass into a short, wide glass, the child also understands gender constancy—that a woman remains a woman whether she wears her hair long or short (Tavris & Wade, 1984). Once children's gender is firmly established, they then use members of their own sex as models for their behavior.

Recall from Chapter 3 that a schema is a concept or framework that organizes and interprets information.

Critics of this *cognitive developmental theory* generally agree that what children think *is* important. But why among all the possible ways of categorizing people do children so consistently do so in terms of gender? Why not eye color? Or religion? Or, in another culture, caste? Is it, as Kohlberg believed, because biological sex differences such as size and strength are obvious? Then, asks Sandra Bem (1987), why even in multiracial societies are children more conscious of gender than they are of race?

Gender Schema Theory To answer these questions, Bem proposed *gender schema theory*, which combines aspects of the cognitive developmental and social learning theories. In agreement with the cognitive developmental view, gender schema theory assumes that children's actions are influenced by their concepts—schemas—of gender, which serve as a lens through which they view themselves and the world. Many languages, including the European languages, use gender schemas to classify objects as either masculine (in French, "*le* train") or feminine ("*la* table"). In English, pronouns classify people by gender. To speak, even a 3-year-old must learn the difference between "she" and "he," "hers" and "his."

But why and how do we acquire these gender schemas? Here Bem agrees with social learning theory: Our conceptions of gender do not come from observing biological sex differences, which actually aren't apparent during the preschool years when children are becoming strongly gender-typed. We instead organize our worlds into female and male categories because of all the diverse and subtle ways in which our culture communicates that sex is a most important category of human life. Preschoolers are constantly being dressed as boys and girls, given boys' or girls' toys to play with, and taught songs in which, for example, the fingers are women (sung with a high pitch) and the thumbs are men (sung with low pitch). Several times a day the culture reminds the child of the distinction between male and female. Small wonder, then, that, given dolls varying in genitalia, physique, and hair length, 4- and 5-year-olds assign sex based on the culturally defined gender difference: hair length (Thompson & Bentler, 1971).

To summarize, gender schema theory suggests that gender-typing occurs as children learn from their culture what it means to be male or female: "I am male—thus masculine, strong, aggressive," or "I am female—therefore feminine, sweet, and helpful" (or whatever are the socially learned associations with one's sex). Comparing themselves to their gender schema, they adjust their behavior accordingly.

Table 5–1
FOUR THEORIES OF GENDER-TYPING

Freud's identification theory

  Sexual anxiety ⟶ Identifying with the same-sex parent ⟶ Gender-typed behavior similar to the parent's

Social learning theory

  Rewards and punishments + observation and imitation of models ⟶ Gender-typed behavior

Cognitive developmental theory

  Child's struggle to comprehend self and world ⟶ Concept of gender ⟶ Imitation of same-sex models ⟶ Gender-typed behavior

Gender schema theory

  Cultural emphasis on gender ⟶ Gender schema (looking at self and world through a gender "lens") ⟶ Gender-organized thinking + gender-typed behavior

GENDER ROLES

Most theories of gender-typing assume that we somehow learn to play the social role of female or male. Like a theatrical role, a social role is a set of prescriptions concerning how those who occupy the role should talk, dress, and act. Knowing someone's role—as professor, student, parent, or child—tells us, in general terms, how others believe that person should behave, which usually strongly influences how that person does behave. Gender roles similarly prescribe behavior, traditionally indicating, for example, that men were expected to initiate the date, drive the car, and pick up the check. Women were expected to cook the meals, buy the children's clothes, and do the laundry.

Such formulas serve to grease the social machinery. They free us from self-conscious preoccupation with awkward little decisions, such as who reaches for the check. When we already know how to act, our attention is freed for other matters.

But these benefits come at a price: Roles also constrain us. When we deviate from them—as when a woman repeatedly initiates formal dates with a man—we may feel anxious or be regarded as weird (Green & Sandos, 1983).

Several experiments show that contemporary men and women do adjust their behavior to fulfill others' gender-role expectations (Deaux & Major, 1987). In one, Mark Zanna and Susan Pack (1975) had college women answer a questionnaire in which they described themselves to a tall, unattached, male senior they expected to meet. Those led to believe that the man had traditional gender-role expectations described themselves as more traditionally feminine than did those who expected to meet a man who liked nontraditional women. Moreover, when given an aptitude test, those who expected to meet the traditional man solved, on average, 15 percent fewer problems. Their more modest performance illustrates how our gender-role expectations can be self-fulfilling. Expectations help create gender differences, especially when people present one self to their own sex and a different self to the other sex. For example, college women are more likely than college men to report having feigned intellectual inferiority on a date (Braito & others, 1981). A gender difference observed in research might therefore be due to men and women exhibiting the behavior they believe is desired of them.

Variations in Gender Roles   Gender roles vary across cultures and over time. Biological sex differences between males and females do not. Clearly, social rather than biological factors create such variations.

Across Cultures   In almost all primitive societies, men predominate in fighting wars and hunting large game, women in gathering food and caring for infants. Sociobiologists have argued that evolution has predisposed this age-old division of labor. In today's industrial societies, where men do not hunt and women do not gather, such gender distinctions may no longer be adaptive. Yet, say the sociobiologists, they persist as relics of our evolutionary past.

Sociobiologists notwithstanding, gender roles vary widely from society to society. In agricultural societies, women stay close to home, working in the fields and tending children, while men roam more freely; nomadic societies have less distinct gender roles (Van Leeuwen, 1978). Among industrialized societies, the roles assigned to men and women vary enormously from country to country. In North America, medicine and dentistry are predominantly male occupations; in Russia, most doctors are women, as are most dentists in Denmark.

"Civilization advances by extending the number of operations which we can perform without thinking about them."
Alfred North Whitehead, 1861–1947

"What happened to Sis? Best skater on the rink, and suddenly she forgot how!"

Over Time   Marcia Guttentag and Paul Secord (1983) analyzed societies from classical Athens to modern America and found that gender roles vary over time as well as across cultures. In times when marriageable women are in short supply, women are protected and marital fidelity is strong. When migration or war creates a relative excess of younger women, men become more sexually promiscuous and women become more self-reliant—more likely to work outside the home and to organize social movements to improve their status.

Consider the changing roles of North American women. Gender roles that may have been adaptive in past eras when women were pregnant or nursing for much of their adult lives may be less adaptive now that most women live longer, bear fewer children, and are employed outside the home.

In some ways, gender roles have changed little. In the 1980s women are still, as in earlier decades, expected to be warm, expressive, and nurturant, and men to be independent, self-reliant, and assertive. Occupationally, nurses, secretaries, and kindergarten teachers are still overwhelmingly women.

In other ways, gender role expectations have shifted dramatically over the past half century. The change is evident first in people's expressed attitudes (*Public Opinion*, 1978, 1980; Wilkins & Miller, 1985). In 1937, 1 in 3 Americans said they would be willing to vote for a qualified woman whom their party nominated for President; in 1984, 4 in 5 said they would. In 1938, only 1 in 5 approved "of a married woman earning money in business or industry if she has a husband capable of supporting her"; by 1978, 3 out of 4 approved. In 1970, Americans were evenly split in favoring or opposing "efforts to strengthen women's status." By 1985, such efforts were approved by a 4 to 1 margin.

The changing role of women is also evident in their changing behavior. Most obvious is the increase in the rate of women's employment (see Figure 4–9 on page 109): In 1960, a third of wives with children were employed; by the mid-1980s, over 50 percent of married women with preschoolers and 60 percent of those with school-aged children worked outside the home (Bianchi & Spain, 1986).

Women's occupations are also changing. When the class of 1989 began college in the fall of 1985, 4 in 10 women were intending to pursue careers in law, business, medicine, or engineering—double the percentage in 1970 (Astin & others, 1987). Since 1972, the percent of doctoral degrees received by American women has also doubled (Howard & others, 1986).

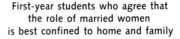

First-year students who agree that the role of married women is best confined to home and family

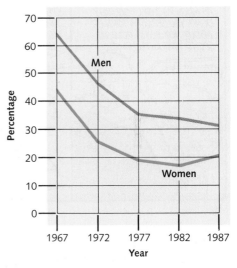

College student endorsement of the traditional view of women's role has declined dramatically. (From Astin & others, 1987.)

The flow of married women into the workforce means that more and more women, like this attorney, occupy multiple roles. A recent study (Cleminshaw, 1988) suggests that the more roles a woman plays, the more satisfied she is with her life.

Joseph Pleck (1987) reports that a slower, more "subtle revolution" has also been occurring in men's roles. Compared with the mid-1960s, men are now devoting more time to family work. Increasingly, men are found in front of the stove, behind the vacuum cleaner, and over the diaper changing table. Still, even in countries that have sought to equalize the roles of women and men, gender distinctions persist. Whether in Russia, China, or Sweden, answers to "Who works in the child care nurseries?," "Who cooks dinner?," and "Who runs the country?" remain nearly as predictable as in the United States and Canada.

Should There Be Gender Roles?   Social scientists' personal concerns motivate their interest in topics such as gender roles, and many share Sandra Bem's (1985) conviction that "human behaviors and personality attributes should no longer be linked with gender." Unlike some parents who are timid about "imposing" their values and beliefs on their children, Bem feels that parents who have deep social, political, or religious convictions should not be bashful about transmitting their convictions to their children. Children are certainly going to absorb an ideology from somewhere—from the culture if not from the home.

Bem suggests how those who share her values might raise children who are less gender-typed. At home, make gender irrelevant to who cooks and does dishes and to what toys are available; when children are young, censor gender-stereotyped books and television programs, and teach them that one's sex entails anatomical and reproductive traits and not much else. In order to help them process what their culture tries to tell them about gender, teach them how individuals differ, how gender roles vary, and how to detect sex discrimination. As they grow older, give boys and girls the same privileges and responsibilities.

Some psychologists doubt that gender roles will ever disappear. Douglas Kenrick (1987), for one, believes that try as we might to reconstruct our gender concepts, "we cannot change the evolutionary history of our species, and some of the differences between us are undoubtedly a function of that history." Bem (1987) agrees there may be "biologically based sex differences in behavior." But she believes that the social construction of gender greatly exaggerates any biological basis. Thus if under egalitarian social conditions, it turns out that more men than women become engineers or that more women than men decide to stay at home with their children, I'll live happily with those sex differences as well as with any others that emerge. But I am willing to bet that the sex differences that emerge under those conditions will not be nearly as large or as diverse as the ones that currently exist in our society.

Those who advocate raising their children without traditional gender schemas believe gender should be irrelevant to who plays with which toys and who does which household tasks.

Alternative Gender Roles   In Bem's ideal world, gender roles would greatly diminish. In the real world they persist. Is this a bad thing? Are people who are less gender-typed mentally healthier and happier? *Androgyny* is the possession of both masculine and feminine qualities. In research studies, androgynous people are those who describe themselves with both traditionally masculine adjectives (independent, assertive, competitive) *and* traditionally feminine adjectives (warm, tender, compassionate). Do such people in fact feel better about themselves than do strongly gender-typed ''masculine'' men and ''feminine'' women?

Initial reports suggested they do, but analyses of dozens of such studies by Marylee Taylor and Judith Hall (1982) and Bernard Whitley (1985) reveal that androgynous people do not consistently exhibit higher self-esteem or better adjustment. Rather, in both men and women, a positive self-concept is linked more strongly to traditional masculine traits. Describing oneself as independent, assertive, and self-confident contributes to high scores on both masculinity and self-esteem scales, and that hints at something deeper: Perhaps the entire culture measures individuals against a male yardstick, thereby valuing masculine traits over feminine traits.

When it comes to relationships, traditional feminine qualities may prove an asset (Kurdek & Schmitt, 1986; Orlofsky & O'Heron, 1987). In a study of 108 Australian married couples, John Antill (1983) found that when either the wife or husband possessed feminine traits such as gentleness, sensitivity, or warmth—or better yet, when *both* did— marital satisfaction was higher. Although traditional masculine traits may boost self-esteem, says Antill, ''they are apparently not the qualities that hold the key to a happy, long-term relationship.''

Should gender roles be preserved? Some say that men's and women's biological differences make their social differences—to some extent at least—not only inevitable but desirable. Yes, they say, the sexes share traits and abilities in common, but each sex also bears special gifts. To distinguish between two wines, composers, or sexes is to appreciate each equally, by discerning their separate virtues. Equality and freedom of individual choice, yes; sameness, no.

Others say that biological differences are socially trivial. Human beings—both women *and* men—should be unshackled from all that constrains their being fully human: assertive and nurturant, self-confident and tender, independent and compassionate. Should gender roles be preserved? Science informs the debate, but personal convictions decide it.

NATURE-NURTURE INTERACTION

Our discussion has proceeded as if the biological and social influences on gender were two opponents in a fencing match. Biology scores points for observed genetic and hormonal sex differences; social influence responds with points scored for the creation of gender and all its cultural variations.

But surely we create a false dichotomy by trying to partition aspects of gender neatly into nature and nurture, for biological and social factors interact. Biological factors that create male and female physical characteristics may predispose different cultural influences on males and females (Harris, 1978). If hormones predispose males to be slightly more aggressive, society may then amplify this difference by encouraging males to be tough and females to be gentle. Such a gender effect would be both a biological and a social effect—culture developing what biology has initiated.

We can conclude by restating the principle in general terms: Biological factors always operate within a social context, and social effects operate on what is biologically given. In the weaving of the human fabric, the biological and social threads act as warp and woof.

"I was a better man as a woman with a woman than I've ever been as a man with a woman." An out-of-work actor (Dustin Hoffman), who masquerades as a woman to land a job, finds his transformation has some surprising consequences for his relationship with a real woman (Jessica Lange) in the movie *Tootsie.*

GENDER DIFFERENCES

Psychology studies many topics that are central to our lives as women and men. The most extensively researched and debated topic of all is how boys and girls, men and women, differ (Walsh, 1987). One book on gender differences synthesized more than a thousand research studies involving a half million participants (Hyde & Linn, 1986). Since 1968, *Psychological Abstracts,* the "reader's guide" to psychological research, has indexed more than 20,000 articles on "human sex differences."

So, how different *are* boys from girls? Young men from young women? Older men from older women? The phrasing of these questions draws our attention to the ways in which the sexes differ, not to their similarities. In many ways—the age of first sitting up, teething, walking, and in generosity, helpfulness, and overall intelligence, to name a few—males and females are not noticeably different (Maccoby, 1980). But because our attention is invariably drawn to how we *differ* from others, such similarities are seldom mentioned. Similarities tend not to require explanation; differences do. In science, as in everyday life, differences excite our interest.

THE POLITICS OF STUDYING GENDER DIFFERENCES

Some critics of psychology are concerned about the study of gender differences. Might the reporting of such studies exaggerate people's perceptions of the differences between women and men? Oblivious to the social construction of gender, might such perceptions in turn lead people to suppose that gender differences are genuine biological sex differences—innate, immutable, and even desirable? Believing the answers to be yes, sociologist Jessie Bernard (1976, p. 13) argued that scientific demonstrations of gender differences therefore serve as "battle weapons against women."

Historically, however, research on gender differences has undermined popular myths about women's inferiority—myths that had the political consequences of limiting women's social power by excluding them from educational and employment opportunities. By reducing overblown gender stereotypes, contends researcher Alice Eagly (1986), recent "gender-difference research has probably furthered the cause of gender equality."

The concern nevertheless remains, because when one group has more status and power than another, differences between them are usually viewed as the less powerful group's deficiencies. Recall from Chapter 4 the caution that women's moral differences are not moral deficits. Similarly, Jacquelynne Eccles (1987a) notes that women's differing educational and vocational choices reflect different but equally important goals and values. Women who choose to become low-paid preschool teachers rather than high-paid business managers surely do reflect our society's definition of gender-appropriate behavior; but they may also reflect women's ethic of care. The differing pay levels for traditionally male and female occupations says more about the values of those who assign wages to work than about the inherent value of women's and men's choices.

> "There should be no qualms about the forthright study of racial and gender differences; science is in desperate need of good studies that . . . inform us of what we need to do to help underrepresented people to succeed in this society. Unlike the ostrich, we cannot afford to hide our heads for fear of socially uncomfortable discoveries."
>
> Developmental psychologist Sandra Scarr (1988)

HOW *DO* MALES AND FEMALES DIFFER?

Just knowing that you are male or female triggers certain perceptions of you in people's minds. Perceived gender differences exceed actual gender differences. This is most obvious in infancy, when boy-girl differences in appearance and behavior are negligible. Without the obvious clues of pink or blue, people will struggle over whether to call the new baby a "he" or a "she." Nevertheless, fathers have been found to rate their day-old daughters as softer, smaller, and more beautiful, and their sons as firmer, stronger, and better coordinated (Rubin & others, 1974). And when John and Sandra Condry (1976) showed people a videotape of a 9-month-old infant reacting strongly to a jack-in-the-box, those told the child was "David" perceived "his" emotion as mostly anger; those told the child was "Dana" perceived "her" identical reaction as mostly fear. Some "gender differences" exist merely in the eyes of their beholders.

Among the gender differences that seem actually to exist between males and females are those involving physical aggression, social dominance, empathy, and spatial ability. Here, as elsewhere in this book, we do well to remember that average differences between groups, such as between males and females, may tell us little about individuals. For the psychological characteristics we are about to consider, the variations among women and among men far exceed those between the average woman and the average man. And that is why judgments about the suitability of people for particular tasks are best made on an

Is this 7-month-old a boy or a girl? (See page 133.) During infancy, boy-girl differences are minimal, but once we know the child's sex we interpret and guide behavior accordingly.

individual basis, without prejudgments based on sex. Could you become a competent engineer? Or child care worker? Knowing that you are a man or a woman tells us little; knowing you as an individual tells us much more.

Aggression By *aggression*, psychologists refer not to assertive, ambitious behavior ("Claire is an aggressive saleswoman") but rather to physical or verbal behavior that is intended to hurt someone. In surveys, men admit to considerably more hostility and aggression than do women. To some extent, such admissions may simply reflect people's acceptance of the common perception that males are more aggressive. But in laboratory experiments that assess *physical* aggression, men indeed behave more aggressively, for example by administering what they think are higher levels of hurtful electric shock (Eagly, 1987; Hyde, 1986a). In everyday American life, men are arrested for violent crimes eight times more often than women (Federal Bureau of Investigation, 1987). Indeed, in every society that has kept crime records, males have committed more physical violence (Kenrick, 1987). Throughout the world, hunting, fighting, and warring are primarily men's activities.

The male sex hormone testosterone seems partly responsible. In various animal species, one can increase aggressiveness by administering testosterone. In humans, violent male criminals average higher than normal testosterone levels (Rubin & others, 1980). Moreover, the aggression difference appears early in life and across many species of mammals. In humans, this may be linked with males' greater physical activity (Eaton & Enns, 1986). (Ninety percent of children diagnosed as rambunctiously hyperactive are boys [McGuinness, 1985].) No one of these findings would be conclusive by itself, but the convergence of evidence suggests that male aggressiveness has biological roots. Without doubt, it also has social roots; as we noted earlier, social learning encourages aggressiveness in boys more than in girls.

Social Dominance Across the world, men are perceived as more dominant. From Finland to France, from Peru to Pakistan, from The Netherlands to New Zealand, people rate men as more dominant, aggressive, and achievement-driven, women as more deferential, nurturant, and affiliative (Williams & Best, 1986). And indeed, in virtually every known society, men *are* socially dominant. When groups are formed, leadership tends to go to males. When people interact, men are more likely to utter opinions, women to express support (Aries, 1987; Wood, 1987). In everyday behavior, men are more likely to act as powerful people do—to talk assertively, to interrupt, to initiate touching, to smile less, to stare (J. Hall, 1987).

Such behaviors help maintain the inequities of social power. When political leaders are elected, they are usually men. When salaries are paid, those in traditionally male occupations are judged more valuable. When asked what pay they deserve, women often expect less than do men with the same qualifications or performance (Major, 1987).

Empathy To have *empathy* is to understand and feel what another feels—to rejoice with those who rejoice, and weep with those who weep. If you are empathic, you identify with others. You are able to imagine what it feels like to live with a handicap, what it must be like to try so hard to impress people, what a thrill it must be to win that award. When surveyed, women are far more likely than men to describe themselves as empathic.

In physical as well as psychological traits, individual differences among men and among women far exceed the small average differences between the sexes. Had he been competing against the women's 500-meter speed skaters in the 1988 Olympics, Erhard Keller, winner of the men's 500-meter race in the 1968 Olympics, would have finished in sixth place, 15 meters behind 1988 gold medalist, Bonnie Blair.

"There is little doubt that we would all be safer if the world's weapon systems were controlled by average women instead of by average men."
Melvin Konner,
The Tangled Wing: Biological Constraints on the Human Spirit, 1982

"When rewards are distributed, the woman gets one half the pay that a man does, and if disgrace is given out she bears it all."
Elbert Hubbard,
The Philistine, 1897

Drawing by Weber; © 1981 The New Yorker Magazine, Inc.

"This feels terrific, *Henry."*

But are they? In the laboratory, females are more likely to cry and to report feeling distressed when observing another's distress, perhaps partly because they are also slightly better than males at reading other people's nonverbal emotional cues (Eisenberg & Lennon, 1983; Hall, 1987). Curiously though, measures such as heart rate, taken while someone observes emotional distress, indicate that women do not consistently exhibit more physiological reaction than males. Similarly, when rating their reactions to pictures or videotapes of babies, women *report* much stronger reactions than men do, but measures of heart rate and perspiration fail to confirm that women physically respond more strongly (Berman, 1980).

Perhaps women respond much as men do but are considered more empathic because they are more aware of their emotional reactions and more willing to report them. If so, that too may help explain why both men and women seem to turn to women for intimacy and understanding (Rubin, 1985), and why women report feeling stronger emotions (Diener & others, 1985).

Differences in aggression, dominance, and empathy peak in late adolescence and early adulthood—the very years most commonly studied. Several studies have found that during middle age, gender differences diminish as women become more assertive and self-confident and men more empathic and less domineering (Helson & Moane, 1987; Turner, 1982). For example, Florine Livson (1976) studied the evolving gender differences among forty females and forty males as young teenagers in Oakland, California, and periodically thereafter up to age 50. During the teen years, the girls became progressively less assertive and more flirtatious, while the boys became more domineering and unexpressive. But by age 50, these differences had diminished. The men were expressing warmer feelings for others, and many of the women had become more assertive. In another study, M. F. Lowenthal and his colleagues (1975) asked married couples, "Who's the boss in your family?" Both husbands and wives were, with age, progressively less likely to single out the husband. Even trivial behaviors such as the customary masculine and feminine ways of carrying books (Figure 5–1) become less predictable in middle age (Jenni & Jenni, 1976).

Women *report* more empathy. Do they actually *feel* more empathy? Studies indicate that women surpass men at sending and reading nonverbal emotional cues. However, society also encourages women to express empathy more freely.

Figure 5–1   The customary masculine and feminine ways of carrying books. (From Jenni & Jenni, 1976.)

Corazón Aquino, shown here with her family—in her own words, "just a housewife"—emerged from 28 years in the shadow of her husband, a slain Philippine political leader, to lead a peaceful revolution that overwhelmed dictator Ferdinand Marcos. When she returned to her college in New York at age 51 to receive an honorary degree, former teachers and classmates were startled by her new self-confidence and authority. "It wasn't the Cory I remembered," said one.

Why do gender differences first increase and then decrease as life progresses? Personality theorist Carl Jung (1933) speculated that both masculine and feminine tendencies exist in everyone, and that during the second half of life people develop their previously repressed feminine or masculine aspects. Others have speculated that during courtship and early parenthood social expectations have traditionally led each sex to deemphasize traits that interfere with their roles at that time. So long as men are expected to provide and protect, they forgo their more dependent and tender sides (Gutmann, 1977), and so long as women are expected to nurture, they forgo their impulses to be assertive and independent. When they graduate from these early adult roles, men and women then become freer to develop and express their previously inhibited tendencies.

"In the long years liker must they grow;
The man be more of woman, she of man."
    Alfred, Lord Tennyson,
    The Princess, 1847

Verbal and Spatial Abilities   Until 1974, studies indicated that females slightly surpassed males on tests of verbal abilities, such as spelling, vocabulary, and comprehending difficult material. Since then, report Janet Hyde and Marcia Linn (1988), studies involving hundreds of thousands of test-takers have found no meaningful gender difference. But among children there is an exception at the low-scoring extreme: Boys more often are slow to develop language. In remedial reading classes, boys outnumber girls by three to one (Finucci & Childs, 1981). Speech defects such as stuttering are also predominantly boys' problems.

On spatial tasks, such as the speed of mentally rotating objects in space, males tend to surpass females (Halpern, 1986; Linn & Peterson, 1986). (See Figure 5–2.) Spatial abilities are helpful when playing chess, mentally rotating suitcases to see how best to fit them into a car trunk, finding one's way around an unfamiliar town, or doing geometry problems. This may help explain the gender difference in mathematics achievement. On the Scholastic Aptitude Test (SAT), males and females score similarly on the verbal test, but on the mathematics test males average about 50 points higher (on a 600-point scale). Males have a similar edge on the American College Testing (ACT) mathematics

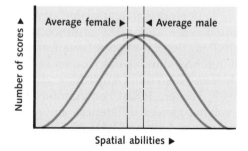

Figure 5–2   The average male's spatial abilities surpass those of the average female. (From Hyde, 1981.) However, given the overlap of scores between the sexes, the small average differences do not completely explain why 96 percent of American architects are men, nor why 96 percent of rated chess players are men (Gilbert, 1986).

test, an edge that is only partly reduced when comparing males with females who have had the same number of math courses (ACT, 1987).

Which two circles contain a configuration of blocks identical to the one in the circle at the left?

Standard   Responses

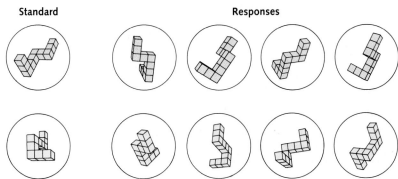

A test of spatial abilities: the mental rotation test. Which two responses show a different view of the standard? (Answers are upside down at the bottom of this page.)

As always when the overlap between the sexes is considerable, small average differences can look bigger when sampling from the extremes of a distribution. Thus among mathematically precocious seventh graders (those scoring above 700 on the SAT mathematics test in nationwide talent searches), boys have outnumbered girls by more than 10 to 1 (Benbow, 1988). These whiz kids, more than others their age, are male, left-handed, nearsighted, and suffer allergies or asthma (see also page 48)—characteristics that brain scientists Norman Geschwind and Peter Behan (1984) attributed to exposure to excess testosterone during prenatal development. But Jacqueline Eccles (1987b) has found that social expectations also shape and constrain boys' and girls' academic and career interests and abilities. Parents more willingly send their sons to computer camps; daughters receive more encouragement in English.

The infant in the photo on page 129 is a girl.

Seventh graders scoring in the 700s on the SAT math test is extreme and unusual. But it is a curious feature of statistical distributions that even a small average difference between two groups (such as in Figure 5–2) can create noticeable differences at the extremes. Only 5 percent of the variation in individuals' activity levels is attributable to gender (Eaton & Enns, 1986), but that's all it takes to make extreme activity—diagnosed as hyperactivity—three times more common in boys than girls. Thus observing the extremes—say, the preponderance of males among the hyperactive, the criminally violent, and the seventh grade math whiz kids—can mislead us into exaggerated perceptions of differences between groups.

What can we conclude? There appear to be detectable differences in the social behavior and cognitive abilities of males and females. But the gender similarities also are impressive, enough so that researcher Lauren Harris (1978) cautioned against thinking of females and males as *opposite* sexes: "Neither in any physiological nor in any psychological sense are males and females 'contrary or antithetical in nature or tendency; diametrically opposed, or altogether different.'" We might instead think of our own sex and the *other* sex as like the two halves of an oyster shell—very similar but not identical, equally important, and fitting together because they grow together and change around each other.

"Today, in the 1980s, there is the growing realization that it is possible for women to be equal and different."
      Psychologist Beatrice B. Whiting (1987)

Answers to the mental rotation test: For the top standard, the first and fourth alternatives; for the bottom standard, the second and third alternatives.

SUMMING UP

Few aspects of our lives are more important to our existence than our being born male or female. Examining the development of our maleness and femaleness, and of the behaviors *expected* of males and females, enables us to see biological and social factors at work and to appreciate how intertwined these factors are.

BIOLOGICAL INFLUENCES ON GENDER: IS BIOLOGY DESTINY?

Hormones   The male hormone testosterone has masculinizing effects on the developing fetus and can influence social behaviors, such as aggressiveness.

Sociobiology   Sociobiologists theorize that evolution favors social behaviors that enable men and women, in their own ways, to survive and reproduce. For males, whose sperm are cheap, this is said to mean being aggressive and taking sexual initiative. For women, whose investment in reproduction is far greater, this is said to mean being selective and then nurturant to their children. Critics maintain that sociobiological explanation often starts with behavior and reasons backward to conjecture an explanation. Furthermore, they say, human behaviors are less constrained by genes and are therefore more varied (adaptable) than those of other species for which sociobiological explanations were first developed. Finally, they point out, the effects of culture must not be ignored.

THE SOCIAL CONSTRUCTION OF GENDER

Theories of Gender-Typing   Theorists have sought to explain how we acquire gender identity and roles. Freud believed that young children resolve sexual anxiety by identifying with their same-sex parent. Social learning theory assumes that children learn gender-linked behaviors by observing and imitating, and being rewarded or punished. Cognitive developmental theory proposes that as children struggle to understand themselves and their world, they form a concept (schema) of gender, which then influences their behavior. Sandra Bem's gender schema theory combines cognitive developmental and social learning views of gender-typing by showing how society influences the child's schema of gender.

Gender Roles   Expectations for men's and women's behavior vary widely across cultures, and across time within a culture. In North America, gender roles have been converging, yet in no culture have they disappeared. Whether they can or should disappear is a debate that science can inform but not decide.

Nature-Nurture Interaction   Biological factors always operate within a social context, and social influences operate upon what is biologically given.

GENDER DIFFERENCES

The Politics of Studying Gender Differences   Differences—even small average differences between overlapping groups of people—catch our attention. Some people worry that studying gender differences may therefore exaggerate people's perceptions of such differences; others argue that such research has debunked gender myths and that men and women can be seen as different, yet be equally valued.

How *Do* Males and Females Differ?   Research studies have shown that males tend to behave more aggressively, to exert more social dominance, and to exhibit greater spatial and math ability. Women tend to show somewhat greater sensitivity to others' nonverbal messages, to report feeling more empathy, and to have fewer language disabilities. In general, men and women differ more in their reports on their social behaviors than is observed in their actual behaviors.

TERMS AND CONCEPTS TO REMEMBER

aggression   Physical or verbal behavior intended to hurt someone.

androgyny (*andros*, man + *gynē*, woman)   Possession of desirable psychological traits traditionally associated with both men and women.

cognitive developmental theory   The theory that gender-typing occurs as children form a concept of gender, which then influences whom they imitate.

empathy   The ability to understand and feel what another feels, to put oneself in someone else's shoes.

gender   The social definition of male and female.

gender identity   One's sense of being male or female. Note: One's gender identity is distinct from one's sexual orientation (as heterosexual or homosexual) and from the strength of one's *gender-typing* (see page 135).

gender role   A set of expected behaviors for males and for females.

gender schema theory   The theory that children learn from their cultures a concept of what it means to be male and female and adjust their behavior accordingly.

gender-typing The acquisition of a masculine or feminine gender identity and role.

identification Freud's term for the presumed process by which a child adopts the characteristics of the same-sex parent. More generally, the process by which people associate themselves with and copy the behavior of significant others.

natural selection The process by which evolution favors individuals within a species best equipped to survive and reproduce.

social learning theory The theory that we learn behavior, such as gender-typed behavior, by observing and imitating, and by being rewarded and punished.

sociobiology The study of the evolution of social behavior using the principles of natural selection. Social behaviors that are genetically based and that contribute to the preservation and spread of one's genes are presumed to be favored by natural selection.

testosterone The most important of the male sex hormones. Both males and females have it, but the additional testosterone in males stimulates the growth of the male sex organs in the fetus and the development of the male sex characteristics during puberty.

FOR FURTHER READING

Doyle, J. A. (1989). *The male experience* (2nd ed.). Dubuque, IA: W. C. Brown.

A book about the male sex role.

Eagly, A. H. (1987). *Sex differences in social behavior: A social-role explanation.* Hillsdale, NJ: Erlbaum.

A state-of-the-art review of how and why men and women are alike and different in aggression, helping, influenceability, and nonverbal behavior.

Hyde, J. (1985). *Half the human experience: The psychology of women* (3rd ed.). Lexington, MA: Heath.

One of several textbooks that provide a comprehensive discussion of the psychology of women.

Tavris, C., & Wade, C. (1984). *The longest war: Sex differences in perspective* (2nd ed.). San Diego, CA: Harcourt Brace Jovanovich.

A provocative and delightfully readable discussion of gender.

Walsh, M. R. (Ed.) (1987). *The psychology of women: Ongoing debates.* New Haven: Yale University Press.

A healthy debating of issues ranging from premenstrual syndrome to the explanation of gender differences in math achievement.

For further information in this text on the psychology of women and men, see:

Adult development of women and men, p. 99
Alcoholism, p. 216
Body image, pp. 358–359
Bonding, pp. 70–72
Breast-feeding, p. 72
Depression, pp. 456, 458, 460
Dreams of men and women, p. 203
Early vs. late maturation of boys and girls, p. 91
Eating disorders, pp. 357–359
Employment of women, p. 109
Fatherhood, p. 73
Generic pronoun "he," p. 309
Heart disease, p. 514

Menarche, p. 90
Menopause, p. 99
Moral development of men and women, p. 95
Pornography, pp. 580–584
Prejudice and stereotyping, pp. 590, 591
Premenstrual syndrome, pp. 526–527
Rape, pp. 244, 580–584, 594–595
Sensitivity to smells, p. 162
Sexual coercion, pp. 215, 581–583
Sexual development, p. 90
Sexuality, pp. 361–362
Smoking by men and women, pp. 531–532
Suicide by men and women, p. 457

PART 3

Experiencing the World

To experience the world around us, we must take in, process, and selectively interpret myriads of messages. Various stimuli that strike our bodies must first be received and transformed into neural messages that reach the brain—a process we investigate in Chapter 6, Sensation. These messages must then be organized and interpreted in meaningful ways, which we consider in Chapter 7, Perception. As we examine how we experience the world, we will touch on such controversial issues as: Can we be affected by stimuli that are too faint to be perceived consciously? What happens when a person is deprived of sensory input? Is there extrasensory perception? Conscious experience can also occur in altered states—states induced by sleep, hypnosis, and drugs, the topics of Chapter 8, States of Consciousness.

CHAPTER 6

Sensation

In a silent, cushioned inner world of utter darkness floats your brain. In the outer world, myriad stimuli continually impinge upon your body. These facts raise a fundamental question, one that predates psychology by thousands of years, one that helped inspire the beginnings of modern psychology some 100 years ago: *How does the world out there get in?*

To put the question in contemporary terms, how do we construct our representations of the external world? How do we manage to experience the world's form and texture, its motion and temperature, its aroma and beauty? And can we be sure that our experiences of sight, sound, touch, taste, and smell really do correspond to what is out there? Some people are able to see a bearded face in Figure 6–1; others are not. So, *is* there a face in the drawing? For that matter, if what we see is merely our visual system's response to electromagnetic energy striking the eye, can we be sure that there really is color out there?

To grasp how the world out there gets represented inside our heads, three computer concepts are useful: input, information processing, and output. As Figure 6–2 illustrates, physical objects emit or reflect stimuli: Our sensory organs detect these stimuli (input) and encode them into neural information that our brains organize and interpret (processing) as a perceptual experience (output) to which we react. As we will see later, our resulting perceptual experiences may affect our actions, which may in turn modify our perceptions. The inexperienced baseball outfielder who runs in too far to catch fly balls soon learns to judge them better.

Figure 6–1 Everyone senses an array of black and white here, but most people require a few minutes before they can perceive anything meaningful.

Figure 6–2 How sensory input is processed.

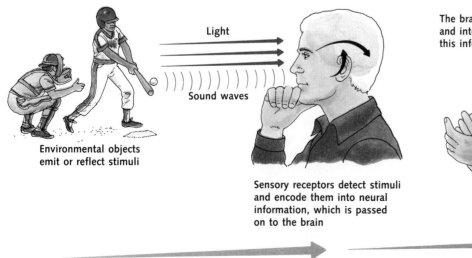 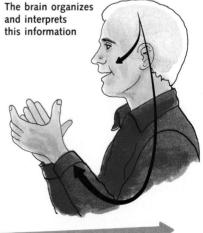

Light

Sound waves

Environmental objects emit or reflect stimuli

Sensory receptors detect stimuli and encode them into neural information, which is passed on to the brain

The brain organizes and interprets this information

SENSATION

PERCEPTION

Perception and sensation are difficult to separate. Nevertheless, we can think of *sensation* as the process by which stimuli are detected and encoded, enabling us to experience the black and white blotches of Figure 6–1. To study sensation is therefore to study how stimuli that strike our bodies are transformed into neural messages received by the brain. *Perception* (our topic in Chapter 7) is the active mental process of organizing and interpreting our sensations, enabling us to see, perhaps, not just blotches but a face in that figure. Roughly speaking, perception takes up where sensation leaves off. So, to recognize, say an A and an ⅄ as *As* and not *Hs* or *Rs*, we must be capable of sensing (detecting, encoding) and perceiving (organizing, interpreting) information.

"Only mind has sight and hearing; all things else are deaf and blind."
Epicharmus,
Fragments, 550 B.C.

SENSING THE WORLD: SOME BASIC PRINCIPLES

Sensory systems enable an organism to obtain the information it needs to function and survive. A frog, which feeds on flying insects, has eyes that include a type of receptor cell that fires only in response to small, moving dark objects—"bug detectors" they have been called (Barlow, 1972; Lettvin & others, 1959). A frog could starve while knee-deep in motionless flies, but let one zoom by and the frog's "bug detectors" are triggered. So sensitive are the male silkworm's receptors to the odor of the female sex-attractant that a single female silkworm moth need only release a billionth of an ounce per second to attract every male silkworm moth within a mile (Sagan, 1979b). Which is why there continue to be silkworms. Humans are similarly designed to detect what are, for them, the important features of their environments. Nature's gifts are suited to the recipients' needs.

(a)

(b)

These two photographs show a flower as it appears (a) to the human eye and (b) to the eye of a bee. The bee's ability to perceive ultraviolet wavelengths enables it to see the "landing field" invisible to the human eye, and makes possible more efficient food gathering.

THRESHOLDS

We exist in a sea of energy. At this moment, you and I are being bombarded with x-rays and radio waves, with ultraviolet and infrared light, with very high and very low frequency sound waves. But to all of them we are blind and deaf. The shades on our senses, our windows on the world, are open just a crack, allowing us only a restricted awareness of this vast sea.

Absolute Thresholds   To some kinds of stimuli we are exquisitely sensitive. Standing atop a mountain on an utterly dark, clear night, we can, given normal senses, see a candle flame atop another mountain 30 miles away. In a silent room, we can hear a watch ticking 20 feet away. We can feel the wing of a bee falling on our cheek and smell a single drop of perfume in a three-room apartment (Galanter, 1962). Our awareness of these faint stimuli illustrates our *absolute thresholds*—the minimum amounts of stimulation necessary for a particular stimulus (light, sound, pressure, odor, taste) to be detected 50 percent of the time. For example, to test our absolute threshold for sounds, a hearing specialist exposes each ear to sounds, some so weak that we never hear them, some so loud that we never miss them. In between is a zone of uncertainty for each pitch, where half the time we will correctly detect the sound and half the time we will not. For each of the senses, that arbitrary fifty-fifty point defines our absolute threshold.

There is no single absolute threshold for *signal detection,* because detecting a weak stimulus (signal) depends not only on the signal strength (such as a tone on a hearing test), but also on our psychological state—our experience, expectations, motivation, and level of fatigue. In a horror-filled wartime situation where failure to detect an intruder may mean death, a sentry standing guard alone at night may notice—and fire at—an almost imperceptible noise. In peacetime, when survival is not threatened, the same sentry will require a stronger signal before sensing danger.

Such variations in one's threshold can have life-or-death consequences when people are responsible for detecting blips on a radar screen, weapons at an airport security checkpoint, or critical signals on the monitoring equipment at a hospital nursing station. Studies of signal detection, in which people must judge whether a faint stimulus is present, indicate that after about 30 minutes of performing on such tasks, people's vigilance tends to diminish. But this depends on the task, on the time of day, and even on whether the subjects are given a chance to exercise (Warm & Dember, 1986).

Subliminal Stimulation   In 1957, a storm of controversy erupted over a report that some movie audiences in New Jersey were unwittingly being influenced by imperceptible flashed messages to "drink Coca-Cola" and "eat popcorn." More than 30 years later the controversy has erupted anew. Advertisers are said to be manipulating consumers by imperceptibly printing the word "sex" on crackers and embedding erotic images in liquor ads. Rock recordings are said to contain "Satanic messages" that are consciously discernible if the recordings are played backward and unconsciously persuasive when played normally. Entrepreneurs offer to help us lose weight, stop smoking, or improve our memories with audiotapes of soothing ocean sounds that contain unheard messages such as "I am thin," "Smoke tastes bad," and "I do well on tests. I have total recall of information." These claims all assume that unconsciously we can sense *subliminal* (literally, "below threshold") stimuli which, without our awareness, have extraordinary suggestive powers.

Do we, in fact, ever sense stimuli that are below the absolute threshold for awareness? In one sense the answer is clearly yes. Remember that the "absolute" threshold is really just a statistically defined point at which we detect a stimulus half the time (Figure 6–3). At or slightly below this threshold we will still detect the stimulus some of the time. The answer is yes in another sense, too. People who plead total ignorance when asked to make some perceptual judgment—for example, when having to decide which of two very similar weights is heavier—may be correct substantially more than 50 percent of the time when forced to guess. Sometimes we know more than we think.

Can we be affected by stimuli that are too weak for us to *ever* notice? Recent experiments hint that, under certain conditions, the answer may again be yes. For example, a group of University of Michigan students was repeatedly shown a series of geometric figures, one at a time, each for less than 0.01 second—long enough to perceive only a flash of light (Kunst-Wilson & Zajonc, 1980). Later the students expressed greater liking for the figures that had been presented than for figures that had not been shown, even though they had no idea which were the repeated ones. When Robert Bornstein and his colleagues (1987) repeated this experiment by subliminally exposing students to a photo of someone, they obtained similar results: The students later felt slightly more liking for the person whose face had been repeatedly

This sentry's survival, and that of his fellow soldiers, may depend on his ability to detect slight changes in the environment.

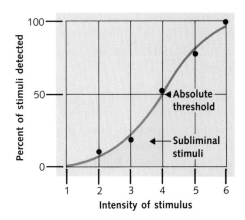

Figure 6–3   The absolute threshold is defined as the intensity at which a stimulus is perceived 50 percent of the times it is presented. As you can see from the graph, to be a subliminal stimulus merely means that it is perceived *less* than 50 percent of the time.

flashed to them. Sometimes we feel what we do not know and cannot describe.

Moreover, researchers have found that "invisible" words (ones flashed too briefly to perceive) may nevertheless prime people to respond appropriately to a later question (Fowler & others, 1981; Greenwald & others, 1988; Marcel, 1983). For instance, Thomas Carr and his colleagues (1987) flashed words on a screen so briefly that their Michigan State University students could not consciously detect whether the flash of light contained a word or not. Nevertheless, when one of the invisible words was presented just before a word that was visible, it affected how fast they read the second word. If the invisible word was "bread," a related word such as "butter" was read faster than were unrelated words such as "bottle" or "bubble." Thus the invisible word's meaning was being processed, though the students were unaware of it.

In hindsight, we can surmise how this might be. Stimuli too weak to cross our thresholds for awareness may nevertheless trigger a weak response in our sense receptors, a response that may even be transmitted to the brain and cross some threshold for feeling or meaning, though not for conscious awareness. Experiments have even detected brain activity that momentarily precedes our awareness of decisions to perform a simple act, such as lifting a finger (Libet, 1985). For these and other reasons, researchers now agree that our brains process much information without our awareness.

Why, then, are most researchers skeptical of subliminal *persuasion?* Perhaps you can detect a difference between the conditions under which subliminal advertising would be likely to occur and the conditions of these last experiments. In the experiments, the subjects' undivided attention was focused on the visual subliminal stimuli; they were straining to glimpse the imperceptible forms or words. When listening to a recording, our attention is focused not on any subliminal stimuli that might be present but on the sounds of which we are *consciously* aware. There is every reason to suppose that stimuli strong enough to command our attention will overpower any effect of subliminal stimuli. Contrary to the claims of purveyors of subliminal tapes, there is no indication that subliminal visual stimuli have an irresistible power to motivate or persuade (Creed, 1987). Moreover, the tapes provide stimuli to the *ear*—a technique for which there is no reliable evidence of subliminal effect (Greenwald, 1987). To summarize, we do process sensory information without awareness. But so far, the research on subliminal persuasion has produced nothing more than subliminal results (Moore, 1982; Tisdell, 1983).

Difference Thresholds   Sensation enables us to get the information we need to function effectively. This requires absolute thresholds low enough to allow us to detect important sights, sounds, tastes, textures, and smells. It also requires the ability to detect small differences among stimuli. A musician must be able to detect minute discrepancies in an instrument's tuning. A wine taster must be able to detect the slight difference in flavor between two vintage wines.

The *difference threshold* (also called the *just noticeable difference,* or *jnd*) is the minimum difference a person can detect between any two stimuli 50 percent of the time. The difference threshold increases with the magnitude of the stimulus. Add 1 ounce to a 10-ounce weight and you will detect the difference; add 1 ounce to a 10-pound weight and you will not, because the difference threshold has increased. More than a century ago, Ernst Weber noted that regardless of their magni-

"Finding the occasional straw of truth awash in a great ocean of confusion and bamboozle requires intelligence, vigilance, dedication and courage. But if we don't practice these tough habits of thought, we cannot hope to solve the truly serious problems that face us—and we risk becoming a nation of suckers, up for grabs by the next charlatan who comes along."
  Carl Sagan (1987)

The LORD is my shepherd;
    I shall not want.
He maketh me to lie down
        in green pastures:
    he leadeth me
        beside the still waters.
He restoreth my soul:
    he leadeth me
        in the paths of righteousness
            for his name's sake.
Yea, though I walk through the valley
        of the shadow of death,
    I will fear no evil:
    for thou art with me;
        thy rod and thy staff
            they comfort me.
Thou preparest a table before me
        in the presence of mine enemies:
    thou anointest my head with oil,
        my cup runneth over.
Surely goodness and mercy
        shall follow me
        all the days of my life:
    and I will dwell
        in the house of the LORD
            for ever.

The difference threshold. In this computer generation of Psalm 23 each line of the type face changes imperceptibly. How many lines are required for you to experience a just noticeable difference?

Members of the National Symphony Orchestra of Washington, DC, and their conductor, Mstislav Rostropovich, must be able to sense slight variations in pitch. The tea taster on the right must distinguish minuscule variations in flavor and aroma.

tude, two stimuli must differ by a constant proportion for their difference to be perceived. This principle—that the difference threshold is not a constant amount but some constant *proportion* of the stimulus—is so simple and so widely applicable that we still refer to it as **Weber's law.** The exact proportion varies, depending on the stimulus (see Table 6–1). For their differences to be perceived by the average person, two objects need to differ in weight by only 2 percent and two tones in frequency by only 0.3 percent.

Table 6–1

SOME COMMON DIFFERENCE THRESHOLDS

To be experienced by the average person as a just noticeable difference,

two	solutions lights objects sounds sounds	must vary in	saltiness intensity weight intensity frequency	by	8% 8% 2% 5% 0.3%

Source: Adapted from "On the exponents of Stevens' law and the constant in Ekman's law," by R. Teghtsoonian, 1971, *Psychology Review, 78,* pp. 71–80.

Weber's law is a rough approximation that works well for nonextreme sensory stimuli. It also parallels some of our life experiences. If the price of a 50-cent candy bar goes up by a nickel, shoppers might note the change; similarly, it might take a $5,000 price hike in a $50,000 Mercedes-Benz to raise the eyebrows of its potential buyers. In both cases, the price went up by 10 percent. Weber's principle: Sensory thresholds for detecting differences (measured as the amount of increased stimulation) are a constant proportion of the magnitude of the original stimulus.

SENSORY ADAPTATION

Upon entering your neighbor's living room, you smell an unpleasant odor; you wonder how she tolerates it, but within minutes you yourself no longer notice it. When the refrigerator motor turns on, you may notice how noisy it is, but only for a moment or two. Jumping into a swimming pool, you shiver and complain how cold it is; a short while later a friend arrives and you exclaim, "C'mon in. Water's lovely!"

"We need above all to know about changes; no one wants or needs to be reminded 16 hours a day that his shoes are on."
Neuroscientist David Hubel (1979)

The body's capacity for sensory adaptation enables this swimmer to tolerate icy water.

These examples illustrate **_sensory adaptation_**—our diminishing sensitivity to an unchanging stimulus. (To experience this phenomenon right now, move your watch up your wrist an inch: You will feel it—but only for a few moments.) After constant exposure to a stimulus, our nerve cells begin to fire less frequently.

Why, then, if we stare at an object without flinching, does it not vanish from sight? The answer is that, unnoticed by us, our eyes are always moving, quivering just enough to guarantee that the retina image is continually changing.

But what if we could stop our eyes from moving? Would sights seem to vanish, as odors do? To answer this question, psychologists have devised ingenious instruments for maintaining a constant or stabilized image on the retina. Imagine that we fitted a subject, Mary, with one of these instruments—a miniature projector mounted on a contact lens (see Figure 6–4a). When Mary's eye moves, the image from the projector moves as well. Thus everywhere that Mary looks the scene is sure to go.

If the profile of a face is projected from such an instrument, what will Mary see? At first she will see the complete profile. But within a few seconds, as her vision receptors begin to fatigue, a strange phenomenon will occur. Bit by bit, the image will vanish, only later to reappear and then disappear—in recognizable fragments or as a whole (see Figure 6–4b). Interestingly, the disappearance and reappearance of an image occurs in meaningful units. Whole portions of the face come and go. If a person is shown a word, it will disappear; and new words made up of parts of the word will appear and then vanish. This phenomenon anticipates a major conclusion about perception that we will consider in the next chapter: Our perceptions are organized by the meanings that our minds impose.

Although sensory adaptation reduces our sensitivity, it offers an important benefit: It enables us to focus our attention on *informative* changes in our environment without being distracted by the uninformative, constant stimulation of garments, odors, and street noise. This reinforces a fundamental lesson of our study of sensation and perception: We perceive the world not exactly as it is, but as it is useful for us to perceive it.

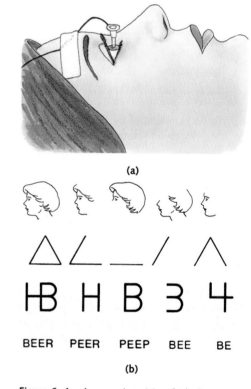

(a)

BEER   PEER   PEEP   BEE   BE

(b)

Figure 6–4 An experiment in which the image moves with the eye. (a) A subject wears a projector mounted on a contact lens; whenever her eye moves so does the projected image. (b) As these sample progressions illustrate, when first projected, the stabilized image is clear, but soon it fades. It reappears in meaningful fragments or as a whole, only to fade and reappear, perhaps in different fragments, again and again. (From ''Stabilized images on the retina'' by R. M. Pritchard. Copyright © 1961 Scientific American, Inc. All rights reserved.)

Absolute threshold, difference threshold, and adaptation are not the only commonalities among the senses. Their common task involves receiving sensory stimulation, transforming it into neural information, and delivering that information to the brain. How do the senses work? Let us find out by beginning with vision, the most thoroughly studied of our windows on the world.

VISION

Our sensory processing model (Figure 6–2, page 139) suggests that the study of any sensory system begins with (1) the analysis of its triggering stimuli, and (2) the process—called *transduction*—by which these stimuli are converted into neural messages. A phonograph needle in a turntable is a transducer: It receives minute vibrations (the triggering stimuli) and transforms (transduces) this energy into electrical signals. Supply another form of energy—shine a light on the needle, warm it up, put perfume on it—and nothing happens. Like each of our sensory receptors, those of the eye transduce a specific type of stimulus energy, electromagnetic waves, into neural activity.

THE STIMULUS INPUT: LIGHT ENERGY

Scientifically speaking, what strikes our eyes is not color but pulses of electromagnetic energy that our visual system experiences as color. What we see as visible light is but a thin slice of the whole spectrum of electromagnetic waves. As Figure 6–5 illustrates, the electromagnetic spectrum varies from the long pulses or waves of radio transmission, to the narrow band of the spectrum that we see, to the extremely short waves of cosmic rays. Other organisms are sensitive to slightly different portions of the spectrum. Bees, for example, cannot see red, but can see ultraviolet light, the part of the spectrum that causes sunburn in humans.

Figure 6–5 The spectrum of electromagnetic energy ranges from radio waves over a mile long to gamma rays as short as the diameter of an atom. The narrow band of wavelengths visible to the human eye (shown enlarged) extends from the longer waves of red light to the shorter waves of blue-violet light. Electromagnetic waves are measured in nanometers—billionths of a meter.

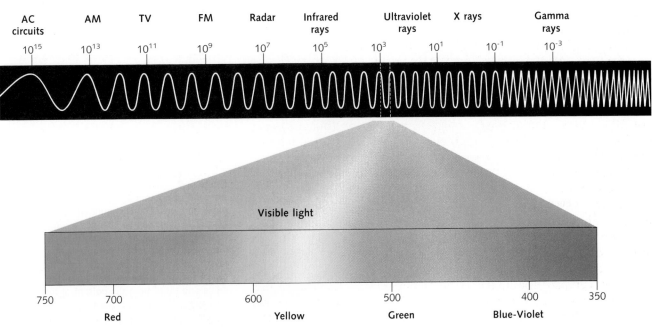

Three physical characteristics of light determine our sensory experience of it. Its *wavelength*—the distance from one wave peak to the next—determines its *hue* (the color that we experience, such as blue or green). The *intensity,* or amount of energy in light waves (determined by their *amplitude*), influences *brightness.* (Wavelength and amplitude are depicted in Figure 6–6.) The *complexity,* or mixture of wavelengths, determines *saturation,* or vividness, of color. Pure wavelengths have little complexity and therefore are highly saturated, vivid colors.

As Figure 6–5 on the previous page shows, the spectrum of light consists of a continuum of wavelengths. However, from infancy we tend to see the visible spectrum not as a continuum but as divided into four basic colors: red, green, yellow, and blue-violet (Lumsden & Wilson, 1983). To understand why this is so, and, more generally, how it is that we manage to see at all, we first need to understand the structure of the visual system.

THE EYE

In some ways, the eye functions like a camera (or, more exactly, the camera functions like the nineteenth-century understanding of the eye). In both eye and camera, light is admitted through a small opening, behind which a lens focuses the incoming rays into an image on a light-sensitive surface (Figure 6–7). The eye's small opening is the *pupil.* Its size, and therefore the amount of light entering the eye, is regulated by the *iris,* the colored muscle that surrounds and dilates or contracts the pupil. The *lens* focuses the incoming rays by changing its curvature in a process referred to as *accommodation.* The light-sensitive surface onto which the rays are focused is the *retina,* the multilayered tissue that lines the inside of the back of the eyeball.

For centuries it was known that when the image of a candle passed through a small opening, it appeared inverted on a dark wall behind. Scholars assumed that we could not see the world right side up if the retina received an upside-down image, so they struggled to conceive

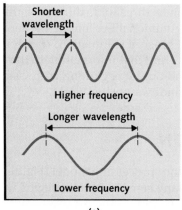

(a)

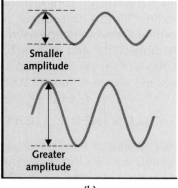

(b)

Figure 6–6 The physical properties of waves. Waves vary in wavelength (a), the distance between successive peaks, and in amplitude or intensity (b), which reflects the difference in height from peak to trough. Frequency, the number of complete wavelengths that can pass a point in a given time, is directly related to the wavelength. The shorter the wavelength, the higher the frequency. These physical properties in turn determine our perceptual experiences of light and sound.

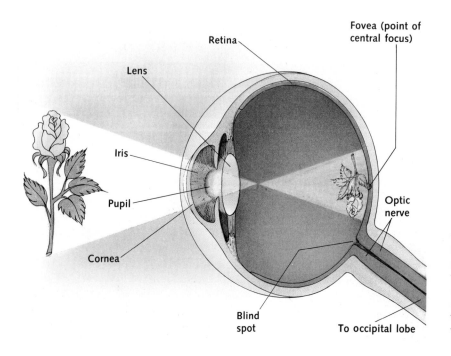

Figure 6–7 The eye. Light rays reflected from the rose pass through the cornea, pupil, and lens. The curvature and thickness of the lens can be changed in order to bring either nearby or distant objects into focus on the retina. Because light rays travel in straight lines, rays from the top of the rose strike the bottom of the retina and those from the bottom of the rose strike the top of the retina. They therefore form an upside-down and reversed image on the retina.

how the retina received an upright image. One idea was that the eye's sensing device is the lens. Realizing this was not so, the ever-curious Leonardo da Vinci theorized that light rays were bent by the eye's watery fluids in such a way that the inverted image was reinverted to the upright position as it reached the retina. The astronomer Johannes Kepler applied the science of optics to vision and in 1604 showed that the retina indeed received upside-down images of the world (Crombie, 1964). And how could we make sense of such a world? "I leave it," said the befuddled Kepler, "to natural philosophers."

The "natural philosophers," who eventually included research psychologists, discovered that the retina includes a layer of millions of receptor cells that convert light energy into neural impulses that are sent to the brain and assembled *there* to create a coherent perceived image—one that is not upside down.

Acuity, or sharpness, of vision can be affected by small distortions in the shape of the eye. Normally the lens focuses the image of any object on the retina (Figure 6–8a). In *nearsightedness,* where the eyeball is longer than normal in relation to its lens or the cornea is too sharply curved, the light rays from distant objects converge in front of the retina (Figure 6–8b) rather than on it. Generally, perception of near objects is clearer than that of distant objects, but people who are extremely nearsighted see nothing clearly. *Farsightedness* is a sort of opposite of nearsightedness. Here, the light rays from near objects entering through the cornea and lens reach the retina before they have converged, producing a blurred image (Figure 6–8c). In children, the eye's ability to accommodate usually makes up for this problem, and they rarely need glasses—but they may suffer eyestrain from overused eye muscles, and some get headaches. People who are only mildly farsighted often do not discover their condition until middle age, when the lens loses its ability to change shape readily, and they begin to have trouble seeing near objects clearly.

"Vision is brought about by a picture of the thing seen being formed on the white concave surface of the retina. That which is to the right outside is depicted on the left on the retina . . . that above, below." Johannes Kepler, *Ad Vitellionem Paralipomena,* 1604

When viewing an eye chart, people with normal 20/20 vision can read material of a certain size from a distance of 20 feet. If standing 20 feet away you can discriminate only what people with normal vision can see at 50 feet, then you have 20/50 vision.

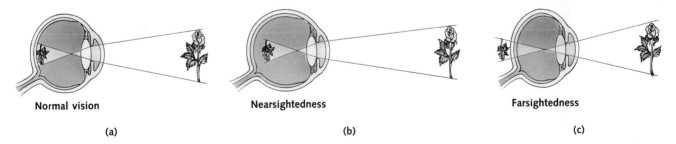

Normal vision (a)   **Nearsightedness** (b)   **Farsightedness** (c)

Figure 6–8 (a) Normal vision. As the diagram shows, rays of light converge on the retina of a normal eye. This occurs for both nearby objects, and, with appropriate readjustments in the curvature of the lens, for objects that are farther away.

(b) Nearsighted vision. The diagram shows that in a nearsighted eyeball, which is longer than normal, the light rays from distant objects are focused in front of the retina. When their image reaches the retina, the rays are spreading out and the

image is blurred. (c) Farsighted vision. As the diagram shows, in the farsighted eyeball, which is shorter than normal, light rays from nearby objects come into focus behind the retina, resulting in blurred images.

In later life the lens hardens, losing some of its ability to thicken, which it must do in order to focus on nearby objects. With age the diameter of the pupil also shrinks and the lens becomes less transparent, reducing the retina's access to light. In fact, the 65-year-old retina receives only about one-third as much light as its 20-year-old counterpart (Kline & Schieber, 1985). To have visual acuity as sharp as that of a 20-year-old when reading, a 65-year-old requires three times as much light (which helps explain why older people often tell younger people, "You need better light for reading").

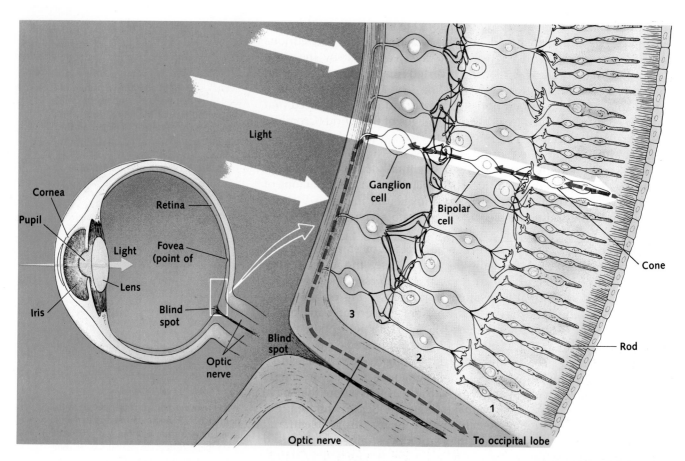

Figure 6–9. Labels: Cornea, Pupil, Light, Iris, Retina, Fovea (point of, Lens, Blind spot, Optic nerve, Blind spot, Optic nerve, Light, Ganglion cell, Bipolar cell, Cone, Rod, 3, 2, 1, To occipital lobe

The Retina   If we were to follow a single particle of light energy into the eye, we would see that it first makes its way through the retina's outer layer of cells to its buried receptor cells, the *rods* and *cones* (see Figure 6–9). When struck by light energy, the rods and cones generate neural signals that activate the neighboring bipolar cells, which in turn activate their neighboring ganglion cells. The axons from the network of ganglion cells converge like the strands of a rope to form an *optic nerve* that carries information to the brain. Nearly a million messages can be transmitted by the optic nerve at once, through nearly 1 million ganglion fibers. Where the optic nerve leaves the eye there are no receptor cells—creating a ***blind spot*** (see Figure 6–10 below).

Most of the estimated 6 million cones are clustered around the *fovea,* the retina's point of central focus (Figure 6–9). In fact, the fovea contains only cones, no rods. Unlike rods, many cones have their own bipolar cells to help relay their individual messages to the cortex. This preserves their precise information, making them better able to detect fine detail. (Rods have no such hot line to the brain; they share bipolar cells with other rods, so their individual messages get combined.) To illustrate, if you pick a word in this sentence and stare directly at it, thereby focusing its image on the cones in your fovea, you will see that words a few inches off to the side appear blurred. This is because their image strikes more peripheral region of your retina, where the 120 million rods predominate.

Figure 6–9   The path of light through the eye. Before signals from the retina reach the brain, they are transformed by a switchboard of neural cells. The ray of light entering the eye triggers a photo-chemical reaction in the rods and cones (1) at the back of the retina behind the other neural layers. The chemical reaction in turn triggers the bipolar cells. (The *amacrine* and *horizontal cells,* shown in yellow, allow information to be shared among the bipolar cells and the ganglion cells). (2) The bipolar cells then activate the ganglion cells (3), which converge to form the optic nerve. The optic nerve transmits information to the occipital lobe of the brain.

Figure 6–10   The blind spot. Where the optic nerve leaves the eye (see Figure 6–9), there are no receptor cells. This creates a blind spot in our vision. To demonstrate its existence in your own eyes, close your left eye, look at the spot, and move the page to a distance from your face (about 9 inches) at which the oncoming car disappears. In everyday vision the blind spot doesn't cause blindness because your eyes are moving and one eye covers what the other misses.

Only cones enable you to see color. As illumination diminishes, the cones adjust quickly, the rods more slowly. However, the rods are keenly sensitive in dim light, to which the cones do not respond (see Figure 6–11). That is why you cannot distinguish colors in dim light. So when we enter a darkened theater or turn off the light at night, the pupil dilates to allow more light to reach the rods in the retina's periphery. In such conditions of sudden light change, it typically takes 20 minutes or more before our eyes are maximally sensitive. This period of dark adaptation seems to be yet another instance of the remarkable adaptiveness of our sensory systems, for it matches the natural twilight transition period between the sun's setting and darkness.

Knowing just this much about the eye, can you imagine why a cat sees so much better at night than you do? There are two reasons: A cat's pupils can open much wider than yours, letting in more light, and a cat has a higher proportion of light-sensitive rods (Moser, 1987). But there is a trade-off: With its fewer cones, a cat can't see details or color as well as a human.

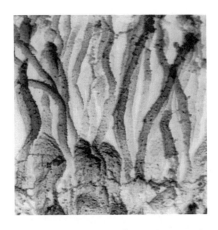

Rods (square-ended) and cones (tapering) as shown by a scanning electron microscope. Rods, which are responsible for black-and-white vision, are more light sensitive than cones, which is why the world becomes colorless to us at night. Some nocturnal animals, such as toads, mice, rats, and bats, have retinas made up almost entirely of rods. Cones, in addition to being responsible for color vision, provide a greater degree of visual precision than rods and are concentrated at the fovea.

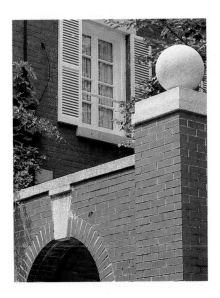 

Figure 6–11   As the light on this brick gateway fades we can still see the structure, but the details of the brickwork and its color are vanishing. In dim light, it is the rods in our retinas that do most of our seeing.

VISUAL INFORMATION PROCESSING

Visual information is processed at progressively more abstract levels. At the entry level, the retina—which is actually a piece of the brain that migrates to the eye during early fetal development—processes information before routing it to the cortex. The retina's neural layers are not just passing along electrical impulses, they also help to encode and analyze the sensory information. Indeed, much of the important processing of visual information takes place in the retina's neural tissues. The third neural layer in a frog's eye, for example, contains cells that fire only in response to specific types of stimulation—recall the "bug detector" cells.

In more complex animals, too, information is processed by the retina's interconnected nerve cells. In human eyes, for example, the information from the retina's approximately 130 million receptor rods and cones is processed by the million or so ganglion cells whose fibers make up the optic nerve. But most information processing occurs in

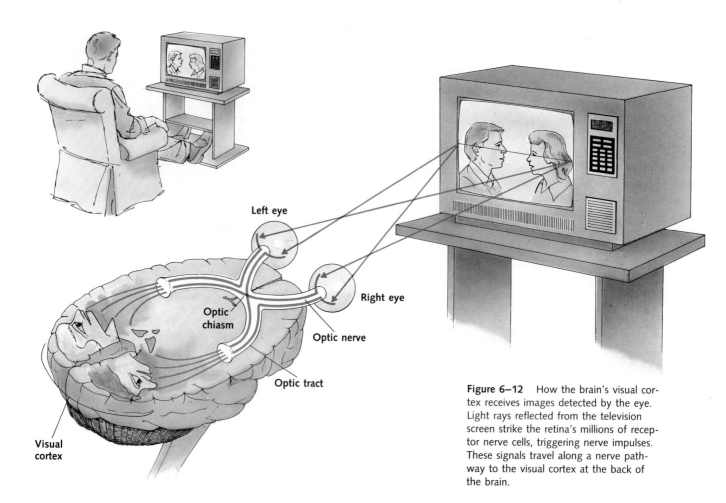

Figure 6–12   How the brain's visual cortex receives images detected by the eye. Light rays reflected from the television screen strike the retina's millions of receptor nerve cells, triggering nerve impulses. These signals travel along a nerve pathway to the visual cortex at the back of the brain.

the brain. Any given area of the retina relays its information to a corresponding location in the visual cortex at the back of the brain (see Figure 6–12).

The sensitivity necessary for the retinal cells to provide accurate information can lead to "error" as well. Turn your eyes to the left, close them, and then gently rub the right side of your right eyelid with your fingertip. You will see a patch of light to the left, moving as your finger moves.

Why do you see light? Why at the left? Your retinal cells are so responsive that even pressure triggers them. But your brain interprets their firing as light. Moreover, it interprets the light as coming from the left—which is where light normally comes from when it activates the right side of the retina. (There is an incidental lesson here: When trying to make sense of unusual neural discharges, the brain may conjure up hallucinations. Thus when disease or drugs disturb our neural functioning, crazy but seemingly real experiences can result.)

Feature Detectors   When individual ganglion cells register information in their region of the visual field, they send signals to the visual cortex. Nobelists David Hubel and Torsten Wiesel (1979) believe that when certain cortical neurons, which they call *feature detectors*, receive this information, they respond only to specific features of what is viewed—to particular bars, edges, and lines. From these elements the brain assembles the perceived image.

For example, Hubel and Wiesel report that a given brain cell might respond maximally to a line flashed at a particular tilt. If the line is tilted further—say from a 2 o'clock to a 3 o'clock or 1 o'clock position—the cell quiets down (see Figure 6–13). Thus the feature detector cells record amazingly specific features that are abstracted from the visual information taken in by the eye. These cells pass this information to other cells that respond only when a more complex pattern, such as a particular angle formed by two lines, is present. Higher level brain cells have even been found that respond selectively to specific complex visual stimuli such as a face or an arm movement in a particular direction. Psychologist David Perrett and his colleagues (1988) report that for biologically important objects and events, monkey brains (and surely ours as well) have a "vast visual encyclopedia" distributed throughout their individual cells.

The precise nature of the features and patterns that brain cells detect is currently being debated. New research suggests that any image, such as a face, can be broken down into simple wave patterns of changing light intensity. These component waves can be mathematically described. Thus in seeing, the brain may actually be processing mathematical-like codes that represent a perceived image (Kosslyn, 1987).

This emerging scientific understanding of vision illustrates why neuropsychologist Roger Sperry (1985) can write that the "insights of science give added, not lessened, reasons for awe, respect, and reverence." Consider: As you look at someone, the visual information is broken down into millions of neural impulses, then reassembled into its component features, and finally—in some as yet mysterious way—composed into a consciously perceived image, which is then compared with previously stored images and recognized as, for example, your grandmother. The whole process (see Figure 6–14) is as complex as taking a car apart, piece by piece, transporting it to a different location, and then having specialized workers reconstruct it. Moreover, the dimensions of vision—color, depth, movement, form—are processed separately before somehow being reunited (Livingstone & Hubel, 1988). That all of this happens instantly, effortlessly, and continuously is indeed awesome.

Figure 6–13 Electrodes record the responses of individual cells in this monkey's visual cortex to different visual stimuli. Hubel and Wiesel won the Nobel Prize for their discovery that most cells in the visual cortex respond only to particular features—for example, to the edge of a surface, or to a line at a 30-degree angle in the upper right part of the field of vision. Higher level detector cells, which integrate information from these simpler ones, are triggered only by more complex features.

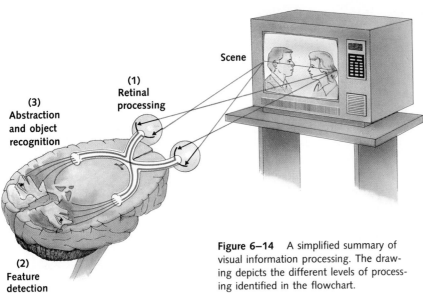

Figure 6–14 A simplified summary of visual information processing. The drawing depicts the different levels of processing identified in the flowchart.

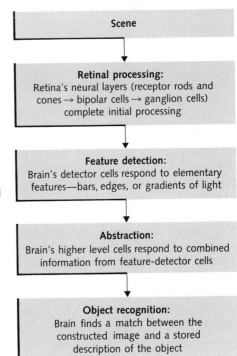

Scene

Retinal processing:
Retina's neural layers (receptor rods and cones → bipolar cells → ganglion cells) complete initial processing

Feature detection:
Brain's detector cells respond to elementary features—bars, edges, or gradients of light

Abstraction:
Brain's higher level cells respond to combined information from feature-detector cells

Object recognition:
Brain finds a match between the constructed image and a stored description of the object

COLOR VISION

In the study of vision, one of the most fundamental and intriguing mysteries is how we see the world in color—and in such a multitude of colors. Our difference threshold for colors is so low that we can discriminate some 7 million differing shades of color (Geldard, 1972).

At least most of us can. The vision of about 1 in 50 people is color deficient—and that person is probably a male, because the defect is genetically sex-linked (Gouras, 1985). To understand why some people have color-deficient vision we must first understand how normal color vision works.

Modern detective work on the mystery of color vision began in the nineteenth century when Hermann von Helmholtz built on the insights of an English physicist, Thomas Young. Recognizing a clue in the fact that any color can be arrived at through some combinations of light waves of three primary colors—red, green, and blue—Young and Helmholtz inferred that the eye must therefore have three types of receptors, one for each of these three primary colors (see Figure 6–15).

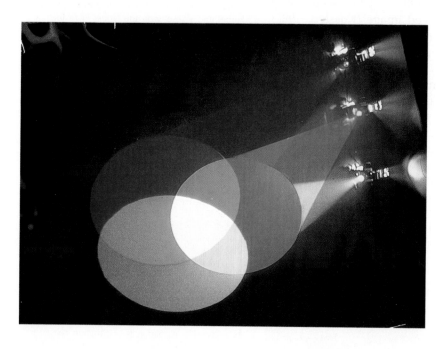

Figure 6–15   The three basic colors of light can be mixed to create other colors. For example, red and green combine to create yellow. All three basic colors combine to create white.

A century later, researchers measured the response of various cones to different color stimuli and confirmed the *Young-Helmholtz trichromatic (three-color) theory,* which simply states that the retina has three types of color receptors, each especially sensitive to one of three colors: red, green, or blue. When combinations of these cones are stimulated, other colors are perceived. For example, there are no receptors for yellow, yet when both red- and green-sensitive cones are stimulated, we see yellow. Most people with color-deficient vision are not actually "color blind"; nearly always they simply lack functioning red- or green-sensitive cones, making it difficult to distinguish red and green as in Figure 6–16 (Boynton, 1979).

Soon after Young and von Helmholtz proposed the trichromatic theory, however, physiologist Ewald Hering pointed out that other parts of the color vision mystery remained unsolved. For example, if we see yellow as a result of stimulation of red- and green-sensitive receptors, how is it that people who are color blind to red and green

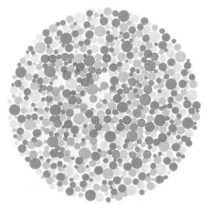

Figure 6–16   Color-deficient vision. People who suffer red-green blindness have trouble perceiving the number within the design above.

can often see yellow? And why does yellow appear to be a pure color and not a mixture of red and green, as purple does of red and blue? Hering found his clue to the answers in the well-known occurrence of afterimages. When you stare at a green square for a while and then look at a white sheet of paper, you will see red, green's "opponent color." Stare at a yellow square and you will later see its opponent color, blue, on the white paper (as in the demonstration of Figure 6–17). Hering surmised that there were two additional color processes, one responsible for red versus green perception, and one for yellow versus blue. (Not so coincidentally, the four opponent colors are the same four colors into which our brains divide the continuum of colors in the color spectrum.)

A century later, researchers have confirmed Hering's **opponent-process theory.** After visual information leaves the receptor cells it is analyzed in terms of the opponent colors red and green and blue and yellow, and also black and white. So if you detect one of these colors at a particular point on the retina, you cannot simultaneously detect the opposing color at the same point; you therefore cannot see a greenish-red.

Psychologist Russell DeValois (DeValois & DeValois, 1975) demonstrated opponent processes in research with monkeys, whose visual system is similar to our own. DeValois measured the activity of single neurons in a portion of the thalamus (where impulses from the retina are relayed en route to the visual cortex) and found that some are turned "on" by red, but turned "off" by green. Others are turned on by green, but off by red.

Opponent processes explain afterimages, such as seeing red stripes after staring at the green-striped flag. White light is made up of light waves of all colors, including green and red. So what happens when we look at white after tiring our green response? Only the red part of the green/red pairing fires normally. And even if we can't discriminate red from green, we will see yellow when the blue component of the blue/yellow system is inhibited.

The present solution to the mystery of color vision is therefore roughly this: Color processing occurs in two stages. The retina's red, green, and blue cones respond in varying degrees to different color stimuli, as the Young-Helmholtz trichromatic theory suggested. Their signals are then processed by the nervous system's opponent-process cells, en route to the visual cortex.

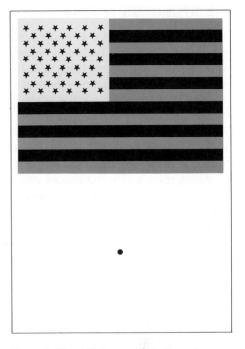

Figure 6–17   Afterimage effect. Stare at the center of the flag for a minute and then shift your eyes to the dot in the white space below it. What do you see?

HEARING

Like all our senses, our hearing, or **audition,** is highly adaptive. We hear a wide range of sounds, but we best hear sounds whose frequency lies within a range that corresponds to the range of the human voice. We are also remarkably sensitive to faint sounds, an obvious boon to our ancestors' survival when hunting or being hunted. (Were our ears any more sensitive, we would hear a constant hiss from the movement of air molecules.) Moreover, we are acutely sensitive to differences in sounds. We can easily detect differences among thousands of human voices, which helps us instantly recognize the voice of almost anyone we know. For hearing as for seeing, the fundamental question is, how do we do it? How do we transduce sound energy into neural messages that the brain interprets as a particular sound coming from a particular place?

THE STIMULUS INPUT: SOUND WAVES

The stimulus energy for hearing is sound waves, air-pressure waves composed of moving bands of compressed and expanded air. These pressure waves are something like the ripples on a pond circling out from where a tossed stone has broken the surface of the water. The height, or *amplitude,* of the waves determines their *loudness;* the greater the amplitude, the louder the sound. For sound as for light, we can tolerate stimulus intensities a trillion times more intense than the faintest detectable stimulus. The length and therefore the *frequency* of these waves determines their *pitch:* The longer the waves, the lower the pitch; the shorter the waves, the higher the pitch. A piccolo produces much shorter waves than a kettledrum.

But rather than being of one pure frequency, most sound waves are a complex mixture of many frequencies. A piano and a clarinet can both produce a pitch of middle C, but neither is pure middle C. It is the *complexity* of mixing in those "other frequencies" that provides the *timbre,* or tone color, of a sound. Complexity enables you to tell that one middle C has come from a piano, the other from a clarinet.

Physical property	Perceptual dimension	
	Color	*Sound*
Wavelength/ Frequency	Hue	Pitch
Amplitude (Intensity)	Brightness	Loudness
Complexity	Vividness of color	Timbre

The *pitch* of a sound corresponds to the *hue* of light (both being determined by *wavelength* and *frequency*); *loudness* corresponds to *brightness* (both being determined by *amplitude*); *timbre* corresponds to *saturation*, or *vividness* (both being determined by *complexity*).

THE EAR

To hear, we must somehow convert sound waves into neural messages. The human ear accomplishes this feat through an intricate mechanical chain reaction (Figure 6–18). First, the visible outer ear channels the sound waves through the auditory canal toward the eardrum, a tight membrane that vibrates in step with the waves. The *middle ear* then amplifies the eardrum's vibrations by transmitting them via a piston made of three tiny bones (the hammer, anvil, and stirrup) to a coiled tube in the *inner ear* called the *cochlea* (KOCK-lee-uh). The incoming vibrations cause the cochlea's membrane (the oval window) to vibrate the fluid that fills this tube. This motion causes ripples in the basilar membrane, which is lined with hair cells, so named because of their tiny hairlike projections. The rippling of the basilar membrane in turn bends these hairs, triggering impulses in the nerve fibers attached to the hair cells. Through this mechanical chain of events, sound waves cause the hair cells of the inner ear to send neural messages up to the brain's auditory cortex (see Figure 2–15 on page 40).

How Do We Perceive Pitch?

How do we know whether a sound is the high-pitched chirp of a bird or the low-pitched roar of a truck? Current thinking on how we discriminate pitch, like current thinking on how we discriminate color, includes aspects of two theories. *Place theory* presumes that we hear different pitches because sound waves of various frequencies trigger activity at different places along the cochlea's basilar membrane. Thus the brain can determine the pitch of a sound by recognizing the place on the membrane from which it receives neural signals. When Georg von Békésy (1957) cut holes in the cochleas of guinea pigs and human cadavers and looked inside with a microscope, he discovered that high-frequency waves triggered activity mostly near the beginning of the cochlea's membrane, a discovery that contributed to his 1961 Nobel Prize. Place theory could thus explain how we hear high-pitched sounds, but it fails to explain how we hear low-pitched sounds, because the neural signals they generate are not so neatly localized in one place on the basilar membrane.

The ear's exquisite sensitivity allows us to detect vibrations of the eardrum as tiny as 0.0000000000003 meter, which is roughly the diameter of a hydrogen molecule (Kaufman, 1979).

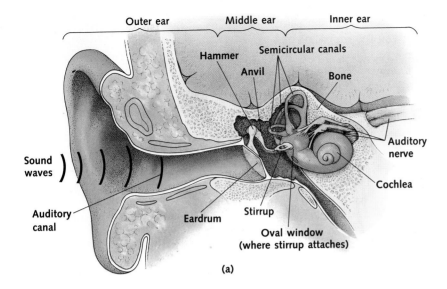

(a)

Figure 6–18   How sound waves are transformed into nerve impulses in the ear. (a) Sound waves are funneled by the outer ear to the eardrum. The bones of the middle ear amplify and relay the eardrum's vibrations through the oval window into the fluid-filled cochlea. (b) The resulting waves in the cochlear fluid cause the basilar membrane to ripple, bending the hair cells on its surface. Hair cell movement sets off impulses in the nerve cells at their bases, whose fibers converge to form the auditory nerve. (For clarity the cochlea is shown partially uncoiled.)

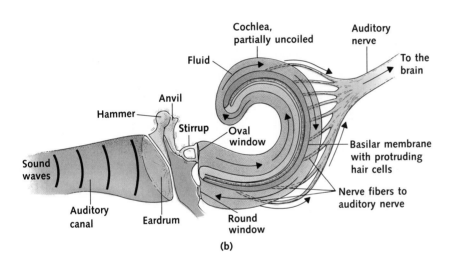

(b)

Frequency theory suggests an equally simple mechanism for the brain's ability to determine pitch. The whole basilar membrane vibrates with the incoming sound wave, thus triggering neural impulses to the brain at the same frequency as the sound wave. If the sound wave has a frequency of 100 waves per second, then 100 pulses per second travel up the auditory nerve. Thus the brain can determine pitch from the frequency of neural impulses. Unlike place theory, frequency theory can explain how we perceive low pitches. But individual neurons cannot fire faster than 1000 times per second, so how can it explain our sensation of sounds with frequencies above 1000 waves per second (roughly the upper third of a piano keyboard and above)? Enter the volley principle: Like soldiers who alternate firing so that some can shoot while others reload, neural cells can alternate firing and thereby achieve a combined frequency well above 1000 times per second.

Place theory best describes how we sense the very high pitches and frequency theory the lower pitches. Some combination of the two processes apparently handles the intermediate range pitches.

How Do We Locate Sounds?   The slightly different messages sensed by the two microphones used in creating a stereophonic recording mimic the slightly different sound messages received by our two ears. As the placement of our eyes allows us to sense depth visually, the placement of our two ears allows us to enjoy stereophonic ("three-dimensional") hearing. If a car to our right honks its horn, our right ear will receive a more intense sound slightly sooner than the left ear. Given that sound travels 750 miles per hour and our ears are but 6 inches apart, the loudness difference and time lag are extremely small. But the sensitivity of our auditory system is such that our two ears can detect extremely small differences (Brown & Deffenbacher, 1979). A just noticeable difference in the direction from which two sounds come corresponds to a time difference of just 0.000027 second!

So how well do you suppose we do at locating a sound that is equidistant from our two ears, such as those that come from directly ahead, behind, overhead, or beneath us? The answer is not very well, because such sounds strike the two ears simultaneously. You can experience this by sitting with eyes closed while a friend snaps fingers at various locations around your head. You easily point to the sound when it comes from either side, but will probably make mistakes when it comes from directly ahead, behind, above, or below. And that is why when trying to pinpoint a sound you find it helpful to cock your head, ensuring that your two ears receive different messages.

HEARING LOSS

The ear's intricate and delicate structure makes it vulnerable to damage. Problems with the mechanical system by which sound wave vibrations reach the cochlea cause *conduction deafness.* For example, if the eardrum is punctured or if the tiny bones of the middle ear lose their flexibility, the ear's conduction of vibrations diminishes. A hearing aid may restore hearing by amplifying the vibrations.

Problems with the cochlea's receptors or with the auditory nerve can cause *nerve deafness.* Once neural tissue is destroyed, no hearing aid can restore its functioning. This type of deafness has three causes—disease, biological changes linked with aging (Figure 6–19), and prolonged exposure to ear-splitting noise or music. Hearing losses with age are especially pronounced in the higher frequencies. To older adults, birds seem to chirp more softly and whispered conversation becomes frustratingly unintelligible.

The barn owl hardly has to cock its head to ensure that each ear receives a different message. The right ear and its opening are directed slightly upward; the left ear and its opening, slightly downward. This built-in asymmetry enables the barn owl to pinpoint location of sound not only horizontally, but vertically as well, making this species the successful nighttime hunter that it is. Even the faint sound of a field mouse scurrying through the grass provides enough information to allow the owl to locate its prey with deadly accuracy.

"One of the strange facts of life is that people, while they are equipped with eyelids, do not have ear lids. Unless they are deaf, they have no escape from the sounds which others make."

Philosopher D. Elton Trueblood (1983)

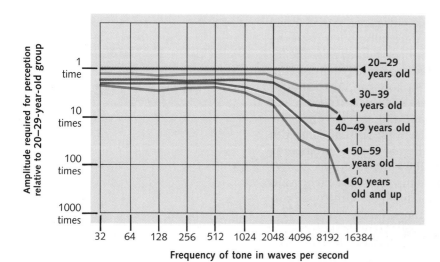

Figure 6–19   Elderly people tend to hear low frequencies well but suffer hearing loss for high frequencies. This high-frequency loss has been linked to nerve degeneration near the beginning of the basilar membrane. Which explanation of hearing does this confirm, place or frequency theory?

NOISE

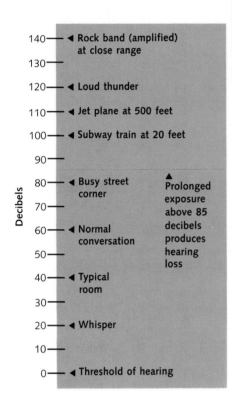

Decibels	
140 —	◄ Rock band (amplified) at close range
130 —	
120 —	◄ Loud thunder
110 —	◄ Jet plane at 500 feet
100 —	◄ Subway train at 20 feet
90 —	
80 —	◄ Busy street corner
70 —	
60 —	◄ Normal conversation
50 —	
40 —	◄ Typical room
30 —	
20 —	◄ Whisper
10 —	
0 —	◄ Threshold of hearing

▲ Prolonged exposure above 85 decibels produces hearing loss

Figure 6–20 The intensity of some common sounds, measured in decibels.

Urban life is noisy. Traffic roars. Factory machines clatter. Jackhammers tear up pavement. Escaping to more pleasant sounds, runners are driven by the beat of intense music over their headphones.

But the intensity of that sound may, in the long run, cause a serious problem. Brief exposure to extremely intense sounds, such as gunfire near one's ear, and prolonged exposure to intense sounds, such as amplified music, can alter or destroy the receptor cells and auditory nerves for sound (Backus, 1977). For some rock musicians, the sad truth is that, while rock and roll is here to stay, their hearing may not be. It has been found that prolonged exposure to sounds above 85 decibels produces hearing loss (see Figure 6–20). (**Decibels** are the physical measure of sound energy. The absolute threshold for hearing is arbitrarily defined as 0 decibels.)

Noise may affect not only our hearing, but our behavior as well. On tasks requiring alert performance, many experiments have shown that people in noisy surroundings work less efficiently and make more errors (Broadbent, 1978). People who live with continual noise in factories, in homes near airports, and in apartments adjacent to trains and highways also suffer elevated rates of stress-related disorders such as high blood pressure, anxiety, and feelings of helplessness (Cohen & others, 1986). But is it the noise that causes the stress?

Laboratory experiments on the psychological effects of noise have suggested an answer. In one such experiment, David Glass and Jerome Singer (1972) recreated the noise of city life by tape-recording the chattering of office machines and of people speaking various languages. While working at various tasks, people heard this noise, played either loudly or softly, either at predictable or unpredictable intervals. Regardless of the conditions, the people soon adapted to the noise and on most tasks performed well. However, having coped with the noise, those who had been exposed to the *unpredictable* loud noise later made more errors on a proofreading task and reacted more quickly to frustration. Results such as these suggest that noise is most stressful when it is unanticipated or uncontrollable. That explains why the unpredictable and uncontrollable blaring of someone else's stereo can be so much more upsetting than the same decibels from your own.

(a)

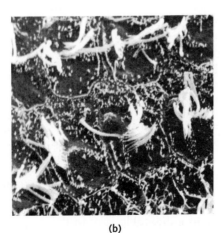

(b)

Warning: Rock concerts can be dangerous to your guinea pig (and you). These scanning electron micrographs of the hair cells of a guinea pig before (a) and after (b) exposure to 24 hours of loud noise (comparable to that of a loud rock concert) testify to its destructive effects.

THE OTHER SENSES

For humans, seeing and hearing are the major senses. We depend on them, particularly for communication. Our brains give these two senses priority in the allocation of cortical tissue. For other animals, the priorities differ. Sharks and dogs rely on their extraordinary senses of smell, which are partly facilitated by the large amount of their cortexes devoted to smell. Nevertheless, without our sense of touch, our senses of taste and smell, and our senses of body motion and position, we humans would be seriously handicapped, and our capacities for enjoying the world would be devastatingly diminished.

TOUCH

Our "sense of touch" is actually a mix of at least four distinct skin senses—pressure, warmth, cold, and pain. Touching various spots on the skin with a soft hair, a warm or cool wire, and a pin point, reveals that some spots are especially sensitive to pressure, others to warmth, others to cold, and still others to pain. Within the skin there are different types of specialized nerve endings. Does that mean that each type is a receptor for one of the basic skin senses, much as the cone receptors of the eye correspond to the basic colors of light?

To answer this question, researchers have compared different sensitive spots on the skin with the particular receptors located at those spots. Surprisingly, there is no simple relationship between what we feel at a given spot and the type of specialized nerve ending found there. Except for pressure, which does have identifiable receptors, the relationship between warmth, cold, and pain and the receptors that respond to them remains a mystery.

Other skin sensations are variations of the basic ones. Stroking adjacent pressure spots creates a tickle. Repeated gentle stroking of a pain spot will create an itching sensation. Touching adjacent cold and pressure spots triggers a sensation of wetness which you can experience for yourself by touching dry but cold metal. Stimulating nearby cold and warmth spots produces a feeling of "hot." Cold spots respond either to very low or very high temperatures. Thus we sense hot when a high temperature activates both warm and cold spots. We have no special "hot spots" (see Figure 6–21).

Pain   Pain is the body's way of telling us that something has gone wrong. It draws our attention to a burn, a break, or a rupture, and tells us to change our behavior immediately. The few people who are born without the ability to feel pain experience severe injury without ever being alerted by pain's danger signals. More numerous are those who endure chronic pain. The suffering of people with persistent or recurring backaches, arthritis, headaches, and cancer-related pain gives a special impetus to finding the answers to two questions: What is pain? How might it be controlled?

What Is Pain?   Pain is not only a property of the senses—of the region where we feel it—but of the brain as well. People who have had limbs amputated may feel pain in their nonexistent limbs. These "phantom limb sensations" indicate that with pain, as with vision, the brain can interpret incoming neural activity as something it is not.

Unlike vision, however, the pain system is not located in a simple neural cord running from a sensing device to a definable spot in the brain. Moreover, there is no one type of stimulus that triggers pains (as

If you had to give up one sense, which would it be? If you could retain only one sense, which would it be?

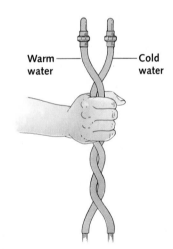

Figure 6–21   Warm + cold = hot. When ice-cold water is passed through one coil and comfortably warm water through another, the combined sensation is perceived as burning hot.

"When belly with bad pains doth swell, It matters nought what else goes well." Sadi, *The Gulistan*, 1258

light triggers vision), and there are no special receptors (as the rods and cones of the retina) for pain. At low intensities, the stimuli that result in pain cause other sensations, including warmth or coolness, smoothness or roughness.

Although no theory of pain explains all the available findings, psychologist Ronald Melzack and biologist Patrick Wall's (1965, 1983) *gate-control theory* remains the most useful model. Melzack and Wall believe that the spinal cord contains a sort of neurological "gate" that either blocks or allows pain signals to pass on to the brain. The spinal cord contains small-diameter nerve fibers that conduct most pain signals and larger fibers that conduct most other sensory signals from the skin. When tissue is injured, the small-diameter fibers activate and open the neural gate, and you feel pain. Activity in the large fibers tends to close the pain gate, turning pain off. Thus, one method of treating chronic pain has been to stimulate (either electrically, by massage, or even by acupuncture) "gate-closing" activity in the large neural fibers. An arthritic patient, for example, may wear a small portable electrical stimulation unit next to a painful area. When the unit stimulates nerves in the area the patient feels a vibrating sensation rather than pain (T. Murphy, 1982).

Melzack and Wall believe that the pain gate can also be closed by information that comes from the brain. These brain-to-spinal cord messages help explain some striking psychological influences on pain. A football player may suffer an injury yet feel no pain until off the field. When we are not attending to pain signals, our experience of pain may be greatly diminished. And pain can stimulate release of the painkilling endorphins described in Chapter 2.

Pain Control   If pain is both a physical and a psychological phenomenon, then it should be treatable through physical and psychological therapies. Depending on the type of symptoms, pain control clinics select one or more therapies from a list that includes drugs, surgery, acupuncture, electrical stimulation, massage, exercise, hypnosis, relaxation training, and thought distraction (Leepson, 1983).

The widely practiced Lamaze method of prepared childbirth combines several of these pain control techniques. They include relaxation (through deep breathing and muscle relaxation), distraction (through focusing attention on, say, a pleasant photograph), and counterstimulation (through gentle massage). After Everett Worthington and his colleagues (1983) trained women in the use of such techniques, the women could more easily tolerate the pain of having their hand in ice water. The women's pain tolerance was even greater when they were encouraged by a trusted "coach," as Lamaze-trained women are by their husbands or an intimate friend during childbirth. Other studies, too, have used the ice water technique for measuring pain tolerance. These studies confirm that distracting people with pleasant images ("think of a warm, comfortable environment") or drawing their attention away from the painful stimulation ("count backward by three's") increases their pain tolerance (McCaul & Malott, 1984).

The same principles operate in health-care situations. A well-trained nurse will distract needle-shy patients with chatter and may ask them to look away as the needle is inserted. For hospitalized patients, a pleasing window view of natural vegetation may have a similarly relaxing and distracting effect. In examining the records of one Pennsylvania hospital, Roger Ulrich (1984) discovered that surgery patients assigned to rooms that looked out on trees required less pain medication and had shorter stays than did those assigned to identical rooms that overlooked a brick wall.

"Pain is increased by attending to it."
Charles Darwin,
Expression of Emotions in Man and Animals, 1872

Although Lamaze training reduces labor pain, most Lamaze patients request a local anesthetic during labor. Some—having expected a "natural, painless birth"—feel needless guilt and failure (Melzack, 1984). Melzack therefore advocates—as does the Lamaze program itself—childbirth training that prepares a woman "to cope with an event which is often extremely painful and, at the same time, one of the most fulfilling peak experiences in her life."

MATTER OVER MIND

The phenomenon of firewalking has become a hot topic in the popular media. For $60 or so we can take a "mind over matter" class that supposedly enables us to alter our body's chemistry. The "proof": walking on red-hot coals without feeling pain or being burned. The psychological result: a newfound capacity to conquer one's fears. "If I can do something that's supposed to be impossible," says the elated firewalker, "I can do almost anything."

Skeptical scientists have taken a cool look at firewalking (Dennett, 1985). The secret, they report, lies not in any mental power to alter the senses but in the poor heat conductivity of the wood coals. Think of a cake baking in a 375° oven. Touch the aluminum cake tin and you'll get burned; touch the cake—like wood, a poor heat conductor—and you'll be okay. Of course, cakes and coals do conduct some heat, so you'd better not stay in touch with them too long or you will get burned. Some have learned the hard way that, indeed, he who hesitates is lost. But the 2 seconds or less that it takes to quickstep across hot embers puts each foot in contact with the coals for only a fraction of a second, and less than a second total time per foot. Confident of these facts—and that wetting the feet before the firewalk provides further insulation—skeptical scientists have themselves performed the feat without the "mind over matter" training.

TASTE

Like our sense of touch, our sense of taste involves four basic sensations—sweet, sour, salty, and bitter (McBurney & Gent, 1979). All other tastes are mixtures of these. Investigators have been frustrated in their search for specialized nerve fibers for each of the four basic taste sensations, but they have found spots on the surface of the tongue that tend to have special sensitivities—the tip of the tongue for sweet and salty tastes, the back of the tongue for bitter (see Figure 6–22).

Taste is a chemical sense. Inside the little bumps on the top and sides of your tongue are 200 or more taste buds. Each contains a pore that catches dissolved food chemicals which are sensed by the fifty taste receptor cells that project antennalike hairs into the pore. Some of these receptors respond mostly to sweet-tasting molecules, others to salty-, sour-, or bitter-tasting ones. It doesn't take much to trigger a response. When a stream of water is pumped across the tongue, the addition of a concentrated salty or sweet taste for but one-tenth of a second can usually be detected (Kelling & Halpern, 1983). When a friend asks for "just a taste" of your soft drink, you can squeeze off the straw after a mere fraction of a second.

Taste receptors reproduce themselves every week, so if you burn your tongue with hot food it matters little. However, as you grow older, the receptors change; their number declines because the number of taste buds decreases, and so taste sensitivity declines as well (Cowart, 1981). (This is one reason why adults enjoy strong-tasting foods that children resist.) The decline in taste sensitivities may be exacerbated by behaviors, such as smoking or alcohol use, that deaden the taste buds.

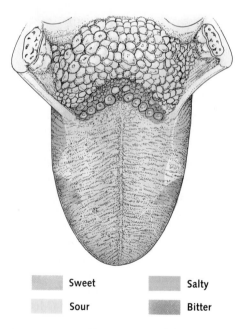

	Sweet		Salty
	Sour		Bitter

Figure 6–22 Different regions of the tongue have extra sensitivity to one or more of the four basic taste sensations—sweet, sour, salty, and bitter.

Although taste buds are essential for taste, there is more to taste than meets the tongue. Hold your nose, close your eyes, and have someone feed you various foods. A piece of apple may then be indistinguishable from a piece of raw potato; a piece of steak may taste like cardboard. To savor a taste, we normally exhale the aroma through the nose—which is why eating is not much fun when you have a bad cold. This is *sensory interaction* at work—the principle that one sense may be influenced by another. Taste is influenced by smell. Similarly, we correctly perceive the location of the voice directly in front of us partly because we also *see* that the person is in front of us, not behind, above, or beneath us.

SMELL

Smell (olfaction) is an intimate sense. To smell someone we must inhale something of that person. Like taste, smell is a chemical sense. We smell something when air-carried molecules of a substance reach a tiny cluster of 5 million receptor cells at the top of each of our nasal cavities (Figure 6–23). These olfactory receptor cells respond selectively to the smell of bacon crackling, to a whisp of smoke, to a friend's fragrance, and instantly alert the brain, switching on one memory after another. Even nursing infants and mothers quickly learn to recognize each others' scents (McCarthy, 1986). The ability to identify scents peaks at about age 20 and gradually declines thereafter (see Figure 6–24 on page 162).

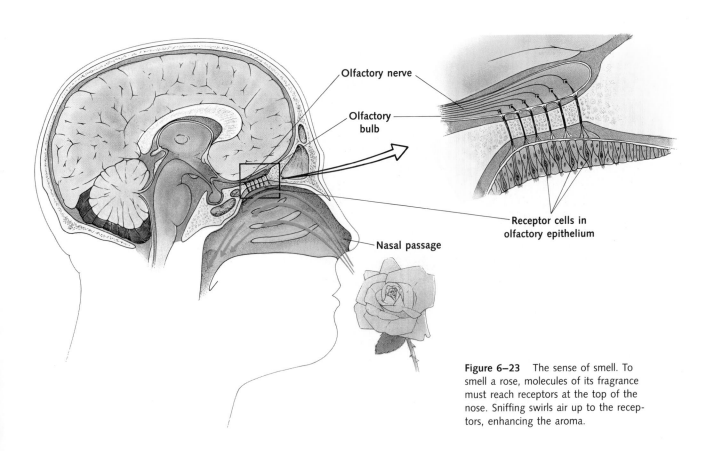

Olfactory nerve

Olfactory bulb

Receptor cells in olfactory epithelium

Nasal passage

Figure 6–23   The sense of smell. To smell a rose, molecules of its fragrance must reach receptors at the top of the nose. Sniffing swirls air up to the receptors, enhancing the aroma.

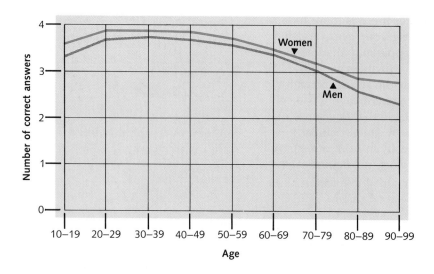

Figure 6–24 Age, sex, and sense of smell. Among the 1.2 million people who responded to a *National Geographic* scratch and sniff survey, women and younger adults most successfully identified six sample odors. (From Wysocki & Gilbert, 1989.)

Precisely how olfactory receptors work is still a mystery. Unlike light, which can be separated into its spectral colors, an odor cannot be separated into more elemental odors. Thus unlike the retina, which can detect myriad colors with sensory cells dedicated to red, green, or blue, olfactory receptors must recognize odors individually.

As any dog or cat with a good nose could tell us, we each have our own identifiable chemical signature (with one noteworthy exception: A dog will follow the tracks of one identical twin as though they had been made by the other [Thomas, 1974]). Animals, which have many olfactory receptors, may also communicate and navigate through their sense of smell. Long before the shark can see its prey, or the moth its mate, odors direct the way.

Our olfactory powers are paltry in comparison to a bloodhound's. Bloodhounds, which have relatively poor eyesight, have followed a person's trail for over 100 miles and can detect someone's scent as much as 3 or 4 days later. Judging by their olfactory nerve endings, bloodhounds are thought to be about 2 million times more sensitive than human beings are to odors.

BODY POSITION AND MOVEMENT

With only the five familiar senses we have so far considered, we would be helpless. We could not put food in our mouths, stand up, or reach out and touch someone. To know just how to move your arms to grasp someone's hand, you first need to know the current position of your arms and hands and then be aware of their changing positions as you move them. To take just one step requires feedback from and instructions to some 200 muscles.

Humans come equipped with millions of such position and motion sensors. They are all over our bodies—in the muscles, tendons, and joints—and they are continually providing our brains with information. If we twist our wrists 1 degree, the sensors immediately report it. This sense of the position and movement of body parts is called *kinesthesis* (kin-ehs-STHEE-sis).

A companion sense called *equilibrium* monitors the position and movement of the whole body. The receptors for our sense of equilibrium are in the inner ear. The *semicircular canals,* which look rather like a three-dimensional pretzel (see Figure 6–18a, page 155), and the *vestibular sacs,* which connect the canals with the cochlea, contain substances that move when the head rotates or tilts. This movement stimulates hairlike receptors in these organs of the inner ear, which trigger messages to the brain that enable us continually to sense our body position and thereby maintain our balance. If you've been twirling around and come to an abrupt halt, the fluid in your semicircular canals and your kinesthetic receptors do not immediately return to their neutral states. This aftereffect fools your dizzy brain with the sensation that you're still spinning.

Olympic gold medalist Brian Boitano demonstrates his highly developed equilibrium and kinesthetic sense.

SENSORY RESTRICTION

Imagine that one of your sensory windows on the world was closed. Would your other senses partially make up for the loss? People with sensory deficits show us the rich potential of the senses. Blind people cope by making greater use of their sense of hearing—for example, by attending to echoes bouncing off obstacles in order to determine their location and size. (Close your eyes and immediately you will notice your attention being drawn to extraneous sounds.)

The loss of a sense is but one type of sensory restrictions. Another is sensory monotony—the relatively unchanging sensory input experienced by prisoners in solitary confinement, nighttime truck drivers and airline pilots, and animals in barren zoos.

To investigate how sensory restriction affects us, experimenters have put several thousand people through controlled, temporary simulations of such conditions. Some have spent several days in monotonous environments—small rooms where light and sound are unchanging. Others have passed time in dark, silent rooms, deprived of normal sensory input. The initial experiments on what was formerly called "sensory deprivation" produced some rather bizarre and widely publicized findings (Heron, 1957). The subjects, lying on beds and wearing translucent goggles to diffuse the light, typically began the experiment in good spirits. Here was a chance to make some easy money while enjoying a time for relaxation and creative thinking. However, before long the subjects became somewhat disoriented, many experienced hallucinations, and some became susceptible to piped-in tape-recorded messages arguing for the reality of ghosts.

As sometimes happens in science, manipulating one factor simultaneously manipulates other hidden factors. Are the effects of spending a day or two in a monotonous environment caused by the sensory restriction, or might they result from social isolation, confinement, or stressful procedures? The dramatic reports from early experiments prompted many more investigations, most of which produced less newsworthy results (Suedfeld & Kristeller, 1982).

"Ears are eyes to the blind."
   Sophocles,
   Oedipus at Colonus, 407 B.C.

Those who lose one means of sensory input generally become more attentive to input from their other senses.

In fact, researchers have found that most people are not negatively affected by sensory restriction. Rather, the experience seems to reduce stress and to help people become more open to being influenced. For example, in experiments with smokers and overweight people at the University of British Columbia, Peter Suedfeld (1980) found that restricted sensory input can help people modify their behavior. Suedfeld (1975) emphasized that during voluntary sensory restriction persuasion does "not reach the awesome proportions which many fiction writers (and some scientists who are writing fiction without knowing it) have indicated." But he also reported that people who wanted to alter their behavior often were able to gain increased self-control after 24 hours of what he aptly called REST—Restricted Environmental Stimulation Therapy.

In one such experiment conducted by Allan Best and Suedfeld (1982), smokers attended antismoking instructional classes and also listened to messages concerning smoking while spending 24 hours lying on beds in quiet, dark rooms (rising only to drink a liquid diet available through tubes or to use toilets next to the beds). In the week that followed, none relapsed to smoking. A year later, two-thirds were still abstaining—double the number of abstainers who had received the instruction without the day of REST.

In other times and places, periods of solitude and sensory restriction have similarly been judged important for human fulfillment. Sensory restriction is a traditional component of the "quiet therapies" of Japan (Reynolds, 1982, 1986). For example, Morita therapy for depressed or anxious people sometimes begins with a week of bed rest and meditation and then progresses to assigned light tasks. The religious visions of Moses, Mohammed, and Buddha are reported to have occurred during times of solitude and contemplation. As living creatures we require sensory stimulation, but there are also times when we can benefit from the peace and relaxation of restricted stimulation.

Sensory restriction can, in small doses, provide healing relaxation. This flotation tank illustrates one way to experience REST.

"It is in silence and not in commotion, in solitude and not in crowds that God best likes to reveal Himself."
   Thomas Merton,
   The Silent Life, 1957

SUMMING UP

To study sensation is to study an ageless question: How does the world out there get represented inside our heads? Put another way, how are the external stimuli that strike our bodies transformed into messages that our brains comprehend?

SENSING THE WORLD: SOME BASIC PRINCIPLES

Thresholds   Each species comes equipped with sensitivities that enable it to survive and thrive. We sense only a portion of the sea of energy that surrounds us, but to this portion we are exquisitely sensitive. Our absolute threshold for any stimulus is the minimum stimulation that is detectable 50 percent of the time. Do we ever react to stimuli that are not only subthreshold (subliminal), but so weak that we could never consciously perceive them? Although recent experiments reveal that we can process some information from stimuli too weak to be recognized, the restricted conditions under which this occurs would not enable unscrupulous opportunists to exploit us with subliminal messages.

To survive and thrive, an organism must also have difference thresholds low enough to detect minute changes in important stimuli. In humans, difference thresholds (also called just noticeable differences, or jnd's) increase as a proportion of the magnitude of the stimulus—a principle known as Weber's Law.

Sensory Adaptation   The phenomenon of sensory adaptation helps to focus our attention on changing stimulation by diminishing our sensitivity to constant or routine odors, sounds, and so forth.

Each of our senses must receive stimulation, transduce (transform) it into neural signals, and transmit the neural signals to the cortex of the brain.

VISION

The Stimulus Input: Light Energy The energies we experience as light are a slice from a broad spectrum of electromagnetic waves. After being admitted into the eye through a cameralike lens, light waves strike the retina. Where the light rays converge in the eye determines sharpness of image, or visual acuity. Acuity is often diminished by distortions in the shape of the eyeball (which cause the focusing problems of nearsightedness and farsightedness) and by other changes linked to aging.

The retina's rods and cones convert the light energy to neural impulses, which are coded by the retina before being transmitted by the optic nerve to the brain. In the cortex, individual cells respond to specific features of the visual stimulus, and their information is apparently pooled by higher level brain cells for interpretation.

Color Vision Research on how we see color supports two theories from the nineteenth century. First, as the Young-Helmholtz three-color theory suggests, the retina contains three types of cones, each of which is most sensitive to one of the three basic colors (red, green, or blue). Second, as opponent-process theory maintains, the nervous system codes the color-related information from the cones into pairs of opponent colors, as demonstrated by the phenomenon of afterimages and as confirmed by measuring opponent processes within visual neurons.

HEARING

The Stimulus Input: Sound Waves The pressure waves we experience as sound vary in frequency and amplitude, and correspondingly in perceived pitch and loudness.

The Ear Through a mechanical chain of events, sound waves traveling down the auditory canal cause minuscule vibrations in the eardrum. Transmitted via the bones of the middle ear to the fluid-filled cochlea, these vibrations create movement in tiny hair cells, triggering neural messages to the brain. Research on how we hear pitch has provided evidence for both the place theory, which best explains the sensation of high-pitched sounds, and frequency theory, which best explains the sensation of low-pitched sound.

We localize sound by detecting minute differences in the loudness and timing of the sounds received by each ear.

Hearing Loss Hearing losses linked to conduction and nerve disorders can be caused by prolonged exposure to loud noise and by diseases and age-related disorders.

THE OTHER SENSES

Touch Our sense of touch is actually four senses—pressure, warmth, cold, and pain—that combine to produce other sensations, such as "hot." One theory of pain is that a "gate" in the spinal cord either opens to permit pain signals traveling up small nerve fibers to reach the brain or closes to prevent their passage. Because pain is both a physiological and psychological phenomenon, it often can be controlled through a combination of medical and psychological treatments.

Taste Taste, a chemical sense, is likewise a composite of four basic sensations—sweet, sour, salty, and bitter—and of the aromas that interact with information from the taste buds.

Smell Like taste, smell is a chemical sense, but there are no basic sensations for smell, as there are for touch and taste.

Body Position and Movement Finally, our effective functioning requires a kinesthetic sense, which notifies the brain of the position and movement of body parts, and a sense of equilibrium, which monitors the position and movement of the whole body.

SENSORY RESTRICTION

People temporarily or permanently deprived of one of their senses typically compensate by becoming more acutely aware of information from the other senses. Temporary experiences of sensory monotony or sensory restriction have somewhat unpredictable effects. However, the reduction of sensory input often evokes a heightened sensitivity to all forms of sensation, and under supervision may provide a therapeutic boost for those seeking control over problems such as smoking.

TERMS AND CONCEPTS TO REMEMBER

absolute threshold The minimum stimulation that a subject can detect 50 percent of the time.

accommodation The process by which the lens of the eye changes shape to focus the image of near or distant objects on the retina.

acuity The sharpness of vision.

amplitude The maximum height (or depth) of a wave, measured from its midpoint.

audition The sense of hearing.

blind spot The point at which the optic nerve leaves the eye, creating a "blind" spot since no receptor cells are located there.

brightness The psychological dimension of color (its brilliance) that is determined mostly by the intensity of light.

cochlea [KOCK-lee-uh] A coiled, bony, fluid-filled tube in the inner ear through which sound waves trigger nerve impulses.

complexity The mixture of different wavelengths of light or sound. Complexity determines the saturation of light and the timbre of sounds (low complexity = purity).

conduction deafness Hearing loss caused by damage to the mechanical system that conducts sound waves to the cochlea.

cones Receptor cells concentrated near the center of the retina that function in daylight or in well-lit conditions. The cones detect fine detail and give rise to color sensations.

decibel A measure of sound intensity.

difference threshold The minimum difference in stimulation that a subject can detect 50 percent of the time. We experience the difference threshold as a just noticeable difference (jnd).

equilibrium The sense of body movement and position, including the sense of balance.

farsightedness A condition in which faraway objects are seen more clearly than near objects because the image of near objects is focused behind the retina.

feature detectors Nerve cells in the brain that respond to specific features of the stimulus, such as movement, angle, or shape.

fovea The central focal point in the retina, around which the eye's cones cluster.

frequency The number of complete wavelengths that can pass a point in a given time.

frequency theory In hearing, the theory that the rate of pulses traveling up the auditory nerve matches the frequency of a tone, thus enabling us to sense its pitch.

gate-control theory Melzack and Wall's theory that the spinal cord contains a neurological "gate" that blocks or allows pain signals to pass on to the brain; the "gate" is opened by the activity of pain signals traveling up small nerve fibers and closed by activity in larger fibers or by information coming from the brain.

hue The dimension of color that is determined by the wavelength of light; what we know as the color names (blue, green, and so forth).

inner ear The innermost part of the ear, containing the cochlea, semicircular canals, and vestibular sacs.

intensity The amount of energy in a light or sound wave, as determined by the wave's amplitude.

iris A ring of muscle tissue that forms the colored portion of the eye around the pupil and controls the size of the pupil opening.

just noticeable difference (jnd) See *difference threshold*.

kinesthesis [kin-ehs-STHEE-sis] The system for sensing body position and the movement of muscles, tendons, and joints.

lens The transparent structure behind the pupil that changes shape to focus images on the retina.

middle ear The chamber between the eardrum and cochlea containing three tiny bones (hammer, anvil, and stirrup) that concentrate the vibrations of the eardrum on the cochlea.

nearsightedness A condition in which nearby objects are seen more clearly than distant objects because the lens focuses the image of distant objects in front of the retina.

nerve deafness Hearing loss caused by damage to the cochlea's receptor cells or to the auditory nerves.

opponent-process theory The theory that color vision depends on pairs of opposing retinal processes (red-green, yellow-blue, white-black). For example, some cells are stimulated by green and inhibited by red; others are stimulated by red and inhibited by green.

optic nerve The nerve that carries neural impulses from the eye to the brain.

perception The process of organizing and interpreting sensory information, enabling us to recognize meaningful objects and events.

pitch The highness or lowness of a tone; depends on frequency.

place theory In hearing, the theory that links the pitch we hear with the place where the cochlea's membrane is stimulated.

pupil The adjustable opening in the center of the eye through which light enters.

retina The light-sensitive inner surface of the eye, containing the receptor rods and cones plus layers of neurons that begin the processing of visual information.

rods Retinal receptors that detect black, white, and gray, especially in peripheral and nighttime vision.

saturation The purity of color, which is greater when complexity (the number of other wavelengths mixed in) is low.

semicircular canals Three curved, fluid-filled structures of the inner ear with receptors that detect body motion.

sensation The process by which certain stimulus energies are detected and encoded.

sensory adaptation Diminished sensitivity with constant stimulation.

sensory interaction The principle that one sense may influence another, as when the smell of food influences its taste.

signal detection The task of judging the presence of a faint stimulus ("signal"). Signal detection researchers assume that there is no single absolute threshold, because the detection of a weak signal depends partly on a person's experience, expectation, motivation, and level of fatigue.

subliminal Below threshold.

timbre The tone color of a sound that distinguishes it from other sounds of the same pitch and loudness, for example the middle C produced by a piano versus the middle C produced by a clarinet.

transduction Conversion of one form of energy into another. In sensation, the transforming of stimulus energies into neural impulses.

vestibular sacs Two structures of the inner ear with receptors that provide the sense of upright body position.

wavelength The distance from the peak of one light or sound wave to the peak of the next. Waves vary in length.

Weber's law The principle that two stimuli must differ by a constant minimum percentage (rather than a constant amount) for their difference to be perceived.

Young-Helmholtz trichromatic (three-color) theory The theory that the retina contains three different color receptors—one most sensitive to red, one to green, one to blue—which in combination can produce the perception of any color.

FOR FURTHER READING

Frisby, J. P. (1980). *Seeing: Illusion, brain and mind.* Oxford: Oxford University Press.

A wonderfully illustrated introduction to the visual system.

Gregory, R. L. (1978). *Eye and brain: The psychology of seeing* (3rd ed.). New York: McGraw-Hill.

The classic popular introduction to vision. An informative and easily readable book.

McBurney, D. H., & Collings, V. B. (1984). *Introduction to sensation and perception* (2nd ed.). Englewood Cliffs, NJ: Prentice-Hall.

A crisp survey, with many everyday examples of how we process sensory information.

CHAPTER 7

Perception

Some 2400 years ago, the philosopher Plato rightly discerned that we perceive objects through the senses with the mind. But *how* does the mind work to create our perceptions? In Chapter 6 we examined the processes by which we sense sights and sounds, tastes and smells. Here our central question is, how do we see not just shapes and colors, but a rose in bloom, a familiar face, a sunset? How do we hear not just a mix of pitches and rhythms, but a child's cry of pain, the hum of distant traffic, a symphony? In short, how do we organize and interpret our sensations so that they become meaningful perceptions?

In the classic version of the now familiar nature-nurture debate, philosophers argued about how these perceptual processes originate—through biological maturation or through experience. On one side were the ***nativists,*** such as the German philosopher Immanuel Kant (1724–1804), who maintained that knowledge comes from our *innate* (inborn) ways of organizing sensory experiences. On the other side were the ***empiricists,*** such as the British philosopher John Locke (1632–1704), who argued that we *learn* how to perceive the world through our experiences of it.

Locke believed that at birth all people's minds are equally blank. If the mind is blank at birth, then all knowledge, including perceptual knowledge, comes through experience. Today, it is generally accepted that perception depends on both nature's endowments and on the experiences that influence what we make of our sensations.

"Let us then suppose the mind to be, as we say, white paper void of all characters, without any ideas:—How comes it to be furnished? . . . To this I answer, in one word, from EXPERIENCE."
John Locke (1690)

PERCEPTUAL ILLUSIONS

During the late 1800s—about the time that psychology was emerging as a distinct discipline—scientists were fascinated with perceptual illusions, and they still are. These misperceptions can provide valuable clues to the ordinary mechanisms of perception. Illusions mislead us by playing on the ways we organize and intepret our sensations. Consider five such perceptual puzzles:

Puzzle 1   Below is the classic illusion created in 1889 by Franz Müller-Lyer. Does either line segment, *AB* or *BC*, appear longer?

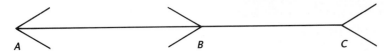

To most people the two segments appear to be the same length. Surprise! They are not. As your ruler can verify, line *AB* is a full one-third longer than line *BC*. Why do our eyes deceive us? (On page 178 we will discover one explanation.)

Puzzle 2 Here we have two unretouched photos of the same boy and dog, in the same room. The camera shows you each of these scenes much as you would see it if you were looking at the room with one eye through a peephole. Why do the boy and dog seem to change size? (Page 179 will reveal why.)

Puzzle 3 Is Gateway Arch in St. Louis taller than it is wide? Or vice versa? To most it appears taller. In truth, its height and width are equal. Once again, seeing is deceiving. Why? (On page 175 we will meet this phenomenon again.)

Puzzle 4 Aircraft pilots, ship captains, and car drivers must judge distances under varying conditions of visibility. To simulate such judgments, psychologist Helen Ross (1975) asked passersby to estimate the distances of white disks she had placed on the lawn at Britain's Hull University. Those who judged the distance in the thick morning fog perceived the disks to be farther away than did those who made their estimates in the midday sunshine. What does this suggest about how we normally judge distances? (Pages 173–176 will discuss distance perception.)

Morning fog

Midday sunshine

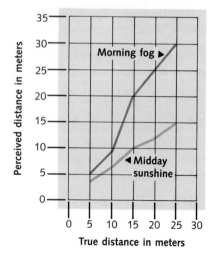

Puzzle 5 Illusions occur with the other senses, too. More than a century ago, the psychologist Wilhelm Wundt was puzzled by the fact that people hear the steady beat of a metronome or clock as if it were a repeating rhythm of two, three, or four beats—not as an unaccented click-click-click-click, which it is, but as, say, CLICK-click CLICK-click

CLICK-click. From the steady beat that strikes the ear, each listener unconsciously shapes an auditory pattern. What perceptual principle is at work here? (See page 180 to find out.)

The mechanisms explaining these illusions will provide an underpinning for our understanding of normal perception. Our emphasis on visual illusions reflects the preeminence of vision among our senses. When there is conflict between visual and other sensory information, vision seems to dominate or "capture" the other senses. We frequently experience this phenomenon of *visual capture* in everyday life. When the sound of a movie comes from a projector behind us, we tend to perceive it as coming from the screen, where we *see* the actors talking. While viewing a roller coaster ride on a giant wraparound movie screen, we may feel the need to brace ourselves, despite the evidence of our motionlessness being supplied by our kinesthetic sense. In both cases, vision captures the other senses.

PERCEPTUAL ORGANIZATION

Early in this century, a number of German psychologists became intrigued with the mind's apparent ability to organize sensations into perceptions. Given a cluster of sensations, the human perceiver tends to organize them into a *gestalt*, a German word meaning a "form" or a "whole." The Gestalt psychologists provided many compelling demonstrations of this ability. Look at Figure 7–1. Note that the individual elements of the figure are really nothing but eight green circles, each containing three white lines. But when we view them all together we see a *whole* form, a "Necker cube." As the Gestalt psychologists were fond of saying, in perception the whole may be different from the sum of its parts. There is far more to perception than meets the senses.

There also is more in this modern version of the Necker cube than you may have noticed. With a little patience in staring at Figure 7–1, you may see several versions and locations of the cube. At first you probably see the X on the front edge of a cube, but after a few moments the cube will reverse and the X will go to the back. Perhaps you see the cube floating in front of the page with the circles behind it (as in Figure 7–2a). But if you stare longer at Figure 7–1, the circles may become holes in the page, through which the cube appears, floating behind it (as in Figure 7–2b). Either way, the position of the cube reverses every few moments. We are looking at eight segmented circles, but organizing them into several coherent images. This demonstrates that a single stimulus can trigger more than one perception. Because the circles can be organized into several coherent images, each equally plausible, the mind switches back and forth from one to the next.

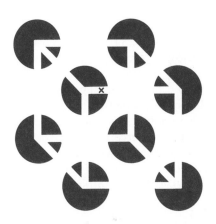

Figure 7–1   What do you see: green circles with white lines or a cube? (From Bradley & others, 1976.)

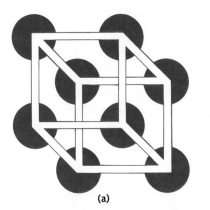

(a)

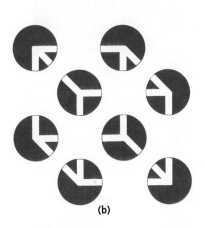

(b)

Figure 7–2   The Necker cube of Figure 7–1 with lines added to clarify its possible locations. Sometimes you perceive the cube in front, with the circles behind it, as in (a). At other times, the cube is floating behind the circles, as in (b). (From Bradley & others, 1976.)

Such demonstrations led the Gestalt psychologists to describe principles by which we organize our sensations into perceptions. As you read about these organizational principles, keep in mind the fundamental truth that they illustrate: Our brains do more than merely register information about the world. Perception is not just opening a shutter and letting a picture print itself on the brain. Always, we are filtering sensory information and constructing our perceptions in ways that make sense to us.

FORM PERCEPTION

To structure incoming sensory information, our minds must perceive objects as separate from other stimuli and as having a meaningful form.

Figure and Ground   When confronted with an object, our perceptual task is to recognize it. To do so, we must first perceive the object, called the *figure,* as distinct from its surroundings, called the *ground.* Among the voices you hear at a party, the one you attend to becomes the figure, all others part of the ground. As you read, the words are the figure; the white paper, the ground. In Figure 7–3, the *figure-ground* relationship continually reverses—but always the stimulus is organized into a figure seen against a ground (either a white vase with a black background or two black profiles on a white background). This reversal demonstrates once more that the same stimulus can trigger more than one perception.

Various artists have studied Gestalt psychology's analysis of the organizational principle of figure and ground and applied it in their art (Teuber, 1974). For example, M. C. Escher's "Day and Night" (Figure 7–4) depicts a slow transformation of ground into figure and figure into ground.

Figure 7–3   The reversible figure-ground relationship. In this vase, created for the 1977 Silver Jubilee of Britain's Queen Elizabeth II, either the profiles of the Queen and Prince Philip (which greet each other from opposite sides of the vase) or the vase itself can be the figure transforming the other element into the background.

Figure 7–4   The transformation of figure into ground. Moving from left to right in M. C. Escher's 1938 woodcut "Day and Night," the figure, the black birds, gradually becomes the ground, the night landscape. Or, from right to left, it is the white birds that begin as figure and become the mirror-image landscape in daylight.

Grouping   Having discriminated figure from ground, we then organize the figure into a meaningful form. To bring order to what we sense and to give it form, our minds seem to follow certain rules for *grouping* stimuli together. Several rules of perceptual organization identified by the Gestalt psychologists illustrate their idea that the perceived whole is different from the mere sum of its parts:

Proximity   If figures are near each other, we tend to group them together. We see below not six separate lines, but three sets of two lines.

Similarity   If figures are similar to each other, we tend to group them together. We see the triangles and circles as columns of similar shapes, not as rows of dissimilar shapes.

Continuity   We tend to perceive smooth, continuous patterns rather than discontinuous ones. This pattern could be a series of alternating semicircles, but we tend to perceive it as a wavy line and a straight line.

Closure   If a figure has gaps, we tend to complete it, filling in the gaps to create a complete, whole object. By filling the gaps we see a whole seashell.

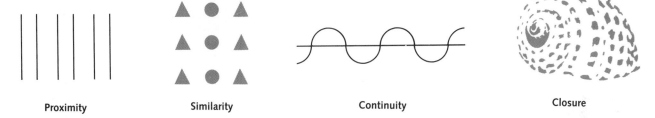

Proximity   Similarity   Continuity   Closure

The grouping principles usually help us perceive reality, but sometimes (see Figure 7–5) they lead us astray.

Reprinted from GAMES Magazine (810 Seventh Avenue, New York, NY 10019). Copyright © 1983 PSC Games Limited Partnership.

Figure 7–5   You probably perceive this doghouse as a gestalt—a whole (though impossible) structure. Actually, as the photo on page 187 indicates, Gestalt principles such as closure lead us to perceive interrupted boards as continuous.

DEPTH PERCEPTION

From the two-dimensional images that fall on our retinas, we somehow manage to organize three-dimensional perceptions. This ability to see objects in three dimensions, called *depth perception,* allows us to estimate their distance from us. At a glance, we can judge the approximate distance of an oncoming car or the depth of the drop-off at the edge of a cliff. This ability seems to be at least partly innate. Eleanor Gibson and Richard Walk (1960) discovered this using a miniature cliff with a drop-off that was covered by sturdy glass. The inspiration for these experiments occurred to Gibson one day as she was eating a picnic lunch at the edge of the Grand Canyon. She wondered if a toddler peering over the rim would perceive the dangerous drop-off and draw back.

Back in their Cornell University laboratory, Gibson and Walk placed infants on the edge of a *visual cliff* (see Figure 7–6) and had their mothers coax them to crawl out on the glass. Most infants refused to do so, preferring to crawl on the "shallow" side, thereby indicating that they could perceive depth. These 6- to 14-month-old infants had had considerable visual experience, but animals with minimal experience—including young kittens, a day-old goat, and newly hatched chicks—responded similarly. What is more, during the first month of life human infants turn to avoid an object coming directly at them but are unbothered by objects approaching at an angle that would not result in a collision (Ball & Tronick, 1971). Thus it seems that part of our ability to perceive depth is innate.

How do we do it? How do we transform two-dimensional retinal images into three-dimensional perceptions? Some of the cues we use require both eyes *(binocular cues),* others are available to each eye separately *(monocular cues).*

Figure 7–6   Eleanor Gibson and Richard Walk devised this miniature cliff with a glass-covered drop-off to determine whether human infants and newborn animals can perceive depth. Even when coaxed, infants are reluctant to venture onto the glass over the cliff, indicating that even the very young can perceive depth.

Binocular Cues   Because our eyes are nearly 3 inches apart, our retinas receive slightly different images of the world. When the brain compares these two images, the amount of *retinal,* or *binocular,* *disparity* (the difference between the two images) provides an important cue to distance. When your finger is held directly in front of your nose, the difference between the two images your retinas receive is great. (You can see this if you close one eye, and then the other.) At greater distance, say when your finger is held at arm's length, the image difference is smaller.

The creators of 3-D movies simulate this disparity by filming two images of the same action simultaneously with two cameras a few inches apart. The two slightly differing movie images of the scene are then projected simultaneously. When viewed with spectacles that allow the left eye to see only the image from the left projector and the right eye the image from the right projector, a 3-D effect is created. The effect mimics the retinal disparity we would have experienced had we been viewing the scene from the two camera perspectives.

Another binocular cue to distance is *convergence,* a muscular cue that indicates the extent to which the eyes turn inward when we look at an object. By noting the angle of convergence, the brain determines whether you are focusing just past your nose, or on this printed page, or on the person across the room.

Monocular Cues   With both eyes open, we can readily and precisely touch the tip of a pen held in front of us; with one eye closed the task becomes noticeably more difficult. This demonstrates the importance of binocular cues in judging the distance of nearby objects. How then do we judge, say, whether a person is 100 feet or 100 yards away? In both cases, each eye receives very similar retinal images while looking straight ahead. At such distances we depend on the following monocular cues to distance:

Relative size   If we assume that two objects are of similar size, we perceive the one that casts the smaller image as farther away.

Overlap   If one object is partially covered by another, we perceive it as farther away. We perceive the smaller deer as closer than the one it partially obscures. (This phenomenon is also called *interposition*.)

Relative size

Overlap

Aerial perspective   We perceive hazy objects as farther away than sharp, clear objects. (Recall from Puzzle 4 the effects of fog on judging distance, page 170.)

Texture gradients   We perceive a gradual but continuous change from a coarser, more distinct to a finer, less distinct textural element as an indication of increasing distance.

Aerial perspective

Texture gradient

Relative height   We perceive objects higher in our field of vision as farther away. This may contribute to the illusion that vertical dimensions are longer than identical horizontal dimensions (as we saw in Puzzle 3, the St. Louis Gateway Arch, page 170). Is the vertical line here longer, shorter, or equal in length to the horizontal line? Measure and see.

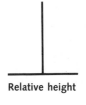

Relative height

Direction of
passenger's motion

Relative motion

Relative motion   As our heads move, stable objects in our environment appear to move relative to us. If while riding in a car you fix your gaze on some object, say a tree, you will see that the objects in front of the tree (the fixation point) appear to be moving backward. The nearer an object is, the faster it will appear to move. Objects beyond the fixation point will appear to be moving in your direction at a speed that decreases as the object gets farther away. Your brain uses these speed and direction clues to determine the objects' relative distances. (This phenomenon is also called *motion parallax*.)

Linear perspective

Linear perspective   We interpret the apparent convergence of parallel lines as a clue to distance. The more the convergence, the greater the perceived distance. Linear perspective can contribute to rail crossing accidents, for example, by leading people to overestimate a train's distance (Leibowitz, 1985). (A train's massive size also makes it appear to be moving more slowly than it is.)

Relative brightness   Nearby objects reflect more light to our eyes. Thus, given two identical objects, the dimmer one will seem farther away. This illusion, too, can contribute to accidents, as when a fog-shrouded vehicle, or one with only its parking lights on, seems farther away than it is.

(a)

(b)

Figure 7–7 (a) This ancient Egyptian wall painting, depicting the wine harvest, lacks the monocular cues that artists have used since to portray depth. (b) By the time that Canaletto (1697–1768) painted this scene of Venice, the techniques for showing perspective were well established. Note the effective use of distance cues such as texture and gradient, overlap, and relative size and height.

To convey depth on a flat canvas (Figure 7–7b), artists make use of these monocular cues, as do people who must gauge depth with but one eye. In 1960, the University of Washington football team won the Rose Bowl, thanks partly to the throwing of star quarterback Bob Schloredt. Schloredt, who was obviously skilled at judging the distance of his pass receivers, must have been extremely sensitive to monocular cues for distance, because he was blind in his left eye.

PERCEPTUAL CONSTANCIES

So far we have seen that we must first perceive an object as a coherent form (not just a disorganized cluster of sensations) and locate it in space. Our next task is to recognize the object, without being deceived by changes in its size, shape, brightness, or color. This perceptual feat— to perceive an object as unchanging while the stimuli from it change— has intrigued perception researchers for decades.

Shape and Size Constancies   Perceptual constancy is our perception that objects have a constant shape, regardless of viewing angle, and a constant size, regardless of distance.

Thanks to *shape constancy* we perceive a familiar object as having a constant form, even while our retinal images of it change. When a door opens, it casts a changing shape on our retinas, yet we manage to perceive the door as having a constant doorlike shape (Figure 7–8).

Figure 7–8 Shape constancy. A door casts an increasingly trapezoidal image on our retinas as it opens, yet we continue to perceive it as rectangular.

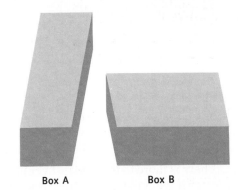

Box A   Box B

Perceiving shape. Do the tops of boxes A and B have different dimensions? They appear to. But if you measure, you will see that they are identical. With both boxes we adjust our perceptions in terms of what we take our viewing angle to be. (From Shepard, 1981.)

Size constancy—the tendency to perceive an object as having a constant size—allows us to perceive a car as big enough to carry people, even when we see it from two blocks away. This illustrates the close connection between an object's perceived *distance* and perceived *size*. Perceiving an object's distance cues us to its size; likewise, knowing its size—that the object is, say, a car—cues us to its distance.

Size-Distance Relationship   The marvel of size perception is how effortlessly it occurs. Given the perceived distance of an object and the size of its retinal image, we instantly and unconsciously infer the object's size. Although the cones in Figure 7–9 cast the same retinal images, the linear perspective cues us that the upper cone is more distant, and we therefore perceive it as larger.

This interplay between perceived size and perceived distance helps explain several well-known illusions. For example, can you imagine why the moon looks larger—up to 50 percent larger—near the horizon than when high in the sky? A partial reason for this "moon illusion" is that cues to the distance of objects at the horizon make the moon, behind them, seem farther away and therefore larger (like the distant cone in Figure 7–9 and distant bar in Figure 7–10). Take away these distance cues—by looking at the horizon moon through a paper tube—and it immediately shrinks.

The size-distance relationship helps us understand two illusions demonstrated at the start of this chapter. Puzzle 1, the Müller-Lyer illusion concerning the length of straight lines between arrow tips has been the subject of more than 1250 scientific publications, but psychologists still debate its explanation. One is that our experience with the corners of rooms or buildings (Figure 7–11) prompts us to interpret vertical line 1 as closer to us and therefore shorter, and vertical line 2 as farther away, and consequently longer.

Figure 7–9   The interplay between perceived size and distance. The monocular cues for distance make the cone that seems more distant look larger. But it isn't. From *The moon illusion* by Lloyd Kaufman and Irving Rock. Copyright © 1962 by Scientific American, Inc. All rights reserved.

Figure 7–10   The two identical orange bars of this "Ponzo illusion" cast identical images on our retinas. We know, however, that a more distant object can only create the same size image if it is larger, so we erroneously infer that the bar that seems more distant is larger.

Figure 7–11   The Müller-Lyer illusion. Richard L. Gregory (1968) suggests that the corners in our rectangularly carpentered world have taught us to interpret "outward" or "inward" pointing arrowheads at the ends of a line as a cue to the line's distance from us and so to its length. The line defined by the corner to the left looks shorter than the line defined by the corner to the right, but if you measure them you will see that both are the same length.

There is more to the Müller-Lyer illusion than size constancy, however, for if we replace the arrowheads with circles and judge whether the black or green line seems longer we still get much the same effect:

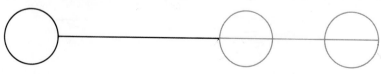

Here, the two line segments are equal. Most people judge the black line to be longer, apparently because they perceptually adjust the lengths of the lines toward the length of the figures of which they are part (Day, 1984). This illustrates how context influences perception.

The size-distance relationship explains Puzzle 2, the shrinking boy and growing dog. As Figure 7–12 reveals, the room is distorted. It was carefully constructed with trapezoidal walls and windows so as to produce, when viewed with one eye through a peephole, images whose shapes are the same as those of a normal rectangular room viewed with both eyes. Presented with the camera's one-eyed view, the brain makes the reasonable assumption that the room *is* normal, and perceives the boy and dog as changing in size.

Figure 7–12 The illusion of the shrinking boy and growing dog. When viewed through a peephole with one eye, this distorted room appears to have a normal rectangular shape with both corners being the same distance away. Thus, anything in the near corner appears disproportionately large compared to anything in the far corner, because we judge their size based on the false assumption that they are the same distance away.

Our occasional misperceptions demonstrate the workings of our normally effective perceptual processes. The perceived relationship between distance and size is generally valid, but under special circumstances can lead us astray—as when helping to create the moon illusion, the Müller-Lyer illusion, and the distorted room illusion. Using distance cues to assess perceived size triggers illusions only if we aren't familiar with the object or if the distance cues are misleading. When the distance cues are correctly interpreted—which normally they are—we perceive the size of objects correctly.

Brightness and Color Constancies   White paper reflects 90 percent of the light falling on it; black paper, only 10 percent. In bright sunlight the black paper may reflect 100 times more light than does the white paper indoors (McBurney & Collings, 1984), but it still looks black. This illustrates *brightness constancy,* the tendency to perceive an object as having a constant amount of brightness even while its illumination varies. Perceived brightness depends on *relative luminance*—how much light an object reflects relative to its surroundings. If you view sunlit black paper through a narrow tube so nothing else is visible it may look gray, because in bright sunshine it reflects a fair amount of light. View it without the tube and it is again black, because in its environmental context, black reflects much less light than the colors around it.

Color constancy also depends on the context. If your view is restricted to only a part of a red apple, without your knowing that the object is an apple, its color will seem to change as the light changes. But if you see the whole apple as one item in a fruit bowl, its color will remain constant as the lighting shifts.

Normally, objects appear to retain their brightness and color, even when the light they reflect changes. However, unusual contexts can trigger illusions of changing brightness and color. The two gray rectangles of Figure 7–13a appear different. Actually each pair is identical. In Figure 7–13b, the color of the diagonal lines appears to change dramatically. In fact, it remains the same. This illustrates the principle that perception is ecological: We perceive objects not in isolation but in their environmental context.

Although we take color constancy for granted, the phenomenon is really quite remarkable. Think about it: A green leaf hanging from a brown branch may, when the illumination changes, now reflect the same light energy that formerly came from the brown branch. Yet to us the leaf stays green rather than turning brown. This demonstrates that our experience of color comes not from the leaf alone—the color is not in the isolated leaf—but from everything around it as well. You and I see color thanks to our brain's computations about the light reflected by any object relative to its surrounding objects.

Form perception, depth perception, and perceptual constancies illustrate how we organize our visual experiences. We experience perceptual organization in ways other than the visual, too, as when the steady clicks of the metronome are grouped into patterns. Listening to an unfamiliar language, we have difficulty telling where one word stops and the next one begins; listening to our own language, we automatically hear distinct sound patterns. This, too, is a form of perceptual organization. But it is more, for even a string of letters—THEDOGATEMEAT—will be organized into words that make an intelligible phrase, more likely as "the dog ate meat" than as "the do gate me at" (McBurney & Collings, 1984). And this process involves not only organization but *interpretation*—finding meaning in what we perceive.

INTERPRETATION

So far we have seen that the nativists were correct (that, for example, depth perception is innate) and evidence that the empiricists were correct (that, for example, through experience we learn to link the distance of an object to its perceived size). But just how important is experience? How radically does it shape our perceptual interpretations?

SENSORY RESTRICTION AND RESTORED VISION

Writing to empiricist John Locke (1690), William Molyneux wondered whether "a man *born* blind, and now adult, taught by his *touch* to distinguish between a cube and a sphere," could, if made to see, visually distinguish the two. Locke's answer was no, because the man would never have *learned* to see.

Molyneux's hypothetical case has since been put to the test in dozens of instances in which adults blind from birth have gained sight (Gregory, 1978; Senden, 1932). Most were patients with cataracts, whose clouded lenses had enabled them to see only diffused light, rather as you or I might see the world if looking through a Ping-Pong ball sliced in half. When the cataracts were surgically removed, the patients could distinguish figure from ground and could sense colors—suggesting that these aspects of perception are innate. But, much as Locke supposed, the formerly blind patients often could not visually recognize objects with which they were tactilely familiar. Learning to perceive shape and form visually was so difficult that some of the patients gave up and returned to living as functionally blind persons.

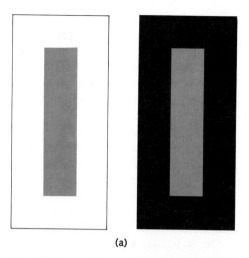

(a)

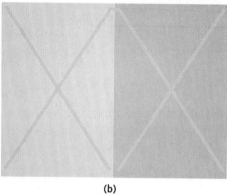

(b)

Figure 7–13   (a) Brightness constancy. Although they are in fact identical, the perceived brightness of the interior rectangles differs depending on the surrounding color—a fact of great significance for artists and interior designers. (b) Color constancy. In this painting by Joseph Albers (1975), the unchanging line seems to vary from yellow to gray as the surrounding context changes.

Perhaps in these cases the patients' visual equipment was not completely restored by the surgery. Seeking to gain more control than can be provided by clinical cases, researchers have conducted Molyneux's imaginary experiment with animals. To discover whether altering a young animal's normal visual experience would permanently alter its perceptual abilities, they gave infant kittens and monkeys simulated cataracts by sewing their eyelids closed or by outfitting them with goggles through which only diffuse, unpatterned light could be seen (Wiesel, 1982). After infancy, when their visual impairments were removed, these animals exhibited perceptual limitations much like those of human cataract patients; they could distinguish colors and brightness, but not the form of a circle from that of a square. Their eyes had not degenerated; their retinas still relayed signals to their visual cortex. But functionally the animals remained blind.

In both humans and animals, a similar period of sensory restriction occurring later in life is not permanently disruptive. If the eye of an animal is covered for several months during adulthood, vision will be unaffected when the eyepatch is removed. If human cataracts that develop *after* early childhood are later removed, the person will enjoy normal vision. The effects of visual experiences during infancy in cats, monkeys, and humans suggest that there is what Chapter 3 termed a *critical period* for normal perceptual development. As we also noted in Chapter 3, experience guides the organization of the brain's neural connections.

The profound effects of early experience on perception are also apparent in experiments in which young animals were reared with severely restricted visual input. In one such study, two Cambridge University researchers, Colin Blakemore and Grahame Cooper (1970), reared kittens in darkness, except for 5 hours each day during which they were placed in a horizontally or vertically striped environment (as in Figure 7–14). Remarkably, kittens raised without exposure to horizontal lines later had difficulty perceiving horizontal bars, and those raised without vertical lines had difficulty seeing vertical bars. When two of these kittens were playing in a room and one of the researchers playfully shook a long black rod, the kitten reared in a world of vertical lines would play with it only when it was held upright. When the rod was held flat, that kitten ignored it while a companion reared in a world of horizontal lines ran to play with it. Eventually, the selective blindness diminished, but the kittens never regained normal sensitivity. By sampling the activity of the kittens' feature-detecting brain cells, Blakemore and Cooper found that whether such cells responded mostly to horizontal or vertical lines depended on the kittens' rearing.

This research provides a partial answer to one of the questions debated in Chapter 4, Adolescence and Adulthood: Does the effect of early experience last a lifetime? Or can we be reshaped by later experiences? For some aspects of visual perception, the answer seems clear. The imprint of early visual experiences—or lack of them—is retained far into the future.

Figure 7–14 The experimental apparatus for the Blakemore and Cooper studies. From the time their eyes first opened to age 5 months, these kittens were removed from darkness each day to spend 5 hours alone in a black and white striped cylinder with a clear glass floor. A stiff collar prevented the kittens from seeing anything else, even their own bodies. Afterward, these kittens were less sensitive to horizontal forms.

"Innate mechanisms endow the visual system with highly specific connections, but visual experience early in life is necessary for their maintenance and full development."

Brain researcher Torsten N. Wiesel (1982)

PERCEPTUAL ADAPTATION

Given a new pair of glasses, we may find ourselves slightly disoriented and dizzy. Within a day or two we *perceptually adapt.* This adjustment to changed visual input makes the world seem normal again. Now imagine a far more dramatic new pair of prescription glasses—one that shifts the apparent location of objects 40 degrees to the left. When you first put them on and toss a ball to a friend, it sails off to the left. Walking forward to shake hands with the person, you veer to the left.

Could you satisfactorily adapt to this distorted world? Chicks cannot. When fitted with such lenses, they peck where food grains *seem* to be (Hess, 1956; Rossi, 1968). But humans wearing such distorting lenses adapt quickly. Within a few minutes your throws would again be accurate, your stride on target. Remove the lenses and you would experience an aftereffect: At first your throws would err in the *opposite* direction, sailing off to the right; but within minutes you would readapt.

Now imagine an even more radical pair of new glasses—one that literally turns the world upside down. The ground is up, the sky is down. Could you adapt? Fish, frogs, and salamanders cannot. When Roger Sperry (1956) surgically turned their eyes upside down, they thereafter reacted to objects by moving in the wrong direction. But, believe it or not, kittens, monkeys, and humans can adapt to an inverted world. The turn-of-the-century psychologist George Stratton (1896) experienced this when he invented and wore for 8 days optical headgear that flipped left to right *and* up to down, making him the first member of our species to experience a right-side-up retinal image while standing upright.

At first, Stratton was disoriented. When he wanted to walk he had to search for his feet, which were now ''up.'' Eating was nearly impossible. He became nauseated and depressed. But Stratton persisted and gradually began to adapt. By the end of the 8 days, he could comfortably reach in the right direction for something and walk without bumping into objects. When the headgear was finally removed it did not take Stratton long to readapt.

Subsequent experiments have replicated Stratton's experience (Dolezal, 1982; Kohler, 1962). After a period of adjustment, people wearing the optical gear have even been able to ride a motorcycle, ski the Alps, and fly an airplane. Is this because through experience they perceptually reinverted their upside-down world to an upright position? No, the street, ski slopes, and runway were still above their heads. But by actively moving about in this topsy-turvy world, they had learned the new relationships between the actual and perceived locations of objects. This learning enabled them to coordinate their movements without being deceived by the inversion.

Dr. Hubert Dolezal views the world through inverted lenses. Remarkably, people can learn to adapt to an upside-down visual world.

PERCEPTUAL SET

As everyone knows, to see is to believe. As many people also know, but do not fully appreciate, to believe is to see. Our assumptions and expectations may give us a *perceptual set,* or mental predisposition, that greatly influences what we perceive. Is the woman in Figure 7–15 young or old? What we see can be influenced by first viewing either of the two unambiguous versions of this drawing (Boring, 1930).

Figure 7–15   Which do you see in the center picture: the old woman or the young woman? Your answer, your interpretation of the ambiguous figure, will be influenced by which of the two unambiguous versions of the picture you might have glanced at first.

Knowing this much, see if you can explain the results of another experiment. A slightly blurred picture was identified correctly by 73 percent of first-time viewers, but only by 25 percent of those who had previously been shown a *badly* blurred version of the picture (Bruner & Potter, 1964). Why do you suppose the second group had so much more trouble perceiving the image?

The evidence indicates that people cannot resist imposing a pattern on unpatterned stimuli. It is strikingly easier to "hang on" to a picture going out of focus than to recognize the same picture coming into focus. Thus, shown a hopelessly blurred picture, people automatically form a preliminary hunch (perceptual set) which then interferes with later perceptions. The point can be generalized: Once you have formed a wrong idea about reality, you have more difficulty seeing the truth.

Expectations predispose perceptions even in science. Confronted with ambiguous information, a scientist will propose a *theory* that serves to organize and interpret the available data. When the "canals" on Mars were first perceived through telescopes, some astronomers and writers assumed them to be the product of intelligent creatures rather than natural landforms. Such assumptions can act as a perceptual set, making it more difficult to assess other possibilities objectively. Thus the canals on Mars did turn out indeed to be the product of intelligent life—but an intelligence on the viewing end of the telescope.

Everyday examples of perceptual set abound. In 1972, a British newspaper published genuine, unretouched photographs of a "monster" in Scotland's Loch Ness—"the most amazing pictures ever taken," stated the paper. If this information creates the same perceptual set in you as it did in most of the paper's readers, you, too, will see the monster in the photo reproduced in Figure 7–16. But when Steuart Campbell (1986) approached the photos with a different perceptual set, he saw a curved tree trunk—very likely the same tree trunk others had seen in the lake the day the photo was shot. Moreover, with this different perceptual set, you may now notice that the object is floating motionless, without any water disturbance or wake around it—hardly what one would expect of a lively monster.

Our perceptual set can also influence what we hear. This principle was painfully learned by the kindly airline pilot who, on a takeoff run, looked over at his depressed copilot and said "cheer up." The copilot heard the usual "gear up" and promptly raised the wheels—before they had left the ground (Reason & Mycielska, 1982). And, when viewing a liquor ad or listening to rock music played backwards, people often perceive a sexual image or evil message *if* specifically told what to look for or listen to (Vokey & Read, 1985).

What determines our perceptual set? As you may recall from Chapter 3, The Developing Child, our experiences help us to develop and to elaborate *schemas*—concepts that we use to organize and interpret information. In order to interpret unfamiliar information, we compare it to our schemas, which are stored in our memories. Our preexisting schemas for young women and old women, for monsters and tree trunks, for airplane lights and UFOs are all available to help us interpret ambiguous sensations. Confronted with an ambiguous moving object in the sky, different people may therefore apply different schemas: "It's a bird." "It's a plane." "It's Superman!"

Children's drawings allow us to glimpse their developing perceptual schemas. A preschooler can draw circles and angled lines but cannot combine them to create an elaborate human figure. Why not? The child's problem is not clumsiness. A right-handed adult asked to draw

"The temptation to form premature theories upon insufficient data is the bane of our profession."
  Sherlock Holmes, in Arthur Conan Doyle's *The Valley of Fear*, 1914

Figure 7–16 Is this the Loch Ness monster or a log? We often see what we expect to see.

In 1988, crew members of the U.S. naval destroyer *Vincennes* were perceptually predisposed to interpret radar signals received during battle as those from an attacking fighter plane. Actually, they were those of an Iranian airliner flying on course to its scheduled destination. The tragic result of this perceptual set: the deaths of the 291 people on board the plane.

with the left hand will create an awkward drawing, but it will be unlike the child's drawing in Figure 7–17. Part of the difference lies in the difficulty that children (and some adults as well) have in representing visually what they see. But the fundamental difference lies in the child's simplified schema for essential human characteristics. For a 3-year-old, a face is a more essential human feature than a body. From ages 3 to 8, children's schemas for bodies become more elaborate, and so in turn do their drawings of bodies.

Our well-established schemas for faces prime us to see facial patterns in cartoonists' caricatures, and even in random configurations. Peter Thompson (1980) at England's University of York discovered that our face recognition is especially attuned to the expressive eyes and mouth—so much so that we have trouble imagining what British Prime Minister Thatcher's inverted eyes and mouth will look like when we turn her face upright (Figure 7–18).

Context Effects   A given stimulus may trigger radically different perceptions, partly because of the differing schemas we develop from our past experiences, but also partly because of the immediate context. Remember that perception is ecological. Whether the speaker is concerned about "cults and sects" or "cults and sex" must be discerned from the context surrounding the words.

The combined effects of perceptual set and context sometimes work to our benefit. In the hospital where I was once an orderly, we occasionally faced the task of transporting a dead body through crowded hallways without alarming the patients or their visitors. Our solution was to create a context that matched people's schemas for sleeping and sedated patients: With face uncovered, and the sheet turned down in normal fashion, an apparently "sleeping" body could be wheeled past the unsuspecting.

The effects of learned schemas and perceptual sets are further evidence that experience influences how we perceive the world. To return to our original question—is perception innate or learned?—we can answer: Our innate sensory equipment makes possible our elementary sensations, and our experiences help us to construct meaningful perceptions from them.

Figure 7–17   Children's drawings reflect their schemas of reality, as well as their abilities to represent what they see. This drawing by a 3-year-old illustrates that the face has far greater importance than the body in young children's schemas of essential human characteristics.

Figure 7–18   Look at Margaret Thatcher's reconstructed face (left) and try to imagine what her face will look like when you turn it upright.

Context effects. What is above the woman's head? In this experiment, nearly all the participants from East Africa thought she was balancing a metal box or can on her head and that the family was sitting under a tree. Westerners, to whom corners and boxlike architecture are more common, were more likely to perceive the family as being indoors, with the woman sitting under a window through which plants can be seen. (Adapted from Gregory & Gombrich, 1973.)

IS THERE PERCEPTION WITHOUT SENSATION?

Can we perceive only what we take in through our senses or, without sensory input, are we capable of *extrasensory perception (ESP)*? Are there people who can read minds, see through walls, or foretell the future? Most Americans believe in the reality of ESP (Greeley, 1987). And the media are full of reports of psychic wonders. Psychics are said to solve crimes that have dumbfounded detectives. Ordinary people are reported to have spontaneous dreams of dreadful events—only to discover their dreams fulfilled.

In laboratory experiments, *parapsychologists* (those who study paranormal—literally, beyond the normal—happenings) have sometimes been astonished at psychics who seem capable of discerning the contents of sealed envelopes, influencing the roll of a die, or drawing a picture of what someone else is viewing at an unknown remote location. Research psychologists and scientists, however, are overwhelmingly skeptical of such claims (McClenon, 1982). If ESP is real, the scientific understanding of human nature—that we are creatures whose minds are tied to our physical brains and whose perceptual experiences of the world are built of sensations—might have to be modified radically. But sometimes our preconceptions are indeed overturned by new evidence. So let's take a look at some of the claims of ESP and then see why scientists remain dubious.

CLAIMS OF ESP

Among the acclaimed paranormal phenomena—including astrological predictions, psychic healings, reincarnation, communication with the dead, and out-of-body travel—the most respectable, testable, and (for a chapter on perception) relevant claims are for the three varieties of ESP:

Telepathy, or mind-to-mind communication—one person sending thoughts to another, or perceiving another's thoughts.

Clairvoyance, or perceiving remote events, such as sensing that a friend's house is on fire.

Precognition, or perceiving future events, such as the death of a political leader.

Closely linked with the claims of ESP are claims of *psychokinesis*, or "mind over matter" acts, such as levitating a table or influencing the roll of a die.

Most people's beliefs about ESP are based on staged performances of psychics, which are quite different from the controlled situation required for a scientist to test for ESP. On stage, the psychic controls what the audience sees and hears. In the laboratory, the experimenter controls what the psychic sees and hears. It is therefore no surprise that the results reported by parapsychologists who test for ESP in the laboratory are modest by comparison to the stage feats of so-called psychics.

Consider a clairvoyance experiment conducted by Bruce Layton and Bill Turnbull (1975) at the University of North Carolina. Layton and Turnbull had a computer generate a randomized 100-item list of the digits 1, 2, 3, 4, and 5 for each of their 179 student participants.

"A psychic is an actor playing the role of a psychic."
Psychologist-magician Daryl Bem (1984)

Each of the students was given such a list in a sealed envelope and was asked to guess which number was in each of the 100 positions.

By chance, 1 guess in 5, or 20 guesses out of the 100, was expected to be correct. However, the average number of correct guesses was 20.66 out of 100 when it was suggested beforehand that ESP was beneficial to people, and only 19.49 when it was said that ESP was harmful. Although such a difference might seem insignificant—indeed you would never have noticed so small a discrepancy had you been observing the experiment—a statistical analysis indicated that a difference that large among so many participants would seldom occur by chance. So the investigators concluded that an ESP effect had occurred.

Bolstered by such experiments, believers in ESP accuse research psychologists of the same sort of skepticism that led eighteenth-century scientists to scoff at the idea that meteorites came from outer space. Novelist Arthur Koestler, who in 1983 left more than $700,000 to fund a British professorship in parapsychology, once complained that today's skeptical scientists resemble the Italian philosophers who refused to look at Jupiter's moons through Galileo's telescope—because they "knew" that such moons did not exist. Skepticism sometimes blinds people to the truth.

> "A man does not attain the status of Galileo merely because he is persecuted; he must also be right."
> Stephen Jay Gould,
> *Ever Since Darwin*, 1973

SKEPTICISM ABOUT ESP

The skeptics reply that the uncritical mind is a gullible mind. They point to the fact that, time and again, so-called psychics have exploited unquestioning audiences with amazing performances in which they appeared to communicate with the spirits of the dead, read minds, or levitate objects—only to have it revealed later that their acts were a hoax, nothing more than the illusions of stage magicians. Indeed, many psychic deceptions have been exposed by magicians, who resent the exploitation of their arts in the name of psychic powers.

> "The most eminent scientist, untrained in magic, is putty in the hands of a clever charlatan."
> Martin Gardner (1983)

Even scientists are vulnerable to being hoodwinked. A notable case involved two teenage magicians, Steve Shaw and Michael Edwards (Randi, 1983a, 1983b). In 1979, this young pair approached Washington University's new parapsychological laboratory, offering to demonstrate their "psychic powers." Over the next three years, the two pretended to defy the laws of nature by seeming to project mental images onto film, causing clocks to slide across a table, effortlessly bending metal objects, affecting objects in sealed jars, and performing other apparently wondrous feats. Although forewarned against trickery by James Randi, the youngsters' magician-adviser, the director of the laboratory ignored the warnings and for a time proclaimed that "these two kids are the most reliable of the people that we've studied" ("Psychic Abscam," 1983).

This parapsychologist's gullibility illustrates how tempting it is to label phenomena *we* don't understand as beyond explanation: "What other explanation could there possibly be but ESP?," the awestruck observer asks. Thus, before bats' echolocation ability was discovered, many people attributed bats' ability to avoid wires in complete darkness to clairvoyance (Gibson, 1979). When the bats were blinded, when their noses were sealed, when their wings were coated with varnish they still could navigate, so what other explanation could there be but ESP?

Magicians Shaw and Edwards with adviser James Randi after revealing their hoax at a news conference.

Premonitions or Pretensions?   Skeptics are equally critical of psychics who claim to see into the future. Those who have taken the trouble to go back and tally unfiltered forecasts of "leading psychics" report meager predictive accuracy. For example, between 1978 and 1985 the New Year's predictions by the *National Enquirer*'s favorite psychics yielded 2 accurate predictions out of 486 (Strentz, 1986). During these years, none of the significant unexpected events—that a woman would run for Vice President of the United States, that famine would devastate Ethiopia, that terrorism would plague Europe—was foreseen by any of the psychics.

The People's Almanac's favorite psychics have fared slightly better. Among 85 predictions 5 were accurate, and these were notably safe bets, such as the prediction that Russia and the United States would "remain as leading world powers" (Donnelly, 1983). Checks on the predictions of visions offered to police departments by psychics revealed that these, too, are no more accurate than guesses made by others (Reiser, 1982). Psychics working with the police do, however, generate dozens or even hundreds of predictions; this increases the odds of an occasional correct guess, which can then be reported to the media.

Are the spontaneous "visions" of ordinary people any more accurate? Consider our dreams. Do they foretell the future? Or do they only seem to because we are more likely to recall or reconstruct dreams that seem to have come true? A test of the prophetic power of dreams was conducted a half-century ago. After the famed aviator Charles Lindbergh's baby was kidnapped and murdered but before the body was discovered, two Harvard psychologists (Murray & Wheeler, 1937) invited the public to send in their dream reports concerning the whereabouts of the child. Of the 1300 dream reports submitted, how many accurately reported that the child was dead? A mere 5 percent. And how many also correctly anticipated the body's location—buried among trees? Only 4 of the 1300. Although this number was surely no better than chance, to those four dreamers the accuracy of their *apparent* precognitions must have seemed uncanny.

Each of us every day imagines numerous good or bad events; occasionally, therefore, an unlikely imagined event is bound to occur and to astonish us when it does. If you tell everyone in a group of 100 people to think "heads" before tossing six coins, someone is likely to get all heads (whether thinking heads or not) and to feel eerie after doing so. Given the billions of events that occur in the world each day, at least a few stunning coincidences are to be expected.

Why do so many people resist the explanation of premonitions as statistical coincidences? And why do two-thirds of American adults report having had a psychic experience (Greeley, 1987)? The skeptics say that after the fact we *selectively recall* past predictions and adjust them to fit the facts. As later chapters will reveal, people also are overly persuaded by misleading but vivid anecdotes and they notice and interpret events in ways that confirm their expectations. As Nostradamus, a sixteenth-century French psychic, explained in an unguarded moment, his ambiguous prophecies "could not possibly be understood till they were interpreted after the event and by it."

Finally, and most important, say the skeptics, is the fact that after tens of thousands of experiments *there has never been discovered a reproducible ESP phenomenon, nor any individual who could convincingly demonstrate psychic ability* (Marks, 1986). British psychologist Mark Hansel (1980, p. 314) noted, "After a hundred years of research, not a single individual has been found who can demonstrate ESP to the satisfaction of independent investigators," and thus, "Today ESP is no nearer to being established than it was a hundred years ago" (1985, p. 124). A

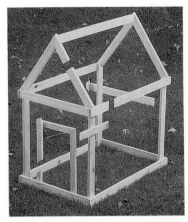

Another view of the impossible doghouse in Figure 7–5 (page 173) reveals the secrets of this illusion.

More recent experiments in which people attempted to send mental images to dreamers produced some intriguing initial results, but these could not be replicated even with the same subjects. Dream telepathy experiments have therefore been discontinued (Hyman, 1986).

recent National Research Council investigation of ESP claims similarly concludes that "the best available evidence does not support the contention that these phenomena exist" (Druckman & Swets, 1988).

One skeptic, magician James Randi, has offered $10,000 to anyone who can demonstrate "*any* paranormal ability" before a group of competent experts. Other similar offers total more than a third of a million dollars (Jones, 1985–1986), and to anyone whose claims could be authenticated the scientific seal of approval would actually be worth far more. Randi's offer has been especially well publicized for two decades, and dozens of people have been tested, sometimes under the scrutiny of an independent panel of judges. To refute those who say there is no ESP, one need only produce a single person who can demonstrate a single reproducible ESP phenomenon. As yet, no one has exhibited any such power.

The Mystique of ESP   In times past there have been all kinds of crazy ideas—that bumps on the head reveal character traits, that bloodletting is a cure for various diseases, that each sperm cell contains a miniature person inside. But a method has been developed for separating the truly crazy ideas from the ideas that sound crazy but are true: Test them to see if they work. This method we know as science. When faced with claims of mind reading or out-of-body travel or mind-over-matter, the appropriate response remains: Test them to see if they work. If they do, so much the worse for our skepticism. If they don't, so much the worse for the ideas.

This scientific attitude was apparent at the 1981 convention of the American Psychological Association, at which two symposia examined the "case for" and the "case against" ESP. Ironically, nearly the same conclusions were expressed at each. Both believers and skeptics agreed: What parapsychology needs to give it credibility is a reproducible phenomenon and a theory to explain it.

Could the Layton and Turnbull clairvoyance experiment (in which students beat chance in guessing numbers in a sealed envelope) provide such a reproducible phenomenon? The skeptical editor of the *Journal of Experimental Social Psychology*, to which Layton and Turnbull submitted their results for publication, wondered. So he made an unusual offer. If they would repeat their experiment, the journal would then publish the results of both experiments, regardless of the outcome. As the offer illustrates, both ESP researchers and skeptics genuinely seek truth and are therefore usually willing to accept valid evidence, no matter which viewpoint it supports.

Layton and Turnbull accepted. The result of the second experiment? Layton and Turnbull summarized succinctly: "No [statistically] significant effects were present."

For all these reasons, but especially in the absence of reproducible results, most research psychologists are skeptical of those who claim to have powers of ESP and are dismayed by the number of shows, books, and magazines offered on paranormal and occult topics. Should we share their skepticism and dismay?

A personal answer: We surely can be skeptical of the pretensions of ESP without being closed to all unprovable claims. We can be open to new ideas without being gullible, critical without being cynical. Knowing that our understanding of nature is incomplete and subject to revision, we can be critical thinkers yet agree with Shakespeare's Hamlet that "There are more things in heaven and earth, Horatio, than are dreamt of in your philosophy."

"At the heart of science is an essential tension between two seemingly contradictory attitudes—an openness to new ideas, no matter how bizarre or counterintuitive they may be, and the most ruthless skeptical scrutiny of all ideas, old and new."
   Carl Sagan (1987)

Even parapsychology advocate Charles Tart (1983) acknowledges that "ESP in the laboratory generally shows up weakly or inconsistently, so it has been hard to study its nature."

Some things that we assume to be true—the reality of another's love, the existence or nonexistence of God, the finality of death or the reality of life after death—are beyond science. That is but one reason why, after clearing the decks of tested and rejected pseudomysteries, we can still retain a humble sense of wonder regarding life's untestable mysteries.

Why are so many people predisposed to believe that ESP exists? In part, such beliefs may stem from understandable misperceptions, misinterpretations, and selective recall. But for some people there also exists an unsatisfied hunger for wonderment, an itch to experience the magical. In Britain and America, the founders of parapsychology were mostly people who, having lost their religious faith, were searching for a scientific basis for believing in the meaningfulness of life and the possibility of life after death (Alcock, 1985; Beloff, 1985).

To be awestruck and to gain a deep reverence for life, we need look no further than our own perceptual system and its capacity for organizing formless nerve impulses into colorful sights, vivid sounds, and evocative smells. Within our ordinary moment-to-moment perceptual experiences lies much that is truly extraordinary—surely much more than has so far been dreamt of in our psychology. A century of research has revealed many of the secrets of sensation and perception, but for future generations of researchers and thinkers there remain profound and genuine mysteries.

"I have uttered what I did not understand, things too wonderful for me. . . ."
Job 42:3

SUMMING UP

The classic debate in perception involved the nativists, who emphasized nature's innate mechanisms for organizing sensory information, and the empiricists, who argued that we learn to perceive the world through our experiences in it.

PERCEPTUAL ILLUSIONS

Visual and auditory illusions have fascinated scientists since the emergence of psychology as a distinct discipline. Explaining illusions required a deeper understanding of how we transform sensory information into meaningful perceptions, so the study of perception became one of the first items on psychology's agenda. Conflict between visual and other sensory information is usually resolved with the mind accepting the visual data. This tendency is known as visual capture.

PERCEPTUAL ORGANIZATION

The early Gestalt psychologists were impressed with the seemingly innate way in which we organize fragmentary sensory data into whole perceptions. Our minds structure the information that comes to us in several demonstrable ways:

Form Perception To recognize an object, we must first perceive it (see it as a figure) as distinct from surrounding stimuli (the ground). We must also organize the figure into a meaningful form. Several Gestalt principles—proximity, similarity, closure, and continuity—describe this process.

Depth Perception Research on the visual cliff suggests that in many species the ability to perceive the world in three dimensions is present at, or very shortly after, birth. We transform two-dimensional retinal images into three-dimensional perceptions by use of binocular cues, such as retinal disparity, and monocular cues, such as the relative sizes of objects.

Perceptual Constancies Having perceived an object as a coherent figure and located it in space, how then do we recognize it—despite the varying images that it may cast on our retinas? The phenomena of size, shape, brightness, and color constancy describe how objects appear to have unchanging characteristics regardless of their distance, shape, or motion. These constancies explain several of the well-known visual illusions.

INTERPRETATION

The most direct tests of the nativism-empiricism issue come from experiments on the modification of human perceptions.

Sensory Restriction and Restored Vision If cataract removal restores eyesight to adults who were blind from birth, they are unable to perceive the world normally. Generally, they can distinguish figure from ground and perceive colors, but even with much effort they are unable to distinguish shapes and forms.

In better controlled experiments, infant kittens and monkeys have been reared with severely restricted visual input. When their visual exposure is returned to normal they, too, suffer enduring visual handicaps. It appears that for many species infancy is a critical period, during which the brain's innate visual mechanisms must be activated through experience.

Perceptual Adaptation Human vision is nevertheless remarkably adaptable. Given glasses that shift the world slightly to the left or right, or even turn it upside down, people manage to adapt their movements and, with practice, to move about with ease.

Perceptual Set Clear evidence that perception is influenced by our learned assumptions and beliefs as well as by sensory input comes from the many demonstrations of perceptual set. The schemas we have stored in memory help us to interpret otherwise ambiguous stimuli, a fact that helps explain why some of us "see" monsters, faces, and UFOs that others do not.

IS THERE PERCEPTION WITHOUT SENSATION?

Many people believe in, and even claim to have experienced, extrasensory perception. Parapsychologists have attempted to document several forms of ESP—telepathy, clairvoyance, and precognition. But for a number of reasons, especially the lack of a reproducible ESP effect, most research psychologists are skeptical of its existence.

TERMS AND CONCEPTS TO REMEMBER

aerial perspective A monocular cue for perceiving distance; distant objects appear hazier, less distinct than nearby objects.

binocular cues Depth cues, such as retinal disparity and convergence, that depend on the use of two eyes.

brightness constancy Perceiving objects as having consistent brightness even when their illumination varies.

closure The perceptual tendency to fill in gaps, thus enabling one to perceive disconnected parts as a whole object.

color constancy Perceiving familiar objects as having consistent color, even if their actual color is altered by changing illumination.

continuity A perceptual tendency to group stimuli into smooth, continuous patterns.

convergence A binocular cue for perceiving depth; the extent to which the eyes converge inward when looking at an object.

depth perception The ability to see objects in three dimensions although the images that strike the retina are two-dimensional; allows us to judge distance.

empiricism The view that perceptions are learned through experience.

extrasensory perception (ESP) The controversial claim that perception can occur apart from sensory input. Said to include telepathy, clairvoyance, and precognition.

figure-ground The organization of the visual field into objects (the figures) that stand out from their surroundings (the ground).

gestalt An organized whole. Gestalt psychologists emphasize our tendency to integrate pieces of information into meaningful wholes.

grouping The tendency to organize stimuli into coherent groups.

linear perspective A monocular cue for perceiving distance; we perceive the converging of what we know to be parallel lines as indicating increasing distance.

monocular cues Distance cues, such as aerial and linear perspective and overlap, available to either eye alone.

nativism The view that important aspects of perception are innate, and thus do not have to be learned through experience.

overlap A monocular cue for perceiving distance; nearby objects partially block our view of more distant objects. (Also called *interposition*, because nearby objects are interposed between our eyes and more distant objects.)

parapsychology The study of paranormal phenomena including ESP and psychokinesis.

perceptual adaptation In vision, the ability to adjust to an artificially displaced or even inverted visual field.

perceptual set A mental predisposition to perceive one thing and not another.

proximity A perceptual tendency to group together visual and auditory events that are near each other.

relative brightness A monocular cue for perceiving distance; dimmer objects seem more distant.

relative height A monocular cue for perceiving distance; we perceive higher objects as farther away.

relative motion A monocular cue for perceiving distance; when we move, objects at different distances change their relative positions in our visual image, with those closest moving most. (Also called *motion parallax*.)

relative size A monocular cue for perceiving distance; when two objects are assumed to be the same size, the one that produces the smaller image appears to be more distant.

retinal disparity A binocular cue for perceiving depth; the greater the disparity (difference) between the two images the retina receives of an object, the closer to us the object is. (Also called *binocular disparity*.)

shape constancy Perceiving familiar objects as having a constant shape, even when their retinal image changes with viewing angle.

similarity A perceptual tendency to group together similar elements.

size constancy Perceiving an object as having a constant size, despite variations in its retinal image.

texture gradient A monocular cue for perceiving distance; a gradual change to a less distinct texture suggests increasing distance.

visual capture The tendency for vision to dominate the other senses; we perceive filmed voices as coming from the screen we see rather than from the projector behind us.

visual cliff A laboratory device for testing depth perception in infants and young animals.

FOR FURTHER READING

Perception

Coren, S., & Girgus, J. S. (1978). *Seeing is deceiving: The psychology of visual illusions*. Hillsdale, NJ: Erlbaum.

This intriguing book presents visual illusions and the perception principles that explain them.

Fineman, M. (1981). *The inquisitive eye*. New York: Oxford University Press.

Written for students in psychology, art, design, and photography, this entertaining book discusses and demonstrates many perceptual phenomena.

Rock, I. (1984). *Perception*. New York: Scientific American Books.

A beautifully illustrated treatment of many of the classic concerns of perception.

ESP

Alcock, J. E. (1981). *Parapsychology: Science or magic? A psychological perspective*. Oxford: Pergamon Press.

A critical analysis of parapsychology that provides psychological explanations of why so many people continue to believe in paranormal phenomena.

Kurtz, P. (1985). *A skeptic's handbook of parapsychology*. Buffalo: Prometheus Books.

Thirty essays by skeptics and parapsychologists provide exposés of pseudopsychics and bungled experiments, and pleas for open-mindedness.

Wolman, B. B., Dale, L. A., Schmeidler, G. R., & Ullman, M. (Eds.). (1985). *Handbook of parapsychology*. New York: Van Nostrand Reinhold.

Parapsychologists summarize their field's research.

CHAPTER 8

States of Consciousness

Most sciences have concepts so fundamental that they are nearly impossible to define. Biologists generally agree on what is alive and what isn't, but they do not agree on precisely what life is. In physics, matter and energy are fundamental concepts that elude simple definition. For psychology, consciousness is a similarly fundamental yet slippery concept. What is consciousness? Is it an awareness of the world? An awareness of one's thoughts? An awareness of one's awareness?

STUDYING CONSCIOUSNESS

At its beginning, psychology was sometimes defined as "the description and explanation of states of consciousness" (Ladd, 1887). But the difficulty of scientifically studying such an elusive concept led many psychologists during the first half of this century to abandon the study of consciousness in favor of direct observations of behavior—an approach favored by an emerging school of psychology called behaviorism (see pages 235–238). By midcentury, psychology was no longer defined as the study of consciousness or "mental life," but rather as the science of behavior. Psychology had nearly lost consciousness.

By 1960, mental concepts began to reenter psychology. Advances in neuroscience made it possible to relate brain activity to various mental states—waking, sleeping, dreaming. Researchers were beginning to study what seemed to be altered states of consciousness induced by hypnosis and drugs. Across psychology, the importance of mental processes (cognition) was again being recognized. Psychology was regaining consciousness.

Although there still is no agreed-upon definition of *consciousness,* we can think of it as *selective attention to ongoing perceptions, thoughts, and feelings.* When learning a complex concept or behavior—say, learning to drive—consciousness focuses our attention on the mechanical tasks of controlling the car and on the traffic conditions around us. With practice, driving becomes automatic and largely unconscious, freeing our consciousness to focus on other tasks.

SELECTIVE ATTENTION

Consciousness comes to us moment by moment, one moment of consciousness vanishing as the next appears. When looking at the Necker cube and figure-ground demonstrations in Chapter 7, we could *know* that two interpretations were possible, yet at any moment we consciously experienced only one of them. This illustrates an important principle: Our conscious attention is *selective.* **Selective attention** means

"Psychology must discard all reference to consciousness."
Behaviorist John B. Watson (1913)

With experience, many tasks, such as driving, become mostly automatic, freeing our conscious attention for other matters.

that at any moment awareness is focused on only a limited aspect of all that we are capable of experiencing. Until reading this sentence you have been unaware that your shoes are pressing against your feet or that your nose is in your line of vision. Now, suddenly, your feet feel encased, your nose stubbornly intrudes on the page before you.

Another example of selective attention is the *cocktail party effect*—the ability to attend selectively to only one voice among many. Imagine being exposed to two conversations over a headset, one to each ear. When your attention is drawn to what's being said in your left ear, what is said in your right ear will generally not be perceived. At the level of conscious awareness, whatever has your attention has your undivided attention.

Similarly, among the immense array of visual stimuli that are constantly before us, only a few are selected for consciousness. Ulric Neisser (1979) and Robert Becklen and Daniel Cervone (1983) demonstrated this dramatically. They showed people a one-minute videotape in which the images of three young men in black shirts passing a basketball were superimposed over the images of three men in white shirts doing the same thing. The viewers were asked to press a key every time the black-shirted players passed the ball. Midway through the tape, a young woman carrying an umbrella sauntered across the screen (see Figure 8–1). Most of the viewers focused their attention so completely on the black-shirted players that they failed to notice the woman. When the researchers replayed the tape for them, they were astonished to see her.

The ability to attend to only one conversation at a time—the cocktail party effect—enables those who work at the New York Stock Exchange to converse coherently in the midst of auditory chaos.

Figure 8–1   In this experiment on selective attention, viewers who were paying careful attention to the basketball being tossed among the black-shirted players usually failed to notice the woman with an umbrella sauntering through.

Can we be affected by such unattended-to stimuli? The answer is yes. In one experiment, women students were asked to listen to a prose passage presented through headphones to one ear, to repeat the words out loud, and to check for errors by comparing them to a written transcript (Wilson, 1979). Meanwhile, some simple, novel tunes were played to the other ear. The stimuli were not subliminal; they could be heard easily. But with their attention selectively focused on the passage, the women were no more aware of the tunes than you normally are of the shoes on your feet. Thus when they later heard these tunes interspersed among similar ones that had not been played previously, they could not recognize them (just as people cannot recall a conversation to which they did not pay attention). Nevertheless, when asked to rate their fondness for each tune, they preferred the ones that had been played previously. Their preferences revealed what their conscious memories could not.

STATES OF CONSCIOUSNESS

Many of our past and future chapter topics (perception, thinking and language, learning, memory, emotion) involve the study of normal waking consciousness. But research in each of these areas reveals that we process much information outside of awareness: We can type proficiently without paying conscious attention to where the letters are on the keyboard. We may change our attitudes or reconstruct our memories with no awareness of having done so. We register and react to stimuli we do not consciously perceive. After a driving lesson we may find ourselves whistling a particular tune and wonder why, not realizing that it was playing on the car radio while we were learning to parallel park. Unlike *un*conscious information processing (which occurs without our awareness), conscious processing takes place in succession (not simultaneously), is relatively slow, and is limited in capacity.

So far as our information processing is concerned, then, consciousness is but the tip of the iceberg. It is the part we are aware of, the part that enables us to exert voluntary control and to communicate our mental states to others (Kihlstrom, 1987b).

Psychologists may be unsure exactly what consciousness is, but they recognize that it occurs in varied states. Thus we have not only alert seeing and hearing, reasoning and remembering, but also the altered (distorted or out-of-the-ordinary) but conscious states that are our focus in this chapter—daydreams and sleep dreams, hypnotic and meditative states, hallucinations and visions.

DAYDREAMS AND FANTASIES

In James Thurber's classic story "The Secret Life of Walter Mitty," the bland existence of mild-mannered Walter Mitty is spiced with gratifying fantasies. As he drives past a hospital, Mitty imagines himself as Dr. Mitty, rushing to an operating room where two renowned specialists plead for his help. Again and again, the bumbling Walter Mitty relieves the tedium of his existence by imagining himself as the triumphant Walter Mitty—now the world's greatest marksman, now a heroic pilot.

The story became a classic because most people can identify with Walter Mitty. From interviews and questionnaire studies with hundreds of adults, clinical psychologist Jerome L. Singer (1975) reported that nearly everyone has daydreams or waking fantasies every day—on the job, in the classroom, walking down the street—in fact, almost anywhere at any time. Compared to older adults, young adults spend more time daydreaming and they admit to more sexual fantasies (Cameron & Biber, 1973; Giambra, 1974).

Not all daydreaming is as overtly escapist or dramatic as Walter Mitty's. Mostly it involves the familiar details of our lives—perhaps imagining an alternative approach to a task we are performing, or picturing ourselves explaining to the course instructor why a paper will be late, or replaying in our minds personal encounters that we particularly enjoyed or wish had gone differently.

Some individuals—perhaps 4 percent of the population—fantasize so vividly as to be called *fantasy-prone personalities.* One study of twenty-six such women found that as children they had enjoyed unusually intense make-believe play with their dolls, stuffed animals, or imaginary companions (Wilson & Barber, 1983). As adults, they reported spending more than half their time fantasizing. They would

André Derain's (1880–1954) painting *La Tasse de Thé* captures the charm of a reflective moment of quiet. The pleasure and relaxation afforded by such moments are part of the adaptive value of daydreams.

relive experiences or imagine scenes so vividly that they would later sometimes have trouble sorting out their remembered fantasies from their memories of actual events. When watching or imagining violent or scary scenes they would sometimes feel ill. Many reported profound mystical or religious experiences. Three-fourths had experienced orgasms solely by sexual fantasy.

Are the hours we spend in fantasy merely a way of escaping rather than facing reality? At times, they are. But daydreaming can also be adaptive. Some daydreams help us prepare for future events by keeping us aware of unfinished business and serving as mental rehearsals. Playful fantasies have enhanced the creativity of scientists, artists, and writers. For children, daydreaming in the form of imaginative play is important to social and cognitive development—a fact that makes the diversion of television watching a matter of concern to some child psychologists (Singer, 1986). Daydreams may also substitute for impulsive behavior. This possibility is suggested by the fact that people prone to delinquency and violent behavior or to seeking the artificial highs of dangerous drugs have fewer vivid fantasies (Singer, 1976). It may be that Walter Mitty's imaginative reveries not only rescued him from boredom but also allowed him to indulge his impulses within the safety of his inner world.

> "When I examined myself, and my methods of thought, I came to the conclusion that the gift of fantasy has meant more to me than my talent for absorbing positive knowledge."
> Albert Einstein

> "The art of living requires us to steer a course between the two extremes of external and internal stimulation."
> Psychologist Jerome L. Singer (1976)

SLEEP AND DREAMS

Sleep—sweet, renewing, mysterious sleep. Sleep—the irresistible tempter to whom we must all succumb. What is it? Why do we need it? How does the lack of it affect us?

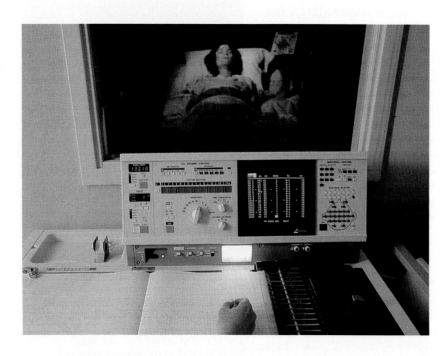

In this sleep laboratory, a researcher electronically monitors the sleeping subject's physiological state. This information, together with observations made of the sleeper's behavior and her reports when awakened at different points in her sleep cycle, provides clues to the mysteries of sleep.

Such questions have intrigued humans for centuries. Now, in our own time, some of the age-old mysteries of sleep have begun to be solved. In laboratories across the world, thousands have slept, attached to modern gadgetry, while others have observed. By recording sleepers' brain waves and muscle movements, by observing sleepers and awakening them at different points in their night's sleep, the sleep-watchers have glimpsed things that a thousand years of common sense never told us. Perhaps you can anticipate some of their discoveries. Are the following statements true or false?

1. When people dream of performing some activity, their limbs often move in concert with the dream (see page 199).

2. Older adults sleep more than young adults (see page 201 and Figure 8–7).

3. After going without sleep for 2 or 3 days, a person's performance on a brief but demanding intellectual task will suffer (see page 200).

4. Sleepwalkers are acting out their dreams (see page 199).

5. Sleep experts recommend an occasional sleeping pill to break a pattern of insomnia (see page 201).

6. The dreams we have before awakening in the morning tend to be quite similar to those we have soon after falling asleep (see page 203).

7. Some people dream every night; others seldom dream at all (see page 200).

Research has shown all these statements (adapted from Palladino & Carducci, 1983) to be false. Let's see how such conclusions have been reached.

THE RHYTHM OF SLEEP

The rhythm of our day has been likened to the rhythm of life—from the rebirth of our waking to a new day to our nightly return to what Shakespeare called "death's counterfeit." Our bodies are synchronized with the 24-hour cycle of day and night through a biological clock known as *circadian rhythm* (from the Latin *circa,* "approximately," and *dies,* "day"). Our body temperature, for example, rises as morning approaches, peaks during the day, and then begins to descend again before we go to sleep. After a long transoceanic or cross-country flight, our circadian rhythm is disrupted and we experience jet lag, mainly because we are awake at a time when our biological clock says "Sleep!"

Researchers are experimenting with drugs and with procedures that make use of bright lights during evening hours in hopes of developing methods for reducing jet lag by allowing us to reset our biological clocks (Czeisler & others, 1986; Turek & Losee-Olson, 1986). Radically altering one's sleeping schedule from weekdays to weekends, as shift workers or college students often do, can also throw the biological clock out of phase. Just as it begins to reset itself to the weekend sleep schedule, a new work (or school) week begins, and the result may be "Sunday night insomnia" and "Monday morning blues."

Mysteriously, when research volunteers are isolated without clocks or daylight, they tend to adopt a 25-hour day. This helps explain why most people find it easier to jet west, with an extended day, than east. When placed in a time-free environment under constant illumination, most animals, too, exceed a 24-hour day.

There is also a biological rhythm during our sleep—a cycle of five distinct sleep stages that we pass through several times during the night. This was unknown until 8-year-old Armond Aserinsky went to bed one night in 1952. His father, Eugene, a University of Chicago graduate student, needed to test an electroencephalograph he had been repairing during the day (Aserinsky, 1988; Seligman, 1987). He placed electrodes near Armond's eyes to catch the electric current produced by the rolling eye movements believed to occur during sleep. Before long, the machine went wild, tracing deep zigzags on the graph paper. Aserinsky thought the machine was still broken. But as the night proceeded, the activity periodically recurred—indicating, Aserinsky finally realized, fast, jerky eye movements accompanied by energetic brain activity. When Armond was awakened during one such episode of *rapid eye movement sleep (REM sleep)*, the boy reported that he was having a dream.

To find out if similar cycles occur during adult sleep, Nathaniel Kleitman (1960) and Aserinsky initiated procedures that have since been followed with thousands of volunteers. To appreciate both the methods and the findings, imagine yourself as a subject in a sleep experiment.

Once you have readied yourself for bed, the researcher tapes electrodes to your scalp (to measure your brain waves) and to the corners of your eyes (to detect eye movements) (Figure 8–2). Other devices allow the researcher to record your heart rate, your respiration rate, your muscle tension, and even the degree of your genital arousal. In this strange environment, with all these instruments attached, and knowing that your waking and sleeping are being observed, you probably have some trouble falling or staying asleep.

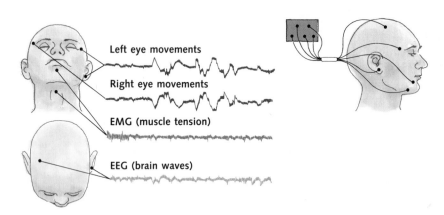

Figure 8–2   How sleep is studied. Researchers measure brain-wave activity, eye movements, and muscle tension, by tapping electrodes to various parts of the head, including the scalp, face, ears, and neck.

The next night the situation is more familiar, you are more tired, and your sleep is therefore more normal. Once you are in bed with your eyes closed, the researcher in the next room sees the relatively slow *alpha waves* of your awake but relaxed state on the EEG (see Figure 8–3). Before long your breathing rate slows and your brain waves slow further and show the irregular pattern of *theta* waves characteristic of Stage 1 sleep. From this light sleep you are easily awakened. In this state, which lasts about 2 minutes, you may experience fantastic images, which are like *hallucinations*—sensory experiences that occur in the absence of a sensory stimulus. You may have a sensa-

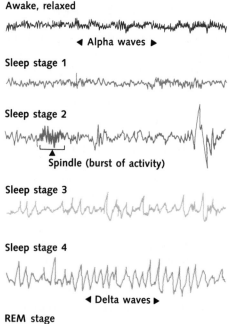

Figure 8–3   Brain waves and sleep stages. The regular alpha waves of an awake, relaxed state are quite different from the slower and much larger rhythmic delta waves of deep Stage 4 sleep. Those of REM sleep are more rapid than Stage 4, resembling the near-waking Stage 1 sleep.

tion of falling (at which moment your body may suddenly jerk) or of floating weightlessly, or you may have a vivid visual image.

Soon, you relax more deeply and begin about 20 minutes of Stage 2 sleep, characterized by the periodic appearance of *sleep spindles—* bursts of brain-wave activity. Although you can still be awakened without too much difficulty during this phase, you are now clearly asleep.

Then for the next few minutes you go through the transitional Stage 3 to the deep sleep of Stage 4. Starting in Stage 3 and increasingly in Stage 4, your brain emits large, slow *delta waves.* Hence, these stages together are sometimes called *delta sleep.* They last for perhaps 30 minutes, during which you are hard to awaken. Curiously, it is during the deep sleep of Stage 4 that we may talk or walk in our sleep, or (as young children) wet the bed. Moreover, even when we are deeply asleep, our brains somehow process the meaning of certain stimuli. We may move around a great deal on our beds, but somehow we manage not to fall out of them. The occasional roar of passing vehicles may leave deep sleep undisturbed, but the cry from a baby's nursery quickly ends it.

About an hour after you first fall asleep, a strange thing happens. Rather than continuing in deep slumber, you go back up the sleep ladder. Returning through stages 3 and 2, you enter the most intriguing sleep phase of all—REM sleep (Figure 8–4). For some 10 minutes, your brain waves become more rapid, like those of the nearly awake Stage 1 sleep. But unlike Stage 1 sleep, your heart rate rises, your breathing becomes more rapid and irregular, your genitals very likely show signs of arousal (either an erection or an increase in vaginal congestion and lubrication), and every half minute or so your eyes dart around in a momentary burst of activity under your closed lids (Figure 8–5). Given that these REM bursts are easily noticed by anyone who patiently watches a sleeper's eyes, it is amazing that science was ignorant of the existence of REM sleep until 1952.

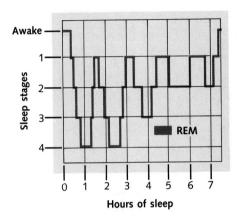

Figure 8–4 The stages in a typical night's sleep. Most people pass through a cycle of the five sleep stages several times, with the periods of Stage 4 sleep and then Stage 3 sleep diminishing and REM sleep periods increasing in duration. (From Cartwright, 1978.)

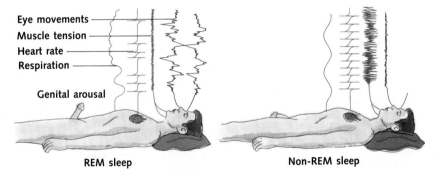

REM sleep   Non-REM sleep

Figure 8–5 REM sleep is paradoxical. Eye movements, heart rate, respiration, and genital activity all suggest arousal. Yet the muscles are deeply relaxed and the sleeper is not easily awakened.

Although your motor cortex is active during REM sleep, its neural messages generally do not reach your muscles, which are therefore very relaxed—so relaxed, in fact, that except for an occasional finger or facial twitch, you are essentially paralyzed. Moreover, you cannot easily be awakened. Thus REM sleep is sometimes called *paradoxical sleep* because internally the body is aroused while externally it appears calm.

Even more intriguing than the paradoxical nature of REM sleep is what the rapid eye movements announce: the beginning of a dream.

The common "morning erection" stems from the last REM period of the night, which often occurs just before waking. Such genital arousal occurs regardless of whether one is dreaming of sexual activity. In young men, sleep-related erections last 30 minutes on average (Karacan & others, 1983). Most men troubled by erectile disorder ("impotence") have morning erections, which indicates a psychological rather than a physical basis for the disorder.

Researcher William Dement (1978) reported that even those who claim they never dream will, when awakened during REM sleep, more than 80 percent of the time recall a vivid dream that, unlike the fleeting images of Stage 1 sleep, is often emotional and usually storylike. (Occasionally people recall dreams when awakened from stages other than REM sleep, but usually these dreams involve only a single incident, such as "I was asking George if I could borrow his hammer.")

Are the eye movements linked to a dream's visual aspects? One suggested answer was that the dreamer is "watching" the dream as if it were a private movie. But some researchers now believe that the darting eyes, like the occasional twitching of muscles, merely reflect the overflow of the dreamer's activated nervous system (Chase & Morales, 1983).

As the night wears on, this sleep cycle repeats itself about every 90 minutes, with the deep Stage 4 sleep becoming briefer and then disappearing and the REM sleep period becoming progressively longer. By morning, some 20 to 25 percent of an average night's sleep—some 100 minutes—has been REM sleep. This means that even those people who claim not to dream actually spend about 600 hours a year experiencing 1500 or so dreams.

WHY DO WE SLEEP?

Sleep commands roughly one-third of our lives. Deprived of it, we begin to feel terrible; our bodies yearn to be taken by it. Obviously, we need sleep. But why?

One might think this question could be answered easily: Just keep people awake for several days and note how they deteriorate. If you were a subject in such an experiment, how do you think it would affect your body and mind? Of course, you would become terribly drowsy at times—especially during the hours when your biological clock programs you to sleep. But could you be physically damaged by lack of sleep? Would your biochemistry or body organs be noticeably altered? Would you become emotionally disturbed? Intellectually disoriented?

The major effect of sleep deprivation, as some chronically fatigued college students know, is sleepiness. Other effects are more subtle: diminished immunity to disease, a slight hand tremor, irritability, occasional moments of inattention or misperceptions on monotonous tasks (Palmblad & others, 1979; Webb, 1982a). With some monotonous tasks, such as long-distance driving, these effects can be devastating. On short, highly motivating tasks, sleep deprivation has little effect. When 17-year-old Randy Gardner made his way into the *Guinness Book of World Records* by staying awake for 11 days, he at times had to keep moving to stay awake. Nevertheless, during his final night of sleeplessness, Gardner managed to beat researcher William Dement 100 straight times in a pinball game. He then slept for 15 hours and awoke feeling fine (Gulevich & others, 1966).

The current record holder, "Ramblin' Rob" McDonald, reportedly stayed awake for 18 days, 22 hours in a 1986 rocking chair marathon.

In a few rare cases, brain-diseased people have lost their ability to sleep, with disastrous results. One recent case involved a 52-year-old man who gradually lost his ability to sleep and became severely fatigued, shaky, disoriented, and incontinent (Lugaresi & others, 1986). He would lapse into a dreamlike stupor from time to time, but without exhibiting the brain waves of sleep. Nine months after the sleep difficulty began, he died.

Why, then, must we sleep? We have few answers, but there is evidence that sleep helps restore body tissues. In one study of runners in a 92-kilometer (57-mile) ultramarathon, the competitors averaged 7 hours sleep during nights before the race, and 8½ hours during the two nights following the race. The night after the run, Stage 4 deep sleep doubled (Shapiro & others, 1981). Sleep may also play a role in the growth process. During deep sleep, the pituitary gland releases a growth hormone. As adults grow older, they release less of this hormone, and they spend less time in deep sleep (Pekkanen, 1982). These physiological discoveries are only beginning to solve the ongoing riddle of sleep. As researcher Dement (1978, p. 83) deadpanned, "we have miles to go before we sleep."

SLEEP DISORDERS

The idea that "Everyone needs 8 hours sleep" is not true. Newborns spend at least two-thirds of their day asleep, the elderly barely more than one-fourth. Age-related differences in average time spent sleeping are rivaled by differences in the normal amount of sleep among individuals at any age. Some people thrive with less than 6 hours of sleep per night; others regularly sleep 9 hours or more. (Among various mammals, the need for sleep varies more widely: Horses and cows sleep only 3 to 4 hours per day; rats and cats, 14 to 15 hours [Webb, 1982b].) Although human sleep differences are not accompanied by striking personality differences (Webb, 1979), sleep patterns may be genetically influenced. When Wilse Webb and Scott Campbell (1983) monitored the pattern and duration of sleep among fraternal and identical twins, only the identical twins were strikingly similar.

Whatever their normal need for sleep, some 15 percent of adults complain of *insomnia*—recurring problems in falling or staying asleep. The emphasis in this sleep disorder is on "recurring." True insomnia is not the occasional inability to sleep that we may experience when we are feeling anxious or excited. Alertness is a natural and adaptive response to stress. We commonly underestimate the amount of sleep we get on restless nights. Even if we've been awake only an hour, we may *think* we've had insomnia much of the night, because that's the part we remember.

The two most common quick fixes for true insomnia, sleeping pills and alcohol, can aggravate the problem. Both tend to reduce REM sleep, and when their use is discontinued, the insomnia may worsen. Sleep experts have other advice:

1. Relax before bedtime.

2. Avoid rich foods around bedtime. (Milk is good, because it aids in the manufacture of serotonin, a neurotransmitter that facilitates sleep.)

3. Sleep on a regular schedule (rise at the same time even after a restless night) and avoid naps.

4. Reassure yourself that the temporary loss of sleep causes no great harm.

Rarer but more severe than insomnia are the sleep disorders narcolepsy and sleep apnea. People with *narcolepsy* suffer periodic overwhelming sleepiness, sometimes at the most inopportune times—perhaps just after taking a terrific swing at a softball or when laughing loudly or shouting angrily (Dement, 1978). The person collapses directly into a brief period of REM sleep, with its accompanying loss of muscular tension. The estimated 100,000 or more Americans who suffer from narcolepsy must live with extra caution.

"This concludes the conscious part of your day. Good night."

"The lion and the lamb shall lie down together, but the lamb will not be very sleepy."
Woody Allen in the movie
Love and Death, 1975

Two uncommon sleep disorders. Narcolepsy sufferers, such as the man pictured at the left, are overcome by sleepiness at inopportune times. The baby on the right suffers from sleep apnea, and is attached to a monitor that sounds an alarm if he stops breathing.

Those who suffer from *sleep apnea* intermittently stop breathing while sleeping (*apnea* means "cessation of respiration"). After an airless minute or so, the decreased oxygen in the blood arouses the sleeper to snort in air for a few seconds. The process is repeated hundreds of times during a night's sleep. Apart from sleepiness during the day—and their mates' complaints about their loud "snoring"—apnea sufferers are often not aware of their disorder. Yet, were they not to become aroused and resume breathing, they would suffocate, as apparently happens to sleeping babies who mysteriously die of Sudden Infant Death Syndrome (SIDS), also known as crib death.

Still other sleepers are afflicted with *night terrors.* The person—often a child—might sit up or walk around, talk incoherently, experience a doubling of heart and breathing rates, and appear terrified (Hartmann, 1981). The night-terror sufferer very seldom awakens fully and recalls little or nothing the next morning—at most a fleeting, frightening image. Unlike nightmares, which typically occur toward morning during REM sleep, but *like* sleepwalking, night terrors usually occur during the first few hours of sleep and during Stage 4 sleep (Figure 8–6).

DREAMS

The discovery of the link between REM sleep and dreaming opened a new era of dream research. Instead of having to trust someone's hazy recall of a dream hours afterward, it became possible to catch dreams as they happen. Researchers could awaken someone during a REM sleep period, or within 5 minutes afterward, and get a vivid account of the dream.

What Do We Dream?   Compared to daydreams, REM dreams are more vivid, more emotional, and more bizarre. In the dream world, events frequently occur in a jumbled sequence, scenes change suddenly, people appear and disappear, and physical laws, such as the law of gravity, may be violated. Yet dreams are so vivid that we may

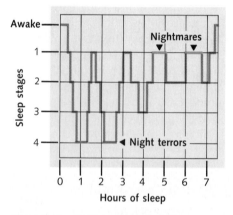

Figure 8–6   Night terrors and nightmares in the sleep laboratory. Night terrors occur within 2 or 3 hours of falling asleep, during Stage 4 sleep. Nightmares occur toward morning, during REM sleep. (From Hartmann, 1984.)

"Why does the eye see a thing more clearly in dreams than in the imagination when awake?"

Leonardo da Vinci, 1452–1519

confuse them with reality. Occasionally, we may be sufficiently lucid during a dream to wonder whether we are, in fact, dreaming. When experiencing such "lucid dreams," some people are able to test their state of consciousness. If they can perform some absurd act, such as floating in the air, then they know they are dreaming.

Although we are more likely to be awakened by and thus to remember our most emotional dreams, many dreams are rather ordinary. When awakened during REM sleep, people report dreams with sexual imagery less often than you might think—in one study, only about 1 in 10 dreams among young men and 1 in 30 among young women had sexual overtones (Hall & Van de Castle, 1966). (Recall that genital arousal accompanies REM sleep, so is usually *not* a consequence of sexual dreams.) More commonly, we dream of events related to our daily lives, such as an incident at work or taking an exam. Most dreams are not notably sweet: People commonly dream of repeatedly failing in an attempt to do something; of being attacked, pursued, or rejected; or of experiencing misfortune (Hall & others, 1982).

Across the world, people of all ages show a curious gender difference in dream content. The average female dreams of males and females equally often, but 65 percent of the average male's dream characters are males. No one is sure why this is so. Whatever its significance, dream researcher Calvin Hall (1984) believed this fact could be added to the short list of apparently universal gender differences noted in Chapter 5.

The story line of our dreams—what Sigmund Freud called their *manifest content*—often incorporates experiences and preoccupations from our day's events, especially in our first dreams of the night. The sensory stimuli of our sleeping environment may also influence dream content. A particular odor or the ringing of an alarm clock or telephone may be instantly and ingeniously woven into the dream story. In one experiment, William Dement and Edward Wolpert (1958) lightly sprayed cold water on dreamers' faces. Compared to sleepers who did not get the cold water treatment, these subjects were more likely to dream about water—about waterfalls, leaky roofs, or even about being sprayed by someone.

"I don't think I'll go in today. I just dreamed a whole day's work, including lunch."

"For what one has dwelt on by day, these things are seen in visions of the night."
  Menander of Athens, 342–292 B.C..
  Fragments

Freud held that a dream's manifest content—what the dreamer experiences and perhaps recalls—is a symbolic version of its hidden, or latent, content.

Why Do We Dream?   In his landmark book *The Interpretation of Dreams*, published in 1900, Freud argued that a dream is a psychic safety valve that harmlessly discharges otherwise unacceptable feelings. According to Freud, a dream's manifest content is but a censored, symbolic version of its deeper ***latent content***, which consists of drives and wishes that would be threatening if expressed directly. Although most dreams do not have overt sexual imagery, Freud nevertheless believed that "most of the dreams of adults are traced back by analysis to *erotic wishes*." In Freud's view, a gun, for example, might actually be a disguised representation of the penis, and a dream in which a person is being robbed at gunpoint might be seen as expressing a wish for sexual surrender.

Although Freud considered dreams the key to understanding the individual's inner conflicts, many of his critics believe that dream interpretation leads down a blind alley. Some contend that even if dreams are symbolic, they can be interpreted almost any way one wishes. Others maintain that there is nothing hidden in dreams. A dream about a gun is, they say, a dream about a gun. Even Freud, who loved to smoke cigars, acknowledged that "Sometimes, a cigar is just a cigar."

Several alternatives to Freud's theory of dreams have recently been offered. One of these sees dreams in terms of an *information-processing* function: Dreams may help sift, sort, and fix in memory our day's experiences. Following stressful experiences or intense learning periods, REM sleep tends to increase (Palumbo, 1978). What is more, a whole series of experiments has produced "consistent and compelling evidence" that REM sleep facilitates memory for unusual or anxiety-arousing material (McGrath & Cohen, 1978). In one experiment, people heard unusual phrases before bedtime and then were given a memory test the next morning. If they were awakened every time they began REM sleep, they remembered less than if they were awakened during other sleep stages (Empson & Clarke, 1970). A night of solid sleep (and dreaming) does, it seems, have a justifiable place in a student's life.

Another proposed explanation of dreams is compatible with the information-processing theory: Dreams may serve a physiological function. Perhaps dreams—or the associated physiological activity of REM sleep—provide the sleeping brain with periodic stimulation. As you may recall from Chapter 3, stimulating experiences develop and preserve the brain's neural pathways. This theory makes sense from a developmental point of view because infants, whose neural networks are just developing, spend the most time in REM sleep (Figure 8–7).

Still other physiological theories propose that dreams are triggered by neural activity that spreads upward from the brainstem. According to one version, this neural activity is random, and dreams are the brain's attempt to make sense out of it (McCarley & Hobson, 1981; Lavie & Hobson, 1986). The limbic system is also active during REM sleep, and it is from this part of the brain that the dream's emotional tone may arise. Psychologists Martin Seligman and Amy Yellen (1987) show how this physiological theory fits with our dream experiences. They note that the seconds-long bursts of rapid eye movements during REM sleep coincide with bursts of activity in the visual cortex. If people are awakened during one of these bursts of visual activity, they report vivid visual experiences, usually dramatic hallucinations.

Seligman and Yellen link these physiological suppositions with our well-established tendencies to impose meanings on even meaningless stimuli. (Recall from Chapter 2 how quickly split-brain patients "ex-

"Dreams are the true interpreters of our inclinations, but art is required to sort and understand them."
Montaigne,
Essays, 1580

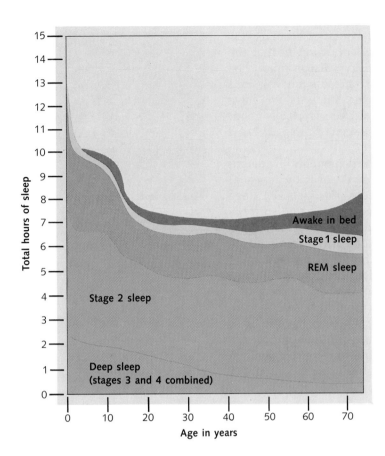

Figure 8–7   As we age our sleep patterns change. During our first few months, we spend progressively less time in REM sleep. During our first 20 years, we spend progressively less time asleep. From middle age on, sleep is seldom sustained through an entire night. Occasional awakenings become the norm, not something to fret over or treat with medication. (Adapted from Williams & others, 1974.)

plained" puzzling actions produced by their right hemisphere. Recall from Chapter 7, too, how readily people can "see" faces, sexual images, or other meaningful patterns in everything from moonscapes to Ritz crackers.) Ergo, say Seligman and Yellen, our ever-active cognitive machinery strings together whatever it has available—residues from our day's experiences, our ongoing concerns, the alarm clock's ringing, or (during REM sleep) the emotional episodes and brief visual hallucinations triggered by brainstem activity plus the emotional tone provided by the limbic system.

Seligman illustrates with one of his own dreams, in which the visual bursts are the striking image of a tomato tree and the faces of several former students. Note, too, how the (real-life) ringing of the telephone in Seligman's bedroom is woven into the narrative fabric:

> I look out the window of the Princeton University library, where I am giving a seminar. I see, to my surprise, a tree with enormous ripe, red tomatoes on its branches. I remark on it to the class. I turn my attention back to the seminar and start speaking about the day's topic. I look around the students in the seminar, and I see several students together in the seminar who are from different eras of graduate school at the University of Pennsylvania. As we begin to talk, the telephone rings, and I notice that my secretary is also in the seminar. She handles the situation with aplomb, picks up the telephone and tells the caller to call back later since Professor Seligman is teaching a seminar. We return again to the topic of interest.

This theory—that dreams originate as unrelated visual bursts which are given their emotional setting by the limbic system and their story line by the mind's relentless effort to make sense of things— explains many of our dream experiences, such as the sudden and bizarre changes in scene (triggered by a new visual burst). Dream reports by Seligman's University of Pennsylvania students confirm that the most vivid dream images tend to be the surprising, discontinuous aspects of the dream; other, less vivid images are presumably conjured up to string the visual bursts together. Moreover, students who have the most coherent and well-integrated dreams also are especially good, while wide awake, at integrating random visual scenes into a coherent story.

The function of dreams is a topic of vigorous debate, but the disputants all agree that we *need* REM sleep. Deprived of it by repeated awakenings, people return more and more quickly to the REM stage after falling back to sleep. When finally allowed to sleep undisturbed, they literally sleep like babies—with increased REM sleep. The withdrawal of REM-suppressing sleeping medications also increases REM sleep, but with accompanying nightmares. This **REM rebound effect** occurs in other mammals as well, most of which share our REM sleep stage. Animals' need for REM sleep is consistent with any of the physiological explanations of REM sleep. But the fact that REM sleep occurs in mammals (and not in animals such as fish, whose behavior is less influenced by learning) also is consistent with the information-processing theory of dreams. All of which serves to remind us once again of a fundamental lesson: Biological and psychological explanations of behavior are partners, not competitors.

This piglet, like her companion, needs REM sleep. Deprived of it, she will replenish this deficiency if allowed to sleep undisturbed.

HYPNOSIS

Imagine you are about to be hypnotized. The hypnotist invites you to sit back, fix your gaze on a spot on the ceiling, and relax. In a quiet, low voice the hypnotist suggests, "Your eyes are growing tired. . . . Your eyelids are becoming heavy . . . now heavier and heavier. . . . They are beginning to close. . . . You are becoming more deeply relaxed. . . . Your breathing is now deep and regular. . . . Your muscles are becoming more and more relaxed. Your whole body is beginning to feel like lead."

After a few minutes of this hypnotic induction, your eyes are probably closed (anyone's eyes will get tired after staring at the ceiling) and you may possibly be undergoing *hypnosis*—a state of heightened suggestibility that enables a hypnotist's coaxings and directions to trigger specific behaviors, perceptions, and perhaps even memories. When it is suggested that "your eyelids are shutting so tight that you cannot open them even if you try," your eyelids will in fact seem beyond your control and will remain closed—if you are hypnotized. Told to forget the number six, you will be puzzled when you count eleven fingers on your hands. Invited to smell a sensual perfume that is actually ammonia, you will linger delightedly over its acrid odor. Asked to describe a nonexistent picture the hypnotist claims to be holding, you will talk about it in detail. Told that you cannot see a certain object, such as a chair, you will indeed report that it is not there, although, curiously, you will manage to avoid the chair when walking around. And if instructed to forget all these happenings once you are out of the hypnotic state, you will later experience *posthypnotic amnesia,* a temporary memory loss rather like being unable to recall a familiar name. The "forgotten" material is nevertheless "in there," for it can affect later behavior and can be recalled at a prearranged signal or upon subtle questioning (Kihlstrom, 1985; Spanos & others, 1985).

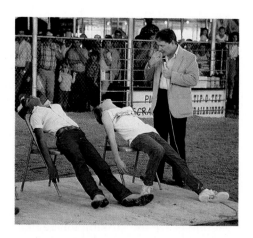

Despite its exploitation by stage performers, hypnosis has become a topic of serious investigation. Researchers disagree, however, as to whether hypnosis is a unique psychological state or merely an extension of normal processes of cognition and social influence.

Although hypnotic techniques have been in use since antiquity, the rediscovery of hypnosis is commonly credited to an Austrian physician, Anton Mesmer (1734–1815), who mistakenly thought he had discovered a universal principle of "animal magnetism." With great flourish, Mesmer passed magnets over the bodies of ailing people, some of whom would lapse into a trancelike *(mesmerized)* state and awaken much improved. As we noted in Chapter 1, the Franklin Commission found no evidence of animal magnetism and attributed the "cures" Mesmer achieved to "mere imagination." Thus, hypnosis—or mesmerism, as it was then called—became linked with quackery and the bizarre. This 200-year-old link can still be seen in the Library of Congress classification scheme: Books on hypnosis are grouped with those on parapsychology, just after the books on phrenology and just before the books on ghosts and witchcraft.

Also working against the "respectability" of hypnosis were the grand claims made by its practitioners. Supposedly, mesmerized people could see with the back of their heads, perceive others' internal organs, and communicate with the dead (Spanos, 1982). Researchers now agree that hypnotized persons cannot perform such feats. They can, however, perform feats that *seem* amazing. Some can become "human planks," their bodies so rigid that when the head and shoulders are placed on one chair and the calves on another, a person can stand on the unsupported trunk (Figure 8–8). But if motivated, almost anyone can become a human plank. Hypnotized subjects can extend their arms for about 6 minutes—but so can unhypnotized subjects.

While hypnosis has now become a respectable topic for scientific study, researchers still disagree on whether the hypnotic state is actually an altered state of consciousness. They do agree, however, that some people can be hypnotized more readily and more deeply than others and that some claims for hypnotic effects are real whereas others are grossly exaggerated. Let us first consider some of the areas of general agreement. Then, with the facts of hypnosis in mind, we can ponder two fundamental and perplexing questions: What is hypnosis? And what does hypnosis tell us about human consciousness?

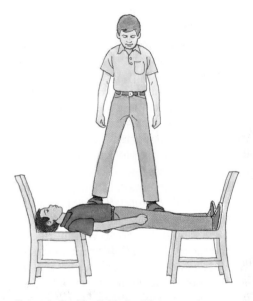

Figure 8–8   The "amazing" hypnotized "human plank." Actually, nonhypnotized people can do the same.

FACTS AND FALSEHOODS

Can Hypnosis Work for Anyone?   Those who study hypnosis agree that its power resides not in the hypnotist but in the subject's capacity to be open to suggestion (Bowers, 1984). To some extent, nearly everyone is suggestible. When people standing upright with their eyes closed are told repeatedly that they are swaying back and forth, most will indeed sway a little. Interestingly, those who sway most tend to be those who can be most easily and deeply hypnotized. In fact, postural sway is one of the items on the Stanford Hypnotic Susceptibility Scale that assesses a person's hypnotizability. During the assessment, a person is given a brief hypnotic induction and is then presented with a series of suggested experiences that range from easy (one's outstretched arms will move together) to difficult (with eyes open one will see a nonexistent person).

Furthermore, those who can be deeply hypnotized—say, the 20 percent who can carry out a suggestion not to smell or react to a bottle of ammonia held under their nose—are likely to still be the most hypnotizable 10 years later (Morgan & others, 1974). These hypnotically susceptible people, like the fantasy-prone people described earlier, usually are able to become deeply absorbed in imaginative activities (Lynn & Rhue, 1986). Typically, they have rich fantasy lives, and they

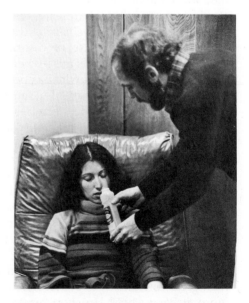

In response to suggestion, this hypnotized subject is outwardly unresponsive to the smell of ammonia.

can easily give themselves over to the imaginary events of a novel or movie. Because the ability to become deeply absorbed in fantasy is in many ways beneficial, it underlies creativity as well as hypnotic responsiveness (Bowers & Bowers, 1979). Many researchers today now refer to hypnotic "susceptibility" as hypnotic *ability,* thereby giving it a label with more positive connotations. Few of us would care to be "susceptible" to hypnosis, but most of us would be glad to have the "ability" to focus our attention totally on a task, to become imaginatively absorbed in it, to entertain fanciful possibilities. And that is what people with hypnotic ability can do.

Can Hypnosis Enhance Recall of Forgotten Events?   Can hypnosis enable people to relive earlier experiences? To recall kindergarten classmates? To retrieve forgotten or suppressed details of a crime? Should testimony obtained under hypnosis be admissible in court?

Most people believe that our past experience is all "in there," that everything that has happened to us is recorded in our brains and could be recalled if only we could break through our own defenses (Loftus, 1980). Testimonies to this come from *age regression* demonstrations, in which subjects supposedly relive experiences from their childhood. But 60 years of research disputes claims of age regression: The behavior of hypnotized people is *not* more genuinely childlike than that of unhypnotized people who are asked to feign childlike behavior (Nash, 1987). Age-regressed people act as they *believe* children would, but typically miss the mark by outperforming real children of the specified age (Silverman & Retzlaff, 1986). Age-regressed people may, for example, *feel* childlike and may print much as they know a 6-year-old would, but they sometimes do so with perfect spelling and typically without any change in their adult brain waves, reflexes, and perceptions.

On a few occasions, the relaxed, focused state of hypnosis has enabled witnesses to produce leads in criminal investigations. On July 15, 1977, 26 children and their bus driver, Ed Ray, were kidnapped and forced into an abandoned trailer truck buried 6 feet underground. After their rescue, Ray was put under hypnosis and was able to recall all but one digit of the kidnapper's license plate. With this crucial information, the abductors were tracked down. Although this ancedote is atypical, most hypnosis researchers agree that hypnosis may have value—or at least do little harm—when used as an investigative tool.

Nevertheless, because of the unreliability of "hypnotically refreshed" memories, perils arise when attempts are made to put a person on the witness stand who has been previously interrogated under hypnosis. Researchers have time and again found that hypnotically refreshed memories tend to combine fact with fiction—findings that have caused a growing list of state courts to curtail testimony derived from hypnosis. Hypnosis typically either fails to boost the recall of information that was previously learned or, worse, *contaminates* one's memory (Dywan & Bowers, 1983; Orne & others, 1984; Smith, 1983). When pressed under hypnosis to recall details, perhaps to "zoom in on your visual memory screen," people will more and more use their imaginations to construct their memories. Without either person being necessarily aware of what is going on, the hypnotist's hints—"Did you hear loud noises?"—can become the subject's memory. Thus, previously hypnotized witnesses may end up testifying confidently, and with great conviction, to events they never actually experienced (Laurence & Perry, 1983). In short, under hypnosis people recall more—both accurately and inaccurately—and become less able to distinguish the one from the other.

"Hypnosis is not a psychological truth serum, and to regard it as such has been a source of considerable mischief."
Kenneth S. Bowers (1987)

A TRUE STORY

Remembrances of Christmases Past? What shall we make of a clever study by Robert True (1949)? He regressed hypnotized volunteers back to Christmases and their birthday parties at ages 10, 7, and 4. In each case, he asked them what day of the week it was. Without hypnosis, the odds that a person could name the correct day of a long-ago date are hardly better than 1 in 7. Remarkably, the hypnotized subjects' answers were 82 percent correct.

Other investigators were unable to obtain similar results when they repeated True's study. When Martin Orne (1982) asked Dr. True why, he replied that *Science*, the journal that published his article, had shortened his key question to "What day is this?" Actually, he had asked his age-regressed subjects, "Is it Monday?, Is it Tuesday?," and so forth until the subject stopped him with a yes. When Orne asked True if he knew the actual day of the week while posing the questions, True granted that he did, but was puzzled as to why Orne would ask him that question.

Can you see why? True's experiment appears to be a beautiful example of how hypnotists can subtly influence the memories of their subjects (and, more generally, of how experimenters can subtly communicate their expectations to their subjects). "Given the eagerness of the hypnotized subject to fulfill the demands placed upon him," surmised Orne, it takes only the slightest change of inflection (in asking "Is it Wednesday?") for the subject to respond, "Yes." The final blow to True's experiment came when Orne simply asked ten 4-year-olds what day of the week it was. To his surprise, none knew. If 4-year-olds typically do not know the day of the week, then True's adults were reporting information that they were unlikely to have known when they were 4.

Remembrances of Lives Past? If people's hypnotic regressions to childhood are partly imagined, then how believable are claims of "regression to past lives"? Nicholas Spanos (1987–1988) reports that when hypnotized, fantasy-prone people who believe in reincarnation will offer vivid details of "past lives." But they nearly always report being their same race—unless the researcher has informed them that different races are common. They often report being someone famous rather than one of the countless "nobodies," and some contradict one another by claiming to have been the same person, such as King Henry VIII (Reveen, 1987–1988). Moreover, they typically do not know things that any person of that historical time would have known. One subject who "regressed" to a "previous life" as a Japanese fighter pilot in 1940 could not name the emperor of Japan and did not know that Japan was at war. Hypnotic regressions to past lives thus offer good stories, but no credible evidence of reincarnation.

MY NAME IS EUNICE. I HAVE LIVED MANY PAST LIVES, MOST OF THEM IN TRENTON, NEW JERSEY....

CHANNELLING ON THE CHEAP

Drawing by M. Stevens; ©1987 The New Yorker Magazine, Inc.

Can Hypnosis Force People to Act Against Their Will?   Researchers Martin Orne and Frederick Evans (1965) demonstrated that hypnotized subjects *could* be induced not only to perform an apparently dangerous act (to briefly dip one hand in fuming acid) but to then throw the "acid" in a research assistant's face. When interviewed a day later they exhibited no memory of their acts and emphatically denied they would follow orders to commit such actions.

Had hypnosis given the hypnotist a special power to control these people against their will? To find out, Orne and Evans included a control group in their experiment—six subjects who were *pretending* to have been hypnotized. The laboratory experimenter was unaware of their presence and treated all subjects in the same manner. The result? In this situation, all six of the *un*hypnotized subjects performed the same acts as the hypnotized ones.

So (as Chapter 19, Social Influence, will emphasize) an authoritative person in a legitimate context can induce people—hypnotized or not—to perform some unusual acts. Hypnosis researcher Nicholas P. Spanos (1982) put it somewhat more succinctly: "The overt behaviors of hypnotic subjects are well within normal limits."

Similarly, another hypnosis researcher, Eugene Levitt (1986), reports that most hypnotized subjects can be induced to cut up an American flag or deface a Bible, and that a few will even cooperate in stealing an exam or selling illegal drugs, but that people asked to simulate hypnosis are no less likely to perform the same acts. However, Levitt also reports that there are a very small number of highly hypnotizable people who, even when offered $100 to resist acting upon a simple hypnotic suggestion, cannot (or will not) resist. With the possible exception of these "hypnotic virtuosos," nonhypnotized and hypnotized people seem to behave similarly.

Generally, then, hypnosis does not surpass other techniques for "controlling" people. Its uniqueness lies mostly in the hypnotized person's inner experience of compelling and subjectively real fantasies—of altered feelings, of seeing what is not there and not seeing what is. As Orne (1984) put it 20 years after his acid experiments, "Hypnosis turns out to be a powerful way to alter experience, but not a powerful way to alter behavior."

"You certainly may not *try to hypnotize me."*

Can Hypnosis Be Therapeutic?   Recently, the clinical use of hypnosis has mushroomed. Hypnotherapists do nothing magical; rather, they attempt to help patients harness their own healing powers (Baker, 1987). *Posthypnotic suggestions* (suggestions to be carried out after the hypnosis session has ended) have alleviated headaches, asthma, warts, and psychosomatic skin disorders. One woman, who had suffered open sores all over her body for more than 20 years, was asked to imagine herself swimming in shimmering, sunlit liquids that would cleanse her skin and to experience her skin as smooth and unblemished. Within 3 months her sores disappeared (Bowers, 1984).

Whether hypnosis per se is therapeutic seems to depend on whether the behavior is voluntary or involuntary. In some studies that apply hypnosis to problems of self-control, such as nail biting or smoking, it has been equally helpful to those who could be deeply hypnotized and to those who could not. This suggests that with voluntary behavior the treatment benefits may be due to something other than hypnotic suggestion. However, with problems unrelated to willpower, such as hypersensitive allergic reactions, the greatest relief *is* experienced by the most hypnotizable people (Bowers & LaBaron, 1986). In such cases, hypnosis seems to be the therapeutic agent.

Can Hypnosis Alleviate Pain?   That pain can be relieved through hypnosis has been well established experimentally (Kihlstrom, 1985). Hypnotized subjects report far less pain than others when their arms are placed in ice water. Moreover, their reports have a consistency that would be hard to fake. For example, if a hypnotic suggestion reduces a low-level pain by half, the same suggestion will also reduce pain twice as strong by about half (Hilgard, 1983). Furthermore, even light hypnosis can reduce fear, and thus hypersensitivity to the pain of, say, dental treatment. And some 10 percent of us can become so deeply hypnotized that even surgery can be performed without anesthesia.

The explanation for pain relief through hypnosis is still being debated. One idea has been that endorphins, the pain-reducing neurotransmitters, might be involved. But when endorphin production is chemically prevented, hypnotic pain relief still occurs (Watkins & Mayer, 1982). Indeed, the person may report feeling no pain even though physiological indicators such as heart rate are responding to the pain stimulus.

How could this be? One theory of hypnotic pain relief involves *dissociation,* a split between different levels of consciousness that allows some mental processes to occur simultaneously. Hypnosis, it suggests, dissociates the sensation of the pain stimulus (of which the subject is aware, whether hypnotized or not) from the emotional suffering that defines our experience of pain. The ice water may be experienced as very cold, but not as painful. Another theory proposes that hypnotic pain relief is due to selective attention, as when an injured athlete, caught up in the heat of competition, feels little or no pain until the game has ended.

Does Hypnosis Block Sensory Input?   Note what both views of pain assume—that at some level the pain stimulus *is* sensed. Indeed, people who report feeling no pain will nevertheless perspire with pounding heart in response to electric shock or a surgeon's knife. Likewise, following a suggestion of deafness, hypnotized people will deny being able to hear their own voices, but will respond as do unhypnotized people when hearing their voice over a headset with a half-second delay: The delayed feedback disrupts their ability to speak fluently. If told they are color blind, hypnotized people will respond to tests of color blindness differently than do people who have vision that is in fact color deficient.

Although the subjects seem genuine in reporting no perception of pain, sound, or color, the stimuli have quite obviously registered within their sensory systems. Similarly, when deeply hypnotized subjects are told to forget having heard certain words they will deny any memory of them; their behavior tells a different story, however, for the stored words will influence the subjects' perceptions of subsequent verbal stimuli in quite normal ways (Kihlstrom & Hoyt, 1988). Researchers debate what hypnosis is, but all agree that it does *not*, as hypnotized subjects and their audiences may think, block sensory input.

The unanswered question, then, of whether hypnosis relieves pain by dissociating the pain sensation from conscious awareness, or merely by focusing attention on other things, brings us to a fundamental issue: Is hypnosis a unique psychological state?

The Lamaze method of childbirth uses several techniques in common with hypnosis, such as relaxation, controlled breathing, eye fixation, and suggestion. Women for whom the Lamaze method effectively lessens pain tend also to have high hypnotic ability (Venn, 1986).

The experience of pain is reduced, even eliminated, at times when one's attention is diverted elsewhere.

DOES MEDITATION PRODUCE A HYPNOTIC STATE?

"Sit down alone and in silence. Lower your head, shut your eyes, breathe out gently, and imagine yourself looking into your own heart. . . . As you breathe out, say 'Lord Jesus Christ, have mercy on me.' . . . Try to put all other thoughts aside. Be calm, be patient and repeat the process very frequently."

Gregory of Sinai, died 1346

Certain meditation practices of both Eastern and Western religions are in some ways similar to hypnosis. Meditators assume a comfortable position in a quiet environment and adopt a receptive, serene attitude. They then focus on their breathing, on a word (in Eastern meditation, a mantra such as *Om*), or on a phrase (in Christianity, perhaps a short prayer). Also like hypnosis, meditation is finding clinical uses, as in the control of pain and stress.

But unlike hypnotized subjects, who are influenced by the hypnotist's suggestions, meditators are under their own control. Also unlike hypnotized subjects, experienced meditators exhibit rapidly decreasing metabolism and changing blood pressure, heart rate, and brain waves, all of which suggest a deeply relaxed state (Alexander & others, 1987; Wallace & Benson, 1972). So, meditation is clearly *not* the same as hypnosis. However, these physiological changes are not unique to meditation; merely resting can produce similar effects (Holmes, 1984). And as we noted in Chapter 6, rest (or, at least, REST—Restricted Environmental Stimulation Therapy) can also be therapeutic.

Drawing by Frascino; ©1975 The Saturday Review of Literature.

IS HYPNOSIS AN ALTERED STATE OF CONSCIOUSNESS?

We have seen that hypnosis involves a heightened state of suggestibility. We have also seen that although hypnosis does not endow a person with special powers, it can sometimes enhance recall of real (and unreal) past events, aid in overcoming psychosomatic ailments, and help to alleviate pain. But just what hypnosis is has been a subject of debate since Mesmer's time.

The word "hypnosis" is derived from the Greek word for sleep. However, the brain waves of hypnotized subjects are like those of a person relaxed and awake, not like those of someone sleeping or dreaming. To some psychologists, this suggests that hypnosis is *not* an altered state of consciousness. But David Spiegel and his colleagues (1985) disagree. They seated deeply hypnotized people before a TV screen and asked them to imagine that a cardboard box was blocking the screen. When a stimulus was flashed on the screen, the subjects' brain waves did not display the normal brain response to the stimulus, which suggests that the hypnosis had affected their brains' information processing. Although other studies have generally found that physiological processes are not affected in any unique way by hypnosis, Spiegel's findings illustrate why the issue is still unsettled.

Hypnosis as a Social Phenomenon   Not only is the physiology of hypnotized subjects largely indistinguishable from that of unhypnotized people, but for the most part, so is their behavior. The fact that a wide range of behaviors that can be produced with hypnosis can also be produced without it suggests that they may be nothing more than the workings of ordinary consciousness (Spanos, 1986a).

In Chapter 7 we saw how powerfully our ordinary perceptions are influenced by our interpretations. Especially in the case of pain, where the effects of hypnosis seem most dramatic, our perceptions depend on where our attention is directed. We have also seen that imaginative people can manufacture vivid perceptions without hypnosis. Perhaps, then, "hypnotized" people are merely acting the role of "good hypnotic subjects," and allowing the hypnotist to direct their fantasies. It's not that the people are consciously faking hypnosis. Rather, like actors who get caught up in their roles, they may begin to feel and behave in ways appropriate to the hypnotic role. And sure enough, it has been shown that the more people like and trust the hypnotist and feel motivated to demonstrate hypnotic behavior, the more they do so (Gfeller & others, 1987). Based on such findings, advocates of the social influence theory contend that the hypnotic phenomena are *not* unique to hypnosis.

Hypnosis as Divided Consciousness   Most hypnosis researchers grant that normal social and cognitive processes play a part in hypnosis, but they believe that hypnosis is more than imaginative acting. For one thing, hypnotized subjects will carry out suggested behaviors on cue, even when they believe no one is watching. Their doing so indicates that more may be at work than merely trying to be a "good subject." Moreover, many researchers remain convinced that certain phenomena *are* unique to hypnosis, and that a special state of consciousness is required to explain hypnotic experiences such as the reduction of pain, the compelling hallucinations, and the relief from allergic reactions, warts, and other physical problems (Bowers, 1989).

To veteran hypnosis researcher Ernest Hilgard (1986), what is at work is a dissociation, a split in consciousness. Hilgard considers the dissociation that occurs during hypnosis to be a more extreme form of the everyday dissociations that occur in our information processing. Putting a child to bed, we might read *Cinderella* for the fourteenth time while mentally organizing a busy schedule for the next day. With practice, it is even possible to read and comprehend a short story while copying dictated words, much as you can doodle while listening to a lecture or much as a skilled pianist can converse while playing a familiar piece (Hirst & others, 1978). Thus, when hypnotized subjects write answers to questions about one topic while talking or reading about a different topic, they are displaying an accentuation of normal cognitive dissociation.

Hilgard's discovery of hypnotic dissociation occurred dramatically. During a class demonstration of hypnosis, he induced deafness in a subject and then set about showing the class that the person was now utterly unresponsive to questions, taunts, and even sudden loud sounds. When a student asked whether some part of the subject might still be able to hear, Hilgard decided to demonstrate that the answer was no. He quietly asked the subject to raise his right index finger if some part of him could still hear. To everyone's surprise—including Hilgard's and the subject's—the finger rose. When the subject's hearing was restored, he explained that "it was a little boring just sitting here . . . when I suddenly felt my finger lift; that is what I want you to explain to me."

This moment of discovery spurred further inquiry. When unhypnotized subjects put their arms in an ice bath, they feel intense pain within 25 seconds. When hypnotized subjects do the same thing after being given suggestions that they will feel no pain, they indeed report feeling little pain. But when asked to press a key if "some part" of them does feel the pain, they invariably press the key. To Hilgard, this suggests that there is a dissociated consciousness, a **hidden observer**, that is passively aware of what is happening.

The divided-consciousness theory of hypnosis is controversial, but this much seems clear: You and I process much information without conscious awareness. We have seen examples of nonconscious information processing in the chapters on sensation and perception, and we will see more in later chapters on learning, memory, and thinking. Without doubt, there is more to thinking than we are aware of. Then again, there is little doubt that social influences do play some role in hypnosis. So might the two views—social influence and divided consciousness—be bridged? Researcher John Kihlstrom (1987a) believes *"there is no contradiction between the two approaches"*; we can understand hypnosis as *both* an extension of normal principles of social influence *and* as an extension of everyday splits in consciousness.

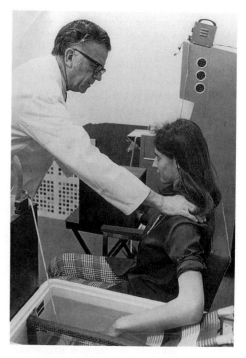

A hypnotized subject being tested by Ernest Hilgard exhibits no pain response when her arm is placed in an ice bath. But when asked to press a key if some part of her feels the pain, she does so.

DRUGS AND CONSCIOUSNESS

If there is controversy about whether hypnosis alters consciousness, there is little dispute that a person's state of consciousness is altered by *psychoactive drugs,* drugs that can change perceptions and moods. The widespread use of legal psychoactive drugs can be dramatized by an imaginary drug user's day: It begins with a wake-up cup of strong coffee. By midday several cigarettes and a prescription tranquilizer have helped calm the nerves. Leaving work early, a happy-hour cocktail provides a relaxing and sociable prelude to a dental appointment, where nitrous oxide makes an otherwise painful experience mildly pleasurable. A diet pill before dinner helps stem the appetite, and its effects can later be partially offset with a sleeping pill. Before drifting off into REM-depressed sleep, our hypothetical drug user is dismayed by news of "rising drug abuse."

Typically, continued use of a psychoactive drug produces *tolerance*—that is, the user requires larger and larger doses in order to experience the drug's effect. A person who rarely drinks alcohol might get tipsy on one can of beer, but an experienced drinker might not get tipsy until the second six-pack. Don't be misled by the word "tolerance": Alcoholics have a high tolerance for alcohol, but their brains, hearts, and livers are damaged by the excessive alcohol they are "tolerating."

Drawing by Sidney Harris.

"Just tell me where you kids got the idea to take so many drugs."

People who stop using a psychoactive drug may experience *withdrawal*—undesirable side effects of discontinued drug use. As the body responds to the drug's absence, the user may feel physical pain and intense cravings for the drug. In such cases, the person has developed an **addiction,** a *physical dependence* on the drug. People can also develop a **psychological dependence,** particularly for drugs used to alleviate stress. While the drug may not be addictive, it nevertheless becomes a very important part of the user's life. With either physical addiction or psychological dependence, the user's primary focus becomes obtaining and using the drug.

There are three broad categories of psychoactive drugs: **depressants,** or "downers," which calm neural activity and slow down body functions; **stimulants,** or "uppers," which, at least temporarily, excite neural activity and arouse body functions; and **hallucinogens,** which distort perception and evoke sensory images in the absence of sensory input. Drugs in all three categories do their work at the synapses of the brain, by stimulating, inhibiting, or mimicking the activity of the brain's chemical messengers, the neurotransmitters.

DEPRESSANTS

Let us look first at drugs such as alcohol, tranquilizers, and opiates, which slow down body functions.

Alcohol   True or false? In large amounts, alcohol is a depressant; in small amounts, it is a stimulant.

False. Small doses of "spirits" may seem to enliven a drinker, but they do so by slowing activity in brain centers that control judgment and inhibitions. Because alcohol decreases control over inhibitions, it facilitates urges that the individual might otherwise resist (Steele & others, 1985; Steele & Southwick, 1985). In experiments, a provoked person will behave more aggressively when under the influence of alcohol; an unprovoked person will not. A strong appeal to help with an unpleasant task gets a more positive response from those under the influence (when there is an urge to help, alcohol reduces inhibitions against helping). Thus, alcohol seems to make us more aggressive or helpful—or self-disclosing or sexually daring—only when such tendencies are already present but are normally restrained in the absence of alcohol. In everyday life, alcohol similarly disinhibits both helpful tendencies, as when restaurant patrons tip more when tipsy (M. Lynn, 1987), and harmful tendencies, as when sexually coercive college men attempt to disinhibit their dates by getting them to drink (Mosher & Anderson, 1986).

Low doses of alcohol relax by slowing the activity of the sympathetic nervous system. With larger doses, alcohol can become a staggering problem: Reactions slow, speech slurs, skilled performance deteriorates. These effects, combined with the lowering of inhibitions, contribute to alcohol's worst consequences—in America, the more than 100,000 lives claimed annually in alcohol-related car accidents and violent crime (Lord, 1987).

Alcohol has an intriguing effect on memory. It impairs neither one's recall for what has just been said nor one's established long-term memories. But it can disrupt the processing of recent experiences into long-term memories. Thus, the day after being intoxicated, heavy drinkers may not recall whom they met or what they said or did the night before. This memory blackout stems partly from an inability to transfer memories from the intoxicated to the sober state (Eich, 1980).

"Take the deaths from every other abused drug, add them together, and they still don't equal the deaths or the cost to society of alcohol alone."
Loran Archer,
Deputy Director, National Institute on Alcohol Abuse and Alcoholism, 1987

This celebration could abruptly turn tragic if the lowered inhibitions (evident here) and slower reactions that result from drinking were to cause an accident.

Blackouts after drinking may also result from the suppression of REM sleep. (Recall that people deprived of REM sleep seem to have difficulty fixing their day's experiences into permanent memories.)

Alcohol has another intriguing effect on consciousness: It reduces self-awareness. Under the influence of alcohol, people are less self-conscious (Hull & others, 1986). Compared to people who feel good about themselves, those who want to suppress the awareness of their failures or shortcomings are more likely to drink.

As with other psychoactive drugs, alcohol's behavioral effects stem not only from its alteration of brain chemistry but also from the user's expectations. Many studies have found that when people *believe* that alcohol affects social behavior in certain ways, and *believe*, rightly or wrongly, that they have been drinking alcohol, they will behave according to their expectations (Critchlow, 1986). For example, alcohol per se has little effect on sexual arousal. But people who believe it promotes arousal and who believe they have been drinking become more responsive to sexual stimuli. From their review of research, Jay Hull and Charles Bond (1986) concluded that for some people alcohol serves "as an excuse to become sexually aroused."

In one experiment by David Abrams and Terence Wilson (1983), Rutgers University men who had volunteered for a study on "alcohol and sexual stimulation" were given either an alcoholic or a nonalcoholic drink. In each group, half the subjects thought they were drinking alcohol and half thought they were not. Regardless of what they drank, after being shown an erotic movie clip, the men who *thought* they had consumed alcohol were more likely to report having strong sexual fantasies and feeling guilt-free. Apparently, being able to attribute their sexual responses to alcohol released their inhibitions—whether they actually had drunk alcohol or not. This illustrates an important principle: A drug's psychological effects are powerfully influenced by the user's psychological state.

Barbiturates The *barbiturate* drugs have effects similar to those of alcohol. Because they depress sympathetic nervous system activity, barbiturates such as Nembutal and Seconal are sometimes prescribed to induce sleep or reduce anxiety. In larger doses, they can lead to

Fact: College students drink more alcohol than their noncollege peers (Atwell, 1986).

Fact: More than 9 in 10 alcoholics are cigarette smokers (Istvan & Matarazzo, 1984).

Fact: Alcoholic tendencies can be inherited. For example, adopted individuals are more susceptible to alcoholism if they had a biological parent who was alcoholic (Holden, 1985).

Fact: Alcoholism plagues more men than women. A recent National Institute of Mental Health survey of 20,000 Americans revealed that roughly 1 in 10 men, but only 1 in 50 women, were problem drinkers at the time of the survey (Helzer, 1987).

Fact: Binge drinking—defined as the consumption of five or more drinks on some occasion during the last month—is reported by 22 percent of American adults. The highest rate of binge drinking—52 percent—is among 18- to 24-year-old males (Centers for Disease Control, 1983).

impaired memory and judgment. In combination with alcohol—as when people take a sleeping pill after an evening of drinking—the total depressive effect on body functions can be lethal. With sufficient doses, the barbiturates by themselves can also cause death, which makes them the drug of choice for those attempting suicide.

Opiates   The *opiates,* opium and its derivatives, morphine and heroin, also depress neural functioning. The pupils constrict, the breathing slows, and the user becomes lethargic. For a few hours, pain and anxiety are replaced by blissful pleasure. But for pleasure one pays a price, which for the heroin user is the gnawing craving for another fix, the need for progressively larger doses, the physical anguish of withdrawal if use is discontinued—and for some the ultimate price, death by overdose.

The pathway to addiction is insidious. When repeatedly flooded with artificial opiates, the brain eventually stops producing its own opiates, the endorphins (see Chapter 2, pages 30–31). Then, when the drug is withdrawn, the brain lacks the normal level of these painkilling neurotransmitters. The result is the raw agony of withdrawal.

Heroin use has been recognized as a major social problem for some time, but in recent years, a new and deadly consequence has appeared—AIDS. Most heroin addicts inject the drug intravenously, and they often share their needles. In the process, small amounts of blood are passed from user to user, spreading the AIDS virus from the infected to the uninfected. According to the Centers for Disease Control (1988), the rate of increase in new AIDS cases reported is highest among intravenous drug users (heroin addicts), their sexual partners, and their infants.

Should needles be distributed free to heroin addicts to help prevent the spread of AIDS?

STIMULANTS

The most widely used stimulants are caffeine, nicotine, the powerful *amphetamines,* and the even more powerful cocaine. Stimulants speed up body functions, hence the nickname "speed" for amphetamines. Strong stimulants increase heart and breathing rates; the pupils dilate; appetite diminishes (because blood sugar rises); and energy and self-confidence rise. For these reasons, stimulants are used to stay awake, lose weight, or boost mood or athletic performance. As with other drugs, the "benefits" of stimulants come with a price. When drug stimulation ends, the user experiences a compensating slowdown and may "crash" into tiredness, headaches, irritability, and depression. Like the depressants, stimulants can be addictive. (For information on nicotine addiction, see page 531.)

The stimulating effect of cocaine is so powerful that even relatively low doses can result in cardiac arrest and death. Nevertheless, in a 1987 national survey, 10 percent of American high school seniors reported having tried cocaine during the past year and 4 percent had smoked crack, an inexpensive, highly potent, and extremely addictive new form of cocaine, which is smoked (Johnston & others, 1988). (These figures may be *under*estimates, as high school dropouts were not included in this survey.) Whether cocaine is sniffed ("snorted") or smoked ("free-based"), it enters the bloodstream quickly, producing a rush of euphoria that lasts 15 to 30 minutes. The "rush" depletes the brain's norepinephrine and dopamine supplies, producing a crash of depression after the effect wears off. Crack works even faster and produces a briefer but more intense high—and a more intense crash.

The cardiac arrest of college basketball great Len Bias (right) shortly after being drafted by the Boston Celtics tragically illustrates the dangers of cocaine.

When cocaine is snorted—and especially when it is injected—it enters the blood-stream quickly, producing a powerful rush. The "crash" that follows is due to the brain's having been depleted of the neurotransmitters dopamine and norepi-nephrine.

Regular cocaine users become both physiologically and psychologically addicted and may experience emotional disturbance, tissue damage, and even convulsions or respiratory failure. As with all psychoactive drugs, cocaine's psychological effects depend on a mix of factors, including not only the dosage and form in which one takes the drug but also one's expectations and personality. Given an inert substance—called a *placebo*—cocaine users who think they are taking cocaine often have a cocainelike experience (Van Dyke & Byck, 1982).

HALLUCINOGENS

Hallucinogens are powerful consciousness-altering drugs that can distort perceptions and evoke vivid images in the absence of sensory input (which is why they are also called *psychedelics*, meaning "mind-manifesting"). Some hallucinogens are natural substances: Mescaline, for example, comes from peyote, a small cactus without spines that grows wild in the southwestern United States and Mexico. Other common hallucinogens are synthetic: Of these, PCP ("angel dust"), a very potent anesthetic that has highly unpredictable and sometimes devastating psychological effects, and LSD are two of the best known.

LSD   The first "acid trip" was taken in 1943 by the creator of *LSD (lysergic acid diethylamide)*, chemist Albert Hofmann. After accidentally ingesting some of the chemical, Hofmann reported that he "perceived an uninterrupted stream of fantastic pictures, extraordinary shapes with intense, kaleidoscopic play of colors" (Siegel, 1984). LSD and other powerful hallucinogens are chemically similar to, and therefore block the actions of, a subtype of the neurotransmitter serotonin (Jacobs, 1987). The emotions that accompany an LSD trip vary from euphoria to detachment to panic.

The LSD experience is usually colored by the person's current mood and expectations. Despite the emotional variations, the resulting hallucinations have certain aspects in common. Research psychologist Ronald Siegel (1982) reports that whether the brain is provoked to hallucinate by loss of oxygen, sensory deprivation, or drugs, "it will hallucinate in basically the same way." The experience typically begins with simple geometric forms, such as a lattice, a cobweb, or a spiral (see Figure 8–9). The next phase consists of more meaningful images; some may be superimposed on a tunnel or funnel, others may involve the replay of past emotional experiences. When the hallucinogenic experience reaches its peak, people frequently feel separated from their bodies and experience dreamlike scenes as if they were real—so real that people may become panic-stricken or may harm themselves, sometimes fatally.

Marijuana   Marijuana consists of the leaves and flowers of the hemp plant, which has been cultivated for some 5000 years for its fiber. It is the most widely used illegal drug, and one of the most popular of psychoactive drugs. By the time marijuana usage peaked in the United States near the end of the 1970s, some 50 million Americans had tried it at least once.

Marijuana's active ingredient is *THC*, the everyday name of the complex organic molecule delta-9-tetrahydrocannabinol. Whether smoked or eaten in such foods as brownies, THC triggers a mixture of effects that makes the drug difficult to classify. (Smoking gets the drug into the brain in only about 7 seconds and produces a greater effect than does eating the drug, which causes its peak concentration to be reached at a slower rate.) Like alcohol, marijuana relaxes, disinhibits, and may produce a euphoric "high." But marijuana is also a mild hallucinogen that can slow the perceived passage of time and amplify one's sensitivity to colors, sounds, tastes, and smells.

As with other drugs, the marijuana user's experience can vary, depending on the situation in which it is taken. If the person is anxious or depressed, taking the drug may intensify these feelings. In other situations, using marijuana can be not only pleasurable but even therapeutic. For those who suffer the pain of glaucoma (caused by pressure within the eyeball) or the severe nausea of cancer chemotherapy, marijuana may spell relief. In acknowledging such benefits, a review of marijuana research published by the National Academy of Sciences (1982) also identified some not-so-pleasant consequences. Like alcohol, marijuana impairs the motor coordination and perceptual skills necessary for safe driving and machine operation. Marijuana also disrupts the transfer of one's experiences into permanent memories and interferes with immediate recall of information learned only a few minutes before. Clearly, being stoned is not conducive to learning.

Unlike alcohol, which is eliminated from the body within hours, THC remains in the body for almost a month. Uncertainty persists about marijuana's physical effects but medical research suggests that long-term marijuana use may depress male sex hormone levels and that it is more damaging to the lungs than cigarette smoking (Wu & others, 1988). Large doses even seem to hasten the loss of brain cells (Landfield & others, 1988). One study that followed 654 junior high students into their early twenties found that adolescent marijuana users developed more health and family problems than did nonusers (Newcomb & Bentler, 1988). Taking all the concerns about marijuana's effects on health into consideration, the National Academy's report concluded that what we know or suspect "justifies serious national concern."

Despite their differences, the psychoactive drugs share a common effect: They trigger aftereffects that offset their immediate effects. The aftereffects illustrate the more general principle that emotions tend to

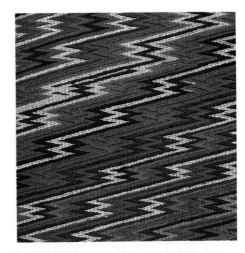

Figure 8–9   Geometric forms, such as those experienced by drug users during drug-induced hallucinations, can be seen in the embroidery of the Huichol, Mexican Indians who use peyote, from which the hallucinogen mescaline is derived.

For those who suffer severe pain or nausea, marijuana may spell relief. But the National Academy of Sciences reports that marijuana also impairs coordination, perception, and memory, and with prolonged use damages lungs and may depress male sex hormone levels.

trigger opposing emotions, which linger after the original emotions disappear; with repetition, the opposing emotions get stronger (see page 397). This emotions-trigger-opposing-emotions principle implies that drug-induced pleasures will wane as nature exacts her compensatory price. And that helps explain tolerance and withdrawal: Because the opposing negative emotions are getting stronger, it takes larger and larger doses to produce the desired high, causing the negative aftereffects to get progressively worse in the absence of the drug. This in turn creates a need to switch off the withdrawal symptoms by taking yet more of the drug.

INFLUENCES ON DRUG USE

Drug use by North American youth increased during the 1970s and has generally declined during the 1980s. The University of Michigan's annual survey of 16,000 high school seniors reveals that the proportion who believe there is "great risk" to regular marijuana use rose from 36 percent in 1977 to 74 percent in 1987 (Johnston & others, 1988). Marijuana use has declined since peaking in 1979 (see Figure 8–10). The American Council on Education's annual survey of new college students similarly reveals that between 1977 and 1987 support for the legalization of marijuana dropped from 53 percent to 19 percent. Similar attitude and usage changes appear in Gallup surveys of Canadian teens (*Behavior Today*, 1984). Unfortunately the picture is not so encouraging when it comes to crack, whose use is increasing in large urban centers. And alcohol remains North America's most common drug of abuse, with no reduction of use in sight.

Why do so many people continue to use psychoactive drugs? Why, for example, did 57 percent of American high school seniors report having tried an illicit drug during the past year (Johnston & others, 1988)? For some adolescents whose focus is on having fun in the here-and-now, occasional drug use may represent thrill-seeking. But why do some and not others become regular drug users?

The reasons are both psychological and social. In their studies of New Jersey and California youth and young adults, Michael Newcomb and L. L. Harlow (1986) found that one psychological factor in drug use is the feeling that one's life is meaningless and directionless, a feeling that is common among school dropouts, who subsist without job skills, without privilege, without hope.

Other studies indicate that regular users of alcohol, marijuana, and cocaine often have experienced significant stress or failure and are depressed. As we noted earlier, alcohol temporarily dulls the pain of self-awareness, which can make it a way to avoid coping with one's problems. One early sign of alcoholism is drinking to relieve depression, anger, anxiety, or insomnia. The relief may be temporary. But as Chapter 9, Learning, explains, behavior is often more controlled by its immediate than by its later consequences.

The social roots of drug use cannot be overestimated, especially for teenagers. Peers influence attitudes about drugs, provide drugs, and establish the social context for their use. If adolescents' friends use drugs, the odds are that they will too; if their friends don't, the temptation may not even arise. Indeed, the peer factor is so powerful that other predictors of adolescent drug use, such as family strength, religiosity, and school adjustment, seem to operate through their effects on peer associations. Teenagers who come from happy families and do well in school tend not to use drugs, partly because they rarely associate with those who do (Oetting & Beauvais, 1987).

"How strange would appear to be this thing that men call pleasure! And how curiously it is related to what is thought to be its opposite, pain! . . . Wherever the one is found, the other follows up behind."

Plato,
Phaedo, 4th century B.C.

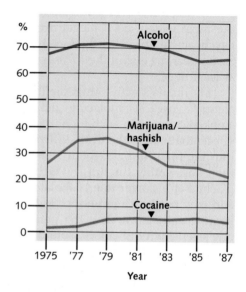

Figure 8–10   The percentage of high school seniors who report having used marijuana or alcohol at least once during the preceding 30 days has declined since the late 1970s. (From Johnston & others, 1988.)

These findings suggest three channels of influence for drug prevention and treatment programs: (1) education about the long-term costs of the temporary pleasures of drug use, (2) efforts to boost people's self-esteem and purpose in life, and (3) attempts to modify peer associations or to "inoculate" youth against peer pressures. Said differently, young people are *very* unlikely to use drugs if they understand the physical and psychological consequences of psychoactive drug use, feel good about themselves and where their lives are heading, and are in a peer group that disapproves of drug use.

NEAR-DEATH EXPERIENCES

A man . . . hears himself pronounced dead by his doctor. He begins to hear an uncomfortable noise, a loud ringing or buzzing, and at the same time feels himself moving very rapidly through a long dark tunnel. After this, he suddenly finds himself outside of his own physical body . . . and sees his own body from a distance, as though he is a spectator. . . . Soon other things begin to happen. Others come to meet and to help him. He glimpses the spirits of relatives and friends who have already died, and a loving, warm spirit of a kind he has never encountered before—a being of light—appears before him. . . . He is overwhelmed by intense feelings of joy, love, and peace. Despite his attitude, though, he somehow reunites with his physical body and lives. (Moody, 1976, pp. 23, 24)

This passage from Raymond Moody's best-selling book, *Life After Life*, is a composite description of a full-blown **near-death experience.** Because reports of these experiences are nearly always positive, they are devoured by those eager for "proof" that there is happiness after death. (Upon being revived, people seldom recall having teetered on the brink of hell.)

What should we make of these reports? Do they prove that we can anticipate bliss on the other side of death? Do they confirm Plato's doctrine that mind—or soul—is separable from body? Do such flights of mind reliably occur to those who face death?

Near-death experiences are more common than you might suspect. Several investigators each interviewed a hundred or more people who had come close to death through such physical traumas as cardiac arrest. In every one of these studies, 30 to 40 percent of those interviewed recalled some sort of near-death experience (Ring, 1980; Schnaper, 1980). When George Gallup, Jr. (1982; Gallup & O'Connell, 1986) interviewed a national sample of Americans, 15 percent reported having experienced a close brush with death. One-third of these people—representing some 8 million people by Gallup's estimate—reported having had a mystical experience in connection with it. Some of these people claim to recall things said while they lay unconscious and near death (but then, some anesthetized patients undergoing major surgery later display similar recall of operating room conversation [Hilgard, 1986]).

Did Moody's description of the "complete" near-death experience sound familiar? The parallels between it and Ronald Siegel's (1977) descriptions of the typical hallucinogenic experience are striking: visions of tunnels or funnels and bright lights or beings of light (Figure 8–11), replay of old memories, out-of-body sensations. In short, the content of the near-death experience is just what one would expect from a knowledge of hallucinations. Moreover, oxygen deprivation

Although some of these people may have been thought "dead," none had suffered true brain death. If they had, they would not have survived to recall their experience—hence the label "near-death."

Figure 8–11   A near-death vision or a hallucination? Psychologist Ronald Siegel (1977) reports that under the influence of hallucinogenic drugs, people often see "a bright light in the center of the field of vision. . . . The location of this point of light create[s] a tunnel-like perspective."

and other insults to the brain are known to produce hallucinations, so it is difficult to resist wondering whether near-death experiences are manufactured by the brain under stress. Patients who have experienced temporal lobe seizures have reported similarly profound mystical experiences, as have solitary sailors and polar explorers while enduring monotony, isolation, and cold (Suedfeld & Mocellin, 1987). Fantasy-prone persons are especially susceptible—or should we say *open*—to near-death and other out-of-body experiences (Wilson & Barber, 1983).

Siegel (1980) concludes that the near-death experience is best understood "as a dissociative hallucinatory activity of the brain"; when external input dims, the brain's own interior activity becomes perceptible. He illustrates with an analogy: When gazing out a window at dusk, we begin to see the reflected interior of the room as if it were outside, either because the light from outside is dimming (as in the near-death experience) or because the inside light is being amplified (as with LSD). When projected on our perceptual window, says Siegel, our mind's internal images can appear as real as images from the outside.

Some investigators of near-death experiences object: People who have experienced both hallucinations and the near-death phenomenon often deny their similarity. Moreover, they often are permanently changed by the experience in ways unlike those who have taken a drug trip; they become kinder, more spiritual, more believing in life after death. Skeptics reply that these effects stem from the death-related context of the experience.

The controversy over interpreting near-death experiences raises some fundamental mind-body issues: Is the mind immaterial? Can it exist separate from body? *Dualists* answer yes. They believe that the mind and body are two distinct entities—the mind nonphysical, the body physical—that somehow interact with each other. As Socrates expresses it in Plato's *Phaedo*, "Does not death mean that the body comes to exist by itself, separated from the soul, and that the soul exists by herself, separated from the body? What is death but that?" For Socrates, as for those today who believe that near-death experiences are proof of immortality, death is not really the death of the person but merely the liberation of that person from the bodily prison. In this sense, death is viewed as an occasion for rejoicing. (Carried to its extreme, this dualistic view has given rise to glorifications of the afterlife trip under such titles as "The Thrill of Dying" and "The Wonderful World of Death.")

Monists answer no to the mind-body questions. They contend that mind and body are different aspects of the same thing. Whether they are scientists who assume the inseparability of mind and brain or theologians who hold to an afterlife that involves some form of bodily resurrection, monists generally believe that death is real and that without bodies we truly are nobodies.

As debates over the significance of fantasy, dreams, hypnotic states, drug-induced hallucinations, and near-death experiences illustrate, science informs our wonderings about human consciousness and human nature. Although there remain questions that it cannot answer, science nevertheless helps fashion our image of who we are, of our human potentials and our human limits.

"**Joan [of Arc]:** I hear voices telling me what to do. They come from God.
Robert: They come from your imagination.
Joan: Of course. That is how the messages of God come to us."
  George Bernard Shaw,
  Saint Joan, 1924

"The mind seems to act independently of the brain in the same sense that a programmer acts independently of his computer."
  Wilder Penfield (1975, p. 79)

"Everything in science to date seems to indicate that conscious awareness is a property of the living functioning brain and inseparable from it."
  Roger W. Sperry (1985)

SUMMING UP

STUDYING CONSCIOUSNESS

Psychology began as the study of consciousness, then turned to the study of observable behavior, and now is again investigating states of mind.

Selective Attention At any moment we are conscious of a very limited amount of all that we are capable of experiencing. The cocktail party effect—the ability to attend to only one voice among many—is one manifestation of our limitation.

States of Consciousness Consciousness can be experienced in various states, all of which involve a focused awareness of perceptions, thoughts, and feelings as they occur. This chapter considers several alternatives to normal waking consciousness.

DAYDREAMS AND FANTASIES

Virtually everyone daydreams, especially fantasy-prone people and especially in times when attention can be freed from the tasks at hand. Daydreaming can be adaptive; it can help us prepare for future events and may substitute for impulsive behavior.

SLEEP AND DREAMS

The Rhythm of Sleep Our daily schedule of waking and sleeping is timed with a body clock known as circadian rhythm. Each night's sleep also has a rhythm of its own, running from transitional Stage 1 sleep to deep Stage 4 sleep and back up to the more internally active REM sleep stage. This cycle is repeated several times during a normal night's sleep, with periods of Stage 4 sleep progressively shortening and of REM sleep lengthening.

Why Do We Sleep? Depriving people of sleep has failed to reveal why, physiologically, we need sleep. Recent research reveals that sleep is linked with the release of pituitary growth hormone and that it may help to restore exhausted tissues.

Sleep Disorders The disorders of sleep include insomnia (recurring wakefulness), narcolepsy (uncontrollable lapsing into REM sleep), and sleep apnea (the cessation of breathing while sleeping).

Dreams Although conscious thoughts can occur during any sleep stage, awakening people during REM sleep yields predictable "dreamlike" reports; awakening during other sleep stages only occasionally yields a fleeting image. Our dreams are mostly of ordinary events; they often relate to everyday experiences and more frequently involve anxiety or misfortune than triumphant achievements.

Freud believed that a dream's manifest content is a censored version of its latent content, which gratifies our unconscious wishes. Newer explanations of why we dream suggest that dreams help process information from the day and fix it in memory, and that dreams serve a physiological function (either by stimulating the sleeping brain or as a means of coping with random activity initiated in the brainstem). Despite their differences, most theorists agree that REM sleep and its associated dreams serve an important function, as shown by the REM rebound that occurs following REM deprivation.

HYPNOSIS

Facts and Falsehoods Although hypnosis has historically been linked with quackery, it has more recently become the subject of serious research. It is now widely agreed that hypnosis is a state of heightened suggestibility; that although hypnosis may help someone to recall something, the hypnotist's beliefs frequently work their way into the subject's recollections; that hypnotized people cannot be made to act against their will any more than nonhypnotized people can; that hypnosis can be at least temporarily therapeutic; that hypnotizable people can enjoy significant pain relief; and that hypnosis can be distinguished from the meditative states.

Is Hypnosis an Altered State of Consciousness? There is debate, however, on whether hypnosis is a by-product of normal social and cognitive processes or whether it is an altered state of consciousness, perhaps involving a dissociation between levels of consciousness.

DRUGS AND CONSCIOUSNESS

Another route to altered consciousness is through psychoactive drugs, including depressants, stimulants, and hallucinogens. Psychoactive drugs often trigger harmful aftereffects that oppose and offset their temporary pleasure.

Depressants Alcohol, barbiturates, and the opiates act by depressing neural functioning. Each offers its pleasures, but at the cost of impaired memory and self-awareness or other physical consequences.

Stimulants Caffeine, nicotine, the amphetamines, and cocaine all act by stimulating neural functioning. As with nearly all psychoactive drugs, they act at the synapses by influencing the brain's neurotransmitters, and their effects depend on dosage and the user's personality and expectations.

Hallucinogens LSD and marijuana can distort the user's judgments of time and, depending on the setting in which they are taken, can alter one's sensations and perceptions.

Influences on Drug Use Although drug use among teenagers and young adults has declined during the 1980s, psychological factors combine with peer influences to lead many people to experiment with—and become dependent on—drugs.

NEAR-DEATH EXPERIENCES

About one-third of those who have survived a brush with death, such as through cardiac arrest, later recall visionary near-death experiences. These experiences have been interpreted by dualists as evidence of human immortality, although monists point out that reports of such experiences closely parallel reports of hallucinations.

TERMS AND CONCEPTS TO REMEMBER

addiction A physical dependence on or need for a drug, with accompanying withdrawal symptoms if the drug is discontinued.

age regression In hypnosis, the supposed reliving of earlier experiences, such as in early childhood; greatly susceptible to false recollections.

alpha waves The relatively slow brain waves of a relaxed, awake state.

amphetamines Drugs that stimulate neural activity, causing speeded-up body functions and associated energy and mood changes.

barbiturates Drugs that depress the activity of the central nervous system, reducing anxiety—and impairing memory and judgment.

circadian rhythm [ser-KAY-dee-an] The biological clock; regular bodily rhythms (for example, of temperature and wakefulness) that occur on a 24-hour cycle.

cocktail party effect The ability to attend selectively to only one voice among many.

consciousness Selective attention to ongoing perceptions, thoughts, and feelings.

delta waves The large, slow brain waves associated with deep sleep.

depressants Drugs (such as alcohol, barbiturates, and opiates) that reduce neural activity and slow down body functions.

dissociation A split in consciousness, which allows some thoughts and behaviors to occur simultaneously with others.

dualism The presumption that mind and body are two distinct entities that interact with each other.

fantasy-prone personality Someone who imagines and recalls experiences with lifelike vividness and who spends considerable time fantasizing.

hallucinations False sensory experiences, such as seeing something in the absence of any external visual stimulus.

hallucinogens Psychedelic ("mind-manifesting") drugs, such as LSD, that distort perceptions and evoke sensory images in the absence of sensory input.

hidden observer Hilgard's term describing a hypnotized subject's awareness of experiences, such as pain, that go unreported during hypnosis.

hypnosis A temporary state of heightened suggestibility in which some people are able to narrow their focus of attention and experience imaginary happenings as if they were real.

insomnia A sleep disorder involving recurring problems in falling or staying asleep.

latent content According to Freud, the underlying but censored meaning of a dream (as distinct from its manifest content). Freud believed that a dream's latent content serves a safety valve function.

LSD (lysergic acid diethylamide) A powerful hallucinogenic drug, also known as *acid*.

manifest content According to Freud, the remembered story line of a dream (as distinct from its latent content).

monism The presumption that mind and body are different aspects of the same thing.

narcolepsy A sleep disorder characterized by uncontrollable sleep attacks in which the sufferer lapses directly into REM sleep, often at inopportune times.

near-death experience An altered state of consciousness reported after a close brush with death (such as through cardiac arrest); often similar to drug-induced hallucinations.

night terrors A sleep disorder characterized by high arousal and an appearance of being terrified; unlike nightmares, night terrors occur during Stage 4 sleep, within 2 or 3 hours of falling asleep, and are seldom remembered.

opiates Opium and its derivatives, such as morphine and heroin, which depress neural activity, temporarily alleviating pain and anxiety.

placebo [pluh-SEE-bo] An inert substance that may, in

an experiment, be administered instead of an active drug; may trigger the effects believed to characterize the actual drug.

posthypnotic amnesia An inability to recall what one experienced during hypnosis, induced by the hypnotist's suggestion.

posthypnotic suggestion A suggestion, made during a hypnotic session, that is to be carried out after the subject is no longer hypnotized; it is used by some clinicians as an aid to controlling undesired symptoms and behaviors.

psychoactive drug A drug that alters mood and perceptions.

psychological dependence A psychological need to use a drug, such as to relieve stress.

REM rebound effect The tendency for REM sleep to increase following REM sleep deprivation (created by repeated awakenings during REM sleep).

REM sleep Rapid eye movement sleep, a recurring sleep stage during which vivid dreams commonly occur. Also known as *paradoxical sleep*, because the muscles are relaxed (except for minor twitches) but the other body systems are active.

selective attention The focusing of conscious awareness on a particular stimulus. (See also *cocktail party effect*.)

sleep apnea A sleep disorder characterized by temporary cessations of breathing during sleep and consequent momentary reawakenings.

sleep spindles Rhythmic bursts of brain activity occurring during Stage 2 sleep.

stimulants Drugs (such as caffeine, nicotine, and the more powerful amphetamines and cocaine) that excite neural activity and speed up body functions.

THC The active ingredient in marijuana and hashish that triggers a variety of effects, including mild hallucinations.

tolerance The diminishing of a drug's effect with regular use of the same dose, requiring the user to take larger and larger doses before experiencing the drug's effect.

withdrawal The physical and psychological distress that follows the discontinued use of addictive drugs.

FOR FURTHER READING

Sleep and Dreams

Coleman, R. (1987). *Wide awake at 3 A.M.* New York: Freeman.

The latest applications of sleep research in business, industry, and even in the Olympics, with practical hints on identifying sleep disorders, coping with jet lag, and simply getting a better night's sleep.

Dement, W. C. (1978). *Some must watch while some must sleep.* New York: Norton.

An easily readable paperback that surveys sleep disorders as well as normal sleeping and dreaming.

Hartmann, E. (1984). *The nightmare: The psychology and biology of terrifying dreams.* New York: Basic Books.

A summary of what we know about bad dreams.

Hypnosis

Hilgard, E. R. (1986). *Divided consciousness: Multiple controls in human thought and action.* New York: Wiley.

An intriguing and provocative introduction to a host of phenomena (possession states, multiple personalities, and hypnotic events) that suggest that consciousness can be divided.

Zilbergeld, B., Edelstien, M. G., & Araoz, D. L. (1986). *Hypnosis: Questions and answers.* New York: Norton.

Eighty-five experts answer 78 questions, from "Are stage hypnotists really doing hypnosis?" to "Can hypnosis enhance athletic performance?"

Drugs

Ray, O. (1986). *Drugs, society, and human behavior* (4th ed.). St. Louis: Mosby.

A thorough textbook introduction to the physical and psychological effects of psychoactive drugs.

Snyder, S. H. (1986). *Drugs and the brain.* New York: Scientific American Library.

An authoritative and beautifully illustrated summary of how psychoactive drugs, both therapeutic and illicit, affect the brain.

For further information in this text regarding drugs, see:

Addiction, explained, p. 397
Alcohol and aggression, p. 577
Alcohol and memory, p. 268
Alcoholism treatment, pp. 236, 485
Drugs and the fetus, p. 61
Drug therapies, pp. 499–501
Smoking (nicotine), pp. 530–532

PART 4

Learning and Thinking

A central question in psychology is how we learn, retain, and use information. Chapter 9, Learning, describes three fundamental types of learning and suggests how they influence our emotions and behavior and how we can use them to our benefit. Chapter 10, Memory, examines the process by which information is taken in, stored, and retrieved, and the factors that sometimes cause us to forget. Chapter 11, Thinking and Language, points out the efficient but sometimes error-prone ways in which we make judgments and decisions, and discusses how we use language to communicate. Chapter 12, Intelligence, describes historical and current attempts to define and assess intelligence.

CHAPTER 9

Learning

When a chinook salmon first emerges from its egg in the gravel bed of a stream, it has in its genes virtually all the behavioral instructions it needs for life. It instinctively knows how to swim, how to navigate, what to eat, how to protect itself from predators. Following this built-in plan, the young salmon soon begins a trek to the sea. After some 4 years in the ocean, the mature salmon undertakes a genetically prede-termined return to its birthplace. It navigates hundreds of miles back to the mouth of its home river, guided by the scent of its home stream, and then begins an upstream odyssey that will take it back to its precise ancestral spawning ground. Once there, the salmon seeks out the exact conditions of temperature, gravel, and water flow that will maximize the success of its breeding, and then mates.

Unlike the salmon, we are not born with a blueprint for life. We must learn many things, and therein lie the seeds of our uniqueness. Although we must struggle to acquire the life directions that a salmon is born with, our learning gives us vastly greater flexibility. We can learn how to build igloos or grass huts or underwater air chambers and thereby adapt to almost any environment. Indeed, nature's most im-portant gift to us may be our adaptability—our ability to learn new behaviors that enable us to cope with ever changing circumstances.

No topic is closer to the heart of psychology than *learning*, a rela-tively permanent change in an organism's behavior due to experience. In earlier chapters we have considered the learning of moral ideas, of gender roles, of visual perceptions. In future chapters we will consider how learning shapes our thought and language, our motivations and emotions, our personalities and attitudes. Learning in all such realms breeds hope. What is learnable can potentially be taught—an assump-tion that encourages animal trainers, athletic coaches, parents, and educators. What has been learned can potentially be changed by new learning—an assumption that is fundamental to counseling, psycho-therapy, and rehabilitation. No matter how unhappy, unsuccessful, or unloving we are, that need not be the end of our story, because we humans are, of all the world's creatures, the most capable of changing our behavior through learning.

Simple animals can learn simple associations. If disturbed by a squirt of water, the sea snail *Aplysia* will protectively withdraw its gill. If this disturbance is continually repeated, as happens naturally in choppy water, the response diminishes. But if the sea snail is repeat-edly given a shock just after being squirted, its withdrawal response to the squirt alone becomes stronger. Somehow the animal has learned to associate the squirt with the impending shock. More complex animals can learn more complicated associations, especially those that bring favorable consequences. Sea lions in an aquarium will repeat behav-

Drawing by Sidney Harris.

"Actually, sex just isn't that important to me."

"Learning is the eye of the mind."
Thomas Drake,
Bibliotheca Scholastica Instructissima,
1633

This chimp has learned that its roller skating routine will be rewarded with food, much as its trainers have learned that training the animal will be rewarded with paychecks.

iors, such as slapping and barking, that prompt people to toss them food. Still more complex animals, such as chimpanzees, can learn behaviors by merely observing others perform them. We humans can learn in all these ways, and through language we can learn things we have neither experienced nor observed.

These ways of learning enable us to adapt to our environments. As this chapter will explain, we learn to anticipate and prepare for significant events such as food or pain—an elementary type of learning called *classical conditioning.* We also learn to repeat acts that bring good results and to avoid acts that bring bad results—a type of learning called *operant,* or *instrumental, conditioning.* And by watching others, we can acquire new behaviors indirectly—a phenomenon called *observational learning.*

The study of how we learn has revealed many facts. It has also stimulated several ongoing lines of inquiry: First, how distinct are these three types of learning? Second, does the learning of animals other than primates and humans involve cognition? For example, do rats learn to *expect* predictable events? Do they *remember* their experiences and the layout of their environments? Third, is one set of learning principles universally applicable to all species? If so, studying any one species would tell us about the others, much as studying the nervous system of one species has revealed principles of nervous system functioning common to all species, including our own.

Keeping these questions in mind, let us review some key discoveries from twentieth-century research on learning.

CLASSICAL CONDITIONING

During the seventeenth and eighteenth centuries, British philosophers such as John Locke and David Hume argued that a key ingredient in learning is association: Our minds naturally assume that events occurring in sequence are connected; we *associate* them. If, after seeing and smelling freshly baked bread, we eat some of it and feel satisfied, then the next time we see and smell a loaf of bread our previous experience will lead us to expect that eating some of this new loaf will likewise be satisfying. Similarly, if we experience certain sounds in conjunction with frightening consequences, then we may be made fearful of the sounds themselves. As one 4-year-old exclaimed after watching a TV character get mugged, "If I had heard that music I wouldn't have gone around the corner!" (Wells, 1981).

Although the idea of learning by association generated much discussion, it was not until the twentieth century that it was verified by some of psychology's most famous research. For many people, the name Ivan Pavlov rings a bell. His experiments are classics, and the phenomenon he explored is today called *classical* (or *Pavlovian*) *conditioning*.

PAVLOV'S EXPERIMENTS

After obtaining a medical degree at age 33, Pavlov was driven by a passion for research. He spent the next two decades studying the digestive system, work that would make him Russia's first Nobel prize winner in 1904. But it was the novel work to which he devoted the last three decades of his life, up to his death at age 86, that earned the feisty Pavlov his place in scientific history.

Pavlov's new direction came when his creative mind seized on an incidental occurrence. Pavlov had been studying salivary secretion in dogs and had already determined that when food was put in a dog's mouth, the animal would invariably salivate. Pavlov also noticed that when he worked with the same dog repeatedly, the dog would salivate in the presence of a number of stimuli that were associated with its food—the mere sight of the food, of the food dish, of the person who regularly brought the food, or even the sound of that person's approaching footsteps. Because these salivary "psychic secretions" interfered with his experiments on digestion, Pavlov considered them an annoyance—until he saw that they represented a simple but important form of learning. From that time forward, Pavlov devoted his efforts to the study of learning, which he hoped might enable him to understand better the workings of the brain.

The basic premise of Pavlov's work on learning arose from his initial distinction between salivation in response to food in the mouth and salivation in response to stimuli that had become associated with food. Pavlov called the salivation in response to the food in the mouth an ***unconditioned response (UCR)*** because its occurrence was not conditional upon the dog's previous experience: Food in the mouth automatically triggered the dog's salivary reflex. It was an innate, or unlearned, response. Because it always had this effect, Pavlov called the food an ***unconditioned stimulus (UCS).***

Salivation in response to something that was associated with food did not occur automatically: Its occurrence was *conditional* upon the dog's developing a connection between the "something" associated with the food and food soon being in the mouth. This learned response is therefore called the ***conditioned response (CR).*** The new stimulus—say, the sight of the food that became associated with the UCS and thereby gained the power to elicit the conditioned response—is called the ***conditioned stimulus (CS).*** You can distinguish between these two kinds of stimuli and responses by remembering that *un*conditioned = *un*learned, and conditioned = learned.

At first, Pavlov and his assistants tried to imagine what the dog was thinking and feeling as it drooled in anticipation of the food. This only got them into fruitless debates. So to attack the phenomenon more objectively, Pavlov decided to experiment. He paired various

Ivan Pavlov (1927): "Experimental investigation . . . should lay a solid foundation for a future true science of psychology."

Remember:

UCS = *Unconditioned Stimulus*
UCR = *Unconditioned Response*
CS = *Conditioned Stimulus*
CR = *Conditioned Response*

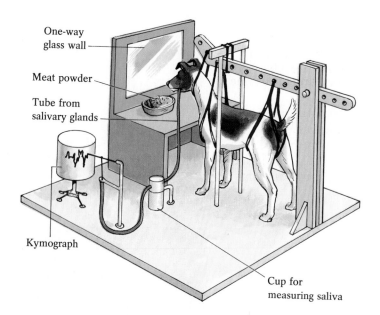

One-way glass wall

Meat powder

Tube from salivary glands

Kymograph

Cup for measuring saliva

Figure 9–1   Pavlov's device for recording salivation. The dog's saliva is collected drop by drop in a tube as it is secreted. The number of drops is recorded on a kymograph, a revolving cylinder outside the chamber. Food is delivered by remote control, and through the window, the experimenter can observe the dog.

neutral stimuli with food in the mouth to see if the dog would eventually begin salivating to the neutral stimuli alone. To eliminate the possible influence of extraneous stimuli, Pavlov isolated the dog in a small room, where it was held securely in place by a harness and attached to a device that diverted its saliva to a measuring instrument (Figure 9–1). From an adjacent room Pavlov could present food—at first by sliding in a food bowl, later by blowing meat powder into the dog's mouth at a precise moment (Gormezano & Kehoe, 1975). If a neutral stimulus—something the dog could see or hear—now regularly signaled the arrival of food, would the dog eventually begin salivating to the neutral stimulus alone?

The answer proved to be yes, as Pavlov demonstrated in his famous experiment that established the procedure for conditioning (Figure 9–2). Just before placing food (the UCS) in the dog's mouth to

Figure 9–2   Pavlov's classic experiment. By presenting a neutral stimulus, the sound of a tone, just before an unconditioned stimulus (UCS), food in mouth, the neutral stimulus became a conditioned stimulus (CS). The CS now triggers a conditioned response (CR), salivation.

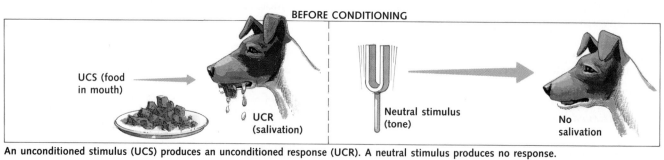

BEFORE CONDITIONING

UCS (food in mouth) → UCR (salivation)

Neutral stimulus (tone) → No salivation

An unconditioned stimulus (UCS) produces an unconditioned response (UCR). A neutral stimulus produces no response.

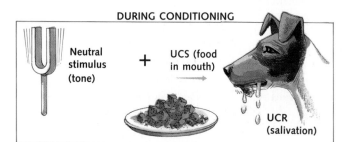

DURING CONDITIONING

Neutral stimulus (tone) + UCS (food in mouth) → UCR (salivation)

The unconditioned stimulus is presented just after a neutral stimulus. The unconditioned stimulus continues to produce an unconditioned response.

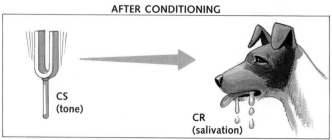

AFTER CONDITIONING

CS (tone) → CR (salivation)

The neutral stimulus now produces a conditioned response (CR), thereby becoming a conditioned stimulus (CS).

produce salivation (the UCR), Pavlov would sound a tone. After several pairings of the tone and the food, the sound of the tone alone (now a CS) caused salivation (the CR). Similarly, if the sound of bacon crackling sets your mouth to watering, then the sound has become a conditioned stimulus; by association with the taste of bacon (UCS), the sound triggers a conditioned response. Using the same procedure, Pavlov was able to condition a dog to salivate to a buzzer, a light, a touch on the leg, even the sight of a circle.

If the experiment was so simple, what did Pavlov do for the next three decades? He explored the determinants and implications of classical conditioning. In the course of his research he distinguished five major conditioning processes: acquisition, extinction, spontaneous recovery, generalization, and discrimination.

Acquisition   Regarding the *acquisition,* or initial learning, of the response there was first a question of timing: How much time should elapse between the presentation of the neutral stimulus (the tone, light, touch, or whatever) and the unconditioned stimulus? Not much. Later work with a variety of species and procedures revealed that half a second often works well. This finding fits the presumption that classical conditioning is biologically adaptive: It helps organisms *prepare* for good or bad events that are about to occur. Because there is no need to prepare for events that have already occurred, preparatory responding does not occur when the neutral stimulus comes after the UCS. When, however, it is presented first, signaling a significant event—say, when a loving tone of voice repeatedly precedes rewarding behavior—it becomes a CS, and we soon begin to respond emotionally in anticipation of what usually follows.

Extinction and Spontaneous Recovery   After conditioning, what happens if the UCS no longer occurs? Will the CS continue to elicit the CR? Pavlov found that when he rang the bell again and again without presenting food, the dogs would salivate less and less. This decline of a CR in the absence of a UCS is called *extinction.* However, Pavlov also found that if he allowed several hours to elapse before ringing the bell again, the conditioned response to the bell ringing would reappear (Figure 9–3). This reappearance of the conditioned response after a rest pause is called *spontaneous recovery.* This phenomenon indicated to Pavlov that extinction was actually inhibition of the CR rather than elimination of it.

Drawing by John Chase.

Figure 9–3 Acquisition, extinction, and spontaneous recovery. In studying classical conditioning, Pavlov distinguished the processes of acquisition, extinction, and spontaneous recovery, as illustrated by these idealized curves. The rising curve shows that the CR rapidly grows stronger as the CS and UCS are repeatedly paired (acquisition), then wanes as the CS is repeatedly presented alone (extinction), but spontaneously recovers after a rest pause.

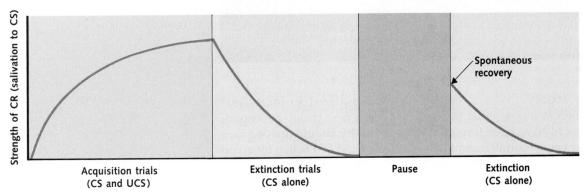

Generalization

Pavlov noticed that a dog conditioned to the ringing of one bell would also respond somewhat to a bell with a different tone or even to a buzzer that had never been paired with food (Figure 9–4). This tendency to respond to stimuli similar to the CS is called *generalization.* Generalization can be adaptive, as when toddlers who are taught to fear moving cars in the street respond similarly to trucks and motorcycles.

Because of generalization, stimuli that are similar to naturally disgusting or appealing objects will, by association, also trigger disgust or liking. Normally desirable foods, such as fudge, are unappealing when presented in a disgusting form, as when shaped to resemble dog feces (Rozin & others, 1986). Adults with childlike facial features (round face, large forehead, small chin, large eyes) are perceived as having greater than usual childlike warmth, submissiveness, and naïveté (Berry & McArthur, 1986). In both cases, people's emotional reactions to one stimulus are generalized to similar stimuli.

Discrimination

The dogs could also learn to respond only to the sound of a particular bell and *not* to other bells. This learned ability to *distinguish* between conditioned stimuli and similar but irrelevant stimuli is called *discrimination.* Like the ability to generalize, the ability to discriminate also has survival value. Sometimes similar but different stimuli are followed by vastly different consequences. Being able to recognize these differences is adaptive. When you are confronted by a pit bull your heart may race; when confronted by a cocker spaniel it does not.

Discrimination training can be used to determine what a nonverbal organism can perceive. Can a dog distinguish between shapes? Can a baby distinguish between sounds? If they can be conditioned to respond to one stimulus and not to the other, then obviously they can perceive the difference.

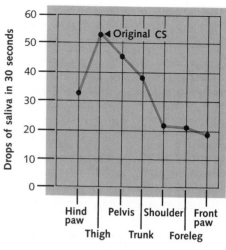

Figure 9–4 Generalization was demonstrated in an experiment in which miniature vibrators were attached to various parts of a dog's body. After salivation had been conditioned to stimulation of the thigh, other areas of the body were stimulated. The closer they were to the original site of stimulation, the stronger the conditioned response. (From Pavlov, 1927.)

University of Windsor psychologist Dale Woodyard is training this manatee to discriminate between objects of different shapes, colors, and sizes for a food reward. The manatee remembers such lessons for as long as a year.

Pavlov's Legacy

Why is Pavlov's work considered so important? Had he taught us only that old dogs can learn new tricks, his experiments would have been forgotten long ago. Why should anyone care that a dog can be conditioned to drool at the sound of a bell, a touch on the leg, or even the sight of a circle? The importance lies first in the fact that many other responses to many other stimuli have subsequently been classically conditioned in many other organisms—in fact, in every species tested, from worms to fish to dogs to monkeys to people (Schwartz, 1984). Thus, classical conditioning is one way that virtually all organisms learn to adapt to their environment.

Classical conditioning has also proved to have many helpful applications to human health and well-being (Domjan, 1987). Paraplegics whose injuries have resulted in a severing of the nerves by which the brain controls the bladder have been able temporarily to condition their lower spinal cords to associate a tickling electric shock to the thigh (a CS) with the strong abdominal shock (a UCS) that automatically triggers urination. For a time thereafter, until the extinction of a CS, they are able to urinate when they choose by giving themselves a light shock on the thigh (Ince & others, 1978).

Finally, Pavlov's work provides an important example of how a significant internal process such as learning can be studied objectively. Pavlov was proud that his method involved virtually no subjective judgments or guesses about what went on in the dogs' minds. The salivary response is an overt behavior that can be measured directly—as so many drops or cubic centimeters of saliva. Pavlov's success therefore suggested a scientific model for how the young discipline of psychology might proceed—by isolating the elementary building blocks of complex behaviors and studying them with objective laboratory procedures.

CLASSICAL CONDITIONING AND BEHAVIORISM

Pavlov's work provided support for the arguments of American psychologist John B. Watson, who in 1913 began to urge that psychology discard references to thoughts, feelings, and hidden motives and focus instead on an organism's response to its environment. In other words, psychology should become a science of *behavior*. Forget the mind, said Watson; psychology's goal is "to be able, given the stimulus, to predict the response."

Watson's position, called **behaviorism,** prevailed throughout much of American psychology during the first half of this century. It was particularly influential in promoting the idea that human behavior could be understood in terms of conditioned responses. In one famous though ethically troublesome study, Watson and Rosalie Rayner (1920; Harris, 1979) showed how specific fears might be conditioned in humans. Their subject was an 11-month-old infant named Albert. "Little Albert," like most infants, feared loud noises, but not white rats. So Watson and Rayner presented him with a white rat and, as he reached to touch it, struck a hammer against a steel bar just behind his head. After seven repetitions of seeing the rat and hearing the frightening noise, Albert burst into tears at the mere sight of the rat. What is more, 5 days later Albert showed generalization of his conditioned response to the rat by reacting with fear when presented with a rabbit, a dog, and a sealskin coat.

Although some psychologists had difficulty repeating these findings with other children, Watson and Rayner's work with Little Albert has had legendary significance for many psychologists, a number of whom have wondered if each of us might not be a walking repository of conditioned emotions. Correspondingly, they have wondered whether our less adaptive emotions might be controlled by the application of extinction procedures or by conditioning new responses to emotion-arousing stimuli. In Chapter 17, Therapy, we will see how behavioral techniques are being used to treat emotional disorders.

Psychologist Gregory Razran (1940) found that when political slogans (a CS) were associated with the eating of food (UCS), people became more approving of them. Similarly, advertisers like to associate their product (a CS) with a naturally pleasing image, such as a sexually attractive model.

John B. Watson (1924, p. 104): "Give me a dozen healthy infants, well-formed, and my own specified world to bring them up in and I'll guarantee to take any one at random and train him to become any type of specialist I might select—doctor, lawyer, artist, merchant-chief and, yes, even beggar-man and thief, regardless of his talents, penchants, tendencies, abilities, vocations, and race of his ancestors."

In Watson's experiment, what was the UCS? The UCR? The CS? The CR? (See page 236.)

BEHAVIORISM RECONSIDERED

The use of scientific methodology advocated by the behaviorists continues to this day in all areas of psychological research. But the behaviorists' disdain for "mentalistic" concepts such as consciousness has given way to a growing realization that (1) cognitive processes—thoughts, perceptions, expectations—have an important place in the science of psychology, and that (2) an organism's capacity for conditioning is constrained by its biological predispositions.

Cognitive Processes The early behaviorists believed that all the learned behaviors of various organisms could be reduced to universal stimulus-response mechanisms. As recently as 30 years ago, the idea that rats and dogs exhibit some cognitive appraisals in connection with the learned associations struck many psychologists as silly. No longer. Classical conditioning experiments by Robert Rescorla and Allan Wagner (1972) revealed that classical conditioning involves something more complex than a new stimulus coming to evoke an old reflex. Animals seem to comprehend the likelihood that the UCS will occur just after the CS. If an electric shock occurs randomly while an animal is repeatedly exposed to a tone, then the shock will by chance occasionally follow the tone. Do such chance pairings serve to "stamp in" an association between tone and shock? If conditioning depends only on how *often* the two are associated, then eventually the animals should become fearful of the tone. But no—the animal becomes conditioned only when the tone *consistently predicts* the shock. The more predictable the association, the stronger the conditioned response.

It's as if what gets "stamped in" is an *expectancy*, an awareness of how likely it is that the UCS will follow the CS. Rescorla (1988) surmises that classical conditioning "is not a stupid process by which the organism willy-nilly forms associations between any two stimuli that happen to occur." Rather, the organism is like an information seeker, using relations among events to form its own adaptive representation of the world. Indeed, says Rescorla, a simple rule of thumb summarizes a host of facts about classical conditioning: Conditioning occurs best when the CS and UCS have just the sort of relationship that would lead a scientist to conclude that the CS *causes* the UCS.

This rule of thumb helps explain why classical conditioning treatments that ignore cognitive appraisals are often not completely successful. When alcoholics are given alcohol spiked with a drug that makes them sick, will they associate alcohol with sickness? If classical conditioning were merely a matter of stamping in stimulus-response associations, we might hope so. And, to some extent, this does occur (as we will see on page 485). However, alcoholics are aware that they can blame their illness on the drug rather than the alcohol. This cognition tends to weaken the association between alcohol and sickness. So, even in classical conditioning, it is not only the simple stimulus-response association but also the thought that counts.

Biological Predispositions Pavlov and the early American behaviorists were highly optimistic about the power and applicability of conditioning principles. Because the basic laws of learning were believed to be essentially similar in all animals, the researchers thought it made little difference whether one studied rats, pigeons, or people. Moreover, it seemed that any natural response could be conditioned to any neutral stimulus. As learning researcher Gregory Kimble proclaimed in

Psychology's "factual and theoretical developments in this century—which have changed the study of mind and behavior as radically as genetics changed the study of heredity—have all been the product of objective analysis—that is to say, behavioristic analysis."

Canadian psychologist D. O. Hebb (1980)

Answer to question on page 235: The UCS was the loud noise; the UCR was the startled fear response; the CS was the rat; the CR was fear.

1956, "just about any activity of which the organism is capable can be conditioned and . . . these responses can be conditioned to any stimulus that the organism can perceive" (p. 195).

Twenty-five years later, Kimble (1981) humbly acknowledged that "half a thousand" scientific reports had shown his pronouncement wrong. Animals are biologically predisposed to learn the particular associations that enhance their species' survival—and not others.

The person most responsible for challenging the prevailing behaviorist view was John Garcia. While researching the effects of radiation on laboratory animals, Garcia and his colleague Robert Koelling (1966) noticed that rats began to avoid drinking water from the plastic bottles in the radiation chambers. He wondered whether their dislike of the water might be a result of classical conditioning. Might the rats have linked the sickness (UCR) induced by the radiation (UCS) to the plastic-tasting water (a CS)?

To test his hunch, Garcia undertook a number of experiments in which rats experienced a particular taste, sight, or sound and were later sickened by radiation or drugs. Two startling findings emerged: First, the rats developed aversions to the tastes, but not to the sights or sounds; this contradicted the behaviorists' idea that any perceivable stimulus could serve as a CS. Second, even if sickened as late as several hours after tasting a particular flavor, the rats thereafter avoided that flavor. This violated the notion that the UCS must follow the CS immediately for conditioning to occur.

The philosopher Schopenhauer once said that important ideas are first ridiculed, then attacked, and finally taken for granted. So it was with Garcia's findings on taste aversion. The leading journals initially refused to publish his work; the findings were impossible, said some critics. But as often happens in science, Garcia's provocative findings stimulated new research, which in this case confirmed and extended the initial findings. Other species are also disposed to learn certain aversions. For example, when coyotes are tempted into eating sheep carcasses laced with a sickening poison, they will develop an aversion to sheep meat (Gustavson & others, 1974). Such findings suggest that predators and agricultural pests might be humanely controlled through taste-aversion procedures. (This is but one instance in which psychological research that began with the suffering of some laboratory animals has contributed to the welfare of many more animals—in this case, *both* of coyotes that might otherwise be killed by ranchers and farmers, and of the sheep.)

Have such results compelled researchers to abandon the search for principles of learning that generalize across species? No, the principles are not wrong, but constrained by biological predispositions. These constraints affirm the deeper principle that learning enables animals to adapt to their environments. The principle of adaptation shows us why animals would be responsive to stimuli that help them to anticipate other significant events, such as food or pain. Animals are predisposed to associate a CS with a UCS that immediately follows, for causes often immediately precede effects. The adaptation principle also helps explain exceptions such as the taste-aversion findings. In these cases, causes need not precede effects immediately—bad food usually causes sickness quite a while after it has been consumed. Similarly, cancer patients who suffer nausea and vomiting beginning more than an hour following chemotherapy often develop classically conditioned nausea to stimuli associated with taking the drug, such as the hospital parking lot, waiting, and nurses (Burish & Carey, 1986).

"Not everything that is incredible is untrue."
Cardinal de Retz,
Memoirs, 1673–1676

Saving coyotes by making them sick. When coyotes were fed poisoned lamb meat, the poison (UCS) made them sick (UCR). As a result, they developed an aversion (CR) to the lamb (CS) and returned to feeding on their natural prey. With their livestock no longer endangered, ranchers were less adamant about destroying the coyotes.

But why did Garcia's rats become conditioned only to tastes and not to sounds or sights? This also has to do with biological constraints. Each organism is better prepared to learn some associations than others. The rats were simply not biologically prepared to associate sights or sounds with their subsequent sickness. This makes adaptive sense, because for rats such stimuli almost never precede sickness. Humans also are more prepared to form some associations than others. People can more readily be conditioned to fear animals (as was Little Albert) than to fear flowers (Cook & others, 1986). Again, this makes sense—humans are frequently harmed by animals but seldom by flowers. The familiar principle that natural selection favors traits that assist survival and reproduction therefore holds: Each species comes prepared to learn those things crucial to its survival.

What, then, remains of Pavlov's ideas about conditioning? A great deal. All the researchers we have met so far in this chapter concur with Pavlov that theories of learning should be tested objectively. They also agree that classical conditioning is an important kind of learning, although one that is constrained by cognitive processes and biological predispositions. Judged by today's knowledge, Pavlov's ideas may seem incomplete. But if we see further than Pavlov did, it is in large measure because we stand on his shoulders.

Birds develop a similar aversion to the *sight* of tainted food (Nicolaus & others, 1983). Once a blue jay has eaten a monarch butterfly (which contains a poison), it will avoid both monarchs and their look-alikes. This, too, makes adaptive sense. Birds hunt by sight, and so are predisposed to learn associations between illness and visual cues.

OPERANT CONDITIONING

We have seen that classical conditioning links simple, involuntary responses with neutral stimuli. How then do we learn more complex voluntary behaviors? It's one thing to teach an animal to salivate at the sound of a bell or a child to avoid cars in the street, and quite another to teach an elephant to walk on its hind legs, a child to learn arithmetic, or a disturbed adult to behave rationally. Behaviorists would reply that through another type of conditioning we can explain and train such behaviors. In what psychologists call *operant,* or *instrumental, conditioning,* a subject becomes more likely to repeat rewarded behaviors and less likely to repeat punished behaviors.

Classical and operant conditioning both involve acquisition, extinction, generalization, and discrimination. Nevertheless, their difference is straightforward: Classical conditioning involves what Skinner calls *respondent behavior*—reflexive behavior that occurs as an automatic *response* to some conditioned stimulus (such as Pavlov's tone). Operant conditioning is the learning of a nonreflexive act, called *operant behavior* because it *operates* on the environment to produce rewarding or punishing stimuli.

We can therefore distinguish classical from operant conditioning by asking, does the controlling stimulus come before the behavior (the CS of classical conditioning) or after (the consequence of operant conditioning)? In classical conditioning it comes before, no matter what the organism is doing, as when the tone comes to elicit salivation. In operant conditioning it comes after, contingent on the animal's behavior, as when a dog performs a trick and obtains food.

Skinner's work elaborated a simple fact of life that the turn-of-the-century psychologist E. L. Thorndike had called the "law of effect": Behavior that is rewarded is likely to recur. Using the law of effect as a starting point, Skinner developed a "behavioral technology" that enabled him to teach pigeons such unpigeonlike behaviors as walking in a figure 8, playing Ping-Pong, and keeping a "guided missile" on course by pecking at a moving target displayed on a screen.

Respondent behavior responds to stimuli.

Operant behavior operates to produce stimuli.

SKINNER'S EXPERIMENTS

B. F. Skinner was a college English major and aspiring writer who, seeking a new direction, entered graduate school in psychology and went on to become the most visible representative of modern behaviorism. For his pioneering studies with rats and later with pigeons, Skinner designed the now famous *Skinner box* (Figure 9–5). The "box" is typically a soundproof chamber with a bar or key that can be manipulated to release a food or water reward, and with devices that electronically record the animal's rate of bar pressing or key pecking.

The experiments of Skinner and other operant researchers did far more than teach us how to pull habits out of a rat. They explored the precise conditions that foster efficient and enduring learning.

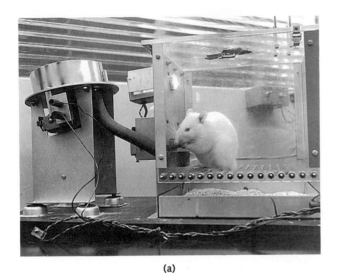

(a)

(b)

Figure 9–5   (a) Inside the Skinner box, the rat presses a bar for a food reward. Note that the grill at the bottom of the box is wired to deliver an electric shock. Conditioning may involve the rat learning to press the lever to shut off the electric shock (negative reinforcement). (b) Outside, a device attached to the bar records the animal's accumulated responses. Figures 9–6 and 9–7 (see pages 241 and 242) depict superimposed model response curves that would be generated by a pigeon on various reward schedules.

Shaping   In his experiments Skinner used a procedure called *shaping,* in which rewards, such as food, are used to guide an animal's natural behavior toward a desired behavior. Imagine that you wanted to condition a rat to press a bar. After observing how the animal naturally behaves before training, you would begin to build upon its existing behaviors. You might, for example, give the rat a food reward each time it approaches the bar. Once the rat is approaching regularly, you would require it to move closer before rewarding it, then closer still, and finally to touch the bar before giving it the reward. With this method of *successive approximations,* responses that are steps toward the desired behavior are rewarded and all other responses are ignored. In this way, the researcher or animal trainer gradually shapes complex behaviors. Similarly, a parent may use rewards to shape good table manners in a developing child by praising eating behavior that is more and more adultlike.

The procedure sounds simple. But let's compare its essential features to what often happens in homes and schools. In the operant conditioning procedure, the trainer builds upon the individual's existing behaviors by immediately rewarding small steps toward the desired new behavior. In everyday life, we are continually rewarding and shaping the behavior of others, says Skinner, often unintentionally. Sometimes we even reward behaviors that are offensive to us. Billy's parents, for example, are annoyed and mystified by his loud whining.

But look at how they typically deal with Billy—by rewarding the very behavior they find so annoying:

Billy: *"Could you tie my shoes?"*

Father: *(Continues reading paper.)*

Billy: *"Dad, I need my shoes tied."*

Father: *"Uh, yeah, just a minute."*

Billy: *"DAAAAD! TIE MY SHOES!"*

Father: *"How many times have I told you not to whine? Now, which shoe do we do first?"*

Or compare the way learning psychologists shape behavior (by continually rewarding small improvements) to the way rewards are administered in some schoolrooms. On a wall chart, the teacher pastes gold stars only after the names of children scoring 100 percent on spelling tests. All children take the same tests. As everyone can then see, some children, the academic all-stars, easily get 100 percent; the others, no matter how hard they try or how much they improve, receive no reinforcement. Better if the teacher would reward poor spellers for gradual improvement or for doing their best.

Principles of Reinforcement   So far, we have referred rather loosely to the power of "rewards." This idea is given a more precise meaning in Skinner's concept of *reinforcer,* which is any event that strengthens the response that it follows.

Varieties of Reinforcers   Although people tend to think of reinforcers as rewards, there actually are two kinds of reinforcers: positive and negative. A *positive reinforcer* is a stimulus that, when presented after a response, will strengthen the response (make its recurrence more likely). Food is typically used as a positive reinforcer for animals; attention, approval, and money are positive reinforcers for most people. A *negative reinforcer* is the termination of an aversive (unpleasant) stimulus. Switching off an electric shock is a rewarding event; it is a negative reinforcer typically used in animal experiments. Stopping nagging (an unpleasant stimulus) is an everyday negative reinforcer for people.

Imagine that whenever a child throws a tantrum the parent gives in for the sake of peace and quiet. The child's behavior will be strengthened by positive reinforcement (the parent gives in), and the parent's behavior will be strengthened by negative reinforcement (the child stops screaming). If after goofing off and getting a bad exam grade a worried student studies harder, the student may be negatively reinforced by the reduction in anxiety and positively reinforced by a good grade on the next exam. Remember: Whether it works by delivering something positive or withdrawing something negative, a reinforcer *strengthens* behavior.

Reinforcers can be further differentiated as either primary or secondary. *Primary reinforcers,* such as food or the termination of shock, are innate; they satisfy basic needs without having to be learned. *Secondary reinforcers* are conditioned; they get their power through association with primary reinforcers. If a rat in a Skinner box has learned that the sound of a buzzer reliably signals that food is coming, the rat will work to turn on the buzzer; the buzzer has become a secondary reinforcer associated with food. Our lives are filled with secondary reinforcers—money, good grades, a tone of voice, a word of praise—each of which has been linked with desirable consequences. Secondary reinforcers greatly enhance our power to influence one another.

The goose won the prize, but it's obviously the boy who has been positively rewarded.

Note that "positive" means presenting a stimulus, and "negative" means withdrawing one. All reinforcers strengthen behavior. Thus the withdrawal of an aversive stimulus (such as nagging) is a negative reinforcer.

Another important distinction is between *immediate* and *delayed* reinforcement. In a typical experiment, an animal will engage in a whole sequence of "unwanted" behaviors—scratching, sniffing, walking about—in addition to performing a "wanted" behavior such as pressing the bar. Whichever of these behaviors immediately precedes the reinforcement becomes more likely to occur again. If the reinforcement for bar pressing is delayed as long as 30 seconds, allowing other behaviors to intervene, virtually no learning of the bar pressing occurs.

Human cognitive abilities—our capacities to recall our past and project our future—enable us to respond to reinforcers that are greatly delayed: the paycheck at the end of the week, the grade at the end of the semester, the trophy at the end of the season. Nevertheless, many of our behaviors are influenced by the immediacy of reinforcement. Smokers, alcoholics, and other drug users may know that the immediate reinforcement accompanying consumption is more than offset by the punishments and dangers that lie in the future. Still, the immediate reinforcements prevail.

Schedules of Reinforcement   So far in our examples, we have mostly assumed **continuous reinforcement:** Every time the desired response occurs, it gets reinforced. Under such conditions, learning occurs rapidly; but when the reinforcement stops—when the food delivery mechanism is disconnected—extinction also occurs rapidly. The rat soon stops pressing the bar. If a normally dependable candy machine fails to deliver a candy bar twice in a row, we stop putting money into it (although a week later we may exhibit spontaneous recovery by trying again).

In real life, continuous reinforcement is rare. A salesperson does not make a sale with every pitch, nor does an angler get a bite with every cast. But they keep on trying because in the past they have been occasionally rewarded for their efforts. Researchers have explored a number of **partial,** or **intermittent, reinforcement** schedules, in which responses are sometimes reinforced, sometimes not. Initial learning is typically slower with partial reinforcement, which makes continuous reinforcement preferable until a behavior has been mastered, but it does produce persistence—a *resistance to extinction* that is not found with continuous reinforcement. Imagine a pigeon that has mastered the pecking of a key to obtain food. When the delivery of food gradually fades out until it occurs only rarely and unpredictably, pigeons have been observed to peck over 150,000 times without a reward (Skinner, 1953). With partial reinforcement, hope springs eternal.

Again, corresponding human examples come readily to mind. Gamblers who play slot machines are rewarded occasionally and unpredictably, and this partial reinforcement affects them much as it affects pigeons: They keep trying. There is a valuable lesson here for parents of children prone to throwing tantrums: Occasionally giving in to such behavior for the sake of peace and quiet puts the child, in effect, on a partial reinforcement schedule—the very best procedure for making the tantrums persist.

Skinner (1961) and his collaborators compared various schedules of partial reinforcement. Some of the schedules were rigidly fixed; some were unpredictably variable. *Fixed-interval schedules* provide a pause after reinforcement, during which time no reinforcements are available; after the specified interval is over the next response is reinforced. Like people checking more frequently for the mail as the delivery time approaches, pigeons on a fixed-interval schedule peck a key more frequently as the anticipated time for reward draws near (Figure 9–6).

"[The child should] gain no request by anger; when he is quiet let him be offered what was refused when he wept" (Seneca, 4 B.C.–A.D. 65).

"The charm of fishing is that it is the pursuit of what is elusive but attainable, a perpetual series of occasions for hope."
Scottish author John Buchan, 1875–1940

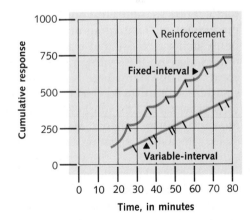

Figure 9–6 Fixed-interval and variable-interval schedules. As these model curves suggest, response rates vary with the reinforcement schedule (slanted lines signify reinforcements). An every-2-minute fixed-interval schedule will produce increased responding as the time for a reinforcement draws near. A variable-interval schedule, with its unpredictable rewards, will produce steady responding. (From Reynolds, 1978.)

Variable-interval schedules eliminate these predictable pauses by reinforcing the first response after *varying* amounts of time. Like the unpredictable pop quiz that reinforces studying or the "hello" that finally rewards persistence in calling back a busy number, variable-interval schedules tend to produce steady responding (Figure 9–6). This makes sense, because there is no way of knowing when the waiting interval will be over. Should the pop quiz become predictable, students will begin the stop-start work pattern that characterizes fixed-interval schedules.

The *fixed-ratio schedule* reinforces behavior after a set number of responses. Like people paid on a piecework basis, say for every thirty pieces of work, laboratory animals may be reinforced on a fixed ratio of, say, one reinforcement to every thirty responses. Typically, the animal will pause after receiving a reinforcement and will then return to a high rate of responding (Figure 9–7). Because resting while on a demanding fixed-ratio schedule results in reduced rewards, employees find piecework arrangements tiring. Thus unions have pressured employers to adopt hourly wage schedules.

Finally, *variable-ratio schedules* provide reinforcement after an unpredictable number of responses. This is similar to the reinforcement schedule that gamblers experience. Like the fixed-ratio schedule, it produces high rates of responding because reinforcements increase as the responding increases (Figure 9–7). And like the equally unpredictable variable-interval schedule, this schedule also creates great resistance to extinction.

Skinner's (1956) behavioristic conviction is that these principles of operant learning are universal. It matters little, he says, what response, what reinforcer, or what species you use. The effect of a given reinforcement schedule is pretty much the same: "Pigeon, rat, monkey, which is which? It doesn't matter. . . . Behavior shows astonishingly similar properties."

Punishment   *Punishment* is the opposite of reinforcement: A punisher is any consequence that *decreases* the recurrence of the behavior that it follows. There is no question that punishment can be a powerful instrument for restraining unwanted behavior—at least under conditions similar to those that make reinforcement effective. Of particular importance are the strength, timing, and consistency of the punishment. Strong, immediate, consistent consequences affect behavior swiftly; weak, delayed, inconsistent consequences do not (Schwartz, 1984). The rat that is shocked after touching the forbidden object and the child who loses a treat after running into the street will learn more quickly to avoid repeating the behavior if punishment is swift and sure.

As powerful as punishment can be, there is much controversy over whether it is a desirable means of controlling behavior. Those who oppose it say that punished behavior is not forgotten; it is suppressed. This temporary suppression of "bad" behavior may reinforce the people who administer the punishment. But if the punishment is avoidable, the punished behavior may reappear as people learn to discriminate the settings where punishment is unlikely. The child who learns through spankings not to swear around the house may do so freely elsewhere. The driver who is hit with a couple of tickets for speeding may buy a fuzz buster and continue to speed freely when no radar patrol is in the area. Teenagers who are punished for telling the truth about where they have been or what they have been doing may begin to lie.

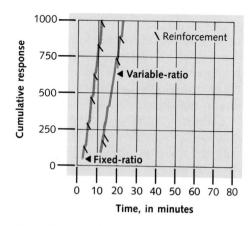

Figure 9–7   Fixed-ratio and variable-ratio schedules. Fixed-ratio schedules produce a high rate of response, with a pause after each reward. The unpredictable variable-ratio schedules produce the highest response rates of all. (From Reynolds, 1978.)

Note: **Punishment** is the delivery of an aversive stimulus that decreases the recurrence of behavior it follows. **Negative reinforcement** is the withdrawal of an aversive stimulus that increases the recurrence of the behavior it follows. Thus the delivery of shock is a punisher; the termination of shock is a negative reinforcer.

What punishment often teaches, says Skinner, is how to avoid punishment. Picture this experimental procedure (Solomon & others, 1953): A dog is placed in a box that is divided into two compartments by a low barrier. Shortly after a light comes on, a powerful shock delivered through an electrified floor sends the dog leaping over the barrier. Because the other compartment is not electrified, the escape behavior is negatively reinforced. This learning to escape an aversive stimulus is called, naturally enough, *escape learning.* On succeeding trials, the dog is again shocked soon after the light comes on unless it learns to leap the barrier immediately, in which case it is reinforced by avoiding the shock altogether. Appropriately, this way of avoiding punishment is called *avoidance learning.*

Punishment is most effective when strong, immediate, and consistent, but it can also have undesirable side effects. This teenager's anger at her mother's scolding might, if this were to become their principal mode of communication, translate into a resistance to listening to her mother.

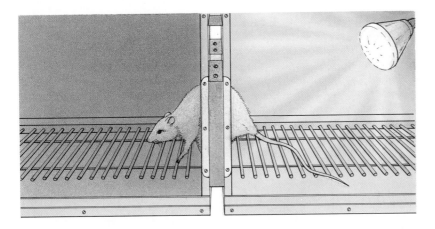

Escape and avoidance learning are often studied using a "shuttle box." When an electric current is transmitted to one compartment, the animal can escape to the other after being shocked. Or it may avoid the shock completely by escaping on a cue, such as a light going on, that signals the shock's impending arrival.

Opponents of punishment also say that it can create fear, and the person receiving the punishment may associate it not only with the undesirable behavior but also with the person who administers it or the situation in which it occurs. Thus, a child may come to fear the punitive teacher and want to avoid school. Worse yet, when punishments are unpredictable and inescapable, both animals and people may develop the sense that events are beyond their control. As a result, they may come to feel helpless, and become passive and depressed. (More on this in later chapters.)

We have seen that swift and sure punishment can suppress unwanted behavior, but that it also teaches how to avoid punishment and may create fear. Yet another way in which punishment, especially physical punishment, is problematic is that it often increases aggressiveness, by demonstrating aggression as a way to cope with problems. Moreover, being painful, physical punishment can arouse anger and hostility. This combination of factors may explain why so many abusive parents turn out to have been abused as children, and why so many aggressive delinquents come from abusive families (Strauss & Gelles, 1980). Within families, violence often breeds violence.

Finally, even when punishment successfully suppresses unwanted behavior, it usually does not guide one toward more desirable behavior. Punishment tells you what *not* to do; reinforcement tells you what to do. (Recall from Chapter 3 that children more easily understand positive instructions than negative ones.) Punishment in combination with reinforcement is, therefore, generally more effective than punishment alone. The dogs in the avoidance learning experiments were both punished for inaction and reinforced for correct action and so learned quickly. Emotionally disabled children who bite themselves or bang their heads may be mildly punished (say, with a squirt of water in the face) whenever they bite themselves, while also rewarded with positive attention and food when behaving well. The teacher whose feedback on a paper says, "No, but try this . . ." and "Yes, that's it!," is eliminating unwanted behavior by reinforcing alternative behaviors.

RAPE AS TRAUMATIC FEAR CONDITIONING

Experiments with dogs reveal that if a painful stimulus is sufficiently powerful, a single event can be sufficient to traumatize the animal when it faces a similar situation. The human counterparts to these experiments can be tragic, as illustrated by one woman's experience of being attacked and raped, and thereby conditioned to a life of fear. Her fear is most powerfully associated with particular locations and people, but it generalizes to other places and people. Note, too, how her traumatic experience has robbed her of the normally relaxing associations with such stimuli as home and bed.

Four months ago I was raped. In the middle of the night I awoke to the sound of someone outside my bedroom. Thinking my housemate was coming home, I called out her name. Someone began walking slowly toward me, and then I realized. I screamed and fought, but there were two of them. One held my legs, while the other put a hand over my mouth and a knife to my throat and said, "Shut up, bitch, or we'll kill you." Never have I been so terrified and helpless. They both raped me, one brutally. As they then searched my room for money and valuables, my housemate came home. They brought her into my room, raped her, and left us both tied up on my bed.

We never slept another night in that apartment, for we were too terrified there. Still, when I go to bed at night—always with the bedroom light left on—the memory of them entering my room repeats itself endlessly. I was an independent person who had lived alone or with other women for four years; now I can't even think about spending a night alone. When I drive by our old apartment, or when I have to go into an empty house, my heart pounds and I sweat. I am afraid of strangers, especially men, and the more they resemble my attackers the more I fear them. My housemate shares many of my fears, and is frightened when entering our new apartment. I'm afraid to stay in the same town, I'm afraid it will happen again, I'm afraid to go to bed. I dread falling asleep.

To sum up, punishment is sometimes effective, and may on occasion cause less pain to a person than does the self-destructive behavior it suppresses. However, punished behavior may reappear if the threatened punishment can be avoided. Punishment can also have undesirable side effects, such as creating fear and teaching aggression, and it often fails to teach how to act positively. Thus, most psychologists join Skinner in favoring an emphasis on positive reinforcement rather than punishment; catch people doing something right and affirm them for it. When you stop to think about it, many of our threats of punishment could be just as forceful, and perhaps more effective, if rephrased posi-

Reinforcement: The process by which consequences *increase behaviors*.

Positive reinforcement: Increasing behaviors by *presenting positive stimuli* (such as food).

Negative reinforcement: Increasing behaviors by *withdrawing negative stimuli* (such as shock).

Punishment: The process by which aversive consequences *decrease behaviors*.

tively: "Johnny, if your room is not cleaned you may not go outside" could become "Johnny, when your room is cleaned you may go outside." "Maria, if you don't get your homework done, there'll be no TV" could become . . .

APPLICATIONS OF OPERANT CONDITIONING

We have already seen numerous everyday applications of operant conditioning principles, and in later chapters we will see how these principles are being applied to problems ranging from high blood pressure to social withdrawal. They have also been applied in many other behavior technologies devised for schools, businesses, and homes. Let's take a look at some examples.

In the Classroom   A generation ago, Skinner and others advocated teaching machines and textbooks that would apply operant principles by shaping learning in small steps and providing immediate reinforcement for correct responses. These machines and texts, it was said, would revolutionize education and free teachers to concentrate on the special needs of their students.

To envision Skinner's dream, imagine two mathematics teachers. Faced with a class of academically diverse students, Teacher A gives the whole class the same math lesson, knowing well that some students already understand the concepts being taught and that others will be frustrated by their inability to comprehend the concepts. When test time comes, the whiz kids breeze through unchallenged, and the slower learners once again experience failure. Faced with a similar class, Teacher B paces the material according to each student's rate of learning and provides prompt feedback with much positive reinforcement to both slow and fast learners. Does the individualized instruction of Teacher B sound like an impossible ideal?

Though the revolution Skinner predicted never occurred, relatively low-cost microcomputers have begun to make the impossible ideal more realistic, and Skinner (1986, 1988) remains hopeful. For some types of educational tasks, such as teaching reading and math, the computer can be Teacher B: engaging the student actively, pacing material according to the student's rate of learning, quizzing the student to find gaps in understanding, providing immediate feedback, and keeping flawless records for the supervising teacher. Experiments comparing computer-assisted instruction (CAI) with traditional instruction suggest that for some "drill and practice" types of tasks the computer can indeed be more effective (Kulik & others, 1980, 1985). As microcomputers have become more widely available, so too have new techniques of CAI, such as educational games and simulations that entice students to explore and discover principles on their own (Lepper, 1982).

Computer-assisted instruction (CAI) can provide individualized instruction with immediate reinforcement for correct responses.

In the Workplace   Believing that people's productivity is influenced by reinforcers, some managers are capitalizing on psychological research. For example, Ed Pedalino and Victor Gamboa (1974) showed how reinforcement could decrease absenteeism. In one manufacturing plant, they invited all workers who showed up on time to pick a card from a poker deck each day. At the end of each week, the worker in each department with the best poker hand won $20. Immediately, absenteeism dropped 18 percent and remained lowered—for as long as the incentive was offered.

Positive reinforcements for jobs well done can also boost productivity. This is especially so when the desired performance is *well-defined*

"How much richer would the whole world be if the reinforcers in daily life were more effectively contingent on productive work?"

B. F. Skinner (1986)

and achievable: Reward specific behaviors, not vaguely defined merit. It's also a good idea to make the reinforcement *immediate.* Thomas Watson, who led IBM during its tremendous growth, would write out a check on the spot for achievements he observed (Peters & Waterman, 1982). But the rewards need not be material, nor so big that they become political and a source of discouragement to those who don't receive them. The effective manager might simply walk the floor and give affirmation for good work, or write unexpected notes of appreciation for a completed project.

Drawing by Stevenson; © 1988 The New Yorker Magazine, Inc.

"Keep up the good work, whatever it is, whoever you are."

TAKING CHARGE OF YOUR OWN BEHAVIOR

Many recent books and articles offer advice on how we can use operant learning principles to strengthen our most desired behaviors and extinguish our least desired behaviors. Here are the step-by-step procedures they recommend.

1. State your goals in measurable terms and make them public— whether they are to stop smoking, lose weight, study more, or get more exercise. You might, for example, aim to boost your study time by an hour a day and announce your goal to friends.

2. Record how often you engage in the behaviors you wish to promote and note how these behaviors are currently being reinforced. You might therefore log your cur-rent study time, noting under what conditions you do and don't study. (When I began writing textbooks, I logged my relevant activities and was astonished to discover how much time I was wasting.)

3. Begin systematically to reinforce the desired behaviors. To increase your study time, allow yourself to eat a snack (or whatever other activity you find reinforcing) only after specified periods of study. Agree with your friends that you will join them for weekend activities *if* you have met your weekly studying goal.

4. As your new behaviors become more habitual, the incentives can gradually be reduced.

In the Home Economists and psychologists also view people's spending behavior as controlled by its consequences (what economists call its costs and benefits). People who live in apartment buildings where energy costs are paid by the landlord use about 25 percent more energy than people who live in comparable buildings but pay their own energy costs, therefore reaping the rewards of their own energy savings. Similarly, home electricity users on an "energy diet" are helped by frequent feedback that shows their current usage compared with their past consumption (Darley & others, 1979). In homes, as in the learning laboratory and workplace, behavior is most effectively modified when it is linked with immediate consequences.

FURTHER RECONSIDERATION OF BEHAVIORISM

B. F. Skinner has been one of the more controversial intellectual figures of our time. The controversy stems mainly from his insistence that external influences, not internal thoughts and feelings, shape behavior and from his proposals that operant principles be used to control people's behavior at home, school, and work. To manage people effectively, Skinner says, we should worry less about their illusions of freedom and dignity. Recognizing that behavior is shaped by its consequences, we should administer rewards in ways that promote more desirable behavior.

Outside of psychology, Skinner's critics object that he dehumanizes people by neglecting their personal freedom and by seeking to control their actions. Skinner and his defenders reply that people's behavior is already controlled by external reinforcers, so why not manipulate those controls for human betterment? In place of the widespread use of punishment in homes, schools, and prisons, would not the use of *positive* reinforcers be more humanitarian? They also suggest that even if it is humbling to think that we are shaped by our histories, this very idea also creates the hope that we may actively shape our future.

B. F. Skinner (1983, p. 25): "I am sometimes asked, 'Do you think of yourself as you think of the organisms you study?' The answer is yes. So far as I know, my behavior at any given moment has been nothing more than the product of my genetic endowment, my personal history, and the current setting."

Within psychology, Skinner has been faulted for ignoring the importance of cognitive processes and for underplaying the extent to which our biological predispositions constrain the environment's power to shape behavior.

Cognitive Processes There have already been several hints that cognitive processes may be involved in operant learning. We have seen, for instance, that animals placed on fixed-interval or fixed-ratio reinforcement schedules respond more and more frequently as they approach the point at which reinforcement will be given, which strongly suggests that the animals have developed an expectancy that repeating the behavior will soon trigger the reward.

Latent Learning Other evidence of cognitive processes comes from studies of rats in mazes. Rats that are given a chance to explore a maze, even when no reinforcement is provided, are somewhat like people who drive around a new town; they develop a *cognitive map,* a mental representation, of the maze. This occurs even if the rats are carried passively through the maze in a wire basket. When a reward is subsequently placed in the goal box of the maze, these rats immediately perform as well as rats that have been reinforced for running the maze, as indicated by Figure 9–8. During their explorations, the rats had obviously experienced some sort of *latent learning*—learning that does

not become apparent until there is some incentive to demonstrate it. This suggests that reinforcement may be more important for triggering performance than for learning.

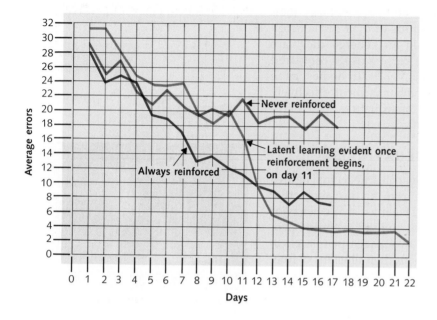

Figure 9–8 Latent learning. Animals, like people, can learn from experience, with or without reinforcement. When rats that had explored a maze for 10 days were then offered a food reward at the end of the maze, they quickly demonstrated their prior learning of the maze—by immediately doing as well as rats that had been reinforced for running the maze. (From Tolman & Honzik, 1930.)

Overjustification The cognitive perspective has also led to an important qualification concerning the power of rewards: Unnecessary rewards carry hidden costs. Most people think that offering tangible rewards is an effective way to boost someone's interest in a task (Boggiano & others, 1987). Actually, promising people a reward for doing a task they already enjoy can undermine its intrinsic interest. People who begin to see the reward as their motive for performing the task may lose their intrinsic enjoyment of it. This phenomenon is called the *overjustification effect* because an already justifiable activity becomes *over*justified by the promise of added reward.

In experiments, children who are promised rewards for playing with an interesting puzzle or toy later exhibit less interest in it than do children who are not paid to play (Deci, 1980; Lepper & Greene, 1979; Newman & Layton, 1984). It is as if the children think, "If I have to be bribed or coerced into doing this, then it must not be worth doing for its own sake."

Wendy Grolnick and Richard Ryan (1987) demonstrated how overjustification can affect teaching and learning. They invited fifth graders to read a passage from a social studies book. Some were instructed in a controlling way: "I'll be grading you on the test to see if you're learning enough." Others, treated in a less controlling manner ("You won't be graded on [the questions]—I'm just interested in what children can remember"), learned as much *and found the passage more interesting.*

Biological Predispositions As with classical conditioning, operant conditioning principles are constrained by each organism's natural predispositions. When reinforced with food, the golden hamster can easily be conditioned to dig or to rear up because these actions are among the animal's natural behaviors when searching for food. Hamster behaviors not normally associated with food or hunger, such as face washing, are difficult to shape with food reinforcement (Shettleworth, 1973). Pigeons have a hard time learning to peck to avoid shock or to flap their wings to obtain food. But they can easily learn to flap to avoid

When the first-grade teacher offers candy each day to children who do their homework, how might this affect their natural eagerness to do schoolwork?

Have you ever thought you'd enjoy learning more if you didn't have to do it for a grade?

shock and peck to obtain food, because they naturally flee with their wings and eat with their beaks. Such constraints on learning are actually predispositions favoring the learning of those associations that are naturally adaptive.

Skinner's former associates, Keller Breland and Marian Breland (1961), came to appreciate biological dispositions while using operant procedures to train animals for circuses, TV shows, and movies—procedures that have since been applied in most trained animal shows (Bailey & Bailey, 1980). They had originally assumed that operant principles could be generalized to almost any response that any animal could make. But after training 6000 animals of 38 different species, from chickens to whales, they concluded that biological predispositions were more important than they had supposed. In one act, pigs were trained to pick up large wooden "dollars" and deposit them in a piggy bank. After learning this behavior, however, the animals began to drift back to their natural ways; they would drop the coin, push it with their snouts as pigs are prone to do, pick it up again, and then repeat the sequence—despite the fact that this delayed their food reinforcement. As this illustrates, "misbehaviors" occurred when the animals reverted to their biologically predisposed patterns.

The last two decades of research have changed our views of both classical and operant conditioning (summarized in Table 9–1). Animals exhibit more sophisticated representations of their worlds than previously seemed likely. And biological predispositions make certain types of learning easier than others.

Animals can most easily learn and retain behaviors that draw on their biological predispositions, such as a raccoon's natural tendency to use its paws.

Table 9–1
COMPARISON OF CLASSICAL AND OPERANT CONDITIONING

	Classical conditioning	**Operant conditioning**
Behavior	Involuntary (reflexive)	Voluntary (nonreflexive)
Procedure	Association of events, such as conditioned and unconditioned stimuli	Association of stimulus (reinforcer or punisher) and response
Cognitive processes	Subjects develop an expectation that the CS signals the arrival of the UCS	Subjects develop an expectation that a given behavior will be reinforced or punished
Biological constraints	Biological predispositions influence what stimuli can be associated with what response	Organisms are biologically predisposed to learn behaviors similar to their natural behaviors; unnatural behaviors drift back toward natural ones

LEARNING BY OBSERVATION

From drooling dogs, running rats, and pecking pigeons we have learned much about the basic processes of learning. However, these animals have not told us the whole story. Among higher animals—us humans, especially—learning does not occur through direct experience alone. *Observational learning,* in which we observe and imitate the behaviors of others, also plays a big part. The process of observing and then imitating a specific behavior is often called *modeling,* and the person observed is referred to as the model. By observing and imitating models we learn, for example, gender roles and problem-solving strategies.

"We are, in truth, more than half what we are by imitation. The great point is, to choose good models and to study them with care."
Lord Chesterfield,
Letters, January 18, 1750

We also learn specific social behaviors through modeling. Picture this scene from a famous experiment devised by Albert Bandura, the pioneering researcher in observational learning (Bandura & others, 1961). A nursery school child is at work on a picture. An adult in another part of the room is working with some Tinker Toys. The adult then gets up and for nearly 10 minutes pounds, kicks, and throws a large inflated Bobo doll around the room, all the while yelling such remarks as "Sock him in the nose. . . . Hit him down. . . . Kick him."

After observing this outburst, the child is taken to another room where there are many appealing toys. But soon the experimenter interrupts the child's play and explains that she has decided to save these good toys "for the other children." The frustrated child is now taken to an adjacent room containing a few toys, including a Bobo doll. Left alone, what does the child do? Compared to other children who were not exposed to the adult model, those children who had observed the aggressive outburst were much more likely to lash out at the doll. Apparently, observing the adult model beating up the doll had lowered their inhibitions. But something more than lowered inhibitions was at work, for the children also imitated the very acts, using the identical words, that they had observed.

The bad news from such studies is that antisocial models—in one's family, neighborhood, TV programs—may have antisocial effects (see pages 579–580). This helps us understand how abusive parents might have aggressive children and why men who batter their wives often had wife-battering fathers (Roy, 1977). The lessons that we learn as children are not easily unlearned as adults, and thus are visited on future generations.

The good news is that **prosocial** (positive, helpful) models can have prosocial effects. People who exemplify nonviolent, helpful behavior can prompt similar behavior in others. Mahatma Gandhi and Martin Luther King, Jr., both drew on the power of modeling, making nonviolent action a powerful force for social change. Separate studies of European Christians who risked their lives to rescue Jews from the Nazis and of the civil rights activists of the late 1950s have revealed that such individuals tended to have had a close relationship with at least one parent who modeled a strong moral or humanitarian concern (London, 1970; Rosenhan, 1970).

Albert Bandura (1977, p. 22): "Learning would be exceedingly laborious, not to mention hazardous, if people had to rely solely on the effects of their own actions to inform them what to do."

"Children need models more than they need critics."
    Joseph Joubert,
    Pensées, 1842

This child is imitating her father—from the tilt of her head to the tilt of her wrist.

Models are most effective when their actions and their words are consistent. Sometimes, however, models preach one thing and do another. Many parents seem to operate according to the principle "Do as I say, not as I do." Experiments suggest that children learn to do both (Rice & Grusec, 1975; Rushton, 1975). When exposed to a hypocrite, they later tend to imitate the hypocrisy by doing what the model did and saying what the model said.

What determines whether we will imitate a model? Bandura believes that reinforcements and punishments—those received by the model as well as by the imitator—help determine whether people will perform a behavior they have observed. We look and we learn. By looking, we learn to anticipate what consequences a behavior might bring in situations like those we are observing. By watching TV programs, for example, children may "learn" that physical intimidation is an effective way to control others, or that free and easy sex brings pleasure without the misery of unwanted pregnancy or disease.

Although our knowledge of learning principles is built on the work of thousands of investigators, this chapter has focused on the ideas of a few pioneers—Pavlov, Watson, Skinner, and Bandura—partly to illustrate the impact that can result from single-minded devotion to a few well-defined problems and ideas. They may have been overenthusiastic about the scope and power of their ideas. Even so, it was they who defined the issues and impressed on us the importance of learning. As their legacy demonstrates, intellectual history is often made by people who, at the risk of overstatement, pursue an idea to its limits.

We more often imitate those we respect and admire, those we perceive as similar to ourselves, and those we perceive as successful.

"I think I'll let my hair grow."

SUMMING UP

All animals, but humans especially, adapt to their environments aided by learning. Through classical conditioning, we learn to anticipate events such as being fed or experiencing pain. Through operant conditioning, we learn to repeat acts that bring desired results and avoid acts that bring punishment. Through observational learning, we learn from the experience and example of others.

CLASSICAL CONDITIONING

Pavlov's Experiments   Although the idea of learning by association had been discussed for two centuries, it remained for Ivan Pavlov to capture the phenomenon in his classic experiments on conditioning. A neutral stimulus (such as a bell) was repeatedly presented just before an unconditioned stimulus (food), which triggered an unconditioned response (salivation). After several repetitions, the neutral stimulus alone (now the conditioned stimulus, CS) began triggering a conditioned response, CR (salivation). Experiments by Pavlov and others revealed that classical conditioning was usually greatest when the CS was presented just before the UCS, thus preparing the organism for what was coming. Further experiments explored the phenomena of extinction, spontaneous recovery, generalization, and discrimination.

Classical Conditioning and Behaviorism   Pavlov's work supported John B. Watson's emerging belief that, to be an objective science, psychology should study only overt behavior, without considering unobservable mental activity. Watson called this position behaviorism.

Behaviorism Reconsidered   The behaviorists' discounting of the importance of mental processes has been strongly challenged by experiments suggesting that for many animals, cognitive appraisals are important for learning; for example, animals appear capable of learning when to "expect" an unconditioned stimulus. The behaviorists' optimism that learning principles would generalize from one response to another and from one species to another has been tempered; conditioning principles, we now know, are constrained by the biological predispositions of each species. For example, rats are biologically prepared to learn associations between the taste of a particular food and the onset of illness, but not between a loud noise and an illness.

OPERANT CONDITIONING

Classical (Pavlovian) conditioning works with involuntary (reflexive) behaviors. Operant (instrumental) conditioning works with voluntary behaviors that actively operate

Drawing by Frascino; © 1986 The New Yorker Magazine, Inc.

on the environment. When followed by positive or negative reinforcement, the behavior is strengthened; when followed by punishment, the occurrence of the behavior is diminished.

Skinner's Experiments   When rats or pigeons are placed in a Skinner box, their actions can be shaped by successive approximations of the desired behavior. Shaping has been used to study the effects of positive and negative reinforcers, primary and secondary reinforcers, and immediate and delayed reinforcers. Partial reinforcement schedules (fixed-interval, fixed-ratio, variable-interval, and variable-ratio) produce slower acquisition of the target behavior than does continuous reinforcement, but much more resistance to extinction. Like reinforcement, punishment is most swiftly effective when strong, immediate, and consistent. However, punishment is not simply the logical opposite of reinforcement, for it can have several undesirable side effects, such as lying to avoid punishment, anger, and fear of the punisher.

Applications of Operant Conditioning   Operant principles are being applied in schools, in businesses, and at home. For example, computer-assisted instruction embodies the operant ideal of individualized shaping and immediate positive reinforcement.

Further Reconsideration of Behaviorism   Many psychologists have criticized behaviorists, such as Skinner, for underestimating the importance of cognitive and biological processes in operant conditioning. Research on cognitive mapping, latent learning, and the overjustification effect points to the importance of cognitive processes in learning. Research has also made it clear that biological predispositions constrain what an animal can be taught.

LEARNING BY OBSERVATION

An important type of learning among higher animals is observational learning, in which learning results from watching others' behavior. In experiments, children tend to imitate both what a model does and says, whether the behavior is prosocial or antisocial.

TERMS AND CONCEPTS TO REMEMBER

acquisition   The initial stage of learning, during which a response is established and gradually strengthened. In classical conditioning, the phase in which a stimulus comes to evoke a conditioned response. In operant conditioning, the strengthening of a reinforced response.

avoidance learning   Learning to prevent an aversive stimulus from occurring.

behaviorism   The view that (1) psychology should be an objective science which (2) studies only overt behavior without reference to mental processes. Most research psychologists today agree with (1) but not (2).

classical conditioning   A type of learning in which an organism comes to associate different events. Thus a neutral stimulus, after being paired with an unconditioned stimulus (UCS), begins to trigger a response that anticipates and prepares for the unconditioned stimulus. (Also known as *Pavlovian*, or *respondent*, *conditioning*.)

cognitive map   A mental representation of the layout of one's environment. For example, once they have explored a maze, rats act as if they have acquired a cognitive map of it.

conditioned response (CR)   In classical conditioning, the learned response to a conditioned stimulus (CS).

conditioned stimulus (CS)   In classical conditioning, an originally neutral stimulus that, after association with an unconditioned stimulus (UCS), comes to trigger a conditioned response.

continuous reinforcement   Reinforcing the desired response every time it occurs.

discrimination   In classical conditioning, the ability to distinguish between a conditioned stimulus and similar stimuli that do not signal an unconditioned stimulus. In operant conditioning, the ability to distinguish between reinforced and nonreinforced behaviors.

escape learning   Learning to withdraw from or terminate an aversive stimulus.

extinction   The diminishing of a response when, in classical conditioning, a conditioned stimulus (CS) is not followed by an unconditioned stimulus (UCS) or when, in operant conditioning, a response is no longer reinforced.

fixed-interval schedule   In operant conditioning, a schedule of reinforcement in which a response is reinforced only after a specified time has elapsed.

fixed-ratio schedule   In operant conditioning, a schedule of reinforcement in which a response is reinforced only after a specified number of responses.

generalization   The tendency, once a response has been conditioned, for stimuli similar to the conditioned stimulus to evoke similar responses.

intermittent reinforcement   See *partial reinforcement*.

latent learning   Learning that occurs but is not apparent until there is an incentive to demonstrate it.

learning   A relatively permanent change in an organism's behavior due to experience.

modeling   The process of observing and then imitating a behavior.

negative reinforcer An aversive stimulus, such as electric shock or nagging, the withdrawal of which strengthens responses that precede it. Like all reinforcers, negative reinforcers strengthen behaviors that trigger them. (Negative reinforcement is not *punishment*.)

observational learning Learning by observing and imitating the behavior of others.

operant behavior Behavior that operates on the environment, producing consequences.

operant conditioning A type of learning in which behavior is strengthened if followed by reinforcement, or diminished if followed by punishment. (Also called *instrumental conditioning*.)

overjustification effect The effect of promising a reward for doing what one already likes doing. The person may now see the reward, rather than intrinsic interest, as the motivation for performing the task.

partial (or **intermittent**) **reinforcement** Reinforcing a response only part of the time; results in slower acquisition of response but much greater resistance to extinction than does continuous reinforcement.

positive reinforcer A rewarding stimulus, such as food, which, when presented after a response, strengthens the response.

primary reinforcer An innately reinforcing stimulus, such as one that satisfies a biological need.

prosocial behavior Positive, constructive, helpful behavior. The opposite of antisocial behavior.

punishment Any event that decreases the behavior that it follows.

reinforcer In operant conditioning, any event that strengthens the behavior that it follows.

respondent behavior Behavior that occurs as an automatic response to some stimulus.

secondary reinforcer A conditioned reinforcer; a stimulus that acquires its reinforcing power by association with another reinforcer, such as a primary reinforcer.

shaping A procedure in operant conditioning that starts with some existing behavior and reinforces closer and closer approximations of a desired behavior.

Skinner box A chamber containing a bar or key that an animal can manipulate to obtain a food or water reinforcer and devices to record the animal's rate of bar pressing or key pecking. Used in operant conditioning research.

spontaneous recovery The reappearance, after a rest period, of an extinguished conditioned response.

successive approximations In operant conditioning, the small steps by which some existing behavior is shaped toward a desired behavior.

unconditioned response (UCR) In classical conditioning, the unlearned, automatic response to the unconditioned stimulus, such as salivation when food is in the mouth.

unconditioned stimulus (UCS) In classical conditioning, a stimulus that naturally and automatically triggers a response without conditioning.

variable-interval schedule In operant conditioning, a schedule of reinforcement in which a response is reinforced at unpredictable time intervals.

variable-ratio schedule In operant conditioning, a schedule of reinforcement in which a response is reinforced after an unpredictable number of responses.

FOR FURTHER READING

Bower, G. H., & Hilgard, E. R. (1981). *Theories of learning* (5th ed.). Englewood Cliffs, NJ: Prentice-Hall.

A classic textbook containing individual chapters on selected theories of learning, including those of Pavlov and Skinner.

Klein, S. B. (1987). *Learning: Principles and applications.* New York: McGraw-Hill.

A contemporary survey of research on learning.

Pryor, K. (1984). *Don't shoot the dog!: How to improve yourself and others through behavioral training.* New York: Simon and Schuster (Bantam Books paperback, 1985).

A practical guide to applying reinforcement principles to various everyday problems, from training animals, managing employees, and dealing with messy roommates, to reforming your own bad habits.

Schwartz, B. (1984). *Psychology of learning and behavior* (2nd ed.). New York: Norton.

A comprehensive textbook summary of research on conditioning.

Skinner, B. F. (1948). *Walden Two.* New York: Macmillan.

A controversial novel by the noted behavioral psychologist, presenting his view of a utopian world guided by an intelligent application of the principles of operant learning.

Williams, R. L., & Long, J. D. (1982). *Toward a self-managed life style* (3rd ed.). Boston: Houghton Mifflin.

This book suggests how learning principles can be applied to one's own life, thereby enhancing self-control.

CHAPTER 10

Memory

Your memory is your mind's storehouse, the reservoir of your accumulated learning. To Cicero, memory was "the treasury and guardian of all things." To a psychologist, *memory* is any indication that learning has persisted over time.

Imagine your life without memory. There would be no savoring the remembrances of joyful moments, no guilt or misery over painful recollections. Each moment would be a fresh experience. But each person would be a stranger, each task—dressing, cooking, biking—a novel challenge, every language a foreign language.

The range of human memory is evident in some fascinating cases:

Conversing with John you would be impressed by his wit, his intelligence (he might tell you the title of his master's thesis in physics), and his skill at tasks such as typing. It might be some time before you noticed that John suffers a tragic defect, caused by a brain injury suffered in a motorcycle accident. John cannot form new memories. Although he retains his memories from before the accident, John otherwise lives in an eternal present. Each morning when his rehabilitation therapist greets him she must reintroduce herself. She must listen patiently as over and over he retells anecdotes from his life before the accident. Each time the need arises, he must inquire, "Where is the bathroom?" and be told anew.

At the other extreme are some special people who probably would have been medal winners in a memory Olympics. One woman, whom psychologist Ulric Neisser (1982) calls MZ, would have been the envy of every student. Until suffering a severe illness at age 29, MZ could recall verbatim anything her teachers wrote on the board and whole sections from her textbooks. When she later worked as a biology technician, her employer would begin each day by giving her detailed instructions on the exact order in which to mount some 150 insects, which MZ would then do without having written anything down.

The gold medalist of our memory Olympics would probably be a Russian, Shereshevskii, or S as he was more simply called by the distinguished Soviet psychologist Alexander Luria (1968). S's memory has earned him a place in virtually every modern book on memory. You and I can repeat back a string of about seven digits—almost surely no more than nine. S could repeat thirty, fifty, or even seventy digits or words, provided they were read about 3 seconds apart in an otherwise silent room. Moreover, he could recall them as easily backward as forward. And his accuracy was unerring even when asked to recall a list as much as 15 years later, after having memorized hundreds of other lists. "Yes, yes," he might recall. "This was a series you gave me once when we were in your apartment. . . . You were sitting at the table and I in the rocking chair. . . . You were wearing a gray suit and you looked at me like this. . . ."

WELL, FOR CRYING OUT LOUD! AL TOWBRIDGE! WHAT IS IT, NINE YEARS, SEVEN MONTHS, AND TWELVE DAYS SINCE I LAST RAN INTO YOU? TEN-THIRTY-TWO A.M., A SATURDAY, FELCHER'S HARDWARE STORE. YOU WERE BUYING SEALER FOR YOUR BLACKTOP DRIVEWAY. TELL ME, AL, HOW DID THAT SEALER WORK? DID IT HOLD UP?

MR. TOTAL RECALL

Do these memory feats make your own memory seem feeble? If so, consider your capacity for remembering countless voices, sounds, and songs; tastes, smells, and textures; faces, places, and happenings. Ralph Haber (1970) demonstrated the enormous capacity of our memories by showing people more than 2500 slides of faces and places. The painstaking effort of the researcher was exceeded only by the patience of his subjects, who over 2 to 4 days viewed each slide once, for 10 seconds. Afterward, the subjects were shown 280 of the pictures again. This time each slide was paired with a previously unseen slide, and the subjects were asked to identify which slide they had seen before. Nine times in ten they could.

Or consider the vividness of your memories of unique and highly emotional moments in your past—perhaps a car accident, your first kiss, or where you were when you heard some tragic news. One such memory of mine is of my only hit in an entire season playing Little League baseball. Most Americans over 40 can tell you exactly what they were doing when they heard the news of President Kennedy's assassination (Brown & Kulik, 1982). You perhaps remember where you were when you learned that the space shuttle *Challenger* had exploded. These clear memories of emotional moments are called *flash-bulb memories,* because it's as if the brain commands "Print this!"

How are such memory feats accomplished? How can we remember things we have not thought of for years, yet forget the name of someone we were introduced to a minute ago? How are memories stored in our brains? Does what we know about memory give us clues to how we could improve our memories? These will be among our questions as we review insights gleaned from a century of research on memory.

> Which is more important—your experiences, or your memories of them?

> "The memory is sometimes so retentive, so serviceable, so obedient; at others, so bewildered and so weak; and at others again, so tyrannic, so beyond control! We are, to be sure, a miracle every way; but our powers of recollecting and forgetting do seem peculiarly past finding out."
> Jane Austen,
> *Mansfield Park*, 1814

FORMING MEMORIES

History is sometimes determined by what people can remember about events. On June 17, 1972, five men were caught trying to tap the telephones of the Democratic National Committee in the Watergate Office Building in Washington, D.C. In 1973, when President Nixon's legal counselor, John Dean, testified before a U.S. Senate committee investigating White House involvement in the Watergate scandal, his recall of conversations with the President was so impressive that some writers called him "the human tape recorder." Ironically, it was later revealed that a secret taping system had actually recorded the conversations that Dean recounted, thus providing a rare opportunity to compare an eyewitness's recollections with the actual event. Dean's recollection concerning the essentials proved correct; the highest ranking members of the White House staff went to prison for doing what John Dean said they had done, and the President was forced to resign.

However, when Ulric Neisser (1981) compared the details in the tapes with the testimony, it became clear that John Dean was far from a human tape recorder. For example, Dean recalled that entering a September 15th meeting, he

> found Haldeman and the President. The President asked me to sit down. Both men appeared to be in very good spirits and my reception was very warm and cordial. The President then told me that Bob—referring to Haldeman—had kept him posted on my handling of the Watergate case. The President told me I had done a good job and he appreciated how difficult a task it had been and the President was pleased that the case had stopped with Liddy.

John Dean testifying before the Senate Watergate Committee. When compared to the White House tapes, John Dean's memory was found to be accurate for the substance of most conversations but not for the details.

But virtually every detail Dean recalled was wrong. The tape of the meeting revealed that the President did not ask Dean to sit down, he did not say Dean had done a good job, he did not say anything about Liddy or the indictments.

Dean's memory was better for a March 15th conversation during which he had delivered a well-prepared report to the President on the unraveling of the White House cover-up. The tape caught Dean saying "We have a cancer within, close to the presidency, that is growing. It is growing daily . . . because (1) we are being blackmailed; (2) people are going to start perjuring themselves. . . . " In his later congressional testimony, Dean recalled "telling the President that there was a cancer growing on the presidency and . . . that it was important that this cancer be removed immediately because it was growing more deadly every day."

How could John Dean have been so right in his basic understanding of the Watergate discussions yet, except for the March 15th conversation, so wrong in recalling the details of most conversations? To understand Dean's memory (and our own) better, we need a model that can help us to organize the many aspects of memory. One helpful model of human memory is that of a dynamic information-processing system such as the computer.

MEMORY AS INFORMATION PROCESSING

Although the ordinary human memory stores more information and is more complex than any computer, both systems can be viewed as processing information in three steps. First, information must be *encoded,* or translated, into some form that enables the system to process it. Keystrokes are encoded into the computer's electronic language, much as sensory messages are encoded into the brain's neural language. Next, information must be *stored,* or retained, by the system over time. A computer might store information magnetically on a disk; a person stores information in the brain. Finally, there must be a method by which information can be *retrieved,* or located and gotten out, when needed. Computers can search their memory stores and present the retrieved information on a screen or in a printout. People remember less exactly, by combining their retrieved information with what they currently assume or believe. Thus, as we will see, a sentence such as "The angry rioter threw the rock at the window" may easily be misrecalled.

These three steps—*encoding, storage, retrieval*—apply not only to human memory and computer systems, but also to other information-processing systems: A library, for example, must have some way of acquiring information, retaining it, and making it available to users. Bear in mind that the danger in using any model of memory is that we may take it too literally. A model can help us organize and simplify a great many observations. But as we learn more, any model is likely to be altered or replaced by another that more accurately reflects how the memory system works. A hundred years from now, most of the current facts and observations about memory almost surely will have survived, but our explanations of them will have changed.

Figure 10–1 summarizes the memory as a human information-processing model. Information that comes in through the senses must be encoded (either automatically or with effort), stored away, and retrieved when needed. First, however, the sensory information must be registered.

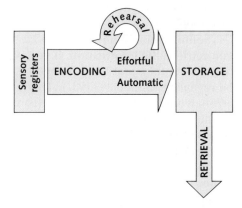

Figure 10-1 A simplified information-processing model of memory. To be remembered, information must be encoded, stored, and retrieved.

SENSORY REGISTERS

Consider what one intriguing memory experiment revealed about how sensory information first enters the memory system. As part of his doctoral research, George Sperling (1960) showed people three rows of three letters each for only 1/20th of a second (see Figure 10–2). It was like trying to read by the flashes of a lightning storm. After the nine letters had disappeared from the screen, the subjects could recall only about half of them.

Why? Was it because they had insufficient time to see them? No, Sperling cleverly demonstrated that even at such lightning-flash speed, people actually *can* see and recall all the letters, but only momentarily. Rather than ask subjects to recall all nine letters at once, Sperling instead would sound a high, medium, or low tone immediately after the nine letters were flashed. This cue directed the subject to report only the letters of the top, middle, or bottom row, respectively. Now the subjects rarely missed a letter. Because they did not know in advance which row would be requested, all nine letters must have been momentarily available for recall.

Sperling's experiment revealed that we do have a fleeting photographic memory called **iconic memory.** For a moment, the eyes register an exact representation of a scene, and can recall any part of it in amazing detail. But only for a moment. If Sperling delayed the tone signal by as much as a second, the iconic memory was gone and the subjects once again recalled only about half of the letters. The visual screen clears quickly, as it must, lest new images be superimposed over old ones. For sound, the auditory sensory image, called **echoic memory,** disappears more slowly. The last few words spoken seem to linger for 3 or 4 seconds. Sometimes, just as you ask "What did you say?," you can hear in your mind the echo of what was said.

ENCODING

How does sensory information, once registered, get encoded and transferred into the memory system? Consider an example of the type of memory most commonly studied—memory for verbal information. As you read this sentence, how do its words get encoded? Did you encode the *image* of the words, a process called **visual encoding**? Did you encode the *sound* of the words, a process called **acoustic encoding**? Or was the sentence coded by its *meaning*, a process called **semantic encoding**?

Some combination of these occurs depending on how long before you retrieve the information. If you were shown a series of letters and then asked to repeat them immediately, your occasional errors would be revealing (Baddeley, 1982). Though you had seen the letters, your errors would be less often visual (confusing a *p* with a *q*) than acoustic (confusing a *b* with a *v*), indicating that you had encoded the list acoustically rather than visually. An hour later, your errors would tend to be semantic rather than acoustic; if you had learned a list of words including the word "labor," it would more likely be misrecalled as "work" rather than as "later," indicating the semantic encoding had been retained.

Some psychologists believe this reflects two very different types of memory storage—(1) a **short-term memory,** where items are often stored acoustically (by sound) before being transferred to (2) a **long-term memory,** where they are more often stored semantically (by meaning). Short-term memory has a limited capacity; except for what is con-

Figure 10-2 Momentary photographic memory. When a group of letters similar to this was flashed for 1/20th of a second, people could recall only about half of the letters. But when signaled to recall a particular row *immediately* after the letters had disappeared, they could do so with near-perfect accuracy.

How many *F*s are in the following sentence? FINISHED FILES ARE THE RESULTS OF YEARS OF SCIENTIFIC STUDY COMBINED WITH THE EXPERIENCE OF YEARS. (See page 260.)

sciously rehearsed, it holds information only briefly. (For computer buffs, short-term memory is comparable to a computer's working memory.) Long-term memory has an essentially unlimited capacity, and it holds information more-or-less permanently. (It is analogous to information stored on a computer's hard disk.)

"The matters about which I'm being questioned, Your Honor, are all things I should have included in my long-term memory but which I mistakenly inserted in my short-term memory."

The short- versus long-term memory distinction is a memory model that to some psychologists no longer seems as useful as it once did. For one thing, even in the short run, we encode meaning as well as sound (we instantly hear "eye-screem" either as "ice cream" or "I scream"); and in the long run, our memory of a poem may be enhanced by its acoustical rhythms and rhymes in addition to its meaning. Although equating short-term memory with acoustic encoding and long-term memory with semantic encoding does not always work, the distinction between fleeting working memories and stored long-term memories remains useful.

Another useful distinction can be made between encoding that tends to be either *automatic* (your memory for your dinner last night) or *effortful* (your processing of this chapter's concepts). Some memory researchers find it helpful to think of our memory systems as being managed by a "central executive." To be effective, business executives must delegate routine activities to subordinates, thus freeing their attention for more important matters. This is also true of your memory executive; it delegates some memory processing to subordinate systems, which function automatically, so that your attention and effort can be devoted to more novel or important tasks.

Automatic Processing With little or no effort, you encode an enormous amount of information about space, time, and frequency: During an exam you may recall the place on the textbook page where the forgotten material appears; you can recreate a sequence of the day's events in order to guess where you left your coat; you may realize that "This is the third time I've run into you this afternoon." Memories like these are formed automatically. In fact, not only does automatic pro-

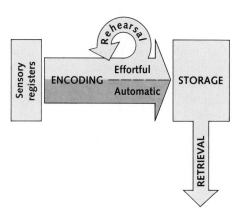

cessing occur effortlessly, but it is also difficult to shut off. When you hear or read a word in your native language, it is virtually impossible not to register its meaning automatically.

Some types of automatic processing, such as the encoding of space, time, and frequency, seem innate to the human information-processing system. But other automatic processes, such as the encoding of word meanings, are learned. Researchers have explored how, through learning, effortful processing can become more automatic. For example, they have trained people to search for a target letter, such as J, among a group of letters (Shiffrin & Schneider, 1977). With practice, subjects find that the processing becomes pretty automatic; the target letter seems to pop out. Similarly, reading reversed sentences at first requires effort:

.citamotua emoceb nac gnissecorp luftroffE

After practice, it begins to be easier, much as reading from right to left becomes easy for students of Hebrew (Kolers, 1975).

So, automatic processing seems to occur with little or no effort, without our awareness and without interfering with our attempts to think about and remember other things. If, indeed, such processing requires no special attention, then asking people to pay special attention to information they encode automatically (to note how frequently, say, specific words appear among a group of words) should be of no benefit. That is just what Lynn Hasher and Rose Zacks (1979) found. In their experiment, one group was warned that they would be asked to judge how frequently a word occurred in a long list of words. Another group was not forewarned. Both groups did equally well. Moreover, reported Hasher and Zacks, not only is memory for space, time, and frequency information unaffected by effort, but it also matters little how old people are, how they feel, or how much they practice. Our automatic processing is genuinely automatic: We cannot switch it off and on at will.

Effortful Processing   We encode and retain other types of information only with effort and attention. During your finger's trip from the phone book to the phone, your memory of a telephone number will disappear unless you work to keep it in consciousness. To find out how quickly it will disappear, Lloyd Peterson and Margaret Peterson (1959) asked people to remember three consonants, such as CHJ. To prevent their rehearsing the letters, the subjects were asked to begin immediately counting aloud backward by threes from some number. As Figure 10–3 indicates (and you can demonstrate with the help of a friend), after 3 seconds the letters were recalled only about half the time; after 12 seconds they were seldom recalled.

The importance of *rehearsal*, or conscious repetition, was demonstrated long ago by the pioneering researcher of verbal memory, German philosopher Hermann Ebbinghaus (1850–1909). Ebbinghaus did for the study of memory what his contemporary Ivan Pavlov did for the study of learning. Impatient with philosophical speculations about memory, Ebbinghaus wanted to study it scientifically. To do so, he decided to study his own learning and forgetting of novel verbal materials.

Where could Ebbinghaus find verbal material that was not familiar? His solution was to form a list of all possible nonsense syllables created by sandwiching a vowel between two consonants; then, for a particular experiment, he would more or less randomly select a sample of the syllables. To get a feel for how Ebbinghaus experimented on

Answer to question on page 258: Partly because your initial processing of the letters was primarily acoustic rather than visual, you probably missed some of the six *F*s, especially those that sound like a *V* rather than an *F*.

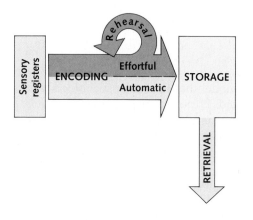

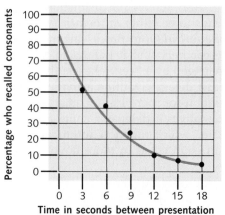

Figure 10-3   Information that is not automatically processed may be quickly forgotten unless rehearsed. (From Peterson & Peterson, 1959.)

himself, rapidly read aloud, eight times over, the following list, and then recall the items (from Baddeley, 1982):

JIH, BAZ, FUB, YOX, SUJ, XIR, DAX, LEQ, VUM, PID, KEL, WAV, TUV, ZOF, GEK, HIW.

After learning the list, Ebbinghaus could recall few of the syllables the following day. But were they entirely forgotten? As Figure 10–4 portrays, the more frequently he repeated the list aloud on day 1, the fewer repetitions he required to relearn the list on day 2. Here, then, was a simple beginning principle: *The amount remembered depends on the time spent learning.* Even after material has been learned, additional repetition, called "overlearning," increases retention. Thus, John Dean recalled almost perfectly his "cancer on the presidency" remarks, which he had written out and rehearsed several times before uttering them to the President.

Harry Bahrick (1984a) confirmed Ebbinghaus's principle when he found that teachers at Ohio Wesleyan University soon forgot the names and faces of most of their former students, whom they saw for only one term. In contrast, these classmates saw each other repeatedly for four years, and this overlearning enabled them a quarter-century later to recognize each other's names and yearbook pictures. As the Roman philosopher Seneca noted in the first century: "The mind is slow in unlearning what it has been long in learning."

The benefits of rehearsal can also be seen in a phenomenon that you probably have experienced. Many experimenters have found that when people are shown a list of items (words, names, dates) and then immediately are asked to recall the items in any order, they remember the last and first items better than those in the middle of the list. This phenomenon is known as the *serial position effect* (Figure 10–5). But after a delay, only the first items tend to be better recalled. As an everyday parallel, imagine that while you are being introduced to a number of people you rehearse all the names as you meet each successive person. By the end you will have spent more time rehearsing the earlier names than the later names; thus even the next day you will probably recall the earlier names better.

Rehearsal will not encode all information equally effectively, however. Sometimes merely repeating information, as with the new phone number we are about to dial, is insufficient to store it for later recall (Craik & Watkins, 1973; Greene, 1987). How, then, do we get information into permanent storage? We must somehow process it. Processing our sensory input is like sorting through the day's mail; we instantly discard some items and open, read, and retain others.

The Processing of Meaning Do you recall (from page 257) the sentence about the rioter? Can you complete the sentence: "The angry rioter threw . . ."?

When we process verbal information for storage we usually encode its meaning by associating it with what we already know or can imagine. Perhaps, then, like the subjects in an experiment by William Brewer (1977), you recalled the rioter sentence not as written ("The angry rioter threw the rock at the window"), but rather as the meaning you encoded when you read it, for example, "The angry rioter threw the rock *through* the window." As such recall indicates, you do not remember things exactly as they were; rather, you remember them as they were encoded, much as after studying for an exam you may remember your lecture notes rather than the lecture itself. This helps us understand (1) John Dean's misrecollections of precisely what the Pres-

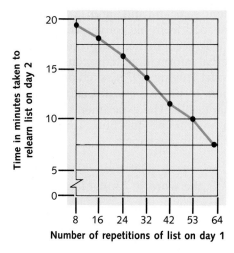

Figure 10-4 Ebbinghaus's retention curve. Ebbinghaus observed that the more times he practiced a list of nonsense syllables on day 1, the fewer repetitions he required to relearn it on day 2. Said simply, the more time spent learning novel information, the more is retained. Ergo, the more you study, the more you'll learn. (From Baddeley, 1982.)

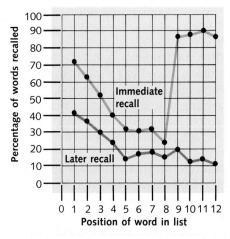

Figure 10-5 The serial position effect. After being presented with a list of words, people immediately recall the last and first items most accurately. But later they recall only the first items most accurately—even if they had repeated the last items for a few moments to keep them in their consciousness. (From Craik & Watkins, 1973.)

ident said and did, and (2) his better recall of the meaning that he encoded from his conversations with the President.

To see whether the processing of meaning yields better memory of verbal information than acoustic or visual processing, Fergus Craik and Endel Tulving (1975) asked people a question that, to answer, required them to process a word either (1) visually, (2) acoustically, or (3) semantically. The experimenters flashed a word and asked the subjects to answer the question. To experience the task, rapidly answer the following questions:

		Flashed word	*Yes*	*No*
1.	Is the word in capital letters?	chair	___	___
2.	Does the word rhyme with train?	BRAIN	___	___
3.	Would the word fit in this sentence: The girl put the ___ on the table.	gun	___	___

Which type of processing would best prepare you to recognize the words a little later? In Craik and Tulving's experiment, the semantic encoding—question 3—yielded much better memory (Figure 10-6).

To experience the importance of meaning for verbal memory, put yourself in the place of the students whom John Bransford and Marcia Johnson (1972) asked to remember the following recorded passage:

> The procedure is actually quite simple. First you arrange things into different groups. Of course, one pile may be sufficient depending on how much there is to do. . . . After the procedure is completed one arranges the materials into different groups again. Then they can be put into their appropriate places. Eventually they will be used once more and the whole cycle will then have to be repeated. However, that is part of life.

When the students heard the paragraph you have just read—without its being placed in a meaningful context—they remembered little of it. When told that the paragraph was about washing clothes (something meaningful to them) they remembered much more of it—as you probably could now after rereading it.

Such research suggests the futility of trying to remember words we do not understand, and the benefits of rephrasing what we read and hear in terms that are meaningful to us. From his experiments on himself, Ebbinghaus estimated that learning *meaningful* material required but one-tenth the effort it took to learn nonsense material. Further, as memory researcher Wayne Wickelgren (1977, p. 346) has noted, "The time you spend thinking about material you are reading and relating it to previously stored material is about the most useful thing you can do in learning any new subject matter." Thus our best recall is of information that we relate to ourselves. People remember adjectives better after judging how well the words describe themselves rather than how well they describe another person (Kuiper & Rogers, 1979).

The Processing of Imagery   We struggle to memorize formulas, definitions, and dates, yet we can easily picture where we were yesterday, who was with us, where we sat, what we wore. Your very earliest memories—probably of something that happened at around age 3 or 4—almost surely involve visual *imagery*, or mental pictures.

In a variety of experiments, researchers have documented the benefits of mental images. For one thing, people who form the most vivid visual images of strangers tend to remember them better than people who do not form vivid images (Swann & Miller, 1982). For another, words that lend themselves to picture images are better remembered

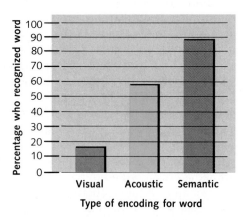

Figure 10-6   Processing a word in terms of its meaning (semantic encoding) produces better recognition of it than does processing it according to its visual or acoustic features. (From Craik & Tulving, 1975.)

"A thing when heard, remember, strikes less keen on the spectator's mind than when 'tis seen."
   Horace,
   Ars Poetica, 8 B.C.

than abstract, low-imagery words. (When I quiz you later—and I will— which three of the following words will you be most likely to recall: typewriter, void, cigarette, inherent, fire, process?) Similarly, you probably still recall the sentence about the rock-throwing rioter, not only because of the meaning you encoded, but also because the sentence lent itself to a visual image. As this example suggests and some memory experts believe (Marschark & others, 1987; Paivio, 1986), memory for concrete nouns is aided by encoding them *both* semantically and visually; two codes are better than one.

The imagery principle—that people have excellent memory for pictures and picture-evoking words—can be applied in teaching, preaching, and writing. Abstract principles become memorable when tied to vivid examples. Consider how difficult it is to remember the statistics of the nuclear age: In 1988, the approximately 10,000-megaton destructive capacity of Soviet and American nuclear weapons was more than 3000 times greater than the 3 megatons of firepower exploded in all of World War II (Bulletin of the Atomic Scientists, 1988). Tomorrow you will probably have trouble recalling these statistics, but I suspect you will remember their visual representation in Figure 10–7.

Visual imagery is at the heart of many memory aids. These *mnemonic* (nih-MON-ik) devices (so named after the Greek word for memory) were developed by ancient Greek scholars and orators as aids to remembering lengthy passages and speeches. They imagined themselves moving through a familiar series of locations, associating each place with a visual representation of the to-be-remembered topic. Then, when speaking, the orator would revisit each location and retrieve the associated image.

A variation on this method employs vivid stories to organize words that are to be memorized. Gordon Bower and Michael Clark (1969) used lists of unrelated nouns, asking one group simply to study the lists and another group to invent stories using the nouns. (A sample made-up story: "A LUMBERJACK DARTed out of a forest, SKATEd around a HEDGE past a COLONY of DUCKs. He tripped on some FURNITURE, tearing his STOCKING while hastening toward the PILLOW where his MISTRESS lay.") After working through twelve lists of ten words each, the group that was instructed merely to study each list struggled to recall 13 percent of the words; the group that invented vivid stories recalled an astounding 93 percent (Figure 10–8).

Other mnemonic devices involve both acoustic and visual codes. For example, the "peg-word" system requires that you first memorize a jingle:

One is a bun; two is a shoe;
Three is a tree; four is a door;
Five is a hive; six is sticks;
Seven is heaven; eight is a gate;
Nine is wine; ten is a hen.

Without much effort, you will soon be able to count by peg-words instead of numbers: bun, shoe, tree . . . and then visually to associate to-be-remembered items with the peg-words. Now you are ready to challenge anyone to give you a grocery list to remember. Carrots? Imagine them stuck into a bun. Milk? Fill the shoe with it. Paper towels? Drape them over the tree branch. With few errors (Bugelski & others, 1968) you will be able to recall the items in any order and to name any given item. The third item? Just retrieve the tree and see what is on it. Such mnemonic systems are often the secret behind the feats of memory experts who repeat long lists of names and objects.

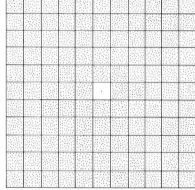

Figure 10-7 Pictures often convey ideas far better than words. The dot in the center square represents all the firepower of World War II. The other dots represent the number of World War II equivalents that exist in nuclear weapons. Just two squares represent enough firepower to destroy all the large and medium-size cities on earth: 300 megatons.

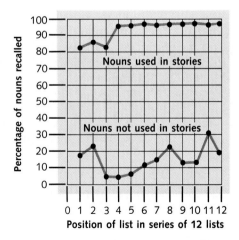

Figure 10-8 Imagery and memory. A group of people who studied twelve lists, each containing ten nouns, soon forgot most of the words on each list. Another group, who studied the same lists by making up stories using the nouns, found that when tested they could remember nearly all of them. (From Bower & Clark, 1969.)

Organization Another way of processing information is to organize it into manageable or meaningful units. Glance for a few seconds at the top row of Figure 10–9, then look away and try to reproduce what you saw. It's nearly impossible. But you can easily reproduce the line segments of the second row, which are no less complex. Similarly, the fourth row is much easier to remember than the third, though both contain the same letters, and the sixth cluster is more easily remembered than the fifth, though both contain the same words.

Chunking As this demonstrates, the more easily remembered information is processed as meaningful units, or chunks. *Chunking* information into meaningful units occurs so naturally that we take it for granted. Consider your ability to reproduce perfectly the 150 or so line segments that make up the sixth cluster of phrases. Surely it would astonish an illiterate person, especially one unfamiliar with the alphabet. You or I might feel similar admiration at the ability of someone literate in Chinese to glance at the ideographs in Figure 10–10 and then to reproduce all the strokes; or for chess masters who, after a 5-second look at the board during a game, can recall the exact positions of most of the pieces (Chase & Simon, 1973); or for varsity basketball players who, given a 4-second glance at a basketball play, can recall the positions of the players (Allard & Burnett, 1985). We all remember information best when it is chunked into familiar units.

Chunking also can aid our recall of unfamiliar material by organizing it into a more familiar form. One such mnemonic technique forms words (called acronyms) or sentences from the first letters of words to be remembered. Should you ever need to recall the names of the five Great Lakes, just remember HOMES (*H*uron, *O*ntario, *M*ichigan, *E*rie, *S*uperior). Want to remember the colors of the rainbow in order? Think of ROY G. BIV (*r*ed, *o*range, *y*ellow, *g*reen, *b*lue, *i*ndigo, *v*iolet). The planets in order? *M*y *v*ery *e*xcellent *m*other *j*ust *s*old *n*uts *u*ntil *P*assover.

By chunking digits, you can increase your recall of them. An impossible string of sixteen numbers—1-4-9-2-1-7-7-6-1-8-1-2-1-9-4-1—becomes easy when chunked into 1492, 1776, 1812, 1941. Two Carnegie-Mellon University students even managed—after more than 200 hours of practice in the laboratory of Anders Ericsson and William Chase (1982)—to increase their memory span from the typical seven digits to more than eighty. In one testing session, Dario Donatelli heard the researcher read one digit per second in a monotonous voice: "15185937655021578416658506120948856867727314181861054629748012-94974965928." Motionless while the numbers were read, Donatelli then sprang alive. He whispered numbers, rubbed his chin, tapped his feet, counted on his fingers, and ran his hands through his hair. "Okay," he announced almost two minutes later. "The first set is 1518. Then 5937 . . ." He repeated all seventy-three digits, in groups of three and four.

How did he do it? By chunking. "First set was a three-mile time," reported Donatelli, an All-American cross-country runner. "Second set was a ten-mile time. Then a mile. Half-mile. Two-mile time. An age. . . . Two mile. Age. Age. Age. Two-mile" (Wells, 1983).

Hierarchies For Donatelli to reach his peak—106 digits—he retrieved the chunks of numbers by clustering them as a hierarchy (Waldrop, 1987). First came "three groups of four," he might think, and so forth. When people develop expertise in an area, they similarly process information not only in chunks, but also in hierarchies composed of a few broad concepts divided into lesser concepts and facts, which are divided into still more specific categories. By organizing their knowledge

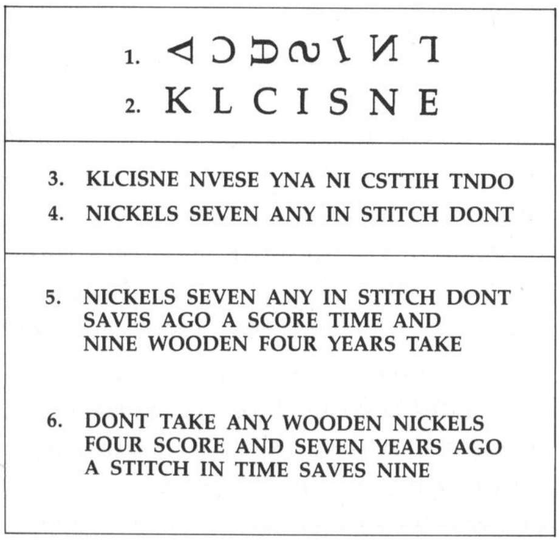

1.	◁Ϲ◿ᗡᑎᑎᑕ⅃
2.	K L C I S N E

| 3. | KLCISNE NVESE YNA NI CSTTIH TNDO |
| 4. | NICKELS SEVEN ANY IN STITCH DONT |

| 5. | NICKELS SEVEN ANY IN STITCH DONT SAVES AGO A SCORE TIME AND NINE WOODEN FOUR YEARS TAKE |
| 6. | DONT TAKE ANY WOODEN NICKELS FOUR SCORE AND SEVEN YEARS AGO A STITCH IN TIME SAVES NINE |

Figure 10-9 Effects of chunking on memory. When information is organized into meaningful units, such as letters, words, and phrases, we recall it more easily. (From *The Psychology of Learning and Memory* by Douglas L. Hintzman. Copyright © 1978 W. H. Freeman and Company. Reprinted with permission.)

Figure 10-10 After looking at these ideographs, can you reproduce them exactly? If so, you are almost certainly literate in Chinese.

in such ways, experts can retrieve information efficiently. This chapter therefore aims not only to teach you the elementary facts of memory, but also to help you organize these facts around broad principles, such as encoding; subprinciples, such as automatic and effortful processing; and still more specific concepts, such as meaning, imagery, and organization (see Figure 10–11).

Gordon Bower and his colleagues (1969) demonstrated the benefits of hierarchical organization by presenting words either randomly or grouped into categories. When the information was hierarchically organized, recall was better—two to three times better. Such results indicate the benefits of organizing what you study—of giving special attention to chapter outlines, headings, topic sentences, and summary paragraphs. If you can master not only the individual concepts of this chapter, but also its overall organization, or if you can fit the information into what you already know, the odds are that, come test time, your recall will be good. Taking lecture and text notes in outline format—a type of hierarchical organization—may also help.

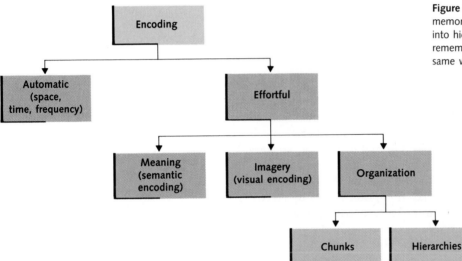

Figure 10-11 Effects of organization on memory. When we see words organized into hierarchical categories, as here, we remember them far better than when the same words are presented randomly.

STORAGE

If an event occurs that you later retrieve as a memory, you must, somehow, have stored it. What is stored lies dormant, waiting to be reawakened by a cue. Storage is difficult to isolate and describe; we cannot see stored memories, but we infer that they exist. What is our mental storage capacity? And just how and where are memories stored in our brains?

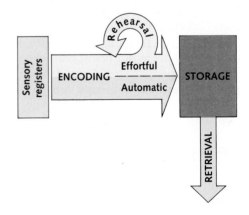

Memory Capacity In Arthur Conan Doyle's *A Study in Scarlet*, Sherlock Holmes offers a popular theory of memory capacity:

> I consider that a man's brain originally is like a little empty attic, and you have to stock it with such furniture as you choose. . . . It is a mistake to think that that little room has elastic walls and can distend to any extent. Depend upon it there comes a time when for every addition of knowledge you forget something that you knew before.

Our short-term, working memory for new information is indeed limited and inelastic. As noted earlier, we can immediately recall roughly seven chunks of information (give or take two), a recall capacity that has been enshrined in psychology as "the Magical Number Seven, plus or minus two" (Miller, 1956). Actually, people's short-term memory spans—the quantity of information they can immediately recall correctly 50 percent of the time—may vary somewhat. Short-term recall is slightly better for random digits (such as those of a phone number) than for random letters, which sometimes have similar sounds. It is slightly better for information we hear rather than see, because echoic memory momentarily outlasts iconic memory. Adults have greater memory spans than children (Chi, 1976). Still, the basic principle holds true: At any given moment, we can process but a very limited amount of information.

Contrary to Sherlock Holmes's supposition, our capacity for storing long-term memories is essentially limitless. By one careful estimate, the average adult has about a billion bits of information in memory; allowing for all the brain must do to encode, store, retrieve, and manipulate this information, its physical storage capacity is probably a thousand to a million times greater (Landauer, 1986). So our brains are *not* like attics, which once filled can only store more by discarding old items. Indeed, the more expertise we have, and therefore the better we can organize and form meaningful associations with new information, the easier it often is both to learn and remember.

But how precise and durable are our stored memories? If we somehow could uncover them, would we find all our past experiences intact, like long-lost books buried on a dusty shelf? Freud thought so. If only we could recover and resolve the painful repressed memories of our childhoods, he thought, emotional healing would follow. When "age-regressed" under hypnosis, some people do offer detailed reports of childhood experiences. But as we noted in Chapter 8, such reports are unreliable and typically contain fabricated material.

For a time, it was thought that brain stimulation during surgery provided evidence that our past experiences are "in there," in complete detail, just waiting to be relived. As you may recall from page 40, brain surgeon Wilder Penfield helped map the motor cortex by electrically stimulating wide-awake patients in order to predict possible side effects of surgery. Occasionally, Penfield's patients would report hearing things, such as "a mother calling her little boy." Penfield (1969) and most people who read about his findings assumed that he was activating long-lost experiences that had been permanently etched on the brain as though a tape recorder had been receiving them all.

On closer scrutiny, memory researchers Elizabeth Loftus and Geoffrey Loftus (1980) discovered that these flashbacks were extremely rare, occurring in but a handful of Penfield's 1100 stimulated patients. Moreover, the content of these few recollections suggested that the experiences were not being relived but invented. As if they had been dreaming, people would recall being in locations they had actually never visited. So, although our storage capacity may be essentially unlimited, the evidence does *not* suggest that we store most information with the exactness of a tape recorder—or a computer.

The Physical Basis of Memory   Contemporary memory research is advancing rapidly on two parallel paths. While cognitive psychologists study our memory "software," neuropsychologists are gaining new insights into our memory "hardware"—how information is physically stored in our brains. And where.

For several decades now, neuropsychologists have searched the brain for physical evidence of memory. The search has at times been exasperating. One psychologist, Karl Lashley (1950), trained rats to solve a maze, then he cut out pieces of the rats' cortices and retested them on their memory of maze running. Eventually, he hoped to find where the memory of the maze was located. Alas, no matter what part of the cortex he removed, the rats retained at least a partial memory of how to solve the maze, forcing Lashley to conclude that memories do not reside in specific spots. (However, that leaves open the possibilities that memories reside in multiple locations within the cortex or outside the cortex completely [Meyer, 1984].)

Are memories instead rooted in the brain's ongoing electrical activity? If so, then temporarily shutting down that activity should eliminate them. To find out, Ralph Gerard (1953) trained hamsters to turn right or left to get food. Then he lowered their body temperature until the brain's electrical activity ceased. When the hamsters were revived and their brains were active again, would they remember which way to turn? Yes. The memory survived the electrical blackout.

Brain Circuits   Since the 1970s, new clues to the physical basis of memory have surfaced rapidly. After a memory-to-be enters the cortex through the senses, it wends its way into the depths of the brain where it is processed for storage. Where it goes depends on the type of information, as strikingly illustrated in the special cases of amnesic patients similar to John, whom we met at the beginning of this chapter. These patients are incapable of learning new facts or recalling anything they have recently done. Nevertheless, in experiments they can be classically conditioned, and with practice they can learn to read mirror-image writing, do a jigsaw puzzle, or even solve a complicated block-stacking brainteaser (L. Squire, 1987). All this they do with absolutely no memory of having learned the skill; indeed, when presented with a block-stacking problem they will deny having seen it before, insist it is silly for them to try, and then proceed to solve it like a practiced expert.

These amnesic patients typically have suffered damage to the *hippocampus* or the *amygdala*, limbic system structures involved in processing *declarative memories* (such as for names, images, or events). That their old memories remain intact shows that the hippocampus and amygdala are way stations that process and feed *new* information to other neural circuits, which store it (Mishkin & Appenzeller, 1987). Destroying these way stations interrupts the circuitry for storing conscious memories. (The reason is unclear—some see the hippocampus as an intermediate storage area—in computerese, a buffer—between short- and long-term memory [Rawlins & others, 1985].)

That an amnesic patient can learn and remember skills but not facts indicates that the two are processed differently. Memories of facts—declarative memories—are processed via the hippocampus (Figure 10–12). Memories of how to do things—*procedural memories*—are processed in the more ancient parts of the brain. (We perhaps should have expected as much—that the learning of simple habits would be processed through the brain's more primitive regions.)

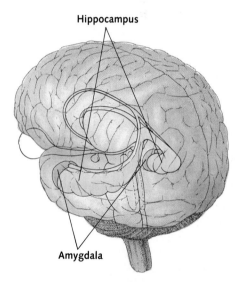

Figure 10-12   In the brain, the hippocampus and amygdala process memories of declarative facts and events. Procedural memories seem to be processed elsewhere.

The ability of some brain-injured patients to learn and remember skills but not facts suggests that skill and fact memories involve different brain mechanisms.

DECLARATIVE MEMORY	PROCEDURAL MEMORY
Facts: easily learned and forgotten	Skills: Learned by repetition and hard to forget
Names, faces Telephone numbers	Sports skills Playing musical instruments

This dual—procedural and declarative—memory system helps to explain, among other phenomena, infantile amnesia. Behaviorally, the reactions and skills we learned during infancy are clearly retained and reach far into our future. Yet as adults we recall nothing of our first 2 years, not only because we index so much of our memory by words that preliterate children have not learned, but also because the hippocampus is one of the last brain structures to mature fully.

Synaptic Changes   Other neuroscientists are analyzing memory on a finer scale, by exploring changes in and between single neurons. Memories begin as messages whizzing through brain circuits but are then somehow consolidated into a permanent neural change. If by passing an electric current through the brain you disrupt its electrical activity, recent memories will be wiped out but earlier memories will still be intact. A blow to the head can do the same. When football players who have been dazed or momentarily knocked unconscious are interviewed a few minutes later, they typically cannot recall the name of the play during which the incident occurred (Yarnell & Lynch, 1970).

Where does the structural change occur that makes memories permanent? The available clues point to the synapses—the sites where nerve cells communicate with one another through their chemical messengers, the neurotransmitters (Lynch & Baudry, 1984). As you may recall from Chapter 3, experience modifies the brain's neural networks. In response to increased activity in a particular pathway or group of converging pathways, neural interconnections form or are preserved and strengthened. Cut these neural pathways, as neuropsychologist Richard Thompson (1985) has done with some conditioned reflex pathways through the cerebellum, and the learned response is destroyed.

To glimpse what changes occur when a neural pathway is repeatedly activated, Eric Kandel and James Schwartz (1982) studied the simplest sort of learning in one of the simplest of animals, the sea snail *Aplysia*, which has only 20,000 nerve cells. Because the snail's simple nervous system nevertheless operates similarly to our own, discovering how snails learn can provide insight into how we learn.

As we noted in Chapter 9, the sea snail can be classically conditioned (with electric shock) to reflexively withdraw its gills at the movement of water. By observing the snail's neural connections before and after conditioning, the researchers were able to pinpoint changes. For example, when learning occurs, the snail releases more of the neurotransmitter serotonin at certain synapses, and these synapses become more efficient at transmitting signals. When neurotransmitters are blocked by drugs, information storage is disrupted (L. Squire, 1987). (Recall, too, that Alzheimer's disease disrupts memory through the loss of brain tissue that secretes important neurotransmitters.)

Eric Kandel (front) and James Schwartz with basins of the subjects of their memory experiments. Their research on memory in these sea snails, *Aplysia*, is shedding light on how human memory works.

Alcohol's disruption of serotonin's messenger activity may explain why alcohol impairs the formation of memories (Weingartner & others, 1983). The morning after a night of heavy drinking, a person may have trouble remembering the previous evening. In general, depressants impede memory formation, whereas the naturally stimulating hormones that humans and animals produce when excited or stressed have an opposite effect: They boost learning and retention. Thus, when a rat is injected with an arousing hormone and receives a mild foot shock, it forms an indelible memory like the one it forms when an intense foot shock naturally triggers release of the same hormone (Gold, 1987). Such hormones apparently act by making more glucose energy available to fuel brain activities. Emotion-triggered hormonal changes are one possible reason why exciting or shocking events, such as the first kiss or a political assassination, are often long remembered. (Another reason is our tendency to rehearse or relive flashbulb memories.)

The Search Continues   Though clues to the physical basis of memory are accumulating, many of the answers remain elusive: Are memories stored at specific synaptic locations, as Kandel and Schwartz's work with sea snails indicates? Or are memories diffused, as Lashley's inability to cut them out suggested? If stored at specific sites, why does presenting a familiar visual cue to a split-brain cat activate (in the hemisphere that had previously learned the scene) more than 5 million neurons (John & others, 1986)? The evidence indicates that different types of memory are stored at specific locations *and* that the processing of each type involves the activity of a complex neural system. In some as yet unknown way, the interaction between the whole system and its subsystems enables us to store residues of a lifetime of experiences with their associated smells, sights, and sounds. Clearly, most of what there is to be known about the physical basis of memory is yet to be discovered.

If and when the biology of memory is understood, will there be any need for a psychology of memory? Yes, because psychology and biology are complementary sciences. Each asks important questions, and both are essential for a complete understanding of memory.

Understanding the physiological basis of memory is of more than academic interest. Discovering the neural and chemical mechanisms of memory may help this woman. Suffering from Alzheimer's disease, she cannot remember the way from bedroom to bathroom. The gate rail guides her, and prevents her from wandering off.

RETRIEVAL

To most people, memory is indicated by *recall,* the ability to retrieve information that is not presently in conscious awareness. To a psychologist, memory is any indication that something learned has been retained, so the ability to *recognize* or more quickly *relearn* information also indicates memory. For example, long after you are unable to recall most of the people in your high school graduating class, you may still recognize their yearbook pictures from a photographic lineup and pick their names out from a list of names. At least that is what Harry Bahrick and his colleagues (1975) found: People who had graduated 25 years earlier could not recall many of their classmates, but they could recognize 90 percent of their old classmates' pictures and names. Also, if you have once learned something and then forgotten it, you will probably relearn it more quickly than you learned it originally. When studying for a final exam or when again learning a language used in early childhood and since forgotten, the relearning comes more easily. Thus, psychologists use tests of *recognition* and time spent *relearning* to reveal that often we remember more than we can recall.

Retrieval Cues   To retrieve a fact from a library of stored information, you need a way to gain access to it. In recognition tests, retrieval cues (such as photographs) provide reminders of information (classmates' names) we could not otherwise recall. Retrieval cues also help us to know where to look. If you want to know what the pyramid on the back of a dollar bill signifies, you might look in *Collier's Encyclopedia* under "dollar," "currency," or "money." But your efforts would be futile. To get the information you want, you would have to look under "Great Seal of the United States" (Hayes, 1981). Like information stored in encyclopedias, memories are inaccessible unless we have cues to use in retrieving them: The more and better learned the retrieval cues, the more accessible the memory.

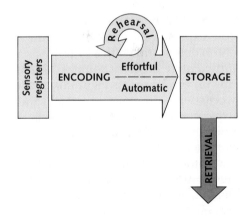

Multiple-choice questions test _____.
(a) recall
(b) recognition
(c) relearning
Fill-in-the-blank questions test _____.
(See page 271.)

You can think of a memory as being held in storage by a web of associations (J. R. Anderson, 1983). To retrieve a specific memory, you first need to identify one of the strands that lead to it, a process called *priming* (Bower, 1986). Philosopher-psychologist William James referred to priming as the "wakening of associations." Often our associations are activated, or primed, without our awareness. Hearing or seeing the word "rabbit" can unconsciously prime people to spell the spoken word "hair" as h-a-r-e. As Figure 10–13 shows, "rabbit" primes associations with "hare" even though we may not recall having heard "rabbit." (Recall from Chapter 6 that even subliminal stimuli can sometimes prime responses to later stimuli.)

How many of the six quiz words on page 262 can you now recall? Of these, how many are high-imagery words? How many are low-imagery?

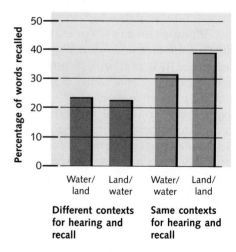

Figure 10-13 Priming. The spreading of associations can unconsciously activate related associations. After seeing or hearing "rabbit," we are later more likely to spell the spoken word "hair" as h-a-r-e. (Adapted from Bower, 1986.)

Can we remember better by activating retrieval cues within our web of associations? Mnemonic devices provide us with handy retrieval cues: ROY G. BIV; HOMES; bun, shoe, tree. We can also expose ourselves to cues that prime our memories for earlier experiences. Before the Watergate hearings, John Dean refreshed his memory "by going through every single newspaper article outlining what had happened and then placing myself in what I had done in a given sequence in time" (Neisser, 1981).

Context Effects   It does help to put yourself back in the context where you experienced something. Duncan Godden and Alan Baddeley (1975) demonstrated this by having scuba divers listen to a list of words in two quite different settings, when either 10 feet underwater or sitting on the beach. As Figure 10–14 illustrates, the divers recalled more words when they were tested in the same place. You have probably experienced similar context effects. Returning to the place you once lived in or the school you once attended, you may have been flooded with retrieval cues, and then with memories.

Odors can be potent retrieval cues. In *Remembrance of Things Past*, the French novelist Marcel Proust describes how the aroma and flavor of a bite of cake soaked in tea resurrected long-forgotten memories of his aunt's bedroom in the old family house. "The smell and taste of things," he notes, "bear unfaltering, in the tiny and almost impalpable drop of their essence, the vast structure of recollection." Laboratory studies confirm that, although it is difficult to recall or to name odors, we do indeed have a remarkable capacity to recognize long-forgotten odors and their associated episodes (Engen, 1987).

Sometimes, being in a context similar to one we've been in before may even trigger the experience of *déjà vu*—that eerie sense that "I've been in this exact situation before." People who pose the question as, "How could I recognize a situation that I'm experiencing for the first time?," may suppose that something paranormal is occurring—perhaps reincarnation ("I must have experienced this in a previous life") or precognition ("I viewed this scene in my mind before experiencing it"). But if we pose the question differently—"Why do I feel as

Figure 10-14 The effects of context on memory are demonstrated by the fact that words heard underwater are best recalled underwater; words heard on land are best recalled on land. (Adapted from Godden & Baddeley, 1975.)

if I recognize this situation?"—we can see how our memory system might produce the déjà vu feeling (Alcock, 1981). If we have previously been in a similar situation, though we can't recall what it was, the current situation may be loaded with cues that unconsciously help us to retrieve the earlier experience. Thus, if you see a stranger who looks and walks like one of your friends, the similarity may give rise to a feeling of recognition. Because the feeling conflicts with your knowing that the person is a stranger, you may think, "I feel I've seen that person before."

Moods and Memories   Words, events, and contexts are not the only retrieval cues. Events in the past may have aroused a specific emotion, which can later prime us to recall its associated events. Cognitive psychologist Gordon Bower (1983) explains: "A specific emotional state is like a specific room in a library into which the subject places memory records, and he can most easily retrieve those records by returning to that same room or emotional state." The things we learn in one state—be it joyful or sad, drunk or sober—are therefore most easily recalled when we are again in the same state, a phenomenon called ***state-dependent memory*** (Figure 10–15). What is learned when drunk, high, or depressed is not recalled well—because drugs and depression interfere with encoding—but it's recalled better when again drunk, high, or depressed.

Some examples: If people are put in a buoyant mood—whether under hypnosis or just by the day's events (a World Cup soccer victory for the West German subjects of one recent study)—they commonly recall the world through rose-colored glasses; thus they judge themselves to be competent and effective, other people to be benevolent, life in general to be wonderful (Forgas & others, 1984; Schwarz & others, 1987). Put in a bad mood, the very same people suddenly see everything more negatively.

The mood-memory link seems strongest with autobiographical recollections of everyday events (called *episodic memory*), because in everyday situations people attribute their emotions to events associated with the emotions (Bower, 1987). Thus *currently* depressed people recall their parents as having been rejecting, punitive, and guilt-promoting, whereas *formerly* depressed people describe their parents no differently than do those who have never suffered from severe depression (Lewinsohn & Rosenbaum, 1987). Being depressed sours memories. You and I may nod our heads knowingly. Yet, curiously, when in a good or bad mood, we persist—and will continue to do so even after learning about state-dependent memory—in attributing our changing judgments and memories to reality rather than to our temporary mood. We perceive the world out there in different ways, depending on our mood.

Moods color both our retrieval of past experiences and our encoding of new experiences (Brown & Taylor, 1986; Johnson & Magaro, 1987; Mayer & Salovey, 1987). Bad moods predispose us to notice and interpret other people's behavior in negative ways. When in a good mood the same actions create a more positive impression.

The effect of mood on encoding and retrieval helps explain why our moods persist. When happy, we recall happy events, which helps prolong the good mood. When depressed, we recall depressing events, which in turn feeds depressing interpretations of current events—all of which, as we will see in Chapter 16, maintains the vicious cycle of depression.

Answers to questions on page 269: Multiple-choice questions test *recognition*. Fill-in-the-blank questions test *recall*.

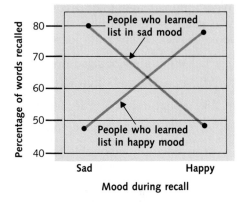

Figure 10-15   The effects of emotional state on memory are demonstrated by the fact that words learned when sad are best recalled when sad; words learned when happy are best recalled when happy. (From Bower, 1981.)

If our current moods color our recall of our childhoods, how might this affect conclusions drawn about the effects of parent-child interactions?

Memory Construction   Picture yourself having the following pleasant experience:

> You decide to go to your favorite restaurant for dinner. You enter the restaurant and are seated at a table with a white tablecloth. You study the menu. You tell the waiter that you want prime rib, medium rare, a baked potato with sour cream, and a salad with blue cheese dressing. You also order some red wine from the wine list. A few minutes later the waiter returns with your salad. Later he brings the rest of the meal, which you enjoy, except that the prime rib is a bit overdone.

Were I immediately to quiz you on this paragraph (from Hyde, 1983), you could surely retrieve considerable detail. For example, without looking back, answer the following questions:

1.   What kind of salad dressing did you order?

2.   Was the tablecloth red checked?

3.   What did you order to drink?

4.   Did the waiter give you a menu?

You were probably able to recall exactly what you ordered, and maybe even the color of the tablecloth. Does retrieval therefore consist merely of "reading" the information stored in our brain's library? We do have an enormous capacity for storing and reproducing the incidental details of our daily experience (Alba & Hasher, 1983). But as we have seen, often we construct our memories as we encode them, and we may also alter our memories as we withdraw them from the memory bank. Like a scientist who infers the appearance of a dinosaur from its remains, we may infer our past, based on stored information plus what we now assume. Did the waiter give you a menu? Not in the paragraph given. Nevertheless, many people answer yes. Why? Their schemas for restaurants direct their memory construction, by filtering information and filling in missing pieces.

Elizabeth Loftus has repeatedly shown how eyewitnesses similarly construct their reports when asked to recall incidents. In one experiment with John Palmer, Loftus showed a film of a traffic accident and then quizzed the viewers about what they saw (Loftus & Palmer, 1973). Those asked "How fast were the cars going when they *smashed* into each other?" gave higher speed estimates than those asked "How fast were the cars going when they *hit* each other?" A week later, the viewers were asked if they recalled seeing any broken glass. Those who had been asked the question with "smashed" were more than twice as likely as those asked the question with "hit" to recall broken glass (Figure 10–16). In fact, there was no broken glass in the film. Summarizing this and other experiments, Loftus (1983) reported that

> when exposed to misleading post-event information, subjects have mis-recalled the colour of a car that was green as being blue, a yield sign as a stop sign, broken glass or tape recorders that never existed, and even recalled something as large and conspicuous as a barn when no barn was ever seen.

The misleading information does not eliminate people's ability to *recognize* what they originally witnessed (the original memory has not been obliterated); rather, it influences their responses when asked to *recall* the event (Zaragoza & others, 1987). The recall problem can be sufficient that people later find it nearly impossible to discriminate between their memories of real and suggested events (Schooler & others, 1986). Unreal memories feel like real memories.

Accident

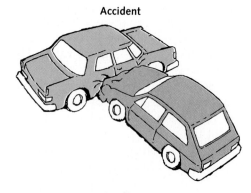

Leading
question:

"About how fast
were the cars going
when they
smashed
into each other?"

Memory
construction

Figure 10-16   *Memory construction. When people who saw the film of a car accident were asked a leading question, they reported a more serious accident than they had witnessed. (From Loftus, 1979.)*

Memory construction helps explain why John Dean's recollections of the Watergate conversations were a mixture of real and imagined events. It explains why "hypnotically refreshed" memories of crimes so easily incorporate errors, some of which originate with the hypnotist's leading questions ("Did you hear loud noises?"). It explains why patients with memory loss, such as those suffering from Alzheimer's disease, so readily "confabulate" (invent) sensible-sounding accounts of their activities. Memory construction explains why dating partners who fall in love tend to overestimate their earlier impressions of one another, while those who break up tend to underestimate their earlier liking (McFarland & Ross, 1987). And it explains why people's confident answers to survey questions—"When you were growing up, how frequently did your father attend religious services?"—often contain inaccuracies (Bradburn & others, 1987).

Knowing What We Know   Sometimes we know more than we are aware of. Other times—perhaps when taking an exam—we discover that we do not know something as well as we thought we did. The difficulties of knowing what you know are strikingly evident in the amnesic patients who know how to do things without knowing that they know. The parallel to learning during infancy is intriguing: We recall nothing, yet what we learn reaches far into our future.

How accurate are we at assessing what we know? John Shaughnessy and Eugene Zechmeister (1989) explored this question in an experiment with two groups of Hope College students. One group was (1) repeatedly shown dozens of factual statements, (2) asked to judge the likelihood that they would later remember each fact, and then (3) actually tested on their recall. Students in this group tended to feel fairly confident of their knowledge, even on the questions they later missed. Instead of constantly reading the statements, students in a second group also spent much of their time evaluating their knowledge by answering practice test questions. These students learned the facts just as well as did the mere-repetition group. What is more, the practice-test group could better discriminate what they did and didn't know. Thus, self-testing not only encourages active rehearsal, it also can help you to know what you know—and thus to focus your study time on what you do not yet know. As the British statesman Benjamin Disraeli once said, "To be conscious that you are ignorant is a great step to knowledge."

"Memory is a great betrayer."
Anais Nin,
The Diary of Anais Nin, 1974

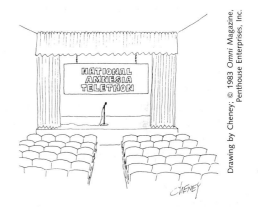

FORGETTING

Amidst all the applause for memory—all the efforts to understand it, all the books on how to improve it—have any voices been heard in praise of forgetting? William James (1890, p. 680) was such a voice: "If we remembered everything, we should on most occasions be as ill off as if we remembered nothing." To discard the clutter of useless or out-of-date information—where we parked the car yesterday, a friend's old phone number, restaurant orders already cooked and served—is surely a blessing (Bjork, 1978). The Russian memory whiz S, whom we met at the beginning of the chapter, was haunted by his junk heap of memories, which continually dominated his consciousness. He found it more difficult than did others with lesser memories to think abstractly—to generalize, to organize, to evaluate. A good memory is beneficial, but so is the ability to forget.

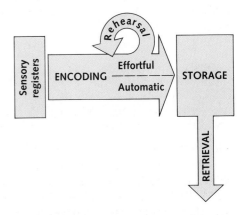

Forgetting can occur at any stage in the memory system.

What causes forgetting? When we forget something, do we fail to *encode* the information? Do we have difficulty *storing* it? Is the memory stored but, for some reason, *irretrievable?* Forgetting is like being unable to find a book in your library—because it was never acquired, or was discarded, or you don't have the information needed to find it.

ENCODING

Most memory failures are simply explained: The information never gets into the memory system. The English novelist-critic C. S. Lewis (1967, p. 107) vividly described why we remember "next to nothing":

> Each of us finds that in his own life every moment of time is completely filled. He is bombarded every second by sensations, emotions, thoughts, which he cannot attend to for multitude, and nine-tenths of which he must simply ignore. . . . The past . . . was a roaring cataract of billions upon billions of such moments: any one of them too complex to grasp in its entirety, and the aggregate beyond all imagination. . . . At every tick of the clock, in every inhabited part of the world, an unimaginable richness and variety of "history" falls off the world into total oblivion.

Indeed, much of what we sense we never notice. For example, if you live in the United States, you have probably looked at thousands of pennies in your lifetime. Can you recall what the side with Lincoln's head looks like? If not, let's make the memory test easier: Can you *recognize* the real thing in Figure 10–17? Raymond Nickerson and Marilyn Adams (1979) found that most people cannot. The details of a penny are not very meaningful (nor are they essential for distinguishing pennies from other coins), and few of us have made the effort to

Drawing by Sidney Harris.

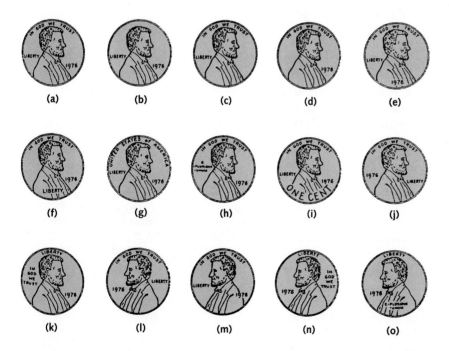

(a)   (b)   (c)   (d)   (e)

(f)   (g)   (h)   (i)   (j)

(k)   (l)   (m)   (n)   (o)

Figure 10-17   Which one of these pennies is the real thing? (From Nickerson & Adams, 1979.) (See page 276.)

encode them. As we noted earlier, we encode some information (such as how frequently we've experienced something) automatically; other types of information require effortful processing. Without effort, the information falls into oblivion.

STORAGE

Even after knowing something well, we sometimes forget it. In one experiment on himself, Ebbinghaus (1885) learned lists of nonsense syllables, and then measured how much less time it took to relearn each list, from 20 minutes to 30 days later. His famous "forgetting curve" (Figure 10–18) indicates that much of what we learn we quickly forget.

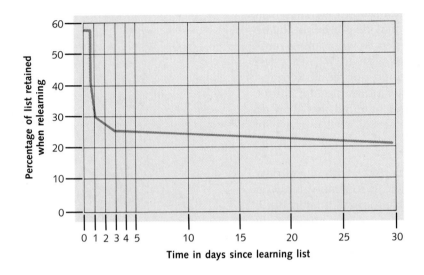

Figure 10-18   Ebbinghaus's forgetting curve. After learning lists of nonsense syllables, Ebbinghaus studied how long it took to relearn each list, from 20 minutes to 30 days later. He found that the retention of novel information drops quickly, then levels out. (Adapted from Ebbinghaus, 1885.)

Harry Bahrick (1984b), a modern-day descendant of the Ebbinghaus tradition, examined the forgetting curve for Spanish learned in school. He used the cross-sectional method (see page 105), by comparing the knowledge of Spanish among people who had just taken Spanish with that of those who had studied Spanish up to 50 years previously. Compared with those just completing a high school or college Spanish course, those who had been out of school for 3 years had forgotten much of what they had learned (Figure 10–19). However, after roughly 3 years, forgetting leveled off; what people remembered then they still remembered 25 years later, even if they had not used their Spanish at all.

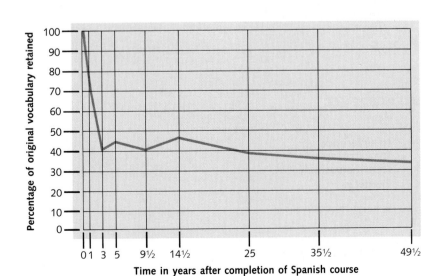

Figure 10-19   The forgetting curve for Spanish vocabulary. Compared with people just completing a Spanish course, those 3 years out of the course remember much less. Compared with the 3-year group, however, those who studied Spanish even longer ago did not forget much more. (Adapted from Bahrick, 1984b.)

One possible explanation for these forgetting curves is that a physical memory trace gradually fades. Too little is known about the physical basis of memory to evaluate the *physical decay* of stored memories. What we do know suggests that memories fade not merely because a physical trace decays as time passes, but also because new information disrupts our retrieval of old information.

Answer to question on page 274: The first penny (a) is the real penny.

RETRIEVAL

Sometimes information gets into our brain and, though we know it is there, we cannot get it out. A person's name may lie poised on the tip of the tongue, waiting to be retrieved. When people who cannot recall information are given retrieval cues ("It begins with an M"), they will often then remember what they previously could not recall. Retrieval problems help explain the occasional memory failures of older adults. Recall from Chapter 4 that older people tend to recall less than do younger adults, but they usually remember just as well if given reminders or a recognition test.

Interference   The learning of some items interferes with our retrieving others, especially when the items are similar. If someone gives you a phone number to remember, you may be able to recall it later. But if two more people give you their numbers, each successive number will be more difficult to recall. Such ***proactive interference*** refers to the disruptive effect of previous learning on the recall of new information. As you accumulate more and more information, your mental closet never fills, but it certainly gets cluttered.

Proactive means forward-acting.

For example, after buying a new combination lock or being assigned a new phone number, the old one may interfere. Benton Underwood (1957) revealed this phenomenon when he found that people who learn different lists of words on successive days have more and more difficulty remembering new lists. This explains why Ebbinghaus, after memorizing countless lists of nonsense syllables during his career, could remember only about one-fourth of a new list of syllables on the day after he learned it—far fewer than you as a novice could remember.

Retroactive interference refers to the disruptive effect of new information on the recall of previous information. For example, the learning of new students' names typically interferes with a professor's recall of names learned in previous classes. Table 10–1 illustrates both types of interference.

Retroactive means backward-acting.

Table 10–1
PROACTIVE AND RETROACTIVE INTERFERENCE

Time 1	Time 2	Test	Interference
Study French	Study Spanish	Recall Spanish	French proactively interferes
Study French	Study Spanish	Recall French	Spanish retroactively interferes

Retroactive interference can be minimized by reducing the number of interfering events—say, by going to sleep shortly after learning new information. This is what John Jenkins and Karl Dallenbach (1924) demonstrated in a classic experiment. Day after day, two people each learned some nonsense syllables, then tried to recall them after up to 8 hours of being awake or asleep. As Figure 10–20 shows, forgetting occurred more rapidly after being awake and involved with other activities. The investigators surmised that "forgetting is not so much a matter of the decay of old impressions and associations as it is a matter of interference, inhibition, or obliteration of the old by the new" (p. 612). Subsequent experiments confirm that the hour before sleep is a good time to commit information to memory (Fowler & others, 1973).

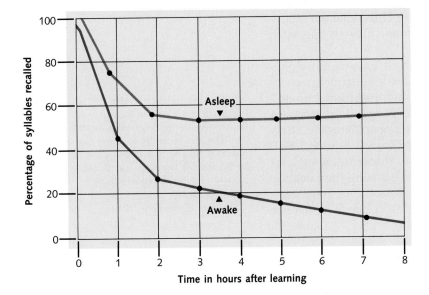

Figure 10-20 Retroactive interference. More forgetting occurs when a person stays awake and learns other new material. (From Jenkins & Dallenbach, 1924.)

Although interference is an important cause of forgetting, we should not overstate the point. Sometimes old information facilitates our learning of new information. Knowledge of Latin may aid one's learning of French—a phenomenon called "positive transfer." It's when the old and new information compete with each other that interference occurs.

Motivated Forgetting Not long ago, the huge cookie jar in our kitchen was jammed with freshly baked chocolate chip cookies. Still more were spread across the cooling racks on the counter. Twenty-four hours later, not a crumb was left. Who had taken them? My wife, three children, and I were the only people in the house during that time. So while memories were still fresh I immediately undertook a little memory test. One son, Andy, confessed that, yes, he may have wolfed as many as 20. Peter admitted eating 15. Laurie guessed that she had stuffed her 6-year-old body with 15 cookies. My wife, Carol, recalled eating 6, and I remembered consuming 15 and taking 18 more to the office. Collectively, our memories sheepishly accepted responsibility for 89 cookies. Still, we had not come close; 160 cookies had been baked.

Why did our memories fail us? How had we failed to notice and encode almost half the instances of our cookie-eating? As noted earlier,

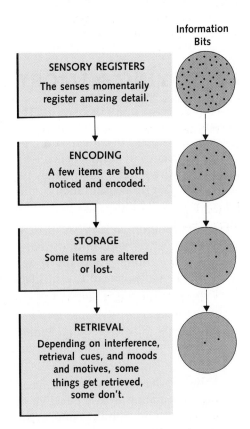

Information Bits

SENSORY REGISTERS
The senses momentarily register amazing detail.

ENCODING
A few items are both noticed and encoded.

STORAGE
Some items are altered or lost.

RETRIEVAL
Depending on interference, retrieval cues, and moods and motives, some things get retrieved, some don't.

Forgetting. As we process information much of it is filtered, altered, or lost.

we encode information about frequency automatically. So was it instead a storage problem? Might our memories of cookies, like Ebbinghaus's memory of nonsense syllables, have vanished almost as fast as the cookies themselves? Or might the information still be intact, but irretrievable because it would be embarrassing to remember?

With his concept of *repression,* Sigmund Freud proposed that our memory systems are indeed self-censoring. In order to protect our self-concepts and to minimize anxiety, we may repress painful memories. But the submerged memory still lingers, said Freud, and with patience and effort may be retrieved during therapy. Evidence of repression comes from clinical cases, such as shock victims who cannot remember their horror-filled moments. The closest laboratory counterpart to repression (and an alternate explanation of it) is found in the studies of state-dependent memory: What is learned in one emotional or physiological state is often forgotten in a different state. Thus what we experience when we are embarrassed or horror-struck may be forgotten when relaxed.

In experiments that more closely parallel the cookie-memory phenomenon, Michael Ross and his colleagues have time and again observed that people unknowingly revise their own histories. Immediately after researchers persuaded a group of people that frequent toothbrushing is desirable, they (more than other people) recalled having frequently brushed their teeth in the past (Ross & others, 1981). Having taken a highly touted study skills course, students tended later to inflate their estimates of self-improvement by *de*flating their evaluations of their previous study habits (Conway & Ross, 1984). To remember our past is often to revise it; by recalling events in a desired manner we protect and enhance our self-images.

> "[It is] necessary to remember that events happened in the desired manner. And if it is necessary to rearrange one's memories . . . then it is necessary to forget that one has done so. The trick of doing this can be learned like any other mental technique. . . . It is called doublethink."
>   George Orwell,
>   *Nineteen Eighty-Four,* 1948

IMPROVING MEMORY

Now and then we are dismayed at our forgetfulness—at our embarrassing inability to recall someone's name, at forgetting to have brought up a point in conversation, at forgetting to bring along something important, at finding ourselves standing in a room unable to recall why we are there (Herrmann, 1982). What can we do to minimize such lapses? Sprinkled throughout this chapter have been suggestions for improving memory. Let us review them:

Study repeatedly to boost long-term recall. To learn a name, say it to yourself after being introduced; wait a few seconds and say it again; wait longer and say it again. To provide many separate study sessions, make use of life's little intervals—riding on the bus, walking across campus, waiting for class to start.

Spend more time rehearsing or actively practicing the material to have better recall. Speed reading (skimming) of complex material—with minimal rehearsal—therefore yields less retention. It pays to study!

Make the material meaningful and make it your own. Mindlessly repeating information is less effective than time spent forming picture images, understanding and organizing information, associating the material with what you already know or have experienced, and putting it in your own words.

Use mnemonic devices to remember a list of unfamiliar items. Associate items with peg-words, make up a story that incorporates vivid images of the items, chunk information into acronyms.

Form as many associations as possible to maximize retrieval cues. Take photographs if you can. These images will later serve as reminders.

Refresh your memory by seeking retrieval cues. Mentally recreate the situation and the mood in which the original learning transpired; return to the same location; jog your memory by allowing one thought to cue the next.

Recall events while fresh, before you encounter possibly misleading information. If you are an eyewitness to an important event, recall it before allowing others to suggest what may have occurred.

Test your own knowledge, both to rehearse it and to help you determine what you do not yet know. If you are required to *recall* information later, do not be lulled into overconfidence by your ability to *recognize* it. For self-testing, the study guides that accompany many texts, including this one, can help.

Minimize interference. Study before sleeping; do not study topics that are likely to interfere with each other—such as Spanish and French—in close proximity.

Several of these techniques for improving memory have been incorporated into a study technique that comes with its own acronym: *SQ3R,* for *Survey, Question, Read, Recite, Review* (Robinson, 1970). To study a chapter, first *survey*—skim the chapter headings and read the summary. This will help you organize its material. As you prepare to read each section, turn the heading into a *question.* For this section, you might ask, "How can I improve my memory?" Then *read,* actively seeking the answer to your question. Having read a section, *recite* in your own words what you have read; test yourself by trying to answer your question, rehearsing what you can recall and then glancing back over what you cannot recall. Finally, *review*: Read your notes, again with an eye on the organization of the whole chapter, and review the chapter again later. Survey, question, read, recite, review. Survey, question, read . . .

Repeated study—a little and often—yields more lasting memory than massed study.

SUMMING UP

FORMING MEMORIES

Memory as Information Processing   Memory is the persistence of learning over time. The computer is a convenient model for thinking about human memory. Both systems must encode, store, and retrieve information.

Sensory Registers   Information first enters the memory system through the senses. We register visual images via iconic memory and sound via echoic memory.

Encoding   Information that is attended to must then be encoded, usually visually, acoustically, or semantically. Some types of information, notably concerning space, time, and frequency, in addition to well-learned information such as words, are encoded automatically. Other types of information, including much of our encoding of meaning, imagery, and organization, require effort. Mnemonic devices depend on the memorability of visual images and of information that is organized into chunks. Organizing information into hierarchies also aids memory.

Storage   In the short run, our memory span for information just presented is very limited—up to about seven or eight items, depending on the information and how it is presented. Our capacity for storing information permanently is essentially unlimited, but how or where we store it is uncertain. The search for the physical basis of memory has recently focused on brain circuits, such as those running through the hippocampus, and on the synapses and their neurotransmitters.

Retrieval   To be remembered, information that is "in there" must be retrieved, with the aid of associations (cues) that serve as reminders. Retrieval is state-dependent: What you learn in one context, mood, or physical state is most easily retrieved when you are again in that state. Apparently, memories are not stored as exact copies, and they certainly are not retrieved as such. Rather, we construct our memories, using both stored and new information. Thus, when eyewitnesses are subtly exposed to misleading details after an event, they often believe they *saw* the misleading details as part of the event.

FORGETTING

Memory failures can be failures of attention and encoding, of storage, or of retrieval (caused by interference, by insufficient cues, or even by motivated forgetting).

IMPROVING MEMORY

Research on memory suggests numerous strategies for improving memory. These include spaced study; active rehearsal; the encoding of well-organized, vivid, meaningful associations; mnemonic techniques; the return to contexts and moods that are rich with associations; self-testing and rehearsal; and the minimizing of interference. Several of these memory aids are incorporated into the SQ3R method of study.

TERMS AND CONCEPTS TO REMEMBER

acoustic encoding   The encoding of sound, especially the sound of words.

automatic processing   Effortless encoding of incidental information, such as space, time, and frequency, and of well-learned information, such as word meanings; not under conscious control.

chunking   Organization of items into familiar, manageable units.

declarative memory   Memory of facts, of information one can "declare."

déjà vu   (From French, literally meaning "already seen.") That eerie sense that "I've experienced this before." Cues from the current situation may subconsciously trigger retrieval of an earlier experience.

echoic memory   A momentary sensory memory of auditory stimuli; if attention is elsewhere, sounds and words can still be recalled within 3 or 4 seconds.

effortful processing   Encoding that requires attention and effort.

encoding   The processing of information into the memory system, for example by extracting meaning.

flashbulb memory   A clear memory of an emotionally significant moment or event.

hippocampus   A neural center in the limbic system that helps process declarative memories for storage.

iconic memory   A momentary sensory memory of visual stimuli; a photographic or picture-image memory lasting no more than a second or so.

imagery Mental pictures. A powerful aid to effortful processing, especially when it is combined with semantic encoding.

long-term memory A relatively permanent and limitless component of the memory system.

memory The persistence of learning over time.

mnemonics [nih-MON-iks] Memory aids, especially those techniques that use vivid imagery and organizational devices.

priming The conscious or unconscious activation of particular associations in memory.

proactive interference The disruptive effect of prior learning on the recall of new information.

procedural memory Memory of skills, of how to do things.

recall A measure of memory in which the person must retrieve information learned earlier, as on a sentence completion test.

recognition A measure of memory in which the person need only identify items previously learned, as on a multiple-choice test.

rehearsal The conscious repetition of information, either simply to maintain information in consciousness or to encode it for storage.

relearning A measure of memory that assesses the amount of time saved when relearning previously learned information.

repression The blocking from consciousness of painful memories and unacceptable impulses.

retrieval The process of getting information out of memory storage.

retroactive interference The disrupting effect of new learning on the recall of old information.

semantic encoding The encoding of meaning, including the meaning of words.

serial position effect Our tendency to recall the last and first items in a list.

short-term memory A component of memory that holds few items briefly, such as the seven digits of a phone number while dialing.

SQ3R An acronym for *Survey*, *Question*, *Read*, *Recite*, *Review*—a method of study.

state-dependent memory The tendency to recall information best when in the same emotional or physiological state one was in when the information was learned.

storage The maintenance of encoded information over time.

visual encoding The encoding of picture images.

FOR FURTHER READING

Allport, S. (1986). *Explorers of the black box: The search for the cellular basis of memory.* New York: Norton.

The story of the race to find the memory trace, and of the motives and emotions of the scientists involved.

Baddeley, A. D. (1982). *Your memory: A user's guide.* New York: Macmillan.

A lavishly illustrated treatment of memory, with practical applications.

Brown, A. S. (1987). *Maximizing memory power: Using recall to your advantage in business.* New York: Wiley.

A practical guide to applying memory principles in everyday work.

CHAPTER 11

Thinking and Language

The debate over the heights of human wisdom versus the depths of human foolishness dates from the very beginnings of recorded history. The psalmist who in a moment of humility wondered, "What is man that thou art mindful of him?," in the next breath rhapsodized that human beings were "little less than God." The poet T. S. Eliot was struck by "the hollow men . . . Headpiece filled with straw." But Shakespeare's Hamlet extolled the human species as "noble in reason! . . . infinite in faculties! . . . in apprehension how like a god!" In the preceding chapters, we too have sometimes marveled at our capabilities and other times at our propensity to err.

We have considered the human brain—a mere 3 pounds of tissue that contains circuitry more complex than all the telephone networks on the planet. We have been surprised at the competence of newborn infants. We have appreciated the human sensory system, which can disassemble visual stimuli into millions of nerve impulses, transmit them to the visual cortex, and reassemble them into clear and colorful perceived images. We have acknowledged the seemingly limitless capacity of human memory and the ease with which we simultaneously process information consciously and unconsciously, effortfully and automatically. Little wonder, then, that our species has had the genius to invent the camera, the car, and the computer; to unlock the atom and crack the genetic code; to travel into space and probe the ocean depths.

At the same time, we have seen that our species is kin to the other animals, influenced by the same principles of learning as rats and pigeons. We have noted that we assimilate reality to our preconceptions, waver in our definitions of gender roles, and succumb to perceptual illusions and distortions. We have seen how easily we deceive ourselves about hypnotic regressions, pseudopsychic claims, and constructed memories. Little wonder, then, that we sometimes imagine we can read minds and travel outside our bodies; that we form distorted images of other ethnic, age, and gender groups; that we are subject to the same biological impulses as "lesser" creatures.

In this chapter, we encounter further instances of these two images of the human condition—the rational and the irrational. Most of the researchers we will encounter are not directly concerned with the implications of their studies for human rationality. Rather, their objectives are simply to describe and to explain specific aspects of thinking and language. Nevertheless, research findings will help us examine the rationality-irrationality debate. Consider some of the questions we will explore in the pages ahead:

What are concepts? How do we form them?

How do we solve problems?

How reasonable are our judgments? When are we most likely to err? How can we improve our judgments?

To what extent can computers simulate human thought?

What are the essential elements of language? How do they develop?

Is language unique to humans, or do some other animals share this capacity?

How do language and thinking affect each other?

The answers to these questions will tell us much about the human condition and will allow us to contemplate further how deserving we are of our name, *Homo sapiens*—wise human.

THINKING

Previous chapters have explained how information is received and perceived, stored and retrieved. Now we consider how our cognitive system uses this information to think and communicate. We begin by considering the logical and sometimes illogical ways in which we create concepts, solve problems, make decisions, and form judgments. First, let's consider the building blocks of thinking: concepts.

CONCEPTS

To think and talk about the countless events, objects, and people in our world, we simplify things by organizing items into mental groupings called **concepts.** Consider the variety of items that are summed up in the concept of "chair"—a baby's high chair, a wing chair, the chairs around a dining room table, folding chairs. When we use a word such as "chair" to refer to a general category of things, we are using it as a concept, our extraction of the features that distinguish a class of items. The relevant features of "chair," for example, are leggedness, having a back, and sit-on-ability.

Imagine life without concepts. We would need a different name for every object and idea. We could not ask a child to "throw the ball" because there would be no concept of ball. Instead of saying "he was angry," we would have to describe the person's facial expression, vocal intensity, and words. Concepts such as "ball" and "angry" provide much information with a minimum of cognitive effort. That is why concepts are the basic building blocks of thought.

We group similar types of information into manageable concepts, and further simplify by organizing concepts into hierarchies. For example, the earliest naturalists sought to simplify and order the overwhelming complexity of some 5 million species of living things by clustering them into two basic categories—the plant kingdom and the animal kingdom. Then they divided these basic categories into smaller and smaller subcategories—vertebrates, fish, and sharks, for instance, in order of increasing specificity.

The urge to classify the world reflects a characteristic human tendency to order our environment into hierarchies of concepts: Cab drivers organize their cities into geographical sections, which are subdivided into neighborhoods and again into blocks; physicists speedily

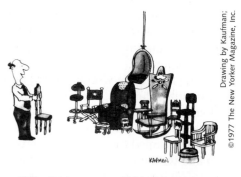

"Attention everyone! I'd like to introduce the newest member of our family."

classify and solve physics problems using fundamental physical principles; chess masters conceptually organize chess games in ways that enable them to see the significance of various game positions (Bransford & others, 1986).

Forming Concepts   How do we form concepts? Sometimes we follow definitional rules. A triangle has three sides, we are told, so we thereafter classify all three-sided geometric forms as triangles. A bird is an animal that has wings, feathers, and hatches from eggs.

More often, we form our concepts by developing a *prototype*—a best example of a particular category (Rosch, 1978). The more closely objects match our prototype of a concept the more readily they are included in the concept. A robin and a goose both satisfy our rule for the concept of "bird," yet people agree more quickly with the statement "a robin is a bird" than with the statement "a goose is a bird." For most of us, the robin is the birdier bird; it looks more like our prototypical image of a bird. This quick and easy way of deciding what belongs to a specific concept is not as logical as the rule-bound method, but it is certainly more efficient.

How Concepts Affect What We Perceive   Given a prototype, such as "bird," we immediately perceive it as having the characteristics that we associate with the prototype, such as wings for flight. Such assumptions are usually correct, but not always. Aware that people's prototypical "hyperactive child" is "noisy" and "moves around," Barry Collins (1986) showed some people a videotaped child. Those who viewed a noisy child (with the TV volume turned up) perceived the child as moving around more than did those who viewed a quiet child (the same taped child with the volume turned down). Once they perceived one component of a prototype ("noisy"), viewers became more likely to "see" other components (such as "moves around"). The concept directed their thinking. (This, by the way, is one reason why oversimplified, stereotyped perceptions of people persist: We perceive and then remember traits that we expect.)

If, however, something fails to match our prototype we may have trouble classifying it. Nonflying animals such as penguins and kiwis may not be recognized as birds. People whose heart attack symptoms don't precisely match their prototype of a heart attack are slow to seek help. We are much quicker to perceive an illness when our symptoms fit one of our disease prototypes (Bishop & others, 1987).

PROBLEM SOLVING

One tribute to our rationality is our ability to form and use concepts. Another is our skill at solving problems—at coping with novel situations for which there is no well-established response. When arriving home without a key and finding the front door locked, when pondering how to organize a term paper, when puzzling over how to test a theory, ingenuity often triumphs. Effective problem solving employs a series of steps: (1) defining the problem (you have no key to the locked front door); (2) developing a specific strategy (try the back door; if it's locked, find an unlocked window); (3) carrying out the strategy; and (4) determining if the strategy is working.

Strategies for Solving Problems   Several different strategies can be used to solve problems. Consider three of the simplest and most important—trial and error, algorithms, and heuristics.

Some rabbits match our rabbit prototype better than others.

Trial and Error   When the possible solutions to a problem are few, we may solve it through *trial and error.* When confronted with a strange television set in a motel room, for instance, we normally try first one button and then another until the set comes on. Unsure which faucet in the motel bathroom is for hot water, we pick one and turn it on; if we err, we know it's the other. Even when we face more complicated problems, trial and error may be useful. Thomas Edison, for example, had no way of knowing what substance would work as a light bulb filament, so he tried thousands before stumbling upon one, carbonized cotton thread, that did (Hunt, M., 1982).

Hypothesis Testing   Sometimes, however, the problem we are faced with may have a large number of possible solutions. In this case, hypothesis testing may be the best strategy. For instance, if the program manual for my computer is unclear about how to exit from a program, I could just start hitting keys hoping some combination might produce the desired effect. But this trial-and-error approach isn't very efficient— there are eighty-five keys on my keyboard. Knowing what keystrokes normally work to exit from a program, and knowing how this particular program operates, I could deduce which alternatives might be most likely to work (form a hypothesis) and just try those (test it).

Algorithms   Problem-solving experts Allan Newell and Herbert Simon (1972) labeled the most systematic problem-solving method the algorithm. *Algorithms* are logical, methodical, step-by-step procedures for solving problems.

If the proper algorithm is used, the correct solution to a problem is guaranteed. Some algorithms, like the formula for finding the area of a rectangle, are simple timesavers. But often the process may take a while, because it involves examining every possible solution in an orderly manner until the correct one is found. For instance, given the challenge of forming another word using all the letters in CINERAMA, we could elect to use an algorithm. The algorithm would involve systematically trying each letter in each position and then checking the resulting combination in a dictionary. If you decide to try this approach, set aside the next few days, for 20,160 combinations of the letters are possible. Allowing 20 seconds to look up each possible solution, you should be finished within 5 days.

Heuristics   For some of the problems we face, algorithms are too laborious; for some other problems no algorithms exist. Because the more formal approaches are often not appropriate, we frequently use simple rule-of-thumb strategies, called *heuristics,* for solving problems. All of us have a repertoire of these strategies based on bits of knowledge we have picked up, rules we have learned, or hypotheses that have worked in the past.

Consider how we might use heuristics to solve the problem of finding a different word in CINERAMA. We know, for instance, that English words never start with the combinations "mc," "nc," "rc," or "nm," and that two "a"s seldom come together. By using such rules of thumb and then applying trial and error, it shouldn't take too long to come up with the correct answer, AMERICAN.

Insight   We can all recall occasions when we puzzled over a problem for some time and then, suddenly, the pieces fell together and we perceived the solution. This facility for sudden flashes of inspiration that allow us to solve problems, often in novel ways, is commonly referred to as *insight.*

Solving complex puzzles like this one is partly a trial-and-error process, partly a step-by-step testing of various possibilities, and partly an application of rules of thumb regarding which types of pieces fit together.

Examples of insight have occasionally been documented in animals. A famous instance was recorded by the German Gestalt psychologist Wolfgang Köhler (1925), who studied the resident chimpanzees on a remote African island. In one experiment with a chimp named Sultan, Köhler placed a piece of fruit and a long stick outside the chimp's cage, well beyond the chimp's reach, and placed a short stick inside the cage. Spying the short stick, Sultan grabbed it and tried to reach the fruit with it. But the stick, by design, was too short. After several unsuccessful attempts, the chimp dropped the stick and paused to survey the whole situation. Then suddenly, as if thinking "Aha!," Sultan jumped up, seized the short stick again, and this time used it to pull in the longer stick—which he then used to reach the fruit. Sultan's actions were not only proof of animal cognition, claimed Köhler, but also evidence that there is more to learning than conditioning. Other apparent instances abound (see Figure 11–1). But what looks like insight may, however, actually be a chain of learned responses, as for the pigeon in Figure 11–2 below.

Whatever the final analysis of bird and chimpanzee insight, the feeling of having had an insight is common in human experience. Köhler described this as the sense of satisfaction that accompanies flashes of inspiration. Satisfying insights are familiar from moments when we have solved a difficult problem or seen how to resolve a conflict with a friend. The joy of a joke may similarly lie in our capacity for insight—in our sudden comprehension of an unexpected ending or a double meaning, as in the story of Professor Smith, who complained to his colleagues that student interruptions had become a problem. "The minute I get up to speak," he explained, "some fool begins to talk."

Figure 11–1 Chimpanzee inventiveness. After learning that he could see himself on TV, Austin apparently wanted to see his throat better. So he picked up a flashlight and shined it in his throat, which he pointed toward the camera. (From Rumbaugh & Savage-Rumbaugh, 1986.)

Figure 11–2 "Insight" in a bird-brained animal. A pigeon, trained by Robert Epstein and his co-researchers (1984), confronts an out-of-reach banana. Having previously been conditioned, separately, (1) to push a box to any designated location, and (2) to climb on a fixed box and peck bananas, the pigeon spontaneously integrated the behaviors. The completion of the first act served as a stimulus for the next: When the box reached the area under the banana, it triggered the previously learned climb-and-peck response. This shows that genuine insight is not essential for spontaneous, complex behaviors.

Obstacles to Problem Solving As inventive as humans can be in solving problems, there are human tendencies that interfere with our problem-solving abilities. Among these obstacles are *confirmation bias* and *fixation.*

Confirmation Bias One of the major obstacles to problem solving is our tendency to search for information that confirms our ideas, a phenomenon known as the **confirmation bias.** In an experiment with British university students, P. C. Wason (1960) demonstrated our reluctance to seek information that might disconfirm our beliefs. He gave students the three-number sequence, 2-4-6, and asked them to guess the rule he had used to devise the series. (The rule was simple: any three ascending numbers.) Before submitting their answers, the students generated their own set of three numbers, and each time Wason would tell them whether or not their set conformed to his rule. Once they had done enough testing to feel certain they had the rule, they were to announce it.

The result? Seldom right but never in doubt! Twenty-three of twenty-nine people convinced themselves of a wrong rule. Typically, they formed an erroneous idea about the rule ("Maybe it's counting by twos") and then searched only for confirming evidence (by testing 6-8-10, 100-102-104, and so forth). Such experiments reveal that we more eagerly seek evidence that will verify our ideas than evidence that might refute them (Klayman & Ha, 1987; Skov & Sherman, 1986). Managers, for example, may confirm their hiring ability by selectively noticing instances of recently hired employees who are doing well. (One tends not to know about rejected applicants who excel elsewhere.)

In other experiments, Wason (1981) found that once people have a wrong idea in mind they often will not budge from their illogic:

> This incorrigible conviction that they are right when they are, in fact, wrong has analogies to real-life crises of belief. . . . Ordinary people evade facts, become inconsistent, or systematically defend themselves against the threat of new information relevant to the issue.

Fixation   Try your hand at some brainteasers that have been drawn from classic experiments.

Arrange the six matches shown in Figure 11–3 so that they form four equilateral triangles.

Suppose that you have a 21-cup jug, a 127-cup jug, and a 3-cup jug. Drawing and discarding as much water as you like, you need to measure out exactly 100 cups of water. How can this be done? This problem is the first of seven presented in Figure 11–4. Solve the remaining problems, too.

"The human understanding, when any proposition has been once laid down . . . forces everything else to add fresh support and confirmation."
Francis Bacon,
Novum Organum, 1620

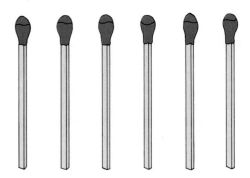

11–3   How would you arrange six matches to form four equilateral triangles? (From "Problem solving" by M. Scheerer. Copyright © 1963 by Scientific American, Inc. All rights reserved.)

Problem	Given jugs of these sizes:			Measure out this much water:
	A	B	C	
1	21	127	3	100
2	14	46	5	22
3	18	43	10	5
4	7	42	6	23
5	20	57	4	29
6	23	49	3	20
7	15	39	3	18

Figure 11–4   Using jugs A, B, and C with the capacities indicated in the table, how would you measure out the volumes indicated in the right-hand column? (From Luchins, 1946.)

Given the box of matches, the thumbtacks, and the candle shown in Figure 11–5, how can you use these materials to mount the candle on a bulletin board?

Figure 11–5 Using these materials, how would you mount the candle on the bulletin board? (From Duncker, 1945.)

Have you tried all of the problems? (It will pay you to do so before reading on.)

A major obstacle to problem solving is *fixation*—the inability to see a problem from a new perspective. For instance, if your attempts to solve the match problem were fixed on two-dimensional solutions, as is usually the case, then the three-dimensional solution shown in Figure 11–6 on page 290 will have eluded you.

We tend to become fixated on certain types of solutions for a very good reason: Solutions that were successful in the past can frequently be applied to new problems. Consider, for instance, the following question:

Given the sequence O-T-T-F-?-?-?, what are the final three letters?

Don't feel bad if you couldn't figure out the answer. Most people have difficulty recognizing that the three final letters are *F*(ive), *S*(ix), and *S*(even). But having learned the type of solution needed for this problem, you may be able to solve the following one:

Given the sequence J-F-M-A-?-?-?, what are the final three letters?

(In case you had difficulty with this one, too, you might ask yourself what month it is.)

Although past successes can help solve present problems, they may also interfere with our taking a fresh approach when faced with problems that demand an entirely new solution. This tendency to repeat solutions that have worked in the past is a type of fixation called *mental set.* We have already seen one example of mental set in the match problem. You may have run into it again in the water jug problems. For the first jug problem, you probably developed the following formula:

B − A − 2C = desired amount of water.

This same formula works for all seven problems. Furthermore, once you developed this mental set, you probably solved the later problems much faster than you did the first. But how did you solve problems 6 and 7? Did the mental set cause you to miss the much simpler solutions (A − C for 6; A + C for 7) shown in Figure 11–7 on page 290?

Another type of fixation, referred to by the awkward but appropriate label *functional fixedness,* is our tendency to perceive the functions of objects as fixed and unchanging. A person may ransack the house for a screwdriver when a dime would have done the job perfectly. You may have experienced functional fixedness when you tried to solve the candle problem. If you thought of the matchbox as having only the function of holding matches, you may have overlooked its potential for serving as a platform for the candle, as shown in Figure 11–8. Indeed, perceiving and relating familiar things in new ways is an important aspect of creativity, a topic we will consider in Chapter 12, Intelligence.

MAKING DECISIONS AND FORMING JUDGMENTS

Our lives are shaped by our daily decisions—whom to date, where to go to school, what career to work toward, how to vote, where to live. Similarly, the judgments we make and the opinions we hold color our lives and lead us to seek out or avoid particular people and experiences.

If we were perfectly rational and had limitless time we might make decisions as professional gamblers often do, by weighing the value of each possible outcome after adjusting for its likelihood. Mathematically, a 50 percent chance of winning $10 has the same value as a sure $5. When making very important decisions, such as what career to prepare for or where to live, it pays to list and weigh the pros and cons systematically, perhaps using the advice offered in "Making Sound Decisions." But for most decisions that takes too long.

Using and Misusing Heuristics   When making each day's hundreds of tiny judgments and decisions—Is it worth the bother to take an umbrella? Can I trust this person? Shall I shoot the basketball or pass to the player who's hot?—we seldom pause to reason systematically. Usually, we follow our intuition. After interviewing policymakers in government, business, and education, social psychologist Irving Janis (1986) concluded that they "often do not use a reflective problem-solving approach. How do they usually arrive at their decisions? If you ask, they are likely to tell you . . . they do it mostly by the *seat of their pants.*"

Although heuristics often enable us to make reasonable seat-of-the-pants judgments, the price we pay for their efficiency can sometimes be costly bad judgments. To gain an idea of how heuristics determine our intuitive judgments—and how they can lead us astray—consider two heuristics identified by cognitive psychologists Amos Tversky and Daniel Kahneman (1974): the *representativeness heuristic* and the *availability heuristic.*

The Representativeness Heuristic   To judge the likelihood of things in terms of how well they represent particular prototypes is to use the *representativeness heuristic.* To illustrate, answer the question below:

> A stranger tells you about a person who is short, slim, and likes to read poetry, and then asks you to guess whether this person is more likely to be a professor of classics at an Ivy League university or a truck driver. Which would be the better guess? (Adapted from Nisbett & Ross, 1980.)

If you are like most people, you answered a professor because the description seems more *representative* of the typical Ivy League scholar than of a truck driver. The representativeness heuristic enabled you to make a snap judgment. But it ignores other relevant information, such

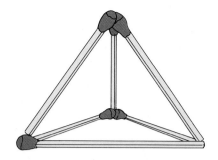

Figure 11–6   Solving the matchstick problem requires breaking a fixation, that of limiting your considerations to two-dimensional solutions. (From "Problem solving" by M. Scheerer. Copyright © 1963 by Scientific American, Inc. All rights reserved.)

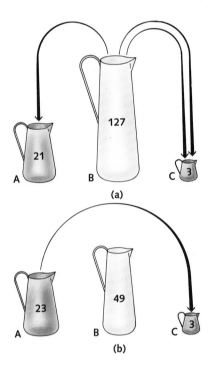

Figure 11–7   (a) The solution to all the three-jug problems is: B − A − 2C = desired volume of water. (b) But simpler solutions exist for problems 6 and 7, such as A − C for problem 6. Did you miss it? (From Luchins, 1946.)

"The information-processing shortcuts—called heuristics—which are normally both highly efficient and immensely time-saving in day-to-day situations, work systematically against us in the marketplace. . . . The tendency to underestimate or altogether ignore past probabilities in making a decision is undoubtedly the most significant problem of intuitive predictions."

David Dreman,
Contrarian Investment Strategy: The Psychology of Stock Market Success, 1979

as the total number of classics professors and truck drivers. When I help people think through this question, their own reasoning usually leads them to an answer that contradicts their immediate intuition. The typical conversation goes something like this:

Question: First, let's figure out how many professors fit the description. How many Ivy League universities do you suppose there are?

Answer: Oh, about ten, I suppose.

Question: How many classics professors would you guess there are at each?

Answer: Maybe four.

Question: Okay, that's forty Ivy League classics professors. What fraction of these are short and slim?

Answer: Let's say half.

Question: And, of these twenty, how many like to read poetry?

Answer: I'd say half—ten professors.

Question: Okay, now let's figure how many truck drivers fit the description. How many truck drivers do you suppose there are?

Answer: Maybe 400,000.

Question: What fraction are short and slim?

Answer: Not many—perhaps 1 in 8.

Question: Of these 50,000, what percent like to read poetry?

Answer: Truck drivers who like poetry? Maybe 1 in 100—oh, oh, I can see where this is going—that leaves me with 500 short, slim, poetry-reading truck drivers.

Question: Yup. So we see that though the person I described may be much more representative of classics professors than of truck drivers, this person is still (even accepting your stereotypes) fifty times more likely to be a truck driver.

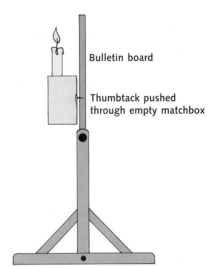

Figure 11–8   Solving the candle-mounting problem requires recognizing that a box need not always serve as a container. (From Duncker, 1945.)

MAKING SOUND DECISIONS

Psychologists Daniel Wheeler and Irving Janis (1980) studied how people arrive at good and bad decisions and devised a system for making a wise decision when faced with a challenge. They recommend five steps:

1. *Accept the challenge.* If the opportunity or the problem is genuine, do not ignore it, do not rationalize ("It can't happen to me"), do not procrastinate ("I'll deal with it later"), do not buckpass ("Let George do it"), and do not panic.

2. *Search for alternatives.* Specify your goals and think up ways to achieve them.

3. *Evaluate the alternatives.* For each reasonable alternative, fill out a balance sheet, such as the one in Figure 11–9. List positive and negative considerations in several categories. Wheeler and Janis reported that people who do so tend later to express fewer regrets and to remain more strongly committed to their choice.

4. *Make a commitment.* Choose the alternative that gives you maximum benefits at minimum costs.

5. *Adhere to the decision.* Anticipate likely difficulties and prepare to deal with them. Assess the consequences and begin the next decision cycle, by accepting the challenge of new problems and opportunities.

Benefits	Costs
1. Gains for self:	1. Losses for self:
2. Gains for others:	2. Losses for others:
3. Self-approval:	3. Self-disapproval:
4. Social approval:	4. Social disapproval:

Figure 11–9   Wheeler and Janis's balance sheet for decision making. Filling in the boxes helps people to think through important decisions and thus to evaluate alternatives more logically.

To sense the power of the representativeness heuristic consider Tversky and Kahneman's (1983) demonstration of the "conjunction fallacy." College students were told that "Bill is 34 years old. He is intelligent but unimaginative, compulsive, and generally lifeless. In school, he was strong in mathematics but weak in social studies and humanities." Based on this description, the students judged that there was virtually no chance that "Bill plays jazz for a hobby." But 87 percent thought there was a somewhat better chance that "Bill is an accountant who plays jazz for a hobby" (because Bill seemed more representative of accountants). If that seems logical, think about it—is there a better chance that Bill *both* plays jazz *and* is an accountant than that he plays jazz alone?

These examples all point to the power of the representativeness heuristic. To judge the likelihood of something, we intuitively compare it to our mental representation of a prototype of that category—of, say, what a truck driver or an accountant is like. If the two match, then that fact usually overrides other considerations of statistics or logic.

The Availability Heuristic   A similar vulnerability to error stems from our use of the *availability heuristic,* which operates when we base our judgments on the availability of information in our memories (Hastie & Park, 1986). If instances of an event are easily available—if they come to mind readily—we tend to presume that such an event is commonplace. Usually it is—but not always. To see this, guess—or ask someone else to guess—whether the letter "k" appears more often as the first letter of words or as the third letter.

Because words beginning with "k" come to mind more easily than words having "k" as their third letter, most people guess that "k" occurs more frequently as the first letter. Actually, "k" is three times more likely to appear as the third letter. So far in this chapter, words such as "know," "kingdoms," and "kin" are outnumbered more than 2 to 1 by words such as "make," "likely," "asked," and "acknowledged."

The judgmental errors influenced by the availability heuristic are frequently harmless, but sometimes they are not. Many important decisions involve judgments of risk. The decision whether to produce energy with nuclear power or by burning coal depends in part on our judgments of the associated risks. Our support for, or opposition to, spending tax dollars on social services is influenced by our judgment of the risk of welfare fraud. Our efforts to prevent various deadly diseases depend on our judgments of the likelihood of their occurrence. Our choice to spend or not to spend money on state lotteries (which return in prizes only about half of each dollar bet) depends on our hunch of the odds of striking it rich (which actually are not much better than the odds of being struck by lightning).

Those who sell life, health, and theft insurance sometimes exploit our tendency to believe that events are more likely if we can readily picture them (Cialdini & Carpenter, 1981). By having people imagine their families in mourning, their cars totaled, or their possessions stolen, sellers of insurance may cause the images of these disasters to linger, making them seem more likely to occur and therefore to be worth insuring against. In one experiment, Larry Gregory and his co-researchers (1982) gave some Arizona residents promotional information about cable TV; other residents were asked to picture themselves enjoying movies on cable TV instead of spending money on babysitters and gas. The latter group, who had pictured themselves with cable TV and therefore had readily available images of themselves as subscribers, were more than twice as likely later to subscribe.

"In creating these problems, we didn't set out to fool people. All our problems fooled us, too."
Amos Tversky (1985)

"Numerous studies show that people (including experts) have great difficulty judging probabilities, making predictions, and otherwise attempting to cope with uncertainty. Frequently these difficulties can be traced to the use of judgmental heuristics, which serve as general strategies for simplifying complex tasks."
Cognitive psychologists Paul Slovic, Baruch Fischoff, and Sarah Lichtenstein (1985)

PERCEIVING RISK: WHEN STATISTICAL REALITY CLASHES WITH THE AVAILABILITY HEURISTIC

Vivid events tend to be more available to memory, and thus seem more common than they are.

With horrific television and magazine images of air crashes in mind, many people, petrified of air travel, prefer the safety of their own cars. However, the statistical reality is that, mile for mile, we are ten times more at risk of death in a car than on a commercial flight. A fully loaded passenger jet would have to crash every day, killing all its passengers, to equal the 46,000 Americans who die in auto accidents each year. During 1986 and 1987, for example, only five scheduled flights out of 13 million—that's one flight in every 2.6 million—involved an accident that caused anyone's death (Hebert, 1988). Still, when this statistical reality is pitted against vivid images of helpless crash victims, many people find the memorable instances more persuasive.

If you think such irrationality frustrates the airlines, imagine how the European tourist industry must have felt when in 1986 a handful of dramatic terrorist incidents persuaded millions of North Americans that their lives would be more endangered by visiting Europe than by staying home and driving their highways. The same fearful public that cancels flights to Britain when a would-be passenger is apprehended with a bomb in her bag continues to drive without seatbelts, smoke billions of cigarettes a year, guzzle alcohol, and wolf down foods that put us at risk for the greatest of killers—heart disease. All because people's *perceptions* of risk are virtually unrelated to actual risk (Slovic, 1987)—a phenomenon due partly to our greater fear of things we cannot control and partly to our overestimating the likelihood of dreaded, publicized, and therefore cognitively available events.

The availability heuristic can also affect our social judgments. In one study (Hamill & others, 1980), people were presented with a single, vivid case of the misuse of welfare. The case involved a long-term welfare recipient, a woman who had a number of unruly children fathered by different men. The statistical fact is that this case was an exception; most Americans who receive welfare do so for 4 years or less (Duncan & others, 1988). Yet when the statistical reality was pitted against the single vivid case, the case proved more memorable and persuasive.

Likewise, in choosing courses, students have been found to be more influenced by two or three in-person testimonials about a course than by the statistically summarized evaluations of a large number of students (Borgida & Nisbett, 1977). An anecdote, it seems, is worth a thousand factual statistics.

Overconfidence Our use of quick and easy heuristics when forming judgments and our bias toward seeking confirmation rather than refutation of our ideas can give rise to the *overconfidence phenomenon,* an overestimation of the accuracy of our current knowledge.

Kahneman and Tversky (1979) asked people factual questions, suggesting that they provide a wide enough estimated range of answers to surely include the actual answer. For example, "I feel 98 percent certain that the number of nuclear power plants operating in the

"The human understanding is most excited by that which strikes and enters the mind at once and suddenly, and by which the imagination is immediately filled and inflated. It then begins almost imperceptibly to conceive and suppose that everything is similar to the few objects which have taken possession of the mind."
Francis Bacon,
Novum Organum, 1620

world in 1980 was more than ____ but fewer than ____." Nearly a third of the time people's estimates made with "98 percent" confidence failed to include the correct answer (189 nuclear power plants in this instance). This finding suggests that we often underestimate our susceptibility to error.

Similarly, people are more confident than correct when answering such questions as "Is absinthe a liqueur or a precious stone?" On questions where people's answers are only 60 percent correct, they will typically feel 75 percent confident. (In case you are wondering, absinthe is a licorice-flavored liqueur.) Even when people feel 100 percent certain of an answer, they err about 15 percent of the time (Fischhoff & others, 1977).

The human tendency to feel overconfident is commonplace in both the scientific laboratory and in everyday life. However, like other cognitive limitations we have studied so far, it has adaptive value. People's failure to appreciate their potential for error when making military, economic, or political judgments can have devastating consequences, but so can *lack* of self-confidence. People who doubt their own capacities may shrink from speaking up or making tough decisions. Moreover, when people are given prompt and clear feedback on the accuracy of their judgments—as weather forecasters are after each day's prediction—they soon learn to assess their accuracy more realistically (Fischhoff, 1982). The wisdom to know when we know a thing and when we do not is born of experience.

Framing Decisions   A further test of rationality in making decisions and forming judgments is whether the same question, posed in two different but equivalent ways, will elicit the same answer. For example, when we are told either that 10 percent will die or that 90 percent will live as a result of a particular medical treatment, the information is mathematically the same. But the effect is not. The risk seems greater when we hear that 10 percent will die. This effect of the way an issue is posed is known as *framing*.

Kahneman and Tversky (1984) explored the effects of framing by setting up situations such as the following:

> Imagine that the United States is preparing for the outbreak of a rare flu that is expected to kill 600 people. Two alternative programs to combat the disease have been proposed.

They then presented one group of people with these two alternatives:

> If Program A is adopted, 200 people will be saved.

> If Program B is adopted, there is 1/3 probability that 600 people will be saved, and 2/3 probability that no people will be saved.

These people favored Program A by about 3 to 1, reasoning that it is better to save those lives that can be saved than to choose the 2/3 chance that no one will be saved.

For another group, the researchers rephrased the alternatives:

> If Program A is adopted, 400 people will die.

> If Program B is adopted, there is 1/3 probability that nobody will die, and 2/3 probability that 600 people will die.

These people favored Program B by 3 to 1, reasoning that it is better to gamble on saving everyone than to consign 400 people to certain

"What do you mean 'Your guess is as good as mine'? My guess is a hell of a lot better *than your guess!"*

"When you know a thing, to hold that you know it; and when you do not know a thing, to allow that you do not know it; this is knowledge."
   Confucius, 551–479 B.C.
   Analects

death. The general rule seems to be that our first priority is to avoid losses. Thus alternatives framed as a possible gain (200 people will be saved) are more attractive than when framed as a possible loss (400 people will die).

Similarly, consumers respond more positively to ground beef described as "75 percent lean" rather than "25 percent fat" (Levin, 1987). A new medical treatment strikes people as more successful and recommendable if described as having a "50 percent success rate" rather than a "50 percent failure rate" (Levin & others, 1988). If our dentist offers a 5 percent discount for immediate cash payment, we do not feel particularly unhappy if we have to pay the full fee when making a late payment. But we would probably feel irritated if the same fee were framed differently—say, if the basic fee were to be lowered 5 percent and an equivalent surcharge on this were to be added for late payment. Somehow a "surcharge" is more irritating than a forfeited "discount," even though they add up to the same thing. And people who say they would drive to another store to save $5 on a pocket calculator typically say they would not do so to save $5 on a $200 stereo. Thus, the way a $5 saving is framed can affect the way we react.

The fact that people's judgments flip-flop so dramatically, even on problems involving life and death, is scary. It suggests that our judgments and the decisions based on them may not be well reasoned, and that those who understand the power of framing can use it to influence our decisions.

REASONING

In order to solve problems, make decisions, and form judgments, we must reason. How, and how well, do we do so? Let us consider the ways humans reason, and some reasons for unreason.

Our beliefs have a tremendous impact on our reasoning. In both science and everyday experience, our beliefs operate like a telescope that selectively brings certain parts of the world into view. Thus, beliefs can powerfully affect what we notice, how we interpret what we notice, and what we remember. In an earlier chapter we noted how our perceptual set can affect what we "see"—a floating log or the Loch Ness monster. We also saw that believers in paranormal phenomena tend to notice and remember incidents that support their beliefs—a dream that comes true, perhaps—and to ignore and forget incidents that refute them—all those dreams that do not come true. Fixation, too, constrains our thinking about a problem.

The Belief Perseverance Phenomenon   Indeed, a major source of irrationality in our reasoning is our tendency, called the *belief perseverance phenomenon,* to cling to our beliefs even in the face of contrary evidence. Belief perseverance often fuels social conflict. Charles Lord and his colleagues (1979) demonstrated how this can happen. They showed two groups of college students, one that favored capital punishment and one that opposed it, two purportedly new research studies. One of the studies supported and the other refuted the crime-deterring effectiveness of the death penalty. Each side was impressed with the study that supported its beliefs, and disputed the study that contradicted them. Showing the two groups the *identical* body of mixed evidence therefore did not narrow their disagreement but actually *increased* it.

"Once you have a belief, it influences how you perceive all other relevant information. Once you see a country as hostile, you are likely to interpret ambiguous actions on their part as signifying their hostility."
Political scientist Robert Jervis (1985)

For those who wish to restrain the belief perseverance phenomenon, a simple remedy exists: *Consider the opposite.* When Lord and his colleagues (1984) repeated the capital punishment study, they added a couple of variations. They asked some of their subjects to be "as *objective* and *unbiased* as possible." The people who received this plea turned out to be every bit as biased in their evaluation of the evidence as those who did not. A third group, however, was asked to consider the opposite—to ask themselves "whether you would have made the same high or low evaluations had exactly the same study produced results on the *other* side of the issue." Having considered the possibility of opposite findings, these people were much less likely to be biased in their evaluations of the evidence.

If ambiguous evidence gets interpreted as supporting a person's preexisting belief, would the belief be demolished by information that clearly discredits its premises? Not necessarily. In some provocative experiments, Craig Anderson and Lee Ross discovered that it can be surprisingly difficult to change a false belief once a person has in mind some ideas in support of it. In one such study with Mark Lepper (1980), they asked people to consider whether risk-prone people or cautious people are better fire fighters. Half of the subjects were shown a case about a risk-taker who was an excellent fire fighter and a case about a cautious person who was a poor fire fighter. From these cases, the subjects surmised that risk-prone people tend to be better fire fighters. When they were asked to explain their belief, a typical response was, "Risk-takers are braver." The other subjects were shown two cases suggesting the opposite conclusion, that cautious people are better fire fighters. They typically reasoned, "Cautious people think before they act, and so are less likely to make foolish mistakes."

The researchers then totally discredited the foundation for the beliefs of both groups by truthfully informing them that the cases were simply made up for the experiment. Did this discrediting of the evidence undermine the subjects' newly formed beliefs? Not by much, because the subjects held on to their explanations for *why* these new beliefs made sense.

Paradoxically, then, the more we come to appreciate why our beliefs *might* be true, the more tightly we cling to them. Once people have explained to themselves why they believe that a child is "gifted" or "learning disabled," that presidential candidate X or Y will be more likely to preserve peace or start a war, or that women are naturally superior or inferior, they tend to ignore evidence that undermines that belief.

Even beliefs about ourselves resist discrediting. Lepper and Ross (with Richard Lau, 1986) demonstrated this by showing California high school students either an effective or a confusing instructional film that taught them how to solve some reasoning problems. Those shown the effective film did well on a subsequent test and felt successful; those shown the useless film did poorly and felt like failures. Apparently, the success or failure triggered recollections of previous successes or failures, which seemed to explain their apparent high or low aptitude at the problem solving. For even when the researchers explained that the confusing film was responsible for their success or failure and showed them the other film as evidence, the students persisted in seeing themselves as either smart or incompetent at that particular type of reasoning problem.

And that, say the researchers, helps explain why early school failures can be so damaging: Even a clear demonstration to children that their poor school performance "may well have been the consequence

Do risk-prone or cautious people make better fire fighters? Once we have been persuaded to have an opinion on such a question and can cite some reasons for our view, we are likely to be reluctant to change it, even if shown that the information on which we formed the opinion is invalid.

"To begin with, it was only tentatively that I put forward the views I have developed . . . but in the course of time they have gained such a hold upon me that I can no longer think in any other way."
Sigmund Freud,
Civilization and Its Discontents, 1930

To prevent subjects from leaving the experiment feeling incompetent, the researchers extensively debriefed and reassured them regarding their competence.

of an inept or biased teacher, a substandard school, or even prior social, cultural, or economic disadvantages" may fail to dent their feelings of incompetence.

The phenomenon of belief perseverance does not mean that people never change their beliefs. Rather, once beliefs are formed and justified, it generally takes more compelling evidence to change them than it did to create them.

Deductive and Inductive Reasoning   We have seen that part of the new thinking about thinking emphasizes our susceptibility to bias. We search for information that can support our hunches (confirmation bias), and we cling to our beliefs even when confronted with mixed evidence or discrediting information (belief perseverance). By reasoning with the tools of logic, can we escape the effects of our beliefs on our reasoning? Let us see.

In *deductive reasoning,* we work "top down"—from the general to the specific. We begin with assumptions that we know or believe to be true and then use them to arrive at particular conclusions. An example: We know as a general truth that all cats meow. We are therefore justified in concluding that Cinder, a cat we do not know, will meow. If the assumptions we begin with are indeed true and if our reasoning is valid, then our conclusions must be true. Mathematics, philosophy, some forms of theology, and law often involve deductive reasoning.

In *inductive reasoning,* we work from the specific to the general. We arrive at a conclusion based on our observations. Inductive reasoning works "bottom up," by *generalizing from specific instances.* For example, if every cat we have ever seen meows, then we can reasonably conclude that Cinder, our friend's new cat, will meow, too. Another instance: The professional football scout sees the quarterback throw six incomplete passes in a row and infers (inductively generalizes) "he's not much of a passer."

Although the deductive/inductive distinction is a tricky one for many students, it really is simple: *deduction* is reasoning downward from the general premise to the specific conclusion; *induction* is reasoning upward from specific instances to the general conclusion. Many thinking tasks involve both types of reasoning. The skills involved in playing chess include a well-practiced ability to reason deductively (from the rules of the game) and inductively (generalizing from past experiences).

Formal Deductive Reasoning   In philosophy, the **syllogism**—an argument in which two or more presumably true statements, called premises, lead to a final statement, the conclusion—is the basis of formal deductive reasoning. Consider the following syllogism:

> All humans are mortal.
> Socrates is human.
> Socrates is mortal.

You can easily see that the conclusion logically follows from the premises.

In philosophy, the task is to assume the premises are true and then to reason from them. In life, however, our preexisting knowledge and beliefs may interfere with our ability to form valid premises and to reach logical conclusions from them. For example, take a look at the following syllogism (adapted from Hunt, 1982a):

> Those who believe in democracy believe in free speech.
> Communists do not believe in democracy.
> Therefore, communists do not believe in free speech.

"I'm happy to say that my final judgment of a case is almost always consistent with my prejudgment of the case."

Deduction: hypothesis → observations
Induction: observations → hypothesis

The skills involved in playing chess include a well-practiced ability to reason deductively (from the rules of the game) and inductively (generalizing from past experience).

Does the conclusion sound logical? If so, consider another syllogism with the same form and logic:

> Robins have feathers.
> Chickens are not robins.
> Therefore, chickens do not have feathers.

In both cases, the reasoning is invalid; the conclusion does not follow from the premises (A is B; X is not A; faulty conclusion: therefore X is not B).

But faulty logic is not the only source of error. Try this syllogism:

> Whatever makes for full employment is socially beneficial.
> War makes for full employment.
> Therefore, war is socially beneficial.

In this case, the conclusion does logically follow from the premises (Any A is B; X is A; therefore X is B). Here what is wrong is not the reasoning but the *false assumption* of the first premise. Thus error can reside either within the premises or the reasoning.

The syllogisms we have just examined illustrate some of the ways our knowledge and beliefs can bias our reasoning. We tend to accept as logical those conclusions that agree with our opinions, such as the idea that communism restricts freedom. But we have a harder time accepting conclusions that run counter to our opinions, such as the idea that war is beneficial.

IN DEFENSE OF OUR THINKING ABILITIES

We have seen how our irrationality, our lapses in logic, can plague our attempts at solving problems, making wise decisions, forming valid judgments, and even reasoning correctly. For this we might be tempted to conclude that our heads are indeed filled with straw. All in all, the findings we have reviewed—and many more that we have not—suggest "bleak implications for human rationality" (Nisbett & Borgida, 1975). What then can we say in defense of our reasoning abilities? How do we generally cope so well? After all, our cognitive abilities are efficient and effective enough to enable us to survive and have some control over our environment.

One reason we function as well as we do is that in many real-life situations, flawed reasoning may nevertheless lead to correct conclusions (Funder, 1987). For example, despite the fact that we arrived at our conclusion illogically, it was correct: Communist countries have restricted free speech.

Another reason we thrive despite flaws in our logic is that we can usually tolerate some inconsistency and uncertainty in our reasoning in exchange for the utility and efficiency of quick, plausible intuitive judgments. Physicians, for example, recognize the similarity between a patient's symptoms and those typical of a particular disease and then proceed to check out their hunch. In effect, their reasoning goes like this (Hunt, M., 1982):

> Disease X is indicated by symptoms A, B, and C.
> This patient has symptoms A, B, and C.
> Therefore, I presume this patient has disease X.

The physician's conclusion may not be accurate. (Other diseases may also have symptoms A, B, and C.) Yet it is efficient and plausible, perhaps even probable. We reason, then, not so much by rigorous logic as by simplified, speedy heuristics, such as, "This situation reminds me of situations I have faced before, so what was true in those situa-

An example of flawed reasoning attributed to Abbott and Costello:
Question: Why is a loaf of bread the mother of airplanes?
Answer: A loaf of bread is a necessity. Airplanes are an invention. Necessity is the mother of invention. Therefore, a loaf of bread is the mother of airplanes.

tions should be true here." Experts in fields other than medicine—even avid racetrack bettors who intuitively calculate the odds on horses (Ceci & Liker, 1986)—are similarly shrewd without necessarily knowing exactly how they reason.

Still, we should not underestimate the importance of sound reasoning. When engaged in such pursuits as deriving scientific hypotheses, playing chess, or debating political issues, it helps to have the powers of reason at our disposal. This is why one of the most important aspects of a college education is learning how to think logically and critically. It is also why psychologists study obstacles to problem solving and biases in reasoning. By learning about our irrational tendencies, we hope to discover how we might learn to reason more logically. We can solve arithmetic problems efficiently *and* rationally because we have been taught to do so. Perhaps we could also teach people how to think through other sorts of problems more efficiently *and* rationally. This is one of the goals of this book's appendix, which explains common flaws in people's statistical intuition and suggests some correctives.

ARTIFICIAL INTELLIGENCE

A tribute to human cognitive powers comes from attempts to simulate human thinking on computers. *Artificial intelligence (AI)* is the science of making computers perform operations that appear intelligent. A hybrid of cognitive psychology and computer science, AI has moved in two directions, one practical, the other theoretical. Thanks to a massive amount of stored information and rules for retrieving it, the practical side of AI has given us chess programs that can beat all but the masters, industrial robots that can sense their environment, and "expert systems" that can carry out chemical analyses, offer tax planning advice, forecast weather, and help physicians diagnose their patients' diseases. The theoretical efforts, pioneered by psychologist Herbert Simon, study how humans think by attempting to make computers mimic or rival human thought processes. The goal is a "unified theory of cognition" embodied in a computer program that can process information, solve problems, learn from experience, and remember much as humans do (Waldrop, 1988).

Artificial intelligence. (a) Expert systems, such as this medical system (dubbed HELP), track patient data and suggest possible diagnoses and treatments. (b) Industrial robots designed to perform routine but often dangerous industrial tasks illustrate another use of artificial intelligence.

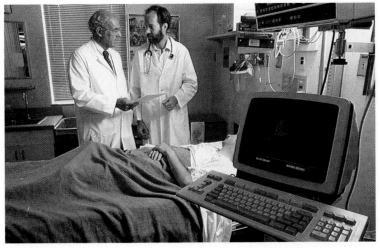

(a)

(b)

Simon's basic assumption is not that the mind is a computer or that computers have minds but rather, that both are information processors. (Recall our memory model in the preceding chapter.) Both receive information from the environment: the computer via keyboards, disks, or tapes; our minds via our senses. Both store this information, retrieve it as needed, and manipulate it in order to perform specific tasks. Both express the results of their information processing as output: The computer displays it on a screen or in a printout; we talk and write. Thus, the issue in artificial intelligence is not whether machines can think, but rather how skillfully can computer programs process information?

Computers can be programmed to use heuristics, which are in large part responsible for our own cognitive efficiency. For instance, a computer programmed to simulate how a human might solve anagrams—remember the CINERAMA puzzle—can be instructed not to consider letter combinations that begin with, say, "nc" or "rc" because English words never start with these letters. Programming a computer to use human problem-solving strategies forces the programmer to be extremely precise. If there is any vagueness included in the steps or if any necessary step is left out, the program will fail.

Can computers mimic our thinking powers? In those areas where humans seem to have the most difficulty—manipulating huge amounts of numerical data or retrieving specific detailed facts from memory—the computer shines. Indeed, such proficiencies have made computers indispensable to banks, libraries, and the space program. Nevertheless, sophisticated computers are dwarfed by the most ordinary of human mental abilities—recognizing a face, distinguishing a cat from a dog, knowing whether the word "line" refers to a rope or a fragment of poetry or a social come-on, and exercising common sense. Moreover, notes Donald Griffin (1984), "Human minds do more than process information; they think and feel. We experience beliefs, desires, fears, expectations, and many other subjective mental states."

Compare also the computer's modes of operation with the brain's. Electricity races through the computer's microchips millions of times faster than our neurons can transmit information. Yet most computers process information serially—one step at a time. Serial processing can be likened to a society in which work can be done only by one person at a time. By contrast, the human brain can process millions of different bits of information simultaneously, a process called parallel processing. One part of the brain is analyzing speech while other parts are recognizing pictures, detecting smells, or planning action. Even within the visual system, information about color, depth, movement, and form are processed in parallel, before being reassembled into the recognized image. Here, too, the brain outclasses the computer. The hope for artificial intelligence therefore lies in a new generation of computers that functions more like the brain's neural networks, by simultaneously processing multiple operations (Fox & Messina, 1987; Kurzweil, 1985; Rumelhart & others, 1986). Thus, while the computer provides a useful but simplified model of how the brain works, more and more the brain is providing a model of how, in the future, computers might work.

Computers provide us with an amazing but narrowly focused intelligence. Their abilities exceed our own at tasks that use their unique strengths such as vast memory and precise logic. But they are far from duplicating the wide-ranging intelligence of a human mind, a mind that can *all at once* converse naturally, perceive the environment, use common sense, experience emotion, and consciously reflect on its own existence.

Imagine a relatively simple task—instructing a computer to discern the difference between these two ads (from Schnitzer, 1984):

1. Car for sale. A classic! Lemon yellow coupe. Exterior is completely rust-proof. Can be delivered upon request. No engine runs better. If the sun is out, you can remove the roof for the feel of the wind in your hair. Go ahead and kick the tires.
2. Car for sale. A classic lemon. Yellow coupe exterior is completely rust. Proof can be delivered upon request! No engine. Runs better if the sun is out. You can remove the roof. For the feel of the wind in your hair, go ahead and kick the tires.

"The things that distinguish us from monkeys—playing chess, for example—are easy for computers to do. But when it comes to doing things we share with the animal kingdom, computers are awful. In computing vision or movement, for example, no computer comes even close to matching the abilities of a fly."

Brain researcher Christof Koch (1988)

LANGUAGE

Perhaps the most tangible indication of the power of human thinking, and definitely one of our species' greatest achievements, is *language*—our words and how we combine them to communicate. Humans have long and proudly proclaimed that language sets us above all other animals. ''When we study human language,'' asserted linguist Noam Chomsky (1972), ''we are approaching what some might call the 'human essence,' the distinctive qualities of mind that are, so far as we know, unique'' to humans. Whether spoken, written, or signed, language enables us to communicate complex ideas from person to person and to transmit civilization's accumulated knowledge from generation to generation.

Language makes possible the oral tradition that transmits cultural knowledge and lore from generation to generation.

LANGUAGE STRUCTURE

Consider how we might go about inventing a language. First, we would need a set of basic sounds, which linguists call *phonemes.* For instance, the ''b,'' ''a,'' and ''t'' sounds that we put together to say the word ''bat'' are all phonemes. So are the ''ch'' sound in ''chat'' and the ''th'' sound in ''that.'' Different languages have different numbers of phonemes. English has about forty; other languages have anywhere from half to twice that many.

Changes in phonemes produce changes in meaning. For example, variations in the vowel sound between a ''b'' and a ''t'' can create eleven different meanings: bat, beat, bit, bait, bet, bite, boot, but, boat, bought, and bout (Fromkin & Rodman, 1983). Generally, though, consonant phonemes carry more information than do vowel phonemes. The treth ef thes stetement shed be evedent frem thes bref demenstretien.

People who grow up learning one set of phonemes usually have difficulty pronouncing the phonemes of another language. Thus, the native English speaker may smile at the native German speaker's difficulties with the ''th'' sound, which often makes ''this'' sound like ''dis.'' But the German speaker can smile in turn at the problems English speakers have rolling the German ''r'' or pronouncing the breathy ''ch'' in ''*Ich,*'' the German word for ''I.''

The next building block of our language is the *morpheme,* which is the smallest unit of speech that carries meaning. In English, a very few morphemes are also phonemes—the personal pronoun "I" and the article "a," for instance—but most are combinations of two or more phonemes. "Bat" is a morpheme made up of the phonemes "b," "a," and "t." Some morphemes are words, but others are only parts of words. Morphemes include prefixes and suffixes, such as the "pro" in "proactive" or the "-ed" that shows past tense. The word "undesirables," for example, has four morphemes—"un," "desire," "able," and "s"—each of which adds to the total meaning of the word.

Finally, our new language must have a *grammar,* a system of rules that enables us to use our language to speak to and understand others. Two important aspects of grammar are *semantics* and *syntax.* **Semantics** refers to the system of rules we use to derive meaning from morphemes, words, and even sentences. A semantic rule tells us that adding "-ed" to "laugh" means that it happened in the past. **Syntax** is the system of rules we use to string words together into proper sentences. For example, one of the rules of English syntax says that adjectives usually come before nouns, so we say "white house." In Spanish, the rule is different; adjectives usually come after nouns, so a Spanish speaker says *"casa blanca."* The English rules of syntax tell us that the sentence "They are hunting dogs" is proper. And, given the context in which the sentence was spoken, semantics tells us whether it refers to people who are looking for some dogs or to dogs that are looking for animals.

Note that language becomes more complex at each succeeding level. In English, the relatively small number of forty or so phonemes can be combined to form more than 100,000 morphemes, which alone or in combination can give us almost half a million words. These words can then be used to create an infinite number of sentences, most of which, like this one, are original. Like the brain that conceives it, language is complexity built of simplicity.

How many morphemes are in the word "cats"? (See page 304.)

LANGUAGE DEVELOPMENT

Make a quick guess: How many words did you learn in one average day during the years between your first birthday and your high school graduation?

The average high school graduate knows some 80,000 words (Miller & Gildea, 1987)—one-quarter the number in the latest Random House unabridged dictionary. That averages to more than 5000 words learned a year, 13 a day, and children with unusually large vocabularies may have picked up words at twice that rate.

How you did it—how the over 5000 words a year you learned could so far outnumber the roughly 200 words a year that your school-teachers consciously taught you—is one of the great wonders of human development. Before children can add two plus two they are creating their own original and grammatically appropriate sentences. Most parents would have trouble stating the rules by which we create and combine words. Yet their preschoolers comprehend and speak with a facility that puts to shame a college student struggling to learn a foreign language or a scientist struggling to simulate natural language on a computer. How does our astonishing facility for language unfold, and how can we explain it?

Although you probably know more than 100,000 words, you use only 150 words for about half of what you say.

Preschoolers have an astonishing capacity to soak up new words and combine them in grammatically sensible sentences.

Describing Language Development   The way a child's language develops mirrors our conception of how language itself is constructed—by moving from simplicity to complexity. By 4 months of age, babies can read lips and discriminate speech sounds. From their preferring to look at a face that matches a sound, we know they can recognize that "ah" comes from wide open lips and "ee" from a mouth with corners pulled back (Kuhl & Meltzoff, 1982). Beginning around the same time, babies enter a *babbling stage,* in which they spontaneously utter a variety of sounds such as "ah-goo." Babbling is not the imitation of adult speech, for it includes phonemes of various languages, even phonemes that do not occur in the language of the household. From this early babbling, a listener could not identify an infant as being, say, French, Korean, or Ethiopian. Deaf infants babble, too, although they obviously are not imitating speech they have heard (Fromkin & Rodman, 1983). Apparently, their playful babble is preprogrammed into the brain.

Babbling, however, soon comes to resemble the characteristic sounds and intonations of the household language. By 10 months of age, the language of an infant's babbling will be identifiable. Phonemes foreign to the infant's native tongue will have begun to disappear.

About the time of the first birthday (the exact age varies from child to child), most children enter the *one-word stage.* Having already learned that sounds can be linked with meanings, they begin to use sounds to communicate meaning. Their first words usually contain but one syllable—"ma" or "da," for instance—and may be barely recognizable. But family members quickly learn to understand the infant's language, and gradually the infant's language conforms more and more to the family's.

Most of the child's first words refer to things that move or can be played with—things such as a ball or a dog, rather than the table or crib that just sits there (Nelson, 1973). At this one-word stage, a word may equal a sentence. "Doggy!" may mean "Look at the dog out there!"

Although some children *begin* speaking in phrases rather than words (Nelson, 1981), most children accumulate more and more single words during the second year, until finally, by about their second birthday, they rather abruptly start uttering two-word sentences. This *two-word stage* exemplifies *telegraphic speech,* because, like telegrams (TERMS ACCEPTED. SEND MONEY), it contains mostly nouns and verbs ("Want juice"). Also like telegrams, there is already syntax; the words are in a sensible order. The English-speaking child will typically say adjectives before nouns—"big doggie" rather than "doggie big."

There seems to be no "three-word stage." Once children move out of the two-word stage, they quickly begin uttering three, four, five, or even more words together (Fromkin & Rodman, 1983). Although the sentences may still sound like a Western Union message, they continue to follow the rules of syntax ("Mommy get ball"). By early elementary school the child understands complex sentences and is beginning to enjoy the humor conveyed by double meanings: "You never starve in the desert because of all the sand-which-is there."

Explaining Language Development   Those who study language acquisition inevitably wonder how we do it. The question is not an easy one to answer, and the attempts that have been made have sparked a spirited intellectual controversy. Basically, this controversy parallels the debate we noted in Chapter 9, Learning, over the behaviorist view of the malleable organism versus the view that each organism is biologically prepared to learn certain associations. The nature-nurture debate surfaces again.

According to behaviorists such as B. F. Skinner (1957), the acquisition of language can be explained by such familiar learning principles as association (of the sights of things with the sounds of words), imitation (of the words and syntax modeled by others), and reinforcement (with success, smiles, and hugs when the child says something right). Thus, the behaviorists argue, babies learn to talk in many of the same ways that animals learn to peck keys and press bars. "Verbal behavior evidently came into existence when, through a critical step in the evolution of the human species, the vocal musculature became susceptible to operant conditioning," Skinner (1985) surmises.

Linguist Noam Chomsky (1959, 1987) sees the behaviorist view of language learning as simplistic and naïve. Surely, says Chomsky, a Martian scientist observing children in a single language community would conclude that language is almost entirely inborn. It isn't, because children do learn the language of their environment. But the rate at which they acquire words and grammar without being taught is too extraordinary to be explained solely by learning principles. Children create all sorts of sentences they have never heard before and therefore could not be imitating. Moreover, many of their errors result from the application of logical grammatical rules. The child who says, "She swimmed across the pool," is overgeneralizing the grammatical rule that says the past tense is normally formed by adding "-ed" to the verb.

Chomsky (1987) likens the behaviorist view of how language develops to filling a bottle with water, and his own to "helping a flower to grow in its own way." Language development, he believes, is akin to sexual maturation—it just "happens to the child." Thanks to their inborn "universal grammar," children are predisposed to learn the grammar of any human language to which they are exposed. Other worlds may have languages that, for us humans, are unlearnable, but not our

Answer to question on page 302: Two—"cat" and "-s."

Drawing by Glenn Bernhardt.

"No, Timmy, not 'I sawed the chair.' It's 'I saw the chair' or 'I have seen the chair.'"

world. Chomsky maintains that we come equipped with a language acquisition capacity that is like a box with grammatical switches which are thrown as children hear their language spoken. Thus, English-speaking children learn to put the object of a sentence last ("John ate an apple"). Japanese-speaking children put the object before the verb ("John an apple ate").

Much as flowers are stunted if not nourished, so children isolated from language during the critical period for its acquisition become linguistically stunted. Consider Genie, who spent most of her early years tied to a chair without being spoken to. When she was discovered by Los Angeles authorities, she was mute and uncomprehending (Curtiss, 1977, 1981). Genie has since learned some individual words but still cannot construct grammatically correct sentences.

To summarize, children are biologically prepared to learn language as they and their caregivers interact. Skinner's emphasis on learning principles helps to explain why infants acquire their parents' language and how they add new words to their vocabularies. Chomsky's emphasis on our built-in readiness to learn grammatical rules helps explain why preschoolers acquire language so readily and use grammar so well. Once again, we see biology and experience working together.

Returning to our debate about humanity's intellectual powers, let's pause to issue a midterm report card. On reasoning, the researchers might give our error-prone species a C+. In problem solving, where humans are inventive yet vulnerable to fixation, we would probably receive better marks, perhaps a B+. On cognitive efficiency, our fallible but quick heuristics earn us an A. And when it comes to learning and using language, the awestruck experts would surely award the human species an A+.

ANIMAL LANGUAGE

If in our use of language we humans are, as the psalmist rhapsodized, "little less than God," where do other animals fit in the scheme of things? Are they "little less than human"? In part, the answer lies in the extent to which animals share our capacity for language. Without doubt, animals can communicate. But do they have language?

The Case of the Honeybee More than 2000 years ago, the Greek philosopher Aristotle observed that once a lone honeybee discovers a source of nectar, other bees soon leave the hive and go straight to the newfound food source. Aristotle surmised that the original explorer must return to the hive and lead other bees back to the food. But he was wrong. In 1901, a clever German researcher followed the explorer bee back to the hive and trapped it as it left to return to the food source. Although deprived of their guide, the new recruits still flew straight to the nectar.

How did the bees know where to go? This question intrigued Austrian biologist Karl von Frisch (1950), so he undertook some experiments in the 1940s for which he ultimately won the Nobel prize. The experiments revealed that the explorer bee communicates with the other worker bees by means of an intricate dance. The direction and duration of the dance, von Frisch discovered, informs other bees of the direction and distance of the food source (see Figure 11–10).

Impressive as it is, the dance of the honeybee hardly challenges the complexity, flexibility, and power of human language. The honeybee communicates, but not with the semantics or syntax of language.

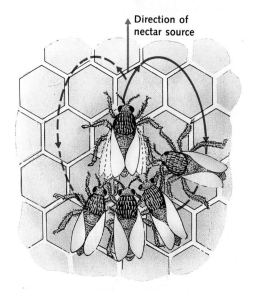

Figure 11–10 The dance of the honeybee. The straight-line part of the dance points in the direction of a nectar source relative to the sun, and its duration indicates the distance. The other bees, who cannot see the dance in the dark hive, huddle close in order to feel what is going on. (From von Frisch, 1974.)

The Case of the Apes   A greater challenge to humanity's claim to be the only language-using species has come from recent reports of apes that "talk" with people. Knowing that chimpanzees could not vocalize more than a few words, University of Nevada researchers Allen and Beatrice Gardner (1969) attempted to teach a chimp named Washoe sign language, as though she were a deaf human child. After 4 years, Washoe could use 132 signs. The Gardners' announcement that their efforts had succeeded aroused enormous scientific and public interest. One reporter for the *New York Times*, whose first language was sign language, which he learned from his deaf parents, visited Washoe and reported, "Suddenly I realized I was conversing with a member of another species in my native tongue."

Washoe, the first sign-language-trained chimpanzee, aroused new interest in the language capabilities of chimps.

During the 1970s, further evidence of "ape language" was even more disturbing to those who believed that the capacity for language set the human species apart from all others. Not only could apes use words, but they could also string words together to form intelligible sentences. Washoe, for instance, was quoted as signing, "You me go out, please." Apes even appeared to be capable of combining words creatively. Washoe designated a swan as a "water bird." Koko, a gorilla trained by Francine Patterson (1978) in California, reportedly described a Pinocchio doll as an "elephant baby." Lana, a chimpanzee who "talked" by punching buttons wired to a computer that translated her punchings into English, wanted her trainer's orange one day, but she had no word for orange. However, she did know her colors and the word for apple, so she improvised: "? Tim give apple which-is orange" (Rumbaugh, 1977).

As reports of the language abilities of apes accumulated, it seemed that the apes might indeed be "little less than human." Although their vocabularies and sentences were simple when compared to ours— corresponding roughly to the capacities of a typical 2-year-old child— apes did seem to share what we humans have considered our unique ability.

But Can Apes Really Talk?   By the late 1970s, the claims of "talking apes" raised a question: Were the chimps language champs or were the

Lana, another chimpanzee, has learned to "speak" by punching word symbols on a computer console in a coherent order.

researchers chumps? The ape language researchers were making monkeys out of themselves, said the skeptics. Consider some of their arguments:

The apes have acquired their limited vocabularies only with great difficulty. They can hardly be compared to children, who effortlessly soak up dozens of new words each week.

Chimps can make signs or push buttons in sequence to get a reward, but so can pigeons—by pecking a sequence of keys to get grain (Straub & others, 1979)—and no one says that the pigeon is "talking."

While apes can certainly use symbols meaningfully, the evidence is far from convincing that they can equal even a 3-year-old's ability to order words with proper syntax. To a child, "you tickle" and "tickle you" communicate different ideas, but a chimp might use the phrases interchangeably.

After training a chimp whom he named Nim Chimpsky, Herbert Terrace (1979) concluded that much of chimpanzees' signing is nothing more than their imitating their trainer's signs.

Presented with ambiguous information, people tend to see what they want or expect to see. (Recall the demonstrations of perceptual set in Chapter 7.) Interpreting chimpanzee signs as language may therefore be little more than wishful thinking on the part of their trainers, claims Terrace. When Washoe signed "water bird," she perhaps was just separately naming "water" and "bird."

"Language is a property of humans. If any other animal had a language capacity, they'd be using it. It's like thinking humans have an undiscovered capacity to fly."
Noam Chomsky (quoted by Wyman, 1983)

Washoe (observing a doll floating in her water) signed, "Baby in my drink."

"Although humans make sounds with their mouths and occasionally look at each other, there is no solid evidence that they actually communicate with each other."

In science as in politics, controversy is the stimulus for progress. The provocative claim that "apes share our capacity for language" and the skeptical rejoinder that "apes no use language" (as Washoe might have put it) have moved psychologists toward a greater appreciation of the remarkable capabilities of the apes on the one hand and of our own genius at using words on the other. Everyone agrees that humans alone possess language, if by the term we mean verbal expression of complex grammar. If we mean, more simply, the ability to communicate through a meaningful sequence of spoken or gestured symbols, then apes are capable of sign language.

Drawing by Sidney Harris.

On reflection, one of chimpanzee Lana's trainers, Duane Rumbaugh (1985, 1987), believes that it is too simplistic to ask, "Do the apes have the capacity for human language—or don't they?" Language "is very complex with many, many dimensions and facets. Our nearest living relatives have some, but not all of those parts."

Although chimpanzees do not have our facility for language, their thinking and communicating abilities continue to impress their trainers. Loulis, a foster son of Washoe, picked up 68 sign language words simply by observing Washoe and three other language-trained chimps. Moreover, Washoe, Loulis, and the others now sign spontaneously when communicating with one another. People who know sign language can eavesdrop on these chimp-to-chimp conversations with near perfect agreement about what the chimps are saying—90 percent of which pertains to social interactions, reassurances, or play (Fouts & Bodamer, 1987).

Lana's instructors have trained two other chimps, Sherman and Austin, to use computer keyboards to communicate with each other. The chimps will ask one another for a specific food (as shown in Figure 11–11) or even for a tool that can be used to obtain food (Rumbaugh & Savage-Rumbaugh, 1986). Also impressive is Savage-Rumbaugh's (1987) recent discovery that pygmy chimpanzees can learn to comprehend spoken English much as a 2-year-old does, without training. Kanzi, one such chimp, behaves intelligently whether asked, "Can you show me the light?," "Can you bring me the light [a flashlight]?," or "Can you turn the light on?"

"[Our] egocentric view that [we are] unique from all other forms of animal life is being jarred to the core."
    Duane Rumbaugh and Sue Savage-Rumbaugh (1978)

Figure 11–11   Chimpanzees using computer-mediated language. After having read Austin's computer-signaled request for bread, Sherman selects the correct food from a tray (left). He then hands the food to Austin (center) and licks his fingers (right).

So, though trained apes' small vocabularies and modest abilities to order words correctly hardly make them "little less than human," their language capacity seems far greater than we once supposed.

THINKING AND LANGUAGE

Thinking and language share this chapter because they are intricately intertwined. Asking which comes first has become one of psychology's chicken-and-egg questions. Do our ideas come first and wait for words to name them? Or are our thoughts conceived in words and unthinkable without them?

LINGUISTIC INFLUENCES ON THINKING

Linguist Benjamin Lee Whorf contended that language determines the way we think. According to Whorf's (1956) *linguistic relativity hypothesis,* different languages impose different conceptions of reality: "Language itself shapes a man's basic ideas."

Whorf's idea seldom occurs to people who speak a single language. To them, language seems only a vehicle for thought. But to those who speak two dissimilar languages, such as English and Japanese, it seems obvious that one thinks differently in different languages (R. Brown, 1986).

Some examples: English has only one word for snow, whereas the Eskimo language has a variety of terms that denote various conditions of snow and ice. This, said Whorf, allows the Eskimos to *perceive* differences in snow that would go unnoticed by people who speak English. The link can also be seen at the level of grammar. The Hopi, for instance, have no past tense for their verbs. Therefore, Whorf contended, the Hopi cannot so readily *think* about the past.

Critics of the idea that language determines thought claim that words reflect rather than create the way we think. The Eskimos' very lives depend on their ability to recognize different conditions of snow and ice, so they need different words for these conditions (as skiers do, using such terms as "sticky snow" or "powder" to describe the slopes). Just because you lack the Eskimos' rich vocabulary for describing snow does not mean that you are incapable of perceiving these differences. Likewise, people who lack our words for shapes and colors nevertheless seem to perceive them as we do (Rosch, 1974).

Although it is therefore too strong to say that language *determines* the *way* we think, our words may *influence what* we think (Hoffman & others, 1986). We therefore do well to choose our words carefully. When people refer to women as "girls"—as in "the girls at the office"—it perpetuates a view of women's lower status, does it not? Or consider the generic pronoun "he." Does it make any difference whether I write "A child learns language as *he* interacts with *his* caregivers" or "Children learn language as *they* interact with *their* caregivers"? Some argue that it makes no difference because every reader knows that "the masculine gender shall be deemed and taken to include females" (as the British Parliament declared in 1850).

But is the generic "he" always taken to include females? Several researchers have concluded that it is not. Janet Hyde (1984), for example, reached this conclusion after she asked children to finish stories for which they were given a first line such as, "When a kid goes to school, _____ often feels excited on the first day." When she filled in the blank with the pronoun "he," the children's stories were nearly always males, whereas "he or she" in the blank resulted in female characters about one-third of the time. Studies with adults (Martyna, 1978; Sniezek & Jazwinski, 1986) have found similar effects of the generic "he." Sentences about "the artist and his work" tend to conjure up images of a man.

In addition, people tend to use the generic pronouns selectively, as in "the doctor . . . he" and "the secretary . . . she" (MacKay, 1983). If the generic masculine pronouns were truly gender-free, it should not startle us to hear that "a nurse must answer his calls" or that "man, like other mammals, nurses his young." That we are startled indicates that the "his" carries a gender connotation that clashes with our idea of "nurse."

"To call forth a concept, a word is needed."
Antoine Lavoisier,
Elements of Chemistry, 1789

"All words are pegs to hang ideas on."
Henry Ward Beecher, 1812–1887
Proverbs from Plymouth Pulpit

The power of language to influence thinking is one reason why vocabulary building is such a crucial part of education. To expand language is to expand the ability to think. David Premack (1983) reported that even among chimpanzees, language training enhances the ability to think abstractly and to reason by analogy. For example, shown a cylinder half filled with water, a chimp not trained in language had difficulty recognizing that half an apple was more like the half-filled cylinder than three-fourths of an apple. But if language-trained, chimps could more readily grasp the analogy. In young children, too, thinking develops hand in hand with language (Gopnik & Meltzoff, 1986). What is true for chimpanzees and preschoolers is true for everyone: *It pays to increase your word power.* This is the reason why most textbooks, including this one, introduce new words to teach new ideas and new ways of thinking.

Increasing one's word power—as this child is doing as his father reads to him—expands one's capacity to think.

THINKING WITHOUT LANGUAGE

When you are alone do you talk to yourself? Is "thinking" simply conversing with yourself? Without a doubt, putting our ideas into spoken or written words can sharpen them. But are there not times when ideas precede words? To turn on the cold water in your bathroom, in which direction do you turn the handle?

To answer this question, you probably thought not in words but with a mental picture. Indeed, thinking in images is not at all uncommon. Artists think in images. So do composers, poets, mathematicians, athletes, and scientists. Albert Einstein reported that he achieved some of his greatest insights through visual images. Only

"Words are but the signs of ideas."
    Samuel Johnson, 1709–1784
    Preface to his *Dictionary of the English Language*

Drawing by Maslin; ©1984 The New York Times Magazine.

later did he put them into words. Words are the containers for the ideas, containers that shape the thoughts poured into them.

Many athletes prepare for contests by imagining themselves performing their events (Suinn, 1986). The wisdom of this advice was demonstrated in a laboratory test of mental practice conducted by Georgia Nigro (Neisser, 1984). The researchers had their subjects make twenty-four dart throws at a target. They then had half of the subjects think through twenty-four throws. Finally, they had all of the subjects again make twenty-four throws. Only those who had mentally practiced showed any improvement. When a National Research Council committee of psychologists recently investigated claims of performance-enhancement techniques for the U.S. Army, most (including ESP and "neurolinguistic programming") were judged to be of no value (Druckman & Swets, 1988). However, based on experiments such as Nigro's, the mental practice of motor skills was deemed useful.

What, then, should we say about the relationship between thinking and language? We have seen that language influences thinking. But if thinking did not also affect language, there would never be any new words. Words are invented to express new ideas. In basketball, the term "slam dunk" was coined after the act itself had become fairly common. So, let us simply say that *thinking affects our language, which then affects our thought.*

To return to the philosophical issue of human rationality, psychological research on thinking and language mirrors the mixed reviews given our species in literature and religion. The human mind is simultaneously capable of striking intellectual failures and of vast intellectual power. On the one hand, our deductive reasoning is often flawed and our inductive reasoning sometimes warps our perceptions of reality. In an age when misjudgments can have disastrous consequences, it is well that we appreciate our capacity for error. On the other hand, our heuristics often serve us well, and they certainly are efficient. Moreover, our ingenuity at problem solving and our extraordinary power of language do surely, among the animals, rank humankind as almost "infinite in faculties."

"Our real first line of defense, wouldn't you agree, is our capacity to reason."

SUMMING UP

Our cognitive system receives, perceives, and retrieves information, which we then use to think and communicate, sometimes wisely, sometimes foolishly. In this chapter we have explored how we form concepts, solve problems, make judgments, and use language.

THINKING

Concepts One of the building blocks of thinking is our concepts, which serve to simplify and order the world by organizing it into a hierarchy of categories. Concepts often form around prototypes, or best examples of a category.

Problem Solving When faced with novel situations for which no well-learned response suffices, we may use any of several strategies, such as trial and error, algorithms, and rule-of-thumb heuristics. Insight, a sudden and often novel realization, can also offer solutions to problems. We do, however, face certain obstacles to successful problem solving. The confirmation bias predisposes us to verify rather than challenge our hypotheses. And fixations such as mental set and functional fixedness may prevent our taking a needed fresh perspective on a problem.

Making Decisions and Forming Judgments Our use of heuristics, such as the representativeness and availability heuristics, provide highly efficient but occasionally misleading guides for making quick decisions and forming intuitive judgments. Our tendencies to seek confirmation of our hypotheses and to use quick and easy heuristics can blind us to our vulnerability to error, a phenomenon known as overconfidence. Also, the way a question is posed, or framed, can significantly affect our responses.

Reasoning As the belief perseverance phenomenon indicates, we sometimes cling to our ideas after their basis has been discredited, because the explanation for their apparent validity lingers in our minds.

Deductive reasoning begins with assumptions or general truths and uses them to derive conclusions. Inductive reasoning is the process of generalizing from observed instances. Even when reasoning with formal syllogisms, people tend to accept as more logical those conclusions that agree with their beliefs.

In Defense of Our Thinking Abilities Despite our capacity for error and our susceptibility to bias, our cognitive mechanisms are remarkably efficient and adaptive. As we gain expertise in a field, we become adept at making quick, shrewd judgments.

Artificial Intelligence Scientists have created computers and robots that perform operations previously thought to require human intelligence. The most notable successes have focused the computer's capacities for memory and precise logic on specific tasks, such as playing chess or diagnosing illnesses. For now, however, the brain's capacity for processing unrelated information simultaneously and the wide range of its abilities dwarf those of the most sophisticated computer.

LANGUAGE

Language—our words and how we combine them to communicate meaning—facilitates and expresses our thought.

Language Structure   Language is built of basic speech sounds, called phonemes; elementary units of meaning, called morphemes; words; and the semantics (meaning) and syntax (rules for word order) that make up grammar.

Language Development   Among the marvels of nature is a child's ability to acquire language. The ease with which children progress from the babbling stage through the one-word stage to the telegraphic speech of the two-word stage and beyond has sparked a lively debate concerning how they do it. The behaviorist explains that language is learned by the familiar principles of association, imitation, and reinforcement. This claim has been challenged by indications that children are biologically prepared to learn words and to organize them according to an inborn readiness to use grammar.

Animal Language   Another vigorously debated issue is whether language is a uniquely human ability. It has been known for some time that bees communicate the location of food through an intricate dance. More recently, several teams of psychologists provoked enormous interest by teaching various apes, including a number of chimpanzees, to communicate with humans by using sign language or by pushing buttons wired to a computer. The animals have developed considerable vocabularies and are able to string words together to express meaning and requests. Skeptics point out significant differences between apes and humans in their facility with language, especially in their respective abilities to order words using proper syntax. Nevertheless, these studies have revealed that apes possess considerable cognitive ability.

THINKING AND LANGUAGE

We have considered thinking and language in the same chapter because they are so difficult to disentangle.

Linguistic Influences on Thinking   There is no disputing that ideas are associated with words, and that different languages can embody different ways of thinking. Although the linguistic relativity hypothesis suggests that language *determines* thought, it is more correct to say that language *influences* thought. Evidence of the influence of words comes from studies of the effects of masculine generic pronouns and of the ability of vocabulary enrichment to enhance thinking.

Thinking Without Language   There is also evidence that some ideas, such as the ability to perceive and remember different colors, do not depend on one's vocabulary. Moreover, we sometimes think in images rather than in words, and we invent new words to describe new ideas. So we might say that our thinking affects our language, which then affects our thought.

TERMS AND CONCEPTS TO REMEMBER

algorithm   A methodical, logical rule or procedure for solving a particular problem. May be contrasted with the usually speedier, but also more error-prone use of *heuristics*.

artificial intelligence (AI)   The science of designing and programming computers to do things that appear intelligent; includes both practical applications (chess playing, industrial robots, expert systems) and theoretically inspired efforts to model thinking.

availability heuristic   A rule of thumb for estimating the likelihood of events in terms of their availability in memory; if instances come readily to mind (perhaps because of their vividness), we presume the thing to be more likely.

babbling stage   The stage in speech development, beginning at about 3 or 4 months, in which the infant spontaneously utters various sounds (which at first are unrelated to the parents' language).

belief perseverance   Clinging to one's initial conceptions after the basis on which they were formed has been discredited.

concept   A mental grouping of similar things, events, and people.

confirmation bias   A tendency to search for information that confirms one's preconceptions.

deductive reasoning   The deriving of conclusions, given certain assumptions.

fixation   The inability to adopt a new perspective on a problem.

framing   The way an issue is posed; it can significantly affect judgments.

functional fixedness   The tendency to think of things only in terms of their usual functions; an impediment to problem solving.

grammar   A system of rules that enables us to use our language to speak to and understand others.

heuristic   A strategy that often allows us to make judgments and to solve problems efficiently.

inductive reasoning The inferring of a general truth from particular examples.

insight A sudden and often novel realization of the solution to a problem; it contrasts with trial-and-error solutions.

language Words and how we combine them to communicate meaning.

linguistic relativity Whorf's hypothesis that language determines the way we think.

mental set A tendency to approach a problem in a particular way, especially a way that has been successful in the past but may or may not be helpful in solving a new problem.

morphemes The smallest speech units that carry meaning; may be words or parts of words (such as a prefix).

one-word stage The stage in speech development, from about age 1 to 2 years, during which a child speaks mostly in single words.

overconfidence phenomenon The tendency to be more confident than correct—to overestimate the accuracy of one's beliefs and judgments.

phonemes A language's smallest distinctive sound units.

prototype The best example of a category; matching new items to the prototype provides a quick and easy method for including items in a category (as when comparing feathered creatures to a prototypical bird, such as a robin).

representativeness heuristic A rule of thumb for judging the likelihood of things in terms of how well they seem to represent, or match, particular prototypes; may lead one to ignore other relevant information.

semantics Meaning (or the study of meaning), as derived from morphemes, words, and sentences.

syllogism The basis of formal deductive reasoning; an argument in which two presumably true statements, called premises, lead to a third true statement, the conclusion.

syntax Rules for combining words into grammatically correct sentences.

telegraphic speech An early speech stage in which the child speaks like a telegram—using mostly nouns and verbs and omitting "auxiliary" words.

trial and error A haphazard problem-solving process in which one solution after another is tried until success is achieved.

two-word stage The stage in speech development, beginning about age 2, during which a child speaks mostly two-word utterances.

FOR FURTHER READING

Beyth-Marom, R., Dekel, S., Gombo, R., & Shaked, M. (1985). *An elementary approach to thinking under uncertainty.* Hillsdale, NJ: Erlbaum.

An educational program, developed originally for Israeli teenagers, that teaches how best to reason when making judgments.

Bransford, J. D., & Stein, B. S. (1984). *The IDEAL problem solver: A guide to improving thinking, learning, and creativity.* New York: Freeman.

This book offers concrete strategies for attacking problems, including academic problems, using the IDEAL system: Identify problem; Define it; Explore strategies for solving it; Act on those strategies; Look at the effects of your efforts.

Halpern, D. F. (1984). *Thought and knowledge: An introduction to critical thinking.* Hillsdale, NJ.: Erlbaum.

A marvelous book that shows how the findings of psychology research can help us to think more rationally and critically.

Hunt, M. (1982). *The universe within: A new science explores the human mind.* New York: Simon & Schuster.

Science journalist Morton Hunt has been thinking about thinking, and the result is perhaps the most engaging and informative book ever written on the subject. Hunt draws on interviews with scores of researchers in presenting his well-documented summary of recent discoveries.

Janis, I. L. (1988). *Crucial decisions: Leadership in policy-making and crisis management.* New York: Free Press.

Analyzes reasons for poor, ill-fated decisions, and suggests four steps that will reduce errors and produce better decisions.

Kahneman, D., Slovic, P., & Tversky, A. (Eds.). (1982). *Judgment under uncertainty: Heuristics and biases.* New York: Cambridge University Press.

Here, many of the researchers whom Morton Hunt discusses in The universe within *speak for themselves, describing various ways in which people's intuitions, predictions, and diagnoses depart from the laws of probability and statistics.*

Nisbett, R., & Ross, L. (1980). *Human inference: Strategies and shortcomings of social judgment.* Englewood Cliffs, NJ: Prentice-Hall.

Is it possible for a book that summarizes psychological research to tickle your funny bone? This book will, as it reveals the pitfalls of human inductive reasoning.

CHAPTER 12

Intelligence

Scott, an energetic kindergartner, acts bored and restless in class. Concerned that he might have a learning disability, Scott's teacher asks the school psychologist to evaluate him. The psychologist's testing reveals that Scott is actually an extraordinarily capable boy who can read like a third grader and add numbers like a second grader. Little wonder that he acts bored; Scott needs activities better suited to his abilities.

Larry and six other California children were also tested by school psychologists; they were then assigned to special education classes for the mentally retarded. Their parents and the San Francisco Bay Area Black Psychology Association were not convinced by the psychologists' judgments. They suspected that the tests used might have been biased against the children, all of whom were black. In 1979 Federal District Court Judge Robert Peckham agreed: Intelligence tests, he ruled, are "racially and culturally biased, have a discriminatory impact on black children, and have not been validated for the purpose of [putting] black children into educationally dead-end, isolated, and stigmatizing classes" (Opton, 1979). In 1986 Judge Peckham reiterated his complete prohibition against using IQ tests in California even "as part of an assessment . . . placing black pupils in special education" (Landers, 1986).

Jennifer and Maria have been close friends throughout high school. Both have grade averages near the top of the class, and both hope to be premed students and attend the same college. In the fall of their senior year they spend a morning taking the Scholastic Aptitude Test. Jennifer does very well and subsequently is admitted to the school she and Maria have chosen. Maria does rather poorly and, despite her excellent high school record, is rejected. "How awful!" they moan. "After three years of making As in the same classes, a 150-minute test separates us!"

Of all psychology's controversies, none has been more heated than the one provoked by the idea that there exists in each person a general mental capacity and that this capacity can be measured and quantified as a number. School boards, courts, and scientists debate the usefulness and fairness of intelligence and aptitude tests. Should they be used to rank individuals and to determine whether they will be allowed to pursue various educational and vocational opportunities?

In this chapter, we will explore the controversy surrounding tests of mental abilities by examining such questions as:

How are intelligence tests used? How are they abused?

What is intelligence?

To what extent is intelligence a product of nature and to what extent of nurture?

What do differences in test scores among individuals and groups really mean?

By the end of the chapter, you should be ready to formulate your own answer to the hotly debated question: Is intelligence testing society's best means of identifying those who would benefit from special opportunities? Or is intelligence testing a potent discriminatory weapon camouflaged as science?

ASSESSING INTELLIGENCE

To understand the concept of intelligence and the impact of intelligence tests, it helps first to know something about the origins and purposes of these tests. The ongoing story of the testing movement reinforces an important lesson—that although science strives for objectivity, scientists can be influenced by their biases.

THE ORIGINS OF INTELLIGENCE TESTS

Some societies are more concerned with the welfare of the family, community, and society than they are with promoting individual opportunity and uniqueness. Other societies emphasize the individual over the group. The latter tradition can be traced to Plato, who more than 2000 years ago wrote in the *Republic* that "No two persons are born exactly alike; but each differs from the other in natural endowments, one being suited for one occupation and the other for another." As heirs to Plato's individualism, people in Western societies are intrigued by questions about how and why individuals differ. It may therefore be surprising that, although testing through civil service exams goes back 3000 years in China, Western attempts to assess individual differences began in earnest only about a century ago.

Civil service testing has a long history in China. These rooms in Nanking, in which hundreds of individuals could be tested at one time, were in use until 1905.

Sir Francis Galton: Quantifying Superiority   In the history of the testing movement, no one has been more preoccupied with measuring and ranking people than the brilliant English scientist Sir Francis Galton (1822–1911). While he was a student at Cambridge University, Galton's letters home revealed a constant concern with how examinations ranked him relative to his fellow students (Fancher, 1979). In time, his fascination with quantification led him to invent methods for measuring boredom, even-temperedness, the beauty of British women, the effects of prayer, and much else.

When his cousin Charles Darwin proposed that nature "selects" successful traits through the "survival of the fittest," Galton concluded that humankind could make conscious use of the same principles. If human traits could be measured, he reasoned, these measurements could be used as the basis for selectively breeding people who possessed superior traits. Those with the greatest "natural ability" should be encouraged to mate with each other, he argued, while those not so well endowed should be discouraged or prevented from reproducing. To promote his plan for human betterment, Galton founded the "eugenics" movement (taking its name from the Greek word *eugenes*, which means "well-born").

Galton assumed that human traits are inherited. He supported this assumption by noting that, like height, social prominence tended to run in families. Unsurprisingly, Galton himself was an eminent child of a well-known upper-class family and he married a "proper" woman, though, ironically, his marriage was childless. Furthermore, although he popularized the phrase "nature and nurture," he was oblivious to the cultural and environmental advantages enjoyed by the upper class

Sir Francis Galton (1892, p. 89): "I have no patience with the hypothesis occasionally expressed, and often implied, especially in tales written to teach children to be good, that babies are born pretty much alike, and that the sole agencies in creating differences between boy and boy, and man and man, are steady application and moral effort. It is in the most unqualified manner that I object to pretensions of natural equality."

in Victorian England (Fancher, 1979). A British male, he also believed in the natural superiority of Caucasian men.

Beginning with his commitment to quantifying human "superiority" and his belief in its heritability, Galton set about trying to measure innate mental capacity. In his 1869 book, *Hereditary Genius,* he toyed with the idea of assessing intelligence by measuring head size, and over the next few years he developed various measures of what he presumed were the biological underpinnings of genius. Galton put his ideas to the test at London's 1884 International Exposition. Over 10,000 visitors to the exposition paid to receive his assessment of their "intellectual strengths," based on such things as reaction time, sensory acuity, muscular power, and body proportions.

How did the tests turn out? Did "superior" individuals (eminent adults and excellent students) outscore those supposedly not so bright? Did they, for instance, process information more swiftly on the tests of reaction time? They did not. Nor did the various measures correlate with one another. Nor did men consistently outscore women.

Although Galton failed in his efforts to invent simple measures of general mental ability, he was an innovative researcher who pioneered some basic statistical techniques. Additionally, he was an influential proponent of the idea that people's mental abilities can be quantitatively measured.

Alfred Binet: Predicting School Achievement   The modern intelligence testing movement began when the pioneering French psychologist Alfred Binet (1857–1911) applied Galton's idea of measuring intellectual abilities to a humanitarian goal. When the French government passed a law requiring all children to attend school, teachers soon found themselves coping with a wider range of individual differences than they could handle. Some of the children seemed incapable of benefiting from the regular school curriculum and appeared to need special classes. But how could the schools objectively identify children with these special needs?

The government was reluctant to trust teachers' subjective judgments of children's learning potential. Academic slowness might merely reflect inadequate prior education. Also, teachers might tend to prejudge children on the basis of their social backgrounds. To remove this potential for bias, the Minister of Public Education in 1904 commissioned Binet to develop an objective test that would identify those children who were likely to have difficulty in the regular classes.

Binet and his collaborator, Théodore Simon, began by assuming that all children follow the same course of intellectual development but that some develop more rapidly than others. "Dull" children, they presumed, were merely "retarded" in their development. On tests, therefore, a dull child should perform like a normal child of a younger age; and a "bright" child should perform like a typical older child.

Binet and Simon's task, then, was to measure what came to be called a child's *mental age,* the age that most typically corresponds to a given level of performance. The average 9-year-old would have a mental age of 9, but many 9-year-olds would have mental ages below or above 9. By comparing a child's mental age with his or her actual age, the researchers reasoned that it should be possible to assess the child's ability to handle normal schoolwork. (Although it did not affect their findings, one of Binet and Simon's assumptions was incorrect. We now know, thanks to cognitive psychologists, that an 11-year-old with a mental age of 9 thinks in a somewhat different fashion than a 7-year-old with a mental age of 9.)

Alfred Binet (Binet & Simon, 1905): "The scale, properly speaking, does not permit the measure of intelligence, because intellectual qualities . . . cannot be measured as linear surfaces are measured."

In attempting to devise a method for measuring mental age, Binet and Simon theorized that intelligence, like athletic coordination, is a general capacity that shows up in various ways. They therefore set about developing various reasoning and problem-solving questions, the answers to which would allow them to predict school achievement better than did Galton's measures of physical and sensory skills. By testing "bright" and "backward" Parisian schoolchildren on these questions, Binet and Simon succeeded in identifying those items that did indeed seem to predict how successfully the children handled regular schoolwork.

Note that Binet and Simon made no assumptions concerning *why* a particular child was slow, average, or precocious. Binet personally leaned toward an environmental explanation. To raise the capacities of children who had low scores he recommended "mental orthopedics" that would train children how to develop their attention span and self-discipline. Binet refused to speculate about what the test was actually measuring. It did not measure inborn intelligence in the way that a yardstick measures height, he insisted. Rather, it had a single practical purpose: to predict which children would probably not succeed in the Paris school system of the early 1900s. Binet was not completely at ease with the test he had devised. His hope was that it would be used to help children improve. His fear was that it would be used to label children and limit their opportunities (Gould, 1981).

Lewis Terman: The Innate IQ

What Binet viewed as merely a practical guide for identifying slow learners who needed special help was soon seen by others to be what Galton had been searching for: a numerical measure of inherited intelligence. After Binet's death in 1911, Stanford University professor Lewis Terman decided to import Binet's test. He soon found, however, that the Paris-developed age norms did not work very well with California schoolchildren. So Terman revised the test. He translated some of Binet's original items, added others, established new age norms, and extended the upper end of the test's range from teenagers to "superior adults." Terman gave his revision the name that through numerous later revisions it retains today—the **Stanford-Binet.**

From Terman's test, German psychologist William Stern derived the famous **intelligence quotient,** or **IQ.** The IQ was simply mental age divided by chronological age and multiplied by 100 to get rid of the decimal point:

$$IQ = \frac{\text{measured mental age}}{\text{chronological age}} \times 100$$

Thus, an 8-year-old who answered questions with the proficiency typical of a 10-year-old was said to have an IQ of 125. Note that by definition an average child would have the same measured mental age and chronological age, and so an IQ of 100.

Current intelligence tests, including the Stanford-Binet itself, no longer compute IQ in this manner. Although the original IQ formula worked fairly well for children, it was not appropriate for adults. Consider: If a 20-year-old does as well on the test as the average 40-year-old, is it reasonable to say this person has an IQ of 200? Obviously, something is out of whack. Today's intelligence tests therefore produce an "IQ score" based on the test-taker's performance relative to the average performance of others the same age. As on the original Stan-

"The IQ test was invented to predict academic performance, nothing else. If we wanted something that would predict life success, we'd have to invent another test completely."
    Robert Zajonc (1984b)

It was not until World War II that the IQ test became fashionable in France—under the name of Terman, not Binet!

Drawing by Sidney Harris.

"You did very well on your IQ test. You're a man of 49 with the intelligence of a man of 53."

ford-Binet, IQ scores are defined so that 100 is average and so that about two-thirds of all people who take IQ tests score between 85 and 115.

Although the term "IQ" is misleading, because there is no longer any intelligence *quotient*, it still lingers in the testing vocabulary as a shorthand expression for "intelligence test score." In addition, the Stanford-Binet has become a standard against which newer tests are often compared. For these reasons and others, Terman's influence reaches into the present.

Sharing Galton's belief that intelligence could be measured, Terman promoted the widespread use of intelligence testing. His motive was to "take account of the inequalities of children in original endowment" by assessing their "vocational fitness" (Terman, 1916). In sympathy with the eugenics movement, Terman (1916, pp. 91–92) lamented what he believed was the "dullness" and "unusually prolific breeding" of certain ethnic groups. He envisioned that the use of intelligence tests would "ultimately result in curtailing the reproduction of feeble-mindedness and in the elimination of an enormous amount of crime, pauperism, and industrial inefficiency" (p. 7).

During the same era, adaptations of Binet's and Terman's tests were used in the United States to evaluate World War I army recruits and newly arriving immigrants. The results of the tests were misinterpreted by some as documenting the inferiority of people not of Anglo-Saxon descent. For instance, following his 1913 study of European immigrants arriving at Ellis Island (many of whom spoke no English), psychologist Henry Goddard claimed that 83 percent of the Jewish immigrants, 80 percent of the Hungarians, 79 percent of the Italians, and 87 percent of the Russians were "feeble-minded" (Eysenck & Kamin, 1981).

That adaptations of his tests were being used to draw such conclusions would surely have horrified Binet. Indeed, such sweeping judgments eventually became an embarrassment to most of those who championed testing, including Terman, who came to appreciate that test scores reflect not only people's innate mental abilities but also their education and their familiarity with the culture assumed by the test. These abuses of the early intelligence tests nevertheless serve to remind us that science can be value-laden. Behind the screen of scientific objectivity, ideology sometimes hides.

Lewis Terman (1916, p. 115): "The children of successful and cultured parents test higher than children from wretched and ignorant homes for the simple reason that their heredity is better."

"The primary concerns of researchers should be to discover . . . the realities that prevail despite shifting politics and policies."
  Arthur R. Jensen (1984)

"Science must be understood as a social phenomenon, a gutsy, human enterprise, not the work of robots programmed to collect pure information."
  Stephen Jay Gould (1981)

When given English-language intelligence tests in the early 1900s, immigrants arriving in the United States often scored poorly because they did not share the culture and language assumed by the test. Nevertheless, there were psychologists and government officials who used the test results as "scientific proof" that the immigrants were intellectually inferior.

MODERN TESTS OF MENTAL ABILITIES

By this point in your life, your mental abilities have undoubtedly been assessed by dozens of different tests: elementary school tests of basic reading and math skills, course examinations, intelligence tests, driver's license examinations, and college entrance examinations, to mention just a few. Traditionally, such tests are classified as either *aptitude tests,* which are intended to predict your ability to learn a new skill, or *achievement tests,* which are intended to measure what you have learned. Thus, a college entrance exam, which seeks to predict how you will do in college, would be called an aptitude test, whereas a final exam covering what you should have learned in this course would be an achievement test.

The differences between aptitude tests and achievement tests are not as clear-cut as their definitions imply. Your score on an aptitude test depends to some extent on your achieved vocabulary. Similarly, your grades on the achievement exams given in this course reflect not only how effectively you have studied but also your aptitude for learning. So think of aptitude and achievement as the two ends of a continuum. Most tests, whether labeled aptitude or achievement, assess both ability and how far that ability has been developed, so they fall somewhere in between. Distinguishing between them is mainly a matter of practicality: Aptitude tests are used to predict future performance, achievement tests to assess current competence.

Tests can also be distinguished by whether they assess abilities that are general or specific. An intelligence test is designed to evaluate general ability by sampling a broad array of mental skills. Conversely, a test to predict the ease with which an individual can learn mechanical tasks assesses a specific aptitude. A typing test given to a prospective employee assesses a specific achievement, whereas a high school competency examination tests for general achievement.

Tests also vary in the procedure by which they are administered. Group tests are very efficient. Individual testing allows the examiner to assess the test-taker's emotional state, to cease asking questions that have become impossibly difficult, and to use more varied materials, such as puzzles.

To get a better feel for modern intelligence-related tests and some of the differences among them, let's look at three tests that are widely used today. We can then refer to these examples as we consider what makes an effective test and how test scores can be used and abused.

An Individual Test of General Ability: The WAIS   Among the early 1900s' tide of supposedly feeble-minded Eastern European immigrants was a 6-year-old Rumanian boy, David Wechsler. Ironically, three decades later it was psychologist David Wechsler who created the most widely used test of intelligence, the *Wechsler Adult Intelligence Scale (WAIS).* Later he developed a similar test for school-age children called the Wechsler Intelligence Scale for Children (WISC), and still later a test for preschool children. The carefully standardized WAIS, which is individually administered, consists of eleven subtests, as illustrated in Figure 12–1. It yields not only an overall IQ score, as does the Stanford-Binet, but also separate "verbal" and "performance" (nonverbal) IQ scores. Striking differences between the two scores may alert the examiner to possible learning problems. For example, a much lower verbal than performance IQ score might indicate a reading disability or a difficulty in comprehending the language of the test.

The Wechsler intelligence test comes in forms suited for adults (WAIS) and for children (WISC).

The Wechsler scales are among the most respected intelligence tests. More than 3000 books and articles have been published about these scales (Anastasi, 1982), and the updated WAIS-R (*R* stands for revised) is used more than any other psychological test (Lubin & others, 1984).

Figure 12–1 Sample items from the Wechsler Adult Intelligence Scale (WAIS) subtests.

VERBAL

General Information
What day of the year is Independence Day?

Similarities
In what way are *wool* and *cotton* alike?

Arithmetic Reasoning
If eggs cost 60 cents a dozen, what does 1 egg cost?

Vocabulary
Tell me the meaning of corrupt.

Comprehension
Why do people buy fire insurance?

Digit Span
Listen carefully, and when I am through, say the numbers right after me.

7 3 4 1 8 6

Now I am going to say some more numbers, but I want you to say them backward.

3 8 4 1 6

PERFORMANCE

Picture Completion
I am going to show you a picture with an important part missing. Tell me what is missing.

'85

SUN	MON	TUE	WED	THU	FRI	SAT
1	2	3	4	5	6	7
8	9	10	11	12	13	14
15	16	17	18	19	20	21
22	23	24	25	26	27	28
29	30					

Picture Arrangement
The pictures below tell a story. Put them in the right order to tell the story.

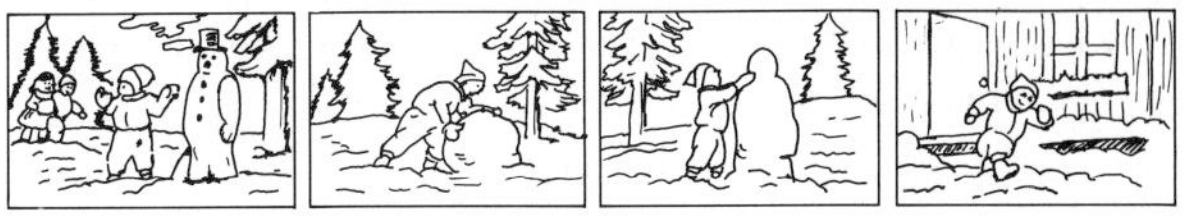

Block Design
Using the four blocks, make one just like this.

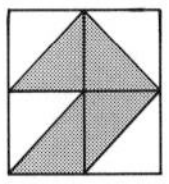

Object Assembly
If these pieces are put together correctly, they will make something. Go ahead and put them together as quickly as you can.

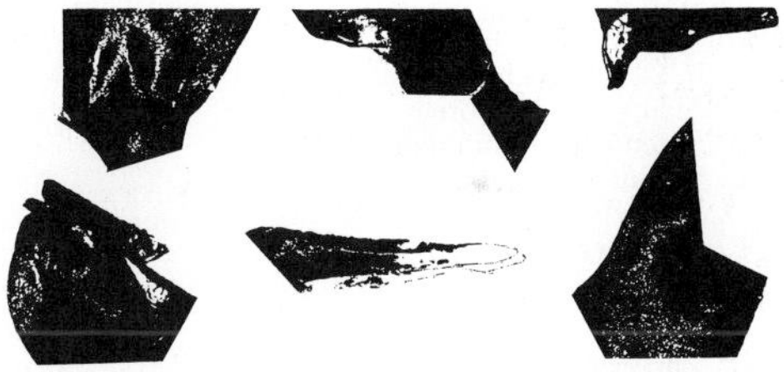

Digit-Symbol Substitution

Code

△	○	▱	×	8
1	2	3	4	5

Test

△	8	×	○	△	▱	8	×	△	8

Group Tests of General Ability: The SAT and ACT Large-scale testing is now efficiently accomplished through the use of multiple-choice tests such as the well-known Scholastic Aptitude Test (SAT), which is taken annually by some 1 million college-bound high school seniors. Like the original Binet test, the SAT attempts to predict academic performance. Unlike the Stanford-Binet and Wechsler tests, however, the SAT yields no overall intelligence score. Rather, it measures verbal and mathematical abilities separately.

Might "intelligence" tests be less controversial had Binet and his followers named them "academic aptitude" tests?

Figure 12–2 Sample items from the Scholastic Aptitude Test (SAT).

VERBAL

Choose the word or phrase that is most nearly *opposite* in meaning to the word in capital letters.

WILT: (A) prevent (B) drain (C) expose (D) revive (E) stick

(93 percent correctly answered D)

GARNER: (A) disfigure (B) hedge (C) connect (D) forget (E) disperse

(26 percent correctly answered E)

Each question below consists of a related pair of words or phrases, followed by five lettered pairs of words or phrases. Select the lettered pair that <u>best</u> expresses a relationship similar to that expressed in the original pair.

PAINTING:CANVAS (A) drawing : lottery (B) fishing : pond (C) writing : paper (D) shading : crayon (E) sculpting : design

(92 percent correctly answered C)

SCOFF : DERISION (A) soothe : mollification (B) slander : repression (C) swear : precision (D) stimulate : appearance (E) startle : speediness

(21 percent correctly answered A)

MATHEMATICAL

If $x^3 + y = x^3 + 5$, then $y =$
(A) -5 (B) $-\sqrt[y]{5}$ (C) $\sqrt[y]{5}$ (D) 5 (E) 5^3

(93 percent correctly answered D)

In a race, if Bob's running speed was 4/5 Alice's and Chris's speed was 3/4 Bob's, then Alice's speed was how many times the average (arithmetic mean) of the other two runners' speeds?
(A) 3/5 (B) 7/10 (C) 40/31 (D) 10/7 (E) 5/3

(10 percent correctly answered D)

In the figure below, one side of the square is a diameter of the circle. If the area of the circle is p and the area of the square is s, which of the following must be true?

I. $s > p$ II. $s \geqq 2p$ III. $s < p$
(A) None (B) I only (C) II only (D) III only (E) I and II

(45 percent correctly answered B)

Figure 12–3 Sample items from the Differential Aptitude Tests (DAT).

VERBAL REASONING

Choose the correct pair of words to fill the blanks. The first word of the pair goes in the blank space at the beginning of the sentence; the second word of the pair goes in the blank at the end of the sentence.

...... is to night as breakfast is to ......
A. supper —— corner
B. gentle —— morning
C. door —— corner
D. flow —— enjoy
E. supper —— morning

The correct answer is E.

NUMERICAL ABILITY

Choose the correct answer for each problem.
Add 13 A. 14 Subtract 30 A. 15
  12 B. 25   20 B. 26
  C. 16   C. 16
  D. 59   D. 8
  N. none of these   N. none of these

The correct answer for the first problem is B and for the second is N.

ABSTRACT REASONING

The four "problem figures" in each row make a series. Find the one among the "answer figures" that would be next in the series.

Problem Figures   Answer Figures

The correct answer is D

MECHANICAL REASONING

Which man has the heavier load? (If equal, mark C.)

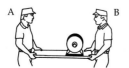

The correct answer is B.

CLERICAL SPEED AND ACCURACY

In each test item, one of the five combinations is underlined. Find the same combination on the answer sheet and mark it.

Test Items   Sample of Answer Sheet

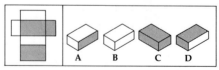

SPACE RELATIONS

Which one of the following figures could be made by folding the pattern at the left? The pattern always shows the outside of the figure. Note the gray surfaces.

The correct answer is D.

SPELLING

Indicate whether each word is spelled right or wrong.
  W. man X. gurl

The correct answer for W is right and for X is wrong.

LANGUAGE USAGE

Decide which of the lettered parts of the sentence contains an error and mark the corresponding letter on the answer sheet. If there is no error, mark N.
  X. Ain't we / going to / the office / next week?
    A   B   C   D

The correct answer is A.

The SAT is a good example of an aptitude test that falls somewhere in the middle of the aptitude-achievement continuum, as can be seen from the sample items in Figure 12–2. More than half of its sixty mathematical questions, for example, presume a basic knowledge of either algebra or geometry. The American College Testing (ACT) exam, taken by a similar number of college-bound high school seniors, is a bit further toward the achievement end of the continuum. On the ACT, the average high school student today would probably outscore Aristotle and other geniuses of the distant past, because the test measures students' "educational development" in English usage, mathematics, social studies, and natural science.

A Group Test of Specific Abilities: The DAT   The Differential Aptitude Tests (DAT) are widely used as an aid to counseling junior and senior high school students. As the sample items in Figure 12–3 illustrate, the DAT evaluates not only such academically related abilities as verbal and mathematical reasoning, spelling, and language usage but also such vocational abilities as clerical speed and mechanical reasoning. Thus, like the SAT, it is an "aptitude" test that also reflects achievement. Combined with other available information, such as student interests, DAT scores are frequently used by counselors to help guide people toward appropriate courses and/or careers.

The Scholastic Aptitude Test (SAT) is a familiar group test, used to predict high school students' potential for academic achievement in college.

PRINCIPLES OF TEST CONSTRUCTION

We can use the three tests just discussed to illustrate three requirements of any good test—standardization, reliability, and validity.

Standardization   Knowing how many questions someone answers correctly on an intelligence test does not tell us whether the person's performance is low, high, or average. To assign a meaningful score to an individual's test performance, we must be able to compare that performance with some sort of standard or norm. So before an intelligence-related test can be used, the test makers must give it to a large, representative sample of people. This process of defining meaningful scores relative to a pretested group is called ***standardization.***

For instance, when Terman realized that the test Binet had created in France did not work so well with California schoolchildren, he revised the test and then standardized the new version by administering it to 2300 white, native-born Americans of all socioeconomic levels. This sample of people comprised the norm against which subsequent takers of the test were compared.

On both the Stanford-Binet and the Wechsler scales, the average score for any age group is set at 100. Within each age group, IQ scores are then assigned according to how much the test-taker's performance deviates above or below this average. For example, a raw score that is higher than 98 percent of all the scores is assigned an IQ score of 130. A raw score that is comparably *below* 98 percent of all the scores is assigned an IQ score of 70.

This method of assigning scores is based on the concept of a ***normal distribution,*** a bell-shaped distribution of scores that forms what is called the ***normal curve*** (Figure 12–4 on page 324). Whether we are measuring people's heights, weights, or mental abilities, most of the values will tend to cluster around the average. As we move away from the average toward either extreme, we find fewer and fewer values.

Terman and his colleagues recognized that a scale standardized on Parisians did not provide a satisfactory standard for evaluating Americans. But, ironically, they proceeded to evaluate nonwhite and immigrant groups based on the native-born white American standard (Van Leeuwen, 1982).

Any individual's score can be expressed in terms of its deviation from the average. The statistical measures of this deviation (standard deviation) and of the average, or mean, score are described in the Appendix.

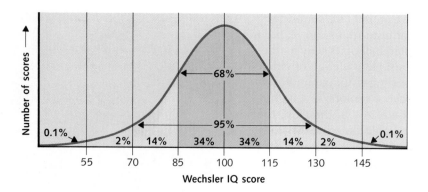

Figure 12–4   The normal curve. When many scores on a test are compiled, they tend to be distributed in a normal, or bell-shaped, curve. On an IQ test, such as the Wechsler scale, the average score is assigned an IQ of 100. The percentages under the curve indicate that about 68 percent of the scores normally fall within about 15 IQ points above or below 100 and about 95 percent within 30 IQ points above and below 100.

Initially, the SAT was standardized using a group of 10,654 students who took the test in April 1941 (Carroll, 1982). The average performance of these students on the verbal and mathematical portions of the SAT was assigned a score of 500 (rather than 100 as on most intelligence tests). The points above and below the average that included 68 percent of all the raw scores were assigned SAT scores of 600 and 400, respectively (see Figure 12–5). All the students in the SAT standardization sample were college-bound and were thus a select group, especially back in 1941. So this sample is not equivalent to the ones used for the Stanford-Binet or the Wechsler scales. A person whose scores average 500 on the two parts of the SAT would probably score well above 100 on an intelligence test.

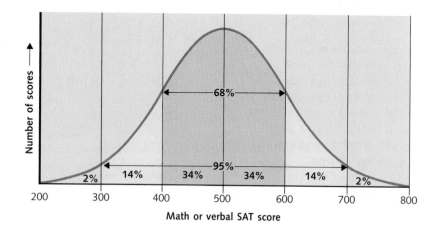

Figure 12–5   When the SAT test was standardized on a normal distribution curve in 1941, the average score for each part was assigned a value of 500. The percentages under the curve indicate that about 68 percent of the scores normally fall within about 100 points above and below 500. Note, however, that an IQ score of 115 on the WAIS is not the equivalent of an SAT score of 600, because the academic ability of the groups on which the tests were standardized was not the same.

If you took the SAT in the past year or so—close to 50 years after those first 10,654 students set the standard, you answered different questions than they did. However, the items on the test you were given had been statistically equated to those that appeared on all previous versions of the test. (Each year students respond not only to the current test but also to items being standardized for use in future tests, which enables current and future items to be equated for difficulty.) Thus your performance could be—and was—measured with the 1941 yardstick.

Because of this comparability, the SAT has become a sort of educational barometer. Between 1963 and 1980, scores on the SAT dropped steadily (see Figure 12–6). Of those who took the test in 1981, only the upper 30 percent did better than the average test-taker in 1963. How can we explain this decline? Does it indicate, as some have surmised, a failure of American education?

One explanation for the drop in SAT scores is that during the 1960s the number of aspiring college students taking the test grew to include a broader range of people, including those with relatively modest academic achievements (Astin & Garber, 1982). But what else might explain the decline, especially during the 1970s when the range of students taking the SAT stabilized? The displacement of reading by the spread of television? A combination of grade inflation, nonacademic electives, simplified textbooks, and reduced homework (Turnbull, 1986)? Decreased adult influence and attention associated with increased family size during the 1950s? All these factors seem to have contributed.

Unlike the SAT, the Stanford-Binet test and the Wechsler scales are periodically restandardized. If you took the WAIS today, your performance would be compared with that of a standardization sample of Americans who took the test between 1976 and 1980, not David Wechsler's initial 1930s standardization sample. We can, however, compare the performance of the most recent standardization sample with that of the 1930s sample. If we did, do you suppose we would find rising or declining test performance? Amazingly—given the decline in SAT scores—test performance has improved (Flynn, 1987). A raw score that would earn you an IQ score of 100 today would have earned a score of 114 in the 1930s! (Similar rising performance has been observed in many other developed nations.)

How can this be? Are the aptitudes of Americans decreasing, as some have inferred from the decline in SAT scores, or are they rising, as the IQ data suggest? Although these conflicting trends seem baffling, we can speculate on some partial explanations. First, remember that the decline in SAT scores can be attributed partly to the greater academic diversity of the students who began taking the test during the 1960s. Conversely, the group of people who take the WAIS, and who are broadly representative of Americans in general, has always been diverse in abilities, much more so than the college-bound SAT takers. Americans—and therefore the IQ standardization group—have become more literate and better educated since the 1930s. Also, the SAT measures higher level academic skills, which seem not to have improved as have the simpler problem-solving skills required by IQ tests. These facts help explain why the scores on the more academically advanced SAT dropped while those on the more basic WAIS rose.

Reliability   A good test must yield dependably consistent scores; in a word, it must have *reliability.* To check *test-retest reliability,* subjects are retested either on the same instrument (which is commonly done with the WAIS or WISC) or on an alternate form of the test (which is commonly done with the SAT). To check *split-half reliability,* which measures internal consistency, scores for the odd and even questions can be compared. If the two scores obtained by either method generally agree (are correlated), the test is said to be reliable.

The higher the correlation between the scores, the higher the reliability of the test. Correlations can vary from −1.0 (which would be perfect disagreement between two sets of scores—as the first score goes up, the second goes down) to 0 (no consistency) to +1.0 (perfect consistency). The tests we have considered so far—the Stanford-Binet, the WAIS and WISC, and the SAT, ACT, and DAT—all have reliabilities of about +.90, which is very high. When retested, people's scores tend to match their first score quite closely.

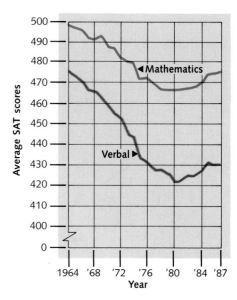

Figure 12–6   Between 1963 and 1980, average SAT scores dropped significantly, with a slight recovery in recent years.

For further information on correlation, see the Appendix.

Drawing by Sidney Harris.

"I'm studying for my IQ test."

COACHING EFFECTS

Suppose that after taking the SAT, the Law School Aptitude Test (LSAT), the Medical College Admission test (MCAT), or the Graduate Record Examination (GRE), you were disappointed by your scores. By enrolling in one of the widely advertised test-preparation courses, could you count on increasing your score if you were to take the test again? Or is your score on the test likely to be unvarying?

Being familiar with a test and knowing how to pace yourself on it does help. But this much you can get from spending an evening with the sample test that is available to anyone who registers for one of these tests. Beyond this, does it pay to sign up for a crash test-preparation course? These courses do often help people to brush up on their academic knowledge, especially in mathematics. They may also provide a few useful tips about how to take the test. For instance, the initial questions in a section are usually answered cor-

rectly by over 80 percent of those who take the test, which means that the most obvious answer is usually correct; on the final questions, which more than 75 percent typically get wrong, the "obvious" answer is often incorrect.

Despite the test-relevant teaching and the test-taking clues that SAT-preparation courses provide, and contrary to advertised claims, three separate research reviews have concluded that the courses increased scores by an average of only 10 to 15 points on the 200 to 800 scale (DerSimonian & Laird, 1983; Kulik & others, 1984; Messick & Jungeblut, 1981). This small boost is greatest on test items that have complex and possibly confusing formats (Powers, 1986). So, if you have studied in your academic courses, brushed up on algebra and geometry, and familiarized yourself with the test, you needn't feel intimidated by those who have taken a test preparation course.

Validity   High reliability does not ensure that a test has *validity*— that it measures what it is supposed to measure or predicts what it is supposed to predict. If you use a shrunken tape measure to measure people's heights, you would obtain values with high reliability (consistency) but low validity. How, then, can we determine whether a test is valid? For some tests, it is sufficient that they have *content validity*, which means that they do indeed tap the behavior they were designed to measure. The road test for a driver's license has content validity because it samples those tasks a driver routinely faces. Your classroom course exams have content validity if they adequately measure your mastery of course material.

Other tests, such as the aptitude tests we have considered, must have *predictive validity*, which is assessed by determining the extent to which the tests predict the future achievements they are intended to predict. Some aptitude tests are created by selecting items that best predict the *criterion* (the behavior the test is designed to predict). During World War II psychologist John Flanagan (1947) gave men who were entering pilot training twenty different tests that he hoped would sample the requirements of successful piloting. Later, knowing which men successfully completed the training (the criterion) and which did not, Flanagan could adapt and score his test so that it gave the best possible estimate of success. When the revised test was actually used to admit people to the training program, the failure rate was cut by more than half. The test had predictive validity.

Is the predictive validity of general aptitude tests as high as their reliability? As critics of aptitude tests are fond of noting, the answer to this question is plainly no. The predictive power of aptitude tests is fairly strong in the early grades, but later it weakens. Intelligence test scores are reasonably good predictors of achievement in elementary school, where the correlation between IQ score and grades is about +.60 (Jensen, 1980). The SAT is less successful in predicting the grades of college freshmen; here, the correlation is only about +.40 (Linn, 1982). By the time we get to the Graduate Record Examination (GRE) aptitude test (a test similar to the SAT for college seniors aspiring to graduate school), the correlation with graduate school grades is typically even more modest. Why does the predictive power of aptitude scores diminish as students move up the educational ladder?

Consider a parallel situation: Among all boxers, body weight correlates with success; heavier boxers usually beat their lighter opponents. To reduce this correlation, weight classes were created. When boxers fight only those of roughly similar weight, the correlation between body weight and boxing success is lower. The narrower the range of weights, the less the predictive power of body weight.

A similar narrowing of range explains why the GRE is only a modest predictor of graduate school grades. If a graduate school takes in only students whose aptitude scores fall within a narrow range—say "heavyweight" students with high scores—it should not surprise us that their aptitude scores will not be highly correlated with their grades. This will be true even if the test is a good predictor of future grades for a sample of students that contains a full spectrum of academic aptitudes. So when a test is validated using a wide range of people but is then used with a restricted range of people, it may lose its predictive validity. A narrowed range of grades—as in graduate school departments that award mostly As and Bs—will similarly reduce the predictive validity.

The best predictor of future grades is past grades, which reflect both aptitude and motivation. More generally, the best predictor of future behavior is a large sample of past behaviors of the same sort. So there is good reason to suppose that Maria and Jennifer (page 315) would do comparably well if attending the same college.

THE NATURE OF INTELLIGENCE

So far in this chapter, we have used the term "intelligence" as though we all naturally agreed on what it means. In reality, defining intelligence is a controversial issue. During the last century psychologists have debated whether intelligence should be defined as an inherent brain capacity, as an achieved level of intellectual functioning, or as an ascribed quality that, like beauty, is in the eye of the beholder.

The experts do agree that intelligence is not a "thing." When we refer to someone's "IQ" as if it were a fixed and objectively real trait like height, we commit a logical error called *reification*—regarding an abstract concept as though it were a real, concrete thing. To reify is to invent a concept, give it a name, and then convince ourselves that such a thing objectively exists in the world.

Intelligence is a concept invented to explain why some people perform better than others on cognitive tasks. In the *Handbook of Human Intelligence*, Robert Sternberg and William Salter (1982, p. 3) report that most experts view **intelligence** as a person's capacity for "goal-directed adaptive behavior"—behavior that, by learning from experience, solving problems, and reasoning clearly, successfully meets challenges and achieves its aims. This definition of intelligence is general enough to be acceptable to most researchers and to leave room for their differences.

"Intelligence is the particular facility a person has to cope with any given situation."
M. S. Michel,
Sweet Murder, 1943

What then are the controversies regarding the nature of intelligence? They concern first, whether intelligence should be considered as culturally defined or as a culture-free ability to solve problems; second, whether intelligence is best considered as an overall ability or as several specific abilities; and third, whether intelligence can be assessed as though it were an information-processing capacity of the brain.

INTELLIGENCE AS CULTURALLY DEFINED OR AS A CULTURE-FREE PROBLEM-SOLVING ABILITY

According to one view, intelligent behavior varies with the situation. For Binet and the later IQ testers, intelligence meant children's adapting successfully to academic demands. For islanders in the South Pacific, it might be the ability to fish and to "read" the ocean. For a manager or salesperson in our society, it might be social skills. For a teen or young adult in a big city ghetto, it might be street smarts.

Those who view intelligence as people's successful adaptation to their environments tend to be skeptical about the prospects for a "culture-free" test of intelligence—a test that is uninfluenced by the culture to which one has adapted. They believe that those who hope for such a test fail to understand that intelligence depends on one's cultural context. It might make sense to talk about a "culture-free" measure of height, but not of intelligence. To say that someone is intelligent necessarily requires making a judgment about what qualities are adaptive in one's cultural environment. As intelligence researcher Howard Gardner has noted, basketball superstar Larry Bird may not have been considered exceptionally intelligent when in school, but in a society of hunters and warriors he would be the gifted one.

Others view intelligence as those cognitive abilities that would help people to solve problems effectively and to achieve their rationally chosen goals in *any* environment (Baron, 1985). The abstract and novel questions asked on intelligence tests provide challenges that are intended to evaluate people's abilities to solve a variety of problems effectively, no matter what their cultural backgrounds may be. The assumption is that people who on the WAIS can remember a string of digits and then recite them in reverse order, or who can find the missing element in a picture, will likely have an edge at solving a variety of other problems, be it taking tests in school or growing corn.

Drawing by Weber; © 1988 The New Yorker Magazine, Inc.

"I've never gotten the hang of hunting. Luckily, we're invited out a lot."

On the Ivory Coast in West Africa, intelligence may mean being capable of learning how to make a good canoe. In northern Alaska, it may mean grasping the finer points of sewing weathertight caribou skins.

INTELLIGENCE AS AN OVERALL ABILITY OR AS SEVERAL SPECIFIC ABILITIES

We are all aware that some people are talented in mathematics, others in creative writing, and still others in art, music, or dance. We might therefore begin to wonder whether people's mental abilities are too diverse to justify the single label "intelligence" or to quantify them with one IQ score. Should we think of intelligence as one general ability or as a collection of specific abilities?

The Factor Analysis Approach   Virtually everyone agrees that there are specific mental abilities. Recall that some intelligence tests, such as the WAIS, distinguish between verbal and performance intelligence, and that aptitude tests, such as the SAT, typically distinguish between verbal and mathematical skills. In your own experience, you may have known a talented artist who was dumbfounded by the simplest mathematical problems or a brilliant math student who seemed to have little aptitude for literary discussion. (Of course, you may also have encountered a mathematically skilled artist or a literary mathematician.)

But are there some common factors that run through our specific mental abilities? In attempts to find out, psychologists have given people questions testing many different kinds of mental abilities and have then correlated the answers to the different questions to see whether various abilities are related to one another.

A statistical procedure called *factor analysis* allows researchers to identify clusters of test items that seem to tap a common ability. For example, people who do well on vocabulary items often do well on paragraph comprehension. This cluster, which also includes other items that pertain to language usage, defines a verbal intelligence factor. Psychologists have identified several such clusters, including a spatial ability factor and a reasoning ability factor.

Charles Spearman (1863–1945), who helped to develop the factor analysis concept and procedure, believed that there was also a *general intelligence,* or *g,* factor that underlies each of the specific factors. People often have special abilities that stand out, Spearman allowed, but those who score high on one factor, such as verbal intelligence, typically score higher than average on other factors such as spatial or reasoning ability. There is at least a small tendency for different abilities to come in the same package. Spearman believed that this commonality, the g factor, underlies all of our intelligent behavior.

This idea that there is a general mental capacity that can be characterized by a single IQ score was controversial in Spearman's day, and it remains so in our own. Opposing Spearman, fellow British psychologist Godfrey Thomson (1881–1955) argued that intelligence is not one but many things, including habits, knowledge, and various mental processes. Another of Spearman's contemporaries, L. L. Thurstone (1887–1955), also believed that each individual has a unique profile of "primary mental abilities." In conducting his research, Thurstone administered fifty-six different tests to people and analyzed the results mathematically. From these analyses, he was able to identify eight different clusters of abilities, such as word fluency, memory, and reasoning, that he believed were distinguishable. Thurstone did not rank his subjects on a single scale of general ability. But when other investigators studied the profiles of his subjects they detected at least a small tendency for those who excelled in one of the eight clusters of abilities to score well on the others also. So they concluded that there was still some evidence of a g factor.

Theories of Multiple Intelligences   More recently, psychologist Howard Gardner (1983) has reaffirmed and expanded upon Thurstone's view. Rather than doing the sort of mathematical analysis that Thurstone performed, Gardner assembled other kinds of evidence. For example, he noted that certain types of brain damage will diminish one type of ability but not others. He analyzed the usefulness of different abilities in different eras and cultures, from hunting societies to Japanese work groups to North American schoolrooms. He studied reports of people with exceptional abilities, including those who excel in only one. *Idiot savants*, for instance, are people who score in the retarded range on intelligence tests but possess incredible specific skills, such as in computation skills, drawing ability, or memory for music (see Figure 12–7). Idiot savants may have virtually no language ability, yet be able to compute numbers as quickly and accurately as an electronic calculator or be capable of identifying almost instantaneously the day of the week that corresponds to any given date in history.

Using such evidence, Gardner argued that we do not have *an* intelligence, but, rather, *multiple* intelligences, each independent of the others. In addition to the verbal and mathematical intelligences assessed by the standard tests, Gardner identified distinct aptitudes (critics would say "talents") for musical accomplishment, for spatially analyzing the visual world, for mastering movement skills such as those characteristic of dance, and for insightfully understanding ourselves and others. According to Gardner, the computer programmer, the poet, the street-smart adolescent who becomes a crafty executive, and the playmaker on the basketball team are each exhibiting a different kind of intelligence.

Robert Sternberg and Richard Wagner (1986, 1987) distinguish more simply among three intelligences: the academic problem-solving skills assessed by IQ tests, the practical intelligence often required for everyday tasks, and the creative intelligence demonstrated in reacting to novel situations. IQ tests predict school grades reasonably well but predict vocational success less well. Success in managerial work, for example, depends less on the abilities assessed by an IQ score (assuming the score is average or above) than on having know-how in managing oneself, one's tasks, and other people. Business executives who score high on Sternberg and Wagner's test of practical managerial intelligence (by knowing how to write effective memos, how to motivate subordinates, when to delegate tasks and responsibilities, and how to promote their own careers) earn higher salaries and receive better performance ratings than those who score low. Likewise, Stephen Ceci and Jeffrey Liker (1986) report that racetrack fans' expertise in handicapping the horses—a practical but complex cognitive task—is unrelated to their IQ scores.

Nancy Cantor and John Kihlstrom (1987) similarly distinguish between academic intelligence and social intelligence—the know-how involved in comprehending social situations and managing oneself successfully. And James Flynn (1987) finds it curious that while performance on IQ tests has increased dramatically during the last generation, rates of inventiveness and scientific discovery seem not to have increased comparably. Although some researchers insist that IQ score *does* predict performance, especially in mentally demanding jobs (Gottfredson, 1988), Sternberg, Wagner, and others are convinced of the distinction between academic, practical, and creative intelligences.

Figure 12–7   Although lacking in language ability, a severely subnormal English girl named Nadia could draw scenes she had witnessed with remarkable skill and accuracy. Nadia drew this horse and rider at age 5.

Drawing by Reilly; © 1988 The New Yorker Magazine, Inc.

"You're wise, but you lack tree smarts."

INTELLIGENCE AS INFORMATION PROCESSING

Recently, a wholly different approach to intelligence has begun to emerge. It asks whether differences in people's performance on intelligence tests can be traced to differences in their more fundamental capacities for processing sensory input and for learning, remembering, and solving problems. And if so, might such differences in how people process information suggest new ways to assess intelligence?

One pioneer of this new approach, Yale psychologist Robert Sternberg, wasted no time getting his career under way (Dorsey, 1987). His first studies of intelligence began as a seventh grader, when he administered IQ tests to other students at his school and did a science project on achievement testing. His senior yearbook quoted him as saying, "Intelligence is the most misunderstood personality trait." A decade and more later, Sternberg was stalking the roots of intelligence by identifying the information-processing procedures people use when taking intelligence tests. To find out what goes on in people's heads, he had subjects read the question portions of multiple-choice analogies, such as "lawyer is to client as doctor is to _____." He then measured how quickly the subjects signaled that they understood the question. Finally he showed the subjects the answer choices, such as (a) patient or (b) medicine, and measured how speedily they responded. Sternberg found that those who score as highly intelligent spend *more* time analyzing the questions than do those who score lower, but they are then able to recognize the correct answer more quickly. Sternberg (1984, 1985) and fellow researcher James Pellegrino (1985) noted that their research findings put a qualification on the common-sense maxim that "smart is fast." High scorers are "quick-witted" *after* they have comprehended a problem.

Examining a more elementary level of cognitive processing, Earl Hunt (1983) and his colleagues found that verbal intelligence scores are also related to the speed with which people retrieve information from memory. Those who score high in verbal ability tend to be slightly quicker than low scorers in recognizing, for example, that "SINK" and "wink" are different words, or that *A* and *a* share the same name.

Philip Vernon (1987) and Hans Eysenck (1982) confirmed that people with high IQ scores react faster than people with low IQ scores on various tests that measure their speed of processing simple information. IQ test items such as "In what way are *wool* and *cotton* alike?" might seem a long way from a measure of mental reaction times or of how quickly a flash of light is registered in someone's brain. But Vernon (1983) speculates that "faster cognitive processing may allow more information to be acquired." Perhaps people who get information into their brain quickly over time accumulate more information—about wool, cotton, and a million other things.

Do Vernon's and Eysenck's attempts to link IQ scores to information-processing speed sound familiar? A century after Galton's futile attempts to gauge intelligence in terms of people's reaction times and sensory abilities, his ideas still live. Will the new efforts be more successful? Will they achieve Galton's aim of reducing what we now call the g factor to simple measures of underlying brain activity? Or are these efforts totally wrongheaded because what we call intelligence is not a single general trait but a multiplicity of culturally defined adaptive skills? As you can see, the controversies surrounding the nature of intelligence are a long way from being resolved.

THE DYNAMICS OF INTELLIGENCE

We have learned a great deal in recent decades about the stability and significance of test scores. This has allowed us to make progress in understanding some of the age-old questions about human intelligence—about its stability over the life span, about mental retardation and brilliance, and about that special mental attribute called creativity.

Stability or Change?   If we were to test people periodically throughout their lives, would their IQ scores be stable? In Chapter 4, we considered the stability of intelligence in later life. What about the stability of intelligence scores early in life? New methods for measuring infants' attention to novel stimuli can modestly predict later intelligence—babies who quickly grow bored with a picture and prefer a new one tend to score well as 5-year-olds (Fagan, 1984; Kolata, 1987a). So, can preschoolers' IQ test performances predict their later performances?

"How are her scores?"

The question is especially interesting to new parents, who may wonder about their baby's intelligence. Those who are anxious about their baby seeming a little slower than others can relax. Except for extreme cases of retardation caused by physical defects, neither casual observation nor IQ tests can reliably predict the future intelligence scores of a child before age 3 (McCall & others, 1973).

After age 3, however, children's performances on intelligence tests begin to predict their adult scores. Although there are anecdotal reports to the contrary—Einstein, for instance, was slow in learning to talk (Quasha, 1980)—precocious adolescents tend to have been precocious preschoolers. One study surveyed the parents of 187 seventh and eighth graders who had taken the SAT as part of a seven-state talent search and had scored considerably higher than most high school seniors. If their parents' memories can be trusted, more than half of these precocious adolescents had begun reading by age 4 and more than 80 percent were reading by age 5 (Van Tassel-Baska, 1983).

After about age 7 stability in IQ scores becomes noteworthy (Bloom, 1964). So, the consistency of IQ scores over time increases with the age of the child. The remarkable stability of aptitude scores by late adolescence is seen in a recent Educational Testing Service study of 23,000 students who took the SAT and then later took the Graduate Record Examination (GRE) (Angoff, 1988). Scores on the SAT verbal test correlated +.86 with GRE verbal scores 4 to 5 years later; an equally high +.86 correlation was obtained between the two math tests. Whatever the SAT is measuring is reliably assessed by the GRE as well.

Ironically, these two exams correlate better with each other than either does with its intended criterion, school achievement.

Extremes of Intelligence   One way to glimpse the validity and significance of any test is to compare people who score at the two extremes of the normal curve. The two groups should differ noticeably, and they do. Let's look at them.

"Giftedness"   In one famous study begun in 1921, Lewis Terman tested more than 1500 California schoolchildren with IQs over 135. Contrary to the popular myth that intellectually "gifted" children are frequently maladjusted because they are "in a different world" from their nongifted peers, Terman's high-scoring children were found to be unusually healthy, well adjusted, and academically successful. When restudied over the next six decades (Goleman, 1980), most of these people had attained high levels of education. While their vocational success was varied, the group included many doctors, lawyers, professors, scientists, and authors of numerous books and articles.

"I'm a gifted child."

Critics nevertheless question many of the assumptions of the currently popular "gifted child" programs—that only some 3 to 5 percent of children are gifted, that it pays to identify and label these special few, to segregate them from the "nongifted," and to give them special opportunities not available to the masses. One recent review of fifty research studies concluded that students grouped by ability had academic achievement scores no higher than students not grouped, and that the ability grouping actually seemed to lower all the students' self-concepts (Noland, 1986). (Why might labeling and separating "gifted" and "nongifted" students affect both groups' self-concepts?)

Sorting children into gifted and nongifted groups often presumes that giftedness is a single trait—usually measured by an IQ test—rather than any one of many potentials. Newspaper and magazine articles advise parents how to spot "the signs of giftedness" in their children, as if giftedness were an objective quality, like blue eyes, that a child either has or lacks. This reifies giftedness—by creating the concept and then presuming that it has a concrete reality. It ignores the fact that we, not nature, decide the criteria of giftedness. The Social Science Research Council's committee on giftedness (1986) argues that, depending on the situation, giftedness might be a talent for mathematics or music or athletics, or even the social skills of an effective leader. Mozart was a genius at composing music, as was Einstein at physics, but we cannot judge from such genius their talent for poetry, painting, or politics. In our humbler ways, each of us is likewise a unique repository of gifts. If, indeed, there is not *an* intelligence but *multiple* intelligences, then one's giftedness cannot be reduced to a single IQ number.

"Alpha children wear grey. They work much harder than we do, because they're so frightfully clever. I'm really awfully glad I'm a Beta, because I don't work so hard. And then we are much better than the Gammas and Deltas. Gammas are stupid."
Aldous Huxley,
Brave New World, 1932

Mental Retardation   At the other extreme of the normal curve are people whose intelligence test scores fall below 70, many of whom are labeled *mentally retarded*. To be so labeled today, a child must have both a low IQ score *and* difficulty adapting to the normal demands of living independently. Only about 1 percent of the population meets both criteria, with males outnumbering females by 50 percent (American Psychiatric Association, 1987). As Table 12-1 indicates, most are "mildly retarded" individuals who suffer no obvious physical defect and who, with support, can be socially and vocationally successful.

Table 12-1
DEGREES OF MENTAL RETARDATION

Level	Percent of the retarded	Typical IQ scores	Adaptation to demands of life
Mild	85%	50–70	May learn academic skills up to sixth-grade level. Adults may, with assistance, achieve self-supporting social and vocational skills.
Moderate	10%	35–49	May progress to second-grade level. Adults may contribute to their own support by labor in sheltered workshops.
Severe	4%	20–34	May learn to talk and to perform simple work tasks under close supervision, but are generally unable to profit from vocational training.
Profound	1%	Below 20	Require constant aid and supervision.

Source: Adapted from the American Psychiatric Association (1987, pp. 32–33).

Indeed, as the idiot savants so strikingly demonstrate, even mentally handicapped individuals may have special gifts.

Severe retardation, characteristic of only 4 percent of the retarded, usually results from known physical causes, such as *Down syndrome,* a disorder normally caused by an extra chromosome in the person's genetic makeup.

During the last two centuries the pendulum of opinion about how best to care for the retarded has made a complete swing. Until the mid-nineteenth century, the mentally handicapped were cared for at home. The most severely retarded often died, but the mildly retarded found a place in a farm-based society. Then, in the United States, residential schools for the retarded were established. By the twentieth century many of these institutions had become warehouses providing no privacy, little attention, and no hope. Parents were often told to separate themselves permanently from a retarded child before they became attached. Now, in the last half of this century, the pendulum has swung back to normalization—allowing retarded people to live in their own communities as normally as their functioning permits. We educate mildly retarded children in less restrictive environments and many are "mainstreamed" (integrated) into regular classrooms. Most grow up with their own families until moving to a group home or some other protected living arrangement. The hope, and often the reality, is a happier and more dignified life.

Mentally handicapped individuals may, with support, live satisfying and productive lives, as do these women helping to prepare dinner in their group home.

Creativity and Intelligence   *Creativity* is the ability to produce ideas that are both novel and valuable. Psychologists have had difficulty constructing tests of creativity that agree with one another or that predict actual creativity in science, invention, and the arts (Jensen, 1980). Tests of creativity assess people's capacity for generating unusual responses to questions such as, "How many uses can you think of for a brick?"

Results from tests of intelligence and creativity suggest that a certain level of intelligence is necessary but not sufficient for creativity. In general, people with high IQ scores tend to do better on creativity tests and in their vocations than people with low scores. But beyond a certain level—an IQ score of about 120—the correlation between IQ scores and creativity disappears. Exceptionally creative architects, mathematicians, scientists, and engineers usually score no higher on intelligence tests than their less creative peers (MacKinnon & Hall, 1972).

Components of Creativity   That people with high IQ scores can be more or less creative hints that intelligence is but one component of creativity. Studies of creative people suggest three other components (Kohn, 1987b; Sternberg, 1988). The first is *expertise*—a well-developed base of knowledge. "Chance favors only the prepared mind," observed Louis Pasteur. The second is *imaginative thinking skills*—an ability to see things in new ways, to recognize patterns, to make connections. The third component is what psychologist Teresa Amabile calls the *intrinsic motivation* principle of creativity: "People will be most creative when they feel motivated primarily by the interest, enjoyment, satisfaction, and challenge of the work itself—and not by external pressures" (Amabile & Hennessey, 1988). Creative people focus not so much on meeting deadlines, impressing people, or making money, as on the pleasure and challenge of their work.

On his way home from picking up a Nobel prize in Stockholm, physicist Richard Feynman stopped in Queens, New York, to look at his high school record. "My grades were not as good as I remembered," he reported, "and my IQ was [an unexceptional] 124" (Faber, 1987).

Amabile's (1983, 1987) experiments illustrate the point: Social conditions that free people from concern about social approval enhance creativity. In one such experiment, college students were asked to make paper collages. Half were told beforehand that their work would be evaluated by experts and half were not told this. The students who were *not* aware that their work would be evaluated produced collages that judges later rated as more creative. In another experiment, Amabile (1985) studied young creative writers. Half were asked to rank intrinsic motives for writing, such as "you enjoy the opportunity for self-expression" and "you achieve new insights through your writing." The other half were asked to rank extrinsic motives, such as "you enjoy public recognition of your work" and "you know that many of the best jobs require good writing skills." When the subjects then wrote poems, those whose attention had been focused on intrinsic motives wrote poems that were rated by experts as more creative.

Managers who wish to foster innovation would do well to keep the intrinsic motivation principle in mind, notes Amabile (1988). They should set employees to work on activities that naturally interest them. And they can emulate managers who have successfully nurtured creativity—by setting goals for the endeavor and providing their subordinates with time, freedom, and support.

More on intrinsic motivation in the next chapter.

THE DETERMINANTS OF INTELLIGENCE

As Sir Francis Galton recognized, intelligence seems to run in families. But why? Is it because intellectual abilities are inherited? Or is it because intellectual abilities are molded by one's environment? These questions about the relative contributions of nature and nurture to academic intelligence have generated one of psychology's stormiest debates. To understand why, consider how people with differing political views have often used the "nature" and "nurture" positions.

If, on the one hand, differences in mental abilities are mainly inherited, and if socioeconomic success tends to reflect those abilities (especially in societies where social position depends more on individual merit than on one's social connections), then people's socioeconomic standings will correspond to inborn differences among them. Thus, those on top may tend to believe that their social positions are justified on the basis of their innate mental superiority. They may even be tempted to remind us that it was Thomas Jefferson, not God, who insisted that all people are created equal.

If, on the other hand, mental abilities are primarily nurtured—by the environment in which individuals are raised and schooled—then children from disadvantaged environments will tend to lead disadvantaged lives because their abilities will not have developed fully. In this case, people's socioeconomic standings will be the result of unequal opportunities, a situation that many regard as basically unjust.

Not surprisingly, those with conservative political viewpoints often tend to favor the nature position, whereas those whose beliefs are labeled liberal tend to find the nurture position closer to their views.

"I am, somehow, less interested in the weight and convolutions of Einstein's brain than in the near certainty that people of equal talent have lived and died in cotton fields and sweatshops."
Stephen J. Gould,
The Panda's Thumb, 1980

Genetic Determinants Virtually everyone now admits that both genes and the environment have some influence on IQ scores. The unresolved question for dispassionate research is "How much?"

Twin Studies Do people who share the same genes tend also to share mental abilities? As you can see from Figure 12–8 on page 336, which

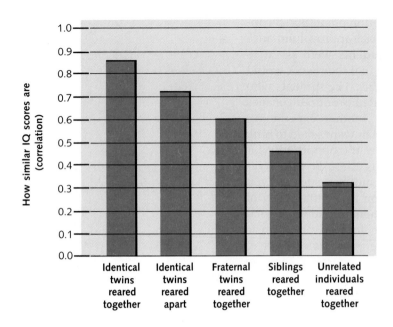

Figure 12–8   Intelligence: nature or nurture? How similar are the IQ test scores of identical twins? Of fraternal twins? Of siblings? Genetic similarity predicts similarity of IQ score, which suggests a substantial genetic contribution. But the correlations also indicate an environmental effect: Note the lower correlation between identical twins who have been reared apart; this can only be due to environmental influence. Remember: 1.0 on the vertical scale indicates a perfect correlation; 0.0 indicates no correlation at all. (From Bouchard, 1982.)

summarizes the accumulated data, the answer is clearly yes. For example, the IQ test scores of identical twins reared together are more similar than those of fraternal twins. What shall we make of these results? Let's eavesdrop on an imaginary conversation between two psychologists—one who believes that heredity powerfully influences intelligence test performance, and one who does not.

Hereditarian: The IQ test scores of identical twins are virtually as similar as those of the same person taking the test twice. In mental ability, as well as in genes, they are carbon copies of one another. By contrast, fraternal twins and other siblings share about half their genes. And, indeed, they are less similar in IQ score.

Environmentalist: Ah, but the identical twins are similar because they are treated similarly. Look at the data again and you'll see that fraternal twins, who are genetically no more alike than any other siblings, nevertheless tend to score more alike. John Loehlin and Robert Nichols (1976) studied hundreds of twins and found that identical twins are more likely than fraternal twins to be dressed alike, to sleep in the same room, to have the same friends and teachers, and so forth. So their greater similarity in IQ scores may be environmental.

Hereditarian: But Loehlin and Nichols also found that identical twins whose parents treated them alike were only slightly more similar than those whose parents did not. Furthermore, even when identical twins are reared separately, they still have IQ scores more alike than do fraternal twins and other siblings reared together. Having the same genes has more effect than having the same environment.

Environmentalist: Leon Kamin analyzed the older studies of separated identical twins and he reported that the separated twins often were selectively placed in similar environments. Storks don't deliver these babies at random, you know. Moreover, as new data accumulate, behavior geneticists are dropping their estimates of the extent to which variation in IQ scores can be attributed to heredity— from earlier estimates of around 80 percent to newer estimates of between 50 percent (Plomin & DeFries, 1980) and 60 percent (Bouchard & Segal, 1988). Certainly, studies of the genetic determinants of behavior can tell us as much about the importance of environment as about the importance of genes.

Adoption Studies   As our imaginary conversation illustrates, psychologists struggle to disentangle genes and environment. Several researchers have therefore asked whether adopted children have IQ scores more like those of their biological parents, from whom they receive their genes, or those of their adoptive parents, who provide their home environment. As Figure 12–9 shows, both correlations turn out to be weak. One reason is that adoptive parents tend to be quite bright, so there is less than the usual variation in their IQ scores. As we saw when we correlated body weight with boxing success, a narrowed range of scores lessens the observed correlations. Most adoptive parents are mental heavyweights.

When a statistical adjustment is made for the similarities in the IQ scores of adoptive parents, the correlation rises, but the conclusions remain the same: Adopted children have IQ scores somewhat more similar to their biological parents' than to their adoptive parents'.

Heritability   To say that the **heritability** of intelligence—the variation in intelligence attributable to genetic factors—is roughly 50 to 60 percent does *not* mean that your genes are responsible for 50 to 60 percent of your intelligence and your environment for the rest. (Likewise, saying that the heritability of height is 90 percent does not mean that a 60-inch-tall woman can credit her genes for 54 inches and her environment for the other 6 inches.) Rather, it means that, *of the variation in intelligence within a group of people,* at least 50 percent can be attributed to heredity. Remember: We can never say how much of an *individual's* intelligence is inherited. The heritability question instead asks, to what extent are the *differences among people* attributable to genes?

Even this conclusion must be qualified. First, the apparent heritability of any trait depends on the context in which that trait is being studied. To see why, imagine two researchers separately investigating whether intelligence is more determined by one's genes or one's life experience. One researcher gives IQ tests to two groups of adopted children, one group the biological offspring of retarded parents, the other of parents who tested at the genius level. Her conclusion: The differences among the children are much more attributable to the intelligence of their biological parents than to the quality of their home environment. Meanwhile, another researcher is comparing another two groups, one the offspring of parents with average intelligence, the other, offspring of parents with slightly above average intelligence. Half of each group of children have been reared in loving homes, the other half in an impoverished orphanage. This researcher finds the quality of the environment to be the primary influence. Meeting at a convention, the first researcher reports that in her study the intelligence differences were primarily genetic; the second researcher reports that in his study they were primarily environmental. Who is right?

They both are, but only for the specific groups they studied under their specified conditions. Let's generalize the point: The heritability of a trait will be low when we compare people with not-so-different heredities in drastically different environments. If everyone had the same heredity, heritability—differences due to genes—would be zero. Conversely, when we compare people with very different heredities from basically similar environments, the heritability of their traits will be greater.

Second, remember that genes and environment are intertwined, not separate. Our genetically influenced traits may trigger responses from people that encourage us to develop our natural gifts and may lead us to select particular environments. Students with a natural aptitude for mathematics are more likely to select math courses in high school, and subsequently to score well on the SAT math test—thanks *both* to their natural math aptitude *and* their math experience. Thus our genes shape the experiences that, in turn, shape us.

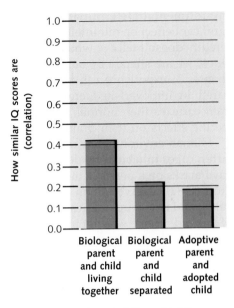

Figure 12–9   The correlations of intelligence test scores between children and their adoptive and biological parents. Adopted children are slightly more similar to their biological than to their adoptive parents, but the data reveal both a genetic and an environmental effect. (From Bouchard & McGue, 1981.)

Environmental Determinants   We have seen that our genes have a significant effect on our intellectual abilities. But we have also seen that heredity doesn't tell the whole story. Within the limits dictated by our genes, we are shaped by our life experiences. As you may recall from Chapter 3, experience can literally leave its mark on the brain: Rats reared in impoverished environments develop lighter and thinner brain cortexes than normal, and particular learning experiences have specific effects on their brains' neural connections.

Human environments are rarely so impoverished as the dark and barren cages inhabited by deprived rats. Yet life experiences may also leave marks on a person's mental abilities, as psychologist J. McVicker Hunt (1982) observed in an Iranian orphanage in Tehran. The typical child could not sit up unassisted at age 2 or walk at age 4. What care the infants did receive was not in response to their crying, cooing, or other behaviors. The infants were therefore not developing any sense of personal control over their environment, and so were becoming passive "glum lumps."

Hunt was well aware of research on the positive benefits of responsive caregiving. So he put the principle into action by instituting a program of "tutored human enrichment." For instance, caregivers were trained to play vocal games with the infants. First, they imitated the babies' babbling, then they led the babies in vocal follow-the-leader by shifting from one familiar sound to another, and then they began to concentrate on sounds from the Persian language.

The results were dramatic. Without exception, all eleven infants who received these language-fostering experiences and whose signs of distress were promptly responded to could name more than fifty objects and parts of the body by the age of 22 months. So charming had the infants become that most of them were adopted—an unprecedented success for the orphanage.

Hunt's findings testify to the importance of environment. But do they indicate how to "give your child a superior intellect"? Some popular books claim that this is possible, but many experts are doubtful. Developmental psychologist Sandra Scarr (1984) agrees that neglectful upbringing can have grave long-term consequences for children. However, she also believes that "as long as an infant has normal human contact and normal exposure to sights, sounds, human speech and so forth, the baby will thrive." As for future intelligence: "Parents who are very concerned about providing special educational lessons for their babies are wasting their time." Parents of children with high IQ scores are more likely to hang mobiles over their cribs, take them to the theater, or whatever. But do such practices have any effect? We don't know, says Scarr (1986b). Parents supply their children with both genes and environments. So even if the environments of children with high IQ scores are noticeably different from those with low scores, we can't be sure how much difference their environments make.

Although Hunt would probably agree with Scarr that extra instruction has little effect on the intellectual development of children from stimulating environments, he is optimistic when it comes to children from disadvantaged environments. Indeed, his views, as expressed in his 1961 book, *Intelligence and Experience*, helped launch Project Head Start in 1965.

Head Start is a family of preschool programs designed for children from educationally disadvantaged environments and funded by the U.S. government. All these programs "share a commitment to enhancing the quality of life for children and families," and to improving children's cognitive and social-emotional development (Zigler & Ber-

''There is a large body of evidence indicating that there is little if anything to be gained by exposing middle-class children to early education.''

Developmental psychologist Edward F. Zigler (1987)

Intelligence experts dispute claims that special lessons (see photo at left) can give preschoolers superior minds. But Project Head Start, which deals with educationally disadvantaged 5-year-olds, has shown itself to aid in adjustment to school.

man, 1983). In 1986, Head Start was serving 452,000 children and their families in over 1300 communities (Washington & Oyemade, 1987). Research studies on its effects initially triggered euphoria over the short-term IQ gains that resulted, and then pessimism because of the lack of longer-term gains. Now, a quarter-century and 1500 studies later, there appears to be a growing consensus that Head Start has been a qualified success. In the words of the Reagan administration official responsible for distilling the accumulated research, "compensatory education has been tried, and it works" (Collins, 1983).

Head Start children do not show large, enduring gains in IQ score. But on other measures they surpass disadvantaged children who have not participated (Lee & others, 1988). Head Start graduates are less likely to repeat grades or require special education classes and more likely to enjoy positive self-esteem and adjust well to school. These benefits occur not because children become fundamentally smarter, but because Head Start helps them cope with the first year or two of school, thus steering them up a pathway of higher expectations (Woodhead, 1988). Such benefits are greatest for children from the most disadvantaged families.

GROUP DIFFERENCES IN INTELLIGENCE TEST SCORES

The issue of hereditary versus environmental determinants of intelligence would not be debated so passionately were there no differences in the average academic aptitude scores among various groups. But there are. As we noted in Chapter 5, males average higher scores than females on math aptitude tests. Recent comparisons have found that Japanese schoolchildren have a slightly higher average than American children on nonverbal items from the WISC-R (Lynn, 1982, 1983) and on mathematics achievement tests (Stevenson, 1983). Asian-Americans, who constitute less than 2 percent of the U.S. population, won 25 percent of the top 120 spots in the Westinghouse Science Talent Search between 1983 and 1985 (Doerner, 1985; McGrath, 1983; Williams, 1984). Similarly, when American blacks have been compared to American whites (neither of which is a random sample of blacks and whites worldwide), blacks have averaged about 15 points lower than whites on IQ tests and a comparable 100 points lower on the SAT verbal and math tests (Loehlin & others, 1975; Jacobson, 1986; Jensen, 1985).

Bear in mind that *average* differences between groups tell us nothing about specific *individuals*. Women outlive men by about 6 years, but

In mathematics, Japanese schoolchildren outperform their American counterparts. What, if anything, does this tell us about the math aptitude of youngsters in the United States relative to those in Japan?

knowing an individual's sex doesn't tell us how long that person is going to live. Similarly, knowledge of your race tells us very little about your likely performance on a mental abilities test.

On the other hand, argues sociologist Linda Gottfredson (1988), "Ignoring or denying the importance of group IQ differences does nothing to blunt their impact on society." We can all wish it were otherwise, but the fact is that the black-white test score gap persists and that high-scoring people are much more likely than low-scoring people to attain high levels of education and high-paying jobs. The hard truth: Using IQ-related tests to select people for school admissions tends to exclude blacks. The racial gaps in academic aptitude test scores therefore raise a potent issue: Do they reflect racial gaps in inherent mental ability?

Let's start with a basic question: If heredity contributes to individual differences in intelligence, does it also contribute to group differences? Not necessarily. Consider the following hypothetical case. Suppose that we were to study math aptitude in an American school and in a Japanese school. Suppose further that we were somehow able to determine that the differences among the children within each school were entirely due to heredity. If we then found that the Japanese children had higher scores than the American children, could we also attribute the differences between the two groups to heredity?

The answer to this question is plainly no, and geneticist Richard Lewontin (1976) has demonstrated why. If a mixture of seeds is sown on poor soil, the differing heights of the resulting plants will be the result of genetic differences among them. If seeds from the same mixture are sown on fertile soil, the differing heights of these plants will again be the result of genetic differences. But, as Figure 12–10 illustrates, the difference in the average heights of the two groups of plants will be due to environmental differences in the soil in which the plants grew. Thus, even if the heritability of a trait is extremely high *within* a particular group, differences in that trait *among* groups may nevertheless have environmental causes.

This point is so important, and so widely misunderstood, that it demands repeating. Consider: If each identical twin were exactly as tall as his or her co-twin, heritability would be 100 percent. Imagine that we then separated some young twins and gave only half of them a nutritious diet, and that the well-nourished twins all grew to be exactly 3 inches taller than their counterparts—an environmental effect comparable to that actually observed in Britain and America where adolescents are several inches taller than they were half a century ago (Angoff, 1987; R. Lynn, 1987). What would the heritability of height be now for our well-nourished twins? Still 100 percent, because the variation in height within the group (or in this case the lack of variation) would remain entirely predictable from the uniform heights of their malnourished siblings. So even perfect heritability within groups would not eliminate the possibility of a strong environmental impact on the different groups.

This is reflected in the belief of most expert psychologists that the racial gap is in large measure environmental (Snyderman & Rothman, 1987). To see why, consider:

1. The average white person in the United States has grown up and been educated in somewhat different conditions than those experienced by the average black person. One attempt at equalizing the educational environments of blacks and whites, desegregation, has generally had only slight effects on the school achievements of black children during its first 30 years. The benefits, though, have been most notable

Might test scores predict job attainment because such scores are used to admit or exclude people from educational opportunities?

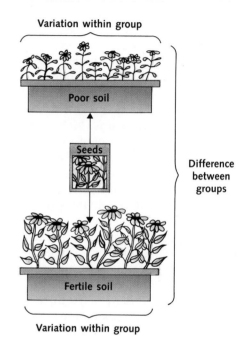

Variation within group

Poor soil

Seeds

Difference between groups

Fertile soil

Variation within group

Figure 12–10   Even if the variation within a group reflects genetic differences (differences between seeds), the average difference between groups may be wholly due to the environment.

Test differences of 15 IQ points can occur between different generations of the same national group—clearly not a genetic effect. Surely equivalent differences among racial groups might also not be genetic.

when desegregation began in kindergarten or the first grade and extended over a number of years (Cook, 1984). As educational opportunities have moved toward more equal opportunity, the black-white SAT difference has shrunk by 20 points on both the verbal and math tests since 1976 (College Board, 1987). Motivate children with rewards for correct answers on IQ tests and the black-white difference shrinks further (Bradley-Johnson & others, 1984).

2. The impact of environment is evident in the mathematical competence of Asian and American children. When psychologist Harold Stevenson and his co-workers (1986, 1987) studied randomly selected elementary schoolchildren in three comparable cities—Sendai in Japan, Minneapolis in the United States, and Taipei in Taiwan—they found that by fifth grade the Asian children were roughly one standard deviation (the equivalent of about 15 IQ points) superior to the American children (Figure 12-11). In fact, in fifth grade the best of the twenty American classes sampled fell below the lowest of the Japanese classes. Among the top 100 students, 1 was American; among the lowest 100, 67 were American.

Compared to elementary school students in Minneapolis, those in Sendai and Taipei attend school 30 percent more days per year, spend much more of their school day studying math, do much more homework, and more strongly believe that "any student can be good at math if he/she works hard enough." Similarly, the current academic success rate of immigrant Asian-Americans is generally attributed not to heredity but to the values they place on hard work, educational achievement, and family cohesiveness (Caplan & others, 1985).

3. Further evidence of environmental impact on intelligence test scores comes from adoption studies. Consider: If black children were reared in privileged, white middle-class homes, would their average IQ score be closer to the average score for black children or for white children? Sandra Scarr and Richard Weinberg (1976) studied 99 such children in Minneapolis. The average IQ score of these children was 110, which is comparable to the average score of white children adopted into similar advantaged families. Thus, being reared as a privileged middle-class child appears to produce middle-class IQ scores.

4. Scarr and her colleagues (1977) also found that having more or less African ancestry bears no relation to scores on cognitive tests within the black population. If the racial difference in IQ is due to racial differences per se, then people of uniform racial heritage should exhibit the IQ difference more strongly. But in this study they didn't. Moreover, children whose mothers were German and whose fathers were black or white American servicemen stationed in Germany after World War II, and who were reared in similar German environments, had nearly identical average IQ scores (Mackenzie, 1984).

5. At different times in history, different ethnic groups have experienced "golden ages," periods of remarkable achievement—2500 years ago it was the Greeks and the Egyptians, then the Romans; in the eighth and ninth centuries, the Arab world; 500 years ago the Aztec Indians, as well as the peoples of northern Europe. Cultures rise and fall over centuries; genes do not. That fact makes it difficult to attribute to any race a "natural" superiority.

Despite all the evidence supporting environmental explanations, suppose that genetic differences do contribute to race and sex differences not only in physical traits and susceptibility to certain diseases, but also in test scores. Would it, or should it, matter? Not to individuals, for whom what matters is their own potential. Not to potential employers, for knowing a person's race or sex does not reveal the

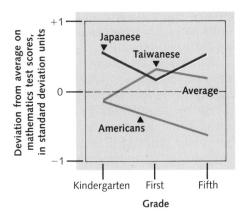

Figure 12-11 Children's mathematics performance in Minneapolis, Sendai, and Taipei. With time in school, math test scores by Minneapolis children fell further and further below the three-city average. (Adapted from Stevenson, 1987.)

Ironically, given the debate over comparable black-white differences, psychologists don't hesitate to explain the poorer math performance of the (mostly white) Americans in terms of environment.

Whether black or white, children raised in privileged middle-class homes tend to have IQ scores typical of the middle class.

applicant's potential. And not to social policy, for the impact of environmental disadvantages would nevertheless unquestionably remain significant.

Finally, we must remember that IQ scores reflect only one aspect of personal competence. Other attributes—motivation, character, social skills, sensitivity, emotional maturity, artistic talent, athletic activity—are also of great importance. In other words, the competence that is sampled by intelligence tests is important, but far from all-inclusive. The spatial ability of the carpenter differs from the logical ability of the computer programmer, which differs from the verbal ability of the poet. Differences are not deficits. Because there are many alternative ways of being successful, our differences—regardless of their origins—are valuable variations on the human theme of adaptability.

THE QUESTION OF BIAS

How we answer the question of whether or not intelligence tests are biased depends on what we mean by the term "bias." One meaning is that the tests are sensitive not only to innate differences in intelligence but also to differences caused by cultural experiences. In this sense, everyone agrees that intelligence tests are biased. No one claims that heritability is 100 percent responsible for the score obtained on any test. An intelligence test measures a person's developed abilities at a particular moment in time, and these abilities necessarily reflect that person's experiences and environment. If people's experiences and backgrounds are unequal, those inequalities will be reflected in the test's results.

You have probably read examples of intelligence test items that make middle-class assumptions (for example, that a cup goes with a saucer or, as in one of the sample test items from the WAIS [page 321], that people buy fire insurance to protect the value of their homes and possessions). Do such items bias the test against those who do not use saucers and whose meager possessions and income hardly warrant the cost of fire insurance? Could such test questions explain the racial differences in test performance? If so, are tests therefore a discriminatory vehicle that could be used to consign potentially capable children to dead-end classes and jobs (as the judge argued in the case of Larry and the six other black children noted at the beginning of this chapter)?

The defenders of aptitude testing respond that racial group differences have been reported on nonverbal items, such as counting digits backward, as well as on verbal items, such as vocabulary knowledge (Jensen, 1983). Moreover, they say that to blame the test for a group's lower scores is comparable to blaming a messenger for bringing the bad news—it is the culture that provides unequal experiences and opportunities to different people. If because of malnutrition the people in a certain country were to suffer stunted growth, would one blame the measuring stick that reveals it? To the extent that unequal past experiences predict unequal future achievements, a valid aptitude test will detect such inequalities.

Another meaning of "bias" hinges on whether a test is less valid for some groups than for others. If the SAT accurately predicts the college achievement of whites but is irrelevant to that of blacks, then the test would be biased. The near consensus among psychologists today, as summarized by the National Research Council's Committee on Ability Testing (Wigdor & Garner, 1982), is that the major aptitude tests are *not* biased in this meaning of the term. The predictive validity of the SAT, for example, is roughly the same for blacks and whites.

"Almost all the joyful things of life are outside the measure of IQ tests."
Madeleine L'Engle,
A Circle of Quiet, 1972

Tests assess one's developed ability, which is influenced by one's life experience. To the extent that a particular environment has hampered or enhanced intellectual growth, a valid test will reflect this effect.

So, it is possible for aptitude tests to be biased in one sense and not in another. For example, if a college's courses and teachers share a particular vocabulary and set of assumptions that make it difficult for people from a foreign culture to excel there, then test scores that accurately predict success in that school will be influenced by a person's cultural background. The test would therefore be culturally biased, because it mirrors the school's cultural bias. Yet the test might be an equally valid predictor of performance for all those who take it, and in this sense not be biased.

Are tests discriminatory? Again, the answer can be yes or no. In one sense, yes, their purpose is to discriminate—to distinguish among individuals. In another sense, their purpose is to reduce discrimination by reducing reliance on the subjective criteria that were once more crucial for school and job placement—criteria such as whom you know, what you look like, or how much the interviewer happens to like your kind of person. Prohibiting the use of aptitude tests simply means that the people who decide admissions and jobs will have to rely more on other considerations, such as their personal opinions. Civil service tests, for example, discriminate among individuals, but were devised to do so more fairly and objectively, by reducing the political discrimination that preceded their use. So perhaps our aim should be to realize the benefits that Alfred Binet foresaw for intelligence tests—to guide individuals toward school opportunities that will be most beneficial for them—while being wary of Binet's fear that test scores might be misinterpreted as measures of a person's worth and fixed potential.

SUMMING UP

ASSESSING INTELLIGENCE

The Origins of Intelligence Tests Attempts to measure individual mental abilities were first undertaken more than a century ago by Sir Francis Galton. Although Galton failed in his efforts to invent simple, quantifiable mea- sures of mental ability, his idea of assessing intellectual capacity was applied by Alfred Binet. Binet developed questions that helped to predict children's future progress in the Paris school system. Like Galton, Lewis Terman of Stanford University was convinced that intelligence was inherited, and, like Binet, he believed his test (called the

Stanford-Binet) could help guide people toward appropriate opportunities. During the early part of this century, intelligence tests were sometimes used in ways that, in hindsight, seemed regrettable even to their designers—to "document" the presumed innate inferiority of certain ethnic and immigrant groups.

Modern Tests of Mental Abilities Tests are commonly classified as either aptitude tests (designed to predict learning ability) or achievement tests (designed to assess current competence), and as assessing either general abilities (as do the Wechsler scales and the SAT) or more specific abilities (as does the DAT).

Principles of Test Construction A good test must be standardized, so that a person's performance can be meaningfully compared to others'; reliable, so that it yields dependably consistent scores (over the short run); and valid, so that it measures what it is supposed to measure. Test scores tend to fall into a normal distribution, with the average score given some arbitrary number (such as 100 on an IQ test). Despite small coaching effects, aptitude tests tend to be highly reliable. Their predictive validity is fairly strong in the early grades but weakens for predicting grades in college and even more so in graduate school, as the range of student abilities becomes restricted.

THE NATURE OF INTELLIGENCE

It is tempting but misleading to reify concepts such as "intelligence" and "giftedness"—to regard these abstract concepts as if they were real, concrete things. Intelligence is most commonly defined by experts as "goal-directed adaptive behavior."

Intelligence as Culturally Defined or as a Culture-Free Problem-Solving Ability Some psychologists argue that intelligent behavior (say, a person's ability to adapt successfully to the demands of school or work) is culturally relative; others contend that intelligence can be viewed as a culture-free ability to solve problems.

Intelligence as an Overall Ability or as Several Specific Abilities Psychologists agree that people possess specific abilities, such as verbal and mathematical aptitudes, but they debate whether a general intelligence (g) factor runs through them all. Factor analysis and studies of special people such as idiot savants have been used to identify people's clusters of mental abilities.

Intelligence as Information Processing More recently, psychologists have linked people's intelligence to their more fundamental capacities for processing information. Some psychologists are studying the components that make up problem-solving skill, others the speed with which people's brains can process information.

The Dynamics of Intelligence The stability of intelligence test scores increases with age, with predictive value beginning at about age 3. Comparing those who score extremely high (the "gifted") or low (the "retarded") will magnify a test's apparent validity. Intelligence is weakly correlated with creativity; increases in intelligence beyond a necessary threshold level are not associated with increased creativity.

The Determinants of Intelligence Because of its political and racial overtones, the nature-nurture debate with regard to intelligence has at times been vehement. Studies of twins, family members, and adopted children all are controversial, yet together point to a significant hereditary contribution to IQ scores. These same studies, plus others that compare children reared in neglectful or enriched environments, indicate that life experiences also significantly influence test performance.

Group Differences in Intelligence Test Scores Like individuals, groups may vary in intelligence scores. The existences of hereditary variation within a group does not justify a hereditary explanation of the differences between groups. In the case of the gap between black and white Americans in average IQ scores, the evidence suggests that environmental differences are largely, perhaps entirely, responsible.

The Question of Bias If by "biased" one means sensitive to differences caused by cultural experience, then aptitude tests are necessarily biased. If by biased one means what psychologists commonly mean—that a test predicts less validly for one group than for another—then the major tests we have considered seem not to be biased.

TERMS AND CONCEPTS TO REMEMBER

achievement tests Tests designed to assess what a person already has learned.

aptitude tests Tests designed to predict a person's future performance; aptitude is the capacity to learn.

content validity The extent to which a test samples the behavior that is of interest (such as a driving test that samples driving tasks).

creativity The ability to produce ideas that are both novel and valuable.

criterion The behavior (such as college grades) that a test (such as the SAT) is designed to predict; thus, the measure used in defining whether the test has predictive validity.

Down syndrome A condition of retardation and associated physical disorders caused by an extra chromosome in one's genetic makeup.

factor analysis   A statistical procedure that identifies clusters of related items (called factors) on a test; used to identify different dimensions of performance that underlie one's total score.

general intelligence (g)   A general underlying intelligence factor believed by Spearman and others to be measured by every task on an intelligence test.

heritability   The extent to which differences in a trait can be attributed to genes. Heritability of a trait may vary, depending on the range of populations and environments studied.

idiot savant   A retarded person who possesses an amazing specific skill, such as in computation or drawing.

intelligence   The capacity for goal-directed adaptive behavior (behavior that successfully meets challenges and achieves its aims). Involves the abilities to profit from experience, solve problems, and reason.

intelligence quotient (IQ)   Defined originally as the ratio of mental age to chronological age multiplied by 100 (thus IQ = MA/CA × 100). Contemporary tests compute IQ score by giving the average performance for a given age a score of 100, with other IQ scores defined in terms of their deviation from the average.

mental age   A measure of intelligence test performance devised by Binet; the chronological age that most typically corresponds to a given level of performance. Thus a child who does as well as the average 8-year-old is said to have a mental age of 8.

mental retardation   A condition of limited mental ability, as assessed by an IQ score below 70, that produces diffi-culty in adapting to the demands of life; varies from mild to profound.

normal curve (or **normal distribution)**   The symmetrical bell-shaped curve that describes the distribution of many physical and psychological attributes (including IQ scores), with most scores falling near the average and fewer and fewer near the extremes.

predictive validity   The success with which a test predicts the behavior it is designed to predict; assessed by computing the correlation between test scores and the criterion behavior.

reliability   The extent to which a test yields consistent results (as assessed by the consistency of scores on two halves of the test, on alternate forms of the test, or on retesting). See *split-half reliability* and *test-retest reliability*.

split-half reliability   A measure of the internal consistency of a test; typically assessed by correlating total scores obtained on the odd- and even-numbered items.

standardization   Defining meaningful scores by comparison with the performance of a representative "standardization group" that has been pretested.

Stanford-Binet   The widely used American revision (by Terman at Stanford University) of Binet's original intelligence test.

test-retest reliability   A measure of the consistency of test scores; assessed by retesting people and correlating these scores with their initial scores.

validity   The extent to which a test measures or predicts what it is supposed to. (See also *content validity* and *predictive validity*.)

Wechsler Adult Intelligence Scale (WAIS)   The most widely used intelligence test; contains a variety of verbal and nonverbal (performance) subtests.

FOR FURTHER READING

Fancher, R. E. (1985).   *The intelligence men*. New York: Norton.

An account of past and current controversies regarding the nature of intelligence and the people who set out to measure it.

Gould, S. J. (1981).   *The mismeasure of man*. New York: Norton.

Offers a provocative, engaging, and sharply critical look at the history of the intelligence testing movement and its abuses.

Sternberg, R. (1986).   *Intelligence applied: Understanding and increasing your intellectual skills*. San Diego: Harcourt Brace Jovanovich.

A leading researcher presents his theory of intelligence to a gen-eral audience and offers "how-to" suggestions for increasing one's practical intelligence.

White, J. L. (1984).   *The psychology of blacks: An Afro-American perspective*. Englewood Cliffs, NJ: Prentice-Hall.

A black psychologist looks at racial differences in intelligence scores and in other traits and behaviors.

Wigdor, A. K., & Garner, W. R. (1982).   *Ability testing: Uses, consequences, and controversies*. Washington, DC: National Academic Press.

A blue-ribbon panel of the U.S. National Research Council offers its analysis of ability testing. An authoritative source of prevailing professional opinion on the major issues.

PART 5

Motivation and Emotion

Our behavior is energized and directed by a complex mixture of motives and emotions. In Chapter 13, Motivation, we consider the nature of motivation by looking closely at the workings of three specific motives—hunger, sex, and the need to achieve. Chapter 14, Emotion, examines feelings such as fear, anger, and happiness that add color to our lives, and shows how each is composed of a mixture of physiological arousal, expressive behaviors, and conscious experiences.

CHAPTER 13

MOTIVATION

In everyday conversation, the question "What motivated you to do that?" is a way of asking "What *caused* you to do that? *Why* did you act that way?" To psychologists—whose discipline aims to reveal the causes of behavior—a ***motivation*** is a need or desire that serves to *energize* behavior and to *direct* it toward a goal. Like intelligence, motivation is a hypothetical concept. We infer motivation from behaviors we observe, as in the following examples:

The yearning for food—

> In the Nazi concentration camps . . . we would get up early, about 4 or 4:30 in the morning, and stand in line. They would give us a hot tea or a coffee which was hot water boiled with some kind of grassy substance. There was no sugar or anything else to put in it. It was just something hot. We downed it and that was our breakfast. . . .
>
> I was so glad I wasn't with my father or brother during this time. You have no idea how a father and son would fight over a piece of bread. Like dogs.
>
> One man in my barracks was about 45. He was dignified in spite of his emaciated state. He had a son about 20 who also lived in the barracks.
>
> One evening the son ate his own bread while the father placed his under a piece of cloth he used as a pillow. The next morning I heard the father scream—his bread was gone. His son had eaten it during the night.
>
> The father went into a deep depression. He kept asking how his son could do such a thing to him. I guess the father lost his will to live, because the next day he was dead. . . .
>
> Hunger does something to you that's hard to describe. I can't believe it myself today, so how can I expect anyone else to understand it?
>
> David Mandel (1983)

The need to achieve—

> Alfredo Gonzales, winner of his community's "man of the year" award and three-time chairperson of Michigan's Commission on the Spanish-speaking, is a successful 40-year-old college administrator with a master's degree from the University of Michigan.
>
> Although born in the United States, Alfredo as a 14-year-old would have been found where he had spent all but the first year of his life—on his grandparents' primitive farm in Mexico, tilling the land with a team of oxen, planting and picking crops, and hauling water from a canal several miles away. Later that year, after Alfredo rejoined his parents in Texas, a school truant officer discovered him picking fruit and ordered him off to the local junior high school.

The longing for sexual intimacy—

> I am sick with love.
> O that his left hand were under
>   my head, and that his right hand
>   embraced me! . . .
> By night on my bed I sought him
>   whom my soul loves: I sought him
>   but I found him not.
> I will rise now, and go about the city
>   in the streets, and in the broad ways
>   I will seek him whom my soul loves:
>   I sought him but I found him not.
>
> * * *
>
> How fair and pleasant you are,
>   O loved one, delectable maiden!
> You are stately as a palm tree,
>   and your breasts are like its clusters.
> I say I will climb the palm tree
>   and lay hold of its branches.
> Oh, may your breasts be like clusters
>   of the vine, and the scent of your
>   breath like apples,
> And your kisses like the best wine
>   that goes down smoothly,
>   gliding over lips and teeth. . . .
>
> *Song of Solomon* (Old Testament)

There, for the first time in his life, Alfredo saw the inside of a school classroom and heard English. "I walked into a room filled mostly with other Mexican-Americans," recalls Gonzales, "all of whom were prohibited from speaking Spanish. Several times I was caught trying to ask a question in Spanish—for which the 'cure' was being beaten with a paddle."

How did the shy, illiterate child of migrant farm workers achieve his present status? Although placed at the lowest skill level by his schools and discouraged from high aspirations, he began to sense, as he still does, that "I could do better. I don't know as much as I could know."

So, while working as a city human relations officer after his release from the army, he completed his college education part-time, became director of a college Upward Bound program, and then Dean. His aim, he says, is to motivate youth by giving them what he obviously developed in himself—"an awareness of their own potential and a desire to achieve it."

In this chapter we will explore motivation by focusing on these three motives—hunger, sex, and achievement. Although many identifiable motives exist (thirst, curiosity, need for approval, and so forth), a close look at just these three will reveal some important principles of motivation, such as the interplay between biological influences and external stimuli. Along the way, we will discover answers to some intriguing questions:

What is the source of gnawing hunger or ardent sexual desire?

Why is the arousal provided by these motives directed toward some targets rather than others, say toward a person of one sex rather than another?

What motivates us to achieve—is it more an inner quest to excel, or a desire for rewards such as social recognition?

First, however, let us look at a few longstanding perspectives on motivation. Like other psychological attributes, motivation can be viewed as resulting from nature and from nurture, from biological "pushes" and from cognitive and cultural "pulls."

CONCEPTS OF MOTIVATION

As the influence of Darwin's theory of evolution grew, people began viewing human behavior less as a product of rational choices and more as a product of biological forces. Sigmund Freud theorized that biologically based sexual and aggressive urges motivated a wide variety of behaviors. Other theorists focused on the instinctive behavior of animals and wondered whether humans might similarly be governed by biological instincts.

To qualify as an *instinct*, a behavior must have a fixed pattern, be characteristic of the whole species, occur in organisms isolated from other members of their species, and develop without practice (Tinbergen, 1951). Thus to be considered instinctive, a human behavior would have to occur in all people, regardless of differing cultures and opportunities for learning. Such behaviors are common in other species (recall the return of salmon to their birthplace to spawn and imprinting in birds). But apart from simple behaviors such as breathing, few human behaviors are sufficiently automatic to meet these criteria.

Nevertheless, early in this century it became fashionable to classify all sorts of behaviors as instincts. If people criticized themselves, it was because of their "self-abasement instinct"; if they boasted, it reflected their "self-assertion instinct." One sociologist compiled a list of 5759

The more complex the nervous system, the more adaptable the organism. The weaver bird's construction skills are instinctual; the human's are learned.

supposed human instincts! Before long, the instinct-naming fad collapsed under its own weight. The early instinct theorists were not explaining human behaviors, but naming them.

There is an important lesson to be learned here. What the instinct theorists did is what we are still sometimes tempted to do: to *explain* a behavior (or fool ourselves into thinking we are explaining it) by *naming* it. The result is a kind of circular reasoning:

> "Why do we spend $3 billion per *day* for arms and armies, while hundreds of millions of people must subsist without adequate food and shelter?"
>
> "It's because of our aggression instinct."
>
> "How do you know we have an aggression instinct?"
>
> "Just look at how much world governments spend on preparing for war—almost $200 per year for every person on earth, millions of whom will never receive $200 in a year!"

While we might agree that these priorities are tragic, this circular explanation of them is no explanation at all. It is like "explaining" a bright child's low grades by saying he or she is an "underachiever." Descriptive labels are an essential part of every science. Nevertheless, to name a behavior, as a supposed instinct or with a diagnostic label, is *not* to explain it.

BIOLOGICAL STATES: THE PUSHES

When the instinct theory of motivation collapsed, it was replaced by the idea that a biological need creates an aroused state, driving an organism to satisfy the need. To psychologists a **need** is a tissue deficit, a deprivation such as a physiological lack of food or water. Food or water deprivation will arouse an organism to replenish its stores. This aroused or activated state is sometimes called a **drive,** and it prompts the organism to reduce the drive by, say, eating or drinking. When a biological need increases, its psychological consequence, a drive, usually increases, too.

The physiological aim of drive reduction is **homeostasis**—which literally means "staying the same"—the maintenance of a balanced or constant internal state. An example of homeostasis is the body's temperature-regulation system, which works much as a thermostat works to keep room temperature at a constant level. Both systems operate through feedback loops, with adjustments based on information that is continually fed back into the system. Sensors detect the temperature of the room or body and feed this information to a control device, which notes any deviations from the desired state and sends instructions that help adjust the temperature. If the room is too cool the furnace comes on. If body temperature cools, blood vessels constrict to conserve warmth, and we may feel driven to put on more clothes or seek a warmer environment. Similarly, if our cellular water level drops, sensors will detect this and thirst will drive us.

COGNITION AND CULTURE: THE PULLS

There are, however, motives that do not seem to satisfy any biological need. Monkeys will monkey around trying to figure out how to unlock a latch that opens nothing or will attempt to open a window that allows them to see outside their room (Butler, 1954). The 9-month-old infant who investigates every accessible corner of the house, the scientists whose work we will be discussing, and the adventurers who first

Curiosity. The activities of these young monkeys and this child powerfully demonstrate the early presence of an insatiable urge to explore—one of the many intrinsic motives that does not fulfill any obvious physiological need.

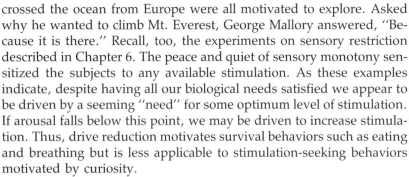

For people who crave the stimulation of ever-increasing tests of their courage or mastery, physical and mental challenges are powerful incentives.

crossed the ocean from Europe were all motivated to explore. Asked why he wanted to climb Mt. Everest, George Mallory answered, "Because it is there." Recall, too, the experiments on sensory restriction described in Chapter 6. The peace and quiet of sensory monotony sensitized the subjects to any available stimulation. As these examples indicate, despite having all our biological needs satisfied we appear to be driven by a seeming "need" for some optimum level of stimulation. If arousal falls below this point, we may be driven to increase stimulation. Thus, drive reduction motivates survival behaviors such as eating and breathing but is less applicable to stimulation-seeking behaviors motivated by curiosity.

As the cognitive perspective gained prominence in psychology, researchers began to appreciate that we are not only pushed by our needs, but pulled by incentives we perceive in the environment. This is where our individual learning histories influence our motives, because an *incentive* is any external stimulus that has come to have positive or negative value in motivating our behavior. Depending on our learning, the aroma of fresh roasted peanuts (or toasted ants), the sight of one's lover, and the threat of disapproval can all motivate behaviors. Behavior is energized and directed by these external incentives, as well as by our internal needs. When there is both a need and an incentive, the experienced drive can be strong. The food-deprived person who smells a sizzling steak feels famished. For each motive we can ask, how much is it motivated by the push of our biological needs and how much by the pull of external incentives?

A HIERARCHY OF MOTIVES

You don't need to read this book to know that some needs take priority over others. At this moment, your needs for air and water are probably satisfied, so other motives—such as your need to achieve—may be energizing and directing your behavior. Let your need for water go unsatisfied, and your thirst will become a preoccupation. Deprive yourself of air, and your thirst will be temporarily forgotten.

As these examples hint, the particular needs that motivate our behavior depend on which needs are unmet and, among those, which are the more fundamental. Abraham Maslow (1970) proposed one possible *hierarchy of needs* (Figure 13–1), at the base of which are our physiological needs, such as for food, water, and shelter. Only if these needs are met are people prompted to meet their need for safety, and then to meet the uniquely human needs to give and receive love, and to enjoy self-esteem. Beyond this, says Maslow, lie the highest order needs: to actualize one's full potential and achieve a spiritual perspective that transcends ordinary experience. (More on self-esteem and self-actualization in Chapter 15, Personality.)

Maslow's specific hierarchy is somewhat arbitrary. Moreover, the order of such needs is not universally fixed (people have, for example, starved themselves to make a political statement). Nevertheless, the simple idea that some motives are more compelling than others—until they are satisfied—is appealing. Let us now consider three representative motives, beginning at the basic, physiological level. In each case, we will see how psychological factors influence what is biologically given.

''Nobody wants to kiss when they are hungry.''
 Dorothea Dix, 1802–1887

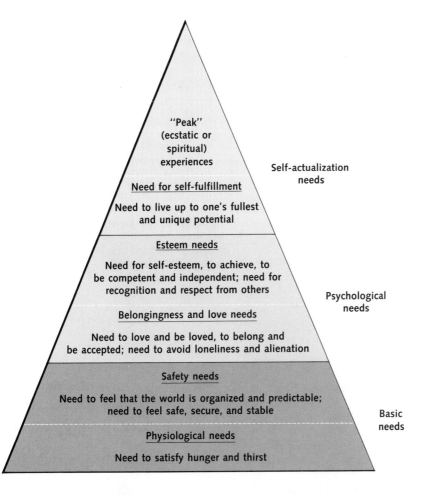

Figure 13–1   Maslow's hierarchy of needs. We are not prompted to satisfy our higher level needs, Maslow believed, until our more fundamental, lower level needs are met.

HUNGER

As reports of starvation in World War II prison camps and occupied areas reached the Allies, they provoked concern for how best to provide relief as territory became liberated. To learn more about the consequences of semistarvation, scientist Ancel Keys and his colleagues (1950) solicited volunteers for an experiment on semistarvation. From among the more than 100 conscientious objectors who applied, they selected 36 men. First, the men were fed just enough to maintain their initial weight. Then, for 6 months, this food level was cut in half.

The physical effects were visible. Soon, without thinking about it, the men began conserving energy; they appeared listless and apathetic. Their body weights dropped rapidly, eventually stabilizing at about 25 percent below their starting weights. The psychological effects were even more dramatic. Consistent with Maslow's idea of a need hierarchy, the subjects became obsessed with food. They talked about food. They daydreamed about food. They collected recipes, read cookbooks, and feasted their eyes on delectable forbidden foods. Meanwhile, they lost their former interests in such things as sex and social activities. They had become preoccupied with their unfulfilled needs. As one subject reported, "If we see a show, the most interesting part of it is contained in scenes where people are eating. I couldn't laugh at the funniest picture in the world, and love scenes are completely dull."

What triggered this gnawing hunger? For that matter, what drives us to eat three times a day?

During Keys's semistarvation experiment with conscientious objectors, food became an obsession.

THE PHYSIOLOGY OF HUNGER

The hunger of Keys's semistarved subjects was the response of a homeostatic system designed to maintain normal body weight and an adequate supply of nutrients. But precisely what is it that triggers hunger? Is it the pangs of an empty stomach? So it feels, and so it seemed after A. L. Washburn, working with Walter Cannon (Cannon & Washburn, 1912), intentionally swallowed a balloon, which, when inflated in his stomach, could transmit his stomach contractions to a recording device (Figure 13–2). While his stomach was being monitored, Wash-

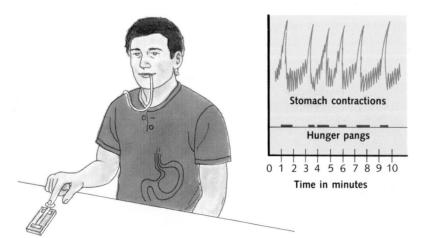

Stomach contractions

Hunger pangs

0 1 2 3 4 5 6 7 8 9 10
Time in minutes

Figure 13–2   The procedure by which Washburn showed that our feelings of hunger (as indicated by a key press) are accompanied by contractions of the stomach (as transmitted through the stomach balloon).

burn would press a key each time he felt hungry. This, too, was transmitted to the recording device, which revealed that Washburn was having powerful contractions of the stomach whenever he said he was hungry. (Some dietary aids reduce this empty stomach feeling by filling the stomach with indigestible fibers that swell as they absorb water.)

Alas, there is more to hunger than an empty stomach, as researchers discovered a quarter century later when they removed some rats' stomachs and attached their esophagi to their small intestines (Tsang, 1938). Without stomach pangs, did hunger persist—did the rats continue to eat regularly? Indeed they did. Hunger persists similarly in humans whose ulcerated or cancerous stomachs have been removed. In fact even a full stomach will not necessarily prevent hunger. Animals that fill their stomachs by eating low-calorie food will eat more than animals that consume a less filling, high-calorie diet (McHugh & Moran, 1978). If the pangs of an empty stomach are not the only source of our hunger, what else is?

Body Chemistry   Hunger is also affected by changes in body chemistry. The fact that people and other animals automatically regulate their caloric intake to maintain a stable body weight suggests that the body is somehow keeping tabs on its available resources. One such resource is blood *glucose* (a type of sugar). We know from experiments that when glucose is injected into the bloodstream and detected by sensors in the brain and liver, hunger decreases. Injecting the hormone *insulin* diminishes blood glucose, partly by converting it to stored fat, thus causing hunger to increase.

Experiments by Judith Rodin (1985) and others indicate that blood insulin levels may also affect hunger directly, and not just by decreasing blood glucose levels. Rodin reports that insulin injections will trigger hunger even when blood glucose levels are held steady by ongoing infusions (Figure 13–3). When their insulin levels are artificially raised, people report that they feel hungrier, they find sweets tastier, and they eat more.

As food is absorbed and hunger diminishes, eating behavior changes. Eliot Stellar (1985) discovered this after outfitting people with a special dental retainer engineered to record each chew and swallow. The device answers questions about "the microstructure of human eating" that you may never have thought to ask. During a meal of sandwich snacks, how often does the average person swallow? Every 13.7 seconds. How many chews on average per swallow? 18.9. How fast do people chew? 1.8 chews per second. As the meal progresses and both hunger and food tastiness decrease, people chew more. Ironically, the better a food tastes, the *less* time people leave it in their mouths.

Some taste preferences (as for sweet and salt) are genetic and universal. Others are conditioned, as when people given highly salted foods develop a great liking for salt (Beauchamp, 1987) or when those who become violently ill following a meal develop a taste aversion. That Bedouins enjoy eating the eye of a camel, which most North Americans would find repulsive, illustrates the power of cultural conditioning. But taste preferences also are influenced by body chemistry. When you are feeling tense or depressed, do you have a hankering for sweet or starchy carbohydrate-laden foods? Carbohydrates help boost levels of the neurotransmitter serotonin, which has calming effects. Given a drug that similarly increases serotonin, carbohydrate cravers

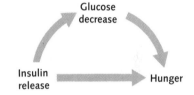

Figure 13–3   Insulin injections increase hunger both directly and indirectly (by decreasing blood glucose).

The increasing popularity of sushi on both coasts of North America shows the effect of familiarity on food preferences. In the central portions of the continent, where fresh fish is largely unavailable, most people reject the very idea of eating raw fish.

lose their cravings—hinting that stress-related cravings might be treatable by providing food substitutes that mimic the biochemical effects of carbohydrates (T. Hall, 1987).

The Hypothalamus   Low blood glucose and high blood insulin are each a source of hunger. But we do not consciously feel our blood chemistry. Rather, information on our body's state is routed to the brain for evaluation. During the 1940s and 1950s, researchers attempted to locate the precise part of the brain where this occurs. They located hunger controls within the hypothalamus, a small but complex neural traffic intersection buried deep in the brain (Figure 13–4).

Experiments suggest that there may be not one but two distinct hypothalamic centers that control eating. Activity in the side areas of the hypothalamus, known as the *lateral hypothalamus,* or *LH,* brings on hunger. When electrically stimulated there, a well-fed animal will begin to eat; when the area is destroyed, even a starving animal has no interest in food. Activity in an area near the bottom and middle of the hypothalamus, known as the *ventromedial hypothalamus,* or *VMH,* depresses hunger. Stimulate this area and an animal will stop eating; destroy it and the animal's stomach and intestines will process food more rapidly, causing it to eat more often and to become grossly fat (Hoebel & Teitelbaum, 1966; Duggan & Booth, 1986).

Can we therefore say that the LH is a simple "hunger on" switch, and the VMH a "hunger off" switch? No, because even animals whose LH has been destroyed will eat if their body weight drops low enough. To biopsychologist Richard Keesey (Keesey & Corbett, 1983), this suggested that the LH and VMH areas of the hypothalamus have opposite influences on the body's "weight thermostat," which predisposes us to keep our body at a particular weight level, called its *set point.* When semistarved rats fall below their normal weight, biological pressures act to restore the lost weight: Hunger increases and energy expenditure decreases. If body weight rises—as happens when rats are force-fed—hunger decreases and energy expenditure increases. This stable weight to which semistarved and overstuffed rats return is their set point.

Despite the day-to-day variations in our eating, our bodies are remarkably good at regulating our weight, much better than we could be through conscious efforts to control food intake precisely. If today you weigh within a pound of what you weighed a year ago, you have managed to keep your average energy intake and expenditure within 10 calories a day of one another. Keep everything the same and add a single carrot per day to caloric input and within a decade you will have gained 30 pounds!

Our bodies regulate weight much as rats' bodies do—through the control of food intake and energy output. If our body weight rises above our set point, we tend not to feel so hungry; if our weight drops below, we tend to eat more. To retain its set-point weight, the body also adjusts its *metabolic rate*—its rate of energy expenditure. By the end of their 24 weeks of semistarvation, the subjects in the World War II experiment had stabilized at three-quarters of their normal weight—while eating half what they previously did. The stabilization resulted from a corresponding reduction in energy expenditure, achieved partly by physical lethargy. But physical activity accounts for only about one-third of our energy use. The other two-thirds are consumed by the maintenance processes that keep us alive even while we rest. And, sure enough, the resting energy expenditure of the semistarving men had dropped 29 percent.

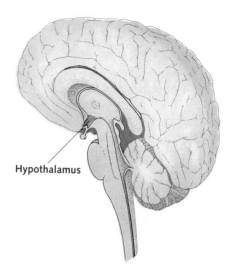

Figure 13–4   As we saw in Chapter 2, the hypothalamus performs various body maintenance functions and influences the endocrine system via the pituitary gland. The hypothalamus is also richly supplied with blood vessels, enabling it to respond to blood chemistry as well as to incoming neural information about the body's state.

Lesioning the ventromedial hypothalamus (VMH) raised this rodent's set point, causing its weight to triple.

EXTERNAL INCENTIVES

Our eagerness to eat is not only pushed by our body state—our body chemistry and hypothalamic activity—but pulled by external stimuli. Like Pavlov's dogs, people learn to salivate in anticipation of appealing foods. When food is abundant, those who are especially responsive to external food stimuli tend to gain the most weight. Consider the 9- to 15-year-old girls at an 8-week summer camp studied by Judith Rodin and Joyce Slochower (1976). During the first week of camp, some girls could not resist munching readily visible M&Ms even after a full meal. Such people, whose eating is triggered more by the presence of food stimuli than by internal factors, are called *externals*. In the 7 weeks that followed, these "external" girls gained the most weight.

In a delicious demonstration of how internal and external factors interact, Rodin (1984) invited people to her laboratory for lunch after they had gone 18 hours without food. While blood samples were being taken, a large, juicy steak was brought in, crackling as it finished grilling. As the hungry subjects sat watching, hearing, and smelling the soon-to-be-eaten steak, Rodin observed their rising blood insulin levels, which were accompanied by increases in their reported feelings of hunger. Those who in prior testing had been found to be "externals" had the greatest insulin response to the sight, sound, and aroma of the steak. This illustrates how our psychological experience of an external incentive (the steak) can affect our inner physiological state.

As those who are involved in preparing, displaying, selling, or advertising food know, few of us are immune to food cues.

EATING DISORDERS

The impact of psychological factors on eating behavior is most strikingly evident in the many people who suffer from an eating disorder. Consider two cases:

Mary is a 5' 3" 15-year-old who, having reached 100 pounds, decided that she needed to lose weight to enhance her attractiveness. After gradually reducing her food intake to a few vegetables a day and then adding a vigorous exercise program, she dropped to 80 pounds. She has been having difficulty sleeping, has at times been depressed, and no longer has regular menstrual periods. Mary is still unhappy about her weight. She is socially inactive and seldom dates, but she is very successful academically. Mary does not regard herself as ill or in need of treatment.

Alice is a 5' 9", 160-pound 17-year-old who says she has always been a little chubby. For the last 5 years, her eating has been characterized by binges followed by vomiting. She will eat a quart of ice cream or an entire pie and then, to control her weight, make herself vomit in secret. Alice wants to date, but doesn't because she is ashamed of her looks. She has at times taken pills to try to lose weight.

Mary's condition is diagnosed as **anorexia nervosa**—a disorder in which a person becomes significantly underweight (typically, 15 percent or more) yet feels fat and is fearful of becoming obese. Even when emaciated, the person continues to restrict food intake. The disorder usually develops in adolescence, and is nine times more common in females than in males.

Alice's condition, which is more common, is diagnosed as **bulimia nervosa**—a disorder characterized by repeated "binge-purge" episodes of overeating followed by vomiting or using a laxative. Most individuals with bulimia are women in their late teens or twenties who, like those with anorexia, are preoccupied with food, fearful of becoming overweight, and experiencing depression or anxiety (Hinz &

Williamson, 1987). The feelings of depression and shame are especially keen during and following binges. About half of those with anorexia also display the binge-purge-depression symptoms of bulimia. But most bulimics fluctuate within or above normal weight ranges, which enables them to keep the condition hidden.

Researchers report that the families of bulimia patients have a higher than usual incidence of alcoholism, obesity, and depression. Anorexia patients often come from families that are high-achieving and protective. Nevertheless, the origins of these disorders are, for now, a mystery.

There is, however, a cultural explanation for the fact that anorexia and bulimia occur so much more frequently in women than in men. Although ideals of beauty have varied over the centuries, women in every era have struggled to make their bodies conform to the ideal of their day. Thus the "sickness" of today's two primary eating disorders lies not just within the victims but also within our weight-obsessed culture—a culture that says in countless ways "fat is bad," that motivates millions of women to be "always dieting," and that effectively encourages eating binges by pressuring women to live in a constant state of semistarvation. Anorexia nervosa always begins as a weight-loss diet, and the self-induced vomiting of bulimics nearly always begins after a dieter has broken diet restrictions and gorged. Obesity researchers Susan Wooley and Orland Wooley (1983) contend that "an increasingly stringent cultural standard of thinness for women has been accompanied by a steadily increasing incidence of serious eating disorders in women."

Consistent with this explanation, the extremely thin women one sees in fashion magazines and advertisements appear to have distorted women's perceptions of what men find attractive. In one study of nearly 500 University of Pennsylvania men and women students, April Fallon and Paul Rozin (1985) found that both women's ideal body weight and the weight they thought men preferred were lighter than both their current weight and the weight men actually preferred (see Figure 13–5). The researchers found no such discrepancies in the men's ratings. The men tended to judge their current weight, their ideal weight, and the man's weight they thought women preferred as all quite similar. Women's greater self-dissatisfaction seems linked with their greater tendency to perceive their cheeks, waist, and hips as

Singer Karen Carpenter's death of cardiac arrest at age 32 was believed to be related to her long struggle with anorexia nervosa.

In recent years, the average weight of women under 30 has increased. Simultaneously—to judge from the decreasing measurements of Miss America contestants, *Playboy* centerfolds, and female magazine models—the cultural ideal has become thinner (Striegel-Moore & others, 1986).

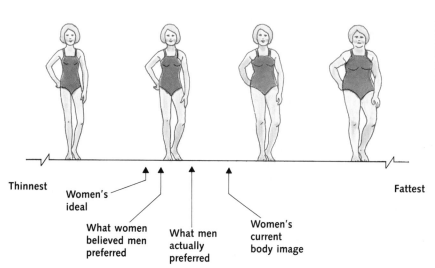

Figure 13–5 Many women tend to idealize, and misperceive men as idealizing, a body shape considerably thinner than their own. (From Fallon & Rozin, 1985.)

Thinnest

Women's ideal

What women believed men preferred

What men actually preferred

Women's current body image

Fattest

looking larger than they do (Thompson, 1986). Women with low self-esteem are particularly likely to have a negative body image and are especially vulnerable to eating disorders (Mintz & Betz, 1986; Striegel-Moore & others, 1986).

SEXUAL MOTIVATION

Part of being human is being sexually motivated. Had this not been so for all your ancestors, right on down to your parents, you would not be reading this book. So what is this thing called sex?

DESCRIBING SEXUAL BEHAVIOR

Before looking at what energizes and directs our sexual arousal, consider the sexual behavior patterns that a theory of sexual motivation must explain.

Sexual Practices   Unable to answer his students' questions about people's sexual practices, Indiana University biologist Alfred Kinsey and his colleagues (1948, 1953) set out to find some answers. Kinsey's confidential interviews with more than 5000 men and nearly 6000 women made history. Although social scientists were quick to point out what Kinsey readily acknowledged—that his nonrandom sample contained an overrepresentation of well-educated, white, urban people from Indiana, Illinois, and several eastern states—his statistics-laden volumes nevertheless became bestsellers. Here one could learn the then surprising news that, among Kinsey's sample at least, most men and nearly half of the women reported having had premarital sexual intercourse, that a majority of women and virtually all men reported they masturbated, and that women who reported masturbating to orgasm before marriage seldom had difficulties experiencing orgasm after marriage. One could also find evidence that sexual behavior is enormously varied. Kinsey found some men and women who said they had never had an orgasm, and others who said they had four or more a day. For those who evaluate themselves by comparisons with others, Kinsey's findings—and others showing wide variations in "normal" sexual behavior around the world—have been reassuring. Given the range of sex drives and the variety of sexual behaviors, your own sexual interest and activities probably fall within the range of "normal."

Because we do not know whether Kinsey's sample accurately represented the nation's sexual practices in the 1940s, let alone those of today, it can be misleading to report his precise findings. But Kinsey's surveys were surely less misleading than some of the haphazard sexual surveys that have been reported more recently in the popular press. When in a national survey of American sexual practices only 20 percent of the people approached agreed to participate (Hunt, 1974), and when popular "sex reports" begin with a biased sample of people (such as subscribers to selected magazines) and receive replies from only 3 percent of this nonrandom sample of people, there is good reason to doubt the generality of their findings. Better information may be on the way, however, thanks to a new national survey of sexual behavior currently being planned by the National Opinion Research Center with the support of the National Institute on Child Health and Human Development (Booth, 1988).

"I lose my respect for the man who can make the mystery of sex the subject of a coarse jest, yet, when you speak earnestly and seriously on the subject, is silent."
   Henry David Thoreau,
   Journal, 1852

Kinsey and his colleagues did not begin their interviews with sexually explicit questions. Rather, they first helped people feel at ease by asking less threatening questions about family background, health, and education.

"The psychologist-asker averages up all the lies . . . and everybody in America feels inferior."
   Psychologist Sol Gordon, born 1923

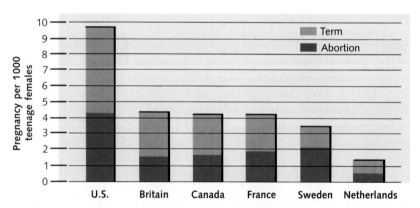

Adolescent Sexuality and Pregnancy   Repeated surveys of high school and college students do, nevertheless, yield some fairly consistent trends. In America the percentage who engaged in premarital sex surged during the 1970s as attitudes became more permissive (peaking in 1979 at 46 percent among 15- to 19-year-old unmarried girls), and then began to taper off during the 1980s as apprehensions grew regarding promiscuous sex (Gerrard, 1987; National Research Council, 1987). Sexual activity is higher among teens who earn low grades, whose parents are not college graduates, and who seldom attend religious services (Harris & Associates, 1986). Sexual behavior patterns vary across place as well as time: In Western Europe the rates of adolescent sexual activity are higher than in the United States. In Japan, the rate is lower—fewer than one-fourth of high school senior boys and one-tenth of girls say they have had intercourse (Tifft, 1985). Likewise in Hong Kong, where a survey at the Chinese University found that 85 percent of the women think that virginity at marriage is essential (Wheeler, 1986).

Because most sexually active teenagers use contraception inconsistently, if at all, the rate of teen pregnancy also surged during the 1970s (Figures 13–6 and 13–7). "Regardless of one's political philoso-

Between 1985 and 1987, the percentage of Americans saying premarital sex is "wrong" rose from 39 to 46 percent (Gallup, 1987).

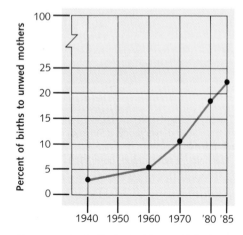

Figure 13–6   In the United States, births to unwed mothers—a majority of them teenagers—have risen sharply since 1960. (National Center for Health Statistics data reported by Cornell, 1987.)

Figure 13–7   American teenagers become pregnant substantially more often than their counterparts in other industrialized countries in the Western Hemisphere, apparently because they are less likely to use contraceptives. (Data from Jones & others, 1985.)

phy or moral perspective, the basic facts are disturbing," reports the National Research Council (1987, p. 1): "More than 1 million teenage girls in the United States become pregnant each year, just over 400,000 teenagers obtain abortions, and nearly 470,000 give birth." (The rest miscarry.)

The epidemic of adolescent pregnancy and the often impoverished futures of teenage mothers and their children have triggered new research on adolescents' use of contraceptives. Short of "just saying no," contraceptives are the surest strategy for preventing pregnancy, yet 27 percent of sexually active 12- to 17-year-old Americans never use birth control and another 34 percent do so only occasionally (Harris, 1986). Why? Among the contributing factors are these:

1. *Ignorance:* In eight surveys, fewer than half the adolescents could correctly identify the safe and risky times of the menstrual cycle (Morrison, 1985). In a more recent national survey, only 40 percent of the 12- to 17-year-olds answered "true" to "The time when a girl is most likely to become pregnant is about two weeks after her menstrual period begins" (Harris, 1986). Ignorance becomes blind optimism in the minds of the many adolescents who report feeling virtually immune to pregnancy.

2. *High sex guilt:* Insofar as they minimize sexual activity, sexual inhibitions work against pregnancy. Ironically, however, these same restraints increase the risks of pregnancy by inhibiting the planning of birth control for those who do engage in sex (Gerrard, 1987; Mosher & Vonderheide, 1985; Whitley & Schofield, 1986). To plan for contraception (to begin taking birth control pills or to carry a diaphragm or condom) is to decide to have intercourse, which sexually conservative teenagers are unlikely to do. When, as sometimes happens, passion overwhelms intentions, the result may be conception.

3. *Minimal communication about birth control* with parents, partners, and peers (Milan & Kilmann, 1987). Teenagers who can talk freely with friends and who are in an exclusive relationship with a partner with whom they communicate openly are more likely to use contraceptives. Although traditional sex education courses might seem an ideal way to reduce ignorance and improve communication, studies indicate that such courses have given only a small boost to teenagers' use of contraceptives (National Research Council, 1987).

4. *Alcohol use:* Sexually active teenagers are typically alcohol-using teenagers (National Research Council, 1987). By depressing brain centers that control judgment, inhibition, and self-awareness, alcohol tends to break down normal restraints. Sexually coercive males commonly exploit this effect by attempting to get their dates under the influence of alcohol (see page 216).

Sexual intercourse without contraception all too frequently ends in unwanted pregnancy. Although there are an increasing number of programs to help both teenage mother and child—like the home for teenage mothers seen here—the large number of births to adolescent mothers creates problems for both the individuals involved and for society.

The Sexual Response Cycle   The headlines created by Kinsey's 1940s surveys were recreated by some 1960s studies in which scientists carefully observed the physiological responses of volunteers who masturbated or had intercourse. With the help of 382 female and 312 male volunteers, gynecologist-obstetrician William Masters and his collaborator Virginia Johnson (1966) monitored or filmed more than 10,000 sexual "cycles."

Their description of the *sexual response cycle* identified four stages, which are essentially similar in men and women (Figure 13–8). During the initial *excitement phase,* the genital areas become engorged with blood, causing the man's penis to become partially erect and the woman's clitoris to swell and the inner lips covering her vagina to open up. Her vagina also expands and secretes lubricant and her breasts and nipples may enlarge.

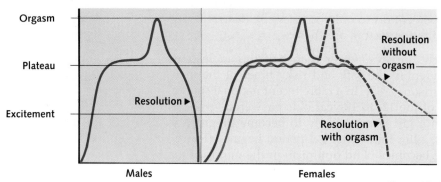

Figure 13–8 The sexual response cycle in men and in women. (From Masters & Johnson, 1966.)

In the *plateau phase,* excitement peaks as breathing, pulse, and blood pressure rates continue to increase. The penis becomes fully engorged and some fluid (possibly containing enough live sperm to enable conception to occur) may appear at the tip of the penis. Vaginal secretion continues to increase, the clitoris retracts, and orgasm feels imminent.

During *orgasm,* Masters and Johnson observed muscle contractions all over the body and even further increases in breathing, pulse, and blood pressure rates. In the excitement of the moment, men and women are hardly aware of all this, but are more aware of their rhythmic genital contractions that create a pleasurable feeling of sexual release. The feeling apparently is much the same for both sexes; in one study, a panel of experts could not reliably distinguish descriptions of orgasm written by men from those written by women (Vance & Wagner, 1976).

After orgasm, the body gradually returns to its unaroused state as the engorged genital blood vessels release their accumulated blood—relatively quickly if orgasm has occurred, relatively slowly otherwise. (It is like the nasal tickle that goes away rapidly if you have sneezed, slowly otherwise.) During this *resolution phase,* a male enters a **refractory period,** lasting from a few minutes to a day or more, during which he is incapable of being aroused to another orgasm. A female does not have a refractory period, which may make it possible for her to have another orgasm if restimulated during resolution.

SEXUAL DYSFUNCTIONS AND THERAPY

Masters and Johnson sought not only to describe the normal sexual response cycle, but to understand and treat the inability to complete it. *Sexual dysfunctions* are problems that consistently impair sexual functioning. Some, but not all, of these dysfunctions are problems in sexual motivation, especially in one's sexual energy and arousability. Men, for example, may experience premature ejaculation (before they or their partners wish) or impotence (the inability to have or maintain an erection). Women more often than men experience orgasmic dysfunction (infrequently or never experiencing orgasm) or low sexual desire.

What causes such problems? The idea that personality disorders are to blame has been largely discounted. Men who experience premature ejaculation seem essentially similar, even in their sexual arousal patterns, to men who do not; they simply ejaculate at lower levels of sexual arousal—something that often occurs with young men who have had long periods of sexual abstinence (Spiess & others, 1984). When Barbara Anderson (1983) reviewed research on the diagnosis and treatment of orgasmic dysfunction in women, she could find no personality dimension that was involved. Furthermore, she reported that attempts to treat orgasmic dysfunction through traditional psychotherapy (as though there were a disorder of personality) have been unsuccessful. On the other hand, she reported a nearly 100 percent success rate with a new treatment that trains women to enjoy their bodies and to give themselves orgasms, with a vibrator if necessary; some of these women can then generalize their new sexual responsiveness to interactions with their mates (LoPiccolo & Stock, 1986; Wakefield, 1987). Success has also been reported in training men to control their ejaculations by repeatedly stimulating the penis and then stopping stimulation (or even firmly squeezing the head of the penis) when the urge to ejaculate arises.

UNDERSTANDING SEXUAL MOTIVATION

Like hunger, sexual arousal depends on the interplay of internal and external stimuli. To understand sexual motivation, we must consider both.

Hormones and Sexual Behavior Sex hormones have two effects. They direct the development of male and female sex characteristics, and (especially in nonhuman animals) they activate sexual behavior. In most mammals, the female becomes sexually receptive ("in heat") if and only if production of the female hormone *estrogen* has peaked, which occurs at ovulation. (In experiments, this can be simulated by injecting females with estrogen.) Male hormone levels are more constant, and the sexual behavior of male animals is not so easily manipulated by hormone treatments (Feder, 1984). Nevertheless, castrated male rats (having lost their testes, where the male hormone testosterone is manufactured) gradually lose much of their interest in receptive females, and gradually regain it if injected with testosterone.

Human sexual behavior is less strictly controlled by hormones. Natural daily and monthly hormone fluctuations do not greatly affect sexual desire. Women's sexual desire is only slightly higher at ovulation (Harvey, 1987), and is actually more responsive to testosterone than to estrogen (Kaplan, 1979; Meyer-Bahlburg, 1980). Normal fluctuations in men's testosterone levels, from man to man and hour to hour, have little effect on their sexual drives (Byrne, 1982). Indeed, such fluctuations are partly a response to sexual stimulation. When James Dabbs and his colleagues (1987) had male collegians converse separately with a male and a female student, the men's testosterone levels rose with the social arousal, but especially after talking with the attractive female. Like the effect of the sizzling steak on insulin level, sexual arousal is both a cause of and a consequence of increased testosterone levels.

Although normal short-term hormonal changes have little effect, large hormone shifts have a bigger effect over the life span. A person's interests in dating and sexual stimulation usually increase with the pubertal surge in sex hormones. If the hormonal surge is precluded—as in the case of *castrati,* prepubertal boys who were castrated during the 1700s and 1800s to preserve their soprano voices for Italian opera—the normal development of sex characteristics and sexual desire does not occur (Peschel & Peschel, 1987). Male sex offenders lose much of their sexual urge when voluntarily taking Depo-Provera, a drug that reduces testosterone levels to that of a prepubertal boy (Money & others, 1983). And in later life, the typical frequency of intercourse declines as sex hormone levels decline.

Hormones help trigger sexual arousal via the hypothalamus, which both monitors variations in blood hormone levels and activates the neural circuits involved in arousal. In rats, destroying a key area of the hypothalamus may eliminate sexual activity; stimulating this area, either electrically or by directly inserting minute quantities of hormones, may activate sexual behavior.

To summarize, we might compare human sex hormones, especially testosterone, to the fuel in a car. Lacking fuel, the car will not run, but if the fuel level is minimally adequate, adding more fuel to the gas tank will not change the way the car runs. The analogy is imperfect, because the interaction between hormones and sexual motivation is two-way. However, the analogy correctly suggests that biology is a necessary but insufficient explanation of human sexual behavior. The biological fuel is essential, but so are the stimuli that will turn on the engine.

External Stimuli   We have seen similarities between hunger and sexual motivation. Both are motivated by internal biological factors, but also are influenced by external stimuli.

In many species of animals, the members of one sex are aroused automatically by odors emitted by the other sex. Are humans also? Despite the millions of dollars spent on advertising scents that are supposed to attract the other sex, attempts to detect unlearned human sexual responses to particular odors have not been very successful (Morris & Udry, 1978). The only unlearned stimulus for human sexual arousal appears to be touch—the pleasurable genital caresses that are a component of foreplay worldwide (Byrne, 1982).

Many studies reveal that men become aroused when they see, hear, or read erotic material. More surprising (in view of the fact that sexually explicit materials are sold mostly to men) is that most women—at least the less inhibited women who volunteer to participate in such studies (Morokoff, 1986)—report similar arousal to the same stimuli (Harrell & Stolp, 1985).

A study by psychologist Julia Heiman (1975) illustrates both the power of such external stimuli and the methods that researchers have used to measure sexual arousal. Much as hunger researchers have developed multiple measures of hunger-related changes (stomach contractions, blood chemistry changes, self-reported hunger, and eating behavior), so sex researchers have developed multiple measures of changes in sexual arousal. These include self-ratings of arousal and direct measures of men's erections and of women's vaginal engorgement.

In Heiman's experiment, instruments that detected arousal (changes in the penis circumference or in vaginal color) were attached

"Ours is a society which stimulates interest in sex by constant titillation. . . . Cinema, television, and all the formidable array of our marketing technology project our very effective forms of titillation and our prejudices about man as a sexy animal into every corner of every hovel in the world."

Germaine Greer (1984)

A Louis Harris and Associates (1988) study for Planned Parenthood found that, per hour, American network programs (not including cable television or rock videos) depicted 10 sexual innuendos, 9 kisses, 5 embraces, 1.8 references to intercourse, and 1.7 references to deviant sexual practices. During the study year 1987–1988, the average TV viewer therefore witnessed 14,000 sexual events.

to sexually experienced university volunteers. Then the students listened to either a sexually explicit erotic tape, a romantic tape (of a couple expressing love, without any indication of physical contact), a combined erotic-romantic tape, or a neutral control tape. Which do you suppose the men were most aroused by? And the women?

Both the men and the women found the tape of explicit sex most arousing, especially when the sex was initiated by a woman and when the depiction centered on her responses. However, the men's verbal reports of arousal tended to correspond more closely to their actual physical arousal, which was easily noticed. The women's sexual responses were more hidden, even to themselves. Later research revealed that this lack of awareness of strong physical responses to erotic stimuli is especially common among women who are sexually inhibited (Morokoff, 1986).

Sexually explicit materials that arouse may be either pleasing or distracting. (If the arousal is distracting, one can usually limit one's exposure to such materials, just as those wishing to control hunger can limit their exposure to tempting cues.) Some explicit materials can have additional effects that are not so harmless. First, those depicting women being sexually coerced—and enjoying it—tend to increase viewers' acceptance of the false idea that women enjoy being raped, and tend to increase male viewers' willingness to hurt women. Second, sexually explicit materials may lead people to devalue their partners and relationships. Several studies (Gutierres & others, 1985; Kenrick & Gutierres, 1980; Weaver & others, 1984) have found that after male college students viewed TV or magazine depictions of sexually attractive women, they rated an average woman, or their own girlfriends or wives, as less attractive than did men who had not experienced this "contrast effect." Viewing X-rated sex films similarly tends to diminish people's satisfaction with their sexual partner (Zillmann & Bryant, 1988). Some sex researchers fear that reading or viewing erotica creates expectations that few men and women can hope to live up to. Sex therapists are sometimes sought out by otherwise normal and satisfied people for the treatment of "problems" such as an inability to have multiple orgasms or "premature" ejaculation after *only* 30 minutes of intercourse (LoPiccolo, 1983).

Sexually explicit materials arouse, but they also may lead to a devaluing of one's romantic or marital partner and distorted perceptions of sexual reality.

Imaginative Stimuli Sexual motivation arises from the interplay of biological factors and external stimuli. But the stimuli inside our heads—our imaginations—also influence our sexual arousal (Figure 13–9). When all the ingredients are present, the sexual chemistry creates arousal.

The brain, it has been said, is our most significant sex organ. People who, because of a spinal cord injury, have no genital sensation, can still feel sexual desire (Willmuth, 1987). Consider, too, the erotic potential of some dreams. As noted on page 199, most dreams do not have overt sexual content, and genital arousal accompanies all types of dreams. But in men and some 40 percent of women (Wells, 1986), dreams sometimes do contain sexual imagery that leads to orgasm. In men, these nocturnal emissions ("wet dreams") are more likely when orgasm has not occurred recently.

When awake, people may become sexually aroused not only by memories of previous sexual interactions but also by fantasies. Fantasies need not correspond to actual behavior. In one survey of masturbation-related fantasies (Hunt, 1974), 13 percent of males and 3 percent of women imagined forcing sex on someone; in the same survey, 19

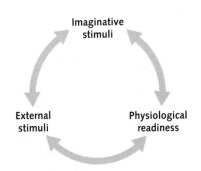

Figure 13–9 Sexual arousal results from the interplay of physiological readiness and external and imaginative stimuli.

percent of women and 10 percent of men imagined being forced to have sex. Fantasy is not reality, however, and to paraphrase Susan Brownmiller (1974), there's a big difference between fantasizing that Robert Redford just won't take no for an answer, and having a stranger actually force himself upon you, hurt you, and kick your teeth out. (See also pages 580–581 and page 595 for a discussion of the "rape myth.")

"There is no difference between being raped and being run over by a truck except that afterward men ask if you enjoyed it."
Marge Piercy,
Rape Poem, 1976

SEXUAL ORIENTATION

To motivate is to energize and direct behavior. So far, we have considered the energizing of sexual motivation but not its direction. The direction of our sexual interest is expressed in our *sexual orientation*—our sexual attraction toward members of a particular sex. Whether their sexual orientation is heterosexual or homosexual, people nearly always have a clear gender identity—they know whether they are male or female. Likewise, researchers have found—contrary to stereotypes of effeminate gay men and masculine lesbian women—that people of either sexual orientation may or may not be strongly gender-typed. For example, knowing that one man displays more traditionally masculine traits than another would not tell you which one is heterosexual.

So far as we know, virtually all cultures in all times have been predominantly heterosexual (Ford & Beach, 1951). Whether homosexuality is condemned and punished or viewed as an acceptable alternative, homosexuality survives and heterosexuality prevails.

How many people are exclusively homosexual? In both Europe and the United States, studies suggest about 4 percent of men and 1 percent of women (Ellis & Ames, 1987; Hyde, 1986b). Some others declare themselves bisexual, but a study of 173 male bisexuals in San Francisco found their behavior to be mostly homosexual: 68 percent reported having had no female sex partners over a 6-month period, while only 14 percent had no male partners during that time (Winkelstein & others, 1987). Nevertheless, many adults—perhaps 25 percent of men and 15 percent of women—report having had some homosexual experience. And most people have had an occasional homosexual fantasy.

What does it feel like to be homosexual in a heterosexual culture? One way for heterosexual people to empathize is to imagine how they

As with heterosexuals, homosexual couples can progress from romantic love to the deep affectionate attachment of companionate love as their relationship matures.

would feel if they were to be ostracized or fired for openly admitting or publicly displaying their feelings toward someone of the other sex, to imagine that people made crude jokes about heterosexual people, or to imagine that family members were pleading with them to change their heterosexual feelings and to enter into a homosexual marriage.

Facing such reactions, homosexual people often struggle with their attachments and desires. At first, they may try to ignore or deny their feelings, hoping they will go away; but they don't. Then they may try to change them, through psychotherapy, willpower, or prayer; but the feelings typically remain as persistent as those of most heterosexual people—who, similarly, are incapable of becoming homosexual. Eventually, they may therefore accept their orientation—by electing celibacy (as do some heterosexuals), by engaging in promiscuous sex (a choice more commonly made by men than women), or by entering into a committed, loving, long-term relationship (a choice more often made by women than men) (Peplau, 1982; Weinberg & Williams, 1974).

There is a growing agreement that one's sexual orientation is neither willfully chosen nor easily changed. Sexual orientation in some ways is like handedness: Most people are one way, some the other, and few are equally ambidextrous; regardless, the way one is endures. Nor is sexual orientation linked with psychological disorder or being a child molester. Some homosexuals do abuse children, but most child molesters are heterosexuals (Gonsiorek, 1982). These facts led the American Psychiatric Association in 1973 to eliminate homosexuality from its list of "mental illnesses."

Understanding Sexual Orientation If our sexual orientation is something we do not choose and cannot change, then where do these preferences come from? When and how do we move toward either a heterosexual or homosexual orientation? See if you can anticipate the consensus that has emerged from hundreds of research studies by responding yes or no to the following questions:

1. Is homosexuality linked with problems in a child's relationships with parents, such as with a domineering mother and a weak, ineffectual father, or a possessive, "seductive" mother and a hostile father?

2. Does homosexuality involve a fear or hatred of the other sex that leads people to direct their sexual desires toward members of their own sex?

3. Is sexual orientation linked with levels of sex hormones in the blood?

4. As children, were many homosexuals molested, seduced by an adult homosexual, or otherwise sexually victimized?

Contrary to widely held ideas about homosexuality, the answers to all these questions are no (Storms, 1983). Consider the findings of lengthy interviews with nearly 1000 homosexuals and 500 heterosexuals conducted by the Kinsey Institute (Bell & others, 1981; Hammersmith, 1982). The investigators assessed every possible psychological cause of homosexuality they could think of—parental relationships, childhood sexual experiences, peer relationships, dating experiences, and even number of brothers and sisters. Their findings: Apart from homosexual feelings and somewhat greater nonconformity, the reported backgrounds of homosexuals and heterosexuals were not discernibly different.

One controversial newer theory proposes that sexual orientation is determined at puberty, as sexual desire emerges (Storms, 1981). It has long been recognized that objects, smells, and sights that are associated with early experiences of sexual pleasure can become conditioned cues for arousal. This helps to explain why some people develop a sexual response to objects that once were associated with sexual arousal or orgasm, and why sexually arousing stimuli are so varied. In laboratory experiments, even a geometric figure can become sexually arousing if it is repeatedly associated with an erotic stimulus (Byrne, 1982). (Note that in this case the geometric figure is a conditioned stimulus, which acquires its power to arouse by repeated pairing with a naturally erotic stimulus.) Perhaps, then, the time when the sex drive matures is a critical period for developing erotic associations with homosexual or heterosexual cues. As their sexual urges intensify, early-maturing individuals are likely to be segregated with others of their own sex. As seventh graders, for example, boys are still associating almost exclusively with other boys. So perhaps a boy who matures early is more likely to associate his developing feelings with other boys, an association that can become a lifelong preference.

It is a simple and logical idea. But the Kinsey researchers doubt it. They found that sexual precocity (as measured by the age at which a person could recall first masturbating, having an orgasm in sleep, and ejaculating) was unrelated to sexual orientation. Their homosexual sample usually recalled having homosexual feelings *before* engaging in any homosexual behavior. Moreover, even growing up in the Sambia tribe of New Guinea, in which homosexual behavior is expected of all boys before marriage, fails to impede heterosexuality (Money, 1987). One member of the Kinsey team therefore proposed a theory that is very nearly the opposite of Storms's theory of erotic attachment. Alan Bell (1982) believes that people develop romantic attachments to those who are *different* from, and thus more fascinating than, the sex they have mostly associated with while growing up. So he speculates that boys who have grown up in a male peer group will find it "virtually impossible" to be fascinated by other males when they reach adolescence.

Newer research hints that sexual orientation may be biologically influenced. We know there is no *simple* biological explanation, because sex hormone levels do not predict sexual orientation and because injections of male hormones do not alter sexual orientation. But many homosexual men do show a feminine-like hormonal response when injected with the female hormone estrogen (Gladue & others, 1984). In animals and some exceptional human cases, sexual orientation has been altered by abnormal prenatal hormone conditions; ewes, for example, will grow up lesbian if their pregnant mothers are injected with testosterone during a critical gestation period (Money, 1987). With humans, a critical period may exist between the middle of the second and fifth months after conception, during which time the brain's neural-hormonal control systems either continue en route to their feminine destiny or are diverted to masculinity (Ellis & Ames, 1987). It seems that exposure to hormone levels typical of females during this time may result in the person (whether female or male) becoming attracted to males. Should this prenatal critical period theory prove correct, it would explain why sexual orientation is so difficult to change.

The bottom line of the conflicting theories is that after 100 years of research on human sexuality, we remain uncertain as to why some people become heterosexual, others homosexual. The determinants of sexual orientation remain, for now, a mystery.

Other types of learned associations with pleasure may also facilitate arousal. Infant male rats that suckle females whose nipples and vagina have been painted with a lemon scent will, as adults, ejaculate more quickly with a female whose vagina has been similarly scented (Fillion & Blass, 1986).

"Were it not for delicately balanced combinations of genetic, neurological, hormonal, and environmental factors, largely occurring prior to birth, each and every one of us would be homosexual."
Lee Ellis and M. Ashley Ames (1987)

AIDS: THE PSYCHOLOGICAL CONSEQUENCES

SAFE SEX

Drawing by Steiner; ©1987 The New Yorker Magazine, Inc.

In the United States, two groups are at ground zero with respect to the devastation of AIDS—Acquired Immune Deficiency Syndrome: One-quarter of its victims have shared needles during intravenous drug use and all but 10 percent of the rest are homosexuals. Also at risk are the unborn children of women who carry the virus, and heterosexuals. (In Central Africa almost all of the victims are heterosexuals and their children.) As the epidemic spreads (the Centers for Disease Control predicts 179,000 deaths in the United States by the end of 1991), what are its psychological consequences?

AIDS and Attitudes   Because AIDS in America has been linked primarily with homosexual practices, there is an interplay of people's attitudes toward AIDS and toward homosexuals. To judge from recent Gallup polls (see Figure 13–10), the AIDS scare has reinforced negative attitudes toward homosexuals. Those who harbor harshly negative

attitudes toward homosexuals tend also to endorse harsh policy measures regarding AIDS, such as favoring tests that exclude AIDS virus carriers from employment or favoring the exclusion of a virus-carrying child from the classroom of one's own child (Omoto & Morier, 1987; Pryor & others, 1988). Indeed, it was only in 1985 when it became apparent that AIDS was not just a rapidly growing homosexual disease, but a heterosexual disease as well, that funding for AIDS research and education sharply increased.

AIDS and Sexual Behavior   The AIDS threat is reducing promiscuity in both the homosexual and heterosexual communities. One ongoing medical study of more than 800 San Francisco men found that the average gay man's number of sexual partners dropped from 10.8 during the first 6 months of 1984 to 4.2 during the first 6 months of 1986. Single heterosexual men dropped from 2.8 to 1.8 sexual partners during the same period (Winkelstein & others, 1987). Similar findings emerged from a study of 637 gay men in Chicago, 93 percent of whom claimed to have changed their behavior to reduce their risk of AIDS and one-third of whom were now either in a monogamous relationship or practicing celibacy (Joseph & others, 1987). Another study of 5000 homosexual men found that between 1984 and 1986 the percent reporting themselves to be either celibate or monogamous rose from 14 to 39 percent (Fineberg, 1988).

There nevertheless remains a tendency for the average gay man to see himself as somehow less vulnerable to AIDS than other gay men—the same sort of unrealistic optimism we noted earlier among sexually active teenagers (Bauman & Siegel, 1987). Such optimism helps explain why among homosexual men studied in Pittsburgh, nearly all of whom knew that condoms reduce the spread of AIDS, 60 percent did not normally use condoms (Fineberg, 1988).

"Do you think homosexual relations between consenting adults should or should not be legal?"

Figure 13–10   Coinciding with growing public awareness of AIDS, there occurred a shift in attitudes toward the legalization of homosexuality among adults. (From *Gallup Report,* 1987.)

SEX AND HUMAN VALUES

Questions of how we ought to act, of what choices we should make, of what ends are desirable, are questions of human values. Recognizing that values are a personal and cultural matter, most sex researchers and educators prefer not to express moral values in their writings on sexuality. As scientists and teachers, their primary aim is simply to help us understand sexual behavior and what motivates it.

Can the study of sex be free of values? Should it be? Critics think not. First, they note that the words we use to describe behavior often reflect our values. When sex researchers label sexually restrained individuals as "erotophobic" and as having "high sex guilt," they express a value judgment. Whether we label sexual acts we do not practice as "perversions," "deviations," or as part of an "alternative sexual lifestyle" depends on our attitude toward the behaviors. Labels both describe and evaluate.

Second, the critics suspect that when sexual information is taught apart from a context of human values, the message some students may get is that sexual intercourse is merely recreational activity, or a biological act that is nothing more than "the depositing of seminal fluid, like squirting jam in a doughnut" (Greer, 1984). Diana Baumrind (1982), a University of California child-rearing expert, suspects that adolescents interpret sex education that pretends to be "value-free" as meaning that adults are neutral about adolescent sexual activity. She feels that such an implication would be unfortunate, because "promiscuous recreational sex poses certain psychological, social, health, and moral problems that must be faced realistically."

On the other hand, some sex researchers have found that teenagers who have had formal sex education are actually no more likely to engage in premarital sex than those who have not (Zelnik & Kim, 1982; Furstenberg & others, 1985). Moreover, consider the benefits we have gained from sex research and education. By knowing ourselves, by realizing that our feelings are shared by others, by understanding what is likely to please or displease our loved one, our lives are enriched. Witness the gradual crumbling of falsehoods about homosexuality. Witness the growing realization that some sexually explicit material can lead us to devalue or hurt other people.

Perhaps we can agree that the knowledge provided by sex research is preferable to ignorance, yet also agree that researchers' hidden values should be stated openly, enabling us to debate them and to reflect upon our own values. We might also remember that while scientific research on sex has answered important questions, it does not aim to define the personal meaning of sex in our lives. One can know every available fact about sex—that the initial spasms of male and female orgasm come at 0.8-second intervals, that the female nipples expand 10 millimeters at the peak of sexual arousal, that systolic blood pressure rises some 60 points and the respiration rate to 40 breaths per minute—but fail to understand the human significance of sexual intimacy.

Surely one significance of sexual intimacy is its expression of our deeply social nature. Sex is a social as well as a biological act. Men and women can have orgasms with just as much pleasurable physical sensation when alone. Yet most people find greater satisfaction in embracing their loved one. As philosopher Bertrand Russell noted in *Marriage and Morals* (1929), "People cannot fully satisfy their sexual instinct without love." Although the yearning for closeness was not part of our description of sexual motivation, this social motive is part of the whole sexual experience. For our predominantly monogamous species, sex is a life-uniting and love-renewing act.

For most adults, sexual intimacy is not only a biological motive but also an emotional one—a sharing of love and intimacy.

"Let us say with all possible emphasis that human sexuality is a very good thing. . . . It is tied in with and expressive of the urgent desire to love."
  Norman Pittenger,
  Making Sexuality Human, 1970

DO TRIAL MARRIAGES REDUCE DIVORCE?

The number of cohabiting unmarried couples in the United States tripled during the 1970s and will have nearly doubled again during the 1980s (Bennett & others, 1988). Similar trends have occurred since 1960 in Scandinavia and throughout much of Western Europe. Premarital cohabitation is viewed by some as a trial marriage that serves to weed out unsuccessful unions before marriage occurs. In a 1987 survey of nearly 300,000 first-year American college students, 52 percent agreed that "a couple should live together before marriage" (American Council on Education, 1988). Might those who are sexually experienced and thoroughly familiar with the living habits of their partner indeed be less likely to stumble into an ill-fated marriage?

The available evidence, although mixed, casts doubt on the idea. Several investigators report that couples who cohabit before marriage have *higher* divorce rates (Kelly & Conley, 1987; Newcomb, 1987; but not White, 1987). One study of 4300 Swedish women found that, compared with those who did not cohabit with their husbands-to-be, those who did were 80 percent more likely to separate or divorce after marriage (Bennett & others, 1988).

Can you imagine why couples who cohabit might be at greater risk for divorce? Researchers offer several possible explanations. One is that people who cohabit are more likely to engage in extramarital sex, which tends to disrupt a marriage. (This analysis has also been used to explain why the number of premarital sexual partners is correlated with marital unhappiness [Newcomb & Bentler, 1981].) Another is that people who cohabit are simply less committed to the institution of marriage. A third possibility is that impulse control and patience are traits that both reduce premarital sex and enhance lasting relationships. (All three explanations suggest only why cohabitation might be *correlated* with divorce risk. None assume a necessary cause-effect connection.)

ACHIEVEMENT MOTIVATION

We have seen that the biological perspective on motivation—the idea that biological needs drive us to satisfy those needs—provides only a partial explanation of what energizes and directs our behavior. There also are motives that, unlike hunger and sex, do not seem to satisfy any biological need. Millionaires may be motivated to make ever more money, movie stars to become ever more famous, politicians to achieve ever more power, daredevils to seek ever greater thrills. Such motives seem not to diminish when they are fed. The more we achieve, the more we may need to achieve.

DESCRIBING ACHIEVEMENT MOTIVATION

Think of two people you know, one who strives to succeed by excelling at any task where evaluation is possible, and one who seems less disciplined and driven. Psychologist Henry Murray (1938) defined the first person's high need for achievement, or *achievement motivation,* as a desire for significant accomplishment; for mastering skills or ideas; for control over things or people; for rapidly attaining a high standard.

What is your greatest achievement to date? What is your greatest future ambition—to attain fame? fortune? creative accomplishment? security? love? power? wisdom? spiritual wholeness?

If we were to study this motive, our first step would probably be to measure it. But how? Recall from the semistarvation studies that people driven by hunger begin to fantasize about food. Recall, too, that our sexual orientation is reflected in our sexual fantasies. Do these examples suggest a way to assess a person's need to achieve?

Murray and investigators David McClelland and John Atkinson presumed that the strength of people's need for achievement would be reflected in their fantasies. So they asked subjects to invent stories about ambiguous pictures. For example, if when shown the daydreaming boy of Figure 13–11, a subject commented that the boy was preoccupied with his pursuit of a goal, that he imagined himself performing a heroic act, or that he was feeling pride in some success, the subject's story was scored as indicating achievement concerns. The researchers regarded people whose stories consistently include achievement themes as having a high need for achievement.

Would you expect people whose stories express a high need for achievement to prefer tasks that are easy, moderately challenging, or very difficult? People whose stories suggest a low need for achievement tend to choose either very easy or very difficult tasks, where failure is either unlikely or unembarrassing (Geen, 1984). Those whose need for achievement is high tend to prefer moderately difficult tasks, for which success is attainable yet attributable to their own skill and effort. In a ring toss game, for instance, they often choose to stand at an intermediate distance from the stake on which the ring is to be tossed; this allows them some successes, yet provides a suitable challenge. People with a strong need to achieve also are more likely to persist with a task when things get difficult (Cooper, 1983).

As you might expect from their persistence and eagerness for realistic challenge, people with high needs for achievement do tend to achieve more. Compared with children of equal ability, they tend to be more successful in business. One study of outstanding athletes, scholars, and artists found that all were highly motivated and self-disciplined, willing to dedicate hours every day to the pursuit of their goals (Bloom, 1985).

When achievement motivation is increased, so is achievement. McClelland (1978) reported that by training the businessmen of a village in India to think, talk, and act like achievement-motivated people, he and his colleagues were able to boost the villagers' business successes. Compared with other businessmen from a comparable nearby town, those trained in achievement motivation started more new businesses and employed over twice as many new people during the ensuing two years.

SOURCES OF ACHIEVEMENT MOTIVATION

Why, despite similar potentials, does one person become more motivated to achieve than another? Researchers have observed that children whose parents encourage their independence from an early age and who are praised and rewarded for their successes tend to become more achievement motivated (Teevan & McGhee, 1972). Such parents encourage their children to dress and feed themselves and to do well in school, and they express their delight when their children achieve. Theorists speculate that the high achievement motivation displayed by such children has both *emotional* roots, as children learn to associate achievement with positive emotions, and *cognitive* roots, as they learn to attribute their achievements to their own competence and effort and so to develop higher expectations of themselves (Dweck & Elliott, 1983).

Figure 13–11   What is this boy daydreaming about? By analyzing responses to ambiguous photos like this, motivation researchers seek clues to people's levels of intrinsic motivation.

"They can because they think they can."
Virgil,
Aeneid, 19 B.C.

These parental influences may also help explain a fascinating finding—that birth order is linked with achievement. In separate studies of children from two-child families who went on to achieve eminence, 64 percent of those described as "distinguished Americans" were firstborn, as were 61 percent of the Rhodes Scholars, 66 percent of the National Merit Scholars, and 64 percent of those in *Who's Who*. Among the *Who's Who* designates and National Merit Scholars who came from three-child families, 52 percent of both groups were firstborn (Altus, 1966). Firstborn and only children also tend to do slightly better in school and on intelligence tests and are more likely to achieve admission to prestigious colleges than are their later born brothers and sisters (Falbo & Polit, 1986). Why?

It is fun to speculate about differences between the experiences of firstborn and later born children. One difference might be the greater parental attention given the firstborn during their years as solo children. Perhaps parents of firstborn children have higher expectations and affirm their children's achievements more than do the more distracted parents of later born children. On the other hand, researchers have found that later born individuals often have their own strengths, such as being more socially relaxed and popular. Having less power than one's older siblings—less size, strength, verbal facility, and experience—apparently fosters more effective social skills (Miller & Maruyama, 1976).

Remember the two friends you chose, one who consistently strives to succeed, the other who seems less concerned with achievement? Is either a firstborn (or only) child?

INTRINSIC MOTIVATION AND ACHIEVEMENT

Two specific types of achievement motivation have been shown to operate in the classroom, at the workplace, on the athletic field. *Intrinsic motivation* is the desire to be effective and to perform a behavior for its own sake; *extrinsic motivation* is being moved by external rewards and punishments.

The Reverend Jesse Jackson's high intrinsic need for achievement has driven him to continually seek out new and more difficult challenges. A phrase from his speech at the 1983 civil rights march on Washington sums it up; "If my mind can conceive it and my heart can believe it, I know I can achieve it."

To sense the difference between extrinsic and intrinsic motivation, you might reflect on your own current experience in this course. Are you feeling pressured to get the reading finished before a deadline? Worried about your course grade? Eager for rewards that depend on your doing well? If your answers are yes, then you are extrinsically motivated (as to some extent students nearly always are). Are you also finding the course material interesting? Does learning it enable you to feel more competent? If there were no grade at stake, might you be curious enough to want to learn the material for its own sake? If your answers are yes, you are also intrinsically motivated.

After studying the motivations and achievements of thousands of college students, scientists, pilots, business people, and athletes, Janet Spence and Robert Helmreich (1983) concluded that intrinsic motivation fuels achievement, while extrinsic motivation (such as the desire for a high-paying career) often does not. Spence and Helmreich identified and assessed three facets of intrinsic motivation: people's quests for *mastery* (as indicated, for example, by their strongly agreeing that "If I am not good at something, I would rather keep struggling to master it than move on to something I may be good at"); their drive to *work* ("I like to work hard"); and their *competitiveness* ("I really enjoy working in situations involving skill and competition").

Despite similar abilities, people oriented toward mastery and hard work tended to achieve more. If students, they tended to get better grades; if MBA graduates, they tended to earn more money; if scientists, their work was more likely to be cited by other scientists. No surprise there. But, surprisingly, those who were most competitive (which is a more extrinsic orientation) often tended to achieve less. As Figure 13–12 illustrates, this was especially true among people who scored high on the mastery and work orientations.

These results illustrate what psychologists call an ***interaction effect***; two factors are said to interact if the effect of one depends on the other. In this case, the effect of competitiveness depends on the degree of work-mastery orientation. Among people who do not intrinsically enjoy mastery and hard work, it pays to be highly competitive; among those who are oriented toward mastery and hard work, it pays to be less competitive.

If intrinsic motivation stimulates achievement, especially in situations where people work independently (as students, executives, and scientists often do), then how might we encourage it? The consistent answer, from hundreds of studies, is first, by providing tasks that challenge and trigger curiosity (Malone & Lepper, 1986) and second, by not snuffing out people's sense of self-determination with an overuse of extrinsic rewards (Deci & Ryan, 1987).

Note that rewards can be used in two ways: to *control* us ("If you clean up your room you can have some ice cream") or to *inform* us of our successes ("That was outstanding—we congratulate you"). Researchers have repeatedly observed that attempts to influence people's behaviors through rewards, deadlines, and surveillance may be successful as long as these controls are present; but if they are taken away, interest in the activity often drops. Ironically, when teachers try hardest to boost their students' achievements on competency tests, they tend to become most controlling, thus undermining their students' intrinsic eagerness for challenge and mastery. (This is similar to the earlier finding that the children of parents who did not encourage independence tend to have lower achievement motivation. Recall, too, from Chapter 9, the principle that unnecessary or excessive rewards can undermine intrinsic interest by "overjustifying" an activity.)

On the other hand, verbal or monetary rewards that inform people when they are doing well can boost their feelings of competence and intrinsic motivation. In one experiment, Thane Pittman and his colleagues (1980) asked college students to work on puzzles. Those who received informative compliments ("Compared to most of my subjects, you're doing really well") were much more likely to continue playing

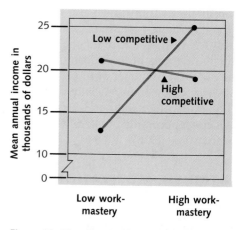

Figure 13–12 Among MBA graduates with a low work-mastery orientation, highly competitive people achieved the highest earnings. Among the high work-mastery group, the less competitive did better. The effect of competitiveness thus depends on ("interacts with") the effect of work and mastery. (From *Achievement and Achievement Motives* by Janet T. Spence. Copyright © 1983 W. H. Freeman and Company. Reprinted with permission.)

with the puzzles when left alone later than were those who received either no praise or a controlling form of praise ("If you keep it up I'll be able to use your data"). So, depending on whether rewards are used to inform or control, they can either raise or lower intrinsic motivation.

Researchers believe there is an important practical principle here. Given that the controlling use of rewards has so widely been shown to undermine intrinsic motivation (and creativity—see pages 334–335), parents, teachers, and managers should take care not to be overcontrolling. It is important to expect, support, challenge, and inform; but if you want to encourage internally motivated, self-directed achievements, do not overly control.

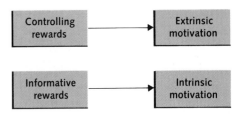

INTRINSIC MOTIVATION AND SPORTS

For most people, participation in sports activities is its own reward. The 20 million American youngsters who participate in organized sports do so not so much for extrinsic rewards as for enjoyment and for the sense of accomplishment it brings. In fact, motivation researchers Edward Deci and Richard Ryan (1985) reported that rewarding children for participating in physical activities can overjustify the activity, making the children less likely to participate again after the rewards are removed.

Another researcher, Dean Ryan (1980), studied football players and found that those on athletic scholarships (who were, in a sense, playing for pay) enjoyed their play less than did nonscholarship players. Apparently, pay and pressure turn play into work. But as other studies of intrinsic motivation show, rewards could also increase intrinsic motivation if their effect was to inform the players of their athletic competence (as with a "most improved player" award).

Researchers have also found that enjoyment of sports is greatest when the activity is neither too easy (and therefore boring) nor too demanding (causing us to worry about our performance). When the challenge is optimally suited to our skills, we experience "flow": Without feeling anxious or self-conscious, we become totally involved in the challenge (Csikszentmihalyi, 1985). This absorption in a game is similar to the "flow" sometimes experienced by dancers, chess players, surgeons, and writers as they become caught up in the task at hand.

Does a competitive orientation enhance or diminish the intrinsic love of sports activities? It all depends, say Deci and Ryan (1985). Like other extrinsic incentives, the lure of victory can be very motivating. Moreover, winning makes us feel competent. So, as long as we are winning, we are still likely to enjoy the activity. Yet in the long run, especially if we begin losing, a competitive orientation may undermine our love of the activity for its own sake.

So, should coaches emphasize extrinsic pressures, rewards, and competition? It depends on what the goal is, report Deci and Ryan. If, as professional football coach Vince Lombardi once said, "Winning isn't everything; it's the only thing," then it may pay to control the players with pressures and rewards for winning. But if the goal is—as it should be for most programs of physical education, fitness, and amateur sports—the promotion of an enduring interest and participation in physical activity, then "external pressures, competitive emphasis, and evaluative feedback are in contradiction to this goal." Thus if Little League coaches want their players to continue playing baseball after Little League, they had best focus not on the urgency of winning, but on the joy of playing well.

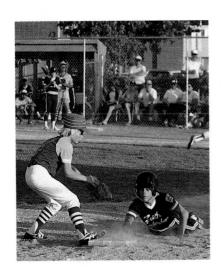

In sports as in other activities, excessive external pressures and incentives can undermine intrinsic enjoyment. Many children who participate in organized sports find their enjoyment of the activity heightened by an emphasis on mastering the game and lessened by excessive pressure to win.

THE MOTIVATING MANAGER

What every manager wants to know, and isn't afraid to ask, is: How can I manage in ways that ensure motivated, productive, and satisfied employees? The growing field of industrial/organizational psychology aims to answer that question, among others. More specifically, it explores how managers might best:

screen and select motivated, well-suited personnel;

match people with suitable work assignments;

create work environments that boost morale and output;

evaluate work and create incentives for excellence; and

promote teamwork and group achievement.

Leadership Style   Whether a directive/autocratic or participative/democratic management style works best depends on the situation and on the manager's intelligence. The best leadership style for leading a discussion may not be the best style for leading the troops on a charge (Fiedler, 1981). In general, if you like to give orders, you had better be bright enough to give good ones (Fiedler, 1987).

Drawing by Anthony; ©1988 The New Yorker Magazine, Inc.

Participative management, in which a leader delegates authority and welcomes input from employees, is often good for morale. Subordinates usually feel more satisfied when they can participate in decision making (Spector, 1986). Moreover, when given some control over their tasks, they are more motivated to achieve (Burger, 1987). In terms of Maslow's hierarchy of needs (page 353), the directive manager—the traditional "boss"—seems to be relying mostly on people's lower level needs to eat and be secure. Participative management capitalizes more on people's needs to enjoy relationships and to actualize their potential.

The world's second largest manufacturer of office furniture is Michigan's Herman Miller, Inc., a much-studied pioneer of participative management. Its chief executive officer, Max DePree (1987), believes that workers want to be effective and productive, to feel they are making a meaningful contribution, to have control over their own destinies, and to be appreciated. When workers share in corporate profits and become part owners they become invested in their company's success. When workers participate in decision making, and know that they and their managers are mutually accountable, labor versus management hostility is replaced by a shared commitment to corporate and personal goals. When workers are respected, cared about, and involved, they find work more satisfying and, thanks to their productivity, their company benefits.

Goal Setting Specific, challenging goals motivate higher achievement, especially when combined with progress reports (Mento & others, 1987; Tubbs, 1986). Clear objectives, such as those you might set in planning your coursework, serve to direct one's attention, promote effort and persistence, and stimulate creative strategies.

Managing with an Eye to People's Motives To motivate people to invest themselves in working toward an organization's goals, Martin Maehr and Larry Braskamp (1986; Braskamp, 1987) advise managers to assess their people's motives and adjust their managerial style accordingly. Employees who value *accomplishment* can be challenged to try new things and to exhibit excellence. Those who value *recognition* can be given attention and reinforced with awards and salary bonuses. Those who value *affiliation* can be placed in a unit that has a trustful family feeling and that shares decision making. Those who value *power* can be motivated with competition and opportunities for triumphant success. Different strokes for different folks, but for each a way to energize and direct—in a word, to motivate—behavior.

> "Good leaders don't ask more than their constituents can give, but they often ask—and get—more than their constituents intended to give or thought it was possible to give."
>
> John W. Gardner,
> *Excellence,* 1984

SUMMING UP

Motivation is the energizing and directing of our behavior, as exemplified in our yearning for food, our longing for sexual intimacy, and our desire to achieve.

CONCEPTS OF MOTIVATION

Under Darwin's influence, behavior came to be viewed as being controlled by biological forces, such as instincts. But when it became clear that people were merely naming various behaviors and calling them instincts, psychologists turned to a drive theory of motivation.

Biological States: The Pushes Most physiological needs create psychological drives that motivate need satisfaction. The aim of drive reduction is internal stability, or homeostasis. Drive reduction motivates survival behaviors such as eating and drinking but seems not so applicable to motives such as sex and curiosity, which involve external stimulation.

Cognition and Culture: The Pulls Not only are we pushed by our internal drives, we are also pulled by external incentives.

A Hierarchy of Motives Maslow's hierarchy of needs expresses the idea that, until satisfied, some motives are more compelling than others.

HUNGER

The Physiology of Hunger The inner push of hunger originates not primarily from the stomach's pangs, but from variations in body chemistry. For example, we are likely to feel hungry when our glucose levels are low and our insulin levels are high. This information is monitored by the lateral and ventromedial areas of the hypothalamus, which regulate the body's weight by influencing our feelings of hunger and satiety. To regain its set-point weight, the body also adjusts its metabolic rate of energy expenditure.

External Incentives Especially in "external" people, food stimuli can trigger hunger and eating, partly by stimulating a rise in insulin level.

Eating Disorders The impact of psychological factors on eating behavior is dramatically manifested in people with anorexia nervosa, who keep themselves on near-starvation rations, and those with bulimia nervosa, who binge and purge in secret.

SEXUAL MOTIVATION

Describing Sexual Behavior Sexual practices in different cultures and surveys on sex by Kinsey and others indicate that sexual behaviors vary from place to place and time to time. In the United States, for example, teen sexual activity rose during the 1970s but tapered off somewhat during the mid-1980s. Biologically, the human sexual response cycle normally follows a pattern of excitement, plateau, orgasm, and resolution.

Sexual Dysfunctions and Therapy Sexual dysfunctions such as premature ejaculation and orgasmic dysfunction are being successfully treated by new methods, which assume that sexual responses are learned and can therefore be modified.

Understanding Sexual Motivation Sex hormones help our bodies develop and function as either male or female. In nonhuman animals, hormones also help to stimulate sexual activity, but in humans, they influence sexual behavior more loosely, especially once minimally sufficient hormone levels are present. External stimuli can trigger sexual arousal in both men and women, although women may be less likely to notice their physiological responses. Sexually explicit materials may also lead people to perceive their partners as comparatively less appealing and to devalue their relationships. In combination with the internal hormonal push and the external pull of sexual stimuli, imagined stimuli (fantasies) help trigger sexual arousal.

Sexual Orientation One's heterosexual or homosexual orientation seems neither willfully chosen nor easily changed. Although it is beginning to look as though biological factors are involved, the reasons one person becomes heterosexual and another homosexual remain shrouded in mystery.

Sex and Human Values Sex research and education are not value-free. Sex-related values should therefore be discussed openly, recognizing the emotional significance of sexual expression.

ACHIEVEMENT MOTIVATION

Some human behaviors are energized and directed without satisfying any apparent biological need. Achieving certain goals, for example, may be motivated by a person's need for competence and self-determination.

Describing Achievement Motivation People with a high need to achieve, as assessed by the stories they make up about an ambiguous photograph, tend to prefer moderately challenging tasks and to persist in accomplishing them.

Sources of Achievement Motivation Many achievement-oriented children have parents and teachers who encourage and affirm independent achievement rather than overly controlling the children with rewards and threats.

Intrinsic Motivation and Achievement Intrinsic motivation is the desire to be effective and to perform a behavior for its own sake. Rewards that are used not to control people but to boost their sense of competence or to inform them of improvement may increase intrinsic motivation.

The Motivating Manager Industrial/organizational psychologists are exploring how best to create a motivated, productive, and satisfied work force.

TERMS AND CONCEPTS TO REMEMBER

achievement motivation A desire for significant accomplishment: for mastery of things, people, or ideas; for attaining a high standard.

anorexia nervosa A disorder in which a normal-weight person (usually an adolescent female) diets to become significantly (15 percent or more) underweight yet, still feeling fat, continues to starve.

bulimia nervosa A disorder characterized by "binge-purge" eating, in which repeated episodes of overeating, usually of highly caloric foods, are followed by vomiting or laxative use.

drive An aroused state that typically arises from an underlying need.

estrogen A sex hormone, secreted in greater amounts by females than males. In nonhuman female mammals, estrogen levels peak during ovulation, rousing sexual receptivity.

extrinsic motivation A desire to perform a behavior due to promised rewards or threats of punishment.

glucose The form of sugar that circulates in the blood and provides the major source of energy for body tissues.

hierarchy of needs Maslow's pyramid of human needs, beginning at the base with physiological needs that must first be satisfied before higher level safety needs and then psychological needs become active.

homeostasis A tendency to maintain a balanced or constant internal state; refers especially to the body's tendency to maintain an optimum internal state for functioning.

incentives Positive or negative environmental stimuli that motivate behavior.

instinct A behavior that is rigidly patterned, characteristic of a whole species, and unlearned.

insulin A hormone that, among its effects, helps body tissues convert blood glucose into stored fat.

interaction effect A result in which the effect of one factor depends on the level of another.

intrinsic motivation A desire to perform a behavior for its own sake and to be effective.

lateral hypothalamus (LH) The side areas of the hypothalamus that, when stimulated, trigger eating and, when destroyed, cause an animal to stop eating.

metabolic rate The body's rate of energy expenditure.

motivation The forces that energize and direct behavior.

need A deprivation that usually rouses a drive to reduce or eliminate the deprivation.

refractory period A resting period after male orgasm during which a man cannot be aroused to another orgasm.

set point The point at which an individual's weight "thermostat" is set. When the body falls below this weight, changes in hunger and metabolic rate act to restore the lost weight.

sexual dysfunction A problem that consistently impairs sexual arousal or functioning.

sexual orientation One's sexual attraction toward members of either one's own sex (homosexual orientation) or the other sex (heterosexual orientation).

sexual response cycle The four stages of sexual responding described by Masters and Johnson—excitement, plateau, orgasm, and resolution.

ventromedial hypothalamus (VMH) The bottom and middle areas of the hypothalamus that, when stimulated, cause the cessation of eating and, when destroyed, cause an animal to overeat.

FOR FURTHER READING

Hunger

Logue, A. W. (1986). *The psychology of eating and drinking.* New York: Freeman.

Why do some foods taste better to you than others? Why do people develop problems related to eating and drinking? Logue provides authoritative and readable answers to these and other questions about hunger and thirst.

Sexuality

Hyde, J. S. (1986). *Understanding human sexuality* (3rd ed.). New York: McGraw-Hill.

A comprehensive overview of every aspect of human sexuality, including sexual orientation and sexual disorders.

Kelley, K. (Ed.) (1987). *Females, males, and sexuality.* Albany: State University of New York Press.

Experts review biological and social influences in male and female sexuality.

Other Motivational Topics

Mook, D. G. (1987). *Motivation: The Organization of Action.* New York: Norton.

Provides a lucid and up-to-date overview of the major topics in motivation.

Steers, R. M., & Porter, L. W. (1987). *Motivation and work behavior.* New York: McGraw-Hill.

Reviews research on maximizing worker motivation and minimizing absenteeism and turnover.

For further information in this text regarding industrial/organizational psychology see:

Absenteeism and age, p. 100
Advertising/persuasion, pp. 292, 562–565
Applicant testing, pp. 423, 435
Conflict management, pp. 605–607
Consumer decisions, p. 295
Creativity encouragement, p. 335
Economic decision making, p. 292
Employee evaluation, p. 549
Employee health/fitness, p. 530
Employee theft, p. 383
Executive/subordinate stress, pp. 434, 513–514
Group decision making, p. 570
Lie detection, pp. 383–385
Loafing, p. 567
Management aptitude, p. 330
Motivating workers, pp. 245–246
Pay schedules, p. 242
Predicting job performance, pp. 424, 453
Risk assessment, p. 293
Stock market predictions, pp. 290, 619
Subliminal ads, pp. 141–142
Women's positions and pay, p. 117
Work motivation, pp. 108–109

CHAPTER 14

Emotion

Feelings—powerful, spontaneous, sometimes unforgettable. Where do feelings come from? Of all the species, we humans seem to be the most emotional (Hebb, 1980). More often than any other creature, we express fear, anger, sadness, joy, love. No one needs to tell you that emotions add color to your life, that in times of stress they can disrupt your life or save it. But what are the ingredients of emotion?

Consider a young basketball player. Thanks to the basket she made in the game's last second, her team has just defeated its archrival. As she leaves the gymnasium to board the team bus for the ride home, she feels elated. Basking in the congratulations of her teammates, she cannot stop smiling. Seldom has she felt more alive, stronger, more confident, or more in control.

Approaching the bus, she becomes aware that a cluster of young men nearby are making loud comments intended for her ears. One questions her team's ability, another snidely impugns her femininity. As she strides past the taunters, she feels a surge of anger. Her heart pounding, her teeth and fists clenched, her face flushed, she controls her impulse to lash back. Once aboard, she throws herself into a seat and seethes: "Those creeps! Where do they get their sick ideas about women athletes?" As the rest of the team boards the bus, whooping and hollering, her attention is drawn back to the thrill of victory, and her intense feelings are rechanneled into celebration.

As this young basketball player's experience illustrates, *emotions* involve a mixture of (1) physiological arousal (heart pounding), (2) expressive behavior (teeth clenched), and (3) conscious experience (interpretations of the men's behavior, and angry feelings). But the puzzle is how these three pieces fit together. For example, did the athlete first notice her pounding heart, her clenched jaw, and *then* feel anger toward the men? Or did the sense of anger come first, stirring her heart and facial muscles to respond? These are difficult questions to answer. Before trying, let us first study the individual aspects of emotion—its physiology, expression, and conscious experience.

Not only emotion, but most psychological phenomena (vision, sleep, memory, sex, and so forth) can be approached these three ways—physiologically, behaviorally, and cognitively.

THE PHYSIOLOGY OF EMOTION

AROUSAL

When you are emotionally aroused, your body is physically aroused. Some body responses are so obvious that you easily notice them. Imagine that, while walking home along a deserted street late at night, a motorcyclist begins stalking you. Hearing the rumble of the bike's engine behind you, your heart begins to race, your muscles tense, your stomach develops butterflies, your mouth becomes dry.

Your body also mobilizes itself for action in less noticeable ways. To provide energy, your liver pours extra sugar into your bloodstream. To help burn the sugar, your respiration rate increases to supply the needed extra oxygen. Your digestion slows, diverting blood from your internal organs to your muscles. Your pupils dilate, letting in more light. To cool your stirred-up body, you perspire more. Should you be wounded, your blood would clot more quickly. Think of this when the next emergency you face is over: Without any conscious effort, your body's response to danger has been wonderfully coordinated and adaptive—preparing you to fight or flee.

Those responses are activated by the sympathetic nervous system. Among other things, it directs the adrenal glands on top of the kidneys to release the hormones epinephrine (adrenaline) and norepinephrine (noradrenaline) that in turn increase heart rate, blood pressure, and blood sugar levels. When the emergency passes, the parasympathetic neural centers become active, calming the body. Even after the parasympathetic nervous system has inhibited further hormone release, those hormones already in the bloodstream linger awhile, so arousal diminishes gradually.

Prolonged arousal, triggered by sustained stress, taxes the body (more on this in Chapter 18, Health). Yet in many situations arousal is adaptive. In fact, both too little arousal (say, being sleepy) and extremely high levels of arousal can disrupt your performance. When you take an exam, it pays to be moderately aroused—alert but not trembling with nervousness.

Generally, performance is best when arousal is moderate. However, the level of arousal for optimal performance varies for different tasks. With easy or well-learned tasks, peak performance comes with relatively high arousal, which enhances the dominant, and usually correct, response. With more difficult or less well rehearsed tasks, the optimal arousal needed is somewhat less. Thus, runners, who are performing a well-learned task, usually achieve their peak performances when highly aroused by competition. But basketball players shooting free throws, which is a less routine skill than running, seem to become slightly *less* accurate when they are highly aroused by fans in a packed fieldhouse (Sokoll & Mynatt, 1984).

PHYSIOLOGICAL STATES ACCOMPANYING SPECIFIC EMOTIONS

Imagine yourself conducting an experiment exploring the physiological indicators of arousal. In each of four different rooms, you have someone watching a movie: In the first, there's a horror show; in the second, a film designed to provoke anger; in the third, a sexually arousing film; and in the fourth, a movie that is utterly boring. You monitor from the control center the physiological responses of each person. By examining the perspiration, breathing, and heart rates of the viewers, could you tell who was frightened, who was angry, who was sexually aroused, who was bored?

With training, you could probably pick out the bored viewer from the other three. Discerning physiological differences among fear, anger, and sexual arousal is much harder (Zillmann, 1986a). Experts even have difficulty distinguishing viewers' physiological responses to sad versus funny movies (apart from the breathing disruption caused by laughter [Averill, 1969]).

"Fear lends wings to his feet."
Virgil,
Aeneid, 19 B.C.

One explanation of sudden death caused by a voodoo "curse" is that the terrified person's parasympathetic nervous system, which calms the body, overreacts to the extreme arousal by slowing the heart to a stop (Seligman, 1974).

Fear, anger, sexual arousal, and sadness certainly *feel* different (and, as we will see, cognitively they *are* different). A terrified person may feel a clutching, sinking sensation in the chest and a knot in the stomach. An angry person may feel "hot under the collar" and will probably experience a pressing, inner tension. The sexually stimulated person will experience a genital response. And the sad person may be choked up and have an empty, drained feeling (Epstein, 1984). Moreover, frightened, angered, and saddened people often *look* different— "paralyzed with fear," "ready to explode," or "down in the dumps." Knowing this, can we pinpoint some distinct physiological indicators of each emotion?

Scientists increasingly agree that different brain regions and distinct patterns of brain activity may underlie different emotions (Panksepp, 1982). As we saw on page 37, when one area of a cat's limbic system is stimulated, it will pull back in apparent terror at the sight of a mouse. Stimulate another limbic area and the cat will become enraged—pupils dilated, fur and tail erect, claws out, hissing furiously. Fear and rage have also been linked with differing hormone secretions (Ax, 1953) and, as we will see, with subtle changes in finger temperature.

To summarize, emotions as different as fear and anger involve a similar general autonomic arousal, thanks to the sympathetic nervous system. The differences we experience are apparently orchestrated by the activity of various brain regions and hormones.

In 1966, a young man named Charles Whitman, after developing what an autopsy later revealed was a tumor in his limbic system, killed his wife and mother and then climbed to the top of a tower at the University of Texas and shot thirty-eight people.

LIE DETECTION

Given the physical indicators of emotion, might we, like Pinocchio, give some telltale sign whenever we lie? The "lie detector," or *polygraph,* was once employed mainly in law enforcement work and national security matters. By the mid-1980s it was used 2 million times a year in the United States, 80 percent of the time in attempts either to screen new employees for honesty or to uncover employee theft (Holden, 1986a). Most such uses were in private corporations. But in 1983, President Reagan signed a directive requiring government employees, if requested, to take lie detector tests during investigations of leaks of classified information (Biddle, 1986).

How does the polygraph work? It does not literally detect lies. Rather, it measures several of the physiological responses that accompany emotion, such as changes in breathing, pulse rate, blood pressure, and perspiration. Assuming that lying is stressful, a person who is lying will become physiologically aroused.

If you are tested, the examiner first tries to convince you that the instrument is highly accurate (to make you fearful of lying). While you are relaxed, the examiner begins by measuring your physiological response as you answer questions. Some of these, called control questions, are designed to make anyone a little nervous. For example, when asked, "In the last 20 years, have you ever taken something that didn't belong to you?" many people will tell a little white lie and say no, but the polygraph may detect slight physiological changes. If your physiological reactions to the critical questions ("Did you ever steal anything from your previous employer?") are weaker than those to the control questions, the examiner infers that you are telling the truth on the critical questions. The assumption is that only the thief would become agitated when denying the theft (see Figure 14–1 on page 384).

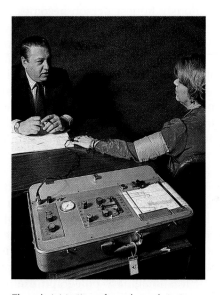

The administration of a polygraph test.

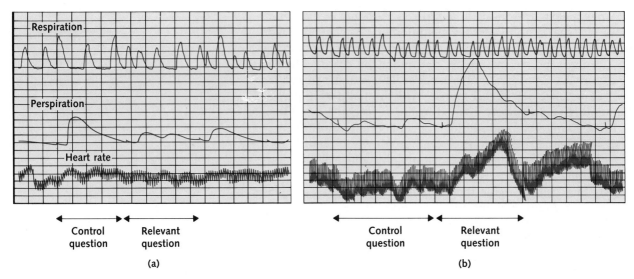

Figure 14–1   Physiological responses to a lie detector test. (a) This is the record of a witness who supported an accused murderer's alibi. She reacted more strongly when answering no to a control question, "Up to age 18, did you ever deceive anyone?," than when answering yes to the relevant question, "Was [the accused] at another location at the time of the murder?" As a result, the examiner concluded that she was telling the truth. (b) This is the record of an accused murderer who was judged to be lying when he pleaded self-defense, because he reacted less strongly in answering no to the control question, "Up to age 18, did you ever physically harm anyone?," than when answering yes to the relevant question, "Did [the deceased] threaten to harm you in any way?"

How well does the polygraph work? That depends on whether liars exhibit anxiety while lying. Some experts suggest that a practiced liar or a hardened criminal might remain relaxed while lying or could learn how to beat the test. An innocent person, on the other hand, might respond with heightened tension to the accusations that are implied by the relevant questions.

A major adversary of the commercial use of lie detector tests is University of Minnesota psychologist David Lykken (1983). He notes that because physiological arousal is much the same from one emotion to another, the polygraph cannot distinguish among anxiety, irritation, and guilt—they all appear as arousal. Thus, these tests err about one-third of the time. They more often label the innocent guilty—when the scrupulously honest person becomes upset by even being asked the relevant question—than the guilty innocent (see Figure 14–2).

Though they are more accurate than a 50-50 coin toss, polygraph tests have been deemed too inaccurate for most state courts, and polygraph evidence is not admissible in half the states (Lykken, 1985). Moreover, a report by the Congressional Office of Technology Assessment (U.S. Congress, 1983, p. 4) warned that "the available research evidence does not establish the scientific validity of the polygraph test for personnel security screening." The American Psychological Association (1986) also "has great reservations about the use of polygraph tests to detect deception."

The congressional report declares that injustices are inevitable in this sort of screening. Imagine that you are an executive of a corporation in which 5 percent of the 1000 employees (50 people) are guilty of misconduct and you hire a polygraph examiner to help you find out who these guilty people are. After the test is administered to all your employees, how many of the 50 guilty persons will be correctly identified? If this imaginary polygraph examiner is right 95 percent of the time, 47 of these people will be correctly identified. So far, so good. But because the examiner errs 5 percent of the time, 5 percent of the 950

Figure 14–2   How often do lie detectors lie? Benjamin Kleinmuntz and Julian Szucko (1984) had polygraph experts study the polygraph data of 50 theft suspects who later confessed to being guilty and 50 suspects whose innocence was later established by the confessions of others. Had the polygraph experts been the judges, more than one-third of the innocent would have been declared guilty, and almost one-fourth of the guilty would have been declared innocent.

innocent employees will be accused wrongly. That is another 48 people. Thus, *even if the polygraph test were 95 percent accurate* (which it is not, especially when evaluating innocent people), one-half of the employees who are labeled "guilty" would be falsely accused. More realistically, if the test were 70 percent accurate, false accusations would outnumber valid ones by 8 to 1. If 1 in every 1000 employees of the government and defense contractors were a spy, hundreds of loyal employees would probably fail the polygraph clearance procedures and be dismissed for every spy who was caught. This, in itself, would be "a victory for the nation's enemies," says Lykken (1987). (Moreover, the KGB has surely taught its spies simple techniques for producing arousal when the control questions are asked, such as biting the tongue or constricting the anal sphincter.)

The polygraph functions more appropriately as a tool in criminal investigation. Police sometimes use the polygraph to induce confessions by criminals who are scared into thinking that their lies are transparent. A more honest approach uses the *guilty knowledge test,* which assesses a suspect's responses to details of a crime known only to the police and the guilty person. For example, if a camera and money were stolen, the polygraph examiner could see whether the suspect reacted strongly to such specific details as the brand name of the camera and the dollar amounts. Presumably, only a guilty person would. Furthermore, given enough such specific probes, an innocent person would be unlikely to be wrongly accused. Nevertheless, critics and advocates alike disapprove widespread commercial use of the polygraph. The truth is that lie detectors sometimes lie, as the U.S. Congress recognized when it passed the Employee Polygraph Protection Act of 1988, prohibiting most nongovernmental polygraph testing.

"If you hang them all, you will get the guilty."
Folksinger Tom T. Hall

EXPRESSING EMOTION

Even if we cannot decipher people's emotions by measuring their body arousal, we can, and often do, use a simpler method: We "read" their bodies, listen to their voices, and look at their faces.

NONVERBAL COMMUNICATION

All of us communicate nonverbally as well as verbally. If irritated, we may tense our bodies, press our lips together, and gesture with our eyebrows. With a gaze, a glance, or a stare we can communicate inti-

Through the silent language of nonverbal expression, the body communicates emotion. Sometimes the message is direct and easily noticed and interpreted, especially if conveyed by the face. Sometimes the message is hopelessly ambiguous. And sometimes, as we all know, it is deceiving. Can you interpret the messages the people's bodies in the photos here and on the next page are sending?

macy, submission, or dominance (Kleinke, 1986). Most of us are good enough at reading nonverbal cues that we can easily detect the emotions being expressed in an old silent film. We are especially good at detecting nonverbal threats. In a crowd of faces a single angry face will "pop out" faster than a happy one (Hansen & Hansen, 1988). Some of us are more sensitive to these cues than others. Robert Rosenthal, Judith Hall, and their colleagues (1979) discovered this by showing hundreds of people brief film clips of portions of a person's emotionally expressive face or body, sometimes with a garbled voice added. For example, a 2-second scene might reveal only the face of an upset woman, and the viewer would be asked whether the woman was expressing anger or discussing a divorce. Rosenthal and Hall reported that some people are much better emotion detectors than others, and that women are generally better at it than men.

The growing awareness that we communicate through the body's silent language has led to research on how judges can nonverbally bias juries, to studies of how job applicants and interviewers communicate (or miscommunicate) nonverbally, and to popular books on how to interpret nonverbal signals, such as posture. The problem with such interpretations is that a given emotion can be expressed with a number of different postures and gestures, and any given posture (such as folded arms) may express different emotions. Furthermore, the meaning of a gesture may vary with the culture. Some years ago, psychologist Otto Klineberg (1938) noted that in Chinese literature people clapped their hands to express worry or disappointment, laughed a great "ho-ho" to express anger, and stuck out their tongues to show surprise. Similarly, the "thumbs up" and "A-OK" signs of American culture would be interpreted as insults in certain other cultures.

Do the facial expressions associated with emotions also vary in different cultures? To find out, two investigative teams, one led by Paul Ekman and Wallace Friesen (1975, 1986) and the other led by Carroll Izard (1977), showed photographs of different facial expressions to people in different parts of the world and asked them to guess the emotion. You can try this yourself. Match the six emotions with the six faces of Figure 14–3 at the top of page 387.

You probably did pretty well. How do you suppose people from Brazil or from Japan did when judging these pictures? About the same

Paul Ekman (Ekman & Friesen, 1975, p. 7): "Emotions are shown primarily in the face, not in the body. There is no specific body movement pattern that always signals anger or fear, but there are facial patterns specific to each emotion."

 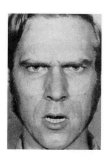 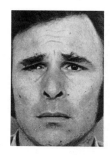   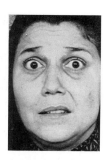

Figure 14–3   Which face expresses: disgust, anger, fear, happiness, sadness, surprise? The answers are on page 388.

as Americans, it turns out. Do people from different cultures make and interpret facial expressions similarly because they are exposed to similar influences such as American movies? Apparently not. Ekman and his team went to an isolated New Guinea tribe and asked its members to display various emotions by saying, for example, "Pretend your child has died." When they showed videotapes of the New Guineans' facial reactions to American college students, the Americans could easily read them. People in various cultures also agree on how a given emotion is conveyed most intensely and on which combinations of two emotions are conveyed by an expression (Ekman & others, 1987). What is more, children's facial expressions—even those of blind children who have not observed others—seem to be universal (Eibl-Eibesfeldt, 1971). The world over, children cry when distressed, shake their heads when defiant, and smile when happy.

The discovery that the facial muscles speak a universal language would come as no surprise to Charles Darwin. He speculated that in prehistoric times, before humans were able to communicate in words, their ability to convey threats, greetings, and submission with facial expressions helped them to survive, as is the case for many animals perhaps including ourselves to this day. For 34 years he developed his thesis that our facial expressions are a product of evolution and are therefore inborn (Izard, 1982). The implication of Darwin's reasoning (which was supported by his initial observations and is reinforced by the newer research just described) is that all humans express the basic emotions by similar facial expressions.

Despite Darwin's interest, the study of emotions fell out of favor for most of this century because subjective emotions were so difficult to measure objectively. Now, armed with new technology and methods, psychologists Izard, Ekman, and their collaborators are continuing Darwin's research. Much as Darwin did more than 100 years ago, for example, they are linking the precise movement of individual facial muscles with different emotions (see Figure 14–4).

Figure 14–4   Ekman's system for classifying a particular smile consists of a specific code for each of the eighty facial muscles used to create it. Notice how different these smiles are: (a) a smile that masks anger (the woman has just been told she is being dismissed); (b) an overly polite smile (the man is telling a patient to enjoy her hospital stay); (c) a smile softening verbal criticism ("I'd appreciate it if you wouldn't come to rehearsal drunk"); and (d) a reluctant, compliant smile ("I guess I don't have any choice, so O.K.").

   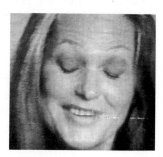

It turns out that the link between experienced emotion and subtle facial movements is hard for people to suppress. Electrodes attached to facial muscles can detect the direction and intensity of people's attitude reactions (Cacioppo & others, 1988). Sometimes just looking at the face tells the story. Ekman (1985) reports that some facial muscles are so hard to control voluntarily that they may provide telltale signs of emotions a person is trying to conceal. The lifting of just the inner part of the eyebrows, which few people can control at will, reveals distress or worry. Eyebrows raised and pulled together signal fear. A feigned smile, such as the Miss America smile, is likely to be switched on and off more quickly than a genuine smile (Bugental, 1986), to be asymmetrical, and to continue more than 4 or 5 seconds, by which time most authentic expressions have faded. Some psychologists believe that these subtle facial indicators of emotion may enable a new behavioral approach to lie detection.

THE EFFECTS OF FACIAL EXPRESSIONS

Expressions not only communicate emotion, they also amplify it. In his 1872 book, *The Expression of the Emotions in Man and Animals,* Darwin contended that "the free expression by outward signs of an emotion intensifies it. . . . He who gives way to violent gestures will increase his rage."

Was Darwin right? I was driving in my car one day when the song "Put On a Happy Face" came on the radio. "How phony," I thought. But I tested Darwin's hypothesis anyway, as you can also: Fake a big grin. Now scowl. Can you feel the difference?

The subjects in dozens of recent experiments could feel a small difference in such expressions (Matsumoto, 1987; McCanne & Anderson, 1987). When James Laird (1974, 1984) subtly induced students to make a frowning expression—by asking them to "contract these muscles," "pull your brows together," and the like—while he attached electrodes to their faces, the students reported feeling a little angry. Compared with the frowners, students who were induced to smile felt happier and found cartoons more humorous. Likewise, German psychologist Fritz Strack and his colleagues (1988) report that people rate cartoons as funnier while holding a pen with their teeth (which activates one of the smiling muscles) than when holding it with their lips (which activates muscles incompatible with smiling). Going through the motions helps awaken the emotions, a fact that may help explain why those who carry out actions suggested by a hypnotist experience compatible emotions.

Why might this be so? Paul Ekman and his colleagues (1983) designed an experiment to find out. Their subjects were professional actors who had been trained in the Stanislavsky method, an acting technique in which actors physically (and psychologically) "become" the characters they are playing. The actors would assume an expression and then hold it for 10 seconds while the researchers measured changes in their heart rates and finger temperatures. When a fearful expression was made, heart rate increased some eight beats per minute and finger temperature was virtually unchanged. When an angry expression was made, both heart rate and finger temperature increased (as though the actor were indeed "hot" with anger). Our facial expressions, it seems, send signals to our autonomic nervous system, which then responds according to the expression.

Answers to the question in Figure 14–3: From left to right: happiness, anger, sadness, surprise, disgust, fear.

This experiment indicates that "facial feedback" can affect our emotions, and it provides evidence that different emotions are linked with subtly different body states. Sara Snodgrass and her associates (1986) observed the same phenomenon with walking behavior. You can duplicate her Skidmore College subjects' experience: Walk for a few minutes while taking short, shuffling steps, keeping your eyes downcast. Now walk around taking long strides, with your arms swinging and your eyes looking straight ahead. Does your mood perceptibly brighten when you shift gaits?

If assuming an emotional expression triggers at least a hint of the emotional feeling, then imitating others' expressions should help us feel what they are feeling. Again, the laboratory evidence is supportive. Kathleen Burns Vaughn and John Lanzetta (1981) asked some students but not others to make a pained expression whenever an electric shock was apparently delivered to someone they were watching. Whenever they thought the shock was given, the grimacing observers perspired more and had a faster heart rate than those not grimacing. So one small way to become more empathic is to let your own face mimic the other person's expression. Acting as another acts helps us feel what another feels.

EXPERIENCING EMOTION

Our feelings are "obscure and confused," noted Benjamin Constant de Rebecque in 1816. But their obscurity has not deterred psychologists from attempting to sort them out. Some psychologists have identified dimensions of emotional experience, such as pleasant versus unpleasant and mild versus intense. (Terror is more frightening than fear, rage is angrier than angry, ecstasy is happier than happy.) Other psychologists have sought to identify the fundamental emotions—emotions that are biologically, facially, and experientially distinct. Carroll Izard (1977) believes there are ten fundamental emotions (interest-excitement, joy, surprise, distress, anger, disgust, contempt, fear, shame, and guilt), most of which are present in infancy (Figure 14–5). Other emotions, he says, are combinations of these (love, for instance, being a mixture of joy and interest-excitement).

Carroll Izard (1977, p. 4): "A complete definition of emotion must take into account (a) the processes that occur in the brain and nervous system, (b) the observable expressive patterns of emotion, particularly those on the face, and (c) the experience or conscious feeling of emotion."

Figure 14–5 Infants' naturally occurring emotions. Carroll Izard has analyzed the facial expressions of very young infants as a means of identifying the emotions present from birth. Shown here are (a) joy (mouth forming smile, cheeks lifted, twinkle in eye); (b) anger (brows drawn together and downward, eyes fixed, mouth squarish); (c) interest (brows raised or knitted, mouth softly rounded, lips may be pursed); (d) disgust (nose wrinkled, upper lip raised, tongue pushed outward); (e) surprise (brows raised, eyes widened, mouth rounded in oval shape); (f) distress (eyes tightly closed; mouth, as in anger, squared angular); (g) sadness (brows' inner corners raised, mouth corners drawn down); and (h) fear (brows level, drawn in and up, eyelids lifted, mouth corners retracted).

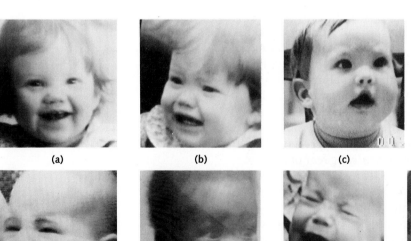

(a)   (b)   (c)

(d)   (e)   (f)   (g)   (h)

Emotions are not just a matter of physiological arousal or facial expression; they are also commonly influenced by our interpretations of the emotion-arousing event. Here, let us examine three of the major emotions: fear, anger, and happiness. (We will consider other emotions, such as hope, depression, and love, in later chapters.) What functions do these emotions serve and what influences our experience of them?

FEAR

Fear is sometimes a poisonous emotion. Fear can torment us, rob us of sleep, and restrict and distract our thinking. People can be literally scared to death. Such maladaptive fear can also be contagious. In 1903, someone yelled "Fire!" as a fire broke out in Chicago's Iroquois Theater. Eddie Foy, the comedian on stage at the time, tried to reassure the crowd by calling out, "Don't get excited. There's no danger. Take it easy!" Alas, the crowd panicked. During the 10 minutes it took the fire department to arrive and quickly extinguish the flames, more than 500 people perished, most of them trampled or smothered in the stampede to escape. In the stairways, bodies were piled seven or eight feet deep, and many of the faces of the dead bore heel marks (Brown, 1965).

More often, fear can be an adaptive response. Fear prepares our bodies to flee danger. Fear of real or imagined enemies binds people together as families, tribes, and nations. Fear of injury protects us from harm. Fear of punishment or retaliation constrains us from harming one another.

"He who fears all snares falls into none."
Publilius Syrus,
Sententiae, 43 B.C.

People can be afraid of almost anything—"afraid of truth, afraid of fortune, afraid of death, and afraid of each other," observed Ralph Waldo Emerson. Why so many fears? Psychologists have noted that we can learn to fear almost anything. Recall from Chapter 9, Learning, that dogs learn to fear neutral stimuli that have been associated with shock, that infants can be conditioned to fear furry objects that are associated with frightening noises, and that adults can become terrified of incidental stimuli linked with traumatic experiences such as rape. Through conditioning, the short list of naturally painful and frightening events can be multiplied into a long list of possible human fears—fear of driving or flying, fear of mice or cockroaches, fear of closed or open spaces, fear of another race or nation, to name just a few.

Chapters 16 and 17 discuss how such phobias develop and are treated.

Learning by observation extends the list even further. Susan Mineka (1985) was intrigued by the fact that nearly all monkeys reared in the wild are afraid of snakes, yet lab-reared monkeys are not. Surely, most wild monkeys have not actually been bitten by snakes. Might they therefore have acquired their fear through observational learning? To find out, Mineka experimented with six wild-reared monkeys (all of which were still strongly fearful of snakes) and their lab-reared offspring (only one of which feared snakes). After repeatedly observing their parents or peers refusing to reach for food in the presence of a snake, the younger monkeys developed a similar strong fear of snakes. When they were retested 3 months later, the learned fear persisted. This suggests that our fears can reflect not only our own past traumas but also the fears of our parents and friends.

Moreover, as we also saw in Chapter 9, we may be biologically prepared to learn some fears more quickly than others. We humans quickly learn and slowly unlearn to fear snakes, spiders, and cliffs—fears that probably helped our ancestors survive. We are less predisposed to fear cars, electricity, and bombs, which in modern society are far more dangerous (Lumsden & Wilson, 1983; McNally, 1987). Stone Age fears leave us unprepared for the dangers of our high-tech world. Some biologically predisposed fears develop with little or no learning. Donald Hebb (1980) recalled being astonished at what happened when he showed a clay model of a chimpanzee head to adult chimpanzees. The animals became panic-stricken. "Some of them screamed, defecated, fled from their outer cages to the inner rooms where they were not within sight of the clay model; those that remained in sight stood at the back of the cage, their gaze fixed on the model held in my hand" (p. 60). The animals' terror is to some extent paralleled by most people's horror the first time they see a dead or dismembered human body.

Of course, some people's fears of specific things, such as spiders, are greater than others'. For a few people, fears of specific objects or situations become so intense that their ability to cope is disrupted. Furthermore, some people seem generally to be more fearful of threatening or embarrassing situations than others. Others—courageous heroes and remorseless criminals—are less fearful. Astronauts and adventurers who have "the right stuff"—who can keep their wits and function coolly and effectively in moments of severe stress—seem to thrive on risk. So, too, do con artists and killers who charm their intended victims without a hint of nervousness, and who in laboratory tests exhibit little fear of a tone that is predictably followed by a painful electric shock. Experience helps shape such fearlessness or fearfulness, but so do our genes. The Minnesota study of separated identical twins found that one twin's level of fearfulness was similar to the other's (Lykken, 1982).

ANGER

Anger is said by the sages to be "a short madness" (Horace, 65–8 B.C.) that "carries the mind away" (Virgil, 70–19 B.C.) and can be "many times more hurtful than the injury that caused it" (Thomas Fuller, 1654–1734). But other sages say that anger "makes any coward brave" (Cato, 234–149 B.C.) and "brings back his strength" (Virgil), so it may be "noble anger" (William Shakespeare, 1564–1616).

What makes us angry? To find out, James Averill (1983) asked many people to recall or keep careful records of their experiences with anger. Most reported becoming at least mildly angry several times a week; some, several times a day. Often the anger was a response to the perceived misdeed of a friend or loved one. Anger was especially common when the other person's act was considered willful, unjustified, and avoidable.

What do people do with their anger? What *should* they do with it? When it fuels physically or verbally aggressive acts that are later regretted, anger is maladaptive. But Averill's subjects recalled that when they were angry they often reacted assertively rather than hurtfully. Their anger frequently led them to talk things over with the offending person and so to alleviate the aggravating situation. Such expressions of anger seemed more adaptive than either hostile outbursts or just keeping the angry feelings inside.

Popular books and articles on aggression sometimes advise that even hostile outbursts can be better than keeping anger pent up, which is a known contributor to high blood pressure (Feshbach, 1986). If first-

One problem with chronic hostility is its link with heart disease (see page 516).

"Anger will never disappear so long as thoughts of resentment are cherished in the mind."
Buddha, c. 500 B.C.

century Roman statesman Seneca was right—"It is hidden anger that harms"—then should we go ahead and curse, retaliate, or tell a person off when we are irritated? Was Ann Landers (1969) right to assert that "youngsters should be taught to vent their anger"?

All such advice presumes that expressing emotion results in emotional release, or *catharsis*. The catharsis hypothesis maintains that anger is reduced after one releases it through aggressive action or fantasy. Experimenters report that sometimes this does occur. When people are allowed to retaliate against someone who has provoked them, they may indeed calm down—*if* the counterattack is directly against the provoker, *if* the retaliation seems justifiable, and *if* the target of the counterattack is not intimidating (Geen & Quanty, 1977; Hokanson & Edelman, 1966). In short, expressing anger can be temporarily calming if it does not leave us feeling guilty or anxious.

But expressing anger can also breed more anger. For one thing, it may trigger retaliation, thus escalating a minor conflict into a major confrontation. For another, expressing anger can magnify anger. (Recall Darwin's suggestion that making violent gestures can increase anger.) Ebbe Ebbesen and his colleagues (1975) observed this when they interviewed 100 frustrated engineers and technicians who had just been laid off by an aerospace company. Some were asked questions that encouraged them to express their hostility toward their employer, such as "What instances can you think of where the company has not been fair with you?" When these people later filled out a questionnaire that assessed their attitudes toward the company, did this opportunity to "drain off" their hostility reduce it? Quite the contrary. Compared with those who had not vented their anger, those who had exhibited more hostility.

> "By controlling the anger of a minute, you may avoid the remorse of a lifetime."
> Chinese proverb

Thus, under some circumstances, "blowing off steam" may temporarily calm an angry person, and under others it may amplify hostility. When outbursts of anger calm us, they may be reinforcing and therefore habit forming. If by berating referees, basketball coaches can drain off some of their tension, then the next time they feel tense with irritation they may be more likely to behave in the same way. Similarly, the next time you are angry you are likely to do whatever has relieved your anger in the past.

How should one best handle anger? Anger experts offer several suggestions. First, bring down the physiological arousal of anger by waiting. "It is true of the body as of arrows," notes Carol Tavris (1982), "what goes up must come down. Any emotional arousal will simmer down if you just wait long enough." Second, deal with anger in a way that involves neither being chronically angry over every little annoyance nor passively sulking, which is merely rehearsing one's reasons for anger.

Indiana University basketball coach Bobby Knight's angry outbursts may be temporarily cathartic. If so, such behavior may be reinforcing and therefore habit forming.

As we noted earlier, anger can benefit relationships—when the grievance is expressed in ways that promote reconciliation rather than retaliation. Civility means not only keeping silent about trivial irritations but also communicating important ones clearly and assertively. A nonaccusing statement of feeling—perhaps letting one's partner know that "I get irritated when you leave your dirty dishes for me to clean up"—can help resolve the conflicts that trigger anger. The poet Blake had the idea:

> "I was angry with my foe,
> I told it not, my wrath did grow,
> I was angry with my friend,
> I told my wrath, my wrath did end."

HAPPINESS

"How to gain, how to keep, how to recover happiness is in fact for most men at all times the secret motive for all they do," observed William James (1902, p. 76). Understandably so, for one's state of happiness or unhappiness colors everything else. People who are happy perceive the world as less dangerous (Johnson & Tversky, 1983), make decisions more easily (Isen & Means, 1983), and report greater satisfaction with their whole life (Schwarz & Clore, 1983). When your mood is gloomy, life as a whole seems depressing; let your mood brighten, and suddenly your relationships, your self-image, and your hopes for the future all seem more promising. Moreover—and this is one of the most consistent findings in all of psychological research—when we feel happy we are more willing to help others. In study after study, people who have had a mood-boosting experience, such as finding money, succeeding on a challenging task, or recalling a happy event, are subsequently more likely to contribute money, pick up someone's dropped papers, volunteer time, and so forth (Myers, 1990).

In searching for the roots of happiness, psychologists have pondered influences upon both our temporary moods and our long-term life satisfaction. When John Eckenrode (1984) studied the daily mood reports of ninety-six women, he found that those who were in good spirits on any given day tended not to have had anything "go wrong" during the day. Similarly, when Arthur Stone and John Neale (1984) studied fifty men, they found that negative events such as an argument with one's spouse or a child's sickness triggered bad moods. Usually the bad mood was gone by the next day, indicating that, short of tragedy, an unwelcome event is but a temporary blow to the spirits.

Apart from prolonged grief over the loss of a loved one or lingering anxiety after a personal trauma such as suffering cancer or rape, even tragedy usually does not permanently depress one's mood. People who become blind or paralyzed tend to recover near-normal levels of self-reported day-to-day happiness. The effect of dramatically positive events is similarly temporary. State lottery winners, though delighted to have won, typically find their life happiness unchanged (Brickman & others, 1978).

Other research confirms that there is much more to well-being than being well off. Many people (including most college freshmen, as Figure 14–6 hints) are convinced they would be happier if they had more

The happiness evident on the faces of these newly naturalized citizens will color their perception of the world around them—at least for a while.

"Weeping may tarry for the night, but joy comes with the morning."
    Psalms 30:5

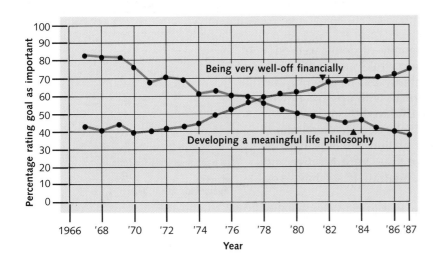

Figure 14–6 Are today's collegians increasingly materialistic? Annual surveys of some 200,000 American college freshmen reveal an increasing desire for wealth. (From Astin & others, 1987a, b.)

money. They probably would be—temporarily. In the long run, increased affluence hardly affects happiness. Those with lots of money are not much happier than those with only enough money to afford life's necessities. Although within a given country there is a slight tendency for the wealthy to be happier than the poor, people in wealthier countries do not generally report feeling more satisfied with their lives than those in poorer countries. Interviews with more than 160,000 Europeans since the mid-1970s reveal that the Danes, Swiss, Irish, and Dutch are much more likely than the French, Greeks, Italians, and West Germans to report themselves happy and satisfied with life. These puzzling national differences are not due to differences in standards of living, in which the West Germans, for example, rank much higher than the Irish (Inglehart & Rabier, 1986). And, although spendable income (income after taxes) in the United States has doubled since the 1950s (adjusting for inflation), personal happiness has remained unchanged; the proportion who declare themselves "very happy" remains at about 1 in 3 (Figure 14–7).

Note that the capacity of people in poor nations to be happy no more justifies poverty than does slaves' capacity to be happy justify slavery.

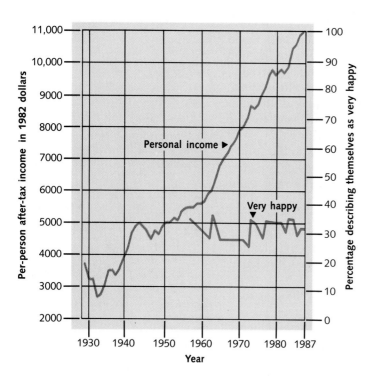

Figure 14–7   Does money buy happiness? It surely helps us to avoid certain types of pain. Yet, though buying power has doubled since the 1950s, self-reported happiness has remained almost unchanged. (Happiness data from Smith, 1979, and personal correspondence.)

Good events, such as obtaining more money or doing well on a school exam, can increase happiness for a short while, and bad events, such as an argument or illness, may temporarily put us down in the dumps. But our moods usually return to normal, with ups and downs reflecting the day's events. Perhaps you have noticed this in your own life. When you are in a bad mood, can you usually depend on rebounding within a day or so? Are your times of elation similarly hard to sustain? Does it seem as if, over a period of time, your positive and negative emotions tend to balance around neutral? If so, have you wondered why?

Two psychological principles that we now look at help us solve this riddle of happiness. Each, in its own way, suggests that happiness is relative.

"No happiness lasts for long."
Seneca,
Agamemnon, A.D. 60

The Adaptation-Level Principle: Happiness Is Relative to Our Prior Experience   The *adaptation-level phenomenon* is based on our tendency to judge various stimuli relative to what we have previously experienced. We adjust our "neutral" levels—the points at which sounds seem neither loud nor soft, lights neither bright nor dim, experiences neither pleasant nor unpleasant—on the basis of past experience. We then notice and react to variations up or down from these levels.

Social psychologists have applied the adaptation-level phenomenon to our emotions. If our income, grades, or social prestige increases, we feel an initial surge of pleasure. We then adapt to this new level of achievement, come to see it as normal, and require something better yet to give us another surge of happiness. From my childhood, I can recall the thrill of watching my family's first 12-inch, black-and-white television set. Now, if the color goes out on our 25-inch TV, I feel deprived. Having adapted upward, I now perceive as negative what I once experienced as positive. Yesterday's luxury has become today's necessity (Figure 14–8). The moral: Satisfaction and dissatisfaction, success and failure—all are relative to our recent experience. "Continued pleasures wear off," notes Dutch emotion theorist Nico Frijda (1988). "Pleasure is always contingent upon change and disappears with continuous satisfaction."

"So the prince and the princess lowered their expectations and lived reasonably contented ever after."

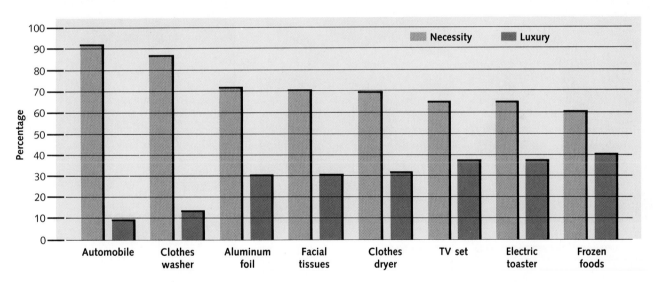

Figure 14–8   Many things once regarded as luxuries are now regarded by most Americans as necessities. (From *Public Opinion*, 1984.)

It follows that we could never create a social paradise on earth (Campbell, 1975). Once our utopia was created, we would soon recalibrate our adaptation level so that we would again sometimes feel gratified (when achievements surpass expectations), sometimes deprived (when they fall below), and sometimes neutral. That helps explain why, despite the realities of triumph and tragedy, million-dollar lottery winners and paraplegics report similar levels of happiness. It also helps explain why material wants can be insatiable—why, for example, Imelda Marcos, wife of the former president of the Philippines, living in splendor amidst nationwide poverty, would acquire 2700 pairs of shoes, more than she could ever wear in her lifetime. When the victor belongs to the spoils and the possessor is possessed by possessions, adaptation level has run amuck.

Because of our capacity to adapt to past events, our emotional ups and downs tend to reflect current happenings.

OPPONENT-PROCESS THEORY OF EMOTION

The adaptation-level principle helps explain why, in the long run, our emotional ups and downs tend to balance. University of Pennsylvania psychologist Richard Solomon (1980) believes that emotions balance in the short run as well, and he has developed a theory to explain why this is so. Solomon was intrigued by the emotional price tag that seems to follow pleasure and the emotional dividends that sometimes compensate for suffering. For the pleasure of a drug high, one pays the price of discomfort when the drug wears off. For the pain of hard exercise or a hot sauna bath, one afterward receives the dividend of a pleasurable feeling of well-being.

Solomon proposes, with support from laboratory studies of human and animal emotions, that *every emotion triggers an opposing emotion*. He calls this the **opponent-process theory.** Imagine that you are about to take your first parachute jump. Solomon would say that the primary emotion you experience before and probably during the jump—fear—triggers an opposing emotion—elation—after the jump is completed. Once the opposing emotion is activated, perhaps to keep the initial emotion under control, we experience a diminishing of the initial emotion's intensity. After the initial emotion subsides, the opposing emotion lingers awhile (Figure 14–9a). For example, after parachutists survive their first free-fall, which for many is a terrifying experience, they typically feel elated. And for women who experience the pain of labor and childbirth, the afterreaction may be euphoria.

Repetitions of the emotion-arousing event strengthen the opposing emotion. Thus the emotional experience, such as the high from drug use or the fear aroused by parachuting, diminishes with repetition and the afterreaction, such as the pain of drug withdrawal or the exhilaration after landing, remains strong or becomes stronger (Figure 14–9b). This helps explain drug tolerance (with repetition the initial pleasure lessens), drug hangovers (the opponent feelings that "knock down" the initial pleasure and linger afterward), and drug addiction (the craving for more of the drug to switch off the pain of withdrawal).

As Solomon wisely notes, opponent-process theory and the research that supports it are good news for puritans and bad news for hedonists. The theory suggests that those who seek pleasure pay for it later and that with repetition their pleasure will lose much of its intensity. An old Spanish saying anticipated opponent-process theory: "'Take what you want,' said God. 'Take it, and pay for it.'" On the other hand, those who suffer will receive their reward and find that, with repetition, their suffering will become more tolerable.

Figure 14–9 Opponent processes in emotion. (a) A primary emotional response to a stimulus triggers an opposing emotion. We experience the difference between the two. (b) With repeated stimulation, the opponent emotion becomes stronger, weakening the experience of the primary emotion and, after the primary emotion subsides, providing a strengthened aftereffect of the opposing emotion. (From Solomon, 1980.)

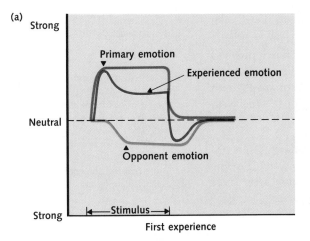

First experience

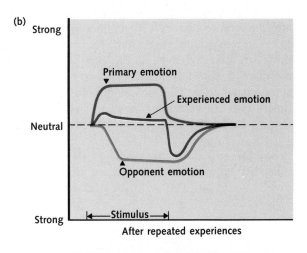

After repeated experiences

The Relative Deprivation Principle: Happiness Is Relative to Others' Attainments   The concept of *relative deprivation* (the sense that we are worse off than others with whom we compare ourselves) was formulated by researchers to explain the frustration expressed by U.S. Air Corps soldiers during World War II. The soldiers were frustrated about promotion rates, even though their promotions at the time were actually rapid (Merton & Kitt, 1950). Apparently, seeing so many others being promoted inflated the soldiers' expectations—and when expectations soar above attainments the result is frustration. Thus, when the Dallas Cowboys signed running back Herschel Walker to a contract worth more than $1 million per year, their other star running back, Tony Dorsett, immediately became frustrated with his suddenly paltry six-figure salary.

The concept of relative deprivation helps us understand why the middle- and upper-income people in a given country tend to be slightly more satisfied with life than the relatively poor, with whom the better-off can compare themselves (Diener, 1984). Nevertheless, once a person reaches a moderate income level, further increases do little to increase happiness. Why? Because as people climb the ladder of success they mostly compare themselves with those who are at or above their current level (Gruder, 1977; Suls & Tesch, 1978). For Tony Dorsett, Herschel Walker was the standard of comparison. As Bertrand Russell (1930, pp. 68–69) observed, "Napoleon envied Caesar, Caesar envied Alexander, and Alexander, I daresay, envied Hercules, who never existed. You cannot, therefore, get away from envy by means of success alone, for there will always be in history or legend some person even more successful than you are."

The bad news about the principles of adaptation level and relative deprivation is that seeking happiness through material achievement requires an ever-increasing abundance of things. At the end of his *Chronicles of Narnia*, writer C. S. Lewis depicts heaven as a place where good things *do* continually increase, where life is a never-ending story "in which every chapter is better than the one before." Here on earth, however, the unavoidable ups and downs of real life preclude perpetual happiness.

The good news is that should we who live in affluent nations choose or be forced to simplify our ways of life, we would undoubtedly adapt. Of course, we would be unhappy at first, but eventually we would recover life's normal balance of joy and sorrow, pleasure and pain. Moreover, by remembering our own low points and by "counting our blessings" when we compare ourselves with those less fortunate, we can increase our contentment. Marshall Dermer and his co-researchers (1979) demonstrated this by asking University of Wisconsin-Milwaukee women to study others' deprivation and suffering. After viewing vivid depictions of how grim life was in Milwaukee in 1900, or after imagining and then writing about various personal tragedies such as being burned and disfigured, the women expressed greater satisfaction with their own lives. In the same way, when people in a depressed mood read about someone who is even more depressed, they feel somewhat better (Gibbons, 1986). Just as comparing ourselves with those who are better off creates envy, so comparing ourselves with those who are less well off boosts contentment.

Predictors of Happiness   If, as the adaptation-level principle implies, our emotions tend to balance around normal, then why do some people seem so filled with joy and others so gloomy day after day?

"I have also learned why people work so hard to succeed: It is because they envy the things their neighbors have. But it is useless. It is like chasing the wind. . . . It is better to have only a little, with peace of mind, than to be busy all the time with both hands, trying to catch the wind."

Ecclesiastes 4:4

This effect of comparison with others helps us understand why students of a given level of academic ability tend to have a higher academic self-concept if they attend a school where most other students are not exceptionally able (Marsh & Parker, 1984). If many of your classmates are brilliant, the comparison may leave you feeling inferior.

What makes one person normally happy and another depressed? In reviewing research on people's feelings of general happiness and well-being, Ed Diener (1984) spotted several predictors of life satisfaction. For example, many studies indicate that religiously active and committed people tend to report greater happiness and life satisfaction (see Figure 14–10 for one such finding). But does religious faith contribute to happiness (by providing a sense of meaning, an inner peace, or a sense of ultimate acceptance)? Or is happiness conducive to religiosity? Table 14–1 indicates that sleeping well is correlated with happiness. Are people happier if they sleep well, or do they sleep better if they're happier? Just knowing the two variables are correlated does not tell us whether one causes the other.

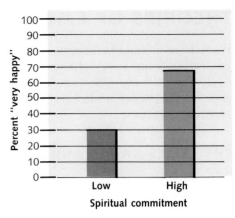

Figure 14–10 Spirituality and happiness. Americans whom George Gallup classifies as high in spiritual commitment are twice as likely as those low in spiritual commitment to say they are "very happy." (From Gallup & O'Connell, 1986.)

Table 14–1
HAPPINESS IS . . .

Researchers have found that happy people tend to:	However, other factors seem unrelated to happiness:
Have high self-esteem	Age
Have a satisfying marriage or other love relationship	Race
Have a meaningful religious faith	Gender (women are more often depressed but also more often joyful)
Be socially outgoing	Educational level
Sleep well	Intelligence
Exercise	Parenthood (having children or not)
Be employed	

Source: Summarized from "Subjective well-being" by E. Diener, 1984, *Psychological Bulletin, 95*, pp. 542–575.

When all the predictors of happiness are taken into account, most of the person-to-person variations in general happiness remain unpredictable. This is partly because random day-to-day fluctuations in our moods color our reports of our general well-being. Our feelings are also colored by how we view our daily activities. Ronald Graef and his colleagues (1983) surmised this after interrupting more than 100 Chicagoans eight times a day with an electronic paging device. Whenever they were beeped, the people would note what they were doing, whether they wanted to be doing what they were doing, and whether they wished they could be doing something else. (How would you answer such questions right now?) Those who frequently enjoyed doing whatever they were doing, even if it was a routine activity, reported being happier overall. Yet they were spending neither more nor less time in leisure activities, at work, or doing housework. The lesson from this, concluded the researchers, is that happiness is usually not to be found in ever-increasing leisure time or even in a different type of work, but in one's state of mind.

"He that thinks himself the happiest man, really is so."
C. C. Colton,
Lacon, 1820

THEORIES OF EMOTION

We have seen that emotions are built from the interplay of physiological arousal, expressive behavior, and conscious experiences. But precisely how? We can gain some insights by looking at one longstanding and one fairly new controversy concerning the sequence of the basic aspects of emotion.

THE JAMES-LANGE AND CANNON-BARD THEORIES

First, the longstanding controversy: Simply put, are you afraid *because* you feel your heart pounding and your muscles quivering?

Common sense tells most people that we cry because we are sad, lash out because we are angry, tremble because we are afraid. However, to pioneering psychologist William James (who once said, "The first psychology lecture I ever heard was the first one I ever gave"), the commonsense view of emotion was 180 degrees out of line. According to James, "we feel sorry *because* we cry, angry *because* we strike, afraid *because* we tremble" (1890, p. 1066). If an oncoming car is in your lane, you will swerve sharply to avoid it; *then* you will notice your racing heart and feel shaken with fright. Thus your feeling of fear follows your body's response (see Figure 14–11).

James's idea, which was independently proposed by Danish physiologist Carl Lange and is therefore called the *James-Lange theory,* struck American physiologist Walter Cannon as implausible. For one thing, Cannon thought that the body's responses were not distinct enough to trigger the different emotions. Does a racing heart indicate fear, anger, or love? For another, changes in heart rate, perspiration, and body temperature seemed to occur too slowly to trigger sudden emotion. Cannon, and later another American physiologist, Philip Bard, concluded that body arousal and the experience of the emotion occur simultaneously: The emotion-arousing stimulus is simultaneously routed (1) to the cortex, causing the subjective awareness of emotion, and (2) to the sympathetic nervous system, causing the body's responses. Thus, said Cannon and Bard in what came to be known as the *Cannon-Bard theory,* your heart begins pounding at the same time you experience fear, but one does not cause the other (see Figure 14–12).

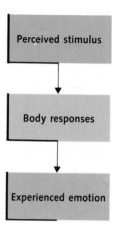

Figure 14–11   The James-Lange theory of emotion.

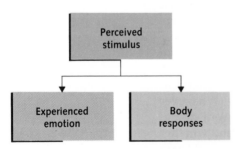

Figure 14–12   The Cannon-Bard theory of emotion.

So long as the evidence suggested that one emotion is much the same as another in terms of arousal, the James-Lange assumption that we experience our emotions through differing body states seemed improbable. With new evidence indicating that there are indeed some subtle but distinct physiological differences among the emotions, the James-Lange theory has become more plausible. As James struggled with his own feelings of depression and grief, he came to believe that emotions can be controlled by going "through the outward motions" of whatever emotion one wants to experience. "To feel cheerful," he advised, "sit up cheerfully, look around cheerfully and act as if cheerfulness were already there." The findings of experiments on the emotional effects of facial expressions are precisely what James might have predicted. One explanation proposes that the muscle movements involved in changing facial expressions alter bloodflow through the face to the brain, thereby influencing the brain's release of mood-affecting neurotransmitters (Zajonc, 1988).

Let's check your understanding of the James-Lange and Cannon-Bard theories. Imagine that your brain is unable to sense your heart pounding or your stomach churning. According to each theory, what effect would this have on your experiencing of emotions?

Cannon and Bard would expect you to experience emotions normally because they believed that the experiencing of emotions occurs separately from (though simultaneously with) the body responses. James and Lange would expect greatly diminished emotions because they believed that to feel emotion you must perceive your body responses.

The imagined situation actually exists in people with severed spinal cords. Psychologist George Hohmann (1966) interviewed twenty-five soldiers who received such injuries in World War II. He asked them to recall emotion-arousing incidents that occurred before and after their spinal cords were severed. Those with injuries in the lower part of the spine, who had lost sensation only in their legs, reported little change in their emotions. But those who could feel nothing below the neck reported a considerable decrease in emotions (just as James and Lange would have expected). These soldiers said they might act much the same as before in emotion-arousing situations, but as one confessed about his anger, "It just doesn't have the heat to it that it used to. It's a mental kind of anger." On the other hand, emotions expressed mostly in body areas above the neck were intensified. Virtually all the men experienced increases in weeping, lumps in the throat, and getting choked up when saying good-bye, worshipping, or watching a touching movie.

Although such evidence has breathed new life into the James-Lange theory, many researchers agree with Cannon and Bard that our experience of emotions also involves cognitive activity of the cortex. Whether or not we fear the man in the dark alley depends entirely on whether we interpret his actions as hostile or friendly. So with James and Lange we can say that our body responses are an important ingredient of emotion, and with Cannon and Bard we can say there is more to the experience of emotion than reading our physiology.

COGNITION AND EMOTION

Now, the new controversy: Put simply, what is the connection between what we *think* and how we *feel*?

We noted in Chapter 10 one instance of how our emotions affect our thinking: Our mood helps trigger memories of events associated with that mood. This partly explains why our moods color our perceptions of life. When we feel like singing "Oh, what a beautiful morning!" we see the world and the people around us as wonderful; if the following day we feel crabby, we perceive the same world and the same people as less wonderful.

There is another explanation: Making a happy face may send feedback to the brain center that physiologically activates mood states. These mood states may make happier memories more accessible, in turn promoting a happier mood.

But does our thinking affect our emotions? Or can we experience emotion apart from thinking? This fundamental issue has practical implications for self-improvement. To change our emotions should we work on changing our thinking, or changing our behavior? (More on this in Chapter 17, Therapy.)

Schachter's Two-Factor Theory of Emotion   Most psychologists today believe that our cognition—our perceptions, memories, and interpretations—is an essential ingredient of emotion. One such theorist is Stanley Schachter, whose influential *two-factor theory* proposes that emotions have two ingredients: physical arousal and a cognitive label (Figure 14–13). Like James and Lange, Schachter presumed that our experience of emotion grows from our awareness of our body's arousal. But he also believed, like Cannon and Bard, that emotions are physiologically similar, so he argued that an emotional experience requires a conscious interpretation of the arousal.

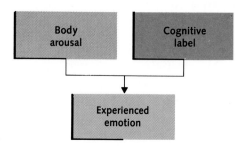

Figure 14–13   A summary of the two-factor theory of emotion. To experience emotion, one must be aroused and must cognitively label the arousal.

It is often hard to disentangle our arousal in response to an event from our interpretation of the event. Imagine that you are aroused and are not sure why, or that you attribute some of your arousal to the wrong source. Perhaps after an invigorating run you arrive home to find a message that you got the job for which you had applied. Would you feel more elated (because you are aroused from your run, but attribute your arousal entirely to the news) than if you had received the same news after awakening from a nap?

To find out, Schachter and Jerome Singer (1962) studied some college men aroused by injections of epinephrine. Picture yourself as one of their subjects: After receiving the injection, you are taken to a waiting room, where you find yourself with another person (actually an accomplice of the experimenters) who is acting either euphoric or irritated. As you observe this person, you begin to feel your heart race, your body flush, and your breathing becoming more rapid. If you were told to expect these effects from the injection, what would you feel? Schachter and Singer's subjects felt little emotion—because they cognitively attributed their arousal to the drug. But if you were told that the injection would produce no effects, what would you feel? Perhaps you would react, as many of the actual subjects did, by "catching" the apparent emotion of the person you are with—becoming happy if the accomplice is acting euphoric and testy if he or she is acting irritated.

This discovery that a stirred-up state can be experienced as one emotion or another, depending on how we interpret and label it, has been replicated in dozens of subsequent experiments. Some of these later experiments indicate that emotional arousal is not as undifferentiated as Schachter believed; nevertheless, the experiments generally confirm that being physically stirred up can intensify just about any emotion (Reisenzein, 1983). For example, if people who have been aroused by pedaling an exercise bike or watching a rock concert film are insulted, they find it easy to misattribute their arousal to the provocation. Thus, they typically feel angrier at being provoked than do similarly provoked people who were not previously aroused. Apparently, arousal originating from emotions as diverse as anger, fear, and sexual excitement can be readily transferred from one emotion to another (Zillmann, 1986a). In anger-provoking situations people who are sexually aroused react with more hostility. Similarly, the arousal that lingers after an intense argument or a frightening experience may intensify sexual passion.

Must Cognition Precede Emotion?   Can we say that we really do not have an emotion until we put a label on our arousal? Robert Zajonc (pronounced ZI-yence) (1980, 1984) contends that the answer is no. He suggests that our emotions are sometimes more instantaneous than our interpretations of a situation, that we feel some emotions *before* we think. (Can you recall immediately liking something or someone without at first knowing why?) Consider some of the evidence that this occurs.

1. In the chapters on sensation and states of consciousness, we reviewed experiments in which people were flashed visual shapes for too short a time to perceive them consciously as anything but flashes of light, or had musical tunes played in one ear while attending to something being read into the other ear. Later, these people preferred the shapes or tunes they had been exposed to over others—despite the fact that they could not recall having been exposed to them. Conscious cognition did not precede their emotional preferences.

2. Although the brain functions as an integrated whole, some of the neural pathways involved in emotion are separate from those involved in thinking and memory. Also, emotional processes are more likely to involve the right hemisphere of the brain. Furthermore, Zajonc reports, there is a neural pathway that runs directly from the eye to one of the brain's emotional control centers, the hypothalamus. Thus, visual stimuli, such as startling flashes of light, might trigger instant emotional responses, such as fear, without involving the cognitive pathways at all.

3. As we have seen, changes in facial expression can affect people's feelings and body states directly, apparently without conscious thought being involved.

Such evidence convinces Zajonc that *some* of our emotional reactions involve no deliberate rational thinking. Cognition, he believes, is not necessary for emotion. The heart is not always subject to the mind.

Emotion researcher Richard Lazarus (1984) disagrees. He concedes that our brains process and react to vast amounts of information without our conscious awareness, and he willingly grants that some emotional responses do not require *conscious* thinking. Nevertheless, he says, even the most instantaneously felt emotions require some sort of quick cognitive appraisal of the situation; otherwise, how do we *know* what we are reacting to? The appraisal may be effortless and we may not be conscious of it, but it is still a function of the mind (Figure 14–14).

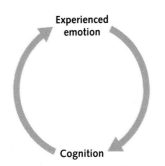

Figure 14–14 Emotion and cognition feed each other. But which is the chicken and which the egg? Lazarus believes that cognition of some kind, either conscious or unconscious, always precedes emotion. Zajonc contends that some of our emotional reactions occur prior to any cognitive processing.

The more important emotions, such as anger, guilt, happiness, and love, clearly arise from our conscious interpretations, memories, and inferences. Whether we attribute a low grade to an unfair exam, bad luck, or our own incompetence or laziness determines whether we feel irritated or depressed (Weiner, 1985). Highly emotional people are intense partly because of their interpretations; they tend to *personalize* events as being somehow directed at them and to *generalize* their experiences by blowing single incidents out of proportion (Larsen & others, 1987).

For us, the important conclusion concerns what Lazarus and Zajonc agree on: Some emotional responses—especially simple likes, dislikes, and fears—involve no conscious thinking. We may fear the spider, even if we "know" it to be harmless. After conditioning, Little Albert was afraid of furry objects. Such responses are hard to alter by changing thinking.

Other emotions—including moods such as depression and complex feelings such as hatred and love—are greatly affected by our interpretations, memories, and expectations. For these emotions, as we will see in Chapter 17, learning to think more positively about ourselves and the world around us makes us feel better.

SUMMING UP

Emotions are psychological responses of the whole organism that involve an interplay among (1) physiological arousal, (2) expressive behaviors, and (3) conscious experience.

THE PHYSIOLOGY OF EMOTION

Arousal   Our performance on a task is usually best when arousal is moderate, though this varies with the difficulty of the task.

Physiological States Accompanying Specific Emotions   The physical arousal that occurs with one emotion is in most ways indistinguishable from that which occurs with another. However, scientists have discovered subtle differences in the brain pathways and hormones associated with different emotions.

Lie Detection   The polygraph measures several physiological indicators of emotion. Can it therefore detect lies by revealing the tension that one might feel while lying? The polygraph does better than chance, but not nearly well enough to justify its widespread use in business and government.

EXPRESSING EMOTION

Nonverbal Communication   Much of our communication is through the silent language of the body. Is such language universal? Gestures appear to be culturally determined, but facial expressions, such as those of happiness and fear, are common the world over.

The Effects of Facial Expressions   Expressions not only communicate emotion, they both amplify the felt emotion and signal the body to respond accordingly.

EXPERIENCING EMOTION

Among various human emotions, we looked closely at three: fear, anger, and happiness.

Fear   Fear is an adaptive emotion, even though it can be traumatic. Although we seem biologically predisposed to acquire some fears, the enormous variety of human fears is best explained by learning.

Anger   Anger is most often aroused by events that are not only frustrating or insulting but also interpreted as willful and unjustified. Although blowing off steam may be temporarily calming, it does not, in the long run, reduce anger. Expressing anger can actually arouse more anger.

Happiness   A good mood boosts people's perceptions of the world and their willingness to help others. The moods triggered by the day's good or bad events seldom last more than that day. Even seemingly significant good events, such as a substantial raise in income, seem not to increase happiness for long. The apparent relativity of happiness can be explained by the adaptation-level and relative-deprivation principles. Nevertheless, some people are usually happier than others, and researchers have identified factors that predict such happiness.

THEORIES OF EMOTION

The James-Lange and Cannon-Bard Theories One of the oldest theoretical controversies regarding emotion is whether we feel emotion after we notice our body responses (as James and Lange proposed) or at the same time that our bodies respond (as Cannon and Bard believed).

Cognition and Emotion Today's number one controversy among emotion researchers concerns whether human emotions can be experienced apart from cognition. Can we feel before we think? Stanley Schachter's two-factor theory of emotion contends that the cognitive labels we put on our states of arousal are an essential ingredient of emotion. Richard Lazarus agrees that cognition is essential: Many important emotions are rooted in our interpretations or inferences, and other emotions require only a simple cognitive appraisal of the emotion-arousing situation. But Robert Zajonc believes that some simple emotional responses occur instantly, not only outside of conscious awareness but before any cognitive processing could occur. The issue has practical implications because to the extent that emotions are rooted in thinking, we can hope to change our emotions by changing our thinking.

TERMS AND CONCEPTS TO REMEMBER

adaptation-level phenomenon The tendency for our judgments (of sounds, of lights, of income, and so forth) to be relative to a "neutral" level that is based on our prior experience.

Cannon-Bard theory The theory that an emotion-arousing stimulus simultaneously triggers (1) physiological responses and (2) the subjective experience of emotion.

catharsis Emotional release. In psychology, the catharsis hypothesis maintains that aggressive urges are relieved by "releasing" aggressive energy (through action or fantasy).

emotion A response of the whole organism, involving (1) physical arousal, (2) expressive behaviors, and (3) conscious experience.

James-Lange theory The theory that our experience of

emotion is a consequence of our physiological responses to emotion-arousing stimuli.

opponent-process theory The theory that every emotion triggers an opposing emotion that fights it and lingers after the first emotion is extinguished.

polygraph A machine, commonly used in attempts to detect lies, that measures several of the physiological responses that accompany emotion (such as perspiration, heart rate, and breathing changes).

relative deprivation The perception that one is worse off relative to those with whom one compares oneself.

two-factor theory The theory that to experience emotion one must (1) be physically aroused and (2) cognitively label the arousal.

FOR FURTHER READING

Carlson, J. G., & Hatfield, E. (1989). *Psychology of emotion.* Belmont, CA: Wadsworth.

A delightfully down-to-earth account of the biology and psychology of emotion, from anger to depression to joy.

Darwin, C. (1872/1965). *The expression of the emotions in man and animals.* Chicago: University of Chicago Press.

The classic description of emotional expressions and their adaptive functions.

Ekman, P. (1985). *Telling lies: Clues to deceit in the marketplace, politics, and marriage.* New York: Norton.

A fascinating book about how our faces and gestures communicate emotion and betray actual feelings.

Izard, C. E., Kagan, J., & Zajonc, R. B. (1984). *Emotions, cognition and behavior.* New York: Cambridge University Press.

Straight from the horses' mouths—leading emotion scholars explain current issues and summarize recent findings.

Tavris, C. (1984). *Anger: The misunderstood emotion.* New York: Simon & Schuster.

A provocative, beautifully written summary of research that points to the dangers of unrestrained expression of anger.

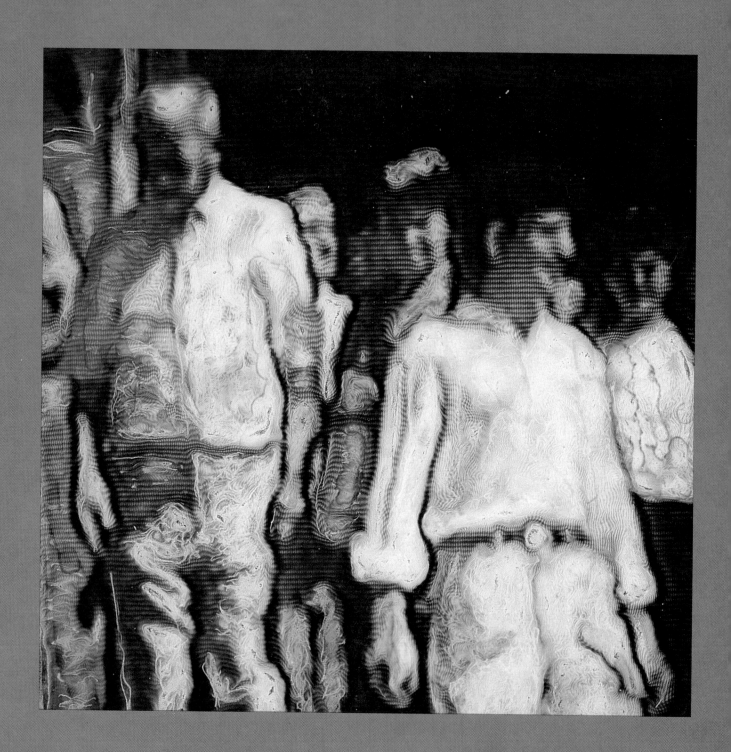

PART 6

Personality, Disorder, and Well-Being

Each of us is unique. In Chapter 15, Personality, we explore four influential perspectives on how we come to have our own unique personalities and how we can best understand and describe human personality. In Chapter 16, Psychological Disorders, we delve into how and why people are labeled "disordered," and we consider the symptoms and causes of major disorders such as depression and schizophrenia. In Chapter 17, Therapy, we review the major approaches to treating psychological disorders and take a hard look at their effectiveness. Finally, in Chapter 18, Health, we describe new research on how our behavior and emotions can affect our health and how we can promote our own health and well-being.

CHAPTER 15

Personality

The novelist William Faulkner was a master at creating characters with vivid personalities, personalities so real they seem to cast shadows.[1] One of his creations, Ike McCaslin, appears at various ages in over a dozen novels and short stories. Ike is highly principled, and consistently so. At the age of 10 he senses within himself a deep reverence for the wilderness and its creatures. At 21 he forfeits what he perceives as a "tainted" inheritance. In his late seventies he counsels his nephew to use his land responsibly. Ike the adult is an extension of Ike the child.

Another Faulkner character, Jason Compson, is a selfish, whining 4-year-old in the opening section of *The Sound and the Fury*, and a selfish, screaming 34-year-old as the novel closes. Head of the Compson household, he verbally abuses his doting mother, his retarded brother, his niece, and the household servants; using blackmail he prevents his sister, Caddy, from seeing her daughter. Lying, threatening, conniving, he is a self-centered adult who developed from a self-centered child.

Faulkner's characters, as they appear and reappear throughout his fiction, exhibit the kinds of distinctiveness and consistency that define personality. Having emphasized in the preceding chapters of this book how we are similar—how we develop, perceive, learn, remember, think, and feel—we now acknowledge that each of us is in some ways unique. This distinctiveness helps define our individual personalities. *Personality* consists of "an individual's enduring response patterns" (Harre & Lamb, 1983). Thus, your personality is defined as your *relatively distinctive and consistent ways of thinking, feeling, and acting.* If your response patterns are unusually distinctive and consistent—if, say, you are strikingly outgoing, whether at a party or in a classroom—people are likely to say that you have a "strong" personality.

Actually, much of this book has to do with personality. We have considered biological influences on personality, personality development across the life span, and personality-related aspects of learning, motivation, and emotion. In later chapters we will study personality disorders, personal and physical well-being, and social influences on personality.

In this chapter we focus on four major perspectives on personality:

Sigmund Freud's *psychoanalytic* theory, with its emphases on the origins of personality in childhood sexuality and the driving force of unconscious motivations.

The efforts of the *trait* theorists to identify specific dimensions of our distinctiveness and consistency.

[1]Faulkner scholar Nancy Taylor assisted with these examples.

The focus of *humanistic* psychologists on our capacities for growth and self-fulfillment.

The concern of *social-cognitive* psychologists with how we are shaped by interaction with our environment.

Each perspective offers a distinctive view of personality that provides valuable insights and, in doing so, reveals limitations of the other perspectives.

THE PSYCHOANALYTIC PERSPECTIVE

According to Freud, all facets of human personality—all emotions, strivings, and ideas—arise from a basic conflict between our aggressive, pleasure-seeking biological impulses and the social restraints against them. In Freud's view, individual personality is the result of each person's attempt to resolve this conflict, to express these impulses in ways that bring satisfaction without also bringing guilt or punishment.

Underlying Freud's conception of personality was his belief that the mind is like an iceberg—mostly hidden. Our conscious thoughts are the part of the iceberg that floats above the surface. Below that is a much larger **unconscious** region containing thoughts, wishes, feelings, and memories of which we are largely unaware. Some of these thoughts are merely stored temporarily in a **preconscious** area, from which they can be retrieved at will into conscious awareness. Of greater interest to Freud was the mass of unacceptable passions and thoughts that we *repress*—forcibly block from our consciousness because they would be so painful to acknowledge. Though we are not consciously aware of these troublesome feelings and ideas, Freud believed them to be powerful shapers of our personalities. In his view our unacknowledged impulses push to be expressed in disguised forms—in the work we do, in the beliefs we hold, in our daily habits, in our troubling symptoms. In such ways, the unconscious leaks through into consciousness.

EXPLORING THE UNCONSCIOUS

Freud wrote about his views, which evolved as he treated patients and analyzed himself, in twenty-four volumes published between 1888 and 1939. Although his first solo book, *The Interpretation of Dreams* (1900), sold but 600 copies in its first 8 years, his ideas gradually began to attract many followers—and intense criticism. For now, let us reserve judgment on his theory and instead try to see things as he did. It is difficult to summarize twenty-four volumes in a few pages, but we can at least highlight Freud's theory, which was the first comprehensive theory of personality.

For most of his life, Freud lived in Vienna, where he earned a medical degree in 1881 and went into private practice, specializing in neurological disorders. He became interested in the hidden aspects of personality when he found himself confronted with certain patients whose apparent disorders made no neurological sense. For example, a patient might have lost all feeling in her hand, or become deaf or blind, with no evidence of physical impairment. (There is no sensory nerve that when damaged would destroy feeling in the entire hand and nothing else.) Noting that such symptoms could also be produced through hypnosis, Freud became intrigued with the idea that they might be psychological rather than physiological in nature. Accordingly, he

Sigmund Freud (1856–1939): "I was the only worker in a new field."

spent several months in Paris studying with Jean Charcot, a French neurologist who was using hypnosis to treat these same kinds of disorders.

When he returned to Vienna, Freud began to use hypnosis with his own patients, encouraging them while in the hypnotic trance to talk freely about themselves and the circumstances surrounding the onset of their symptoms. Typically the patients responded openly, at times becoming quite agitated during the hypnotic experience. Sometimes they would later find their symptoms had disappeared or at least were much relieved.

It was in this way that Freud "discovered" the unconscious. Piecing together his patients' accounts of their lives, he decided that the loss of feeling in one's hand might be caused by, say, the fear of touching one's genitals; that blindness or deafness might be caused by not wanting to see or hear something that aroused intense anxiety. In time Freud began to see patients with a wide variety of symptoms, and he abandoned hypnosis in favor of *free association*—in which the patient was merely told to relax and say whatever came to mind, no matter how embarrassing or trivial. Freud believed this procedure produces a chain of thought leading into the patient's unconscious, thereby retrieving and releasing painful unconscious memories. Freud called the procedure *psychoanalysis.* The theory of personality that he created to explain his observations is called "psychoanalytic theory."

Freud believed he glimpsed the unconscious not only in people's free associations and in their symptoms but also in their dreams and slips of the tongue and pen. For Freud the determinist, nothing was ever accidental. Dreams, he contended, are a major outlet for people's unconscious wishes. The remembered content of dreams (their "manifest content") he believed to be a censored expression of those wishes (the dream's "latent content") (see pages 203–204). For Freud, dreams were the "royal road to the unconscious." By analyzing people's dreams, Freud believed he could help reveal the nature of their inner conflicts and release their troublesome tensions. Slips while reading, writing, and speaking further suggested that what we say and do may reflect the workings of our unconscious minds. Consider Freud's example of his financially stressed patient who, not wanting any large pills, said "Please do not give me any bills, because I cannot swallow them."

Personality Structure   For Freud, personality was composed of three interacting systems: id, ego, and superego (Figure 15–1). Like other abstract psychological concepts such as intelligence and memory, id, ego, and superego are only, as Freud said, "useful aids to understanding" that he invented to help explain his view of the mind's dynamics.

The *id* is a reservoir of unconscious psychic energy that constantly strives to satisfy instinctual drives to survive, reproduce, and aggress. The id operates on the *pleasure principle:* It seeks immediate gratification, totally unconstrained by reality. Think of the newborn infant, who, governed by the id, cries out for satisfaction the moment a need is felt, with no recognition of the conditions and demands that may exist in the outside world.

The *ego* develops gradually as the infant learns to cope with the real world. It operates on the *reality principle,* which seeks to gratify the id's impulses in realistic ways that will bring long-term pleasure rather than pain or destruction. Imagine what would happen if, lacking an ego, we expressed our unrestrained sexual or hostile impulses whenever we felt them. The ego, which contains our mostly conscious perceptions, thoughts, judgments, and memories, is said to be the

Drawing by Fradon; © 1983 The New Yorker Magazine, Inc.

"Good morning, beheaded—uh, I mean beloved."

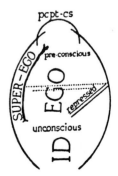

Figure 15–1   Freud's (1933, p. 111) sketch of the mind's structure. "Pcpt.-cs." refers to the perceptual-conscious, or more simply, the conscious.

"executive" of personality because it decides on our actions as it intervenes between the impulsive demands of the id and those of the external world. Beginning at around age 4 or 5, the ego recognizes the demands of a newly emerging psychic system, the superego.

The *superego* is like a voice of conscience that forces the ego to consider not only the real but the ideal: Its sole focus is on how one *ought* to behave. It develops as we internalize the morals and values of parents and society, thereby providing both our sense of right and wrong and our *ideal* standards. The superego strives for perfection and judges our actions, accompanied by feelings of guilt or pride. Someone with an exceptionally strong superego may be continually upright yet guilt-ridden, while another with a weak superego may be wantonly self-indulgent. Because the superego's demands are often in opposition to those of the id, the ego must struggle to reconcile the two, as when a chaste student who is sexually attracted to someone joins a volunteer organization in order to work alongside the desired person, thus satisfying the demands of id and superego.

Personality Development   Freud's analysis of his patients' problems and memories convinced him that personality is decisively shaped in the first few years of life. Again and again his patients' symptoms appeared to him to be rooted in unresolved conflicts that originated in early childhood. He concluded that children pass through a series of *psychosexual stages* of development (Table 15–1)—stages during which the id's pleasure-seeking energies are focused on different pleasure-sensitive areas of the body called "erogenous zones."

During the *oral stage*, which lasts throughout the first 18 months of life, the infant's sensual pleasures focus on sucking, biting, and chewing.

During the *anal stage*, from about age 18 months to 3 years, the sphincter muscles become sensitive and controllable and bowel and bladder retention and elimination become a source of gratification.

During the *phallic stage*, from roughly ages 3 to 6 years, the pleasure zone shifts to the genitals. During this stage Freud believed that children seek genital stimulation and develop both unconscious sexual desires for the parent of the other sex and feelings of jealousy and hatred for the rival parent of the same sex. Children also develop feelings of guilt and a fear that the rival parent will punish them; boys, for example, supposedly fear castration by their father. Freud called this collection of feelings the *Oedipus complex* after the Greek legend of Oedipus, who unknowingly killed his father and married his mother. In girls, similar feelings are called the *Electra complex* after the Greek legend of Electra, who helped kill her mother.

Children eventually cope with these threatening feelings by repressing them and by identifying with (by trying to become like) the rival parent. It is through this *identification* process, in which children incorporate many of their parents' values, that the superego gains strength. As we noted on page 121, Freud also believed that identification with the same-sex parent provides our gender identity.

With their sexual feelings repressed, children enter a *latency period*, during which sexuality is dormant and children play mostly with peers of the same sex.

At puberty, latency gives way to the final stage, the *genital stage*, as youths begin to experience sexual feelings toward others.

In Freud's view, maladaptive behavior in the adult results from unresolved conflicts that originated during the course of these psychosexual stages. At any point in these stages, strong conflict could lock,

"Fifty is plenty."

"Hundred and fifty."

Drawing by Woodman; © 1987 The New Yorker Magazine, Inc.

Table 15–1

FREUD'S PSYCHOSEXUAL STAGES

Stage	Focus
Oral (0 to 18 months)	Oral pleasures—sucking, biting, chewing
Anal (18 to 36 months)	Anal pleasures; coping with demands for control
Phallic (3 to 6 years)	Genitals; coping with incestuous sexual feelings
Latency (6 to puberty)	Repressed sexual feelings
Genital (puberty on)	Maturation of sexual interests

or *fixate,* the person's pleasure-seeking energies in that stage. Thus, people who were either orally overindulged or deprived (perhaps by abrupt, early weaning) might be fixated at the oral stage as adults. Orally fixated people are said to exhibit either passive dependence (like that of a nursing infant) or an exaggerated denial of this dependence— perhaps by acting tough and indulging in biting sarcasm. They might also continue to seek oral gratification through excessive smoking and eating. Those who never quite resolve the anal conflict, between the desire to eliminate at will and the demands of toilet training, may as adults become either messy and disorganized ("anal expulsive") or highly controlled and compulsively neat ("anal retentive"). In such ways, believed Freud, the twig of personality is bent at an early age.

Personality Dynamics   To live in social groups, we cannot act out our sexual and aggressive impulses willy-nilly. We must control them. When the ego fears losing control of the inner war between the demands of the id and the superego, the result is anxiety. Anxiety, said Freud, is the price we pay for civilization.

Unlike the specific fears discussed in Chapter 14, Emotion, the dark cloud of anxiety need not be focused on one specific object. It is therefore hard for us to cope with, as when we feel unsettled but are not sure why. Freud proposed that the ego protects itself against anxiety with what he called ego *defense mechanisms.* Defense mechanisms reduce anxiety *unconsciously,* by distorting reality.

Repression banishes anxiety-arousing thoughts and feelings from consciousness. According to Freud, repression underlies the other defense mechanisms, all of which serve to disguise threatening impulses and keep them from reaching consciousness. Freud believed that repression explains why we do not remember our childhood lust for our parent of the other sex. However, he also believed that the repression is often not complete, and the repressed urges seep out in dream symbols and slips of the tongue.

Another means of coping with anxiety is through *regression—* retreating to an earlier, more infantile stage of development where some of our psychic energies are still fixated. Thus, when facing the anxious first days of school, a child may regress to the oral comfort of thumb sucking or nail biting. Even juvenile monkeys, when anxious, retreat to infantlike clinging to their mothers or to one another (Suomi, 1987).

In *reaction formation,* the ego unconsciously makes unacceptable impulses look like their opposites. En route to consciousness, the unacceptable proposition "I hate him" becomes "I love him." Timidity becomes daring. Feelings of inadequacy become bravado. According to the principle behind this defense mechanism, vehement social crusaders, such as those who rail against gay rights, may be motivated by the very sexual desires against which they are crusading.

Projection disguises threatening impulses by attributing them to others. Thus "He hates me" may be a projection of the actual feeling "I hate him" or "I hate myself." According to Freudian theory, racial prejudice may be the result of projecting one's own unacceptable impulses or characteristics onto members of another group.

The familiar mechanism of *rationalization* lets us unconsciously generate self-justifying explanations so we can hide from ourselves the real reasons for our actions. Thus, habitual drinkers may explain that they drink with their friends "just to be sociable." Students who fail to study may rationalize that "All work and no play makes Jack [or Jill] a dull person."

Displacement diverts one's sexual or aggressive impulses toward a more psychologically acceptable object than the one that aroused them. Children who do not feel free to express anger against their parents will sometimes displace their anger onto someone or something else, such as the family pet.

Sublimation is transforming impulses into socially valued motivations. Sublimation is therefore socially adaptive and may even be a wellspring for great cultural and artistic achievements. Freud suggested that Leonardo da Vinci's paintings of Madonnas were a sublimation of his longing for intimacy with his mother, from whom he had been separated at an early age.

Note again that all these defense mechanisms function indirectly and unconsciously. They reduce anxiety by disguising our threatening impulses. We never say, "I'm feeling anxious; I'd better project my sexual or hostile feelings onto someone else." Defense mechanisms would not work were we to recognize them. Just as the body unconsciously defends itself against disease, so, believed Freud, the ego unconsciously defends itself against anxiety.

Freud's Descendants and Dissenters   Although controversial, Freud's writings soon attracted a group of followers, some of whom later broke away to establish their own versions of psychoanalytic theory. These "neo-Freudians," as they were called, accepted Freud's basic ideas about the personality structures of id, ego, and superego; the importance of the unconscious; the shaping of personality in childhood; and the dynamics of anxiety and the defense mechanisms. They differed in their view of these concepts by placing somewhat more emphasis on the role of the conscious mind in interpreting experience and coping with the environment. Moreover, they doubted that sex and aggression were all-consuming instincts, and they placed more emphasis on social relationships.

Alfred Adler and Karen Horney agreed with Freud that childhood is important. But they believed that the social, not the sexual, tensions of childhood are crucial for personality formation. Adler, who himself struggled to overcome childhood illnesses and accidents, said that behind much of our behavior lies an attempt to vanquish childhood feelings of inferiority, feelings that trigger strivings for superiority and power. (We have Adler to thank for the still popular idea of the "inferiority complex.") Horney said that childhood anxiety, caused by a sense of helplessness, triggers the desire for love and for security.

Erich Fromm and other "ego psychologists" agreed with Freud that the ego is important. But in deemphasizing the role of sexual and aggressive impulses, they viewed the ego as more than a mediator between id and superego. The ego, they said, strives for unity and love, for truth and freedom; such conscious strivings are not merely a sublimation of baser motives.

Erik Erikson agrees with Freud that development proceeds through a series of critical stages. But he believes these are psycho*social*, not psycho*sexual*, stages. As we noted in Chapters 3 and 4, Erikson also believes that life's developmental stages encompass the whole life span. He maintains that infancy is a time for establishing basic trust, and adolescence for establishing identity, and proposes that in adulthood people strive first for intimacy, then for generativity (a feeling of productivity through family and work), and finally for integrity, a sense that their lives have been meaningful.

Unlike these other neo-Freudians, Freud's disciple-turned-

Alfred Adler (*Problems of Neurosis*, 1964): "The individual feels at home in life and feels his existence to be worthwhile just so far as he is useful to others and is overcoming feelings of inferiority."

dissenter, Carl Jung, placed less emphasis on social factors and agreed with Freud that the unconscious exerts a powerful influence. But he contended that the unconscious contains more than a person's repressed thoughts and feelings. There is also a *collective unconscious,* he believed, a reservoir of images derived from our early ancestors' universal experiences. This inherited unconscious includes deep-rooted spiritual concerns and explains why people in different cultures share certain myths and images, such as that of the mother as a symbol of nurturance. (Recall from Chapter 5 that sociobiologists also believe that our ancestral past endows us with some shared dispositions, for reasons having to do with natural selection.)

Carl Jung *(Symbols of Transformation,* 1912): "We can keep from a child all knowledge of earlier myths, but we cannot take from him the need for mythology."

ASSESSING THE UNCONSCIOUS

Researchers who study personality and mental health professionals who provide therapy for troubled persons need methods for evaluating personality characteristics. Different theories of personality imply different methods of describing and assessing personality.

Psychoanalytic theory maintains that the most significant influences on our personalities arise from the unconscious, which contains residues from early childhood experiences. Practitioners of this perspective therefore dismiss objective agree-disagree or true-false questionnaires as merely tapping the conscious surface. What is needed is a sort of psychological x-ray—a test that can see through our surface pretensions and reveal our hidden conflicts and impulses.

Drawing by Sidney Harris.

"The forward thrust of the antlers shows a determined personality, yet the small sun indicates a lack of self-confidence. . . ."

One type of test designed to provide such a view is the *projective test,* in which a person is presented with an ambiguous stimulus and then asked to describe it or tell a story about it. The stimulus has no inherent meaning, so whatever meaning people read into it is presumed to reflect their interests, biases, and conflicts. Henry Murray (1933) demonstrated a possible basis for such a test at a house party hosted by his 11-year-old daughter. Murray got the children to play a frightening game called "Murder." When he showed them some photographs after the game, Murray found that the children perceived the photos as more malicious than they had before the game. The children, it seemed to Murray, had *projected* their inner feelings into the pictures. A few years later, Murray introduced the *Thematic Apperception Test*

The hopes, fears, interests, and biases revealed in this boy's descriptions of a series of ambiguous pictures in the Thematic Apperception Test (TAT) are presumed to be projections of his inner feelings. As such, they provide valuable leads for the psychologist making the assessment.

(TAT)—ambiguous pictures about which people are asked to make up stories. As you may recall from page 372, one use of the TAT has been to assess achievement motivation. Shown a daydreaming boy, those who imagine him fantasizing an achievement are presumed to be projecting their own achievement concerns.

There are now a variety of other projective tests. They ask subjects to draw a person, to complete sentences ("My mother . . ."), or to provide the first word that comes to mind after the examiner says a test word. More widely used than any of these is the famous *Rorschach inkblot test,* introduced in 1921 by Swiss psychiatrist Hermann Rorschach. The Rorschach test provides ten inkblots, the assumption being that what we see in them is a projection of our inner feelings and conflicts. If we see fierce animals or weapons, for example, the examiner may infer that we have aggressive tendencies.

Is this a reasonable assumption? If so, can the psychologist who administers the test use the Rorschach to understand one's personality and to help diagnose any emotional disorder? Recall from our discussion of intelligence tests the two primary criteria of a good test: reliability and validity. On those criteria, how good is the Rorschach?

Not very good. There is no one accepted system for scoring the test, so unless two raters have been trained in the same scoring system, their agreement on the results of any given test may be minimal. There is also no set system for interpretation. In effect, a subject's inkblot interpretations are themselves ambiguous stimuli, which different examiners may interpret differently. Nor is the test very successful at predicting behavior or at discriminating between groups (for example, identifying who is homosexual and who is heterosexual). Writing in *The Eighth Mental Measurements Yearbook,* Rolf Peterson (1978) summed up 50 years of research and 5000 articles and books by concluding that "the general lack of predictive validity for the Rorschach raises serious questions about its continued use in clinical practice."

Although not as popular as it once was, the test nevertheless remains one of the most widely used psychological instruments (Lubin & others, 1984). Some clinicians continue to be confident of the test's validity—not as a device that by itself can provide a diagnosis, but as a source of suggestive leads that can be supplemented with other infor-

This girl is taking the most familiar projective test, the Rorschach. Although its reliability and validity are being questioned, the Rorschach test is still widely used and some researchers are working to make its scoring and interpretation more objective.

mation. Other clinicians believe that even if the Rorschach scoring systems have little validity, the test is still an icebreaker and a revealing interview technique. Promising new research-based, computer-aided scoring and interpretation may improve agreement between raters and may enhance the validity of this venerable test (Exner, 1986). But Freud himself would probably have been uncomfortable with such attempts to assign each patient a score, and more interested in the therapist-patient interactions that took place during the course of the test.

EVALUATING THE PSYCHOANALYTIC PERSPECTIVE

Having sought to understand Freud's ideas, let us now listen to his critics. Bear in mind that we do so from the perspective of the late twentieth century, a perspective that is itself subject to revision. Freud died in 1939 without the benefit of all that we have since learned about human development, thinking, and emotion and without today's tools for research. To criticize Freud's theories by comparing them with current concepts is rather like comparing the Model T with today's Ford Escort.

Freud's Ideas in Light of Modern Research   The criticisms occur at two levels. First, many of Freud's specific ideas are contradicted by more recent theory and research. His idea that conscience and gender identity are formed by the child's resolving the Oedipus or Electra complex at age 5 or 6 is questioned by newer work in developmental psychology. Developmental research indicates that human development is lifelong, not fixed in childhood (see Chapters 3 to 5). Freud's ideas of childhood sexuality arose from his rejection of stories of childhood sexual abuse told by his female patients—stories he thought were an expression of their own childhood sexual wishes and conflicts but that today we might not dismiss. And his ideas that women have weak superegos and suffer "penis envy" are now discounted—even by many psychoanalysts—and are considered sexist as well.

As we saw in Chapter 8, Freud's belief that dreams are disguised wish fulfillments that can be interpreted by skilled analysts has been disputed by newer conceptions of dreams (pages 202–206). His belief that repression causes forgetting is somewhat supported by reports of memory loss among victims of war trauma and sexual abuse, but the evidence indicates that other mechanisms of forgetting account for most memory loss (see pages 274–278). Even slips of the tongue can be explained as competition between similar verbal choices in our memory network (page 270). Freud's surmise that people protect themselves against painful self-knowledge by projecting their own unrecognized negative traits onto others has generally not been supported by research (Holmes, 1978, 1981).

History has been kinder to Freud's "iceberg" view of the mind, at least in part. Research confirms that our access to what goes on in our minds is very limited (Erdelyi, 1985, 1988). However, the "iceberg" notion held by today's research psychologists differs from that of Freud. As we saw in earlier chapters, many researchers think of the unconscious not in terms of seething passions and repressive censoring but of information processing that occurs without our awareness. To them, the unconscious involves the schemas that automatically control our perceptions and interpretations; the processing of stimuli to which we have not consciously attended; the right hemisphere activity that enables the split-brain patient's left hand to carry out an instruc-

"Two passengers leaned against the ship's rail and stared at the sea. 'There sure is a lot of water in the ocean,' said one. 'Yes,' answered his friend, 'and we've only seen the top of it.'"
Psychologist George A. Miller (1962)

tion the patient cannot verbalize. This understanding of unconscious information processing is more like the pre-Freudian view of the unconscious—in which spontaneous creative ideas were viewed as the surfacing of an underground stream of thought.

Freud's Ideas as Scientific Theory   The second level at which Freud's theory is criticized is not about its specific concepts but about its scientific shortcomings. As we noted in Chapter 1, good scientific theories make sense of observations and offer testable hypotheses. Freud's theory, say the critics, rests on relatively few objective observations and offers few hypotheses that one can verify or reject. (For Freud, his own interpretations of patients' free associations, dreams, and slips were evidence enough.)

The most serious problem with Freud's theory, according to critics, is that it offers after-the-fact explanations of any characteristic (of one person's smoking, another's fear of horses, another's sexual orientation), yet it fails to *predict* such behavior and traits. If you feel angry at your mother's death, you support the theory because "your unresolved childhood dependency needs are threatened." If you do not feel angry, you again support the theory because "you are repressing your anger." That, said Calvin Hall and Gardner Lindzey (1978, p. 68), "is like betting on a horse after the race has been run." After-the-fact interpretation is perfectly appropriate for historical and literary scholarship, which helps explain Freud's currently greater influence on literary criticism than on psychological research. But in science a good theory makes testable predictions.

Such criticisms of Freud's specific concepts and after-the-fact interpretations have led some modern critics to scorn his theory totally. Peter Medawar (1982, pp. 71–72) compared it to "a dinosaur . . . one of the saddest and strangest of all landmarks in the history of twentieth-century thought." Perhaps we can evaluate Freud less harshly, for three reasons:

1. To criticize Freudian theory for failing to satisfy the criteria of predictive science is like criticizing baseball for not being an aerobic exercise. Is it fair to fault something for not being what it was never intended to be? Freudian sociologist Phillip Rieff explains (1979, p. 130):

    > Freud never made for psychoanalysis the fundamental claim of modern science: the power of prediction. Psychoanalysis, he maintained, is a retrospective science, never a predictive one. . . . Neurotic states of mind are systematically meaningful—which is what Freud meant by causation—whether we can predict them or not.

2. Some of Freud's ideas are enduring. It was Freud who drew our attention to the unconscious and the irrational, to anxiety and our struggle to cope with it, to the importance of human sexuality, and to the tension between our biological impulses and our social well-being. It was Freud who challenged our self-righteousness, punctured our pretensions, and reminded us of our potential for evil. Few dispute that Freud's ideas were creative, courageous, and comprehensive.

3. Correctly, or incorrectly, Freud influenced our view of human nature. Some ideas that many of us assume to be true—that childhood experiences mold personality, that many behaviors have disguised motives, that dreams have symbolic meaning—

"We are arguing like a man who should say, 'If there were an invisible cat in that chair, the chair would look empty; but the chair does look empty; therefore there is an invisible cat in it.'"
C. S. Lewis,
Four Loves, 1958

are partly Freud's legacy, which lives on in our own ideas. As Peter Drucker (1982) remarked, "[Many] psychologists have no use for Freud, and I have some grave doubts about him, but he is the only one who created vision and insight and changed our view of ourselves and of the world." For that, Sigmund Freud continues to rank as one of the towering intellectual figures of modern history.

THE TRAIT PERSPECTIVE

Psychoanalytic theory defines personality in terms of the dynamics that underlie behavior. It always seems to be peering beneath the surface in search of hidden motives. In 1919, Gordon Allport, a curious 22-year-old psychology student, discovered when he interviewed Freud in Vienna just how preoccupied the founder of psychoanalysis was with finding hidden motives for behavior:

> Soon after I had entered the famous red burlap room with pictures of dreams on the wall, he summoned me to his inner office. He did not speak to me but sat in expectant silence, for me to state my mission. I was not prepared for silence and had to think fast to find a suitable conversational gambit. I told him of an episode on the tram car on my way to his office. A small boy about four years of age had displayed a conspicuous dirt phobia. He kept saying to his mother, "I don't want to sit there . . . don't let that dirty man sit beside me." To him everything was *schmutzig* (filthy). His mother was a well-starched *Hausfrau,* so dominant and purposive looking that I thought the cause and effect apparent.
>
> When I finished my story Freud fixed his kindly therapeutic eyes upon me and said, "And was that little boy you?" Flabbergasted and feeling a bit guilty, I contrived to change the subject. While Freud's misunderstanding of my motivation was amusing, it also started a deep train of thought (1967, pp. 7–8).

That train of thought ultimately led Allport to do what Freud did not do—describe personality in terms of fundamental *traits*—people's characteristic behaviors and conscious motives (such as the professional curiosity that actually motivated Allport to see Freud). "This experience," said Allport, "taught me that depth psychology, for all its merits, may plunge too deep, and that psychologists would do well to

Personality traits can be fundamental to job performance. The outgoing temperament so vital to being a standup comedian would probably not be necessary to a naturalist.

give full recognition to manifest motives before probing the unconscious." Allport therefore developed *trait theory*, which defines personality in terms of the behaviors themselves. It takes behavior more or less at face value. Trait theorists are less concerned with *explaining why* we differ from one another, and more concerned with *describing how* we differ.

Once more, it is important to remember the distinction between explanation and description. To say that someone is generally talkative *because* he or she has an outgoing personality is merely to describe behavior with a trait name, not to explain it. Description is, however, an important starting point for any science. How do psychologists describe and classify personalities? An analogy may help. Imagine that you want to describe and classify apples. Someone might correctly say that every apple is unique. Still, you might find it useful to begin by classifying apples by *types*—Delicious, Jonathan, McIntosh, and so forth.

That is how the ancient Greeks described personality—by classifying people according to four types. Depending on which of one's bodily "humors," or fluids, was believed to predominate, people were said to be either melancholic (depressed), sanguine (cheerful), phlegmatic (unemotional), or choleric (irritable). Although this classification system seems humorous now, other more recent attempts have classified people according to their body types. Santa Claus typifies what psychologist William Sheldon (1954) called the plump "endomorph": relaxed and jolly. Superman typifies the muscular "mesomorph": bold and physically active. Sherlock Holmes typifies the thin "ectomorph": high strung and solitary.

Are different body types actually associated with different personalities? It is conceivable. However, when people's body types and personalities are assessed separately, the actual linkage is modest. The stereotypes of the chubby, happy-go-lucky person and of the muscular, confident person turn out to be just that—stereotypes that exaggerate a kernel of truth (Tucker, 1983).

DESCRIBING TRAITS

If classifying people as one type or another fails to capture their individuality, how else can we describe their personalities? To return to our analogy, you might decide to describe each apple in terms of several trait dimensions—as relatively large or small, red or yellow, sweet or sour. Similarly, the trait perspective seeks to describe and classify people in terms of their predispositions to behave in certain ways. By viewing people on several dimensions simultaneously, trait psychologists can describe countless individual variations. If this seems surprising, recall from Chapter 6 that the hundreds of thousands of color variations we can distinguish may each be described on just three color dimensions (hue, saturation, and brightness).

But what trait dimensions describe personality? Trait theorist Allport and his associate H. S. Odbert (1936) literally counted all the possible words in an unabridged dictionary that could be used to describe people. The list numbered almost 18,000 words! How, then, could psychologists condense the list to a manageable number of basic traits?

One way has been to propose traits, such as anxiety, that appear to be basic according to clinical judgment or to a particular psychological theory. A newer technique is *factor analysis*, the statistical procedure we saw used in Chapter 12 to identify clusters of test items that tap basic

In our consideration of intelligence in Chapter 12, we confronted a similar distinction between psychologists who seek to *explain* intelligence (in terms of genes and experience) and those who seek to *describe* the components or dimensions of intelligence.

components of intelligence (such as spatial ability, reasoning ability, or verbal skill). Imagine you find that people who describe themselves as outgoing also tend to say that they like excitement and practical jokes, and that they do not like quiet reading. Such a statistically correlated cluster of behaviors might be viewed as reflecting a basic trait, or factor. In this particular case, the identified items are part of a cluster that make up a trait called *extraversion.*

Raymond Cattell (1973) used factor analysis to reveal sixteen personality traits—traits such as outgoingness, assertiveness, and stability. The degree to which a person embodies each of the sixteen basic traits forms a unique pattern, called a personality profile. British psychologists Hans and Michael Eysenck believe that many of our individual variations can be reduced to only two genetically influenced dimensions: *extraversion-introversion* and *emotional stability-instability.* Extraverts, they contend, are predisposed to seek stimulation because their normal level of brain arousal is relatively low. Emotionally stable people are said to react calmly because their autonomic nervous system is not so reactive as that of unstable people. The Eysencks also note that the four combinations of these two trait dimensions resemble the personality types proposed by the ancient Greeks (see Figure 15–2).

Recently, several researchers have concurred that while the Eysencks' two dimensions don't tell the whole story of someone's personality, Cattell's sixteen factor dimensions could be simplified. An intermediate number of factors—dubbed the "Big Five"—seem to describe the major features of personality (Digman & Inouye, 1986; Goldberg, 1981; Noller & others, 1987). If a test specifies where you are on the five dimensions of Table 15–2, it has said much of what there is to say about your personality.

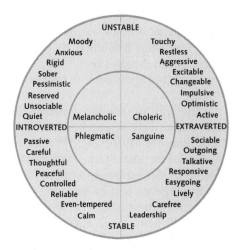

Figure 15–2 In this chart, various combinations of the Eysencks' two primary personality factors—extraversion-introversion and stability-instability—are used to define other, more specific traits. The four basic combinations of the two factors coincidentally resemble the personality types proposed by the ancient Greeks, which are noted in the center of the chart. (From Eysenck & Eysenck, 1963.)

Table 15–2
THE "BIG FIVE" PERSONALITY FACTORS

Factor	Description
Emotional stability	Calm versus anxious Secure versus insecure Self-satisfied versus self-pitying
Extraversion	Sociable versus retiring Fun-loving versus sober Affectionate versus reserved
Openness	Imaginative versus practical Preference for variety versus preference for routine Independent versus conforming
Agreeableness	Soft-hearted versus ruthless Trusting versus suspicious Helpful versus uncooperative
Conscientiousness ("the will to achieve")	Well-organized versus disorganized Careful versus careless Self-disciplined versus weak willed

Source: Adapted from "Clinical assessment can benefit from recent advances in personality psychology" by R. McCrae & P. T. Costa, Jr., 1986, *American Psychologist, 41,* p. 1002.

ASSESSING TRAITS

Assessment techniques derived from trait theory aim not to reveal the hidden dynamics of someone's personality—which is the intent of projective tests—but to provide a profile of a person's traits. Some measures provide a quick assessment of a single trait, such as sociability, anxiety, or self-confidence. By administering *personality inventories*—longer questionnaires on which people report their feelings and behaviors—psychologists seek to measure several important aspects of personality.

One way to develop a personality inventory is illustrated by the most extensively researched and widely used of all personality tests, the *Minnesota Multiphasic Personality Inventory (MMPI).* One of the creators of the test, Starke Hathaway (1960), compared his effort to that utilized by Alfred Binet, who, as we saw in Chapter 12, developed the first intelligence test by selecting items that successfully discriminated between children who were and were not progressing in Paris schools. The MMPI items were also *empirically derived*—that is, from a large pool of items those that were found to differentiate among particular groups were selected. Hathaway and his colleagues initially administered hundreds of true-false statements ("No one seems to understand me," "I get all the sympathy I should," "I like poetry") both to different groups of psychologically disordered patients and to "normal" people. Those that a patient group answered differently from the normal group were retained for the test, no matter how silly they sounded. "Nothing in the newspaper interests me except the comics" may seem senseless, but it just so happened that depressed people were more likely to answer "true" to that statement.

The MMPI that resulted contains ten such "clinical scales" (see Figure 15–3). It also has several "validity scales," including a "lie scale" that assesses the extent to which a person is faking a good impression (by responding "false" to statements such as "I get angry sometimes").

Figure 15–3   Minnesota Multiphasic Personality Inventory (MMPI) test profile of a group of depressed patients from the Minneapolis VA hospital. The relatively high scores on the first three scales are typical of depressed people. Roughly two-thirds of people taking the MMPI have a T-score between 40 and 60 on any scale. (A T-score of 50, like an IQ score of 100, is the designated mean of this nearly bell-shaped distribution of scores.) (Adapted from Rosen, 1958.)

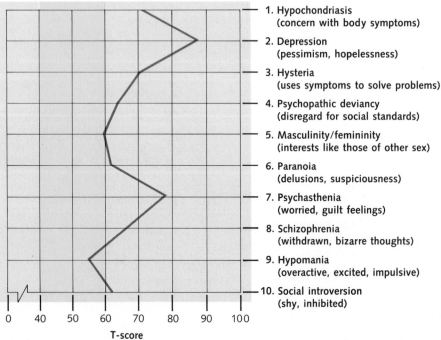

1. **Hypochondriasis**
   (concern with body symptoms)
2. **Depression**
   (pessimism, hopelessness)
3. **Hysteria**
   (uses symptoms to solve problems)
4. **Psychopathic deviancy**
   (disregard for social standards)
5. **Masculinity/femininity**
   (interests like those of other sex)
6. **Paranoia**
   (delusions, suspiciousness)
7. **Psychasthenia**
   (worried, guilt feelings)
8. **Schizophrenia**
   (withdrawn, bizarre thoughts)
9. **Hypomania**
   (overactive, excited, impulsive)
10. **Social introversion**
    (shy, inhibited)

0   40   50   60   70   80   90   100

T-score

Other investigators have administered the 566 revised MMPI items to countless other clearly differentiated groups (for example, successful and unsuccessful nurses) in hopes of empirically deriving a scale for use in selecting or evaluating people. Hundreds of such MMPI scales now exist. However, most experts believe that the test is more appropriately used for its original purpose—assessing troubled people by comparing their test profiles with those of others who are troubled.

In contrast to the subjectivity of projective tests, these personality inventories are objective—so objective that they can be administered and scored by a computer. (The computer can also provide descriptions of people who have previously responded similarly.) Objectivity does not, however, guarantee validity; for example, sophisticated test-takers can create a false good impression if taking the MMPI for employment purposes (by answering in socially desirable ways, except on those items where nearly anyone would admit to being imperfect). Moreover, the ease of computerized testing tempts untrained administrators—including many personnel officers, educational admissions officers, and physicians—to expand the use of the test beyond the purposes for which it has been validated (Matarazzo, 1983). Nevertheless, for better or worse, the objectivity of the MMPI has contributed to its rising popularity (Lubin & others, 1984), to its translation into 124 languages, and to a forthcoming revision with updated and more representative norms.

EVALUATING THE TRAIT PERSPECTIVE: HOW CONSISTENT ARE WE?

Do we indeed possess stable and enduring traits? Or does our behavior depend on where we are and whom we are with at the time? As we noted earlier, William Faulkner, who strove to reconstruct his own reality in fiction, created characters, like the self-centered Jason Compson, whose personal traits were consistently expressed at different times and places. The Italian playwright Luigi Pirandello had a different view of the nature and consistency of personality. For him, personality was ever-changing, tailored to the particular role or situation in which we find ourselves. Consider Lamberto Laudisi's description of himself to Signora Sirelli in Pirandello's play *It Is So! (If You Think So)*: "I am really what you take me to be; though, my dear madam, that does not prevent me from also being really what your husband, my sister, my niece, and Signora Cini take me to be—because they also are absolutely right!" To which she responds, "In other words you are a different person for each of us."

Who best represents human personality, Faulkner's consistent Jason Compson or Pirandello's inconsistent Laudisi? Most of us agree that this is not strictly an either/or question: Our behavior is influenced by our inner disposition, and it is also responsive to the environment. The real question—one of the most important and longstanding questions in all psychology—is which is *more* important? Are we *more* as Faulkner or as Pirandello imagines us to be? Forced to choose, most people would probably side with Faulkner. Until recently, most psychologists would have too. After all, isn't it obvious that some people are dependably conscientious and others unreliable, some cheerful and others dour, some outgoing and others shy?

Remember, to be a genuine personality trait a characteristic must *both* endure over time and persist across situations. If friendliness is a trait, friendly people must act friendly at different times and places. Do they? In Chapter 4, we considered the research of those who have

"There is as much difference between us and ourselves, as between us and others."
  Michel de Montaigne,
  Essays, 1588

Roughly speaking, the temporary, external influences on behavior are the focus of social psychology, and the enduring, inner influences are the focus of personality psychology.

followed lives over time. We noted that although some researchers have been most impressed with personality change (especially those who have begun by studying infants), others have been struck by the stability of important traits from adolescence through adulthood. If people's temperaments are rated in young adulthood and then rated again several decades later, their basic temperamental traits seem to persist. Faulkner would not have been surprised.

The consistency of *behavior* from one situation to the next is another matter, however. As Walter Mischel (1968, 1984) points out, people seem not to act with predictable consistency from one situation to the next. In one of the first studies to suggest this, Hugh Hartshorne and Mark May (1928b) gave thousands of children a variety of opportunities to lie, cheat, and steal while at home, at play, and in the classroom. Were some children consistently honest, others dishonest? Generally not. "Most children will deceive in certain situations and not in others," the researchers reported. A child's "lying, cheating, and stealing as measured by the test situations used in these studies are only very loosely related" (p. 411). More than a half century later, Mischel's studies of college students' conscientiousness revealed a similar finding. There was virtually no relationship between a student's being conscientious on one occasion (say, showing up for class on time) and being similarly conscientious on another occasion (say, turning in assignments on time). Pirandello would not have been surprised.

Mischel also points out that people's scores on personality tests are only mildly predictive of their behaviors. For example, people's scores on an extraversion test are not closely related to how sociable they actually are on any given day. If we remember such results, says Mischel, we will be more cautious about trying to label and pigeonhole individuals. We will be more restrained when asked to predict if someone is likely to violate parole, commit suicide, or be an effective employee. Years in advance, science can tell us the phase of the moon for any given date, but we're a long way from being able to predict how you will feel and act tomorrow.

In defense of trait theory, personality psychologist Seymour Epstein (1983a, 1983b) maintains that trying to predict a specific act on the basis of a personality test is like trying to predict your answer to a single test question on the basis of an intelligence test. Your answer to any given question is largely unpredictable because it depends on so many variables (your reading of the question, your understanding of the topic, your concentration level at the moment, luck). Your *average* accuracy over many questions on several tests is more predictable. Similarly, says Epstein, people's *average* outgoingness, happiness, or carelessness over *many* situations is somewhat predictable. This consistency enables people who know someone well to agree when rating behavioral traits, such as how shy the person is (Kenrick & Funder, 1988). As our best friends can verify, we *do* have personality traits.

To sum up, we can say that at any moment a person's behavior is powerfully influenced by the immediate situation, especially when the situation is clear and unambiguous, demanding only particular behaviors from us. We can better predict drivers' behavior at traffic lights from knowing the color of the lights than from knowing their personalities. Even Gordon Allport, whom many regard as the original trait theorist, expected an individual's traits to be expressed only in particular situations (Zuroff, 1986). Thus, professors may perceive a student as subdued, while friends may perceive her as rather wild. By averaging people's behavior across many different situations, we see evidence of distinctive and consistent personalities.

"Every man is more the man of the day than a regular and consequential character."
Lord Chesterfield, 1694–1733

THE HUMANISTIC PERSPECTIVE

By 1960, some prominent personality psychologists had become discontented both with the deterministic negativity of Freud's views and with the seeming irrelevance of what was derisively termed behavioristic "rat psychology." In place of Freud's emphasis on the unconscious sexual and aggressive impulses of "sick" people, these "humanistic psychologists" emphasized the strivings of "healthy" people for self-determination and self-realization. In place of behaviorism's mechanistic analysis, which seemed to belittle subjective experience and reduce human behavior to a chain of conditioned responses, they urged that the whole personality be studied, including personal experiences of sorrow and joy, alienation and intimacy, frustration and fulfillment. These emphases on positive human potential and seeing the world through the person's (not the experimenter's) eyes are illustrated in the viewpoints of two pioneering theorists, Abraham Maslow (1908–1970) and Carl Rogers (1902–1987).

EXPLORING THE SELF

Abraham Maslow's Self-Actualizing Person   As you may recall from page 353, Maslow proposed that humans are motivated by a hierarchy of needs. If our physiological needs are met, we become concerned with personal safety; if we achieve a sense of security, we then are motivated to love, to be loved, and to love ourselves. After we achieve our need for self-esteem, we ultimately seek *self-actualization,* the process of fulfilling one's potential, of becoming the self one is capable of becoming.

Unlike many theorists before him, Maslow (1970) developed his ideas by studying healthy, creative people rather than clinical cases. His description of self-actualization was based on a study of acquaintances and historical figures who seemed notable for the richness and productiveness of their lives—Abraham Lincoln, Thomas Jefferson, and Eleanor Roosevelt among them. These people seemed to share a number of characteristics. Maslow reported that they were self-aware and self-accepting, open and spontaneous, loving and caring, and not paralyzed by others' opinions. Being secure in their sense of who they were as individuals, they tended to be problem-centered rather than self-centered. Often they focused their energies on a particular task that they regarded as their mission in life. Many had been moved by spiritual or ecstatic "peak experiences" that surpassed ordinary consciousness. Most enjoyed a few deep relationships rather than many superficial ones.

These are mature adult qualities, said Maslow, ones likely to be found in those individuals who have learned enough about life to be compassionate, to have outgrown their mixed feelings toward their parents, to have found their calling, to have "acquired enough courage to be unpopular, to be unashamed about being openly virtuous, etc." Maslow's work with college students led him to speculate that those likely to become self-actualizing adults tended to be likable, caring, "privately affectionate to those of their elders who deserve it," and "secretly uneasy about the cruelty, meanness, and mob spirit so often found in young people."

Abraham Maslow (1970, p. 33): "Any theory of motivation that is worthy of attention must deal with the highest capacities of the healthy and strong person as well as with the defensive maneuvers of crippled spirits."

Carl Rogers' Person-Centered Perspective   Fellow humanistic psychologist Carl Rogers agreed with much of Maslow's thinking. Rogers believed that people are basically good and are endowed with inherent self-actualizing tendencies: Each of us is like an acorn, containing the potential for tremendous growth and fulfillment, unless thwarted by an environment that inhibits growth. Rogers (1980) thought that a "growth-promoting" climate required three conditions—genuineness, acceptance, and empathy.

According to Rogers, people nurture growth, first, by being *genuine*—by being open with their own feelings, by dropping their facades, by being transparent and self-disclosing. People nurture our growth, second, by being *accepting*—by offering us what Rogers called **unconditional positive regard.** This is an attitude of grace, an attitude that values us, even knowing our failings. Have you ever experienced the relief of having dropped your pretenses, confessed your worst feelings, and discovered that you were still accepted? This gratifying experience we sometimes enjoy in a good marriage or in an intimate friendship, where we no longer feel the need to explain ourselves and are free to be spontaneous without fear of losing the other's esteem.

People nurture our growth, third, by being *empathic*—by sensing and nonjudgmentally reflecting our feelings and meanings. "Rarely do we listen with real understanding, true empathy," said Rogers. "Yet listening, of this very special kind, is one of the most potent forces for change that I know."

These three conditions—genuineness, acceptance, and empathy— are the water, the sun, and the nutrients that enable people to grow like strong, vigorous oak trees. For "as persons are accepted and prized," Rogers (1980, p. 116) continued, "they tend to develop a more caring attitude toward themselves." As persons are empathically heard, "it becomes possible for them to listen more accurately to the flow of inner experiencings." Rogers would have been pleased by a study, published shortly after his death, which found that preschool children whose parents exhibited such attitudes grew to exhibit considerable creativity as adolescents (Harrington & others, 1987).

For Maslow, and even more for Rogers, a central feature of personality is one's **self-concept**—all the thoughts and feelings we have in response to the question, "Who am I?" If our self-concept is positive, we tend to act and perceive the world positively. If it is negative—if in our own eyes we fall far short of our "ideal self"—said Rogers, we feel dissatisfied and unhappy. A real goal for parents, teachers, helpers, and friends is to help all individuals know, accept, and be true to themselves.

Being open and sharing confidences is easy when you have an empathic listener.

Although Rogers' experience as a therapist fostered his recognition of genuineness, acceptance, and empathy for nurturing growth, he believed they applied equally well to relations between parent and child, leader and group, teacher and student, administrator and staff member— in fact, any two human beings.

ASSESSING THE SELF

Humanistic psychologists sometimes assess personality with questionnaires that measure people's self-concepts. One questionnaire, inspired by Carl Rogers, asks people to describe themselves both as they ideally would like to be and as they actually are. When the ideal and the actual self are nearly alike, the self-concept is considered positive. Thus Rogers used the growing similarity of the client's successive ratings of actual and ideal self as a way to assess personal growth during therapy.

Other humanistic psychologists believe that any formal, objective assessment of personality tends to be depersonalizing. Even a questionnaire detaches the psychologist from the living human who is being studied. Rather than forcing the person to respond to narrow categories, these humanistic psychologists believe that interviews and intimate conversation can get closer to the person's own thoughts, perceptions, and feelings—and thus to a better understanding of the person's unique experiences.

EVALUATING THE HUMANISTIC PERSPECTIVE

One thing said of Freud can also be said of the humanistic psychologists: Their impact has been pervasive. Their ideas have found their way into counseling, education, child-rearing, and management. They have also influenced—sometimes in ways they did not intend—much of the popular psychology proclaimed in the media.

It is also through the media that many of us have absorbed some of what Maslow and Rogers have so effectively taught. Partly due to their influence, many people assume that a positive self-concept is a key to happiness and success, that acceptance and empathy help nurture positive feelings about oneself, and that people are basically good and capable of self-improvement. The National Opinion Research Center (1985) reports that by a 4 to 1 margin, Americans believe that "human nature is basically good" rather than "fundamentally perverse and corrupt." Humanistic psychologists might also take satisfaction in the dramatically different responses today from those of 50 years ago to one of the MMPI statements (Holden, 1986c): In the 1930s, only 9 percent of the rural Minnesotans on whom the test was standardized agreed that "I am an important person." In the mid-1980s, more than half of Americans in the new normative sample agreed with the statement.

Criticism of Humanistic Psychology   The prominence of the humanistic perspective set off a backlash of criticism. First, said the critics, its concepts are vague and subjective. Consider the description of self-actualizing people as open, spontaneous, loving, self-accepting, and productive. Is this really a scientific description of human fulfillment? Or is it merely a description of Maslow's personal values and ideals? What Maslow did, noted M. Brewster Smith (1978), was to pick his own personal heroes and offer his impressions of them. Had some other theorist (with different values and ideals) begun with a different set of heroes—perhaps people like Napoleon, Alexander the Great, and John D. Rockefeller, Sr.—the resulting picture of the self-actualizing person would have probably included descriptives such as "undeterred by the needs of others," "motivated to achieve," and "obsessed with power."

Second, some critics object to the idea that, as Carl Rogers put it, "The only question which matters is, 'Am I living in a way which is deeply satisfying to me, and which truly expresses me?'" (quoted by Wallach & Wallach, 1985). They fear that the priorities encouraged by humanistic psychology—self-fulfillment, trusting and acting on one's feelings, being true to oneself—have encouraged self-indulgence, selfishness, and an erosion of moral restraints (Campbell & Specht, 1985; Wallach & Wallach, 1983). Those who focus not on themselves but beyond themselves are most likely to experience social support, to enjoy life, and to cope effectively with stress (Crandall, 1984). Humanistic psychologists reject such objections. They counter that belligerence, hostility, and insensitivity are often traceable to a poor self-concept and that self-love is actually the first step toward loving others.

"We do pretty well when you stop to think that people are basically good."

"Man is not a solitary animal, and so long as social life survives, self-realization cannot be the supreme principle of ethics."
Bertrand Russell, 1872–1970

Finally, the humanistic psychologists have been accused of failing to appreciate reality and the perils of the human capacity for evil. Faced with assaults on the environment, overpopulation, and threats of nuclear war, apathy can develop from at least two rationalizations. One is a naïve optimism that denies the threat ("People are basically good; everything will work out"). The other is a dark despair ("It's hopeless; why try?"). Action requires enough realism to fuel concern and enough optimism to provide hope. Humanistic psychology, say the critics, encourages the needed hope, but not the equally necessary realism.

MINI-DEBATE

Does Human Nature Contain Evil?
Two Humanistic Psychologists Debate

Rollo May: YES

The culture admittedly has powerful effects upon us. But it could not have these effects were these tendencies not already present in us. Who makes up the culture except persons like you and me? The culture is evil as well as good because we, the human beings who constitute it, are evil as well as good. We are bundles of both evil and good potentialities.

Some people who join and lead the humanistic movement do so in order to find a haven, a port in the storm, a community of like-minded persons who also are playing possum to the evils about us. Life, to me, is not a requirement to live out a preordained pattern of goodness, but a challenge coming down through the centuries out of the fact that each of us can throw the lever toward good or toward evil. This seems to me to require the age-old religious truths of mercy and forgiveness and it leaves no place for self-righteousness. (Excerpted from May [1982]. Reprinted with permission.)

Carl Rogers: NO

Though I am very well aware of the incredible amount of destructive, cruel, malevolent behavior in today's world—from the threats of war to the senseless violence in the streets—I do not find that this evil is inherent in human nature. In a psychological climate which is nurturant of growth and choice, I have never known an individual to choose the cruel or destructive path. Choice always seems to be in the direction of greater socialization, improved relationships with others. So my experience leads me to believe that it is cultural influences which are the major factor in our evil behaviors. The rough manner of childbirth, the infant's mixed experience with the parents, the constricting, destructive influence of our educational system, the injustice of our distribution of wealth, our cultivated prejudices against individuals who are different—all these elements and many others warp the human organism in directions which are antisocial. So I see members of the human species, like members of other species, as essentially constructive in their fundamental nature, but damaged by their experience. (From Rogers [1981]. Reprinted with permission.)

Research on the Self Psychology's concern with people's sense of self dates back at least to William James, who devoted more than 100 pages of his 1890 *Principles of Psychology* to the topic. By 1943 Gordon Allport lamented that the self had become "lost to view." Although humanistic psychology's emphasis on the self did not instigate much scientific research, it did help renew the concept of the self and keep it alive. Now, a century after James, the self has become one of psychology's most vigorously researched topics. Studies are being conducted on many different aspects: "self-esteem," "self-disclosure," "self-awareness," "self-schemas," "self-monitoring," and so forth. During 1987 the word "self" appeared in 4778, or 11 percent, of the article and book summaries appearing in *Psychological Abstracts*, the "reader's guide" to psychological research—more than double the percentage of 15 years earlier.

One example of the new thinking about self is the concept of "possible selves" put forth by Hazel Markus and her University of Michigan colleagues (Markus & Nurius, 1986; Inglehart & others, 1987). Your possible selves include your visions of the self you dream of becoming—the rich self, the thin self, the loved and admired self—and of the self you fear becoming—the unemployed self, the alcoholic self, the academically failed self. Such possible selves motivate us by providing specific goals to pursue and the energy to work toward them. Olympian Carl Lewis concentrated on the achievements of Olympic hero Jesse Owens to give form to his aspirations. Similarly, University of Michigan students in a combined undergraduate/medical school program earned higher grades than their equally able classmates if they underwent the program with a clear vision of themselves as successful doctors. Those who dream most, achieve most.

Underlying this research is the assumption of humanistic psychologists that the self, as organizer of our thoughts, feelings, and actions, is a pivotal aspect of personality (Markus & Wurf, 1987). We even remember things better when the information is encoded in terms of ourselves: When asked whether specific words such as "friendly" describe us, we later recall those words better than if we had been asked whether they describe someone else.

How we *feel* about ourselves is also important. Research studies bear witness first to the personal benefits of positive self-esteem and second to the social and personal costs of self-righteous pride.

The Benefits of Self-Esteem High *self-esteem*—a feeling of self-worth—pays dividends. People who feel good about themselves tend to have fewer ulcers and less insomnia, are less likely to become drug addicted, are more independent of pressures to conform, and are more persistent at difficult tasks (Brockner & Hulton, 1978; Greenwald & Pratkanis, 1984).

Low self-esteem exacts great costs. People who feel they are falling short of their hoped-for ideal are vulnerable to depression, and those whose self-image falls short of what they think they *ought* to be are more vulnerable to anxiety (Higgins, 1987). Psychotherapy researcher Hans Strupp (1982, pp. 64–65) reflected that

> As soon as one listens to a patient's story, one encounters unhappiness, frustration, and despair which find expression in diverse forms of psychopathology including psychosomatic symptoms, neurotic symptoms, and maladaptive character styles. . . . Basic to all these difficulties are impairments in self-acceptance and self-esteem.

What possible future selves do you envision? To what extent do these imagined selves motivate you in the here and now?

"What you think of yourself is much more important than what others think of you." Seneca, *Ad Lucilium*, A.D. 64

These correlational links between low self-esteem and life problems have other possible interpretations (maybe life problems cause low self-esteem). However, an effect of low self-esteem has been demonstrated in experiments. People whose self-image is temporarily deflated (say, by being told they did poorly on an aptitude test or by having their personality disparaged) are, at such a time, more likely to disparage other people or even to express heightened racial prejudice. People who are negative about themselves also tend to be negative about others (Crocker & Schwartz, 1985; Wills, 1981). While some "love their neighbors as themselves," others loathe their neighbors as themselves.

In several related experiments, Teresa Amabile (1983a; Amabile & Glazebrook, 1982) captured a happening she had noticed in everyday life. Insecure people, it seemed to her, were often excessively critical, as if to impress others with their own brilliance. When Amabile asked college students to assess the intellect of someone who was interviewed on videotape, who do you suppose were the more scathing in their judgments—the students who were made to feel *insecure* (compared with the experimenter who they thought was a doctoral student), or those who were made to feel *secure* (by having the experimenter declare herself to be a fellow undergraduate)? Amabile reported that the first group—those who thought their opinions would be judged by a person of higher status—were more critical.

Although few of these researchers would call themselves humanistic psychologists, their findings are consistent with Maslow's and Rogers's presumptions that a "healthy" self-image is beneficial.

The Pervasiveness of Self-Serving Bias   The benefits of a healthy self-image, however, are tempered by another phenomenon: people tend not to judge themselves harshly, as might be supposed, but favorably, a tendency called *self-serving bias.*

Carl Rogers (1958) once objected to the religious doctrine that humanity's problems originate in excessive self-love, or pride, by noting that most people he had known "despise themselves, regard themselves as worthless and unlovable." Actually, researchers find that although some people express low self-esteem, most of us have a good reputation with ourselves. Furthermore, suggest social psychologists John Darley (1983) and Abraham Tesser (1988), we have several strategies for protecting our self-esteem even when we fail at a task—strategies that Freud might label rationalization. We can deny that our poor performance reflects our ability ("I had an off day," "I didn't have time to study"). We can say the ability is irrelevant ("Who cares about sports, anyway?"). We can even reverse the scale, so that to be good at that would be bad ("Who wants to be an egghead?"). Only when we are trapped in an environment that insists on telling us we are no good does self-esteem become chronically low.

Social psychologists have documented self-serving bias in several ways (Pyszczynski & Greenberg, 1987):

1. People typically accept more responsibility for success than for failure, for good deeds than for bad. Time and again, experimenters have found that people readily accept credit when told they have succeeded (attributing the success to their own ability and effort), yet attribute failure to such uncontrollable factors as bad luck or the "impossibility" of the task. Athletes often privately credit their victories to their own prowess, but are more likely to attribute losses to bad breaks, bad officiating, or the other team's exceptional effort.

"To love oneself is the beginning of a life-long romance."
  Oscar Wilde,
  An Ideal Husband, 1895

And who do you suppose are quickest to spot flaws in an exam—the highest scoring students who presumably know best? No, a half dozen recent studies have found that after receiving an exam grade, students tend to judge the exam as a good test of their competence if they did well and as a poor test if they did not. "What have I done to deserve this?" is a question we ask of our troubles, not our successes—those we assume we deserve. "It is only our bad temper that we put down to being tired or worried or hungry," noted C. S. Lewis. "We put our good temper down to ourselves."

2. Most people see themselves as relatively superior on nearly any dimension that is both subjective and socially desirable. For example, most American business people see themselves as more ethical than their average counterpart. Most community residents see themselves as less prejudiced than others in their communities. Most drivers—even those drivers who have been hospitalized as a result of accidents—believe themselves to be more skillful than the average driver. Most employees rate themselves among the top third of their colleagues. Most high school seniors rate themselves in the top 10 percent of seniors in their "ability to get along with others."

   Added to the above are the following observations (Myers, 1990; Steele, 1988):

3. We tend to justify our past actions.

4. We have an inflated confidence in the accuracy of our beliefs and judgments.

5. We overestimate how desirably we would act in situations in which most people are known to behave less than admirably.

6. We are more willing to believe flattering descriptions of ourselves than unflattering ones.

7. We prefer to gather and seek confirmation of information that is likely to be self-affirming.

8. We "remember" our own past in self-enhancing ways.

9. We exhibit a wide-eyed optimism about our personal futures.

10. We guess that physically attractive people have personalities more like our own than do unattractive people.

While the reasons for our self-serving bias can be debated, and may include the inner turmoil of insecurity and self-doubt, the phenomenon certainly exists.

Many of us object to this conclusion: Like Carl Rogers, we know people who seem to despise themselves, who feel worthless and unlovable. Indeed, all of us some of the time, and some of us much of the time, *do* feel inferior—especially when comparing ourselves with those who are a step or two higher on the ladder of status, grades, looks, income, or agility. And some people—especially those who are depressed and oppressed—*do* suffer chronic low self-esteem.

It is important to recognize what humanistic psychologists have emphasized: For the individual, self-affirming thinking is generally adaptive; such thinking maintains self-confidence and minimizes depression. Moreover, genuine self-acceptance enables us to view others with compassion and understanding.

"People experience life through a self-centered filter."
  Social psychologist Anthony Greenwald (1984)

Drawing by Koren; © 1986 The New Yorker Magazine, Inc.

"Call it vanity, call it narcissism, call it egomania. I love you."

"If you compare yourself with others, you may become vain and bitter; for always there will be greater and lesser persons than yourself."
  Desiderata
  Found in Old St. Paul's Church, 1692

But it is also important to recognize the reality of self-serving bias and the harm that self-righteousness can wreak upon relationships. Expressed high self-esteem can coexist with a self-righteous disdain for people outside one's circle of friends (J. Brown, 1986; Falbo & Shepperd, 1986). Such tendencies are especially dangerous in group settings. Group pride may exhibit itself as prejudice—as racism, sexism, or nationalism, each of which assumes that "my group" (my race, my sex, my country) is superior to yours. The Nazi atrocities were fueled by "Aryan" pride. The nuclear arms race is fed by a national self-righteousness that leads both sides to say, "Your weapons threaten us, ours are only for defense." Understandably, both religion and literature therefore have emphasized the perils of pride. The big question is, how can we encourage self-acceptance while discouraging the pretensions of self-righteousness?

"Then we're in agreement. There's nothing rotten here in Denmark. Something is rotten everywhere else."

THE SOCIAL-COGNITIVE PERSPECTIVE

Our fourth major perspective on personality is derived from the principles of social learning and cognition. Called the *social-cognitive perspective* by psychologist Albert Bandura (1986), its proponents emphasize the importance of external events. Like social learning theorists, they believe that some of our behaviors are acquired by conditioning as well as by observing others and modeling our behavior after them. As we noted in Chapter 9, they also believe that we learn through direct reinforcement. In addition, they emphasize the importance of internal events—how we think and feel about the situations we find ourselves in affects our behavior. So instead of focusing solely on how our environment controls us (behaviorism), social-cognitive theorists focus on how we and our environment interact: How do we interpret and respond to external events? How do our schemas, our memories, and our expectations influence our responses?

EXPLORING BEHAVIOR IN SITUATIONS

Reciprocal Influences   Bandura (1986) believes that interacting with our environment involves *reciprocal determinism*—in which "behavior, internal personal factors, and environmental influences all operate as interlocking determinants of each other" (see Figure 15–4). For example, children's behavior is influenced by television (an environmental factor), which is influenced by their personal preferences (an internal personal factor), which are influenced by their past viewing behaviors. The influences are all mutual.

Consider some of the ways in which environments and people interact. First, different people choose different environments. The college you attend, the reading you do, the television you watch, the music you listen to, the neighborhood you live in, the friends you associate with—all are an environment you have chosen, based partly on your dispositions. You choose it and it shapes you.

Second, our personality shapes how we interpret and react to events. Anxious people are more likely to be attuned to potentially threatening events than are nonanxious people (Eysenck & others, 1987). Thus anxious people perceive the world as more threatening, and react accordingly.

Third, our personalities help create the situations to which we react. Many experiments reveal that how we view and treat our fami-

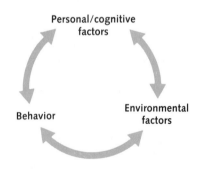

Figure 15–4   Reciprocal determinism. The social-cognitive perspective proposes that our personalities are shaped by the interaction of our situations, our thoughts and feelings, and our behaviors.

lies, roommates, and friends influences how they in turn treat us. If we expect someone to be angry with us, we may treat the person less warmly and more defensively than usual, touching off the very behavior we expect.

We are therefore both the products and the architects of our environments. If all this has a familiar ring, it may be because it parallels and reinforces what may be psychology's greatest lesson: Behavior is best understood in terms of the interplay of internal and external influences. *At every moment* our behavior is determined by our genes *and* our experiences, our personalities *and* our environments.

This interactive, reciprocal perspective has inspired researchers to study how the environment shapes personal factors such as self-control and self-concept, and how these in turn influence behavior. Unlike some humanistic psychologists, social-cognitive theorists do not assume that one's "self" is innate, waiting to be "discovered" or "actualized." Rather, they assume that our self-understandings are shaped by the environment.

Personal Control   One important aspect of our self-concept pertains to whether we learn to see ourselves as in control of, or controlled by, our environments. Numerous studies of people's sense of personal control have demonstrated that behavior is affected by whether people perceive the control of their lives as internal (in themselves) or external (at the mercy of the outside world). Unlike the feelings of control that come from adjusting one's behavior to fit the environment—a process more valued in Japan than in North America (Weisz & others, 1984)—personal control refers to the individual's perceived power to change the environment.

As with most personality factors, there are two ways to study personal control: (1) by *measuring individual differences* in people's feelings of control and then *correlating* these measurements with their behaviors and achievements; and (2) by *experimentally* raising or lowering people's perceptions of control and observing the effects.

Locus of Control   Do you feel that your life is beyond your control? That the world is run by a few powerful people? That getting a good job depends mainly on being in the right place at the right time? Or do you more strongly believe that what happens to you is your own doing? That the average person can influence government decisions? That being a success is a matter of hard work, not luck?

Hundreds of studies have compared people who perceive what psychologist Julian Rotter has called an *external locus of control*—that their fate is determined by chance or by outside forces—with those who perceive an *internal locus of control*—that to a great extent they control their own destinies. In study after study, "internals" have been observed to achieve more in school (Findley & Cooper, 1983), to be more independent, to be better able to delay gratification, and to be better able to cope with various stresses, including marital problems (Lefcourt, 1982; Miller & others, 1986).

Learned Helplessness Versus Self-Efficacy   If indeed the person-environment interaction is reciprocal, then people's perceptions of control may both affect and be affected by their environments. Helpless, oppressed people often perceive that control is external, and this perception may deepen their feelings of resignation. Those who experience their actions as making a difference may perceive that control is internal, and this perception may strengthen their persistence and assertiveness.

Unbearable crisis or exhilarating challenge? Our individual personalities are expressed in the distinctive ways we perceive and react to situations.

This is precisely what researcher Martin Seligman (1975) and others found in experiments with both animals and people. When dogs are strapped in a harness and given repeated shocks, with no opportunity to avoid them, they learn a sense of helplessness. When later they are placed in another situation where they *could* escape the punishment by merely leaping a hurdle, they fail to do so. When faced with repeated traumatic events over which they have no control, people, too, come to feel helpless, hopeless, and depressed. This passive resignation is called *learned helplessness* (Figure 15–5).

In contrast, animals that are able to escape the shocks in the first situation learn "personal" control and are easily able to escape the shocks in the new situation. In research on personal control in humans, Ellen Langer (1983), Judith Rodin (1986), and their associates have found something similar. When the aged, the infirm, and those facing stress are led to think they can influence and control the happenings in their environment (often by actually giving them more control), they become more alert, effective, and happy. Nursing-home patients—normally the passive recipients of staff care—who were given some responsibility for their own care and made aware of opportunities to change their environments, showed improved health during the ensuing 3 weeks. The patients who received the usual kindhearted care, over which they had no control, continued to decline.

Similarly, prisoners who by moving chairs and controlling TV sets and room lights feel some control over their environment experience less stress, exhibit fewer health problems, and commit less vandalism (Ruback & others, 1986; Wener & others, 1987). Workers who are given leeway in how to carry out tasks and are provided with opportunities to participate in decision making experience increases in morale (Miller & Monge, 1986). "Perceived control is basic to human functioning," Langer concludes. Thus, "we must create environments, for the young and old alike, that foster feelings of mastery" (p. 291).

People who have such feelings of mastery and competence—who have what Bandura calls a sense of *self-efficacy*—therefore cope with life more successfully. They are more persistent, less anxious and depressed, and more academically successful (Maddux & Stanley, 1986). One measure of how helpless or effective we feel is how we characteristically explain negative events. Perhaps you have known students who blame poor grades on situations beyond their control—their lack of ability ("I can't do this") or "bad" teachers, textbooks, or exam ques-

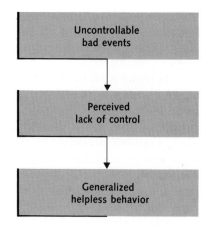

Figure 15–5   Learned helplessness.

See also pages 513–514.

Self-efficacy: The sense that one is a competent, effective person.

Self-esteem: One's feelings of self-worth.

Nursing-home patients who take an active part in their care and pursue their own interests are more alert and happy than those who do not.

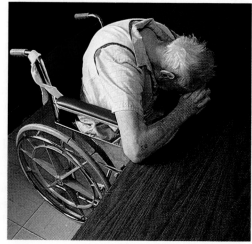

tions. Such students are more likely to persist in getting low grades than are students who adopt the more hopeful attitude that effort, good study habits, and self-discipline can make a difference (Noel & others, 1987; Peterson & Barrett, 1987). Similarly, new life insurance salespeople who habitually explain failures as uncontrollable ("I always fail," or "This is impossible") have been observed to sell fewer policies and be twice as likely as their more optimistic peers to quit during their first year (Seligman & Schulman, 1986). The optimists are more likely to see setbacks as a fluke or to think "I need to try a different approach."

If positive thinking in the face of adversity pays dividends, so, too, can a realistic dash of pessimism. Anxiety over contemplated failure can fuel energetic efforts to avoid the dreaded fate (Goodhart, 1986; Norem & Cantor, 1986; Showers & Ruben, 1987). Students who are overconfident and underprepared often perform less well than their equally able peers who, fearing they are going to bomb the upcoming exam, proceed to study furiously and then get fabulous grades. Success, it seems, requires neither positive nor negative thinking alone, but a fine mix of enough optimism to provide hope, enough pessimism to prevent complacency, and enough realism to discriminate those things that can be controlled from those that cannot.

ASSESSING BEHAVIOR IN SITUATIONS

Social cognition researchers have a keen interest in discerning the effect of differing situations on people's behavior and attitudes. They study, for example, how viewing different aggressive or nonaggressive models affects behavior. They assess the impact of dehumanizing situations on people's sense of self. And they examine people's consistency in varying circumstances.

An ambitious example that predates social-cognitive theory is the U.S. Army's World War II strategy for assessing candidates for spy missions. Rather than attempt to do so with paper-and-pencil tests, the army psychologists subjected the candidates to simulated undercover conditions that tested their ability to handle stress, solve problems, maintain leadership, and withstand intense interrogation without blowing their covers. Although time-consuming and expensive, the assessment of behavior in a realistic situation helped predict later success on real spy missions (OSS Assessment Staff, 1948).

Business, military, and educational organizations are continuing this strategy in their evaluations of several hundred thousand persons each year. The American Telephone and Telegraph Company sends prospective managers to assessment centers for 1 to 3 days. There they are closely observed while engaging in simulated managerial work (Bray, 1982). Many colleges assess potential faculty members' teaching abilities by observing them teach. The army assesses its soldiers by observing them during military exercises.

These procedures attempt to exploit the principle that one of the best ways to predict people's future behavior is to observe their past behavior in similar situations (Mischel, 1981). So long as the situation remains much the same, the best predictor of future job performance is past job performance; the best predictor of future grades is past grades; the best predictor of future aggressiveness is past aggressiveness; the best predictor of drug use in young adulthood is high school drug use. If you can't check the person's past behavior, the next best thing is to create an assessment situation that simulates the task demands so that you can see how the person handles them.

"O God, give us grace to accept with serenity the things that cannot be changed, courage to change the things which should be changed, and the wisdom to distinguish the one from the other."
Reinhold Niebuhr,
"The Serenity Prayer," 1943

PSEUDO-ASSESSMENT: HOW TO BE A "SUCCESSFUL" ASTROLOGER OR PALM READER

Some personality assessment techniques have minimal validity, yet are strongly believed in by their devotees. Ray Hyman (1981), palm reader turned research psychologist, helps us to see why, by revealing the methods by which astrologers, palm readers, and crystal-ball gazers can persuade so many believers that they can accurately assess their personalities and problems.

The first technique, the "stock spiel," builds on the truth of the observation that each of us is in some ways like no one else and in other ways like everyone. The fact that some things are true of nearly all of us enables the "seer" to offer statements that seem impressively accurate: "I sense that you're nursing a grudge against someone; you really ought to let that go." "You worry about things more than you let on, even to your best friends." "You are adaptable to social situations and your interests are wide-ranging."

Such generally true statements can be combined into a personality description. Imagine that you take a personality test and then receive the following character sketch:

> You have a strong need for other people to like and to admire you. You have a tendency to be critical of yourself. . . . You pride yourself on being an independent thinker and do not accept other opinions without satisfactory proof. You have found it unwise to be too frank in revealing yourself to others. At times you are extraverted, affable, sociable; at other times you are introverted, wary, and reserved. Some of your aspirations tend to be pretty unrealistic.

In experiments, college students have received stock assessments like the one above. When they thought the bogus feedback was prepared just for them and when it was generally favorable, they nearly always rated the description as either "good" or "excellent." This acceptance is called the

Drawing by Frascino; © 1982 The New Yorker Magazine, Inc.

"Ah-ha! You are not happy."

Barnum effect, named in honor of master showman P. T. Barnum's dictum that "There's a sucker born every minute." So powerful is the Barnum effect that when given a choice between this stock spiel and an individualized personality description actually based on an established test, most people choose the phony description as being more accurate. Astrologers and palm readers sprinkle their assessments with stock statements, as in the description just quoted, which was drawn from a newsstand astrology book.

The second technique is to "read" the person's clothing, physical features, nonverbal gestures, and reactions to what you are saying. Imagine yourself as the character reader who was visited by a young woman in her late twenties or early thirties. Hyman describes the woman as "wearing expensive jewelry, a wedding band, and a black dress of cheap material. The observant reader noted that she was wearing shoes which were currently being advertised for people with foot trouble." Do these clues suggest anything?

Drawing on these observations, the character reader proceeded to amaze his client with his insights. He assumed that the woman had come to see him, as did most of his female customers, because of a love or financial problem. The black dress and the wedding band led him to reason that her husband had died recently. The expensive jewelry suggested that she had been financially

French psychologist Michel Gauguelin placed an ad in a Paris newspaper offering a free personal horoscope. Ninety-four percent of those receiving the horoscope later praised the description as accurate. Actually, all had received the horoscope of France's Dr. Petiot, a notorious mass murderer (Kurtz, 1983).

comfortable during marriage, but the cheap dress indicated that her husband's death had left her penniless. The therapeutic shoes signified that she was now standing on her feet more than she was used to, implying that she was working to support herself since her husband's death.

If you are not so shrewd as this character reader (who correctly guessed that the woman was wondering if she should marry in order to end her economic hardship), no matter, says Hyman. Just tell people what they want to hear. Memorize some Barnum statements from astrology and for-

tune-telling manuals and use them liberally. Tell people it is their responsibility to cooperate by relating your message to their specific experiences, and later they will recall that you predicted the specifics. Phrase statements as questions, and when you detect a positive response assert the statement strongly. Be a good listener, and later, in different words, reveal to people what they earlier revealed to you.

Better yet, beware of fortune-tellers, who, by exploiting people with these techniques, become fortune-takers.

While astronomers scoff at the naïveté of astrology, psychologists ask a different question: Does it work? Are birth dates correlated with character traits? Given someone's birth date, can astrologers surpass chance when asked to identify the person from a short lineup of different personality descriptions? Can people pick out their own horoscopes from a lineup of horoscopes? The consistent answers have been: no, no, no, and no (e.g., Carlson, 1985).

EVALUATING THE SOCIAL-COGNITIVE PERSPECTIVE

The social-cognitive perspective has sensitized researchers to how situations affect, and are affected by, individuals. More than the other perspectives, it can also be credited with building upon the broad base of psychological research on learning and cognition.

One criticism is that the theory works *too* well, after the fact. In hindsight, anything can be "explained" as a product of cognition and the social environment. Another criticism is that the theory has focused so much on the situation that the inner traits of the person are not fully appreciated. Where is the *person* in this view of personality? ask the dissenters (Carlson, 1984). Granted, the situation guides our behavior. But in many instances our unconscious motives and pervasive traits shine through, they say. And so do genetic influences. Twin and adoption studies indicate that some personality traits, such as extraversion, aggressiveness, and even helpfulness, are influenced by heredity (Hewitt, 1984; Rushton & others, 1986).

And that brings us back to the thought with which we began our review of the major personality theories—that each offers a perspective that can teach us something. The psychoanalytic perspective draws our attention to the unconscious and irrational aspects of human existence. The trait perspective systematically describes and measures important components of personality. The humanistic perspective reminds us of our healthy potential and of the pivotal importance of our sense of self. The social-cognitive perspective applies psychology's basic concepts of learning and thinking and teaches us that we always act in the context of situations that we may help to create. The four perspectives are summarized in Table 15–3 on page 438.

In life seldom does one perspective give us the complete picture. Our subject—the workings of human personality—is like a kaleidoscope, mysterious and complex enough to reveal different aspects when viewed with different perspectives. The best we can do, as most psychologists have done, is to allow each perspective to enlarge our vision of the whole.

TABLE 15–3
THE FOUR PERSPECTIVES ON PERSONALITY

Perspective	Where behavior springs from	Assessment techniques	Evaluation
Psychoanalytic	Processing unconscious conflicts between pleasure-seeking impulses and social restraints	Projective tests aim to reveal unconscious motivations	A speculative, hard-to-confirm theory with enormous cultural impact
Trait	Expressing consistent psychological dispositions, such as extraversion or introversion	Objective inventories assess the strength of different traits	A descriptive theory criticized as sometimes underestimating the variability of behavior from situation to situation
Humanistic	Processing conscious feelings about oneself in light of one's experiences	(a) Questionnaire assessments of self-concept (b) Empathic understandings of people's unique experiences	A humane theory that reinvigorated contemporary interest in the self; criticized as subjective and sometimes naïvely self-centered and optimistic
Social-Cognitive	Reciprocal influences between people and their situations, as influenced by perceptions of control	(a) Questionnaire assessments of people's feelings of control (b) Observations of people's behavior in particular situations	An interactive theory that integrates research on learning, cognition, and social behavior; criticized as underestimating the importance of the unconscious and of enduring traits

SUMMING UP

Like intelligence, personality is an abstract concept that cannot be seen, touched, or directly measured. To psychologists, personality is one's relatively distinctive and consistent pattern of thinking, feeling, and acting. We have examined four major perspectives on personality, each valuable for the light it sheds on our complex workings.

THE PSYCHOANALYTIC PERSPECTIVE

Exploring the Unconscious Sigmund Freud's treatment of emotional disorders led him to believe they resulted from the unconscious dynamics of personality, dynamics which he sought to analyze through his own and his patients' free associations and dreams. Freud saw personality as composed of a reservoir of pleasure-seeking psychic impulses (the id), a reality-oriented executive (the ego), and an internalized set of ideals (the superego).

Freud believed that children develop through several formative psychosexual stages, which he labeled the oral, anal, phallic, latency, and genital stages. He suggested

that people's later personalities were influenced by how they resolved conflicts associated with these stages and whether they remained fixated at any stage.

To cope with anxiety caused by the tensions between the demands of id and superego, the ego has protective defense mechanisms, of which repression is the most basic. Neo-Freudians Alfred Adler, Karen Horney, Erich Fromm, and Erik Erikson accepted many of Freud's ideas, as did Carl Jung, but argued that we have more positive motives than sex and aggression.

Assessing the Unconscious Psychoanalytic assessment techniques attempt to reveal aspects of personality that are thought to be hidden in the unconscious. However, some projective tests such as the Rorschach inkblots have been criticized for their minimal reliability and validity.

Evaluating the Psychoanalytic Perspective Many of Freud's specific ideas have been criticized as implausible or have not been validated. His theory has also been faulted for offering after-the-fact explanations. Nevertheless, Freud drew psychology's attention to the unconscious, to the struggle to cope with anxiety and sexuality, and to the conflict between biological impulses and social restraints. Moreover, his cultural impact has been enormous.

THE TRAIT PERSPECTIVE

Describing Traits Rather than explain the hidden aspects of personality, trait theorists have described the predispositions that underlie our actions. For example, through factor analysis, these theorists have isolated distinct dimensions of personality.

Assessing Traits To assess traits, psychologists have devised objective personality inventories such as the empirically derived MMPI. Computerized testing has made these inventories widely available; however, they are still most helpful when used to assess those who are emotionally troubled.

Evaluating the Trait Perspective: How Consistent Are We? Critics of trait theory question the consistency with which traits are expressed. Although people's traits do seem to persist through time, human behavior varies widely from situation to situation. Despite these variations, people's average behavior across different situations is fairly consistent.

THE HUMANISTIC PERSPECTIVE

Humanistic psychologists have sought to turn psychology's attention to the growth potential of healthy people, as seen through the individual's own experiences.

Exploring the Self Abraham Maslow believed that if more basic human needs are fulfilled, people will strive to actualize their highest potential. To describe self-actualization, he studied some exemplary personalities and summarized his impressions of their qualities. To nurture growth in others, Carl Rogers advised being genuine, accepting, and empathic. In such a climate, people can develop a deeper self-awareness and a more realistic and positive self-concept.

Assessing the Self Humanistic psychologists assess personality through questionnaires that rate self-concept and by seeking to understand others' subjective personal experiences in therapy.

Evaluating the Humanistic Perspective Humanistic psychology's critics complain that its concepts are vague and subjective, its values self-centered, and its assumptions naïvely optimistic. Nevertheless, humanistic psychology has helped to renew psychology's interest in the concept of self, which is now being vigorously researched through studies of phenomena such as self-esteem and self-serving bias.

THE SOCIAL-COGNITIVE PERSPECTIVE

The social-cognitive perspective applies principles of social learning and cognition to personality, with particular emphasis on the ways in which our personalities are influenced by our interaction with the environment.

Exploring Behavior in Situations This perspective deals with reciprocal determinism—how personal-cognitive factors combine with the environment to influence people's expectations regarding their situations. By studying variations among people in their perceived locus of control and in their experiences of learned helplessness or self-efficacy, researchers have found that an inner locus of control helps people to cope with life.

Assessing Behavior in Situations Social-cognitive researchers study how people's behaviors and beliefs both affect and are affected by their situations. They have found that the best way to predict someone's behavior in a given situation is to observe that person's behavior in similar situations.

Evaluating the Social-Cognitive Perspective Though faulted for underemphasizing the importance of unconscious dynamics and inner traits, the social-cognitive perspective builds on psychology's well-established concepts of learning and cognition and reminds us of the power of social situations.

TERMS AND CONCEPTS TO REMEMBER

anal stage The second of Freud's psychosexual stages, during which pleasure is focused on bowel and bladder elimination and retention.

Barnum effect The tendency to accept as valid those favorable descriptions of one's personality that are generally true of everyone, such as those found in astrology books and horoscopes.

collective unconscious Carl Jung's concept of inherited memory traces from our species' history.

defense mechanisms In psychoanalytic theory, the ego's methods of reducing anxiety by unconsciously distorting reality.

displacement In psychoanalytic theory, the shifting of one's impulses toward a more acceptable or less threatening object or person, as when redirecting anger toward a safer outlet.

ego The largely conscious, "executive" part of personality that, according to Freud, mediates between the demands of the id and superego and reality.

Electra complex See *Oedipus complex.*

empirically derived test An inventory (such as the MMPI) that is developed by testing a pool of items and then selecting those that differentiate groups of interest.

external locus of control The belief that one's fate is determined by chance or outside forces that are beyond one's personal control.

fixation According to Freud, a lingering focus of pleasure-seeking energies at an earlier psychosexual stage.

free association A psychoanalytic method of exploring the unconscious in which the person relaxes and says whatever comes to mind, no matter how trivial or embarrassing.

genital stage The final of Freud's psychosexual stages, beginning in puberty, during which pleasure is sought through sexual contact with others.

id The instinctual drives that, according to Freud, supply psychic energy to personality.

identification The process by which, according to Freud, children incorporate their parents' values into their developing superegos.

internal locus of control The belief that one can control one's own fate.

latency stage The fourth of Freud's psychosexual stages, from about age 6 to puberty, during which sexual impulses are repressed.

learned helplessness Passive resignation that is learned when an animal or human has been unable to avoid repeated aversive events.

Minnesota Multiphasic Personality Inventory (MMPI) The most widely researched and used of all personality inventories, containing ten scales of clinical dimensions and other validity scales and subscales. Originally developed to distinguish among emotionally troubled people—still considered its most appropriate use—this test is now used for many other screening purposes.

Oedipus [ed-uh-puss] **complex** According to Freud, the 3- to 5- or 6-year-old child's sexual desires toward the parent of the other sex and feelings of jealousy and hatred for the rival parent of the same sex. In girls, sometimes called the *Electra complex.*

oral stage The first of Freud's psychosexual stages, during which pleasure centers on the mouth.

personality An individual's relatively distinctive and consistent patterns of thinking, feeling, and acting.

personality inventories Questionnaires (often with true-false or agree-disagree items) on which people report their customary feelings and behaviors; used to assess personality traits.

phallic stage The third of Freud's psychosexual stages, during which the pleasure zone is focused on the genitals and sexual feelings arise toward the parent of the other sex.

pleasure principle The id's demand for immediate gratification.

preconscious Information that is not currently conscious, but is retrievable into conscious awareness.

projection In psychoanalytic theory, the defense mechanism by which people disguise their own threatening impulses by imputing them to others.

projective tests Personality tests, such as the Rorschach and TAT, that provide ambiguous stimuli designed to trigger projection of one's inner dynamics.

psychoanalysis The technique of treating disorders by analyzing unconscious tensions. Freud's psychoanalytic theory of personality sought to explain what he observed during psychoanalysis.

psychosexual stages The developmental stages (oral, anal, phallic, latency, genital) during which, according to Freud, the id's pleasure-seeking energies are focused on different erogenous zones.

rationalization In psychoanalytic theory, a defense mechanism in which self-justifying explanations are offered in place of the real, more threatening, unconscious reasons for one's actions.

reaction formation In psychoanalytic theory, the ego's unconscious switching of unacceptable impulses into their opposites. Thus people may express feelings that are the opposite of their anxiety-arousing unconscious feelings.

reality principle The ego's tendency to satisfy the id's desires in ways that will realistically bring pleasure rather than pain.

reciprocal determinism The mutual influences among personal factors, environmental factors, and behavior.

regression In psychoanalytic theory, an individual's retreat, when faced with anxiety, to an earlier, more comfortable stage of development.

repression In psychoanalytic theory, the basic defense mechanism that banishes anxiety-arousing thoughts and feelings from consciousness.

Rorschach inkblot test A test designed by Hermann Rorschach that uses people's interpretation of inkblots in an attempt to identify their projected feelings.

self-actualization According to Maslow, the final psychological need that arises when basic physical and psychological needs are met; the process of fulfilling one's potential as one achieves qualities such as self-acceptance, spontaneity, love, mastery, and creativity.

self-concept All our thoughts and feelings about ourselves which answer the question, "Who am I?"

self-efficacy A sense that one is competent and effective.

self-esteem One's feelings of high or low self-worth.

self-serving bias The bias of perceiving oneself favorably.

social-cognitive perspective Applies interactive principles of social learning and cognition to study how the environment shapes people's behavior and beliefs, and how these in turn influence people's situations.

sublimation In psychoanalytic theory, the defense mechanism by which people rechannel their unacceptable impulses into socially approved activities.

superego The part of personality that, according to Freud, represents internalized ideals, thus providing standards for judgment (conscience) and for future aspirations.

Thematic Apperception Test (TAT) A projective test in which people make up stories about ambiguous scenes.

trait theory Describes personality in terms of behaviors, as scored on various scales, each of which represents a personality dimension.

traits Our predispositions to behave in given ways, assessed by personality inventories.

unconditional positive regard According to Rogers, an attitude of total acceptance toward another person.

unconscious According to Freud, a reservoir of mostly unacceptable thoughts, wishes, feelings, and memories. According to contemporary research psychologists, information processing of which we are unaware.

FOR FURTHER READING

Bandura, A. (1986). *Social foundations of thought and action. A social-cognitive theory.* Englewood Cliffs, NJ: Prentice-Hall.

The definitive introduction to the social-cognitive perspective.

Freud, S. (1933). *Introductory lectures on psychoanalysis.* Published separately in 1966, J. Strachey (Ed. & trans.). New York: Liveright. Also published in 1963, in J. Strachey (Ed. & trans.), *The standard edition of the complete psychological works of Sigmund Freud.* London: Hogarth.

One of Freud's most popular works, introducing his ideas about human motivation, dream interpretation, slips of the tongue, and psychoanalytic therapy.

Goleman, D. (1985). *Vital lies, simple truths: The psychology of self-deception and shared illusions.* New York: Simon & Schuster.

A popular, engaging account of how self-deception helps us avoid anxiety, but not without costs.

Hall, C. S., Lindzey, G., Loehlin, J. C., & Manosevitz, M. (1985). *Introduction to theories of personality.* New York: Wiley.

A revision of the classic text summary of personality theories, from Freud to the modern social-cognitive perspective.

Rogers, C. R. (1961). *On becoming a person.* Boston: Houghton Mifflin.

A warm and readable introduction to Carl Rogers' view of the person and of how to nurture personal growth.

CHAPTER 16

Psychological Disorders

Most people are fascinated by things out of the ordinary—by exceptional occurrences, unusual experiences, and abnormal behaviors. "The sun shines and warms and lights us and we have no curiosity to know why this is so," observed Ralph Waldo Emerson, "but we ask the reason of all evil, of pain, and hunger, and mosquitoes and silly people."

One reason for this fascination with disturbed people is that in them we often see something of ourselves. At some time, all of us feel, think, or act as disturbed people do much of the time: We, too, may be anxious, depressed, withdrawn, suspicious, deluded, or antisocial. "Abnormal" people share these characteristics with "normal" people—but their experience is intensified and more enduring. Studying psychological disorders may therefore at times evoke an eerie sense of self-recognition that illuminates our own personality dynamics.

Another reason for our curiosity is that so many of us have been touched, either personally or through friends or family members, by the bewilderment and pain of a psychological disorder. In all likelihood, you or someone you care about has been at some time disabled by unexplained physical symptoms, overwhelmed by irrational fears, or paralyzed by the feeling that life is not worth living. Each year there are nearly 2 million admissions to U.S. mental hospitals and psychiatric units (Bureau of the Census, 1987); others seek help in community mental health centers or in private counseling; many more—as many as 1 in 5 Americans according to one government study—are judged to need such help (Robins & others, 1984). Few of us go through life unacquainted with the reality of psychological disturbance.

"We are all mad at some time or another."
Battista Mantuanus,
Eclogues, 1500

PERSPECTIVES ON PSYCHOLOGICAL DISORDERS

Most people would agree that someone who is too depressed to get out of bed for weeks at a time is suffering from a psychological disorder. But what about those who, having experienced a loss, are unable to resume their usual social activities? Where should we draw the line between normality and abnormality? In other words, how should we *define* psychological disorders? Equally important, how should we *understand* disorders—as sicknesses that need to be diagnosed and cured or as natural responses to a troubling environment? Finally, how should we describe and *classify* disordered personalities? Can we do so in a way that allows us to help disturbed people and not merely stigmatize them with labels?

DEFINING PSYCHOLOGICAL DISORDERS

James Oliver Huberty had been hearing voices. He "talked with God," his wife reported. Although he had never been to Vietnam, he strode into a San Ysidro, California, McDonald's restaurant one summer day in 1984 screaming, "I've killed a thousand in Vietnam and I'll kill a thousand more." In the next few minutes, before being gunned down by police, Huberty proceeded to slaughter twenty-one people.

At the end of World War II, James Forrestal, the first U.S. Secretary of Defense, became convinced that Israeli secret agents were following him. His suspiciousness struck his physicians as bizarre; they diagnosed him as mentally ill and confined him to an upper floor of Walter Reed Army Hospital. From there he plunged to his death. Although Forrestal had other problems, it was later discovered that he was, in fact, being followed by Israeli agents, who were worried that he might secretly negotiate with representatives of Arab nations (Sagan, 1979b).

Both the voices that Huberty heard and the degree of anxiety that Forrestal experienced were deviations from the normal. These were "ab-normal" *(atypical)* perceptions. Being different from most other people is *part* of what it takes to be defined as disordered. As the reclusive poet Emily Dickinson observed in 1862,

> Assent—and you are sane—
> Demur—you're straightaway dangerous—
> and handled with a Chain.

Clearly, there is more to being disordered than being atypical. Olympic gold medalists are abnormal in their physical capabilities, and they are heroes. To be considered disordered, the atypical behavior must also be *disturbing* to other people, if not to the person exhibiting the behavior. In most times and places the atypical behavior of a James Oliver Huberty would be disturbing. But standards of acceptability for behaviors do vary. In some cultures people routinely behave in ways (such as going about naked) that in other cultures would get them arrested. In some cultural contexts even mass killing may be viewed as heroic. One person's homicidal "terrorist" is another person's "freedom fighter."

Standards of acceptability vary not only from culture to culture but also from time to time. Thus in the latest edition of the American Psychiatric Association's manual on psychological disorders, some disorders were added and some eliminated, reflecting changes in our standards of acceptability. Heavy smoking, for example, has lost its acceptability now that it is known to be both addictive and the cause of serious health problems. Smokers who have tried unsuccessfully to stop smoking or who have developed these health problems are now diagnosed as suffering from tobacco dependence, a psychological disorder. In contrast, homosexuality is no longer regarded as a psychological disorder (unless the person feels distressed by it).

As these examples suggest, atypical and disturbing behaviors are more likely to be considered disordered when judged as harmful. Indeed, many clinicians define disorders as behaviors that are *maladaptive*—as when a smoker's nicotine dependence produces physical damage or emotional distress. Accordingly, even typical behaviors, such as the occasional despondency that many college students feel, may signal a psychological disorder if they become disabling.

Although most of us would readily perceive this man's behavior as abnormal, we might be hard pressed to say just why. Clinical definition attempts to establish criteria for such judgments.

Finally, a person exhibiting abnormal behavior is most likely to be considered disordered when others find that person's behavior to be rationally *unjustifiable*. Forrestal's suspicions were attributed to his imagination—and he was declared disordered. Had he managed to convince others that his suspicions were based on real events, he might have been helped, not merely labeled. James Oliver Huberty claimed to hear voices and to talk with God, and we presume he was deranged. On the other hand, Shirley MacLaine can wear a crystal on her neck and say, "See the outer bubble of white light watching you. It is part of you," and she is not considered disordered because enough people take her seriously (Friedrich, 1987). It is acceptable to be different from others if both you and they can justify or are not disturbed by the difference.

So, behavior is labeled ***psychologically disordered*** when it is judged to be *atypical, disturbing, maladaptive*, and *unjustifiable*. James Oliver Huberty's clearly meets these criteria and so we have few doubts about our judgment of the man.

"If a man is in a minority of one, we lock him up."
Oliver Wendell Holmes, 1841–1935

UNDERSTANDING PSYCHOLOGICAL DISORDERS

Imagine yourself living hundreds or thousands of years ago. How might you have accounted for the behavior of a James Oliver Huberty? To explain puzzling behavior, our ancestors often presumed that strange forces—the movements of the stars, godlike powers, or evil spirits—were at work. "The devil made him do it," you might have said. The cure might then have been to get rid of the evil force—by exorcising the demon or even by chipping a hole in the skull to allow the evil spirit to escape (Figure 16–1). Until the last two centuries, "mad" people were sometimes caged under zoolike conditions or given "therapies" appropriate to a demon, including:

> beatings, whippings, blistering the shaved head, burning, and scarring fingers. Surgically, the mentally disordered have had lengths of intestines removed and teeth pulled, they have been castrated, hysterectomies have been performed, the clitoris has been cauterized, they have had animal blood tranfused into their veins, and their own blood has been removed. (Farina, 1982, p. 306)

The Medical Perspective   In response to such brutal treatment, reformers such as Philippe Pinel (1745–1826) insisted that madness was not demon possession but a disease that, like other diseases, could be treated and cured. For Pinel, treatment meant boosting patients' morale by talking with them and by providing humane living conditions. When it was later discovered that an infectious disease, syphilis, produced a particular psychological disorder, people came to believe in physical causes for disorders and to search for medical treatments.

Today, the medical perspective of Pinel and his followers is familiar to us in the terminology of the mental *health* movement: A mental *illness* (also called a psycho*pathology*) needs to be *diagnosed* on the basis of its *symptoms* and *cured* through *therapy*, which may include *treatment* in a psychiatric *hospital*. In the 1800s, the assumption of this ***medical model***—that psychological disorders are sicknesses—provided the impetus for much needed reforms. The "sick" were unchained and asylums were replaced by hospitals.

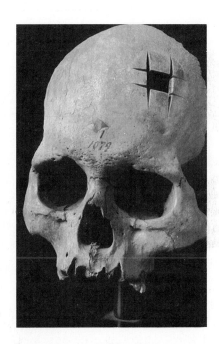

Figure 16-1   A skull found in Peru, showing a hole chipped through the cranium to allow evil spirits to escape. One wonders whether this patient survived the cure.

THE INSANITY DEFENSE ON TRIAL

In discussing what psychological disorders are, we have made no mention of insanity. That is because *sanity* and **insanity** are legal, not psychological, terms, ones that must be judged either/or. You can be a little depressed or greatly depressed; you cannot be judged a little insane.

The insanity defense was established in 1843 when a deluded Scotsman, Daniel M'Naghten, tried to shoot the British Prime Minister (who he thought was persecuting him) and killed the Prime Minister's secretary by mistake. A furor erupted after M'Naghten was acquitted as insane and sent to a mental hospital rather than to prison. When the M'Naghten verdict was upheld, an insanity rule emerged that limited the insanity defense to cases where persons were judged not to have known what they were doing or not to have known that it was wrong.

By the time John Hinckley came to trial in 1982 for shooting President Reagan and his press secretary, the insanity defense had been broadened. The prosecution was required to prove that Hinckley was sane, which under the Model Penal Code meant his having "a substantial capacity" not merely to "know" his act was wrong but to "appreciate" its wrongfulness and to act accordingly.

The prosecution was unable to prove sanity to the jurors' satisfaction, and so Hinckley, like M'Naghten, was sent to a mental hospital. As in the first insanity case, the public was outraged. One newspaper headlined "Hinckley Insane, Public Mad." The outrage stemmed partly from the fact that, like others declared not guilty by reason of insanity, Hinckley will be released when declared sane and no longer dangerous—conceivably earlier, but possibly later, than his release from a prison would have occurred.

Following the verdict, some news commentators complained that the heinousness of a crime had become the very basis for evading responsibility for it, "like the person who kills his parents and demands mercy because he is an orphan." Are "sick crimes" necessarily the products of sick minds that need treatment, not punishment? Must the genuinely bad be truly mad? If so, said one commentator, then modern society has become like Aldous Huxley's nightmarish *Brave New World*, in which when someone commits a crime the correct response is, "I did not know he was ill."

In defense of the insanity plea, psychologist David Rosenhan (1983a, 1983b) noted that, actually, such a plea is entered only about 2 times in every 1000 felony cases. In 85 percent of those cases, all parties—mental health experts, prosecutor, and defense attorney—agree that the sadly deranged person was not responsible. In fact, the most important issues that involve psychology and law are not the rare disputes over insanity but the far more frequent cases concerning child custody (judging who will be the better parent), involuntary commitment to mental hospitals, and predictions about a criminal's future behavior made at the time of sentencing or parole.

On the strength of recommendations from the American Bar Association and the American Psychiatric Association, the insanity defense has survived in the United States in a restricted format (under a 1984 law) that shifts the burden of proving insanity to the defense (as is the case in Canada). Now defendants must establish that they did not understand the wrongfulness of their acts.

By 1987, thirteen states had instituted a verdict of "guilty but mentally ill." This verdict recognizes a need for treatment but holds people responsible and returns them to prison if they are judged recovered before their sentence is over (Rosenfeld, 1987). Jurors seem to find the verdict a viable option. In mock trials, defendants who would otherwise have been found either innocent or not guilty by reason of insanity are often judged guilty but mentally ill (Savitsky & Lindblom, 1986).

A posed self-portrait of John W. Hinckley, Jr., President Reagan's would-be assassin.

When psychiatrists and psychologists have predicted violence they have been wrong more often than they have been right (Monahan, 1983; Faust & Ziskin, 1988). Thus even the American Psychiatric Association has argued that predictions of dangerousness should be barred from court, because such predictions give "the appearance of being based on expert medical judgment, when in fact no such expertise exists" (Tierney, 1982).

Equating psychological disorders with sickness does, however, have its critics, among them psychiatrist Thomas Szasz, who, beginning with his 1961 book, *The Myth of Mental Illness*, has argued that, unlike cancer and tuberculosis, "problems in living" are not diseases. Szasz believes that mental "illnesses" are socially, not medically, defined. When some psychiatrists judged 1964 Republican presidential candidate Barry Goldwater as having "paranoid" tendencies and when Soviet psychiatrists diagnosed dissident citizens as "psychotic," they were using medical metaphors to disguise their contempt for these people's political ideas. Szasz (1984, 1987) concludes that psychiatrists and other mental health practitioners have assumed too much authority in today's society. When people are demeaned with the label "mentally ill," they may begin to view themselves as "sick" and therefore become unable to take responsibility for coping with their problems. As we will see, labels can become self-fulfilling prophecies.

Despite such criticisms, the medical perspective has survived and even gained renewed credibility from recent discoveries. As we will also see, genetically influenced disorders in brain biochemistry have been linked with two of the most prevalent and troubling psychological disorders, depression and schizophrenia, both of which are often treated medically.

Some clinicians, such as those who adopt Freud's psychoanalytic perspective, agree that psychological disorders are sicknesses that have diagnosable and treatable causes. However, they insist that these causes may include psychological as well as physical factors. Such factors are seen most clearly in the lingering emotional aftereffects of traumatic stresses, such as those caused by rape (see page 244) or combat (see pages 524–525).

Alternative Perspectives Other clinicians find the "sickness" idea, and all the terminology that has grown up around it, unnecessary and misleading. They contend that *all* behavior, whether called normal or disordered, arises from the interaction of nature (genetic and physiological factors) and nurture (past and present experiences). To presume that a person is "mentally ill" attributes the condition solely to an internal problem—to a "sickness" that must be found and cured. Maybe there *is* no deep, internal problem. Maybe there is instead a growth-blocking difficulty in the person's environment, in the person's current interpretations of events, or in the person's bad habits and poor social skills.

When Native Americans were banished from their lands, forced onto reservations to live in poverty and unemployment, and deprived of feelings of personal control, the result was a rate of alcoholism more than five times that of other Americans (May, 1986). Because only some Native Americans become alcoholic, the medical model would incline one to attribute such alcoholism to an individual Indian's "sickness." A more psychological perspective would emphasize the interaction between the individual and the environment.

Evidence of environmental effects comes from well-established links between culture and disorder. Although major disorders such as schizophrenia are universal, others, such as anorexia in Western countries, are culture-bound (Carson & others, 1988). Different cultures have different stresses and produce different ways of coping.

Most mental health workers today assume that the disordered are indeed influenced by genetic predispositions and physiological states. And by inner psychological dynamics. And by social circumstances. To get the whole picture we need an interdisciplinary "bio-psycho-social" perspective.

"According to official data, nearly 5 million people are listed on the psychiatric register in the Soviet Union. During the next two years, the authorities intend to take up to 2 million of them off the register. . . . To be on it officially permits a healthy person to be placed in a psychiatric prison at any time and to be deprived of all rights."

Sergei Grigoryants, chief editor of *Glasnost* magazine, February 23, 1988

"It's no measure of health to be well adjusted to a profoundly sick society."

Krishnamurti, 1895–1986

Should the high incidence of alcoholism among Native Americans be viewed primarily as individual sicknesses to be treated by therapy, or is it more a social problem that should be dealt with by environmental changes?

CLASSIFYING PSYCHOLOGICAL DISORDERS

In biology and the other sciences, classification creates order. To classify an animal as a mammal says a great deal—that its young are nourished by milk, that it has hair or fur, that it has a relatively high body temperature. In psychiatry and psychology, classification also provides a way of ordering and describing clusters of symptoms. To classify a person's disorder as "schizophrenic" suggests that the person talks incoherently, has hallucinations or delusions (bizarre beliefs), shows either little emotion or inappropriate emotion, or is socially withdrawn. Thus, the diagnostic label provides a handy shorthand for describing a complex disorder.

In both medicine and psychology, diagnostic classification seeks to describe a disorder and to predict its future course, as well as to facilitate research about its causes and treatment. Indeed, naming and describing a disorder is the first step in studying it. In the United States, the authoritative scheme for classifying psychological disorders is the American Psychiatric Association's *Diagnostic and Statistical Manual of Mental Disorders (Third Edition–Revised)*, nicknamed **DSM-III-R.** This volume and the book of case illustrations that accompanies it provide the basis for much of the material in this chapter. The World Health Organization's international classification of mental disorders is generally compatible with the DSM-III-R diagnostic categories.

Although the task force that prepared DSM-III-R included not only psychiatrists (who are medical doctors) but clinical psychologists as well, DSM-III-R was shaped by the medical model. The very idea of "diagnosing" people's problems in terms of their "symptoms" seems to assume the existence of mental "disease." Although some practitioners are not enthralled with this medical terminology (Smith & Kraft, 1983), most find DSM-III-R a helpful and practical tool. In any event, most North American health insurance companies require a DSM-III-R diagnosis before paying for therapy.

The DSM was revised to describe disorders without presuming to explain them. Thus the once popular term "neurosis" is no longer a diagnostic category, because neurosis was Freud's term for the process by which he believed that unconscious conflicts create anxiety. DSM-III-R does mention *neurotic disorders*—psychological disorders that, while distressing, still allow one to think rationally and function socially. But even this term is so vague that psychologists now use it only minimally, usually as a contrast to *psychotic disorders,* which are severely debilitating and involve bizarre behavior and thinking.

Instead of emphasizing the old neurotic/psychotic distinction, DSM-III-R groups some 230 psychological disorders and conditions into seventeen major categories of "mental disorder." There are diagnoses for almost every conceivable complaint. In fact, some critics fault DSM-III-R for bringing "almost any kind of behavior within the compass of psychiatry" (Eysenck & others, 1983)—from irrational fear of humiliation and embarrassment (social phobia) to persistently breaking rules at home or school (conduct disorder) to being drawn into situations or relationships that cause one to suffer (self-defeating personality disorder). The range of human problems that can be fit into DSM-III-R is evident in a National Institute of Mental Health survey of 10,000 Americans, which suggested that 1 in 5 adults suffers a recognizable psychological disorder (Myers & others, 1984).

The most important concern with DSM-III-R categories, however, is their reliability. If one psychologist or psychiatrist diagnoses some-

Drawing by Sidney Harris.

"I'm always like this, and my family was wondering if you could prescribe a mild depressant."

"Saying one out of every five people has a mental disorder is like saying the average person is crazy. The average person isn't crazy. He or she may act crazy sometimes but that's all part of being normal."

Andy Rooney,
Tribune Media Series, October 10, 1984

one as having, say, a "catatonic schizophrenic disorder," what are the chances that another clinician would independently give the same diagnosis? With previous diagnostic schemes, reliability has been modest. For broad diagnostic groupings, such as "schizophrenic disorders," the agreement averaged 70 percent or better in most studies. For more specific diagnoses, such as "catatonic schizophrenia," agreement was not much above 50 percent (Eysenck & others, 1983).

The DSM-III-R system for classifying disorders is designed to improve reliability. Instead of requiring a subjective assessment of the patient's condition, it bases diagnoses on observable behaviors. By asking clinicians a series of questions with yes or no answers (such as, "Is the person afraid to leave home?"), it attempts to guide them to diagnoses that can be reached with greater consensus. In one study, sixteen psychologists used this structured interview procedure to diagnose seventy-five patients at a psychiatric center as suffering either (1) depression, (2) generalized anxiety, or (3) some other disorder (Riskind & others, 1987). Without knowing the first psychologist's diagnosis, another psychologist then viewed a videotape of each interview and offered a second opinion. For 83 percent of the patients, the two opinions agreed.

Let us now consider a few of the most prevalent and perplexing disorders, remembering that these disorders afflict real people, not mere curiosities—people who are troubled and whose loved ones are troubled for them.

Other chapters discuss substance abuse (Chapters 8 and 18), sexual dysfunctions and eating disorders (Chapter 13), and post-traumatic stress disorder (Chapter 18).

ANXIETY DISORDERS

When speaking in front of a class, when peering down from a ledge, when waiting for a big game to begin, any one of us might feel anxious. At one time or another most of us feel enough anxiety in some social situation that we fail to make eye contact or we avoid talking to someone—"shyness" we call our social anxiety. According to the National Institute of Mental Health (Regier & others, 1984), however, for about 1 in 12 people, anxiety becomes so distressing and persistent that they are said to suffer an *anxiety disorder.*

Anxiety is a part of our everyday experiences. Fortunately for most of us, it does not entail the intense suffering endured by those with anxiety disorders, of which there are three important types: *generalized anxiety disorder,* in which a person, for no apparent reason, feels uncontrollably tense and uneasy; *phobic disorder,* in which the person feels irrationally afraid of a specific object or situation; and *obsessive-compulsive disorder,* in which the person is troubled by repetitive thoughts and actions.

GENERALIZED ANXIETY DISORDER

Tom, a 27-year-old electrician, seeks help, complaining of dizziness, sweating palms, heart palpitations, and ringing in the ears. He feels edgy and sometimes finds himself shaking. With reasonable success he tries to hide his symptoms from his family and co-workers. Nevertheless, he has had few social contacts since the symptoms began 2 years ago. Worse, he has had to leave work occasionally. His family doctor and neurologist can find no physical problem, and a special diet for those with low blood sugar has not helped.

Tom's chronic, unfocused anxiety suggests a generalized anxiety disorder. The symptoms of this disorder are commonplace; their persistence is not. The sufferers are continually tense and jittery, apprehensive and worrying about bad things that might happen, and experiencing all the symptoms of autonomic nervous system arousal (racing heart, clammy hands, butterflies in the stomach). The tension and apprehension may be apparent to others through furrowed brows, twitching eyelids, or fidgeting.

One of the worst characteristics of a generalized anxiety disorder is that the person cannot identify, and therefore cannot avoid, its cause. To use Freud's term, the anxiety is "free-floating." Indeed, for no apparent reason the anxiety may at times suddenly escalate into a terrifying *panic attack*—an episode of intense dread, usually lasting several minutes, that is typically accompanied by chest pain, choking or smothering sensations, trembling, dizziness, or fainting. The experience is unpredictable and so frightening that the sufferer may then avoid situations where attacks have previously occurred.

We can only speculate about the causes of generalized anxiety disorder. Psychoanalysts believe it illustrates what happens when the ego's defense mechanisms are weak: If the ego is unable to cope with the demands of the id, the reprimands of the superego, and the pressures of living in a complex world, the result is anxiety.

Biological factors also contribute to anxiety. When anxious individuals face a threat, stress hormones surge to very high levels. High doses of caffeine (as from several cups of coffee) can further amplify anxiety. In monkeys, and probably in humans as well, the anxiety response is genetically influenced. Monkeys show more behavioral and physiological reactivity to stress if their close genetic relatives are anxiously reactive (Suomi, 1986).

Learning researchers suggest that anxiety is a response to helplessness. Drawing on animal research (see page 513), they note that one can create the disorder in the laboratory by giving rats unpredictable electric shocks (Schwartz, 1984). After experiencing such aversive events without forewarning, the animals become chronically anxious and often develop ulcers. Never knowing when something bad will happen, they seem apprehensive whenever they are in their laboratory environment. (They are in some ways like the rape victim described on page 244, who reported being terrified of her old apartment and anxious about approaching the neighborhood where she was attacked.) On the other hand, when similar shocks are preceded by a conditioned stimulus, the animals become fearful of only *that stimulus* and can relax in its absence. They are more like people who suffer phobic disorders.

PHOBIC DISORDERS

Phobic anxiety is focused on some specific object, activity, or situation. (See Figure 16-2 for a ranking of some common fears.) Phobias—irrational fears—are a common psychological disorder that people usually accept and live with. Some phobic disorders are debilitating. Marilyn, a 28-year-old homemaker, is so frightened of thunderstorms that she feels anxious as soon as a weather forecaster mentions the possibility of storms later in the week. If her husband is away and a storm is forecast, she sometimes stays with a close relative. During a storm, she hides from windows and buries her head to avoid seeing the lightning. She is otherwise healthy and happy.

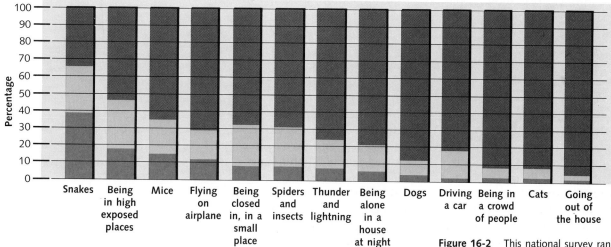

Afraid of it   **Bothers slightly**   **Not at all afraid of it**

Figure 16-2 This national survey ranks the relative fear levels of Americans to some common sources of anxiety. (From *Public Opinion*, 1984.)

Other people with phobic disorders suffer from irrational fears of specific animals or of airplanes or elevators or even public places such as department stores. Sometimes it is possible to avoid the fear-arousing stimulus: One can hide during thunderstorms or avoid air travel. With other phobias, such as an intense fear of being scrutinized by other people ("social phobia"), avoiding fear-arousing situations may dictate never leaving home.

There are several theories about the causes of phobic disorders. The psychoanalytic explanation is that phobia sufferers are actually anxious about their own impulses. When repression of these impulses is incomplete, anxiety surfaces and becomes displaced to a harmless stimulus. One of Freud's classic cases concerned a 5-year-old boy known as Little Hans, whose phobia of horses prevented, in those days before cars, his going outdoors. Freud concluded that Little Hans's fear of horses was but an expression of his underlying fear of his father, whom Hans perceived as a rival for his mother's affections.

Few people enjoy being in a crowded subway. But only people suffering from a severe phobia are incapacitated, their lives crippled by their attempts to avoid situations that to them are terrifying.

The learning explanation is that phobias are conditioned fears—fears that can also be *un*learned through extinction or counterconditioning. Recently, my car was struck by another whose driver failed to notice a stop sign. Now, every time I see a car approaching a stop sign on a cross street ahead of me, I feel a twinge of unease. Perhaps Marilyn had a terrifying or painful experience at an earlier time during a thunderstorm.

These conditioned fears may remain long after the initial experiences that caused them are forgotten (Jacobs & Nadel, 1985). A person can be afraid of airplanes, however, without ever having flown. Perhaps the fear response has generalized from, say, a fear of heights (due to a fall) to a fear of flying. Perhaps the fear has instead been learned from observing others' fears and frightening experiences, as when parents transmit their fears to their children. Or perhaps the fear stems from low self-efficacy, causing people to doubt their ability to cope with specific challenges (Williams, 1987a,b). Regardless, avoiding or escaping the feared situation reduces anxiety, which reinforces the phobic behavior.

Biological predispositions also contribute to phobic disorders, or at least to their persistence (McNally, 1987). As we noted on page 390, human beings seem biologically prepared to develop fears of heights, storms, snakes, and insects—dangers that our ancestors surely faced. Some psychologists even believe that our individual genetic makeup predisposes us to particular fears. Identical twins who have been raised separately sometimes develop identical phobias (Eckert & others, 1981). One pair of 35-year-old female twins independently developed claustrophobia and also became so fearful of water that they would gingerly wade backward into the ocean, only up to their knees.

OBSESSIVE-COMPULSIVE DISORDER

As with the generalized anxiety and phobic disorders, we can see aspects of ourselves in the obsessive-compulsive disorder. We may at times be obsessed with senseless or offensive thoughts that will not go away. Or we may engage in compulsive, rigid behavior—checking several times to see if the door is locked, stepping over the cracks in the sidewalk, or lining up our books and pencils "just so" before studying.

Obsessive thoughts and compulsive behaviors cross the fine line between normality and disorder when they become so persistent that they interfere with the way we live or when they cause us or others great distress. Checking to see that the doors are locked is normal; checking the door ten times is disordered. Hand washing is normal; hand washing so often that one's skin becomes raw is disordered. Billionaire Howard Hughes, once the anxiety-ridden child of an anxious mother, would compulsively dictate the same phrases over and over again. Under stress, he also developed an obsessive fear of germs. He became reclusive and insisted that his assistants carry out elaborate hand-washing rituals and wear white gloves when handling documents he would later touch. He ordered tape around doors and windows and forbade his staff to touch or even look at him. "Everybody carries germs around with them," he explained. "I want to live longer than my parents, so I avoid germs" (Fowler, 1986).

Again, the psychoanalytic and learning perspectives offer differing explanations for the disorder. In the Freudian view, obsessive

"He always times '60 Minutes.'"

thoughts may be a thinly disguised expression of forbidden impulses. These thoughts may prompt the person to perform compulsive acts that counter the forbidden impulse. Repetitive hand washing, for example, may help to suppress anxiety over one's "dirty" urges.

In the learning view, obsessive thoughts create anxiety, and compulsive behaviors reduce it, thereby reinforcing the behavior. If hand washing relieves anxiety, the person may repeat this behavior when again feeling anxious.

The anxiety of the obsessive-compulsive disorder is measurable as a biological state of overarousal (Turner & others, 1985). PET scans (see Figure 16-3) reveal elevated brain activity in a forward portion of the left frontal lobe (Baxter & others, 1987). Studies of twins suggest that a genetic predisposition to an anxious, aroused state may lead the obsessive-compulsive person to overreact to threatening stimuli and therefore to take actions that control perceived threats.

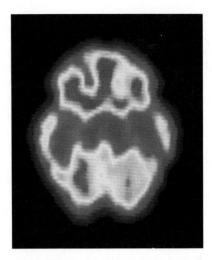

Figure 16-3 A PET scan of a person with obsessive-compulsive disorder reveals abnormally high metabolic activity in a region of the left hemisphere's frontal lobe that is involved in directing attention—a major component of obsessing—to specific objects.

SOMATOFORM DISORDERS

Ellen becomes dizzy and nauseated in the late afternoon—shortly before her husband is expected home. Neither her family doctor nor a neurologist has been able to identify a physical cause for her dizzy spells, and it seems likely that they have an unconscious psychological origin, possibly triggered by her mixed feelings about her husband. In *somatoform disorders,* such as Ellen's, the distressing symptoms take a somatic (bodily) form, without apparent physical causes. One person may have a variety of complaints—vomiting, dizziness, blurred vision, difficulty in swallowing, and so forth. Another may experience severe and prolonged pain. The problem is a familiar one: To a lesser extent, we have all experienced inexplicable physical symptoms under stress. It is little comfort to be told that the problem is "all in your head"; although the symptoms may be psychological in origin, they are nevertheless genuinely felt.

One type of somatoform disorder, more common in Freud's day than ours, is *conversion disorder,* so called because anxiety was presumed to be converted into a very specific physical symptom. As we noted in Chapter 15, Freud's effort to treat and understand psychological disorders stemmed from his puzzlement over ailments for which no physiological basis could be found. A patient would lose sensation in a way that made no neurological sense. Yet the physical symptoms were real; one could stick pins in the affected area without getting a response. Others experienced unexplained paralysis, blindness, or an inability to swallow and were strangely indifferent to their problems.

As you can imagine, somatoform disorders send people not to a psychologist or psychiatrist but to a physician. This is especially true of those who experience *hypochondriasis.* In this relatively common somatoform disorder, people interpret normal sensations (a stomach cramp today, a headache tomorrow) as symptoms of a dreaded disease, for which they may be reinforced with sympathy or relief from some of the demands of life. No amount of reassurance by any physician convinces the patient not to worry, so the patient may move on to another physician, seeking and receiving more medical attention—but failing to confront the psychological root of the disorder.

"He was a dreadful hypochondriac."

DISSOCIATIVE DISORDERS

Among the most uncommon and most intriguing of the psychological disorders are the *dissociative disorders,* in which the patient experiences a sudden loss of memory or change in identity. Under extreme stress, conscious awareness becomes *dissociated,* or separated, from previous memories, thoughts, and feelings.

AMNESIA

Amnesia, the failure to recall events, can be caused by head injuries or alcoholic intoxication. But psychogenic amnesia—a dissociative disorder—usually begins as a response to intolerable psychological stress. One 18-year-old victim was rescued from his sailboat by the Coast Guard and brought to a hospital. He knew he had gone sailing with friends and that he was a college student, but he could not recall what had happened to his friends. Moreover, he kept forgetting that he was in the hospital; each time he was reminded, he seemed surprised. Later, with the aid of a drug that relaxed him, he was able to recall that a ferocious storm had washed his companions overboard.

As this case illustrates, the forgetfulness of amnesia tends to be selective: The young man forgot what was intolerably painful. Those with amnesia may be somewhat disoriented and may forget who they are, but they will remember how to drive, count, and talk. Typically, the amnesia vanishes as abruptly as it began and rarely recurs.

FUGUE

Like amnesia, *fugue* (pronounced *fewg,* meaning "flight") involves forgetting, but it is also associated with fleeing one's home and identity for days, months, or years. When suddenly "awakening" from a fugue state, people will remember their old identities but will have no memory for what transpired during the fugue. Such was the self-reported experience of Steven Kubacki, a Hope College senior who, on a cold February afternoon in 1978, went hiking on the ice over Lake Michigan and failed to return. Eventually, his parents presumed him dead and his college awarded him a posthumous degree. The next thing he knew he was awakening in a field in Massachusetts on a warm spring day. Beside him was a backpack with someone's running shoes, swimming goggles, and glasses. "What the hell's going on here?" he reports wondering. Fourteen months of his life had vanished.

MULTIPLE PERSONALITY

Even more mysterious is the massive dissociation of self from ordinary consciousness in those with *multiple personality disorder.* Such people have two or more distinct personalities. The first is usually rather restrained and dull, the second more impulsive and uninhibited. The person may be prim and proper one moment and loud and flirtatious the next. Each personality has its own voice and mannerisms, and the original one is typically unaware of the other.

Although people diagnosed as having multiple personality disorder are usually nonviolent, there have been cases in which the person reportedly became dissociated into a "good" and a "bad" or aggressive personality—a Dr. Jekyll/Mr. Hyde split of the sort immortalized in Robert Louis Stevenson's story. Freud would say that, rid of the original "good" personality's awareness, the wanton second personality is free to discharge forbidden impulses. One unusual case that for a time seemed to support this interpretation involved Kenneth Bianchi, who was convicted of the "Hillside Strangler" rapes and murders of ten California women. During a hypnosis session with psychologist John Watkins (1984), Bianchi revealed a highly sadistic second personality.

Watkins first told Bianchi that hypnosis can be used as a tool for uncovering hidden aspects of personality. He then "called forth" a hidden personality:

> I've talked a bit to Ken, but I think that perhaps there might be another part of Ken that I haven't talked to, another part that maybe feels somewhat differently from the part that I've talked to. . . . Would you talk with me, Part, by saying, "I'm here"?

Bianchi answered "yes" and engaged in the following interchange:

Watkins: Part, are you the same thing as Ken, or are you different in any way?
Bianchi: I'm not him.
Watkins: You're not him? Who are you? Do you have a name?
Bianchi: Steve. You can call me Steve.

"Hillside Strangler" Kenneth Bianchi at his trial.

While speaking as Steve, Bianchi stated that he hated Ken because Ken was nice and that he (Steve), with the help of a cousin, had murdered a number of women. He also claimed that Ken knew nothing about his existence and that Ken was innocent of the murders.

Was Bianchi's second personality a ruse, simply a way of disavowing responsibility for his actions? The psychologist who diagnosed Bianchi believes he is a genuine case of multiple personality. Others doubt the diagnosis. They believe either that Bianchi, a consistent rule-breaker and liar since childhood, was consciously faking it to save his own skin (Orne, 1984), or that to dissociate himself from his impulses and actions he unconsciously created the multiple personality during the hypnotic session (Allison, 1984).

To see if normal people might act as if they had a multiple personality, one such skeptic, Nicolas Spanos (1986b), asked college students to pretend they were accused murderers being examined by a psychiatrist. When given the same hypnotic treatment that Bianchi received, most spontaneously expressed a second personality. Spanos wonders if clinicians who discover multiple personalities are merely triggering people to enact a role, whether consciously or unconsciously. If so, can such people then be convinced of the authenticity of their own role enactments?

"Pretense may become reality."
Chinese proverb

You may recall from Chapter 8 a similar question concerning whether hypnosis is a unique state of consciousness or a social phenomenon. People diagnosed as multiple personality typically are able to drift spontaneously into a hypnotic state, and they may have distinct brain and body states associated with each of their personalities (Goleman, 1985b). As yet, however, the issue of whether most diagnosed cases of multiple personalities are genuine is unresolved. Skeptics find it suspicious that the disorder has just recently become rather popular. There have been three times more cases of the disorder reported since 1970 than in the previous 150 years (Orne & others, 1984)—just the sort of fad one might expect now that the role of multiple personality has been well publicized in books such as *The Three Faces of Eve* and *Sybil*. Moreover, the vast majority of clinicians have never encountered a multiple personality, but a few claim to encounter them regularly (Levitt, 1988).

With the dissociative disorders as with the anxiety and somatoform disorders, the psychoanalytic and learning perspectives both view the symptoms as ways of dealing with anxiety—as defenses against the anxiety evolved by the eruption of unacceptable impulses (as Freud would say) or as behaviors that have been reinforced by anxiety reduction (as a learning theorist would say). Others view dissociative disorders as hypnotic-like states into which people lapse as a protective response to traumatic childhood experiences. Most people diagnosed as multiple personality are said to have suffered physical, sexual, or emotional abuse as children (Kluft, 1987). Perhaps, then, multiple personalities are the desperate efforts of the traumatized to flee inward. Maladaptive as they may be, such psychological disorders are expressions of our human struggle to cope with and survive the stresses of life.

"Though this be madness, yet there is method in 't."
William Shakespeare,
Hamlet, 1600

MOOD DISORDERS

The *mood disorders,* which are characterized by emotional extremes, come in two principal forms: (1) *major depression,* in which the person experiences the hopelessness and lethargy of prolonged depression until eventually rebounding to normalcy; and (2) *bipolar disorder,* in which the person alternates between depression and *mania,* an overexcited, hyperactive state.

MAJOR DEPRESSION

Possibly you know what depression feels like. If you are like most of the college students studied by Aaron Beck and Jeffrey Young (1978), at some time during this year you will probably experience a few of the symptoms of depression—by feeling deeply discouraged about the future, dissatisfied with your life, isolated from people, saddened by you're-not-sure-what; by lacking energy; by being unable to concentrate, eat, or sleep normally; by wondering if you would be better off dead. Perhaps academic success came easily to you in high school, and now you find that disappointing grades jeopardize your career goals. Maybe conflicting parental and peer pressures seem almost intolerable. Perhaps social difficulties such as loneliness or the breakup of a romantic relationship have plunged you into despair. And maybe your brooding has at times only worsened your self-torment.

If so, you are not alone. Depression has been called "the common cold" of psychological disorders—an expression that well states its pervasiveness but not its seriousness. Studies in the United States and Europe suggest that at some time during their lives 5 to 10 percent of men and twice that many women will suffer a major depressive episode. Among people born since World War II depression has increased dramatically—tenfold, reports Martin Seligman (1988).

The line between life's normal "downs" and major depression is difficult to define. Joy, contentment, sadness, and despair are different points on a continuum, points at which any of us may be found at any given moment. Depression can be an appropriate response to profoundly sad events, such as a significant loss or bereavement. When signs of depression (poor appetite, insomnia, lethargy, feelings of worthlessness, or loss of interest in family, friends, and activities) last 2 weeks or more without there being any discernible cause, the depressed mood is likely to be diagnosed as major depression.

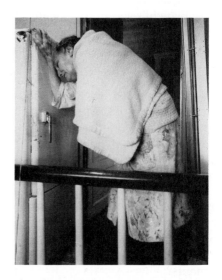

The attitude of this woman's body eloquently testifies to the loss of energy and sense of isolation that accompany a major depression.

"My life had come to a sudden stop. I was able to breathe, to eat, to drink, to sleep. I could not, indeed, help doing so; but there was no real life in me."
Leo Tolstoy,
My Confession, 1887

SUICIDE

Contrary to popular opinion, there are *fewer* suicides on holidays such as Thanksgiving and Christmas than at other times of the year (Phillips & Wills, 1988).

But life, being weary of these worldly bars,
Never lacks power to dismiss itself.

> William Shakespeare,
> *Julius Caesar,* 1599

Each year in the United States, some 25,000 to 30,000 wearied, despairing people will say no to life by electing a permanent solution to what may be a temporary problem. In retrospect, their family and friends may recall signs that they now believe should have forewarned them—the suicidal talk, the giving away of possessions, or the withdrawal and preoccupation with death. One-third of those who now succeed will have tried suicide before.

Actually, few of those who think suicidal thoughts (a number that includes perhaps one-third of all college students) actually attempt suicide, and few of these succeed in killing themselves (Westefeld & Furr, 1987). Most individuals who commit suicide have talked of it, and any who do talk about it are at least sending a signal of their desperate or despondent feelings.

To find out who commits suicide, researchers have compared the suicide rates of different groups (see Figure 16–4). National differences are puzzling: The suicide rates of Ireland, Italy, and Israel are half that in the United States; those of Austria, Denmark, and Switzerland are nearly double (Bureau of the Census, 1987). Racial differences are intriguing: In the United States, whites kill themselves twice as often as blacks. Group differences are suggestive: Suicide rates have tended to be higher among the rich, the non-religious, and the unmarried (including the widowed and divorced [Stengel, 1981]). Gender differences are dramatic: Women are much more likely than men to attempt suicide; depending on the country, however, men are two to three times more likely to succeed. (Men are more likely to use foolproof methods, such as putting a bullet into the brain.) Age differences have vanished: The suicide rate among 15- to 24-year-olds has more than doubled since 1955 and now equals the traditionally higher suicide rate among older adults (Figure 16–5).

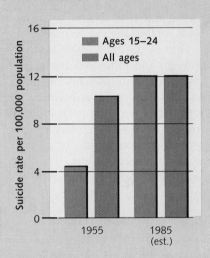

Figure 16-5   Teen and young adult suicide has soared since 1955. (National Center for Health Statistics data from Wilentz, 1987.)

Suicide often occurs not when the person is in the depths of depression, when energy and initiative are lacking, but when the person begins to rebound, becoming capable of following through. Teenage suicides may follow a traumatic event such as a romantic breakup or antisocial act, and often are linked with drug and alcohol abuse (Fowler, 1986; Kolata, 1986b). In the elderly, suicide is sometimes chosen as an alternative to future suffering. In people of all ages, suicide is not necessarily an act of hostility or revenge, as many people think, but a way of switching off unendurable and seemingly inescapable pain (Shneidman, 1987).

Social suggestion may also initiate the final act: Known suicides as well as fatal auto "accidents" and private airplane crashes increase following highly publicized suicides (see pages 551–552).

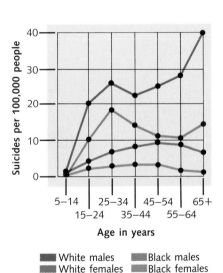

Figure 16-4   In the United States, suicide rates are higher among whites than blacks, and males than females. (From Bureau of the Census, 1987.)

BIPOLAR DISORDER

After days, weeks, or months, depressive episodes usually are self-terminating without therapy. Depressed people nearly always rebound—usually by returning to their previous normal behavior. However, some people rebound to the opposite emotional extreme—to a euphoric, hyperactive, wildly optimistic state called *mania.* People who alternate between depression and mania are said to suffer from bipolar disorder. If the depression they experience is like living in slow motion, the mania is like a speeded-up movie. During the manic phase of a bipolar disorder, the person is typically overtalkative, elated (*and* easily irritated if crossed), has little need for sleep, and shows few sexual inhibitions. Speech is loud, flighty, and hard to interrupt.

One of the most maladaptive symptoms of mania is a grandiose optimism and inflated self-esteem that may lead to recklessness, such as spending and investment sprees. Like other disordered people, individuals exhibiting mania may need to be protected from the consequences of their own poor judgments, although they will be irritated with those who try to provide advice or guidance. In milder forms, the energy, sensitive reactivity, and free-flowing thinking characteristic of mania can fuel creativity. This fact may help explain the high rate of bipolar disorders among creative writers, especially poets (Holden, 1987a).

It is as true of emotions as of other things: What goes up generally comes down. Before long, the mood either returns to normal or plunges into a brief depression. Though equally as maladaptive as depression, bipolar disorder is much less common, occurring in about 1 percent of the U.S. population.

"All the people in history, literature, art, whom I most admire: Mozart, Shakespeare, Homer, El Greco, St. John, Chekhov, Gregory of Nyssa, Dostoevsky, Emily Brontë: not one of them would qualify for a mental-health certificate."
Madeleine L'Engle,
A Circle of Quiet, 1972

EXPLAINING MOOD DISORDERS

Because depression affects so many people so powerfully, it has been the subject of thousands of studies. Psychologists are working to develop a theory of depression that, by identifying its causes, will suggest ways to treat or prevent it. Researcher Peter Lewinsohn and his colleagues (1985) have summarized the facts that any theory of depression must explain. Among them are the following:

1. Many behavioral and cognitive changes accompany depression. Depressed people tend to be inactive, unmotivated, sensitive to negative happenings, expecting negative outcomes, and more likely to recall negative information. When the depression lifts, these behavioral and cognitive accompaniments disappear.

2. The commonality of depression (Lewinsohn estimates that actually 25 percent or more of us will experience at least one depressive episode during our lifetime) suggests that its causes must be common.

3. Women, especially women who have previously been depressed, are at greatest risk for depression. Curiously, the gender difference in depression rates does *not* exist in college students or among bereaved persons (Nolen-Hoeksema, 1987).

4. Most depressive episodes last less than 3 months, and most people return to normal without professional assistance.

5. Stressful events related to work, marriage, and close relationships tend to precede depression.

About 50 percent of those who recover from depression will suffer another episode within 2 years. Recovery is more likely to be enduring the longer patients stay well, the fewer their previous episodes, the less stress they experience, and the more social support they have (Belsher & Costello, 1988).

As you might expect, researchers understand and interpret these facts in ways that reflect their different perspectives.

The Psychoanalytic Perspective   As we noted in Chapter 15, Freud assumed the importance of early childhood experiences and of unconscious feelings and impulses. The psychoanalytic theory of depression applies these assumptions. It suggests that depression in adulthood can be triggered by significant losses that evoke feelings associated with earlier losses experienced in childhood. Loss of a romantic relationship or job might evoke feelings associated with the loss of the intimate relationship with one's mother. Unresolved anger toward one's parents is also a factor, Freud believed. Some losses, such as the death of a loved one, may evoke the anger once felt toward parents who were similarly "abandoning" or "rejecting." Since this anger is unacceptable to the superego, the emotion may be turned inward against the self. The net result of this reaction to loss and internalized anger is said to be depression.

The Biological Perspective   The research on psychological disorders that has attracted most of the U.S. government's mental health research dollars of late has to do with biological factors in mood disorders (Sullivan, 1987). It has long been known that mood disorders run in families. The data suggest that if an identical twin is diagnosed as having a bipolar disorder, the chances are nearly 2 in 3 that the other twin will at some point be diagnosed similarly; if an identical twin is diagnosed as suffering from a major depression, the chances are about 2 in 5 that sometime the other twin will be, too.

Among fraternal twins, the corresponding odds are only 10 to 15 percent (Allen, 1976). The risk of becoming depressed is increased if you have a parent or sibling who became depressed in adolescence or young adulthood, especially if their depression struck before age 30 (Weissman & others, 1986). Moreover, adopted people who suffer a mood disorder are much more likely than normal to have close biological relatives who suffer mood disorders, become alcoholic, or commit suicide (Wender & others, 1986).

Mood disorders run in certain families among the Older Order Amish in Lancaster County, Pennsylvania. It's "in the blood" the Amish say, noting that all twenty-six suicides that occurred in their community between 1880 and 1980 took place in only four extended families. Janice Egeland and her colleagues (1987) studied the family history and the chromosomes of nineteen Amish people suffering bipolar disorder, which is easily diagnosed in a community noted for its sober, quiet ways. Using new genetic techniques, the researchers compared gene segments from affected and unaffected family members and discovered that all nineteen had an identifiable abnormality within the eleventh chromosome.

This is among the first discoveries of a genetic anomaly linked with a major psychological disorder. But this particular difference seems involved only in bipolar disorders among the Lancaster County Amish. And even in this Amish community, only 63 percent of those carrying the gene exhibit the disorder. Apparently, experience influences the expression of this genetic disorder. Given the critical genetic predisposition, people may be pushed into a depression by significant stress.

Genes act by directing biochemical events that, down the line, influence behavior. Through what biochemical processes might genes predispose mood disorders? Recall that among the body's most important biochemicals are the neurotransmitters, the messenger molecules that shuttle signals between nerve cells. These biochemicals have been implicated in depression. Norepinephrine, a neurotransmitter that increases arousal and boosts mood, appears to be overabundant during mania and in short supply during depression. A second neurotransmitter, serotonin, appears scarce in a particular type of depression. Drugs that alleviate mania tend to reduce norepinephrine; drugs that relieve depression tend to increase norepinephrine or serotonin by blocking their uptake (Schmeck, 1988). This hints that low levels of norepinephrine may cause depression and that keeping norepinephrine within normal bounds might be one way to alleviate depression.

But the story is more complicated. Other biochemical links with depression also are emerging. Researchers are studying the role of the neurotransmitters serotonin, dopamine, and their neural receptors (McNeal & Cimbolic, 1986). Their hope is that we may eventually be able to identify those vulnerable to mood disorders and to take protective steps by psychological interventions and/or by counteracting the disorder's biological underpinnings.

The Social-Cognitive Perspective   Biological factors do not operate in a vacuum: As Figure 16–6 suggests, they are correlated with psychological reactions to particular experiences. In recent years some exciting research in the psychology of depression has come from social-cognitive psychologists, whose findings indicate that depression is rooted in negative perceptions, beliefs, and thoughts. For example, psychiatrist Aaron Beck's (1982) work with depressed patients convinced him that depression is linked with *self-defeating beliefs*. Depressed people view life through dark glasses. Their intensely negative assumptions about themselves, their situations, and their futures lead them to magnify bad experiences and minimize good ones. As one occasionally depressed young woman put it (Burns, 1980, pp. 28–29):

> My thoughts become negative and pessimistic. As I look into the past, I become convinced that everything that I've ever done is worthless. Any happy period seems like an illusion. My accomplishments appear as genuine as the false facade of a Western movie. I become convinced that the real me is worthless and inadequate. I can't move forward with my work because I become frozen with doubt.

Self-defeating beliefs may arise from *learned helplessness*. As we saw in Chapter 15, both dogs and humans act depressed, passive, and withdrawn after experiencing uncontrollable events that persuade them their actions are futile. Society has more often rendered women than men helpless to control their lives, which helps to explain why women have been twice as vulnerable to depression as men (Nolen-Hoeksema, 1987).

Maladaptive Explanations Feed Depression   Why do life's unavoidable failures lead some people, but not others, to become depressed? The difference lies partly with people's *attributions* of blame. The fact is that we have some choice of whom or what to blame for our failures. If you fail a test and blame it on yourself, you may conclude that you are stupid and feel depressed. However, if you attribute your failure to an unfair test, you are more likely to feel angry.

In more than 100 studies involving some 15,000 subjects (Sweeney & others, 1986), depressed people have been more likely to explain bad events in terms that are *stable* ("it's going to last forever"), *global* ("it's

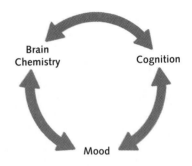

Figure 16-6   Depression—an ailing mind in an ailing body. Altering any component of the chemistry-cognition-mood circuit can alter the others.

"I have learned to accept my mistakes by referring them to a personal history which was not of my making."
B. F. Skinner (1983)

going to affect everything I do''), and *internal* (''it's all my fault''). Lyn Abramson, Gerald Metalsky, and Lauren Alloy (1989) theorize that the result of these pessimistic, overgeneralized, self-blaming attributions is a depressing sense of hopelessness. Martin Seligman (1988) argues that depression is now rife among young Americans because of epidemic hopelessness, which stems from the rise of individualism and the decline of commitment to religion and family. When facing failure or rejection, contends Seligman, the self-focused individual takes on personal responsibility for problems and has nothing to fall back on for hope.

Negative Moods Feed Negative Thoughts and Actions   There is, however, a chicken-and-egg problem with the cognitive explanation of depression. Self-blame and negative attributions surely do support depression, but do they cause it? Peter Barnett and Ian Gotlib (1988) note that such cognitions are better *indicators* than predictors of depression. Depressing thoughts *coincide* with a depressed mood; before or after being depressed, people's thoughts are less negative. Perhaps this is because, as we noted in our discussion of state-dependent memory (page 271), a depressed mood triggers negative thoughts. If you temporarily put people in a bad or sad mood, their memories, judgments, and expectations are suddenly more pessimistic.

Joseph Forgas and his associates (1984) provide a striking demonstration of the mood effect. After being put in a good or bad mood via hypnosis, subjects watched a videotape (made the day before) of themselves talking with someone. The happy subjects detected in themselves more instances of positive than negative behavior; the unhappy subjects more often saw themselves behaving negatively (see Figure 16–7). Thus, even when viewing themselves on videotape, people judge themselves more negatively when they are feeling depressed.

The Vicious Cycle of Depression   Depression is often brought on by stressful experiences—losing a job, being criticized or rejected, physical trauma—anything that disrupts your sense of who you are and why you are a worthy human being (Dohrenwend & others, 1987; Oatley & Bolton, 1985). But bad events per se don't cause depression, for not everyone is depressed by them. Those who are depressed typically have a negative explanatory style that becomes self-focused (Pyszczynski & Greenberg, 1987a). Brooding over their problems produces self-blame and amplifies their depressed mood, which in turn triggers all the other cognitive and behavioral symptoms of depression.

Moreover, being withdrawn, passive, and complaining tends to elicit more social rejection (Gurtman, 1986; Pietromonaco & Rook, 1987). In one study, researchers Stephen Strack and James Coyne (1983) observed that ''depressed persons induced hostility, depression, and anxiety in others and got rejected. Their guesses that they were not accepted were not a matter of cognitive distortion.'' Weary of the

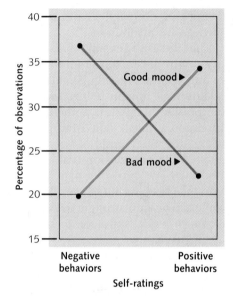

Figure 16-7 A happy or depressed mood strongly influences people's rating of their own behavior. In this experiment, those in a hypnotically induced good mood detected many more positive than negative behaviors. The reverse was true for those in a bad mood. (From Forgas & others, 1984.)

''Man never reasons so much and becomes so introspective as when he suffers, since he is anxious to get at the cause of his sufferings.''
  Luigi Pirandello,
  Six Characters in Search of an Author,
  1922

Drawings by Charles Shultz; © 1956 United Feature Syndicate, Inc.

depressed person's fatigue, hopeless attitude, and never wanting to do anything, a spouse may threaten to leave or a boss may begin to question the person's competence.

We can now assemble the pieces of the depression puzzle (Figure 16–8): (1) Stressful events interpreted through (2) a pessimistic explanatory style create (3) a hopeless, depressed state that (4) hampers the way the person thinks and acts. This, in turn, fuels (1) more negative experiences. On the brighter side, one can break the cycle of depression at any of these points—by engaging in more pleasant activities and more competent behavior, by turning one's attention outward, by moving to a different environment, or by reversing one's self-blame and negative attributions.

That there are several points at which the cycle can be broken helps explain why several different therapy methods have been found effective and why depression is usually of relatively short duration. It also explains why human beings are not necessarily defeated by depression, poison though it is to the human spirit. Winston Churchill called depression a "black dog" that periodically hounded him. Poet Emily Dickinson was so afraid of bursting into tears that she spent much of her adult life in seclusion (Patterson, 1951). Abraham Lincoln was so withdrawn and brooding as a young man that his friends feared he might take his own life (Kline, 1974). As each of these lives reminds us, people can and do struggle out of depression and regain their capacity to love, to work, and even to succeed at the highest levels.

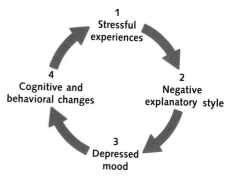

Figure 16-8 The vicious cycle of depression can be broken at any point.

LONELINESS

Loneliness—the painful awareness that one's social relationships are deficient—is both a contributor to depression and a problem in itself. The deficiency stems from a mismatch between one's social contacts and one's desire for contact. Although one person may feel lonely when isolated and another may feel lonely in a crowd (Peplau & Perlman, 1982), people who are alone —unmarried and unattached—are more likely to feel lonely. Dutch psychologist Jenny de Jong-Gierveld (1987) therefore speculates that the modern emphasis on individual fulfillment and the downgrading of the importance of satisfactory and stable relationships and of the importance of commitment to others are "loneliness-provoking factors."

College students commonly experience one or more of four types of loneliness (Beck & Young, 1978). To be lonely is to feel *excluded* from a group you would like to belong to; to feel *unloved* and uncared about by those around you; to feel *constricted* and unable to share your private concerns with anyone; or to feel *alienated*, or different from, those in your community. Like depressed people, lonely people tend to blame themselves, attributing their deficient social relationships to their own inadequacies (Snodgrass, 1987). There may be a basis for this self-blame: Chronically lonely people tend to be shy, self-conscious, and lacking in self-esteem. They often find it hard to introduce themselves, make phone calls, and participate in groups (Rook, 1984; Spitzberg & Hurt, 1987). In addition, their belief in their social unworthiness tends to restrict them from taking steps that would reduce their loneliness. Thus, factors that work to create and maintain the cycle of depression can also produce the cycle of loneliness.

SCHIZOPHRENIC DISORDERS

One in 100 people will develop schizophrenia, joining the millions who have suffered one of humanity's most dreaded disorders. Schizophrenia is the foremost psychotic disorder—a disorder in which a person loses contact with reality by experiencing grossly irrational ideas and distorted perceptions—a devastating ailment that typically strikes an adolescent or young adult. Although it tends to be diagnosed more frequently in the lower socioeconomic classes, it knows no national boundaries and it affects the two sexes about equally.

SYMPTOMS OF SCHIZOPHRENIA

Schizophrenia literally translated means "split mind"—not a Dr. Jekyll/ Mr. Hyde multiple-personality split, but rather a *split from reality* that shows itself in disorganized thinking, disturbed perceptions, and inappropriate emotions and actions.

Disorganized Thinking   Imagine trying to communicate with Sylvia Frumkin, a young woman whose thoughts spill out in no logical order. Her biographer, Susan Sheehan (1982, p. 25), observed her saying aloud to no one in particular,

> "This morning, when I was at Hillside [Hospital], I was making a movie. I was surrounded by movie stars. The X-ray technician was Peter Lawford. The security guard was Don Knotts. That Indian doctor in Building 40 was Lou Costello. I'm Mary Poppins. Is this room painted blue to get me upset? My grandmother died four weeks after my eighteenth birthday." Miss Frumkin laughed.

As this strange monologue illustrates, the schizophrenia patient's thinking is fragmented, bizarre, and distorted by false beliefs, called ***delusions*** ("I'm Mary Poppins"). Jumping from one idea to another may even occur within sentences, creating a sort of "word salad," as in the case of the young man who begged for "a little more allegro in the treatment," and who suggested that "liberationary movement with a view to the widening of the horizon" will "ergo extort some wit in lectures."

Many psychologists believe that the disorganized thoughts result from a breakdown in the normal human capacity for selective attention. As we noted on pages 193–194, we normally have a remarkable capacity for selective attention—for, say, giving our undivided attention to one voice at a party while filtering out competing sensory stimuli. Schizophrenia sufferers seem to have impaired attention (Gjerde, 1983). Thus, they are easily distracted by an irrelevant stimulus or an extraneous part of the preceding thought. As one former schizophrenia patient recalled, "What had happened to me . . . was a breakdown in the filter, and a hodge-podge of unrelated stimuli were distracting me from things which should have had my undivided attention" (MacDonald, 1960, p. 218).

Disturbed Perceptions   The schizophrenia victim experiences an altered world. Minute stimuli, such as the grooves on a brick or the inflections of a voice, may distract attention, disrupting the person's perception of the whole scene or of the speaker's meaning. Worse, the person may perceive things that are not there.

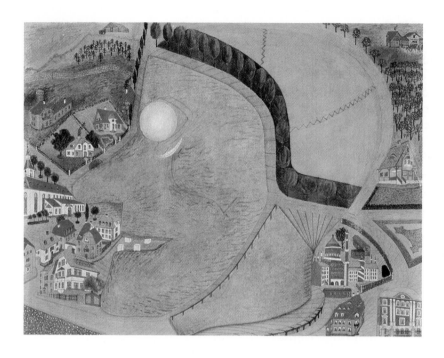

In reviewing a showing of artworks by schizophrenia patients, such as the paintings shown here, poet John Ashbery wrote: ''The lure of the work is strong, but so is the terror of the unanswerable riddles it proposes.''

Such *hallucinations* (sensory experiences without sensory stimulation) are most commonly auditory. The person may hear voices that seem to come from outside the head and that make insulting statements or give orders. The voices may, for example, tell the patient that she is bad or that he must burn himself with a cigarette lighter. Less commonly, people may see, feel, taste, or smell things that are not there. Such hallucinations have been likened to dreams breaking into waking consciousness. The unreal has become real, and the resulting perceptions are at best bizarre and at worst terrifying.

Inappropriate Emotions and Actions   The emotions of people with schizophrenia are often utterly inappropriate to what they have said or heard. Sylvia Frumkin's emotions seemed split off from reality; she laughed after recalling her grandmother's death. On occasion, she would become angry for no apparent reason or cry when others would laugh. Other schizophrenia victims sometimes lapse into a flat, zombielike state of emotionless apathy.

Motor behavior also tends to be inappropriate. The person may perform senseless repetitive acts, such as continually rocking or rubbing an arm, or may remain motionless for hours on end.

Needless to say, disorganized thinking, disturbed perceptions, and inappropriate emotions and actions disrupt normal social relationships. During their worst periods, schizophrenia sufferers live in a private inner world, preoccupied with illogical ideas and unreal images. Indeed, although some people suffer schizophrenia only intermittently, others remain socially withdrawn and isolated throughout much of their lives.

TYPES OF SCHIZOPHRENIA

We have described schizophrenia as if it were a single disorder. Actually, it is a cluster of disorders that have common features but also some distinguishing symptoms. ''Active'' schizophrenia patients, for example, are conspicuously disorganized and deluded in their talk or prone to inappropriate laughter, tears, or rage. "Passive" schizophrenia patients have toneless voices, expressionless faces, or mute and rigid bodies. The finer distinctions among the schizophrenia disorders listed in Table 16–1 are hazy. Nevertheless, we should not think of schizophrenia as one disorder for which there is one set of causes. A number of psychologists believe that paranoid schizophrenia, like mania and alcohol abuse and *un*like the other schizophrenias, is a defense against an underlying depression and loss of self-worth (Zigler & Glick, 1988). Thus, individuals with paranoid delusions can reassure themselves that "Far from being inadequate, I must be very important if everyone is so interested in me."

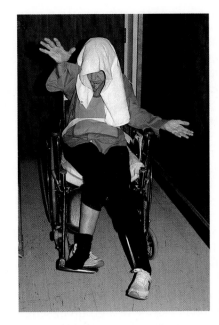

People who suffer from schizophrenia often withdraw into an inner world of bizarre thoughts and disturbed perceptions. Their inappropriate behaviors demonstrate their loss of contact with reality.

Table 16–1 THE SCHIZOPHRENIAS	
Type	**Characteristics**
Disorganized	Incoherent speech and inappropriate, often silly, emotion. The individual may be extremely withdrawn and behavior may include odd grimaces and mannerisms.
Catatonic	Bizarre physical movements, ranging from motionless stupor to violent hyperactivity and sometimes alternating between these two extremes.
Paranoid	Delusions of persecution or grandeur. The individual may trust no one and may be anxious or angry about supposed tormentors.
Undifferentiated	Delusions, hallucinations, and incoherence typical of schizophrenia; however, the individual does not neatly fit any of the other types.
Residual	Minor symptoms of schizophrenia lingering after a serious episode.

Sometimes, as in the case of Sylvia Frumkin, schizophrenia develops gradually, emerging from a long history of social inadequacy (which partially explains why those predisposed to schizophrenia often end up in the lower socioeconomic levels, or even as homeless street people). At other times, it appears more suddenly, seemingly as a reaction to stress. Shortly after his parents split up, his girlfriend took off with another man, and his father became "outlandishly famous," Mark Vonnegut (1975), son of the writer Kurt Vonnegut, suffered a schizophrenia disorder. There is a rule of thumb that holds true across the world (World Health Organization, 1979): When a previously well-adjusted person develops schizophrenia rapidly, as a reaction to particular life stresses, the chances for recovery are bright; when the schizophrenic disorder is a slow-developing process, the chances for recovery are not so bright. After his schizophrenia abated, Mark Vonnegut was able to enter medical school (Gorman, 1984).

UNDERSTANDING SCHIZOPHRENIA

Schizophrenia is not only the most dreaded psychological disorder but also one of the most heavily researched over the years. Some of the most important new discoveries have linked schizophrenia with biological factors.

Brain Abnormalities   The idea that imbalances in brain chemistry might underlie schizophrenia has intrigued scientists for a long while. After all, strange behaviors have been known to be caused by chemicals. The saying "mad as a hatter" refers to the psychological deterioration of British hatmakers who, it was later discovered, were being slowly poisoned as they moistened the brims of mercury-laden felt hats with their lips (Smith, 1983). As we saw on page 218, scientists are coming to understand the mechanism by which chemicals such as LSD produce hallucinations. Such discoveries have increased the hope that a biochemical key to schizophrenia might be found.

The search has turned up many leads, some of which have turned out to be dead ends. One researcher may discover an abnormality in the blood or urine of a group of schizophrenia patients. Upon further investigation the abnormality may turn out to be a product of the hospital diet, or perhaps a *consequence* of the disorder itself or of its treatment with drugs.

Nevertheless, the process of debate and testing by which science sifts truth from falsehood has identified neurotransmitter abnormalities that seem involved in some types of schizophrenia. For example, when the brain tissue of schizophrenia patients is examined after death, it has been found to have an excess of receptors for the neurotransmitter dopamine (Wong & others, 1986). Drugs that block dopamine receptors often alleviate symptoms of schizophrenia (although more slowly than would be the case if schizophrenia were caused solely by excess dopamine activity). Drugs that increase dopamine levels sometimes exacerbate schizophrenia symptoms (Swerdlow & Koob, 1987). Such dopamine overactivity may be what makes schizophrenia victims overreactive to irrelevant external and internal stimuli.

Modern techniques of scanning the brain have revealed that many chronic schizophrenia patients have a detectable brain abnormality, such as a shrinkage of cerebral tissue and enlarged fluid-filled chambers, or an abnormal pattern of low brain activity in the frontal lobes (Andreasen, 1988) (Figure 16–9). Patients with diminished brain tissue tend also to have less of an enzyme that converts dopamine to norepinephrine, thereby providing another hint that excess dopamine may be linked with schizophrenia (van Kammen & others, 1983).

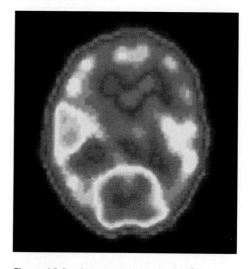

Figure 16-9   Large green areas near the top of this PET scan of the brain of a patient afflicted with schizophrenia indicate abnormally low levels of metabolism in the frontal lobes.

Genetic Factors   Naturally, scientists wonder whether the abnormalities in brain chemistry, structure, and activity are inherited. The evidence strongly suggests that there is a genetic predisposition to schizophrenia. The 100 to 1 odds against any person's being diagnosed with schizophrenia become 10 to 1 among those who have an afflicted sibling or parent, and almost 50-50 among those who have an identical twin who has been diagnosed with schizophrenia (Figure 16-10). Moreover, although there are only a dozen relevant cases, it appears that an identical twin of a schizophrenia victim retains that 50-50 chance whether reared with or apart from the twin with schizophrenia.

Adoption studies also suggest a genetic link (Faraone & Tsuang, 1985). Children who are adopted by someone who develops schizo-

"It is a common observation that men born of parents that are sometimes wont to be mad, will be obnoxious [susceptible] to the same disease."
  Thomas Willis, 1685

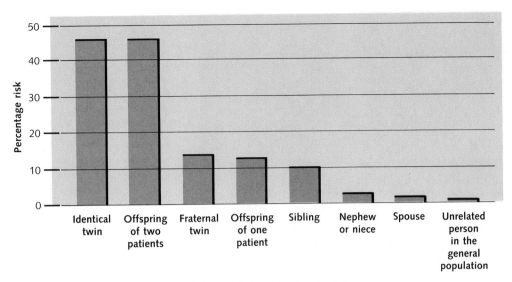

Relationship to schizophrenia victim

Figure 16-10 The lifetime risks of being diagnosed as suffering from schizophrenia are linked with one's genetic relatedness to someone having this disorder. (From Nicol & Gottesman, 1983.)

phrenia are unlikely to "catch" the disorder; but adopted children do have an elevated risk if they have a biological parent diagnosed as having schizophrenia.

The genetic contribution to schizophrenia is beyond question. Nonetheless, the genetic role is not so straightforward as the heritability of eye color. After all, about half the identical twins whose twins develop schizophrenia do *not* develop the disorder. Thus, behavior geneticists Susan Nicol and Irving Gottesman (1983) conclude that some people "have a genetic predisposition to the disorder but that this predisposition by itself is not sufficient for the development of schizophrenia."

Psychological Factors If, by themselves, genetically predisposed physiological abnormalities do not cause schizophrenia, neither do psychological factors alone. Nicol and Gottesman report that "no environmental causes have been discovered that will invariably, or even with moderate probability, produce schizophrenia in persons who are not related to a schizophrenic."

Nevertheless, if genes predispose some people to *react* to particular experiences by developing a schizophrenia disorder, then there must be identifiable triggering experiences. Researchers have asked: Can stress, such as that experienced by Mark Vonnegut, trigger schizophrenia? Can difficulties in family communications also be a contributing factor?

The answer to each question is perhaps. The psychological triggers of schizophrenia have proved somewhat elusive, partly because they may vary with the type of schizophrenia and whether it is slow-developing and chronic schizophrenia, or a more sudden, acute reaction to stress. It is true that young people with schizophrenia tend to have disturbed communications with their parents, but is this a cause or a result of their disorder? It is true that stressful experiences, biochemical abnormalities, and schizophrenia's symptoms often occur together. But the traffic between brain biochemistry and psychological experiences is two-way, so cause and effect are difficult to sort out. It is true that schizophrenic withdrawal often occurs in adolescence or early

The odds of all four identical quadruplets being diagnosed as having schizophrenia are 1 in 2 billion. But Nora, Iris, Myra, and Hester Genain, shown here at their fifty-first birthday party, were. Problems for the sisters began in high school. Since then they have been in and out of hospitals. Of course, these women shared not only identical genes but also a similar environment.

adulthood, coinciding with the stresses of having to become independent, to assert oneself, and to achieve social success and intimacy. So is schizophrenia the maladaptive coping reaction of biologically vulnerable people?

Hoping to identify the psychological causes of schizophrenia, several investigators are now following the development of "high-risk" children, such as those who were born to a parent suffering from schizophrenia (Asarnow & Goldstein, 1986). By comparing the experiences of those who develop schizophrenia with the experiences of high- and low-risk children who do not, these researchers are beginning to spot the early warning signs of schizophrenia and to identify the environments that are most likely to worsen the condition. So far, these signs include:

having a mother whose schizophrenia was severe and long-lasting;

having had complications at birth;

having been separated from parents;

having short attention spans and poor muscle coordination; and having created disturbances in school.

Most of us can relate to the ups and downs of the mood disorders. The strange thoughts, perceptions, and behaviors of schizophrenia are much harder to identify with. Sometimes our thoughts do jump around, but we do not talk nonsensically. Occasionally we feel unjustly suspicious of someone, but we do not fear that the world is plotting against us. Often our perceptions are distorted, but rarely do we see or hear things that are not there. We have felt regret after laughing at someone's misfortune, but generally we do not giggle in response to bad news. From time to time we just want to be alone, but we do not live in social isolation. However, millions of people around the world do talk strangely, suffer delusions of persecution, hear nonexistent voices, see things that are not there, laugh or cry at inappropriate times, or withdraw into their private imaginary worlds. So long as this is true, the quest to solve the cruel puzzle of schizophrenia will continue.

The annual U.S. government research spending, per patient, has been $10,000 for muscular dystrophy, but only $10 for depression and $14 for schizophrenia (Holden, 1986b).

PERSONALITY DISORDERS

Maladaptive personality traits, or *personality disorders,* are enduring character problems that sometimes coexist with one of the other disorders we have discussed but need not involve any apparent anxiety, depression, or loss of contact with reality. Examples range from the attention-getting emotionality of those with a "histrionic personality disorder" to the self-aggrandizement of those with a "narcissistic personality disorder," who fantasize about their unlimited successes and overreact to criticism.

For society, the most troubling of these disorders is the *antisocial personality* disorder. The person (who used to be called a *sociopath* or a *psychopath*) is typically a male whose lack of conscience becomes apparent before age 15, as he begins to display lying, stealing, fighting, or unrestrained sexual behavior. In adulthood, additional problems may include being unable to keep a job, irresponsible marital and parental behavior, and a record of assaults or other criminal behaviors. When the antisocial personality combines a keen intelligence with amorality, the result may be a charming and clever con artist.

Despite their antisocial behavior, most criminals do not fit the description of those with an antisocial personality disorder. For example, most criminals show some responsible concern for their friends and family members; antisocial personalities seem to have little feeling for anyone and to fear almost nothing. They lie, cheat, and steal without remorse. In extreme cases, the results can be tragic. Henry Lee Lucas reported that at age 13 he strangled a woman who refused him sex. He at one time confessed to having bludgeoned, suffocated, stabbed, shot, or mutilated some 360 women, men, and children over the course of his 32 years of crime. During the last 6 years of his reign of terror, Lucas teamed with Elwood Toole, who slaughtered about 50 people whom he "didn't think was worth living anyhow." It ended when Lucas confessed to stabbing and dismembering his 15-year-old common-law wife, who was Toole's niece.

The antisocial personality expresses little regret over violating others' rights. "Once I've done a crime, I just forget it," said Lucas. Toole was equally matter of fact: "I think of killing like smoking a cigarette, like another habit" (Darrach & Norris, 1984).

As with mood disorders and schizophrenia, the antisocial personality is apparently woven of biological as well as psychological strands. Researchers have also found that when those with antisocial personality disorders await aversive events such as electric shocks or loud noises, they show much less autonomic nervous system arousal than do normal people (Hare, 1975). It simply takes more to excite them.

Charles Manson is perhaps this country's best known example of someone with an extreme antisocial personality disorder.

SHOULD PEOPLE BE LABELED? THE POWER OF PRECONCEPTIONS

As we noted earlier, the practice of attaching diagnostic labels to people has provoked controversy. With broad categories—such as the distinction between mood disorders and schizophrenic disorders—one therapist's diagnosis has more often than not agreed with another's. It is when the diagnoses become more specific—such as disorganized versus undifferentiated schizophrenia—that the labels prove less relia-ble. Critics say that the labels are at best arbitrary and at worst value judgments that, thanks to the medical model, masquerade as science. It is better, they say, to study the roots of specific symptoms, such as delusions or hallucinations, than to study catchall categories such as schizophrenia (Persons, 1986).

Despite the uncertainty that surrounds diagnostic labels, most cli-nicians believe that classification helps in describing, treating, and re-searching the causes of disorders. Critics respond that these benefits come at a cost. Once a diagnostic label is attached, we view the person differently (Farina, 1982). Labels create preconceptions that can bias our perceptions and interpretations.

In the most controversial demonstration of the biasing power of diagnostic labels, David Rosenhan (1973) and seven of his friends and Stanford University colleagues went to mental hospital admissions of-fices, complaining of "hearing voices" that were saying "empty," "hol-low," and "thud." Apart from this complaint and giving false names and occupations, they truthfully answered all the questions. All eight were diagnosed as psychotic, seven of them as suffering from schizo-phrenia.

That these normal people were misdiagnosed is not surprising. As one psychiatrist noted, if someone swallowed some blood, went to an emergency room, and spit it up, would we fault the doctor for diagnos-ing a bleeding ulcer? More startling is the fact that although the "pa-tients" exhibited no further symptoms after being admitted, the clini-cians were able to "discover" the causes of their disorders after analyzing their (quite normal) life histories. One person was said to be reacting to mixed emotions about his parents. Furthermore, before being released (an average of 19 days later) the normal behaviors of the "patients," such as note-taking, were often either overlooked or misin-terpreted as symptoms.

Other studies confirm that a label can affect how we perceive someone. Ellen Langer and her colleagues (1974, 1980) had people evaluate an interviewee they thought was either normal (such as a job applicant) or out of the ordinary (such as a psychiatric patient or a cancer patient). When all subjects were shown the identical videotape, interviewees who carried no special label were perceived as normal people. But those who had been labeled were frequently perceived by laypeople as "different from most people," and by therapists (who thought they were evaluating a patient) as "frightened of his own ag-gressive impulses," "passive, dependent type," and so forth. Thus, while a label can serve a useful purpose, it can, as Rosenhan discov-ered, have "a life and an influence of its own."

Labels can also affect people's self-images and stigmatize them in others' eyes. Senator Thomas Eagleton experienced this when, in 1972, he was dumped as the Democratic party's vice-presidential candidate after it was discovered that he had been treated with electroshock ther-apy for being depressed. The same stigma was revealed when a female associate of psychologist Stewart Page (1977) called 180 people in To-ronto who had advertised furnished rooms for rent. When she merely asked if the room was still available, the answer was nearly always yes. When she said that she was about to be released from a mental hospi-tal, the answer three times out of four was no (as it was, incidentally, when she said she was calling for her brother who was about to be released from jail). When some of those who answered no were called by a second person who simply asked if the room was still available, the advertiser nearly always revealed that it still was.

"One of the unpardonable sins, in the eyes of most people, is for a man to go about unlabelled. The world regards such a person as the police do an unmuzzled dog, not under proper control."
T. H. Huxley,
Evolution and Ethics, 1893

If people form their impressions of psychological disorder from the media, such findings are hardly surprising. Television researcher George Gerbner (1985) reports that 1 in 5 prime-time and daytime programs depicts a psychologically disordered person, and the odds are 7 in 10 that this character is portrayed as a violent person or a criminal. More than a few schizophrenia-prone people do commit crimes (Silverton, 1988), and there do indeed exist some disordered people who are amoral and antisocial. However, most disordered people are *not* dangerous. They are instead anxious, depressed, or withdrawn.

Labels not only bias perceptions (the "to believe is to see" effect), they can also change reality. When teachers are told that certain students are "gifted," when students expect someone to be "hostile," or when interviewers check to see whether someone is indeed "extraverted," they often act in ways that elicit the very behavior expected (Snyder, 1984). Labels can serve as self-fulfilling prophecies.

But let us also remember the benefits of diagnostic labels. As Robert Spitzer (1975), the chief author of DSM-III-R, explains:

> There is a purpose to psychiatric diagnosis. It is to enable mental health professionals to (a) communicate with each other about the subject matter of their concern, (b) comprehend the pathological processes involved in psychiatric illness, and (c) control psychiatric outcomes.

We need not dismiss psychological labels to be encouraged by the fact that many successful people—including Leonardo da Vinci, Isaac Newton, and Leo Tolstoy—endured psychological difficulties while pursuing brilliant careers. The bewilderment, fear, and sorrow caused by psychological disorders are real. As we will see in the next chapter, the hope that these conditions can be alleviated is real as well.

SUMMING UP

PERSPECTIVES ON PSYCHOLOGICAL DISORDERS

Defining Psychological Disorders Between normality and abnormality there is not a gulf, but a fine and somewhat arbitrarily drawn line. Where the line is drawn is usually based on a variety of criteria, such as how atypical, disturbing, maladaptive, and unjustifiable a person's behavior is. Insanity, on the other hand, is a legal term that is now applied in rare cases where defendants are judged not to have known that what they were doing was wrong.

Understanding Psychological Disorders The medical model's assumption that psychological disorders are mental illnesses has displaced earlier views that demons and evil spirits were to blame. However, critics question the medical model's labeling of psychological disorders as sicknesses; they argue that the disorders are socially defined and that the labels may be self-fulfilling.

Classifying Psychological Disorders Many psychiatrists and psychologists believe that a system for naming and describing psychological disorders facilitates treatment and research. In the United States, the revised third edition of the *Diagnostic and Statistical Manual of Mental Disorders* (DSM-III-R) is the authoritative classification scheme

ANXIETY DISORDERS

Those who suffer an anxiety disorder may for no apparent reason feel uncontrollably tense and uneasy (generalized anxiety disorder). They may be irrationally afraid of a specific object or situation (phobic disorder), or troubled by repetitive thoughts and actions (obsessive-compulsive disorder).

SOMATOFORM DISORDERS

The somatoform disorders involve a somatic (bodily) symptom—a physiologically unexplained but genuinely felt ailment. Freud was particularly fascinated by conversion disorders, in which anxiety seemed to be converted to a symptom that had no physiological basis. Today, hypochondriasis (interpreting one's normal sensations as symptoms of a dreaded disease) is a much more common disorder.

DISSOCIATIVE DISORDERS

Under stress a person's conscious awareness will sometimes become dissociated, or separated, from previous memories, thoughts, and feelings. Dissociative amnesia usually involves selective forgetting in response to stress. Fugue involves not only forgetting one's identity but fleeing one's home. Most mysterious of all dissociative disorders are cases of multiple personality in which a person is said to have two or more distinct personalities, with the original typically unaware of the other(s).

MOOD DISORDERS

Major Depression   In major depression, the person—without apparent reason—descends for weeks or months into deep unhappiness, lethargy, and feelings of worthlessness before rebounding to normality.

Bipolar Disorder   In the less common bipolar disorder, the person alternates between the hopelessness and lethargy of depression and the hyperactive, wildly optimistic, impulsive phase of mania.

Explaining Mood Disorders   Current research on depression is vigorously exploring (1) genetic predispositions and neurotransmitter abnormalities and (2) cyclic self-defeating beliefs, learned helplessness, negative attributions, and aversive experiences.

SCHIZOPHRENIC DISORDERS

Symptoms of Schizophrenia   Schizophrenia shows itself in disordered thinking (nonsensical talk and delusions, which may stem from a breakdown of selective attention); disturbed perceptions (including hallucinations); and inappropriate emotions and actions.

Types of Schizophrenia   Schizophrenia is actually a set of disorders (classified as disorganized, catatonic, paranoid, undifferentiated, and residual) that emerge either gradually from a long history of social inadequacy (in which case the outlook is dim) or suddenly in reaction to stress (in which case the prospects for recovery are brighter).

Understanding Schizophrenia   As they have for depression, researchers have identified brain abnormalities (such as in the neurotransmitter dopamine) that seem linked with certain forms of schizophrenia. Twin and adoption studies also point to a genetic predisposition that, in conjunction with environmental factors, may bring about a schizophrenia disorder.

PERSONALITY DISORDERS

Personality disorders are enduring, maladaptive personality traits. For society, the most troubling of these is the remorseless and fearless antisocial personality.

SHOULD PEOPLE BE LABELED? THE POWER OF PRECONCEPTIONS

Critics of diagnostic classification point out that for the benefits we derive from labeling people we pay a price. Labels facilitate mental health professionals' communications and research. But they also create preconceptions that bias our perceptions of people's past and present behavior and unfairly stigmatize people.

TERMS AND CONCEPTS TO REMEMBER

amnesia   Loss of memory. Psychogenic amnesia, a dissociative disorder, is selective memory loss often brought on by extreme stress.

antisocial personality   A personality disorder in which the person (usually a male) exhibits a lack of conscience for wrongdoing, even toward friends and family members. May be aggressive and ruthless or a clever con artist.

anxiety disorders   Psychological disorders characterized by distressing, persistent anxiety or maladaptive behaviors that reduce anxiety. See *generalized anxiety disorder*, *phobic disorder*, and *obsessive-compulsive disorder*.

bipolar disorder   A mood disorder in which the person alternates between the hopelessness and lethargy of depression and the overexcited, hyperactive, wildly optimistic state of mania.

conversion disorder   Now rare, a somatoform disorder in which a person experiences very specific genuine physical symptoms for which no physiological basis can be found.

delusions   False beliefs, often of persecution or grandeur, that may accompany psychotic disorders.

dissociative disorders   Disorders in which conscious awareness becomes separated (dissociated) from previous memories, thoughts, and feelings. See *amnesia*, *fugue*, and *multiple personality*.

DSM-III-R   The American Psychiatric Association's *Diagnostic and Statistical Manual of Mental Disorders (Third Edition–Revised)*, a widely used system for classifying psychological disorders.

fugue [fewg]   A dissociative disorder in which amnesia is accompanied by physical flight from one's home and identity.

generalized anxiety disorder An anxiety disorder in which a person is continually tense, apprehensive, and in a state of autonomic nervous system arousal.

hypochondriasis A somatoform disorder in which a person misinterprets normal physical sensations as symptoms of a disease.

insane A legal term for someone who has committed a crime but is judged not to have understood that the act was wrong at the time of the crime.

major depression A mood disorder in which a person, for no apparent reason, experiences two or more weeks of depressed moods, feelings of worthlessness, and diminished interest or pleasure in most activities.

mania A hyperactive, wildly optimistic state.

medical model The concept that diseases have physical causes and that they can be diagnosed, treated, and, in most cases, cured. When applied to psychological disorders, the medical model assumes that these "mental" illnesses can be diagnosed on the basis of their symptoms and cured through therapy, which may include treatment in a psychiatric hospital.

mood disorders Psychological disorders characterized by emotional extremes. See *major depression* and *bipolar disorder*.

multiple personality disorder A formerly rare dissociative disorder in which a person exhibits two or more distinct and alternating personalities.

neurotic disorders Psychological disorders that are usually distressing, but allow one to think rationally and function socially. The neurotic disorders are usually viewed as ways of dealing with anxiety.

obsessive-compulsive disorder An anxiety disorder in which a person is troubled by unwanted repetitive thoughts (obsessions) and/or actions (compulsions).

panic attack An episode of intense dread in which a person experiences terror and accompanying chest pain, choking, or other frightening sensations for a number of minutes.

personality disorders Psychological disorders characterized by enduring, maladaptive character traits. See *antisocial personality*.

phobic disorder An anxiety disorder in which a person is troubled by a phobia—a persistent, irrational fear of a specific object or situation.

psychological disorder Behavior that is typically defined on the basis of being atypical, disturbing, maladaptive, and unjustifiable.

psychotic disorders Psychological disorder in which a person loses contact with reality, experiencing irrational ideas and distorted perceptions.

schizophrenia A group of psychotic disorders characterized by disorganized thinking, disturbed perceptions, and inappropriate emotions and actions.

somatoform disorders Psychological disorders in which the symptoms take a somatic (bodily) form without apparent physical cause. See *conversion disorder* and *hypochondriasis*.

FOR FURTHER READING

Diagnostic and statistical manual of mental disorders (3rd ed., revised, 1987). Washington, DC: American Psychiatric Association.

Provides the most widely accepted definitions and descriptions of the categories of psychological disorder, including those described in this chapter.

Neale, J. M., Oltmann, T. F., & Davison, G. C. (1986). *Case studies in abnormal psychology* (2nd ed.). New York: Wiley.

Describes the development and treatment of psychological disorders, including cases of depression, school phobia, bulimia, and psychosexual disorders.

Sheehan, S. (1982). *Is there no place on earth for me?* Boston: Houghton Mifflin.

This Pulitzer prize–winning biography chronicles the transformation of "Sylvia Frumkin" from a highly intelligent grade-school student through her subsequent 17 years in mental institutions. Sheehan, who followed Sylvia as she journeyed in and out of mental hospitals, and in and out of reality, writes skillfully and compassionately.

Torrey, E. F. (1984). *Surviving schizophrenia: A family manual.* New York: Harper & Row.

A comprehensive and caring guide to coping with schizophrenia, written for laypeople.

CHAPTER 17

Therapy

The history of our attempts to treat psychological disorders reveals how mystifying and intractable we have found these problems to be. In other realms of science our record of progress is impressive; in the 2200 years since Eratosthenes correctly estimated the earth's circumference, we have charted the heavens, explored the solar system, reconstructed the basic history of life on earth, cracked the genetic code, and eliminated or found cures for all sorts of diseases. Meanwhile, we have attempted to alleviate psychological disorders with a bewildering variety of methods, harsh and gentle: by cutting holes in the head and by giving warm baths and massages; by restraining, bleeding, or "beating the devil" out of people and by placing them in sunny, serene environments; by administering drugs and electric shocks and by talking—talking about childhood experiences, about current feelings, about maladaptive thoughts and behaviors.

We can now state with certainty the chemical composition of Jupiter's atmosphere, but when it comes to understanding and treating what is much closer to home—the psychological disorders described in Chapter 16—we are only beginning to make real progress. The therapies clinicians favor depend on the most persuasive explanations of the disorder. Those who believe that a particular disordered behavior is learned tend to favor a psychological therapy. Those who view a disorder as biologically rooted are likely to advocate medication, too. Those who believe that certain disorders are a response to social conditions will also want to reform the "sick" environment.

Treatment of mental disorders in the eighteenth century. William Hogarth's (1697–1764) famous engraving (left) of St. Mary of Bethlehem hospital in London (commonly called Bedlam). Patients were treated like animals. Hospitals were unheated and basic human amenities were neglected. This chair (right) was designed by Benjamin Rush (1746–1813) "for the benefit of maniacal patients." Rush, considered by many the father of the American movement for more humane treatment of the mentally ill, believed that they required care to regain their sensibilities.

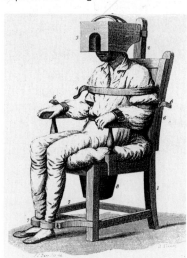

A catalog of all the therapies that have been tried at one time or another can, however, be organized with only two main sections: the psychological therapies (therapies that involve verbal interaction between a trained professional and a client with a problem) and the biomedical therapies (therapies that alter the structure or functioning of the nervous system).

THE PSYCHOLOGICAL THERAPIES

Psychological therapy, or *psychotherapy,* is "a planned, emotionally charged, confiding interaction between a trained, socially sanctioned healer and a sufferer" (Frank, 1982). From among the 250 or more types of psychotherapy (Parloff, 1987), we will consider only the most widespread. Each technique is distinctive, yet common threads run through them all. Therapists who view disorders as an interplay of biopsychosocial influences may welcome a combination of treatments. Indeed, half of all psychotherapists describe themselves as *eclectic*—as using a blend of therapies (D. Smith, 1982). Depending on the client and the problem, an eclectic therapist will use or mix a variety of techniques. Let us first consider the basic theoretical perspectives upon which the aims and techniques of each therapy are built—the psychoanalytic, humanistic, behavioral, and cognitive perspectives first introduced in Chapter 1.

PSYCHOANALYSIS

Although most of today's therapists do not practice as Sigmund Freud did, his psychoanalytic techniques for treating psychological disorders warrant our attention. *Psychoanalysis* is part of our modern vocabulary, and its assumptions influence many other therapies.

Aims   As we noted in our consideration of Freud in Chapters 15 and 16, psychoanalysis assumes that psychological problems are fueled by unconscious impulses and conflicts, many of which develop and are repressed in childhood. Psychoanalysts attempt to bring these repressed feelings into conscious awareness so that they can be dealt with. By gradually gaining conscious insight into the origins of the disorder—by fulfilling the ancient imperative to "know thyself" in a deep way—the person in analysis "works through" the buried feelings. This is said to release the energy that was previously devoted to id-ego-superego conflicts, allowing it to be redirected toward healthier, more anxiety-free living.

Methods   Psychoanalysis probes the past in hopes of unraveling the present. But how? When Freud discarded hypnosis, he turned to free association. Imagine yourself as a patient using the free association technique: The analyst invites you to relax in a comfortable position, perhaps by lying on a couch. He or she will probably sit out of your line of vision, helping you to focus attention on your internal thoughts and feelings. Beginning with a childhood memory, a dream, or a recent experience, you say aloud whatever comes to your mind from moment to moment. It sounds easy, but soon you become aware how often you edit your thoughts as you speak, by omitting material that seems trivial, irrelevant, or shameful. Even in the relatively safe presence of the analyst, you may pause momentarily before uttering an embarrassing

In this classical Freudian setting, the psychoanalyst minimizes distraction from the inward journey by sitting out of view of the patient on the couch.

thought. You may make a joking remark or change the subject to something less threatening. Sometimes your mind may go blank or you may find yourself unable to remember important details.

To the psychoanalyst, these blocks in the flow of your free associations are *resistances.* They hint that anxiety lurks and that sensitive material is being repressed. The analyst will want to explore these sensitive areas, first by making you aware of your resistances, and later by helping you to interpret their underlying meaning. The analyst's *interpretations*—suggestions of hidden feelings and conflicts—are considered an important avenue to insight. If offered at the right moment, the analyst's interpretation of what your avoidance of a particular topic—say, your not wanting to talk about your mother—really might mean may help you become aware of what you are avoiding. You may then discover more about what your resistances mean and how they fit with other pieces of your psychological puzzle.

Freud believed that another clue to repressed impulses is the *latent content* of our dreams (see page 204). Thus, after inviting you to report a dream, the analyst may suggest its hidden meaning, thereby adding yet another piece to your developing self-portrait.

Drawing by Miller; © 1983 The New Yorker Magazine, Inc.

After many such sessions you will likely have disclosed more of yourself to your analyst than you have ever revealed to anyone. Because psychoanalytic theory emphasizes the formative power of childhood experiences, much of what you reveal will pertain to your childhood. You will also probably find yourself experiencing strong positive or negative feelings for your analyst, feelings that express the dependency or mingled love and anger that you earlier experienced toward family members or other important people in your life. When this happens, Freud would say that you are actually "transferring" to the analyst your strongest feelings from those other relationships. Analysts and other therapists believe that this *transference* exposes long-repressed feelings, giving you a belated chance to work through them with your analyst's help. By examining your feelings toward the analyst you may also gain insight into your current relationships with others.

Critics say that psychoanalysts' after-the-fact interpretations are hard to disprove. If, in response to the analyst's suggested interpretation, you say, "Yes! I see now," your acceptance confirms the analyst's interpretation. If you emphatically say, "No! That doesn't ring true," your denial may be taken to reveal more resistance, which would also confirm the interpretation. Although psychoanalysts acknowledge that their interpretations cannot be proved or disproved, they insist that they often are of great help to patients.

Second, traditional psychoanalysis is criticized for being a long, hard, expensive process. It generally requires up to several years of several sessions a week with a highly trained and well-paid analyst. Only those with a high income or generous health benefits can afford such treatment.

Third, psychoanalysis has been criticized for rationalizing the oppression of women. Freud suggested that women's "penis envy" made it difficult for them to develop the strong superego necessary for making important social contributions. Psychoanalysts who agree with Freud that anatomy is destiny may therefore influence women to adjust to a status quo that assumes their biological and social inferiority.

Although there are relatively few classical psychoanalysts, many therapists are influenced by psychoanalytic assumptions. This influence can be seen in any therapist who tries to understand patients' current symptoms by exploring their childhood experiences; who probes for repressed, emotion-laden information; who seeks to help people gain insight into the unconscious roots of problems and work through newly resurrected feelings. Although influenced by psycho-analysis, these therapists may talk to people face-to-face (rather than out of the line of vision) once a week (rather than several times weekly) and only for a few weeks or months (rather than several years).

One such therapist is David Malan, who in the following session with a depressed woman seeks to help her gain insight into the source of her problems. Note how Malan interprets the woman's earlier re-marks and suggests that she is repeating a characteristic pattern of behavior in her relationship with him (1978, pp. 133–134):

> *Malan: I get the feeling that you're the sort of person who needs to keep active. If you don't keep active, then something goes wrong. Is that true?*
>
> *Patient: Yes.*
>
> *Malan: I get a second feeling about you and that is that you must, underneath all this, have an awful lot of very strong and upsetting feelings. Somehow they're there but you aren't really quite in touch with them. Isn't this right? I feel you've been like that as long as you can remember.*
>
> *Patient: For quite a few years, whenever I really sat down and thought about it I got depressed, so I tried not to think about it.*
>
> *Malan: You see, you've established a pattern, haven't you? You're even like that here with me, because in spite of the fact that you're in some trouble and you feel that the bottom is falling out of your world, the way you're telling me this is just as if there wasn't anything wrong.*

Although in this therapy session the couch has disappeared, the influence of psycho-analytic theory probably has not, especially if the therapist probes for the origin of the patient's symptoms by analyzing repressed information from her past.

HUMANISTIC THERAPIES

As we noted in Chapter 15, the humanistic perspective emphasizes people's inherent potential for self-fulfillment. Not surprisingly, then, humanistic therapists attempt to facilitate self-fulfillment by helping people grow in self-awareness and self-acceptance. Unlike psychoana-lytic therapists, humanistic therapists tend to focus on:

the present instead of the past;

becoming aware of feelings as they occur rather than achieving insights into the childhood origins of the feelings;

conscious rather than unconscious material;

taking immediate responsibility for one's feelings and actions rather than uncovering the hidden obstacles to doing so; and

promoting growth and fulfillment instead of curing illness.

Person-Centered Therapy   The best known and most widely used humanistic therapy is an outgrowth of Carl Rogers' (1961, 1980) person-centered perspective on personality. Because the therapist seeks to focus on the person's own conscious self-perceptions rather than the therapist's interpretations, the therapy is called ***person-centered*** (or, as Rogers formerly called it, *client-centered*). Rather than directing the client toward certain insights, the therapist listens, with-out judgment or interpretation. This therapy has therefore also been called *nondirective* therapy.

Believing that people already possess within themselves the re-sources for growth, Rogers encouraged therapists to exhibit *genuine-ness, acceptance,* and *empathy,* which he believed would enable clients to accept themselves and fulfill their potential (see Chapter 15). When

Carl Rogers, at right, actively listening to a client during a group therapy session.

therapists drop their facades and genuinely express their true feelings, when they enable their clients to feel unconditionally accepted, and when they empathically sense and reflect their clients' feelings, the clients may increase their self-understanding and self-acceptance. Rogers (1980, p. 10) explained:

> Hearing has consequences. When I truly hear a person and the meanings that are important to him at that moment, hearing not simply his words, but him, and when I let him know that I have heard his own private personal meanings, many things happen. There is first of all a grateful look. He feels released. He wants to tell me more about his world. He surges forth in a new sense of freedom. He becomes more open to the process of change.
>
> I have often noticed that the more deeply I hear the meanings of the person, the more there is that happens. Almost always, when a person realizes he has been deeply heard, his eyes moisten. I think in some real sense he is weeping for joy. It is as though he were saying, "Thank God, somebody heard. Someone knows what it's like to be me."

"Hearing" refers to Rogers' technique of *active listening*— echoing, restating, and seeking clarification of what the person has said, and acknowledging the expressed feelings. Active listening has become an accepted part of therapeutic counseling practices in many schools, colleges, and clinics. The counselor listens attentively and interrupts only to restate and confirm feelings that the client has expressed, to indicate acceptance of what the client is expressing, or to ask for clarification. In fact, active listening is so easily described (though not so easily practiced) that computer scientist Joseph Weizenbaum developed a delightful computer program named ELIZA that simulates a Rogerian counselor. A few moments ago I (DGM) sat before a computer terminal and had the following conversation with ELIZA:

"We have two ears and one mouth that we may listen the more and talk the less."
Zeno, 335–263 B.C.
Diogenes Laertius

ELIZA: *How do you do. Please state your problem.*

DGM: *Hi, I guess I am feeling just a little nervous.*

ELIZA: *How long have you been feeling a little nervous?*

DGM: *I suppose that when I am writing I am always a little anxious.*

ELIZA: *Can you think of a specific example?*

DGM: *Well, I'm wondering whether students will find this stuff as interesting as I do.*

ELIZA: *Why do you believe it isn't normal to be wondering whether students will find this stuff as interesting as you do?*

DGM: *Maybe it is normal. I guess every author must feel the same. . . .*

ELIZA: *What are your feelings now?*

DGM: *Glad that you are willing to listen.*

ELIZA: *Why would you confide in someone who is willing to listen?*

DGM: *Sometimes it just helps to talk things over.*

ELIZA: *What does that suggest to you?*

DGM: *Perhaps that I should share my feelings more openly.*

ELIZA: *Your feelings more openly.*

DGM: *Yes.*

ELIZA: *I understand, please go on.*

DGM: *Do you understand?*

ELIZA: *Oh, I do understand at times.*

Although ELIZA is infinitely patient and nonjudgmental, she does not understand; she is nothing more than what Weizenbaum programmed—a parody of a nonjudgmental, person-centered therapist. Real interaction requires what the computer lacks—a sensitivity to meaning and an ability to clarify by reflecting meanings in *different* words. Compare ELIZA's conversation with me to the interaction between Carl Rogers and a quiet, troubled, 28-year-old male client (Meador & Rogers, 1984, p. 167):

Client: *I just ain't no good to nobody, never was, and never will be.*

Rogers: *Feeling that now, hm? That you're just no good to yourself, no good to anybody. Never will be any good to anybody. Just that you're completely worthless, huh?—Those really are lousy feelings. Just feel that you're no good at all, hm?*

Client: *Yeah. (Muttering in low, discouraged voice) That's what this guy I went to town with just the other day told me.*

Rogers: *This guy that you went to town with really told you that you were no good? Is that what you're saying? Did I get that right?*

Client: *M-hm.*

Rogers: *I guess the meaning of that if I get it right is that here's somebody that— meant something to you and what does he think of you? Why, he's told you that he thinks you're no good at all. And that just really knocks the props out from under you. (Client weeps quietly.) It just brings the tears. (Silence of 20 seconds)*

Client: *(Rather defiantly) I don't care though.*

Rogers: *You tell yourself you don't care at all, but somehow I guess some part of you cares because some part of you weeps over it.*

As this brief therapy excerpt illustrates, the person-centered counselor seeks to provide a psychological mirror that helps clients to see themselves more clearly. But can a therapist be a perfect mirror, without selecting and interpreting what is reflected? Rogers concedes that one cannot be *totally* nondirective but that the most important contribution the therapist can make is to accept and understand the client. In this nonjudgmental environment people can come to accept even the ugly or unwanted parts of themselves and feel valued and whole.

Gestalt Therapy   Another influential humanistic therapy, developed by Fritz Perls (1969), joins the psychoanalytic emphasis on bringing unconscious feelings and conflicts into awareness with the humanistic emphasis on getting in touch with oneself and taking responsibility for oneself in the present. Perls's *Gestalt therapy* aims to make people whole by breaking through their defenses and helping them sense and express their moment-to-moment feelings. "All therapy that has to be done can only be done in the now," said Perls (1970). "Nothing exists except in the now."

Eavesdropping on a Gestalt therapy session, we might hear the therapist using any one of several techniques for getting people to express their real feelings and to "own responsibility" for them. One way is to train people to speak in the first person (Passons, 1975, p. 79):

Client: *When you go skiing you feel healthy and vigorous. You have this sense of excitement.*

Therapist: *Sue, try saying the same thing only substituting the word "I" for "you."*

Client: *Why?*

Therapist: *Because I believe you're saying something about yourself except you're not sounding that way.*

Client: *When I'm skiing I feel healthy and excited.*

Therapist: *Do you hear the difference?*

Client: *Yes. The second one is what I really meant.*

To get people to take responsibility for their feelings, the Gestalt therapist might get people to change their verbs—to say "I want" instead of "I need," "I choose to" instead of "I have to," and "I won't" instead of "I can't" (Passons, 1975, p. 82):

Client: *Every day I just sit there and feel like a stooge. I just can't speak up in that class.*

Therapist: *You say you can't.*

Client: *That's right. I've tried and I know I should, I mean I know the stuff, that's not the problem. I just can't get the words out.*

Therapist: *Try saying "I won't talk" instead of "I can't talk."*

Client: *I won't talk in that class.*

Therapist: *Let yourself feel how you are refusing to talk.*

Client: *I guess I am holding myself back a little.*

Therapist: *What are your objections to speaking up?*

Client: *Well, everyone else in there seems to be talking just to talk. I don't like doing that.*

Gestalt therapists also capitalize on the power of actions to affect thoughts and feelings (see also Chapter 19, Social Influence). The therapist may ask people to role-play different aspects of their relationships, or to act out suppressed feelings. The ultimate goal—to become better aware of and able to express one's own feelings—exemplifies the humanistic value of being true to oneself, a value that some critics believe promotes self-centeredness. This value is epitomized in Perls's Gestalt credo (1972, p. 70):

I do my thing, and you do your thing.
I am not in this world to live up to your expectations.
And you are not in this world to live up to mine.
You are you and I am I,
And if by chance we find each other, it's beautiful.
If not, it can't be helped.

Group Therapies   Most of the therapies we are considering in this chapter may also occur in therapist-led groups of usually eight to ten people. While it does not provide the same degree of involvement by the therapist in each client's concern, group therapy saves therapists' time and clients' money. More important, the social context allows people to discover that other people have problems similar to their own and to try out new ways of behaving. As you have perhaps experienced, it can be a relief to find that you are not alone—to learn that

It's not always true that "misery loves company." But as often happens in group therapy, it helps to realize that others' fears of disapproval and rejection are much like our own.

others, despite their seeming composure, share your problems and your feelings of loneliness, inadequacy, or anger. Such has been the experience of a wide range of people, from cancer patients to dieters to alcoholics (Yalom, 1985).

One popular form of group experience for those not seriously disturbed began as sensitivity training groups ("T-groups" for short) in which teachers, executives, and others practiced ways of relating to one another more sensitively and openly. In groups of between twelve and twenty that met for limited periods of time, people were encouraged to be less inhibited and defensive in their interactions with others, to "talk straight" and to listen empathically. Before long, Carl Rogers (1970) and others were offering *encounter groups*—groups in which emotion-laden and confrontational experiences were honest and open. Although encounter groups are not as popular today as they were during the 1970s, they set the stage for the emergence of various sorts of self-help and support groups—for substance abusers, divorced people, the bereaved, as well as for those who are simply seeking personal growth.

BEHAVIOR THERAPIES

So far, all the therapies we have considered assume that psychological problems diminish as self-awareness grows. When the psychoanalyst helps people gain insight into their unresolved and unconscious tensions, or when the humanistic therapist enables people to "get in touch with their feelings," symptoms are expected to subside. Behavior therapists, however, doubt that self-awareness is the key. They assume that the symptoms *are* the problems. You can, for example, become aware of why you are highly anxious during exams and still be anxious. So instead of trying to alleviate distressing symptoms by resolving a presumed underlying problem, *behavior therapy* applies learning principles to the elimination of the unwanted behavior.

Symptoms such as phobias, sexual dysfunctions, or depression, for example, can be viewed as products of learning. The aim of behavior therapy is to eliminate the problem thoughts and maladaptive behaviors and replace them with more constructive ways of thinking and acting, without delving deep below the surface looking for inner causes.

Classical Conditioning Therapies   One cluster of behavior therapies is derived from principles developed in Pavlov's classic experiments on the conditioning of dogs. As Pavlov and others demonstrated, various behaviors and emotions can be acquired through classical conditioning. If a maladaptive symptom, such as claustrophobic fear of elevators, is assumed to be a conditioned response to the stimulus of being in an enclosed space, then by applying extinction principles, the fear response might be unlearned. Even better, by using *counterconditioning,* the stimulus could be paired with a new response that is incompatible with fear. If an adaptive, relaxed response can be paired repeatedly with the enclosed space of the elevator, the fear response might be displaced. Two such counterconditioning techniques are *systematic desensitization* and *aversive conditioning.*

Systematic Desensitization   Picture this scene reported in 1924 by Mary Cover Jones, an associate of the behaviorist John B. Watson. Three-year-old Peter is woefully afraid of various objects, including animals such as rabbits and rats. (Unlike Little Albert's laboratory-conditioned fear of white rats, described in Chapter 9, Peter's fears have arisen over the course of his life at home and are more intense.) Jones's aim is to replace the fear with a conditioned response that is incompatible with fear. Her strategy: to associate a fear-evoking rabbit with the pleasurable, relaxed response associated with eating.

As the hungry child begins eating his midafternoon snack, Jones introduces a caged rabbit on the other side of the huge room. Peter hardly notices as he eagerly munches his crackers and milk. On succeeding days, the rabbit is gradually moved closer and closer. Within 2 months, Peter not only tolerates the rabbit in his lap, but he strokes it with one hand while he eats with the other. Moreover, his fear of other furry objects subsides as well, having been "countered" or replaced by a relaxed state that cannot coexist with fear (Fisher, 1984; Jones 1924).

Unfortunately for those who might have been helped by her counterconditioning procedures, Jones's story of Peter and the rabbit did not immediately become part of psychology's lore. It was not until more than 30 years later that her technique was refined by psychiatrist Joseph Wolpe (1958, 1982) into what has become the most widely used method of behavior therapy: *systematic desensitization.* Wolpe assumed, as did Jones, that you cannot simultaneously be anxious and relaxed. Therefore, if you can repeatedly relax when faced with anxiety-provoking stimuli, you will gradually eliminate your anxiety. The trick is to proceed gradually.

Let's see how this might work with a common phobia—fear of public speaking. If you were troubled by this fear, a behavior therapist might first ask your help in constructing a hierarchy of anxiety-triggering speaking situations. Your anxiety hierarchy could range from mildly anxiety-provoking situations, such as speaking up in a small informal group of friends, to panic-provoking situations such as having to address a large audience.

The therapist would then train you in relaxation. You learn to relax one muscle group after another, until you achieve a drowsy state of complete relaxation and blissful comfort. Then, with your eyes closed, the therapist asks you to imagine a situation listed on your hierarchy that is mildly anxiety-arousing. Perhaps you are having coffee with a group of your friends, and you are deciding whether or not to speak up. If imagining the scene causes you to feel any anxiety at all you signal your tension by raising your finger, and the therapist instructs you to switch off the mental image and go back to deep relaxation.

Behavior therapies have been particularly successful in dealing with phobias. The lives of the women in each of these photos will be greatly improved by successful treatment. The woman on the right in the top photo is being helped to overcome a fear of heights so severe that she is unable to walk down a flight of steps. The woman at the right in the bottom photo is participating in a desensitization group for people who are afraid to fly. Her therapist, left, is encouraging her. The treatment has progressed to the point where group members are able to tolerate sitting in a grounded airplane.

This scene is imagined over and over until you can feel completely relaxed while imagining it, with no trace of anxiety. Gradually but systematically over several therapy sessions, the therapist progresses up your anxiety hierarchy, using the relaxed state to desensitize you to each imagined situation. Next you practice the imagined behaviors in actual situations, beginning with relatively easy tasks and gradually moving to more anxiety-filled ones (see Figure 17–1). Conquering your anxiety in an actual situation, not just in your imagination, can raise your feelings of self-efficacy (Foa & Kozak, 1986; Williams, 1987b). Eventually, you actually may be able to speak in public without fear.

Systematic desensitization is sometimes combined with other techniques. With phobias, desensitization techniques may be supplemented by having someone model appropriate behavior in a fear-arousing situation. For example, if you were afraid of snakes, you would first observe someone handling a snake and then would be coaxed in gradual steps to approach, touch, and handle it yourself (Bandura & others, 1969). By applying this principle of observational learning, therapists have helped people overcome disruptive fears of snakes, spiders, and dogs.

Notice that the systematic desensitization procedure makes no attempt to help you achieve insight into the underlying cause of the fear.

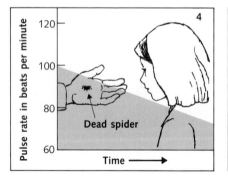

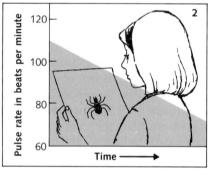

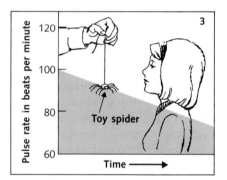

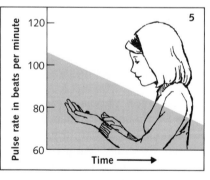

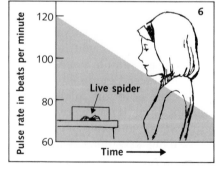

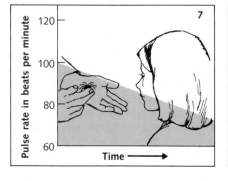

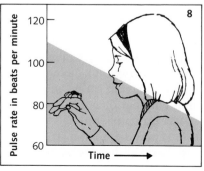

Figure 17–1   Desensitization of a phobia. Beverly, who is terribly afraid of spiders, is gradually able to relax—as shown by her decreasing pulse rate as she spends time in the presence of the aversive object—first at the sight of a spider, then in the presence of a toy spider, a dead spider, and a live one. (From Gilling & Brightwell, 1982.)

If you are afraid of heights, the therapist will not be particularly concerned with the first time you experienced this fear or what may have caused it. Nor do behavior therapists worry that if your fear of heights is eliminated, an underlying problem may still remain and be expressed now as, say, a fear of elevators. On the contrary, they argue, overcoming maladaptive symptoms helps people to feel better about themselves in general and to begin acting in ways that bring greater life satisfaction.

Aversive Conditioning   In systematically desensitizing a patient, the therapist seeks to substitute a positive (relaxed) response for a negative (fearful) response to a harmless stimulus. In *aversive conditioning,* the therapist attempts to replace a positive response to an attractive but harmful stimulus with a negative (aversive) response. Aversive conditioning is thus the reverse of systematic desensitization.

The procedure is simple: It associates unwanted behavior with unpleasant experiences. For example, in treating an alcoholic, aversion therapists administer a drug that produces violent nausea when alcohol is consumed. By linking the drinking of alcohol with violent nausea, the therapist seeks to transform the alcoholic's reaction to alcohol from positive to negative (Figure 17–2). Similarly, by giving child molesters electric shocks as they view photos of nude children, aversion therapists have tried to eliminate the molesters' sexual response to children. And by giving withdrawn and self-abusing autistic children harmless ''aversives,'' such as a spray of cold water in the face, such therapists hope to suppress self-injury while reinforcing more appropriate behavior. Because this therapy involves an unpleasant experience, it is practiced sparingly and only with the parent's or patient's consent.

Does aversive conditioning work? In the short run it may. But, as we saw in Chapter 9, the problem is that conditioning is influenced by cognition. People know that outside the therapist's office they can drink without fear of nausea or engage in sexually deviant behavior without fear of shock. The person's ability to discriminate between the situation in which the aversive conditioning occurs and all other situations can limit the treatment's effectiveness.

Aversive conditioning of alcoholics has recently enjoyed renewed popularity. For example, Arthur Wiens and Carol Menustik (1983) studied 685 alcoholic patients who completed an aversion therapy program at a Portland, Oregon, hospital. One year later, after returning for several booster treatments of alcohol–sickness pairings, 63 percent were still successfully abstaining. Three years later, 33 percent remained totally abstinent.

A milder form of classical conditioning, invented by learning psychologist O. H. Mowrer, exists for chronic bedwetters. The child sleeps on a liquid-sensitive pad connected to an alarm. Moisture on the pad triggers the alarm that awakens the child. With repetitions, this association of urinary relaxation with awakening serves to eliminate the bedwetting. Usually, the treatment is permanently effective, providing a boost to the child's self-image (Sherman & Levin, 1979).

Operant Conditioning Therapies   As we saw in Chapter 9, voluntary behaviors are strongly influenced by their consequences. This simple fact enables behavior therapists to influence behavior by controlling its consequences. They reinforce desired behaviors, while withholding reinforcement for undesired behaviors. Such applications of operant conditioning to solve specific behavior problems are sometimes called **behavior modification,** a therapy that has raised hopes for some who

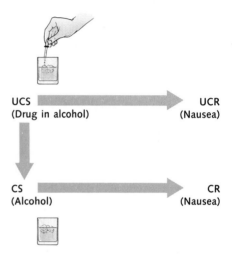

Figure 17–2   Aversion therapy for alcoholics. After repeatedly imbibing an alcoholic drink mixed with a drug that produces severe nausea, some patients develop at least a temporary conditioned aversion to alcohol.

The best candidates for alcoholism treatment programs are people with good jobs, stable relationships, and no history of treatment failures (Holden, 1987a).

What might a psychoanalyst say about this therapy for bedwetting? How might a behavior therapist reply?

were thought hopeless. Retarded children have been taught to care for themselves, autistic children have been induced to interact, and people with schizophrenia have been helped to behave more rationally.

In extreme cases, the treatment must be intensive—a 2-year 40-hour-a-week shaping program plus the involvement of trained parents for the nineteen withdrawn, uncommunicative 3-year-old autistic children in one recent study (Lovaas, 1987). But the combination of positive reinforcement of desired behaviors and the ignoring or punishing of aggressive and self-abusive behaviors worked wonders: By first grade half of these children were functioning successfully in school and exhibiting normal intelligence. Only 1 of the 40 comparable children who did not undergo this treatment showed similar improvement.

The rewards vary. With some people the reinforcing power of attention or praise is sufficient. With others, a more concrete reward such as food is required. In institutional settings, a *token economy* is sometimes established. When people display appropriate behavior, such as getting out of bed, washing, dressing, eating, talking coherently, cleaning up their rooms, or playing cooperatively, they receive a token of some sort, such as a plastic coin (Kazdin, 1982). The accumulated tokens can later be exchanged for various rewards, such as candy, television watching, trips to town, or better living quarters. Tokens can also be used to shape behavior in the step-by-step manner described on pages 239–240. Token economies have been successfully applied in various settings (classrooms, hospitals, and homes for the delinquent) and with various populations (disturbed children, the mentally retarded, schizophrenic patients).

Critics of behavior modification express two main concerns. The first is practical: What happens when the reinforcements stop, as when the person leaves the institution? Might the person have become so dependent on the extrinsic rewards that the appropriate behaviors quickly disappear? If so, how can behavior therapists make the appropriate behaviors more likely to endure? First, they may wean patients from the token rewards by shifting them toward rewards, such as social approval, that are typical of life outside the institution. They may also train patients to behave in ways that are intrinsically rewarding. As a withdrawn person becomes more socially competent, for example, the intrinsic satisfactions of social interaction may help to maintain the behavior.

The second concern is ethical: Is it right for one human to control another's behavior? Those who set up token economies must first deprive people of something they desire and then decide which behaviors will be reinforced. To critics, the whole behavior modification process has a totalitarian taint. Advocates reply that behavior modification increases *self*-control. They argue that treatment with positive rewards is more humane than remaining institutionalized or being punished, and that the right to effective treatment and to an improved life justifies temporary deprivation.

If this boy completes his work before the timer goes off, he will be rewarded with one of the tokens in the cup on the desk—tokens he can later exchange for special privileges. This form of behavior modification is effective in overcoming specific behavior problems.

COGNITIVE THERAPIES

We have seen how behavior therapies are used in the treatment of specific fears and problem behaviors. But how do behavior therapies deal with major depression or unfocused anxiety? After all, it is difficult to make a hierarchy of anxiety-triggering situations when the anxiety is unfocused. The "cognitive revolution" that has so changed psychology during the last two decades has influenced how therapists treat these less clearly defined psychological problems.

The *cognitive therapies* assume that our feelings and responses to events are strongly influenced by our thinking (see pages 402–404 and Figure 17–3). As we noted in the last chapter's discussion of depression, self-blaming and overgeneralized explanations of bad events are an integral part of the vicious cycle of depression. And if our characteristic thinking patterns are learned, then surely they can be relearned. Thus, cognitive therapists try in various ways to teach people new, more constructive ways of thinking.

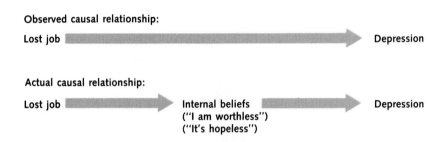

Observed causal relationship:

Lost job ──────────────────────────▶ Depression

Actual causal relationship:

Lost job ──────▶ Internal beliefs ──────▶ Depression
                 ("I am worthless")
                 ("It's hopeless")

Figure 17–3 A cognitive perspective on psychological disorders. The person's emotional reactions are produced not directly by the event, but by the person's thoughts in response to the event.

Rational-Emotive Therapy   According to Albert Ellis (1962, 1987), the creator of *rational-emotive therapy,* one cause of many problems is irrational thinking. For example, he describes (1984, p. 198) a disturbed woman who

> does not merely believe it is *undesirable* if her love partner is rejecting. She tends to believe, also, that (1) it is *awful;* (2) she *cannot stand it;* (3) she *should not,* must not be rejected; (4) she will *never* be accepted by any desirable partner; (5) she is a *worthless person* because one lover has rejected her; and (6) she *deserves to be damned* for being so worthless. Such common covert hypotheses are nonsensical. . . . They can be easily elicited and demolished by any scientist worth his or her salt; and the rational-emotive therapist is exactly that: an exposing and nonsense-annihilating scientist.

Does this sound like the opposite of the warm, caring, reflective acceptance of feelings expressed by Carl Rogers? It very nearly is. Ellis intends to "make mincemeat" of people's illogical ideas—that we must be loved by everyone, that we must be thoroughly competent and successful at everything, that it is a disaster when things do not go as we wish. Change people's thinking by revealing the "absurdity" of their self-defeating ideas, he believes, and you will change their self-defeating feelings and actions. Let's eavesdrop as tart-tongued Ellis exhibits his confrontational style with a 25-year-old female client (1984, p. 219):

> ***Ellis:*** *The same crap! It's always the same crap. Now if you would look at the crap—instead of "Oh, how stupid I am! He hates me! I think I'll kill myself!"— then you'd get better right away.*
>
> ***Client:*** *You've been listening! (laughs)*
>
> ***Ellis:*** *Listening to what?*
>
> ***Client:*** *(laughs) Those wild statements in my mind, like that, that I make.*
>
> ***Ellis:*** *That's right! Because I know that you have to make those statements— because I have a good theory. And according to my theory, people couldn't get upset unless they made those nutty statements to themselves. . . . Even if I loved you madly, the next person you talk to is likely to hate you. So I like brown eyes and he likes blue eyes, or something. So you're then dead! Because you really think: "I've got to be accepted! I've got to act intelligently!" Well, why?*
>
> ***Client:*** *(very soberly and reflectively) True.*
>
> ***Ellis:*** *You see?*
>
> ***Client:*** *Yes.*

Ellis: *Now, if you will learn that lesson, then you've had a very valuable session. Because you don't have to upset yourself. As I said before: if I thought you were the worst [expletive] who ever existed, well that's my opinion. And I'm entitled to it. But does it make you a turd?*

Client: *(reflective silence)*

Ellis: Does *it?*

Client: No.

Ellis: *What makes you a turd?*

Client: Thinking *that you are.*

Ellis: *That's right! Your* belief *that you are. That's the only thing that could ever do it. And you never have to believe that. See? You control your thinking. I control my thinking—my belief about you. But you don't have to be affected by that. You* always *control what you think.*

MINI-DEBATE

Values in Psychotherapy

To what extent do therapists' personal attitudes, beliefs, and values influence their advice to and interactions with clients? What values prevail in psychotherapy and what values should prevail? Two sharply contrasting positions are offered by psychotherapists Allen Bergin (co-editor of the *Handbook of Pychotherapy and Behavior Change*) and Albert Ellis (rational-emotive therapist). Bergin and Ellis disagree more radically than most therapists regarding what values are healthiest. In so doing, however, they illustrate what they agree upon: that values are an inevitable part of psychotherapy that should be acknowledged more openly.

Albert Ellis

Bergin does not properly represent the views of nondogmatic atheistic clinicians like myself who tend to believe that human disturbance largely springs from absolutistic thinking—from dogmatism, inflexibility, and devout shoulds, oughts, and musts—and that extreme religiosity is essentially emotional disturbance. I assume that a) no one and nothing is supreme, b) relationships with others do not define self-worth (nothing does—self-acceptance can be had for the asking), c) self-gratification is encouraged with mutually chosen partners, with or without long-term responsibilities, and d) meaning is derived from personal desire and validated by test and by reason.

I therefore offer the following alternative hypotheses: (1) That devout, orthodox, or dogmatic religion is significantly correlated with emotional disturbance, because devoutly religious persons tend to be inflexible, closed, intolerant, and unchanging. (2) The elegant therapeutic solution to emotional problems is to be quite unreligious and have no degree of dogmatic faith that is unfounded or unfoundable in fact. (3) There is no intrinsic connection between religion and

Allen Bergin

The dominant values in psychotherapy can be contrasted with those of a theistic approach that roots values in faith in God. The prevailing clinical-humanistic values assume that a) because humans are supreme, the individual self should be liberated from external authority, b) self-expression and self-gratification are to be encouraged, c) self-worth is defined through relationships with others, and d) meaning and purpose are derived from one's own reason and intellect. By contrast, theistic values assume that a) because God is supreme, humility and the acceptance of divine authority are virtues, b) self-control and committed love and self-sacrifice are to be encouraged, c) self-worth is defined through relationship with God, and d) meaning and purpose are derived from spiritual insight.

Drawing from my own religious values, I offer some testable hypotheses: (1) Religious communities that provide both a belief structure and a network of loving support should manifest lower rates of emotional disorder. (2) Those who endorse high standards of impulse control will suffer lower than average rates of alcoholism, addiction, divorce, and emotional instability. (3) Infidelity to any interpersonal commitment, especially marriage, leads to harmful consequences. (4) Teaching clients love, commitment, service, and sacrifice for others will help heal interpersonal difficulties and reduce intrapsychic distress. (5) Improving male commitment, caring, and responsibility in families will reduce marital and familial conflict and associated psychological disorders.

morality, and one can be a highly moral atheist or a distinctly immoral religionist (or vice versa). (4) Unequivocal and eternal fidelity to any interpersonal commitment, especially marriage, leads to harmful consequences. (5) Teaching clients unselective, universal, and unequivocal love, commitment, service, and sacrifice for others will help sabotage interpersonal relations and increase intrapsychic distress.

Source: Adapted, with permission, from an exchange in the *Journal of Consulting and Clinical Psychology,* 1980, Vol. 48, pp. 102–103, 635, 637–638.

Cognitive Therapy for Depression   Like Ellis, cognitive therapist Aaron Beck was originally trained in Freudian techniques. As Beck analyzed his depressed patients' dreams, negative themes such as loss, rejection, and abandonment seemed to recur and to extend into their waking thoughts. So in his form of cognitive therapy, Beck and his colleagues (1979) seek to reverse clients' catastrophizing beliefs about themselves, their situations, and their futures. Although Beck shares with Ellis the goal of getting depressed people to take off the dark glasses through which they view life, his technique is a gentler questioning that aims to help people discover their irrationalities for themselves (Beck & others, 1979, pp. 145–146):

Patient: *I agree with the descriptions of me but I guess I don't agree that the way I think makes me depressed.*

Therapist: *How do you understand it?*

Patient: *I get depressed when things go wrong. Like when I fail a test.*

Therapist: *How can failing a test make you depressed?*

Patient: *Well, if I fail I'll never get into law school.*

Therapist: *So failing the test means a lot to you. But if failing a test could drive people into clinical depression, wouldn't you expect everyone who failed the test to have a depression? . . . Did everyone who failed get depressed enough to require treatment?*

Patient: *No, but it depends on how important the test was to the person.*

Therapist: *Right, and who decides the importance?*

Patient: *I do.*

Therapist: *And so, what we have to examine is your way of viewing the test (or the way that you* think *about the test) and how it affects your chances of getting into law school. Do you agree?*

Patient: *Right.*

Therapist: *Do you agree that the way you interpret the results of the test will affect you? You might feel depressed, you might have trouble sleeping, not feel like eating, and you might even wonder if you should drop out of the course.*

Patient: *I have been thinking that I wasn't going to make it. Yes, I agree.*

Therapist: *Now what did failing mean?*

Patient: (tearful) *That I couldn't get into law school.*

Therapist: *And what does that mean to you?*

Patient: *That I'm just not smart enough.*

Therapist: *Anything else?*

Patient: *That I can never be happy.*

Therapist: *And how do these* thoughts *make you feel?*

Patient: *Very unhappy.*

Therapist: *So it is the meaning of failing a test that makes you very unhappy. In fact, believing that you can never be happy is a powerful factor in producing unhappiness. So, you get yourself into a trap—by definition, failure to get into law school equals "I can never be happy."*

A new variation of cognitive therapy utilizes the finding (described on pages 460–461) that depressed people often attribute their failures to themselves and their successes to external circumstances, whereas nondepressed people usually take credit for their successes and blame circumstances when things go wrong. In one attempt to teach depressed people to change their thinking, Adele Rabin and her colleagues (1986) put 235 depressed adults through a ten-session program that first explained the advantages of interpreting events as nondepressed people do and then trained them to reform their habitually negative patterns of thinking and labeling. For example, the patients were given homework assignments that required them to keep a record of each day's positive events and to write down how they had contributed to each. Compared with depressed people who remained on a waiting list, those who went through the positive thinking exercises became much less depressed (see Figure 17–4).

Donald Meichenbaum (1977, 1985) similarly advocates training people to think more adaptively. His "stress-inoculation training" helps people to identify and change their maladaptive reasoning. Because we often think in words, getting people to change what they say to themselves is an effective way to change their thinking (Dush & others, 1983). For example, perhaps you can identify with the anxious students who before an exam make matters worse with self-defeating thoughts: "This exam is probably going to be impossible. All these other students seem so relaxed and self-confident. I wish I were better prepared. Anyhow, I'm so nervous I'll forget everything." To change such negative patterns, Meichenbaum trains people to restructure the way they think in stressful situations. Sometimes it may be enough simply to say more positive things to oneself: "Relax. The exam may be hard, but it will be hard for everyone else, too. I studied harder than most people. Besides, I don't need a perfect score to get a good grade."

Cognitive therapists often combine these attempts to reverse irrational, self-defeating thinking with standard behavioral techniques such as systematic desensitization. Debate continues on whether the

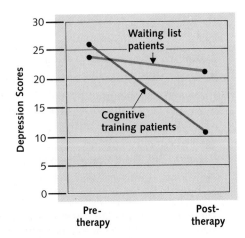

Figure 17–4   Cognitive therapy for depression. After undergoing a program that trained them to think more like nondepressed people—by noticing and taking personal credit for good events and by not taking blame for or overgeneralizing from bad events—the scores of 235 patients on the Beck Depression Inventory dropped dramatically. (From Rabin & others, 1986.)

success of such treatment, sometimes called *cognitive-behavior* therapy, is due more to the cognitive or behavioral component (Latimer & Sweet, 1984).

EVALUATING PSYCHOTHERAPIES

Advice columnist Ann Landers frequently advises letter writers to get themselves to a mental health professional for psychological repair. One response concluded by urging the writer "not to give up. Hang in there until you find someone [a psychotherapist] who fills the bill. It's worth the effort." The same day's second letter writer is advised, "There are many excellent mental health facilities in your city. I urge you to make an appointment at once" (Farina & Fisher, 1982).

Many people apparently share Ann Landers' confidence in the effectiveness of psychotherapy. Between the mid-1950s and the mid-1980s the percentage of Americans who had ever sought psychological counseling more than doubled, from 13 to almost 30 percent (Meredith, 1986). The National Institute of Mental Health estimates that 15.5 million Americans now undergo psychotherapy each year (Trafford, 1988). Before 1950, psychiatrists were the main providers of professional mental health treatment. Since then the demand has been growing faster than the psychiatric profession, and most psychotherapy is now done by clinical psychologists; clinical social workers; pastoral, marital, abuse, and school counselors; and psychiatric nurses (see Table 17–1). All told the estimated number of therapists mushroomed from 60,000 in 1975 to 160,000 in 1985 (Goleman, 1985).

Table 17–1
A CONSUMER'S GUIDE TO PSYCHOTHERAPISTS

To choose a therapist, you may wish to shop around by having a preliminary consultation with two or three therapists, during which you can describe your problem, gather information about their treatment approaches, credentials, and fees, and assess your feelings about each.

Type	Description	Number Practicing in U.S.	Average Hourly Fee
Psychiatrists	Physicians who specialize in the treatment of psychological disorders. Not all psychiatrists have had extensive training in psychotherapy, but as M.D.s they alone can prescribe medications. Thus they tend to see those with the most serious problems. Most have a private practice.	21,000	$75 +
Clinical psychologists	Ph.D. psychologists with expertise in research, testing, and therapy, usually supplemented by a supervised internship. About half work in agencies and institutions, half in private practice.	50,000	$70
Clinical or psychiatric social workers	A 2-year Master of Social Work graduate program plus postgraduate supervision prepares some social workers to offer psychotherapy, mostly to people with everyday personal and family problems. About half have earned the National Association of Social Workers designation of clinical social worker.	34,000	$55
Other therapists	Marriage and family counselors specialize in problems arising from family relations. Pastoral counselors, some certified by the American Association of Pastoral Counselors, provide counseling to countless people. Abuse counselors work with abusers and their victims.	55,000 +	0–$60

Note: Most numbers and fees from Hunt (1987).

Is the faith that Ann Landers and millions of other Americans have placed in psychotherapy justified? To pose the question as government and private health insurance programs do, "Is psychotherapy an effective treatment?"

Is Psychotherapy Effective?   The question, though simply put, is not simply answered. For one thing, measuring the effectiveness of therapy is not like taking your temperature with a thermometer. If you and I were to undergo psychotherapy, how would we gauge its effectiveness? In terms of how we feel about our progress? How our therapist feels about it? How our friends and family feel about it? How another clinician would independently judge us? How our behavior has changed?

Clients' Perceptions   If clients' testimonials were the only measure, we could strongly affirm the effectiveness of psychotherapy. In the more than two dozen available studies of consumer satisfaction with psychotherapy, 3 out of 4 clients reported themselves satisfied and 1 in 2 said they were "very satisfied" (Lebow, 1982). We have their word for it—and who should know better?

We should not dismiss these testimonials lightly. If after entering therapy because they were suffering, people leave feeling better about themselves, that is not inconsequential. But there are several reasons why client testimonials do not persuade skeptics. First, people often enter therapy when they are in crisis. When with the normal ebb and flow of events the crisis passes, they may attribute the improvement to the therapy.

Second, clients may have a need to believe the therapy was worth the effort. To admit investing time and money in something that was doing no good is like admitting having one's car serviced repeatedly by a mechanic who never fixed it. Self-justification is a powerful human motive.

Third, clients generally like their therapists and speak kindly of them. Even if the clients' problems remain, say the therapy critics, "they work hard to find something positive to say. The therapist had been very understanding, the client had gained a new perspective, he learned to communicate better, his mind was eased, anything at all so as not to have to say treatment was a failure" (Zilbergeld, 1983, p. 117).

There is ample evidence that such testimonials can be misleading. As earlier chapters have documented, we are prone to selective and biased recall and to making judgments that confirm our beliefs. Consider a massive experiment with over 500 Massachusetts boys, aged 5 to 13 years, many of whom seemed bound for delinquency. By the toss of a coin, half the boys were assigned to a treatment program for 5 years: They were visited twice a month by counselors; they were involved in community programs such as Boy Scouts; and, as the need arose, they received academic tutoring, medical attention, and family assistance. By 1979, some 30 years after the end of the program, Joan McCord (1978, 1979) managed to locate 97 percent of the participants and to assess the impact of the treatment by questionnaire and by a check of public records from courts, mental hospitals, and other sources.

Assessing the treatment program with client testimonials yielded encouraging results. Many of the men offered glowing reports. Some even noted that had it not been for their counselors, "I would probably be in jail," "My life would have gone the other way," or "I think I would have ended up in a life of crime." The court records offered apparent support for these testimonials. Even among the "difficult" boys in the program, 66 percent had no official juvenile crime record.

But for every boy who was counseled there was a similar boy in a control group who was not. McCord tracked down these untreated people and found that among the predelinquent boys in the control group, 70 percent had no juvenile record. Moreover, on some measures, such as a record of having committed a second crime, alcoholic tendencies, death rate, and job satisfaction, the treated men exhibited slightly *more* problems. The glowing testimonials of those treated had been deceiving. Perhaps, McCord speculated, the intervention had created a dependency, or maybe it had generated such high expectations that greater frustration was experienced later, or perhaps it had led the boys to view themselves as requiring help.

Clinicians' Perceptions   If clinicians' perceptions accurately reflected their own therapeutic effectiveness, we would have even more reason to celebrate. Case studies of successful treatment abound. Furthermore, every therapist treasures compliments from clients as they say goodbye or later express their gratitude. The problem is that clients tend to justify entering psychotherapy by emphasizing their woes, to justify leaving therapy by emphasizing their well-being, and to stay in touch only if they are satisfied. Therapists are aware of failures, mostly the failures of *other* therapists—therapists whose clients, having experienced only temporary relief, are now seeking a new therapist for their recurring problems. Thus the same person, with the same recurring difficulty—the same old weight problem, depression, or marital difficulty—may represent "success" stories in several therapists' files.

Outcome Research   In hopes of better assessing the effectiveness of psychotherapy, psychologists have turned to controlled research studies. Similar research in the 1800s transformed medicine from concocted treatments (bleeding, purging, infusions of plant and metal substances) into a science. The transformation occurred when skeptical physicians began to realize that many patients got better on their own, that most of the fashionable treatments were doing no good, and that sorting sense from nonsense required close observations of the course of an illness—with and without a particular treatment.

In psychology, the opening volley in what has become a spirited debate over such research was fired by British psychologist Hans Eysenck (1952). After summarizing the data available from studies of eclectic psychotherapy, he concluded that after undergoing psychotherapy approximately two-thirds of those suffering neurotic disorders had improved markedly. To this day, no one disputes that optimistic estimate.

So why are we still debating psychotherapy's effectiveness? Because Eysenck also reported a similar improvement rate among *untreated* "neurotic" persons, such as those who were on waiting lists. With or without psychotherapy, he said, roughly two-thirds improved noticeably. The avalanche of criticism prompted by Eysenck's analysis revealed shortcomings in his work. For one thing, those in the untreated control group were not exactly comparable to those who were treated. When clinical researchers Allen Bergin and Michael Lambert (1978) reanalyzed Eysenck's data, they found that the **spontaneous remission** rate (the rate of improvement *without* treatment) was actually only 43 percent. (Even this rate of spontaneous remissions is heartening evidence of our capacity to overcome our miseries.)

Despite its weaknesses, Eysenck's paper was a historic prod. It raised such questions as: How can we objectively measure the effectiveness of psychotherapy? What types of people and problems are most likely to be helped, and by what type of psychotherapy? The

Although many suicide-prone people have turned to suicide-prevention centers for help, such centers have not been found to affect community suicide rates (Dew & others, 1987).

The U.S. government's total investment in psychotherapy research since 1948 is roughly equal to the annual budget for military bands (Fisher, 1986b).

"Fortunately, [psycho]analysis is not the only way to resolve inner conflicts. Life itself still remains a very effective therapist."
  Karen Horney,
  Our Inner Conflicts, 1945

questions have both academic and personal relevance. If you or some-one you care about suffers a psychological disorder, how likely is it that psychotherapy will help?

In 1952, Eysenck could find only twenty-four studies of psycho-therapy outcomes to analyze. Today, there are hundreds. In the best of these, people on a waiting list for therapy are randomly assigned to alternative treatments or to no treatment. Afterward, everyone is eval-uated using tests and the reports of their close associates or of psychol-ogists who do not know whether therapy was given. The results of such studies are then digested by a technique called *meta-analysis,* a procedure for statistically combining the results of many different stud-ies as if they were one huge study with thousands of participants.

In the first reported meta-analysis of psychotherapy outcome stud-ies, Mary Lee Smith and her colleagues (1980) combined the results of 475 investigations. For psychotherapists, the welcome result was that "The evidence overwhelmingly supports the efficacy of psychother-apy" (p. 183). Figure 17–5 depicts their finding—that the average ther-apy client ends up better off than 80 percent of the untreated individu-als on waiting lists. Although the claim is more modest than first appears—50 percent of the untreated people also are better off than the average untreated person—Smith and her collaborators concluded that "Psychotherapy benefits people of all ages as reliably as school-ing educates them, medicine cures them, or business turns a profit" (p. 183).

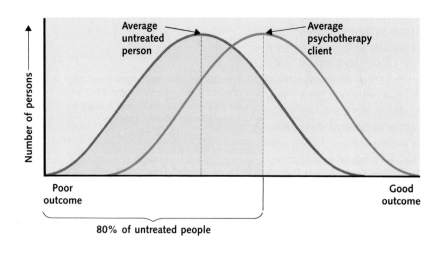

Figure 17–5   The two normal distribu-tion curves based on data from 475 stud-ies show the improvement of untreated people and psychotherapy clients. The outcome for the average therapy client surpasses that for 80 percent of the un-treated people.

The most ambitious psychotherapy study yet is a recent National Institute of Mental Health evaluation of three depression treatments: cognitive therapy, interpersonal therapy (which focuses on social rela-tions), and a standard drug therapy. Twenty-eight experienced thera-pists at three research sites—the University of Oklahoma, George Washington University, and the University of Pittsburgh—were trained in one of the three methods and randomly assigned their share of the 240 depressed patients who participated. After an average of 13 weeks of treatment, patients in all three groups improved more than did those in a control condition who received merely a placebo medica-tion and supportive encouragement and advice. Among patients who completed a full 16-week treatment program, slightly over half the pa-tients in each treatment group—but only 29 percent of those in the control group—were no longer depressed (Elkin, 1986). This verdict echoes the results of the earlier outcome studies: Those not undergoing therapy improved, but those undergoing therapy improved more.

So, while extravagant expectations that psychotherapy will transform your life and personality seem unwarranted (despite the conviction of many former patients that it has), Eysenck's pessimism also seems unwarranted. On the average, psychotherapy is somewhat effective—and is also cost-effective compared with the greater costs of unnecessary medical treatment for psychological ailments (Turkington, 1987). But note that "on the average" refers to no one therapy in particular. It is like saying "surgery is somewhat effective," or like reassuring lung cancer patients that "on the average" medical treatment of health problems is effective. What people want to know is not the effectiveness of therapy in general, but the effectiveness of particular treatments for their particular problems.

Certain problems seem more amenable to change through therapy. In general, the best results are obtained when the problem is clear-cut and specific (Singer, 1981). Those who suffer phobias, who are impeded by a lack of assertiveness, or who are frustrated by premature ejaculation or orgasmic dysfunction can hope for improvement. Those who have been chronically schizophrenic or who wish to change their personalities are unlikely to benefit from psychotherapy (Zilbergeld, 1983).

The Relative Effectiveness of Different Therapies   Those who are considering therapy will want to know not only whether psychotherapy is likely to be effective for their problem but *which* psychotherapy will be most effective. The meta-analysis conducted by Mary Lee Smith and her colleagues (1977, 1980) allowed a comparison of the effectiveness of different therapies. What do you suppose they found? Did one therapeutic technique get the best results? Did people benefit more from group or individual therapy? From sustained or short-term therapy? From therapy with experienced or novice therapists?

Despite claims of superiority by advocates of different therapies, Smith's comparison of the therapies revealed no clear winner. No one type of therapy proved consistently superior. Moreover—and more astonishing—it seemed to make no discernible difference whether the therapy was group or individual, whether many or few sessions were offered, or how well trained and experienced the therapist was.

Some therapies do, however, seem well suited to particular disorders. With specific behavior problems such as phobias, compulsions, or sexual dysfunctions, behavioral conditioning therapies have achieved especially favorable results; with depression, the cognitive therapies have proved successful (Bowers & Clum, 1988; Giles, 1983; Shapiro & Shapiro, 1982). Just as physicians offer particular treatments for particular problems rather than treating every complaint with the same drug or surgical procedure, so psychotherapists increasingly offer particular treatments for particular problems, rather than treating everyone with, say, psychoanalysis or cognitive therapy (Stiles & others, 1986).

Given the roughly 230 psychological disorders defined in DSM-III-R, the research questions are almost limitless: What specific therapeutic techniques are helpful with what problems for what types of people under what conditions? As answers become available, it is becoming possible to integrate different therapies and to guide people toward those that are likely to be most effective for them.

Commonalities Among Psychotherapies   Some clinicians believe that the reason no one therapeutic method seems to be generally superior or inferior to another is because, despite their apparent differences, each therapy's effectiveness derives from underlying commonalities. Jerome Frank (1982), Marvin Goldfried (Goldfried & Padawer, 1982), and Hans Strupp (1986), three psychologists who have studied the common ingredients of the various therapies, suggest that they all offer the following benefits: hope for demoralized people, a new perspective on oneself and the world, and an empathic, trusting, caring relationship. Let's take a closer look at each.

Hope for Demoralized People   People who seek therapy typically are anxious, depressed, or lacking in self-esteem, and feel incapable of turning things around. What any therapy offers is the expectation that things can and will get better. Quite apart from the particular therapeutic technique, this belief may itself be sufficient to promote improved morale, new feelings of self-efficacy, and diminished symptoms (Prioleau & others, 1983). This beneficial effect of a person's belief in a treatment is called the *placebo effect.* As we saw in Chapter 8, a placebo is an inert treatment often used as a control treatment in drug experiments. The placebo has no effect apart from a person's believing it does. In psychotherapy experiments, the placebo treatment may be listening to tapes, attending group discussions, or taking a fake pill.

The finding that placebo-treated people improve more than do untreated people, and nearly as much as those receiving actual psychotherapy, does not mean the psychotherapies are ineffective, only that part of the reason they help seems to be the hope that they offer. In their individual ways, each therapy may harness the person's own healing powers. And this, says psychiatrist Jerome Frank, helps us understand why all sorts of treatments—including some folk healing rites and medical practices now known to be powerless apart from the patient's belief—may in their own time and place produce cures.

A New Perspective on Oneself and the World   Every therapy offers people a plausible explanation of their symptoms and an alternative way of looking at themselves or responding to their worlds. Therapy also offers new learning experiences that help people to change their views of themselves and their behaviors.

An Empathic, Trusting, Caring Relationship   To say that all therapies are about equally effective is not to say that all *therapists* are equally effective. Regardless of their therapeutic technique, effective therapists are empathic people who can understand another's experience; whose care and concern are felt by the client; and whose respectful listening, reassurance, and advice earn the client's trust and respect.

The notion that all therapies offer hope through the fresh perspective offered by a concerned and sensitive person gains support from a meta-analysis of thirty-nine studies that compared treatment offered by professional therapists with the help offered by laypeople. These included friendly professors, people who have had a few hours' training in empathic listening skills, and college students who are being supervised by a professional clinician. The result? The "paraprofessionals," as these briefly trained people are called, typically proved as effective as the professionals (Berman & Norton, 1985; Hattie & others, 1984). Although most of the problems they treated were mild, the trained paraprofessionals seemed as effective as professionals even when dealing with more disturbed adults, such as those who were seriously depressed.

Effective therapists are those capable of forming a bond of trust with their clients, be they adults or children.

Self-help groups, like this one for Vietnam veterans, often are started by a person who has experienced a tragedy—a serious illness or accident, loss of a spouse or a child, a problem with drinking or drugs—and who believes that by mutual sharing and support such traumas can be eased. Such groups provide support for many who would not seek or could not afford professional therapy.

Research confirms that people who seek help usually improve. So do many of those who do not receive psychotherapy, and that perhaps is a tribute to our human resourcefulness and to our capacity to care for one another. Nevertheless, though it appears not to matter much which type of therapy is practiced, how much is received, or how experienced the therapist, those who receive at least some psychotherapy often improve more than those who receive none. Especially likely to improve are mature, articulate people with specific emotional or behavior problems.

Part of what all therapies offer is hope and an empathic, caring relationship. That may explain why, for mild problems at least, the empathy and friendly counsel of paraprofessionals are so often as helpful as professional psychotherapy. And that may also explain why those who are supported by close relationships—who enjoy the fellowship and friendship of caring people—are less likely to need or seek therapy (Frank, 1982; O'Connor & Brown, 1984).

"I believe we are entering an era in which the claims and aspirations of psychotherapy will become more circumscribed and more focused. It may also spell a return to greater modesty, from which we should never have departed."

Clinical psychologist Hans Strupp

THE BIOMEDICAL THERAPIES

Psychotherapy is one type of treatment for psychological disorders. The other is to alter the brain's functioning—by disconnecting its circuits through psychosurgery, by overloading its circuits with electroconvulsive shock, or by altering its electrochemical transmissions with drugs.

PSYCHOSURGERY

Because its effects are irreversible, *psychosurgery*—surgery that removes or destroys brain tissue in an effort to change behavior—is the most drastic biomedical intervention. In the 1930s, Portuguese physician Egas Moniz developed what became the best known psychosurgical operation: the *lobotomy*. Moniz found that when he surgically cut the nerves that connect the frontal lobes with the emotion-controlling centers of the inner brain, uncontrollably emotional and violent patients were calmed. During the 1940s and 1950s, literally tens of thousands of severely disturbed people were "lobotomized," and Moniz was honored with a Nobel prize (Valenstein, 1986).

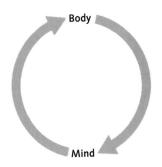

The biomedical therapies are based on the belief that mind and body are a unity: Affect one and you probably will affect the other.

Although the intention was simply to disconnect emotion from thought, the effect was often more drastic: The lobotomy produced a permanently lethargic, immature personality. When during the 1950s calming drugs became readily available, psychosurgery was largely abandoned. Today, lobotomies are no longer performed and other psychosurgery is used only in extreme cases. For example, if a patient suffers uncontrollable seizures, surgeons can deactivate the specific nerve clusters that cause or transmit the convulsions, as done in the split-brain operations described in Chapter 2. Even such apparently beneficial operations are irreversible, however, and so are used only as a last resort.

ELECTROCONVULSIVE THERAPY

A less drastic manipulation of the brain occurs with the controversial practice of shock treatment, or *electroconvulsive therapy (ECT).* When ECT was first introduced in 1938, the wide-awake patient was strapped to a table and jolted with roughly 100 volts of electricity to the brain, producing wracking convulsions and momentary unconsciousness. ECT therefore acquired a barbaric image that lingers to the present. Today, however, the patient is first given a general anesthetic and a muscle relaxant to prevent injury from convulsions. Then the shock is administered to the unconscious patient for a fraction of a second. Within 30 minutes the patient awakens and remembers nothing of the treatment or of the hours preceding.

The medical use of electricity is actually an ancient practice. The Roman Emperor Claudius (10 B.C.–A.D. 54) was treated for headaches by pressing electric eels to his temples.

ECT is used to treat severely depressed patients. (It has been found ineffective in treating other disorders such as schizophrenia.) After three such treatments a week for 2 to 4 weeks, depressed people often improve markedly and without discernible brain damage (Scovern & Kilmann, 1980; Weiner, 1984). "A miracle had happened in two weeks," reported noted research psychologist Norman Endler (1982) after ECT alleviated his deep depression. A 1985 panel of the National Institutes of Health reported that for others the effect may be less than a miracle but nonetheless an effective treatment for severe depression that has not responded to drug therapy (Kolata, 1985b). Thus, in recent years ECT has been regaining respectability.

How does ECT work? After 50 years of use, the process remains a mystery. ECT affects the brain, endocrine glands, and muscles. The difficulty lies in discerning which changes are linked to its antidepressant effect and which are irrelevant. One possible explanation is that shock triggers increased release of norepinephrine, the neurotransmitter that elevates arousal and mood and seems in short supply during depression. Another is that depression is linked with the overactivity of certain brain areas that may become less active as the brain reacts against the hyperactivity of the shock-induced seizure (Sackheim, 1985).

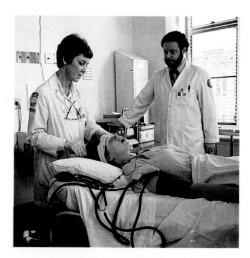

Electroconvulsive therapy remains a controversial treatment that may, however, provide relief from depression.

Although ECT is believed to have saved thousands from suicide and is now used on some 100,000 Americans a year (S. Squire, 1987), its Frankenstein-like image continues. No matter how impressive the results, the idea of electrically shocking people into convulsions does seem barbaric to many, especially given our ignorance about why ECT works. Nevertheless, electroconvulsive therapy is, in the minds of many psychiatrists and patients, a lesser evil than the misery, anguish, and risk of suicide that are associated with major depression.

In 1982, the voters of Berkeley, California, banned the use of ECT within their city, a vote that was later overturned in court.

DRUG THERAPIES

By far the most widely used biomedical treatments are the drug therapies. Introduced in the 1950s, they have reduced the need for psychosurgery and in many cases have reduced the need for hospitalization. New discoveries in *psychopharmacology* (the study of the effect of drugs on mind and behavior) have revolutionized the treatment of severely disordered people, enabling thousands to be liberated from confinement in mental hospitals. Thanks to drug therapy—and to political and legal efforts to minimize involuntary hospitalization and to return hospitalized people to their communities—the resident population of state and county mental hospitals is today but a quarter of what it was 30 years ago (Figure 17–6). For those still unable to care for themselves, however, release from hospitals has meant not liberation but homelessness. One careful study of Chicago's homeless revealed that 47 percent were depressed and another 23 percent psychotic (Rossi & others, 1987).

"The mentally ill were out of the hospital, but in many cases they were simply out on the streets, less agitated but lost, still disabled but now uncared for."
Lewis Thomas,
Late Night Thoughts on Listening to Mahler's Ninth Symphony, 1983

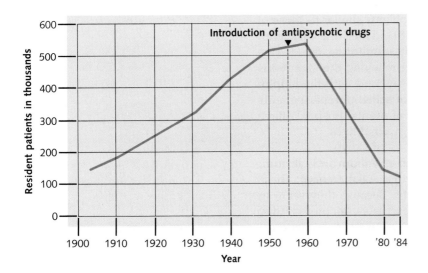

Figure 17–6 The emptying of America's mental hospitals. After the widespread introduction of antipsychotic drugs, starting in about 1955, the number of residents in state and county mental hospitals began to decline and has been dropping sharply ever since. The new drugs and efforts to "normalize" patients' environments were primarily responsible, but political concerns about the rights of involuntarily hospitalized patients have also had an effect. This rush to "deinstitutionalize" the mentally ill has unfortunately left many people who are ill-equipped to care for themselves homeless on city streets. (Data from NIMH.)

With almost any new treatment—drug therapy included—there is initially a wave of enthusiasm as many people recover. But that enthusiasm often diminishes after researchers subtract the rate of (1) normal recovery among untreated persons, and (2) recovery due to the placebo effect, which arises from expectations of improvement on the part of patients and staff alike. So, to evaluate the effectiveness of any new drug, researchers use a *double-blind* experiment. Half the patients are given the drug, the other half a similar-appearing placebo. Neither the staff nor the patients know whether a given patient has received the drug or the placebo; both groups are "blind." In double-blind studies, several categories of drugs have been found useful in treating psychological disorders.

Psychopharmacologist Solomon Snyder (1986a) reports that although "there are easily a hundred, probably two hundred, neurotransmitters, . . . all the psychiatric drugs we use today act through the three or four transmitter systems we've known about for twenty years." But that may change as new drugs are designed to mimic or block other, more recently discovered, neurotransmitters.

Antipsychotic Drugs   The revolution in drug therapy for psychological disorders began when it was accidentally discovered that certain drugs, which were being used for other medical purposes, also served to calm psychotic patients. Some schizophrenia victims—notably those with the negative symptoms of apathy and withdrawal—do not respond to these drugs. But many, especially those experiencing the positive symptoms of auditory hallucinations and paranoia, are helped by antipsychotic drugs that dampen their responsiveness to irrelevant stimuli.

The drug molecules, which are similar to molecules of the neurotransmitter dopamine, occupy receptor sites for dopamine, thus blocking its activity and decreasing its production (Pickar & others, 1984). This finding that antipsychotic drugs block dopamine receptors reinforces the idea that, as Snyder (1984b) put it, "dopamine systems in the brain are closely related to whatever is fundamentally abnormal in schizophrenic brains—either an excess of dopamine formation or perhaps a supersensitivity of dopamine receptors."

The antipsychotics are powerful drugs that can produce sluggishness, tremors, and muscular coordination problems similar to those of Parkinson's disease (Kaplan & Saddock, 1981). Thus, the task with every drug and every patient is, by carefully monitoring the dosage and its effects, to tread the fine line between relieving the symptoms and causing unpleasant side effects. In this way, and with the help of supportive people, hundreds of thousands of schizophrenia patients who had been consigned to the back wards of mental hospitals have been able to return to jobs and to lead near-normal lives.

Antianxiety Drugs   Antianxiety drugs, such as Valium and Librium, are among the most heavily prescribed drugs. Like alcohol, these drugs depress central nervous system activity. Because they seem to reduce tension and anxiety without causing excessive sleepiness, they have been prescribed even for minor emotional stresses. Sometimes, too, an antianxiety drug used in combination with other therapy can help a person learn to cope successfully with fear-arousing situations. Calmed with the help of a drug, the person may be able to face anxiety-triggering stimuli and learn to lessen the anxiety response.

The criticism sometimes made of the behavior therapies—that they reduce symptoms without resolving underlying problems—has also been made of antianxiety drugs, which, unlike the behavior therapies, may be used as a continuing treatment. Routinely "popping a Valium" at the first sign of tension can produce psychological dependence on the drug. Apart from its temporary calming effect, a study of Valium users suggests that the drug does less to reduce ongoing anxiety than its users believe (Caplan & others, 1984). When one's anxiety level is high it tends to come down within a few weeks, as quickly for those not using Valium as for those who are.

Antidepressant Drugs   If the antianxiety drugs can be said to calm anxious people down, the antidepressants could be said to lift depressed people up. These drugs apparently increase the availability of the neurotransmitters norepinephrine and serotonin, which appear to be scarce during depression. Most recently, drugs affecting dopamine have shown themselves useful with some of the roughly 30 percent of patients who do not respond to more standard drug treatments (Schmeck, 1988).

For those suffering the manic-depressive mood swings of a bipolar disorder, the chemical *lithium* is often an effective mood stabilizer. An Australian physician, John Cade, discovered this in the 1940s when he administered lithium to a severely manic patient. Although his reason for doing so was totally misguided—he thought lithium had calmed excitable guinea pigs when actually it made them sick—Cade nevertheless found that in less than a week the patient became perfectly well (Snyder, 1986b). Follow-up research has confirmed that with continued lithium use, the emotional highs and lows are typically leveled and usually do not recur. By bringing emotions under control, the antianxiety and antidepressant drugs can also facilitate the process of psychotherapy.

The effectiveness of the biomedical therapies reminds us of a fundamental lesson: Although we find it convenient to talk of separate psychological and biological influences, everything psychological *is* biological. Every thought and feeling depends on the functioning brain. Every creative idea, every moment of joy or anger, every period of depression emerges from the electrochemical activity of the brain.

PREVENTING PSYCHOLOGICAL DISORDERS

Psychotherapies and biomedical therapies tend to locate psychological disorders within people and thus seek to remedy the disorder by changing the person. We infer that people who act cruelly must be cruel and that people who act "crazy" must be "sick." We attach labels to such people, thereby distinguishing them from "normal" folks. It follows, then, that we try to treat "abnormal" people by giving them insight into their problems, by changing their thinking, or by controlling them with drugs.

Another way to view many psychological disorders is as an understandable response to a disturbed and stressful society. According to this view, it is not just the individual who needs treatment, but also the social context in which the individual acts. Better to prevent the problem by reforming a sick situation than to await and treat the problem.

FAMILY THERAPY

The fundamental assumption of *family therapy* is that no person is an island. Because we live and grow in relationship to others, especially our families, our problem behaviors often can be understood as our responses to others and as our attempts to influence them. Consequently, family therapists work in various ways to heal broken family relationships, by helping family members discover the role they play within their family's social system and how they affect each other. Family therapists also aim—usually with some success, research suggests (Hazelrigg & others, 1987)—to open up communication within the family or to help family members discover new ways of preventing or resolving conflicts. This excerpt from family therapist Virginia Satir (1967, pp. 98–100) illustrates the process:

Therapist: As far as you know, have you ever been in that same spot before, that is, were you puzzled by something Alice said or did?

Husband: Hell, yes, lots of times.

Therapist: Have you ever told Alice you were puzzled when you were?

Wife: He never says anything.

Therapist: (smiling, to Alice) Just a minute, Alice, let me hear what Ralph's idea is of what he does. Ralph, how do you think you have let Alice know when you are puzzled?

In family therapy the entire family unit is the client. The therapist helps family members understand how the ways they relate to each other create problems for one or more of them. The emphasis of treatment is on changing relationships and interactions, not individuals.

Husband: *I think she knows.*

Therapist: *Well, let's see. Suppose you ask Alice if she knows.*

Husband: *This is silly.*

Therapist: *(smiling) I suppose it might seem so in this situation, because Alice is right here and certainly has heard what your question is. She knows what it is. I have the suspicion, though, that neither you nor Alice are very sure about what the other expects, and I think you have not developed ways to find out. Alice, let's go back to when I commented on Ralph's wrinkled brow. Did you happen to notice it, too?*

Wife: *(complaining) Yes, he always looks like that.*

Therapist: *What kind of message did you get from that wrinkled brow?*

Wife: *He don't want to be here. He don't care. He never talks. Just looks at television or he isn't home.*

Therapist: *I'm curious. Do you mean that when Ralph has a wrinkled brow that you take this as Ralph's way of saying, "I don't love you, Alice. I don't care about you, Alice"?*

Wife: *(exasperated and tearfully) I don't know.*

Therapist: *Well, maybe the two of you have not yet worked out crystal-clear ways of giving your love and value messages to each other. Everyone needs crystal-clear ways of giving their value messages. (To son) What do you know, Jim, about how you give your value messages to your parents?*

Son: *I don't know what you mean.*

Therapist: *Well, how do you let your mother, for instance, know that you like her, when you are feeling that way? Everyone feels different ways at different times. When you are feeling glad your mother is around, how do you let her know?*

Son: *I do what she tells me to do. Work and stuff. . . .*

Therapist: *Let's check this out and see if you are perceiving clearly. Do you, Alice, get a love message from Jim when he works around the house?*

Wife: *I s'pose—he doesn't do very much.*

Therapist: *So from where you sit, Alice, you don't get many love messages from Jim. Tell me, Alice, does Jim have any other ways . . . that say to you he is glad you are around?*

Wife: *(softly) The other day he told me I looked nice.*

PREVENTIVE MENTAL HEALTH

Some therapists look beyond the family to the even larger social context in which both families and individuals act. Their concerns are illustrated in a story about the rescue of a drowning person from a river. Having successfully administered first aid, the rescuer spots another struggling person and pulls her out, too. After a half dozen repetitions, the rescuer suddenly turns and starts running away while yet another person is seen floundering. "Aren't you going to rescue that fellow?" asks a bystander. "Heck no," the rescuer replies. "I'm going upstream to find what's pushing all these people in."

Preventive mental health is upstream work. It seeks to prevent psychological casualties by identifying and alleviating the conditions that cause them. George Albee (1986), a past president of the American Psychological Association, contends that there is abundant evidence that poverty, meaningless work, constant criticism, unemployment, racism, and sexism undermine people's sense of competence, personal control, and self-esteem. Such experiences increase their risk of psychological disorders—of depression, alcoholism, and suicide.

Albee contends that those who care about preventing psychological casualties should therefore support programs that alleviate poverty and other demoralizing situations. Smallpox was eliminated not by treating the afflicted but by inoculating the unafflicted. Prevention means empowering those who have learned an attitude of helplessness, changing environments that breed loneliness, and bolstering parents' and teachers' skills at nurturing children's self-esteem. Indeed, "Everything aimed at improving the human condition, at making life more fulfilling and meaningful, may be considered part of primary prevention of mental or emotional disturbance" (Kessler & Albee, 1975, p. 557).

SUMMING UP

THE PSYCHOLOGICAL THERAPIES

The major psychotherapies are derived from the familiar psychoanalytic, humanistic, behavioral, and cognitive perspectives on psychology.

Psychoanalysis   The goal of psychoanalysts is to help people gain insight into the unconscious origins of their disorders and to work through the accompanying feelings. To do so, analysts draw on techniques such as free association and the interpretation of dreams, resistances, and the transference to the therapist of long-repressed feelings. Like psychoanalytic theory, psychoanalysis is criticized for its after-the-fact interpretations and for being time-consuming and costly. Although traditional psychoanalysis is not practiced widely, its influence can be seen in therapists who explore childhood experiences, who assume that defense mechanisms repress emotion-laden information, and who seek to help their clients achieve insight into the root of their problems.

Humanistic Therapies   Unlike psychoanalysts, humanistic therapists tend to focus on clients' current conscious feelings and on their taking responsibility for their own growth. Carl Rogers, in his person-centered therapy, used active listening to express genuineness, acceptance, and empathy. With Gestalt therapy, Fritz Perls sought to break down people's defenses and to make them accept responsibility for their feelings. Many therapeutic techniques can also be applied in group therapy.

Behavior Therapies   Behavior therapists worry less about promoting self-awareness and more about directly modifying problem behaviors. Thus they may countercondition behaviors through systematic desensitization or aversive conditioning. Or they may apply operant conditioning principles with behavior modification techniques such as token economies.

Cognitive Therapies   The newer cognitive therapies, such as Ellis's rational-emotive therapy, Beck's cognitive therapy for depression, and Meichenbaum's stress-inoculation training, all aim to change self-defeating thinking by training people to look at themselves in new, more positive ways.

Evaluating Psychotherapies   Because the positive testimonials of clients and therapists cannot prove that therapy is actually effective, psychologists have conducted hundreds of studies of the outcomes of psychotherapy. These studies indicate that (1) people who remain untreated often improve (a phenomenon called spontaneous remission); (2) those who receive psychotherapy are somewhat more likely to improve, regardless of what kind of therapy they receive and for how long; (3) mature, articulate people with specific behavior problems often receive the greatest benefits from therapy; but (4) placebo treatments or the sympathy and friendly counsel of paraprofessionals also tend to produce more improvement than occurs with untreated people.

THE BIOMEDICAL THERAPIES

Psychosurgery   Although brain surgery is occasionally performed to alleviate specific problems, the effects of radical psychosurgical procedures such as lobotomy are irreversible and potentially drastic. Thus, psychosurgery is seldom performed.

Electroconvulsive Therapy   Although controversial, a growing body of evidence indicates that ECT is an effective treatment for many severely depressed people who do not respond to drug therapy.

Drug Therapies   The most widely used of biomedical therapies are the antipsychotic, antianxiety, and antidepressant drugs.

PREVENTING PSYCHOLOGICAL DISORDERS

Family Therapy   Rather than locating psychological problems within individuals, family therapists treat the family system, out of which they believe problem behaviors arise.

Preventive Mental Health   Psychologists concerned with preventive mental health argue that many psychological disorders could be prevented by changing oppressive, esteem-destroying environments into more benevolent, nurturing environments that would foster individual growth and self-esteem.

TERMS AND CONCEPTS TO REMEMBER

active listening   Empathic listening in which the listener echoes, restates, and clarifies. A feature of Rogers' person-centered therapy.

aversive conditioning   A type of counterconditioning that associates an unpleasant state (such as nausea) with an unwanted behavior (such as drinking alcohol).

behavior modification   The application of operant conditioning principles to the modification of human behavior. (Sometimes also used as a synonym for *behavior therapy*.)

behavior therapy   Therapy that applies learning principles to the elimination of unwanted behaviors.

cognitive therapy   Therapy that teaches people new, more adaptive ways of thinking and acting; based on the assumption that thoughts intervene between events and our emotional reactions.

counterconditioning   A behavior therapy procedure that conditions new responses to stimuli that trigger unwanted behaviors; based on classical conditioning. See also *systematic desensitization* and *aversive conditioning*.

double-blind procedure   An experimental procedure in which both the patient and the staff are ignorant (blind) as to whether the patient has received the treatment or a placebo. Commonly used in drug evaluation studies.

eclectic   Using what appears to be the best of various theories and methods; eclectic therapists draw techniques from the various forms of therapy, depending on the client's problems.

electroconvulsive therapy (ECT)   Shock treatment. A biomedical therapy in which a brief electric current is sent through the brain; used to treat severely depressed patients.

encounter groups   Gatherings of twelve to twenty people whose emotion-laden experiences are characterized by honesty and openness, through which the participants hope to grow in self-awareness and social sensitivity.

family therapy   Therapy that treats individuals within their family system. Views unwanted behaviors as engendered by or directed at other family members; encourages family members to mend relationships and improve communication.

Gestalt therapy   Developed by Fritz Perls, therapy that combines the psychoanalytic emphasis on bringing unconscious feelings to awareness and the humanistic emphasis on getting "in touch with oneself"; aims to help people become more aware of and able to express their feelings, and to take responsibility for their feelings and actions.

interpretation In psychoanalysis, the analyst's assisting the patient to note and understand resistances and other significant behaviors in order to promote insight.

lithium A chemical that provides an effective drug therapy for the mood swings of bipolar (manic-depressive) disorders.

lobotomy A psychosurgical procedure once used to calm uncontrollably emotional or violent patients. In this procedure the nerves that connect the frontal lobes to the emotion-controlling centers of the inner brain are cut. Also called frontal (or prefrontal) lobotomy.

meta-analysis A procedure for statistically combining the results of many different research studies.

person-centered therapy A humanistic therapy, developed by Carl Rogers, in which the therapist attempts to facilitate clients' growth by offering a genuine, accepting, empathic environment.

placebo effect The beneficial effect of a person's *expecting* that a treatment will be therapeutic. A placebo is a neutral treatment (such as an inactive pill) that may nevertheless promote change because of the hope and confidence placed in it.

psychoanalysis Sigmund Freud's therapy technique, in which the patient's free associations, resistances, dreams, and transferences—and the therapist's interpretations of them—are the means by which previously repressed feelings are released, allowing the patient to gain self-insight.

psychopharmacology The study of the effects of drugs on mind and behavior.

psychosurgery Surgery that removes or destroys brain tissue in an effort to change behavior.

psychotherapy An emotionally charged, confiding interaction between a trained therapist and someone who suffers a psychological difficulty.

rational-emotive therapy A confrontational cognitive therapy developed by Albert Ellis that vigorously challenges people's illogical, self-defeating attitudes and assumptions.

resistance In psychoanalysis, the blocking from consciousness of anxiety-laden material.

spontaneous remission Improvement without treatment. In psychotherapy, symptom relief without psychotherapy.

systematic desensitization A type of counterconditioning that associates a pleasant, relaxed state with gradually increasing anxiety-triggering stimuli. Commonly used to treat phobias.

token economy An operant conditioning procedure in which a token of some sort, which can be exchanged later for various privileges or treats, is given as a reward for desired behavior.

transference In psychoanalysis, the patient's transfer to the analyst of emotions linked with other relationships (such as love or hatred for a parent).

FOR FURTHER READING

Corsini, R. J. (Ed.). (1989). *Current psychotherapies* (4th ed.). Itasca, IL: Peacock.

Prominent therapists of various persuasions describe their techniques of psychotherapy in their own words.

Endler, N. S. (1982). *Holiday of darkness.* New York: Wiley.

A psychologist's account of his own struggle with depression. Discusses various attempts at treatment, including electroconvulsive therapy.

Garfield, S. L., & Bergin, A. E. (Eds.). (1986). *Handbook of psychotherapy and behavior change* (3rd ed.). New York: Wiley.

An authoritative source of research information. Contains expertly written chapters on every major therapeutic approach and on scientific issues regarding psychotherapy.

Zilbergeld, B. (1983). *The shrinking of America: Myths of psychological change.* Boston: Little, Brown.

One clinical psychologist's analysis of psychotherapy and its limitations. Challenges myths about the need for and practicality of personal change and reassures readers about accepting their own uniqueness.

CHAPTER 18

HEALTH

No one needs to be told that psychological states can cause physical reactions. Nervous about an important exam, we feel butterflies in the stomach. Anxious over a public speaking assignment, we make frequent trips to the bathroom. Smoldering over a conflict with a family member, we develop a splitting headache. If such psychological states are prolonged, they may also bring on (in those who are physiologically predisposed) a skin rash, an asthma attack, or an ulcer.

Many people are less aware, however, of the part their own behaviors play in determining whether they will become victims of one of the four leading causes of serious illness and death in the United States today: heart disease, cancer, stroke, and accidents (Figure 18–1). In fact, according to the National Academy of Sciences' Institute of Medicine (1982), half the mortality from the *ten* leading causes of death in the United States can be traced to people's behavior—to cigarette smoking, excessive alcohol consumption, maladaptive responses to stress, nonadherence to doctors' orders, insufficient exercise, use of illicit drugs, and poor nutrition. If we could understand and modify the behavioral sources of illness, we could greatly alleviate suffering and increase life expectancy. It is in pursuit of these goals that the interdisciplinary field of *behavioral medicine* has arisen—a field that integrates behavioral and medical knowledge to fight disease and promote health (Miller, 1983a).

Research psychologists Mary Jasnoski and Gary Schwartz (1985) contrast traditional efforts to link specific diseases to single causes (genes, germs, or emotions) with behavioral medicine's "systems theory" perspective. Every level of our existence is both composed of subsystems and itself a subcomponent of a larger system. Thus if we are interested in an individual's health, we must take account of transactions among these biological, psychological, and social systems. Your body organs, for example, are part of a larger system—you—and you are a part of your family, your community, your culture, and so forth. Your internal organs, in turn, are composed of subsystems—cells— which are composed of biochemicals. Virtually every level of our existence is both a component of larger systems and an aggregate of smaller systems. Instead of assuming that illness has *either* a physical *or* a psychological cause, systems theorists presume that illness results from the interaction of all these interdependent systems (as studied by physiologists, psychologists, and sociologists, among others).

Health psychology is a relatively new subfield that provides psychology's contribution to the interdisciplinary science of behavioral medicine. One indicator of health psychology's explosive growth is the number of psychologists working in medical schools. In 1953, there were 255; by the late 1980s, there were about 3000 (Matarazzo & others,

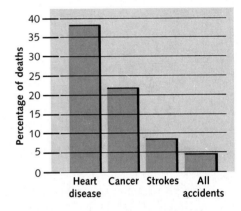

Figure 18–1 The four leading causes of death are all strongly influenced by people's behavior—by their patterns of consumption, their reactions to stress, and their health-related behaviors.

"All the parts of the universe are so linked together that it seems to me impossible to know one apart from another or from the whole."
  Blaise Pascal,
  Pensées, 1670

"Health has its science as well as disease."
  Elizabeth Blackwell,
  Medicine as a Profession for Women, 1860

1981; Thompson, 1987). Another indicator is the growth of the American Psychological Association's division of health psychology from its inception in 1979 to 2900 members in 1988.

Health psychology's key issues are this chapter's questions:

Are our emotions and our responses to stressful events linked with heart disease, strokes, and other diseases?

How can we reduce or control stress?

How do people decide whether they are sick, and what steps can be taken to facilitate their treatment?

What life-style changes would promote health and well-being?

STRESS AND ILLNESS

Walking along the path toward her Rocky Mountain campsite, Karen hears a rustle in the grass off to the left. As she glimpses a rattlesnake slithering toward her, her body mobilizes for fight or flight: her muscles tense, her adrenaline flows, her heart pounds. Flee she does, racing to the security of camp. Once there, Karen's muscles gradually relax and her heart rate and breathing ease.

Karl leaves his suburban apartment one morning and, delayed by road construction, arrives at the parking lot of the commuter train station just in time to see the 8:05 pull away. Catching the next train, he arrives in the city late and has to elbow his way through the crowds of rush-hour pedestrians. Once at his bank office, he apologizes to his first client, who is wondering where he has been and is irritated that his quarterly investment report is not ready. Karl does his best to mollify the client. When he has gone, Karl notices the effects of his own pent-up emotion—his tense muscles, clenched teeth, and churning stomach.

Karen's response to stress saved her life; Karl's, if chronic, could increase his risk of heart disease and high blood pressure and could make him more vulnerable to a variety of other stress-linked illnesses. Moreover, feeling under pressure, he might sleep and exercise less and smoke and drink more, further endangering his long-term health.

According to the American Academy of Family Physicians, two-thirds of office visits to family doctors are prompted by symptoms related to stress (Wallis, 1983).

WHAT IS STRESS?

Stress is a slippery concept. It is used sometimes to describe threats or challenges ("Karl was under considerable stress") and sometimes to describe our responses to threats or challenges ("When Karen saw the rattler she experienced acute stress"). To encompass both these meanings, we will define *stress* as the whole process by which we appraise and respond to events, called *stressors,* that threaten or challenge us. Stressors can have positive effects, by arousing and motivating us to conquer problems. Championship athletes, successful entertainers, and great teachers and leaders all thrive and excel when aroused by a challenge. But when stress is severe or prolonged, it may also cause mental or physical harm.

The Stress Response System   Although medical interest in stress can be traced back to Hippocrates (460–377 B.C.), it was not until the 1920s that physiologist Walter Cannon (1929) confirmed that the stress response is part of a unified mind-body system. He observed that a

Tragedies, like the destruction of this couple's house by a tornado, can cause stress. So too can major life events, like the birth of a baby.

variety of stressors—extreme cold, lack of oxygen, emotion-arousing incidents—trigger an outpouring of epinephrine and norepinephrine (commonly known as *adrenaline* and *noradrenaline*) into the bloodstream from sympathetic nerve endings in the inner part of the adrenal glands. As we saw in Chapter 14 in the discussion of emotional arousal, this is but one part of a general response mediated by the sympathetic nervous system. When alerted by any of a number of brain pathways, the sympathetic nervous system increases heart rate and respiration, diverts blood to the deep muscle tissue, and releases fat from the body's stores to prepare the body for what Cannon called "fight or flight." All in all, this response struck Cannon as a wonderfully adaptive system. More recently, physiologists have identified that the secretion of the hormone cortisol in response to signals from the cortex is the one characteristic reaction to stress. It is usually but not always accompanied by the increase in sympathetic nervous system activity (Figure 18–2) that Cannon thought was "the" stress response.

Canadian scientist Hans Selye's (1936, 1976) 40 years of research on stress extended Cannon's findings and helped make stress a major concept in both psychology and medicine. The story of how Selye arrived at his concept of the stress response is one worth remembering in times of intellectual discouragement. Hoping to discover a new sex hormone, Selye injected rats with extracts of hormone-rich ovary tissue. He detected three effects: enlargement of the adrenal cortex, shrinkage of the thymus gland (which contains disease-fighting white blood cells), and development of bleeding ulcers in the stomach and intestines. No known hormone had ever produced such symptoms, so Selye was elated. "At the age of 28, I seemed to be already on the track of a new hormone."

Before long, though, Selye's elation was transformed into great disappointment. Other tissue extracts had exactly the same effect. What is more, when he injected the rats with toxic fluids not derived from living tissue, the adrenal enlargement, thymus shrinkage, and development of bleeding ulcers were even more pronounced. Alas, Selye was forced to conclude that the effects were *not* due to a new sex hormone. Selye recalled that:

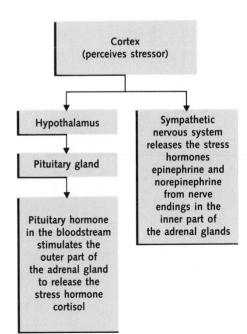

Figure 18–2 Stress hormones are released by the adrenal glands (atop the kidneys) on orders received through a dual-track system.

All my dreams of discovering a new hormone were shattered. All the time and all the materials that went into this long study were wasted. . . . I became so depressed that for a few days I could not do any work at all. I just sat in my laboratory, brooding. . . . The ensuing period of introverted contemplation turned out to be the decisive factor in my whole career; it pointed the way for all my subsequent work. . . . As I repetitiously continued to go over my ill-fated experiments and their possible interpretation, it suddenly struck me that one could look at them from an entirely different angle. If there was such a thing as a single nonspecific reaction of the body to damage of any kind, . . . the general medical implications of the syndrome would be enormous! (1976, pp. 24–26)

To verify his hunch, Selye studied animals' reactions to a variety of other stressors, such as electric shock, surgical trauma, and immobilizing restraint. He discovered that these, too, had similar physiological effects. In fact, the body's adaptive response to stress seemed so general—like a single burglar alarm that would sound off no matter what intruded—that he called it the **general adaptation syndrome (GAS)**. Selye saw the GAS as having three phases (Figure 18–3). Let's say you suffer a physical or emotional trauma. In Phase 1, you first experience an *alarm reaction* due to the sudden activation of your sympathetic nervous system. You will go into a temporary state of shock (normally relatively minor, but sometimes serious if the trauma is particularly severe). In Phase 2, the *stage of resistance*, your body responds with an outpouring of stress hormones; your temperature, blood pressure, heart rate, and respiration all increase. Now your body's resources are mobilized to cope with the stressor. If the stress persists, your body's reserves may become depleted and your tissues may suffer wear and tear, causing you to enter Phase 3, the *stage of exhaustion*. During this phase, you are especially vulnerable to diseases or even, in extreme cases, collapse and death.

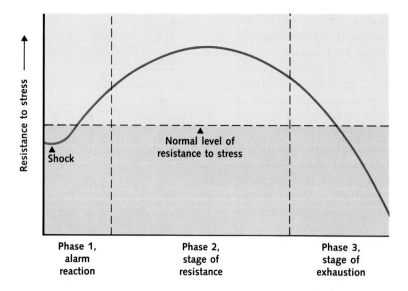

Figure 18–3 Selye's general adaptation syndrome. After a trauma, the body enters a temporary state of shock (Phase 1), during which resistance to the stressor drops below normal. From this, it rebounds and resistance to the stressor rises (Phase 2). But if the stress persists, wear and tear on the body may lead to exhaustion and increasing vulnerability (Phase 3). (From Cox, 1978.)

Although newer research reveals subtle differences in the body's reactions to different stressors, few medical experts today quarrel with Selye's basic point that prolonged stress can produce physical deterioration. This leads to the practical concerns of today's health psychologists: What causes stress? What are the effects of stress? And how can those effects be alleviated?

Stressful Life Events The level of stress we experience largely depends on how we appraise the big and little traumas of our lives. One person alone in a house dismisses its creaking sounds and experiences no stress; someone else appraises them as signaling the possible presence of an intruder and becomes alarmed. Research has focused on the health consequences of our reactions to three types of stresses: catastrophes, significant life changes, and daily hassles.

Catastrophes Catastrophes are unpredictable, large-scale events such as acts of war, nuclear accidents, and natural disasters. Although people often provide one another with comfort and assistance after such events, the health consequences can be significant. Paul and Gerald Adams (1984) documented such consequences in their study of the aftermath of the Mount Saint Helens eruption and ashfall in the nearby town of Othello, Washington. Compared with the same period during the previous year, emergency room visits rose 34 percent during the 7 months following the eruption, deaths rose 19 percent, and stress-related illness complaints at the local mental health clinic doubled (Figure 18–4).

"It's not the large things that send a man to the madhouse . . . no, it's the continuing series of small tragedies . . . not the death of his love but a shoelace that snaps with no time left."

Charles Bukowski (cited by Lazarus in Wallis, 1983)

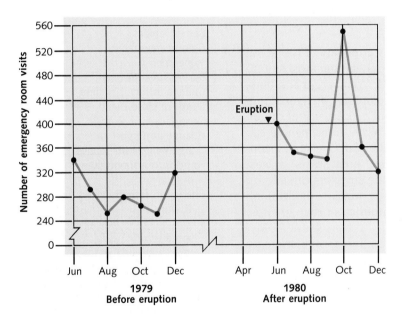

Figure 18–4 Health consequences of a cataclysmic event. During the 7 months following the May 18, 1980, eruption of Mount Saint Helens, emergency room visits in nearby Othello, Washington, rose 34 percent compared to the same 7-month period during the previous year. (From Adams & Adams, 1984.)

Significant Life Changes The second type of life event stressor is personal life changes such as the death of a loved one, the loss of a job, marriage or divorce, the birth of a child. The health effects of such changes have been studied either by following people over time to see if these changes precede illnesses, or by comparing the life changes recalled by those who have or have not suffered a specific health problem such as a heart attack. A review of these studies commissioned by the National Academy of Sciences (Dohrenwend & others, 1982) revealed that people who have recently been widowed, fired, or divorced are indeed more vulnerable to disease. A recent study of 96,000 widowed people in Finland found that their risk of death doubled in the week following their partner's death (Kaprio & others, 1987). Experiencing a cluster of such events puts one even more at risk.

The increasing number of magazine articles on stress (over 500 from 1983 to 1988 in the United States alone) often lists stressful life changes on a sliding scale inventory, such as the Social Readjustment

Rating Scale (SRRS) shown in Table 18–1, in which each item is assigned a certain number of life-change "stress points." By totaling your stress points on the inventory, you supposedly have an indication of your risk of getting a stress-related illness in the next year. For the SRRS, a score of more than 200 points is said to indicate increased risk of health problems. A student version of a life-change stress scale would add points for low grades, troubles with roommates, a change in vocational plans, and so forth.

As popular as such scales are, total scores are only modest predictors of future health problems (Depue & Monroe, 1986; Maddi & others, 1987). If stress has the effects that Selye and others believe it does, why aren't such scales better predictors? Stress researchers suggest several reasons: First, the stressors that most people face are seldom life's major crises (relatively few of us have recently been married, widowed, divorced, or fired). Second, it is not the events themselves but how we appraise them that determines their stressfulness (retirement may increase stress for one person, reduce it for another). Third, how we react to life changes may be influenced by other factors—how easygoing we are, the degree of self-efficacy and vigor we feel in stressful situations, the amount of caring support we have during difficult times, or health habits such as exercise (Holahan & Moos, 1986; O'Leary, 1987).

Daily Hassles   For many of us, those everyday annoyances we face at school, on the job, and in our family relations may be the most significant sources of stress (Lazarus & Folkman, 1984; Weinberger & others, 1987). These daily hassles include such things as rush-hour traffic, aggravating housemates, long lines at the bank or grocery store, or getting caught in the rain without an umbrella. While some people can simply shrug them off, others are "driven up the wall" by such inconveniences; in fact, 6 in 10 Americans say they feel "great stress" at least once a week (Harris, 1987). Over time, these little stressors can add up and take a toll on health and well-being. Hypertension (high blood pressure) is common among the residents of America's urban ghettos, who endure the daily stresses that accompany poverty, unemployment, single parenting, and overcrowding. There is a correspondingly low rate of heart attacks among those who live the relatively peaceful monastic life (Henry & Stephens, 1977).

For many people the hassles of daily living add up to more stress than is frequently experienced during life's occasional crises.

Table 18–1
SOCIAL READJUSTMENT RATING SCALE (SRRS)

Life event	Life-change units
Death of spouse	100
Divorce	73
Marital separation	65
Jail term	63
Death of close family member	63
Personal injury or illness	53
Marriage	50
Being fired	47
Marital reconciliation	45
Retirement	45
Change in health of family member	44
Pregnancy	40
Sex difficulties	39
Gain of new family member	39
Business readjustment	39
Change in financial state	38
Death of close friend	37
Change line of work	36
Change in number of arguments with spouse	35
Foreclosure of mortgage or loan	30
Change in responsibilities at work	29
Son or daughter leaving home	29
Trouble with in-laws	29
Outstanding personal achievement	28
Wife begins or stops work	26
Begin or end school	26
Change in living conditions	25
Revision of personal habits	24
Trouble with boss	23
Change in work hours or conditions	20
Change in residence	20
Change in school	20
Change in recreation	19
Change in church activities	19
Change in social activities	18
Change in sleeping habits	16
Change in eating habits	15
Vacation	13
Christmas	12
Minor violations of the law	11

Source: Adapted from Holmes and Rahe (1967).

One source of everyday stress comes from the conflicts we face between our different motives. Easiest are the *approach-approach* conflicts, in which we are pulled by two attractive but incompatible goals—to go to a sporting event or out for pizza, to take sociology or anthropology, to wear the green or the beige sweater.

At other times we face an *avoidance-avoidance* conflict between two undesirable alternatives. Do you avoid studying a disliked subject or do you avoid failure by opening the book? Do you suffer someone's wrath for admitting the truth or feelings of guilt for having told a fib?

In times of *approach-avoidance* conflict we are both attracted and repelled at the same time. Some things you may adore about a person you are dating, and other things you dislike. Compared to the approach tendency, the avoidance tendency grows more rapidly as one approaches the goal (see Figure 18–5). Thus, we vacillate. From a distance, the goal—a happy relationship—looks pretty good. Up close, we feel a desire to escape the undesirable aspects. When we step back, the negative aspects fade and we again feel attracted. The situation may be further complicated by several approach-avoidance conflicts occurring simultaneously—regarding whom to date, which school to attend, which job to accept—multiplying the stress of decision making.

Perceived Control Whether natural catastrophes, important life changes, or accumulating daily hassles and conflicts, events are especially stressful when we appraise them as both negative *and* uncontrollable. An "executive" rat that can switch off the electric shocks it receives (see Figure 18–6) is not likely to develop ulcers. A "subordinate" rat that receives these same shocks in a nearby cage but has no control over them is more vulnerable to ulcers and develops lowered immunity to disease (Laudenslager & Reite, 1984; Weiss, 1977).

Similar findings have been observed in humans: People who perceive a loss of control over their lives are more likely to suffer ill health. As we noted in Chapter 15, elderly people who are placed in nursing homes without their consent and thereby lose control over their day-to-day activities tend to decline more rapidly and die sooner than do those who help decide where they will live and take more control over their activities (Rodin, 1986).

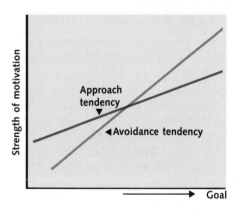

Figure 18–5 Approach-avoidance conflict. As people approach the goal, their avoidance tendency often rises faster than their approach tendency, causing them to vacillate.

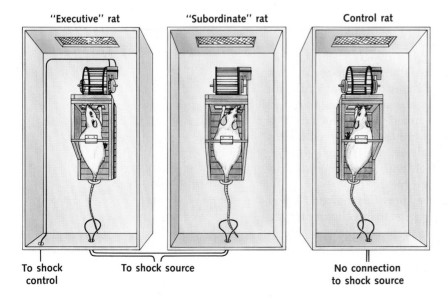

"Executive" rat "Subordinate" rat Control rat

To shock control To shock source No connection to shock source

Figure 18–6 The health consequences of a loss of control. The "executive" rat at the left can switch off the tail shock by turning the wheel. Because it has control over the shock, it is no more likely to develop ulcers than the unshocked control rat at the right. The "subordinate" rat in the center receives the identical shocks as the executive rat. Because it has no control over the shocks, the subordinate rat is more likely to develop ulcers. (From Weiss, 1977.)

Another factor that influences our vulnerability to stress is optimism. Psychologists Michael Scheier and Charles Carver (1987) report that optimists—people who have a generally positive outlook ("In uncertain times, I usually expect the best")—cope with stressful events more actively and successfully and enjoy better health. During the last month of a semester, students who previously tested as optimistic report less fatigue and fewer coughs, aches, and pains. Optimists also respond to stress with smaller increases in blood pressure and recover faster from heart bypass surgery. They are the "hardy" types—stress-resistant people whom psychologists Suzanne Kobasa (1982) and Salvatore Maddi and his colleagues (1987) observed approaching life with vigor and self-confidence.

Why do lack of control and a negative outlook contribute to health problems? Animal studies indicate—and human studies confirm—that losing control triggers an outpouring of stress hormones. When rats cannot control shock or when humans feel unable to control their environment, cortisol levels rise and immune responses drop (Rodin, 1986). The crowding that can occur in high-density neighborhoods, prisons, and college dorms is one source of diminished control—and of increased levels of stress hormones and blood pressure (Fleming & others, 1987; Ostfeld & others, 1987). So also are the time pressures, competition, and hostilities associated with many jobs.

STRESS AND HEART DISEASE

Although infrequent before this century, *coronary heart disease*—the narrowing of the vessels that nourish the heart muscle—had become North America's leading cause of death by the 1950s. In the United States alone, more than half a million people die annually from the resulting heart attacks. Why did this dramatic increase in coronary deaths occur? Clearly, people live longer now, and older people are simply more vulnerable to heart attacks. (The virtual elimination of some causes of death, such as smallpox or polio, has elevated the frequency of others.) But changing longevity does not explain why more younger adults are dying of heart disease (Chesney, 1984).

Thousands of research studies have now identified factors that increase the risk of heart disease—smoking, obesity, family history of the disease, high fat diet, physical inactivity, elevated blood pressure, and elevated cholesterol level. Even taking all these factors together still leaves most instances of heart disease unexplained. Many inactive, overweight smokers do not suffer the disease and many who have heart attacks are active, slender nonsmokers.

So what else might be involved? In 1956, cardiologists Meyer Friedman, Ray Rosenman, and their colleagues stumbled upon an idea (Friedman & Ulmer, 1984). While studying the eating behavior of San Francisco Junior League women and their husbands, Friedman and Rosenman discovered that the women consumed just as much cholesterol and fat as their husbands, yet they were far less susceptible to heart disease. Was it because of their female sex hormones? No, the researchers surmised, because black women with the same sex hormones are as prone to heart disease as their husbands.

The Junior League president thought she knew the answer. "If you really want to know what is going to give our husbands heart attacks, I'll tell you. It's stress," she said sadly, "the stress they have to face in their businesses, day in, day out. Why, when my husband comes home at night, it takes at least one martini just to unclench his jaws."

Although the medical textbooks of the day never hinted that stress might be a killer, Friedman and Rosenman were already wondering whether stress affected the heart. They sent out questionnaires to hundreds of industrialists and physicians, asking them what they thought had caused the heart attacks their friends or patients had suffered. Both groups suspected that the stresses of meeting deadlines and competing for success had helped precipitate the heart attacks of the victims they knew.

To test the idea that stress and heart disease are related, Friedman and Rosenman measured the blood cholesterol level and blood-clotting speed of forty tax accountants. From January through March, both of these coronary warning indicators were completely normal. Then, as the accountants began scrambling to finish their clients' tax returns before the April 15th filing deadline, their cholesterol and clotting measures rose to dangerous levels. In May and June, with the deadline past, the measures returned to normal. The researchers' hunch had paid off: Stress was linked with indications of heart attack risk.

The stage was thus set for what was to become Friedman and Rosenman's classic 9-year study of more than 3000 healthy men, 35 to 59 years of age. At the start of the study, each man was interviewed for 15 minutes about his work and eating habits. During the interview, the man's manner of talking and other behavioral patterns were noted. Those who seemed the most competitive, hard-driving, impatient, time-conscious, supermotivated, verbally aggressive, and easily angered were called *Type A.* Those who were more easygoing were called *Type B.* Which group do you suppose turned out to be the most coronary-prone? By the time the study was complete, 257 of the men had suffered heart attacks, 178 of whom were Type A. Thus, compared to the Type B men, the Type As were more than twice as vulnerable. Moreover, not one of the "pure" Type Bs—the most mellow and laid-back of their group—had suffered a heart attack.

As often happens in science, this exciting discovery provoked enormous public interest: Millions of people have by now analyzed and labeled themselves and their friends with the aid of newspaper and magazine checklists such as the one in Figure 18–7. But after the honeymoon period, in which the finding seemed definitive and revolutionary, other researchers begin the necessary labor of replicating and refining the conclusions.

As with all such classifications, people vary along a continuum from "pure" Type A to "pure" Type B.

In both India and America, Type A bus-drivers are literally hard-driving; they brake, pass, and honk their horns more often than their more easygoing Type B colleagues (Evans & others, 1987).

Self-evaluation:
Which type are you?

Type A	Type B
1. Very competitive	1. Noncompetitive
2. Always on the go, in a hurry	2. Relaxed, in control
3. Hard-driving	3. Easygoing
4. Demands perfection	4. Understanding, forgiving
5. Ambitious, wants quick promotions	5. Confident and happy in job
6. Is a "workaholic" —even at play	6. Enjoys leisure and weekends

Figure 18–7 One of the many questionnaires found in the popular press for evaluating whether your behavior patterns are more those of a Type A or Type B personality. (From "How to Cope Better with Stress," *Reader's Digest,* March 1984.)

Why may Type A people be more prone to heart disease? There are at least two possibilities: First, such individuals tend to smoke more, sleep less, and drink less milk and more caffeinated drinks (Hicks & others, 1982, 1983a, b), all of which are behaviors that may contribute to coronary risk. Second, their temperament seems to contribute directly to heart disease. In relaxed situations, the hormonal secretions, pulse rate, and blood pressure of Type As and Type Bs are no different. When harassed, given a difficult challenge, or threatened with a loss of freedom and control, Type A individuals are more physiologically reactive. Their hormonal secretions, pulse rate, and blood pressure tend to soar, whereas those of Type Bs remain at moderate levels (Krantz & Manuck, 1984). For example, when Redford Williams and his associates (1982) asked Duke University men to begin with the number 7683 and repeatedly subtract 13 (with a prize to go to the fastest), the Type A students' stress hormone levels rose at least twice as high as those of their Type B classmates. These hormones are believed to accelerate the buildup of plaques (scarlike masses formed by cholesterol deposits) on the artery walls, producing atherosclerosis, or "hardening" of the arteries.

These findings suggest that during the course of a day the reactive Type A individuals are more often "combat ready." At such times, their active sympathetic nervous system redistributes bloodflow to the muscles and away from the internal organs, including the liver, which removes cholesterol and fat from the blood. Thus, their blood may contain excess cholesterol and fat that later get deposited around the heart. In such ways, the hearts and minds of people interact.

Now, can we safely say that Type A behavior leads to heart attacks? No, because follow-up studies have sometimes found little relationship between Type A personality and later heart disease. Type A people are not only reactive, they also seek out challenge, value productivity and success, and like to know how well they are doing (Smith & Anderson, 1986; Strube, 1987). Does some particular aspect of the Type A personality predict coronary risk? Perhaps time urgency? Competitiveness? Irritability?

Newer research reveals that heart disease is not linked with a fast-paced, time-conscious life-style or with high ambitions. The crucial component of Type A seems rather to be negative emotions, especially the anger associated with an aggressively reactive temperament (Booth-Kewley & Friedman, 1987; Matthews, 1988). The effect is usually observed only in studies where people are interviewed because interviewers can assess verbal assertiveness and intensity. (If you pause in the middle of a sentence, an anger-prone person may jump in and finish it for you.) Among young and middle-age adults, those who react with anger over little things are the most coronary-prone. Furthermore, people who suppress their anger are prone to hypertension, another risk factor for heart attacks (see Figure 18–8). As Charles Spielberger and Perry London (1982) put it, rage "seems to lash back and strike us in the heart muscle."

Drawing by Fradon; © 1985 The New Yorker Magazine, Inc.

"At ten-thirty, you have an appointment to get even with Ward Ingram. At twelve, you're going to get even with Holus Wentworth at lunch. At three, you're getting even with the Pro-Tech Company at their annual meeting. And at five you're going to get even with Fred Benton over drinks."

"My tongue will tell the anger of my heart, or else my heart, concealing it, will break."
    William Shakespeare,
    The Taming of the Shrew, 1594

"The fire you kindle for your enemy often burns you more than him."
    Chinese proverb

STRESS AND RESISTANCE TO DISEASE

Not so long ago, the term "psychosomatic" was used to describe psychologically caused physical symptoms. To laypeople, the term implied that the symptoms were not real—they were "merely" psychosomatic. To avoid such connotations and to describe better the genuine physiological effects of psychological states, most experts today refer instead to **psychophysiological** ("mind-body") **illnesses.** These ill-

THE ANGER-IN SCALE

Directions: For each item circle the number which seems to best describe how you *generally* act or feel when you are *angry* or *furious*.

When angry or furious, . . .	Almost never	Some-times	Often	Almost always
I keep things in	1	2	3	4
I pout or sulk	1	2	3	4
I withdraw from people	1	2	3	4
I boil inside, but I don't show it	1	2	3	4
I tend to harbor grudges that I don't tell anyone about	1	2	3	4
I am secretly quite critical of others	1	2	3	4
I am angrier than I am willing to admit	1	2	3	4
I am irritated a great deal more than people are aware of	1	2	3	4

Scoring: Add up the points (1–4) for each item to get your total "Anger-In" Score, somewhere between 8 and 32. Most American college students tested by Charles Spielberger score between 10 and 18. High school students tend to score higher.

Source: The Anger-In Scale is a subscale of the Anger Expression Scale. Copyright © 1982 by C. D. Spielberger, E. H. Johnson, and G. A. Jacobs. Reprinted with permission.

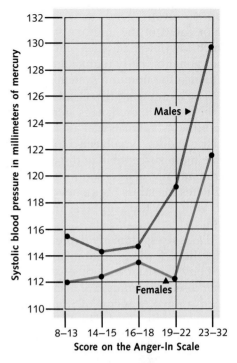

Figure 18–8 People who suppress their anger (as measured by a high score on the Anger-In Scale to the left) tend to have higher blood pressure than those who do not. Each data point on this graph (from Spielberger & others, 1985) represents approximately 100 high school students.

nesses, which include certain forms of hypertension, ulcers, and headaches, are not caused by any known physical disorder but instead seem to be linked, in varying degrees, to stress. In people with reactive temperaments, chronic stress produces various changes. In one person, prolonged resentment, anger, or anxiety may stimulate an excess of digestive acids that may eat away parts of the lining of the stomach or small intestine, creating ulcers. Another person under stress may retain excess sodium and fluids, which together with constriction of the arteries' muscle walls contributes to increased blood pressure (Light & others, 1983). If the stress is continual, the elevated blood pressure may develop into chronic hypertension, putting the person at greater risk for stroke, heart attack, or kidney failure.

Stress and the Immune System   Perhaps the strongest indication that psychophysiological ailments are real comes from dozens of new experiments that are revealing the influence of the nervous and endocrine systems on the body's immune system—its mechanisms for fighting disease. The immune system is a complex surveillance system that defends the body by isolating and destroying bacteria, viruses, and other foreign substances (Pomerleau & Rodin, 1986). It includes two types of white blood cells, called *lymphocytes.* B lymphocytes form in the bone marrow and release antibodies that fight bacterial infections. T lymphocytes form in the spleen and other lymphatic tissue and, among other duties, attack cancer cells, viruses, and foreign sub-

When organic causes of illness are unknown, it is tempting to invent psychological explanations. Before the germ that causes tuberculosis was discovered, personality explanations of TB were popular (Sontag, 1978).

"Each patient carries his own doctor inside him."
    Albert Schweitzer, 1875–1965

stances—even "good" ones, such as in tissue transplants. Another major agent of the immune system is the macrophage ("big eater"), which identifies, pursues, and ingests harmful invaders. Age, nutrition, genetics, body temperature, and—we now know—stress can all influence the immune system's activity.

The immune system is not a headless horseman; like other systems of the body, it exchanges information with the brain. In laboratory experiments, animals that are physically restrained, given unavoidable electric shocks, or subjected to loud noises or crowded conditions become more susceptible to disease (Jemmott & Locke, 1984). These experiments reveal a reason for the stress-disease connection: The brain regulates the stress hormones epinephrine, norepinephrine, and cortisol, which in turn suppress the disease-fighting lymphocytes (Marx, 1985).

Does stress similarly depress the immune system of humans? Consider the following: Accumulating evidence indicates that stress lowers the body's resistance to tuberculosis, upper respiratory infections, and other diseases (Jemmott & Locke, 1984). A 1984 report by a panel of the U.S. National Academy of Sciences indicates that the grief and depression that frequently follow the death of a spouse can have physiological counterparts—not only increased risk of a heart attack or stroke but also decreased protection against disease by the immune system. In three separate Skylab missions, the immune systems of the astronauts showed reduced effectiveness immediately after the excitement of re-entry and splashdown (Kimzey, 1975; Kimzey & others, 1976). Other studies indicate that students' disease-fighting mechanisms are weaker during high-stress times, such as exam weeks, and on days when they are upset (Jemmott & Locke, 1984; Stone & others, 1987). In one experiment, a stressful experience even increased the severity of symptoms experienced by volunteers who were knowingly infected with a cold virus (Dixon, 1986).

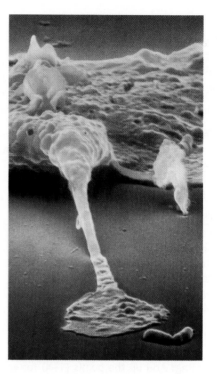

A large macrophage (at top) about to trap and ingest a tiny bacterium (lower right). Macrophages constantly patrol the body in their search for invaders, such as this *Escherichia coli* bacterium, and for debris, such as worn-out red blood cells.

Stress and Cancer   Even more provocative are controversial new findings that link stress to cancer. Several investigators have reported that states of depression, helplessness, or bereavement are sometimes followed a year or so later by the appearance of cancer. For example, cancer occurs more often than usual among those who are widowed, divorced, or separated. One study of the husbands of women with terminal breast cancer pinpointed a possible reason: During the first 2 months after the death of their wives, the bereaved men's lymphocyte responses dropped (Schleifer & others, 1979). Another study administered the MMPI personality test to 2018 middle-aged men employed by the Western Electric Company in 1958. Over the next 20 years, 7 percent of those not depressed and 12 percent of those somewhat depressed died of cancer—a difference not attributable to differences in their age, smoking, drinking, or physical characteristics (Persky & others, 1987). What is more, there are indications that cancer patients who bottle up their negative emotions may have less chance of survival than those who express them (Derogatis & others, 1979; Jensen, 1987).

To understand better the stress-cancer link, experimenters have inoculated rodents with tumor cells or given them carcinogens. Those rodents that are also exposed to uncontrollable stress, such as inescapable electric shocks, are less resistant to cancer (Sklar & Anisman, 1981). Because their immune systems are weakened, their tumors develop sooner and grow larger.

It is important not to overstate the link between emotions and cancer. Researcher Alan Justice (1985) notes that stress does not cause cancer but rather affects its growth by weakening the body's natural defenses against a few malignant cells. A relaxed, hopeful state may enhance these same defenses. Mastectomy patients who display a determination to conquer their breast cancer are more likely to survive than those who are stoic or feel hopeless (Hall & Goldstein, 1986; Pettingale & others, 1985).

One danger in publicizing such reports is that they may lead some patients to blame themselves for their cancer—"If only I had been more expressive, relaxed, hopeful." Unfortunately, the biological processes at work in advanced cancer are *not* likely to be derailed by a relaxed but determined spirit. Moreover, though there are some things we can do to control our experiences of stress, our emotional reactivity is partly inherited (recall pages 80–81). As theologian Reinhold Niebuhr recognized in his famous prayer (page 435), we therefore do well to accept those things about ourselves that we cannot change, to change those things that we can, and to seek the wisdom to discern the difference. By studying the interplay among emotions, the brain, and the immune system, health psychologists want to provide us with the wisdom we need to distinguish between pseudoscientific hocus-pocus and the genuine links between emotions and health.

The Immune Response and Conditioning   A hay fever sufferer sees the flower on the restaurant table and, not realizing it is plastic, begins to sneeze. Such experiences hint that stress is not the sole psychological influence upon the body's ailments. Simple classical conditioning, generalized to similar stimuli, may be an added influence. This raises an intriguing question: If conditioning affects the body's overt physiological responses, might it not affect the immune system as well?

Psychologist Robert Ader together with immunologist Nicholas Cohen (1985) discovered that the answer is yes. Ader came upon this discovery while researching taste aversion in rats. He paired the rats' drinking of saccharin-sweetened water with injections of a drug that causes stomachaches. Not surprisingly, the rats developed a taste aversion for sweetened water, an aversion the experimenter could extinguish only by force-feeding the rats nothing but sweetened water for several days. About 40 days after the experiment, some of the animals unexpectedly died. Ader subsequently learned that the drug injected into the rats was known to suppress immune functioning. "It dawned on me that at the same time we were conditioning an aversion to saccharin, we might be inadvertently conditioning a suppression of immune response" (quoted by Anderson, 1982). Further experiments confirmed that animals can indeed be conditioned to suppress their own immune systems by associating the taste of saccharin (the conditioned stimulus) with the immune suppressing effects of the drug (the unconditioned stimulus) (Figure 18–9).

Many questions about the role of the immune system and how to harness its healing potential remain unanswered. If it is possible to condition a suppression of the immune system, should it not also be possible to condition an enhancement of it? Might this be one way in which placebos—treatments that are actually inert—promote healing? Can a placebo sometimes elicit the same healthful state triggered by an actual drug? Research now under way may soon answer such questions.

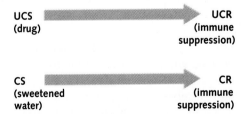

Figure 18–9   The conditioning of immune suppression. When an inert substance is associated with a drug that causes immune suppression, the immune response comes to be triggered by the inert substance alone.

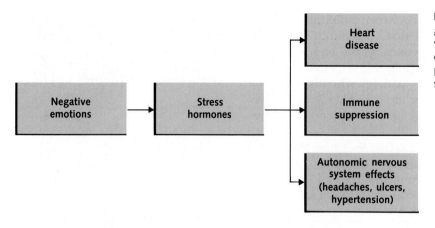

Figure 18–10   Negative emotions triggered by stressful life events can have a variety of health-related consequences, especially when experienced by ''disease-prone'' angry, depressed, or anxious persons (Friedman & Booth-Kewley, 1987).

For now, we can view the toll that stress sometimes takes on our resistance to disease as a price we pay for the adaptive benefits of the stress response (Figure 18–10). Stress, as we noted earlier, invigorates our lives by arousing and motivating us. An unstressed life would hardly be challenging or productive. Expending our resources in fighting or fleeing an external challenge aids our immediate survival, but sometimes at the cost of diminished resources for fighting internal challenges to the body's health.

COPING WITH STRESS

Coping with stress can mean confronting or escaping the problem and taking steps to prevent its recurrence. Yet stress is an unavoidable ingredient of modern life. This fact, coupled with the growing realization that recurring stress is linked with heart disease, lowered immunity, and other bodily ailments, gives us a clear message: If the stress cannot be eliminated by changing the situation, we had best learn to cope with the stressful events effectively and positively. Among the extensively studied coping mechanisms are aerobic exercise, biofeedback, relaxation, and social support networks.

Aerobic Exercise   Recent research indicates that *aerobic exercise*—sustained exercise, such as jogging, that increases heart and lung fitness—can reduce stress, depression, and anxiety. Some studies simply report that people who exercise regularly cope with stressful events better and are less depressed than those who do not. But stated the other way around—stressed and depressed people exercise less—cause and effect become unclear.

New experiments resolve the ambiguity by randomly assigning stressed, depressed, or anxious people either to aerobic exercise treatments or to other treatments. In one such experiment, Lisa McCann and David Holmes (1984) assigned one-third of a group of mildly depressed women students to a program of aerobic dancing and running and another third to a treatment of relaxation exercises; the remaining third received no treatment and served as controls. The students' self-reported depression levels were reassessed 10 weeks later. As Figure 18–11 illustrates, the women in the aerobic exercise program experienced the greatest decrease in depression.

Other research confirms the benefits of exercise. Shipboard sailors report less stress if assigned to an exercise routine (Pavett & others, 1987). One 16-year study of 17,000 middle-aged Harvard alumni found that those who exercised regularly were likely to live longer (Paf-

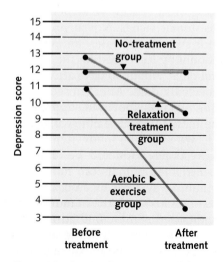

Figure 18–11   Aerobic exercise and depression. Mildly depressed college students who participated in an aerobic exercise program showed markedly reduced depression compared to those who participated in a treatment of relaxation exercises or received no treatment. (From McCann & Holmes, 1984.)

Studies of stress, anxiety, and depression reveal that aerobic exercise strengthens the spirit as well as the body.

fenbarger & others, 1986). Another study of 15,000 Control Data Corporation employees found that those who exercised had 25 percent fewer hospital days than those who didn't (Anderson & Jose, 1987). And an analysis of data from forty-three studies revealed that, compared to people who exercise vigorously, inactive adults have twice the risk of heart attack (Powell & others, 1987). Even a daily 10-minute walk raises energy levels and lowers tension for 2 hours (Thayer, 1987). Off your duffs, couch potatoes!

Researchers are now wondering *why* aerobic exercise alleviates the effects of stress and negative emotions. They know that exercise strengthens the heart and lowers both blood pressure and the blood pressure reaction to stress (Perkins & others, 1986; Roviario & others, 1984). Does exercise trigger increased production of mood-boosting neurotransmitters such as the endorphins? Are the emotional benefits a side effect of the increased body warmth that occurs during exercise or the muscle relaxation and sounder sleep that occur afterward? Does a sense of accomplishment and an improved physique enhance one's emotional state? Such are some of the suggested explanations (Martinsen, 1987).

"Gentlemen, please! I'm sure we can all agree that both the rowing machine and the stationary bicycle have a place in any serious program of cardiovascular exercise."

Drawing by Lorenz; © 1984 The New Yorker Magazine, Inc.

Biofeedback When a few psychologists started experimenting with ways to train people to bring their internal functions, such as heart rate and blood pressure, under conscious control, many of their colleagues thought them foolish. These functions are, after all, controlled by the autonomic ("involuntary") nervous system. Then, in the late 1960s, ingenious experiments by respected psychologists began to make the doubters change their minds. Neal Miller, for example, found that rats could learn to control their heartbeats if given pleasurable brain stimulation when they increased or decreased their heart rate. Later research revealed that paralyzed humans (who cannot use their skeletal muscles) could also learn to control their blood pressure (Miller & Brucker, 1979).

Miller was experimenting with *biofeedback*, a system of electronically recording, amplifying, and feeding back information about subtle physiological responses. Biofeedback instruments have been likened to a mirror (Norris, 1986). The instruments no more provide a means for achieving bodily self-control than a mirror provides a means for combing one's hair. Rather, they reflect the results of a person's own efforts, allowing an individual to assess which techniques are most effective in controlling a particular physiological response.

In the example in Figure 18–12, a sensor records tension in the forehead muscle of a headache sufferer. This biological information is processed by a computer and instantly fed back to the person in some easily understood image. As the forehead muscle relaxes, a line on a screen may go lower or a light may grow brighter. The patient's task is to learn to control the line or the light and thereby learn how to control voluntarily the tension in the forehead muscle and the accompanying headaches.

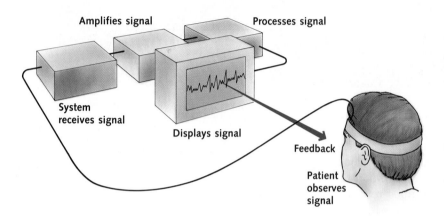

Amplifies signal   Processes signal

System receives signal

Displays signal

Feedback

Patient observes signal

Figure 18–12   Biofeedback systems such as this one, which records tension in the forehead muscle of a headache sufferer, allow people to monitor one or another of their subtle physiological responses in an attempt to modify that response.

Initially, biofeedback researchers and practitioners reported that people could be trained through such procedures to increase their production of alpha brain waves, warm their heads, and lower their blood pressure—all signs of a more relaxed state. But a decade later, when researchers stepped back to assess the results of hundreds of experiments, the initial claims for biofeedback were found to have been overblown and oversold (Miller, 1985). During biofeedback training, people do enjoy a calm, tranquil, relaxing experience, but this comes about mostly from accompanying factors such as restricted sensory input (Plotkin, 1979). Biofeedback does enable some people to influence their finger temperature and forehead-muscle tension, and it can help somewhat in reducing the intensity of migraine headaches and chronic pain (King & Montgomery, 1980; Qualls & Sheehan, 1981; Turk & others, 1979). But other, simpler methods of relaxation—for which no expensive equipment is required—produce many of the same benefits and results.

Today, biofeedback is often used in combination with other techniques to help patients control the physical symptoms of stress (Miller, 1983a). Patients in one hypertension program at the Menninger Foundation in Kansas were placed on a drug that reduced their blood pressure. Biofeedback was then used in an effort to wean the patients from the medication while maintaining or further lowering their blood pressure. With biofeedback, 65 percent of patients treated between 1975 and 1983 were successfully weaned from the medication (Fahrion & others, 1986).

Relaxation   If relaxation is an important component of biofeedback, then might not relaxation exercises alone be an even more natural antidote to stress? Cardiologist Herbert Benson (1976 to 1987) became intrigued with this possibility when he found that experienced meditators were able to decrease their blood pressure, heart rate, and oxygen consumption and raise their fingertip temperature. You can experience the essence of this "relaxation response," as Benson called it, right now by following a few simple steps: Assume a comfortable position, close your eyes, breathe deeply, and relax your muscles from foot to face. Now, concentrate on a single phrase—a word, such as "one," or perhaps a prayer, such as "Lord, have mercy." Let other thoughts drift away when they intrude as you repeat this phrase continually for 10 to 20 minutes. Simply by setting aside a quiet time or two each day, many people report enjoying a greater sense of tranquillity and inward stillness. In experiments, people who practice relaxation also commonly exhibit lowered blood pressure and strengthened immune defenses (Jasnoski & others, 1986).

If Type A heart attack victims could be taught to relax, might not their risk of another attack be reduced? Couldn't the better management of one's emotions do as much as controlled exercise and an altered diet to prevent heart attacks? To find out, Meyer Friedman and his colleagues randomly assigned hundreds of middle-aged heart attack survivors in San Francisco to one of two groups: The first group received standard advice from cardiologists concerning medications, diet, and exercise habits; the second group received similar advice plus continuing counseling on how to slow down and relax—by walking, talking, and eating more slowly; smiling at others and laughing at themselves; admitting mistakes; taking time to enjoy life; and renewing their religious faith. As Figure 18–13 indicates, over the ensuing 3 years the second group experienced half as many repeat heart attacks as the first group. This, wrote the exuberant Friedman, is "a spectacular reduction in their cardiac recurrence rate. No drug, food, or exercise program ever devised, not even a coronary bypass surgical program, could match the protection against recurrent heart attacks" (Friedman & Ulmer, 1984, p. 141).

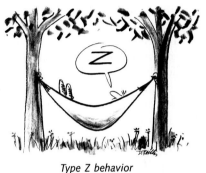

Type Z behavior

Drawing by Reilly; © 1987 The New Yorker Magazine, Inc.

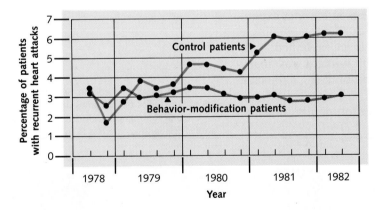

Figure 18–13   In the San Francisco Recurrent Coronary Prevention Project, heart attack survivors who received counseling aimed at modifying their Type A behavior suffered fewer repeat heart attacks over the ensuing years than those in the control group who received only counseling from a cardiologist. (From Friedman & Ulmer, 1984.)

It remains for other researchers to do the painstaking work of identifying which of Friedman's dozens of stress reduction drills are actually beneficial. Even while Friedman was collecting his data, other investigators were at work studying specific stress buffers. For example, laughter seems to work in ways similar to exercise—it arouses us and then leaves us feeling more relaxed (Robinson, 1983). This may help explain findings that people who laugh readily and have a sense of humor are less disturbed by stressful life events (Lefcourt & Martin, 1986; Nezu & others, 1988). Although it would probably be an overstatement to suggest that "Laughter is the best medicine," there is reason to suspect that, indeed, he who laughs, lasts.

"A cheerful heart is a good medicine, but a downcast spirit dries up the bones."
Proverbs 17:22

Social Support   Yet another stress buffer is the support enjoyed by those who have sustained close relationships with friends, kin, or fellow members of close-knit religious or other organizations. Six massive investigations, each of which studied thousands of people across several years, provide strong evidence that social relations affect health: People who enjoy close relationships are less likely to die prematurely than are those with few social ties (Cohen, 1988; House & others, 1988). The conflicts and responsibilities associated with close relationships can also be a source of stress. Generally, though, close relationships help to buffer major stressors such as unemployment, surgery, or bereavement.

There are several possible explanations for the link between social support and health. Perhaps people with strong social ties eat better, exercise more, and smoke and drink less. Perhaps social relationships provide aid in evaluating and overcoming stressful events, such as social rejection. Perhaps they help bolster our threatened self-esteem. When wounded by someone's dislike or the loss of a job, a friend's advice, assistance, and reassurances may be good medicine (Cutrona, 1986; Rook, 1987).

Close relationships also provide the opportunity to confide painful feelings. In one study, health psychologists James Pennebaker and Robin O'Heeron (1984) contacted the surviving spouses of people who had committed suicide or died in car accidents. Those who bore their grief alone had more health problems than those who openly expressed it. Talking about things that trouble us can be therapeutic. In a simulated confessional, Pennebaker asked volunteers to share with an experimenter who was hidden behind a screen some upsetting events that had been preying on their minds. Some of the volunteers were asked to describe a trivial event before they divulged the troubling one. Physiological measures revealed that their bodies remained tense the whole time they talked about the trivial event; they relaxed only when they later confided the cause of their turmoil. Even writing about personal traumas in a diary can help. When volunteers in another experiment did this, they had fewer health problems during the ensuing 6 months (Pennebaker & Beall, 1984). As one subject explained, "Although I have not talked with anyone about what I wrote, I was finally able to deal with it, work through the pain instead of trying to block it out. Now it doesn't hurt to think about it."

Sometimes suppressed traumas eat away at us for months or years.

"Friendship is a sovereign antidote against all calamities."
    Seneca,
    Of a Happy Life, A.D. 54

Friendships are good medicine. Several long-term studies of thousands of people have found that people with close supportive relationships are less likely to die prematurely.

Such has been the experience of many combat veterans of the Vietnam war (Kaylor & others, 1987) and victims of sexual assault who suffer from *posttraumatic stress disorder,* symptoms of which include haunting memories, social withdrawal, and anxiety or depression. To pin down the frequency of such problems, the Centers for Disease Control (1988) compared 7000 Vietnam combat veterans with 7000 noncombat veterans who served during the same years. The combat stress more than doubled a veteran's risk of suffering alcohol abuse, depression, or anxiety.

Traumatic stress can also have long-term effects on physical health. When Pennebaker surveyed more than 700 undergraduate women, he found that about 1 in 12 reported a traumatic sexual experience in childhood. Compared with women who had experienced nonsexual traumas, such as parental death or divorce, the sexually abused women, especially those who had kept their secret to themselves, reported more health problems, such as headaches and stomach ailments.

Summing up, we can say that although stressful events can sometimes be debilitating, the level of stress depends on the person and the environment. Because nothing is stressful until it is appraised as such, our personalities influence how we react when stressful things happen. Moreover, the negative impacts of stressful events can be buffered by a relaxed, healthy life-style and by the comfort and aid provided by supportive friends and family (Figure 18–14).

REACTIONS TO ILLNESS

Health psychologists study not only the links between stress and illness but also how we cope with illness. In a perfect world, people would behave rationally at each step in the decision scheme for seeking and complying with medical treatment shown in Figure 18–15. First, they would notice and realistically evaluate the seriousness of their aches and pains; second, they would seek medical care when it is needed; and third, they would follow the prescribed treatment. But most people do not do this. To find out why, health psychologists are studying people's behaviors at each of the three steps.

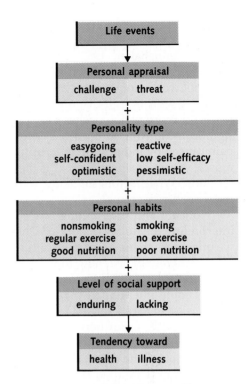

Figure 18–14   Coping with stress. Life events can be debilitating or not, depending on whether the stresses are buffered by a stress-resistant disposition, healthy habits, and enduring social support.

Figure 18–15   The three steps in the decision scheme for seeking and complying with medical treatment. (From Safer & others, 1979.)

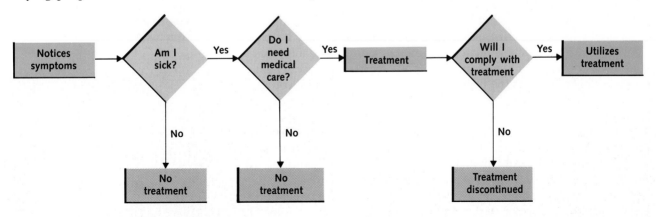

AM I SICK? NOTICING AND EXPLAINING SYMPTOMS

The typical physical complaints of college students include headache, stomachache, nasal congestion, sore muscles, ringing in the ears, excess perspiration, cold hands, racing heart, dizziness, stiff joints, and diarrhea or constipation. In fact, the chances are good that you have recently experienced one or more of these symptoms to at least a slight degree (Pennebaker, 1982). Such symptoms require your interpretation. Are you coming down with the flu or a cold? Or are the symptoms not worthy of your attention? Hardly a week goes by without our playing doctor by self-diagnosing the meaning of some symptom.

With more serious aches and pains, the questions become more significant. Is your stubbed toe bruised or broken? Is your abdominal pain caused by indigestion or a ruptured appendix? Is the chest pain a muscle spasm or a heart attack? Is the small lump a meaningless cyst or a tumor? What factors influence whether we notice and how we explain such symptoms?

Noticing and interpreting our body's signals is like noticing and interpreting the noises of our car. Unless the signals are loud and clear, we often miss them. Most of us cannot tell whether our car needs an oil change merely by listening to its engine. Similarly, most of us are not very accurate judges of our heart rate, blood-sugar level, or blood pressure. People guess at their blood pressure based on how they feel, which is often barely related to their actual blood pressure (Baumann & Leventhal, 1985). Furthermore, the early signs of many illnesses, including cancer and heart disease, are subtle and often go unnoticed. Half or more of heart attack victims die before seeking and receiving medical help (DiMatteo & Friedman, 1982).

As we saw in the discussion of normal consciousness in Chapter 8, our ability to attend consciously to different inputs is limited. We usually attend selectively to only one thing at a time, say, one voice at a party. Thus, if external stimuli command our attention, our internal cues do not. When students in one experiment were working comfortably on an arithmetic task, they were unlikely to notice bursts of air on their forearms (Pennebaker & Brittingham, 1982). In another experiment, students ran faster when jogging through a beautiful wooded environment than when running the same distance around a track, apparently because the distractions of the woods made them less aware of their fatigue (Pennebaker & Lightner, 1980) (Figure 18–16). In general, we are more likely to notice such symptoms as fatigue when we are in quiet, uneventful environments than when our minds are engaged.

Once we notice symptoms, we tend to interpret them according to familiar disease schemas. In medical schools, this can have amusing results. As part of their training, medical students learn the symptoms associated with various diseases. At the same time, they may be experiencing a variety of stress-related symptoms. Understandably, many students attribute their symptoms to recently learned disease schemas ("Maybe this wheeze is the beginnings of pneumonia"). (As you may have already discovered, psychology students are vulnerable to this same effect as they read about psychological disorders.)

Once people form the idea that their symptoms match those of a particular disease schema, they often become selectively attuned to sensory information. And that, researchers Diane Ruble and Jeanne Brooks-Gunn (1979, 1987) maintain, helps explain why many women believe that they are more depressed, tense, irritable, and uncomfortable during the time prior to menstruation. As we saw in Chapter 11, people tend to notice and remember instances that confirm their beliefs and not to notice instances that contradict them. Thus, a woman who feels tense the day before her period is due to begin may attribute the tension to her being premenstrual. But if the woman feels similarly

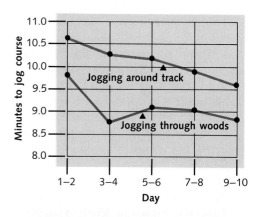

Figure 18–16   Joggers run faster when distracted from their fatigue by the beauty of a course in the woods than when running the same distance around a track. (From Pennebaker & Lightner, 1980.)

tense 2 weeks later or does not feel tense the day her next period is about to start, she may be less likely to notice and remember these instances, which would *dis*confirm her premenstrual syndrome schema. Many researchers are now persuaded that some women do indeed experience not only menstrual discomfort but also premenstrual tension (Bancroft & Backstrom, 1985; Haemmerlie & Montgomery, 1987; McMillan & Pihl, 1987). Nevertheless, anxiety and depression seem not as strongly related to the premenstrual phase as many people believe (Brooks-Gunn & Ruble, 1986). And contrary to the presumptions of some employers, women's physical and mental skills do not fluctuate noticeably with their menstrual cycles.

Taken together, these examples indicate that people's sensitivity to being aware of and interpreting bodily symptoms varies from a life-threatening failure to notice the symptoms of serious illness to hypochondriasis—the persistent conviction of being ill. Generally speaking, though, people are prone to optimistic denials of health problems. John Jemmott and his colleagues (1986) demonstrated such optimism experimentally after they "tested" students for the presence of a fictitious enzyme deficiency. Compared with students who were told they did not have the deficiency, those who were told they did dismissed it as a less serious problem. Moreover, contrary to the common belief that elderly people tend to overreport medical complaints, Paul Costa and Robert McCrae (1985) found that, although the elderly do have more health problems, they usually complain only when they are actually ill.

SEEKING TREATMENT

Once people notice a symptom and interpret it as possibly serious, the decision to seek medical care is influenced by a variety of factors. People are more likely to seek treatment if they believe their symptoms have a physical rather than a psychological cause (Bishop, 1987). However, if they feel embarrassed about their ailment, if they think the likely benefits of medical attention or counseling will not be worth the anticipated cost and inconvenience, or if they dread and want to avoid a potentially devastating diagnosis, they may delay seeking help.

The U.S. National Center for Health Statistics reports a gender difference in decisions to seek medical treatment: Women report more symptoms, visit physicians more often, and use more prescription and nonprescription drugs. Are women, in fact, more often sick? Actually, there is evidence that men may be more disease-prone. Among other problems, men have higher rates of hypertension, ulcers, and cancer as well as shorter life expectancies (Pennebaker, 1982). Why the difference? Perhaps males are more focused on the external environment and are therefore less attentive to their internal state. Perhaps they perceive as many symptoms as women yet are more reluctant to admit "weakness" and seek help (Bishop, 1984). Or perhaps those women who are not employed full-time simply feel freer to make time for a doctor's appointment (Marcus & Siegel, 1982).

THE PATIENT ROLE

As she approaches the hospital, Mrs. Hernandez anxiously wonders whether a woman in her seventies should really be having heart surgery. After filling out the admission forms, she is given the standard hospital gown to wear and is put in a bare, white-walled room with

"When a man can't explain a woman's actions, the first thing he thinks about is the condition of her uterus."
Clare Boothe Luce,
Slam the Door Softly, 1970

three other patients. From time to time—she can never predict when—nurses or technicians come in to stick her with a needle or cart her off for another unexplained test. Many of the staff members talk to her in ways she is unaccustomed to, as if she were a child or not all there. "Climb up on this table, dear," the x-ray technician orders, "so we can have a little look inside your tummy." With visits by friends and family members prohibited during some hours and occurring unpredictably during others, Mrs. Hernandez feels no more control over her social contacts than over her hospital regimen.

Certainly, Mrs. Hernandez's experience does not describe that of all hospital patients. Such treatment is typical enough, however, to draw psychologists' attention to people's reactions to their loss of control in hospital settings. As we noted earlier, having no control over what you do and what others do to you can make unpleasant events profoundly stressful. In hospitals, people who adopt what psychologist Shelley Taylor (1979) called the *good-patient role*—being cooperative, undemanding, and unquestioning—experience the greatest loss of control. Thus, "good" behavior can be bad for the docile patient if that patient is actually feeling helpless, anxious, and depressed. Because most people are reasonably good patients, doctors generally underestimate how much information their patients really desire (Krupat, 1986). Tape recordings of doctor-patient conversations reveal that doctors also greatly overestimate how much time they spend providing their patients with information.

Those who adopt the more uncooperative, complaining, demanding *bad-patient role* may not be much better off because, as we have seen, anger and hostility can also have harmful consequences. Moreover, in some cases nurses avoid disagreeable patients or subdue them with medication. On a more positive note, the stress experienced by both the helpless "good" patient and the angry "bad" patient can be lessened when patients actively participate by helping to decide which course of treatment to pursue and then monitoring their own progress (Pomerleau & Rodin, 1986).

Can anything be done to alleviate the stress caused by medical procedures? Imagine that you have just been admitted to the hospital and that tomorrow you will undergo surgery. Should the doctor give you kindhearted reassurances that "it really won't be so bad"? Or should the doctor let you know what you can honestly expect afterward so that you can prepare yourself for any pain and not be surprised when it occurs? Several studies indicate that providing patients with realistic information about what they can expect before, during, and after a medical procedure, together with instructions on how to cope with any discomfort, reduces their distress later (Janis, 1983). When patients know that things are going according to plan, they are less anxious, and when they are less anxious, they are better able to cope with discomfort (Figure 18–17). As a patient in one study explained, "I knew there might be some bad pains, so when my side started to ache, I told myself that this didn't mean anything had gone wrong" (Janis, 1969, p. 98).

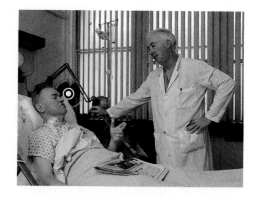

Realistic information about medical procedures helps patients prepare for and cope with the stress and discomfort of hospitalization and its aftermath.

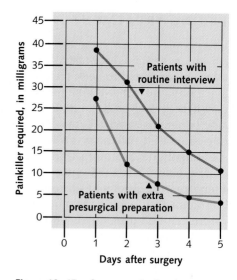

Figure 18–17 Surgery patients who were fully informed about the consequences of abdominal surgery and how to cope required less painkilling morphine after the surgery than patients not so informed. (From Egbert & others, 1964.)

PATIENT ADHERENCE TO TREATMENT

For years, it was widely assumed that the doctor ordered and the patient dutifully obeyed. Then, between 1974 and 1977, some 250 research studies revealed that as many as half of all patients fail to follow their doctors' recommendations (Adler & Stone, 1984). Patients stop taking their prescribed medications, ignore suggestions for adopting more healthful life-styles, and fail to report recurrences of symptoms. Of people with dangerously high blood pressure who seek treatment, only about half adhere to the prescribed treatment regimen (Leventhal & others, 1984). Even among women who have had breast cancer, fewer than half follow their doctors' recommendation of breast self-examination (Taylor & others, 1984).

As we will see in the next chapter, Social Influence, people under the direct orders of authority figures in experiments will comply to the point of supposedly giving painful electric shocks to others. But once patients are away from their doctors' surveillance, they may fail to comply even with orders to take pills that will prevent them from going blind. The questions for social psychologists are made-to-order: Why don't patients follow their doctors' orders when doing so is in their own best interest? And what can physicians do to get their patients to comply more fully?

Studies of the doctor-patient relationship offer some answers (DiMatteo & Friedman, 1982). For one thing, surprising numbers of patients simply do not understand either their illnesses or their doctors' instructions. Patients told to take prescribed medication "as needed for water retention" can understand this to mean they should take the pill when they need to retain water (Mazullo & others, 1974). And sometimes instructions *are* confusing. Does "take one pill every 6 hours" apply only to waking hours—that is, three pills a day? The solution is greater clarity on the part of the doctor. When medical orders are given in vivid, nontechnical language along with easy-to-follow written instructions, patient compliance increases (Gatchel & Baum, 1983).

Patient response is also affected by how recommendations are framed. When asked to imagine they had 1 year to live, nearly all said they would choose to undergo an operation that might extend their life expectancy to 5 years, given "a 40 percent chance of surviving it"; however, most said they would *not* want the surgery given "a 60 percent chance of not surviving" (Wilson & others, 1987).

Health care providers' communication skill influences patients' decisions to comply with treatment regimens. Both the boy learning about his diabetes from his nurse and the man getting advice from his doctor will be more likely to follow clearly explained instructions.

In addition, patients' adherence to treatment instructions improves when they have a warm relationship with their doctor and when they are involved in planning their own regimen of diet, exercise, and medication (Janis, 1982b). Fortunately, the doctor-patient relationship can be warmed considerably with only a small effort on the part of the doctor—speaking to patients by name, explaining procedures while they are occurring, smiling, and saying good-bye (DiMatteo & DiNicola, 1982).

Finally, although patients may understand that their behaviors are harmful, when the delayed rewards of a more healthful life-style must compete with the immediate discomfort or inconvenience of exercising, flossing their teeth, or giving up smoking, the immediate consequences often win out. Recall from Chapter 9, Learning, that immediate reinforcements are more effective than delayed ones. We can *know* that in the long run smoking is harmful and hardly worth the pleasure it provides, yet continue to smoke. We can *know* that high blood pressure is dangerous and still ignore the problem, especially if our hypertension medication has immediate side effects, such as sexual impotence. Thus, to be effective, strategies for increasing patients' compliance need to offer immediate rewards for compliant behavior.

PROMOTING HEALTH

Traditionally, people have sought out medical doctors only for the diagnosis and treatment of disease. That, say the advocates of behavioral medicine, is like ignoring your car's maintenance and going to a mechanic only when the car breaks down. Now that we realize many of our medical problems are intimately related to our behaviors, attention is being focused more and more on health maintenance—on ways of preventing illness and promoting well-being.

Researchers are only beginning to compute the cost-effectiveness of various health-promotion programs (Kaplan, 1984; Taylor, 1987). But most are optimistic that creating programs to prevent disease by modifying people's personal habits will cost far less than it now costs to treat their diseases. With North America's annual health care expenditures now at over one-half trillion dollars, even modestly successful health-promotion programs could prove cost-effective. The economic costs of alcohol abuse, for example, exceed $100 billion annually, counting everything from medical bills to lost workdays (Desmond, 1987). Any program that reduces alcohol abuse would certainly save more money than its abuse now costs.

Businesses pay half of America's health care costs (Cohen, 1985), so many of them are introducing health-promotion programs for their employees. Some are even setting up on-site clinics that offer health-related testing and counseling. The workplace is an ideal location for the promotion of health and vitality because most employees are there regularly. In addition, employers can actively encourage healthy behaviors by creating and maintaining healthy work environments, providing social support, arranging for competition between work groups, and awarding bonuses or days off for sticking to an exercise or smoking cessation regimen (Abrams & Wilson, 1986; Cataldo & Coates, 1986). At work sites where Control Data Corporation implemented its StayWell health program, smoking dropped 20 percent compared to other work sites, the number of overweight employees dropped 25 percent, and the number not exercising dropped 32 percent—with corresponding reductions in health care claims and sick leave (Anderson & Jose, 1987).

In the earlier discussion on coping with stress, we noted things people can do to improve their health. Let's now examine some additional behaviors that strongly affect our health—namely, smoking, nutrition, and weight control.

SMOKING

In 1980, the U.S. Public Health Service announced that smoking is "clearly the largest preventable cause of illness and premature death." By 1988, the U.S. Surgeon General declared that tobacco products are just as addictive as heroin and cocaine. Given that 30 percent of all cancer deaths and 30 percent or more of the deaths caused by heart disease in the United States are linked with cigarette smoking, the elimination of the habit would do more to increase life expectancy than any other single preventive measure (Surgeon General, 1983). The reality of smoking's destructiveness has prompted psychologists to study the factors that influence people to start smoking, what it is about tobacco that keeps people smoking, and the effectiveness of efforts to stop or prevent smoking.

Increasingly, North American corporations recognize that good health is good business, as exemplified in this aerobic workout session for Ford employees.

Ironically, the same government that warns us of 350,000 tobacco-related deaths a year and seems determined to remove other less harmful substances from our foods, provides subsidies to tobacco growers (Centers for Disease Control, 1987).

When and Why Do People Start Smoking? Smoking most often begins during early adolescence and is especially common among those whose friends, parents, and siblings are smokers (Chassin & others, 1988). If you are still a nonsmoker, the odds are overwhelming that you will forever remain so.

The vulnerability of adolescents to the allure of smoking can be understood with the help of social-cognitive theory, which explains how behaviors are acquired through the models we imitate and the social rewards we receive (see pages 249–251). Teenage smokers tend to be perceived by other teenagers as tough, precocious, and sociable (Barton & others, 1982). Self-conscious adolescents, who tend to think the world is watching their every move, may therefore begin smoking to imitate those tough, cool models, to receive the social reward of being accepted by them, and to project a mature image (Covington & Omelich, 1988).

Why Do People Continue Smoking? Most adults who smoke cigarettes would rather not (Surgeon General, 1988). However, once influenced to begin smoking, addiction to nicotine makes it difficult to quit. The smoking habit is hard to break because the craving, hunger, and irritability that accompany nicotine withdrawal are aversive states that can be relieved by a cigarette. After an hour or a day without smoking, the habitual smoker finds a cigarette powerfully reinforcing. In fact, if given low-nicotine cigarettes, the smoker will smoke more of them in order to maintain a roughly constant level of nicotine in the blood.

Behavioral medicine researchers Ovide and Cynthia Pomerleau (1984) reported that smoking not only serves as a negative reinforcer—by terminating the aversive craving—but also as a pleasureful positive reinforcer. Nicotine triggers the release of epinephrine and norepinephrine, which in turn diminish appetite and boost alertness and mental efficiency. More significantly, nicotine also stimulates the central nervous system to release acetylcholine and beta-endorphin, neurotransmitters that serve to calm anxiety and reduce sensitivity to pain. These "positive" rewards of smoking, when combined with the relief smoking provides from the unpleasantness of withdrawal, keep people smoking even when they wish they could stop—even when they know that they are committing "slow-motion suicide."

How Effective Are Programs to Stop Smoking? Efforts to help people stop smoking have used a variety of techniques, including public health warnings, counseling, drug treatments, hypnosis, aversive conditioning (for example, having people rapidly smoke cigarette after cigarette until they are literally sickened), operant conditioning, cognitive therapy, and support groups. Although these treatments are often effective in the short run, the bad news is that all but one-third to one-quarter of the participants eventually succumb to the habit again (Pomerleau & Rodin, 1986). During a 3-week smoking-cessation program sponsored by a TV evening news program, 50,000 Chicagoans picked up free stop-smoking manuals—but only 20 percent were successfully abstaining 1 year later (Jason, 1986).

That does mean, however, there were 10,000 successful quitters. And better news comes from a Surgeon General's report (1988): America's 51 million smokers are now almost equaled by its 41 million ex-smokers. The American Council on Education reports that the 1985 smoking rate among first-year college students was just over 8 percent—

For early adolescents, the decision to smoke is usually influenced by a need for acceptance by their peers and by a desire to project the images they see in cigarette ads.

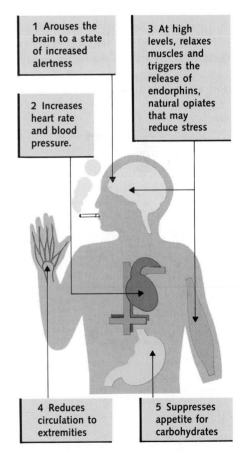

1 Arouses the brain to a state of increased alertness

3 At high levels, relaxes muscles and triggers the release of endorphins, natural opiates that may reduce stress

2 Increases heart rate and blood pressure.

4 Reduces circulation to extremities

5 Suppresses appetite for carbohydrates

The physiological effects of nicotine. Nicotine mimics the action of the neurotransmitter acetylcholine, rapidly producing the effects indicated above.

half that of 20 years before—with the greatest decline evident in male students' smoking (Astin & others, 1987). Although women are now nearly as likely to smoke as men, this reflects a greater drop in the rate of male smoking rather than a rise in the rate of female smoking. Because so many people have stopped smoking and because the number of adolescents who never begin is rising, the net result is a steady decline in the percentage of Americans who smoke (Figure 18–18). Thanks in part to such trends, the death rate due to coronary heart disease has declined by about 30 percent since the mid-1960s.

How Can We Prevent Smoking?   It is vastly easier never to begin smoking than to stop once addicted. Drawing upon social psychological analyses of why youngsters start smoking, several research teams have devised strategies for interrupting the behavior pattern that leads to smoking (Evans & others, 1984; Murray & others, 1984). In one such study, a research team led by Alfred McAlister (1980) had high school students help prepare seventh graders to resist peer pressure to smoke. The youngsters were taught to respond to ads implying that liberated women smoke by observing, "She's not really liberated if she is hooked on tobacco." They also role-played being called "chicken" for not trying a cigarette and practiced responding with statements like, "I'd be a real chicken if I smoked just to impress you." After several sessions during both the seventh and eighth grades, these students were half as likely to begin smoking compared with a control group at a neighboring junior high school, even though the parents of both sets of students had the same smoking rate (Figure 18–19). From this experiment and others like it have evolved specific curricular programs that teachers can implement easily and inexpensively, with the hope of significantly reducing future smoking rates.

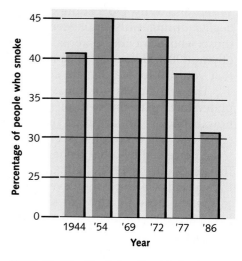

Figure 18–18   The Gallup Organization's (1986) periodic survey of smoking behavior revealed that in 1986 smoking was at its lowest level in four decades.

To guess which of two people is a high school dropout and which is a college student, observe who smokes—as most dropouts, but fewer than 1 in 10 college students, do (Johnston, 1988).

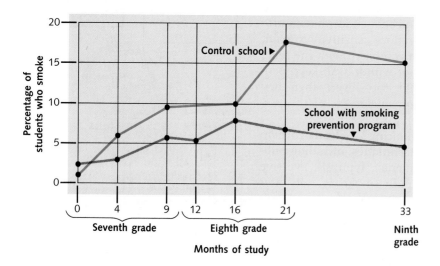

Figure 18–19   Junior high school students who participated in a smoking prevention program that prepared them to cope with smoking ads and peer pressures were much less likely to begin smoking than were students at a matched control school. (From McAlister & others, 1980.)

NUTRITION

Is the way you feel and act affected by what you eat? The discovery that specific neurotransmitters affect emotion and behavior has fueled speculation that eating foods which provide the biochemical building blocks for those neurotransmitters may affect mood and behavior. For example, the body synthesizes the neurotransmitter serotonin from the amino acid tryptophan. Several studies have found that high-carbohydrate foods (such as bread, potatoes, and pasta) can increase the relative amount of tryptophan reaching the brain, which serves to raise the level of serotonin, which facilitates feeling relaxed, sleepy, and less sensitive to pain (Spring, 1988). When we desire food for thought, a low-carbohydrate, high-protein meal seems to improve concentration and alertness.

Other nutritional issues are now the subject of vigorous research and debate. Are children and prisoners hyped up by a diet high in sugar and calmed by one that is low in sugar? Researchers now doubt this folk wisdom (Spring & others, 1987). Do diets high in cholesterol literally eat your heart out? Researchers are still debating this, although men with high cholesterol levels who take a cholesterol-reducing drug and go on a low cholesterol diet are indeed less likely to suffer heart disease (Roberts, 1987). What are the links between diet and high blood pressure? The findings indicate that hypertensive people tend to have not only higher than normal salt intake but also lower than normal calcium intake (Feinleib & others, 1984; McCarron & others, 1984).

Even clearer are the links between diet and cancer. Throughout most of its history, our species has existed on a low-fat, high-fiber diet, a diet that is still common in hunter-gatherer societies that have survived into the present. For the rest of us, our Stone Age physiology must now contend with a more sedentary way of life and a diet that is much higher in fat and lower in fiber. Dietary fat accounts for an unhealthy 37 percent of Americans' calorie intake, according to a 1988 report of the Surgeon General. Such a diet contains more of the biochemicals that promote the growth of cancerous cells and less of the dietary elements, such as those found in broccoli, cabbage, and cauliflower, that inhibit such growth (Cohen, 1987).

One of the consequences of a high-fat diet can be seen in Figure 18–20, which displays the strong positive correlation between different nations' fat consumption and their death rates from breast cancer. These correlational data are strengthened by laboratory experiments in which mice on a high-fat diet are twice as likely as other mice to de-

Figure 18–20 Diet and cancer. As a nation's fat intake increases, so also does its rate of breast cancer deaths. (From ''Diet and Cancer'' by L. A. Cohen. Copyright © 1987 by Scientific American, Inc. All rights reserved.)

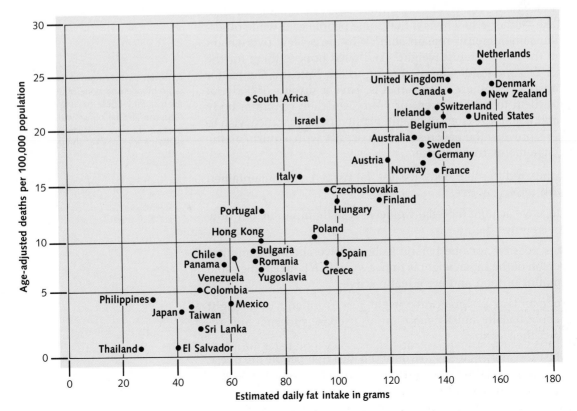

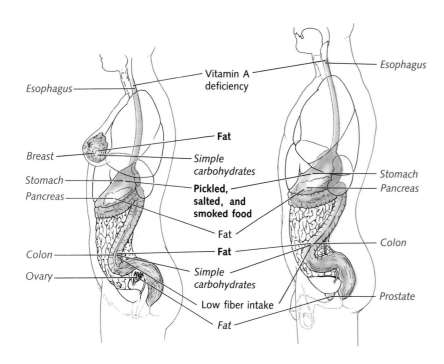

Figure 18–21   Components of diet and specific cancers. Correlations are indicated in the center of the figure: The strongest links are shown in boldface type, weaker ones in regular type, and weakest ones in italic type. (From "Diet and Cancer" by L. A. Cohen. Copyright © 1987 by Scientific American, Inc. All rights reserved.)

velop mammary tumors. Additional studies with humans and experiments with rodents suggest how diet can contribute to other forms of cancer as well (Figure 18–21).

OBESITY AND WEIGHT CONTROL

A heightened cancer rate is not the only consequence of a high-fat diet. Another consequence can be obesity. But there is more to obesity than caloric intake—otherwise why is it that some people gain while others who eat the same amount remain slim? Why do so few overweight people win the battle against weight? And what hope is there for the one-quarter of Americans who, according to the National Center for Health Statistics (1985), are *obese*—that is, have a surplus of body fat that causes them to be 20 percent or more over their optimum body weight—and who for reasons of health, vitality, or appearance wish to reduce? Let's preview the new research on obesity with a quiz: Are the following statements true or false?

One can be over normal weight—due to large muscle and bone mass—and not be even slightly obese (having excess fat). One can also be obese without being overweight (U.S. Department of Health and Human Services, 1983b).

1.   Compared to other body tissues, fat tissue can be maintained with fewer calories.

2.   Once we acquire fat cells, we never lose them, no matter how severely we diet.

3.   It is possible for one person to be overweight while another person of the same height is thin, even when both eat the same amount of food and are equally active.

4.   To maintain a significant weight loss, formerly overweight people usually must remain on an exercise program and restrict their eating.

5.   Most researchers today discount the idea that people are obese because they lack normal willpower or turn to food as a substitute for other satisfactions.

See if you can spot the truth or falsity of these statements in what follows.

First, the good news about fat. Fat is an ideal form of stored energy that provides the body with a high caloric fuel reserve to carry it through periods when food is scarce—a common occurrence in the feast-or-famine existence of our prehistoric ancestors. Eating three meals each and every day is a relatively recent phenomenon and a luxury hundreds of millions of people still do not enjoy. In circumstances of alternating feast and famine, overeating and storing the excess as fat is adaptive; it prepares the body to withstand periods of starvation.

The bad news is that in those parts of the world where food and sweets are now abundantly available, the adaptive tendency to store fat has become maladaptive. According to the National Institutes of Health, obesity increases the risk of diabetes, high blood pressure and heart disease, gallstones, arthritis, and certain types of cancer (Kolata, 1985a).

Obesity is not just a threat to physical health: It can also affect how obese people are treated and how they feel about themselves. Many people think that fat people are gluttons. They see obesity as a matter of choice or as a reflection of a personality problem (a maladjusted way of reducing anxiety, dealing with guilt, or gratifying an "oral fixation"). If being obese signifies either a lack of self-discipline or a personality problem, then who would want to hire, date, or associate with such people? And if obese people believe such things about themselves, how could they feel anything but unworthy and undesirable?

Recent research on obesity has discredited certain myths about its causes.

The Physiology of Obesity   As most overweight people know, the arithmetic of obesity is simple. People get fat by consuming more calories than they expend, and the energy equivalent of a pound of fat is 3500 calories. Therefore, dieters have been told for years that a pound will be lost for every 3500-calorie reduction in diet. Surprise: This conclusion turns out to be untrue. To see why, we must assemble the pieces of the obesity puzzle.

Fat Cells   The immediate determinants of our body fat are the size and number of our fat cells. A typical adult has about 30 billion of these miniature fuel tanks, only about half of which lie near the skin's surface. A fat cell can vary from relatively empty, like a deflated balloon, to overly full; in the obese, fat cells may enlarge two or three times their normal size and then divide. Once the number of fat cells increases— due to genetic predisposition, early childhood eating patterns, or adult overeating—it never decreases. On a diet, fat cells may shrink, but they do not disappear (Sjostrom, 1980).

The unyielding nature of our fat cells is but one way in which, once we become fat, our bodies are able to maintain our fat. Another way is that the metabolic rate of fat is lower than that of other tissue: Fat tissue takes less food energy to maintain. Thus, once we become fat, we require less food to maintain our weight than we did to attain it.

Body Chemistry   For the would-be dieter there are more reasons why being fat works to keep a person fat. In Chapter 13 we noted that insulin is a short-term determinant of hunger that (1) helps convert blood sugar to fat, (2) triggers hunger, and (3) is secreted in response to tempting food stimuli, particularly in people who are most responsive to external food cues. Because they are often dieting, obese people are more responsive to external food cues, such as a waitress's appetizing description of a dessert (Herman & others, 1983).

Set Points and Metabolism   There is still another reason why those who are fat find it so difficult to become and stay thin. Their bodies' weight thermostats are generally set to maintain a higher than average set-point weight. As we saw in Chapter 13, the body does this by controlling hunger and metabolism—the process by which food is transformed into energy. As many a dieter can testify, the drop in resting metabolic rate can be particularly frustrating. After the rapid weight losses that occur during the initial 3 weeks or so of a rigorous diet, further drops in weight come slowly. In one experiment (Bray, 1969), obese patients whose daily food intake was reduced from 3500 to 450 calories lost only 6 percent of their weight—partly because their metabolic rates dropped 15 percent (see Figure 18–22). Thus, the body adapts to starvation by burning off fewer calories and to extra calories by burning off more. That is why reducing your food intake by 3500 calories may not reduce your weight by 1 pound. And that is why when a diet is over and the body is still conserving energy through a reduced metabolic rate, amounts of food that only maintained weight before the diet may now be fattening.

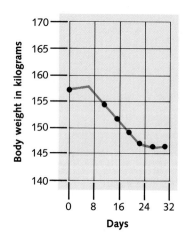 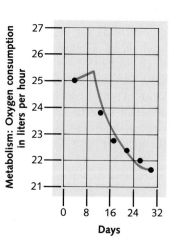 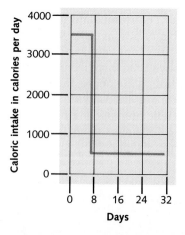

Figure 18–22   The effects of a severe diet on obese patients' body weight and metabolism. After 7 days on a 3500 calorie diet, six obese patients were given only 450 calories a day for the next 24 days. Body weight declined only 6 percent and then leveled off, because metabolism dropped 15 percent. (From Bray, 1969.)

Person-to-person differences in resting metabolism explain why—contrary to the stereotype of the overweight glutton—it is possible for two people of the same height and age to maintain the same weight and activity level, even if one of them eats *twice* what the other does, or why it is possible for a person to eat less than another similarly active person, yet weigh more (Rose & Williams, 1961). One study of young adult Pima Indians in Arizona followed those with low or high metabolic rates for up to 4 years. Those with relatively high metabolic rates did not gain significant weight; of those with low metabolic rates, almost 30 percent had added at least 22 pounds within 2 years (Ravussin & others, 1988).

A genetic influence on body weight set point is apparent from studies of adoptees and twins. The fatness of adopted people correlates with that of their biological parents, not with that of their adoptive parents (Price, 1987). Among 3-month-old babies, those who burn the most calories weigh less as 1-year-olds and have slimmer biological mothers (Roberts & others, 1988). Moreover, identical twins have closely similar weights, even if reared apart (Eckert & others, 1987).

Genes aren't the whole story, however. Weight resemblance is somewhat less among identical twin women than among men, hinting that females are more responsive to social pressures concerning desirable weight levels. And something other than genes must explain why obesity is six times more common among lower-class than upper-class women, more common among Americans than Japanese and Europeans, and more common among Americans in 1988 than in 1900.

Losing Weight   Perhaps you are shaking your head in sympathy with obese people: "Slim chance they (or we) have of becoming and staying thin. If they lose weight on a diet, their metabolism slows and their hungry fat cells cry out 'feed me!'" Indeed, the condition of an overweight person who has reduced to normal weight is much like that of a normal-weight person who has been semistarved: Because both bodies are being held under their normal set point, each "thinks" it is starving.

Having lost weight, formerly obese people look normal, but their fat cells may be abnormally small, their caloric expenditure 25 percent below normal, and their minds obsessed with food. Which explains why most people who succeed on a weight loss program will eventually gain it all back (Wing & Jeffery, 1979). One study followed 207 obese patients who had lost large amounts of weight during a 2-month hospital fast (Johnson & Drenick, 1977). Half gained back all the weight they had lost within 3 years, and virtually all were again obese within 9 years (Figure 18–23). So although health clubs and commercial weight loss programs are justified in proclaiming that they help people lose weight, the loss is usually temporary. For most people the only long-term result is a thinner wallet.

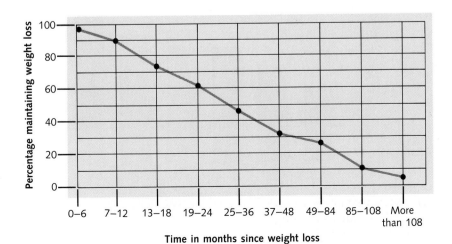

Figure 18–23   Obese patients successfully lost weight on a hospital fast, but few were able to maintain their weight loss permanently. (From Johnson & Drenick, 1977.)

Dieting failure rates become poignant when viewed on a personal level. Consider Ray Goldsmith (WGBH, 1983), a 5'6½'' man who dropped from 300 to 170 pounds:

> When I lost the weight, I was just obsessed about the fact of not putting it back on. So I literally did just about everything: I went into behavior modification, I tried slowing down my eating patterns, and that kind of thing. And then, at one point, where I saw myself still binging and still eating, I actually fasted a couple days a week, just to try to keep it off. I would sit there and eat six apples to try to . . . make it work. I mean I got really fanatic and very scared about putting the weight back on. I was very, very nervous about that, but I also found that I was not in control. . . . I even went to a hypnotist to try to stop eating and that worked for 3 days.
>
> It took me about a year and a half to put the 130 pounds back on. I mean, I fought it. I tried to fight it like a son of a gun. . . . I did it. I lost 130 pounds. I was able to do it. So clearly, it can be done. And I probably could have kept it off somehow, but I never found out the way to.

HELPFUL HINTS FOR DIETERS

Figure 18–24   A correlational study of TV watching and obesity. In one study of 6671 12- to 17-year-olds, obesity was more common among those who watched the most television. Of course, overweight people may avoid activity, preferring to sit and watch TV. But the association between TV watching and obesity remained when many other factors were controlled, suggesting to the researchers that the inactivity of TV watching contributes to obesity. (From Dietz & Gortmaker, 1985.)

For those who are determined to lose weight, research on hunger and obesity suggests some helpful hints:

Minimize exposure to tempting food cues. All of us to some extent, and some of us to a great extent, have our hunger accentuated by tempting food cues. So keep tempting foods out of the house, or at least stored out of sight, and only go to the supermarket on a full stomach.

Take steps to boost your metabo- *lism.* Remember, the only way to lose weight is to burn more calories than you take in. One way to do this is by exercising. Sustained exercise, such as running and swimming, not only empties fat cells, builds muscle, and makes you feel better, it can also temporarily speed up metabolism (Kolata, 1987b; Thompson & others, 1982). Thus, sustained exercise can be a weapon against the body's normal metabolic slowdown when dieting (Figure 18–24).

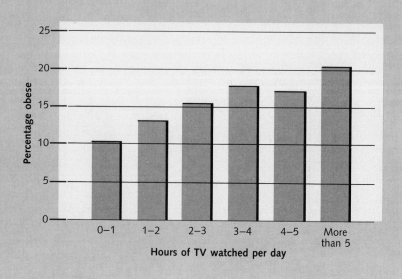

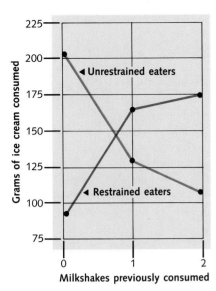

Figure 18–25 A laboratory eating binge. Normally unrestrained eaters (nondieters) ate less ice cream if they had first consumed one or two milkshakes. Restrained eaters (dieters) ate more ice cream after having their restraint broken with a milkshake or two, a tendency that has been dubbed the "what-the-hell phenomenon." (From Herman & Mack, 1975.)

Modify both your hunger and your metabolic rate by changing the food you eat. New findings suggest that eating carbohydrates increases metabolism more than eating fats (Rodin, 1979, 1985). Among the fats, saturated fats (those, like animal fat, that turn hard when left standing) seem to be the worst culprits. Also, some foods do more than others to boost postmeal insulin levels and thereby cause hunger to return sooner and stronger. After you ingest a sugar drink, your insulin levels rise, causing your blood sugar levels to fall within 2 or 3 hours. When the ingested sugar is glucose (as is found in pancake syrup), the rise in insulin and the resulting fall in blood sugar is especially steep, causing the average subject in one experiment to wolf down 1400 calories from a buffet of foods offered little more than 2 hours later. After ingesting an equal number of calories in the form of fructose (the sugar found in fruits), the insulin rise is smaller, and the average subject was content enough to eat only 869 calories from the buffet (Spitzer, 1983). Sucrose—table sugar—has effects like those of glucose. Foods such as potatoes and rice trigger less of the hunger-producing insulin jump. So how hungry you are by lunchtime will depend not just on how much but also on *what* you had for breakfast.

Don't starve all day and eat one big meal at night. This eating pattern, which is common among overweight people, slows down metabolism.

Beware of the binge. Among people who consciously restrain their eating (as the overweight often do), drinking alcohol or feeling either anxious or depressed can unleash the urge to eat (Herman & Polivy, 1980). Stress can also break down one's normal restraints. Temporarily going off a diet, by eating just a little of a forbidden food, can do the same. In several "taste testing" experiments, Peter Herman, Janet Polivy, and their colleagues (Herman & Mack, 1975; Polivy & others, 1986) asked Northwestern University students to drink zero, one, or two milkshakes and then to taste-test ice cream, helping themselves to as much as they wished. Those who normally restrained their eating ate more ice cream than normally unrestrained eaters *if* their restraint was first broken with the milkshakes (Figure 18–25). Thus, dieting—now the "normal" eating behavior for about half of North American women—is often self-defeating because, once the diet is broken, it may trigger binging (Polivy & Herman, 1985, 1987). A lapse can cause a collapse.

Set realistic goals. As we noted on page 377, goal setting can motivate achievement, especially when combined with feedback on progress. A realistic objective—such as losing a pound a week—will promote effort and persistence toward winning the battle against weight.

Nevertheless, the battle of the bulge rages more intensely than ever. Americans spend $5 billion a year trying to lose weight, and during 1985 at least one diet-fitness guide made the bestseller list every week (Toufexis, 1986). Louis Harris (1987) reported that 56 percent of men and 78 percent of women say they would like to change their weight. In 1986 the National Center for Health Statistics reported that 27 percent of men and 46 percent of women said they were currently trying to lose weight. James Rosen and Janet Gross (1987) found the gender difference to be even more striking among a large, diverse sample of high school students: 16 percent of boys and 63 percent of girls (most of whom were actually normal weight) reported they were currently dieting. With fat cells, blood chemistry, set points, metabolism, and genetic factors all tirelessly conspiring to make losing weight a big problem, what advice can we offer to those who wish to shed excess pounds?

Before age 13, 10 percent of boys and 80 percent of girls report they have been on a weight-loss diet (Hawkins & others, 1983). Janet Polivy and Peter Herman (1987) believe widespread, chronic dieting among basically normal-weight girls and women represents the seeds of eating disorder on a massive scale.

We should advise first assessing the costs. There are no easy routes to permanent weight loss. Maintaining weight loss will be difficult, and the more weight fluctuates up and down from going on and off a diet, the more quickly the body will begin its energy-saving metabolic slowdown each time one diets. Kelly Brownell and his associates (1986) confirmed this effect of yo-yo dieting by making rats obese, putting them on a diet, and then repeating the cycle of weight gain and loss. On the first diet, the rats lost their excess weight in 21 days and took 46 days to regain it. The second time, eating precisely the same amount of food, they took 46 days to lose the weight and 14 days to regain it. It's as if the body learns from previous diets how to defend its set-point weight, thereby protecting itself from what it interprets as the threat of starvation. So rather than following the principle of "If at first you don't succeed, try, try again," a dieter's motto should be, "Get it right the first time." Begin a diet only if you are sure you are motivated and self-disciplined enough to restrict your eating permanently.

Although preserving weight loss will be a constant challenge, Stanley Schachter (1982) is not as pessimistic as most obesity researchers about the likelihood of doing it successfully. He recognizes the overwhelming rate of failure among patients in structured weight loss programs, but he also notes that these are a special group of people, probably people who have been unable to help themselves. Moreover, the failure rates recorded for these programs are based on single attempts at weight loss. Perhaps when people make repeated attempts to lose weight, more eventually succeed, despite the negative consequences of repeated dieting. When Schachter interviewed a haphazard sample of people, some of whom had surely been in structured weight-loss programs, he found that one-fourth of them had at one time been more than 15 percent overweight and had tried to lose weight. Of these, 6 out of 10 had *succeeded* in that they weighed at least 10 percent less than their maximum pre-diet weight (average loss = 35 pounds) and were no longer obese. These findings must be interpreted cautiously, however, for they come from a limited sample of people. Two other studies found less encouraging results: Fewer than a third of formerly overweight people were no longer overweight (Jeffery & Wing, 1983; Rzewnicki & Forgays, 1987). But the findings do hint that prospects for losing weight may be somewhat brighter than the dismal conclusions indicated by follow-up studies of patients who underwent a single weight-loss program.

If all this has a familiar ring, recall that stop-smoking programs tend to be (1) effective in the short run and (2) ineffective in the long run, but that (3) many people are former smokers. Perhaps smoking-cessation and weight-reduction programs attract the people who are least able to succeed on their own, or perhaps those who don't succeed on any given effort often do on a later attempt.

There is, however, another option for overweight people, the one chosen by 13 percent of the people Schachter interviewed—simply to accept one's weight. Perhaps the new research on obesity can help us all to be more accepting of overweight people. And note what researchers have *not* identified as causes of obesity: guilt, hostility, oral fixation, or any similar personality maladjustment. Nor is obesity simply a matter of no willpower. If obese people are more likely to binge when under stress or after breaking their diets, this may be more a consequence of their constant dieting than a cause of their obesity. "Fat is not a four-letter word," proclaims the National Association to Aid

Weight-conscious people may struggle valiantly to restrain their eating. This dieter wears a mask to control nibbling during meal preparation.

The statements in the obesity quiz on page 534 are all true.

Fat Americans. Although this motto disregards the health risks linked with significant obesity, it does convey a valid point: It may be better to accept oneself as a little chubby than to diet and binge and feel continually out of control and guilty.

As researchers work to clarify further the precise relationships among diet, behavior, and health, health psychologists will continue their efforts to persuade people to adopt healthier life-styles. Doing so is quite a challenge, however. People tend to see themselves as relatively invulnerable to health problems, especially those that might arise from their own actions (Weinstein, 1987). They also typically think that their own life-style is healthier than other people's—that they drink less alcohol, consume less fat and cholesterol, and get more exercise. Often they are fooling themselves. For instance, most people will tell you they eat properly, even though 38 percent of adults admit to skipping breakfast on any given day (Roper, 1987). Furthermore, many individuals who admit to behaviors known to increase health risks will deny that the behaviors actually make them personally more vulnerable to illness or injury. Smokers, for example, may claim that they get enough exercise to counteract the negative effects of smoking. Thus, the first hurdle that health promotion programs must surmount is to get people to realize their individual vulnerability to stress- and behavior-related health problems. Only then will people make an effort to control stress, stop smoking, moderate their drinking, eat wisely, exercise regularly, and even buckle their seat belts.

Society's increasing obsession with thinness defines an ideal that most people cannot achieve.

SUMMING UP

People's behaviors and stress responses are now recognized as major influences on health and disease. Health psychology contributes to the interdisciplinary field of behavioral medicine, which provides new avenues for the prevention and treatment of illness. Among the concerns of health psychology are the effects of stress, the seeking of medical treatment, the adherence to health-enhancing regimens, and the promotion of healthier ways of living.

STRESS AND ILLNESS

What Is Stress? Stress, the process by which we appraise and respond to events that challenge or threaten us, was conceptualized by Walter Cannon as a "fight or flight" system and by Hans Selye as a three-stage, general adaptation syndrome (alarm/resistance/exhaustion). Modern research on stress has assessed the health consequences of cataclysmic events, significant life changes, and daily hassles. Events are especially stressful when perceived as both negative and uncontrollable.

Stress and Heart Disease Coronary heart disease, the number one cause of death in the United States, has been linked with the competitive, hard-driving, impatient, and

(especially) anger-prone Type A personality. Under stress, the body of the reactive, Type A person secretes more of the "stress hormones" that are believed to accelerate the buildup of plaques on the heart's artery walls.

Stress and Resistance to Disease In addition to contributing to heart disease and a variety of psychophysiological illnesses, stress can suppress the immune system, making a person more vulnerable to infections and malignancy. New experiments indicate that the immune system's responses can be influenced by conditioning.

Coping with Stress Among the components of stress management programs are training in aerobic exercise, biofeedback, and relaxation. Although the degree of mind control over the body that can be gained through biofeedback has fallen short of early expectations, biofeedback has become one accepted method for helping people control ailments such as tension headaches and high blood pressure. Simple relaxation exercises offer some of the same benefits. Counseling Type A heart attack survivors to slow down and relax has helped them lower their rate of recurring attacks. Social support also helps people cope, partly by buffering the impact of stress.

REACTIONS TO ILLNESS

Am I Sick? Noticing and Explaining Symptoms   Our body provides us with a variety of ambiguous signals. If they catch our attention, we often interpret them according to familiar disease schemas.

Seeking Treatment   If the symptoms seem to fit one of our disease schemas, we must decide whether medical care is warranted, based on our evaluation of anticipated costs and benefits.

The Patient Role   Feelings of loss of control—a common experience of those who adopt the good-patient role—can trigger an outpouring of stress hormones just as hostility can for those who adopt the bad-patient role. When given realistic information before stressful medical procedures and advice on how to cope, patients endure medical trauma more effectively.

Patient Adherence to Treatment   The realization that patients often ignore doctors' instructions has stimulated social psychologists to study ways to increase patients' compliance. How and what the physician communicates and the immediate incentives for adhering to or discontinuing treatment regimens are among the most important influences on the patient's behavior.

PROMOTING HEALTH

It is far better to prevent illness than to treat it once it occurs. What steps can be taken to prevent illness and promote health?

Smoking   The largest preventable cause of death in North America is cigarette smoking, a fact that has prompted psychologists to study the social influences that motivate adolescents to start smoking, the negative and positive reinforcers that maintain the habit once it is established, and possible ways to stop and prevent smoking.

Nutrition   Researchers are now exploring how specific foods, by providing the building blocks for specific neurotransmitters, can affect mood and behavior.

Obesity and Weight Control   Fat is a concentrated fuel reserve that is stored in fat cells. The number and size of these cells determine one's body fat. Obese people find it difficult to lose weight permanently because the number of fat cells is not reduced by a diet, because the rate of energy expenditure necessary for tissue maintenance is lower in fat than in other tissues, and because the overall metabolic rate decreases when body weight drops below the set point. Those who wish to diet anyhow are advised to minimize exposure to food cues, boost energy expenditure through exercise, and modify eating patterns.

TERMS AND CONCEPTS TO REMEMBER

aerobic exercise   Sustained exercise that increases heart and lung fitness; may also alleviate depression and anxiety.

bad-patient role   Uncooperative, complaining, demanding patient behavior.

behavioral medicine   An interdisciplinary field that integrates and applies behavioral and medical knowledge to health and disease.

biofeedback   A system for electronically recording, amplifying, and feeding back information regarding a subtle physiological state, such as blood pressure or muscle tension.

coronary heart disease   The narrowing of the vessels that nourish the heart muscle; the leading cause of death in the United States.

general adaptation syndrome (GAS)   Selye's concept of the body's adaptive response to stress as composed of three stages—alarm, resistance, exhaustion.

good-patient role   Cooperative, unquestioning, undemanding patient behavior, sometimes exhibited by anxious, helpless, depressed patients.

health psychology   A subfield of psychology that provides psychology's contribution to behavioral medicine.

lymphocytes   The two types of white blood cells that are part of the body's immune system: B lymphocytes form in the bone marrow and release antibodies that fight bacterial infections; T lymphocytes form in the thymus and, among other duties, attack cancer cells, viruses, and foreign substances.

obesity   A surplus of body fat that causes one to be 20 percent or more overweight.

psychophysiological illness   Literally, "mind-body" illness; any illness that is not caused by any known physical disorder; certain forms of hypertension, ulcers, and headaches are often linked with stress.

stress   The whole process by which we perceive and respond to certain events, called *stressors,* that we appraise as threatening or challenging us.

Type A   Friedman and Rosenman's term for competitive, hard-driving, impatient, verbally aggressive, and anger-prone people.

Type B   Friedman and Rosenman's term for easygoing, relaxed people.

FOR FURTHER READING

Benson, H., & Proctor, W. (1984). *Beyond the relaxation response: How to harness the healing power of your personal beliefs.* New York: Times Books.

A physician's advice on how to relax, manage stress, and harness your body's healing powers.

Friedman, M., & Ulmer, D. (1984). *Treating Type A behavior—and your heart.* New York: Knopf.

Easy to read, this book summarizes the results of a massive experiment in heart attack prevention and offers advice on how life-style changes can help minimize one's risk of heart attack.

Ornstein, R., & Sobel, D. (1987). *The healing brain.* New York: Simon & Schuster.

A nontechnical summary of the new discoveries about how the brain normally works to keep us healthy.

Polivy, J., & Herman, C. P. (1983; paperback, 1985). *Breaking the diet habit: The natural weight alternative.* New York: Basic Books.

Two psychologists who are obesity researchers question the practice of dieting and instead recommend realizing one's "natural weight" with an "undiet" that meets needs and discourages eating when hunger is satisfied.

Taylor, S. E. (1986). *Introduction to health psychology.* New York: Random House.

A leading researcher explores work on stress, health-related behaviors, and the management of pain and chronic illness.

PART 7

Social Behavior

Social psychologists study interpersonal behavior—how we relate to one another. They investigate the origins and consequences of attitudes and beliefs, conformity and independence, love and hate. Chapter 19, Social Influence, examines the social forces that affect our willingness to comply, our openness to persuasion, and our behavior in groups. Chapter 20, Social Relations, explores human hurting and helping, prejudice and attraction, conflict and peacemaking.

CHAPTER 19

Social Influence

Social psychology's great lesson—the enormous power of social influences on our decisions, beliefs, attitudes, and actions—is easy to overlook. But consider some illustrative phenomena.

Suggestibility   Suicides, bomb threats, airplane hijackings, and UFO sightings have a curious tendency to come in waves. One well-publicized incident—say, the suicide of a famous movie star—can inspire imitation. Copycat actions are *not* restricted to the spectacular or the bizarre. We all know that laughter, even canned laughter, can be contagious. Bartenders and street musicians know to "seed" their tip cups with money to make it appear that others have already given.

Role Playing   A group of decent young men volunteered to spend time in a simulated prison devised by psychologist Philip Zimbardo (1972). Some were randomly designated as guards; they were given uniforms, billy clubs, and whistles and were instructed to enforce certain rules. The remainder became prisoners; they were locked in barren cells and forced to wear humiliating outfits. After a day or two of self-consciously "playing" their roles, the simulation became very real—too real, in fact. The guards devised cruel and degrading routines, and one by one the prisoners either broke down, rebelled, or became passively resigned, causing Zimbardo to call the study off after only 6 days. Meanwhile, in real life, another group of men was being trained by the military junta then in power in Greece to become torturers (Staub, 1989). The men's indoctrination into their roles occurred in small steps. First, the trainee stood guard outside the interrogation cells. Next, he stood guard inside. Only then was he ready to become actively involved in the questioning and torture.

Persuasion   In late October 1980, presidential candidate Ronald Reagan trailed incumbent Jimmy Carter by 8 percentage points in a Gallup poll. On November 4, after a 2-week media blitz and a presidential debate, Reagan, "the great communicator," emerged victorious by a stunning 10 percentage points. The Reagan landslide caused many people to wonder what qualities made Ronald Reagan so persuasive and his audience so persuadable.

Group Influence   Buoyed by a string of successful space shuttle launches, the NASA management team approached the 1985 *Challenger* mission brimming with confidence, though frustrated by launch delays. When the engineers who designed the rocket booster opposed the launch because of dangers posed by freezing temperatures, group pressures to go ahead effectively silenced their warnings. Unless the engineers could *prove* that the rocket seals would not hold, the management group would not agree to another delay. Moreover, the NASA executive who made the final "go" decision was never informed of the warnings. Assuming, therefore, that there was unanimous support for a launch, he sent the space shuttle *Challenger* off on its one-way flight to annihilation.

This chapter examines these phenomena. First, though, let's consider the extent to which people are aware of the power of social influences.

EXPLAINING OUR OWN AND OTHERS' BEHAVIOR

When visiting another culture, we are sometimes struck by how "they" think and act. A Westerner in China may at first be puzzled when the gracious performer claps while being applauded. To Latin American dinner guests, their North American host may seem curiously offended by their not having arrived on time. A preppy in a punk setting, a small-town student at an urban university, and a Methodist at a Roman Catholic mass may feel like fish out of their cultural waters. We may also be struck by how alike "they all" are. We may, for example, perceive the Japanese as polite, the students at Medfield College as party types, New Yorkers as aggressive.

Within our own familiar environment, we hardly notice commonly accepted behaviors; we are more aware of differences among individuals. In class, we notice that Jack doesn't say much; over coffee, Julie seems to engage in conversation nonstop. Thus we may decide that Jack is shy and Julie is outgoing, thereby attributing their behaviors to their personal dispositions. Such *attributions*—explanations for people's behavior—are sometimes valid; in earlier chapters we saw that individuals do have enduring personality traits. However, we frequently overestimate the influence of people's personalities and underestimate the impact of their situations. In class, Julie may be as quiet as Jack. This underestimation of social influences is called the *fundamental attribution error.*

An experiment by David Napolitan and George Goethals (1979) illustrates the fundamental attribution error. The researchers had Williams College students talk, one at a time, with a young woman who acted either aloof and critical or warm and friendly. Beforehand, half the students were told that the woman's behavior would be spontaneous. The other half were told the truth—that for the purposes of the experiment she had been instructed to *act* friendly (or unfriendly). What effect do you suppose this information had? Believe it or not, none.

The students disregarded the information. If the woman acted friendly to them, they inferred that she really was a warm person; if she acted unfriendly to them, they inferred that she really was a cold person. In other words, they attributed her behavior to her personal disposition, *even when told that she was merely acting that way for purposes of the experiment.*

To know about the fundamental attribution error is to be forewarned. But committing it is almost irresistibly easy. In a high school play I attended recently, the part of a bitter old woman was played convincingly by a talented 16-year-old girl—so convincingly that, although I reminded myself of the fundamental attribution error, I assumed that the young actor had been typecast because she was so

"There was a serious flaw in the decision-making process." *Report of the Presidential Commission on the Space Shuttle Challenger Accident,* 1986

People see themselves acting differently in different situations, and so are aware that their behavior depends on the situation in which they find themselves. Observers may see a particular person in but one type of situation and infer that that person's behavior is a reflection of his or her inner traits. Most of Rock Hudson's public were unaware that his heterosexual movie persona was just that—mere role playing.

well-suited for the part. Thus I was surprised when, meeting her later at a cast party, I discovered she actually had a very pleasant disposition. I then remembered that several months earlier I had seen her play the part of a charming 10-year-old in *The Sound of Music*. Leonard Nimoy of *Star Trek* fame would not have been surprised by my error; he entitled one of his books *I Am Not Spock*.

WHO OR WHAT IS TO BLAME? A QUESTION OF ATTRIBUTION

In everyday life we often struggle to explain why others act as they do. A jury must decide whether a shooting was malicious or in self-defense. An unhappy wife and husband each ponder why the other behaves so selfishly. An interviewer must judge whether the applicant's geniality is genuine. When making such judgments, our attributions—either to individuals' dispositions or to their situations—can have important consequences.

Consider: How do you explain poverty or unemployment? Researchers in Britain, India, Australia, and the United States (Furnham, 1982; Pandey & others, 1982; Wagstaff, 1983) report that political conservatives tend to attribute these and other social problems to the personal dispositions of the poor and unemployed themselves: "People generally get what they deserve; people who don't work and have little money are usually lazy and undeserving." Po-

litical liberals are less likely to attribute such problems to dispositions and are more likely to blame past and current situations: "If you or I had to live with the same overcrowding, poor education, lack of meaningful opportunity, and outright discrimination, would we be any better off?"

In evaluating employees, managers must also make attributions. They are likely to attribute the poor performance of workers to personal factors such as low ability or lack of motivation. The workers who are doing poorly on a job more easily recognize situational influences: inadequate supplies, poor working conditions, difficult co-workers, impossible or ambiguous demands (Rice, 1985).

A point to remember: Our attributions—to individuals' dispositions or to their situations—have important practical consequences.

"Judge not" may be our ideal, but most of us cannot resist judging. Is this woman's poverty best attributed to her own disposition or to an oppressive or hopeless situation? Conservatives and liberals tend to offer differing explanations.

You, too, have probably committed the fundamental attribution error. In judging, say, whether your psychology instructor is shy or outgoing, you perhaps inferred from your experience in class that he or she has an outgoing personality. But you know your instructor only from the classroom, a situation that demands outgoing behavior. The instructor, on the other hand, observes his or her own behavior in many different situations—in the classroom, in meetings, at home, and the like—and so might say, "Me, outgoing? It all depends on the situation. When I'm in class or with good friends, yes, I'm outgoing. But at conventions and meetings I'm really rather shy."

So, when explaining *our own* behavior, we are usually sensitive to how our behavior depends on the changing situations that we encounter. However, when explaining the behavior of others, particularly after observing them in but one type of situation, we often commit the fundamental attribution error by disregarding the situation and leaping to unwarranted conclusions about their personality traits. The attribution difference can be seen in our language (McGuire & McGuire, 1986). When talking about ourselves, we generally use words that describe our *actions* and *reactions* ("I get upset when . . . ; I feel good when . . ."); when talking about others, we more often use words that describe what that person *is* ("He is irritable; she is demanding").

Recall from Chapter 15 that personality psychologists study the enduring, inner determinants of behavior that help to explain why different people act differently in a given situation. Social psychologists study the social influences that help explain why a person will act differently in different situations.

CONFORMITY AND COMPLIANCE

Social influences are important, but what exactly are these influences? How do they operate? To find out, social psychologists often create laboratory simulations of everyday social situations. In the miniature social world of the experiment, researchers will hold constant all the factors that might influence our behavior, except for one or two. These they vary to pinpoint how changes in them affect us. Let's see how social psychologists work by imagining ourselves as participants in some classic experiments.

SUGGESTIBILITY

You've witnessed the contagiousness of behavior often. One person giggles, coughs, or yawns, and others in the group are soon doing the same. A cluster of people stand gazing upward, and passersby pause to do likewise. The suggestibility apparent in these examples is a subtle form of **conformity,** adjusting our thinking or behavior to bring it into line with some group standard.

Muzafer Sherif (1937) designed a simple social situation to study people's suggestibility. As a participant in one of Sherif's experiments, you would first be seated by yourself in a dark room, staring at a pinpoint of light about 15 feet in front of you. The light seems to be moving, but you cannot be sure. After a few seconds the light disappears, and Professor Sherif asks you how far it moved from its original position. The light's movements seemed small and erratic, and there are no guides for estimating distance in the dark room, so you hesitate before guessing "8 inches." After making similar estimates on repeated tests, you are done for the day.

The next day you are joined by two other experimental subjects from the day before, and the three of you repeat the experiment, this time together. After the first appearance and disappearance of light, the first person calls out "1 inch," and the second says, "2 inches." You scratch your head, shrug your shoulders, and guess aloud, "6 inches."

Drawing by Handelsman; © 1984 The New Yorker Magazine, Inc.

"The person we have to thank is Arthur here. He's the one with the infectious grin."

As you repeat the tests with the other subjects on this and succeeding days, will you continue to change your responses? Probably. As Figure 19–1 indicates, the estimates of the light's movement made by the Columbia University students Sherif tested converged. Actually, the light never moved. Sherif had taken advantage of a perceptual illusion called the autokinetic (self-movement) phenomenon: In utter darkness, a stationary point of light will appear to move.

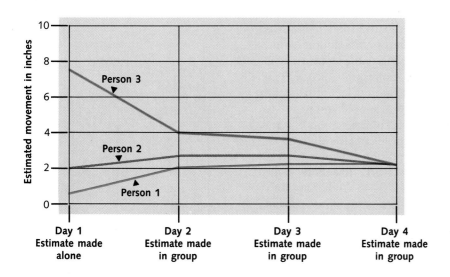

Figure 19–1 In this sample group from Sherif's study of suggestibility, the three individuals' guesses converged as they repeatedly estimated the apparent movement of a point of light, first alone and then together in a group. (From Sherif & Sherif, 1969.)

Did his subjects actually believe their new estimates, or were they just "going along"? Apparently, the new responses were genuine. When retested alone as much as a year later, the subjects still held to their revised judgments.

In real life, the effects of suggestibility are sometimes devastating. Sociologist David Phillips (1985) found that known suicides as well as fatal auto accidents and airplane crashes (some of which are disguised suicides) increase following a highly publicized suicide (Figure 19–2). These increases occur only in areas where the suicide is publicized; the number of deaths increases with the amount of media coverage; and the victims tend to be about the same age as the person in the publicized suicide. For example, following film star Marilyn Monroe's Au-

"I often marvel that while each man loves himself more than anyone else, he sets less value on his own estimate than on the opinions of others."
  Marcus Aurelius, A.D. 121–180, *Meditations*

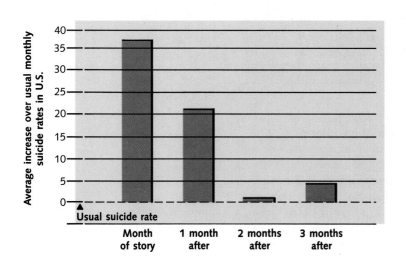

Figure 19–2 Imitative suicides? During the 2 months following each of 35 highly publicized suicides between 1947 and 1968, an average of 58 more people than usual killed themselves. (From Phillips, 1974.)

gust 6, 1962, suicide, there were 200 more August suicides in the United States than normal. Suicides on soap operas—and even well-intentioned dramas dealing with the issue—can escalate rates (Gould & Shaffer, 1986; Phillips, 1982; Phillips & Carstensen, 1986). Such shocking outbreaks of copycat suicides may help to explain the clusters of teenage suicides that occasionally occur in some communities.

GROUP PRESSURE AND CONFORMITY

Faced with an ambiguous reality, Sherif's subjects were unsure of the truth, so it is easy to understand why they adjusted their responses toward those of the others. But what would happen if people could easily judge the truth for themselves? Would they still conform to a group standard if it was clearly incorrect? Solomon Asch (1955) thought not. To test his assumption and to examine factors that he thought might affect conformity, Asch devised a simple test.

As one of his subjects, you arrive at the experiment location in time to take a seat at the end of a row where four people are already seated. You are all asked which of the three comparison lines in Figure 19–3 is identical in length to the standard line. You see clearly that the answer is line 2 and await your turn to say so after the others. Your boredom with this experiment begins to show when the next set of lines proves equally easy.

Now comes the third trial, and the correct answer seems just as clear-cut as before, but the first person gives what strikes you as a wrong answer: "line 3." When the second person and then the third give the same wrong answer, you sit straight up and squint at the lines. When the fourth person agrees with the first three, you can feel your heart begin to pound. Professor Asch then looks to you for your answer. Torn between the unanimity of your four fellow subjects and the evidence of your own eyes, you feel tense and much less sure of yourself than you were moments ago. You hesitate before answering, wondering whether you should suffer the discomfort of being viewed as an oddball. What answer do you give?

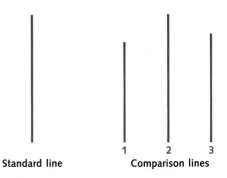

Standard line   Comparison lines

Figure 19–3 An example of the perceptual judgments made in Asch's conformity experiments. Which of the three comparison lines is equal to the standard line? What do you suppose most people would say after hearing four others say "line 3"? (From "Opinions and social pressure," by S. E. Asch. Copyright © 1955 by Scientific American, Inc. All rights reserved.)

In this photo from the Asch experiment, the subject (center) shows the severe discomfort that comes from disagreeing with the responses of other group members.

In the experiments conducted by Asch and others after him, thousands of college students have experienced this conflict. Answering such questions alone, they erred less than 1 percent of the time. When several others—who were actually confederates working for the experimenter—answered wrongly, Asch reports that his "intelligent and well-meaning" college subjects were "willing to call white black" more than one-third of the time by going along with the group.

"It is too easy to go over to the majority."
    Seneca,
    Ad Lucilium Epistula, A.D. 63–65

Conditions That Strengthen Conformity Asch's procedure became the model for many subsequent investigations. Although more recent experiments have not always found such a high degree of blind conformity, they have revealed that conformity is heightened when:

We are made to feel incompetent or insecure.

The group has at least three people. (Further increases in the group size yield smaller increases in conformity.)

The group is unanimous. (The support of a single fellow dissident greatly increases our social courage.)

We admire the group's status and attractiveness.

We have made no prior commitment to any response.

Our behavior will be observed by the others in the group.

We have been socialized by a culture that strongly encourages respect for social standards.

Thus, we might predict the behavior of Joe, an eager but insecure new member of a prestigious fraternity: Noting that the other members appear to be unanimous in their agreement about plans for an upcoming fund-raiser, Joe is unlikely to voice his dissent.

Reasons for Conforming Why do people comply with social pressure? Why do we clap when others clap, eat as others eat, believe what others believe, even see what others see? Frequently, it is to avoid rejection or to gain social approval. In such cases we are responding to what social psychologists call *normative social influence*. We are sensitive to social *norms*—understood rules for accepted and expected behavior—because the price we pay for being an oddball may be severe.

But there is another reason why we are open to social influence: The group can provide valuable information. When we accept others' opinions about reality we are responding to *informational social influence*. As a subject in the Sherif experiment—feeling very unsure about how far the light had moved—would it not have seemed reasonable to be open to others' judgments?

As the concept of informational social influence suggests, conformity is sometimes adaptive. "Those who never retract their opinions love themselves more than they love truth," observed Joseph Joubert, an eighteenth-century French essayist. Even normative conformity can be viewed positively. In today's Western culture, to be called a "conformist" may be taken as an insult; it calls up images of spineless submissiveness. In a less individualistic culture, the conforming person may be seen as socially sensitive or even selfless. Whereas Western observers might see the Japanese as "excessively conforming" and "overly sensitive to disapproval," others see in the Japanese a "serenity that comes to people who know exactly what to expect from each other" (Weisz & others, 1984).

OBEDIENCE

Social psychologist Stanley Milgram (1974) knew that people often comply when social pressures are subtle. But how would they respond to outright commands? To find out, he undertook what have become social psychology's most famous and controversial experiments. Imagine yourself as one of the nearly 1000 people who participated in one of Milgram's twenty experiments.

Drawing by Richter; © 1983 The New Yorker Magazine, Inc.

"The way to get along,' I was told when I entered Congress, 'is to go along.' "
John F. Kennedy,
Profiles in Courage, 1956

These workers in Tokyo are participating in a mandatory exercise class at work. Japanese companies expect their employees to participate in many company-sponsored activities, from exercise classes to weekend retreats. North Americans have traditionally regarded the idea of company involvement in their personal lives as an invasion of privacy. However, the productivity of Japanese society has given Westerners a growing respect for Japan's tradition of conformity and group identification.

Responding to an advertisement, you come to Yale University's psychology department to participate in an experiment, which Professor Milgram's assistant explains is a study of the effect of punishment on learning. You and another subject draw slips out of a hat to see who will be the "teacher" (which your slip says) and who will be the "learner." The learner is then led to an adjoining room and strapped into a chair that is wired through the wall to an electric shock machine. You sit down in front of the machine, which has switches labeled with voltages. Your task: to teach and then test the learner on a list of word pairs. You are to punish the learner for wrong answers by delivering brief electric shocks, beginning with a switch labeled "15 Volts—Slight Shock." After each error by the learner you are to move up to the next higher voltage. With each flick of a switch, lights flash, relay switches click on, and an electric buzzing fills the air.

If you comply with the experimenter's instructions, you hear the learner grunt when you flick the third, fourth, and fifth switches. After you activate the eighth switch (labeled "120 Volts"), the learner shouts out that the shocks are painful; after the tenth switch ("150 Volts—Strong Shock"), he cries, "Experimenter, get me out of here! I won't be in the experiment anymore! I refuse to go on!" You draw back when you hear these pleas, but the experimenter prods you: "Please continue—the experiment requires that you continue." If you still resist, he insists, "It is absolutely essential that you continue," or "You have no other choice, you *must* go on."

If you obey, you hear the learner's protestations escalate to shrieks of agony as you continue to raise the shock level with each succeeding error. After the 330-volt level, the learner refuses to answer and soon falls silent. Still, the experimenter pushes you toward the final, 450-volt switch, ordering you to ask the questions and, if a correct answer is not given, to administer the next level of shock.

How far do you think you would go in complying with the experimenter's commands? When Milgram surveyed people before conducting the experiment, most declared that they would have stopped playing such a sadistic role soon after the learner first indicated pain and certainly before he was shrieking in agony. This was also the prediction made by every psychiatrist Milgram asked to guess the outcome of his experiment. When Milgram actually conducted this experiment with men aged 20 to 50, he was astonished to find that 63 percent complied fully—right up to the last switch.

Did the teachers figure out the hoax—that no shock was actually being delivered? Did they guess that the learner was actually a confederate who only pretended to feel the shocks? Did they realize that the experiment was really testing the teachers' willingness to comply with commands to inflict punishment? No, the teachers typically displayed genuine agony: They sweated, trembled, laughed nervously, and bit their lips. Perhaps the subjects complied because the learners' protests were not convincing. To preclude this possibility, Milgram repeated the experiment. This time his confederate mentioned a "slight heart condition" as he was being strapped into the chair and then complained and screamed more intensely as the shocks became more punishing. When forty new teachers were tested, 65 percent complied fully (see Figure 19–4).

In succeeding experiments, Milgram discovered that when he varied the social conditions, the proportion of subjects who were fully compliant varied from 0 to 93 percent. Obedience was nil to an experimenter who insisted the subject go on, when a second experimenter said to stop. Obedience was highest under certain conditions:

Stanley Milgram (1933–1984), whose obedience experiments now "belong to the self-understanding of literate people in our age" (Sabini, 1986).

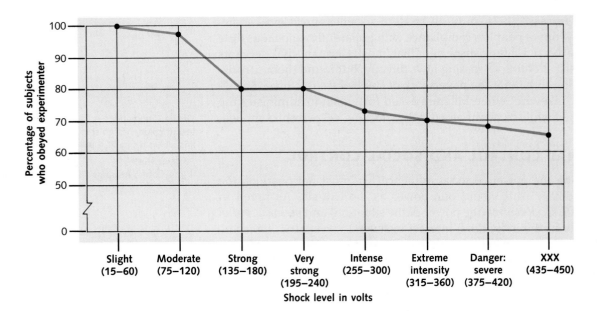

Shock level in volts

Figure 19–4 In Milgram's follow-up obedience experiment, 65 percent of the adult male subjects fully complied with the experimenter's commands to continue, despite hearing cries of protest after 150 volts and agonized protests after 330 volts. (Data from Milgram, 1974.)

The one giving the orders was close at hand and was perceived as a legitimate authority figure.

The authority figure was in turn supported by a prestigious institution. (Milgram obtained somewhat less compliance when he dissociated his experiments from Yale University.)

The victim was depersonalized or at a distance, as in another room. (Similarly, in combat with an enemy they can see, many soldiers either do not fire their rifles or do not aim them properly. Such refusals to kill are rare among those who operate the more distant weapons of artillery or aircraft [Padgett, 1986].)

There were no role models for defiance; that is, none of the other subjects were seen to disobey the experimenter.

LESSONS FROM THE CONFORMITY AND OBEDIENCE STUDIES

What do these experiments teach us about ourselves? How does guessing the movement of a point of light, judging a line length, or flicking a shock switch relate to everyday social behavior? Recall from Chapter 1 that the aim of psychological experiments is not to recreate the literal behaviors of everyday life but to capture and explore the underlying processes that shape those behaviors. Sherif, Asch, and Milgram devised experiments in which the subjects had to choose between holding to their own standards and being responsive to others, a dilemma we all face frequently. In Milgram's experiments, subjects were also torn between what they should respond to—the pleas of the victim or the orders of the experimenter. Their moral sense warned them not to harm another, but it also prompted them to obey the experimenter and to be a good subject. When kindness and obedience were put on a collision course, obedience often won.

These experiments demonstrate that social influences can be strong enough to make people conform to falsehoods or capitulate to cruelty. "The most fundamental lesson of our study," Milgram noted, is that "ordinary people, simply doing their jobs, and without any particular hostility on their part, can become agents in a terrible de-

"Drive off the cliff, James, I want to commit suicide."

"I was only following orders."
Adolf Eichmann,
Director of Nazi deportation of Jews to concentration camps

structive process'' (1974, p. 6). In modern societies, great evils sometimes grow out of people's compliance with apparently innocuous little evils. The Nazi leaders suspected that most German civil servants would resist shooting or gassing Jews directly, but found them surprisingly willing to handle the paperwork of the Holocaust (Silver & Geller, 1978). Likewise, when Milgram asked forty men to administer the learning test while someone else did the shocking, 93 percent complied.

PERSONAL CONTROL AND SOCIAL CONTROL

In affirming the power of social influence, we must not overlook the complementary truth about our power as individuals. As noted in Chapter 15, *social control* (the power of the situation) and *personal control* (the power of the individual) interact in several ways. First, the same situation will affect different people differently. At a party, some people closely monitor their own behavior in order to create a good impression; others are less concerned with managing the impressions they create (Snyder, 1987). Second, we often choose the ideas and social situations that influence us—where we go to college, where we live, what we read, and the people with whom we talk. Third, we are the creators as well as the creatures of our social worlds. Thus, our expectations of others may be self-fulfilling. If we expect people to be uncooperative and hostile, we may treat them in ways that trigger such behavior.

An experiment by Mark Snyder, Elizabeth Tanke, and Ellen Berscheid (1977) illustrates self-fulfilling expectations. The researchers had male students talk privately on the phone with a woman. Unknown to the women the men were shown a picture of another woman, either a beautiful or an unattractive one, who had nothing to do with the experiment. The women involved in the experiment were not aware that the men had this erroneous idea of their looks.

Snyder and his colleagues later analyzed and rated the women's comments during the telephone conversations. They discovered that the women who were presumed attractive actually spoke in a warmer, more likable way than did the women who were presumed unattractive. Can you imagine why? The men's expectations had become self-fulfilling; they led the men to talk to the women in ways that influenced the women to fulfill the expectation that beautiful people are warm and charming.

The interaction of social and personal control is also apparent in the human tendency to react against constraints. Romeo and Juliet's love was intensified, not weakened, by their families' opposition. Ex-

> "If the Commander in Chief tells this lieutenant colonel to go stand in the corner and sit on his head, I will do so."
>
> Oliver North,
> Iran-Contra hearings, Summer, 1987

THE ETHICS OF RESEARCH THROUGH DECEPTION

Many people, including many social psychologists, were disturbed not only by Milgram's findings but also by his methods. More than one-third of social-psychological studies—and virtually all those that investigate conformity and compliance—temporarily mislead subjects concerning the purpose of the research, the accuracy of the information they are given, or the true identity of a confederate they believe is a fellow subject (Vitelli, 1988). But rarely does such deception cause research subjects as much mental anguish as Milgram's experiments did.

In defense of his use of deception, Milgram pointed out that there was no other way we could have learned all that we did about the conditions under which people will participate in cruelty. Moreover, after learning of the deception and the actual purposes of the research, his subjects voiced their support of his efforts to study obedience. When surveyed, 84 percent of them said they were glad to have helped, and virtually none said they regretted participating. When forty of the subjects who had agonized most were later interviewed by a psychiatrist, none appeared to be suffering emotional aftereffects.

Nevertheless, one result of the controversy over experiments involving deception has been the development of stricter ethical guidelines and the establishment of university and foundation committees to see that they are followed. Ethical guidelines established by the American Psychological Association now urge researchers to tell potential subjects enough about the experiment to enable them to give their "informed consent" to participate; to use deception sparingly—only for an important purpose and only when there is no alternative; to protect people from harm and significant pain; and to explain the experiment afterward so that the subjects feel at least as good about themselves after the experiment as they did before they participated. Thus experiments such as Milgram's that even temporarily frighten or embarrass people are today generally considered unacceptable.

"... the assaulting quality of the Milgram experiment is really a valuable attack on the denial and indifference of all of us. Whatever upset follows facing the truth, we must eventually face up to the fact that so many of us are, in fact, available to be genociders or their assistants."

Israel W. Charny (1982, p. 16)
Executive Director, International Conference on the Holocaust and Genocide

perimenters have found that when people are unintimidated by someone who is trying to coerce them, they often do the *opposite*, thereby protecting their freedom of action from social control; this phenomenon is called *reactance* (Brehm & Brehm, 1981). Similarly, people who are made to feel commonplace, by being told their opinions are just like everyone else's, will alter their opinions to restore their sense of uniqueness (Snyder & Fromkin, 1980). Thus, nonconformity can make us feel uncomfortable, but so, too, can attempts to rob us of our freedom of action and our sense of personal uniqueness.

"To do just the opposite is also a form of imitation."

Georg Christoph Lichtenberg, 1742–1799
Aphorisms

ATTITUDES AND ACTIONS

In the history of social psychology, the single most important concept has been that of *attitudes*. **Attitudes** are beliefs and feelings that may predispose our responses to objects, people, and events. A common assumption is that our attitudes and actions are interconnected. If we *believe* that someone is mean, for example, we may *feel* dislike for the person and therefore *act* unfriendly. First, let's examine the influence of attitudes on actions. Then we will see how actions can influence attitudes.

Actions

Attitudes

DO OUR ATTITUDES GUIDE OUR ACTIONS?

During the 1960s, dozens of research studies challenged the conventional wisdom that our attitudes and actions are interconnected. People's expressed attitudes toward cheating, the church, and racial minorities were observed to be surprisingly unrelated to their reluctance to cheat, their church attendance, and their behavior in an actual interracial situation. What is more, persuasive appeals that changed people's attitudes seemed to have little effect on their behavior. These results were so discouraging that one respected social psychologist wondered whether it might be "desirable to abandon the attitude concept" (Wicker, 1971).

Is there really so little relation between our attitudes and actions, between what we profess to believe and what we do, between our words and deeds? If so, what hope is there for influencing people through preaching, teaching, and other forms of persuasion? The findings of the 1960s provoked hundreds of studies during the 1970s and 1980s. Social psychologists wanted to know why people's actions so seldom reflect their expressed attitudes and to learn the circumstances under which attitudes and actions do correspond.

WHEN DO OUR ATTITUDES GUIDE OUR ACTIONS?

Studies over the last two decades reveal that our attitudes *do* predict our actions—under the following conditions:

First, our attitudes guide our behavior when *other influences that affect our attitudes and our actions are minimized.* Often, these other influences blur the connection between our attitudes and actions. Because we may adjust what we say in order to please our listeners, our expressed attitudes are sometimes not our real attitudes. Our automatic cordial answer to the restaurant cashier's question, "How was your meal?" may reflect neither our actual attitude toward the meal nor our probable future behavior toward the restaurant. Moreover, as we learned in the studies of conformity and compliance, social expectations have a major influence on our actions (Figure 19–5). The need to please others and to conform to social expectations is especially strong during adolescence. Thus, as we saw in Chapter 4, high school students' future decisions regarding smoking marijuana can be better predicted from the number of their friends who smoke it than from their expressed attitudes toward smoking it (Andrews & Kandel, 1979).

Second, our attitudes guide our behavior when *the attitude is specifically relevant to the behavior.* People easily profess general beliefs and feelings that are inconsistent with their actions. They may proclaim love while practicing hate, value good health while overeating and smoking, or cherish honesty while cheating on their income tax returns. Yet when the attitude pertains specifically to a given behavior, people usually do what they say. Our attitudes toward particular political candidates, for example, accurately predict our voting behavior.

Third, our attitudes guide our behavior when *we are keenly aware of our attitudes.* In familiar situations, we often act according to well-learned scripts without stopping to think about what we are really doing. However, attitudes become potent guides to our actions when we are reminded of them before we act. For example, Martha Powell and Russell Fazio (1984) had people repeatedly remind themselves of their attitudes regarding gun control, the Equal Rights Amendment, and certain other issues by rating their attitudes on a variety of scales. The researchers found that repeatedly stating an attitude made that

"Thinking is easy, acting difficult, and to put one's thoughts into action, the most difficult thing in the world."
    Goethe, 1749–1832

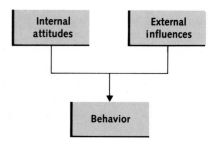

Figure 19–5   Our behavior is affected both by our attitudes and by social influences.

Attitudes predict behavior when they are specifically relevant to the behavior. The political attitudes of these Young Republicans at the University of Iowa readily translate into their actions of political recruitment.

attitude come more quickly to mind. In subsequent experiments, Fazio (1986) found that attitudes that come quickly to mind are more likely to guide our behavior. Our attitudes also are more readily brought to mind if we are made self-conscious, say, by looking in a mirror, or if the attitudes have been strongly forged through life experience rather than by mere hearsay. To be true to yourself, you must know what you believe and be conscious of its implications for your actions.

Do the three conditions under which attitudes guide behavior seem obvious? In hindsight, we may think we knew them all along. But they were not obvious to researchers in 1970. Nor were they obvious to the West German university students who were unable to guess the outcomes of published studies on attitude-behavior consistency (Six & Krahe, 1984). As so often happens, the research outcomes did not seem obvious—until they were obtained and explained.

DO OUR ACTIONS AFFECT OUR ATTITUDES?

We have seen that under certain conditions people will indeed stand up for what they believe. Now we turn to a less obvious but equally valid principle: People tend to believe in what they have stood up for. One of social psychology's most consistent findings is that our actions shape our attitudes. Many streams of evidence converge to establish the principle that attitudes follow behavior. Consider two.

"One does what one is; one becomes what one does."
Robert Musil,
Kleine Prosa, composed 1930

Role Playing Affects Attitudes   In psychology, as in the theater, a **role** refers to a set of prescribed actions—behaviors expected of those who occupy particular social positions. When you start college, begin a new job, or become a parent, you are expected to behave according to certain social prescriptions. At first, the behaviors may feel phony because you are *acting* the role. Before long, however, your behavior no longer feels forced. What began as play-acting in the theater of life has become you. As happened to the prisoners and guards in the prison simulation described earlier, you have absorbed the role.

Researchers have confirmed this effect by assessing people's attitudes before and after they adopt a role, either in everyday situations such as before and after taking a job, or in experimental situations. In one of these experiments, Kenneth Gergen (1965) interviewed women students from Duke University a month after they had taken a self-esteem test. Before the interview, some of the women were encouraged to describe themselves as accurately as possible, others to make a positive impression. Women in the first group therefore gave modest self-descriptions; those in the second group presented themselves as more likable, sensitive, and intelligent.

What do you think Gergen found when all the women retook the self-esteem test after the interviews? The women's self-images were unchanged in the "accuracy" group but had improved considerably in the second group. Putting on a positive face had led those in the second group to feel better about themselves. As the nineteenth-century writer Nathaniel Hawthorne noted, "No man, for any considerable period, can wear one face to himself and another to the multitude without finally getting bewildered as to which may be true." A social psychologist might say that the women in the experiment avoided bewilderment by reevaluating themselves more favorably after positive role playing. As we noted on pages 489–490, cognitive therapists often treat depression by encouraging patients to replace the tendency to think and speak negatively about themselves with more upbeat and positive self-characterizations.

Both the obedient recruit and the abusive sergeant may have begun by consciously adopting the behavior expected of them in these roles, but they often end up becoming the characters they are playing.

Saying and Doing Become Believing   Dozens of experiments have revealed that people who are coaxed into acting against their attitudes or violating their moral standards will begin to rationalize their behavior by persuading themselves that they were justified in saying or doing what they did. If people are induced to speak or write on behalf of a point of view they have doubts about, they begin to believe their own words. A notorious example is the "brainwashing" that American prisoners of war underwent during the Korean war. Typically, the prisoner would first be asked to write a trivially negative statement such as "The United States is not perfect." Then the captors would up the ante; the prisoner might be asked to list some flaws in American democracy or culture and to sign his name to the list. Later, the prisoner might be goaded to expand these ideas into an essay or speech. Aware that his behavior had not been brutally coerced and that his statements were being shown to others, the prisoner's attitudes would often shift toward consistency with what he had said (Schein, 1956). Saying became believing.

Similarly, subjects who are induced to harm an innocent victim—by making cutting comments or by delivering electric shocks—typically begin to disparage the victim. The obedient subjects in Milgram's experiments were entrapped step by step. They were first asked to perform only a slightly hurtful act—to deliver just a little tickle of electricity to the victim. Only gradually did the shocks they were delivering become more severe. By the time the "learner" first indicated mild discomfort, the "teachers" had already behaved obediently on several occasions and had repeatedly justified their actions to themselves. Milgram reported that at the end of the experiment, many of the subjects blamed the victim with harsh comments, such as, "He was so stupid and stubborn he deserved to get shocked." As with the torturers-in-training, their actions had gradually affected their attitudes. In such ways as this, doing can become believing.

Fortunately, the attitudes-follow-behavior principle works as well for good deeds as for bad. In the years immediately following the introduction of school desegregation and the passage of the U.S. Civil Rights Act of 1964, white Americans expressed diminishing racial prejudice. And as Americans in different regions came to act more alike—thanks to more uniform national standards against discrimination—they began to think more alike. Similarly, experiments indicate that moral action has positive effects on the actor and that doing favors for another person often leads to greater liking for that person. We love people for the good we do them as well as for the good they do us. Researchers have also found that children who are gently induced to resist temptation—say, not to play with a desirable but forbidden toy—tend to internalize their conscientious behavior. Evil acts shape the self, but so do moral acts.

The attitudes-follow-behavior principle has heartening implications. Although we cannot directly control all our feelings, we can influence them by altering our behavior. If we are unloving, we can become more loving by behaving as if we were so—by doing thoughtful acts, expressing affection, giving affirmation. If we are down in the dumps, we can do as cognitive therapists advise and talk in more positive, self-accepting ways, with fewer self put-downs. The moral: We can as easily act ourselves into a way of thinking as think ourselves into a way of acting.

"No new truth is ever really learned until it is acted upon."
Father John Powell, S.J., born 1925

WHY DO OUR ACTIONS AFFECT OUR ATTITUDES?

Although the principle that attitudes follow behavior is now well established, its explanation is not. One idea is that people, wanting to make a good impression, may merely make their attitude statements *appear* consistent with their actions. This does happen, but experiments indicate that genuine attitude change also occurs. If you have ideas about *why* our actions influence our attitudes, you can now compare them to two theories proposed by social psychologists.

Self-Justifying Our Actions: Cognitive Dissonance Theory   One explanation is that we are motivated to justify our actions. We want to relieve the discomfort we feel when our behavior differs noticeably from what we think and feel. This is the implication of *cognitive dissonance theory*. The theory was developed by Leon Festinger as he wondered why people living just outside an earthquake disaster zone in India spread rumors of disasters to come. Festinger suspected that the rumors served to justify the anxieties the people were feeling. Generalizing from this case, he proposed that people adjust their view of the world to fit how they have responded to the world.

Cognitive dissonance, argued Festinger, is the tension we feel when two of our thoughts (cognitions) are inconsistent. Our cognitions include the knowledge we have of our own behavior. Thus, we may experience cognitive dissonance when we think one way but act in another and are aware of the discrepancy. Dissonance, like hunger, motivates its own reduction. The theory therefore offers an intriguing prediction: If you can get people to choose to behave in a way that is contrary to their usual attitudes, they will feel the discomfort of cognitive dissonance. They can reduce this discomfort by bringing their attitudes more into line with what they have done. "If I chose to do it," they might rationalize, "it must have been worth doing." (Note, however, that cognitive dissonance is minimal when people feel that their action was coerced, which allows them to disclaim responsibility.)

Dissonance theory has been confirmed by many experiments in which people were either coaxed or forced into complying with some disagreeable request. Robert Croyle and Joel Cooper (1983) conducted one such study with Princeton University men, all of whom had indicated they were opposed to the banning of alcohol from the Princeton campus. The men were asked to write forcefully all the arguments they could think of in *support* of the ban, supposedly to provide information to a committee that was studying the issue. Half of the writers were first reminded that their participation was "completely voluntary"; the other half were merely ordered to begin writing down their arguments. Afterward, Croyle and Cooper had the men again indicate their actual attitudes toward the ban. The men were less opposed to the ban after writing the arguments. But for whom was this especially so?—those who could not easily attribute their behavior to the experimenter's coercion. If you argue for a point without feeling coerced, you are likely to see the rationale for it more clearly.

Inferring Our Attitudes: Self-Perception Theory   Cognitive dissonance theory assumes that our need to maintain a consistent and positive self-image motivates us to adopt attitudes that justify our actions.

"Aw, come on, guys! We've marketed worse candidates!"

Drawing by Fisher; © 1988 The New Yorker Magazine, Inc.

Assuming no such motive, *self-perception theory* says simply that when our attitudes are unclear to us, we observe our behaviors and then infer our attitudes from them.

In proposing this theory, Daryl Bem (1972) assumed that we make inferences about our own attitudes much as we make inferences about others' attitudes. Were we to see someone freely volunteer to write arguments in favor of a drinking ban, we would likely infer that the person is in favor of the ban. Perhaps before writing their pro-ban arguments, many of the Princeton men were not sure how they felt, so they inferred their attitudes from what they wrote. And so it goes as we observe our own behavior. What we freely say and do can be self-revealing. As we noted in Chapter 14, Emotion, even our facial expressions help define our feelings.

Self-perception theory also helps explain the overjustification effect described on page 248. Recall that promising people a reward for doing a task they already enjoy can lead them to infer that their behavior is due to the reward, thereby undermining their intrinsic enjoyment. Dissonance theory cannot explain this phenomenon: When an already justifiable activity is *overjustified* by the promise of added reward, there is no dissonance because the person is not doing anything that is contrary to his or her prevailing attitudes.

The debate over these and other explanations of the attitudes-follow-behavior principle has inspired hundreds of experiments that have shown the conditions under which dissonance and self-perception processes operate. To summarize the findings: Dissonance theory best explains what happens when our actions openly contradict our well-defined previous attitudes. When, say, we hurt someone we like, we feel tension, which we may reduce by liking the person less. Self-perception theory explains what happens when we are unsure of our attitudes: We simply infer them by observing our uncoerced actions. If we lend our new neighbors a cup of sugar, our helpful behavior may engender warm feelings toward them. As often happens in science, each of the theories provides a partial explanation of a complex reality.

PERSUASION

We have seen that behavior can affect attitudes, sometimes turning prisoners into collaborators, enemies into friends, or doubters into believers. But change occurs by effective persuasion as well. The health fitness movement has persuaded 30 percent of American adults to become ex-smokers and many formerly sedentary people to take up jogging, biking, or swimming.

What makes for effective persuasion? If you want to communicate your beliefs more effectively, sell a product or idea, or simply sharpen your awareness of the persuasion techniques that people use to influence you, what should you know? Social psychologists have broken down the process of persuasion into four elements: the communicator, the message, the medium, and the audience; or *who* says *what* by *what means* to *whom*.

WHO SAYS? THE COMMUNICATOR

In the 1920s, Edward Bernays, an enterprising public relations expert working for the American Tobacco Company, was assigned the task of convincing American women, few of whom smoked, that smoking

"I can watch myself and my actions, just like an outsider."
Anne Frank,
The Diary of a Young Girl, 1947

"A man should never be ashamed to own that he has been in the wrong, which is but saying, in other words, that he is wiser today than he was yesterday."
Jonathan Swift,
Thoughts on Various Subjects, 1711

was acceptable (Cunningham, 1983). His strategy: to present examples of attractive or respectable women smokers. Bernays hired models to smoke in the lobby of New York's Waldorf-Astoria Hotel and persuaded debutantes to smoke while walking in the New York City Easter Parade. He also placed advertisements in magazines portraying enviable women smoking cigarettes or featuring stage and screen stars attesting to the pleasures of smoking. By the 1940s, the number of women smokers was rising dramatically.

What makes for an effective communicator? As Bernays recognized, *attractiveness* is important, especially on matters of personal preference rather than fact. In preferences that have to do with lifestyle, tastes, and values, an appealing communicator—one who is attractive physically or whose characteristics are similar to those of the audience—is most persuasive.

On matters of fact, the *credibility* of the communicator becomes more important. Credible sources are those perceived as both expert and trustworthy. Experimenters have found that these perceived qualities are enhanced when communicators look the listener straight in the eye, talk fairly rapidly, and argue against their self-interest or expected beliefs. In one study, researchers Wendy Wood and Alice Eagly (1981) found that university students were persuaded more by antipornography arguments attributed to someone generally opposed to censorship than attributed to someone who favored censorship. When the anticensorship communicator argued an unexpected position, such as calling for a ban of pornography, people attributed his position to compelling evidence rather than to personal bias.

WHAT IS SAID? THE MESSAGE

Is a message more persuasive when it differs from the audience's existing opinions by a great deal or by only a little? Will the arms reduction advocate accomplish more by arguing for total disarmament or for a 10 percent reduction in military contracts? Experiments suggest that highly credible sources cause greater opinion change when they argue a relatively extreme position rather than a moderate one. Less credible people may be discredited when they take extreme positions, so they are more effective when they advocate points of view closer to those of the audience.

Should the message argue your side only, or should it also acknowledge and refute opposing positions? Researchers report that it depends on the listeners. If the audience already tends to agree with the message and is unlikely ever to hear opposing arguments, then a one-sided appeal will be most persuasive. To persuade more sophisticated and well-informed audiences, however, speakers need to address the opposing arguments.

If both sides of an issue are presented, does the side going first or second have the advantage? Often, the side going first has an edge, especially when the first speaker can affect how people will interpret what the second speaker says. But if a time gap separates the two presentations and if a decision is made immediately after hearing both messages, the second side is more likely to have the advantage. For good reason, campaigning is not allowed near places of voting.

Is a tightly reasoned message more powerful than one that arouses emotion? It would be nice if logic usually won out, but here, too, the human reality is complex. The answer depends on the interaction of reason and emotion with other factors, including the listener's knowledge and interest. For example, people who are both informed and

Our responsiveness to a frank appeal, to a trustworthy look directed exclusively at us, and to a well-known, physically attractive individual help make this an effective advertisement.

concerned about the topic tend to respond thoughtfully to the accuracy and logic of the presentation. And as we noted earlier, attitudes that we consciously examine tend to be long-lasting and to guide our behavior. People who are uninformed or uninterested are persuaded more effectively by emotional approaches. They usually form attitudes based on their response to the appeal of the communicator or to emotional associations with the message (Petty & Cacioppo, 1986).

Evidence that emotional factors are important for persuasion comes from a variety of studies. Associating a message with the good feelings we have while eating, drinking, or listening to music can make the message more convincing (which is perhaps why so many business deals are made over lunch). Messages that arouse fear can also be effective. Such messages are often vivid, and vivid information tends to be more readily available in memory than information that is matter-of-fact. When various teams of researchers sampled the audience of 100 million Americans before and again several weeks after the telecast of the 1983 nuclear-war film *The Day After,* they found that concern over nuclear war had risen (Oskamp & others, 1985; Schofield & Pavelchak, 1985). When it comes to memory and persuasion, an emotional image can indeed be worth a thousand words.

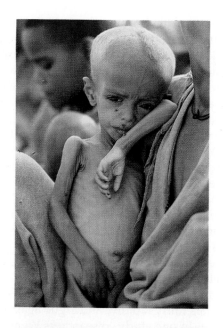

Heartrending images, like this photo of a child in an Ethiopian refugee camp, and rousing appeals by well-known entertainers, moved many people who had been vaguely aware of the long-existing drought and famine in Africa to contribute desperately needed millions for famine relief. This illustrates findings that those who are less concerned or informed about an issue are more responsive to a vivid emotional message or one delivered by an appealing communicator.

BY WHAT MEANS? THE MEDIUM

Which media are the most effective for changing attitudes: the mass media, direct mail, or face-to-face appeals? If you are campaigning for a cause or a candidate, is your time spent more effectively leaving leaflets at many houses or going to fewer houses and taking the time to talk with people?

On relatively minor or unfamiliar issues, the mass media and mailings can be a powerful tool. Advertisers can easily persuade us to choose one brand of aspirin over a chemically identical brand, but getting us to change our basic values is usually difficult. Although Ronald Reagan's triumph over incumbent President Carter demonstrated that people can sometimes be persuaded to change their leanings in an important election, people can be more easily persuaded to choose one unknown candidate over another for a less important office, such as water commissioner.

Generally, face-to-face appeals are more persuasive than media appeals and mailings. This was demonstrated over 30 years ago in Ann Arbor, Michigan, where citizens intending to vote against a revision of the city charter were split into three groups (Eldersveld & Dodge, 1954). Of those who were exposed only to mass media advertisements for the revision, 19 percent voted for it on election day. Of those who received four mailings supporting the revision, 45 percent voted for it. But of those visited personally and appealed to face-to-face, 75 percent were persuaded to cast their votes for the revision.

TO WHOM? THE AUDIENCE

The final ingredient in our recipe for persuasion is the audience. The ultimate determinant of persuasion is not the message itself but what thoughts it triggers. When a message seems important to its listeners, they will not just soak it up, they will mentally agree or counterargue. More than 300 years ago in his *Pensées,* French philosopher and mathematician Blaise Pascal anticipated the findings of many recent experiments on persuasion: "People are usually more convinced by reasons they discover themselves than by those found by others."

In an extensive series of experiments, Richard Petty and John Cacioppo (1986) found that when a message evokes the desired sort of thoughts, it becomes even more persuasive if techniques are used to enhance the audience's thinking about it. Asking rhetorical questions is one such technique, as illustrated by Ronald Reagan's potent question at the end of his 1980 debate with President Carter: "Are you better off than you were four years ago?"

The audience's personal characteristics also affect their openness to persuasion. People whose opinions are not strongly defined are, quite naturally, more open to persuasion than are those whose opinions are well formed. Thus, political canvassers are advised to bypass people who either strongly favor or strongly oppose their candidate or cause and to focus their energies instead on those in the middle. Because many of their opinions are not yet well defined, teenagers and young adults seem to be good candidates for persuasion. When researchers survey and resurvey the social attitudes of groups of younger and older people over several years, they generally find that younger people's attitudes change more (Sears, 1979). For this reason, the influences that people subject themselves to during these years—the peers they spend time with; the schools they attend; the media they read, hear, and watch; the commercials they view; the groups they join—can have lasting impacts.

Older audiences and those with well-formed opinions are typically harder to persuade.

GROUP INFLUENCE

How do the groups we belong to affect our behavior? Social psychologists have explored this question by studying the influences that operate in the simplest of groups—one person in the presence of another—and those that operate in larger, more complex groups, such as families, athletic teams, and decision-making committees.

INDIVIDUAL BEHAVIOR IN THE PRESENCE OF OTHERS

Social Facilitation Appropriately, the simplest of all social-psychological questions was one of the first to be investigated: How are we influenced by the mere presence of others—by people either watching us or joining us as we engage in various activities? Having noticed that cyclists' racing times were faster when they competed against each other directly than when they competed against a clock, Norman Triplett (1898) guessed that the presence of others boosts performance. To test his hypothesis, Triplett had adolescents wind a fishing reel as rapidly as possible. He discovered that they wound faster in the presence of a *coactor*, someone who works simultaneously on the same task. The phenomenon Triplett observed—the better or faster performance of tasks in the presence of others—is called *social facilitation.* Drivers, for example, take about 15 percent less time to travel the first 100 yards after a light turns green when another car is beside them at the intersection than when they are alone (Towler, 1986).

For a while, social facilitation was viewed as a universal principle, an effect that always occurred. Researchers were therefore mystified when they began to find the opposite effect: On tasks such as learning nonsense syllables or solving complex multiplication problems, people did less well when observers or coactors were present. Some 300 studies and 25,000 subjects later, the mystery has been solved (Guerin, 1986). The Sherlock Holmes in this scientific detective story was social psychologist Robert Zajonc. As he wondered why the presence of others would sometimes help and sometimes hurt task performance, Zajonc (1965) recalled the effect of arousal on performance (page 382): Arousal facilitates the most likely response—the correct one on an easy task, an incorrect one on a difficult task. If performing tasks in the presence of others causes people to become aroused, reasoned Zajonc, then easy tasks should become easier and difficult tasks should become harder.

Performers, whether amateur or professional, often find they are only really "on" before an audience. The presence of onlookers inspires them to turn in a better performance. This illustrates the principle that emotional arousal leads to better performance on well-learned tasks.

A variety of carefully controlled laboratory studies have confirmed Zajonc's hunch. When observed by others, people do become aroused (Geen & Gange, 1983; Moore & Baron, 1983). With arousal, they do perform well-learned tasks more quickly and more accurately and unmastered tasks more slowly and less accurately. The effect is usually small, but it can be noticeable in everyday activities. James Michaels and his associates (1982) found that expert pool players who made 71 percent of their shots while being unobtrusively observed made 80 percent when four people came up to watch them. However, poor shooters, who made 36 percent of their shots when they thought they were unobserved, made only 25 percent when they knew they were being watched. The moral: What you do well, you are likely to do even better in front of an audience; what you normally find difficult may seem impossible when others are watching.

People who anonymously pool their efforts toward a group goal tend to "free ride" on the group by exerting less effort than when they are individually accountable for attaining the goal.

Social Loafing The social facilitation experiments evaluate people's *individual* efforts in tasks ranging from winding fishing reels to shooting pool. But what happens in situations that require a team effort to achieve a common goal? In a team tug-of-war do you suppose people would individually exert more, less, or the same effort as they would in a one-on-one tug-of-war?

To find out, Alan Ingham and his fellow researchers (1974) asked blindfolded University of Massachusetts students to "pull as hard as you can" on a rope. When the students were fooled into believing that three others were also pulling behind them, they exerted only 82 percent as much effort as when they knew they were pulling alone.

Bibb Latané and his colleagues (1981; Jackson & Williams, 1988) coined the term *social loafing* to describe this diminished effort by those submerged in a group. It has been documented on various tasks in more than four dozen experiments conducted in the United States, India, Thailand, Japan, and Taiwan (Gabrenya & others, 1983). In some of these experiments, blindfolded subjects seated in a group were asked to clap or shout as loud as they could while listening through headphones to the sound of loud clapping or shouting. When the subjects were told they were doing it with others, they produced about one-third less noise than when they thought their individual efforts were identifiable.

How do we explain social loafing? First, people acting as part of a group feel less accountable and are therefore less worried about what others think. Second, they may view their contribution as dispensable (Kerr & Bruun, 1983). And, as many leaders of organizations know, if group members share equally in the group's benefits regardless of how much they contribute, they may slack off and "free ride" on the other group members' efforts.

Deindividuation We have seen that the presence of others can arouse people (as in the social facilitation experiments) or can diminish their feelings of responsibility (as in the social loafing experiments). Sometimes the presence of others both arouses people *and* diminishes their sense of responsibility, causing unrestrained behavior that can range from a food fight in the dining hall or screaming at a basketball referee to vandalism or rioting. The abandonment of normal restraints to the power of the group is called *deindividuation.* To become deindividuated is to become less self-conscious and less inhibited in a group situation.

Deindividuation often occurs when group participation makes people feel aroused and anonymous. In one experiment, New York University women who were dressed in depersonalizing Ku Klux Klan–style hoods delivered twice as much electric shock to a victim as

Deindividuation. Whether in experiments or in real life, people made anonymous act on their impulses with less restraint.

did women who were identifiable (Zimbardo, 1970). (The "victim" did not actually receive the shocks.) Similarly, tribal warriors who depersonalize themselves with face paints or masks are more likely than those with exposed faces to kill, torture, or mutilate captured enemies (Watson, 1973). Whether in a mob, at a rock concert, at a dance, or at worship, to lose one's self-consciousness (to become deindividuated) is to become more responsive to the group experience and—for better or for worse—to give up some self-control.

Crowding   Sometimes the density of other people (the number of people per unit space) becomes so great that we feel crowded. If someone invades our *personal space*—the buffer zone we like to maintain around our bodies—we may become uncomfortable. We are especially likely to feel crowded if we feel constrained and lacking control. In one experiment, Judith Rodin and her fellow researchers (1978) jockeyed passengers in a crowded elevator to positions either away from or in front of the elevator controls. When leaving the elevator, the passengers were approached to complete a survey on elevator design. Those who had been standing away from the controls reported feeling more crowded.

Experimenters have found that crowding sometimes amplifies people's reactions. For example, friendly people who sit close to experimental subjects are liked even more, but unfriendly people who sit close are liked even less (Schiffenbauer & Schiavo, 1976; Storms & Thomas, 1977). Why? Perhaps we are simply more aware of and therefore more responsive to others when they are close to us. Or perhaps we become more physiologically aroused when others are nearby and this arousal intensifies our reactions—which might explain a funny effect of crowding: Comedy records that are mildly amusing to people in a large, uncrowded room seem funnier to people in a small, densely packed room (Aiello & others, 1983; Freedman & Perlick, 1979).

If conditions of high density are indeed arousing, do people who have lived under crowded conditions for many years suffer ill effects? Densely populated urban areas do have higher rates of crime and mental disorder than do small towns, but these effects could be due to other factors, such as lower levels of income and education and higher noise levels in these areas. To investigate whether crowding itself causes ill effects, we need a self-contained physical environment in

"The use of self-control is like the use of brakes on a train. It is useful when you find yourself going in the wrong direction, but merely harmful when the direction is right."
   Bertrand Russell,
   Marriage and Morals, 1929

Personal space is influenced by culture. Middle Easterners typically require less personal space than North Americans.

which the population density varies over time. In such an environment would behavior and health problems rise and fall with changes in population density?

Paul Paulus and his co-researchers (1988) identified one such environment—prisons—and analyzed the records of four state prison systems. They discovered that the rates of death, suicide, disciplinary problems, and psychiatric commitment are higher in prisons with higher population density than in prisons with fewer inmates, and that these rates go up as a prison's population increases. Moreover, the more inmates per cell (and therefore the less privacy each inmate has) the greater their problems. Even blood pressure and complaints of illness are higher among inmates who are living under crowded prison conditions (Figure 19–6).

EFFECTS OF GROUP INTERACTION

We have examined the conditions under which the presence of others can fuel mob violence and enhance humor, make easy tasks easier and difficult tasks harder, tempt people to free-ride on the efforts of others and motivate them to jog faster. Research shows that group interaction also can have both bad and good effects.

Group Polarization Educational researchers have long been intrigued by the fact that, over time, initial differences between groups of college students often become accentuated. If the first-year students at College X are more intellectually oriented than those at College Y, chances are the difference between the students will be even more pronounced by the time they are seniors. Similarly, if the political conservatism of students who join fraternities and sororities is greater than that of students who do not, the gap in the political attitudes of the two groups will likely widen as they progress through college (Wilson & others, 1975).

This enhancement of a group's prevailing tendencies—called *group polarization*—occurs when people within a group discuss attitudes that most of them favor or oppose. For example, Serge Moscovici and Marisa Zavalloni (1969) found that group discussion strengthened French students' initially positive attitudes toward their premier as well as their initially negative attitudes toward Americans. Similarly, George Bishop and I (Myers & Bishop, 1970) discovered that when groups of prejudiced high school students discussed racial issues, their opinions became even more prejudiced, whereas those low in prejudice became even less prejudiced (Figure 19–7).

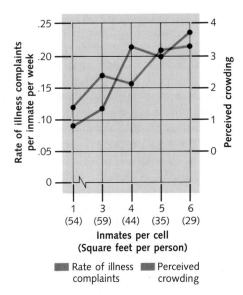

Figure 19–6 Studies of prison records clearly show the ill effects of crowding: greater incidence of death, suicide, disciplinary infraction, and psychiatric commitment. In one study, inmates living six per cell felt much more crowded and experienced more illness than those in individual cells. (From *Prison crowding: A psychological perspective*, by P. B. Paulus [with the collaboration of V. C. Cox & G. McCain]. Copyright © 1988 Springer-Verlag.)

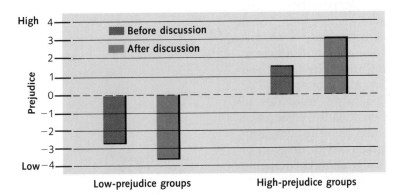

Figure 19–7 If a group is like-minded, discussion strengthens its prevailing opinions. Talking over racial issues increased prejudice in a high-prejudice group of high school students and decreased it in a low-prejudice group. (From Myers & Bishop, 1970.)

Group polarization can have beneficial results, as when it strengthens the resolve of members of a self-help group. But it can also have dire consequences, both for the members of the group and for society as a whole. From their analysis of terrorist organizations around the world, psychologists Clark McCauley and Mary Segal (1987) note that the terrorist mentality does not erupt suddenly. Rather, it arises among people who have come together because of a grievance and who, as they interact in isolation from moderating influences, gradually become more and more extreme.

Groupthink   Does the polarization that often occurs when like-minded people discuss their concerns ever distort important group decisions? Social psychologist Irving Janis thought so when he first read historian Arthur M. Schlesinger, Jr.'s account of how President John Kennedy and his advisers blundered into an ill-fated plan to invade Cuba with 1400 CIA-trained Cuban exiles. When the invaders were easily captured and soon linked to the American government, Kennedy wondered aloud, "How could we have been so stupid?"

To find out, Janis (1982a) studied the decision-making procedures that led to the fiasco. He discovered that the high morale of the recently elected President and his advisers fostered a sense that the plan had to succeed. To preserve the good group feeling, dissenting views were suppressed or self-censored, especially after the President voiced his enthusiasm for the scheme. When no one spoke sharply against the idea, everyone assumed there was consensus support for it. Janis used the term *groupthink* to describe this harmonious but unrealistic group thinking.

As Janis examined other historical fiascoes—the failure to anticipate the attack on Pearl Harbor, the escalation of the Vietnam war, the Watergate cover-up—he discovered more and more evidence that groupthink is fed by such psychological processes as conformity, self-justification, and group polarization. Yet he was also aware of experiments indicating that to solve some types of problems, two heads are indeed better than one. So Janis also studied instances in which American presidents and their advisers collectively made good decisions. Examples were the Truman administration's formulation of the Marshall Plan for getting Europe back on its feet after World War II and the Kennedy administration's actions to keep the Soviets from installing missiles in Cuba. In such instances, groupthink was prevented by a leader who welcomed various shades of opinion, invited experts' critiques of developing plans, or even assigned people to identify possible problems.

"One's impulse to blow the whistle on this nonsense was simply undone by the circumstances of the discussion."
Arthur M. Schlesinger, Jr. (1965, p. 255)

MINORITY INFLUENCE

Let us close this chapter with a reminder that the powers of social influence include the individual's power to influence the group. Social history is often made by a minority that sways the majority. Were this not so, women would still lack the right to vote, communism would not have spread beyond Marx and Engels, and Christianity would be a small Middle Eastern sect. Technological history, too, is often made by innovative minorities who overcome the majority's resistance to change. The railroad was first viewed as a nonsensical idea; some farmers even feared that the noise from trains would prevent hens from laying eggs. Robert Fulton's steamboat was greeted with derision as "Fulton's Folly." As Fulton later said, "Never did a single encouraging remark, a bright hope, a warm wish, cross my path." Much the same type of reaction greeted the printing press, the telegraph, the incandescent lamp, and the typewriter (Cantril & Bumstead, 1960).

To understand better how minorities can sway majorities, social psychologists in Europe have investigated groups in which an individual or two consistently expresses a controversial attitude or an unusual perceptual judgment. One repeated finding of this research is that a minority (especially a minority of more than one person) that unswervingly holds to its position is far more successful in swaying the majority than is a minority that waffles. Holding consistently to a minority opinion will not make you popular, but it may make you influential, especially if your self-confidence stimulates others to consider why you react as you do. Although people often comply publicly with the majority view, they may privately develop sympathy for the minority view. So even when a minority's influence is not yet visible, it may be persuading some members of the majority to rethink their views (Maass & Clark, 1984; Nemeth, 1986).

The principles of social influence examined in this chapter can help us understand how people are persuaded to buy certain products, vote for particular candidates, or join religious cults. The combined powers of social pressure to conform, of actions affecting attitudes, of persuasion, and of group influence are indeed enormous. But so are the powers of the individual. We all choose or create many of the situations that influence us. We also reassert our sense of freedom and uniqueness when we feel threatened. And minority opinions can move empires.

Finally, we do well to remember that explaining *why* someone has adopted a particular belief says nothing about the belief's truth or falsity. To know why someone does or does not believe that running benefits health does not tell us whether running is, in fact, beneficial. To know why one person is a devout religious believer and another a nonbeliever does not tell us whether God, in fact, exists. So let no one say to you and do not say to anyone, "Your convictions are silly. You believe them because of social influence." The second statement may be true, but it can never justify the first.

"If the single man plant himself indomitably on his instincts, and there abide, the huge world will come round to him."

Ralph Waldo Emerson,
Addresses and Lectures, 1849

As the life of Mahatma Gandhi (1869–1948) powerfully testifies, a consistent and persistent minority voice can sometimes sway the majority. Gandhi was often vilified and imprisoned. But his appeals and fasts on behalf of nonviolence in the struggle for India's independence eventually won that independence.

SUMMING UP

Social psychology's great lesson is that our attitudes and behaviors are powerfully affected by social influences such as suggestibility, role playing, persuasion, and group influence.

EXPLAINING OUR OWN AND OTHERS' BEHAVIOR

We generally explain people's behavior by attributing it either to internal dispositions or to external situations. In accounting for others' actions, we tend to underestimate the influence of the situation, thus committing the fundamental attribution error. When we explain our own behavior, however, we more often point to the situation and not to ourselves.

CONFORMITY AND COMPLIANCE

Suggestibility   As Sherif's pioneering studies demonstrated, when we are not sure about our judgments, we are likely to adjust them toward the group standard.

Group Pressure and Conformity   Solomon Asch and others learned that under certain conditions people will conform to a group's judgment even when it is clearly incorrect.

Obedience   In Milgram's famous experiments, people who were torn between obeying an experimenter and responding to another's pleas usually chose to obey orders, even though obedience supposedly meant harming another person.

Lessons from the Conformity and Obedience Studies These classic experiments demonstrate the potency of social forces, and they indicate that we may conform either to gain or to protect social approval (normative social influence) or because we depend on the information that others provide (informational social influence).

Personal Control and Social Control People choose many of the situations that influence them. If not intimidated, they will react against the pressures of social control that constrain their freedom and that reduce their feeling of uniqueness.

ATTITUDES AND ACTIONS

Do Our Attitudes Guide Our Actions? When Do Our Attitudes Guide Our Actions? Initially, social psychologists agreed with the popular wisdom that attitudes determine behavior. Now they note that attitudes predict behavior only under certain conditions, such as when other influences are minimized, when the attitude is specific to the behavior, and when people are aware of their attitudes.

Do Our Actions Affect Our Attitudes? Studies of role playing and of performing uncharacteristic acts reveal that our actions can modify our attitudes, especially when we feel responsible for those actions.

Why Do Our Actions Affect Our Attitudes? Cognitive dissonance theorists explain that behavior shapes attitudes because people feel discomfort when their actions go against their feelings and beliefs; they reduce the discomfort by bringing their attitudes more into line with what they have done. Self-perception theorists explain that actions shape attitudes for a simpler reason: When uncertain about their feelings or beliefs, people will look to their own behavior to determine their attitudes, much as an outside observer would.

PERSUASION

Experiments on persuasion have focused on four ingredients in the persuasion process: the attractiveness and credibility of the communicator, the characteristics of the message, the effectiveness of the medium (mass appeal versus face-to-face encounters), and the nature of the audience.

GROUP INFLUENCE

Individual Behavior in the Presence of Others Experiments on social facilitation indicate that the presence of either observers or coactors can arouse individuals, slightly boosting their performance on easy tasks but hindering it on difficult ones. When people pool their efforts toward a group goal, social loafing may occur as individuals free-ride on others' efforts. When people are aroused and made anonymous by a group, they may become less self-aware and self-restrained, a psychological state known as deindividuation. To be with others in situations that constrain our sense of control may give rise to feelings of crowding.

Effects of Group Interaction Discussions with like-minded others often produce group polarization, an enhancement of the group's prevailing attitudes. This is one cause of groupthink, the tendency for harmony-seeking groups to make unrealistic decisions after suppressing unwelcome information.

Minority Influence The power of the group is great, but so can be the power of a minority, especially when its views are expressed consistently.

TERMS AND CONCEPTS TO REMEMBER

attitude A belief and feeling that may predispose one to respond in a particular way to objects, people, and events.

attribution A causal explanation for someone's behavior, such as an explanation in terms of the situation or the person's disposition.

coactors People who are simultaneously at work on the same noncompetitive task.

cognitive dissonance theory The theory that we act to reduce the discomfort (dissonance) we feel when two of our thoughts (cognitions) are inconsistent—as when we respond to the fact that we have chosen to act in a manner that contradicts our attitudes by changing our attitude.

conformity Adjusting one's behavior or thinking to coincide with a group standard.

deindividuation The loss of self-awareness and self-restraint occurring in group situations that foster arousal and anonymity.

fundamental attribution error The tendency for observers, when analyzing another's behavior, to underestimate the impact of the situation and to overestimate the impact of personal disposition.

group polarization The enhancement of a group's prevailing attitudes through discussion.

groupthink The mode of thinking that occurs when the desire for harmony in a decision-making group overrides a realistic appraisal of alternatives.

informational social influence Influence resulting from accepting others' opinions about reality.

normative social influence Influence resulting from a person's desire to gain approval or avoid disapproval.

norms Understood rules for accepted and expected behavior. Norms prescribe "proper" behavior.

personal space The buffer zone we like to maintain around our bodies.

reactance The tendency to protect or restore one's sense of freedom from social control, often by doing the opposite of what has been demanded.

role A set of expectations about a social position, defining how those in the position ought to behave.

self-perception theory The theory that when we are unsure of our attitudes we infer them by looking at our behavior and the circumstances under which it occurs, much as an outside observer would.

social facilitation Improved performance of tasks in the presence of others; occurs with simple or well-learned tasks but not with tasks that are difficult or not yet mastered.

social loafing The tendency for each person in a group to exert less effort when they are pooling their efforts toward attaining a common goal than when they are each individually accountable.

FOR FURTHER READING

Cialdini, R. B. (1988). *Influence: science and practice* (2nd ed.). Glenview, IL: Scott, Foresman.

A delightful, captivating introduction to six "weapons of influence." Cialdini brings to life the lessons of social-psychological research on persuasion with riveting everyday examples of influence—from Tupperware parties to cult indoctrination programs.

Janis, I. L. (1982). *Groupthink: Psychological studies of policy decisions and fiascoes.* Boston: Houghton Mifflin.

A provocative, readable analysis of the group decision making that led to several historical fiascoes, from the failure to anticipate the Pearl Harbor attack to the Watergate cover-up. Janis beautifully interweaves basic concepts in social psychology with recent American history, explains how debilitating groupthink occurs, and suggests how to avoid it.

Lindzey, G., & Aronson, E. (Eds.). (1985). *Handbook of social psychology* (3rd ed., Vols. 1 and 2). New York: Random House.

The authoritative overview of the methods and findings of social psychology—two volumes and nearly 2000 pages contributed by leading researchers.

Milgram, S. (1974). *Obedience to authority.* New York: Harper & Row.

The full description of Milgram's controversial research on obedience, complete with reflections on the dilemmas of obedience and the ethics of such research.

Staub, E. (1989). *The roots of evil: The psychological and cultural sources of genocide.* New York: Cambridge University Press.

How can human beings kill, brutalize, and torture other human beings? By analyzing genocide during the Holocaust and in countries around the world, Staub exposes the roots and evolution of mass killing and cruelty.

CHAPTER 20

Social Relations

"We cannot live for ourselves alone," remarked the novelist Herman Melville, for "our lives are connected by a thousand invisible threads." These connecting threads may strain with tension, vibrate with joy, or lie peacefully calm. In our day-to-day relations with one another, we sometimes harm and sometimes help, we sometimes hate and sometimes love, we are sometimes in conflict and sometimes at peace.

In this concluding chapter we will look at the two-sided aspects of social relations—at aggression and altruism, prejudice and attraction, conflict and peacemaking. Why and when do we act one way or the other? And what steps can we take to transform the closed fists of aggression, prejudice, and conflict into the open arms of altruism, attraction, and peace?

AGGRESSION

In psychology, *aggression* has a more precise meaning than it does in everyday usage. The assertive salesperson who is irritatingly persistent is not displaying aggression. Nor is the dentist who makes you wince with pain. Both the person who passes along a vicious rumor about you and the attacker who mugs you are. Aggression is any physical or verbal behavior that is intended to hurt or destroy, whether done out of hostility (as when someone angrily attacks another) or as a calculated means to an end (as when a "hit man" calmly assaults or murders another for pay). Some of the 20,000 murders and 855,000 assaults committed in the United States during 1987 (Federal Bureau of Investigation, 1988) were cool, calculated acts; more were hostile outbursts.

Time and again, we have seen that behavior emerges from the interaction of nature and nurture. Research on aggression reinforces that theme. For a gun to fire, the trigger must be pulled; with some people, as with some guns, the trigger is pulled more easily. Let us look first at biological factors that influence our thresholds for aggressive behavior. Then we will examine the psychological factors that can arouse or restrain our aggressive impulses.

THE BIOLOGY OF AGGRESSION

Is Aggression an Instinctive Drive?   According to one view, argued by both Sigmund Freud and animal behavior theorist Konrad Lorenz, our species has volcanic potential to erupt in aggression. Freud thought that, along with positive survival instincts, we harbor a self-destructive "death instinct" that usually gets redirected toward others as aggression. Lorenz believed that aggressive energy wells up instinctively from within until released by appropriate stimuli or inhibited by gestures of submission. But now our "aggression instinct" has been armed with weapons that can cause injury and death to unseen victims miles away. These potential victims cannot inhibit their attackers with white flags or hands held high, as in the days of hand-to-hand combat. How, then, can we keep the human volcano from erupting? One way, said Freud and Lorenz, is by channeling pent-up aggressive energy into socially approved activities, from painting to competitive sports.

How do today's research psychologists view the idea that aggression is an *instinctive drive*—an unlearned behavior pattern that is characteristic of a whole species? Not very favorably. For one thing, to "explain" aggression (or any other human behavior) by calling it an instinct is usually no explanation at all. Some behaviors—the nest building of birds, for instance—do qualify as instinctive. Most human behaviors do not. Because aggressiveness varies so widely from culture to culture and person to person, it can hardly be considered an unlearned characteristic of our species. The Iroquois Indians who lived peacefully before the arrival of European settlers offer a dramatic contrast to the present-day warring tribes of South American Yanomamö Indians, nearly half of whose surviving males over age 25 have been involved in a killing (Chagnon, 1988). Moreover, the reasoning that attributes human behavior to instinct is often circular: "Why do people act violently?" "Because of their aggression instinct." "How do you know that?" "Well, just look at all their aggressive acts!"

This photo from Vietnam is poignant testimony to the horrors of warfare. Has our inventiveness for new and more deadly weapons outstripped our ability to inhibit our aggressive impulses, leaving us an endangered species?

Physiological Influences on Aggression   Although aggression may not be an instinctive drive, our aggressive reactions are biologically influenced. The external stimuli that influence our behaviors operate through our biological system. We can look for physiological influences on aggression at three levels—the genetic, the neural, and the biochemical: Our genes engineer our individual nervous systems, which are biochemically influenced.

Genetic Influences   Many strains of animals have been bred for aggressiveness, sometimes for sport, sometimes for research. Finnish psychologist Kirsti Lagerspetz (1979) showed the power of genetic influences on aggressive tendencies. She took a group of normal mice and bred the most aggressive with one another and the least aggressive with one another. After repeating this selective breeding for another twenty-five generations, she had a group of vicious mice that would attack immediately when put together and a group of docile mice that, no matter what she did to them, would refuse to fight. Twin studies suggest that aggressiveness is genetically influenced among humans as well (Rushton & others, 1986). If one identical twin admits to "having a violent temper," the other twin will often independently admit the same. Fraternal twins are much more likely to respond differently.

Neural Influences   According to aggression researcher Kenneth Moyer (1983), there is "abundant evidence" that animal and human brains have neural systems which, when stimulated, produce aggressive behavior. Some sample findings:

A cat lives harmoniously with a rat until one day a specific spot in its hypothalamus is stimulated via an implanted electrode. Immediately, the cat attacks its cage-mate and kills it precisely as would a wild, predatory cat, by biting through its spinal cord at the neck.

A mild-mannered woman has an electrode implanted deep in her brain's limbic system (in the amygdala) by neurosurgeons who are seeking to diagnose a disorder. Because the brain has no sensory receptors, she cannot feel any stimulation. But at the flick of a switch she snarls, "Take my blood pressure. Take it now," and then stands up and begins to strike the doctor.

The domineering leader of a caged monkey colony has a radio-controlled electrode implanted in an area of his neural system that, when stimulated, inhibits aggression. When the button that activates the electrode is placed in the colony's cage, one small monkey learns to push it every time the boss becomes threatening, thereby calming him down.

Biochemical Influences   The neural systems that activate and inhibit aggression are influenced in turn by hormones and other substances in the blood. A raging bull will become a gentle Ferdinand when its testosterone level is reduced through castration. The same thing occurs with castrated mice. If the mice are then injected with testosterone, they will again become aggressive. Although humans are less sensitive to such hormonal changes, violent criminals tend to be muscular young males with lower than average IQs and higher than average testosterone levels (Dabbs & others, 1987; Wilson & Herrnstein, 1985). Drugs that diminish testosterone levels tend to subdue the aggressive tendencies of violent males.

For both physical and psychological reasons, alcohol unleashes aggressive responses to provocation (Taylor & Leonard, 1983). Police data and prison surveys confirm the link between alcohol and aggression. One study of state prisoners by the U.S. Bureau of Justice Statistics found "an alcohol problem of staggering size": One-fourth of the 12,000 inmates interviewed acknowledged drinking heavily just before committing their crimes (Rosewicz, 1983).

Without disputing genetic, neural, and hormonal influences on aggression, social scientists worry that many people are convinced that

"He that is naturally addicted to Anger, let him Abstain from Wine; for it is but adding Fire to Fire."
  Seneca,
  De Ira, A.D. 49

A 1985 riot at a soccer game in Brussels left 38 dead and 437 injured. English fans, aroused by the competition and loaded with alcohol, lost all restraint when provoked by Italian fans. They attacked the Italians, who retreated and were then crushed against a wall.

aggression is so biologically intrinsic to human nature that peace is therefore unattainable. To counter such pessimism, the Council of Representatives of the American Psychological Association and the directors of the International Council of Psychologists unanimously endorsed a "Statement on Violence" (Adams & others, 1987) that was drafted in 1986 by scientists from a dozen nations. The statement declares it "scientifically incorrect" to say that "war or any other violent behavior is genetically programmed into our human nature," that "humans have a 'violent brain,'" or that "war is caused by 'instinct' or any single motivation."

THE PSYCHOLOGY OF AGGRESSION

So far we have seen that genetic, neural, and biochemical factors influence the ease with which the aggression trigger can be pulled. But what kind of events lead to aggression? Does learning buffer or amplify these events?

Aversive Events   Although suffering sometimes builds character, it may also bring out the worst in us. Studies in which animals or humans are subjected to a variety of unpleasant experiences reveal that those made miserable will often make others miserable in turn (Berkowitz, 1983).

Initially, investigators thought that being unable to achieve some goal increased people's readiness to behave aggressively. This observation led to the *frustration-aggression theory:* Frustration creates anger, which may generate aggression. When social psychologists later realized that physical pain, personal insults, and other unpleasant events also instigate aggression, they saw that frustrations are simply instances of aversive events. Foul odors, hot temperatures, cigarette smoke, and a host of other aversive stimuli can also lead people to react with hostility (Figure 20–1).

This confrontation is not only the result of a near collision but also of each driver's belief that the other is at fault.

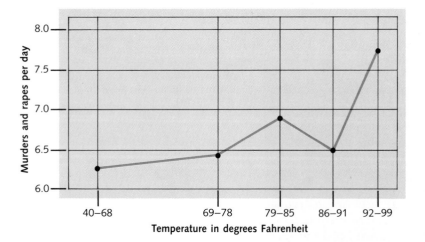

Temperature in degrees Fahrenheit

Figure 20–1   Uncomfortably hot weather can elicit and heighten aggressive reactions. More violent crimes occur in summer than in winter, in hot years than in cooler years, in hot cities than in cooler cities, and on hotter days than on cooler days (Anderson, 1987). For example, between 1980 and 1982 in Houston, Texas, murders and rapes were more common on days over 91°. This finding is consistent with those from laboratory experiments in which people working in a hot room reacted to provocations with greater hostility. (From Anderson & Anderson, 1984.)

Whether we actually respond aggressively to an aversive event depends partly on our interpretation of it. Imagine that you are walking along a noisy sidewalk when someone comes out from a doorway and trips you with a stick. You fall, are bruised, and rise up in anger only to discover you tripped over the cane of a now dismayed blind person. Instantly your urge to say or do something hurtful is transformed by your understanding.

Learning to Express and Inhibit Aggression   Aggression may be a natural response to aversive events, especially when it is biologically sensitized. But natural reactions can be altered by learning. Animals naturally eat when they are hungry, but if appropriately rewarded or punished, they can be taught to overeat or to starve.

Human reactions, too, are more likely to be aggressive in situations where experience has taught us that aggression pays. Children whose aggression successfully intimidates other children may become more aggressive. Violent demonstrations that draw attention to the demonstrators' grievances may be reinforcing.

Aggressive behavior can be learned through direct rewards, as when animals that have fought successfully to obtain food or mates become increasingly ferocious. It can also be learned through observation (see Chapter 9, Learning). Children who grow up observing physically aggressive models often imitate the behaviors they see. To Leonard Eron and Rowell Huesmann (1984), these ways of learning aggression suggest how it might be counteracted. The family and other socializing agents could use the power of rewards to socialize males—who commit most of the physical violence—to be more gentle and compassionate. Eron and Huesmann explain:

> If we want to reduce the level of aggression in society, we should also discourage boys from aggression very early on in life and reward them for other behaviors. . . . Boys should be . . . encouraged to develop socially positive qualities like tenderness, sensitivity to feelings, nurturance, cooperativeness, and empathy. Such prosocial behaviors and attitudes are incompatible with aggressive behaviors.

We could also teach better parenting skills. Studies by Gerald Patterson and his associates (1982) reveal that parents of delinquent youngsters tend to be unaware of their children's whereabouts; not to discipline their children effectively for antisocial behavior; and to rely on spankings and beatings, thereby modeling the use of aggression as a method of dealing with problems. Once established, aggressive behavior patterns are difficult to modify. Patterson therefore recommends using teachers' and parents' reports to identify children who seem headed for delinquency. The parents of these youngsters would then be taught how to monitor their own behavior and that of their children, how to punish antisocial behavior consistently but nonphysically, and how to model and reinforce positive behavior.

Television Watching and Aggression   We have seen that aggression is triggered by aversive events but that the effect of such events is influenced by one's physiology and learning. Let us now consider in more depth one way in which aggressive behavior may be learned.

The facts are these: The average American household has its TV set on 7 hours a day, and the average household member watches it for about 4 of those hours. Thus, during the first 18 years, most children spend more time watching television than they spend in school. Prime-time programs offer about five violent acts per hour; the average Saturday cartoon, about twenty (Gerbner & others, 1986a). During their impressionable elementary and junior high school years, the average young person will view some 13,000 murders.

Does viewing such acts influence some people to commit them? The answer is still disputed. The National Institute of Mental Health indicated in its 1982 summary of *Television and Behavior* (and the American Psychological Association affirmed in a 1985 resolution), "The consensus among most of the research community is that violence on television does lead to aggressive behavior by children and teenagers who watch the programs."

The glorification of war in the media has yielded new heroes for children—among them, the angry but patriotic Rambo. By observing such aggressive models, children readily learn aggressive methods of coping with conflict.

After the violent Vietnam war movie *The Deer Hunter* was telecast, high school student Christopher Mahan put a bullet in his father's handgun, spun the barrel, pulled the trigger, and killed himself, becoming the thirty-fifth person known to have lost while reenacting the movie's climactic game of Russian roulette (Radecki, 1984).

This conclusion emerges from correlational and experimental studies involving more than 100,000 participants (Hearold, 1986). Correlational studies have established a link between the amount of TV violence young boys watch and their later combativeness as teenagers and young adults (Eron, 1987; Turner & others, 1986). Critics respond that the link between violence-viewing and aggressiveness is modest and that aggressive children prefer violent programs. They also argue that, despite efforts to extract the effects of other factors (such as poverty) that are linked with both TV viewing and aggression, these studies have not shown that viewing violence *causes* aggression (Freedman, 1988; McGuire, 1986).

Experimenters have tried to pin down causation by exposing some viewers to an episode of violence and others to an entertaining nonviolent episode and then observing the reactions of both groups. Does viewing murder and mayhem make people more willing to do something cruel when made to feel irritated? More often than not, frustrated or angry people who are exposed to cruelty are indeed more likely to commit a hurtful act. The effect seems due to a combination of factors—to having been *aroused* by the excitement of violence, to the triggering of violence-related *ideas*, to the erosion of one's *inhibitions*, and to *imitating* others' violent behavior (Geen & Thomas, 1986).

Television's unreal world—in which acts of assault greatly outnumber acts of affection—can also affect our thinking about the real world. Prolonged exposure to violence desensitizes viewers; they become more indifferent to it when later viewing a brawl, whether on TV or in real life (Rule & Ferguson, 1986). Indeed, suggests Edward Donnerstein and his co-researchers (1987), an evil psychologist could hardly imagine a more perfect way to make people indifferent to brutality than to expose them to a graded series of scenes, from fights to killings to the sorts of mutilation observed in slasher movies. Furthermore, those who have watched a great deal of prime-time crime on television tend to regard the world as more dangerous (Heath & Petraitis, 1987; Singer & Singer, 1986).

But TV's greatest effect may stem from what it displaces. Children and adults who spend 4 hours a day watching television spend 4 fewer hours in active pursuits—talking, studying, playing, reading, or socializing with friends. What would you have done with your extra time if you had never watched television?

Pornography and Aggression   The spread of the VCR has spelled death for three-fourths of America's X-rated theaters in the last 10 years, but it has been a boon to the X-rated movie business. Between 1983 and 1986 sales of hard-core video cassettes doubled, peaking at almost one-half billion dollars a year and enabling as many people to see pornography in a single night as did in a week a decade ago (Leerhsen, 1986; Siskel, 1987).

The Content of Pornography   What do people who watch pornography see? Mostly quick, casual sex between strangers. One analysis of 160 pornographic films did not find a single instance of loving, caring sexual relations between two married or otherwise committed adults (NCTV, 1987). Mainly at issue in studies of pornography and aggression are materials that are sexually violent or degrading to women. About 15 percent of X-rated films and 30 percent of "adult" books portray violence such as bondage, mutilation, or rape (Malamuth & Briere, 1986). In a typical depiction of rape, the victim flees, resists, or fights her attacker. Despite her protests, she gradually becomes sexu-

Most researchers believe that children's behaviors and attitudes can be affected by the thousands of aggressive acts they view each year on television.

In the days before television

Drawing by Gary Larson: "The Far Side" cartoon is reprinted by permission of Chronicle Features, San Francisco.

ally aroused and eventually finds herself in ecstasy. In less graphic form, the same unrealistic, women-enjoy-being-taken myth is commonplace on TV programs and in romance novels. The woman who at first pushes the insistent man away ends up passionately kissing him.

The Effects of Pornography   In Joyce, Washington, Eugene Pyles picked up a teenage girl and drove her to a remote area where he raped and stabbed her. He left briefly, returning to smash her head with a rock. Miraculously, the girl survived. When Pyles was arrested, a cache of pornographic magazines and videos depicting violent sexual acts against women was found in his room.

Such an anecdote makes us wonder: How exceptional is this? Does pornography influence as well as entertain? To find out, researchers have conducted experiments in which they first expose young adults to a particular type of pornography and then provide them with an opportunity to indicate their attitudes or to deliver what they think is electric shock to someone who provokes them. A 1986 conference of twenty-one social scientists, including many of the researchers who conducted these experiments, produced a consensus that:

Being able to watch an X-rated movie in the comfort and privacy of the home rather than at a movie theater has made the viewing of pornographic films both easier and more respectable.

> "Pornography that portrays sexual aggression as pleasurable for the victim increases the acceptance of the use of coercion in sexual relations."

> "In laboratory studies measuring short-term effects, exposure to violent pornography increases punitive behavior toward women" (Surgeon General, 1986).

In one study, Edward Donnerstein and Daniel Linz (1984) exposed University of Wisconsin men to sexually violent "slasher" movies, such as *Texas Chainsaw Massacre*. After watching one such movie a day for 5 days, the men no longer found the violent scenes as offensive as they had at first. And they were more likely than men who had not seen the films to devalue the victim in a reenacted rape trial and to judge her injury as not severe.

To experiment with nonviolent pornography, Dolf Zillmann and Jennings Bryant (1984) showed forty male and forty female undergraduates either three or six brief, sexually explicit films a week for 6 weeks. A control group of men and women was shown nonerotic films during the same 6-week period. Three weeks later, all three groups were asked to read a newspaper report about a man who had been convicted of raping a hitchhiker but had not yet been sentenced. When asked to suggest an appropriate prison term, those who had seen six sexually explicit films a week recommended sentences half as long as the control group's. In a follow-up study, Zillmann (1986b) found that men and women who were massively exposed to pornography became more accepting of premarital and extramarital affairs, of women's sexual submission to men, and even of a man's seducing a 12-year-old girl.

These experimental studies are complemented by correlational studies of pornography and aggression in everyday life. (Remember, a correlation does not necessarily indicate causation.) John Court (1984) noted that the incidence of reported rapes rose sharply during the 1960s and 1970s as pornography became much more available in the United States and around the world. There are exceptions, such as in Japan, where violent pornography is readily available but rape is infrequent. But in general, countries and areas where pornography has been controlled have not experienced this steep rise in reported rapes.

Just as people who see a lot of televised crime perceive the world as more dangerous, those who see a lot of pornography see the world as more sexual. Zillmann (1986a) reports that people who are massively exposed to sexually explicit films offer greatly increased estimates of various sexual practices, such as extramarital and group sex.

Alaska and Nevada, which have had the highest sales rates of sexually explicit magazines, have also had the highest rape rates—even after controlling for other factors, such as the proportion of young males in the population (Baron & Straus, 1984, 1986). In Hawaii, the number of reported rapes rose by 900 percent between 1964 and 1974, then dropped when restraints on pornography were temporarily imposed, then rose again when the restraints were lifted (Figure 20–2).

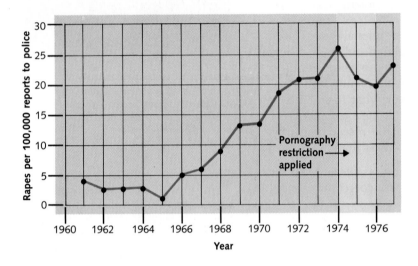

Figure 20–2   During a 2-year period when pornography was restricted in Hawaii, a downturn in reported rapes occurred. (From Court, 1984.)

Media Violence, Pornography, and Society   We must be careful not to oversimplify the complex causes of violent crime. Murders and assaults were common before television, and rape predated pornographic books and movies. There is a principle here worth remembering: Virtually every significant behavior has many determinants and any single explanation is inevitably an oversimplification.

Still, if viewing pornography can lead viewers to trivialize rape, misperceive normal sexuality, and devalue their partners (see page 365), and if viewing sexual violence can foster attitudes and behaviors that degrade women, then the questions surrounding pornography are indeed sobering. During the few minutes it has taken you to read about the new pornography research, chances are that at least one North American woman has called the police or visited a hospital emergency room to report being raped. Recent surveys of both women and men reveal that unreported rapes greatly outnumber those reported and that most rapes are committed by dates or acquaintances. In most such surveys, about half of women report some form of unwanted sexual coercion and most report having been sexually harassed verbally (Sandberg & others, 1985).

In a nationwide study of 6200 college students, Mary Koss and her colleagues (1987, 1988) found that 27.5 percent of the women reported an experience that met the legal definition of rape or attempted rape. Only 1 out of 4 victims of stranger rape and 1 out of 30 victims of acquaintance rape reported the incident to the police. When Diana Russell (1984) surveyed a random sample of 930 San Francisco adult women, she found that 44 percent said they had experienced an attempted or completed rape but only 8 percent had reported the experience to police. In eight different surveys, about two-thirds of young males say there is no circumstance under which they would rape, even if they were sure of not being punished (Stille & others, 1987)—which means that one-third admit to the possibility! And in Koss's national sample of college men, almost 1 in 10 admitted attempting or committing rape. Such findings, in combination with the spread of violent pornography and the new research on its effects, have sparked a vigorous debate over what, if anything, to do about it.

MINI-DEBATE

Should Pornography Be Controlled?

Aryeh Neier, former national executive director of the American Civil Liberties Union, currently vice chair of Helsinki Watch and Americas Watch: NO

Two weeks ago, in a displaced-persons camp in El Salvador, I talked to a group of women, every one of whom had been raped; some told me of friends who had been killed after they were raped. Pornography was not a factor. There isn't any pornography in El Salvador. . . .

That a majority of the people in a given community say they don't want to hear or see something is no legal basis for suppressing it. You could suppress virtually anything if all you had to do was submit it to a vote. But our Constitution says that "Congress shall make no law"—that is, the democratic process shall not be a basis for prohibiting speech or expression. . . .

One has to ask a simple question of those who favor censorship: What do you regard as an intellectually honest method of distinguishing between material you find offensive and other forms of expression? We need a persuasive argument that regulating pornography would not at the same time allow the regulation of other forms of communication. . . .

Susan Brownmiller, a founder of Women Against Pornography and author of *Against Our Will: Men, Women, and Rape:* YES

Pornography is propaganda against women, and propaganda is a very powerful spur to action—think of the anti-Semitic propaganda in Hitler's Germany. In an age when women are putting forward their aspirations toward equality in a healthy, positive way, pornography is working to increase hostility toward women, and therefore to increase tensions between the sexes. I find this unbearable; and I don't think there's any danger that if we limit pornography we will eventually ban *Leaves of Grass* or *Ulysses* or even Henry Miller's *Tropic of Cancer.* Those battles were fought and won a long time ago. . . .

I don't want to spend my time fighting against pornography. I would much rather be gardening, or writing my books. But someone has to do it, and feminists have brought new ideas to the struggle. Someone has to make society recognize that pornography is a problem—that it is in fact anti-female propaganda that presents a distorted picture of female sexuality. We've got to do something about it. The question is, how do we do it while protecting our important right of free speech? One way to start is by restricting the public display of pornography. And restricting public display obviously means restricting public access.

Source: Excerpted from "Forum on pornography," *Harper's Magazine,* pp. 31–45, November 1984. Copyright © 1984 *Harper's Magazine.* All rights reserved. Reprinted by permission.

Media Control   Surveys reveal that a wide majority of people favor some forms of censorship of the media. Ninety-two percent of Americans favor a total ban on video cassettes featuring sexual acts involving children, and 96 percent favor laws that ban the distribution of pornography to those under age 18 (*Gallup Report*, 1986; *Public Opinion*, 1987b). On the other hand, only 36 percent favor a total ban of all X-rated video cassettes. And even the president of the National Coalition Against Pornography supports the constitutional First Amendment right to distribute sexually explicit materials (Kirk, 1986).

The main issues are materials that are sexually violent or degrading to women. Gallup polls show that 3 of 4 Americans favor a ban on sexual violence in magazines and movies. In Canada, a national commission has recommended distinguishing three levels of pornography (Linz & others, 1986): Distributing child pornography would be a criminal offense. "Sexually violent and degrading pornography" that depicts the mistreatment of women would be a criminal offense. Except to minors, other "visual pornographic material" would be saleable with a warning. In the United States, control of pornography has varied with the enthusiasms of local prosecutors. Thus, New York City and Seattle have adults-only establishments aplenty, while Cincinnati and Fort Wayne do not.

Media Awareness Training   Recognizing the problems with censorship, many psychologists favor an approach that would limit the media's influence by educating children and adults. An American Psychological Association pamphlet advises parents not only to limit their children's TV watching and to "ban some programs" but also to watch and discuss TV programs with their children (Murray & Lonnborg, 1985). Despairing that the TV networks would ever "face the facts and change their programming," Leonard Eron and Rowell Huesmann (1984) taught 170 young children in suburban Chicago that television portrays the world unrealistically, that aggression is neither as common nor as effective as it appears to be on TV, and that such behavior is wrong. When restudied 2 years later, these children were found to be less influenced by viewing violent programs than were untrained children.

Likewise, pornography researchers debrief, resensitize, and educate their subjects regarding how the media distort women's actual responses to sexual coercion (Donnerstein & Linz, 1986). When surveyed later, these research subjects are *less* likely than other people to agree that "Being roughed up is sexually stimulating to many women." Perhaps, then, future education will counteract pornography by promoting critical viewing skills while sensitizing people to issues of sexual harassment, coercion, and violence.

New experiments on the effects of viewing pornography and of the increasing availability of hard-core and violent pornography have raised concerns about society's acceptance of pornography's degradation of women.

"What we're trying to do is raise the level of awareness of violence against women and pornography to at least the level of awareness of racist and Ku Klux Klan literature."

Gloria Steinem (1988)

ALTRUISM

Altruism—an unselfish regard for the welfare of others—became a major concern of social psychologists after Kitty Genovese, walking from a train station parking lot to her nearby Queens, New York, apartment at 3:20 A.M. on March 13, 1964, was murdered by a knife-wielding stalker. "Oh, my God, he stabbed me!" she screamed into the early-morning stillness. "Please help me!" Windows opened and lights went on as thirty-eight of her neighbors heard her screams. One couple even pulled chairs up to the window and turned out the light to see better. Her attacker fled and then returned to stab her eight more times and sexually molest her. Not until he departed for good did anyone so much as call the police. It was then 3:50 A.M.

The incident is not isolated. A 20-year-old Trenton, New Jersey, woman was raped in full view of twenty-five employees of a nearby roofing company. As the employees watched intently, not one responded to her screams for help. Later one workman explained, "We thought, well, if we went up there, it might turn out to be her boyfriend or something like that" (Shotland & Goodstein, 1984).

Could these reactions be typical? Harold Takooshian and Herzel Bodinger (1982) decided to ask volunteers from a social psychology class, many of whom had been victims of street crime, to simulate the burglary of a volunteer's parked car. In full view of passersby, the "burglar" would inspect a row of parked cars in a Manhattan business district, spend a minute forcing open the door of one with a coat hanger, remove a large valuable object such as a fur coat, relock the car, and hurry away.

Expecting that they would be apprehended, the "burglars" understandably felt queasy; their hands shook, and they felt a desire to quit the experiment (despite having full identification and proof of ownership). But after 214 "burglaries," their fears were allayed. The more than 3000 passersby who saw them often paused to stop, stare, or snicker, and some even offered to help. Only six people, three of them police officers, raised any question about the activity. The "break-ins" were restaged in seventeen other U.S. and Canadian cities. While bystanders were somewhat more likely to intervene in these other cities, 9 times out of 10 the "burglars" were unchallenged.

"Probably no single incident has caused social psychologists to pay as much attention to an aspect of social behavior as Kitty Genovese's murder."
R. Lance Shotland (1984)

BYSTANDER INTERVENTION

Reflecting on the Genovese murder, most commentators lamented the bystanders' "apathy" and "indifference." Rather than blaming them, social psychologists John Darley and Bibb Latané (1968b) attributed their inaction to an important situational factor—the presence of others. Given the right circumstances, they suspected, most of us might behave like the witnesses to the Genovese murder.

In one of Takooshian and Bodinger's experiments, a "burglar" breaks into a car and walks away with a fur coat, while bystanders either ignore or merely watch the event. This was the typical reaction in several cities.

After staging emergencies under various conditions, Darley and Latané assembled their findings into a decision scheme: We will help if and only if the situation enables us first to *notice* the incident, then to *interpret* it as an emergency, and finally to *assume responsibility* for helping (Figure 20–3). At each step the presence of other bystanders can turn people away from the path that leads to helping. In laboratory experiments and in street situations such as the car break-ins, people in groups of strangers are more likely than solitary individuals to keep their eyes on what they are doing or where they are going and thus not to notice an unusual situation. Some who did notice the car break-ins—and also observed the blasé reactions of the other passersby—perceived the burglar as a locked-out car owner.

Figure 20–3 The decision-making process for bystander intervention. (From Darley & Latané, 1968b.)

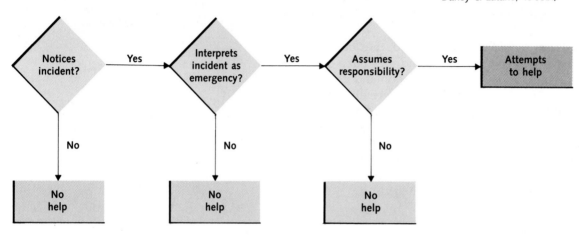

But sometimes, as with the Genovese murder, the emergency is unambiguous and people still fail to help. The witnesses looking out through their windows noticed the incident, correctly interpreted the emergency, *and* failed to assume responsibility. To find out why, Darley and Latané (1968a) simulated a physical emergency in their laboratory. University students participated in a discussion over an intercom. Each student was in a separate cubicle, and only the person whose microphone was switched on could be heard. One of the students was an accomplice of the experimenters. When his turn came, he was heard calling for help and making sounds as though he were being overcome by an epileptic seizure.

How do you think the other students reacted? As Figure 20–4 indicates, those who believed that they were the only one who could hear the victim—and therefore thought they bore total responsibility for helping—usually went to his aid. Those who thought others could also hear were more likely to react as did Kitty Genovese's neighbors. And the more the responsibility for helping was shared, the less likely it was that any single listener would help.

In hundreds of additional experiments psychologists have studied the factors that influence bystanders' willingness to relay an emergency phone call, to aid a stranded motorist, to donate blood, to pick up dropped books, to contribute money, and to give time to someone. For example, Latané, James Dabbs (1975), and 145 collaborators took 1497 elevator rides in three American cities and "accidentally" dropped coins or pencils in front of 4813 fellow passengers. The women coin-droppers were more likely to receive help than the men—a gender difference often reported by other researchers (Eagly & Crowley, 1986).

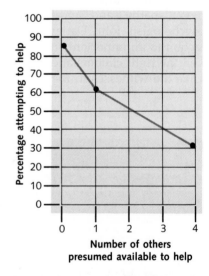

Figure 20–4 When people thought they alone heard an epileptic seizure victim calling for help, they usually helped. But when they thought four others were hearing it, too, fewer than a third responded. (From Darley & Latané, 1968a.)

We often walk by derelicts on our city streets. We may wonder, "Are they drunk or on drugs or are they sick? Will they be abusive? What can I do for them, anyway?" Although these questions tend to excuse our inaction, sometimes we do stop to help. What prompts us to do so in one instance and not in others?

But the major finding of all this research was the *bystander effect*—that any particular bystander is less likely to give aid if other bystanders are present. Thus, when one other person was on the elevator, those who dropped the coins were helped 40 percent of the time. When there were six passengers, help came less than 20 percent of the time.

From their observations of behavior in tens of thousands of such "emergencies," altruism researchers have discerned some patterns. The odds of our helping someone are best when:

We have just observed someone else being helpful.
We are not in a hurry.
The victim appears to need and deserve help.
The victim is in some way similar to ourselves.
We are in a small town or rural area.
We are feeling guilty.
We are focused on others and not preoccupied.
We are in a good mood.

This last result, that happy people are helpful people, is one of the most consistent findings in all psychology. No matter how people are put in a good mood—whether by having been made to feel successful and intelligent, by thinking happy thoughts, by finding money, or even by receiving a posthypnotic suggestion—they become more generous, more eager to help (Carlson & others, 1988).

WHY DO WE HELP?

To answer the question "Why do we help?" we need to examine both the psychological and the biological dimensions of altruism.

The Psychology of Helping   One widely held view is that self-interest is at the basis of all human interactions, that is, that our constant goal is to maximize rewards and minimize costs. As we exchange either material or social goods, we weigh the costs and benefits of doing so. Economic theorists call it cost-benefit analysis. Philosophers call it utilitarianism. Social psychologists call it *social exchange theory.* If you are pondering whether to donate blood, you may weigh the costs of doing so (time, discomfort, and anxiety) against the benefits (reduced

"Oh, make us happy and you make us good!"
   Robert Browning,
   The Ring and the Book, 1868

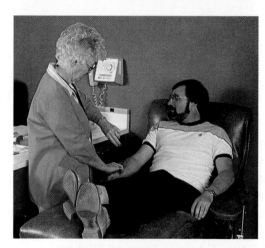

guilt, social approval, good feelings). If the anticipated rewards of helping exceed the anticipated costs, you are likely to help.

Social exchange theory helps to explain why we are most likely to help those whose approval we seek or who can reciprocate favors in the future. In such cases, the subtle, perhaps unconscious, calculations of costs and benefits motivate us to give aid.

Perhaps you are wondering, "Doesn't social exchange theory suggest that helping is not truly altruistic but is rather a disguised form of selfishness?" If we helped merely to feel good, the answer might be yes. But to gain pleasure from helping others is surely more a virtue than a vice. Moreover, many people regardless of age exhibit a natural empathy for others—we feel distress when we observe someone in distress and relief when suffering is alleviated (Batson, 1987). In an experiment in which women subjects were supposedly going to receive mild electric shocks, an accomplice of the experimenter revealed to the others that she was frightened by the prospect. She said she expected the shock to be painful because of an electrical accident she had experienced as a child. Although the other subjects were free to leave the laboratory at this point in the experiment, most willingly agreed to substitute for the frightened woman.

What motivates these volunteers—tutoring, advising a younger child, assisting in a hospital, donating blood, teaching a fatherless child how to bat? If the rewards, whether psychological or social, are greater than the costs, these volunteers are likely to continue.

Social norms also influence helping. Norms prescribe how we ought to behave, often to our mutual benefit. Through socialization, we learn the "reciprocity norm," the expectation that we should return help, not harm, to those who have helped us. In our relations with others of similar status the reciprocity norm compels us to give (in favors, gifts, or social invitations) about as much as we receive. With young children, the disabled, and others who cannot give as much as they receive, we also learn to apply a "social responsibility norm"—that we should help those who need our help, even if the costs outweigh the benefits.

The Biology of Helping   Are altruistic psychological processes predisposed by our genes? Sociobiologists suspect they are. As we saw in Chapter 5, Gender, sociobiologists use the principles of natural selection to study social behavior. Their main assumption is that any behavior that helps perpetuate our genes will tend to be selected in the competition for gene survival. Self-sacrifice is generally *not* favored because those who give their lives for another are less likely to leave descendants who will perpetuate their "unselfish" genes.

Sociobiologists remind us, however, that some forms of altruism do help to perpetuate our genes. The most obvious example is devotion to our children—the carriers of our genes. Natural selection predisposes parents to care deeply about the survival and welfare of their children. Empathy is usually felt toward other relatives, too, in proportion to their genetic closeness to us. People also empathize with strangers who are similar to themselves. In experiments, strangers perceived as similar to the subjects are offered more help and friendship than those perceived as dissimilar (Rushton & others, 1984).

That we may be genetically biased to behave altruistically toward our kin and toward similar strangers (in order to enhance the chances of our shared genes surviving) is a mixed blessing. Writes sociobiologist E. O. Wilson (1978, p. 167): "Altruism based on kin selection is the enemy of civilization. If human beings are to a large extent guided . . . to favor their own relatives and tribe, only a limited amount of global harmony is possible."

Social psychologist Daniel Batson (1983) notes that religion has sometimes accentuated the division of people into the "believers" within the group (for whom concern is felt) and the "heathen" on the outside (for whom contempt is felt). Nevertheless, Batson believes that the religious theme of "brotherly love" toward the entire human "family"—the "children of God"—serves to extend family-linked altruism beyond one's immediate biological relatives. And there is some evidence that devotion to such religious precepts does indeed correlate with long-term altruism. Among Americans whom George Gallup (1984) classified as "highly spiritually committed," 46 percent said they were presently working among the poor, the infirm, or the elderly—a significantly higher rate of altruism than reported by people classified as "moderately committed" (36 percent), "moderately uncommitted" (28 percent), or "highly uncommitted" (22 percent).

Evidence of at least a limited form of genetically programmed altruism comes from instances among insects and animals. The clearest case of altruistic behavior is the self-sacrifice of worker ants, honeybees, and termites, all of whom are sterile. The altruistic worker bee that gives its life by stinging an intruder is helping to perpetuate its genes, which are transmitted by the queen bee. Higher animals, too, will sometimes perform altruistic acts. Porpoises have been observed

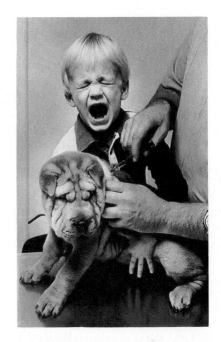

Empathy. Many people witnessing distress will feel compassion.

"Human history can be viewed as a slowly dawning awareness that we are members of a larger group. Initially our loyalties were to ourselves and our immediate family, next, to bands of wandering hunter-gatherers, then to tribes, small settlements, city-states, nations. We have broadened the circle of those we love. We have now organized what are modestly described as superpowers, which include groups of people from divergent ethnic and cultural backgrounds working in some sense together—surely a humanizing and character-building experience. If we are to survive, our loyalties must be broadened further, to include the whole human community, the entire planet Earth."

Carl Sagan (1980, p. 339)

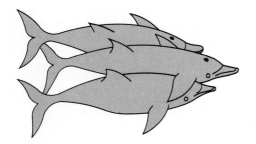

Porpoises cooperating to aid an injured porpoise. (From Siebenaler & Caldwell, 1956.)

to cooperate in giving aid to an injured porpoise (Hebb, 1980). Consider an act by Washoe, one of the first chimps to receive language training. One day Washoe observed another chimp, Cindy, leap the electric fence around their island compound. Cindy landed in the water, went under, came to the surface, thrashed, and went under again. Washoe immediately leaped the electric fence and reached out to Cindy with one hand while holding on to the grass at the water's edge with the other. When Cindy resurfaced, Washoe grabbed her and pulled her to safety and then sat with her. "Washoe's act gave me a new perspective on chimpanzees," reported her caretaker, Roger Fouts (1984). "I was impressed with her heroism in risking her life on the slippery banks. She cared about someone in trouble; someone she didn't even know that well."

It would be naïve to think that such devotion to others is common among animals or humans. Among us humans, however, social learning encourages reciprocity, social learning, and the sense of kinship that makes genuine altruism possible. To strangers in great need, people will sometimes give blood, food, and money and ask nothing in return. Heroes among us have risked their lives in helping others. On a hillside in Jerusalem, 800 trees line the Avenue of the Righteous (Hellman, 1980). Beneath each is a plaque bearing the name of a European Christian who, during the Holocaust, gave refuge to one or more Jews. These people knew that if the refugees were discovered, both host and refugee would suffer a common fate—as many did.

PREJUDICE

Prejudice means prejudgment. It is an unjustifiable and usually negative attitude toward a group and its members. Like all attitudes, prejudice is a mixture of beliefs (often overgeneralized and called ***stereotypes***), feelings (hostility, envy, or fear), and predispositions to action (discrimination). To generalize that overweight people are gluttonous, to feel contempt for an overweight person, and to be hesitant to hire or date an overweight person, is to be prejudiced.

Prejudice can be assessed by noting what people say and do. To judge by what Americans say, attitudes regarding blacks and women have improved since the 1940s (see Figure 20–5). Americans have achieved a virtual national consensus that white and black children should attend the same schools and that women and men who are doing the same job should receive equal pay.

Despite this consensus, subtle—and not so subtle—forms of racial and gender prejudice persist. Many white people still admit to discomfort while in socially intimate settings (such as dancing and dating) with someone of a different race. Race can also influence how a given behavior gets interpreted. In one experiment, most white observers perceived a white man shoving a black as "horsing around," whereas the same behavior by the black man toward the white was more likely

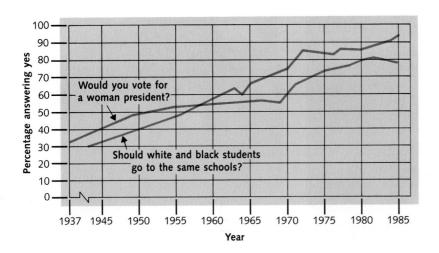

Figure 20–5 Americans today express much less racial and gender prejudice than two and three decades ago. But if our actions are to be judged, many subtle forms of prejudice still abound. (Responses to the racial question are from whites only.) (From *Public Opinion*, October/November, 1984; and *Gallup Report*, 228/229, 1984.)

to be seen as ''violent'' (Duncan, 1976). Moreover, people tend to choose those of their own race for neighbors and friends (Schofield, 1982). Studies of subtle forms of gender prejudice reveal a similar lingering but potentially potent bias in people's beliefs, feelings, and actions regarding women, as in the hope of most prospective parents that their first child will be a boy (Frieze & others, 1978).

Most of us deny we feel prejudice and insist that prejudice is morally wrong. Although we strongly support the principle of racial or sexual equality, we are typically less enthusiastic about specific methods of furthering it. And we often react prejudicially when our actions— our failure to help, to hire, or to invite—can be attributed to something other than race or gender. If white bystanders to an emergency can attribute their inaction to the presence of other bystanders, they are less likely to help black than white victims (Dovidio & Gaertner, 1986). Such prejudice is fed by complex social, emotional, and cognitive factors.

SOCIAL ROOTS OF PREJUDICE

Once established, prejudice is maintained largely by the inertia of social influence—by conformity to established norms of prejudice and by the support prejudice finds in our social institutions. But how does prejudice arise in the first place?

Social Inequalities   If some people have money, power, and prestige and others do not, the ''haves'' are likely to develop attitudes about the ''have nots'' that justify and help preserve the difference in their status. Slaves were perceived as being lazy and irresponsible—as having the very traits that justified enslaving them. Women are still seen as weak and emotional, and therefore fit only for the menial tasks they often perform. In short, prejudice rationalizes inequalities.

Discrimination can lead to increased prejudice through the reactions it provokes in its victims. In his classic book *The Nature of Prejudice*, Gordon Allport noted that being a victim of discrimination can trigger either self-blame and self-deprecation or anger and rebellion. Both reactions may create new grounds for prejudice through the classic ''blame the victim'' dynamic, in which the victims' plight is turned against them. For example, if the circumstances of ghetto life breed a higher crime rate, the higher crime rate can then be used to justify continuing the discrimination that has helped to create the ghetto.

''Prejudice is never easy unless it can pass itself off for reason.''
   William Hazlitt,
   On Prejudice, 1839

''It is understandable that the suppressed people should develop an intense hostility towards a culture whose existence they make possible by their work, but in whose wealth they have too small a share.''
   Sigmund Freud,
   The Future of an Illusion, 1927

Groups often preserve their social status by rationalizing the prejudicial system that supports it. The South African government strives to maintain white supremacy by enforcing apartheid laws, as illustrated (upper left) by the separate "public conveniences" for whites and nonwhites (formerly referred to as "Europeans" and "non-Europeans"). Although the Indian caste system was officially abolished in 1949, it still dominates the lives of millions of Indians in rural areas. The outcastes shown here (upper right) are often called "untouchables" because even to be touched by their shadows is considered a form of pollution by higher castes. In 1987 in Howard Beach, New York, a young black man was chased by a group of white youths onto a highway, where he was struck and killed by a car. The incident exposed deep-seated racial tensions in the community and sparked a series of highly charged demonstrations (lower left). The plight of this fisherman (lower right), a Vietnamese refugee whose boat has been burned, displays the bias of "native" Gulf Coast fishermen to protect interests of their own group.

Us and Them: Ingroup and Outgroup   The social definition of who we are—our race, sex, and group memberships—also indicates who we are not. The circle that defines and includes "us" excludes "them." Indeed, the very act of being put in a group triggers an *ingroup bias*—a tendency to favor one's own group.

British psychologist Henri Tajfel (1982) conducted a series of studies showing that ingroup bias occurs even when the we-they distinction is trivial. In the initial experiment, boys sat together in groups of eight and watched slides with dots flash on a screen. After individually guessing how many dots had been flashed on each slide, four of the boys were taken aside and told that they tended to overestimate. The other four were told that they tended to underestimate. Later, each of the eight boys was given some money to divide between two of the other boys, one a fellow overestimator or underestimator, the other not. It wasn't much to respond to, but it was enough; the boys gave more money to those who shared their own label.

In this experiment—and in later ones with people of various ages, sexes, and nationalities—temporarily forming people into inconsequential groups was enough to produce ingroup favoritism (Wilder, 1981). In more natural situations, too, people are strongly biased to favor their own groups (Hinkle & Schopler, 1986). Students at most schools are convinced that their school is better than the other schools in town. Even chimpanzees have been observed to wipe clean the spot where a chimp from another group has touched them (Goodall, 1986).

"I'm surprised, Marty. I thought
you were one of us."

EMOTIONAL ROOTS OF PREJUDICE

Prejudice can spring from the passions of the heart as well as the biases of the mind. For one thing, prejudice may express anger. When things go wrong, finding someone to blame can provide an outlet for anger. Evidence for this **scapegoat theory** of prejudice comes from surveys of economically frustrated people, who exhibit heightened prejudice, and from experiments in which people who are temporarily frustrated express intensified prejudice. Nazi leader Hermann Rausching once explained the Nazis' need to scapegoat: "If the Jew did not exist, we should have to invent him" (quoted by Koltz, 1983).

Despised outgroups not only provide a handy outlet for anger, they can also boost self-esteem. To see ourselves as high in status, it helps to have others to look down on. For this reason, the misfortune of a rival may sometimes provide a twinge of pleasure. In experiments, students who have just experienced failure or who are made to feel insecure will often alleviate their self-doubts by disparaging a rival school or another person (Cialdini & Richardson, 1980; Crocker & others, 1987). More generally, people who have difficulty accepting themselves tend to be less affirming of others (page 430).

"If the Tiber reaches the walls, if the Nile does not rise to the fields, if the sky doesn't move or the earth does, if there is famine, if there is plague, the cry is at once: 'The Christians to the lion!'"
    Tertullian,
    Apologeticus, A.D. 197

"I blame everything on the Russians, except for
the few things, Stacey, I blame on you."

COGNITIVE ROOTS OF PREJUDICE

So far, we have noted some of the social and emotional roots of prejudice. Recent research has focused on another source: Stereotyped beliefs may be a natural by-product of our normal ways of cognitively simplifying our complex world.

Categorization   One way we simplify our world is to categorize things. A chemist classifies molecules as organic and inorganic. A mental health professional classifies people's psychological disorders by types. Such categories help us to organize our thoughts and speed our thinking.

One price we pay for categorizing things and people into groups is a tendency to overestimate the similarity of people within groups other than our own. "They"—the members of some other group—seem to look and act alike, but "we" are diverse. To us on the outside, the members of fraternity X are jocks and those in fraternity Y are intellectuals. Of course, the men in each fraternity see diversity among their fellow members.

Vivid Cases   As noted in Chapter 11, Thinking and Language, we tend to judge the frequency of events in terms of instances that readily come to mind. If asked whether blacks can run faster than whites, many people may think of Jesse Owens, Carl Lewis, and Florence Griffith Joyner and overgeneralize from such vivid but exceptional cases that "Yes, blacks seem to be faster."

That we overgeneralize from vivid, memorable cases has been verified in experiments by Myron Rothbart and his colleagues (1978). In one study, University of Oregon students were divided into two groups, each of which was shown a list of fifty men, including ten who had committed crimes. The ten criminals in the first group's list had committed nonviolent crimes such as forgery. Those in the second group's list had committed violent crimes such as rape. When both groups were tested for recall and were asked how many men on their list had committed any sort of crime, which group do you suppose overestimated the actual number? The group whose list included violent criminals. Vivid cases, being readily available to memory, powerfully influence the generalizations we make.

The Just-World Phenomenon   Earlier we noted that oppressors tend to justify their acts by blaming their victims. Impartial observers also tend to blame victims, by assuming that the world is just and that people therefore get what they deserve. In laboratory experiments, merely observing someone receive painful shocks led many of the observers to think less of the victim (Lerner, 1980). This *just-world phenomenon* is reflected in an idea we commonly teach our children—that good is rewarded and evil is punished. From this it is a short leap to assume that those who are rewarded must be good and those who suffer must likewise deserve their fate. Such reasoning enables the rich to see their wealth, and the poor's misfortune, as justly deserved. As one German civilian remarked after being shown the concentration camp at Bergen-Belsen at the close of World War II, "What terrible criminals these prisoners must have been to receive such treatment."

The hindsight bias (the I-knew-it-all-along phenomenon) is also at work here. Have you ever heard people say that rape victims, abused spouses, or people with AIDS have gotten what they deserved? It happens all the time. An experiment by Ronnie Janoff-Bulman and her collaborators (1985) illustrates this: People who were given an account of

Overgeneralized stereotypes appear in people's simplified judgments of the past (Silka, 1988). "Last winter was warm, the winter before was cold," a person may think, "but this winter the temperatures are up and down." "Last year's basketball team was pretty consistent, but this year's team has hot and cold streaks." The past seems more uniform, the present more variable.

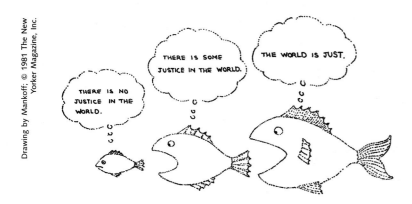

a date that ended with the woman being raped perceived the woman as partly to blame; in hindsight, they thought, "She should have known better." But others who were given the same account without the rape did not perceive the woman as having invited rape. Only when she was believed to be a victim was she faulted for her behavior.

The Cognitive Consequences of Stereotypes   Like other forms of prejudgment, prejudices are schemas that influence what we notice, interpret, and remember. If told that a friendly person they are about to meet is unfriendly, people may treat the person with kid gloves. Later they assume that it was their gentle handling that led the "unfriendly" person to act so well (Ickes & others, 1982).

In one of his last research projects, Stanley Milgram (1984) demonstrated the biasing power of preconceptions by creating "cyranoids"—people who, like a character under the influence of Cyrano de Bergerac in the play of the same name, echo someone else's thoughts. In one experiment, high school teachers were invited to interview an 11- and a 12-year-old boy, both of whom echoed whatever the 50-year-old Milgram transmitted to them through a wireless radio receiver in their ear. Thus, without realizing it, the teachers were actually talking to one of America's most brilliant scholars, who was literally speaking through the mouths of sixth and seventh graders. The teachers were asked to probe the limits of each child's knowledge in science, literature, and current events "so that you would be able to recommend a grade level for each subject."

Although the teachers were impressed with the children and recognized them as above average, their impressions were constrained by their preconceptions. As Milgram noted,

> The opinions teachers formed of our child cyranoids depended as much on the teacher as on the child, and the questions asked and avoided. Teachers varied in how they approached their questions, the best of them allowing the cyranoids' responses to guide their interview, the worst never seeing beyond the possibilities of an average 11-year-old.
>
> Moreover, we see how general preconceptions did not allow the teachers to get anywhere near the appropriate grade level of the cyranoid in some subjects. After all, to assign a Ph.D. to a 10th grade class of social studies does no great honor to his Harvard degree. . . . As the source, I was hoping they would ask the cyranoid about Freud, Jung, Adler or at least Darwin and Wittgenstein, but some teachers stuck to fractions and parts of speech.

We see then that prejudice not only is nurtured by its social, emotional, and cognitive roots, but it also bears cognitive fruits. Our preconceived ideas about people—as formed by labels such as "gifted" or "schizophrenic"—bias the impressions we form of them. To believe is to see.

ATTRACTION

Pause a moment and think about your relationships with two people—a close friend and someone who either now or in the past has stirred you to feel romantic love. What factors led you into these relationships and helped you sustain them?

We endlessly wonder what makes our affections flourish and fade and how we can win the affection of others. In literature, song lyrics, and social commentary we can find a variety of possible explanations. Do birds of a feather flock together, or do opposites attract? Does familiarity breed contempt or liking? Does absence make the heart grow fonder—or is out of sight out of mind? Social-psychological studies suggest some answers.

LIKING

What is the psychological chemistry that binds two people together in a friendship so deep that it helps them cope with all their other relationships? More simply, what factors help predict whether two people will become friends?

Proximity   Before friendships can become deep, they must first be initiated. Proximity—geographic nearness—is perhaps the most powerful predictor of friendship. Of course, proximity also provides opportunities for assaults, rapes, and murders. But much more often it instigates liking. Study after study reveals that people are most likely to like, and even to marry, those who live in the same neighborhood, have a nearby dorm room or apartment, sit nearby in class, work in the same office, or share the same parking lot.

Why is proximity so conducive to liking? Obviously, part of the answer is the greater availability of those we encounter often. But there is more to it than that. For one thing, being repeatedly exposed to novel stimuli—whether they be Chinese characters, nonsense syllables, musical selections, geometric figures, human faces, or the letters found in our own name—increases our liking for them (Moreland & Zajonc, 1982; Nuttin, 1987). This phenomenon is known as the *mere exposure effect.* Within certain limits, familiarity breeds not contempt but fondness.

The mere exposure effect applies even to ourselves. Have you ever noticed that you never look quite right in photographs? An experiment by Theodore Mita and his colleagues (1977) with women at the University of Wisconsin, Milwaukee, revealed why. The researchers photo-

The Johnny Carson we know and like is at the left. But, if asked, Carson would probably prefer the self at the right, the one he sees in the mirror every day.

graphed each woman and then showed her and a close friend the actual photo along with a mirror-image copy. Most of the friends preferred the actual photo, which portrayed the woman's face the way they were used to seeing it. Most of the subjects, however, preferred the mirror-image photo, which reflected the way they were used to seeing themselves.

Physical Attractiveness   Once proximity has brought you into contact with someone, what most affects your first impressions: the person's sincerity? intelligence? personality? Hundreds of experiments reveal that it is likely to be something more superficial: appearance.

For people taught that "beauty is only skin deep" and that "appearances can be deceiving," the power of physical attractiveness is unnerving. In one early study, Elaine Hatfield and her co-workers (Walster & others, 1966) randomly matched University of Minnesota freshmen for a "Welcome Week" dance. All were given a battery of personality and aptitude tests prior to the dance. On the night of the blind date, the couples danced and talked for more than 2 hours and then took a brief intermission to evaluate their dates. What determined whether they liked each other? So far as the researchers could determine, only one thing mattered: physical attractiveness (which had been rated by the researchers beforehand). Both the men and the women liked good-looking dates best.

Subsequent studies revealed that people's physical attractiveness is linked with the frequency of their dating, their feelings of popularity, and the impressions others form about their personalities. Attractive people, including children and those of one's own sex, are perceived as happier, more sensitive, more successful, and more socially skilled (Dion, 1986; Hatfield & Sprecher, 1986). Attractive and well-dressed people are also more likely to make a favorable impression on potential employers (Cash & Janda, 1984; Solomon, 1987). To judge from their gazing times, even babies prefer attractive over unattractive faces (Langlois & others, 1987).

If looks matter so much, who dates and marries those who are less attractive? Although people might prefer someone superattractive, they tend not to approach those who are "out of their league." Thus, less attractive people tend eventually to match up with people who are about as attractive as they are (Murstein, 1986). In exceptional cases where partners are noticeably unequal in attractiveness, the less physically attractive person often has compensating assets, such as greater wealth or status. This helps explain why beautiful young women often marry older men whose social status is higher than their own (Elder, 1969).

That looks can be so important may seem unfair and unenlightened. Two thousand years ago the Roman statesman Cicero felt the same way: "The final good and the supreme duty of the wise man is to resist appearance." Cicero might be reassured by two other findings about attractiveness.

First, people's attractiveness is surprisingly unrelated to their self-esteem (Major & others, 1984). One reason may be that few people view themselves as very unattractive. (Thanks, perhaps, to the mere exposure effect, most of us become accustomed to our face.) Another reason is that strikingly attractive people are sometimes suspicious that the praise they receive may be simply a reaction to their looks; when less attractive people are praised for their work, they are less likely to discount it as flattery. In fact, attraction researcher Ellen Berscheid (1981) reported that those who have improved their appearance by

"Personal beauty is a greater recommendation than any letter of introduction."
Aristotle,
Apothegems, 330 B.C.

"Love comes in at the eye."
William Butler Yeats,
"A Drinking Song," 1909

Dating and married couples tend to be matched in attractiveness. If unmatched, the less attractive member often has compensating assets.

cosmetic surgery are often disturbed to discover the extent to which this favorably influences how people react to them.

Cicero might also find comfort in knowing that judgments about attractiveness are relative. They depend not only on one's time and place and the standards of beauty to which one has been socialized but also on one's feelings about the person. In a Rodgers and Hammerstein musical, Prince Charming asks Cinderella, "Do I love you because you are beautiful, or are you beautiful because I love you?" Chances are it is both. As we discover someone's similarities to us, see them again and again, and come to like them, their physical imperfections usually grow less noticeable and their attractiveness grows more apparent (Beaman & Klentz, 1983; Gross & Crofton, 1977). E.T. is as ugly as Darth Vader, until you get to know him.

"The thin, narrow-shouldered ectomorph who was yesterday's spinster librarian is today's high fashion model; the plump and buxom endomorph who was a Victorian romantic ideal today is eating cottage cheese and grapefruit, and weighing in every Tuesday at Weight Watchers."
Phyllis Bronstein-Burrows (1981)

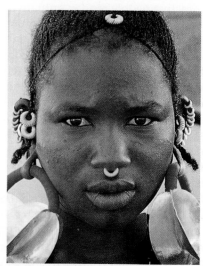

These beauties from around the world illustrate different cultural ideas of what is attractive.

Similarity Let us say that proximity has brought you into contact with someone and that your appearance has made a favorable first impression. What now influences whether acquaintances develop into friends? For example, as you get to know someone better, is liking more probable if you are opposites or if you are alike?

It makes a good story—extremely different types living in harmonious union: Rat, Mole, and Badger in *The Wind in the Willows*, Frog and Toad in Arnold Lobel's books. The stories delight us by expressing what we seldom experience, for in fact we tend to dislike dissimilar people (Rosenbaum, 1986). In real life birds who flock together are usually of the same feather. Friends and couples are far more likely than randomly paired people to share common attitudes, beliefs, and interests (or, for that matter, age, religion, race, education, intelligence, smoking behavior, and economic status). Moreover, the greater the similarity, the more likely it is the relationship will endure (Byrne, 1971).

Proximity, attractiveness, and similarity are not the only determinants of liking, however. We also tend to like those who like us, especially when our self-image is low. And when we *believe* someone likes us, we respond to them more warmly, which leads them to like us even more (Curtis & Miller, 1986). To be liked is powerfully rewarding. Indeed, a simple reward theory of attraction—that we will like those whose behavior is rewarding to us and that we will continue relationships that offer more rewards than costs—can explain all the findings we have so far considered. When a person lives or works in close proximity with someone else, it costs less time and effort to develop the friendship and enjoy its benefits. Attractive people are aesthetically pleasing, and associating with them can be socially rewarding. Those with similar views reward us by validating our own.

Prince Charles loves opera, art museums, and vacations in Scotland; Princess Diana loves rock concerts, nightclubs, and London. Royalty watchers worry: Can a marriage flourish between two people so different in age and interests?

LOVING

Occasionally, people progress from initial impressions to friendship to the more intense, complex, and mysterious state of romantic love. Elaine Hatfield (1988) distinguishes two types of love: the temporary passionate love and the more enduring "companionate" love.

Passionate Love The state of intense positive absorption in another is known as ***passionate love.*** Noting that emotional arousal is a key ingredient of passionate love, Hatfield suggests that the *two-factor theory of emotion* (pages 402–403) can help us understand it. The theory assumes that emotions have two ingredients—physical arousal plus a cognitive label—and that arousal from any source can facilitate one emotion or another, depending on how we interpret and label the arousal.

In tests of this theory, college men have been aroused by being frightened, by running in place, by viewing erotic materials, or by listening to humorous or repulsive monologues. They are then introduced to an attractive woman and asked to rate her, or are simply asked to rate their girlfriends. Compared with unaroused men, those who are stirred up are likely to attribute some of their arousal to the woman or girlfriend and to report more positive feelings toward her (Carducci & others, 1978; Dermer & Pyszczynski, 1978; White & Kight, 1984; White & others, 1981).

Outside the laboratory, Donald Dutton and Arthur Aron (1974) staked out two bridges across British Columbia's rocky Capilano River.

One was a swaying footbridge 230 feet above the rocks; the other was a low, solid bridge. An attractive young female accomplice intercepted men coming off each bridge, sought their help in filling out a short questionnaire, and then offered her phone number in case they wanted to hear more about her project. Far more of those who had just crossed the high bridge—which had left their hearts pounding—accepted the number and later called the woman. To be revved up and to attribute that arousal to a desirable person is to feel the pull of passion. As lovers who take a thrilling roller coaster ride together know, adrenaline makes the heart grow fonder.

> "When two people are under the influence of the most violent, most insane, most delusive, and most transient of passions, they are required to swear that they will remain in that excited, abnormal, and exhausting condition continuously until death do them part."
> George Bernard Shaw,
> *Man and Superman*, 1903

Companionate Love   "Love makes the time pass and time makes love pass," goes a French saying. The passionate fires of love burn hot, and then, in a relationship that endures, usually cool to a warm afterglow that Hatfield calls *companionate love*—a strong, affectionate attachment. As a marriage proceeds, the initial elation of passionate love usually subsides (though it may rebound after the children leave home [Hatfield & others, 1984; Mathes & Wise, 1983]). Granted, the affection of companionate love may also dwindle as a relationship ages, but under favorable circumstances, it deepens.

One key to a gratifying and enduring relationship is *equity:* Both partners receive in proportion to what they contribute. If equity exists and if decision-making power is shared, the chances for sustained and satisfying companionate love are good (Gray-Little & Burks, 1983; Matthews & Clark, 1982). Indeed, equitable giving and receiving—mutually sharing self and possessions, giving and getting emotional support, promoting and caring about one another's welfare—are at the core of every type of loving relationship, whether with a lover, a parent or child, or an intimate friend (Sternberg & Grajek, 1984).

Another vital ingredient for loving relationships is intimacy (Sternberg, 1986). A strong friendship or marriage permits *self-disclosure,* a revealing of intimate details about ourselves—what we like and don't like, what we feel proudest of and most ashamed of, what we spend most time dreaming or worrying about. "When I am with my friend," noted the Roman statesman Seneca, "methinks I am alone, and as much at liberty to speak anything as to think it. . . ." Self-disclosure grows as a relationship deepens; as one person reveals a little, the other reciprocates, the first person reveals more, and on and on, as friends or lovers move to ever deeper levels of intimacy.

The quality of love changes as a relationship matures from passionate absorption to deep affectionate attachment.

CONFLICT AND PEACEMAKING

Conflict, a perceived incompatibility of actions, goals, or ideas, is a normal part of social relations. When people are involved with one another, their needs and desires occasionally clash. If conflict is managed well, it can provide an opportunity for improving relations by identifying and eliminating irritations. Conflict can also bring out the worst in us. Our human capacity for destructive aggression and mean-spirited discrimination makes conflict potentially dangerous—whether between individuals (a married couple, roommates, parents and child), between groups (blacks and white, labor and management, teachers and students), or between nations (Israel and Syria, Iran and Iraq, the United States and Soviet Union).

What initiates conflict? And what steps can be taken to resolve conflict peacefully to the mutual satisfaction of both parties?

CONFLICT

The elements of conflict are much the same in any situation, whether involving individuals, groups, or nations. To examine these elements, let us focus on one situation: the nuclear arms race. Writing on the prevention of nuclear holocaust, psychologist M. Brewster Smith (1982) noted that

> all other questions of human value and social controversy are dwarfed in comparison. If psychology as a science and profession is to be concerned with the promotion of human welfare, if indeed it is to persist as a science, there must be surviving human beings!

International conflict springs from tensions between nations with differing histories, ideologies, and economies. To understand why every thinking person dreads nuclear war while most technologically advanced nations plan for it, we need insight from many disciplines. Psychology contributes by helping us understand how—as the United Nations Educational, Scientific, and Cultural Organization (UNESCO) motto declares—"wars begin in the minds of men."

When psychiatrist Robert Jay Lifton (1982) went to Hiroshima in 1962 to study the psychological aftereffects of the atomic bomb blast, he encountered an emotional defense process that he called "psychic numbing." The survivors of the blast itself recalled seeing "people dying around them, they knew they were dying, they knew something horrible was happening, but they suddenly ceased to feel, underwent what one woman writer described as a 'paralysis of the mind.'" Lifton now believes that psychic numbing occurs in the minds of those who today collaborate to plan, produce, and prepare to use nuclear weapons, as well as in the minds of the majority of us who cannot imagine what nuclear war would be like or simply do not wish to think about it. One way to "break out of the numbing," Lifton urges, is to be mindful of the truth.

The truth is that the world's spending for arms and armies now approaches $2 million per minute or nearly $3 billion per *day* (Associated Press, 1986). Moreover, all the conventional bombs dropped in all of World War II are now equaled in power by a *single* run-of-the-mill thermonuclear bomb—"one bomb [has] the destructive force of the Second World War," noted Carl Sagan (1980, p. 320). "But there are tens of thousands of nuclear weapons."

"My God, what have we done!"
Robert A. Lewis, co-pilot of the B-29 *Enola Gay*, August 7, 1945, as he watched the blast created by the atom bomb his plane had just dropped on Hiroshima

Nuclear facts from the *Bulletin of the Atomic Scientists* (1988): There are 55,000 nuclear weapons in the world, which on average pack 15 times the wallop of the Hiroshima bomb. The Soviet Union has 12,000 warheads capable of being fired at the United States. The twelve-thousandth largest city in the United States is Roxie, Mississippi, population 640.

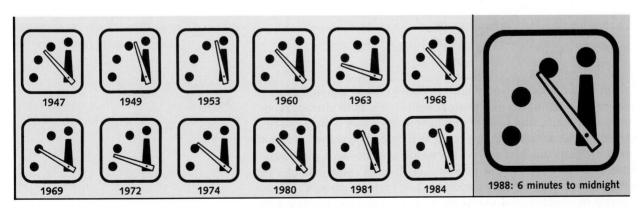

The closeness of the minute hand to midnight on the "Doomsday Clock" symbolizes how close the editors of the *Bulletin of the Atomic Scientists* believe the world is to nuclear war. In 1984, the editors, after consultation with a committee of forty-seven world-renowned scientists, advanced the clock to 3 minutes to midnight—the closest the world has been to nuclear holocaust since 1953. In January 1988, following an arms reduction agreement, the clock was turned back to 6 minutes to midnight.

Social psychologists believe that the arms race, like many other conflicts, arises from destructive social processes by which even well-meaning persons become enmeshed in a web of hostilities that no one really wants. Psychologist Morton Deutsch (1986) has identified several of these "malignant social processes." Here we will consider two: social traps and mirror-image perceptions.

Social Traps   In some situations, we can contribute to our collective well-being by pursuing our own self-interest. As the eighteenth-century capitalist economist Adam Smith wrote in *The Wealth of Nations,* "It is not from the benevolence of the butcher, the brewer, or the baker, that we expect our dinner, but from their regard to their own interest." In other situations, the parties involved—be they individuals or nations—may become caught up in mutually harmful behavior as they pursue their own ends. Such situations are called *social traps.*

Consider the simple game matrix in Figure 20–6, which is similar to those used in experiments with thousands of people. Pretend that you are person 1, and that you and person 2 will each receive the amount of money indicated in the matrix after separately choosing either A or B. (You might invite someone to look at the matrix with you and to take the role of person 2.) Which do you choose—A or B?

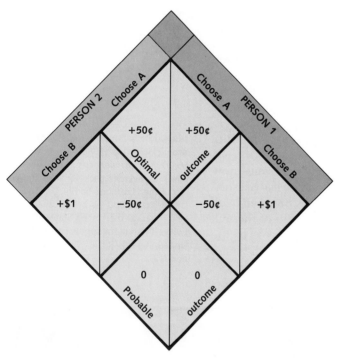

Figure 20–6   By pursuing our best interests and not trusting others, we can end up losers. To illustrate this, play the game to the left. The beige triangles indicate the outcomes for person 1, which depend on the choices made by both persons. If you were person 1, would you choose A or B? (This game is called a "non-zero-sum game," because the outcomes need not add up to zero; both sides can win or both can lose.)

As you play the game, you will soon discover that you and person 2 are caught in a dilemma. You both benefit if you both choose A, by making 50 cents each, and neither of you benefits if you both choose B, for you both make nothing. However, it will quickly become clear that your own interests are best served if you always choose B, no matter what the other person does. If person 2 chooses A, you make $1 by choosing B but only 50 cents by choosing A. If person 2 chooses B, you lose nothing by choosing B, but lose 50 cents by choosing A. Moreover, you can bet the other person will realize that, no matter what you do, his or her personal interests are similarly best served by always choosing B. Hence, the malignant social trap. The predicament becomes maddening, for as long as neither of you trusts the other to choose A and so both pursue your own best interest and choose B, you will both end up with nothing instead of 50 cents.

The arms race can be understood as a social trap. The leaders of both the United States and the U.S.S.R. recognize that, as President Eisenhower once said, "Every gun that is made, every warship launched, every rocket fired signifies, in the final sense, a theft from those who hunger and are not fed, those who are cold and are not clothed." To both countries' mutual detriment, the arms race has continued. An adapted game matrix helps us understand why (Figure 20-7). Strategists in each nation figure that if the other nation is arming, then so must we; a military buildup is the only way to avoid the disaster that might come if they secretly arm while we disarm. To deter them from attacking we must have a capacity to retaliate. Indeed, in laboratory simulations of the arms race, those who use a pacifist strategy of unconditional disarmament in playing the game are usually exploited (Reychler, 1979). And those who arm themselves stimulate reciprocation. As social psychologist George Levinger (1987) observes, "When multiplied by 2, a national policy of Peace Through Strength leads inevitably to an arms race."

"I can calculate the motions of the heavenly bodies, but not the madness of people."

 Sir Isaac Newton, 1642–1727

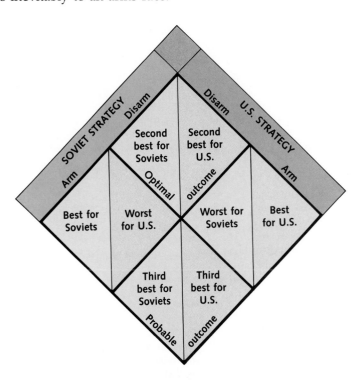

Figure 20–7 The arms race: When America and Russia each protect their self-interest and distrust the other, the result is mutually defeating.

Social traps challenge us to find ways of reconciling our right to pursue our personal well-being with our responsibility for the well-being of all. Psychologists are therefore exploring ways to convince people to cooperate for their mutual betterment—through establishing agreed-upon regulations, through developing better communication with one another, and through promoting an increased awareness of our responsibilities toward our community, our country, and the whole of humanity (Dawes, 1980; Linder, 1982; Sato, 1987).

Mirror-Image Perceptions   Guess who the following news story, reported by the Associated Press, was about.

> The [President/Premier] acknowledged that [Washington's/the Kremlin's] military might had grown in the last decade, but said the [United States/Soviet Union] had been compelled to strengthen itself because of the "feverish [U.S.S.R./U.S.] effort to establish bases near [American/Soviet] territory" and to counter "the [U.S.S.R./U.S.] military superiority for which [Moscow/Washington] is now pining so much."

THE COMMONS DILEMMA

Another social trap is what ecologist Garrett Hardin (1968) called the "tragedy of the commons." The "commons" was a pasture that was once maintained at the center of many rural communities and to which all the town's residents had grazing rights. If 100 farmers share a commons that is capable of sustaining 100 cows, and each grazes one cow, then the pasture is fully utilized without being overgrazed. The commons could just as well be air, water, food, whales, or any other shared and limited resource. If all restrain their use of the resource, it replenishes itself as fast as it is used, and there continues to be enough for all.

Now, imagine a farmer who reasons, "If I put a second cow in the pasture, I'll double my milk production, and the cost of the one percent overgrazing caused by my cow will be shared by everybody." So the farmer adds a second cow. But each of the farmer's neighbors reasons the same and also adds a second cow. As a result, the pasture is stripped bare—the tragedy of the commons.

The commons dilemma arises in many real-life situations when people pit their individual interests against the well-being of the community. Individual whalers reasoned that the few whales they took didn't threaten the species and that if they didn't take them others would anyway. The result: A species of whales becomes endangered. The individual polluter reasons, "It would cost me lots of money to buy expensive pollution controls for my car. Besides, my car's defective exhaust system, by itself, doesn't noticeably harm the air in my city." If everyone reasons the same way, the collective result is environmentally devastating.

The words were those of the Soviet leader. But if you imagine U.S. leaders saying them, they sound familiar. Indeed, psychologists (such as Ralph White, 1984) and political scientists (such as Robert Jervis, 1985b) have noted a curious tendency for those in conflict to form diabolical images of each other. These distorted images are so similar that they are called *mirror-image perceptions:* As we see them—as untrustworthy and evil intentioned—so they see us. Thus, during the early 1980s, the American government viewed the Communist support of guerrillas trying to overthrow the government of El Salvador as evidence of an "evil empire" at work. Meanwhile, the Soviets saw the American support of guerrillas trying to overthrow the government of Nicaragua as the work of "imperialist warmongers." Such mirror-image perceptions extend to the arms race: "Our nuclear weapons are defensive," each nation declares. "And unlike those who build aggressive weapons in hopes of dominating us and who propose arms control for propaganda purposes, we really desire peace. But we would be foolhardy to disarm while they are striving for military superiority."

Elsewhere in this book, and especially in the preceding chapter, we considered the psychological roots of such biased thinking. The *self-serving bias* leads us—political leaders included—to accept credit for our good deeds and to shuck the blame for, or to *self-justify,* our bad deeds. Although both nations admit to a buildup of military forces, the *fundamental attribution error* leads each to see the other's actions as arising from its aggressive disposition, whereas its own buildup is seen as a necessary response to a threatening situation. Information about one

"Why do you see the speck that is in your brother's eye, but do not notice the log that is in your own eye?"
Jesus,
The Gospel According to Luke 6:41–42

"If the experience of the past 25 years has proved anything, it has taught us to beware of the false promise that unilateral concessions on our side will produce matching concessions from the other."
Kenneth L. Adelman (1987)
Director, U.S. Arms Control and Disarmament Agency

another's actions is then filtered, interpreted, and remembered in accordance with preconceived *stereotypes*. Group interaction among like-minded policymakers may *polarize* these tendencies, leading to a *group-think* tendency to see one's own group as moral and one's opposition as less than fully human, with motives and behaviors that fully justify whatever one does to retaliate.

The end result of such perceptions is a vicious cycle of hostility. Recall that people treat more warmly someone they believe likes them and are treated more warmly by them in return. Liking begets liking. Similarly, hostility begets hostility. If John believes Mary is annoyed at him, he may snub her, causing her to act in ways that justify his perception. As it is with individuals, so it is with countries. Perceptions tend to be self-confirming by triggering the other country to react in ways that seem to justify the perceptions.

CONFLICT RESOLUTION

Come, my friends,
'Tis not too late to seek
a newer world.

Alfred, Lord Tennyson

Although conflicts are easily ignited and sustained by social traps and misperceptions, it is possible for acts of retaliation to be replaced by peaceful gestures. Such transformations are most likely in situations characterized by cooperation, communication, and conciliation.

Cooperation Does it help to put two conflicting parties into close contact so that they might get to know and like each other? It depends. When the contact is noncompetitive and between parties of equal status, such as store clerks, it may indeed help. Initially prejudiced co-workers of different races have, in such circumstances, learned to accept one another (Pettigrew, 1969). However, mere contact is sometimes not enough. In most desegregated junior high schools, whites and blacks resegregate themselves in the lunchrooms and on the school grounds (Schofield, 1982).

Mere contact was not enough to defuse the intense conflict that Muzafer Sherif (1966) instigated when he placed twenty-two Oklahoma City boys in two separate areas of a Boy Scout camp and then put the two groups through a series of competitive activities, with prizes going to the victors. Before long, each group became intensely proud of itself and hostile to the "sneaky," "smart-alecky" "stinkers" in the other group. Dining hall food wars broke out, cabins were ransacked, and fistfights had to be broken up by members of the camp staff. When the two groups were brought together, they avoided talking to one another, except to threaten and taunt.

Nevertheless, within a few days, Sherif managed to transform these young enemies into jovial comrades by giving them some ***super-ordinate goals***—shared goals that overrode their differences and required them to cooperate. A disruption of the camp water supply necessitated all twenty-two boys working together to restore water. Renting a movie required them to pool their resources. A stalled truck was restarted by all the boys pulling and pushing together to get it moving. Having used isolation and competition to make strangers into enemies, Sherif used shared predicaments and goals to reconcile the enemies and make them friends. Thus, Sherif showed that what reduces conflict is not contact itself but cooperative contact.

Where is this? Media coverage of Soviet life during the 1988 Reagan-Gorbachev summit in Moscow showed North Americans that Russians—as in this street scene in Leningrad—are not so different.

Cooperative efforts to achieve superordinate goals break down barriers between people.

During the 1970s, several teams of educational researchers simultaneously wondered: If successful, cooperative contacts between members of rival groups encourage more positive attitudes, could this principle be applied in desegregated schools? Could interracial friendships be promoted by replacing competitive classroom situations with cooperative ones? That it could has now been confirmed by many experiments (Johnson & Johnson, 1987). The members of interracial groups who work and play together on projects and athletic teams typically come to feel friendly toward those of the other race, as are those who engage in cooperative learning activities in the classroom. So encouraging are these results that more than 25,000 teachers have already introduced interracial cooperative learning into their classrooms (Kohn, 1987b).

The power of cooperative activity to make friends of former enemies has led psychologists to urge that international exchange and cooperation be increased (Klineberg, 1984). As we engage in mutually beneficial trade, as we work to protect our common destiny on this fragile planet Earth, and as we become more aware that our hopes and fears are shared, we can begin to change the misperceptions that fuel international conflict.

Communication   In the conflict game matrices we considered earlier, people were distrustful and pursued their individual interests as a defense against exploitation. When allowed to communicate—to discuss the dilemma they shared and to negotiate a commitment to cooperate—cooperation usually rose (Jorgenson & Papciak, 1981).

"You cannot shake hands with a clinched fist."
  Indira Gandhi, 1971

*"To begin with, I would like to express my sincere thanks
and deep appreciation for the opportunity to meet with you.
While there are still profound differences between us,
I think the very fact of my presence here today is a major breakthrough."*

When conflicts are intense, a third-party mediator—a marriage counselor, a labor mediator, a diplomat, a community volunteer—may facilitate communication (Pruitt & Rubin, 1987). Mediators help each party to voice its viewpoint and, in the process, to understand the other's. Such understanding is most needed, yet least likely, in times of crisis (Tetlock, 1988). When conflicts grow intense—as would happen during a nuclear crisis—our images of one another become more distorted and oversimplified, communication becomes more difficult, and judgments become more premature and rigid.

Conciliation   When tension and suspicion run high, cooperation and communication become impossible. Each party is likely to threaten, coerce, or retaliate—the very actions that will worsen the conflict. At the same time, both parties recognize that appeasement through unconditional cooperation is politically naïve and likely to invite exploitation.

Under such conditions, is there an alternative to war or surrender? Social psychologist Charles Osgood (1962, 1980) advocates a strategy of "Graduated and Reciprocated Initiatives in Tension-reduction," nicknamed *GRIT.* In applying GRIT, one side first announces its recognition of mutual interests and its intent to reduce tensions. It then initiates one or more small, conciliatory acts. Without weakening one's retaliatory capability, this modest beginning opens the door for reciprocation by the other party. Should the enemy respond with hostility, this would be reciprocated in kind. But so would any conciliatory response. In laboratory experiments, GRIT is the most effective strategy found thus far for increasing trust and cooperation (Lindskold & others, 1978 to 1988). Even in times of intense personal conflict, when communication is nonexistent, a conciliatory gesture—a smile, a touch, a word of apology—may be all that is needed to allow both people to begin edging down the tension ladder to a safer rung where communication and mutual understanding can begin.

The closest thing to an application of GRIT to international relations was the "Kennedy experiment." In 1963 President John F. Kennedy proclaimed "A Strategy for Peace." He announced that, as a gesture of conciliation, the United States was stopping all atmospheric nuclear tests (Etzioni, 1967). This offer initiated a series of reciprocated conciliatory acts that culminated in an atmospheric test-ban treaty that has endured to the present.

By the 1980s, the U.S. nuclear arsenal included thirty strategic submarines, each with missiles targeted at and capable of destroying 160 Soviet cities, to say nothing of the cruise missiles, intermediate-range missiles, ICBMs, aircraft, and weapons now on the drawing board. The Soviets have a huge stockpile of various weapons of their own that are similarly targeted at the United States. In their 1988 treaty reducing medium-range missiles, both nations, without sacrificing their retaliatory capabilities, agreed to give up a small part of their overkill capability. Might further gestures of mutual conciliation bring about a series of reciprocated conciliatory acts?

We must not oversimplify complex questions of diplomatic and military policy. Neither should we ignore their psychological components. Because of our hostile tendencies and prejudiced perceptions, our endangered species teeters at the edge of oblivion. We have equipped ourselves with the power to exterminate ourselves. After passing the baton of life from generation to generation across the ages of time, the most critical social-relations question lies before us: Will we act to preserve the world so that the baton of life can be handed on to our children and our children's children?

Mikhail Gorbachev, in a toast at the 1988 summit meeting in Moscow: "As we see it . . . habitual stereotypes stemming from enemy images have been shaken loose."

"It is . . . our intention to challenge the Soviet Union, not to an arms race, but to a peace race; to advance step by step, stage by stage, until general and completed disarmament has actually been achieved."

   John F. Kennedy (1962)

"But can they save themselves?"

Drawing by Dedini; © 1983 The New Yorker Magazine, Inc.

SUMMING UP

We have considered both undesirable and desirable social relations: aggression and altruism, prejudice and attraction, conflict and peacemaking.

AGGRESSION

The Biology of Aggression   Aggressive behavior, like all behavior, is a product of both nature and nurture. Although the idea that aggression is an instinctual drive is not looked upon favorably, there is ample evidence that aggressiveness is genetically influenced; that certain areas of the brain, when stimulated, activate or inhibit aggression; and that these areas are biochemically influenced.

The Psychology of Aggression   A variety of aversive events are known to heighten people's hostility. Such stimuli are especially likely to trigger aggression in those who have been rewarded for aggression in the past or who have observed role models acting aggressively. Violent television and violent pornographic films present numerous aggressive models. Viewers of such media are somewhat more likely, when provoked, to behave aggressively, and they tend to become desensitized to the cruelties depicted.

ALTRUISM

Bystander Intervention   In response to incidents of bystander nonintervention in emergency situations, social psychologists undertook experiments that revealed a bystander effect—any given bystander is less likely to help if others are present. The bystander effect is especially true in situations where the presence of others inhibits one's noticing the event, interpreting it as an emergency, or assuming responsibility for helping. Many factors, including mood, also influence willingness to help someone in distress.

Why Do We Help?   Both psychological and biological explanations have been offered for why we help others. Social exchange theory proposes that our social behaviors—even our helpful acts—are based on calculations, often unconscious, of how we can maximize our benefits (which may include our own good feelings) and minimize our costs. Our desire to help is also affected by social norms, which prescribe reciprocating the help we ourselves receive and being socially responsible toward those in need. Sociobiologists suggest that such psychological processes are based on an underlying genetic predisposition to preserve our own genes through devotion to those with whom we share genes.

PREJUDICE

Prejudice toward a group or its members is an unjustifiable attitude that usually is supported by stereotyped beliefs. Although overt prejudice against racial minorities and women has declined in the United States since the 1940s, subtle and sometimes not-so-subtle prejudice still exists. Such prejudice arises from an interplay of social, emotional, and cognitive factors.

Social Roots of Prejudice   Prejudice often arises as those who enjoy social and economic superiority attempt to justify the status quo. Even the temporary assignment of people to groups can cause an ingroup bias. Once established, the inertia of social influence can help maintain prejudice.

Emotional Roots of Prejudice   Prejudice may also serve the emotional functions of draining off the anger caused by frustration and of boosting self-esteem.

Cognitive Roots of Prejudice   Newer research reveals how our ways of processing information—for example, by overestimating similarities when we categorize people or by noticing and remembering vivid cases—work to create stereotypes.

ATTRACTION

Liking   Three factors are known to influence our liking for one another. Geographical proximity is conducive to attraction, partly because mere exposure to novel stimuli enhances liking. Physical attractiveness influences both social opportunities and the way one is perceived. As acquaintanceship moves toward friendship, similarity of attitudes and interests greatly increases liking.

Loving   Passionate love can be viewed as a temporary aroused state that we cognitively label as love. The strong affection of companionate love, which often emerges as a relationship matures, is enhanced by an equitable relationship and by intimate self-disclosure.

CONFLICT AND PEACEMAKING

Conflict   Conflicts often arise from malignant social processes that include social traps, in which each party, by protecting and pursuing its self-interest, creates a result that no one wants. The vicious spiral of conflict both feeds and is fed by distorted mirror-image perceptions, in which each party views itself as moral and the other as untrustworthy and full of evil intentions.

Conflict Resolution   Enemies sometimes become friends, especially when the circumstances favor cooperation toward superordinate goals, understanding through communication, and reciprocated conciliatory gestures.

TERMS AND CONCEPTS TO REMEMBER

altruism Unselfish regard for the welfare of others.

bystander effect The tendency for any given bystander to be less likely to give aid if other bystanders are present.

companionate love The deep affectionate attachment we feel for those with whom our lives are intertwined.

conflict A perceived incompatibility of actions, goals, or ideas.

equity A condition in which people receive from a relationship in proportion to what they contribute to it.

frustration-aggression theory The theory that frustration—the blocking of an attempt to achieve some goal—creates anger, which can generate aggression.

GRIT Graduated and Reciprocated Initiatives in Tension-reduction—a strategy designed to decrease international tensions.

ingroup bias The tendency to favor one's own group.

just-world phenomenon The tendency of people to believe the world is just and that people therefore get what they deserve and deserve what they get.

mere exposure effect The phenomenon that repeated exposure to novel stimuli increases liking of them.

mirror-image perceptions Distinct but similar views of one another often held by parties in conflict; each views itself as moral and peace-loving and the other as evil and aggressive.

passionate love An aroused state of intense positive absorption in another, usually present at the beginning of a relationship.

prejudice An unjustifiable attitude toward a group and its members. Prejudice generally involves stereotyped beliefs, negative feelings, and a predisposition to discriminatory action.

scapegoat theory The theory that prejudice provides frustrated people with an outlet for their anger by providing someone to blame.

self-disclosure Revealing intimate aspects of oneself to others.

social exchange theory The theory that our social behavior is an exchange process, the aim of which is to maximize benefits and minimize costs.

social traps Situations in which the conflicting parties, by each rationally pursuing their self-interest, become caught in mutually destructive behavior.

stereotype A generalized (often overgeneralized) belief about a group of people.

superordinate goals Shared goals that override differences among people and require their cooperation.

FOR FURTHER READING

Brehm, S. S. (1985). *Intimate relationships.* New York: Random House.

Draws on social, clinical, and developmental psychology to describe the life cycle of close relationships, from acquaintance to intimacy and sometimes to breakup. Discusses ways to improve intimate relationships.

Groebel, J., & Hinde, R. (Eds.). (1988). *Aggression and war: Their biological and social bases.* New York: Cambridge University Press.

Leading researchers on aggression from around the world summarize current knowledge about the biological, psychological, and cultural roots of aggression.

Pruitt, D. G., & Rubin, J. Z. (1986). *Social conflict: Escalation, stalemate, and settlement.* New York: Random House.

Social psychologists Pruitt and Rubin draw on examples from both research and everyday life to explain how conflicts arise, escalate, and are resolved.

Wagner, R. V., de Rivera, J., & Watkins, M. (Eds.). (1988). *Psychology and the promotion of peace.* Special Issue of *Journal of Social Issues, 44,* No. 2.

Psychologists offer research-based strategies for peacemaking and disarmament.

White, R. K. (1986). *Psychology and the prevention of nuclear war.* New York: New York University Press.

Leading conflict researchers explore the psychology of war and peace.

Wollman, N. (Ed.). (1985). *Working for peace: A handbook of practical psychology and other tools.* San Luis Obispo, CA: Impact.

Thirty-five short chapters offer practical suggestions for organizing peace groups, changing attitudes, and reducing conflict.

APPENDIX:

Statistical Reasoning in Everyday Life

Science fiction writer H. G. Wells once predicted that "statistical thinking will one day be as necessary for efficient citizenship as the ability to read and write." If by statistical thinking Wells meant not a technical knowledge of how to compute statistics but rather an understanding of the principles of statistical reasoning, then that day has arrived.

Virtually every college—including yours, I would wager—requires its psychology majors to study statistics. Statistics are tools that help us see and interpret what the unaided eye might miss. That is why, if you become a psychology major, you will be taught how to see data through the lens of statistics.

Chances are, however, that you will not major in psychology. Therefore, my aims in this appendix are these:

> To explain how to use the power of statistical reasoning in your own everyday thinking to organize and interpret the events you observe;
>
> To show you how to generalize from instances more realistically;
>
> To improve your critical thinking skills; and
>
> To become a more discerning consumer of research reported in the media.

First, I will introduce you to a few basic statistical concepts and formulas. If you are not mathematically inclined, stay with me, rereading where necessary. You will be amazed at how easy it is to grasp the basics.

DESCRIBING DATA

Researchers or not, we all make observations or obtain data that must be organized and interpreted.

> Laura is a college admissions officer. Attempting to predict which applicants will be most likely to succeed at her school, she sorts through their high school grades, aptitude scores, biographical statements, and letters of recommendation.
>
> Andrew is a governmental official. To determine the level of poverty in the various small towns in his region, he gathers data about the residents' incomes.
>
> Peter is the punter on his college football team. To keep track of his progress, he carefully records the distance of each of his punts.

Let's see how these three people might go about their tasks by considering some of the ways they can describe, organize, and interpret the raw information available to them.

DISTRIBUTIONS

To gain a sense of the past academic performance of her pool of applicants, Laura could thumb through their files and form some impressions. But there is too much information to remember. Moreover, she knows that impressions are influenced by the information that is most available to memory, which tends to be the vivid or extreme instances (see the "availability heuristic," pages 292–293). So instead of trusting her impressions, she begins by organizing the applicants' high school grade point averages (GPAs) into a *frequency distribution*, as shown in the table at the right. To do this, she breaks the entire range of scores into equal intervals and then counts the number of scores that fall in each interval. (The table, in fact, presents a frequency distribution of the actual high school GPAs of fifty randomly selected sophomores at my own college.)

To make the general picture easier to see, Laura displays this frequency distribution in a graph called a *histogram* (Figure A–1). Here the frequency of scores within a particular interval is represented as a bar. This histogram also helps Laura see about where any particular student's score falls relative to the others. Any student's ranking may be expressed more exactly as a *percentile rank*, which is simply the percentage of the total number of scores that fall below a particular score. So a student whose percentile rank is 99 has a GPA that exceeds those of 99 percent of all the students. (You can never have a percentile rank of 100; your score can never exceed those of 100 percent of the people because you are one of them.)

A note of caution: Take care when reading statistical graphs. Depending on what people want to emphasize, they can make the same difference seem small or big by how they design the graph. For example, Laura can make the difference in the average high school GPAs of male and female students seem small or large depending on the units she chooses for the vertical axis (Figure A–2).

The moral: When looking at statistical graphs in books and magazines and on TV ads and news broadcasts, always read the labels.

FREQUENCY DISTRIBUTION OF THE HIGH SCHOOL GPAS OF 50 COLLEGE STUDENTS

Interval	Number of persons in interval
3.51–4.00	23
3.01–3.50	6
2.51–3.00	16
2.01–2.50	5

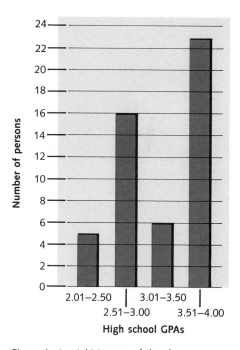

Figure A–1 A histogram of the above table's frequency distribution of the high school GPAs of fifty students.

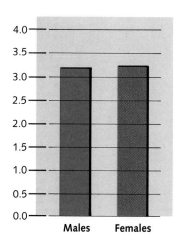

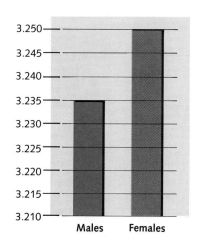

Figure A–2 Two histograms comparing the average high school GPAs of males and females in a sample of fifty students. Notice how a difference in the vertical dimension of the two graphs can make the gap seem either (a) small or (b) large.

FLORENCE NIGHTINGALE: PIONEER IN THE USE OF STATISTICS

Florence Nightingale (1820–1910)

Figure A–3   Florence Nightingale's histogram comparing peacetime death rates of British soldiers and civilian males illustrates her innovative approach to the presentation of statistics.

Florence Nightingale is remembered as a pioneering nurse and hospital reformer. Less well known is her equally pioneering use of statistics to persuade people. In advocating medical reform, Nightingale also promoted statistical description: She developed a uniform procedure for hospitals to report statistical information. She invented the pie chart, in which proportions are represented as wedges of a circular diagram. And she struggled to get the study of statistics introduced into higher education.

One of Nightingale's analyses compared the peacetime death rates of British soldiers and civilians. She discovered and showed that the soldiers, who lived in barracks under unhealthy conditions, were twice as likely to die as civilians of the same age and sex (Figure A–3). She then used the soldiers' 2 percent death rate to persuade the Queen and the Prime Minister to establish a Royal Commission on the Health of the Army. It is just as criminal, she wrote, for the Army to have a mortality of 20 per 1000 "as it would be to take 1,100 men per annum out upon Salisbury Plain and shoot them."

I. Bernard Cohen (1984) reports that "Nightingale's commitment to statistics transcended her interest in health care reform, and it was closely tied to her religious convictions. To her, laws governing social phenomena, 'the laws of our moral progress,' were God's laws, to be revealed by statistics."

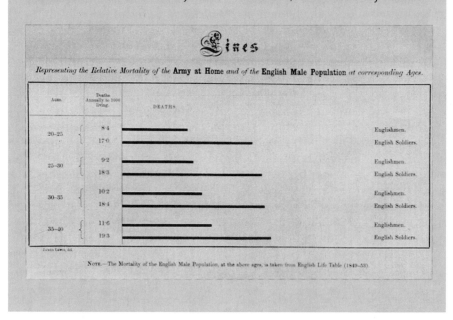

CENTRAL TENDENCIES

Now let's see how Andrew, the government official, might examine and describe the incomes earned by the residents in the small towns of his region. To simplify things, he might decide first to calculate the typical income level or *central tendency* for each town. There are three commonly used measures of the central tendency of a distribution of scores (in this case, incomes). The simplest of these is the **mode,** which is the most frequently occurring score. The most commonly reported measure is the arithmetic average, or *mean;* it is the total sum of all the scores divided by the number of scores. The *median* is the midmost score—the 50th percentile; if you arrange all the scores in order from the highest to the lowest, half will be above the median and half will be below it.

When the distribution of scores (or incomes) is not symmetrical, the three measures of central tendency tell very different stories. Suppose, for instance, that the mean annual family income in the first town Andrew studies is $19,000 whereas mean income in the second town is only $13,000. At first Andrew might assume there are more families living in poverty in the second town. But as Figure A–4 indicates, the first town, in which a few wealthy employers and quite a few poorly paid employees live, actually has many families struggling to live on less than $10,000.

"The poor are getting poorer, but with the rich getting richer it all averages out in the long run."

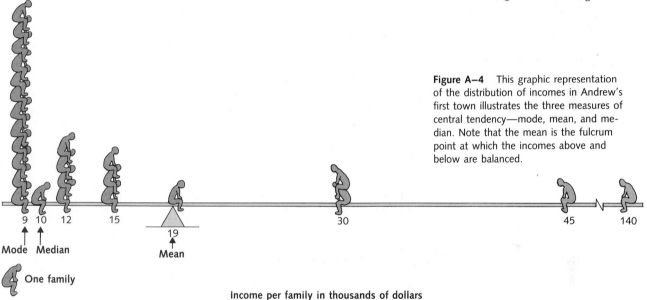

Mode   Median

Mean

One family

Income per family in thousands of dollars

Figure A–4 This graphic representation of the distribution of incomes in Andrew's first town illustrates the three measures of central tendency—mode, mean, and median. Note that the mean is the fulcrum point at which the incomes above and below are balanced.

The moral: Always take note of which measure of central tendency is being reported and consider—could a few atypical scores be distorting it?

In Brazil, the mean income in 1984 was $1720 and the median income was $808. What does this tell you about the distribution of income in Brazil?

VARIATION

It is useful to know how much variation there is in a distribution, that is, whether the scores tend to be similar or widely spread out. The *range* of scores—the gap between the lowest and highest score—provides only a crude estimate of variation because one extreme score in an otherwise uniform group will create a deceptively large range. If, in a small class, all the scores on an exam were between 70 and 80 except for one score of 20, the range of 60 (80 − 20 = 60) would mislead us about the actual amount of variation.

The more standard measure of how much scores deviate from one another is the *standard deviation,* which makes the term easy to remember. Although this measure, like the range, is influenced by extreme scores, it is a better gauge of whether scores are packed together or dispersed because it uses information from each score. The standard deviation is important and surprisingly simple to compute: (1) calculate the difference, or deviation, between each score and the mean; (2) square these deviations; (3) find their average; and (4) find the square root of this average.

As an example, let's take our punter, Peter. He does not trust his gut-level impression of how consistent his punting is. After his first football game, Peter therefore calculates the standard deviation for his four punts:

Punting distance	Deviation from mean (40 yards)	Deviation squared
36	−4	16
38	−2	4
41	+1	1
45	+5	25
Mean = 160/4 = 40		Sum of (deviations)² = 46

Thus,

$$\text{Standard deviation} = \sqrt{\frac{\text{Sum of (deviations)}^2}{\text{Number of scores}}} = \sqrt{46/4} = 3.4 \text{ yards}$$

To grasp the meaning of this statistic, Peter would need to understand how scores tend to be distributed. In nature, large amounts of data—heights, weights, IQ scores, grades, punt distances (though not incomes)—often form a roughly symmetrical, bell-shaped distribution, with most cases falling near the mean and fewer cases falling near either extreme. This bell-shaped distribution is so typical that the curve it forms is called the *normal curve.* As Figure A–5 indicates, a useful property of the normal curve is that roughly 68 percent of the cases fall within 1 standard deviation on either side of the mean—in Peter's case within 3.4 yards of his 40-yard average. Ninety-five percent of cases fall within 2 standard deviations. Thus, as we note in Chapter 12, Intelligence, about 68 percent of people taking an intelligence test will score within ±15 points (1 standard deviation) of 100 and about 95 percent will score within ±30 points (2 standard deviations).

CORRELATION

In this book we often ask about the degree to which two things are related—how closely the personality scores of twins are related to one another, how well IQ scores predict school grades, how closely stress is linked with certain diseases. To get a feel for whether one set of scores is related to a second set, let's once again begin graphically, with a *scatterplot.* For example, Figure A–6a depicts the actual relationship between SAT scores and college freshman GPAs for the fifty college students we met earlier. Each point on the graph represents these two numbers for one student. Figure A–6b is a scatterplot of the relationship between these students' high school and college freshman GPAs.

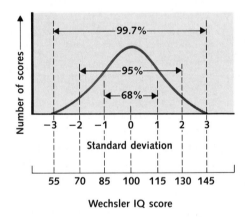

Figure A–5 The normal curve. Data are often distributed in a normal or bell-shaped curve in which 68 percent of the cases fall within 1 standard deviation of the mean and 95 percent fall within 2 standard deviations. For example, on an IQ test such as the WAIS, the mean is assigned a value of 100 and the standard deviation is 15 points; therefore 68 percent of the scores fall between 85 and 115, and 95 percent fall between 70 and 130.

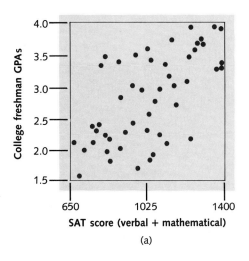

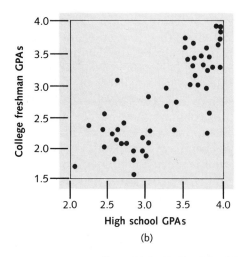

The ***correlation coefficient*** is a statistical measure of how strongly related any two sets of scores are. It can range from

+1.00, which means that one set of scores increases in direct proportion to the other

through 0.00, meaning that the scores are not related at all

to −1.00, which indicates that one set of scores goes up precisely as the other goes down.

Figure A–6   Scatterplots of (a) the relationship between total SAT scores (verbal and mathematical) and college freshman GPAs and (b) the closer relationship between high school and freshman GPAs of fifty college students. Each point represents the data for one student.

Perfect positive correlation

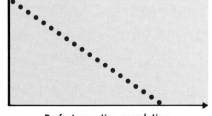

Perfect negative correlation

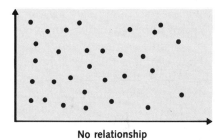

No relationship

(Note that a correlation being negative has nothing to do with its strength or weakness; a negative correlation means two things are inversely related. A weak correlation, indicating little or no relationship, is one that has a coefficient near zero.) Now look again at the scatterplots in Figure A–6. Do the correlations look as if they were positive or negative?

In each scatterplot in Figure A–6, the upward slope of the cluster of points as one moves to the right indicates that the two sets of scores tend to rise together. This means the correlations are positive: +.64 for the SAT–college freshman GPA relationship shown in A–6a, and a stronger +.80 for the high school GPA–college freshman GPA relationship shown in A–6b. As SAT scores and, especially, high school grades go up, so do college grades. (The GPA–GPA relationship, incidentally, illustrates the common finding that the best predictor of people's future behavior is usually their behavior in similar situations in the past. Still, people can and do change.)

I said at the beginning that statistics can help us see what the naked eye sometimes misses. To demonstrate this for yourself, try to determine what, if any, relationship exists between two sets of scores that have not been organized into a scatterplot. For example, Elaine wonders whether men's heights are related to their temperaments. She

Some examples of positive correlations:
  Child abuse and children's aggressiveness
  Education and income
  Achievement motivation and grades
Some examples of negative correlations:
  Self-esteem and depression
  Age and deep sleep
  Stress and health

measures the height of twenty men, has someone else independently assess their temperament (from 0 for extremely calm and placid to 100 for highly reactive), and obtains the data in the table at right.

With all the relevant data right in front of you, can you tell whether there is (1) a positive correlation between height and reactive temperament, (2) very little or no correlation, or (3) a negative correlation?

Comparing the columns in the table, you can probably detect very little relationship between height and temperament. In fact, the correlation in this imaginary example is moderately positive, +.57, as you could see if you made a scatterplot of the data. If we fail to see a relationship when the data are presented as systematically as in this table, how much less likely are we to notice them in everyday life? To see what is right in front of us, we sometimes need statistical illumination. People can easily see evidence of sex discrimination when given statistically summarized information about job level, seniority, performance, sex, and salary, but will often see no sex discrimination when the same information dribbles in, case by case (Twiss & others, in press).

The moral: The correlation coefficient tells us nothing about cause and effect, but it can help us see the world more clearly by revealing the actual extent to which two things are related.

Illusory Correlations   We sometimes also "see" relationships that do not exist. A correlation that is perceived but does not really exist is called an ***illusory correlation.*** When we believe there is a relationship between two things, we are likely to notice and recall instances that confirm rather than deny our belief (Trolier & Hamilton, 1986). In one experiment, a group of people were shown the results of a hypothetical 50-day cloud-seeding experiment (Ward & Jenkins, 1965). For each of the 50 days, the subjects were told whether or not the clouds had been seeded and whether or not it had rained. The "results" given were actually random; they showed no relationship between cloud seeding and rainfall. Nevertheless, the subjects typically were convinced—in keeping with what they expected—that they really had observed a positive relationship between cloud seeding and rainfall.

Because we are especially sensitive to dramatic or unusual events, the occurrence of two such events in sequence—say, a premonition of an unlikely phone call followed by the call—is likely to be noticed and remembered. When the call does not follow the premonition, we are less likely to take note of that fact and remember it.

The moral: When we notice and remember vivid, random events, we may forget that they are random and see them as correlated. Thus we can easily be deceived into missing what is there or seeing what is not there.

Regression Toward the Average   Illusory correlations can feed another illusion—that chance events are subject to our personal control. Gamblers, remembering their lucky rolls, may come to believe that they can influence the roll of the dice by again doing what they did then—breathing on the dice or throwing softly for low numbers and hard for high numbers. The illusion that uncontrollable events are correlated with our actions is also fed by a statistical phenomenon called ***regression toward the average.*** Average results are more typical than extreme results. Thus after an unusual event, things tend to return toward their average level; that is, extraordinary happenings tend to be followed by more ordinary happenings. Basketball players who make or miss all their shots in the first half of the game are likely to "regress" (fall back) to their more usual performance level during the second half. Students

HEIGHT AND TEMPERAMENT OF 20 MEN		
Subject	**Height in inches**	**Temperament**
1	80	75
2	63	66
3	61	60
4	79	90
5	74	60
6	69	42
7	62	42
8	75	60
9	77	81
10	60	39
11	64	48
12	76	69
13	71	72
14	66	57
15	73	63
16	70	75
17	63	30
18	71	30
19	68	84
20	70	39

who score much lower or higher on an exam than they usually do are likely, when retested, to regress toward their average. Unusual ESP subjects who defy chance when they are first tested seem to lose their "psychic powers" when retested (a phenomenon that parapsychologists have called the "decline effect").

The point may seem obvious, yet we regularly miss it and instead attribute what may be a normal statistical regression to something we have done. If, after doing miserably on the first test, we stop reading the chapter summaries before reading the chapters and then do better on the second test, we may attribute our improvement to the new study technique. If, after a sudden crime wave, the town council initiates a "stop crime" drive and the crime rate then returns to previous levels, the drive may appear to have had more impact than it actually did. Coaches who yell at their players after an unusually bad first half may feel rewarded for having done so when the team's performance improves during the second half.

On the other hand, scientists who win a Nobel prize often have diminished accomplishments thereafter, leading some to wonder whether winning a Nobel hinders creativity. Some people also believe there is a *"Sports Illustrated* jinx"—that athletes whose peak performances get them on the cover of the magazine will then suffer a decline in their performance. In each of these cases, it is possible that the effect is genuine. It is more likely, however, that these represent the natural tendency for behavior to regress from the unusual to the more usual.

Failure to recognize regression is the source of many superstitions and some ineffective practices as well. When day-to-day behavior has a substantial element of chance fluctuation, we may observe that others' behavior improves (regresses toward average) after we criticize them for very bad performance and worsens (regresses toward average) after we warmly praise them for an exceptionally fine performance. Ironically, then, regression toward the average can lead us to feel rewarded for having criticized others and punished for having praised them (Tversky & Kahneman, 1974).

The moral: When a fluctuating behavior returns to normal, there is no need to invent fancy explanations for why it does: Regression toward the average is probably at work.

> "Once you become sensitized to it, you see regression everywhere."
> Daniel Kahneman (1985)

GENERALIZING FROM INSTANCES

So far we have seen how statistical reasoning can help us to digest and describe information more accurately. Statistical reasoning can also help us in a second important way: to make correct leaps of understanding from our sample of information to what is generally true.

POPULATIONS AND SAMPLES

A *population* is the whole group we are interested in. For convenience, we often limit our observations to a small sample drawn from a population and then generalize about the population itself. We meet a few students and attend a few classes during a visit to a college and infer from those instances how friendly the campus is and how good the teaching is. We observe the weather during a week-long visit to Seattle and then tell our friends about the climate there. But we have to be careful when drawing conclusions from specific people or events. Let's take a look at some principles that can guide us when generalizing from instances.

Principle 1: Representative Samples Are Better Than Biased Samples It is often tempting to overgeneralize from highly select samples. For example, we can delude ourselves about the actual difference between two groups when we compare members of those groups drawn only from their extremes. In the 1988 Olympics, the competitors in the finals of the men's 100-meter dash were predominantly black. But how much does this tell us about the sprinting abilities of the different races? As you can see from the hypothetical illustration in Figure A–7, even if the Olympic finalists are all members of Race Y, knowing that any individual is a member of Race X or Race Y tells you virtually nothing about the person's sprinting abilities. The same is true when the superstars in some nonathletic pursuit come mostly from a given race, culture, or gender. Though it seems obvious, this principle is often missed in everyday life (Nisbett & Ross, 1980).

We are particularly prone to overgeneralize when the extremes are vivid cases. Given a statistical summary of the evaluations of all of Professor Zeno's students and the more vivid, specific comments of two irate students, the administrator's impression of the professor may be as much influenced by the two unhappy students as by the generally favorable evaluations of the many. Driving into Chicago from the south, many people see the miles of tenement houses near the highway and think, "What an ugly city this is." Standing in the checkout line at the supermarket, George sees the woman in front of him pay with food stamps and then drive away in a Cadillac. "What an easy life these welfare bums have!" he later tells his friends. In each of these situations, the temptation to generalize from a few unrepresentative but vivid cases is nearly irresistible.

The moral: The best basis for generalizing is not from the exceptional cases one finds at the extremes—however vivid—but from a representative sample of cases.

Principle 2: Random Sequences May Not Look Random As we noted in Chapter 1, gathering a *random* sample—one in which each person in the population has an equal chance of being selected—is a formal technique for making the sample representative. As chance would have it, though, random sequences often do not look random. If someone were to flip a coin six times, would one of the following sequences of heads (H) and tails (T) be more likely than the other two: HHHTTT or HTTHTH or HHHHHH?

Daniel Kahneman and Amos Tversky (1972) reported that most people believe that HTTHTH would be the most likely random sequence. Actually, all possible sequences are equally likely to occur (or, you might say, equally unlikely). A bridge or poker hand in which all the cards were of one suit would seem extraordinary; actually, it would be no more or no less likely to occur than would any other specific hand of cards.

The failure to recognize random, coincidental occurrences for what they are can predispose people to seek extraordinary explanations for ordinary events. Imagine that on one warm spring day, 4000 college students gather for a coin-tossing contest. Their task is to flip heads. On the first toss, 2000 students do so and advance to the second round. As you might expect, about 1000 of these progress to a third round, 500 to a fourth, 250 to a fifth, 125 to a sixth, 62 to a seventh, 31 to an eighth, 15 to a ninth, and 8 amazing individuals, having flipped heads nine times in a row with ever-increasing displays of concentration and effort, advance to the tenth round.

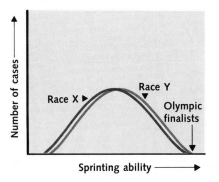

Figure A–7 Hypothetical normal curves for sprinting ability for two races. As you can see, sampling from the extremes is not the best basis for inferring general racial differences.

Your chances of being dealt either of these exact hands is precisely the same: 1 in 2,598,960.

WHEN YOU'RE HOT YOU'RE HOT, RIGHT? RANDOM SEQUENCES THAT DON'T LOOK RANDOM

Hospital workers sometimes notice streaks of male births or female births. Not realizing that random sequences usually contain such streaks, they may attribute them to mysterious forces, such as phases of the moon.

Every basketball player and fan "knows" that players have hot and cold streaks. Players who have "hot hands" can't seem to miss while those who have "cold" ones can't find the center of the hoop. When Thomas Gilovich, Robert Vallone, and Amos Tversky (1985) interviewed team members of the Philadelphia 76ers, the players estimated they were about 25 percent more likely to make a shot after they had just made one than after a miss. Nine in ten basketball fans surveyed concurred that a player "has a better chance of making a shot after having just *made* his last two or three shots than he does after having just *missed* his last two or three shots." Believing in shooting streaks, players will feed a teammate who has just made two or three shots in a row, and many coaches bench the player who has just missed three in a row. When you're hot you're hot (Figure A–8).

The only trouble is, it isn't true. When Gilovich and his collaborators studied detailed individual shooting records, they found that the 76ers—and the Boston Celtics, the New Jersey Nets, the New York Knicks, and Cornell University's men's and women's basketball players—were equally likely to score after a miss as after a basket. Fifty percent shooters average 50 percent after just missing three shots, and 50 percent after just making three shots.

Why, then, do players and fans alike believe that players are more likely to score after scoring and miss after missing? In any series of twenty shots by a 50 percent shooter (or twenty flips of a coin), there is a 50-50 chance of four baskets (or heads) in a row, and it is quite possible that 1 person out of 5 will have a streak of five or six. Players and fans notice these random streaks and so form the myth that "when you're hot you're hot."

The same type of thing happens with investors who believe that a fund is more likely to perform well after a string of good years than after a string of bad years. But, as economist Burton Malkiel (1985) documents in *A Random Walk Down Wall Street*, past performances of mutual funds do not predict their future performance. When funds have streaks of several good or bad years, we may nevertheless be fooled into thinking that past success predicts future success.

The moral: Whether watching basketball, choosing stocks, or flipping coins, remember the statistical principle that random sequences often don't look random. Even when the next outcome cannot be predicted from the preceding ones, streaks are to be expected.

Figure A–8   Who is the chance shooter? Here are twenty-one consecutive shots, each scoring either a basket or a miss, by two players who each shoot 50 percent. Within this sample of shots, which player's sequence looks more like what we would expect in a random sequence? (See page 620.) (Adapted from Barry Ross, *Discover*, 1987.)

By now, the crowd of losers is in awestruck silence as these expert coin tossers prepare to display their amazing ability yet again. The finalists are the center of celebration and adulation. The proceedings are temporarily halted so that a panel of impartial scientists can be called in to observe and document the incredible achievement of these gifted individuals. Alas, on the next tosses they each freeze up and flip tails. (They regress to normal.) "But, of course," their admirers say, "coin tossing is a highly sensitive skill. The tense, pressured atmosphere created by the scientific scrutiny has disturbed their fragile gift."

The moral: By chance, exceptional events must occasionally be expected. Because it is natural for some events to lie far from the hump of the normal curve, such ordinary events needn't have extraordinary explanations.

Principle 3: More Cases Are Better Than Fewer   I have seen it happen often: An eager high school senior visits two college campuses, each for a day. At the first, the student randomly visits three classes and discovers each instructor to be witty and engaging. At the next campus, the three instructors sampled seem dull and uninspiring. Returning home, the student tells friends what "great teachers" there are at the first school, and what "bores" the faculty are at the second school. Again, we know it but we ignore it: Small samples provide less reliable estimates of the average than do large samples. For example, the proportion of heads in samples of 10 coin tosses varies more than in samples of 100 tosses.

We can actually estimate the reliability of an observed average, given the number and variability of the scores on which the average is based. Without describing this computational procedure, we can state the principle that it illustrates: *averages based on more cases are more reliable* (less variable) than averages based on only a few cases. Knowing this, maybe you will come up with different answers to a question posed by Christopher Jepson, David Krantz, and Richard Nisbett (1983) to University of Michigan introductory psychology students:

> The registrar's office at the University of Michigan has found that there are usually about 100 students in Arts and Sciences who have a 4.00 GPA at the end of their first term at the University. However, only about 10–15 students graduate with a 4.00 GPA. What do you think is the most likely explanation for the fact that there are more 4.00 GPAs after one term than at graduation?

Most of the students come up with plausible causes for the drop in GPA, such as, "Students tend to work harder at the beginning of their college careers than toward the end." Fewer than a third of the students recognized the statistical phenomenon clearly at work: Averages based on fewer courses are more variable, which guarantees a greater number of extremely low and high GPAs at the end of the first term.

The moral: Don't be overly impressed by a few anecdotes. Generalizations based on only a few cases are unreliable.

Principle 4: Less Variable Observations Are Better Than Highly Variable Observations   Averages derived from scores with low variability (such as Peter's punts, which varied by only 9 yards) tend to be more reliable than averages based on scores with high variability. If Peter's four punts in the first game had ranged from 20 to 60 yards, we should be less confident that his 40-yard average would be close to the average of his punts in the next game.

Intuitively, you know this to be the case. You might therefore respond much as did the students in another experiment by Nisbett and

Answer to Figure A–8: Player B, whose outcomes may *look* more random, actually has *fewer* streaks than would be expected by chance. For these players, chance shooting, like chance coin tossing, should produce a change in outcome about 50 percent of the time. But 70 percent of the time (14 times out of 20) Player B's outcome changes on successive shots. Player A, on the other hand, is scoring randomly; 10 times out of 20, Player A's next outcome is different.

his colleagues (1983): Imagine that you are an explorer who has landed on a little known island in the southeastern Pacific. You encounter three natives, each of whom is obese and brown-skinned. What percentage of all the natives on the island would you expect to be obese and what percentage would you expect to be brown-skinned? Knowing that body weight tends to be more variable than skin color within a geographical group, the students in the experiment were much more likely to infer that all the people of the island were brown than that all of them were obese.

Well and good. The problem comes when we falsely assume groups to be relatively homogeneous, which is typically the case with unfamiliar "outgroups." As demonstrated in numerous experiments, we tend to perceive groups we don't know as being more homogeneous than groups we know well.

With this in mind, put yourself in the place of the Princeton students to whom George Quattrone and Edward Jones (1980) showed a videotape of a subject who chose to wait either alone or with others for an experiment to begin. Some of the Princeton students were told the subject attended Princeton and the rest that the subject attended Rutgers. When they were asked to guess what percentage of the other subjects in the experiment chose to wait alone or with others, they were much more willing to generalize from the single case when the supposed subject came from the other school. For example, if the videotaped subject chose to wait with others and was said to be from Rutgers, the Princeton viewers formed an impression of Rutgers students as a sociable group and guessed that most of the Rutgers subjects chose to wait with others. (Rutgers students were similarly more likely to overgeneralize from the behavior of a supposed Princeton student than from the behavior of a supposed Rutgers student.)

The moral: Less variable observations do indeed provide a better basis for generalizing than highly variable observations; nevertheless, we often misperceive people in other groups as being more uniform than they are.

TESTING DIFFERENCES

We have seen that we can have more confidence in the generalizations we make from samples that are (1) representative of the population we wish to study, (2) larger rather than smaller, and (3) less rather than more variable. These principles extend to the inferences we make about differences between groups. So, when can we justifiably generalize from a difference we have observed—say, from the difference between the male and female grade point averages in Figure A–2 to the whole campus population of males and females?

Statistical tests help us decide by indicating the reliability of such differences. You needn't understand how they are computed to understand the logic behind them, which is basically as follows: When *averages* from two samples are each judged to be *reliable* measures of their respective populations (as when each is based on a large number of observations that have a small standard deviation), then the difference observed between the samples is likely to be reliable. When the *difference* between the averages for the two samples is *large*, we have even more confidence that the difference between them reflects a real difference in their populations. In short, to the extent that the sample averages are reliable and the difference between them is large, we can say (as psychologists often do) that the difference has ***statistical significance.*** This simply means that the difference very likely reflects a real difference and is not due to chance variation between the samples.

When reading about research, you should remember that, given large enough or homogeneous enough samples, a difference between them may be "significant" yet unimportant. For example, when comparing the IQs among several hundred thousand firstborn and later-born individuals, there is a highly significant tendency for firstborn individuals within a family to have higher average scores than their later-born siblings, but only by a single IQ point or two (Zajonc & Markus, 1975).

The moral: "Statistical significance" does not equal importance; rather, it means the results are probably not due to chance.

Using the basic statistical tools discussed in this appendix can help you to think critically—to see more clearly what you might otherwise miss or misinterpret and to generalize more accurately from your observations. When you understand and use the principles of statistics, you think more rationally (Nisbett & others, 1987). It requires training and practice, but developing the ability to think clearly and critically is part of becoming an educated person. The report of the Project on Redefining the Meaning and Purpose of Baccalaureate Degrees (1985) eloquently asserts why there are few higher priorities in a college education:

> If anything is paid attention to in our colleges and universities, thinking must be it. Unfortunately, thinking can be lazy. It can be sloppy. It can be reactive rather than active. It can be inert. It can be fooled, misled, bullied. . . . Students possess great untrained and untapped capacities for logical thinking, critical analysis, and inquiry, but these are capacities that are not spontaneous: they grow out of wide instruction, experience, encouragement, correction, and constant use.

SUMMING UP

To be an educated person today is to be able to apply simple statistical principles to everyday reasoning. One needn't remember complicated formulas to think more clearly and critically about data.

From our consideration of how we can organize and describe data—by constructing distributions and computing measures of central tendency, variation, and correlation—we derived five practical morals for intelligent statistical reasoning:

1. When looking at statistical graphs in books and magazines and on TV ads and news broadcasts, always read the labels.

2. Note which measure of central tendency is actually being reported, and consider—could a few atypical scores be distorting it?

3. The correlation coefficient tells us nothing about cause and effect, but it *can* help us see the world more clearly by revealing the actual extent to which two things are related.

4. When we notice and remember vivid, random events, we may see them as correlated. Thus we can easily be deceived into missing what is there or seeing what is not there.

5. When a fluctuating behavior returns to normal, there is no need to invent fancy explanations for why it does. Regression toward the average is likely at work.

From our consideration of how we can appropriately leap from samples of data to conclusions about what is generally true we derived six more practical morals:

6. The best basis for generalizing is not from the exceptional, though vivid, cases one finds at the extremes but from a representative sample of cases.

7. Whether watching basketball, choosing stocks, or flipping coins, remember the statistical principle that random sequences often don't look random. Even when the next outcome cannot be predicted from the preceding ones, streaks are to be expected.

8. By chance, exceptional events must occasionally be expected. Because it is natural for some events to lie far from the hump of the normal curve, such ordinary events needn't have extraordinary explanations.

9. Don't be overly impressed by a few anecdotes. Generalizations based on only a few cases are unreliable.

10. Less variable observations provide a better basis for generalizing than highly variable observations; nevertheless, we often misperceive people in other groups as being more uniform than they actually are.

11. "Statistical significance" does not equal importance; rather, it means the results are not likely to be due to chance.

TERMS AND CONCEPTS TO REMEMBER

correlation coefficient A measure of the direction and extent of the relationship between two sets of scores. Scores with a *positive correlation coefficient* go up and down together (as with high school and college GPAs). A *negative correlation coefficient* indicates that one score falls as the other rises (as in the relationship between self-esteem and depression).

frequency distribution A listing of the number of individual scores that occur within each equal-sized interval into which the entire range of scores has been divided.

histogram A bar graph that depicts a frequency distribution.

illusory correlation The perception of a relationship where none exists.

mean The arithmetic average of a distribution, which is obtained by adding the scores and dividing by their number.

median The middle score in a distribution; half the scores are above it and half are below it.

mode The most frequently occurring score in a distribution.

normal curve (or normal distribution) A symmetrical, bell-shaped curve that describes the distribution of many types of data; most scores fall near the mean (68 percent fall within 1 standard deviation of it) and fewer and fewer near the extremes.

percentile rank The percentage of the scores in a distribution that a given score exceeds.

population All the cases in a group, from which samples may be drawn for study.

range The difference between the highest and lowest scores in a distribution.

regression toward the average The tendency for extreme or unusual scores to fall back (regress) toward the average.

scatterplot A graphed cluster of dots, each of which represents the values of two variables (such as a student's high school and college GPAs). The slope of the points suggests the degree and direction of the relationship between the two variables. (Also called a *scattergram* or *scatter diagram*.)

standard deviation A measure of variability of the scores in a distribution; computed by squaring the deviation of each score from the mean and finding the square root of their average.

statistical significance A statistical statement of how small the likelihood is that an obtained result occurred by chance.

FOR FURTHER READING

Huff, D. (1954). *How to lie with statistics.* New York: Norton.

A delightful, easy-to-read little book on the uses and abuses of statistics. It suggests how to recognize and see through the deceptive ways people use statistics.

Nisbett, R., & Ross, L. (1980). *Human inference: Strategies and shortcomings in social judgments.* Englewood Cliffs, NJ: Prentice-Hall.

This provocative and playful book, written by two prominent social psychologists, reveals the common errors of thinking we can fall into when we fail to use the principles of statistical reasoning. Recommended reading for anyone who wishes to think more clearly and critically.

Shaughnessy, J. J., & Zechmeister, E. B. (1985; 2nd ed., 1990). *Research methods in psychology.* New York: Knopf.

An excellent, gentle introduction to basic statistical methods and procedures used by psychologists; shows how our everyday use of them can sharpen our reasoning.

Glossary

absolute threshold The minimum stimulation that a subject can detect 50 percent of the time. (p. 140)

accommodation 1. Adapting one's current understandings (schemas) to incorporate new information. (p. 65) 2. The process by which the lens of the eye changes shape to focus the image of near or distant objects on the retina. (p. 146)

acetylcholine [ah-seat-el-KO-leen] **(ACh)** A neurotransmitter that, among its functions, triggers muscle contraction. (p. 30)

achievement motivation A desire for significant accomplishment: for mastery of things, people, or ideas; for attaining a high standard. (p. 371)

achievement tests Tests designed to assess what a person already has learned. (p. 320)

acoustic encoding The encoding of sound, especially the sound of words. (pp. 257–259)

acquisition The initial stage of learning, during which a response is established and gradually strengthened. In classical conditioning, the phase in which a stimulus comes to evoke a conditioned response. In operant conditioning, the strengthening of a reinforced response. (p. 233)

active listening Empathic listening in which the listener echoes, restates, and clarifies. A feature of Rogers' person-centered therapy. (p. 479)

acuity The sharpness of vision. (p. 147)

adaptation-level phenomenon The tendency for our judgments (of sounds, of lights, of income, and so forth) to be relative to a "neutral" level that is based on our prior experience. (p. 395)

addiction A physical dependence on or need for a drug, with accompanying withdrawal symptoms if the drug is discontinued. (p. 215)

adolescence The period from puberty to independent adulthood; in industrialized nations, roughly the teen years. (pp. 89–97)

adrenal [ah-DREEN-el] glands A pair of endocrine glands just above the kidneys. The adrenals secrete the hormones epinephrine (adrenaline) and norepinephrine (noradrenaline), which help to arouse the body in times of stress. (p. 31)

aerial perspective A monocular cue for perceiving distance; distant objects appear hazier, less distinct than nearby objects. (p. 175)

aerobic exercise Sustained exercise that increases heart and lung fitness; may also alleviate depression and anxiety. (p. 520)

age regression In hypnosis, the supposed reliving of earlier experiences, such as in early childhood; greatly susceptible to false recollections. (p. 208)

aggression Physical or verbal behavior intended to hurt someone. (p. 130)

algorithm A methodical, logical rule or procedure for solving a particular problem. May be contrasted with the usually speedier, but also more error-prone use of *heuristics*. (p. 286)

all-or-none response The principle that at any moment, like a gun, a neuron either fires or does not. (pp. 28–30)

alpha waves The relatively slow brain waves of a relaxed, awake state. (p. 198)

altruism Unselfish regard for the welfare of others. (p. 584)

Alzheimer's disease A progressive and irreversible brain disorder characterized by gradual deterioration of memory, reasoning, language, and finally, of physical function. (p. 101)

amnesia Loss of memory. Psychogenic amnesia, a dissociative disorder, is selective memory loss often brought on by extreme stress. (p. 454)

amphetamines Drugs that stimulate neural activity, causing speeded-up body functions and associated energy and mood changes. (p. 217)

amplitude The maximum height (or depth) of a wave, measured from its midpoint. (p. 154)

amygdala [ah-MIG-dah-la] Two almond-shaped neural centers in the limbic system that are linked to emotion. (p. 37)

anal stage The second of Freud's psychosexual stages, during which pleasure is focused on bowel and bladder elimination and retention. (p. 412)

androgyny (*andros*, man + *gynē*, woman) Possession of desirable psychological traits traditionally associated with both men and women. (p. 127)

anorexia nervosa A disorder in which a normal-weight person (usually an adolescent female) diets to become significantly (15 percent or more) underweight yet, still feeling fat, continues to starve. (p. 357)

antisocial personality A personality disorder in which the person (usually a male) exhibits a lack of conscience for wrongdoing, even toward friends and family members. May be aggressive and ruthless or a clever con artist. (p. 469)

anxiety disorders Psychological disorders characterized by distressing, persistent anxiety or maladaptive behaviors that reduce anxiety. See *generalized anxiety disorder, phobic disorder,* and *obsessive-compulsive disorder.* (p. 449)

aphasia Impairment of language, usually caused by left hemisphere damage either to Broca's area (impairing speaking) or to Wernicke's area (impairing understanding). (p. 42)

aptitude tests Tests designed to predict a person's future performance; aptitude is the capacity to learn. (p. 320)

artificial intelligence (AI) The science of designing and programming computers to do things that appear intelligent; includes both practical applications (chess playing, industrial robots, expert systems) and theoretically inspired efforts to model thinking. (p. 299)

assimilation Interpreting one's new experience in terms of one's existing schemas. (p. 65)

association areas Areas of the cerebral cortex that are involved not in primary motor or sensory functions, but rather in higher mental functions such as learning, remembering, thinking, and speaking. (p. 41)

attachment An emotional tie with another person; evidenced in young children by their seeking closeness to the caregiver and showing distress on separation. (p. 71)

attitude A belief and feeling that may predispose one to respond in a particular way to objects, people, and events. (p. 557)

attribution A causal explanation for someone's behavior, such as an explanation in terms of the situation or the person's disposition. (p. 548)

audition The sense of hearing. (p. 153)

automatic processing Effortless encoding of incidental information, such as space, time, and frequency, and of well-learned information, such as word meanings; not under conscious control. (p. 259)

autonomic [aw-tuh-NAHM-ik] **nervous system** The part of the peripheral nervous system that controls the glands and the muscles of the internal organs (such as the heart). Its sympathetic division arouses; its parasympathetic division calms. (p. 26)

availability heuristic A rule of thumb for estimating the likelihood of events in terms of their availability in memory; if instances come readily to mind (perhaps because of their vividness), we presume the thing to be more likely. (p. 292)

aversive conditioning A type of counterconditioning that associates an unpleasant state (such as nausea) with an unwanted behavior (such as drinking alcohol). (p. 483)

avoidance learning Learning to prevent an aversive stimulus from occurring. (p. 243)

axon The extension of a neuron ending in branching terminal fibers through which messages are sent to other neurons or to muscles or glands. (p. 28)

babbling stage The stage in speech development, beginning at about 3 or 4 months, in which the infant spontane-

ously utters various sounds (which at first are unrelated to the parents' language). (p. 303)

bad-patient role Uncooperative, complaining, demanding patient behavior. (p. 528)

barbiturates Drugs that depress the activity of the central nervous system, reducing anxiety—and impairing memory and judgment. (p. 216)

Barnum effect The tendency to accept as valid those favorable descriptions of one's personality that are generally true of everyone, such as those found in astrology books and horoscopes. (p. 436)

basic trust According to Erik Erikson, a sense that the world is predictable and trustworthy; said to be formed during infancy by experiences with responsive caregivers. (p. 74)

behavior modification The application of operant conditioning principles to the modification of human behavior. (Sometimes also used as a synonym for *behavior therapy.*) (p. 485)

behavior therapy Therapy that applies learning principles to the elimination of unwanted behaviors. (p. 482)

behavioral medicine An interdisciplinary field that integrates and applies behavioral and medical knowledge to health and disease. (p. 507)

behavioral perspective Emphasizes environmental influences on observable behaviors. (p. 6)

behaviorism The view that (1) psychology should be an objective science which (2) studies only overt behavior without reference to mental processes. Most research psychologists today agree with (1) but not (2). (p. 235)

belief perseverance Clinging to one's initial conceptions after the basis on which they were formed has been discredited. (pp. 295–297)

binocular cues Depth cues, such as retinal disparity and convergence, that depend on the use of two eyes. (p. 174)

biofeedback A system for electronically recording, amplifying, and feeding back information regarding a subtle physiological state, such as blood pressure or muscle tension. (p. 521)

biological perspective Emphasizes the influences of heredity and physiology upon our behaviors, emotions, memories, and sensory experiences. (p. 6)

biological psychology A branch of psychology concerned with the links between biology and behavior. (Some biological psychologists call themselves *behavioral neuroscientists, neuropsychologists, physiological psychologists,* or *biopsychologists.*) (p. 7)

bipolar disorder A mood disorder in which the person alternates between the hopelessness and lethargy of depression and the overexcited, hyperactive, wildly optimistic state of mania. (p. 458)

blind spot The point at which the optic nerve leaves the eye, creating a "blind" spot since no receptor cells are located there. (p. 148)

brainstem The central core of the brain, beginning where the spinal cord swells as it enters the skull; it is the oldest part of the brain, and is responsible for automatic survival functions. (p. 35)

brightness The psychological dimension of color (its brilliance) that is determined mostly by the intensity of light. (p. 146)

brightness constancy Perceiving objects as having consistent brightness even when their illumination varies. (p. 179)

Broca's area An area of the left frontal lobe that directs the muscle movements involved in speech. (p. 42)

bulimia nervosa A disorder characterized by "binge-purge" eating, in which repeated episodes of overeating, usually of highly caloric foods, are followed by vomiting or laxative use. (p. 357)

bystander effect The tendency for any given bystander to be less likely to give aid if other bystanders are present. (p. 587)

Cannon-Bard theory The theory that an emotion-arousing stimulus simultaneously triggers (1) physiological responses and (2) the subjective experience of emotion. (pp. 400–401)

case study An observational technique in which one person is studied in depth in the hopes of revealing things universally true. (pp. 10–11)

CAT (computerized axial tomograph) scan A series of x-ray photographs taken from different angles and combined by computer into a composite three-dimensional representation of a slice through the body at whatever angle is desired. (p. 34)

catharsis Emotional release. In psychology, the catharsis hypothesis maintains that aggressive urges are relieved by "releasing" aggressive energy (through action or fantasy). (p. 392)

central nervous system (CNS) The brain and spinal cord. (p. 26)

cerebellum [sehr-uh-BELL-um] The "little brain" attached to the rear of the brainstem; it helps to coordinate voluntary movement and balance. (p. 36)

cerebral [seh-REE-bruhl] **cortex** The intricate fabric of interconnected neural cells that covers the cerebral hemispheres; the body's ultimate control and information-processing center. (p. 39)

chromosomes Threadlike structures made of DNA molecules that contain the genes. A human cell has twenty-three pairs of chromosomes, one member of each pair coming from each parent. (p. 59)

chunking Organization of items into familiar, manageable units. (p. 264)

circadian rhythm [ser-KAY-dee-an] The biological clock; regular bodily rhythms (for example, of temperature and wakefulness) that occur on a 24-hour cycle. (p. 197)

classical conditioning A type of learning in which an organism comes to associate different events. Thus a neutral stimulus, after being paired with an unconditioned stimulus (UCS), begins to trigger a response that anticipates and prepares for the unconditioned stimulus. (Also known as *Pavlovian*, or *respondent, conditioning*.) (p. 230)

clinical psychology A branch of psychology involving the assessment and treatment of those with psychological disorders. (p. 8)

closure The perceptual tendency to fill in gaps, thus enabling one to perceive disconnected parts as a whole object. (p. 173)

coactors People who are simultaneously at work on the same noncompetitive task. (p. 566)

cochlea [KOCK-lee-uh] A coiled, bony, fluid-filled tube in the inner ear through which sound waves trigger nerve impulses. (p. 154)

cocktail party effect The ability to attend selectively to only one voice among many. (p. 194)

cognition All the mental activities associated with thinking, knowing, and remembering. (p. 65)

cognitive developmental theory The theory that gender-typing occurs as children form a concept of gender, which then influences whom they imitate. (p. 122)

cognitive dissonance theory The theory that we act to reduce the discomfort (dissonance) we feel when two of our thoughts (cognitions) are inconsistent—as when we respond to the fact that we have chosen to act in a manner that contradicts our attitudes by changing our attitude. (p. 561)

cognitive map A mental representation of the layout of one's environment. For example, once they have explored a maze, rats act as if they have acquired a cognitive map of it. (p. 247)

cognitive perspective Emphasizes how we process, store, and retrieve information and how we use it to reason and solve problems. (p. 6)

cognitive therapy Therapy that teaches people new, more adaptive ways of thinking and acting; based on the assumption that thoughts intervene between events and our emotional reactions. (p. 487)

collective unconscious Carl Jung's concept of inherited memory traces from our species' history. (p. 415)

color constancy Perceiving familiar objects as having consistent color, even if their actual color is altered by changing illumination. (p. 179)

companionate love The deep affectionate attachment we feel for those with whom our lives are intertwined. (p. 600)

complexity The mixture of different wavelengths of light or sound. Complexity determines the saturation of light and the timbre of sounds (low complexity = purity). (p. 146)

concept A mental grouping of similar things, events, and people. (p. 284)

concrete operational stage In Piaget's theory, the stage of cognitive development (from about 7 to 12 years of age) during which children acquire the mental operations that enable them to think logically about concrete events. (p. 69)

conditioned response (CR) In classical conditioning, the learned response to a conditioned stimulus (CS). (p. 231)

conditioned stimulus (CS) In classical conditioning, an originally neutral stimulus that, after association with an unconditioned stimulus (UCS), comes to trigger a conditioned response. (p. 231)

conduction deafness Hearing loss caused by damage to the mechanical system that conducts sound waves to the cochlea. (p. 156)

cones Receptor cells concentrated near the center of the retina that function in daylight or in well-lit conditions. The cones detect fine detail and give rise to color sensations. (p. 148)

confirmation bias A tendency to search for information that confirms one's preconceptions. (p. 287)

conflict A perceived incompatibility of actions, goals, or ideas. (p. 600)

conformity Adjusting one's behavior or thinking to coincide with a group standard. (p. 550)

consciousness Selective attention to ongoing perceptions, thoughts, and feelings. (p. 193)

conservation The principle (which Piaget believed to be a part of concrete operational reasoning) that properties such as mass, volume, and number remain the same despite changes in the forms of objects. (p. 69)

content validity The extent to which a test samples the behavior that is of interest (such as a driving test that samples driving tasks). (p. 326)

continuity A perceptual tendency to group stimuli into smooth, continuous patterns. (p. 173)

continuous reinforcement Reinforcing the desired response every time it occurs. (p. 241)

control condition The condition of an experiment in which the experimental treatment is absent; serves as a comparison for evaluating the effect of the treatment. (p. 14)

convergence A binocular cue for perceiving depth; the extent to which the eyes converge inward when looking at an object. (p. 174)

conversion disorder Now rare, a somatoform disorder in which a person experiences very specific genuine physical symptoms for which no physiological basis can be found. (p. 453)

coronary heart disease The narrowing of the vessels that nourish the heart muscle; the leading cause of death in the United States. (p. 514)

corpus callosum [kah-LOW-sum] The largest bundle of nerve fibers connecting and carrying messages between the two brain hemispheres. (p. 44)

correlation A statistical index that indicates the extent to which two factors vary together and thus how well one factor can be predicted from knowing the other. (pp. 12–13)

correlation coefficient A measure of the direction and extent of the relationship between two sets of scores. Scores with a *positive correlation coefficient* go up and down together (as with high school and college GPAs). A *negative correlation coefficient* indicates that one score falls as the other rises (as in the relationship between self-esteem and depression). (p. 615)

counterconditioning A behavior therapy procedure that conditions new responses to stimuli that trigger unwanted behaviors; based on classical conditioning. See also *systematic desensitization* and *aversive conditioning*. (p. 483)

creativity The ability to produce ideas that are both novel and valuable. (p. 334)

criterion The behavior (such as college grades) that a test (such as the SAT) is designed to predict; thus, the measure used in defining whether the test has predictive validity. (p. 326)

critical period A restricted time period during which an organism must be exposed to certain influences or experiences if proper development is to occur; in humans there appear to be critical periods for the formation of attachments and the learning of language. (p. 71)

cross-sectional study A study in which people of different ages are tested or observed at a given time. (p. 103)

crystallized intelligence One's accumulated information and verbal skills; tends to increase with age. (p. 104)

decibel A measure of sound intensity. (p. 157)

declarative memory Memory of facts, of information one can "declare." (p. 267)

deductive reasoning The deriving of conclusions, given certain assumptions. (p. 297)

defense mechanisms In psychoanalytic theory, the ego's methods of reducing anxiety by unconsciously distorting reality. (p. 413)

deindividuation The loss of self-awareness and self-restraint occurring in group situations that foster arousal and anonymity. (p. 567)

déjà vu (From French, literally meaning "already seen.") That eerie sense that "I've experienced this before." Cues from the current situation may subconsciously trigger retrieval of an earlier experience. (p. 270)

delta waves The large, slow brain waves associated with deep sleep. (p. 199)

delusions False beliefs, often of persecution or grandeur, that may accompany psychotic disorders. (p. 463)

dendrite The bushy, branching extensions of a neuron that receive messages and conduct impulses toward the cell body. (p. 28)

dependent variable The variable that is being measured; in an experiment, the variable that may change in response to manipulations of the independent variable. (p. 14)

depressants Drugs (such as alcohol, barbiturates, and opiates) that reduce neural activity and slow down body functions. (p. 215)

depth perception The ability to see objects in three dimensions although the images that strike the retina are two-dimensional; allows us to judge distance. (p. 173)

developmental psychology A branch of psychology that studies physical, cognitive, and social change throughout the life cycle. (p. 8)

difference threshold The minimum difference in stimulation that a subject can detect 50 percent of the time. We experience the difference threshold as a just noticeable difference (jnd). (p. 142)

discrimination   In classical conditioning, the ability to distinguish between a conditioned stimulus and similar stimuli that do not signal an unconditioned stimulus. In operant conditioning, the ability to distinguish between reinforced and nonreinforced behaviors. (p. 234)

displacement   In psychoanalytic theory, the shifting of one's impulses toward a more acceptable or less threatening object or person, as when redirecting anger toward a safer outlet. (p. 414)

dissociation   A split in consciousness, which allows some thoughts and behaviors to occur simultaneously with others. (p. 211)

dissociative disorders   Disorders in which conscious awareness becomes separated (dissociated) from previous memories, thoughts, and feelings. See *amnesia, fugue,* and *multiple personality.* (p. 454)

DNA (deoxyribonucleic acid)   In cells, a complex molecule containing genetic information. (p. 59)

double-blind procedure   An experimental procedure in which both the patient and the staff are ignorant (blind) as to whether the patient has received the treatment or a placebo. Commonly used in drug evaluation studies. (p. 499)

Down syndrome   A condition of retardation and associated physical disorders caused by an extra chromosome in one's genetic makeup. (p. 334)

drive   An aroused state that typically arises from an underlying need. (p. 351)

DSM-III-R   The American Psychiatric Association's *Diagnostic and Statistical Manual of Mental Disorders (Third Edition–Revised),* a widely used system for classifying psychological disorders. (pp. 448–449)

dualism   The presumption that mind and body are two distinct entities that interact with each other. (p. 222)

echoic memory   A momentary sensory memory of auditory stimuli; if attention is elsewhere, sounds and words can still be recalled within 3 or 4 seconds. (p. 258)

eclectic   Using what appears to be the best of various theories and methods; eclectic therapists draw techniques from the various forms of therapy, depending on the client's problems. (p. 476)

effortful processing   Encoding that requires attention and effort. (p. 259)

ego   The largely conscious, "executive" part of personality that, according to Freud, mediates between the demands of the id and superego and reality. (p. 411)

egocentrism   In Piaget's theory, the inability of the preoperational child to take another's point of view. (p. 68)

Electra complex   See *Oedipus complex.*

electroconvulsive therapy (ECT)   Shock treatment. A biomedical therapy in which a brief electric current is sent through the brain; used to treat severely depressed patients. (p. 498)

electroencephalogram (EEG)   An amplified recording of the waves of electrical activity that sweep across the brain's surface. These waves are measured by placing electrodes on the scalp. (p. 33)

embryo   The early developmental stage of an organism after fertilization; in human development, the prenatal stage from about 2 weeks to 2 months. (p. 60)

emotion   A response of the whole organism, involving (1) physical arousal, (2) expressive behaviors, and (3) conscious experience. (p. 381)

empathy   The ability to understand and feel what another feels, to put oneself in someone else's shoes. (p. 130)

empirically derived test   An inventory (such as the MMPI) that is developed by testing a pool of items and then selecting those that differentiate groups of interest. (p. 422)

empiricism   The view that perceptions are learned through experience. (p. 169)

encoding   The processing of information into the memory system, for example by extracting meaning. (pp. 257–259)

encounter groups   Gatherings of twelve to twenty people whose emotion-laden experiences are characterized by honesty and openness, through which the participants hope to grow in self-awareness and social sensitivity. (p. 482)

endocrine [EN-duh-krin] **system**   The body's "slow" chemical communication system; a set of glands that secrete hormones into the bloodstream. (p. 31)

endorphins [en-DOR-fins]   "Morphine within"—natural, opiatelike neurotransmitters linked to pain control and pleasure. (p. 30)

equilibrium   The sense of body movement and position, including the sense of balance. (p. 163)

equity   A condition in which people receive from a relationship in proportion to what they contribute to it. (p. 600)

escape learning   Learning to withdraw from or terminate an aversive stimulus. (p. 243)

estrogen   A sex hormone, secreted in greater amounts by females than males. In nonhuman female mammals, estrogen levels peak during ovulation, rousing sexual receptivity. (p. 363)

experiment   A research method in which the investigator manipulates one or more factors (independent variables) to observe their effect on some behavior (the dependent variable) while controlling other relevant factors. (p. 13)

experimental condition   The condition of an experiment in which subjects are exposed to the treatment, that is, to the independent variable. (p. 14)

external locus of control   The belief that one's fate is determined by chance or outside forces that are beyond one's personal control. (p. 433)

extinction   The diminishing of a response when, in classical conditioning, a conditioned stimulus (CS) is not followed by an unconditioned stimulus (UCS) or when, in operant conditioning, a response is no longer reinforced. (p. 233)

extrasensory perception (ESP)   The controversial claim that perception can occur apart from sensory input. Said to include telepathy, clairvoyance, and precognition. (p. 185)

extrinsic motivation A desire to perform a behavior due to promised rewards or threats of punishment. (p. 373)

factor analysis A statistical procedure that identifies clusters of related items (called factors) on a test; used to identify different dimensions of performance that underlie one's total score. (p. 329)

family therapy Therapy that treats individuals within their family system. Views unwanted behaviors as engendered by or directed at other family members; encourages family members to mend relationships and improve communication. (p. 501)

fantasy-prone personality Someone who imagines and recalls experiences with lifelike vividness and who spends considerable time fantasizing. (pp. 195–196)

farsightedness A condition in which faraway objects are seen more clearly than near objects because the image of near objects is focused behind the retina. (p. 147)

feature detectors Nerve cells in the brain that respond to specific features of the stimulus, such as movement, angle, or shape. (pp. 150–151)

fetus The developing human organism from 9 weeks after conception to birth. (p. 60)

figure-ground The organization of the visual field into objects (the figures) that stand out from their surroundings (the ground). (p. 172)

fixation 1. According to Freud, a lingering focus of pleasure-seeking energies at an earlier psychosexual stage. (p. 413) 2. The inability to adopt a new perspective on a problem. (p. 283)

fixed-interval schedule In operant conditioning, a schedule of reinforcement in which a response is reinforced only after a specified time has elapsed. (p. 241)

fixed-ratio schedule In operant conditioning, a schedule of reinforcement in which a response is reinforced only after a specified number of responses. (p. 242)

flashbulb memory A clear memory of an emotionally significant moment or event. (p. 256)

fluid intelligence One's ability to reason abstractly; tends to decrease during later adulthood. (p. 104)

formal operational stage In Piaget's theory, the stage of cognitive development (normally beginning about age 12) during which people learn to think logically about abstract concepts. (p. 92)

fovea The central focal point in the retina, around which the eye's cones cluster. (p. 148)

framing The way an issue is posed; it can significantly affect judgments. (pp. 294–295)

fraternal twins Twins who develop from separate eggs and sperm cells, thus ordinary brothers and sisters who have shared the fetal environment. (p. 81)

free association A psychoanalytic method of exploring the unconscious in which the person relaxes and says whatever comes to mind, no matter how trivial or embarrassing. (p. 411)

frequency The number of complete wavelengths that can pass a point in a given time. (p. 154)

frequency distribution A listing of the number of individual scores that occur within each equal-sized interval into which the entire range of scores has been divided. (p. 611)

frequency theory In hearing, the theory that the rate of pulses traveling up the auditory nerve matches the frequency of a tone, thus enabling us to sense its pitch. (p. 155)

frontal lobes The portion of the cerebral cortex lying behind the forehead; involved in speaking and muscle movements and in making plans and judgments. (p. 39)

frustration-aggression theory The theory that frustration—the blocking of an attempt to achieve some goal—creates anger, which can generate aggression. (p. 578)

fugue [fewg] A dissociative disorder in which amnesia is accompanied by physical flight from one's home and identity. (p. 454)

functional fixedness The tendency to think of things only in terms of their usual functions; an impediment to problem solving. (p. 290)

fundamental attribution error The tendency for observers, when analyzing another's behavior, to underestimate the impact of the situation and to overestimate the impact of personal disposition. (p. 548)

gate-control theory Melzack and Wall's theory that the spinal cord contains a neurological "gate" that blocks or allows pain signals to pass on to the brain; the "gate" is opened by the activity of pain signals traveling up small nerve fibers and closed by activity in larger fibers or by information coming from the brain. (p. 159)

gender The social definition of male and female. (p. 117)

gender identity One's sense of being male or female. Note: One's gender identity is distinct from one's sexual orientation (as heterosexual or homosexual) and from the strength of one's *gender-typing* (see page 135). (p. 117)

gender role A set of expected behaviors for males and for females. (p. 117)

gender schema theory The theory that children learn from their cultures a concept of what it means to be male and female, and adjust their behavior accordingly. (p. 123)

gender-typing The acquisition of a masculine or feminine gender identity and role. (p. 121)

general adaptation syndrome (GAS) Selye's concept of the body's adaptive response to stress as composed of three stages—alarm, resistance, exhaustion. (p. 510)

general experimental psychology A branch of psychology that uses experimental methods to discover principles of behavior, such as those underlying sensation and perception, learning and memory, motivation and emotion. (p. 8)

general intelligence (g) A general underlying intelligence factor believed by Spearman and others to be measured by every task on an intelligence test. (p. 329)

generalization The tendency, once a response has been conditioned, for stimuli similar to the conditioned stimulus to evoke similar responses. (p. 234)

generalized anxiety disorder An anxiety disorder in which a person is continually tense, apprehensive, and in a state of autonomic nervous system arousal. (pp. 449–450)

generativity In Erikson's theory, the impulse to be productive, such as by raising children and doing creative work; a major focus during middle adulthood. (p. 105)

genes The biochemical units of heredity that make up the chromosomes; a segment of DNA capable of synthesizing a protein. (p. 58)

genital stage The final of Freud's psychosexual stages, beginning in puberty, during which pleasure is sought through sexual contact with others. (p. 412)

gestalt An organized whole. Gestalt psychologists emphasize our tendency to integrate pieces of information into meaningful wholes. (p. 171)

Gestalt therapy Developed by Fritz Perls, therapy that combines the psychoanalytic emphasis on bringing unconscious feelings to awareness and the humanistic emphasis on getting "in touch with oneself"; aims to help people become more aware of and able to express their feelings, and to take responsibility for their feelings and actions. (p. 480)

glucose The form of sugar that circulates in the blood and provides the major source of energy for body tissues. (p. 355)

good-patient role Cooperative, unquestioning, undemanding patient behavior, sometimes exhibited by anxious, helpless, depressed patients. (p. 528)

grammar A system of rules that enables us to use our language to speak to and understand others. (p. 302)

GRIT Graduated and Reciprocated Initiatives in Tension-reduction—a strategy designed to decrease international tensions. (p. 606)

group polarization The enhancement of a group's prevailing attitudes through discussion. (p. 569)

grouping The tendency to organize stimuli into coherent groups. (p. 172)

groupthink The mode of thinking that occurs when the desire for harmony in a decision-making group overrides a realistic appraisal of alternatives. (p. 570)

hallucinations False sensory experiences, such as seeing something in the absence of any external visual stimulus. (p. 198)

hallucinogens Psychedelic ("mind-manifesting") drugs, such as LSD, that distort perceptions and evoke sensory images in the absence of sensory input. (pp. 215, 218–219)

health psychology A subfield of psychology that provides psychology's contribution to behavioral medicine. (p. 507)

heritability The extent to which differences in a trait can be attributed to genes. Heritability of a trait may vary, depending on the range of populations and environments studied. (p. 337)

heuristic A rule-of-thumb strategy that often allows us to make judgments and to solve problems efficiently. (p. 286)

hidden observer Hilgard's term describing a hypnotized subject's awareness of experiences, such as pain, that go unreported during hypnosis. (p. 214)

hierarchy of needs Maslow's pyramid of human needs, beginning at the base with physiological needs that must first be satisfied before higher level safety needs and then psychological needs become active. (p. 353)

hippocampus A neural center in the limbic system that helps process declarative memories for storage. (p. 267)

histogram A bar graph that depicts a frequency distribution. (p. 611)

homeostasis A tendency to maintain a balanced or constant internal state; refers especially to the body's tendency to maintain an optimum internal state for functioning. (p. 351)

hormones Chemical messengers, such as those manufactured by the endocrine glands, that are produced in one tissue and affect another. (p. 31)

hospice Organizations whose largely volunteer staff members provide support for dying people and their families either in special facilities or in people's own homes. (p. 111)

hue The dimension of color that is determined by the wavelength of light; what we know as the color names (blue, green, and so forth). (p. 146)

humanistic perspective Emphasizes people's capacities for choice and growth; studies people's subjective experiences. (p. 6)

hypnosis A temporary state of heightened suggestibility in which some people are able to narrow their focus of attention and experience imaginary happenings as if they were real. (p. 206)

hypochondriasis A somatoform disorder in which a person misinterprets normal physical sensations as symptoms of a disease. (p. 453)

hypothalamus [hi-po-THAL-uh-muss] A neural structure lying below (hypo) the thalamus; it directs several maintenance activities (eating, drinking, body temperature), helps govern the endocrine system via the pituitary gland, and is linked to emotion and reward. (p. 37)

hypothesis A testable prediction, often derived from a theory. (p. 10)

iconic memory A momentary sensory memory of visual stimuli; a photographic or picture-image memory lasting no more than a second or so. (p. 258)

id The instinctual drives that, according to Freud, supply psychic energy to personality. (p. 411)

identical twins Twins who develop from a single fertilized egg that splits in two, creating two genetic replicas. (p. 81)

identification 1. Freud's term for the presumed process by which a child adopts the characteristics of the same-sex parent. More generally, the process by which people associate themselves with and copy the behavior of significant others. (p. 121) 2. The process by which, according to Freud, children incorporate their parents' values into their developing superegos. (p. 412)

identity One's sense of self. According to Erikson, the adolescent's task is to form a sense of self by integrating various roles. (p. 95)

idiot savant A retarded person who possesses an amazing specific skill, such as in computation or drawing. (p. 330)

I-knew-it-all-along phenomenon The tendency to believe one would have foreseen how something turned out, *after* learning the outcome. (Also known as *hindsight bias*.) (pp. 20–21)

illusory correlation The perception of a relationship where none exists. (p. 616)

imagery Mental pictures. A powerful aid to effortful processing, especially when it is combined with semantic encoding. (pp. 262–263)

imprinting The process by which certain birds and mammals form attachments during a critical period very early in life. (p. 72)

incentives Positive or negative environmental stimuli that motivate behavior. (p. 352)

independent variable The experimental factor; the manipulated variable whose effect is being studied. (p. 14)

inductive reasoning The inferring of a general truth from particular examples. (p. 297)

industrial/organizational psychology A branch of psychology that studies behavior in the workplace and the marketplace; it seeks to enhance the former and influence the latter. (p. 8)

informational social influence Influence resulting from accepting others' opinions about reality. (p. 553)

ingroup bias The tendency to favor one's own group. (p. 592)

inner ear The innermost part of the ear, containing the cochlea, semicircular canals, and vestibular sacs. (p. 154)

insane A legal term for someone who has committed a crime but is judged not to have understood that the act was wrong at the time of the crime. (p. 446)

insight A sudden and often novel realization of the solution to a problem; it contrasts with trial-and-error solutions. (p. 286)

insomnia A sleep disorder involving recurring problems in falling or staying asleep. (p. 201)

instinct A behavior that is rigidly patterned, characteristic of a whole species, and unlearned. (p. 350)

insulin A hormone that, among its effects, helps body tissues convert blood glucose into stored fat. (p. 355)

integrity In Erikson's theory, the positive outcome of later life: a nondespairing sense that one's life has been meaningful and worthwhile. (p. 105)

intelligence The capacity for goal-directed adaptive behavior (behavior that successfully meets challenges and achieves its aims). Involves the abilities to profit from experience, solve problems, and reason. (p. 327)

intelligence quotient (IQ) Defined originally as the ratio of mental age to chronological age multiplied by 100 (thus IQ = MA/CA × 100). Contemporary tests compute IQ score by giving the average performance for a given age a score of 100, with other IQ scores defined in terms of their deviation from the average. (p. 318)

intensity The amount of energy in a light or sound wave, as determined by the wave's amplitude. (p. 146)

interaction effect A result in which the effect of one factor depends on the level of another. (p. 374)

intermittent reinforcement See *partial reinforcement*.

internal locus of control The belief that one can control one's own fate. (p. 433)

interneurons Central nervous system neurons that intervene between the sensory inputs and motor outputs. (p. 27)

interpretation In psychoanalysis, the analyst's assisting the patient to note and understand resistances and other significant behaviors in order to promote insight. (p. 477)

intimacy In Erikson's theory, the ability to form close, loving relationships; the primary developmental task of early adulthood. (p. 96)

intrinsic motivation A desire to perform a behavior for its own sake and to be effective. (p. 373)

iris A ring of muscle tissue that forms the colored portion of the eye around the pupil and controls the size of the pupil opening. (p. 146)

James-Lange theory The theory that our experience of emotion is a consequence of our physiological responses to emotion-arousing stimuli. (pp. 400–401)

just noticeable difference (jnd) See *difference threshold*.

just-world phenomenon The tendency of people to believe the world is just and that people therefore get what they deserve and deserve what they get. (p. 594)

kinesthesis [kin-ehs-STHEE-sis] The system for sensing body position and the movement of muscles, tendons, and joints. (p. 163)

language Words and how we combine them to communicate meaning. (p. 301)

latency stage The fourth of Freud's psychosexual stages, from about age 6 to puberty, during which sexual impulses are repressed. (p. 412)

latent content According to Freud, the underlying but censored meaning of a dream (as distinct from its manifest content). Freud believed that a dream's latent content serves a safety valve function. (pp. 203–204)

latent learning Learning that occurs but is not apparent until there is an incentive to demonstrate it. (pp. 247–248)

lateral hypothalamus (LH) The side areas of the hypothalamus that, when stimulated, trigger eating and, when destroyed, cause an animal to stop eating. (p. 356)

learned helplessness Passive resignation that is learned when an animal or human has been unable to avoid repeated aversive events. (p. 434)

learning A relatively permanent change in an organism's behavior due to experience. (p. 229)

lens The transparent structure behind the pupil that changes shape to focus images on the retina. (p. 146)

lesion [LEE-zhuhn] Tissue destruction. A brain lesion is a naturally or experimentally caused destruction of brain tissue. (p. 33)

limbic system A doughnut-shaped system of neural structures at the border of the brainstem and cerebral hemispheres; associated with emotions such as fear and aggression and drives such as those for food and sex. (p. 37)

linear perspective A monocular cue for perceiving distance; we perceive the converging of what we know to be parallel lines as indicating increasing distance. (p. 176)

linguistic relativity Whorf's hypothesis that language determines the way we think. (p. 309)

lithium A chemical that provides an effective drug therapy for the mood swings of bipolar (manic-depressive) disorders. (p. 500)

lobotomy A psychosurgical procedure once used to calm uncontrollably emotional or violent patients. In this procedure the nerves that connect the frontal lobes to the emotion-controlling centers of the inner brain are cut. Also called frontal (or prefrontal) lobotomy. (p. 497)

longitudinal study Research in which the same people are restudied over a long period of time. (p. 103)

long-term memory A relatively permanent and limitless component of the memory system. (p. 258)

LSD (lysergic acid diethylamide) A powerful hallucinogenic drug, also known as *acid*. (p. 218)

lymphocytes The two types of white blood cells that are part of the body's immune system: B lymphocytes form in the bone marrow and release antibodies that fight bacterial infections; T lymphocytes form in the thymus and, among other duties, attack cancer cells, viruses, and foreign substances. (p. 517)

major depression A mood disorder in which a person, for no apparent reason, experiences two or more weeks of depressed moods, feelings of worthlessness, and diminished interest or pleasure in most activities. (p. 456)

mania A hyperactive, wildly optimistic state. (p. 458)

manifest content According to Freud, the remembered story line of a dream (as distinct from its latent content). (pp. 203–204)

maturation Biological growth processes that enable orderly changes in behavior, relatively uninfluenced by experience. (p. 58)

mean The arithmetic average of a distribution, which is obtained by adding the scores and dividing by their number. (p. 613)

median The middle score in a distribution; half the scores are above it and half are below it. (p. 613)

medical model The concept that diseases have physical causes and that they can be diagnosed, treated, and, in most cases, cured. When applied to psychological disorders, the medical model assumes that these "mental" illnesses can be diagnosed on the basis of their symptoms and cured through therapy, which may include treatment in a psychiatric hospital. (p. 445)

medulla [muh-DUL-uh] The base of the brainstem; controls heartbeat and breathing. (p. 35)

memory The persistence of learning over time. (p. 255)

menarche [meh-NAR-key] The first menstrual period. (p. 90)

menopause The cessation of menstruation. Also used loosely to refer to the biological and psychological changes during the several years of declining ability to reproduce. (p. 99)

mental age A measure of intelligence test performance devised by Binet; the chronological age that most typically corresponds to a given level of performance. Thus a child who does as well as the average 8-year-old is said to have a mental age of 8. (p. 317)

mental retardation A condition of limited mental ability, as assessed by an IQ score below 70, that produces difficulty in adapting to the demands of life; varies from mild to profound. (p. 333)

mental set A tendency to approach a problem in a particular way, especially a way that has been successful in the past but may or may not be helpful in solving a new problem. (p. 289)

mere exposure effect The phenomenon that repeated exposure to novel stimuli increases liking of them. (p. 596)

meta-analysis A procedure for statistically combining the results of many different research studies. (p. 494)

metabolic rate The body's rate of energy expenditure. (p. 356)

middle ear The chamber between the eardrum and cochlea containing three tiny bones (hammer, anvil, and stirrup) that concentrate the vibrations of the eardrum on the cochlea. (p. 154)

Minnesota Multiphasic Personality Inventory (MMPI) The most widely researched and used of all personality inventories, containing ten scales of clinical dimensions and other validity scales and subscales. Originally developed to distinguish among emotionally troubled people—still considered its most appropriate use—this test is now used for many other screening purposes. (p. 422)

mirror-image perceptions Distinct but similar views of one another often held by parties in conflict; each views itself as moral and peace-loving and the other as evil and aggressive. (pp. 603–604)

mnemonics [nih-MON-iks] Memory aids, especially those techniques that use vivid imagery and organizational devices. (p. 263)

mode The most frequently occurring score in a distribution. (p. 612)

modeling The process of observing and then imitating a behavior. (p. 249)

monism The presumption that mind and body are different aspects of the same thing. (p. 222)

monocular cues Distance cues, such as aerial and linear perspective and overlap, available to either eye alone. (p. 176)

mood disorders Psychological disorders characterized by emotional extremes. See *major depression* and *bipolar disorder*. (p. 456)

morphemes The smallest speech units that carry meaning; may be words or parts of words (such as a prefix). (p. 302)

motivation The forces that energize and direct behavior. (p. 349)

motor cortex An area at the rear of the frontal lobes that controls voluntary movements. (p. 40)

motor neurons The neurons that carry outgoing information from the central nervous system to the muscles and glands. (p. 27)

MRI (magnetic resonance imaging) A technique that uses magnetic fields and radio waves to produce computer-generated images that distinguish between different types of soft tissue; allows us to see structures within the brain. (p. 34)

multiple personality disorder A formerly rare dissociative disorder in which a person exhibits two or more distinct and alternating personalities. (pp. 454–456)

myelin [MY-uh-lin] **sheath** A layer of fatty cells segmentally encasing the axons of many neurons; makes possible vastly greater transmission speed of neural impulses. (p. 28)

narcolepsy A sleep disorder characterized by uncontrollable sleep attacks in which the sufferer lapses directly into REM sleep, often at inopportune times. (p. 201)

nativism The view that important aspects of perception are innate, and thus do not have to be learned through experience. (p. 169)

natural selection The process by which evolution favors individuals within a species best equipped to survive and reproduce. (p. 119)

naturalistic observation Observing and recording behavior in naturally occurring situations, without trying to manipulate and control the situation. (p. 12)

nature-nurture issue The longstanding controversy over the relative contributions of genes and experience to the development of psychological traits and behaviors. (p. 58)

near-death experience An altered state of consciousness reported after a close brush with death (such as through cardiac arrest); often similar to drug-induced hallucinations. (p. 221)

nearsightedness A condition in which nearby objects are seen more clearly than distant objects because the lens focuses the image of distant objects in front of the retina. (p. 147)

need A deprivation that usually rouses a drive to reduce or eliminate the deprivation. (p. 351)

negative reinforcer An aversive stimulus, such as electric shock or nagging, the withdrawal of which strengthens responses that precede its withdrawal. Like all reinforcers, negative reinforcers strengthen behaviors that trigger them. (Negative reinforcement is not *punishment*.) (p. 240)

nerve deafness Hearing loss caused by damage to the cochlea's receptor cells or to the auditory nerves. (p. 156)

nervous system The body's electrochemical communication system, consisting of all the nerve cells of the peripheral and central nervous systems. (p. 25)

neuron A nerve cell; the basic building block of the nervous system. (p. 27)

neurotic disorders Psychological disorders that are usually distressing, but allow one to think rationally and function socially. The neurotic disorders are usually viewed as ways of dealing with anxiety. (p. 448)

neurotransmitters Chemical messengers that traverse the synaptic gaps between neurons. When released by the sending neuron, neurotransmitters travel across the synapse and bind to receptor sites on the receiving neuron, thereby influencing whether it will fire. (p. 29)

night terrors A sleep disorder characterized by high arousal and an appearance of being terrified; unlike nightmares, night terrors occur during Stage 4 sleep, within 2 or 3 hours of falling asleep, and are seldom remembered. (p. 202)

normal curve (or normal distribution) The symmetrical bell-shaped curve that describes the distribution of many physical and psychological attributes (including IQ scores), with most scores falling near the mean (68 percent within 1 standard deviation) and fewer and fewer near the extremes. (pp. 323–324, 614)

normative social influence Influence resulting from a person's desire to gain approval or avoid disapproval. (p. 553)

norms Understood rules for accepted and expected behavior. Norms prescribe "proper" behavior. (p. 553)

obesity A surplus of body fat that causes one to be 20 percent or more overweight. (p. 534)

object permanence The awareness that things continue to exist even when they are not perceived. (p. 67)

observational learning Learning by observing and imitating the behavior of others. (p. 249)

obsessive-compulsive disorder An anxiety disorder in which a person is troubled by unwanted repetitive thoughts (obsessions) and/or actions (compulsions). (pp. 452–453)

occipital [ahk-SIP-uh-tuhl] **lobes** The portion of the cerebral cortex lying at the back of the head; includes the visual areas, each of which receives visual information from the opposite visual field. (p. 39)

Oedipus [Ed-uh-puss] **complex** According to Freud, the 3- to 5- or 6-year-old child's sexual desires toward the parent of the other sex and feelings of jealousy and hatred for the rival parent of the same sex. In girls, sometimes called the *Electra complex*. (p. 412)

one-word stage The stage in speech development, from

about age 1 to 2 years, during which a child speaks mostly in single words. (p. 303)

operant behavior   Behavior that operates on the environment, producing consequences. (p. 238)

operant conditioning   A type of learning in which behavior is strengthened if followed by reinforcement, or diminished if followed by punishment. (Also called *instrumental conditioning*.) (p. 230)

opiates   Opium and its derivatives, such as morphine and heroin, which depress neural activity, temporarily alleviating pain and anxiety. (p. 217)

opponent-process theory   1. The theory that every emotion triggers an opposing emotion that fights it and lingers after the first emotion is extinguished. (p. 397)   2. The theory that color vision depends on pairs of opposing retinal processes (red-green, yellow-blue, white-black). For example, some cells are stimulated by green and inhibited by red; others are stimulated by red and inhibited by green. (pp. 152–153)

optic nerve   The nerve that carries neural impulses from the eye to the brain. (p. 148)

oral stage   The first of Freud's psychosexual stages, during which pleasure centers on the mouth. (p. 412)

overconfidence phenomenon   The tendency to be more confident than correct—to overestimate the accuracy of one's beliefs and judgments. (p. 293)

overjustification effect   The effect of promising a reward for doing what one already likes doing. The person may now see the reward, rather than intrinsic interest, as the motivation for performing the task. (p. 248)

overlap   A monocular cue for perceiving distance; nearby objects partially block our view of more distant objects. (Also called *interposition*, because nearby objects are interposed between our eyes and more distant objects.) (p. 175)

ovum   The female reproductive cell, or egg, which after fertilization develops into a new individual. (p. 59)

panic attack   An episode of intense dread in which a person experiences terror and accompanying chest pain, choking, or other frightening sensations for a number of minutes. (p. 456)

parapsychology   The study of paranormal phenomena including ESP and psychokinesis. (p. 185)

parasympathetic nervous system   The division of the autonomic nervous system that calms the body, conserving its energy. (p. 27)

parietal [puh-RYE-uh-tuhl] **lobes**   The portion of the cerebral cortex lying at the top of the head and toward the rear; includes the sensory cortex. (p. 39)

partial (or intermittent) reinforcement   Reinforcing a response only part of the time; results in slower acquisition of response but much greater resistance to extinction than does continuous reinforcement. (p. 240)

passionate love   An aroused state of intense positive absorption in another, usually present at the beginning of a relationship. (p. 599)

percentile rank   The percentage of the scores in a distribution that a given score exceeds. (p. 611)

perception   The process of organizing and interpreting sensory information, enabling us to recognize meaningful objects and events. (p. 140)

perceptual adaptation   In vision, the ability to adjust to an artificially displaced or even inverted visual field. (p. 181)

perceptual set   A mental predisposition to perceive one thing and not another. (p. 182)

peripheral nervous system (PNS)   The part of the nervous system that lies outside of the central nervous system. It consists of the sensory neurons, which carry messages to the central nervous system from the body's sense receptors, and the motor neurons, which carry messages from the central nervous system to the muscles and glands. (p. 26)

personal space   The buffer zone we like to maintain around our bodies. (p. 568)

personality   An individual's relatively distinctive and consistent patterns of thinking, feeling, and acting. (p. 409)

personality disorders   Psychological disorders characterized by enduring, maladaptive character traits. See *antisocial personality.* (p. 469)

personality inventories   Questionnaires (often with true-false or agree-disagree items) on which people report their customary feelings and behaviors; used to assess personality traits. (p. 422)

personality psychology   A branch of psychology that studies how individuals are influenced by relatively enduring inner factors. (p. 8)

person-centered therapy   A humanistic therapy, developed by Carl Rogers, in which the therapist attempts to facilitate clients' growth by offering a genuine, accepting, empathic environment. (p. 478)

PET (positron emission tomograph) scan   A visual display of brain activity that detects where a radioactive form of glucose goes while the brain performs a given task. (p. 34)

phallic stage   The third of Freud's psychosexual stages, during which the pleasure zone is focused on the genitals and sexual feelings arise toward the parent of the other sex. (p. 412)

phobic disorder   An anxiety disorder in which a person is troubled by a phobia—a persistent, irrational fear of a specific object or situation. (pp. 450–452)

phonemes   A language's smallest distinctive sound units. (p. 301)

phrenology   A discarded nineteenth-century theory, proposed by Franz Gall, that the shape of the skull reveals one's abilities and character. (p. 25)

pitch   The highness or lowness of a tone; depends on frequency. (p. 154)

pituitary gland   The endocrine system's most influential gland. Under the influence of the hypothalamus, the pituitary regulates growth and controls other endocrine glands. (p. 31)

place theory   In hearing, the theory that links the pitch we hear with the place where the cochlea's membrane is stimulated. (p. 154)

placebo [pluh-SEE-bo]   An inert substance that may, in an experiment, be administered instead of an active drug; may trigger the effects believed to characterize the actual drug. (p. 218)

placebo effect   The beneficial effect of a person's *expecting* that a treatment will be therapeutic. A placebo is a neutral treatment (such as an inactive pill) that may nevertheless promote change because of the hope and confidence placed in it. (p. 218)

plasticity   The brain's capacity for modification, as evident in brain reorganization following damage (especially in children) and in experiments on the effects of experience on brain development. (p. 49)

pleasure principle   The id's demand for immediate gratification. (p. 411)

polygraph   A machine, commonly used in attempts to detect lies, that measures several of the physiological responses that accompany emotion (such as perspiration, heart rate, and breathing changes). (p. 383)

population   All the cases in a group, from which samples may be drawn for study. (p. 617)

positive reinforcer   A rewarding stimulus, such as food, which, when presented after a response, strengthens the response. (p. 240)

posthypnotic amnesia   An inability to recall what one experienced during hypnosis, induced by the hypnotist's suggestion. (p. 206)

posthypnotic suggestion   A suggestion, made during a hypnotic session, that is to be carried out after the subject is no longer hypnotized; it is used by some clinicians as an aid to controlling undesired symptoms and behaviors. (p. 210)

preconscious   Information that is not currently conscious, but is retrievable into conscious awareness. (p. 410)

predictive validity   The success with which a test predicts the behavior it is designed to predict; assessed by computing the correlation between test scores and the criterion behavior. (p. 326)

prejudice   An unjustifiable attitude toward a group and its members. Prejudice generally involves stereotyped beliefs, negative feelings, and a predisposition to discriminatory action. (p. 590)

preoperational stage   In Piaget's theory, the stage (from about 2 to 7 years of age) during which a child learns to use language but does not yet comprehend the mental operations of concrete logic. (pp. 68–69)

primary reinforcer   An innately reinforcing stimulus, such as one that satisfies a biological need. (p. 240)

primary sex characteristics   The body structures (ovaries and gonads) that make sexual reproduction possible. (p. 90)

priming   The conscious or unconscious activation of particular associations in memory. (p. 270)

proactive interference   The disruptive effect of prior learning on the recall of new information. (p. 276)

procedural memory   Memory of skills, of how to do things. (p. 267)

projection   In psychoanalytic theory, the defense mechanism by which people disguise their own threatening impulses by imputing them to others. (p. 413)

projective tests   Personality tests, such as the Rorschach and TAT, that provide ambiguous stimuli designed to trigger projection of one's inner dynamics. (p. 415)

prosocial behavior   Positive, constructive, helpful behavior. The opposite of antisocial behavior. (p. 250)

prototype   The best example of a category; matching new items to the prototype provides a quick and easy method for including items in a category (as when comparing feathered creatures to a prototypical bird, such as a robin). (p. 285)

proximity   A perceptual tendency to group together visual and auditory events that are near each other. (p. 173)

psychiatry   A branch of medicine dealing with psychological disorders practiced by physicians and sometimes involving medical (for example, drug) treatments as well as psychological therapy. (p. 8)

psychoactive drug   A drug that alters mood and perceptions. (pp. 214–215)

psychoanalysis   1. Sigmund Freud's therapy technique, in which the patient's free associations, resistances, dreams, and transferences—and the therapist's interpretations of them—are the means by which previously repressed feelings are released, allowing the patient to gain self-insight. (p. 476)   2. The technique of treating disorders by analyzing unconscious tensions. Freud's psychoanalytic theory of personality sought to explain what he observed during psychoanalysis. (p. 411)

psychoanalytic perspective   Builds on Freud's ideas that behavior arises from unconscious drives and conflicts, many of which may stem from childhood experiences. (p. 6)

psychological dependence   A psychological need to use a drug, such as to relieve stress. (p. 215)

psychological disorder   Behavior that is typically defined on the basis of being atypical, disturbing, maladaptive, and unjustifiable. (p. 445)

psychology   The science of behavior and mental processes. (p. 4)

psychopharmacology   The study of the effects of drugs on mind and behavior. (p. 499)

psychophysiological illness   Literally, "mind-body" illness; any illness that is not caused by any known physical disorder; certain forms of hypertension, ulcers, and headaches are often linked with stress. (p. 516)

psychosexual stages   The developmental stages (oral, anal, phallic, latency, genital) during which, according to Freud, the id's pleasure-seeking energies are focused on different erogenous zones. (p. 412)

psychosurgery   Surgery that removes or destroys brain tissue in an effort to change behavior. (p. 497)

psychotherapy   An emotionally charged, confiding interaction between a trained therapist and someone who suffers a psychological difficulty. (p. 476)

psychotic disorder A psychological disorder in which a person loses contact with reality, experiencing irrational ideas and distorted perceptions. (p. 448)

puberty The early adolescent period of rapid growth and sexual maturation. (p. 90)

punishment Any event that decreases the behavior that it follows. (p. 242)

pupil The adjustable opening in the center of the eye through which light enters. (p. 146)

random assignment Assigning subjects to experimental and control conditions by chance, thus minimizing preexisting differences between those assigned to the different groups. (p. 15)

random sample A sample that is representative of some larger group because every person has an equal chance of being included. (p. 15)

range The difference between the highest and lowest scores in a distribution. (p. 613)

rational-emotive therapy A confrontational cognitive therapy developed by Albert Ellis that vigorously challenges people's illogical, self-defeating attitudes and assumptions. (p. 487)

rationalization In psychoanalytic theory, a defense mechanism in which self-justifying explanations are offered in place of the real, more threatening, unconscious reasons for one's actions. (p. 413)

reactance The tendency to protect or restore one's sense of freedom from social control, often by doing the opposite of what has been demanded. (p. 557)

reaction formation In psychoanalytic theory, the ego's unconscious switching of unacceptable impulses into their opposites. Thus people may express feelings that are the opposite of their anxiety-arousing unconscious feelings. (p. 413)

reality principle The ego's tendency to satisfy the id's desires in ways that will realistically bring pleasure rather than pain. (p. 411)

recall A measure of memory in which the person must retrieve information learned earlier, as on a sentence completion test. (p. 269)

reciprocal determinism The mutual influences among personal factors, environmental factors, and behavior. (p. 432)

recognition A measure of memory in which the person need only identify items previously learned, as on a multiple-choice test. (p. 269)

reflex A simple, automatic, inborn response to a sensory stimulus, such as the knee-jerk response. (p. 27)

refractory period A resting period after male orgasm during which a man cannot be aroused to another orgasm. (p. 362)

regression In psychoanalytic theory, an individual's retreat, when faced with anxiety, to an earlier, more comfortable stage of development. (p. 413)

regression toward the average The tendency for extreme or unusual scores to fall back (regress) toward the average. (p. 616)

rehearsal The conscious repetition of information, either simply to maintain information in consciousness or to encode it for storage. (p. 260)

reinforcer In operant conditioning, any event that strengthens the behavior that it follows. (p. 240)

relative brightness A monocular cue for perceiving distance; dimmer objects seem more distant. (p. 176)

relative deprivation The perception that one is worse off relative to those with whom one compares oneself. (p. 398)

relative height A monocular cue for perceiving distance; we perceive higher objects as farther away. (p. 176)

relative motion A monocular cue for perceiving distance; when we move, objects at different distances change their relative positions in our visual image, with those closest moving most. (Also called *motion parallax*.) (p. 176)

relative size A monocular cue for perceiving distance; when two objects are assumed to be the same size, the one that produces the smaller image appears to be more distant. (p. 175)

relearning A measure of memory that assesses the amount of time saved when relearning previously learned information. (p. 269)

reliability The extent to which a test yields consistent results (as assessed by the consistency of scores on two halves of the test, on alternate forms of the test, or on retesting). See *split-half reliability* and *test-retest reliability*. (p. 325)

REM rebound effect The tendency for REM sleep to increase following REM sleep deprivation (created by repeated awakenings during REM sleep). (p. 206)

REM sleep Rapid eye movement sleep, a recurring sleep stage during which vivid dreams commonly occur. Also known as *paradoxical sleep*, because the muscles are relaxed (except for minor twitches) but the other body systems are active. (p. 198)

replication Repeating the essence of an experiment, usually with different subjects in different situations, to see whether the basic finding generalizes to other people and circumstances. (p. 9)

representativeness heuristic Judging the likelihood of things in terms of how well they seem to represent, or match, particular prototypes; may lead one to ignore other relevant information. (p. 290)

repression 1. In psychoanalytic theory, the basic defense mechanism that banishes anxiety-arousing thoughts and feelings from consciousness. (p. 413) 2. The blocking from consciousness of painful memories and unacceptable impulses. (p. 278)

resistance In psychoanalysis, the blocking from consciousness of anxiety-laden material. (p. 477)

respondent behavior Behavior that occurs as an automatic response to some stimulus. (p. 238)

reticular activating system A nerve network (also called the *reticular formation*) in the brainstem that plays an important role in controlling arousal and attention. (p. 36)

retina   The light-sensitive inner surface of the eye, containing the receptor rods and cones plus layers of neurons that begin the processing of visual information. (p. 146)

retinal disparity   A binocular cue for perceiving depth; the greater the disparity (difference) between the two images the retina receives of an object, the closer to us the object is. (Also called *binocular disparity*.) (p. 174)

retrieval   The process of getting information out of memory storage. (p. 257)

retroactive interference   The disrupting effect of new learning on the recall of old information. (p. 276)

rods   Retinal receptors that detect black, white, and gray, especially in peripheral and nighttime vision. (p. 148)

role   A set of expectations about a social position, defining how those in the position ought to behave. (p. 559)

rooting reflex   A baby's tendency, when touched on the cheek, to open the mouth and search for the nipple. (pp. 61–62)

Rorschach inkblot test   A test designed by Hermann Rorschach that uses people's interpretation of inkblots in an attempt to identify their projected feelings. (p. 416)

saturation   The purity of color, which is greater when complexity (the number of other wavelengths mixed in) is low. (p. 146)

scapegoat theory   The theory that prejudice provides frustrated people with an outlet for their anger by providing someone to blame. (p. 593).

scatterplot   A graphed cluster of dots, each of which represents the values of two variables (such as a student's high school and college GPAs). The slope of the points suggests the degree and direction of the relationship between the two variables. (Also called a *scattergram* or *scatter diagram*.) (p. 614)

schema   A concept or framework that organizes and interprets information. (p. 65)

schizophrenia   A group of psychotic disorders characterized by disorganized thinking, disturbed perceptions, and inappropriate emotions and actions. (pp. 463–464)

secondary reinforcer   A conditioned reinforcer; a stimulus that acquires its reinforcing power by association with another reinforcer, such as a primary reinforcer. (p. 240)

secondary sex characteristics   Nonreproductive sexual characteristics such as female breasts and hips, male voice quality, and body hair. (p. 90)

selective attention   The focusing of conscious awareness on a particular stimulus. (See also *cocktail party effect*.) (pp. 193–194)

self-actualization   According to Maslow, the final psychological need that arises when basic physical and psychological needs are met; the process of fulfilling one's potential as one achieves qualities such as self-acceptance, spontaneity, love, mastery, and creativity. (p. 425)

self-concept   All our thoughts and feelings about ourselves which answer the question, "Who am I?" (p. 426)

self-disclosure   Revealing intimate aspects of oneself to others. (p. 600)

self-efficacy   A sense that one is competent and effective. (p. 434)

self-esteem   One's feelings of high or low self-worth. (p. 432)

self-perception theory   The theory that when we are unsure of our attitudes we infer them by looking at our behavior and the circumstances under which it occurs, much as an outside observer would. (p. 562)

self-serving bias   The bias of perceiving oneself favorably. (p. 430)

semantic encoding   The encoding of meaning, including the meaning of words. (pp. 257–259)

semantics   Meaning (or the study of meaning), as derived from morphemes, words, and sentences. (p. 302)

semicircular canals   Three curved, fluid-filled structures of the inner ear with receptors that detect body motion. (p. 163)

sensation   The process by which certain stimulus energies are detected and encoded. (p. 140)

sensorimotor stage   In Piaget's theory, the stage (from birth to about 2 years of age) during which infants know the world mostly in terms of their sensory impressions and motor activities. (pp. 67–68)

sensory adaptation   Diminished sensitivity with constant stimulation. (pp. 143–144)

sensory cortex   The area at the front of the parietal lobes that registers and processes body sensations. (p. 41)

sensory interaction   The principle that one sense may influence another, as when the smell of food influences its taste. (p. 161)

sensory neurons   Neurons that carry incoming information from the body's sense receptors to the central nervous system. (p. 27)

serial position effect   Our tendency to recall the last and first items in a list. (p. 261)

set point   The point at which an individual's weight "thermostat" is set. When the body falls below this weight, changes in hunger and metabolic rate act to restore the lost weight. (p. 356)

sexual dysfunction   A problem that consistently impairs sexual arousal or functioning. (pp. 362–363)

sexual orientation   One's sexual attraction toward members of either one's own sex (homosexual orientation) or the other sex (heterosexual orientation). (p. 366)

sexual response cycle   The four stages of sexual responding described by Masters and Johnson—excitement, plateau, orgasm, and resolution. (p. 362)

shape constancy   Perceiving familiar objects as having a constant shape, even when their retinal image changes with viewing angle. (p. 177)

shaping   A procedure in operant conditioning that starts with some existing behavior and reinforces closer and closer approximations of a desired behavior. (p. 239)

short-term memory   A component of memory that holds few items briefly, such as the seven digits of a phone number while dialing. (p. 258)

signal detection The task of judging the presence of a faint stimulus ("signal"). Signal detection researchers assume that there is no single absolute threshold, because the detection of a weak signal depends partly on a person's experience, expectation, motivation, and level of fatigue. (p. 141)

similarity A perceptual tendency to group together similar elements. (p. 173)

size constancy Perceiving an object as having a constant size, despite variations in its retinal image. (p. 177)

Skinner box A chamber containing a bar or key that an animal can manipulate to obtain a food or water reinforcer and devices to record the animal's rate of bar pressing or key pecking. Used in operant conditioning research. (p. 239)

sleep apnea A sleep disorder characterized by temporary cessations of breathing during sleep and consequent momentary reawakenings. (p. 202)

sleep spindles Rhythmic bursts of brain activity occurring during Stage 2 sleep. (p. 199)

social clock The culturally preferred timing of social events such as marriage, childbearing, and retirement. (p. 106)

social exchange theory The theory that our social behavior is an exchange process, the aim of which is to maximize benefits and minimize costs. (p. 588)

social facilitation Improved performance of tasks in the presence of others; occurs with simple or well-learned tasks but not with tasks that are difficult or not yet mastered. (pp. 565–566)

social learning theory The theory that we learn behavior, such as gender-typed behavior, by observing and imitating, and by being rewarded and punished. (p. 121)

social loafing The tendency for each person in a group to exert less effort when they are pooling their efforts toward attaining a common goal than when they are each individually accountable. (p. 567)

social psychology The study of how people influence and relate to one another. (p. 8)

social traps Situations in which the conflicting parties, by each rationally pursuing their self-interest, become caught in mutually destructive behavior. (p. 602)

social-cognitive perspective Applies interactive principles of social learning and cognition to study how the environment shapes people's behavior and beliefs, and how these in turn influence people's situations. (p. 432)

sociobiology The study of the evolution of social behavior using the principles of natural selection. Social behaviors that are genetically based and that contribute to the preservation and spread of one's genes are presumed to be favored by natural selection. (p. 119)

somatic [so-MAT-ik] **nervous system** The division of the peripheral nervous system that receives information from various sense receptors and controls the skeletal muscles of the body. (p. 26)

somatoform disorders Disorders in which the symptoms take a somatic (bodily) form without apparent physical cause. See *conversion disorder* and *hypochondriasis*. (p. 453)

split-brain Describing a condition in which the two hemispheres of the brain are isolated by cutting the connecting fibers between them (mainly those of the corpus callosum). (p. 44)

split-half reliability A measure of the internal consistency of a test; typically assessed by correlating total scores obtained on the odd- and even-numbered items. (p. 325)

spontaneous recovery The reappearance, after a rest period, of an extinguished conditioned response. (p. 233)

spontaneous remission Improvement without treatment. In psychotherapy, symptom relief without psychotherapy. (p. 493)

SQ3R An acronym for *Survey, Question, Read, Recite, Review*—a method of study. (p. 279)

standard deviation A measure of variability of the scores in a distribution; computed by squaring the deviation of each score from the mean and finding the square root of their average. (p. 613)

standardization Defining meaningful scores by comparison with the performance of a representative "standardization group" that has been pretested. (p. 323)

Stanford-Binet The widely used American revision (by Terman at Stanford University) of Binet's original intelligence test. (p. 318)

state-dependent memory The tendency to recall information best when in the same emotional or physiological state one was in when the information was learned. (p. 271)

statistical significance A statistical statement of how small the likelihood is that an obtained result occurred by chance. (p. 621)

stereotype A generalized (often overgeneralized) belief about a group of people. (p. 590)

stimulants Drugs (such as caffeine, nicotine, and the more powerful amphetamines and cocaine) that excite neural activity and speed up body functions. (p. 215)

storage The maintenance of encoded information over time. (p. 257)

stranger anxiety The fear of strangers that infants commonly display beginning at about 8 months of age. (p. 68)

stress The whole process by which we perceive and respond to certain events, called *stressors*, that we appraise as threatening or challenging us. (p. 507)

sublimation In psychoanalytic theory, the defense mechanism by which people rechannel their unacceptable impulses into socially approved activities. (p. 414)

subliminal Below threshold. (p. 141)

successive approximations In operant conditioning, the small steps by which some existing behavior is shaped toward a desired behavior. (p. 239)

superego The part of personality that, according to Freud, represents internalized ideals, thus providing standards for judgment (conscience) and for future aspirations. (p. 412)

superordinate goals Shared goals that override differences among people and require their cooperation. (p. 605)

survey A technique for ascertaining the self-reported attitudes or behaviors of people by questioning a representative (random) sample of them. (pp. 11–12)

syllogism   The basis of formal deductive reasoning; an argument in which two presumably true statements, called premises, lead to a third true statement, the conclusion. (p. 297)

sympathetic nervous system   The division of the autonomic nervous system that arouses the body, mobilizing its energy in stressful situations. (p. 26)

synapse [SIN-aps]   The junction (also called the *synaptic gap*) between the axon tip of the sending neuron and the dendrite or cell body of the receiving neuron. (p. 29)

syntax   Rules for combining words into grammatically correct sentences. (p. 302)

systematic desensitization   A type of counterconditioning that associates a pleasant, relaxed state with gradually increasing anxiety-triggering stimuli. Commonly used to treat phobias. (p. 483)

telegraphic speech   An early speech stage in which the child speaks like a telegram—using mostly nouns and verbs and omitting "auxiliary" words. (p. 304)

temperament   A person's characteristic emotional reactivity and intensity. (p. 80)

temporal lobes   The portion of the cerebral cortex lying roughly above the ears; includes the auditory areas, each of which receives auditory information primarily from the opposite ear. (p. 39)

teratogens   Agents, such as chemicals and viruses, that can reach the embryo or fetus during prenatal development and cause harm. (p. 61)

testosterone   The most important of the male sex hormones. Both males and females have it, but the additional testosterone in males stimulates the growth of the male sex organs in the fetus and the development of the male sex characteristics during puberty. (p. 118)

test-retest reliability   A measure of the consistency of test scores assessed by retesting people and correlating these scores with their initial scores. (p. 325)

texture gradient   A monocular cue for perceiving distance; a gradual change to a less distinct texture suggests increasing distance. (p. 175)

thalamus [THAL-uh-muss]   The brain's sensory switchboard, located on top of the brainstem; directs messages to the sensory receiving areas in the cortex and transmits replies to the cerebellum and medulla. (p. 36)

THC   The active ingredient in marijuana and hashish that triggers a variety of effects, including mild hallucinations. (p. 219)

Thematic Apperception Test (TAT)   A projective test in which people make up stories about ambiguous scenes. (pp. 415–416)

theory   An integrated set of principles that organizes, explains, and predicts observations. (p. 10)

threshold   The level of stimulation required to trigger a neural impulse. (p. 28)

timbre   The tone color of a sound that distinguishes it from other sounds of the same pitch and loudness, for example the middle C produced by a piano versus the middle C produced by a clarinet. (p. 154)

token economy   An operant conditioning procedure in which a token of some sort, which can be exchanged later for various privileges or treats, is given as a reward for desired behavior. (p. 486)

tolerance   The diminishing of a drug's effect with regular use of the same dose, requiring the user to take larger and larger doses before experiencing the drug's effect. (p. 214)

trait theory   Describes personality in terms of behaviors as scored on various scales, each of which represents a personality dimension. (p. 420)

traits   Our predispositions to behave in given ways, assessed by personality inventories. (p. 419)

transduction   Conversion of one form of energy into another. In sensation, the transforming of stimulus energies into neural impulses. (p. 145)

transference   In psychoanalysis, the patient's transfer to the analyst of emotions linked with other relationships (such as love or hatred for a parent). (p. 477)

trial and error   A haphazard problem-solving process in which one solution after another is tried until success is achieved. (p. 286)

two-factor theory   The theory that to experience emotion one must (1) be physically aroused and (2) cognitively label the arousal. (pp. 402–403)

two-word stage   The stage in speech development, beginning about age 2, during which a child speaks mostly two-word utterances. (p. 304)

Type A   Friedman and Rosenman's term for competitive, hard-driving, impatient, verbally aggressive, and anger-prone people. (p. 515)

Type B   Friedman and Rosenman's term for an easygoing person. (p. 515)

unconditional positive regard   According to Rogers, an attitude of total acceptance toward another person. (p. 426)

unconditioned response (UCR)   In classical conditioning, the unlearned, automatic response to the unconditioned stimulus, such as salivation when food is in the mouth. (p. 231)

unconditioned stimulus (UCS)   In classical conditioning, a stimulus that naturally and automatically triggers a response without conditioning. (p. 231)

unconscious   According to Freud, a reservoir of mostly unacceptable thoughts, wishes, feelings, and memories. According to contemporary research psychologists, information processing of which we are unaware. (p. 410)

validity   The extent to which a test measures or predicts what it is supposed to. (See also *content validity* and *predictive validity*.) (p. 326)

variable-interval schedule   In operant conditioning, a

schedule of reinforcement in which a response is reinforced at unpredictable time intervals. (p. 242)

variable-ratio schedule In operant conditioning, a schedule of reinforcement in which a response is reinforced after unpredictable numbers of responses. (p. 242)

ventromedial hypothalamus (VMH) The bottom and middle areas of the hypothalamus that, when stimulated, cause the cessation of eating and, when destroyed, cause an animal to overeat. (p. 356)

vestibular sacs Two structures of the inner ear with receptors that provide the sense of upright body position. (p. 163)

visual capture The tendency for vision to dominate the other senses; we perceive filmed voices as coming from the screen we see rather than from the projector behind us. (p. 171)

visual cliff A laboratory device for testing depth perception in infants and young animals. (p. 174)

visual encoding The encoding of picture images. (pp. 257–259)

wavelength The distance from the peak of one light or sound wave to the peak of the next. Waves vary in length. (p. 146)

Weber's law The principle that two stimuli must differ by a constant minimum percentage (rather than a constant amount) for their difference to be perceived. (p. 143)

Wechsler Adult Intelligence Scale (WAIS) The most widely used intelligence test; contains a variety of verbal and nonverbal (performance) subtests. (p. 320)

Wernicke's area An area of the left hemisphere involved in language comprehension. (p. 42)

withdrawal The physical and psychological distress that follows the discontinued use of addictive drugs. (p. 215)

X **sex chromosome** The sex chromosome found in both men and women. Females have two *X* chromosomes; males have one. An *X* chromosome from each parent produces a female. (p. 59)

Y **sex chromosome** The sex chromosome found only in males. When it pairs with an *X* sex chromosome from the mother, a male is produced. (p. 59)

Young-Helmholtz trichromatic (three-color) theory The theory that the retina contains three different color receptors—one most sensitive to red, one to green, one to blue—in combination producing the perception of any color. (p. 152)

zygote The fertilized egg; it enters a 2-week period of rapid cell division and develops into an embryo. (p. 60)

REFERENCES

Abbey, A. (1987). Misperceptions of friendly behavior as sexual interest: A survey of naturally occurring incidents. *Psychology of Women Quarterly, 11,* 173–194. (p. 119)

Abrams, D. B., & Wilson, G. T. (1983). Alcohol, sexual arousal, and self-control. *Journal of Personality and Social Psychology, 45,* 188–198. (pp. 216, 530)

Abramson, L. Y., Metalsky, G. I., & Alloy, L. B. (1989). Hopelessness depression: A theory-based subtype. *Psychological Review,* in press. (p. 461)

ACT (1987, July). Are standardized admissions tests biased against women. *ACT Activity,* p. 8. (p. 132)

Adams, D., & 19 others (1987). Statement on violence. *Medicine and War, 3,* 191–193. (p. 578)

Adams, P. R., & Adams, G. R. (1984). Mount Saint Helens's ashfall: Evidence for a disaster stress reaction. *American Psychologist, 39,* 252–260. (p. 511)

Adelman, K. L. (1987). Arms control: A slow and frustrating business. *Vital Speeches of the Day, 53*(8), 226–229. (p. 604)

Adelmann, P. K. (1988). Work and psychological well-being: A meta-analysis. Unpublished manuscript, University of Michigan. (p. 109)

Ader, R., & Cohen, N. (1985). CNS–immune system interactions: Conditioning phenomena. *Behavioral and Brain Sciences, 8,* 379–394. (p. 519)

Adler, N., & Stone, G. (1984). Psychology and the health system. In J. Ruffini (Ed.), *Advances in medical social science.* New York: Gordon & Breach. (p. 529)

Aiello, J. R., Thompson, D. D., & Brodzinsky, D. M. (1983). How funny is crowding anyway? Effects of room size, group size, and the introduction of humor. *Basic and Applied Social Psychology, 4,* 193–207. (p. 568)

Ainsworth, M. D. S. (1973). The development of infant-mother attachment. In B. Caldwell & H. Ricciuti (Eds.), *Review of child development research* (Vol. 3). Chicago: University of Chicago Press. (p. 72)

Ainsworth, M. D. S. (1979). Infant-mother attachment. *American Psychologist, 34,* 932–937. (pp. 72–73)

Ainsworth, M. D. S., Blehar, M. C., Waters, E, & Wall, S. (1978). *Patterns of attachment: A psychological study of the strange situation.* Hillsdale, NJ: Erlbaum. (p. 72)

Alba, J. W., & Hasher, L. (1983). Is memory schematic? *Psychological Bulletin, 93,* 203–231. (p. 272)

Albee, G. W. (1986). Toward a just society: Lessons from observations on the primary prevention of psychopathology. *American Psychologist, 41,* 891–898. (p. 503)

Alcock, J. E. (1981). *Parapsychology: Science or magic?* Oxford: Pergamon. (p. 271)

Alcock, J. E. (1985, Spring). Parapsychology: The "spiritual" science. *Free Inquiry,* pp. 25–35. (p. 189)

Alexander, C. N., Cranson, R. W., Boyer, R. W., & Orme-Johnson, D. W. (1987). Transcendental consciousness: A fourth state of consciousness beyond sleep, dreaming and waking. In J. Gackenbach (Ed.), *Sleep and dreams: A sourcebook.* New York: Garland Press. (p. 212)

Allard, F., & Burnett, N. (1985). Skill in sport. *Canadian Journal of Psychology, 39,* 294–312. (p. 264)

Allen, M. (1983). Models of hemispheric specialization. *Psychological Bulletin, 93,* 73–104. (p. 47)

Allen, M. G. (1976). Twin studies of affective illness. *Archives of General Psychiatry, 33,* 1476–1478. (p. 459)

Allison, R. B. (1984). Difficulties diagnosing the multiple personality syndrome in a death penalty case. *International Journal of Clinical and Experimental Hypnosis, 32,* 102–117. (p. 455)

Alloy, L. B., & Abramson, L. Y. (1988). Depressive realism: Four theoretical perspectives. In L. B. Alloy (Ed.), *Cognitive processes in depression.* New York: Guilford. (p. 461)

Allport, G. W. (1967). Gordon W. Allport. In E. G. Boring & G. Lindzey (Eds.), *A history of psychology in autobiography* (Vol. V). New York: Appleton-Century-Crofts. (p. 419)

Allport, G. W., & Odbert, H. S. (1936). Trait-names: A psycho-lexical study. *Psychological Monographs, 47* (1) (p. 420)

Altus, W. D. (1966). Birth order and its sequelae. *Science, 151,* 44–49. (p. 373)

Amabile, T. M. (1983). *The social psychology of creativity.* New York: Springer-Verlag. (pp. 335, 430)

Amabile, T. M. (1985). Motivation and creativity: Effects of motivational orientation on creative writers. *Journal of Personality and Social Psychology, 48,* 393–399. (p. 335)

Amabile, T. M. (1987). The motivation to be creative. In S. Isaksen (Ed.), *Frontiers in Creativity: Beyond the Basics.* Buffalo, NY: Bearly Limited. (p. 335)

Amabile, T. M. (1988). From individual creativity to organizational innovation. In K. Gronhaug & G. Kaufmann (Eds.),

Innovation: A crossdisciplinary perspective. Oslo: Norwegian University Press. (p. 335)

Amabile, T. M., & Glazebrook, A. H. (1982). A negativity bias in interpersonal evaluation. *Journal of Experimental Social Psychology, 18*, 1–22. (p. 430)

Amabile, T. M., & Hennessey, B. A. (1988). The motivation for creativity in children. In A. K. Boggiano & T. Pittman (Eds.), *Achievement and motivation: A social-developmental perspective*. New York: Cambridge University Press. (p. 334)

American Council on Education (1988, February 1). Freshman interest in teaching continues to increase. *Higher Education and National Affairs, 37*(1), pp. 3, 12. (p. 371)

American Psychiatric Association (1987). *Diagnostic and statistic manual of mental disorders (Third Edition—Revised)*. Washington, DC: American Psychiatric Association. (p. 333)

American Psychological Association (1986). Council of Representatives statement cited by N. Abeles, Proceedings of the American Psychological Association, Incorporated, for the Year 1985: Minutes of the annual meeting of the Council of Representatives August 22 and 25, 1985, Los Angeles, California, and January 31–February 2, 1986, Washington, DC *American Psychologist, 41*, 633–663. (p. 384)

Anastasi, A. (1982). *Psychological testing*. New York: Macmillan. (p. 321)

Anderson, A. (1982, December). How the mind heals. *Psychology Today*, pp. 51–56. (p. 519)

Anderson, B. L. (1983). Primary orgasmic dysfunction: Diagnostic considerations and review of treatment. *Psychological Bulletin, 93*, 105–136. (p. 363)

Anderson, C. A. (1987). Temperature and aggression: Effects on quarterly, yearly, and city rates of violent and nonviolent crime. *Journal of Personality and Social Psychology, 52*, 1161–1173. (p. 578)

Anderson, C. A., & Anderson, D. C. (1984). Ambient temperature and violent crime: Tests of the linear and curvilinear hypotheses. *Journal of Personality and Social Psychology, 46*, 91–97. (p. 578)

Anderson, C. A., Lepper, M. R., & Ross, L. (1980). Perseverance of social theories: The role of explanation in the persistence of discredited information. *Journal of Personality and Social Psychology, 39*, 1037–1049. (p. 296)

Anderson, D. R., & Jose, W. S., II (1987, December). Employee lifestyle and the bottom line: Results from the StayWell evaluation. *Fitness in Business*, 86–91. (pp. 521, 530)

Anderson, J. R. (1983). Retrieval of information from long-term memory. *Science, 220*, 25–30. (p. 270)

Andreasen, N. C. (1988). Brain imaging: Applications in psychiatry. *Science, 239*, 1381–1388. (p. 466)

Andrews, K. H., & Kandel, D. B. (1979). Attitude and behavior: A specification of the contingent consistency hypothesis. *American Sociological Review, 44*, 298–310. (p. 558)

Angoff, W. H. (1987). The nature-nurture debate, aptitudes, and group differences. Presidential address to American Psychological Association Division 5. (pp. 332, 340)

Antill, J. K. (1983). Sex role complementarity versus similarity in married couples. *Journal of Personality and Social Psychology, 45*, 145–155. (p. 127)

Arendt, H. (1963). *Eichmann in Jerusalem: A report on the banality of evil*. New York: Viking Press. (p. 94)

Aries, E. (1987). Gender and communication. In P. Shaver & C. Henrick (Eds.), *Review of Personality and Social Psychology, 7*, 177–200. (p. 130)

Asarnow, J. R., & Goldstein, M. J. (1986). Schizophrenia during adolescence and early adulthood: A developmental perspective on risk research. *Clinical Psychology Review, 6*, 211–235. (p. 468)

Asch, S. E. (1955). Opinions and social pressure. *Scientific American, 193*, 31–35. (p. 552)

Aserinsky, E. (1988, January 17). Personal communication. (p. 198)

Asher, J. (1987, April). Born to be shy? *Psychology Today*, pp. 56–64. (p. 81)

Associated Press (1986, November 24). Global weapons bill is $1.7 million a minute. *Grand Rapids Press*, p. A4. (p. 601)

Astin, A. W., Green, K. C., & Korn, W. S. (1987). The American freshman: Twenty year trends. (A report of the Cooperative Institutional Research Program sponsored by the American Council on Education.) Los Angeles, CA: Higher Education Research Institute, Graduate School of Education, UCLA. (pp. 125, 531)

Astin, G. R., & Garber, H. (1982). *The rise and fall of national test scores*. New York: Academic Press. (p. 325)

Atwell, R. H. (1986, July 28). Drugs on campus: A perspective. *Higher Education & National Affairs*, p. 5. (p. 216)

Averill, J. R. (1969). Autonomic response patterns during sadness and mirth. *Psychophysiology, 5*, 399–414. (p. 382)

Averill, J. R. (1983). Studies on anger and aggression: Implications for theories of emotion. *American Psychologist, 38*, 1145–1160. (p. 391)

Ax, A. F. (1953). The physiological differentiation of fear and anger in humans. *Psychosomatic Medicine, 15*, 433–442. (p. 383)

Bachman, J. G. (1987, July). An eye on the future. *Psychology Today*, pp. 6–7. (p. 97)

Bachman, J. G., Johnston, L. D., and O'Malley, P. M. (1987). *Monitoring the future: Questionnaire responses from the nation's high school seniors, 1986*. Ann Arbor, MI: Institute for Social Research, The University of Michigan. (p. 97)

Bachman, J. G., O'Malley, P. M., & Johnston, L. D. (1984). Drug use among young adults: The impacts of role status and social environment. *Journal of Personality and Social Psychology, 47*, 629–645. (p. 97)

Backus, J. (1977). *The acoustical foundations of music* (2nd ed.). New York: Norton. (p. 157)

Baddeley, A. D. (1982). *Your memory: A user's guide*. New York: Macmillan. (pp. 258, 260–261)

Badenhoop, M. S. & Johansen, M. K. (1980). Do reentry women have special needs? *Psychology of Women Quarterly, 4*, 591–595. (p. 102)

Bahrick, H. P. (1984a). Memory and people. In J. Harris (Ed.), *Everyday memory, actions, and absentmindedness.* Orlando, FL: Academic Press. (p. 261)

Bahrick, H. P. (1984b). Semantic memory content in permastore: 50 years of memory for Spanish learned in school. *Journal of Experimental Psychology: General, 113,* 1–29. (p. 275)

Bahrick, H. P., Bahrick, P. O., & Wittlinger, R. P. (1975). Fifty years of memory for names and faces: A cross-sectional approach. *Journal of Experimental Psychology: General, 104,* 54–75. (p. 269)

Bailey, R. E., & Bailey, M. B. (1980). A view from outside the Skinner box. *American Psychologist, 35,* 942–946. (p. 249)

Bairagi, R. (1987). Food crises and female children in rural Bangladesh. *Social Science, 72,* 48–51. (p. 117)

Baker, E. L. (1987). The state of the art of clinical hypnosis. *International Journal of Clinical and Experimental Hypnosis, 35,* 203–214. (p. 210)

Ball, W., & Tronick, E. (1971). Infant responses to impending collision: Optical and real. *Science, 171,* 818–820. (p. 174)

Bancroft, J., & Backstrom, T. (1985). Premenstrual syndrome. *Clinical Endocrinology, 22,* 313–336. (p. 527)

Bandura, A. (1977). *Social learning theory.* Englewood Cliffs, NJ: Prentice-Hall. (p. 250)

Bandura, A. (1982). The psychology of chance encounters and life paths. *American Psychologist, 37,* 747–755. (p. 107)

Bandura, A. (1986). *Social foundations of thought and action: A social-cognitive theory.* Englewood Cliffs, NJ: Prentice-Hall. (p. 431)

Bandura, A., Blanchard, E. B., & Ritter, B. (1969). Relative efficacy of desensitization and modeling approaches for inducing behavioral, affective, and attitudinal changes. *Journal of Personality and Social Psychology, 13,* 173–199. (p. 484)

Bandura, A., Ross, D., & Ross, S. A. (1961). Transmission of aggression through imitation of aggressive models. *Journal of Abnormal and Social Psychology, 63,* 575–582. (p. 250)

Barlow, H. B. (1972). Single units and sensations: A neuron doctrine for perceptual psychology? *Perception, 1,* 371–394. (p. 140)

Barnett, P. A., & Gotlib, I. H. (1988). Psychosocial functioning and depression: Distinguishing among antecedents, concomitants, and consequences. *Psychological Bulletin, 104,* 97–126. (p. 461)

Baron, J. (1985). *Rationality and intelligence.* New York: Cambridge University Press. (p. 328)

Baron, L., & Straus, M. A. (1984) Sexual stratification, pornography, and rape in the United States. In N. M. Mamamuth & E. Donnerstein (Eds.), *Pornography and sexual aggression.* Orlando, FL: Academic Press. (p. 582)

Baron, L., & Straus, M. A. (1986). Rape and its relation to social disorganization, pornography, and sexual inequality in the United States. Unpublished manuscript, Yale University. Cited by E. Donnerstein, D. Linz, & S. Penrod (1987). *The question of pornography.* New York: Free Press. (p. 582)

Barton, J., & Chassin, L., Presson, C. C., & Sherman, S. J. (1982). Social image factors as motivators of smoking initiation in early and middle adolescence. *Child Development, 53,* 1499–1511. (p. 531)

Baruch, G. K., & Barnett, R. (1986). Role quality, mulitple role involvement, and psychological well-being in midlife women. *Journal of Personality and Social Psychology, 51,* 578–585. (p. 109)

Batson, C. D. (1983). Sociobiology and the role of religion in promoting prosocial behavior: An alternative view. *Journal of Personality and Social Psychology 45,* 1380–1385. (p. 589)

Batson, C. D. (1987). Prosocial motivation: Is it ever truly altruistic? In L. Berkowitz (Ed.), *Advances in experimental social psychology* (Vol. 20). Orlando, Fla: Academic Press. (p. 588)

Bauman, L. J., & Siegel, K. (1987). Misperception among gay men of the risk for AIDS associated with their sexual behavior. *Journal of Applied Social Psychology, 17,* 329–350. (p. 369)

Baumann, L. J., & Leventhal, H. (1985). "I can tell when my blood pressure is up, can't I?" *Health Psychology, 4,* 203–218. (p. 526)

Baumeister, R. F., & Tice, D. M. (1986). How adolescence became the struggle for self: A historical transformation of psychological development. In J. Suls & A. G. Greenwald (Eds.), *Psychological perspectives on the self* (Vol. 3). Hillsdale, N.J.: Erlbaum. (p. 89)

Baumrind, D. (1982). Adolescent sexuality: Comment on Williams' and Silka's comments on Baumrind. *American Psychologist, 37,* 1402–1403. (p. 370)

Baumrind, D. (1983). Rejoinder to Lewis's reinterpretation of parental firm control effects: Are authoritative families really harmonious? *Psychological Bulletin, 94,* 132–142. (pp. 78–79)

Baxter, L. R., Jr., Phelps, M. E., Mazziotta, J. C., Guze, B. H., Schwartz, J. M., Selin, C. E. (1987). Local cerebral glucose metabolic rates in obsessive-compulsive disorder. *Archives of General Psychiatry, 44,* 211–218. (p. 453)

Beaman, A. L., & Klentz, B. (1983). The supposed physical attractiveness bias against supporters of the women's movement: A meta-analysis. *Personality and Social Psychology Bulletin, 9,* 544–550. (p. 598)

Beauchamp, G. K. (1987). The human preference for excess salt. *American Scientist, 75,* 27–33. (p. 355)

Beck, A. T. (1982). *Depression: Clinical, experimental, and theoretical aspects.* New York: Harper & Row. (p. 460)

Beck, A. T., Rush, A. J., Shaw, B. F., & Emery, G. (1979). *Cognitive therapy of depression.* New York: Guilford Press. (p. 489)

Beck, A. T., & Young, J. E. (1978, September). College blues. *Psychology Today,* pp. 80–92. (pp. 456, 462)

Becklen, R., & Cervone, D. (1983). Selective looking and the noticing of unexpected events. *Memory and Cognition, 11,* 601–608. (p. 194)

Behavior Today Staff (1984, November 26). Canada: Recent study shows decline in marijuana use among teenagers. *Behavior Today,* pp. 7–8. (p. 220)

Békésy, G., von. (1957, August). The ear. *Scientific American,* pp. 66–78. (p. 154)

Bell, A. P. (1982, November/December). Sexual preference: A postscript. (SIECUS Report, 11, No. 2) *Church and Society,* pp. 34–37. (p. 368)

Bell, A. P., Weinberg, M. S., & Hammersmith, S. K. (1981). *Sexual preference: Its development in men and women.* Bloomington: Indiana University Press. (p. 367)

Beloff, J. (1985, Spring). Science, religion and the paranormal. *Free Inquiry,* pp. 36–41. (p. 189)

Belsher, G., & Costello, C. G. (1988). Relapse after recovery from unipolar depression: A critical review. *Psychological Bulletin, 104,* 84–96. (p. 458)

Belsky, J. (1984). Two waves of day care research: Developmental effects and conditions of quality. In R. Ainslie (Ed.), *The child and the day care setting.* New York: Praeger. (p. 76)

Belsky, J. (1988). The "effects" of infant day care reconsidered. *Early Childhood Research Quarterly* (Vol. III). 235–272 (p. 77)

Belsky, J., Lang, M., & Huston, T. L. (1986). Sex typing and division of labor as determinants of marital change across the transition to parenthood. *Journal of Personality and Social Psychology, 50,* 517–522. (p. 108)

Bem, D. J. (1972). Self-perception theory. In L. Berkowitz (Ed.), *Advances in experimental social psychology* (Vol. 6). New York: Academic Press. (p. 562)

Bem, D. J. (1984). Quoted in the *Skeptical Inquirer, 8,* 194. (p. 185)

Bem, S. L. (1985). Androgeny and gender schema theory: A conceptual and empirical integration. *Nebraska Symposium on Motivation, 32,* 179–226. (p. 126)

Bem, S. L. (1987). Masculinity and femininity exist only in the mind of the perceiver. In J. M. Reinisch, L. A. Rosenblum, & S. A. Sanders (Eds.), *Masculinity/femininity: Basic perspectives.* New York: Oxford University Press. (pp. 123, 126)

Benbow, C. P. (1988). Sex differences in mathematical reasoning ability in intellectually talented preadolescents: Their nature, effects, and possible causes. *Behavioral and Brain Sciences,* in press. (p. 133)

Bennett, N. G., Blanc, A. K., & Bloom, D. E. (1988). Commitment and the modern union: Assessing the link between premarital cohabitation and subsequent marital stability. *American Sociological Review, 53,* 127–138 (p. 371)

Bergin, A. E., & Lambert, M. J. (1978). The evaluation of therapeutic outcomes. In S. L. Garfield & A. E. Bergin (Eds.), *Handbook of psychotherapy and behavior change: An empirical analysis* (2nd ed.). New York: Wiley. (p. 493)

Berkowitz, L. (1983). Aversively stimulated aggression: Some parallels and differences in research with animals and humans. *American Psychologist, 38,* 1135–1144. (p. 578)

Berkowitz, M. W., Mueller C. W., Schnell, S. V., & Padberg, M. T. (1986). Moral reasoning and judgments of aggression. *Journal of Personality and Social Psychology, 51,* 885–891. (p. 93)

Berman, J. S., & Norton, N. C. (1985). Does professional training make a therapist more effective? *Psychological Bulletin, 98,* 401–407. (p. 496)

Berman, P. W. (1980). Are women more responsive than men to the young? A review of developmental and situational variables. *Psychological Bulletin 88,* 668–695. (p. 131)

Bernard, J. (1976). *Sex differences: An overview.* New York: MSS Modular Publications. (p. 129)

Berry, D. S., & McArthur, L. Z. (1986). Perceiving character in faces: The impact of age-related craniofacial changes on social perception. *Psychological Bulletin, 100,* 3–18. (p. 234)

Berscheid, E. (1981). An overview of the psychological effects of physical attractiveness and some comments upon the psychological effects of knowledge of the effects of physical attractiveness. In G. W. Lucker, K. Ribbens, & J. A. McNamara (Eds.), *Psychological aspects of facial form* (Craniofacial growth series). Ann Arbor: Center for Human Growth and Development, University of Michigan. (p. 597)

Best, J. A., & Suedfeld, P. (1982). Restricted environmental stimulation therapy and behavioral self-management in smoking cessation. *Journal of Applied Social Psychology, 12,* 408–419. (p. 164)

Bianchi, S. M., & Spain, D. (1986). *American women in transition.* New York: Russell Sage Foundation. (p. 125)

Biddle, W. (1986, March). The deception of detection. *Discover,* pp. 24–33. (p. 383)

Binet, A., & Simon, T. (1905; reprinted 1916). New methods for the diagnosis of the intellectual level of subnormals. In A. Binet & T. Simon, *The development of intelligence in children.* Baltimore: Williams & Wilkins. (p. 317)

Bishop, G. D. (1984). Gender, role, and illness behavior in a military population. *Health Psychology, 3,* 519–534. (p. 527)

Bishop, G. D. (1987). Lay conceptions of physical symptoms. *Journal of Applied Social Psychology, 17,* 127–146. (p. 527)

Bishop, G. D., Briede, C., Cavazos, L., Grotzinger, R., & McMahon, S. (1987). Processing illness information: The role of disease prototypes. *Basic and Applied Social Psychology, 8,* 21–43. (p. 285)

Bishop, G. D., McMahon, S., Grotzinger, R., Cavazos, L., Briede, C., Wood, R., Wodkins, M., Rodriguez, L., & Doyle, D. (1985). *Disease prototypes: Speed of processing and associations.* Paper presented at the meeting of the American Psychological Association. (p. 285)

Bjork, R. A. (1978). The updating of human memory. In G. H. Bower (Ed.), *The psychology of learning and motivation* (Vol. 12). New York: Academic Press. (p. 273)

Blake, C., & Cohen, H. (1985, May). A meta-analysis of sex differences in moral development. *Resources in Education,* Document ED251749. (p. 95)

Blakemore, C., & Cooper, G. F. (1970). Development of the brain depends on the visual environment. *Nature, 228,* 477–478. (p. 181)

Blasi, A. (1980). Bridging moral cognition and moral action: A critical review of the literature. *Psychological Bulletin, 88,* 1–45. (p. 94)

Blass, E. (1987). Research reported at a National Institute of Child Health and Human Development workshop, June 30 and July 1, 1987; reported by G. Kolata, What babies know, and noises parents make. *Science, 237,* 726. (p. 62)

Block, J. (1981).   Some enduring and consequential structures of personality. In A. I. Rabin (Ed.), *Further explorations in personality.* New York: Wiley. (pp. 112–113)

Bloom, B. J. (1964).   *Stability and change in human characteristics.* New York: Wiley. (p. 332)

Bloom, B. S. (Ed.) (1985).   *Developing talent in young people.* New York: Ballantine. (p. 372)

Boggiano, A. K., Barrett, M., Weiher, A. W., McClelland, G. H., & Lusk, C. M. (1987).   Use of the maximal-operant principle to motivate children's intrinsic interest. *Journal of Personality and Social Psychology, 53,* 866–879. (p. 248)

Booth, W. (1988).   The long, lost survey on sex. *Science, 239,* 1084–1086. (p. 359)

Booth-Kewley, S., & Friedman, H. S. (1987).   Psychological predictors of heart disease: A quantitative review. *Psychological Bulletin, 101,* 343–362. (p. 516)

Borgida, E., & Nisbett, R. E. (1977).   The differential impact of abstract vs. concrete information on decisions. *Journal of Applied Social Psychology, 7,* 258–271. (p. 293)

Boring, E. G. (1930).   A new ambiguous figure. *American Journal of Psychology, 42,* 444–445. (p. 182)

Bornstein, R. F., Leone, D. R., & Galley, D. J. (1987).   The generalizability of subliminal mere exposure effects: Influence of stimuli perceived without awareness on social behavior. *Journal of Personality and Social Psychology, 53,* 1070–1079. (p. 141)

Botwinick, J. (1977)   Intellectual abilities. In J. E. Birren and K. W. Schaie (Eds.), *Handbook of the psychology of aging.* New York: Van Nostrand Reinhold. (p. 104)

Bouchard, T. J., Jr. (1981, December 6). Interview on *Nova: Twins* [program broadcast by the Public Broadcasting Service]. (p. 83)

Bouchard, T. J., Jr. (1982).   Twins—Nature's twice told tale. In *1983 Yearbook of science and the future.* Chicago: Encyclopaedia Britannica. (p. 336)

Bouchard, T. J., Jr. (1984). Twins reared together and apart: What they tell us about human diversity. In S. W. Fox (Ed.), *Individuality and determinism.* New York: Plenum Press. (p. 83)

Bouchard, T. J., Jr., & McGue, M. (1981).   Familial studies of intelligence: A review. *Science, 212,* 1055–1059. (p. 337)

Bouchard, T. J., Jr., & Segal, N. L. (1988).   Heredity, environment, and IQ. In *Instructor's Resource Manual* to accompany G. Lindzey, R. Thompson, & B. Spring, *Psychology* (3rd ed.).   New York: Worth Publishers. (p. 336)

Bower, G. H. (1981, June). Mood and memory. *Psychology Today,* pp. 60–69. (p. 271)

Bower, G. H. (1983).   Affect and cognition. *Philosophical Transaction: Royal Society of London, Series B, 302,* 387–402. (p. 271)

Bower, G. H. (1986).   Prime time in cognitive psychology. In P. Eelen (Ed.), *Cognitive research and behavior therapy: Beyond the conditioning paradigm.* Amsterdam: North Holland Publishers. (p. 270)

Bower, G. H. (1987).   Commentary on mood and memory. *Behaviour Research and Therapy, 25,* 443–455. (p. 271)

Bower, G. H., & Clark, M. C. (1969).   Narrative stories as mediators for serial learning. *Psychonomic Science, 14,* 181–182. (p. 263)

Bower, G. H., Clark, M. C., Lesgold, A. M., & Winzenz, D. (1969).   Hierarchical retrieval schemes in recall of categorized word lists. *Journal of Verbal Learning and Verbal Behavior, 8,* 323–343. (p. 265)

Bower, T. G. R. (1977).   *A primer of infant development.* San Francisco: Freeman. (p. 62)

Bowers, K. S. (1983).   *Hypnosis for the seriously curious.* New York: Norton. (p. 13)

Bowers, K. S. (1984).   Hypnosis. In N. Endler & J. M. Hunt (Eds.), *Personality and behavioral disorders* (2nd ed.). New York: Wiley. (pp. 207, 210)

Bowers, K. S. (1987, July).   Personal correspondence. (p. 208)

Bowers, K. S. (1989, in press).   Unconscious influences and hypnosis. In J. E. Singer (Ed.), Repression: Defense mechanism and personality style. Chicago: University of Chicago Press. (p. 213)

Bowers, K. S., & LeBaron, S. (1986).   Hypnosis and hypnotizability: Implications for clinical intervention. *Hospital and Community Psychiatry, 37,* 457–467. (p. 211)

Bowers, P. G., & Bowers, K. S. (1979).   Hypnosis and creativity: A theoretical and empirical rapprochement. In E. Fromm & R. E. Shor (Eds.), *Hypnosis: Developments in research and new perspectives.* New York: Aldine. (p. 208)

Bowers, T. G., & Clum, G. A. (1988).   Relative contribution of specific and nonspecific treatment effects: Meta-analysis of placebo-controlled behavior therapy research. *Psychological Bulletin, 103,* 315–323, (p. 495)

Bowlby, J. (1973).   *Separation: Anxiety and anger.* New York: Basic Books. (p. 76)

Boynton, R. M. (1979).   *Human color vision.* New York: Holt, Rinehart and Winston. (p. 152)

Bradburn, N. M., Rips, L. J., & Shevell, S. K. (1987).   Answering autobiographical questions: The impact of memory and inference on surveys. *Science, 236,* 157–161. (p. 273)

Bradley, D. R., Dumais, S. T., & Petry, H. M. (1976).   Reply to Cavonius. *Nature, 261,* 78. (p. 171)

Bradley-Johnson, S., Johnson, C. M., Shanahan, R. H., Rickert, V. L., & Tardona, D. R. (1984).   Effects of token reinforcement on WISC-R performance of black and white, low-socioeconomic second graders. *Behavioral Assessment, 6,* 365–373. (p. 341)

Braito, R., Dean, D., Powers, E., & Bruton, B. (1981). The inferiority games: Perceptions and behavior. *Sex Roles, 7,* 65–72. (p. 124)

Bransford, J. D., & Johnson, M. K. (1972).   Contextual prerequisites for understanding: Some investigations of comprehension and recall. *Journal of Verbal Learning and Verbal Behavior, 11,* 717–726. (p. 262)

Bransford, J., Sherwood, R., Vye, N., & Rieser, J. (1986). Teaching thinking and problem solving. *American Psychologist, 41,* 1078–1089. (p. 285)

Braskamp, L. A. (1987). Spectrum: Utility for educational selection and organizational development. Paper presented at the American Psychological Association convention. (p. 377)

Bray, D. W. (1982). The assessment center and the study of lives. *American Psychologist, 37,* 180–189. (p. 435)

Bray, G. A. (1969). Effect of caloric restriction on energy expenditure in obese patients. *Lancet, 2,* 397–398. (p. 536)

Brehm, S., & Brehm, J. W. (1981). *Psychological reactance: A theory of freedom and control.* New York: Academic Press. (p. 557)

Breland, K., & Breland, M. (1961). The misbehavior of organisms. *American Psychologist, 16,* 661–664. (p. 249)

Brewer, W. F. (1977). Memory for the pragmatic implications of sentences. *Memory & Cognition, 5,* 673–678. (p. 261)

Brickman, P., Coates, D., & Janoff-Bulman, R. J. (1978). Lottery winners and accident victims: Is happiness relative? *Journal of Personality and Social Psychology, 36,* 917–927. (p. 393)

Broadbent, D. E. (1978). The current state of noise research: Reply to Poulton. *Psychological Bulletin, 85,* 1052–1067. (p. 157)

Brockner, J., & Hulton, A. J. B. (1978). How to reverse the vicious cycle of low self-esteem: The importance of attentional focus. *Journal of Experimental Social Psychology, 14,* 564–578. (p. 429)

Bronstein-Burrows, P. (1981). *Introductory psychology: A course in the psychology of both sexes.* Paper presented at the meeting of the American Psychological Association. (p. 598)

Brooks-Gunn, J. (1986). Pubertal processes and girls' psychological adaptation. In R. M. Lerner & T. T. Foch (eds.), *Biological-psychosocial interactions in early adolescence: A life-span perspective.* Hillsdale, NJ: Erlbaum. (p. 91)

Brooks-Gunn, J., & Ruble, D. N. (1986). Men's and women's attitudes and beliefs about the menstrual cycle. *Sex Roles, 14,* 287–299. (p. 527)

Brown, E. L., & Deffenbacher, K. (1979). *Perception and the senses.* New York: Oxford University Press. (p. 156)

Brown, J. D. (1986). Evaluations of self and others: Self-enhancement biases in social judgments. *Social Cognition, 4,* 353–376. (p. 432)

Brown, J. D., & Taylor, S. E. (1986). Affect and the processing of personal information: Evidence for mood-activated self-schemata. *Journal of Experimental Social Psychology, 22,* 436–452. (p. 271)

Brown, R. (1965). *Social psychology.* New York: Free Press. (pp. 92, 390)

Brown, R. (1986). Linguistic relativity. In S. H. Hulse and B. F. Green, Jr. (Eds.), *One hundred years of psychological research in America.* Baltimore: Johns Hopkins University Press. (p. 309)

Brown, R., & Kulik, J. (1982). Flashbulb memories. In U. Neisser (Ed.), *Memory observed.* San Francisco: Freeman. (p. 256)

Browne, A., & Finkelhor, D. (1986). Impact of child sexual abuse: A review of the research. *Psychological Bulletin, 99,* 66–77. (p. 75)

Brownell, K. D., Greenwood, M. R. C., Stellar, E., & Shrager, E. E. (1986). The effects of repeated cycles of weight loss and regain in rats. *Physiology and Behavior, 38,* 459–464. (p. 540)

Brownmiller, S. (1975). *Against our will: Men, women, and rape.* New York: Simon and Schuster. (p. 582)

Bruner, J. S., & Potter, M. C. (1964). Interference in visual recognition. *Science, 144,* 424–425. (p. 183)

Bugelski, B. R., Kidd, E., & Segmen, J. (1968). Image as a mediator in one-trial paired-associate learning. *Journal of Experimental Psychology, 76,* 69–73. (p. 263)

Bugental, D. B. (1986). Unmasking the ''polite smile'': Situational and personal determinants of managed affect in adult-child interaction. *Personality and Social Psychology Bulletin, 12,* 7–16. (p. 388)

Bulletin of the Atomic Scientists (1988, January/February). U.S. and Soviet strategic nuclear forces, end of 1987, 56. (p. 263)

Bulletin of the Atomic Scientists (1988, April). Nuclear pursuits, 60. (p. 601)

Bureau of the Census (1987). *Statistical abstract of the U.S.* Washington, DC: Superintendent of Documents, U.S. Government Printing Office. (pp. 107, 443, 457)

Burger, J. M. (1987). Increased performance with increased personal control: A self-presentation interpretation. *Journal of Experimental Social Psychology, 23,* 350–360. (p. 376)

Buri, J. R., Louiselle, P. A., Misukanis, T. M., & Mueller, R. A. (1988). Effects of parental authoritarianism and authoritativeness on self-esteem. *Personality and Social Psychology Bulletin, 14,* 271–282. (p. 78)

Burish, T. G., & Carey, M. P. (1986). Conditioned aversive responses in cancer chemotherapy patients: Theoretical and developmental analysis. *Journal of Counseling and Clinical Psychology, 54,* 593–600. (p. 237)

Burns, D. D. (1980). *Feeling good: The new mood therapy.* New York: Signet. (p. 460)

Butler, R. A. (1954, February). Curiosity in monkeys. *Scientific American,* pp. 70–75. (p. 351)

Byrne, D. (1971). *The attraction paradigm.* New York: Academic Press. (p. 599)

Byrne, D. (1982). Predicting human sexual behavior. In A. G. Kraut, *The G. Stanley Hall Lecture Series* (Vol. 2). Washington, DC: American Psychological Association. (pp. 363–364, 368)

Cacioppo, J. T., Martzke, J. S., Petty, R. E., & Tassinary, L. G. (1988). Specific forms of facial EMG response index emotions during an interview: From Darwin to the continuous flow hypothesis of affect-laden information processing. *Journal of Personality and Social Psychology, 54,* 592–604. (p. 387)

Cameron, P., & Biber, H. (1973). Sexual thought throughout the life-span. *Gerontologist, 13,* 144–147. (p. 195)

Campbell, A. (1981). *The sense of well-being in America*. New York: McGraw-Hill. (p. 109)

Campbell, B. A., & Coulter, X. (1976). The ontogenesis of learning and memory. In M. R. Rosenzweig & E. L. Bennet (Eds.), *Neural mechanisms of learning and memory*, pp. 209–235. Cambridge, MA: MIT Press. (p. 63)

Campbell, D. T. (1975). On the conflicts between biological and social evolution and between psychology and moral tradition. *American Psychologist, 30*, 1103–1126. (p. 395)

Campbell, D. T., & Specht, J. C. (1985). Altruism: Biology, culture, and religion. *Journal of Social and Clinical Psychology. 3*(1), 33–42. (p. 427)

Campbell, S. (1986). *The Loch Ness Monster: The evidence*. Willingborough, Northamptonshire, U.K.: Acquarian Press. (p. 183)

Candee, D., & Kohlberg, L. (1987). Moral judgment and moral action: A reanalysis of Haan, Smith, and Block's (1968) Free Speech Movement data. *Journal of Personality and Social Psychology, 52*, 554–564. (p. 93)

Cannon, W. B. (1929). *Bodily changes in pain, hunger, fear, and rage*. New York: Branford. (p. 508)

Cannon, W. B., & Washburn, A. (1912). An explanation of hunger. *American Journal of Physiology, 29*, 441–454. (p. 354)

Cantor, N., & Kihlstrom, J. F. (1987). *Personality and social intelligence*. Englewood Cliffs, NJ: Prentice-Hall. (p. 330)

Cantril, H., & Bumstead, C. H. (1960). *Reflections on the human venture*. New York: New York University Press. (p. 571)

Caplan, N., Whitemore, J., Bui, Q., & Traupmann, M. (1985). *Scholastic achievement among the children of Southeast Asian refugees*. Ann Arbor: University of Michigan, Institute for Social Research. (p. 341)

Caplan, R. D., Abbey, A., Abramis, D. J., Andrews, F. M., Conway, T. L., & French, J. R. P., Jr. (1984). *Tranquillizer use and well-being: A longitudinal study of social and psychological effects*. Ann Arbor: Institute for Social Research, University of Michigan. (p. 500)

Carducci, B. J., Cosby, P. C., & Ward, C. D. (1978). Sexual arousal and interpersonal evaluations. *Journal of Experimental Social Psychology, 14*, 449–457. (p. 599)

Carlson, M., Charlin, V., & Miller, N. (1988). Positive mood and helping behavior: A test of six hypotheses. *Journal of Personality and Social Psychology, 55*, 211–229. (p. 587)

Carlson, R. (1984). What's social about social psychology? Where's the person in personality research? *Journal of Personality and Social Psychology, 47*, 1304–1309. (p. 437)

Carlson, S. (1985). A double-blind test of astrology. *Nature, 318*, 419–425. (p. 437)

Carr, T. H., Kontowicz, A., & Dagenbach, D. (1987). Subthreshold priming and the cognitive unconscious. Invited paper presented to the Midwestern Psychological Association convention. (p. 142)

Carroll, J. B. (1982). The measurement of intelligence. In R. J. Sternberg (Ed.), *Handbook of human intelligence*. New York: Cambridge University Press. (p. 324)

Carson, R. C., Butcher, J. N., & Coleman, J. C. (1988). *Abnormal psychology and modern life* (8th ed.). Glenview, IL: Scott, Foresman. (p. 447)

Cartwright, R. D. (1978). *A primer on sleep and dreaming*. Reading, MA: Addison-Wesley. (p. 199)

Cash, T., & Janda, L. H. (1984, December). The eye of the beholder. *Psychology Today*, pp. 46–52. (p. 597)

Caspi, A., Elder, Jr., G. H., & Bem, D. J. (1987). Moving against the world: Life-course patterns of explosive children. *Developmental Psychology, 23*, 308–313. (p. 113)

Cataldo, M. F., & Coates, T. J. (1986). *Health and industry: A behavioral medicine perspective*. New York: Wiley. (p. 530)

Cattell, R. B. (1973, July). Personality pinned down. *Psychology Today*, pp. 40–46. (p. 421)

Ceci, S. J., & Liker, J. K. (1986). A day at the races: A study of IQ, expertise, and cognitive complexity. *Journal of Experimental Psychology: General, 115*, 255–266. (pp. 299, 330)

Centers for Disease Control (1983). Behavioral risk factor prevalence surveys—United States. Reported in *Behavior Today Newsletter*, October 29, 1984, p. 7. (p. 216)

Centers for Disease Control (1987). *Smoking, tobacco, and health: A fact book*. Washington, D.C.: U.S. Government Printing Office. (p. 530)

Centers for Disease Control Vietnam Experience Study (1988). Health status of Vietnam veterans. *Journal of the American Medical Association, 259*, 2701–2709. (p. 525)

Center for Education Statistics (1987). *The condition of education*. Washington, DC: U.S. Department of Education. (For sale by Superintendent of Documents, U.S. Government Printing Office.) (p. 102)

Cerella, J. (1985). Information processing rates in the elderly. *Psychological Bulletin, 98*, 67–83. (p. 104)

Chagnon, N. A. (1988). Life histories, blood revenge, and warfare in a tribal population. *Science, 239*, 985–992. (p. 576)

Charny, I. W. (1982). *How can we commit the unthinkable? Genocide: The human cancer*. Boulder, CO: Westview Press. (p. 557)

Chase, M. H., & Morales, F. R. (1983). Subthreshold excitatory activity and motoneuron discharge during REM periods of active sleep. *Science, 221*, 1195–1198. (p. 200)

Chase, W. G., & Simon, H. A. (1973). Perception in chess. *Cognitive Psychology, 4*, 55–81. (p. 263)

Chassin, L., Presson, C. C., Sherman, S. J., & McGrew, J. (1987). The changing smoking environment for middle and high school students: 1980–1983. *Journal of Behavioral Medicine, 10*, 581–593. (p. 531)

Chesney, M. A. (1984). *Behavioral factors in coronary heart disease separating benign from malignant*. Paper presented at the meeting of the American Psychological Association. (p. 514)

Chi, M. T. H. (1976). Short-term memory limitations in children: Capacity or processing deficits. *Memory & Cognition, 4*, 559–572. (p. 266)

Chomsky, N. (1959). Review of B. F. Skinner's *Verbal behavior. Language, 35*, 26–58. (p. 304)

Chomsky, N. (1972). *Language and mind.* New York: Harcourt Brace Jovanovich. (p. 301)

Chomsky, N. (1987). Language in a psychological setting. Sophia Linguistic Working Papers in Linguistics, No. 22, Sophia University, Tokyo. (p. 304)

Chugani, H. T., & Phelps, M. E. (1986). Maturational changes in cerebral function in infants determined by ^{18}FDG Positron Emission Tomography. *Science, 231,* 840–843. (p. 65)

Cialdini, R. B., & Carpenter, K. (1981). The availability heuristic: Does imagining make it so? In P. H. Reingen & A. G. Woodside (Eds.), *Buyer-seller interactions: Empirical issues and normative issues.* Chicago: American Marketing Association. (p. 292)

Cialdini, R. B., & Richardson, K. D. (1980). Two indirect tactics of image management: Basking and blasting. *Journal of Personality and Social Psychology, 39,* 406–415. (p. 593)

Clark, M., & Gelman, D. (1987, January 12). A user's guide to hormones. *Newsweek,* pp. 50–59. (p. 31)

Cleminshaw, H. K.; Zarski, J. J.; Heckroth, J.; & Newman, I. (March 1988). Educated women adapting to social change. Paper presented at the Annual Conference of the American Orthopsychiatric Association. (p. 125)

Cohen, I. B. (1984, March). Florence Nightingale. *Scientific American,* pp. 128–137. (p. 612)

Cohen, L. A. (1987, November). Diet and cancer. *Scientific American,* pp. 42–48. (pp. 533–534)

Cohen, S. (1988). Psychosocial models of the role of social support in the etiology of physical disease. *Health Psychology,* Vol. 7 269–297. (p. 524)

Cohen, S., Evans, G. W., Stokols, D., & Krantz, D. S. (1986). *Behavior, health, and environmental stress.* New York: Plenum. (p. 157)

Cohen, W. S. (1985). Health promotion in the workplace: A prescription for good health. *American Psychologist, 40,* 213–216. (p. 530)

Coile, D. C., & Miller, N. E. (1984). How radical animal activists try to mislead humane people. *American Psychologist, 39,* 700–701. (p. 18)

Coleman, J. C. (1980). *The nature of adolescence.* London: Methuen. (p. 90)

Coleman, P. D., & Flood, D. G. (1986). Dendritic proliferation in the aging brain as a compensatory repair mechanism. In D. F. Swaab, E. Fliers, M. Mirmiram, W. A. Van Gool, & F. Van Haaren (Eds.), *Progress in brain research* (Vol. 20). New York: Elsevier. (p. 101)

College Board (1987). 1987 profile of SAT and achievement test takers. Princeton, NJ: Educational Testing Service. (p. 341)

Collins, B. E. (1986). Towing a fragment of abnormal behavior into the mainstream of social psychology: Hyperactivity. *Journal of Social and Clinical Psychology, 4,* 488–496. (p. 285)

Collins, R. C. (1983, Summer). Head start: An update on program effects. *Newsletter, Society for Research in Child Development,* pp. 1–2. (p. 339)

Colombo, J. (1982). The critical period concept: Research,

methodology, and theoretical issues. *Psychological Bulletin, 91,* 260–275. (p. 72)

Condry, J., & Condry, S. (1976). Sex differences: A study in the eye of the beholder. *Child Development, 47,* 812–819. (p. 129)

Conley, J. J. (1984). The hierarchy of consistency: A review and model of longitudinal findings on adult individual differences in intelligence, personality, and self opinion. *Personality and Individual Differences, 5,* 11–26. (p. 113)

Conley, J. J. (1985). Longitudinal stability of personality traits: A multitrait-multimethod-multioccasion analysis. *Journal of Personality and Social Psychology, 49,* 1266–1282. (p. 113)

Converse, P. E., & Traugott, M. W. (1986). Assessing the accuracy of polls and surveys. *Science, 234,* 1094–1098. (p. 11)

Conway, M., & Ross, M. (1984). Getting what you want by revising what you had. *Journal of Personality and Social Psychology, 47,* 738–748. (p. 278)

Cook, E. W., III, Hodes, R. L., & Lang, P. J. (1986). Preparedness and phobia: Effects of stimulus content on human visceral conditioning. *Journal of Abnormal Psychology, 95,* 195–207. (p. 238)

Cook, S. W. (1984). The 1954 social science statement and school desegregation—A reply to Gerard. *American Psychologist, 39,* 819–832. (p. 341)

Cooper, W. H. (1983). An achievement motivation nomological network. *Journal of Personality and Social Psychology, 44,* 841–861. (p. 372)

Coopersmith, S. (1967). *The antecedents of self-esteem.* San Francisco: Freeman. (p. 78)

Cornell, G. W. (1987, October 24). Churches concerned about unwed births. Associated Press release. (p. 360)

Costa, P. T., Jr., & McCrae, R. R. (1980). Still stable after all these years: Personality as a key to some issues in adulthood and old age. In P. B. Baltes & O. Brim, Jr. (Eds.), *Life-span development and behavior* (Vol. 3). New York: Academic Press. (p. 106)

Costa, P. T., Jr., & McCrae, R. R. (1985). Hypochondriasis, neuroticism, and aging: When are somatic complaints unfounded? *American Psychologist, 40,* 19–28. (p. 527)

Costa, P. T., Jr., Zonderman, A. B., McCrae, R. R., Cornoni-Huntley, J., Locke, B. Z., & Barbano, H. E. (1987). Longitudinal analyses of psychological well-being in a national sample: Stability of mean levels. *Journal of Gerontology, 42,* 50–55. (p. 110)

Cotman, C. W., & Nieto-Sampedro, M. (1982). Brain function, synapse renewal, and plasticity. *Annual Review of Psychology, 33,* 371–401. (p. 49)

Court, J. H. (1984). Sex and violence: A ripple effect. In N. M. Malamuth & E. Donnerstein (Eds.), *Pornography and sexual aggression.* Orlando, FL: Academic Press. (p. 581)

Covington, M. V., & Omelich, C. L. (1988). I can resist anything but temptation: Adolescent expectations for smoking cigarettes. *Journal of Applied Social Psychology, 18,* 203–227. (p. 531)

Cowart, B. J. (1981). Development of taste perception in

humans: Sensitivity and preference throughout the life span. *Psychological Bulletin, 90,* 43–73. (p. 160)

Cowley, G. (1988, May 23).   The wisdom of animals. *Newsweek,* pp. 52–60. (p. 306)

Cox, T. (1978) *Stress.* London: Macmillan. (p. 510)

Craik, F. I. M. (1977).   Age differences in human memory. In J. E. Birren & K. W. Schaie (Eds.), *Handbook of the psychology of aging.* New York: Van Nostrand Reinhold. (p. 102)

Craik, F. I. M., & Tulving, E. (1975).   Depth of processing and the retention of words in episodic memory. *Journal of Experimental Psychology: General, 104,* 268–294. (pp. 261–262)

Craik, F. I. M., & Watkins, M. J. (1973).   The role of rehearsal in short-term memory. *Journal of Verbal Learning and Verbal Behavior, 12,* 599–607. (p. 261)

Crandall, J. E. (1984).   Social interest as a moderator of life stress. *Journal of Personality and Social Psychology, 47,* 164–174. (p. 427)

Creed, T. L. (1987).   Subliminal deception: Pseudoscience on the college lecture circuit. *Skeptical Inquirer, 11,* 358–366. (p. 142)

Critchlow, B. (1986).   The powers of John Barleycorn: Beliefs about the effects of alcohol on social behavior. *American Psychologist, 41,* 751–764. (p. 216)

Crocker, J., & Schwartz, I. (1985).   Effects of self-esteem on prejudice and ingroup favoritism in a minimal intergroup situation. *Personality and Social Psychology Bulletin, 11*(4). (p. 430)

Crocker, J., Thompson, L. L., McGraw, K. M., & Ingerman, C. (1987).   Downward comparison, prejudice, and evaluation of others: Effects of self-esteem and threat. *Journal of Personality and Social Psychology, 52,* 907–916. (p. 593)

Crombie, A. C. (1964, May).   Early concepts of the senses and the mind. *Scientific American,* pp. 108–116. (p. 147)

Croyle, R. T., & Cooper, J. (1983).   Dissonance arousal: Physiological evidence. *Journal of Personality and Social Psychology, 45,* 782–791. (p. 561)

Csikszentmihalyi, M. (1985).   Reflections on enjoyment. *Perspectives in Biology and Medicine, 28,* 489–497. (p. 375)

Csikszentmihalyi, M., & Larson, R. (1984).   *Being adolescent: Conflict and growth in the teenage years.* New York: Basic Books. (p. 110)

Cunningham, S. (1983, November).   Not such a long way, baby: Women and cigarette ads. *APA Monitor,* p. 15. (p. 563)

Curtis, R. C., & Miller, K. (1986).   Believing another likes or dislikes you: Behaviors making the beliefs come true. *Journal of Personality and Social Psychology, 51,* 284–290. (p. 599)

Curtiss, S. (1977).   *Genie: A psycholinguistic study of a modern-day "wild child."* New York: Academic Press. (p. 305)

Curtiss, S. (1981).   Dissociations between language and cognition: Cases and implications. *Journal of Autism and Developmental Disorders, 11,* 15–30. (p. 305)

Cutrona, C. E. (1986).   Behavioral manifestations of social support: A microanalytic investigation. *Journal of Personality and Social Psychology, 51,* 201–208. (p. 254)

Czeisler, C. A., Allan, J. S., Strogatz, S. H., Ronda, J. M.,

Sanchez, R., Rios, C. D., Freitag, W. O., Richardson, G. S., & Kronauer, R. E. (1986).   Bright light resets the human circadian pacemaker independent of the timing of the sleep-wake cycle. *Science, 233,* 667–671. (p. 197)

Dabbs, J. M., Jr., Frady, R. L., Carr, T. S., & Besch, N. F. (1987).   Saliva testosterone and criminal violence in young adult prison inmates. *Psychosomatic Medicine, 49,* 174–182. (p. 577)

Dabbs, J. M., Jr., Ruback, R. B., & Besch, N. F. (1987).   Male saliva testosterone following conversations with male and female partners. Paper presented at the American Psychological Association convention. (p. 363)

Damon, W., & Hart, D. (1982).   The development of self-understanding from infancy through adolescence. *Child Development, 53,* 841–864. (pp. 77–78)

Darley, J. (1983).   *Self-esteem and social comparison.* Paper presented to the meeting of the Society for Experimental Social Psychology. (p. 430)

Darley, J. M., & Latané, B. (1968a).   Bystander intervention in emergencies: Diffusion of responsibility. *Journal of Personality and Social Psychology, 8,* 377–383. (p. 586)

Darley, J. M., & Latané, B. (1968b, December).   When will people help in a crisis? *Psychology Today,* pp. 54–57, 70–71. (pp. 585, 586)

Darley, J. M., Seligman, C., & Becker, L. J. (1979, April).   The lesson of twin rivers: Feedback works. *Psychology Today,* pp. 16, 23–24. (p. 247)

Darrach, B., & Norris, J. (1984, August).   An American tragedy. *Life,* pp. 58–74. (p. 469)

Dawes, R. M. (1980).   Social dilemmas. *Annual Review of Psychology, 31,* 169–193. (p. 603)

Day, R. H. (1984).   The nature of perceptual illusions. *Interdisciplinary Science Reviews, 9,* 47–58. (p. 179)

Deaux, K., & Major, B. (1987).   Putting gender into context: An interactive model of gender-related behavior. *Psychological Review, 94,* 369–389. (p. 124)

Deci, E. L. (1980).   *The psychology of self-determination.* Lexington, MA: Lexington Books. (p. 248)

Deci, E. L. (1984, April 4).   Personal communication. (p. 248)

Deci, E. L., & Ryan, R. M. (1985).   *Intrinsic motivation and self-determination in human behavior.* New York: Plenum Press. (p. 375)

Deci, E. L., & Ryan, R. M. (1987).   The support of autonomy and the control of behavior. *Journal of Personality and Social Psychology, 53,* 1024–1037. (p. 374)

de Jong-Gierveld, J. (1987).   Developing and testing a model of loneliness. *Journal of Personality and Social Psychology, 53,* 119–128. (p. 462)

Delgado, J. M. R. (1969).   *Physical control of the mind: Toward a psychocivilized society.* New York: Harper & Row. (p. 40)

DeLoache, J. S. (1987).   Rapid change in the symbolic functioning of very young children. *Science, 238,* 1556–1557. (p. 68)

Dement, W. C. (1978). *Some must watch while some must sleep.* New York: Norton. (pp. 200, 201)

Dement, W. C., & Wolpert, E. A. (1958). The relation of eye movements, body mobility, and external stimuli to dream content. *Journal of Experimental Psychology, 55,* 543–553. (p. 203)

Dennett, M. R. (1985, Fall). Firewalking: reality or illusion? *Skeptical Inquirer, 10,* 36–40. (p. 160)

Denney, N. W. (1982). Aging and cognitive changes. In B. B. Wolman (Ed.), *Handbook of developmental psychology.* Englewood Cliffs, NJ: Prentice-Hall. (p. 104)

Dennis, W. (1940). Does culture appreciably affect patterns of infant behavior? *Journal of Social Psychology, 12,* 305–317. (p. 64)

De Pree, M. (1987). *Leadership is an art.* East Lansing, MI: Michigan State University Press. (p. 376)

Depue, R. A., & Monroe, S. M. (1986). Conceptualization and measurement of human disorder in life stress research: The problem of chronic disturbance. *Psychological Bulletin, 99,* 36–51. (p. 512)

Dermer, M., Cohen, S. J., Jacobsen, E., & Anderson, E. A. (1979). Evaluative judgments of aspects of life as a function of vicarious exposure to hedonic extremes. *Journal of Personality and Social Psychology, 37,* 247–260. (p. 398)

Dermer, M., & Pyszczynski, T. A. (1978). Effects of erotica upon men's loving and liking responses for women they love. *Journal of Personality and Social Psychology, 36,* 1302–1309. (p. 599)

Derogatis, L. R., Abeloff, M., & Melasaratos, N. (1979). Psychological coping mechanisms and survival time in metastatic breast cancer. *Journal of the American Medical Association, 242,* 1504–1508. (p. 518)

DerSimonian, R., & Laird, N. M. (1983). Evaluating the effect of coaching on SAT socres: A meta-analysis. *Harvard Educational Review, 53,* 1–15. (p. 326)

Desmond, E. W. (1987, November 30). Out in the open. *Time,* pp. 80–90. (p. 530)

Deutsch, J. A. (1972, July). Brain reward: ESP and ecstasy. *Psychology Today,* pp. 46–48. (p. 39)

Deutsch, M. (1986). The malignant (spiral) process of hostile interaction. In R. K. White (Ed.), *Psychology and the prevention of nuclear war: A book of readings.* New York: New York University Press. (p. 602)

DeValois, R. L., & DeValois, K. K. (1975). Neural coding of color. In E. C. Carterette & M. P. Friedman (Eds.), *Handbook of perception: Vol. V. Seeing.* New York: Academic Press. (p. 153)

DeValois, R. L., & DeValois, K. K. (1980). Spatial vision. *Annual Review of Psychology, 31,* 309–341. (p. 153)

Dew, M. A., Bromet, E. J., Brent, D., & Greenhouse, J. B. (1987). A quantitative literature review of the effectiveness of suicide prevention centers. *Journal of Consulting and Clinical Psychology, 55,* 239–244. (p. 493)

Diamond, J. (1986). Variation in human testis size. *Nature 320,* 488–489. (pp. 60, 81)

Diamond, M. C. (1978) The aging brain: Some enlightenment and optimistic results. *American Scientist, 66,* 66–71. (p. 63)

Dickie, J. R. (1987). Interrelationships within the mother-father-infant triad. In P. W. Berman & F. A. Pedersen (Eds.), *Men's transitions to parenthood: Longitudinal studies of early family experience.* Hillsdale, NJ: Erlbaum. (p. 73)

Dickson, D. (1986). EEC to cut animal use. *Science, 234,* 1494. (p. 18)

Diener, E. (1984). Subjective well-being. *Psychological Bulletin, 95,* 542–575. (pp. 398–399)

Diener, E., Emmons, R. A., & Sandvik, E. (1986). The dual nature of happiness: Independence of positive and negative moods. Unpublished manuscript, University of Illinois. (p. 110)

Diener, E., Sandvik, E., & Larsen, R. J. (1985). Age and sex effects for emotional intensity. *Developmental Psychology, 21,* 542–546. (p. 131)

Dietz, W. H., Jr., & Gortmaker, S. L. (1985). Do we fatten our children at the television set? Obesity and television viewing in children and adolescents. *Pediatrics, 75,* 807–812. (p. 538)

Digman, J. M., & Inouye, J. (1986). Further specification of the five robust factors of personality. *Journal of Personality and Social Psychology, 50,* 116–123. (p. 421)

DiMatteo, M. R., & DiNicola, D. D. (1982). *Achieving patient compliance: The psychology of the medical practitioner's role.* New York: Pergamon Press. (p. 529)

DiMatteo, M. R., & Friedman, H. S. (1982). *Social psychology and medicine.* Cambridge, MA: Oelgeschlager, Gunn, & Hain. (pp. 526, 529)

Dion, K. K. (1986). Stereotyping based on physical attractiveness: Issues and conceptual perspectives. In C. P. Herman, M. P. Zanna, & E. T. Higgins (Eds.), *Physical appearance, stigma, and social behavior: The Ontario symposium on personality and social psychology* (Vol. 3). Hillsdale, NJ: Erlbaum. (p. 596)

Dixon, B. (1986, April). Dangerous thoughts: How we think and feel can make us sick. *Science 86,* pp. 63–66. (p. 518)

Doerner, W. R. (1985, July 8). To America with skills. *Time,* pp. 42, 44. (p. 339)

Dohrenwend, B., Pearlin, L., Clayton, P., Hamburg, B., Dohrenwend, B. P., Riley, M., & Rose, R. (1982). Report on stress and life events. In G. R. Elliott & C. Eisdorfer (Eds.), *Stress and human health: Analysis and implications of research* (A study by the Institute of Medicine/National Academy of Sciences). New York: Springer. (p. 511)

Dohrenwend, B. P., Levav, I., Shrout, P. E., Link, B. G., Skodol, A. E., & Martin, J. L. (1987). Life stress and psychopathology: Progress on research begun with Barbara Snell Dohrenwend. *American Journal of Community Psychology,* Vol. 15, 677–715. (p. 461)

Dolezal, H. (1982). *Living in a world transformed.* New York: Academic Press. (p. 182)

Domjan, M. (1987). Animal learning comes of age. *American Psychologist, 42,* 556–564. (p. 235)

Donaldson, M. (1979, March). The mismatch between

school and children's minds. *Human Nature*, pp. 60–67. (p. 70)

Donnelly, F. K. (1983, Spring). *People's Almanac* predictions: Retrospective check of accuracy. *Skeptical Inquirer*, pp. 48–52. (p. 187)

Donnerstein, E., & Linz, D. (1984, January). Sexual violence in the media: A warning. *Psychology Today*, pp. 14–15. (p. 581)

Donnerstein, E., & Linz, D. (1986). Techniques designed to mitigate the impact of mass media sexual violence on adolescents and adults. Background paper for *The Surgeon General's workshop on pornography and public health*, June 22–24. Report prepared by E. P. Mulvey & J. L. Haugaard and released by Office of the Surgeon General on August 4, 1986. (p. 584)

Donnerstein, E., Linz, D., & Penrod, S. (1987). *The question of pornography*. New York: Free Press. (p. 580)

Dorsey, G. (1987, February 8). The love doctor. *Hartford Courant/Northeast*, pp. 12–21, 33–35. (p. 331)

Doty, R. L., Shaman, P., Applebaum, S. L., Giberson, R., Siksorski, L., & Rosenberg, L. (1984). Smell identification ability: Changes with age. *Science, 226*, 1441–1443. (p. 100)

Dovidio, J. F., & Gaertner, S. L. (Eds.) (1986). *Prejudice, discrimination and racism: Theory and research*. Orlando, FL: Academic Press. (p. 591)

Drucker, P. F. (1982, December). A conversation with Peter F. Drucker. *Psychology Today*, pp. 60–67. (p. 419)

Druckman, D., & Swets, J. A. (Eds.) (1988). *Enhancing human performance: Issues, theories, and techniques*. Washington, D.C.: National Academy Press. (pp. 188, 310)

Duggan, J. P., & Booth, D. A. (1986). Obesity, overeating, and rapid gastric emptying in rats with ventromedial hypothalamic lesions. *Science, 231*, 609–611. (p. 356)

Duncan, B. L. (1976). Differential social perception and attribution of intergroup violence: Testing the lower limits of stereotyping of blacks. *Journal of Personality and Social Psychology, 34*, 590–598. (p. 590)

Duncan, G. J., Hill, M. S., & Hoffman, S. D. (1988). Welfare dependence within and across generations. *Science, 239*, 467–471. (p. 293)

Duncker, K. (1945). On problem solving. *Psychological Monographs, 58* (Whole no. 270). (pp. 289, 291)

Dush, D. M., Hirt, M. L., & Schroeder, H. (1983). Self-statement modification with adults: A meta-analysis. *Psychological Bulletin, 94*, 408–422. (p. 490)

Dutton, D. G., & Aron, A. P. (1974). Some evidence for heightened sexual attraction under conditions of high anxiety. *Journal of Personality and Social Psychology, 30*, 510–517. (p. 599)

Dweck, C. S., & Elliott, E. S. (1983). Achievement motivation. In P. Mussen & E. M. Hetherington (Eds.), *Handbook of child psychology* (Vol. IV). New York: Wiley. (p. 372)

Dywan, J., & Bowers, K. (1983). The use of hypnosis to enhance recall. *Science, 222*, 184–185. (p. 208)

Eagly, A. H. (1986). Some meta-analytic approaches to examining the validity of gender-difference research. In J. S.

Hyde & M. C. Linn (Eds.), *The psychology of gender: Advances through meta-analysis*. Baltimore: John Hopkins University Press. (p. 129)

Eagly, A. H. (1987). *Sex differences in social behavior: A social-role interpretation*. Hillsdale, NJ: Erlbaum. (p. 130)

Eagly, A. H., & Crowley, M. (1986). Gender and helping behavior: A meta-analytic review of the social psychological literature. *Psychological Bulletin, 100*, 283–308. (p. 587)

Eaton, W. O., & Enns, L. R. (1986). Sex differences in human motor activity level. *Psychological Bulletin, 100*, 19–28. (p. 133)

Ebbesen, E. B., Duncan, B., & Konecni, V. J. (1975). Effects of content of verbal aggression on future verbal aggression: A field experiment. *Journal of Experimental Social Psychology, 11*, 192–204. (p. 392)

Ebbinghaus, H. (1885). *Über das Gedachtnis*. Leipzig: Duncker & Humblot. Cited in R. Klatzky (1980), *Human memory: Structures and processes*. San Francisco: Freeman. (p. 275)

Eccles, J. S. (1987a). Gender roles and achievement patterns: An expectancy value perspective. In J. M. Reinisch, L. A. Rosenblum, & S. A. Sanders (Eds.), *Masculinity/femininity: Basic perspectives*. New York: Oxford University Press. (p. 129)

Eccles, J. S. (1987b). Gender roles and women's achievement-related decisions. *Psychology of Women Quarterly, 11*, 135–172. (p. 133)

Eckenrode, J. (1984). Impact of chronic and acute stressors on daily reports of mood. *Journal of Personality and Social Psychology, 46*, 907–918. (p. 393)

Eckert, E. D., Bouchard, T. J., Jr., Segal, N. L., Lykken, D. T., & Heston, L. L. (1987). Sex differences in genetic influence on body weight in monozygotic twins reared apart. Unpublished manuscript, University of Minnesota. (p. 537)

Eckert, E. D., Heston, L. L., & Bouchard, T. J., Jr. (1981). MZ twins reared apart: Preliminary findings of psychiatric disturbances and traits. In L. Gedda, P. Paris, & W. D. Nance (Eds.), *Twin research; Vol. 3. Pt. B: Intelligence, personality, and development*. New York: Alan Liss. (p. 452)

Edwards, C. P. (1981). The comparative study of the development of moral judgement and reasoning. In R. H. Munroe, R. L. Munroe, & B. B. Whiting (Eds.), *Handbook of cross-cultural human development*. New York: Garland Press. (p. 95)

Edwards, C. P. (1982). Moral development in comparative cultural perspective. In D. A. Wagner & H. W. Stevenson (Eds.), *Cultural perspectives on child development*. San Francisco: Freeman. (p. 95)

Egbert, L. D., Battit, G. E., Welch, C. E., & Bartlett, M. K. (1964). Reduction of postoperative pain by encouragement and instruction of patients. *New England Journal of Medicine, 270*, 825–827. (p. 528)

Egeland, J., Gerhard, D. S., Pauls, D. L., Sussex, J. N., Kidd, K. K., Allen, C. R., Hostetter, A. M., & Housman, D. E. (1987). Bipolar affective disorders linked to DNA markers on chromosome 11. *Nature, 325*, 783–787. (p. 459)

Ehrhardt, A. A. (1987). A transactional perspective on the development of gender differences. In J. M. Reinisch, L. A. Rosenblum, & S. A. Sanders (Eds.), *Masculinity/femininity: Basic perspectives*. New York: Oxford University Press. (p. 118)

Ehrhardt, A., & Money, J. (1967). Progestin-induced hermaphroditism: IQ and psycho-sexual identity in a study of ten girls. *Journal of Sex Research, 3,* 83–100. (p. 121)

Eibl-Eibesfeldt, I. (1971). *Love and hate: The natural history of behavior patterns.* New York: Holt, Rinehart & Winston. (p. 387)

Eich, J. E. (1980). The cue-dependent nature of state-dependent retrieval. *Memory and Cognition, 8,* 157–173. (p. 215)

Eisenberg, N., & Lennon, R. (1983). Sex differences in empathy and related capacities. *Psychological Bulletin, 94,* 100–131. (p. 131)

Ekman, P. (1985). *Telling lies: Clues to deceit in the marketplace, politics, and marriage.* New York: Norton. (p. 388)

Ekman, P., & Friesen, W. V. (1975). *Unmasking the face.* Englewood Cliffs, NJ: Prentice-Hall. (p. 381)

Ekman, P., Friesen, W. V., O'Sullivan, M., Chan, A., Diacoyanni-Tarlatzis, I., Heider, K., Krause, R., LeCompte, W. A., Pitcairn, T., Ricci-Bitti, P. E., Scherer, K., Tomita, M., & Tzavaras, A. (1987). Universals and cultural differences in the judgments of facial expressions of emotion. *Journal of Personality and Social Psychology, 53,* 712–717. (pp. 386–387)

Ekman, P., Levenson, R. W., & Friesen, W. V. (1983). Autonomic nervous system activity distinguishes among emotions. *Science, 221,* 1208–1210. (p. 388)

Elder, G. H., Jr. (1969). Appearance and education in marriage mobility. *American Sociological Review, 34,* 519–533. (p. 597)

Eldersveld, S. J., & Dodge, R. W. (1954). Personal contact or mail propaganda? An experiment in voting turnout and attitude change. In D. Katz, D. Cartwright, S. Eldersveld, & A. M. Lee (Eds.), *Public opinion and propaganda.* New York: Dryden Press. (p. 564)

Elkin, I. (1986). Outcome findings and therapist performance. Paper presented at the American Psychological Association convention. (p. 495)

Ellis, A. (1962). *Reason and emotion in psychotherapy.* Secaucus, NJ: Citadel Press. (p. 487)

Ellis, A. (1984). Rational-emotive therapy (3rd ed.). In R. J. Corsini (Ed.), *Current psychotherapies.* Itasca, IL: Peacock. (p. 487)

Ellis, A. (1987). The impossibility of achieving consistently good mental health. *American Psychologist, 42,* 364–375. (p. 487)

Ellis, L., & Ames, M. A. (1987). Neurohormonal functioning and sexual orientation: A theory of homosexuality-heterosexuality. *Psychological Bulletin, 101,* 233–258. (pp. 365, 368)

Empson, J. A. C., & Clarke, P. R. F. (1970). Rapid eye movements and remembering. *Nature, 227,* 287–288. (p. 204)

Endler, N. S. (1982). *Holiday of darkness: A psychologist's personal journey out of his depression.* New York: Wiley. (p. 498)

Engen, T. (1987). Remembering odors and their names. *American Scientist, 75,* 497–503. (p. 270)

Ennis, R. H. (1982). Children's ability to handle Piaget's propositional logic: A conceptual critique. In S. Modgil &

C. Modgil (Eds.), *Jean Piaget: Consensus and controversy.* New York: Praeger. (p. 92)

Epstein, R., Kirshnit, C. E., Lanza, R. P., & Rubin, L. C. (1984). "Insight" in the pigeon: Antecedents and determinants of an intelligent performance. *Nature, 308,* 61–62. (p. 287)

Epstein, S. (1983a). Aggregation and beyond: Some basic issues on the prediction of behavior. *Journal of Personality, 51,* 360–392. (p. 424)

Epstein, S. (1983b). The stability of behavior across time and situations. In R. Zucker, J. Aronoff, & A. I. Rabin (Eds.), *Personality and the prediction of behavior.* San Diego: Academic Press. (p. 424)

Epstein, S. (1984). Controversial issues in emotions. In P. Shaver (Ed.), *Review of Personality and Social Psychology.* Beverly Hills, CA: Sage. (p. 383)

Erdelyi, M. H. (1985). *Psychoanalysis: Freud's cognitive psychology.* New York: Freeman. (p. 417)

Erdelyi, M. H. (1988). Repression, reconstruction, and defense: History and integration of the psychoanalytic and experimental frameworks. In J. Singer (Ed.), *Repression: Defense mechanism and cognitive style.* Chicago: University of Chicago Press. (p. 417)

Ericsson, K. A., & Chase, W. G. (1982). Exceptional memory. *American Scientist, 70,* 607–615. (p. 263)

Erikson, E. H. (1963). *Childhood and society.* New York: Norton. (pp. 95, 105)

Erikson, E. H. (1983, June). A conversation with Erikson (by E. Hall). *Psychology Today,* pp. 22–30. (p. 74)

Eron, L. D. (1987). The development of aggressive behavior from the perspective of a developing behaviorism. *American Psychologist, 42,* 435–442. (pp. 113, 580)

Eron, L. D., & Huesmann, L. R. (1984). The control of aggressive behavior by changes in attitudes, values and the conditions of learning. In R. J. Blanchard & C. Blanchard (Eds.), *Advances in the study of aggression* (Vol. 1). Orlando, FL: Academic Press. (pp. 113, 579, 584)

Etzioni, A. (1967). The Kennedy experiment. *The Western Political Quarterly, 20,* 361–380. (p. 607)

Evans, G. W., Palsane, M. N., & Carrere, S. (1987). Type A behavior and occupational stress: A cross-cultural study of blue-collar workers. *Journal of Personality and Social Psychology, 52,* 1002–1007. (p. 515)

Evans, R. I., Raines, B. E., & Hanselka, L. (1984). Developing data-based communications in social psychological research: Adolescent smoking prevention. *Journal of Applied Social Psychology, 14,* 289–295. (p. 532)

Exner, J. E., Jr. (1986). *The Rorschach: A comprehensive system. Volume 1: Basic Foundations* (2nd ed.). New York: Wiley. (p. 417)

Eysenck, H. J. (1952). The effects of psychotherapy: An evaluation. *Journal of Consulting Psychology, 16,* 319–324. (p. 493)

Eysenck, H. J. (1963). The validity of questionnaire and rating assessments of extraversion and neuroticism, and their factorial stability. *British Journal of Psychology, 54,* 51–62. (p. 421)

Eysenck, H. J. (1982). *A model for intelligence.* Berlin: Springer-Verlag. (p. 331)

Eysenck, H. J. & Kamin, L. (1981). *The intelligence controversy: H. J. Eysenck vs. Leon Kamin.* New York: Wiley. (p. 319)

Eysenck, H. J., Wakefield, J. A., Jr., & Friedman, A. F. (1983). Diagnosis and clinical assessment: The DSM-III. *Annual Review of Psychology, 34,* 167–193. (pp. 448–449)

Eysenck, M. W., MacLeod, C., & Mathews, A. (1987). Cognitive functioning and anxiety. *Psychological Research, 49,* 189–195. (p. 452)

Faber, N. (1987, July). Personal glimpse. *Reader's Digest,* p. 34. (p. 334)

Fagan, J. F. (1984). The intelligent infant: Theoretical implications. *Intelligence, 8,* 1–9. (p. 332)

Fahrion, S., Norris, P., Green, A., Green, E., & Snarr, C. (1986). Biobehavioral treatment of essential hypertension: A group outcome study. *Biofeedback and Self-Regulation, 11,* 257–277. (p. 522)

Falbo, T., & Polit, D. F. (1986). Quantitative review of the only child literature: Research evidence and theory development. *Psychological Bulletin, 100,* 176–189. (p. 373)

Falbo, T., & Shepperd, J. A. (1986). Self-righteousness: Cognitive, power, and religious characteristics. *Journal of Research in Personality, 20,* 145–157. (p. 432)

Fallon, A. E., & Rozin, P. (1985). Sex differences in perceptions of desirable body shape. *Journal of Abnormal Psychology, 94,* 102–105. (p. 358)

Fancher, R. E. (1979). *Pioneers of psychology.* New York: Norton. (pp. 316–317)

Fantz, R. L. (1961, May). The origin of form perception. *Scientific American,* pp. 66–72. (p. 61)

Faraone, S. V., & Tsuang, M. T. (1985). Quantitative models of the genetic transmission of schizophrenia. *Psychological Bulletin, 98*(1) 41–66. (p. 466)

Farina, A. (1982). The stigma of mental disorders. In A. G. Miller (Ed.), *In the eye of the beholder.* New York: Praeger. (pp. 445, 470)

Farina, A., & Fisher, J. D. (1982). Beliefs about mental disorders: Findings and implications. In G. Weary & H. L. Mirels (Eds.), *Integrations of clinical and social psychology.* New York: Oxford University Press. (p. 491)

Farrell, P. A., Gates, W. K., Maksud, M. G., & Morgan, W. P. (1982). Increases in plasma beta-endorphin/beta-lipotropin immunoreactivity after treadmill running in humans. *Journal of Applied Physiology, 52,* 1245–1249. (p. 30)

Faust, D., & Ziskin, J. (1988). The expert witness in psychology and psychiatry. *Science, 241,* 31–35. (p. 446)

Fazio, R. H. (1986). How do attitudes guide behavior? In R. M. Sorrentino & E. T. Higgins (Eds.), *The handbook of motivation and cognition: Foundations of social behavior.* New York: Guilford Press. (p. 559)

Fechner, G. (1860). Cited in O. Zangwill (1974), Conscious-

ness and the cerebral hemispheres. In S. Dimond and G. Beaumont (Eds.), *Hemispheric function in the human brain.* New York: Halsted Press. (p. 44)

Feder, H. H. (1984). Hormones and sexual behavior. *Annual Review of Psychology, 35,* 165–200. (p. 363)

Federal Bureau of Investigation (1987). *Uniform crime reports for the United States.* Washington, DC: U.S. Government Printing Office. (p. 130)

Federal Bureau of Investigation (1988). *Uniform crime reports for the United States.* Washington, DC: U.S. Government Printing Office. (p. 575)

Feeney, D. M. (1987). Human rights and animal welfare. *American Psychologist, 42,* 593–599. (p. 19)

Feinleib, M., Lenfant, C., & Miller, S. A. (1984). Hypertension and calcium. *Science, 226,* 384–385. (p. 533)

Fergusson, D. M., Horwood, L. J., & Shannon, F. T. (1987). Breastfeeding and subsequent social adjustment in six- to eight-year-old children. *Journal of Child Psychology & Psychiatry & Allied Disciplines, 28*(3), 379–386. (p. 72)

Feshbach, S. (1986). Reconceptualizations of anger: Some research perspectives. *Journal of Social and Clinical Psychology, 4,* 123–132. (p. 391)

Fiedler, F. E. (1981). Leadership effectiveness. *American Behavioral Scientist, 24,* 619–632. (p. 376)

Fiedler, F. E. (1987, September). When to lead, when to stand back. *Psychology Today,* pp. 26–27. (p. 376)

Field, T. M. (1987, May). Baby research comes of age. *Psychology Today,* p. 46. (p. 62)

Field, T. M., Schanberg, S. M., Scafidi, F., Bauer, C. R., Vega-Lahr, N., Garcia, R., Nystrom, J., & Kuhn, C. M. (1986). Tactile/kinesthetic stimulation effects on preterm neonates. *Pediatrics, 77,* 654–658. (p. 63)

Field, T. M., Woodson, R., Greenberg, R., & Cohen, D. (1982). Discrimination and imitation of facial expressions by neonates. *Science, 218,* 179–181. (p. 62)

Fields, C. M. (1984, September 5). Psychologists emphasize their commitment to humane use of animals in research. *Chronicle of Higher Education,* pp. 5, 12. (p. 19)

Fillion, T. J., & Blass, E. M. (1986). Infantile experience with suckling odors determines adult sexual behavior in male rats. *Science, 231,* 729–731. (p. 368)

Findley, M. J., & Cooper, H. M. (1983). Locus of control and academic achievement: A literature review. *Journal of Personality and Social Psychology, 44,* 419–427. (p. 433)

Fineberg, H. V. (1988). Education to prevent AIDS: Prospects and obstacles. *Science, 239,* 592–596. (p. 369)

Finn, S. E. (1986). Stability of personality self-ratings over 30 years: Evidence for an age/cohort interaction. *Journal of Personality and Social Psychology, 50,* 813–818. (p. 113)

Finucci, J. M., & Childs, B. (1981). Are there really more dyslexic boys than girls? In A. Ansara, N. Geschwind, A. Galaburda, M. Albert, & N. Gartrell (Eds.), *Sex differences in dyslexia.* Townson, MD: The Orton Dyslexia Society. (p. 132)

Fischhoff, B. (1982). Debiasing. In D. Kahneman, P. Slovic,

& A. Tversky (Eds.), *Judgment under uncertainty: Heuristics and biases.* New York: Cambridge University Press. (p. 294)

Fischhoff, B., Slovic, P., & Lichtenstein, S. (1977). Knowing with certainty: The appropriateness of extreme confidence. *Journal of Experimental Psychology: Human Perception and Performance, 3,* 552–564. (p. 293)

Fischman, J. (1986, June). The wounds of war. *Psychology Today,* pp. 8–9. (p. 43)

Fisher, H. T. (1984). Little Albert and Little Peter. *Bulletin of the British Psychological Society, 37,* 269. (p. 483)

Fisher, K. (1986a, March). Animal research. *APA Monitor,* pp. 16–17. (p. 18)

Fisher, K. (1986b, July). Debate. *APA Monitor,* p. 6. (p. 493)

Flanagan, J. C. (1947). Scientific development of the use of human resources: Progress in the Army Air Forces. *Science, 105,* 57–60. (p. 326)

Fleming, I., Baum, A., & Weiss, L. (1987). Social density and perceived control as mediator of crowding stress in high-density residential neighborhoods. *Journal of Personality and Social Psychology, 52,* 899–906. (p. 514)

Floderus-Myrhed, B., Pedersen, N., & Rasmuson, I. (1980). Assessment of heritability for personality, based on a short-form of the Eysenck Personality Inventory: A study of 12,898 twin pairs. *Behavior Genetics, 10,* 153–162. (pp. 81–82)

Flynn, J. R. (1987). Massive IQ gains in 14 nations: What IQ tests really measure. *Psychological Bulletin, 101,* 171–191. (pp. 325, 330)

Foa, E. B., & Kozak, M. J. (1986). Emotional processing of fear: Exposure to corrective information. *Psychological Bulletin, 99,* 20–35. (p. 484)

Ford, C. S., & Beach, F. A. (1951). *Patterns of sexual behavior.* New York: Harper & Row. (p. 366)

Forgas, J. P., Bower, G. H., & Krantz, S. E. (1984). The influence of mood on perceptions of social interactions. *Journal of Experimental Social Psychology, 20,* 497–513. (pp. 271, 461)

Fouts, R. S. (1984, November). *Friends of Washoe letter.* Central Washington University, Ellensburg, WA. (p. 590)

Fouts, R. S., & Bodamer, M. (1987). Preliminary report to the National Geographic Society on: "Chimpanzee intra-personal signing." *Friends of Washoe, 7(1),* 4–12. (p. 308)

Fowler, C. A., Wolford, G., Slade, R., & Tassinary, L. (1981). Lexical access with and without awareness. *Journal of Experimental Psychology: General, 110,* 341–362. (p. 142)

Fowler, M. J., Sullivan, M. J., & Ekstrand, B. R. (1973). Sleep and memory. *Science, 179,* 302–304. (p. 277)

Fowler, R. C., Rich, C. L., & Young, D. (1986). San Diego suicide study: II. Substance abuse in young cases. *Archives of General Psychiatry, 43,* 962–965. (p. 457)

Fowler, R. D. (1986, May). Howard Hughes: A psychological autopsy. *Psychology Today,* pp. 22–33. (pp. 452, 457)

Fox, G. C., & Messina, P. C. (1987, October). Advanced computer architectures. *Scientific American,* pp. 66–74. (p. 300)

Fox, J. L. (1984). The brain's dynamic way of keeping in touch. *Science, 225,* 820–821. (p. 41)

Fozard, J. L., & Popkin, S. J. (1978). Optimizing adult development: Ends and means of an applied psychology of aging. *American Psychologist, 33,* 975–989. (p. 100)

Frank, J. D. (1982). Therapeutic components shared by all psychotherapies. In J. H. Harvey & M. M. Parks (Eds.), *The Master Lecture Series: Vol. 1. Psychotherapy research and behavior change.* Washington, DC: American Psychological Association. (pp. 476, 496–497)

Frank, M. G., & Gilovich, T. (1988). The dark side of self and social perception: Black uniforms and aggression in professional sports. *Journal of Personality and Social Psychology, 54,* 74–85. (pp. 15–16)

Freedman, D. G. (1979). *Human sociobiology: A holistic approach.* New York: Free Press. (p. 81)

Freedman, J. L. (1978). *Happy people.* San Diego: Harcourt Brace Jovanovich. (p. 109)

Freedman, J. L. (1988). Television violence and aggression: What the evidence shows. In S. Oskamp (Ed.), *Television as a social issue.* Newbury Park, CA: Sage. (p. 580)

Freedman, J. L., & Perlick, D. (1979). Crowding, contagion, and laughter. *Journal of Experimental Social Psychology, 15,* 295–303. (p. 568)

Freud, S. (1888–1939; reprinted 1963). In J. Strachey (Ed. & trans.), *The standard edition of the complete psychological works of Sigmund Freud.* London: Hogarth Press. (p. 121)

Freud, S. (1933). *New introductory lectures on psycho-analysis.* New York: Carlton House. (p. 411)

Freud, S. (1935; reprinted 1960). *A general introduction to psychoanalysis.* New York: Washington Square Press. (p. 107)

Friedman, H. S., & Booth-Kewley, S. (1987). The "disease-prone personality": A meta-analytic view of the construct. *American Psychologist, 42,* 539–555. (p. 520)

Friedman, M., & Ulmer, D. (1984). *Treating Type A behavior—and your heart.* New York: Knopf. (pp. 514, 523)

Friedman, W. J., Robinson, A. B., & Friedman, B. L. (1987). Sex differences in moral judgments? A test of Gilligan's theory. *Psychology of Women Quarterly, 11,* 37–46. (p. 95)

Friedrich, O. (1987, December 7). New age harmonies. *Time,* pp. 62–72. (p. 445)

Frieze, I. H., Parsons, J. E., Johnson, P. B., Ruble, D. N., & Zellman, G. L. (1978). *Women and sex roles: A social psychological perspective.* New York: Norton. (pp. 121, 591)

Frijda, N. H. (1988). The laws of emotion. *American Psychologist, 43,* 349–358. (p. 395)

Fritsch, G., & Hitzig, E. (1870; reprinted 1960). On the electrical excitability of the cerebrum. In G. Von Bonin (Trans.), *Some papers on the cerebral cortex.* Springfield, IL: Charles C Thomas. (pp. 39–40)

Fromkin, V., & Rodman, R. (1983). *An introduction to language* (3rd ed.). New York: Holt, Rinehart & Winston. (pp. 301, 303–304)

Fuchs, V. R. (1986). Sex differences in economic well-being. *Science, 232,* 459–464. (p. 117)

Funder, D. C. (1987). Errors and mistakes: Evaluating the accuracy of social judgment. *Psychological Bulletin, 101*, 75–90. (p. 298)

Furstenberg, F. F., Jr., Moore, K. A., & Peterson, J. L. (1985). Sex education and sexual experience among adolescents. *American Journal of Public Health 75*, 1331–1332 (p. 370)

Gabrenya, W. K., Jr., Latané, B., & Wang, Y-E. (1983). Social loafing in cross-cultural perspective. *Journal of Cross-Cultural Psychology, 14*, 368–384. (p. 567)

Galanter, E. (1962). Contemporary psychophysics. In R. Brown, E. Galanter, E. H. Hess, & G. Mandler (Eds.), *New directions in psychology*. New York: Holt, Rinehart & Winston. (p. 140)

Gallatin, J. (1980). Political thinking in adolescence. In J. Adelson (Ed.), *Handbook of adolescent psychology*. New York: Wiley. (p. 97)

Gallup, G. G., Jr. (1982). *Adventures in immortality*. New York: McGraw-Hill. (p. 221)

Gallup, G. G., Jr. (1984, March). Religion in America. *The Gallup Report*, No. 222. (p. 589)

Gallup, G. G., Jr., & O'Connell, G. (1986). *Who do Americans say that I am?* Philadelphia, PA: Westminster Press. (pp. 221, 399)

Gallup, G. G., Jr., & Suarez, S. D. (1985). Alternatives to the use of animals in psychological research. *American Psychologist, 40*, 1104–1111. (p. 18)

Gallup, G. G., Jr., & Suarez, S. D. (1986). Self-awareness and the emergence of mind in humans and other primates. In J. Suls & A. G. Greenwald (Eds.), *Psychological perspectives on the self* (Vol. 3.). Hillsdale, NJ: Erlbaum. (p. 78)

Gallup Organization (1986, June). Cigarette smoking audit. *Gallup Report*, No. 249, p. 3. (p. 532)

Gallup Organization (1987, August). Premarital sex: More today than in 1985 say premarital sex is wrong. *The Gallup Report* No. 263, pp. 20–21. (p. 360)

Gallup Report (1984, August/September). Women in politics, pp. 2–14. (p. 591)

Gallup Report (1986, August). Pornography. Report No. 251, pp. 2–12. (p. 584)

Gallup Report (1987). Legalized gay relations. *Gallup Report*, No. 254, p. 25. (p. 369)

Galton, F. (1892). *Hereditary genius* (2nd ed.). London: Macmillan. (p. 317)

Garcia, J., & Koelling, R. A. (1966). Relation of cue to consequence in avoidance learning. *Psychonomic Science, 4*, 123–124. (p. 237)

Gardner, H. (1983). *Frames of mind: The theory of multiple intelligences*. New York: Basic Books. (p. 330)

Gardner, J. W. (1984). *Excellence: Can we be equal and excellent too?* New York: Norton. (pp. 108–109, 377)

Gardner, M. (1983, Summer). Lessons of a landmark PK hoax. *Skeptical Inquirer*, pp. 16–19. (p. 186)

Gardner, R. A., & Gardner, B. I. (1969). Teaching sign language to a chimpanzee. *Science, 165*, 664–672. (p. 306)

Gash, D. M., Notter, M. F. D., Okawara, S. H., Kraus, A. L., & Joynt, R. J. (1986). Amniotic neuroblastoma cells used for neural implants in monkeys. *Science, 233*, 1420–1421. (p. 50)

Gatchel, R. J., & Baum, A. (1983). *An introduction to health psychology*. Reading, MA: Addison-Wesley. (p. 529)

Gazzaniga, M. S. (1967, August). The split brain in man. *Scientific American*, pp. 24–29. (pp. 44–45)

Gazzaniga, M. S. (1983). Right hemisphere language following brain bisection: A 20-year perspective. *American Psychologist, 38*, 525–537. (p. 46)

Gazzaniga, M. S. (1985, November). The social brain. *Psychology Today*, pp. 29–38. (p. 47)

Geen, R. G. (1984). Human motivation: New perspectives on old problems. In A. M. Rogers & C. J. Scheirer (Eds.), *The G. Stanley Hall Lecture Series* (Vol. 4). Washington, DC: American Psychological Association. (p. 372)

Geen, R. G., & Gange, J. J. (1983). Social facilitation: Drive theory and beyond. In H. H. Blumberg, A. P. Hare, V. Kent, & M. Davies (Eds.), *Small groups and social interaction* (Vol. 1). New York: Wiley. (p. 566)

Geen, R. G., & Quanty, M. B. (1977). The catharsis of aggression: An evaluation of a hypothesis. In L. Berkowitz (Ed.), *Advances in experimental social psychology* (Vol. 10). New York: Academic Press. (p. 392)

Geen, R. G., & Thomas, S. L. (1986). The immediate effects of media violence on behavior. *Journal of Social Issues, 42*(3), 7–28. (p. 580)

Geiwitz, J. (1980). *Psychology: Looking at ourselves* (2nd ed.). Boston: Little, Brown. (p. 103)

Geldard, F. A. (1972). *The human senses* (2nd ed.). New York: Wiley. (p. 152)

Gelman, R. (1979). Preschool thought. *American Psychologist, 34*, 900–905. (p. 70)

Gerard, R. W. (1953, September). What is memory? *Scientific American*, pp. 118–126. (p. 267)

Gerbner, G. (1985). Dreams that hurt: Mental illness in the mass media. Keynote address to the First Rosalynn Carter Symposium on Mental Health Policy, Emory University School of Medicine, Atlanta. (p. 471)

Gerbner, G., Gross, L., Signorielli, N., & Morgan, M. (1986). Television's mean world: Violence profile No. 14–15. Philadelphia: Annenberg School of Communications, University of Pennsylvania. (p. 579)

Gergen, K. J. (1965). The effects of interaction goals and personalistic feedback on the presentation of self. *Journal of Personality and Social Psychology, 1*, 413–424. (p. 559)

Gerrard, M. (1987a). Emotional and cognitive barriers to effective contraception: Are males and females really different. In K. Kelley (Ed.), *Females, males, and sexuality: Theories and research*. Albany: State University of New York Press. (p. 361)

Gerrard, M. (1987b). Sex, sex guilt, and contraceptive use revisited: The 1980s. *Journal of Personality and Social Psychology, 52,* 975–980. (p. 360)

Geschwind, N. (1979, September). Specializations of the human brain. *Scientific American,* pp. 180–199. (pp. 42–43)

Geschwind, N., & Behan, P. O. (1984). Laterality, hormones, and immunity. In N. Geschwind & A. M. Galaburda (Eds.), *Cerebral dominance: The biological foundations.* Cambridge, MA: Harvard University Press. (pp. 48, 133)

Gfeller, J. D., Lynn, S. J., & Pribble, W. E. (1987). Enhancing hypnotic susceptibility: Interpersonal and rapport factors. *Journal of Personality and Social Psychology, 52,* 586–595. (p. 213)

Giambra, L. M. (1974). Daydreaming across the life span: Late adolescent to senior citizen. *Aging and Human Development, 5,* 115–140. (p. 195)

Gibbons, F. X. (1986). Social comparison and depression: Company's effect on misery. *Journal of Personality and Social Psychology, 51,* 140–148. (p. 398)

Gibbs, J. C., & Schnell, S. V. (1985). Moral development "versus" socialization. *American Psychologist, 40,* 1071–1080. (p. 94)

Gibson, E. J., & Walk, R. D. (1960, April). The "visual cliff." *Scientific American,* pp. 64–71. (pp. 173–174)

Gibson, H. B. (1979). The 'Royal Nonesuch' of parapsychology. *Bulletin of the British Psychological Society, 32,* 65–67. (p. 186)

Gilbert, L. C. (1986). Chessplayers: Gender, myth, and psychological research. Paper presented to the American Psychological Association convention. (p. 132)

Giles, T. R. (1983). Probable superiority of behavioral interventions—II: Empirical status of the equivalence of therapies hypothesis. *Journal of Behavior Therapy and Experimental Psychiatry, 14,* 189–196. (p. 495)

Gilligan, C. (1982). *In a different voice: Psychological theory and women's development.* Cambridge, MA: Harvard University Press. (pp. 95, 96, 106)

Gilling, D. & Brightwell, R. (1982). *The human brain.* New York: Facts on File. (p. 484)

Gilovich, T., Vallone, R., & Tversky, A. (1985). The hot hand in basketball: On the misperception of random sequences. *Cognitive Psychology, 17,* 295–314. (p. 619)

Gjerde, P. F. (1983). Attentional capacity dysfunction and arousal in schizophrenia. *Psychological Bulletin, 93,* 57–72. (p. 463)

Gladue, B. A., Green, R., & Hellman, R. E. (1984). Neuroendocrine response to estrogen and sexual orientation. *Science, 225,* 1496–1499. (p. 368)

Glass, D. C., & Singer, J. E. (1972). *Urban stress.* New York: Academic Press. (p. 157)

Godden, D. R., & Baddeley, A. D. (1975). Context-dependent memory in two natural environments: On land and underwater. *British Journal of Psychology, 66,* 325–331. (p. 270)

Gold, M., & Yanof, D. S. (1985). Mothers, daughters, and girlfriends. *Journal of Personality and Social Psychology, 49,* 654–659. (p. 97)

Gold, P. E. (1987). Sweet memories. *American Scientist, 75,* 151–155. (p. 268)

Goldberg, L. R. (1981). Language and individual differences: The search for universals in personality lexicons. In L. Wheeler (Ed.), *Review of personality and social psychology* (Vol. 2). Beverly Hills, CA: Sage. (p. 421)

Goldberg, S. (1983). Parent-infant bonding: Another look. *Child Development, 54,* 1355–1382. (p. 72)

Goldfried, M. R., & Padawer, W. (1982). Current status and future directions in psychotherapy. In M. R. Goldfried (Ed.), *Converging themes in psychotherapy: Trends in psychodynamic, humanistic, and behavioral practice.* New York: Springer. (p. 496)

Goldsmith, H. H., & Alansky, J. F. (1987). Maternal and infant temperamental predictors of attachment: A meta-analytic review. *Journal of Consulting and Clinical Psychology, 55,* 805–816. (p. 74)

Goleman, D. (1980, February). 1,528 little geniuses and how they grew. *Psychology Today,* pp. 28–53. (p. 332)

Goleman, D. (1985a, April 30). Social workers vault into a leading role in psychotherapy. *New York Times,* pp. C1, C9. (p. 491)

Goleman, D. (1985b, May 21). New focus on multiple personality. *The New York Times,* pp. C1, C6. (p. 455)

Goleman, D. (1987, February 24). Terror's children: Mending mental wounds. *New York Times,* pp. C1, C12. (p. 75)

Golub, S. (1983). *Menarche: The transition from girl to woman.* Lexington, MA: Lexington Books. (p. 90)

Gonsiorek, J. C. (1982). Summary and conclusions. In W. Paul, J. D. Weinrich, J. C. Gonsiorek, & M. E. Hotvedt (Eds.), *Homosexuality: Social, psychological, and biological issues.* Beverly Hills, CA: Sage. (p. 367)

Goodall, J. (1986). *The chimpanzees of Gombe: Patterns of behavior.* Cambridge, MA: Harvard University Press. (p. 593)

Goodchilds, J. (1987). Quoted by Carol Tavris, Old age is not what it used to be. *New York Times Magazine: Good Health Magazine,* September 27, pp. 24–25, 91–92. (p. 99)

Goodhart, D. E. (1986). The effects of positive and negative thinking on performance in an achievement situation. *Journal of Personality and Social Psychology, 51,* 117–124. (p. 435)

Goodman, W. (1982, August 9). Of mice, monkeys and men. *Newsweek,* p. 61. (p. 18)

Gopnik, A., & Meltzoff, A. N. (1986). *Child Development, 57,* 1040–1053. (p. 310)

Gorman, M. E. (1984). Using the *Eden Express* to teach introductory psychology. *Teaching of Psychology, 11,* 39–40. (p. 465)

Gormezano, I., & Kehoe, E. J. (1975). Classical conditioning: Some methodological-conceptual issues. In W. K. Estes (Ed.), *Handbook of learning and cognitive processes: Vol. 2. Conditioning and behavior theory.* Hillsdale, NJ: Erlbaum. (p. 232)

Gottfredson, L. S. (1988). Intelligence versus training: Job performance and black-white occupational inequality. *Personality and Individual Differences,* in press. (pp. 330, 340)

Gould, M. S., & Shaffer, D. (1986). The impact of suicide in television movies: Evidence of imitation. *New England Journal of Medicine, 315,* 690–694. (p. 552)

Gould, S. J. (1981). *The mismeasure of man.* New York: Norton. (pp. 318–319)

Gould, S. J. (1987, January). Darwinism defined: The difference between fact and theory. *Discover,* pp. 64–70. (p. 7)

Gouras, P. (1985). Color vision. In E. R. Kandel & J. H. Schwartz (Eds.), *Principles of neural science.* New York: Elsevier. (p. 152)

Graef, R., Csikszentmihalyi, M., & Gianinno, S. M. (1983). Measuring intrinsic motivation in everyday life. *Leisure Studies, 2,* 155–168. (p. 399)

Grant, W. V., & Snyder, T. D. (1986). *Digest of education statistics 1985–86.* Washington, DC: Superintendent of Documents, U.S. Government Printing Office. (p. 102)

Gray-Little, B., & Burks, N. (1983). Power and satisfaction in marriage: A review and critique. *Psychological Bulletin, 93,* 513–538. (p. 600)

Greeley, A. W. (1987, January-February). Mysticism goes mainstream. *American Health,* pp. 47–49. (pp. 185, 187)

Green, S. K. & Sandos, P. (1983). Perceptions of male and female intiators of relationships. *Sex Roles, 9,* 849–852. (p. 124)

Greene, R. L. (1987). Effects of maintenance rehearsal on human memory. *Psychological Bulletin, 102,* 403–413. (p. 261)

Greenough, W. T., Black, J. E., & Wallace, C. S. (1987). Experience and brain development. *Child Development, 58,* 539–559. (p. 63)

Greenwald, A. G. (1984, June 12). Quoted by D. Goleman, A bias puts self at center of everything. *The New York Times,* pp. C1, C4. (p. 431)

Greenwald, A. G. (1987, December 2). Personal communication. (p. 142)

Greenwald, A. G., & Pratkanis, A. R. (1984). The self. In R. S. Wyer, & T. K. Srull (Eds.), *Handbook of social cognition.* Hillsdale, NJ: Erlbaum. (p. 429)

Greenwald, A. G., Pratkanis, A. R., Leippe, M. R., & Baumgardner, M. H. (1986). Under what conditions does theory obstruct research progress? *Psychological Review, 93,* 216–229. (pp. 9, 142)

Greer, G. (1984, April). The uses of chastity and other paths to sexual pleasures. *MS,* pp. 53–60, 96. (pp. 364, 370)

Gregory, R. L. (1968, November). Visual illusions. *Scientific American,* pp. 66–76. (p. 178)

Gregory, R. L. (1978). *Eye and brain: The psychology of seeing* (3rd ed.). New York: McGraw-Hill. (p. 180)

Gregory, R. L., & Gombrich, E. H. (Eds.). (1974). *Illusion in nature and art.* New York: Charles Scribner's Sons. (p. 184)

Gregory. W. L., Cialdini, R. B., & Carpenter, K. M. (1982). Self-relevant scenarios as mediators of likelihood estimates and compliance: Does imagining make it so? *Journal of Personality and Social Psychology, 43,* 89–99. (p. 292)

Greif, E. B., & Ulman, K. J. (1982). The psychological impact of menarche on early adolescent females: A review of the literature. *Child Development, 53,* 1413–1430. (p. 90)

Griffin, D. R. (1984). Animal thinking. *American Scientist, 72,* 456–464. (p. 300)

Grobstein, C. (1979, June). External human fertilization. *Scientific American,* pp. 57–67. (p. 60)

Grolnick, W. S., & Ryan, R. M. (1987). Autonomy in children's learning: An experimental and individual difference investigation. *Journal of Personality and Social Psychology, 52,* 890–898. (p. 248)

Gross, A. E., & Crofton, C. (1977). What is good is beautiful. *Sociometry, 40,* 85–90. (p. 598)

Gruder, C. L. (1977). Choice of comparison persons in evaluating oneself. In J. M. Suls & R. L. Miller (Eds.), *Social comparison processes.* New York: Hemisphere. (p. 398)

Guerin, B. (1986). Mere presence effects in humans: A review. *Journal of Personality and Social Psychology, 22,* 38–77. (p. 566)

Gulevich, G., Dement, W., & Johnson, L. (1966). Psychiatric and EEG observations on a case of prolonged (264 hours) wakefulness. *Archives of General Psychiatry, 15,* 29–35. (p. 200)

Gurtman, M. B. (1986). Depression and the response of others: Reevaluating the reevaluation. *Journal of Abnormal Psychology, 95,* 99–101. (p. 461)

Gustavson, C. R., Garcia, J., Hankins, W. G., & Rusiniak, K. W. (1974). Coyote predation control by aversive conditioning. *Science, 184,* 581–583. (p. 237)

Gutierres, S. E., Kenrick, D. T., & Goldberg, L. (1985). *Adverse influence on exposure to popular erotica: Effects on judgments of others and judgments of one's spouse.* Paper presented at the meeting of the Midwestern Psychological Association. (p. 365)

Gutmann, D. (1977). The cross-cultural perspective: Notes toward a comparative psychology of aging. In J. E. Birren & K. Warner Schaie (Eds.), *Handbook of the psychology of aging.* New York: Van Nostrand Reinhold. (p. 132)

Guttentag, M., & Secord, P. F. (1983). *Too many women? The sex ratio question.* Beverly Hills, CA: Sage. (p. 125)

Haber, R. N. (1970, May). How we remember what we see. *Scientific American,* pp. 104–112. (p. 256)

Haemmerlie, F. M., & Montgomery, R. L. (1987). Psychological state and the menstrual cycle. *Journal of Social Behavior and Personality, 2,* 233–242. (p. 527)

Hahn, W. K. (1987). Cerebral lateralization of function: From infancy through childhood. *Psychological Bulletin, 101,* 376–392. (p. 49)

Hall, C. S. (1984). "A ubiquitous sex difference in dreams" revisited. *Journal of Personality and Social Psychology, 46,* 1109–1117. (p. 202)

Hall, C. S., Dornhoff, W., Blick, K. A., & Weesner, K. E. (1982). The dreams of college men and women in 1950 and 1980: A comparison of dream contents and sex differences. *Sleep, 5,* 188–194. (p. 202)

Hall, C. S., & Lindzey, G. (1978). *Theories of personality* (2nd ed.). New York: Wiley. (p. 418)

Hall, C. S., & Van de Castle, R. L. (1966). *The content analysis of dreams.* New York: Appleton-Century-Crofts. (p. 202)

Hall, G. S. (1904). *Adolescence: Its psychology and its relations to physiology, anthropology, sex, crime, religion and education* (Vol. I). New York: Appleton-Century-Crofts. (p. 90)

Hall, J. A. (1987). On explaining gender differences: The case of nonverbal communication. In P. Shaver & C. Hendrick (Eds.), *Review of Personality and Social Psychology, 7,* 177–200. (pp. 130–131)

Hall, N. R., & Goldstein, A. L. (1986, March/April). Thinking well: The chemical links between emotions and health. *The Sciences,* pp. 34–40. (p. 519)

Hall, T. (1987, September 27). Cravings: Does your body know what it needs? *New York Times Magazine: Good Health Magazine,* pp. 23, 62–65. (p. 356)

Halpern, D. F. (1986). *Sex differences in cognitive abilities.* Hillsdale, NJ: Erlbaum. (p. 132)

Hamill, R., Wilson, T. D., & Nisbett, R. E. (1980). Insensitivity to sample bias: Generalizing from atypical cases. *Journal of Personality and Social Psychology, 39,* 578–589. (p. 293)

Hammersmith, S. K. (1982, August). *Sexual preference: An empirical study from the Alfred C. Kinsey Institute for Sex Research.* Paper presented at the meeting of the American Psychological Association, Washington, D.C. (p. 367)

Hansel, C. E. M. (1980). *ESP and parapsychology: A critical reevaluation.* Buffalo, NY: Prometheus. (p. 187)

Hansel, C. E. M. (1985). The search for a demonstration of ESP. In P. Kurtz (Ed.), *A skeptic's handbook of parapsychology.* Buffalo, NY: Prometheus. (p. 187)

Hansen, C. H., & Hansen, R. D. (1988). Finding the face-in-the-crowd: An anger superiority effect. *Journal of Personality and Social Psychology, 54,* 917–924. (p. 386)

Hardin, G. (1968). The tragedy of the commons. *Science, 162,* 1243–1248. (p. 604)

Hare, R. D. (1975). Psychophysiological studies of psychopathy. In D. C. Fowles (Ed.), *Clinical applications of psychophysiology.* New York: Columbia University Press. (p. 469)

Harlow, H. F., Harlow, M. K., & Suomi, S. J. (1971). From thought to therapy: Lessons from a primate laboratory. *American Scientist, 59,* 538–549. (p. 71)

Harre, R., & Lamb, R. (1983). *The encyclopedic dictionary of psychology.* Cambridge, MA: MIT Press. (p. 409)

Harrell, T. H., & Stolp, R. D. (1985). Effects of erotic guided imagery on female sexual arousal and emotional response. *Journal of Sex Research, 21,* 292–304. (p. 364)

Harrington, D. M., Block, J. H., & Black, J. (1987). Testing aspects of Carl Rogers's theory of creative environments: Child-rearing antecedents of creative potential in young adolescents. *Journal of Personality and Social Psychology, 52,* 851–856. (p. 426)

Harris, B. (1979). Whatever happened to Little Albert? *American Psychologist, 34,* 151–160. (p. 235)

Harris, L. (1987). *Inside America.* New York: Random House. (pp. 11, 512, 539)

Harris, L., & associates (1986). American teens speak: Sex, myths, TV, and birth control: The Planned Parenthood Poll. Available from Planned Parenthood, 810 Seventh Avenue, New York, NY 10019. (pp. 360–361)

Harris, L., & associates (1988, January 26). Sexual material on American network television during the 1987–88 season. Conducted for Planned Parenthood Federation of America, New York. (p. 364)

Harris, L. J. (1978). Sex differences in spatial ability: Possible environmental, genetic, and neurological factors. In M. Kinsbourne (Ed.), *The asymmetrical function of the brain.* New York: Cambridge University Press. (pp. 128, 133)

Harris, R. L., Ellicott, A. M., & Holmes, D. S. (1986). The timing of psychosocial transitions and changes in women's lives: An examination of women aged 45 to 60. *Journal of Personality and Social Psychology, 51,* 409–416. (p. 106)

Hart, D. (1988). The development of personal identity in adolescence: A philosophical dilemma approach. *Merrill-Palmer Quarterly, 34,* 105–114. (p. 96)

Hartmann, E. (1981, April). The strangest sleep disorder. *Psychology Today,* pp. 14, 16, 18. (p. 202)

Hartmann, E. (1984). *The nightmare: The psychology and biology of terrifying dreams.* New York: Basic Books. (p. 202)

Hartshorne, H., & May, M. A. (1928b). *Studies in deceit.* New York: Macmillan. (p. 424)

Harvey, S. M. (1987). Female sexual behavior: Fluctuations during the menstrual cycle. *Journal of Psychosomatic Research, 31,* 101–110. (p. 363)

Hasher, L., & Zacks, R. T. (1979). Automatic and effortful processes in memory. *Journal of Experimental Psychology: General, 108,* 356–388. (p. 260)

Hastie, R., & Park, B. (1986). The relationship between memory and judgment depends on whether the judgment task is memory-based or on-line. *Psychological Bulletin, 93,* 258–268. (p. 292)

Hatfield, E. (1988). Passionate and companionate love. In R. J. Sternberg & M. L. Barnes (Eds.), *The psychology of love.* New Haven: Yale University Press. (p. 599)

Hatfield, E., & Sprecher, S. (1986). *Mirror, mirror . . . The importance of looks in everyday life.* Albany: State University of New York Press. (p. 597)

Hatfield, E., Traupmann, J., & Sprecher, S. (1984). Older women's perceptions of their intimate relationships. *Journal of Social and Clinical Psychology, 2,* 108–124. (p. 600)

Hathaway, S. R. (1960). *An MMPI Handbook* (Vol. 1, Foreword). Minneapolis: University of Minnesota Press. (Revised edition, 1972) (p. 422)

Hattie, J. A., Sharpley, C. F., & Rogers, H. J. (1984). Comparative effectiveness of professional and paraprofessional helpers. *Psychological Bulletin, 95,* 534–541. (p. 496)

Hawkins, R. C., Jr., Turell, S., & Jackson, L. J. (1983). Desirable and undesirable masculine and feminine traits in relation to students' dietary tendencies and body image dissatisfaction. *Sex Roles, 9,* 705–724. (p. 539)

Hayes, J. R. (1981). *The complete problem solver.* Philadelphia: Franklin Institute Press. (p. 269)

Hazan, C., & Shaver, P. (1987). Romantic love conceptualized as an attachment process. *Journal of Personality and Social Psychology 52,* 511–524. (p. 74)

Hazelrigg, M. D., Cooper, H. M., & Borduin, C. M. (1987). Evaluating the effectiveness of family therapies: An integrative review and analysis. *Psychological Bulletin, 101,* 428–442. (p. 501)

Hearold, S. (1986). A synthesis of 1043 effects of television on social behavior. In G. Comstock (Ed.), *Public communication and behavior.* New York: Academic Press. (p. 580)

Heath, L., & Petraitis, J. (1987). Television viewing and fear of crime: Where is the mean world? *Basic and Applied Social psychology, 8,* 97–123. (p. 580)

Hebb, D. O. (1980). *Essay on mind.* Hillsdale, NJ: Erlbaum. 9–16. (pp. 236, 381, 391, 590)

Hebert, H. J. (1988, January 13). Airlines hit 5–year high in fatalities. *Detroit Free Press,* pp. 1A, 16A. (p. 293)

Heckler, M. M. (1985). The fight against Alzheimer's disease. *American Psychologist, 40,* 1240–1244. (p. 101)

Heiman, J. R. (1975, April). The physiology of erotica: Women's sexual arousal. *Psychology Today,* 90–94. (p. 364)

Hellman, P. (1980). *Avenue of the righteous of nations.* New York: Atheneum. (p. 590)

Helson, R., & Moane, G. (1987). Personality change in women from college to midlife. *Journal of Personality and Social Psychology, 53,* 176–186. (p. 131)

Helzer, J. E. (1987). Epidemiology of alcoholism. *Journal of Consulting and Clinical Psychology, 55,* 284–292. (p. 216)

Henry, J. P., & Stephens, P. M. (1977). *Stress, health, and the social environment.* New York: Springer-Verlag. (p. 512)

Herman, C. P., & Mack, D. (1975). Restrained and unrestrained eating. *Journal of Personality, 43,* 647–660. (p. 539)

Herman, C. P., Olmsted, M. P., & Polivy, J. (1983). Obesity, externality, and susceptibility to social influence: An integrated analysis. *Journal of Personality and Social Psychology, 45,* 926–934. (p. 536)

Herman, C. P., & Polivy, J. (1980). Restrained eating. In A. J. Stunkard (Ed.), *Obesity.* Philadelphia: Saunders. (p. 539)

Heron, W. (1957, January). The pathology of boredom. *Scientific American,* pp. 52–56. (p. 163)

Herrmann, D. (1982). Know thy memory: The use of questionnaires to assess and study memory. *Psychological Bulletin, 92,* 434–452. (p. 278)

Hess, E. H. (1956, July). Space perception in the chick. *Scientific American,* pp. 71–80. (p. 182)

Hetherington, E. M. (1979). Divorce: A child's perspective. *American Psychologist, 34,* 851–858. (p. 79)

Hewitt, J. K. (1984). Normal components of personality variation. *Journal of Personality and Social Psychology, 47,* 671–675. (p. 437)

Hicks, R. A., & Gaus, W. (1983a). Type A–Type B behavior and daily milk consumption in college students. *Bulletin of the Psychonomic Society, 21,* 259. (p. 516)

Hicks, R. A., Kilcourse, J., & Sinnott, M. A. (1983b). Type A-B behavior and caffeine use in college students. *Psychological Reports, 52,* 338. (p. 516)

Hicks, R. A., & Pellegrini, R. J. (1982). Sleep problems and Type A-B behavior in college students. *Psychological Reports, 51,* 196. (p. 516)

Higgins, E. T. (1987). Self-discrepancy: A theory relating self and affect. *Psychological Review, 94,* 319–340. (p. 429)

Hilgard, E. R. (1983, August). *Dissociation theory and hypnosis.* Paper presented at the meeting of the American Psychological Association, Anaheim, CA. (p. 211)

Hilgard, E. R. (1986). *Divided consciousness: Multiple controls in human thought and action.* New York: Wiley. (pp. 213, 221)

Hinde, R. A. (1984). Why do the sexes behave differently in close relationships? *Journal of Social and Personal Relationships, 1,* 471–501. (p. 119)

Hines, M. (1982). Prenatal gonadal hormones and sex differences in human behavior. *Psychological Bulletin, 92,* 56–80. (p. 119)

Hinkle, S., & Schopler, J. (1986). Bias in the evaluation of in-group and out-group performance. In S. Worchel & W. G. Austin (Eds.), *Psychology of intergroup relations* (2nd ed.). Chicago: Nelson-Hall. (p. 593)

Hintzman, D. L. (1978). *The psychology of learning and memory.* San Francisco: Freeman. (p. 264)

Hinz, L. D., & Williamson, D. A. (1987). Bulimia and depression: A review of the affective variant hypothesis. *Psychological Bulletin, 102,* 150–158. (pp. 357–358)

Hirst, W., Neisser, U., & Spelke, E. (1978, June). Divided attention. *Human Nature,* pp. 54–61. (p. 213)

Hoebel, B. G., & Teitelbaum, P. (1966). Effects of force-feeding and starvation on food intake and body weight in a rat with ventromedial hypothalamic lesions. *Journal of Comparative and Physiological Psychology, 61,* 189–193. (p. 356)

Hoffman, C., Lau, I., & Johnson, D. R. (1986). The linguistic relativity of person cognition: An English-Chinese comparison. *Journal of Personality and Social Psychology, 51,* 1097–1105. (p. 309)

Hohmann, G. W. (1966). Some effects of spinal cord lesions on experienced emotional feelings. *Psychophysiology, 3,* 143–156. (p. 401)

Hokanson, J. E., & Edelman, R. (1966). Effects of three social responses on vascular processes. *Journal of Personality and Social Psychology, 3,* 442–447. (p. 392)

Holahan, C. J., & Moos, R. H. (1986). Personality, coping, and family resources in stress resistance: A longitudinal analysis. *Journal of Personality and Social Psychology, 51,* 389–395. (p. 512)

Holden, C. (1980a). Identical twins reared apart. *Science, 207,* 1323–1325. (p. 82)

Holden, C. (1980b, November). Twins reunited. *Science 80,* pp. 55–59. (p. 82)

Holden, C. (1986a). Days may be numbered for polygraphs in the private sector. *Science, 232,* 705. (p. 383)

Holden, C. (1986b). Giving mental illness its research due. *Science, 232,* 1084–1085. (p. 468)

Holden, C. (1986c). Researchers grapple with problems of updating classic psychological test. *Science, 233,* 1249–1251. (p. 427)

Holden, C. (1987a, April). Creativity and the troubled mind. *Psychology Today,* pp. 9–10. (p. 458)

Holden, C. (1987b). Is alcoholism treatment effective? *Science, 236,* 20–22. (p. 485)

Holden, C. (1987c). OTA cites financial disaster of Alzheimer's. *Science, 236,* 253. (p. 101)

Holmes, D. S. (1978). Projection as a defense mechanism. *Psychological Bulletin, 85,* 677–688. (p. 417)

Holmes, D. S. (1981). Existence of classical projection and the stress-reducing function of attributive projection: A reply to Sherwood. *Psychological Bulletin, 90,* 460–466. (p. 417)

Holmes, D. S. (1984). Meditation and somatic arousal reduction: A review of the experimental evidence. *American Psychologist, 39,* 1–10. (p. 212)

Holmes, T. H., & Rahe, R. H. (1967). The social readjustment rating scale. *Journal of Psychosomatic Research, 11,* 213–218. (p. 512)

Hooper, J., & Teresi, D. (1986). *The Three-Pound Universe.* New York: Macmillan. (p. 39)

Hooykaas, R. (1972). *Religion and the rise of modern science.* Grand Rapids, MI: Eerdmans. (p. 9)

Horn, J. L. (1982). The aging of human abilities. In J. Wolman (Ed.), *Handbook of developmental psychology.* Englewood Cliffs, NJ: Prentice-Hall. (p. 104)

Horner, K. L., Rushton, J. P., & Vernon, P. A. (1986). Relation between aging and research productivity of academic psychologists. *Psychology and Aging, 1,* 319–324. (p. 104)

House, J. S., Landis, K. R., & Umberson, D. (1988). Social relationships and health. *Science, 241,* 540–545. (p. 524)

Howard, A., Pion, G. M., Gottfredson, G. D., Flattau, P. E., Oskamp, S., Pfafflin, S. M., Bray, D. W., & Burstein, A. G. (1986). The changing face of American psychology: A report from the committee on employment and human resources. *American Psychologist, 41,* 1311–1327. (p. 125)

Hubel, D. H. (1979, September). The brain. *Scientific American,* pp. 45–53. (p. 143)

Hubel, D. H., & Wiesel, T. N. (1979, September). Brain mechanisms of vision. *Scientific American,* pp. 150–162. (pp. 35, 150–151)

Hugo, G. (1987). Aging in the third world. *Social Science, 72,* 57–60. (p. 100)

Hull, J. G., & Bond, Jr., C. F. (1986). Social and behavioral consequences of alcohol consumption and expectancy: A meta-analysis. *Psychological Bulletin, 99,* 347–360. (p. 216)

Hull, J. G., Young, R. D., & Jouriles, E. (1986). Applications of the self-awareness model of alcohol consumption: Predicting patterns of use and abuse. *Journal of Personality and Social Psychology, 51,* 790–796. (pp. 216, 338)

Hunt, E. (1983). On the nature of intelligence. *Science, 219,* 141–146. (p. 331)

Hunt, J. M. (1982). Toward equalizing the developmental opportunities of infants and preschool children. *Journal of Social Issues, 38*(4), 163–191. (p. 338)

Hunt, M. (1974). *Sexual behavior in the 1970s.* Chicago: Playboy Press. (pp. 359, 365)

Hunt, M. (1982). *The universe within.* New York: Simon and Schuster. (pp. 286, 297)

Hunt, M. (1987, August 30). Navigating the therapy maze. *New York Times Magazine,* pp. 28–49. (p. 491)

Hunziker, U. A., & Barr, R. B. (1986). Increased carrying reduces infant crying: A randomized controlled trial. *Pediatrics, 77,* 641–648. (p. 71)

Hyde, J. S. (1981). How large are cognitive gender differences? A meta-analysis using w^2 and *d. American Psychologist, 36,* 892–901. (p. 132)

Hyde, J. S. (1983, November). *Bem's gender schema theory.* Paper presented at GLCA Women's Studies Conference, Rochester, IN. (p. 272)

Hyde, J. S. (1984, July). Children's understanding of sexist language. *Developmental Psychology, 20*(4), 697–706. (p. 308)

Hyde, J. S. (1986a). Gender differences in aggression. In J. S. Hyde & M. C. Linn (Eds.), *The psychology of gender: Advances through meta-analysis.* Baltimore: Johns Hopkins University Press. (p. 130)

Hyde, J. S. (1986b). *Understanding human sexuality* (3rd ed.). New York: McGraw-Hill. (p. 366)

Hyde, J. S., & Linn, M. C. (1986). *The psychology of gender: Advances through meta-analysis.* Baltimore: Johns Hopkins University Press. (p. 128)

Hyde, J. S., & Linn, M. C. (1988). Gender differences in verbal ability: A meta-analysis. *Psychological Bulletin, 104,* 53–69. (p. 131)

Hyman, R. (1981). Cold reading: How to convince strangers that you know all about them. In K. Frazier (Ed.), *Paranormal borderlands of science.* Buffalo, NY: Prometheus. (pp. 436–437)

Hyman, R. (1986). Maimonides dream-telepathy experiments. *Skeptical Inquirer, 11,* 91–92. (p. 107)

Ickes, W., Patterson, M. L., Rajecki, D. W., & Tanford, S. (1982). Behavioral and cognitive consequences of reciprocal versus compensatory responses to preinteraction expectancies. *Social Cognition, 1,* 160–190. (p. 595)

Ince, L. P., Brucker, B. S., & Alba, A. (1978). Conditioned responding of the neurogenic bladder. *Psychosomatic Medicine, 40,* 14–24. (p. 235)

Inglehart, M. R., Markus, H., Brown, D. R., & Moore, W. (1987). The impact of possible selves on academic achievement: A longitudinal analysis. Paper presented at the Midwestern Psychological Association convention. (p. 429)

Ingelhart, R., & Rabier, J-R. (1986). Aspirations adapt to situations—but why are the Belgians so much happier than the French? A cross-cultural analysis of the subjective quality of life. In F. M. Andrews (Ed.), *Research on the quality of life*. Ann Arbor, MI: Institute for Social Research, University of Michigan. (pp. 9, 104, 394)

Ingham, A. G., Levinger, G., Graves, J., & Peckham, V. (1974). The Ringelmann effect: Studies of group size and group performance. *Journal of Experimental Social Psychology, 10,* 371–384. (p. 567)

Inhelder, B., & Piaget, J. (1958). *The growth of logical thinking.* New York: Basic. (p. 92)

Insel, P. M., & Roth, W. T. (1976). *Health in a changing society.* Palo Alto, CA: Mayfield. (p. 99)

Isen, A. M., & Means, B. (1983). The influence of positive affect on decision-making strategy. *Social Cognition, 2,* 28–31. (p. 393)

Istvan, J. & Matarazzo, J. D. (1984). Tobacco, alcohol, and caffeine use: A review of their interrelationships. *Psychological Bulletin, 95,* 301–326. (p. 216)

Izard, C. E. (1977). *Human emotions.* New York: Plenum Press. (p. 386)

Izard, C. E. (1982). The psychology of emotion comes of age on the coattails of Darwin. *Contemporary Psychology, 27,* 426–429. (pp. 387–388)

Jackson, J. M., & Williams, K. D. (1988). Social loafing: A review and theoretical analysis. Unpublished manuscript, Fordham University. (p. 567)

Jackson, L. A., Ialongo, N., & Stollak, G. E. (1986). Parental correlates of gender role: The relations between parents' masculinity, femininity, and child-rearing behaviors and of their children's gender roles. *Journal of Social and Clinical Psychology, 4,* 204–224. (p. 121)

Jacobs, B. L. (1987). How hallucinogenic drugs work. *American Scientist, 75,* 386–392. (p. 218)

Jacobs, W. J., & Nadel, L. (1985). Stress-induced recovery of fears and phobias. *Psychological Bulletin, 92,* 512–531. (p. 52)

Jacobson, R. L. (1986, September 3). Number of blacks taking SAT drops 5 pct. in 5 years. *Chronicle of Higher Education,* p. 108. (p. 339)

James, W. (1890). *The principles of psychology* (Vol. 2). New York: Holt. (pp. 27, 273, 400, 429)

James, W. (1902; reprinted 1958). *Varieties of religious experience.* New York: Mentor Books. (p. 393)

Janis, I. L. (1969). *Stress and frustration.* New York: Harcourt Brace Jovanovich. (p. 528)

Janis, I. L. (1982a). *Groupthink: Psychological studies of policy decisions and fiascoes.* Boston: Houghton Mifflin. (p. 570)

Janis, I. L. (Ed.) (1982b). *Counseling on personal decisions: Theory and research on short-term helping relationships.* New Haven: Yale University Press. (p. 529)

Janis, I. L. (1983). Stress inoculation in health care: Theory and research. In D. Meichenbaum & M. E. Jaremko (Eds.), *Stress reeducation and prevention.* New York: Plenum Press. (p. 528)

Janis, I. L. (1986). Problems of international crisis manage-

ment in the nuclear age. *Journal of Social Issues, 42* (2), 201–220. (p. 290)

Janoff-Bulman, R., Timko, C., & Carli, L. L. (1985). Cognitive biases in blaming the victim. *Journal of Experimental Social Psychology, 21,* 161–177. (p. 594)

Jarvik, L. F. (1975). Thoughts on the psychobiology of aging. *American Psychologist, 30,* 576–583. (p. 101)

Jasnoski, M. L., Kugler, J., & McClelland, D. C. (1986). Power imagery and relaxation affect psychoneuroimmune indices. Paper presented at the American Psychological Association convention. (p. 523)

Jasnoski, M. L., & Schwartz, G. E. (1985). A synchronous systems model for health. *American Behavioral Scientist, 28,* 468–485. (p. 507)

Jason, L. A. (1986). Implementing large-scale behavioral interventions at the community level. Presidential address to the Behavior Analysis Society of Illinois. (p. 531)

Jeffery, R. W., & Wing, R. R. (1983). Recidivism and self-cure of smoking and obesity: Data from population studies. *American Psychologist, 38,* 852. (p. 540)

Jemmott, J. B., III, Ditto, P. H., & Croyle, R. T. (1986). Judging health status: Effects of perceived prevalence and personal relevance. *Journal of Personality and Social Psychology, 50,* 899–903. (p. 527)

Jemmott, J. B., III, & Locke, S. E. (1984). Psychosocial factors, immunologic mediation, and human susceptibility to infectious diseases: How much do we know? *Psychological Bulletin, 95,* 78–108. (p. 518)

Jenkins, J. G., & Dallenbach, K. M. (1924). Obliviscence during sleep and waking. *American Journal of Psychology, 35,* 605–612. (p. 277)

Jenni, D. A., & Jenni, M. A. (1976). Carrying behavior in humans: Analysis of sex differences. *Science, 194,* 859–860. (p. 131)

Jensen, A. R. (1980). *Bias in mental testing.* New York: The Free Press. (pp. 327, 334)

Jensen, A. R. (1983, August). *The nature of the black-white difference on various psychometric tests: Spearman's hypothesis.* Paper presented at the meeting of the American Psychological Association, Anaheim, CA. (p. 342)

Jensen, A. R. (1984, March). Political ideologies and educational research. *Phi Delta Kappan,* pp. 460–462. (p. 319)

Jensen, A. R. (1985). The nature of the black-white difference on various psychometric tests: Spearman's hypothesis. *Behavioral and Brain Sciences, 8,* 193–263. (p. 339)

Jensen, M. R. (1987). Psychobiological factors predicting the course of breast cancer. *Journal of Personality, 55,* 317–342. (p. 577)

Jepson, C., Krantz, D. H., & Nisbett, R. E. (1983). Inductive reasoning: Competence or skill. *The Behavioral and Brain Sciences, 3,* 494–501. (p. 620)

Jervis, R. (1985a, April 2). Quoted by D. Goleman, Political forces come under new scrutiny of psychology. *The New York Times,* pp. C1, C4. (p. 295)

Jervis, R. (1985b). Perceiving and coping with threat: Psychological perspectives. In R. Jervis, R. N. Lebow, & J. Stein (Eds.), *Psychology and deterrence*. Baltimore: Johns Hopkins University Press. (p. 604)

John, E. R., Tang, Y., Brill, A. B., Young, R., & Ono, K. (1986). Double-labeled metabolic maps of memory. *Science, 233*, 1167–1175. (p. 269)

Johnson, D., & Drenick, E. J. (1977). Therapeutic fasting in morbid obesity. Long-term follow-up. *Archives of Internal Medicine, 137*, 1381–1382. (p. 537)

Johnson, D. W., & Johnson, R. T. (1987). *Learning together and alone: Cooperative, competitive, and individualistic learning* (2nd ed.). Englewood Cliffs, NJ: Prentice-Hall. (p. 606)

Johnson, E. J., & Tversky, A. (1983). Affect, generalization, and the perception of risk. *Journal of Personality and Social Psychology, 45*, 20–31. (p. 393)

Johnson, M. H., & Magaro, P. A. (1987). Effects of mood and severity on memory processes in depression and mania. *Psychological Bulletin, 101*, 28–40. (p. 271)

Johnston, L. D. (1988, January 13). Summary of 1987 drug study results. Media statement delivered in the Offices of the Secretary of Health and Human Services. (p. 532)

Johnston, L. D., O'Malley, P. M., & Bachman, J. G. (1988). *Illicit drug use, smoking, and drinking by America's high school students, college students, and young adults, 1975–1987*. Rockville, MD: National Institute on Drug Abuse. (pp. 217, 220)

Jones, E. F., Forrest, J. D., Goldman, N., Henshaw, S. K., Lincoln, R., Rosoff, J. I., Westoff, C. F., & Wulf, D. (1985, March/April). Teenage pregnancy in developed countries: Determinants and policy implications. *Family Planning Perspectives, 17*, 53–64. (p. 360)

Jones, L. (1985–86). CSICOP's international conference in London: Investigation and belief, past lives and prizes. *Skeptical Inquirer, 10*, 98–104. (p. 188)

Jones, M. C. (1924). A laboratory study of fear: The case of Peter. *Journal of Genetic Psychology, 31*, 308–315. (p. 483)

Jones, M. C. (1957). The later careers of boys who were early or late maturing. *Child Development, 28*, 113–128. (p. 91)

Jones, W. H., Carpenter, B. N., & Quintana, D. (1985). Personality and interpersonal predictors of loneliness in two cultures. *Journal of Personality and Social Psychology, 48*, 1503–1511. (pp. 17, 360)

Jorgenson, D. O., & Papciak, A. S. (1981). The effects of communication, resource feedback, and identifiability on behavior in a simulated commons. *Journal of Experimental Social Psychology, 17*, 373–385. (p. 606)

Joseph, J. G., Montgomery, S. B., Emmons, C-A., Kirscht, J. P., Kessler, R. C., Ostrow, D. G., Wortman, C. B., O'Brien, K., Eller, M., & Eshleman, S. (1987). Perceived risk of AIDS: Assessing the behavioral and psychosocial consequences in a cohort of gay men. *Journal of Applied Social Psychology, 17*, 231–250. (p. 369)

Jung, C. (1933). *Modern man in search of a soul*. New York: Harcourt Brace Jovanovich. (pp. 100, 132)

Justice, A. (1985). Review of the effects of stress on cancer in laboratory animals: Importance of time of stress application and type of tumor. *Psychological Bulletin, 98*, 108–138. (p. 519)

Kagan, J. (1976). Emergent themes in human development. *American Scientist, 64*, 186–196. (p. 75)

Kagan, J. (1978, January). The baby's elastic mind. *Human Nature*, pp. 66–73. (p. 112)

Kagan, J. (1982, July). The fearful child's hidden talents (interview with E. Hall). *Psychology Today*, pp. 50–59. (p. 112)

Kagan, J. (1984). *The nature of the child*. New York: Basic Books. (p. 68)

Kagan, J. (1988, May). Quoted by A. J. Hostetler, Rethinking how personality flowers. *APA Monitor*, pp. 12–13. (p. 112)

Kagan, J., Reznick, J. S., & Snidman, N. (1988). Biological bases of childhood shyness. *Science, 240*, 167–171. (p. 80)

Kahn, S., Zimmerman, G., Csikszentmihalyi, M., & Getzels, J. W. (1985). Relations between identity in young adulthood and intimacy in midlife. *Journal of Personality and Social Psychology, 49*, 1316–1322. (p. 96)

Kahneman, D. (1985, June). Quoted by K. McKean, Decisions, decisions. *Discover*, pp. 22–31. (p. 617)

Kahneman, D., & Tversky, A. (1979). Intuitive prediction: Biases and corrective procedures. *Management Science, 12*, 313–327. (pp. 293–294)

Kahnenan, D., & Tverksy, A. (1984). Choices, values, and frames. *American Psychologist, 39*, 341–350. (p. 294)

Kandel, E. R., & Schwartz, J. H. (1982). Molecular biology of learning: Modulation of transmitter release. *Science, 218*, 433–443. (p. 268)

Kantrowitz, B. (1986, September 1). Three's a crowd. *Newsweek*, pp. 68–76. (pp. 107–108)

Kaplan, H. I., & Saddock, B. J. (1981). *Modern synopsis of comprehensive textbook of psychiatry* (3rd ed.). Baltimore: Williams & Wilkins. (p. 500)

Kaplan, H. S. (1979). *Disorders of sexual desire*. New York: Brunner/Mazel. (p. 363)

Kaplan, R. M. (1984). The connection between clinical health promotion and health status: A critical overview. *American Psychologist, 39*, 755–765. (p. 530)

Kaprio, J., Koskenvuy, M., & Rita, H. (1987). Mortality after bereavement: A prospective study of 95,647 widowed persons. *American Journal of Public Health, 77*, 283–287. (p. 511)

Karacan, I., Aslan, C., & Hirshkowitz, M. (1983). Erectile mechanisms in man. *Science, 220*, 1080–1082. (p. 199)

Kaufman, J., & Zigler, E. (1987). Do abused children become abusive parents? *American Journal of Orthopsychiatry, 57*, 186–192. (p. 75)

Kaufman, L. (1979). *Perception: The world transformed*. New York: Oxford University Press. (p. 154)

Kaylor, J. A., King, D. W., & King, L. A. (1987). Psychological effects of military service in Vietnam: A meta-analysis. *Psychological Bulletin, 102*, 257–271. (p. 525)

Kazdin, A. E. (1982). The token economy: A decade later. *Journal of Applied Behavior Analysis, 15*, 431–445. (p. 486)

Keesey, R. E., & Corbett, S. W. (1983). Metabolic defense of the body weight set-point. In A. J. Stunkard & E. Stellar (Eds.), *Eating and its disorders.* New York: Raven Press. (p. 356)

Kelling, S. T., & Halpern, B. P. (1983). Taste flashes: Reaction times, intensity, and quality. *Science, 219,* 412–414. (p. 160)

Kelly, E. L. (1955). Consistency of the adult personality. *American Psychologist, 10,* 659–681. (p. 112)

Kelly, E. L., & Conley, J. J. (1987). Personality and compatibility: A prospective analysis of marital stability and marital satisfaction. *Journal of Personality and Social Psychology, 52,* 27–40. (p. 371)

Kempe, R. S., & Kempe, C. C. (1978). *Child abuse.* Cambridge, MA: Harvard University Press. (p. 75)

Kennell, J. N., & Klaus, M. (1982). *Parent-infant bonding.* St. Louis: C. V. Mosby. (p. 72)

Kenrick, D. T. (1987). Gender, genes, and the social environment. In P. C. Shaver & C. Hendrick (Eds.), *Review of Personality and Social Psychology, 8,* 14–43. (pp. 126, 130)

Kenrick, D. T., & Funder, D. C. (1988). Profiting from controversy: Lessons from the person-situation debate. *American Psychologist, 43,* 23–34. (p. 424)

Kenrick, D. T., & Gutierres, S. E. (1980). Contrast effects and judgments of physical attractiveness: When beauty becomes a social problem. *Journal of Personality and Social Psychology, 38,* 131–140. (p. 365)

Kenrick, D. T., & Trost, M. R. (1987). A biosocial theory of heterosexual relationships. In K. Kelly (Ed.), *Females, males, and sexuality.* Albany: State University of New York Press. (p. 119)

Kerr, N. L., & Bruun, S. E. (1983). Dispensability of member effort and group motivation losses: Free-rider effects. *Journal of Personality and Social Psychology, 44,* 78–94. (p. 567)

Kessler, M., & Albee, G. (1975). Primary prevention. *Annual Review of Psychology, 26,* 557–591. (p. 503)

Kett, J. F. (1977). *Rites of passage: Adolescence in America, 1790 to the present.* New York: Basic Books. (p. 89)

Keys, A., Brozek, J., Henschel, A., Mickelsen, O., & Taylor, H. L. (1950). *The biology of human starvation.* Minneapolis: University of Minnesota Press. (p. 354)

Kihlstrom, J. F. (1985). Hypnosis. *Annual Review of Psychology, 36,* 385–418. (pp. 206, 211)

Kihlstrom, J. F. (1987a). Strong inferences about hypnosis. *Brain and Behavioral Sciences, 9,* 474–475. (p. 214)

Kihlstrom, J. F. (1987b). The cognitive unconscious. *Science, 237,* 1445–1452. (p. 195)

Kihlstrom, J. F., & Harachkiewicz, J. M. (1982). The earliest recollection: A new survey. *Journal of Personality, 50,* 134–148. (p. 62)

Kihlstrom, J. F., & Hoyt, I. P. (1988). Hypnosis and the psychology of delusions. In T. F. Oltmanns & B. A. Maher (Eds.), *Delusional beliefs.* New York: Wiley. (p. 211)

Kimble, G. A. (1956). *Principles of general psychology.* New York: Ronald Press. (pp. 236–237)

Kimura, D. (1973, March). The asymmetry of the human brain. *Scientific American,* pp. 70–78. (p. 49)

Kimzey, S. L. (1975). The effects of extended spaceflight on hematologic and immunologic systems. *Journal of the American Medical Women's Association, 30*(5), 218–232. (p. 518)

Kimzey, S. L., Johnson, P. C., Ritzman, S. E., & Mengel, C. E. (1976, April). Hematology and immunology studies: The second manned Skylab mission. *Aviation, Space, and Environmental Medicine,* pp. 383–390. (p. 518)

King, N. J., & Montgomery, R. B. (1980). Biofeedback-induced control of human peripheral temperature: A critical review of the literature. *Psychological Bulletin, 88,* 738–752. (p. 522)

Kinsey, A. C., Pomeroy, W., & Martin, C. (1948). *Sexual behavior in the human male.* Philadelphia: Saunders. (p. 359)

Kinsey, A. C., Pomeroy, W., Martin, C., & Gebhard, P. (1953). *Sexual behavior in the human female.* Philadelphia: Saunders. (p. 359)

Kirk, J. (1986, August 11). Deciding morality (Letters column). *Time,* p. 9. (p. 584)

Klayman, J., & Ha, Y-W. (1987). Confirmation, disconfirmation, and information in hypothesis testing. *Psychological Review, 94,* 211–228. (p. 288)

Kleinke, C. L. (1986). Gaze and eye contact: A research review. *Psychological Bulletin, 100,* 78–100. (p. 386)

Kleinmuntz, B., & Szucko, J. J. (1984). A field study of the fallibility of polygraph lie detection. *Nature, 308,* 449–450. (p. 384)

Kleitman, N. (1960, November). Patterns of dreaming. *Scientific American,* pp. 82–88. (p. 198)

Kline, D., & Schieber, F. (1985). Vision and aging. In J. E. Birren & K. W. Schaie (Eds.), *Handbook of the psychology of aging.* New York: Van Nostrand Reinhold. (p. 147)

Kline, N. S. (1974). *From sad to glad.* New York: Ballantine Books. (p. 462)

Klineberg, O. (1938). Emotional expression in Chinese literature. *Journal of Abnormal and Social Psychology, 33,* 517–520. (p. 386)

Klineberg, O. (1984). Public opinion and nuclear war. *American Psychologist, 39,* 1245–1253. (p. 606)

Kluckhohn, C., & Murray, H. A. (1956). Personality formation: The determinants. In C. Kluckhohn, H. A. Murray, & D. Schneider (Eds.), *Personality in nature, society, and culture* (2nd ed.). New York: Knopf. (p. 57)

Kluft, R. P. (1987). An update on multiple personality disorder. *Hospital and Community Psychiatry, 38,* 363–373. (p. 456)

Kluver, H., & Bucy, P. C. (1939). Preliminary analysis of functions of the temporal lobes in monkeys. *Archives of Neurology and Psychiatry, 42,* 979–1000. (p. 37)

Knapp, R. J. (1987, July). When a child dies. *Psychology Today,* pp. 60–67. (p. 110)

Kobasa, S. C. (1982). The hardy personality: Toward a social psychology of stress and health. In G. S. Sanders & J. Suls (Eds.), *Social psychology of health and illness.* Hillsdale, NJ: Erlbaum. (p. 514)

Koch, C. (1988, June 17). Quoted in W. F. Allman, How the brain really works its wonders. *U.S. News & World Report*, pp. 46–54. (p. 300)

Kohlberg, L. (1966). A cognitive-developmental analysis of children's sex-role concepts and attitudes. In E. E. Maccoby (Ed.), *The development of sex differences*. Stanford, CA: Stanford University Press. (pp. 122–123)

Kohlberg, L. (1981). *The philosophy of moral development: Essays on moral development* (Vol. I). San Franscisco: Harper & Row. (p. 92)

Kohlberg, L. (1984). *The psychology of moral development: Essays on moral development* (Vol. II). San Francisco: Harper & Row. (pp. 92, 93)

Kohler, I. (1962, May). Experiments with goggles. *Scientific American*, pp. 62–72. (p. 182)

Köhler, W. (1925; reprinted 1957). *The mentality of apes*. London: Pelican. (p. 287)

Kohn, A. (1987a, September). Art for art's sake. *Psychology Today*, pp. 52–57. (p. 606)

Kohn, A. (1987b, October). It's hard to get left out of a pair. *Psychology Today*, pp. 53–57. (p. 334)

Kolata, G. (1985a). Obesity declared a disease. *Science, 227*, 1019–1020. (p. 535)

Kolata, G. (1985b). A guarded endorsement for shock therapy. *Science, 228*, 1510–1511. (p. 498)

Kolata, G. (1986a). New growth industry in human growth hormone? *Science, 234*, 22–24. (p. 32)

Kolata, G. (1986b). Youth suicide: New research focuses on a growing social problem. *Science, 233*, 839–841. (p. 457)

Kolata, G. (1987a). Early signs of school age IQ. *Science, 236*, 774–775. (p. 332)

Kolata, G. (1987b). Metabolic catch–22 of exercise regimens. *Science, 236*, 146–147. (p. 538)

Kolers, P. A. (1975). Specificity of operations in sentence recognition. *Cognitive Psychology, 7*, 289–306. (p. 260)

Koltz, C. (1983, December). Scapegoating. *Psychology Today*, pp. 68–69. (p. 593)

Konner, M. (1982). *The tangled wing: Biological restraints on the human spirit*. New York: Holt, Rinehart & Winston. (p. 130)

Koss, M. P., Dinero, T. E., Seibel, C. A., & Cox, S. L. (1988). Stranger and acquaintance rape: Are there differences in the victim's experience? *Psychology of Women Quarterly, 12*, 1–24. (p. 582)

Koss, M. P., Gidycz, C. A., & Wisniewski, N. (1987). The scope of rape: Incidence and prevalence of sexual aggression and victimization in a national sample of higher education students. *Journal of Consulting and Clinical Psychology, 55*, 162–170. (p. 582)

Kosslyn, S. M. (1987). Seeing and imagining in the cerebral hemispheres: A computational approach. *Psychological Review, 94*, 148–175. (p. 151)

Krantz, D. S., & Manuck, S. B. (1984). Acute psychophysiologic reactivity and risk of cardiovascular disease: A review and methodologic critique. *Psychological Bulletin, 96*, 435–464. (p. 516)

Krech, D. (1978). Quoted in M. C. Diamond, The aging brain: Some enlightening and optimistic results. *American Scientist, 66*, 66–71. (p. 104)

Krupat, E. (1986, November). A delicate imbalance. *Psychology Today*, pp. 22–26. (p. 528)

Kübler-Ross, E. (1969). *On death and dying*. New York: Macmillan. (p. 111)

Kuhl, P. K., & Meltzoff, A. N. (1982). The bimodal perception of speech in infancy. *Science, 218*, 1138–1141. (p. 303)

Kuiper, N. A., & Rogers, T. B. (1979). Encoding of personal information: Self-other differences. *Journal of Personality and Social Psychology, 37*, 499–514. (p. 262)

Kulik, J. A., Bangert-Drowns, R. L., & Kulik, C-L. C. (1984). Effectiveness of coaching for aptitude tests. *Psychological Bulletin, 95*, 179–188. (p. 326)

Kulik, J. A., Kulik, C. C., & Cohen, P. A. (1980). Effectiveness of computer-based college teaching: A meta-analysis of findings. *Review of Educational Research, 50*, 525–544. (p. 245)

Kulik, J. A., Kulik, C. C., & Gangert-Drowns, R. L. (1985). Effectiveness of computer-based education in elementary schools. *Computers in Human Behavior, 1*, 59–74. (p. 245)

Kunst-Wilson, W. R., & Zajonc, R. B. (1980). Affective discrimination of stimuli that cannot be recognized. *Science, 207*, 557–558. (p. 141)

Kurdek, L. A., & Schmitt, J. P. (1986). Interaction of sex role self-concept with relationship quality and relationship beliefs in married, heterosexual cohabiting, gay, and lesbian couples. *Journal of Personality and Social Psychology, 51*, 365–370. (p. 127)

Kurtz, P. (1983, Spring). Stars, planets, and people. *The Skeptical Inquirer*, pp. 65–68. (p. 436)

Kurzweil, R. (1985). What is artificial intelligence anyway? *American Scientist, 73*, 258–264. (p. 300)

Labbe, R., Firl, A., Jr., Mufson, E. J., & Stein, D. G. (1983). Fetal brain transplants: Reduction of cognitive deficits in rats with frontal cortex lesions. *Science, 221*, 470–472. (p. 50)

Labouvie-Vief, G., & Schell, D. A. (1982). Learning and memory in later life. In B. B. Wolman (Ed.), *Handbook of developmental psychology*. Englewood Cliffs, NJ: Prentice-Hall. (p. 103)

Ladd, G. T. (1887). *Elements of physiological psychology*. New York: Scribner's. (p. 193)

Lagerspetz, K. (1979). Modification of aggressiveness in mice. In S. Feshbach & A. Fraczek (Eds.), *Aggression & behavior change: Biological & social processes*. New York: Praeger. (pp. 81, 576)

Lagerweij, E., Nelis, P. C., van Ree, J. M., & Wiegant, V. M. (1984). The twitch in horses: A variant of acupuncture. *Science, 225*, 1172–1174. (p. 30)

Laird, J. D. (1974). Self-attribution of emotion: The effects of expressive behavior on the quality of emotional experience. *Journal of Personality and Social Psychology, 29*, 475–486. (p. 388)

Laird, J. D. (1984). The real role of facial response in the experience of emotion: A reply to Tourangeau and Ellsworth, and others. *Journal of Personality and Social Psychology, 47,* 909–917. (p. 388)

Lamb, M. (1979, June 17). Quoted by G. Collins, A new look at life with father. *New York Times Magazine,* pp. 30–31, 48–52, 65. (p. 73)

Lamb, M. (1982, April). Second thoughts on first touch. *Psychology Today,* pp. 9–11. (p. 72)

Lamb, M. E. (1987). Predictive implications of individual differences in attachment. *Journal of Consulting and Clinical Psychology, 55,* 817–824. (p. 74)

Lancioni, G. (1980). Infant operant conditioning and its implications for early intervention. *Psychological Bulletin, 88,* 516–534. (p. 62)

Landauer, T. K. (1986). How much do people remember? Some estimates of the quantity of learned information in long-term memory. *Cognitive Science, 10,* 477–493. (p. 266)

Landers, A. (1969, April 8). Syndicated newspaper column. Cited by L. Berkowitz, The Case for bottling up rage. *Psychology Today,* September, 1973, pp. 24–31. (p. 392)

Landers, S. (1986, December). Judge reiterates I.Q. test ban. *APA Monitor,* p. 18. (p. 315)

Landfield, P., Cadwallader, L. B., & Vinsant, S. (1988). Quantitative changes in hippocampal structure following long-term exposure to Delta–9–tetrahydrocannabinol: Possible mediation by glucocorticoid systems. *Brain Research,* Vol. 443, 47–62. (p. 219)

Langer, E. J. (1983). *The psychology of control.* Beverly Hills, CA: Sage. (p. 434)

Langer, E. J., & Abelson, R. P. (1974). A patient by any other name . . .: Clinician group differences in labeling bias. *Journal of Consulting and Clinical Psychology, 42,* 4–9. (p. 470)

Langer, E. J., & Imber, L. (1980). The role of mindlessness in the perception of deviance. *Journal of Personality and Social Psychology, 39,* 360–367. (p. 470)

Langlois, J. H., Roggman, L. A., Casey, R. J., Ritter, J. M., Rieser-Danner, L. A., & Jenkins, V. Y. (1987). Infant preferences for attractive faces: Rudiments of a stereotype? *Developmental Psychology, 23,* 363–369. (p. 597)

Larrance, D. T., & Twentyman, C. T. (1983). Maternal attributions and child abuse. *Journal of Abnormal Psychology, 92,* 449–457. (p. 68)

Larsen, R. J., & Diener, E. (1987). Affect intensity as an individual difference characteristic: A review. *Journal of Research in Personality, 21,* 1–39. (p. 80)

Larsen, R. J., Diener, E., & Cropanzano, R. S. (1987). Cognitive operations associated with individual differences in affect intensity. *Journal of Personality and Social Psychology, 53,* 767–774. (p. 404)

Lashley, K. S. (1950). In search of the engram. In *Symposium of the Society for Experimental Biology* (Vol. 4). New York: Cambridge University Press. (pp. 266–267)

Latané, B. (1981). The psychology of social impact. *American Psychologist, 36,* 343–356. (p. 567)

Latané, B., Dabbs, J. M., Jr. (1975). Sex, group size and helping in three cities. *Sociometry, 38,* 180–194. (p. 586)

Latimer, P. R., & Sweet, A. A. (1984). Cognitive versus behavioral procedures in cognitive-behavior therapy: A critical review of the evidence. *Journal of Behavior Therapy and Experimental Psychiatry, 15,* 9–22. (p. 491)

Laudenslager, M. L., & Reite, M. L. (1984). Losses and separations: Immunological consequences and health implications. *Review of Personality and Social Psychology, 5,* 285–312. (p. 513)

Laurence, J-R., & Perry, C. (1983). Hypnotically created memory among highly hypnotizable subjects. *Science, 222,* 523–524. (p. 208)

Lavie, P., & Hobson, J. A. (1986). Origin of dreams: Anticipation of modern theories in the philosophy and physiology of the eighteenth and nineteenth centuries. *Psychological Bulletin, 100,* 229–240. (p. 204)

Layton, B. D., & Turnbull, B. (1975). Belief, evaluation, and performance on an ESP task. *Journal of Experimental Social Psychology, 11,* 166–179. (pp. 185, 188)

Lazarus, R. S. (1984). On the primacy of cognition. *American Psychologist, 39,* 124–129. (p. 403)

Lazarus, R. S., & Folkman, S. (1984). *Stress, appraisal, and coping.* New York: Springer. (p. 512)

Lebow, J. (1982). Consumer satisfaction with mental health treatment. *Psychological Bulletin, 91,* 244–259. (p. 492)

Lee, V. E., Brooks-Gunn, J., & Schnur, E. (1988). Does Head Start work? A 1-year follow-up comparison of disadvantaged children attending Head Start, no preschool, and other preschool programs. *Developmental Psychology, 24,* 210–22. (p. 339)

Leepson, M. (1983, May 27). Chronic pain: The hidden epidemic. *Editorial Research Reports, 1*(20). (Published by Congressional Quarterly, Inc.) (p. 159)

Leerhsen, C. (1986, August 4). Aging Playboy. *Newsweek,* pp. 50–56. (p. 580)

Lefcourt, H. M. (1982). *Locus of control: Current trends in theory and research.* Hillsdale, NJ: Erlbaum. (p. 433)

Lefcourt, H. M., & Martin, R. A. (1986). *Humor and life stress.* New York: Springer-Verlag. (p. 523)

Lehman, D. R., Wortman, C. B., & Williams, A. F. (1987). Long-term effects of losing a spouse or child in a motor vehicle crash. *Journal of Personality and Social Psychology, 52,* 218–231. (p. 110)

Leibowitz, H. W. (1985). Grade crossing accidents and human factors engineering. *American Scientist, 73,* 558–562. (p. 176)

Lenneberg, E. H. (1967). *Biological foundations of language.* New York: Wiley. (p. 63)

Lepper, M. R. (1982). *Microcomputers in education: Motivational and social issues.* Paper presented at the meeting of the American Psychological Association. (p. 245)

Lepper, M. R., & Greene, D. (Eds.). (1979). *The hidden costs of reward.* Hillsdale, NJ: Erlbaum. (p. 248)

Lepper, M. R., Ross, L., & Lau, R. R. (1986). Persistence of inaccurate beliefs about the self: Perseverance effects in the classroom. *Journal of Personality and Social Psychology, 50,* 482–491. (p. 296)

Lerner, M. J. (1980). *The belief in a just world: A fundamental delusion.* New York: Plenum Press. (p. 594)

Lettvin, J. Y., Maturana, H. R., McCulloch, W. S., & Pitts, W. H. (1959). What the frog's eye tells the frog's brain. *Proceedings of the Institute of Radio Engineers, 47,* 1940–1951. (p. 140)

Leventhal, H., Zimmerman, R., & Gutmann, M. (1984). Compliance: A self-regulation perspective. In D. Gentry (Ed.), *Handbook of behavioral medicine.* New York: Guilford Press. (p. 529)

Levin, I. P. (1987). Associative effects of information framing. *Bulletin of the Psychonomic Society, 25,* 85–86. (p. 295)

Levin, I. P., Schnittjer, S. K., & Thee, S. L. (1988). Information framing effects in social and personal decisions. *Journal of Experimental Social Psychology,* in press. (p. 295)

Levinger, G. (1987). The limits of deterrence: An introduction. *Journal of Social Issues, 43*(4), 1–4. (p. 603)

Levinson, D. J. (1986). A conception of adult development. *American Psychologist, 41,* 3–13. (p. 106)

Levinson, D. J., Darow, C. N., Klein, E. B., Levinson, M. H., & McKee, B. (1978). *The seasons of a man's life.* New York: Knopf. (p. 106)

Levitt, E. E. (1986). Coercion, voluntariness, compliance and resistance: The essence of hypnosis twenty-seven years after Orne. Invited address to the American Psychological Association convention. (p. 210)

Levitt, E. E. (1988). Questions about multiple personality. *Harvard Medical School Mental Health Letter, 4*(10), 8. (p. 455)

Levy, J. (1983). Language, cognition, and the right hemisphere: A response to Gazzaniga. *American Psychologist, 38,* 538–541. (p. 46)

Levy, J. (1985, May). Right brain, left brain: Fact and fiction. *Psychology Today,* pp. 38–44. (p. 47)

Levy, J. (1987). Hemispheric assymetry and integration in the normal human brain. Address to the Eastern Psychological Association convention, April 11th. (p. 46)

Lewin, R. (1987). Brain grafts benefit Parkinson's patients. *Science, 236,* 149; Dramatic results with brain grafts, *Science, 237,* 245–247. (p. 50)

Lewis, C. C. (1981). The effects of parental firm control: A reinterpretation of findings. *Psychological Bulletin, 90,* 547–563. (p. 79)

Lewis, C. S. (1967). *Christian reflections.* Grand Rapids, MI: Eerdmans. (p. 274)

Lewinsohn, P. M., Mischel, W., Chaplin, W., & Barton, R. (1980). Social competence and depression: The role of illusory self-perceptions. *Journal of Abnormal Psychology, 89,* 203–212. (p. 488)

Lewinsohn, P. M., & Rosenbaum, M. (1987). Recall of parental behavior by acute depressives, remitted depressives, and nondepressives. *Journal of Personality and Social Psychology, 52,* 611–619. (p. 271)

Lewontin, R. (1976). Race and intelligence. In N. J. Block & G. Dworkin (Eds.), *The IQ controversy: Critical readings.* New York: Pantheon. (p. 340)

Libet, B. (1985). Unconscious cerebral initiative and the role of conscious will in voluntary action. *Behavioral and Brain Sciences, 8,* 529–566. (p. 142)

Lifton, R. J. (1982). Beyond nuclear numbing: A call to teach and learn. In *Proceedings of the Symposium on the Role of the Academy in Addressing the Issues of Nuclear War.* Geneva, NY: Hobart and William Smith Colleges. (p. 601)

Light, K. C., Koepke, J. P., Obrist, P. A., & Willis, P. W., Jr. (1983). Psychological stress induces sodium and fluid retention in men at high risk for hypertension. *Science, 220,* 429–431. (p. 517)

Linder, D. (1982). Social trap analogs: The tragedy of the commons in the laboratory. In V. J. Derlega & J. Grzelak (Ed.), *Cooperative and helping behavior: Theories and research.* New York: Academic Press. (p. 603)

Lindskold, S. (1978). Trust development, the GRIT proposal, and the effects of conciliatory acts on conflict and cooperation. *Psychological Bulletin, 85,* 772–793. (p. 607)

Lindskold, S. (1986). GRIT: Reducing distrust through carefully introduced conciliation. In S. Worchel & W. G. Austin (Eds.), *Psychology of intergroup relations,* (2nd ed.). Chicago: Nelson-Hall. (p. 607)

Lindskold, S., & Han, G. (1988). GRIT as a foundation for integrative bargaining. *Personality and Social Psychology Bulletin, 14,* 335–345. (p. 607)

Lindskold, S., Han, G., & Betz, B. (1986). Repeated persuasion in interpersonal conflict. *Journal of Personality and Social Psychology, 51,* 1183–1188. (p. 607)

Lindskold, S., Walters, P. S., & Koutsourais, H. (1983). Cooperators, competitors, and response to GRIT. *Journal of Conflict Resolution, 27,* 521–532. (p. 607)

Linn, M. C., & Peterson, A. C. (1986). A meta-analysis of gender differences in spatial ability: Implications for mathematics and science achievement. In J. S. Hyde & M. C. Linn (Eds.), *The psychology of gender: Advances through meta-analysis.* Baltimore: Johns Hopkins University Press. (p. 132)

Linn, R. L. (1982). Ability testing: Individual differences, prediction, and differential prediction. In A. K. Wigdor & W. R. Garner (Eds.), *Ability testing: Uses, consequences, and controversies* (Part II). Washington, DC: National Academy Press. (p. 327)

Linz, D., Penrod, S., & Donnerstein, E. (1986). Issues bearing on the legal regulation of violent and sexually violent media. *Journal of Social Issues, 42,* 171–194. (p. 584)

Littlefield, C. H., & Rushton, J. P. (1986). When a child dies: The sociobiology of bereavement. *Journal of Personality and Social Psychology, 51,* 797–802. (p. 110)

Livingstone, M., & Hubel, D. (1988). Segregation of form, color, movement, and depth: Anatomy, physiology, and perception. *Science, 240,* 740–749. (p. 151)

Livson, F. B. (1976, October). Coming together in the middle years: A longitudinal study of sex role convergence. In B. F. Turner (Chair), *The double standard of aging: A question of sex differences.* Symposium conducted at the Annual Scientific

Meeting of the Gerontological Society, New York, NY. (p. 131)

Locke, J. (1690; reprinted 1964). *An essay concerning human understanding.* New York: Meridian. (p. 180)

Loehlin, J. C., Lindzey, G., & Spuhler, J. N. (1975). *Race differences in intelligence.* San Francisco: Freeman. (p. 339)

Loehlin, J. C., & Nichols, R. C. (1976). *Heredity, environment, and personality.* Austin: University of Texas Press. (pp. 82, 336)

Loehlin, J. C., Willerman, L., & Horn, J. M. (1982). Personality resemblances between unwed mothers and their adopted-away offspring. *Journal of Personality and Social Psychology, 42,* 1089–1099. (p. 83)

Loehlin, J. C., Willerman, L., & Horn, J. M. (1985). Personality resemblances in adoptive families when the children are late-adolescent or adult. *Journal of Personality and Social Psychology, 48,* 376–392. (p. 83)

Loehlin, J. C., Willerman, L., & Horn, J. M. (1987). Personality resemblance in adoptive families: A 10-year follow-up. *Journal of Personality and Social Psychology, 53,* 961–969. (p. 83)

Loftus, E. F. (1979). The malleability of human memory. *American Scientist, 67,* 313–320. (p. 272)

Loftus, E. F. (1980). *Memory: Surprising new insights into how we remember and why we forget.* Reading, MA: Addison-Wesley. (p. 208)

Loftus, E. F. (1983). Misfortunes of memory. *Philosophical Transactions. Royal Society of London. Series B. Biological Sciences, 302,* 413–421. (p. 272)

Loftus, E. F., & Loftus, G. R. (1980). On the permanence of stored information in the human brain. *American Psychologist, 35,* 409–420. (p. 266)

Loftus, E. F., & Palmer, J. C. (1973). Reconstruction of automobile destruction: An example of the interaction between language and memory. *Journal of Verbal Learning and Verbal Behavior, 13,* 585–589. (p. 272)

London, P. (1970). The rescuers: Motivational hypotheses about Christians who saved Jews from the Nazis. In J. Macaulay & L. Berkowitz (Eds.), *Altruism and helping behavior.* New York: Academic Press. (p. 250)

LoPiccolo, J. (1983). Challenges to sex therapy. In C. M. Davis (Ed.), *Challenges in sexual science: Current theoretical issues and research advances.* Philadelphia: Society for Scientific Study of Sex. (p. 365)

LoPiccolo, J. L., & Stock, W. E. (1986). Treatment of sexual dysfunction. *Journal of Consulting and Clinical Psychology, 54,* 158–167. (p. 363)

Lord, C. G., Lepper, M. R., & Preston, E. (1984). Considering the opposite: A corrective strategy for social judgement. *Journal of Personality and Social Psychology, 47,* 1231–1247. (pp. 295–296)

Lord, C. G., Ross, L., & Lepper, M. (1979). Biased assimilation and attitude polarization: The effects of prior theories on subsequently considered evidence. *Journal of Personality and Social Psychology, 37,* 2098–2109. (p. 295)

Lord, L. J. (1987, November 30). Coming to grips with alcoholism. *U.S. News and World Report,* pp. 56–63. (p. 215)

Lorenz, K. (1937). The companion in the bird's world. *Auk, 54,* 245–273. (p. 72)

Lorenz, K. (1966). *On aggression.* London: Metheun. (p. 72)

Lovaas, O. I. (1987). Behavioral treatment and normal educational and intellectual functioning in young autistic children. *Journal of Consulting and Clinical Psychology, 55,* 3–9. (p. 486)

Lowenthal, M. F., Thurnher, M., Chiriboga, D., Beefon, D., Gigy, L., Lurie, E., Pierce, R., Spence, D., & Weiss, L. (1975). *Four stages of life.* San Francisco: Jossey-Bass. (p. 131)

Lubin, B., Larsen, R. M., & Matarazzo, J. D. (1984). Patterns of psychological test usage in the United States: 1935–1982. *American Psychologist, 39,* 451–454. (pp. 321, 416, 422)

Luchins, A. S. (1946). Classroom experiments on mental set. *American Journal of Psychology, 59,* 295–298. (pp. 288, 290)

Lugaresi, E., Medori, R., Montagna, P., Baruzzi, A., Cortelli, P., Lugaresi, A., Tinuper, P., Zucconi, M., & Gambetti, P. (1986). Fatal familial insomnia and dysautonomia with selective degeneration of thalamic nuclei. *New England Journal of Medicine, 315,* 997–1003. (p. 200)

Lumsden, C. J., & Wilson, E. O. (1983). *Promethean fire: Reflections on the origin of mind.* Cambridge, MA: Harvard University Press. (pp. 146, 391)

Luria, A. M. (1968). In L. Solotaroff (Trans.), *The mind of a mnemonist.* New York: Basic Books. (p. 255)

Lykken, D. T. (1982, September). Fearlessness: Its carefree charm and deadly risks. *Psychology Today,* pp. 20–28. (p. 391)

Lykken, D. T. (1983, April). Polygraph prejudice. *APA Monitor,* p. 4. (p. 384)

Lykken, D. T. (1985). The probity of the polygraph. In S. M. Kassin & L. S. Wrightsman (Eds.), *The psychology of evidence and trial procedure.* Beverly Hills, CA: Sage. (p. 384)

Lykken, D. T. (1987, Spring). The validity of tests: Caveat emptor. *Jurimetrics Journal,* pp. 263–270. (p. 385)

Lynch, G., & Baudry, M. (1984). The biochemistry of memory: A new and specific hypothesis. *Science, 224,* 1057–1064. (p. 268)

Lynn, M. (1988). The effects of alcohol consumption on restaurant tipping. *Personality and Social Psychology Bulletin, 14,* 87–91. (p. 215)

Lynn, R. (1982). I.Q. in Japan and the United States shows a growing disparity. *Nature, 297,* 222–223. (p. 339)

Lynn, R. (1983). Lynn replies. *Nature, 306,* 292. (p. 339)

Lynn, R. (1987). Japan: Land of the rising IQ. A reply to Flynn. *Bulletin of the British Psychological Society, 40,* 464–468. (p. 340)

Lynn, S. J., & Rhue, J. W. (1986). The fantasy-prone person: Hypnosis, imagination, and creativity. *Journal of Personality and Social Psychology, 51,* 404–408. (p. 207)

Maass, A., & Clark, R. D., III. (1984). Hidden impact of minorities: Fifteen years of minority influence research. *Psychological Bulletin, 95,* 428–450. (p. 571)

Maccoby, E. (1980). *Social development: Psychological growth* *and the parent-child relationship.* New York: Harcourt Brace Jovanovich. (pp. 71, 73, 76, 78, 79, 128)

MacDonald, N. (1960). Living with schizophrenia. *Canadian Medical Association Journal, 82,* 218–221. (p. 463)

MacFarlane, A. (1978, February). What a baby knows. *Human Nature,* pp. 74–81. (p. 61)

Macfarlane, J. W. (1964). Perspectives on personality consistency and change from the guidance study. *Vita Humana, 7,* 115–126. (p. 90, 112)

MacKay, D. G. (1983). Prescriptive grammar and the pronoun problem. In B. Thorne, C. Kramarae, & N. Henley (Eds.), *Language, gender and society.* Rowley, MA: Newbury House. (p. 309)

Mackenzie, B. (1984). Explaining race differences in IQ: The logic, the methodology, and the evidence. *American Psychologist, 39,* 1214–1233. (p. 341)

MacKinnon, D. W., & Hall, W. B. (1972). Intelligence and creativity. *Preceedings, XVIIth International Congress of Applied Psychology* (Vol. 2, pp. 1883–1888). Brussels: Editest. (p. 334)

Maddi, S. R., Bartone, P. T., & Puccetti, M. C. (1987). Stressful events are indeed a factor in physical illness: Reply to Schroeder and Costa (1984). *Journal of Personality and Social Psychology, 52,* 833–843. (pp. 512, 514)

Maddux, J. E., & Stanley, M. A. (1986). Self-efficacy theory in contemporary psychology: An overview. *Journal of Social and Clinical Psychology, 4,* 249–255. (p. 434)

Maehr, M. L., & Braskamp, L. A. (1986). *The motivation factor: A theory of personal investment.* Lexington, MA: Lexington Books. (p. 377)

Major, B. (1987). Gender, justice, and the psychology of entitlement. In P. Shaver & C. Hendrick (Eds.), *Sex and gender.* Beverly Hills, CA: Sage. (p. 130)

Major, B., Carrington, P. I., & Carnevale, P. J. D. (1984). Physical attractiveness and self-esteem: Attribution for praise from an other-sex evaluator. *Personality and Social Psychology Bulletin, 10,* 43–50. (p. 597)

Malamuth, N. M., & Briere, J. (1986). Sexual violence in the media: Indirect effects on aggression against women. *Journal of Social Issues, 42,* 75–92. (p. 580)

Malan, D. H. (1978). "The case of the secretary with the violent father." In H. Davanloo (Ed.), *Basic principles and techniques in short-term dynamic psychotherapy.* New York: Spectrum. (p. 477)

Malkiel, B. (1985). *A random walk down Wall Street* (4th ed.). New York: Norton. (p. 619)

Malone, T. W., & Lepper, M. R. (1986). Making learning fun: A taxonomy of intrinsic motivations for learning. In R. E. Snow & M. J. Farr (Eds.), *Aptitude, learning, and instruction: III. Cognitive and affective process analysis.* Hillsdale, NJ: Erlbaum. (p. 374)

Mandel, D. (1983, March 13). One man's holocaust: Part II. The story of David Mandel's journey through hell as told to David Kagan. *Wonderland Magazine* (Grand Rapids Press), pp. 2–7. (p. 349)

Marcel, A. (1983). Conscious and unconscious perception:

Experiments on visual masking and word recognition. *Cognitive Psychology, 15,* 197–237. (p. 142)

Marcus, A. C., & Siegel, J. M. (1982). Sex differences in the use of physician services: A preliminary test of the fixed role hypothesis. *Journal of Health and Social Behavior, 23,* 186–197. (p. 527)

Mark, V., & Ervin, F. (1970). *Violence and the brain.* New York: Harper & Row. (p. 37)

Marks, D. F. (1986). Investigating the paranormal. *Nature, 320,* 119–124. (p. 187)

Markus, H., & Nurius, P. (1986). Possible selves. *American Psychologist, 41,* 954–969. (p. 429)

Markus, H., & Wurf, E. (1987). The dynamic self-concept: A social psychological perspective. *Annual Review of Psychology, 38,* 299–337. (p. 429)

Marschark, M., Richman, C. L., Yuille, J. C., & Hunt, R. R. (1987). The role of imagery in memory: On shared and distinctive information. *Psychological Bulletin, 102,* 28–41. (p. 263)

Marsh, H. W., & Parker, J. W. (1984). Determinants of student self-concept: Is it better to be a relatively large fish in a small pond even if you don't learn to swim as well? *Journal of Personality and Social Psychology, 47,* 213–231. (p. 398)

Martinsen, E. W. (1987). The role of aerobic exercise in the treatment of depression. *Stress Medicine, 3,* 93–100. (p. 521)

Martyna, W. (1978). What does "he" mean? Use of generic masculine. *Journal of Communication, 28*(1), 131–138. (p. 309)

Marx, J. L. (1985). The immune system "belongs in the body." *Science, 227,* 1190–1192. (p. 518)

Maslow, A. H. (1968). *Toward a psychology of being* (2nd ed.). Princeton, NJ: Van Nostrand Reinhold. (pp. 107, 353–354)

Maslow, A. H. (1970). *Motivation and personality* (2nd ed.). New York: Harper & Row. (p. 425)

Masters, W. H., & Johnson, V. E. (1966). *Human sexual response.* Boston: Little, Brown. (pp. 361–362)

Matarazzo, J. D. (1983). Computerized psychological testing. *Science, 221,* 323. (p. 423)

Matarazzo, J. D., Carmody, T. P., & Gentry, W. D. (1981). Psychologists on the faculties of United States schools of medicine: Past, present and possible future. *Clinical Psychology Review, 1,* 293–317. (p. 507)

Mathes, E. W., & Wise, P. S. (1983). Romantic love and the ravages of time. *Psychological Reports, 53,* 839–846. (p. 600)

Matsumoto, D. (1987). The role of facial response in the experience of emotion: More methodological problems and a meta-analysis. *Journal of Personality and Social Psychology, 52,* 769–774. (p. 388)

Matthews, C., & Clark, R. D., III (1982). Marital satisfaction: A validation approach. *Basic and Applied Social Psychology, 3,* 169–186. (p. 100)

Matthews, K. A. (1988). CHD and Type A behaviors: Update on and alternative to the Booth-Kewley and Friedman quantitative review. *Psychological Bulletin, 104,* in press. (p. 516)

Maugh, T. H., II (1988, January). Mexican medicine to change your mind. *Discover*, pp. 39–40. (p. 50)

May, P. A. (1986). Alcohol and drug misuse prevention programs for American Indians: Needs and opportunities. *Journal of Studies on Alcohol, 47*, 187–195. (p. 447)

May, R. (1982). The problem of evil: An open letter to Carl Rogers. *Journal of Humanistic Psychology, 22*, 10–21. (p. 428)

Mayer, J. D., & Salovey, P. (1987). Personality moderates the interaction of mood and cognition. In K. Fiedler & J. Forgas (Eds.), *Affect, cognition, and social behavior*. Toronto: Hogrefe. (p. 271)

Mazullo, J., Lasagna, L., & Grinar, P. (1974). Variations in interpretation of prescription instructions. *Journal of the American Medical Association, 227*, 929–931. (p. 529)

McAlister, A., Perry, C., Killen, J., Slinkard, L. A., & Maccoby, N. (1980). Pilot study of smoking, alcohol and drug abuse prevention. *American Journal of Public Health, 70*, 719–721. (p. 532)

McBurney, D. H., & Collings, V. B. (1984). *Introduction to sensation perception* (2nd ed.). Englewood Cliffs, NJ: Prentice-Hall. (pp. 179–180)

McBurney, D. H., & Gent, J. F. (1979). On the nature of taste qualities. *Psychological Bulletin, 86*, 151–167. (p. 160)

McCall, R. B., Appelbaum, M. I., & Hogarty, P. S. (1973). Developmental changes in mental performance. *Monographs of the Society for Research in Child Development, 38*(3, Serial No. 150). (p. 332)

McCann, I. L., & Holmes, D. S. (1984). Influence of aerobic exercise on depression. *Journal of Personality and Social Psychology, 46*, 1142–1147. (p. 520)

McCanne, T. R., & Anderson, J. A. (1987). Emotional responding following experimental manipulation of facial electromyographic activity. *Journal of Personality and Social Psychology, 52*, 759–768. (p. 388)

McCarley, R. W., & Hobson, E. (1981). REM sleep dreams and the activation-synthesis hypothesis. *American Journal of Psychiatry, 138*, 904–912. (p. 204)

McCarron, D. A., Morris, C. D., Henry, H. J., & Stanton, J. L. (1984). Blood pressure and nutrient intake in the United States. *Science, 225*, 1392–1398. (p. 533)

McCarthy, P. (1986, July). Scent: The tie that binds? *Psychology Today*, pp. 6, 10. (p. 161)

McCaul, K. D., & Malott, J. M. (1984). Distraction and coping with pain. *Psychological Bulletin, 95*, 516–533. (p. 159)

McCauley, C. R., & Segal, M. E. (1987). Social psychology of terrorist groups. In C. Hendrick (Ed.), *Group processes and intergroup relations*. Beverly Hills, CA: Sage. (p. 570)

McClelland, D. C. (1978). Managing motivation to expand human freedom. *American Psychologist, 33*, 201–210. (p. 372)

McClenon, J. (1982). A survey of elite scientists: Their attitudes toward ESP and parapsychology. *Journal of Parapsychology, 46*, 127–152. (p. 185)

McCord, J. (1978). A thirty-year follow up on treatment effects. *American Psychologist, 33*, 284–289. (p. 492)

McCord, J. (1979). Following up on Cambridge-Somerville. *American Psychologist, 34*, 727. (p. 492)

McCrae, R. R., & Costa, P. T., Jr. (1982). Self-concept and the stability of personality: Cross-sectional comparisons of self-reports and ratings. *Journal of Personality and Social Psychology, 43*, 1282–1292. (pp. 113, 421)

McCrae, R. R., & Costa, P. T., Jr. (1986). Clinical assessment can benefit from recent advances in personality psychology. *American Psychologist, 41*, 1001–1003. (p. 421)

McFarland, C., & Ross, M. (1987). The relation between current impressions and memories of self and dating partners. *Psychological Bulletin, 13*, 228–238. (p. 273)

McGhee, P. E. (1976). Children's appreciation of humor: A test of the cognitive congruency principle. *Child Development, 47*, 420–426. (p. 69)

McGrath, E. (1983, March 28). Confucian work ethic. *Time*, p. 52. (p. 339)

McGrath, M. J., & Cohen, D. G. (1978). REM sleep facilitation of adaptive waking behavior: A review of the literature. *Psychological Bulletin, 85*, 24–57. (p. 204)

McGuinness, D. (1985). *When children don't learn: Understanding the biology and psychology of learning disabilities*. New York: Basic Books. (p. 130)

McGuire, W. J. (1986). The myth of massive media impact: Savings and salvagings. In G. Comstock (Ed.), *Public communication and behavior*. Orlando, FL: Academic Press. (p. 580)

McGuire, W. J., & McGuire, C. V. (1986). Differences in conceptualizing self versus conceptualizing other people as manifested in contrasting verb types used in natural speech. *Journal of Personality and Social Psychology, 51*, 1135–1143. (p. 550)

McHugh, P. R., & Moran, T. H. (1978). Accuracy of the regulation of caloric ingestion in the rhesus monkey. *American Journal of Physiology, 235*, R29–34. (p. 355)

McKean, K. (1987, January). The orderly pusuit of pure disorder. *Discover*, pp. 72–81. (p. 619)

McMillan, M. J., & Pihl, R. O. (1987). Premenstrual depression: A distinct entity. *Journal of Abnormal Psychology, 96*, 149–154. (p. 527)

McNally, R. J. (1987). Preparedness and phobias: A review. *Psychological Bulletin, 101*, 283–303. (pp. 391, 452)

McNeal, E. T., & Cimbolic, P. (1986). Antidepressants and biochemical theories of depression. *Psychological Bulletin, 99*, 361–374. (p. 460)

Meador, B. D., & Rogers, C. R. (1984). Person-centered therapy. In R. J. Corsini (Ed.), *Current psychotherapies* (3rd ed.). Itasca, IL: Peacock. (p. 480)

Meaney, M. J., Aitken, D. H., Van Berkel, C., Bhatnagar, S., & Sapolsky, R. M. (1988). Effect of neonatal handling on age-related impairments associated with the hippocampus. *Science, 239*, 766–768. (p. 63)

Medawar, P. (1982). *Pluto's republic*. New York: Oxford University Press. (p. 418)

Meichenbaum, D. (1977). *Cognitive-behavior modification: An integrative approach*. New York: Plenum Press. (p. 490)

Meichenbaum, D. (1985). *Stress inoculation training.* New York: Pergamon. (p. 490)

Meltzoff, A. N. (1987, May). Baby research comes of age. *Psychology Today*, p. 47. (p. 62)

Meltzoff, A. N., & Moore, M. K. (1983). Newborn infants imitate adult facial gestures. *Child Development, 54,* 702–709. (p. 62)

Meltzoff, A. N., & Moore, M. K. (1985). Cognitive foundations and social functions of imitation and intermodal representation in infancy. In J. Mehler & R. Fox (Eds.), *Neonate cognition: Beyond the blooming, buzzing confusion.* Hillsdale, NJ: Erlbaum. (p. 62)

Melzack, R., & Wall, P. D. (1965). Pain mechanisms: A new theory. *Science, 150,* 971–979. (p. 159)

Melzack, R., & Wall, P. D. (1983). *The challenge of pain.* New York: Basic Books. (p. 159)

Mento, A. J., Steel, R. P., & Karren, R. J. (1987). A meta-analytic study of the effects of goal setting on task performance: 1966–1984. *Organizational Behavior and Human Decision Processes, 39,* 52–83. (p. 377)

Meredith, N. (1986, June). Testing the talking cure. *Science,* pp. 31–37. (p. 491)

Merton, R. K. (1938; reprinted 1970). *Science, technology and society in seventeenth-century England.* New York: Fertig. (p. 9)

Merton, R. K., & Kitt, A. S. (1950). Contributions to the theory of reference group behavior. In R. K. Merton & P. F. Lazarsfeld (Eds.), *Continuities in social research: Studies in the scope and method of the American soldier.* Glencoe, IL: Free Press. (p. 398)

Messick, S., & Jungeblut, A. (1981). Time and method in coaching for the SAT. *Psychological Bulletin, 89,* 191–216. (p. 326)

Meyer-Bahlburg, H. F. L. (1980). Sexuality in early adolescence. In B. B. Wolman & J. Money (Eds.), *Handbook of human sexuality.* Englewood Cliffs, NJ: Prentice-Hall. (p. 363)

Meyer, D. R. (1984). The cerebral cortex: Its roles in memory storage and remembering. *Physiological Psychology, 12,* 81–88. (p. 267)

Michaels, J. W., Bloomel, J. M., Brocato, R. M., Linkous, R. A., & Rowe, J. S. (1982). Social facilitation and inhibition in a natural setting. *Replications in Social Psychology, 2,* 21–24. (p. 566)

Michel, G. F. (1981). Right-handedness: A consequence of infant supine head-orientation preference? *Science, 212,* 685–687. (p. 48)

Milan, R. J., Jr., & Kilmann, P. R. (1987). Interpersonal factors in premarital contraception. *Journal of Sex Research, 23,* 289–321. (p. 361)

Milgram, S. (1974). *Obedience to authority.* New York: Harper & Row. (pp. 553, 555–556)

Milgram, S. (1984). *Cyranoids.* Paper presented at the meeting of the American Psychological Association. (p. 595)

Miller, G. A. (1956). The magical number seven, plus or minus two: Some limits on our capacity for processing information. *Psychological Review, 63,* 81–97. (p. 265)

Miller, G. A. (1962). *Psychology: The science of mental life.* New York: Harper & Row. (p. 417)

Miller, G. A., & Gildea, P. M. (1987, September). How children learn words. *Scientific American*, pp. 94–99. (p. 302)

Miller, K. I., & Monge, P. R. (1986). Participation, satisfaction, and productivity: A meta-analytic review. *Academy of Management Journal, 29,* 727–753. (p. 434)

Miller, N. E. (1983a). Behavioral medicine: Symbiosis between laboratory and clinic. *Annual Review of Psychology, 34,* 1–31. (pp. 507, 522)

Miller, N. E. (1983b). Value and ethics of research on animals. Paper presented at the meeting of the American Psychological Association. (p. 18)

Miller, N. E. (1985, February). Rx: biofeedback. *Psychology Today*, pp. 54–59. (p. 522)

Miller, N. E., & Brucker, B. S. (1979). A learned visceral response apparently independent of skeletal ones in patients paralyzed by spinal lesions. In N. Birbaumer & H. D. Kimmel (Eds.), *Biofeedback and self-regulation.* Hillsdale, NJ: Erlbaum. (p. 521)

Miller, N., & Maruyama, G. (1976). Ordinal position and peer popularity. *Journal of Personality and Social Psychology, 33,* 123–131. (p. 373)

Miller, P. C., Lefcourt, H. M., Holmes, J. G., Ware, E. E., & Saleh, W. E. (1986). Marital locus of control and marital problem solving. *Journal of Personality and Social Psychology, 51,* 161–169. (p. 433)

Mills, M., & Melhuish, E. (1974). Recognition of mother's voice in early infancy. *Nature, 252,* 123–124. (p. 61)

Mineka, S. (1985). The frightful complexity of the origins of fears. In F. R. Brush & J. B. Overmier (Eds.), *Affect, conditioning and cognition: Essays on the determinants of behavior.* Hillsdale, NJ: Erlbaum. (p. 390)

Mineka, S., & Suomi, S. J. (1978). Social separation in monkeys. *Psychological Bulletin, 85,* 1376–1400. (p. 76)

Minkoff, H. L. (1987). Care of pregnant women infected with human immunodeficiency virus. *Journal of the American Medical Association, 258,* 2714–2717. (p. 61)

Mintz, L. B., & Betz, N. E. (1986). Sex differences in the nature, realism, and correlates of body image. *Sex Roles, 15,* 185–195. (p. 359)

Mischel, W. (1968). *Personality and assessment.* New York: Wiley. (p. 424)

Mischel, W. (1981). Current issues and challenges in personality. In L. T. Benjamin, Jr. (Ed.), *The G. Stanley Hall Lecture Series* (Vol. 1). Washington, DC: American Psychological Association. (p. 435)

Mischel, W. (1984). Convergences and challenges in the search for consistency. *American Psychologist, 39,* 351–364. (p. 424)

Mishkin, M. (1986). Physiological psychology and the future: An optimist's view. Paper presented at the American Psychological Association convention. (p. 32)

Mishkin, M., & Appenzeller, T. (1987, June). The anatomy of memory. *Scientific American*, pp. 80–89. (p. 267)

Mita, T. H., Dermer, M., & Knight, J. (1977). Reversed facial images and the mere-exposure hypothesis. *Journal of Personality and Social Psychology, 35,* 597–601. (p. 596)

Monahan, J. (1983). *Predicting violent behavior: An assessment of clinical techniques.* Beverly Hills, CA: Sage. (p. 446)

Money, J. (1987). Sin, sickness, or status? Homosexual gender identity and psychoneuroendocrinology. *American Psychologist, 42,* 384–399. (pp. 118, 368)

Money, J., Berlin, F. S., Falck, A., & Stein, M. (1983). *Antiandrogenic and counseling treatment of sex offenders.* Baltimore: Department of Psychiatry and Behavioral Sciences, The Johns Hopkins University School of Medicine. (p. 364)

Money, J., Hampson, J. G., & Hampson, J. L. (1957). Imprinting and the establishment of gender role. *AMA Archives of Neurology and Psychiatry, 77,* 333–336. (p. 121)

Moody, R. (1976). *Life after life.* Harrisburg, PA: Stackpole Books. (p. 221)

Mook, D. G. (1983). In defense of external invalidity. *American Psychologist, 38,* 379–387. (p. 17)

Moore, D. L., & Baron, R. S. (1983). Social facilitation: A physiological analysis. In J. T. Cacioppo & R. Petty (Eds.), *Social psychophysiology.* New York: Guilford Press. (p. 566)

Moore, T. E. (1982). Subliminal advertising: What you see is what you get. *Journal of Marketing, 46,* 38–47. (p. 142)

Moreland, R. L., & Zajonc, R. B. (1982). Exposure effects in person perception: Familiarity, similarity, and attraction. *Journal of Experimental Social Psychology, 18,* 395–415. (p. 596)

Morgan, A. H., Johnson, D. L., & Hilgard, E. R. (1974). The stability of hypnotic susceptibility: A longitudinal study. *International Journal of Clinical and Experimental Hypnosis, 22,* 249–257. (p. 207)

Morokoff, P. J. (1986). Volunteer bias in the psychophysiological study of female sexuality. *Journal of Sex Research, 22,* 35–51. (pp. 364–365)

Morris, N. M., & Udry, J. R. (1978). Pheromonal influences on human sexual behavior: An experimental search. *Journal of Biosocial Science, 10,* 147–157. (p. 364)

Morrison, D. M. (1985). Adolescent contraceptive behavior: A review. *Psychological Bulletin, 98,* 538–568. (p. 361)

Moruzzi, G. & Magoun, H. W. (1949). Brain stem reticular formation and activation of the EEG. *Electroencephalography and Clinical Neurophysiology, 1,* 455–473. (p. 36)

Moscovici, S., & Zavalloni, M. (1969). The group as a polarizer of attitudes. *Journal of Personality and Social Psychology, 12,* 124–135. (p. 569)

Moser, P. W. (1987, May). Are cats smart? Yes, at being cats. *Discover,* pp. 77–88. (p. 149)

Mosher, D. L., & Anderson, R. D. (1986). Macho personality, sexual aggression, and reactions to guided imagery of realistic rape. *Journal of Research in Personality, 20,* 77–94. (p. 215)

Mosher, D. L., & Vonderheide, S. G. (1985). Contributions of sex guilt and masturbation guilt to women's contraceptive attitudes and use. *Journal of Sex Research, 21,* 24–39. (p. 361)

Moss, H. A., Susman, E. J. (1980). Longitudinal study of personality development. In O. G. Brim, Jr. & J. Kagan (Eds.), *Constancy and change in human development.* Cambridge, MA: Harvard University Press. (p. 113)

Moyer, K. E. (1983). The physiology of motivation: Aggression as a model. In C. J. Scheier & A. M. Rogers (Eds.), *G. Stanley Hall Lecture Series* (Vol. 3). Washington, DC: American Psychological Association. (p. 576)

Murphy, E. A. (1982). Muddling, meddling, and modeling. In V. E. Anderson, W. A. Hauser, J. K. Penry, & C. F. Sing (Eds.), *Genetic basis of the epilepsies.* New York: Raven Press. (p. 46)

Murphy, T. N. (1982). Pain: Its assessment and management. In R. J. Gatchel, A. Baum & J. E. Singer (Eds.), *Handbook of psychology and health: Vol I. Clinical psychology and behavioral medicine: Overlapping disciplines.* Hillsdale, NJ: Erlbaum. (p. 159)

Murray, D. M., Johnson, C. A., Luepker, R. V., Mittelmark, M. B. (1984). The prevention of cigarette smoking in children: A comparison of four strategies. *Journal of Applied Social Psychology, 14,* 274–288. (p. 532)

Murray, H. (1938). *Explorations in personality.* New York: Oxford University Press. (p. 371)

Murray, H. A. (1933). The effect of fear upon estimates of the maliciousness of other personalities. *Journal of Social Psychology, 4,* 310–329. (p. 415)

Murray, H. A., & Wheeler, D. R. (1937). A note on the possible clairvoyance of dreams. *Journal of Psychology, 3,* 309–313. (p. 187)

Murray, J. P., & Lonnborg, B. (1985). *Violence on TV: What do children learn? What can parents do?* Washington, DC: American Psychological Association. (p. 584)

Murstein, B. L. (1986). *Paths to marriage.* Newbury Park, CA: Sage. (p. 597)

Myers, B. J. (1984a). Mother-infant bonding: The status of the critical period hypothesis. *Developmental Review, 4,* 240–274. (p. 72)

Myers, B. J. (1984b). Mother-infant bonding: Rejoinder to Kennell and Klaus. *Developmental Review, 4,* 283–288. (p. 72)

Myers, D. G. (1990). *Social psychology* (3rd ed.). New York: McGraw-Hill, in press. (p. 393, 431).

Myers, D. G., & Bishop, G. D. (1970). Discussion effects on racial attitudes. *Science, 169,* 778–779. (p. 569)

Myers, J. K., Weissman, M. M., Tischler, G. L., Holzer, C. E., III, Leaf, P. J., Orvaschel, H., Anthony, J. C., Boyd, J. H., Burke, J. D., Kramer, M., & Stoltzman, R. (1984). Six-month prevalence of psychiatric disorders in three communities. *Archives of General Psychiatry, 41,* 959–967. (p. 448)

Nash, M. (1987). What, if anything, is regressed about hypnotic age regression? A review of the empirical literature. *Psychological Bulletin, 102,* 42–52. (p. 208)

National Academy of Sciences, Institute of Medicine (1982). *Marijuana and health.* Washington, DC: National Academic Press. (pp. 219, 507)

National Centers for Health Statistics (1985). *Health: United States, 1985.* DHHS Pub. No. (PHS) 86–1232. Washington, D.C.: U.S. Government Printing Office. (p. 534)

National Council on the Aging (1976). *The myth and reality of aging in America.* Washington, DC. (p. 101)

National Opinion Research Center (1985, October/November). Images of the World. *Public Opinion*, p. 38. (p. 427)

National Research Council (1987). *Risking the future: Adolescent sexuality, pregnancy, and childbearing.* Washington, DC: National Academy Press. (p. 361)

NCTV News (1987, July-August). More research links harmful effects to non-violent porn. National Coalition on Television Violence, p. 12. (p. 580)

Neisser, U. (1979). The control of information pickup in selective looking. In A. D. Pick (Ed.), *Perception and its development: A tribute to Eleanor J. Gibson.* Hillsdale, NJ: Erlbaum. (p. 194)

Neisser, U. (1981). John Dean's memory: A case study. *Cognition, 9*, 1–22. (pp. 256, 270)

Neisser, U. (1982). Memorists. In U. Neisser (Ed.), *Memory observed: Remembering in natural contexts.* San Francisco: Freeman. (p. 255)

Neisser, U. (1984). The role of invariant structures in the control of movement. In M. Frese & J. Sabini (Eds.), *Goal directed behavior: The concept of action in psychology.* Hillsdale, NJ: Elbaum. (p. 310)

Nelson, K. (1973). Structure and strategy in learning to talk. *Monographs of the Society for Research in Child Development, 38*(1 & 2, Serial No. 149). (p. 303)

Nelson, K. (1981). Individual differences in language development: Implications for development and language. *Developmental Psychology, 17*, 170–187. (p. 304)

Nemeth, C. J. (1986). Differential contributions of majority and minority influence. *Psychological Review, 93*, 23–32. (p. 571)

Neugarten, B. L. (1974). The roles we play. In American Medical Association, *Quality of Life: The Middle Years.* Acton, MA: Publishing Sciences Group. (p. 108)

Neugarten, B. L. (1979). Time, age and the life cycle. *American Journal of Psychiatry, 136*, 887–894. (p. 107)

Neugarten, B. L. (1980, February). Must everything be a midlife crisis? *Prime Time*, pp. 45–48. (pp. 107, 112)

Neugarten, B. L., Wood, V., Kraines, R. J., & Loomis, B. (1963). Women's attitudes toward the menopause. *Vita Humana, 6*, 140–151. (p. 99)

Newcomb, M. D. (1987). Cohabitation and marriage: A quest for independence and relatedness. In S. Oskamp (Ed.), *Family processes and problems: Social psychological aspects.* Newbury Park, CA: Sage. (p. 371)

Newcomb, M. D., & Bentler, P. M. (1981). Marital breakdown. In S. Duck & R. Gilmour (Eds.), *Personal relationships: Vol. 3. Personal relationships in disorder.* London: Academic Press. (p. 371)

Newcomb, M. D., & Bentler, P. M. (1988). Impact of adolescent drug use and social support on problems of young adults: A longitudinal study. *Journal of Abnormal Psychology, 97*, 64–75. (pp. 219, 371)

Newcomb, M. D., & Harlow, L. L. (1986). Life events and substance use among adolescents: Mediating effects of perceived loss of control and meaninglessness in life. *Journal of Personality and Social Psychology, 51*, 564–577. (p. 220)

Newell, A., & Simon, H. A. (1972). *Human problem solving.* Englewood Cliffs, NJ: Prentice-Hall. (p. 286)

Newman, B. (1982). Mid-life development. In B. B. Wolman (Ed.), *Handbook of developmental psychology.* Englewood Cliffs, NJ: Prentice-Hall. (p. 99)

Newman, J., & Layton, B. D. (1984). Overjustification: A self-perception perspective. *Personality and Social Psychology Bulletin, 10*, 419–425. (p. 248)

Nezu, A. M., Nezu, C. M., & Blissett, S. E. (1988). Sense of humor as a moderator of the relation between stressful events and psychological distress: A prospective analysis. *Journal of Personality and Social Psychology, 54*, 520–525. (p. 523)

Nickerson, R. S., & Adams, M. J. (1979). Long-term memory for a common object. *Cognitive Psychology, 11*, 287–307. (p. 274)

Nicol, S. E., & Gottesman, I. I. (1983). Clues to the genetics and neurobiology of schizophrenia. *American Scientist, 71*, 398–404. (p. 467)

Nicolaus, L. K., Cassel, J. F., Carlson, R. B., & Gustavson, C. R. (1983). Taste-aversion conditioning of crows to control predation on eggs. *Science, 220*, 212–214. (p. 238)

Nisbett, R. E., & Borgida, E. (1975). Attribution and the psychology of prediction. *Journal of Personality and Social Psychology, 32*, 932–943. (p. 298)

Nisbett, R. E., Fong, G. T., Lehman, D. R., & Cheng, P. W. (1987). Teaching reasoning. *Science, 238*, 625–631. (pp. 620, 622)

Nisbett, R. E., & Ross, L. (1980). *Human inference: Strategies and shortcomings of social judgment.* Englewood Cliffs, NJ: Prentice-Hall. (pp. 290, 618)

Noel, J. G., Forsyth, D. R., & Kelley, K. N. (1987). Improving the performance of failing students by overcoming their self-serving attributional biases. *Basic and Applied Social Psychology, 8*, 151–162. (p. 435)

Noland, T. K. (1986). The effects of ability grouping: A meta-analysis of research findings. *Dissertation Abstracts 46*(10), 2909-A. (p. 333)

Nolen-Hoeksema, S. (1987). Sex differences in unipolar depression: Evidence and theory. *Psychological Bulletin, 101*, 259–282. (p. 460)

Noller, P., Law, H., & Comrey, A. L. (1987). Cattell, Comrey, and Eysenck personality factors compared: More evidence for the five robust factors? *Journal of Personality and Social Psychology, 53*, 775–782. (p. 421)

Norem, J. K., & Cantor, N. (1986). Defensive pessimism: Harnessing anxiety as motivation. *Journal of Personality and Social Psychology, 51*, 1208–1217. (p. 435)

Norris, P. A. (1986). On the status of biofeedback and clinical practice. *American Psychologist, 41*, 1009–1010. (p. 521)

Nuttin, Jr., J. M. (1987). Affective consequences of mere ownership: The name letter effect in twelve European languages. *European Journal of Social Psychology, 17,* 381–402. (p. 596)

Oatley, K., & Bolton, W. (1985). A social-cognitive theory of depression in reaction to life events. *Psychological Review, 92,* 382–388. (p. 461)

O'Connor, P., & Brown, G. W. (1984). Supportive relationships: Fact or fancy? *Journal of Social and Personal Relationships, 1,* 159–175. (p. 497)

Oetting, E. R., & Beauvais, F. (1987). Peer cluster theory, socialization characteristics, and adolescent drug use: A path analysis. *Journal of Counseling Psychology, 34,* 205–213. (p. 220)

Olds, J. (1958). Self-stimulation of the brain. *Science, 127,* 315–324. (p. 38)

Olds, J. (1975). Mapping the mind onto the brain. In F. G. Worden, J. P. Swazey, & G. Adelman (Eds.), *The neurosciences: Paths of discovery.* Cambridge, MA: MIT Press. (p. 38)

Olds, J., & Milner, P. (1954). Positive reinforcement produced by electrical stimulation of the septal area and other regions of rat brain. *Journal of Comparative and Physiological Psychology, 47,* 419–427. (p. 38)

O'Leary, A. (1987). Perceived self-efficacy and health. Paper presented to the American Psychological Association convention. (p. 512)

O'Malley, P. M., & Bachman, J. G. (1983). Self-esteem: Change and stability between ages 13 and 23. *Developmental Psychology, 19,* 257–268. (p. 96)

Omoto, A. M., & Morier, D. M. (1987). Thinking about AIDS: The role of attitudes toward male homosexuals. Paper presented at the Midwestern Psychological Association convention. (p. 369)

Opton, E., Jr. (1979, December). A psychologist takes a closer look at the recent landmark Larry P. opinion. *American Psychological Association Monitor,* pp. 1, 4. (p. 315)

Orlofsky, J. L., & O'Heron, C. A. (1987). Stereotypic and nonstereotypic sex role trait and behavior orientations: Implications for personal adjustment. *Journal of Personality and Social Psychology, 52,* 1034–1042. (p. 127)

Orne, M. T. (1982, April 28). Affidavit submitted to State of Pennsylvania. (p. 209)

Orne, M. T. (1984). *Compliance, responsibility, and fantasy in hypnotic responding.* Paper presented at the meeting of the American Psychological Association. (pp. 210, 455)

Orne, M. T. (1987, March 22). Quoted in D. G. Savage, High court to review validity of hypnosis in legal cases. *Los Angeles Times* news report in *Grand Rapids Press,* p. A13. (p. 209)

Orne, M. T., Dinges, D. F., & Orne, E. C. (1984). On the differential diagnosis of multiple personality in the forensic context. *International Journal of Clinical and Experimental Hypnosis, 32,* 118–169. (p. 455)

Orne, M. T., & Evans, F. J. (1965). Social control in the psychological experiment: Antisocial behavior and hypnosis. *Journal of Personality and Social Psychology, 1,* 189–200. (p. 210)

Orne, M. T., Soskis, D. A., Dinges, D. F., & Orne, E. C. (1984). Hypnotically induced testimony. In G. L. Wells & E.

F. Loftus (Eds.), *Eyewitness testimony: Psychological perspectives.* New York: Cambridge University Press. (p. 208)

Osgood, C. E. (1962). *An alternative to war or surrender.* Urbana: University of Illinois Press. (p. 607)

Osgood, C. E. (1980). GRIT: *A strategy for survival in mankind's nuclear age?* Paper presented at the Pugwash Conference on New Directions in Disarmament. (p. 607)

Osherson, D. N., & Markman, E. (1974–1975). Language and the ability to evaluate contradictions and tautologies. *Cognition, 3,* 213–226. (p. 92)

Oskamp, S., King, J. C., Burn, S. M., Konrad, A. M., Pollard, J. A., & White, M. A. (1985). The media and nuclear war: Fallout from TV's "The Day After." In S. Oskamp (Ed.), *Applied Social Psychology Annual* (Vol. 6). Beverly Hills, CA: Sage. (p. 564)

OSS Assessment Staff (1948). *The assessment of men.* New York: Rinehart. (p. 435)

Ostfeld, A. M., Kasl, S. V., D'Atri, D. A., & Fitzgerald, E. F. (1987). *Stress, crowding, and blood pressure in prison.* Hillsdale, NJ: Erlbaum. (p. 514)

Padgett, V. R. (1986). Predicting violence in totalitarian organizations: An application of 11 powerful principles of obedience from Milgram's experiments on obedience to authority. Unpublished manuscript, Marshall University. (p. 555)

Paffenbarger, R. S., Jr., Hyde, R. T., Wing, A. L., & Hsieh, C-C. (1986). Physical activity, all-cause mortality, and longevity of college alumni. *New England Journal of Medicine, 314,* 605–612. (p. 520)

Page, S. (1977). Effects of the mental illness label in attempts to obtain accommodation. *Canadian Journal of Behavioral Science, 9,* 84–90. (p. 470)

Paivio, A. (1986). *Mental representations: A dual coding approach.* New York: Oxford University Press. (p. 263)

Palladino, J. J., & Carducci, B. J. (1983). *"Things that go bump in the night": Students' knowledge of sleep and dreams.* Paper presented at the meeting of the Southeastern Psychological Association. (p. 197)

Palmblad, J., Petrini, B., Wasserman, J., & Akerstedt, T. (1979). Lymphocyte and granulocyte reactions during sleep deprivation. *Psychosomatic Medicine, 41,* 273–278. (p. 200)

Palmore, E. B. (1981). The facts on aging quiz: Part two. *The Gerontologist, 21,* 431–437. (p. 100)

Palumbo, S. R. (1978). *Dreaming and memory: A new information-processing model.* New York: Basic Books. (p. 204)

Panksepp, J. (1982). Toward a general psychobiological theory of emotions. *Behavioral and Brain Sciences, 5,* 407–467. (p. 383)

Parke, R. D. (1981). *Fathers.* Cambridge, MA: Harvard University Press. (p. 73)

Parloff, M. B. (1987, February). Psychotherapy: An import from Japan. *Psychology Today,* pp. 74–75. (p. 476)

Passons, W. R. (1975). *Gestalt approaches to counseling.* New York: Holt, Rinehart & Winston. (p. 481)

Patterson, F. (1978, October). Conversations with a gorilla. *National Geographic,* pp. 438–465. (p. 306)

Patterson, G. R. (1986). Performance models for antisocial boys. *American Psychologist, 41,* 432–444. (p. 79)

Patterson, G. R., Chamberlain, P., & Reid, J. B. (1982). A comparative evaluation of parent training procedures. *Behavior Therapy, 13,* 638–650. (p. 579)

Patterson, R. (1951). *The riddle of Emily Dickinson.* Boston: Houghton Mifflin. (p. 461)

Paulus, P. B. (with the collaboration of V. C. Cox & G. McCain) (1988). *Prison crowding: A psychological perspective.* New York: Springer-Verlag. (p. 569)

Pavett, C., M., Butler, M., Marcinik, E. J., & Hodgdon, J. A. (1987). Exercise as a buffer against organizational stress. *Stress Medicine, 3,* 87–92. (p. 520)

Pavlov, I. P. (1927). In G. V. Anrep (Trans.), *Conditioned reflexes.* London: Oxford University Press. (pp. 231–235)

Pedalino, E., & Gamboa, V. U. (1974). Behavior modification and absenteeism. *Journal of Applied Psychology, 59,* 694–698. (p. 245)

Pekkanen, J. (1982, June). Why do we sleep? *Science, 82,* p. 86. (p. 201)

Pellegrino, J. W. (1985, October). Anatomy of analogy. *Psychology Today,* pp. 49–54. (p. 331)

Penfield, W. (1958). Functional localization in temporal and deep sylvian areas. *Research Publications—Association for Research in Nervous and Mental Disease, 36,* 210–226. (p. 40)

Penfield, W. (1969). Consciousness, memory, and man's conditioned reflexes. In K. Pigram (Ed.), *On the biology of learning.* New York: Harcourt, Brace & World. (p. 265)

Penfield, W. (1975). *The mystery of the mind.* Princeton: Princeton University Press. (p. 222)

Pennebaker, J. W. (1982). *The psychology of physical symptoms.* New York: Springer-Verlag. (pp. 526, 527)

Pennebaker, J. W., & Beall, S. (1984). *Cognitive, emotional, and physiological components of confiding: Behavioral inhibition and disease.* Unpublished manuscript, Southern Methodist University. (p. 524)

Pennebaker, J. W., & Brittingham, G. L. (1982). Environmental and sensory cues affecting the perception of physical symptoms. In A. Baum & J. Singer (Eds.), *Advances in environmental psychology* (Vol. 4). Hillsdale, NJ: Erlbaum. (p. 526)

Pennebaker, J. W., & Lightner, J. M. (1980). Competition of internal and external information in an exercise setting. *Journal of Personality and Social Psychology, 39,* 165–174. (p. 526)

Pennebaker, J. W., & O'Heeron, R. C. (1984). Confiding in others and illness rate among spouses of suicide and accidental death victims. *Journal of Abnormal Psychology, 93,* 473–476. (p. 524)

Peplau, L. A. (1982). Research on homosexual couples: An overview. *Journal of Homosexuality, 8*(2), 3–8. (p. 367)

Peplau, L. A., & Gordon, S. L. (1985). Women and men in love: Gender differences in close heterosexual relationships. In V. E. O'Leary, R. K. Unger, & B. S. Wallston (Eds.),

Women, gender, and social psychology. Hillsdale, NJ: Erlbaum. (p. 121)

Peplau, L. A., & Perlman, D. (1982). *Loneliness: A sourcebook of current theory, research and therapy.* New York: Wiley. (p. 462)

Perkins, K. A., Dubbert, P. M., Martin, J. E., Faulstich, M. E., & Harris, J. K. (1986). Cardiovascular reactivity to psychological stress in aerobically trained versus untrained mild hypertensives and normotensives. *Health Psychology, 5,* 407–421. (p. 521)

Perlmutter, M. (1983). Learning and memory through adulthood. In M. W. Riley, B. B. Hess, & K. Bond (Eds.), *Aging in society: Selected reviews of recent research.* Hillsdale, NJ: Erlbaum. (p. 103)

Perls, F. S. (1969). *Ego, hunger and aggression: The beginning of Gestalt therapy.* New York: Random House. (p. 480)

Perls, F. S. (1970). Four lectures. In J. Fagan & I. L. Shepherd, *Gestalt therapy now.* Palo Alto, CA: Science and Behavior Books. (p. 480)

Perls, F. S. (1972). Gestalt therapy [interview]. In A. Bry (Ed.), *Inside psychotherapy.* New York: Basic Books. (p. 481)

Perrett, D. I., Harries, M., Mistlin, A. J., & Chitty, A. J. (1988). Three stages in the classification of body movements by visual neurons. In H. B. Barlow, C. Blakemore, & M. Weston Smith (Eds.), *Images and understanding.* Cambridge: Cambridge University Press. (p. 151)

Persky, V. W., Kempthorne-Rawson, J., & Shekelle, R. B. (1987). Personality and risk of cancer: 20-year follow-up of the Western Electric study. *Psychosomatic Medicine, 49,* 435–449. (p. 518)

Persons, J. B. (1986). The advantages of studying psychological phenomena rather than psychiatric diagnoses. *American Psychologist, 41,* 1252–1260. (p. 470)

Pert, C. (1986). Quoted in J. Hooper & D. Teresi, *The three-pound universe.* New York: Macmillan. (pp. 38, 50)

Pert, C. B., & Snyder, S. H. (1973). Opiate receptor: Demonstration in nervous tissue. *Science, 179,* 1011–1014. (p. 30)

Peschel, E. R., & Peschel, R. E. (1987). Medical insights into the castrati in opera. *American Scientist, 75,* 578–583. (p. 364)

Peters, T. J., & Waterman, R. H., Jr. (1982). *In search of excellence: Lessons from America's best-run companies.* New York: Harper & Row. (p. 246)

Petersen, A. C. (1987, September). Those gangly years. *Psychology Today,* pp. 28–34. (p. 91)

Peterson, C., & Barrett, L. C. (1987). Explanatory style and academic performance among university freshmen. *Journal of Personality and Social Psychology, 53,* 603–607. (p. 435)

Peterson, C., Peterson, J., & Skevington, S. (1986). Heated argument and adolescent development. *Journal of Social and Personal Relationships, 3,* 229–240. (p. 92)

Peterson, L. R., & Peterson, M. J. (1959). Short-term retention of individual verbal items. *Journal of Experimental Psychology, 58,* 193–198. (p. 260)

Peterson, R. (1978). Review of the Rorschach. In O. K.

Buros (Ed.), *The eighth mental measurements yearbook* (Vol. I). Highland Park, NJ: Gryphon Press. (p. 416)

Pettigrew, T. F. (1969). Racially separate or together? *Journal of Social Issues, 25*, 43–69. (p. 605)

Pettingale, K. W., Morris, T., Greer, S., & Haybittle, J. L. (1985, March 30). Mental attitudes to cancer: An additional prognostic factor. *Lancet*, p. 750. (p. 519)

Petty, R. E., & Cacioppo, J. T. (1986). The elaboration likelihood model of persuasion. In L. Berkowitz (Ed.), *Advances in experimental social psychology* (Vol. 19). Orlando, FL: Academic Press. (pp. 564–565)

Pfeiffer, E. (1977). Sexual behavior in old age. In E. W. Busse & E. Pfeiffer (Eds.), *Behavior and adaptation in late life* (2nd ed.). Boston: Little, Brown. (p. 101)

Phelps, M. E., & Mazziotta, J. C. (1985). Positron emission tomography: Human brain function and biochemistry. *Science, 228*, 799–809. (p. 34)

Phillips, D., McCartney, K., & Scarr, S. (1987). Child-care quality and children's social development. *Developmental Psychology, 23*, 537–543. (p. 76)

Phillips, D. P. (1974). The influence of suggestion on suicide: Substantive and theoretical implications of the Werther effect. *American Sociological Review, 39*, 340–354. (p. 551)

Phillips, D. P. (1982). The impact of fictional television stories on U.S. adult fatalities: New evidence on the effect of the mass media on violence. *American Journal of Sociology, 87*, 1340–1359. (p. 552)

Phillips, D. P. (1985). Natural experiments on the effects of mass media violence on fatal aggression: Strengths and weaknesses of a new approach. In L. Berkowitz. (Ed.), *Advances in experimental social psychology* (Vol. 19). Orlando, FL: Academic Press. (p. 551)

Phillips, D. P., & Carstensen, L. L. (1986). Clustering of teenage suicides after television news stories about suicide. *New England Journal of Medicine, 315*, 685–689. (p. 552)

Phillips, D. P., & Wills, J. S. (1987). A drop in suicides around major national holidays. *Suicide and Life-Threatening Behavior, 17*, 1–12. (p. 457)

Phillips, J. L. (1969). *Origins of intellect: Piaget's theory.* San Francisco: Freeman. (p. 69)

Piaget, J. (1930). *The child's conception of physical causality.* London: Routledge & Kegan Paul. (p. 65)

Piaget, J. (1932). *The moral judgement of the child.* New York: Harcourt, Brace & World. (p. 92)

Piaget, J. (1972). Intellectual evolution from adolescence to adulthood. *Human Development, 15*, 1–12. (p. 92)

Pickar, D., Labarca, R., Linnoila, M., Roy, A., Hommer, D., Everett, D., & Payl, S. M. (1984). Neuroleptic-induced decrease in plasma homovanillic acid and antipsychotic activity in schizophrenic patients. *Science, 225*, 954–957. (p. 500)

Pietromonaco, P. R., & Rook, K. S. (1987). Decision style in depression: The contribution of perceived risks versus benefits. *Journal of Personality and Social Psychology, 52*, 399–408. (p. 461)

Pittman, T. S., Davey, M. E., Alafat, K. A., Vetherill, K. V.,

& Kramer, N. A. (1980). Informational versus controlling verbal rewards. *Personality and Social Psychology Bulletin, 6*, 228–233. (p. 374)

Pleck, J. H. (1981). *Three conceptual issues in research on male roles.* Working paper no. 98, Wellesley College Center for Research on Women, Wellesley, MA. (p. 126)

Pleck, J. H. (1987). The contemporary man. In M. Scher et al. (Eds.), *Handbook of counseling and psychology with men.* Beverly Hills, CA: Sage. (p. 126)

Plomin, R., & Daniels, D. (1987). Why are children in the same family so different from one another? *Behavioral and Brain Sciences, 10*, 1–60. (p. 83)

Plomin, R., & DeFries, J. C. (1980). Genetics and intelligence: Recent data. *Intelligence, 4*, 15–24. (p. 336)

Plomin, R., & DeFries, J. C. (1985). *The origins of individual differences in infancy.* Orlando, Fla.: Academic Press. (p. 83)

Plomin, R., Loehlin, J. C., & DeFries, J. C. (1985). Genetic and environmental components of "environmental" influences. *Developmental Psychology, 21*, 391–402. (p. 74)

Plotkin, W. B. (1979). The alpha experience revisited: Biofeedback in the transformation of psychological state. *Psychological Bulletin, 86*, 1132–1148. (p. 522)

Polivy, J., & Herman, C. P. (1985). Dieting and binging: A causal analysis. *American Psychologist, 40*, 193–201. (p. 539)

Polivy, J., & Herman, C. P. (1987). Diagnosis and treatment of normal eating. *Journal of Personality and Social Psychology, 55*, 635–644. (p. 539)

Polivy, J., Herman, C. P., Hackett, C. P., & Kuleshnyk, I. (1986). The effects of self-attention and public attention on eating in restrained and unrestrained subjects. *Journal of Personality and Social Psychology, 50*, 1253–1260. (p. 539)

Pomerleau, O. F., & Pomerleau, C. S. (1984). Neuroregulators and the reinforcement of smoking: Towards a biobehavioral explanation. *Neuroscience and Biobehavioral Reviews, 8*, 503–513. (p. 531)

Pomerleau, O. F., & Rodin, J. (1986). Behavioral medicine and health psychology. In S. L. Garfield & A. E. Bergin (Eds.), *Handbook of psychotherapy and behavior change* (3rd ed.). New York: Wiley. (pp. 517, 528, 531)

Poon, L. W. (1987). Myths and truisms: Beyond extant analyses of speed of behavior and age. Address to the Eastern Psychological Association convention. (p. 104)

Powell, M. C., & Fazio, R. H. (1984). Attitude accessibility as a function of repeated attitudinal expression. *Personality and Social Psychology Bulletin, 10*, 139–148. (p. 558)

Powell, K. E., Thompson, P. D., Caspersen, C. J., & Kendrick, J. S. (1987). Physical activity and the incidence of coronary heart disease. *Annual Review of Public Health, 8*, 253–287. (p. 521)

Powers, D. E. (1986). Relations of test item characteristics to test preparation/test practice effects: A quantitative summary. *Psychological Bulletin, 100*, 67–77. (p. 326)

Premack, D. (1983). The codes of man and beasts. *The Behavioral and Brain Sciences, 6*, 125–167. (p. 310)

Price, R. A. (1987). Genetics of human obesity. *Annals of Behavioral Medicine, 9,* 9–14. (p. 537)

Prioleau, L., Murdock, M., & Brody, N. (1983). An analysis of psychotherapy versus placebo studies. *The Behavioral and Brain Sciences, 6,* 275–310. (p. 496)

Pritchard, R. M. (1961, June). Stabilized images on the retina. *Scientific American,* pp. 72–78. (p. 144)

Pruitt, D. G., & Rubin, J. Z. (1986). *Social conflict: Escalation, stalemate, and settlement.* New York: Random House. (p. 607)

Pryor, J. B., Reeder, G. D., Vinacco, R., Jr., & Kott, T. L. (1988). The instrumental and symbolic functions of attitudes toward persons with AIDS. *Journal of Applied Social Psychology,* in press. (p. 369)

Psychic Abscam (1983, March). *Discover,* p. 10. (p. 186)

Public Opinion (1978, September/October). New women's roles welcomed, p. 36. (p. 125)

Public Opinion (1980, December/ January). Women in the 70's, p. 33. (p. 125)

Public Opinion (1984, August/ September). Phears and phobias, p. 32. (pp. 395, 451)

Public Opinion (1984, October/November). Racial prejudice curve, p. 15. (p. 591)

Public Opinion (1986b, December/January). Household tasks: Divisions of Labor, p. 30. (p. 117)

Public Opinion (1986a, December/January). Fertility data from U. S. National Center for Health Statistics, p. 30.(p. 108)

Public Opinion (1987a, May/June, p. 32). Teen angels. (Report of University of Michigan survey.) (p. 90)

Public Opinion (1987b, September/October). Pornography (report of survey by National Opinion Research Center), p. 27. (p. 584)

Pyszczynski, T., & Greenberg, J. (1987a). Self-regulatory perseveration and the depressive self-focusing style: A self-awareness theory of reactive depression. *Psychological Bulletin, 102,* 122–138. (p. 461)

Pyszczynski, R., & Greenberg, T. (1987b). Toward an integration of cognitive and motivational perspectives on social inference: A biased hypothesis-testing model. In L. Berkowitz (Ed.), *Advances in experimental social psychology* (Vol. 20). Orlando, Fla: Academic Press. (p. 430)

Qualls, P. J., & Sheehan, P. W. (1981). Electromyograph biofeedback as a relaxation technique: A critical appraisal and reassessment. *Psychological Bulletin, 90,* 21–42. (p. 522)

Quasha, S. (1980). *Albert Einstein: An intimate portrait.* New York: Forest. (p. 332)

Quattrone, G. A., & Jones, E. E. (1980). The perception of variability within in-groups and out-groups: Implications for the law of small numbers. *Journal of Personality and Social Psychology, 38,* 141–152. (p. 621)

Rabin, A. S., Kaslow, N. J., Rehm, L. P. (1986). Aggregate outcome and follow-up results following self-control therapy for depression. Paper presented at the American Psychological Association convention. (p. 490)

Radecki, T. (1984). Deerhunter continues to kill, 35th victim—31 dead. *NCTV News, 5*(3–4), 3. (p. 579)

Ramón y Cajal, S. (1917). *Recollections of my life.* Cited by M. Jacobson (1970), *Developmental neurobiology.* New York: Holt, Rinehart, & Winston. (p. 29)

Randi, J. (1983a, Summer). The Project Alpha experiment: Part 1. The first two years. *Skeptical Inquirer,* pp. 24–33. (p. 186)

Randi, J. (1983b, Fall). The Project Alpha experiment: Part 2. Beyond the laboratory. *Skeptical Inquirer,* pp. 36–45. (p. 186)

Raskin, D. C., & Podlesny, J. A. (1979). Truth and deception: A reply to Lykken. *Psychological Bulletin, 86,* 54–59. (p. 385)

Ravussin, E., Lillioja, S., Knowler W. C., Christin, L., Freymond, D., Abbott, W. G. H., Voyce, V., Howard, B. V., & Bogardus, C. (1988). Reduced rate of energy expenditure as a risk factor for body-weight gain. *New England Journal of Medicine, 318,* 467–472. (p. 537)

Rawlins, J. N. P. (with replies by others). (1985). Associations across time: The hippocampus as a temporary memory store. *Behavioral and Brain Sciences, 8,* 479–496. (p. 267)

Raymond, C. A. (1987). Birth defects linked with specific level of maternal alcohol use, but abstinence still is the best policy. *Journal of the American Medical Association, 258,* 177–178. (p. 61)

Razran, G. H. S. (1940). Conditioned response changes in rating and appraising sociopolitical solutions. *Psychological Bulletin, 37,* 481. (p. 235)

Reagan, N., & Libby, B. (1980). *Nancy.* New York: Morrow. (p. 107)

Reason, J., & Mycielska, K. (1982). *Absent-minded? The psychology of mental lapses and everyday errors.* Englewood Cliffs, NJ: Prentice-Hall. (p. 183)

Regier, D. A., Myers, J. K., Kramer, M., Robins, L. N., Blazer, D. G., Hough, R. L., Eaton, W. W., & Locke, B. Z. (1984, October). The NIMH epidemiologic catchment area program: Historical contact, major objectives, and study population characteristics. *Archives of General Psychiatry, 41*(10), 934–941. (p. 449)

Reisenzein, R. (1983). The Schachter theory of emotion: Two decades later. *Psychological Bulletin, 94,* 239–264. (p. 403)

Reiser, M. (1982). *Police psychology.* Los Angeles: LEHI. (p. 187)

Renner, M. J., & Rosenzweig, M. R. (1987). Enriched and impoverished environments: Effects on brain and behavior. New York: Springer-Verlag. (p. 63)

Rescorla, R. A. (1988). Pavlovian conditioning: It's not what you think it is. *American Psychologist, 43,* 151–160. (p. 236)

Rescorla, R. A., & Wagner, A. R. (1972). A theory of Pavlovian conditioning: Variations in the effectiveness of reinforcement and nonreinforcement. In A. H. Black & W. F. Perokasy (Eds.), *Classical conditioning II: Current theory.* New York: Appleton-Century-Crofts. (p. 236)

Reveen, P. J. (1987–88). Fantasizing under hypnosis: Some experimental evidence. *Skeptical Inquirer, 12*, 181–183. (p. 209)

Reychler, L. (1979). The effectiveness of a pacifist strategy in conflict resolution. *Journal of Conflict Resolution, 23*, 228–260. (p. 603)

Reynolds, D. K. (1982). *The quiet therapies.* Honolulu: University of Hawaii Press. (p. 164)

Reynolds, D. K. (1986). *Even in summer the ice doesn't melt: Japan's Morita Therapy.* New York: Morrow (Quill paperback). (p. 164)

Reynolds, G. S. (1978). *A primer of operant conditioning.* Glenview, IL: Scott, Foresman. (p. 241–242)

Rheingold, H. L. (1985). Development as the acquisition of familiarity. *Annual Review of Psychology, 36*, 1–17. (pp. 71–72)

Rhodes, S. R. (1983). Age-related differences in work attitudes and behavior: A review and conceptual analysis. *Psychological Bulletin, 93*, 328–367. (p. 100)

Rice, M. E., & Grusec, J. E. (1975). Saying and doing: Effects on observer performance. *Journal of Personality and Social Psychology, 32*, 584–593. (p. 251)

Ridenour, M. (1982). Infant walkers: Developmental tool or inherent danger. *Perceptual and Motor Skills, 55*, 1201–1202. (p. 64)

Rieff, P. (1979). *Freud: The mind of a moralist* (3rd ed.). Chicago: University of Chicago Press. (p. 418)

Ring, K. (1980). *Life at death: A scientific investigation of the near-death experience.* New York: Coward, McCann & Geoghegan. (p. 221)

Riskind, J. H., Beck, A. T., Berchick, R. J., Brown, G., & Steer, R. A. (1987). Reliability of *DSM-III* diagnoses for major depression and generalized anxiety disorder using the structured clinical interview for *DSM-III. Archives of General Psychiatry, 44*, 817–820. (p. 449)

Roberts, L. (1987). Study bolsters case against cholesterol. *Science, 237*, 28–29. (p. 533)

Roberts, S. B., Savage, J., Coward, W. A., Chew, B., & Lucas, A. (1988). Energy expenditure and intake in infants born to lean and overweight mothers. *New England Journal of Medicine, 318*, 461–466. (p. 537)

Robins, L. N., Helzer, J. E., Weissman, M. M., Orvaschel, H., Gruenberg, E., Burke, J. D., Jr., & Regier, D. A. (1984). Lifetime prevalence of specific psychiatric disorders in three sites. *Archives of General Psychiatry, 41*, 949–958. (p. 443)

Robinson, D. N. (1981). *An intellectual history of psychology* (rev. ed.). New York: Macmillan. (p. 5)

Robinson, F. P. (1970). *Effective study.* New York: Harper & Row. (p. 279)

Robinson, V. M. (1983). Humor and health. In P. E. McGhee & J. H. Goldstein (Eds.), *Handbook of humor research: Vol. II. Applied studies.* New York: Springer-Verlag. (p. 523)

Rodin, J. (1979). *Obesity theory and behavior therapy: An uneasy couple?* Paper presented at the meeting of the Association for the Advancement of Behavior Therapy. (p. 539)

Rodin, J. (1984, December). A sense of control [interview]. *Psychology Today,* pp. 38–45. (p. 357)

Rodin, J. (1985). Insulin levels, hunger and food intake: An example of feedback loops in body weight regulation. *Health Psychology, 4*, 1–18. (pp. 355, 539)

Rodin, J. (1986). Aging and health: Effects of the sense of control. *Science, 233*, 1271–1276. (pp. 434, 513–514)

Rodin, J., & Slochower, J. (1976). Externality in the non-obese: Effects of environmental responsiveness on weight. *Journal of Personality and Social Psychology, 33*, 338–344. (p. 357)

Rodin, J., Solomon, S. K., & Metcalf, J. (1978). Role of control in mediating perceptions of density. *Journal of Personality and Social Psychology, 36*, 988–999. (p. 568)

Rogers, C. R. (1958). Reinhold Niebuhr's *The self and the dramas of history:* A criticism. *Pastoral Psychology, 9*, 15–17. (p. 430)

Rogers, C. R. (1961). *On becoming a person: A therapist's view of psychotherapy.* Boston: Houghton Mifflin. (p. 477)

Rogers, C. R. (1970). *Carl Rogers on encounter groups.* New York: Harper & Row. (p. 482)

Rogers, C. R. (1980). *A way of being.* Boston: Houghton Mifflin. (pp. 426, 477–478)

Rogers, C. R. (1981, Summer). Notes on Rollo May. *Perspectives, 2*(1), p. 16. (p. 428)

Rook, K. S. (1984). Promoting social bonding: Strategies for helping the lonely and socially isolated. *American Psychologist, 39*, 1389–1407. (p. 462)

Rook, K. S. (1987). Social support versus companionship: Effects on life stress, loneliness, and evaluations by others. *Journal of Personality and Social Psychology, 52*, 1132–1147. (p. 524)

Roper Organization (1987, May/June). All in a day. *Public Opinion,* p. 40. (p. 540)

Rosch, E. (1974). Linguistic relativity. In A. Silverstein (Ed.), *Human communication: Theoretical perspectives.* New York: Halsted Press. (p. 309)

Rosch, E. (1978). Principles of categorization. In E. Rosch & B. L. Lloyd (Eds.), *Cognition and categorization.* Hillsdale, NJ: Erlbaum. (p. 285)

Rose, G. A., & Williams, R. T. (1961). Metabolic studies on large and small eaters. *British Journal of Nutrition, 1*, 1–9. (p. 536)

Rose, R. J., Koskenvuo, M., Kaprio, J., Sarna, S., & Langinvainio, H. (1988). Shared genes, shared experiences, and similarity of personality: Data from 14,228 adult Finnish co-twins. *Journal of Personality and Social Psychology, 54*, 161–171. (pp. 81–82)

Rosen, A. (1958). Differentiation of diagnostic groups by individual MMPI scales. *Journal of Consulting Psychology, 22*, 453–457. (p. 422)

Rosen, J. C., & Gross, J. (1987). Prevalence of weight reducing and weight gaining in adolescent girls and boys. *Health Psychology, 6*, 131–147. (p. 539)

Rosenbaum, M. (1986). The repulsion hypothesis: On the nondevelopment of relationships. *Journal of Personality and Social Psychology, 51*, 1156–1166. (p. 599)

Rosenfeld, S. P. (1987, March 29). Insanity defense is riskier now and can turn winners to losers. Associated Press release (*Grand Rapids Press*, p. A17). (p. 446)

Rosenhan, D. L. (1973). On being sane in insane places. *Science, 179*, 250–258. (p. 470)

Rosenhan, D. L. (1983a). Psychological abnormality and law. In C. J. Scheirer & B. C. Hammonds (Eds.), *The master lecture series: Vol. 2. Psychology and the law.* Washington, DC: American Psychological Association. (p. 446)

Rosenhan, D. L. (1983b). *Psychological realities and judicial policy.* Paper presented at the meeting of the American Psychological Association. (pp. 250, 446)

Rosenthal, R., Hall, J. A., Archer, D., DiMatteo, M. R., & Rogers, P. L. (1979). The PONS test: Measuring sensitivity to nonverbal cues. In S. Weitz (Ed.), *Nonverbal communication* (2nd ed.). New York: Oxford University Press. (p. 386)

Rosenzweig, M. R. (1984a). Experience, memory, and the brain. *American Psychologist, 39*, 365–376. (p. 63)

Rosenzweig, M. R. (1984b). U.S. psychology and world psychology. *American Psychologist, 39*, 877–884. (p. 41)

Rosenzweig, M. R., Bennett, E. L., & Diamond, M. C. (1972, February). Brain changes in response to experience. *Scientific American*, 22–29. (p. 63)

Rosewicz, B. (1983, January 31). Study finds grim link between liquor and crime: Figures far worse than officials expected. *Detroit Free Press*, pp. 1A, 4A. (p. 577)

Ross, H. (1975, June 19). Mist, murk, and visual perception. *New Scientist*, pp. 658–660. (p. 170)

Ross, M., McFarland, C., & Fletcher, G. J. O. (1981). The effect of attitude on the recall of personal histories. *Journal of Personality and Social Psychology, 40*, 627–634. (p. 278)

Rossi, P. J. (1968). Adaptation and negative aftereffect to lateral optical displacement in newly hatched chicks. *Science, 160*, 430–432. (p. 182)

Rothbart, M., Fulero, S., Jensen, C., Howard, J., & Birrell, P. (1978). From individual to group impressions: Availability heuristics in stereotype formation. *Journal of Experimental Social Psychology, 14*, 237–255. (p. 594)

Rothbart, M. K., Hanley, D., & Albert, M. (1986). Gender differences in moral reasoning. *Sex Roles, 15*, 645–653. (p. 95)

Rothstein, W. G. (1980). The significance of occupations in work careers: An empirical and theoretical review. *Journal of Vocational Behavior, 17*, 328–343. (p. 108)

Rovee-Collier, C. (1988). The joy of kicking: Memories, motives, and mobiles. In P. R. Solomon, G. R. Goethals, C. M. Kelley, and B. R. Stephens (Eds.), *Perspectives on memory research.* New York: Springer Verlag. (p. 63)

Roviaro, S., Holmes, D. S., & Holmsten, R. D. (1984). Influence of a cardiac rehabilitation program on the cardiovascular, psychological, and social functioning of cardiac patients. *Journal of Behavioral Medicine, 7*, 61–81. (p. 521)

Rowe, D. C. (1987). Resolving the person-situation debate: Invitation to an interdisciplinary dialogue. *American Psychologist, 42*, 218–227. (p. 83)

Rowe, J. W., & Kahn, R. L. (1987). Human aging: Usual and successful. *Science, 237*, 143–149. (p. 101)

Roy, M. (1977) A current survey of 150 cases. In M. Roy (Ed.), *Battered Women.* New York: Van Nostrand. (p. 250)

Rozin, P., Millman, L., & Nemeroff, C. (1986). Operation of the laws of sympathetic magic in disgust and other domains. *Journal of Personality and Social Psychology, 50*, 703–712. (p. 234)

Ruback, R. B., Carr, T. S., & Hopper, C. H. (1986). Perceived control in prison: Its relation to reported crowding, stress, and symptoms. *Journal of Applied Social Psychology, 16*, 375–386. (p. 434)

Rubin, J. Z., Provenzano, F. J., & Luria, Z. (1974). The eye of the beholder: Parents' views on sex of newborns. *American Journal of Orthopsychiatry, 44*, 512–519. (pp. 129, 130)

Rubin, L. B. (1979). *Women of a certain age: The midlife search for self.* New York: Harper & Row. (p. 108)

Rubin, L. B. (1985). *Just friends: The role of friendship in our lives.* New York: Harper & Row. (p. 131)

Ruble, D. N., & Brooks-Gunn, J. (1979). Menstrual symptoms: A social cognition analysis. *Journal of Behavioral Medicine, 2*, 171–194. (p. 526)

Ruble, D. N., & Brooks-Gunn, J. (1987). In B. F. Carter & B. E. Ginsburg (Eds.), *Legal and ethical implications of the biobehavioral sciences: Premenstrual syndrome.* New York: Plenum. (p. 526)

Rule, B. G., & Ferguson, T. J. (1986). The effects of media violence on attitudes, emotions, and cognitions. *Journal of Social Issues, 42(3)*, 29–50. (p. 580)

Rumbaugh, D. M. (1977). *Language learning by a chimpanzee: The Lana project.* New York: Academic Press. (p. 306)

Rumbaugh, D. M. (1985). Comparative psychology: Patterns in adaptation. In A. M. Rogers & C. J. Scheirer (Eds.), *The G. Stanley Hall Lecture Series* (Vol. 5). Washington, DC: American Psychological Association. (p. 308)

Rumbaugh, D. M. (1987, September 17). Personal communication. (p. 308)

Rumbaugh, D. M., & Savage-Rumbaugh, S. (1978). Chimpanzee language research: Status and potential. *Behavior Research Methods & Instrumentation, 10*, 119–131. (pp. 287, 308)

Rumbaugh, D. M., & Savage-Rumbaugh, S. (1986)., Reasoning and language in chimpanzees. In R. J. Hoage & L. Goldman (Eds.), *Animal intelligence.* Washington, D.C.: Smithsonian Institution Press. (p. 308)

Rumelhart, D. E., McClelland, J. L., and the PDP Research Group (1986). *Parallel distributed processing: Explorations in the microstructure of cognition, Vol. 1. Foundations.* Cambridge, MA: MIT Press. (p. 300)

Ruopp, R. R., & Travers, J. (1982). Janus faces day care: Perspectives on quality and cost. In E. F. Zigler & E. W. Gordon (Eds.), *Day care: Scientific and social policy issues.* Boston, MA: Auburn House. (p. 76)

Rushton, J. P. (1975). Generosity in children: Immediate and long-term effects of modeling, preaching, and moral judgment. *Journal of Personality and Social Psychology, 31*, 459–466. (p. 251)

Rushton, J. P., Fulker, D. W., Neale, M. C., Nias, D. K. B., & Eysenck, H. J. (1986). Altruism and aggression: The heritability of individual differences. *Journal of Personality and Social Psychology, 50,* 1192–1198. (pp. 437, 576)

Rushton, J. P., Russell, R. J. H., & Wells, P. A. (1984). Genetic similarity theory: Beyond kin selection. *Behavior Genetics, 14,* 179–193. (p. 589)

Russell, B. (1930/1985). *The conquest of happiness.* London: Unwin Paperbacks. (p. 398)

Russell, D. E. H. (1984). *Sexual exploitation: Rape, child sexual abuse, and workplace harassment.* Beverly Hills, CA: Sage (p. 582)

Rutter, M. (1979). Maternal deprivation, 1972–1978: New findings, new concepts, new approaches. *Child Development, 50,* 283–305. (p. 75)

Ryan, E. D. (1980). Attribution, intrinsic motivation, and athletics: A replication and extension. In C. H. Nadeau, W. R. Halliwell, K. M. Newell, & G. C. Roberts (Eds.), *Psychology of motor behavior and sport—1979.* Champaign, IL: Human Kinetics Press. (p. 375)

Rzewnicki, R., & Forgays, D. G. (1987). Recidivism and self-cure of smoking and obesity: An attempt to replicate. *American Psychologist, 42,* 97–100. (p. 540)

Sabini, J. (1986). Stanley Milgram (1933–1984). *American Psychologist, 41,* 1378–1379. (p. 554)

Sackheim, J. A. (1985, June). The case for ECT. *Psychology Today,* pp. 36–40. (p. 498)

Sagan, C. (1979a). *Broca's brain.* New York: Random House. (pp. 9, 32)

Sagan, C. (1979b). *Dragons of Eden.* New York: Random House. (pp. 140, 444)

Sagan, C. (1980). *Cosmos.* New York: Random House. (pp. 589, 601)

Sagan, C. (1987, February 1). The fine art of baloney detection. *Parade.* (pp. 142, 188)

Sandberg, G. G., Jackson, T. L., & Petretic-Jackson, P. (1985). *Sexual aggression and courtship violence in dating relationships.* Paper presented at the meeting of the Midwestern Psychological Association. (p. 582)

Satir, V. (1967). *Conjoint family therapy.* Palo Alto, CA: Science and Behavior Books. (p. 501)

Sato, K. (1987). Distribution of the cost of maintaining common resources. *Journal of Experimental Social Psychology, 23,* 19–31. (p. 603)

Savage-Rumbaugh, S. (1987). Communication, symbolic communication, and language: Reply to Seidenberg and Petitto. *Journal of Experimental Psychology: General, 116,* 288–292. (p. 308)

Savitsky, J. C., & Lindblom, W. D. (1986). The impact of the guilty but mentally ill verdict on juror decisions: An empirical analysis. *Journal of Applied Social Psychology, 16,* 686–701. (p. 446)

Sayre, R. F. (1979). The parents' last lessons. In D. D. Van Tassel (Ed.), *Aging, death, and the completion of being.* Philadelphia: University of Pennsylvania Press. (p. 101)

Scanzoni, L. D., & Scanzoni, J. (1981). *Men, women, and change: A sociology of marriage and family.* New York: McGraw-Hill. (p. 106)

Scarr, S. (1982). Development is internally guided, not determined. *Contemporary Psychology, 27,* 852–853. (pp. 58, 83)

Scarr, S. (1984, May). What's a parent to do? [Conversation with E. Hall.] *Psychology Today,* pp. 58–63. (p. 338)

Scarr, S. (1986). *Mother care/other care.* New York: Basic Books. (pp. 76, 338)

Scarr, S. (1988). Race and gender as psychological variables: Social and ethical issues. *American Psychologist, 43,* 56–59. (p. 129)

Scarr, S., & McCartney, K. (1983). How people make their own environments: A theory of genotype → environment effects. *Child Development, 54,* 424–435. (p. 85)

Scarr, S., Pakstis, A. J., Katz, S. H., & Barker, W. B. (1977). The absence of a relationship between degree of white ancestry and intellectual skills within a black population. *Human Genetics, 39,* 69–86. (p. 341)

Scarr, S., Webber, P. L., Weinberg, R. A., & Wittig, M. A. (1981). Personality resemblance among adolescents and their parents in biologically related and adoptive families. *Journal of Personality and Social Psychology, 40,* 885–898. (p. 83)

Scarr, S., & Weinberg, R. A. (1976). IQ test performance of black children adopted by white families. *American Psychologist, 31,* 726–739. (p. 341)

Scarr, S., & Weinberg, R. A. (1983). The Minnesota adoption studies: Genetic differences and malleability. *Child Development, 54,* 260–267. (p. 83)

Scarr, S., & Weinberg, R. A. (1986). The early childhood enterprise: Care and education of the young. *American Psychologist, 41,* 1140–1146. (p. 76)

Schachter, S. (1982). Recidivism and self-cure of smoking and obesity. *American Psychologist, 37,* 436–444. (p. 540)

Schachter, S., & Singer, J. E. (1962). Cognitive, social and physiological determinants of emotional state. *Psychological Review, 69,* 379–399. (p. 402)

Schaie, K. W. (1987). Old dogs can learn new tricks: Intellectual decline and its remediation in later adulthood. Address to the Eastern Psychological Association convention. (p. 104)

Schaie, K. W., & Geiwitz, J. (1982). *Adult development and aging.* Boston: Little, Brown. (pp. 103, 106)

Schaie, K. W., & Strother, C. R. (1968). A cross-sequential study of age changes in cognitive behavior. *Psychological Bulletin, 70,* 671–680. (p. 103)

Scheerer, M. (1963, April). Problem solving. *Scientific American,* pp. 118–128. (pp. 288–289)

Scheier, M. F., & Carver, C. S. (1987). Dispositional optimism and physical well-being: The influence of generalized outcome expectancies on health. *Journal of Personality, 55,* 169–210. (p. 514)

Schein, E. H. (1956). The Chinese indoctrination program for prisoners of war: A study of attempted brainwashing. *Psychiatry, 19,* 149–172. (p. 560)

Schiele, B. C., & Brozek, J. (1956). ''Experimental neurosis'' resulting from semistarvation in man. In G. S. Welsh & W. G. Dahlstrom (Eds.), *Basic reading on the MMPI in psychology and medicine.* Minneapolis: University of Minnesota Press. (p. 422)

Schiffenbauer, A., & Schiavo, R. S. (1976). Physical distance and attraction: An intensification effect. *Journal of Experimental Social Psychology, 12,* 274–282. (p. 568)

Schleifer, S. J., Keller, S. E., McKegney, F. P., & Stein, M. (1979). *The influence of stress and other psychosocial factors on human immunity.* Paper presented at the 36th Annual Meeting of the American Psychosomatic Society. (p. 518)

Schlesinger, A. M., Jr. (1965). *A thousand days.* Boston: Houghton Mifflin. (p. 570)

Schmeck, H. M., Jr. (1988, February 16). Depression: Studies bring new drugs and insights. *New York Times,* pp. C1, C10. (pp. 460, 500)

Schmeck, H. M., Jr. (1988, March (p. 8). Studies find abnormal burning of energy in patients' brains. *New York Times,* pp. C1, C11. (p. 500)

Schnaper, N. (1980). Comments germane to the paper entitled ''The reality of death experiences'' by Ernst Rodin. *Journal of Nervous and Mental Disease, 168,* 268–270. (p. 221)

Schneider, W., & Shiffrin, R. M. (1977). Controlled and automatic human information processing: I. Detection, search, and attention. *Psychological Review, 84,* 1–66. (p. 360)

Schnitzer, B. (1984, May). Repunctuated message. *Games,* pp. 57, 62. (p. 300)

Schofield, J. (1982). *Black and white in school.* New York: Praeger. (pp. 590, 605)

Schofield, J., & Pavelchak, M. (1985). The day after: The impact of a media event. *American Psychologist, 40,* 542–548. (p. 564)

Schonfield, D., & Robertson, B. A. (1966). Memory storage and aging. *Canadian Journal of Psychology, 20,* 228–236. (p. 102)

Schooler, J. W., Gerhard, D., & Loftus, E. F. (1986). Qualities of the unreal. *Journal of Experimental Psychology: Learning, Memory, and Cognition, 12,* 171–181. (p. 272)

Schwartz, B. (1984). *Psychology of learning and behavior* (2nd ed.). New York: Norton. (pp. 235, 242, 450)

Schwarz, J. (1987, September 15). Mapping the mind. *American Way,* 18–20. (p. 33)

Schwarz, N., & Clore, G. L. (1983). Mood, misattribution, and judgments of well-being: Informative and directive functions of affective states. *Journal of Personality and Social Psychology, 45,* 513–523. (p. 393)

Schwarz, N., Strack, F., Kommer, D., & Wagner, D. (1987). Soccer, rooms, and the quality of your life: Mood effects on judgments of satisfaction with life in general and with specific domains. *European Journal of Social Psychology, 17,* 69–79. (p. 271)

Scovern, A. W., & Kilmann, P. R. (1980). Status of electro-convulsive therapy: Review of the outcome literature. *Psychological Bulletin, 87,* 260–303. (p. 498)

Scribner, S. (1977). Modes of thinking and ways of speaking: Culture and logic reconsidered. In P. N. Johnson-Laird & P. C. Wason (Eds.), *Thinking: Readings in cognitive science.* New York: Cambridge University Press. (p. 92)

Sears, D. O. (1979, May 3–5). *Life stage effects upon attitude change, especially among the elderly.* Paper presented at the Workshop on the Elderly of the Future, Committee on Aging, National Research Council, Annapolis, MD. (p. 565)

Seligman, M. E. P. (1974, May). Submissive death: Giving up on life. *Psychology Today,* pp. 80–85. (pp. 198, 382)

Seligman, M. E. P. (1975). *Helplessness: On depression, development and death.* San Francisco: Freeman. (p. 434)

Seligman, M. E. P. (1988). Why is there so much depression today? The waxing of the individual and the waning of the commons. G. Stanley Hall Lecture to the American Psychological Association convention. (pp. 456, 461)

Seligman, M. E. P., & Schulman, P. (1986). Explanatory style as a predictor of productivity and quitting among life insurance sales agents. *Journal of Personality and Social Psychology, 50,* 832–838. (p. 435)

Seligman, M. E. P., & Yellen, A. (1987). What is a dream? *Behavior Research and Therapy, 25,* 1–24. (pp. 204–205)

Selye, H. (1936). A syndrome produced by diverse nocuous agents. *Nature, 138,* 32. (p. 509)

Selye, H. (1976). *The stress of life.* New York: McGraw-Hill. (pp. 509–510)

Senden, M., von (1932; reprinted 1960). In P. Heath (Trans.), *Space and sight: The perception of space and shape in the congenitally blind before and after operation.* Glencoe, IL: Free Press. (p. 180)

Shapiro, C. M., Bortz, R., Mitchell, D., Bartel, P., & Jooste, P. (1981). Slow-wave sleep: A recovery period after exercise. *Science, 214,* 1253–1254. (p. 201)

Shapiro, D. A., & Shapiro, D. (1982). Meta-analysis of comparative therapy outcome studies: A replication and refinement. *Psychological Bulletin, 92,* 581–604. (p. 495)

Shaughnessy, J. J., & Zechmeister, E. B. (1989). Memory-monitoring accuracy as influenced by the distribution of retrieval practice. *Bulletin of the Psychonomic Society,* in press. (p. 273)

Sheehan, S. (1982). *Is there no place on earth for me?* Boston: Houghton Mifflin. (p. 463)

Sheldon, W. H. (1954). *Atlas of man: A guide for somatotyping the adult male of all ages.* New York: Harper & Row. (p. 420)

Shepard, R. N. (1981). Psychophysical complementarity. In M. Kubovy & J. R. Pomerantz (Eds.), *Perceptual organization.* Hillsdale, NJ: Erlbaum. (p. 177)

Sherif, M. (1937). An experimental approach to the study of attitudes. *Sociometry, 1,* 90–98. (p. 550)

Sherif, M. (1966). *In common predicament: Social psychology of intergroup conflict and cooperation.* Boston: Houghton Mifflin. (p. 605)

Sherman, A. R., & Levin, M. P. (1979). *In vivo* therapies for compulsive habits, sexual difficulties, and severe adjustment problems. In A. P. Goldstein & F. H. Kanfer (Eds.), *Maximizing treatment gains: Transfer enhancement in psychotherapy*. New York: Academic Press. (p. 485)

Shettleworth, S. J. (1973). Food reinforcement and the organization of behavior in golden hamsters. In R. A. Hinde & J. Stevenson-Hinde (Eds.), *Constraints on learning*. London: Academic Press. (p. 248)

Shiffrin, R. M., & Schneider, W. (1977). Controlled and automatic human information processing: II. Perceptual learning, automatic attending, and a general theory. *Psychological Review, 84*, 127–190. (p. 260)

Shneidman, E. (1987, March). At the point of no return. *Psychology Today*, pp. 54–58. (p. 457)

Shotland, L. (1984, March 12). Quoted by Maureen Dowd, 20 years after the murder of Kitty Genovese, the question remains: Why? *The New York Times*, p. B1 (p. 585)

Shotland, R. L., & Craig, J. M. (1988). Can men and women differentiate between friendly and sexually interested behavior? *Social Psychology Quarterly, 51*, 66–73. (p. 119)

Shotland, R. L., & Goodstein, L. I. (1984). The role of bystanders in crime control. *Journal of Social Issues, 40*, 9–26. (p. 585)

Showers, C. & Ruben, C. (1987). Distinguishing pessimism from depression: Negative expectations and positive coping mechanisms. Paper presented at the American Psychological Association convention. (p. 435)

Siebenhaler, J. B., & Caldwell, P. K. (1956). Cooperation among adult dolphins. *Journal of Mammalogy, 37*, 126–128. (p. 590)

Siegel, L. S., & Hodkin, B. (1982). The garden path to the understanding of cognitive development: Has Piaget led us into the poison ivy? In S. Modgil & C. Modgil (Eds.), *Jean Piaget: Consensus and controversy*. New York: Praeger. (p. 70)

Siegel, R. K. (1977, October). Hallucinations. *Scientific American*, pp. 132–140. (p. 221)

Siegel, R. K. (1980). The psychology of life after death. *American Psychologist, 35*, 911–931. (p. 222)

Siegel, R. K. (1984, March 15). Personal communication. (p. 218)

Siegel, R. K. Quoted by J. Hooper (1982, October), Mind tripping. *Omni*, pp. 72–82, 159–160. (p. 218)

Silka, L. (1988). *Intuitive judgments of change*. New York: Springer-Verlag. (p. 594)

Silver, M., & Geller, D. (1978). On the irrelevance of evil: The organization and individual action. *Journal of Social Issues, 34*, 125–136. (p. 556)

Silverman, P. S., & Retzlaff, P. D. (1986). Cognitive stage regression through hypnosis: Are earlier cognitive stages retrievable? *International Journal of Clinical and Experimental Hypnosis, 34*, 192–204. (p. 208)

Silverton, L. (1988). Crime and the schizophrenia spectrum: A study of three Danish cohorts. In T. E. Moffitt & S. A. Mednick (Eds.), *Biological contributions to crime causation*. New York: Martinus-Nijhoff. (p. 471)

Singer, J. L. (1975). Navigating the stream of consciousness: Research in daydreaming and related inner experience. *American Psychologist, 30*, 727–738. (p. 195)

Singer, J. L. (1976, July). Fantasy: The foundation of serenity. *Psychology Today*, pp. 32–37. (p. 196)

Singer, J. L. (1981). Clinical intervention: New developments in methods and evaluation. In L. T. Benjamin, Jr. (Ed.), *The G. Stanley Hall Lecture Series*, (Vol. 1). Washington, DC: American Psychological Association. (p. 495)

Singer, J. L. (1986). Is television bad for children? *Social Science, 71*, 178–182. (p. 198)

Singer, J. L., & Singer, D. G. (1986). Family experiences and television viewing as predictors of children's imagination, restlessness, and aggression. *Journal of Social Issues, 42*(3), 7–28. (p. 580)

Siskel, G. (1987, September 9). Porn turns to video rentals for livelihood. Tribune Media Services. (p. 580)

Six, B., & Krahe, B. (1984). Implicit psychologists' estimates of attitude-behaviour consistencies. *European Journal of Social Psychology, 14*, 79–86. (p. 55)

Sjostrom, L. (1980). Fat cells and bodyweight. In A. J. Stunkard (Ed.), *Obesity*. Philadelphia: Saunders. (p. 535)

Skinner, B. F. (1953). *Science and human behavior*. New York: Macmillan. (p. 241)

Skinner, B. F. (1956). A case history in scientific method. *American Psychologist, 11*, 221–233. (p. 242)

Skinner, B. F. (1957). *Verbal behavior*. Englewood Cliffs, NJ: Prentice-Hall. (p. 304)

Skinner, B. F. (1961, November). Teaching machines. *Scientific American*, pp. 91–102. (p. 241)

Skinner, B. F. (1983, September). Origins of a behaviorist. *Psychology Today*, pp. 22–33. (pps. 247, 460)

Skinner, B. F. (1984). The shame of American education. *American Psychologist, 39*, 947–954. (p. 245)

Skinner, B. F. (1985). *Cognitive science and behaviorism*. Unpublished manuscript, Harvard University. (p. 304)

Skinner, B. F. (1986). What is wrong with daily life in the western world? *American Psychologist, 41*, 568–574. (p. 245)

Skinner, B. F. (1987, August 25). Quoted in D. Goleman, Embattled giant of psychology speaks his mind. *New York Times*, pp. C1, C3. (p. 329)

Skinner, B. F. (1988). The school of the future. Address to the American Psychological Association convention. (p. 245)

Sklar, L. S., & Anisman, H. (1981). Stress and cancer. *Psychological Bulletin, 89*, 369–406. (p. 518)

Skov, R. B., & Sherman, S. J. (1986). Information-gathering processes: Diagnosticity, hypothesis-confirmatory strategies, and perceived hypothesis confirmation. *Journal of Experimental Social Psychology, 22*, 93–121. (p. 288)

Slovic, P. (1987). Perception of risk. *Science, 236*, 280–285. (p. 293)

Slovic, P., & Fischhoff, B. (1977). On the psychology of experimental surprises. *Journal of Experimental Psychology: Human Perception and Performance, 3*, 544–551. (p. 20)

Slovic, P., Fischhoff, B., & Lichtenstein, S. (1985). Regulation of risk: A psychological perspective. In R. Noll (Ed.), *Social science and regulatory policy*. Berkeley, CA: University of California Press. (p. 292)

Smith, A. (1987). Personal communication. (p. 49)

Smith, A., & Sugar, O. (1975). Development of above normal language and intelligence 21 years after left hemispherectomy. *Neurology, 25,* 813–818. (p. 49)

Smith, D. (1982). Trends in counseling and psychotherapy. *American Psychologist, 37,* 802–809. (p. 476)

Smith, D., & Kraft, W. A. (1983). DSM-III: Do psychologists really want an alternative? *American Psychologist, 38,* 777–785. (p. 448)

Smith, M. B. (1978). Psychology and values. *Journal of Social Issues, 34,* 181–199. (p. 427)

Smith, M. B. (1982). *Psychologists and peace*. Paper presented at the meeting of the American Psychological Association. (p. 601)

Smith, M. C. (1983). Hypnotic memory enhancement of witnesses: Does it work? *Psychological Bulletin, 94,* 387–407. (p. 208)

Smith, M. L., & Glass, G. V. (1977). Meta-analysis of psychotherapy outcome studies. *American Psychologist, 32,* 752–760. (p. 495)

Smith, M. L., Glass, G. V., & Miller, R. L. (1980). *The benefits of psychotherapy*. Baltimore: Johns Hopkins Press. (pp. 494–495)

Smith, T. W. (1979). Happiness: Time trends, seasonal variations, intersurvey differences, and other mysteries. *Social Psychology Quarterly, 42,* 18–30. (p. 394)

Smith, T. W., & Anderson, N. B. (1986). Models of personality and disease: An interactional approach to Type A behavior and cardiovascular risk. *Journal of Personality and Social Psychology, 50,* 1166–1173. (p. 516)

Snarey, J. (1987, June). A question of morality. *Psychology Today*, pp. 6–7. (p. 95)

Snarey, J. R. (1985). Cross-cultural universality of social-moral development: A critical review of Kohlbergian research. *Psychological Bulletin, 97,* 202–233. (p. 95)

Sniezek, J. A., & Jazwinski, C. H. (1986). Gender bias in English: In search of fair language. *Journal of Applied Social Psychology, 16,* 642–662. (p. 309)

Snodgrass, M. A. (1987). The relationships of differential loneliness, intimacy, and characterological attributional style to duration of loneliness. *Journal of Social Behavior and Personality, 2,* 173–186. (p. 462)

Snodgrass, S. E., Higgins, J. G., & Todisco, L. (1986). The effects of walking behavior on mood. Paper presented at the American Psychological Association convention. (p. 389)

Snyder, C. R., & Fromkin, H. (1980). *Uniqueness: The human pursuit of difference*. New York: Plenum Press. (p. 557)

Snyder, M. (1984). When belief creates reality. In L. Berkowitz (Ed.), *Advances in experimental social psychology* (Vol. 18). New York: Academic Press. (p. 471)

Snyder, M. (1987). *Public appearances: Private realities*. New York: Freeman. (p. 556)

Snyder, M., Tanke, E. D., & Berscheid, E. (1977). Social perception and interpersonal behavior: On the self-fulfilling nature of social stereotypes. *Journal of Personality and Social Psychology, 35,* 656–666. (p. 556)

Snyder, S. H. (1984). Neurosciences: An integrative discipline. *Science, 225,* 1255–1257. (p. 29)

Snyder, S. H. (1986a). Quoted in J. Hooper & D. Teresi, *The 3-pound universe*. New York: Laurel/Dell. p. 76. (p. 499)

Snyder, S. H. (1986b). *Drugs and the brain*. New York: Scientific American Library. (p. 501)

Snyderman, M., & Rothman, S. (1987). Survey of expert opinion on intelligence and aptitude testing. *American Psychologist, 42,* 137–144. (p. 340)

Social Science Research Council (1986). Report for 1985–86 of the Committee on Development, Giftedness, and the Learning Process. *Annual Report 1985–86*. New York: Social Science Research Council. (p. 333)

Sokoll, G. R., & Mynatt, C. R. (1984). *Arousal and free throw shooting*. Paper presented at the meeting of the Midwestern Psychological Association. (p. 382)

Solomon, M. (1987, December). Standard issue. *Psychology Today*, pp. 30–31. (p. 597)

Solomon, R. L. (1980). The opponent-process theory of acquired motivation: The costs of pleasure and the benefits of pain. *American Psychologist, 35,* 691–712. (p. 397)

Solomon, R. L., Kamin, L. J., & Wynne, L. C. (1953). Traumatic avoidance learning: The outcomes of several extinction procedures with dogs. *Journal of Abnormal and Social Psychology, 48,* 291–302. (p. 243)

Sontag, S. (1978). *Illness as metaphor*. New York: Farrar, Straus, & Giroux. (p. 517)

Spanos, N. P. (1982). A social psychological approach to hypnotic behavior. In G. Weary & H. L. Mirels (Eds.), *Integrations of clinical and social psychology*. New York: Oxford. (pps. 207, 210)

Spanos, N. P. (1986a). Hypnotic behavior: A social-psychological interpretation of amnesia, analgesia, and "trance logic." *Brain and Behavioral Sciences, 9,* 449–502. (p. 213)

Spanos, N. P. (1986b). Hypnosis, nonvolitional responding, and multiple personality: A social psychological perspective. *Progress in Experimental Personality Research, 14,* 1–62. (p. 455)

Spanos, N. P. (1987–88). Past-life hypnotic regression: A critical view. *Skeptical Inquirer, 12,* 174–180. (p. 209)

Spanos, N. P., Radtke, L., Bertrand, L. D. (1985). Hypnotic amnesia as a strategic enactment: Breaching amnesia in highly susceptible subjects. *Journal of Personality and Social Psychology, 47,* 1155–1169. (p. 206)

Spector, P. E. (1986). Perceived control by employees: A meta-analysis of studies concerning autonomy and participation at work. *Human Relations, 39,* 1005–1016. (p. 376)

Spence, J. T., & Helmreich, R. L. (1983). Achievement-related motives and behavior. In J. T. Spence (Ed.), *Achieve-*

ment and achievement motives: Psychological and sociological approaches. New York: Freeman. (p. 374)

Sperling, G. (1960). The information available in brief visual presentations. *Psychological Monographs, 74* (Whole No. 498). (p. 258)

Sperry, R. W. (1956, May). The eye and the brain. *Scientific American,* pp. 48–52. (p. 182)

Sperry, R. W. (1964). *Problems outstanding in the evolution of brain function.* James Arthur Lecture, American Museum of Natural History, New York. Cited by R. Ornstein (1977), *The psychology of consciousness* (2nd ed.) New York: Harcourt Brace Jovanovich. (p. 46)

Sperry, R. W. (1968). Hemisphere deconnection and unity in conscious awareness. *American Psychologist, 23,* 723–733. (pp. 45–46, 47)

Sperry, R. W. (1982). Some effects of disconnecting the cerebral hemispheres. *Science, 217,* 1223–1226. (pp. 43–44, 47)

Sperry, R. W. (1985). Changed concepts of brain and consciousness: Some value implications. *Zygon, 20,* 41–57. (pp. 151–222)

Spiegel, D., Cutcomb, S., Ren, C., & Pribram, K. (1985). Hypnotic hallucination alters evoked potentials. *Journal of Abnormal Psychology, 94,* 249–255. (p. 213)

Spielberger, C. D., Johnson, E. H., Russell, S. F., Crane, R. J., Jacobs, G. A., & Worden, T. J. (1985). The experience and expression of anger. In M. A. Chesney, S. E. Goldston, & R. H. Rosenman (Eds.), *Anger and hostility in behavioral medicine.* New York: Hemisphere/McGraw-Hill. (p. 517)

Spielberger, C., & London, P. (1982). Rage boomerangs. *American Health, 1,* 52–56. (p. 516)

Spiess, W. F. J., Greer, J. H., & O'Donohue, W. T. (1984). Premature ejaculation: Investigation of factors in ejaculatory latency. *Journal of Abnormal Psychology, 93,* 242–245. (p. 363)

Spitzberg, B. H., & Hurt, H. T. (1987). The relationship of interpersonal competence and skills to reported loneliness across time. *Journal of Social Behavior and Personality, 2,* 157–172. (p. 462)

Spitzer, L. (1983). *The effects of type of sugar ingested on subsequent eating behavior.* Unpublished doctoral dissertation, Yale University. (p. 539)

Spitzer, R. L. (1975). On pseudoscience in science, logic in remission, and psychiatric diagnosis: A critique of Rosenhan's "On being sane in insane places." *Journal of Abnormal Psychology, 84,* 442–452. (p. 471)

Spring, B. (1988). Foods, brain and behavior: New links. *Harvard Medical School Mental Health Letter, 4*(7), 4–6. (p. 533)

Spring, B., Chiodo, J., & Bowen, D. J. (1987). Carbohydrates, tryptophan, and behavior: A methodological review. *Psychological Bulletin, 102,* 234–256. (p. 533)

Springer, S. P., & Deutsch, G. (1985). *Left brain, right brain.* San Francisco: W. H. Freeman. (p. 47)

Squire, L. R. (1987). *Memory and brain.* New York: Oxford University Press. (pp. 267–268)

Squire, S. (1987, November 22). Shock therapy's return to respectability. *New York Times Magazine,* pp. 78–89. (p. 498)

Sroufe, L. A. (1978, October). Attachment and the roots of competence. *Human Nature, 1*(10), 50–57. (p. 74)

Sroufe, L. A., Fox, N. E., & Pancake, V. R. (1983). Attachment and dependency in developmental perspective. *Child Development, 54,* 1615–1627. (p. 74)

Stapp, J., Tucker, A. M., & VandenBos, G. R. (1985). Census of psychological personnel: 1983. *American Psychologist, 40,* 1317–1351. (pp. 4, 7)

Staub, E. (1989). *The roots of evil: The psychological and cultural sources of genocide.* New York: Cambridge University Press. (p. 547)

Steele, C. M. (1988). The psychology of self-affirmation: Sustaining the integrity of the self. In L. Berkowitz (Ed.), *Advances in experimental social psychology.* Orlando, FL: Academic Press (p. 431)

Steele, C. M., Critchlow, B., & Liu, T. J. (1985). Alcohol and social behavior II: The helpful drunkard. *Journal of Personality and Social Psychology, 48,* 35–46. (p. 215)

Steele, C. M., & Southwick, L. (1985). Alcohol and social behavior I: The psychology of drunken excess. *Journal of Personality and Social Psychology, 48,* 18–34. (p. 215)

Steinberg, L. (1987, September). Bound to bicker. *Psychology Today,* pp. 36–39. (p. 97)

Steinem, G. (1988). Six great ideas that television is missing. In G. Comstock (Ed.), *Public communication and behavior.* New York: Academic Press. (p. 584)

Stein, J. A., Newcomb, M. D., & Bentler, P. M. (1986). Stability and change in personality: A longitudinal study from early adolescence to young adulthood. *Journal of Research In Personality, 20,* 276–291. (p. 113)

Stellar, E. (1985). Hunger in animals and humans. Distinguished lecture to the Eastern Psychological Association convention. (p. 355)

Stengel, E. (1981). Suicide. In *The new encyclopaedia britannica, macropaedia* (Vol. 17, pp. 777–782). Chicago: Encyclopaedia Britannica. (p. 457)

Sternberg, R. J. (1984). Testing intelligence without IQ tests. *Phi Delta Kappan, 65*(10), 694–698. (p. 331)

Sternberg, R. J. (1985). *Beyond IQ: A triarchic theory of human intelligence.* New York: Cambridge University Press. (p. 331)

Sternberg, R. J. (1986). A triangular theory of love. *Psychological Review, 93,* 119–135. (p. 600)

Sternberg, R. J., & Grajek, S. (1984). The nature of love. *Journal of Personality and Social Psychology, 47,* 312–329. (p. 600)

Sternberg, R. J., & Salter, W. (1982). Conceptions of intelligence. In R. J. Sternberg (Ed.), *Handbook of human intelligence.* New York: Cambridge University Press. (p. 327)

Sternberg, R. J., & Wagner, R. K. (1987). Tacit knowledge: An unspoken key to managerial success. (p. 330)

Sternberg, R. J., & Wagner, R. K. (Eds.). (1986). *Practical intelligence: Origins of competence in the everyday world.* New York: Cambridge University Press. (p. 330)

Stevenson, H. W. (1983). *Making the grade: School achievement in Japan, Taiwan, and the United States.* Stanford, CA: Center for Advanced Study in the Behavioral Sciences (Annual Report). (p. 339)

Stevenson, H. W. (1988). Culture and schooling: Influences on cognitive development. In E. M. Hetherington, R. Lerner & M. Perlmutter (Eds.) *Child development and a life-span perspective.* Hillsdale NJ: Erlbaum. (p. 341)

Stevenson, H. W., Lee, S. Y., & Stigler, J. W. (1986). Mathematics achievement of Chinese, Japanese, and American children. *Science, 231,* 693–699. (p. 341)

Stiles, W. B., Shapiro, D. A., & Elliott, R. (1986). "Are all psychotherapies equivalent?" *American Psychologist, 41,* 165–180. (p. 495)

Stille, R. G., Malamuth, N., & Schallow, J. R. (1987). Prediction of rape proclivity by rape myth attitudes and hostility toward women. Paper presented at the American Psychological Association convention. (p. 583)

Stock, W. A., Okun, M. A., Haring, M. J., & Witter, R. A. (1983). Age and subjective well-being: A meta-analysis. In R. J. Light (Ed.), *Evaluation studies: Review annual* (Vol. 8). Beverly Hills, CA: Sage. (p. 109)

Stone, A. A., Cox, D. S., Valdimarsdottir, H., Jandor, L., & Neale, J. M. (1987). Evidence that secretory IgA antibody is associated with daily mood. *Journal of Personality and Social Psychology, 52,* 988–993. (p. 518)

Stone, A. A., & Neale, J. M. (1984). Effects of severe daily events on mood. *Journal of Personality and Social Psychology, 46,* 137–144. (p. 393)

Storms, M. D. (1981). A theory of erotic orientation development. *Psychological Review, 88,* 340–353. (p. 368)

Storms, M. D. (1983). *Development of sexual orientation.* Washington, DC: Office of Social and Ethical Responsibility, American Psychological Association. (p. 367)

Storms, M. D., & Thomas, G. C. (1977). Reactions to physical closeness. *Journal of Personality and Social Psychology, 35,* 412–418. (p. 568)

Strack, F., Martin, L., & Stepper, S. (1988). Inhibiting and facilitating conditions of the human smile: A nonobtrusive test of the facial feedback hypothesis. *Journal of Personality and Social Psychology, 54,* 768–777. (p. 388)

Strack, S., & Coyne, J. C. (1983). Social confirmation of dysphoria: Shared and private reactions to depression. *Journal of Personality and Social Psychology, 44,* 798–806. (p. 461)

Stratton, G. M. (1896). Some preliminary experiments on vision without inversion of the retinal image. *Psychological Review, 3,* 611–617. (p. 182)

Straub, R. O., Seidenberg, M. S., Bever, T. G., & Terrace, H. S. (1979). Serial learning in the pigeon. *Journal of the Experimental Analysis of Behavior, 32,* 137–148. (p. 307)

Straus, M. A., & Gelles, R. J. (1980). *Behind closed doors: Violence in the American family.* New York: Anchor/Doubleday. (p. 243)

Strentz, H. (1986, January 1). Become a psychic and amaze your friends! *Atlanta Journal,* p. 15A. (p. 187)

Striegel-Moore, R. H., Silberstein, L. R., & Rodin, J. (1986). Toward an understanding of risk factors for bulimia. *American Psychologist, 41,* 246–263. (pps. 358–359)

Strube, M. J. (1987). A self-apprisal model of the Type A behavior pattern. In R. Hogan & W. H. Jones (Eds.), *Perspectives in personality: A research annual* (Vol. 2). Greenwich, CT: JAI Press. (p. 516)

Strupp, H. H. (1982). The outcome problem in psychotherapy: Contemporary perspectives. In J. H. Harvey & M. M. Parks (Eds.), *The master lecture series: Vol. 1. Psychotherapy research and behavior change.* Washington, DC: American Psychological Association. (p. 429)

Strupp, H. H. (1986). Psychotherapy: Research, practice, and public policy (How to avoid dead ends). *American Psychologist, 41,* 120–130. (p. 496)

Suedfeld, P. (1975). The benefits of boredom: Sensory deprivation reconsidered. *American Scientist, 63,* 60–69. (p. 164)

Suedfeld, P. (1980). *Restricted environmental stimulation: Research and clinical applications.* New York: Wiley. (p. 164)

Suedfeld, P., & Kristeller, J. L. (1982). Stimulus reduction as a technique in health psychology. *Health Psychology, 1,* 337–357. (p. 163)

Suedfeld, P., & Mocellin, J. S. P. (1987). The "sensed presence" in unusual environments. *Environment and Behavior, 19,* 33–52. (p. 222)

Suinn, R. M. (1986). *Seven steps to peak performance.* Toronto: Hogrefe. (p. 310)

Sullivan, F. (1987). The future of mental health research. Invited address (by the Acting Director of NIMH) to the Eastern Psychological Association convention. (p. 459)

Suls, J. M., & Tesch, F. (1978). Students' preferences for information about their test performance: A social comparison study. *Journal of Experimental Social Psychology, 8,* 189–197. (p. 398)

Suomi, S. J. (1983). Social development in rhesus monkeys: Consideration of individual differences. In A. Oliverio & M. Zappella (Eds.), *The behavior of human infants.* New York: Plenum Press. (pp. 80–81)

Suomi, S. J. (1986). Anxiety-like disorders in young non-human primates. In R. Gettelman (Ed.), *Anxiety disorders of childhood.* New York: Guilford Press. (p. 450)

Suomi, S. J. (1987). Genetic and maternal contributions to individual differences in rhesus monkey biobehavioral development. In N. A. Krasnegor & others (Eds.), *Perinatal development: A psychobiological perspective.* Orlando, Fla.: Academic Press. (p. 413)

Super, C. M. (1981). Behavioral development in infancy. In R. H. Munroe, R. L. Munroe, & B. B. Whiting (Eds.), *Handbook of cross-cultural human development.* New York: Garland Press. (p. 64)

Surgeon General. (1983). *The health consequences of smoking: Cardiovascular disease.* Washington, DC: Government Printing Office. (p. 530)

Surgeon General (1986). *The Surgeon General's workshop on pornography and public health,* June 22–24. Report prepared by E. P. Mulvey & J. L. Haugaard and released by Office of the Surgeon General on August 4, 1986. (p. 581)

Surgeon General (1988). *The health consequences of smoking:*

Nicotine addiction. Rockville, MD: U.S. Department of Health and Human Services. (pp. 530–531, 533)

Swann, W. B., Jr., & Miller, L. C. (1982). Why never forgetting a face matters: Visual imagery and social memory. *Journal of Personality and Social Psychology, 43,* 475–480. (p. 262)

Sweeney, P. D., Anderson, K., & Bailey, S. (1986). Attributional style in depression: A meta-analytic review. *Journal of Personality and Social Psychology 50,* 974–991. (p. 460)

Swerdlow, N. R., & Koob, G. F. (1987). Dopamine, schizophrenia, mania, and depression: Toward a unified hypothesis of cortico-stiato-pallido-thalamic function (with commentary). *Behavioral and Brain Sciences, 10,* 197–246. (p. 466)

Szasz, T. (1984). *The therapeutic state: Psychiatry in the mirror of current events.* Buffalo, NY: Prometheus. (p. 447)

Szasz, T. (1987). *Insanity: The idea and its consequences.* New York: Wiley. (p. 447)

Tajfel, H. (Ed.). (1982). *Social identity and intergroup relations.* New York: Cambridge University Press. (p. 592)

Takooshian, H., & Bodinger, H. (1982). Bystander indifference to street crime. In L. Savitz & N. Johnston (Eds.), *Contemporary criminology.* New York: Wiley. (p. 585)

Tanner, J. M. (1978). *Fetus into man: Physical growth from conception to maturity.* Cambridge, MA: Harvard University Press. (p. 90)

Tart, C. T. (1983). *OpenMind, 1*(1), 6. (p. 188)

Tavris, C. (1982, November). Anger defused. *Psychology Today,* pp. 25–35. (p. 392)

Tavris, C., & Baumgartner, A. I. (1983, February). How would your life be different if you'd been born a boy? *Redbook,* pp. 92–95. (p. 117)

Tavris, C., & Wade, C. (1984). *The longest war: Sex differences in perspective* (2nd ed.). San Diego: Harcourt Brace Jovanovich. (p. 122)

Taylor, M. C., & Hall, J. A. (1982). Psychological androgyny: Theories, methods and conclusions. *Psychological Bulletin, 92,* 347–366. (p. 127)

Taylor, S. E. (1979). Hospital patient behavior: Reactance, helplessness, or control? *Journal of Social Issues, 35,* 156–184. (p. 528)

Taylor, S. E. (1987). The process and prospects of health psychology: Tasks of a maturing discipline. *Health Psychology, 6,* 73–87. (p. 530)

Taylor, S. E., Lichtman, R. R., Wood, J. V., Bluming, A. Z., Dosik, G. M., & Leibowitz, R. L. (1984). Breast self-examination among diagnosed breast cancer patients. *Cancer, 54,* 2528–2532. (p. 529)

Taylor, S. P., & Leonard, K. E. (1983). Alcohol and human physical aggression. In R. Geen & E. Donnerstein (Eds.), *Aggression: Theoretical and empirical reviews* (Vol. 1). New York: Academic Press. (p. 577)

Teevan, R. C., & McGhee, P. E. (1972). Childhood development of fear of failure motivation. *Journal of Personality and Social Psychology, 21,* 345–348. (p. 372)

Teghtsoonian, R. (1971). On the exponents of Stevens' Law and the constant in Ekman's Law. *Psychology Review, 78,* 71–80. (p. 143)

Tellegen, A., Lykken, D. T., Bouchard, T. J., Jr., Wilcox, K. J., Segal, N. L., & Rich, S. (1988). Personality similarity in twins reared apart and together. *Journal of Personality and Social Psychology, 54,* 1031–1039. (p. 83)

Terman, L. M. (1916). *The measurement of intelligence.* Boston: Houghton Mifflin. (p. 319)

Terrace, H. S. (1979, November). How Nim Chimpsky changed my mind. *Psychology Today,* pp. 65–76. (p. 307)

Tesser, A. (1988). Toward a self-evaluation maintenance model of social behavior. In L. Berkowitz (Ed.), *Advances in experimental social psychology.* Orlando, FL: Academic Press. (p. 430)

Tetlock, P. E. (1988). Monitoring the integrative complexity of American and Soviet policy rhetoric: What can be learned? *Journal of Social Issues, 44,* 101–131. (p. 607)

Teuber, M. L. (1974, July). Sources of ambiguity in the prints of Maurits C. Escher. *Scientific American,* pp. 90–104. (p. 172)

Thatcher, R. W., Walker, R. A., & Giudice, S. (1987). Human cerebral hemispheres develop at different rates and ages. *Science, 236,* 1110–1113. (pp. 65, 111)

Thayer, R. E. (1987). Energy, tiredness, and tension effects of a sugar snack versus moderate exercise. *Journal of Personality and Social Psychology, 52,* 119–125. (p. 521)

Thoma, S. J. (1986). Estimating gender differences in the comprehension and preference of moral issues. *Developmental Review, 6,* 165–180. (p. 95)

Thomas, A., & Chess, S. (1986). The New York Longitudinal Study: From infancy to early adult life. In R. Plomin & J. Dunn (Eds.), *The study of temperament: Changes, continuities, and challenges.* Hillsdale, NJ: Erlbaum. (pp. 80, 112)

Thomas, L. (1974). *The lives of a cell.* New York: Viking Press. (p. 162)

Thomas, L. (1983). *The youngest science: Notes of a medicine watcher.* New York: Viking. (p. 31)

Thompson, J. K. (1986, April). Larger than life. *Psychology Today,* pp. 38–44. (p. 359)

Thompson, J. K., Jarvie, G. J., Lahey, B. B., & Cureton, K. J. (1982). Exercise and obesity: Etiology, physiology, and intervention. *Psychological Bulletin, 91,* 55–79. (p. 538)

Thompson, P. (1980). Margaret Thatcher: A new illusion. *Perception, 9,* 483–484. (p. 184)

Thompson, R. F. (1985). *The brain.* New York: W. H. Freeman. (p. 268)

Thompson, R. J., Jr. (1987, October 15). Personal correspondence from the President, Association of Medical School Professors of Psychology. (p. 508)

Thompson, S. K., & Bentler, P. M. (1971). The priority of cues in sex discrimination by children and adults. *Developmental Psychology, 5,* 181–185. (p. 123)

Tierney, J. (1982, June). Doctor, is this man dangerous? *Science 82,* pp. 28–31. (p. 446)

Tifft, S. (1985, December 9). The virtue of openness. *Time*, p. 34. (p. 360)

Timmer, S. G., Eccles, J., & O'Brien, K. (1985–1986, Winter). How families use time. *ISR Newsletter* (University of Michigan), pp. 3–4. (p. 77)

Tinbergen, N. (1951). *The study of instinct*. Oxford: Clarendon. (p. 350)

Tisdell, P. (1983, September). Mixed messages. *Science 83*, pp. 84–85. (p. 142)

Tolman, E. C., & Honzik, C. H. (1930). Introduction and removal of reward, and maze performance in rats. *University of California publications in psychology, 4*, 257–275. (p. 248)

Toufexis, A. (1986, January 20). Dieting: The losing game. *Time*, pp. 42–48. (p. 539)

Towler, G. (1986). From zero to one hundred: Coaction in a natural setting. *Perceptual and Motor Skills, 62*, 377–378. (p. 566)

Trafford, A. (1988, August 11). Why the beef? Psychotherapy gets bad rap in political campaigns. *Grand Rapids Press* (via *Washington Post*), p. A11. (p. 491)

Triplett, N. (1898). The dynamogenic factors in pacemaking and competition. *American Journal of Psychology, 9*, 507–533. (p. 565–566)

Trolier, T. K., & Hamilton, D. L. (1986). Variables influencing judgments of correlational relations. *Journal of Personality and Social Psychology, 50*, 879–888. (p. 616)

Troll, L. E. (1987). Mother-daughter relationships through the life span. In S. Oskamp (Ed.), *Family processes and problems: A social psychological analysis*. Newbury Park, CA: Sage. (p. 95)

True, R. M. (1949). Experimental control in hypnotic age regression states. *Science, 110*, 583–584. (p. 209)

Trueblood, D. E. (1983). *Quarterly Yoke Letter, 25*(4), p. 2. (p. 156)

Tsang, Y. C. (1938). Hunger motivation in gastrectomized rats. *Journal of Comparative Psychology, 26*, 1–17. (p. 355)

Tubbs, M. E. (1986). Goal setting: A meta-analytic examination of the empirical evidence. *Journal of Applied Psychology, 71*, 474–483. (p. 377)

Tucker, D. M. (1981). Lateral brain function, emotion, and conceptualization. *Psychological Bulletin, 89*, 19–46. (pp. 46–47)

Tucker L. A. (1983). Muscular strength and mental health. *Journal of Personality and Social Psychology, 45*, 1355–1360. (p. 420)

Turek, F. W., & Losee-Olson, S. (1986). A benzodiazepine used in the treatment of insomnia phase-shifts in the mammalian circadian clock. *Nature, 321*, 167–168. (p. 147)

Turk, D. C., Meichenbaum, D. H., & Berman, W. H. (1979). Application of biofeedback for the regulation of pain: A critical review. *Psychological Bulletin, 86*, 1322–1338. (p. 522)

Turkington, C. (1987, August). Help for the worried well. *Psychology Today*, pp. 44–48. (p. 495)

Turnbull, W. W. (1986). *Student change, program change: Why SAT scores kept falling*. College Board Publications, Box 886, New York City 10101. (p. 325)

Turner, B. F. (1982). Sex-related differences in aging. In B. B. Wolman (Ed.), *Handbook of developmental psychology*. Englewood Cliffs, NJ: Prentice-Hall. (p. 131)

Turner, C. W., Hesse, B. W., & Peterson-Lewis, S. (1986). Naturalistic studies of the long-term effects of television violence. *Journal of Social Issues, 42*(3), 7–28. (p. 580)

Turner, S. M., Beidel, D. C., & Nathan, R. S. (1985). Biological factors in obsessive-compulsive disorders. *Psychological Bulletin, 97*, 430–450. (p. 453)

Tversky, A. (1985, June). Quoted by K. McKean, Decisions, decisions. *Discover*, pp. 22–31. (p. 292)

Tversky, A., & Kahneman, D. (1974). Judgment under uncertainty: Heuristics and biases. *Science, 185*, 1124–1131. (pp. 290, 617)

Tversky, A., & Kahneman, D. (1980). Causal schemas in judgments under uncertainty. In M. Fishbein (Ed.), *Progress in social psychology*. Hillsdale, NJ: Erlbaum. (p. 292)

Tversky, A., & Kahneman, D. (1983). Extensional versus intuitive reasoning: The conjunction fallacy in probability judgement. *Psychological Review, 90*, 293–315. (p. 292)

Twiss, C., Tabb, S., & Crosby, F. (in press). Affirmative action and aggregate data: The importance of patterns in the perception of discrimination. In F. Blanchard & F. Crosby (Eds.), *Affirmative action: Social psychological perspectives*. New York: Springer-Verlag. (p. 616)

Ulrich, R. S. (1984). View through a window may influence recovery from surgery. *Science, 224*, 420–421. (p. 159)

Underwood, B. J. (1957). Interference and forgetting. *Psychological Review, 64*, 49–60. (p. 276)

United Nations (1980). *Demographic yearbook*. New York. (p. 106)

U.S. Congress, Office of Technology Assessment (1983, November). *Scientific validity of polygraph testing: A research review and evaluation—A technical memorandum*, p. 4. Washington, DC: U.S. Government Printing Office. (p. 384)

U.S. Department of Health and Human Services (1983a, September/October). *Smoking and health bulletin*. Washington, DC: U.S. Government Printing Office. (p. 61)

U.S. Department of Health and Human Services (1983b). *Vital and health statistics* (Series 11, No. 230, pp. 4–5). Washington, DC: U.S. Government Printing Office. (p. 534)

U.S. Public Health Service (1980). *Smoking, tobacco & health: A fact book*. Washington, DC: U.S. Government Printing Office. (p. 530)

Valenstein, E. S. (1986). *Great and desperate cures: The rise and decline of psychosurgery*. New York: Basic Books. (pp. 37, 497)

Vance, E. B., & Wagner, N. N. (1976). Written descriptions of orgasm: A study of sex differences. *Archives of Sexual Behavior, 5*, 87–98. (p. 362)

Van Dyke, C., & Byck, R. (1982, March). Cocaine. *Scientific American*, pp. 128–141. (p. 218) van Kammen, D. P., Mann, L. S., Sternberg, D. E., Scheinin, M., Ninan, P. T., Marder, S. R., van Kammen, W. B., Rieder, R. O., & Linnoila, M. (1983). Dopamine-B-hydroxylase activity and homovanillic acid in spinal fluid of schizophrenics with brain atrophy. *Science, 220,* 974–977. (p. 466)

Van Leeuwen, M. S. (1978). A cross-cultural examination of psychological differentiation in males and females. *International Journal of Psychology, 13,* 87–122. (p. 124)

Van Leeuwen, M. S. (1982). I.Q.ism and the just society: Historical background. *Journal of the American Scientific Affiliation, 34,* 193–201. (p. 323)

VanTassel-Baska, J. (1983). Profiles of precocity: The 1982 Midwest Talent Search finalists. *Gifted Child Quarterly, 27,* 139–145. (p. 332)

Vaughn, K. B., & Lanzetta, J. T. (1981). The effect of modification of expressive displays on vicarious emotional arousal. *Journal of Experimental Social Psychology, 17,* 16–30. (p. 389)

Vernon, P. A. (1983). Speed of information processing and general intelligence. *Intelligence, 7,* 53–70. (p. 331)

Vernon, P. A. (Ed.). (1987). *Speed of information-processing and intelligence.* Norwood, NJ: Ablex. (p. 331)

Vitelli, R. (1988). The crisis issue assessed: An empirical analysis. *Basic and Applied Social Psychology, 9,* 301–309. (p. 557)

Vokey, J. R., & Read, J. D. (1985). Subliminal messages: Between the devil and the media. *American Psychologist, 40,* 1231–1239. (p. 183)

von Frisch, K. (1950). *Bees: Their vision, chemical senses, and language.* Ithaca, NY: Cornell University Press. (p. 305)

von Frisch, K. (1974). Decoding the language of the bee. *Science, 185,* 663–668. (p. 305)

Von Ginlow, M. A. (1986). Reported by A. M. Morrison, R. P. White, & E. Van Velsor (1987, August), Executive women: Substance plus style. *Psychology Today,* pp. 18–26. (p. 117)

Vonnegut, M. (1975). *The Eden express: A personal account of schizophrenia.* New York: Praeger. (p. 465)

Wakefield, J. C. (1987). The semantics of success: Do masturbation exercises lead to partner orgasm? *Journal of Sex and Marital Therapy, 13,* 3–14. (p. 363)

Waldrop, M. M. (1987). The workings of working memory. *Science, 237,* 1564–1567. (p. 264)

Waldrop, M. M. (1988). Toward a unified theory of cognition. *Science, 241,* 27–29; and Soar: A unified theory of cognition. *Science, 241,* 296–298. (p. 299)

Walker, L. J. (1986). Sex differences in the development of moral reasoning: A rejoinder to Baumrind. *Child Development, 57,* 522–526. (p. 95)

Wallace, R. K., & Benson, H. (1972, February). The physiology of meditation. *Scientific American,* pp. 84–90. (p. 212)

Wallach, M. A., & Wallach, L. (1983). *Psychology's sanction for selfishness: The error of egoism in theory and therapy.* New York: Freeman. (p. 427)

Wallach, M. A., & Wallach, L. (1985, February). How psychology sanctions the cult of the self. *Washington Monthly,* pp. 46–56. (p. 427)

Wallis, C. (1983, June 6). Stress: Can we cope? *Time,* pp. 48–54. (p. 510)

Wallis, C. (1987, October 12). Back off, buddy: A new Hite report stirs up a furor over sex and love in the '80s. *Time,* pp. 68–73. (p. 121)

Walsh, M. R. (1987). Introduction. In M. R. Walsh (Ed.), *The psychology of women: Ongoing debates.* New Haven: Yale University Press. (p. 128)

Walster (Hatfield), E., Aronson, V., Abrahams, D., & Rottman, L. (1966). Importance of physical attractiveness in dating behavior. *Journal of Personality and Social Psychology, 4,* 508–516. (p. 597)

Ward, W. C., & Jenkins, H. M. (1965). The display of information and the judgment of contingency. *Canadian Journal of Psychology, 19,* 231–241. (p. 616)

Warm, J. S., & Dember, W. N. (1986, April). Awake at the switch. *Psychology Today,* pp. 46–53. (p. 141)

Washington, V., & Oyemade, U. J. (1987). *Project Head Start: Past, present, and future trends in the context of family needs.* New York: Garland Publishing. (p. 339)

Wason, P. C. (1960). On the failure to eliminate hypotheses in a conceptual task. *Quarterly Journal of Experimental Psychology, 12,* 129–140. (pp. 287–288)

Wass, H., Christian, M., Myers, J., & Murphey, M. (1978–1979). Similarities and dissimilarities in attitudes toward death in a population of older persons. *Omega, 9,* 337–354. (p. 111)

Waterman, A. S., Geary, P. S., & Waterman, C. K. (1974). A longitudinal study of changes in ego identity status during the freshman to the senior year in college. *Developmental Psychology, 10,* 387–392. (p. 96)

Watkins, J. G. (1984). The Bianchi (L.A. Hillside Strangler) case: Sociopath or multiple personality? *International Journal of Clinical and Experimental Hypnosis, 32,* 67–101. (p. 455)

Watkins, L. R., & Mayer, D. J. (1982). Organization of endogenous opiate and nonopiate pain control systems. *Science, 216,* 1185–1192. (p. 211)

Watson, J. B. (1913). Psychology as the behaviorist views it. *Psychological Review, 20,* 158–177. (p. 193)

Watson, J. B. (1924). *Behaviorism.* New York: Norton. (p. 235)

Watson, J. B., & Rayner, R. (1920). Conditioned emotional reactions. *Journal of Experimental Psychology, 3,* 1–14. (p. 235)

Watson, R. I., Jr. (1973). Investigation into deindividuation using a cross-cultural survey technique. *Journal of Personality and Social Psychology, 25,* 342–345. (p. 568)

Weaver, J. B., Masland, J. L., & Zillmann, D. (1984). Effect of erotica on young men's aesthetic perception of their female sexual partners. *Perceptual and Motor Skills, 58,* 929–930. (p. 365)

Webb, W. B. (1982a). Sleep and biological rhythms. In W. B. Webb (Ed.), *Biological rhythms, sleep, and performance* (pp. 87–110). Chichester, England: Wiley. (p. 200)

Webb, W. B. (1982b). Sleep and dreaming. In *Encyclopedia of Science and Technology* (pp. 470–474). New York: McGraw-Hill. (p. 201)

Webb, W. B., & Campbell, S. S. (1983). Relationships in sleep characteristics of identical and fraternal twins. *Archives of General Psychiatry, 40,* 1093–1095. (p. 201)

Webb, W. G. (1979). Are short and long sleepers different? *Psychological Reports, 44,* 259–264. (p. 201)

Wechsler, D. (1972). "Hold" and "Don't Hold" tests. In S. M. Chown (Ed.), *Human aging.* New York: Penguin. (p. 103)

Weinberg, M. S., & Williams, C. (1974). *Male homosexuals: Their problems and adaptations.* New York: Oxford University Press. (p. 367)

Weinberger, M., Hiner, S. L., & Tierney, W. M. (1987). In support of hassles as a measure of stress in predicting health outcomes. *Journal of Behavioral Medicine, 10,* 19–31. (p. 512)

Weiner, B. (1985). An attributional theory of achievement motivation and emotion. *Psychological Review, 92,* 548–573. (p. 404)

Weiner, R. D. (1984). Does electroconvulsive therapy cause brain damage? *The Behavioral and Brain Sciences, 7,* 1–53. (p. 498)

Weingartner, H. (1986, January). The roots of failure. *Psychology Today,* pp. 6–7. (p. 101)

Weingartner, H., Rudorfer, M. V., Buchsbaum, M. S., & Linnoila, M. (1983). Effects of serotonin on memory impairments produced by ethanol. *Science, 221,* 472–473. (p. 268)

Weinstein, N. D. (1987). Unrealistic optimism about susceptibility to health problems: Conclusions from a community-wide sample. *Journal of Behavioral Medicine,* Vol 10, 481–500. (p. 541)

Weiss, J. M. (1977). Psychological and behavioral influences on gastrointestinal lesions in animal models. In J. D. Maser & M. E. P. Seligman (Eds.), *Psychopathology: Experimental models.* San Francisco: Freeman. (p. 513)

Weissman, M. M., Merikangas, K. R., Wickramaratne, P., Kidd, K. K., Prusoff, B. A., Leckman, J. F., & Pauls, D. L. (1986). Understanding the clinical heterogeneity of major depression using family data. *Archives of General Psychiatry, 43,* 430–434. (p. 459)

Weisz, J. R., Rothbaum, F. M., & Blackburn, T. C. (1984). Standing out and standing in: The psychology of control in America and Japan. *American Psychologist, 39,* 955–969. (p. 553)

Wells, B. L. (1986). Predictors of female nocturnal orgasms: A multivariate analysis. *Journal of Sex Research, 22,* 421–437. (p. 365)

Wells, C. (1983, March). Teaching the brain new tricks. *Esquire,* pp. 49–57. (p. 264)

Wells, G. L. (1981). Lay analyses of causal forces on behavior. In J. Harvey (Ed.), *Cognition, social behavior and the environment.* Hillsdale, NJ: Erlbaum. (p. 231)

Wender, P. H., Kety, S. S., Rosenthal, D., Schulsinger, F., Ortmann, J., & Lunde, I. (1986). Psychiatric disorders in the biological and adoptive families of adopted individuals with affective disorders. *Archives of General Psychiatry, 43,* 923–929. (p. 459)

Wener, R., Frazier, W., & Farbstein, J. (1987, June). Building better jails. *Psychology Today,* pp. 40–49. (p. 434)

Westefeld, J. S., & Furr, S. R. (1987). Suicide and depression among college students. *Professional Psychology: Research and Practice, 18,* 119–123. (p. 457)

WGBH (1983, March 22). *Fat chance in a thin world.* Transcript of *Nova* PBS program. (Available from WGBH, 125 Western Avenue, Boston, Mass. 02134). (p. 538)

Wheeler, D. D., & Janis, I. L. (1980). *A practical guide for making decisions.* New York: Free Press. (p. 291)

Wheeler, L. (1986). My year in Hong Kong: Some observations about social behavior. Presidential address to Division 8, American Psychological Association convention. (p. 360)

White, G. L., Fishbein, S., & Rutsein, J. (1981). Passionate love and the misattribution of arousal. *Journal of Personality and Social Psychology, 41,* 56–62. (p. 599)

White, G. L., & Kight, T. D. (1984). Misattribution of arousal and attraction: Effects of salience of explanations for arousal. *Journal of Experimental Social Psychology, 20,* 55–64. (p. 599)

White, J. M. (1987). Premarital cohabitation and marital stability in Canada. *Journal of Marriage and the Family, 49,* 641–647. (p. 371)

White, R. K. (1984). *Fearful warriors: A psychological profile of U.S.-Soviet Relations.* New York: Free Press. (p. 604)

Whiting, B. B. (1987). An introduction to biocultural approach to sex differences. *Contemporary Psychology, 32,* 811. (p. 133)

Whitley, Jr., B. E. (1985). Sex-role orientation and psychological well-being: Two meta-analyses. *Sex Roles, 12,* 207–225. (p. 127)

Whitley, B. E., Jr., & Schofield, J. W. (1986). A meta-analysis of research on adolescent contraceptive use. *Population and Environment, 8,* 173–203. (p. 361)

Whorf, B. L. (1956). Science and linguistics. In J. B. Carroll (Ed.), *Language, thought, and reality: Selected writings of Benjamin Lee Whorf.* Cambridge, MA: MIT Press. (p. 309)

Wickelgren, W. A. (1977). *Learning and memory.* Englewood Cliffs, NJ: Prentice-Hall. (p. 262)

Wicker, A. W. (1971). An examination of the "other variables" explanation of attitude-behavior inconsistency. *Journal of Personality and Social Psychology, 19,* 18–30. (p. 558)

Wiens, A. N., & Menustik, C. E. (1983). Treatment outcome and patient characteristics in an aversion therapy program for alcoholism. *American Psychologist, 38,* 1089–1096. (p. 485)

Wiesel, T. N. (1982). Postnatal development of the visual cortex and the influence of environment. *Nature, 299,* 583–591. (p. 181)

Wigdor, A. K., & Garner, W. R. (1982). *Ability testing: Uses, consequences, and controversies.* Washington, DC: National Academy Press. (p. 342)

Wilder, D. A. (1981). Perceiving persons as a group: Categorization and intergroup relations. In D. L. Hamilton (Ed.),

Cognitive processes in stereotyping and intergroup behavior. Hillsdale, NJ: Erlbaum. (p. 593)

Wilkins, S., & Miller, T. A. W. (1985, October/November). Working women: How it's working out. *Public Opinion*, pp. 44–48. (p. 125)

Wilentz, A. (1987, March 23). Teen suicide: Two death pacts shake the country. *Time*, p. 12. (p. 457)

Williams, D. (1984, April 23). A formula for success. *Newsweek*, pp. 77–78. (p. 339)

Williams, J. E., & Best, D. L. (1986). Sex stereotypes and intergroup relations. In S. Worchel & W. G. Austin (Eds.), *Psychology of intergroup relations*. Chicago: Nelson-Hall. (p. 130)

Williams, R. B., Jr., Lane, J. D., Kuhn, C. M., Melosh, W., White, A. D., & Schanberg, S. M. (1982). Type A behavior and elevated physiological and neuroendocrine responses to cognitive tasks. *Science, 218,* 438–485. (p. 205)

Williams, S. L. (1987a). On anxiety and phobia. *Journal of Anxiety Disorders, 1,* 161–180. (p. 452)

Williams, S. L. (1987b). Self-efficacy and mastery-oriented treatment for severe phobias. Paper presented to the American Psychological Association convention. (pp. 452, 484)

Willmuth, M. E. (1987). Sexuality after spinal cord injury: A critical review. *Clinical Psychology Review, 7,* 389–412. (p. 365)

Wills, T. A. (1981). Downward comparison principles in social psychology. *Psychological Bulletin, 90,* 245–271. (p. 431)

Wilson, D. K., Kaplan, R. M., Schneiderman, L. J. (1987). Framing of decisions and selections of alternatives in health care. *Social Behaviour, 2,* 51–59. (p. 529)

Wilson, E. O. (1975, October 12). Human decency is animal. *The New York Times Magazine*, pp. 38–50. (p. 120)

Wilson, E. O. (1978). *On human nature.* Cambridge, MA: Harvard University Press. (p. 589)

Wilson, J. Q., & Herrnstein, R. J. (1985). *Crime and human nature.* New York: Simon & Schuster. (p. 577)

Wilson, R. C., Gaft, J. G., Dienst, E. R., Wood, L., & Bavry, J. L. (1975). *College professors and their impact on students.* New York: Wiley. (p. 569)

Wilson, R. S. (1978). Synchronies in mental development: An epigenetic perspective. *Science, 202,* 939–948. (p. 64)

Wilson, R. S., & Matheny, A. P., Jr. (1986). Behavior-genetics research in infant temperament: The Louisville twin study. In R. Plomin & J. Dunn (Eds.), *The study of temperament: Changes, continuities, and challenges.* Hillsdale, NJ: Erlbaum. (p. 80)

Wilson, S. C., & Barber, T. X. (1983). The fantasy-prone personality: Implications for understanding imagery, hypnosis, and parapsychological phenomena. In A. A. Sheikh (Ed.), *Imagery: Current theory, research, and applications.* New York: Wiley. (pp. 195, 222)

Wilson, W. R. (1979). Feeling more than we can know: Exposure effects without learning. *Journal of Personality and Social Psychology, 37,* 811–821. (p. 194)

Wing, R. R., & Jeffery, R. W. (1979). Outpatient treatments of obesity: A comparison of methodology and clinical results. *International Journal of Obesity, 3,* 261–279. (p. 537)

Winkelstein, W., Jr., Samuel, M., Padian, N. S., & Wiley, J. A. (1987). Selected sexual practices of San Francisco heterosexual men and risk of infection by the human immunodeficiency virus. *Journal of the American Medical Association, 257,* 1470. (pp. 366, 369)

Witelson, S. F. (1985). The brain connection: The corpus callosum is larger in left-handers. *Science, 229,* 665–667. (p. 48)

Wolpe, J. (1958). *Psychotherapy by reciprocal inhibition.* Stanford, CA: Stanford University Press. (p. 483)

Wolpe, J. (1982). *The practice of behavior therapy.* New York: Pergamon. (p. 483)

Wong, D. F., & associates (1986). Positron emission tomography reveals elevated D2 dopamine receptors in drug-naive schizophrenics. *Science, 234,* 1558–1563. (p. 466)

Wood, G. (1979). The knew-it-all-along effect. *Journal of Experimental Psychology: Human Perception and Performance, 4,* 345–353. (p. 20)

Wood, W. (1987). Meta-analytic review of sex differences in group performance. *Psychological Bulletin, 102,* 53–71. (p. 130)

Wood, W., & Eagly, A. H. (1981). Stages in the analysis of persuasive messages: The role of causal attributions and message comprehension. *Journal of Personality and Social Psychology, 40,* 246–259. (p. 563)

Woodhead, M. (1988). When psychology informs public policy: The case of early childhood intervention. *American Psychologist, 43,* 443–454. (p. 339)

Woodruff-Pak, D. S. (1989). Aging and intelligence: Changing perspectives in the twentieth century. *Journal of Aging Studies*, in press. (pp. 103, 339)

Woods, N. F., Dery, G. K., & Most, A. (1983). Recollections of menarche, current menstrual attitudes, and premenstrual symptoms. In S. Golub (Ed.), *Menarche: The transition from girl to woman.* Lexington, MA: Lexington Books. (p. 90)

Wooley, S., & Wooley, O. (1983). Should obesity be treated at all? *Psychiatric Annals, 13*(11), 884–885, 888. (p. 358)

World Health Organization (1979). *Schizophrenia: An international follow-up study.* Chicester, England: Wiley. (p. 465)

Worthington, E. L., Jr., Martin, G. A., Shumate, M., & Carpenter, J. (1983). The effect of brief Lamaze training and social encouragement on pain endurance in a cold pressor tank. *Journal of Applied Social Psychology, 13,* 223–233. (p. 159)

Wortman, C. B., & Silver, R. C. (1987). Coping with irrevocable loss. In G. R. VandenBos & B. K. Bryant (Eds.), *Cataclysms, crises, and catastrophes: Psychology in action.* Washington, DC: American Psychological Association. (p. 110)

Wu, T–C., Tashkin, D. P., Djahed, B., & Rose, J. E. (1988). Pulmonary hazards of smoking marijuana as compared with tobacco. *New England Journal of Medicine, 318,* 347–351. (p. 219)

Wyman, A. (1983, October 25). Animal talk: Instinct or intelligence? *Detroit Free Press*, pp. 1B, 2B. (p. 307)

Yalom, I. D. (1985). *The theory and practice of group psychotherapy* (3rd ed.). New York: Basic Books. (p. 482)

Yarnell, P. R., & Lynch, S. (1970, April 25). Retrograde memory immediately after concussion. *Lancet,* pp. 863–865. (p. 268)

Yarrow, L. J., Goodwin, M. S., Manheimer, H., & Milowe, I. D. (1973). Infancy experience and cognitive and personality development at ten years. In L. J. Stone, H. T. Smith, & L. B. Murphy (Eds.), *The competent infant.* New York: Basic Books. (p. 76)

Zacks, R. T., & Hasher, L. (1988). Capacity theory and the processing of inferences. In L. Light & D. Burke (Eds.), *Language, memory, and aging.* New York: Cambridge University Press. (p. 102)

Zaidel, E. (1983). A response to Gazzaniga: Language in the right hemisphere. *American Psychologist, 38,* 542–546. (p. 46)

Zajonc, R. B. (1965). Social facilitation. *Science, 149,* 269–274. (p. 565)

Zajonc, R. B. (1980). Feeling and thinking: Preferences need no inferences. *American Psychologist, 35,* 151–175. (p. 403)

Zajonc, R. B. (1984a). On the primacy of affect. *American Psychologist, 39,* 117–123. (p. 403)

Zajonc, R. B. (1984b, July 22). Quoted by D. Goleman, Re-thinking I.Q. tests and their value. *The New York Times,* p. D22. (p. 318)

Zajonc, R. B. (1989). The face as a primary instrument of social process. In R. B. Zajonc & S. Moscovici (Eds.), *Social psychology and the emotions.* Cambridge: Cambridge University Press, in press. (p. 401)

Zajonc, R. B., & Markus, G. B. (1975). Birth order and intellectual development. *Psychological Review, 82,* 74–88. (p. 622)

Zanna, M. P., & Pack, S. J. (1975). On the self-fulfilling nature of apparent sex differences in behavior. *Journal of Experimental Social Psychology, 11,* 583–591. (p. 124)

Zaragoza, M. S., McCloskey, M., & Jamis, M. (1987). Misleading postevent information and recall of the original event: Further evidence against the memory impairment hypothesis. *Journal of Experimental Psychology: Learning, Memory, and Cognition, 13,* 36–44. (p. 272)

Zelnick, M., & Kim, Y. J. (1982). Sex education and its association with teenage sexual activity, pregnancy, and contraceptive use. *Family Planning Perspectives, 14*(3). (p. 370)

Zigler, E. F. (1986, February). Quoted in D. Meredith, Day care: The nine-to-five dilemma. *Psychology Today,* pp. 36–39, 42–44. (p. 77)

Zigler, E. F. (1987). Formal schooling for four-year-olds? No. *American Psychologist, 42,* 254–260. (p. 338)

Zigler, E. F., & Berman, W. (1983). Discerning the future of early childhood intervention. *American Psychologist, 38,* 894–906. (p. 338)

Zigler, E. F., & Glick, M. (1988). Is paranoid schizophrenia really camouflaged depression? *American Psychologist, 43,* 284–290. (p. 465)

Zilbergeld, B. (1983). *The shrinking of America: Myths of psychological change.* Boston: Little, Brown. (p. 492)

Zillmann, D. (1986a). Effects of prolonged consumption of pornography. Background paper for *The Surgeon General's workshop on pornography and public health,* June 22–24. Report prepared by E. P. Mulvey & J. L. Haugaard and released by Office of the Surgeon General on August 4, 1986. (pp. 382, 403, 581)

Zillmann, D. (1986b). In D. Byrne & K. Kelley (Eds.), *Alternative approaches to the study of sexual behavior.* Hillsdale, NJ: Erlbaum. (p. 581)

Zillmann, D., & Bryant, J. (1984). Effects of massive exposure to pornography. In N. Malamuth & E. Donnerstein (Eds.), *Pornography and sexual aggression.* Orlando, FL: Academic Press. (pp. 365, 581)

Zimbardo, P. G. (1970). The human choice: Individuation, reason, and order versus deindividuation, impulse, and chaos. In W. J. Arnold & D. Levine (Eds.), *Nebraska Symposium on Motivation, 1969.* Lincoln, NE: University of Nebraska Press. (p. 568)

Zuroff, D. C. (1986). Was Gordon Allport a trait theorist? *Journal of Personality and Social Psychology, 51,* 993–1000. (p. 424)

Illustration Credits

Part Openers Manipulated Polaroid photography by Jim Finlayson

CHAPTER 1

Opener © Alan Hochman/Int'l. Stock Photo **Fig. 1–1** Wundt, Hall, James, Thorndike, Freud, Binet, Watson: Brown Brothers; Ebbinghaus: The Bettmann Archive; Calkins: Wellesley College Archives; Pavlov: Sovfoto; Washburn: National Library of Medicine **p. 6** © Martin M. Rotker/Taurus Photos **p. 7** © Roe Di Bona **p. 8** © Louis Fernandez/ Black Star **p. 11** © Peter Menzel/Stock, Boston **p. 12** © Anthro-Photo **p. 13** Historical Pictures Service **p. 15** Movie Still Archives **Fig. 1–4** Frank, M. G., & Gilovich, T. (1988). The dark side of self and social perceptions: Black uniforms and aggression in professional sports. *Journal of Personality and Social Psychology, 54,* 74–85. **p. 18** © Jim Amos/ Photo Researchers

CHAPTER 2

Opener © Stuart Cohen/Comstock **p. 25** The Bettmann Archive **p. 30** © MacDonald Photography/The Picture Cube **p. 32** © A. Glauberman/ Photo Researchers **Fig. 2–7** © Alexander Tsiaras/Medichrome **Fig. 2–8** © David York/Medichrome **Fig. 2–9** Courtesy of Drs. Michael Phelps and John C. Mazziota, U.C.L.A. School of Medicine **Fig. 2–10** © CNRI/Science Photo Library, Photo Researchers **p. 37** © Frank Siteman/Taurus Photos **Fig. 2–13** Adapted from Gazzaniga, M. S., Steen, D., & Volpe, B. T. (1979). *Functional neuroscience* (p. 278). New York: Harper & Row. Copyright © 1979 by Harper & Row, Publishers, Inc. Reprinted by permission of Harper & Row, Publishers, Inc. **Fig. 2–17** Rose, S. (1983). *The conscious brain.* New York: Alfred A. Knopf. Copyright © 1983 by Alfred A. Knopf. **p. 42** The Warren Anatomical Museum, Harvard Medical School **p. 43** Courtesy of Dr. Michael Vannier, Washington University School of Medicine **Fig. 2–19** © Martin M. Rotker/Taurus Photos **Fig. 2–22** Gazzaniga, M. S. (1983). Right hemisphere language following brain bisection. *American Psychologist, 38,* 525–537. Copyright © 1983 by the American Psychological Association. **p. 49** Courtesy of Drs. Michael Phelps and John C. Mazziota, U.C.L.A. School of Medicine

CHAPTER 3

Opener © Ida Wyman/Int'l. Stock Photo **p. 57** *(both)* © William Hubbell/Woodfin Camp & Associates **p. 58** © Eric Kroll/Taurus Photos **Fig. 3–2** © Per Sundström/Gamma-Liaison **Fig. 3–3** *(a–c)* © Petit Format/Science Source, Photo Researchers; *(d)* © Donald Yeager/Camera MD Studios **p. 61** © Enrico Ferorelli/DOT **p. 62** © Enrico Ferorelli/ DOT **Fig. 3–4** Conel, J. L. (1939–1963). *The postnatal development of the human cerebral cortex* (Vols. I–VI). Cambridge, MA: Harvard University Press. Reprinted by permission. **Fig. 3–5** Rosenzweig, M. R., Bennett, E. L., & Diamond, M. C. (1972). *Brain changes in response to experience.* Copyright © 1972 Scientific American, Inc. **Fig. 3–6** Adapted from Frankenburg, W. K., & Dodds, J. B. (1967). The Denver developmental screening test. *Journal of Pediatrics, 71*(2), 181–191. **p. 65** *(top)* © Bill Anderson/Monkmeyer Photo Service; *(bottom)* Coren, S., Porac, C., & Ward, L. M. (1984). *Sensation and perception* (2nd edition), p. 490. Orlando, FL: Academic Press. **p. 66** *(left)* Pierre Dupuis, *Still Life with Grapes,* c. 1650, Louvre, Paris. Photo: Scala/Art Resource; *(right)* Gino Severini, *The Basket of Fruit,* 1919, Private Collection, Florence. Photo: Scala/Art Resource **p. 67** *(left)* © P. Price/Stock, Boston; *(right)* © Patrick Grace/Taurus Photos **p. 68** © Hazel Hankin **p. 69** © Hazel Hankin **p. 70** *(left)* © Alice Kandell; *(right)* © Elizabeth Crews/Stock, Boston **Fig. 3–7** University of Wisconsin Primate Laboratory **p. 72** © Peter Menzel/Stock, Boston **p. 73** *(top)* University

of Wisconsin Primate Laboratory; *(bottom)* © Elizabeth Crews **Fig. 3–8** Kagan, J. (1976). Emergent themes in human development. *American Scientist, 64,* 186–196. **p. 75** *(bottom)* University of Wisconsin Primate Laboratory **p. 77** © Alan Carey/The Image Works **p. 78** © Elizabeth Crews **p. 79** © Frank Siteman/The Picture Cube **p. 80** *(top)* © Rick Friedman/Black Star; *(bottom)* University of Wisconsin Primate Laboratory **p. 81** *(top)* © Doris Pinney **Fig. 3–10** Diamond, J. (1986). Variation in human testis size. *Nature, 320,* 488–489. Reprinted by permission from *Nature.* Copyright © 1986 Macmillan Journals Limited. **p. 82** *(top)* © Lenore Weber/Taurus Photos; *(bottom)* © Enrico Ferorelli/ DOT **p. 84** © Erika Stone

CHAPTER 4

Opener © Joe Epstein/Design Conceptions **p. 89** The Bettmann Archive **Fig. 4–1** Tanner, J. M. (1978). *Fetus into man: Physical growth from conception to maturity.* Cambridge, MA: Harvard University Press. Reprinted by permission. **p. 91** © Elizabeth Crews **p. 92** © Elizabeth Crews **p. 94** AP/Wide World Photos **p. 96** *(top left)* © Bob Daemmrich/The Image Works; *(top right)* © Lenore Weber/Taurus Photos; *(bottom right)* © Topham/The Image Works **p. 97** © Pam Hasegawa/Taurus Photos **Fig. 4–3** Johnston, L. D., & Bachman, J. G. (1980) and Bachman, J. G., Johnston, L. D., & O'Malley, P. M. (1987). *Monitoring the future.* Ann Arbor, MI: Institute for Social Research, The University of Michigan. **Fig. 4–4** Adapted from Insel, P. M., & Roth, W. T. (1976). *Health in a changing society,* p. 98. Mountain View, CA: Mayfield. **p. 99** © McDonough/Focus on Sports **p. 100** Adapted from Doty, R. L. et al. (1984). Smell identification ability: Changes with age. *Science, 226,* 1441–1443. Copyright © 1984 by the American Association for the Advancement of Science. **p. 101** *(top)* © Alan Carey/The Image Works; *(bottom)* © Frank Siteman/The Picture Cube **Fig. 4–5** Schonfield, D., & Robertson, B. A. (1966). Memory storage and aging. *Canadian Journal of Psychology, 20,* 228–236. Copyright © 1966 Canadian Psychological Association. **p. 102** © Paul S. Conklin/Monkmeyer Press Photo Service **Fig. 4–6** Geiwitz, J. (1980). *Psychology: Looking at ourselves.* Boston: Little, Brown, & Co. **Fig. 4–7** Schaie, K. W., & Strother, C. R. (1968). A cross-sequential study of age changes in cognitive behavior. *Psychological Bulletin, 70,* 671–680. Copyright © 1968 by the American Psychological Association. Reprinted by permission of the author. **p. 104** *(top)* © Lester Sloan/Woodfin Camp & Associates; *(bottom)* Sarah Putnam/NYT Pictures **Fig. 4–8** Levinson, D. J., Darow, C. N., Klein, E. B., Levinson, M. H., & McKee, B. (1978). *The seasons of a man's life.* New York: Alfred A. Knopf. Copyright © 1978 by Alfred A. Knopf. **p. 106** © Joe McNally/Wheeler Pictures **p. 107** *(left)* © Arlene Collins/Monkmeyer Press Photo Service; *(right)* © Greg Smith/ Stock, Boston **p. 108** *(bottom left)* © Liane Enkelis/Stock, Boston; *(bottom center)* © Spencer Grant/The Picture Cube; *(top right)* © Joe McNally/Wheeler Pictures; *(bottom right)* © Paul S. Conklin/Monkmeyer Press Photo Service **p. 110** *(top)* © John Dominis/Wheeler Pictures; *(bottom)* © Anthony Suau/Black Star **p. 111** © Linda Bartlett **Fig. 4–10** Adapted from Eron, L., & Huesman, R. (1984). The control of aggressive behavior by changes in attitudes, values and the conditions of learning. In R. J. Blanchard & C. Blanchard (Eds.), *Advances in the study of aggression* (Vol. I). Orlando: Academic Press.

CHAPTER 5

Opener © Comstock **p. 118** © Sylvia Johnson/Woodfin Camp & Associates **p. 119** © Tom McHugh/Photo Researchers **p. 120** *(left to right, top to bottom)* © Ira Kirschenbaum/Stock, Boston; © Carol Palmer/ The Picture Cube; © Roland and Sabrina Michaud/Woodfin Camp &

Associates; © John Moss/Black Star; © Thomas & Gitte Nebbia/ Woodfin Camp & Associates; © Owen Franken/Stock, Boston; © Thomas Nebbia/Woodfin Camp & Associates; © Jodi Cobb/Woodfin Camp & Associates **p. 121** © Elizabeth V. Gemmette **p. 122** *(left)* © Bill Stanton/Int'l. Stock Photo; *(right)* © Bob Krist/Black Star **p. 125** *(top)* Astin, A. W., Green, K. C., & Korn, W. S. (1987). *The American freshman: National norms for Fall 1987.* Los Angeles: Higher Education Research Institute, Graduate School of Education, University of California; *(bottom)* © Elizabeth Crews **p. 127** *(left)* © Bill Stanton/Int'l. Stock Photo; *(right)* © Elizabeth Crews **p. 128** Movie Still Archives **p. 129** © Betsy Lee/Taurus Photos **p. 130** © Focus on Sports **p. 131** © Gale Zucker/Stock, Boston **Fig. 5–1** Jenni, D. A., & Jenni, M. A. (1976). Carrying behavior in humans: Analysis of sex differences. *Science, 194,* 859–860. Copyright © 1976 by the American Association for the Advancement of Science. **p. 132** © Diana Walker, Time Inc. **Fig. 5–2** Adapted from Hyde, J. S. (1981). How large are cognitive gender differences? A meta-analysis using w^2 and d. *American Psychologist, 36,* 892–901. Copyright © 1981 by the American Psychological Association. Adapted by permission of the author. **p. 133** Vandenberg, S. G., & Kuse, A. R. (1978). Mental rotations, a group test of three-dimensional spatial visualization. *Perceptual and Motor Skills, 47,* 599–604. Reprinted with permission of authors and publisher.

CHAPTER 6

Opener © Mark Bolster/Int'l. Stock Photo **Fig. 6–1** Porter, B. P. (1954). Another puzzle picture. *American Journal of Psychology, 67,* 550–551. Copyright © 1954 by the Board of Trustees and the University of Illinois. **p. 140** Dr. Thomas Eisner **p. 141** © A. Keler/Sygma **p. 142** Knuth, D. B. (1982). The concept of a meta-font. *Visible Language, 16(1),* p. 15. Reprinted by permission from *Visible Language.* Copyright © 1982 by *Visible Language,* Rhode Island School of Design, Providence, RI 02903. **p. 143** *(left)* © Bill Pierce/Rainbow; *(right)* © Marcia Weinstein **p. 144** © Jeffrey Cardenas/Sygma **p. 149** © Ralph Eagle/Science Source, Photo Researchers **Fig. 6–11** © Joel Gordon **Fig. 6–12** Adapted from Frisby, J. P. (1980). *Seeing: Illusion, brain and mind,* (p. 157). New York: Oxford University Press. Reprinted by permission of the publisher. **Fig. 6–13** Fritz Goro, LIFE Magazine © 1971 Time Inc. **Fig. 6–15** Fritz Goro, LIFE Magazine © 1944 Time Inc. **Fig. 6–16** Richmond Products, Boca Raton, FL **p. 156** © Stan Schroeder/Animals Animals **Fig. 6–19** Wever, E. G. (1949). *Theories of hearing.* New York: Wiley. **p. 157** Robert Preston, courtesy of J. E. Hawkins, Kresge Hearing Research Institute, University of Michigan Medical School **p. 160** © Joel Gordon **Fig. 6–24** Wysocki, C. J., & Gilbert, A. N. (in press - Spring 1989). In C. Murphy & W. S. Cain (Eds.), *Proceedings of the conference on nutrition and the chemical senses in aging (Annals of the New York Academy of Sciences.)* New York: New York Academy of Sciences. **p. 162** © Mary Bloom/Peter Arnold **p. 163** *(top)* © Focus on Sports; *(bottom)* © Charles Gupton/Stock, Boston **p. 164** Flotation REST session in FLOATARIUM® tank. Courtesy of Enrichment Enterprises, Inc., Babylon, New York

CHAPTER 7

Opener Mural designed by Richard Haas, 1983. The Brotherhood Building, Kroger Co., Cincinnati, OH. Photo: Peter Mauss **p. 170** *(top)* © Norman Snyder 1985; *(center)* © Dario Perla/Int'l. Stock Photo; *(bottom)* Photos courtesy Helen E. Ross from Ross, H. E. (1975). Mist, murk and visual perception. *New Scientist, 66,* 658–660. **Fig. 7–1** and **Fig. 7–2** Bradley, D. R., et al. (1976). Reply to Cavonius. *Nature, 261,* 78. Copyright © 1976 by Macmillan Journals Limited. Reprinted by permission from *Nature.* **Fig. 7–3** Kaiser Porcelain Ltd. **Fig. 7–4** © 1988 M. C. Escher Heirs/Cordon Art—Baarn—Holland **Fig. 7–5** Walter Wick **Fig. 7–6** *(left)* Gibson, E. J., & Walk, R. D. (1950). The visual cliff. *Scientific American, April 1950,* 170. Copyright © 1950 by Scientific American, Inc. All rights reserved; *(right)* © Enrico Ferorelli/ DOT **p. 175** *(top left)* © Nik Wheeler/Black Star; *(top right)* © Ron Watts/Black Star; *(bottom left)* © Joel Gordon; *(bottom right)* © Francis de Richemond/The Image Works **p. 176** © Bob Daemmrich/Stock, Boston **Fig. 7–7** *(a) Wine Harvest, Tomb of Night.* Scala/Art Resource; *(b)* Canaletto, detail from *Il Canale Grande e Palazzo Bembo,* 1730–1731. Woburn Abbey, Collection of the Duke of Bedford. Scala/Art Resource **Fig. 7–8** McBurney, D. H., & Collings, V. B. (1984). *Introduction to sensation/perception* (2nd ed.). Englewood Cliffs, NJ: Prentice-Hall. Adapted by permission of Prentice-Hall, Inc. **p. 177** *(bottom right)* Shepard, R. N. (1981). Psychophysical complementarity. In M. Kubovy

and J. R. Pomerantz (Eds.), *Perceptual organization* (pp. 279–341). Hillsdale, NJ: Lawrence Erlbaum. Copyright © 1981 by Lawrence Erlbaum Associates, Inc. **Fig. 7–10** © Alan Choisnet/The Image Bank **Fig. 7–12** *(right)* © Norman Snyder 1985 **Fig. 7–13** *(b)* Josef Albers, *Interaction of Color.* From Albers, J. (1975). *The interaction of color,* revised pocket edition (Plate VI-3). New Haven: Yale University Press. Photo courtesy of the Josef Albers Foundation **Fig. 7–14** Blakemore, C. R., & Cooper, G. F. (1970). Development of the brain depends on the visual environment. *Nature, 228,* 447–448. Copyright © 1970 by Macmillan Journals Limited. Reprinted by permission from *Nature.* **Fig. 7–15** Adapted from Leeper, R. W. (1935). A study of a neglected portion of the field of learning: The development of sensory organization. *Journal of Genetic Psychology, 46,* 41–75. Reprinted with permission of the Helen Dwight Reid Educational Foundation. Published by Heldref Publications, 4000 Albemarle St., N.W., Washington, D.C. 20016. Copyright © 1935. **Fig. 7–16** © Frank Searle, photo supplied by Steuart Campbell **Fig. 7–18** Courtesy Dr. Peter Thompson, York University **p. 184** *(bottom)* Adapted from Gregory, R. L., & Gombrich, E. H. (Eds.) (1974). *Illusion in nature and art.* New York: Charles Scribner's Sons. Copyright © 1973 by C. Blakemore, J. D. Deregowski, E. H. Gombrich, R. L. Gregory, H. P. Hinton, & R. Primrose. Reprinted by permission of Charles Scribner's Sons. **p. 186** © Dana Fineman/Sygma **p. 187** Walter Wick

CHAPTER 8

Opener © Joel Gordon **p. 193** © John Blaustein/Woodfin Camp & Associates **p. 194** © Tom Sobolik/Black Star **Fig. 8–1** Neisser, U. (1979). The control of information pickup in selective looking. In A. D. Pick (Ed.), *Perception and its development: A tribute to Eleanor J. Gibson.* Hillsdale, NJ: Lawrence Erlbaum. Copyright © 1979 by Lawrence Erlbaum Associates, Inc. **p. 195** André Derain, *La Tasse de Thé,* 1935. Gallery of Modern Art, Paris. SEF/Art Resource **p. 196** © Patrick L. Pfister/Medichrome **Fig. 8–2** and **Fig. 8–3** Dement, W. (1978). *Some must watch while some must sleep.* New York: Norton. Copyright © 1972, 1976, 1978 by William C. Dement **Fig. 8–4** Cartwright, R. D. (1978). *A primer on sleep and dreaming* (Fig. 1–6). Reading, MA: Addison-Wesley. Reprinted by permission. **Fig. 8–5** Van de Castle, R. L. (1971). *The psychology of dreaming.* Morristown, NJ: General Learning Press. Copyright © 1971 General Learning Corporation **p. 202** *(left)* © Louis Fernandez/Black Star; *(right)* © Yoav/Phototake **Fig. 8–6** Hartmann, E. (1984). *The nightmare: The psychology and biology of terrifying dreams.* New York: Basic Books. Reprinted by permission. **p. 203** © Peter Angelo Simon/Phototake **Fig. 8–7** Williams, R. L., Karacan, I., Hursch, C. J. (1974). *Electroencephalography (EEG) of human sleep: Clinical applications.* New York: Wiley. **p. 206** *(top)* © Susan Copen Oken/DOT; *(bottom)* © Bob Daemmrich/Stock, Boston **p. 207** © Mimi Forsyth/Monkmeyer Press Photo Service **p. 211** © Focus on Sports **p. 214** Courtesy News and Publications Service, Stanford University **p. 216** *(left)* © John Annerino/Gamma-Liaison *(right)* Courtesy The Advertising Council, Inc. **p. 217** © Focus on Sports **p. 218** *(left)* © Lawrence Migdale; *(right)* © Frank Micelotta/Time Magazine **Fig. 8–9** Ronald K. Siegel **p. 219** © Mike Kagan/Monkmeyer Press Photo Service **Fig. 8–10** Johnston, L. D. (1988). Summary of 1987 drug study results. Media statement delivered in the offices of the Secretary of Health and Human Services. **Fig. 8–11** Siegel, R. K. (1977). Hallucinations. *Scientific American,* October 1977. Copyright © 1977 by Scientific American. All rights reserved.

CHAPTER 9

Opener © Margot Granitsas/Photo Researchers **p. 230** © Alon Reininger/Contact, Woodfin Camp & Associates **p. 231** Sovfoto **Fig. 9–1** Garrett, H. E. (1951). *Great experiments in psychology.* New York: Appleton-Century-Crofts. Reprinted by permission. **Fig. 9–4** Data from I. P. Pavlov (1927). In G. P. Anrep (Trans.), *Conditioned reflexes* (p. 185). London: Oxford University Press. Reprinted by permission of the publisher. **p. 234** © Fred Bavendam/Peter Arnold **p. 235** Brown Brothers **p. 237** © Ed Cesar/NAS, Photo Researchers **Fig. 9–5** *(a)* Sybil Shelton/Monkmeyer Press Photo Service; *(b)* Gerbrands Corporation **p. 240** © Jean-Claude Lejeune/Stock, Boston **p. 241** © Jack Prelutsky/Stock, Boston **Fig. 9–6** and **Fig. 9–7** Reynolds, G. S. (1978). *A primer of operant conditioning.* Glenview, IL: Scott Foresman. Reprinted by permission. **p. 243** *(right)* © Willie Hill, Jr./ The Image Works **p. 245** © Bob Daemmrich/The Image Works **p. 247** © Joe McNally/Wheeler Pictures **Fig. 9–8** Tolman, E. C., & Honzik, C. H. (1930). Introduction and removal of reward, and maze performance in rats. *University of California Publications in Psychology, 4,* 257–275. Reprinted by permission of the University of California Press. **p. 249** *(top)* © Zig Leszczynski/Animals Animals; *(right)* Courtesy Animal Behavior Enterprises **p. 250** *(top)* Courtesy News and Publications Service, Stanford University; *(bottom)* © Anthony Jalandoni/Monkmeyer Press Photo Service

CHAPTER 10

Opener © Mike Yamashita/Woodfin Camp & Associates, **p. 256** © Steve Northup/Black Star **Fig. 10–3** Peterson, L. R., & Peterson, M. J. (1959). Short-term retention of individual verbal items. *Journal of Experimental Psychology, 58,* 193–198. Copyright © 1959 by the American Psychological Association. Reprinted by permission of the authors. **Fig. 10–4** Data from H. Ebbinghaus, 1885. Graph from Baddeley, A. D. (1982). *Your memory: A user's guide.* New York: Macmillan. Copyright © 1982 by Macmillan Publishing Co., Inc. Reprinted by permission. **Fig. 10–5** Craik, F. I. M., & Watkin, M. J. (1973). The role of rehearsal in short-term memory. *Journal of Verbal Learning and Verbal Behavior, 12,* 599–607. **Fig. 10–6** Craik, F. I. M., & Tulving, E. (1975). Depth of processing and the retention of words in episodic memory. *Journal of Experimental Psychology: General, 104,* 268–294. Copyright © 1975 by the American Psychological Association. Reprinted by permission of the authors. **Fig. 10–7** *(top)* AP/Wide World Photos; *(bottom)* From *Physics and Society,* 12(4), October 1983. Reprinted by permission. **Fig. 10–8** Bower, G. H., & Clark, M. C. (1969). Narrative stories as mediators for serial learning. *Psychonomic Science, 14,* 181–182. Copyright © 1969 by G. H. Bower and M. C. Clark. Reprinted by permission of the Psychonomic Society, Inc. **Fig. 10–11** Bower, G. H., et al. (1969). Hierarchical retrieval schemes in recall of categorized word lists. *Journal of Verbal Learning and Verbal Behavior, 8,* 323–342. **p. 268** © Nubar Alexanian **p. 269** © Lynn Johnson/Black Star **Fig. 10–13** Adapted from Bower, G. H. (1986). Prime time in cognitive psychology. In P. Eelen (Ed.), *Cognitive research and behavior therapy; Beyond the conditioning paradigm.* Amsterdam: North Holland Publishers. **Fig. 10–14** Adapted from Godden, D. R., & Baddeley, A. D. (1975). Context-dependent memory in two natural environments: On land and underwater. *British Journal of Psychology, 66,* 325–331. **Fig. 10–15** Bower, G. (1981). Mood and memory. *Psychology Today,* June 1981, 60–69. Reprinted with permission of *Psychology Today* Magazine. Copyright © 1981 by the American Psychological Association. **Fig. 10–16** Loftus, E. F. (1979). The malleability of human memory. *American Scientist, 67,* 313–320. Reprinted by permission of *American Scientist,* Journal of Sigma XI. **Fig. 10–17** Nickerson, R. S., & Adams, M. J. (1979). Long-term memory for a common object. *Cognitive Psychology, 11,* 287–307. **Fig. 10–18** Adapted from Ebbinghaus, E. (1885). *Über das Gedächtnis.* Leipzig: Duncker. Cited in R. Klatzky (1980). *Human memory: Structures and processes.* Copyright © 1980 by W. H. Freeman and Company. All rights reserved. **Fig. 10–19** Adapted from Bahrick, H. P. (1984). Semantic memory content in permastore: 50 years of memory for Spanish learned in school. *Journal of Experimental Psychology: General, 113,* 1–29. **Fig. 10–20** Jenkins, J. G., and Dallenbach, K. M. (1924). Obliviscence during sleep and waking. *American Journal of Psychology, 35,* 605–612. Copyright © 1924 by the Board of Trustees and the University of Illinois. **p. 279** © Donald Dietz/Stock, Boston

CHAPTER 11

Opener © Phil Schultz/Black Star **p. 285** © Stephen Green-Armitage **p. 286** © Dave Schaefer/Monkmeyer Press Photo Service **Fig. 11–1** Rumbaugh, D. M., & Savage-Rumbaugh, S. (1986). Reasoning and language in chimpanzees. In R. J. Hoage & L. Goldman (Eds.), *Animal intelligence.* Washington, D. C.: Smithsonian Institution Press. **Fig. 11–2** Norman Baxley © DISCOVER Magazine 1984, Time Inc. **Fig. 11–3** Scheerer, M. (1962). Problem solving. *Scientific American,* April, 118–128. Copyright © 1963 by Scientific American, Inc. All rights reserved. **Fig. 11–4** and **Fig. 11–7** Adapted from Luchins, A. S. (1946). Classroom experiments on mental set. *American Journal of Psychology, 59,* 295–298. Copyright © 1946 by the Board of Trustees of the University of Illinois. Reprinted by permission of the University of Illinois Press. **p. 293** © Chip Peterson/Sygma **p. 296** © Thomas Wanstall/The Image Works **p. 297** © Joel Gordon **p. 299** *(left)* © Tim Kelly; *(right)* © Peter Menzel/Stock, Boston **p. 301** © M. & E. Bernheim/Woodfin Camp & Associates **p. 303** © Camilla Smith/Rainbow **Fig. 11–10** von Frisch, K. (1974). Decoding the language of the bee. *Science, 185,* 663–668. Copyright © The Nobel Foundation 1974. **p. 306** *(left)* © Paul Fusco/Magnum Photos; *(right)* Language Research Center/Yerkes Regional

Primate Research Center **Fig. 11–11** Language Research Center/Yerkes Regional Primate Research Center **p. 310** © Michal Heron/Woodfin Camp & Associates

CHAPTER 12

Opener © Anthony Howarth/Woodfin Camp & Associates **p. 316** *(top)* © 1927 National Geographic Society; *(bottom)* National Library of Medicine **p. 317** Brown Brothers **p. 319** *(top)* Courtesy News and Publications Service, Stanford University; *(bottom)* Brown Brothers **p. 320** *(both)* © Mimi Forsyth/Monkmeyer Press Photo Service **Fig. 12–1** Thorndike, A. L., & Hagen, E. P. (1977). *Measurement and evaluation in psychology and education.* New York: Macmillan. Reprinted with permission of Macmillan Publishing Company. **Fig. 12–2** College Entrance Examination Board (1983). Sample SAT questions from *10 SATs.* Copyright © 1983 Educational Testing Service, Princeton, NJ. Reprinted by permission. **Fig. 12–3** Sample items from the Differential Aptitude Tests. (1982, 1972). Copyright © 1982, 1972 by The Psychological Corporation. Reproduced by permission. All rights reserved. **Fig. 12–6** Data from The College Board (1984). Figure from *The Chronicle of Higher Education, Vol. XXIX (5).* **p. 328** *(left)* © Enrico Ferorelli/DOT; *(right)* © David Hiser/Photographers Aspen **Fig. 12–7** From Selfe, L. (1979). *Nadia.* New York: Academic Press. Reprinted by permission. **p. 334** © Alan Carey/The Image Works **Fig. 12–8** Bouchard, T. J. Jr. (1983). Twins—Natures twice-told tale. In *1983 Yearbook of Science and the Future.* Chicago: Encyclopaedia Britannica. Reprinted with permission from Encyclopaedia Britannica, Inc. **Fig. 12–9** Data summarized by T. J. Bouchard, Jr. and M. McGue (1981). Familial studies of intelligence: A review. *Science, 212,* 1055–1059. Copyright © 1988 by the American Association for the Advancement of Science. **p. 339** *(top left)* © Jacques Chenet/Woodfin Camp & Associates; *(top right)* © Paul S. Conklin/Monkmeyer Press Photo Service; *(bottom)* © Peter Dublin/Stock, Boston **Fig. 12–10** Lewontin, R. (1976). Race and intelligence. In N. J. Block and D. Dworken (Eds.), *The IQ controversy: Critical readings.* New York: Pantheon. Copyright © 1976 by Pantheon Books. Reprinted by permission. **Fig. 12–11** Stevenson, H. W. et al. (1986). Mathematics achievement in Chinese, Japanese, and American children. *Science, 231,* 693–699. Copyright © 1986 by the American Association for the Advancement of Science. **p. 341** © Alec Duncan/Taurus Photos **p. 343** *(left)* © Paul S. Conklin; *(right)* © Tim Carlson/Stock, Boston

CHAPTER 13

Opener © Bob Krist/Black Star **p. 350** *(top)* © Tony Brandenburg/Bruce Coleman, Inc.; *(bottom)* © Peter Vandermark/Stock, Boston **p. 351** *(top)* University of Wisconsin Primate Lab; *(bottom)* © George Goodwin/Monkmeyer Press Photo Service **p. 352** *(top left)* © Steve Lissau/Rainbow; *(top right)* © Michael Melford/Wheeler Pictures; *(bottom left)* © Steve Lissau/Rainbow; *(bottom right)* © Art Stein/Photo Researchers **Fig. 13–1** Maslow, A. H. (1970). *Motivation and personality* (2nd ed.). New York: Harper & Row. Copyright © 1970 by Harper & Row, Publishers. Reprinted by permission. **p. 354** Wallace Kirkland, LIFE Magazine © 1945 Time Inc. **Fig. 13–2** Adapted from Cannon, W. B. (1929). *Bodily changes in pain, hunger, fear, and rage.* New York: Branford. **p. 355** © Burt Glinn/Magnum Photos **p. 356** *(bottom)* Richard Howard, © DISCOVER Magazine 1981, Family Media Inc. **p. 357** © Freda Leinwand/Monkmeyer Press Photo Service **p. 358** © Schiffman/Gamma-Liaison **Fig. 13–5** Fallon, A. E., & Rozin, P. (1985). Sex differences in perception of desirable body shape. *Journal of Abnormal Psychology, 94,* 102–105. **Fig. 13–6** National Center for Health Statistics data reported by Cornell, G. W. (1987). In *Churches concerned about unwed births.* Associated Press release. **Fig. 13–7** Jones, E. F., et al. (1985). Teenage pregnancy in developed countries: Determinants and policy implications. *Family Planning Perspectives, 17,* 53–64. **p. 361** © D. Fineman/Sygma **Fig. 13–8** Masters, W. H., & Johnson, V. E. (1966). *Human sexual response.* Boston: Little, Brown and Co. Copyright © 1966 by Little, Brown and Co. Reprinted by permission of the publisher. **p. 365** © Joel Gordon **Fig. 13–9** Adapted from Byrne, D. (1982). Predicting human sexual behavior. In A. G. Kraut, *The G. Stanley Hall Lecture Series* (Vol. 2). Copyright © 1982 by the American Psychological Association. Reprinted by permission of the author. **p. 366** *(left)* © Joel Gordon; *(right)* © Herb Snitzer/The Stock Shop **p. 370** © Michael Abramson/Black Star **Fig. 13–11** McClelland, D. C., et al. (1953). The achievement motive. New York: Appleton-Century-Crofts. Reprinted with permission of Irvington Publishers, New York. **p. 373** © Carl Andon/Black Star **Fig. 13–12** Spence, J. T., &

Helmreich, R. L. (1983). Achievement-related motives and behavior. In J. T. Spence (Ed.), *Achievement and achievement motives: Psychological and sociological approaches.* New York: Freeman. Copyright © 1983 by W. H. Freeman and Company. Reprinted with permission.   **p. 375** © M. D. Fenton/Taurus Photos

CHAPTER 14

Opener © Christopher Morrow/Black Star   **p. 383** © Bernard Gotfryd/Woodfin Camp & Associates   **Fig. 14–1** Courtesy David Raskin, University of Utah, as shown in *Science '82,* June, 24–27.   **Fig. 14–2** Kleinmuntz, B., & Szucko, J. J. (1984). A field study of the fallibility of polygraph lie detection. *Nature, 308,* 449–450. Reprinted by permission of *Nature.* Copyright © 1984 Macmillan Journals Limited.   **p. 385** *(left)* © Michal Heron/Monkmeyer Press Photo Service; *(center)* © Bob Daemmrich; *(right)* © Harriet Gans/The Image Works   **p. 386** *(top left)* © Bob Daemmrich/Stock, Boston; *(top right)* © Carol Lee/The Picture Cube; *(bottom)* © Benjamin E. Boblett   **Fig. 14–3** Courtesy Dr. Paul Ekman from Ekman, P. & Friesen, W. V. (1984). *Unmasking the face,* reprint edition. Palo Alto, CA: Consulting Psychologists Press.   **Fig. 14–4** Courtesy Dr. Paul Ekman, University of California at San Francisco   **p. 389** Courtesy Carroll Izard, University of Delaware   **Fig. 14–5** Courtesy Carroll Izard, University of Delaware   **p. 392** © Focus on Sports   **p. 393** © Bob Daemmrich/Stock, Boston   **Fig. 14–6** Astin, A. W., et al. (1987). *The American freshman: National norms for Fall 1987.* Los Angeles: University of California Higher Research Institute.   **Fig. 14–7** Smith, T. W. (1979). Happiness: Time trends, seasonal variations, intersurvey differences, and other mysteries. *Social Psychology Quarterly, 42,* 18–30.   **Fig. 14–8** Roper report 84-1, December 3–10, 1983. *Public Opinion, August/September 1984,* 25. Reprinted with permission of American Enterprise Institute for Public Policy Research.   **p. 396** *(top left)* © Brad Trent/DOT; *(top right)* © Bob Daemmrich; *(center left)* © Bob Daemmrich; *(center)* © Bob Krist/Black Star; *(center right)* © Bob Daemmrich; *(bottom left)* © Bob Daemmrich; *(bottom center)* © Michael Baytoff/Black Star; *(bottom right)* © Dan McCoy/Rainbow   **Fig. 14–9** Adapted from Solomon, R. L. (1980). The opponent-process theory of acquired motivation: The costs of pleasure and the benefits of pain. *American Psychologist, 35,* 691–712. Copyright © 1980 by the American Psychological Association. Reprinted by permission of the author.   **Fig. 14–10** Adapted from Gallup, G., Jr., & O'Connell, G. (1986). *Who do Americans say that I am?* Philadelphia: Westminster/John Knox Press. Copyright © 1986 George Gallup, Jr. and George O'Connell. Used by permission of The Westminster/John Knox Press.

CHAPTER 15

Opener © Hank Morgan/Rainbow   **p. 410** Culver Pictures   **p. 414** UPI/Bettmann Newsphotos   **p. 415** © Karsh/Woodfin Camp & Associates   **p. 416** *(left)* © Sing-Si Schwartz; *(right)* © Sepp Seitz/Woodfin Camp & Associates   **p. 419** *(left)* © Ellis Herwig/Taurus Photos; *(right)* © Gerd Ludwig/Visum, Woodfin Camp & Associates   **Fig. 15–2** Eysenck, S. B. G., & Eysenck, H. J. (1963). The validity of questionnaire and rating assessments of extraversion and neuroticism, and their factorial stability. *British Journal of Psychology, 54,* 51–62, Fig. 1.   **Fig. 15–3** Adapted from Rosen, A. (1958). Differentiation of diagnostic groups by individual MMPI scales. *Journal of Consulting Psychology, 22,* 453–457.   **p. 425** Ted Polumbaum, LIFE Magazine © 1968 Time Inc.   **p. 426** © Lenore Weber/Taurus Photos   **p. 428** *(left)* Alfred Eisenstaedt, LIFE Magazine © Time Inc.; *(right)* Michael Rougier, LIFE Magazine © Time Inc.   **Fig. 15–4** Adapted from Bandura, A. (1978). The self-system in reciprocal determinism. *American Psychologist, 33,* 344–358. Copyright © 1978 by the American Psychological Association. Adapted by permission of the author.   **p. 433** © Frank Siteman/Taurus Photos   **p. 434** *(left)* © Joe McNally/Wheeler Pictures; *(right)* © Bob Daemmrich

CHAPTER 16

Opener © Philippe Gontier/The Image Works   **p. 444** © Mark Antman/The Image Works   **Fig. 16–1** American Museum of Natural History   **p. 446** AP/Wide World Photos   **p. 447** © Ellis Herwig/Stock, Boston   **Fig. 16–2** Roper report 84-3, February 11–25, 1984. *Public Opinion, August/September,* 25. Reprinted with permission of American Enterprise Institute for Public Policy Research.   **p. 451** © Christopher Morris/Black Star   **Fig. 16–3** Baxter, L. R. *Archives of General Psychology, 44*(3). Copyright © AMA.   **p. 455** AP/Wide World Photos   **p. 456** © Norman Hurst/Stock, Boston   **Fig. 16–4** Bureau of the Census (1987). *Statistical abstract of the United States.* Washington, D.C.: Superintendent of Documents, United States Government Printing Office.   **Fig. 16–5**

National Center for Health Statistics data from Wilentz (1987). *Time,* p. 457.   **Fig. 16–7** Forgas, J. P. et al. (1984). The influence of mood on perceptions of social interactions. *Journal of Experimental Social Psychology, 20,* 497–513. Orlando, FL: Academic Press, Journals Division.   **Fig. 16–8** Adapted from Lewinsohn et al., (1985). An integrative theory of depression. In S. Reiss and R. Bootzin (Eds.). *Theoretical issues in behavior therapy.* Orlando, FL: Academic Press.   **p. 464** *(left)* August Natterer, *Witch's Head.* The Prinzhorn Collection, University of Heidelberg; *(right)* Berthold L., *Untitled.* The Prinzhorn Collection, University of Heidelberg. Photos: Krannert Museum, University of Illinois at Urbana   **p. 465** © Grunnitus/Monkmeyer Press Photo Service   **Fig. 16–9** Courtesy Brookhaven National Laboratory, N.Y.U. Medical Center   **Fig. 16–10** Nicol, S. E., & Gottesman, I. I. (1983). Clues to the genetics and neurobiology of schizophrenia. *American Scientist, 71,* 398–404. Reprinted by permission of *American Scientist,* journal of Sigma XI.   **p. 468** National Institute of Mental Health   **p. 469** © Nuel Emmons/Sygma

CHAPTER 17

Opener © Jeffrey Muir Hamilton/Stock, Boston   **p. 475** *(left)* The Bettmann Archive; *(right)* Snark/Art Resource   **p. 476** © Judith D. Sedwick/The Picture Cube   **p. 478** © Bernard Gotfryd/Woodfin Camp & Associates   **p. 479** Michael Rougier, LIFE Magazine © Time Inc.   **p. 482** *(left)* © Dave Schaefer/The Picture Cube; *(right)* © Louis Fernandez/Black Star   **p. 483** *(top)* © James Wilson/Woodfin Camp & Associates; *(bottom)* © Rick Friedman/Black Star   **Fig. 17–1** Gilling, D., & Brightwell, R. (1982). *The human brain.* Copyright © 1982 by D. Gilling and R. Brightwell. Reprinted by permission of Facts on File, Inc., New York.   **p. 486** © Sybil Shelton/Monkmeyer Press Photo Service   **Fig. 17–3** Adapted from Ellis, A. (1984). Rational-emotive therapy. In R. J. Corsini (Ed.), *Current psychotherapies* (3rd ed.). Itasca, IL: F. E. Peacock. Reproduced by permission of the publisher.   **p. 488** *(left)* Courtesy University of Oregon; *(right)* Courtesy Institute for Rational-Emotive Therapy   **Fig. 17–4** Rabin, A. S., et al. (1986). *Aggregate outcome and follow-up results following self-control therapy for depression.* Paper presented at the American Psychological Association convention.   **Fig. 17–5** Adapted from Smith, M. L., et al. (1980). *The benefits of psychotherapy,* p. 88. Baltimore: John Hopkins Press. Reprinted by permission.   **p. 496** © Hugh Rogers/Monkmeyer Press Photo Service   **p. 497** © J. P. Laffont/Sygma   **p. 498** © Will McIntyre/Photo Researchers   **Fig. 17–6** Data from NIMH - PSC Collaborative Study I; *(photo)* © Judy Sloan/Gamma-Liaison   **p. 502** © Louis Fernandez/Black Star

CHAPTER 18

Opener © Mike Magnuson/Int'l. Stock Photo   **p. 509** *(left)* Nancy Pierce/Black Star; *(right)* © Jon Feingersh/Stock, Boston   **Fig. 18–3** Selye's general adaptation syndrome. In T. Cox, *Stress.* Copyright © 1978 by Tom Cox. Reprinted by permission of Macmillan, London and Basingstoke.   **Fig. 18–4** Adams. P. R., & Adams, G. R. (1984). Mount St. Helens's ashfall: Evidence for a disaster stress reaction. *American Psychologist, 29,* 252–260. Copyright © 1984 by the American Psychological Association. Reprinted by permission of the authors.   **p. 512** © Peter Glass/Monkmeyer Press Photo Service   **Fig. 18–5** *(photo)* © Ellis Herwig/Stock, Boston   **Fig. 18–6** Weiss, J. M. (1977). Psychological and behavioral influences on gastrointestinal lesions in animal models. In J. D. Maser and M. E. P. Seligman (Eds.), *Psychopathology: Experimental models.* Copyright © 1977 by W. H. Freeman and Company. All rights reserved.   **Fig. 18–7** Courtesy of the Campbell Soup Company   **Fig. 18–8** Spielberger, C. D., et al. (1985). The experience and expression of anger. In M. A. Chesney, S. E. Goldston, & R. H. Rosenman (Eds.), *Anger and hostility in behavioral medicine.* New York: Hemisphere.   **p. 518** Lennart Nilsson © Boehringer Ingelheim International GmbH   **Fig. 18–10** Friedman, H. S., & Booth-Kewley, S. (1987). The "disease-prone personality": A meta-analytic view of the construct. *American Psychologist, 42,* 539–555. Reprinted by permission.   **Fig. 18–11** Adapted from McCann, I. L., & Holmes, D. S. (1984). Influence of aerobic exercise on depression. *Journal of Personality and Social Psychology, 46,* 1142–1147. Copyright © 1984 by the American Psychological Association. Reprinted by permission of the authors.   **p. 521** *(left)* © Addison Geary/Stock, Boston; *(center)* © David Lissy/The Picture Cube; *(right)* © Gregg Mancuso/Stock, Boston   **Fig. 18–12** *(photo)* © Dan McCoy/Rainbow   **Fig. 18–13** Friedman, M., & Ulmer, D. (1984). *Treating type A behavior—and your heart.* New York: Alfred A. Knopf, Inc. Reprinted by permission.   **p. 524** *(left)* © Bill Anderson/Monkmeyer Press Photo Service; *(right)* © Cary Wolinsky/Stock, Boston   **Fig. 18–15** Adapted from Safer, M. A., et al. (1979). Determinants of three stages of delay in seeking care at a medical clinic. *Medical Care, 17*(1), 11–28. Reprinted by permission of the publisher.   **Fig. 18–16** Pennebaker, J. W., and Lightner, J. M. (1980). Competition of internal and external information in an exercise setting. *Journal of Personality and Social Psychology, 39,* 165–174. Copyright © 1980 by the American Psychological Association. Reprinted by permission of the author; *(photo)* © Mimi Forsyth/Monkmeyer Press Photo Service   **p. 528** © Joe McNally/Wheeler Pictures   **Fig. 18–17** Egbert, L. D., et al. (1964). Reduction of postoperative pain by encouragement and instruction of patients. *New England Journal of Medicine, 270.* 825–827. Reprinted by permission.   **p. 529** *(top)* © Siu/Photo Researchers; *(bottom)* © John Griffin/The Image Works   **p. 530** © Michael Abramson/Woodfin Camp & Associates   **p. 531** *(top)* © Rob Nelson/Stock, Boston; *(bottom)* Adapted from Pomerleau, O. (1988). In C. Gorman, Why it's so hard to quit smoking. *Time,* May 30, 1988, p. 56.   **Fig. 18–18** Gallup Organization (June 1986). Cigarette smoking audit. *Gallup Report, No. 249,* 3.   **Fig. 18–19** Data from McAlister, A., et al. (1980). Pilot study of smoking, alcohol and drug abuse prevention. *American Journal of Public Health, 70,* 719–721. Data also from Telch, M. J. et al. (1982). Long-term follow-up of a pilot project on smoking prevention with adolescents. *Journal of Behavioral Medicine, 5,* 1–7.   **Fig. 18–20** Cohen, L. A. (1987). Diet and cancer. *Scientific American, 257*(5), 42–48. Copyright © 1987 by Scientific American, Inc. All rights reserved.   **p. 535** *(top)* © MacDonald/The Picture Cube; *(center)* © Eastcott, Momatiuk/The Image Works; *(bottom)* © Lincoln Russell/Stock, Boston   **Fig. 18–22** Bray, G. A. (1969). Effect of caloric restriction on energy expenditure in obese patients. *Lancet, 2,* 397–398.   **Fig. 18–23** Adapted from Johnson, D., & Drenick, E. J. (1977). Therapeutic fasting in morbid obesity. Long term follow-up. *Archives of Internal Medicine, 137,* 1381–1382. Reprinted by permission of the American Medical Society.   **Fig. 18–24** *(photo)* © Steve Takatsuno; Dietz, W. H., Jr., & Gortmaker, S. L. (1985). Do we fatten our children at the television set? Obesity and television viewing in children and adolescents. *Pediatrics, 75,* 807–812. Reproduced by permission.   **Fig. 18–25** Herman, C. P., & Mack, D. (1975). Restrained and unrestrained eating. *Journal of Personality, 43*(4), 647–660. Copyright © 1975 Duke University Press.   **p. 540** © Arnold J. Kaplan/The Picture Cube   **p. 541** © Steven R. Krous/Stock, Boston

CHAPTER 19

Opener © Ethan Hoffman/Archive Pictures   **p. 547** AP/Wide World Photos   **p. 548** Movie Still Archives   **p. 549** © Joe Rodriguez/Black Star   **Fig. 19–1** From Sherif, M., & Sherif, C. W. (1969). *Social psychology.* Copyright © 1969 by Muzafer Sherif and Carolyn W. Sherif. Reprinted by permission of Harper & Row.   **Fig. 19–2** Phillips, D. P. (1974). The influence of suggestion on suicide: Substantive and theoretical implications of the Werther effect. *American Sociological Review, 39,* 340–354. Reprinted by permission of the American Sociological Association.   **Fig. 19–3** Asch, S. E. (1955). Opinions and social pressure. *Scientific American,* November 1955, 31–35. Copyright © 1955 by Scientific American, Inc. All rights reserved.   **p. 552** William Vandivert and *Scientific American*   **p. 553** © Diego Goldberg/Sygma   **p. 554** Courtesy Graduate School and University Center of the City University of New York   **Fig. 19–4** From Milgram, S. (1974). *Obedience to authority.* Copyright © 1974 by S. Milgram. Reprinted by permission of Harper & Row.   **p. 558** © Paul S. Conklin/Monkmeyer Press Photo Service   **p. 559** © Bob Krist/Black Star   **p. 563** Courtesy DDB Needham Worldwide   **p. 564** *(both)* © Anthony Suau/Black Star;   **p. 565** © Roger Dollarhide/Monkmeyer Press Photo Service   **p. 566** © Terry E. Eiler/

Stock, Boston   **p. 567** *(top)* Courtesy The Henry Ford Museum, Dearborn, MI; *(bottom)* © Owen Franken/Sygma   **p. 568** © Robert Azzi/Woodfin Camp & Associates   **p. 569** Paulus, P. B. (with the collaboration of V. C. Cox & G. McCain) (1988). *Prison crowding: A psychological perspective.* New York: Springer-Verlag.   **Fig. 19–7** Data from Myers, D. G., & Bishop, G. D. (1970). Discussion effects on racial attitudes. *Science,* 778–779. Copyright © 1988 by the American Association for the Advancement of Science.   **p. 571** Margaret Bourke-White, LIFE Magazine © 1946 Time Inc.

CHAPTER 20

Opener © Jim Sugar/Black Star   **p. 576** © Bill Strode/Woodfin Camp & Associates   **p. 577** © Presse-Sports   **p. 578** © Serge de Sazo/Rapho, Photo Researchers   **Fig. 20–1** Anderson, C. A., & Anderson, D. C. (1984). Ambient temperature and violent crime: Tests of the linear and curvilinear hypotheses. *Journal of Personality and Social Psychology, 46,* 91–97. Copyright © 1984 by the American Psychological Association. Reprinted by permission of the author.   **p. 579** © Ralph Lewin Studio   **p. 580** © Alan Carey/The Image Works   **p. 581** © Rick Brady/The Stock Shop   **Fig. 20–2** Court, J. H. (1984). Sex and violence: A ripple effect. In N. M. Malamuth & E. Donnerstein (Eds.), *Pornography and sexual aggression* (Fig. 5–2). Orlando, FL: Academic Press.   **p. 583** *(left)* Courtesy Americas Watch; *(right)* © Nancy Crampton   **p. 584** © Joel Gordon   **p. 585** © Michael Abramson/Gamma-Liaison   **Fig. 20–3** Adapted from Darley, J. M., & Latané, B. (1968). Bystander intervention in emergencies: Diffusion of responsibility. *Journal of Personality and Social Psychology, 8,* 377–383. Copyright © 1968 by the American Psychological Association. Reprinted by permission of the authors.   **Fig. 20–4** Data from Darley, J. M., & Latané, B. (1968). When will people help in a crisis? *Psychology Today,* December 1968, 54–57. Reprinted by permission of *Psychology Today* magazine. Copyright © 1968 by the American Psychological Association.   **p. 587** *(left)* © Christopher Morrow/Black Star; *(right)* © Ida Wyman/Monkmeyer Press Photo Service   **Fig. 20–5** (racial prejudice curve) Data from *Public Opinion,* October/November 1984, p. 15, the National Opinion Research Center; (gender prejudice curve) Data from *Gallup Report 228/229,* August/September 1984, p. 13. Reprinted by permission.   **p. 588** *(top left)* © Sybil Shackman/Monkmeyer Press Photo Service; *(top right)* © Bob Daemmrich; *(center left)* © James D. Wilson/Woodfin Camp & Associates; *(center right)* © Larry Mulvehill/Photo Researchers; *(bottom)* © Paul S. Conklin/Monkmeyer Press Photo Service   **p. 589** © Janet Kelly, Reading Eagle/Times   **p. 592** *(top left)* © Ian Berry/Magnum Photos; *(top right)* © Eddie Adams/Sygma; *(bottom left)* © Tannenbaum/Sygma; *(bottom right)* © Shelly Katz/Black Star   **p. 596** © B. Bartholemew/Black Star   **p. 597** *(top)* © Will McIntyre/Photo Researchers; *(bottom)* © Joel Gordon   **p. 598** *(top row)* © Nik Wheeler/Black Star; *(bottom row, left to right)* © David Austen/Stock, Boston; © Soames Summerhaup/Photo Researchers; © Wendy V. Watriss/Woodfin Camp & Associates   **p. 599** © Wildlight, Johns/Black Star   **p. 600** *(top)* © Bob Daemmrich; *(bottom)* © Carol Lee/The Picture Cube   **p. 601** Reprinted by permission of the *Bulletin of Atomic Scientists,* a magazine of science and world affairs. Copyright © 1947 by the Educational Foundation for Nuclear Science, 6042 S. Kimbark Ave., Chicago, IL 60637   **p. 605** © Peter Turnley/Black Star   **p. 606** *(left)* © Bob Daemmrich; *(right)* © James Carroll   **p. 607** © Sygma

APPENDIX

p. 612 The Bettmann Archive   **Fig. A–3** Tom Pantages, Courtesy the Harvard College Library   **Fig. A–8** Adapted from Ross, B. (1987). In K. McKean. The orderly pursuit of pure disorder. *Discover,* January, 72–81.

Name Index

Abbey, A., 119, 500
Abbott, W. G. H., 537
Abeloff, M., 518
Abelson, R. P., 470
Abrahams, D., 597
Abramis, D. J., 500
Abrams, D. B., 216
Abramson, L. Y., 461
Adams, D., 528
Adams, G. R., 511
Adams, M. J., 274
Adelman, K. L., 604
Adelmann, P. K., 109
Ader, R., 519
Adler, A., 414, 438
Adler, N., 529
Aiello, J. R., 568
Ainsworth, M. D. S., 72–73
Aitken, D. H., 63
Akerstedt, T., 200
Alafat, K. A., 374
Alansky, J. F., 74
Alba, A., 235, 272
Albee, G. W., 504
Albert, M., 95
Alcock, J. E., 189, 271
Alexander, C. N., 212
Allan, J. S., 197
Allard, F., 264
Allen, C. R., 459
Allen, M., 47
Allen, M. G., 459
Allison, R. B., 455
Alloy, L. B., 461
Allport, G. W., 419–420, 424, 429, 591
Altus, W. D., 373
Amabile, T. M., 334–335, 430
Ames, M. A., 366, 368
Anastasi, A., 321
Anderson, A., 519
Anderson, B. L., 363
Anderson, C. A., 296, 578
Anderson, D. C., 578
Anderson, D. R., 521
Anderson, E. A., 398
Anderson, J. A., 388
Anderson, J. R., 270
Anderson, K. E., 460
Anderson, N. B., 516
Anderson, R. D., 215
Andreasen, N., 466

Andrews, F. M., 500
Andrews, K. H., 558
Angoff, W. H., 332, 340
Anisman, H., 518
Anthony, J. C., 448
Antill, J. K., 127
Appelbaum, M. I., 332
Appenzeller, T., 267
Applebaum, S. L., 100
Archer, D., 386
Archer, L., 215
Arendt, H., 94
Aries, E., 130
Aristotle, 5, 305
Aronson, V., 597
Asarnow, J. R., 468
Asch, S. E., 552–553, 555
Aserinsky, E., 198
Asher, J., 81
Aslan, C., 199
Astin, A. W., 125, 531
Astin, G. R., 325
Atwell, R. H., 216
Averill, J. R., 382, 392
Ax, A. F., 383

Bachman, J. G., 96, 97, 217, 220
Backstrom, T., 527
Backus, J., 157
Bacon, F., 287, 293
Baddeley, A. D., 258, 260–261, 270
Badenhoop, M. S., 102
Bahrick, H. P., 269, 275
Bahrick, P. O., 269
Bailey, M. B., 249
Bailey, R. E., 249
Bailey, S., 460
Bairagi, R., 117
Ball, W., 174
Baltes, P. B., 104
Bancroft, J., 527
Bandura, A., 107, 250–251, 432, 484
Bangert-Drowns, R. L., 326
Barbano, H. E., 110
Barber, T. X., 195, 222
Bard, P., 400–402, 405
Barker, W. B., 341
Barlow, H. B., 140
Barnet, P. A., 461
Barnett, R., 109, 461
Baron, J., 328, 582

Baron, R. S., 566
Barr, R. B., 71
Barrett, L. C., 435
Barrett, M., 248
Bartel, P., 201
Bartlett, M. K., 528
Barton, J., 531
Barton, R., 458
Bartone, P. T., 512, 514
Baruch, G. K., 109
Baruzzi, A., 200
Batson, C. D., 588
Battit, G. E., 528
Baudry, M., 268
Bauer, C. R., 63
Baum, A., 514, 529
Bauman, L. J., 369
Baumann, L. J., 526
Baumeister, R. F., 89
Baumgardner, M. H., 9, 142
Baumgartner, A. I., 117
Baumrind, D., 78–79, 370
Bavry, J. L., 569
Baxter, L. R., Jr., 453
Beach, F. A., 366
Beall, S., 524
Beaman, A. L., 598
Beauchamp, G. K., 355
Beauvais, F., 97, 220
Beck, A. T., 449, 457, 460, 462, 489, 503
Becker, L. J., 247
Becklen, R., 194
Beefon, D., 131
Behan, P. O., 48, 133
Beidel, D. C., 453, 580
Békésy, G. von, 154
Bell, A. P., 367–368
Beloff, J., 189
Belsher, G., 458
Belsky, J., 76, 77, 108
Bem, D. J., 113, 185, 562
Bem, S. L., 123, 126, 134
Benbow, C. P., 133
Bennett, E. L., 63
Bennett, N. G., 371
Benson, H., 522–523
Bentler, P. M., 113, 123, 219, 371
Berchick, R. J., 449
Berger, H., 33
Bergin, A. E., 488, 493
Berkel, C. Van, see Van Berkel, C.

Subject Index